D1000565

THE LAIRD LEGACY

A Biography of Melvin R. Laird

⌒

DALE VAN ATTA

Foreword by President Gerald R. Ford

Copyright © 2008

Marshfield Clinic / Laird Center for Medical Research
1000 North Oak Avenue
Marshfield, Wisconsin 54449

All rights reserved

Published by Marshfield Clinic

Edited by Daryl Gibson

Designed and composed by Jane Tenenbaum

ISBN 978-0-9815707-0-9

This book has been published in a limited edition of 500 copies.
An abridged edition, entitled *With Honor: Melvin Laird in War, Peace, and Politics*
(ISBN 978-0-299-22680-0), is published by the University of Wisconsin Press.

Printed in the United States of America by Worzalla Publishing Company,
located in Melvin Laird's former Congressional district

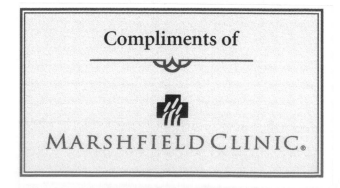

Compliments of

MARSHFIELD CLINIC.

TO THE AMERICAN SOLDIERS, SAILORS, AIRMEN,
AND WOMEN WHO SERVED OUR COUNTRY
COURAGEOUSLY AND HONORABLY IN VIETNAM.

CONTENTS

ACKNOWLEDGMENTS

Mel Laird never intended to write a book about his life, and it took me three long years to talk him into letting me write an authorized biography. My first approach to Laird was in early 1994. We crossed paths at the *Reader's Digest* Washington, D.C., office where he was the senior counselor for international affairs and I was a contributing editor. In several conversations with Bill Schulz, the *Digest* Washington bureau chief, I became intrigued with his accounts of how former secretary of defense Laird had survived, honor intact, the Nixon administration. As I looked deeper it became clear to me that Laird was largely responsible for ending U.S. involvement in the Vietnam War.

My two chief mentors at the time were also surprisingly high on Laird. One was Dick Brown, a longtime friend and top official with the General Accounting Office. He could not say enough good things about Laird, whom he had come to know through his boss, GAO Comptroller General Chuck Bowsher, who had worked under Laird at the Pentagon. And there was Jack Anderson, my partner on a nationally syndicated column. Jack had won a Pulitzer Prize uncovering the duplicity of Richard Nixon and Henry Kissinger over the Indo-Pakistan war and was at the top of Nixon's enemies list. When I mentioned I was thinking about a Laird biography, Jack slapped my back and said, "Do it!" He told me Laird was one of the most honest, effective, and yet unheralded politicians the country had seen in the last century.

Sy Hersh, the *New York Times* reporter and author of the Kissinger biography *The Price of Power,* vouched for Laird's integrity. David Broder of the *Washington Post* and CBS's Bob Schieffer were equally effusive. Both said Laird's contribution to American history had been too long overlooked. Dozens of others of all political stripes, from Hillary Rodham Clinton to Dick Cheney to Colin Powell, said the same.

Finally in 1997, when Mel turned seventy-five, Bill Schulz and I persuaded him it was time. *Reader's Digest* generously funded the initial research. It took another two years to secure enough funding to begin the project on solid ground. That came from Laird's beloved Marshfield Clinic, whose nonprofit Heritage Foundation agreed to back the project for three years. Once Laird was in, he was all in. His memory was extraordinary, as was his attention to detail. He had a long list of people to interview, and a huge cache of material about the Nixon administration that had never before been made public. The fact that it took so many years to finish the book had as much to do with Laird's insistence on fairness and perfection as with my personal commitment to tell his whole story well and accurately.

When a book project lasts more than a decade, the list of those who should be thanked is voluminous. At the top of the list are five individuals who were with this project from the beginning and without whom it would have been impossible: Mel Laird; Robert Froehlke who is Laird's oldest and closest friend and served him as secretary of the army; Robert Pursley, Laird's military assistant at the Pentagon; Daryl Gibson, my friend and colleague for thirty-five years and a freelance book editor; and Kathy Weaver, Laird's executive assistant.

Reed Hall, executive director of the Marshfield Clinic, has been a champion of this work in recent years. His loyalty to Laird has been both touching and tenacious as numerous obstacles to the book's final publication arose. The Laird family was also gracious and unswervingly helpful, beginning with his wife, Carole Howard Laird. His three children—John, Alison, and David—and his stepdaughter, Kimberly, were also cheerfully helpful and encouraging. He is justifiably proud of all of them.

More than three hundred people were interviewed for this book, and I am grateful for all their contributions. Former presidents Gerald Ford, George H. W. Bush, Jimmy Carter, Ronald Reagan, and Bill Clinton all offered their insights on Laird, as did Vice President Dick Cheney. Also granting interviews out of respect for Laird were ten former secretaries of defense: Robert S. McNamara (1961–68), Clark M. Clifford (1968–69), Elliot L. Richardson (1973), James R. Schlesinger (1973–75), Donald H. Rumsfeld (1975–77, 2001–06), Harold Brown (1977–81), Caspar Weinberger (1981–87), Dick Cheney (1989–93), William J. Perry (1994–97), and William S. Cohen (1997–2001). Many of the military leaders of those various eras, including the joint chiefs of staff, also contributed.

Among the other hundreds interviewed, those who went above and beyond in their assistance included but are not limited to (alphabetically): Senator John Chafee, who granted an interview two days before he unexpectedly died; former secretary of state Larry Eagleburger, a fellow Wisconsinite and loyal friend; Jerry Friedheim, whose anecdotes and "lists" of things the book should cover were superb; Laurie Hawley, Laird's congressional and defense department executive assistant, who thankfully preserved all the appointment books; Henry Kissinger, who gave of his time even though he knew some of the book's themes would be critical of him; Jack Mills, raconteur and Laird buddy; former Japanese prime minister Yasuhiro Nakasone; former West German chancellor Helmut Schmidt; Donna Shalala, former Clinton health and human services secretary; and Senator John Warner, one of Laird's favorite protégés and friends.

A debt is also owed to various historians, among them David Horrocks of the Gerald R. Ford Presidential Library, and Dr. Alfred Goldberg and Stuart Rochester, historians for the Office of the Secretary of Defense. There were also

Barbara Constable, Dwight D. Eisenhower Presidential Library; Carol Hegeman, Eisenhower National Historic Site; as well as archivists at the John F. Kennedy Presidential Library, Lyndon Baines Johnson Presidential Library, Richard Nixon Library, and the Nixon Presidential Materials section of the National Archives. The folks at my local Loudoun County library in Ashburn, Virginia, were unstintingly helpful and understanding as I spent many months at the corner table that became my satellite office. The bibliography of this book includes many journalists and historians who are long-standing experts on Laird's period in world history, and whose work prepared me with countless words of background. Among the most notable are military historians Lewis Sorley and Bruce Palmer.

Finally, no author can work more than a decade without help from friends, a few of whom I acknowledge here: the aforementioned Dick Brown and his wife, Hazie, Mike Binstein, Lynn Chapman, Clark and Kathy Kidd, Ryan McIlvain (my unpaid "intern"), Shad and Tiffany McPheters, Phil and Joni Broderick, Warren and Anne Cordes, and Paul Smith.

The most miraculous thing about my wife, Lynne, is that I am still privileged to call her that at the end of this project, which had its shares of ups and downs. She unfailingly supported me with love and patience.

The final miracle of this book is the greatest tribute this world-weary and cynical investigative reporter can offer Mel Laird: after exhaustively reviewing his life, I respect and admire him more at the end of this process than when I began.

Dale Van Atta

FOREWORD

Jimmy Carter once said, "Of all the Cabinet officers who served in the first Nixon term, Mel Laird, with his quiet and somewhat modest demeanor, as well as absence of self-promotion, was the most underestimated." Henry Kissinger and I often remarked how underrated and certainly underappreciated have been the enormous contributions of this remarkable man. This book is long overdue, since no respectable historian tracing the evolution of this country during the second half of the twentieth century can afford to overlook the life and legacy of this Man from Marshfield, who so thoroughly changed the course of America's history.

Without Melvin Laird as our country's tenth secretary of defense, there likely would have been no end during the Nixon administration to the Vietnam War, no end to the draft, no steady military modernization during the country's most virulent antimilitary years, and no arms control treaties with the Soviet Union. This laudatory list does not include all that the Honorable U.S. Congressman Laird did in the sixteen years before becoming defense secretary.

I was not surprised on that January 1953 day in the House Chamber when Speaker Sam Rayburn swore in this thirty-year-old political prodigy from central Wisconsin. Months earlier, members of the Wisconsin delegation—Johnny Byrnes and Glenn Davis—had tipped me off to an outstanding young state senator from Marshfield whom they were absolutely convinced would be elected in the House in 1952. For Mel it was the first of nine triumphs at the polls. Over the next sixteen years he more than lived up to the advance billing given to me.

From the outset Mel was a highly effective member of the House Committee on Appropriations, serving on both the Defense and Health subcommittees, which together controlled two-thirds of the federal budget. I was his seat mate on the Defense Appropriations Subcommittee, where I was the ranking member and he was right behind that. With his quick mind and endless capacity for hard work, Mel quickly became one of the best-informed House members on military affairs. He was our sharpest and most relentless interrogator of the defense establishment when they came testifying. Mel was the only congressman who so rattled Defense Secretary Bob McNamara that he lunged across the witness table when Mel called him out on a lie. He was a tower of strength for us on that subcommittee.

But his best work was on the Health, Education, and Welfare Subcommittee.

As the senior member on the Republican side, he won the respect and confidence of the members on both sides of the political aisle. Long before today's talk of a health crisis in America, Mel Laird was legislating in hopes of averting such a crisis. Among many significant achievements, he and the chairman, Representative John Fogarty, worked closely to legislate a vast and rapid expansion of the National Institutes of Health. It's no exaggeration to refer to health care's renaissance from 1953 through 1969 as the Fogarty-Laird years.

Though Mel often exemplified the epitome of bipartisanship, he was a committed, progressive Republican who was always intensely interested in electing a Republican majority so we would have a Republican Speaker of the House. In the late 1950s, when a group of so-called Young Turks joined forces to overthrow Joe Martin in favor of Congressman Charlie Halleck of Indiana, Mel and I were a part of that group. Then, in the wake of the Goldwater debacle in 1964, history repeated itself. Only this time around, these by-now Middle-Aged Turks were looking for a candidate to challenge Halleck. Mel urged me to run, and thanks in no small part to his efforts, I won that election by the landslide margin of 73 to 67.

Mel became the Republican Conference chairman. For the next four years, we worked in tandem on legislative programs that helped revitalize the Republican Party and elect Dick Nixon president in 1968.

To Mel, politics is the "art and science of government." More than almost anyone I've known, Mel has the political equivalent of perfect pitch; he has a long-range view of what's going to happen, and he knows what to do about it. He's a prodigious worker. He was abrasive at times and enjoyed scheming—not for any sinister reason, but to keep the pot boiling. He is an idea man; he pushed hard, and I responded to that kind of challenge. Ours was a good combination: we respected one another and confided in one another. We were the closest of friends; we played together and often prayed together. I never made a serious move in the House or the White House without consulting this friend and partner.

I well remember a day in December 1968 when we found ourselves in Palm Springs, California, attending a Republican governors conference. It was there I learned that Nixon intended to appoint Mel as his secretary of defense. I felt sadness for my friend and myself. It would be a grisly job for him, coming at a terrible time of trauma in American history. And I didn't look forward to the House without him. But knowing of his impressive military record in the navy in World War II and his subsequent service with me on the Defense Appropriations Subcommittee, I believed that Mel would be of enormous help to President Nixon and get us honorably out of the morass of Vietnam. In my judgment Nixon was very, very lucky to have Mel working with him and Henry Kissinger to extricate us from Vietnam.

With due credit to Henry for the Paris Accords, it was Mel who really brought our troops home. He unilaterally began withdrawing them faster than

Nixon and Henry wanted to, but slower than Mel wanted to. There was not a single month while he was secretary of defense that the number of American troops in Vietnam increased. Mel was lampooned by editorial cartoonists as a "missile head," while too many missed the fact that he was adroitly doing the heavy lifting in the Nixon administration on all things military. He deftly negotiated the crosscurrents of the views of the uniformed military leadership, the White House, Congress, and the American public. To keep American defense strong in the face of the Soviet military threat while ending the draft and conducting myriad other initiatives was no small feat.

At a time when our returning soldiers were being spat upon by their fellow Americans, and some on Capitol Hill seemed to have lost their common sense, Mel stood strong for the defense of America and never lost one vote in Congress. At a time when obsessive secrecy in the Nixon administration was actively undermining the good it would do, Mel was the most open, candid, and fearless of the Cabinet officers. At a time when it was not easy to hold onto one's integrity and honor and pride, Mel was able to do that not only for himself but for all who served with him. Few public servants have been so tested by events as Mel Laird in those days of tumult and challenge, and fewer still have come out unblemished.

Mel announced during his confirmation hearings that he would serve only one term as secretary of defense; the taxi to take him home was already ordered. But by then he was Washington's Indispensable Man, so President Nixon immediately drafted him as presidential counselor for domestic affairs when the unraveling Watergate scandal forced the resignation of John Ehrlichman and H. R. Haldeman. During his year at the White House, as Mel kept the necessary budget-making gears of government working, he once again stood out as a model of personal and political integrity.

The October 1973 resignation of Vice President Agnew touched off speculation over who Nixon might choose to replace him, and it was Mel behind the scenes who was maneuvering to get Nixon to choose me. Two days after Agnew's departure, my wife, Betty, and I were at home in Alexandria, Virginia, having a quiet family dinner when the telephone rang. It was Mel calling. He told me that the Democrat-controlled House and Senate were very unlikely to confirm Nelson Rockefeller, Ronald Reagan, or Nixon's favorite choice, John Connally, for the job. He asked whether I would be interested. My ambition was to be Speaker of the House, not vice president, but that evening, Betty and I agreed those three and one-half years as vice president would be a nice way to end my political career in the nation's capital. I assumed that would be history's footnote for me.

But history doesn't stop for anyone—not for Mel and not for me. I became president, and Mel became a key member of my unofficial "Kitchen Cabinet." He has been quietly but forcefully advising every president and secretary of defense since. He exemplifies a magical blend of principle and pragmatism that is sorely needed in our country today. In fact, it is what Americans want. Most Americans are pragmatists. We want to make things work. We value authenticity at least as much as ideology. As far as Mel and I are concerned, there are no enemies in politics—just adversaries who disagree with you on one vote and might be with you on the next. We've always thought that you had to listen before you could lead, and it's hard to listen if you're screaming at one another. It's even harder to hear the voice of those who sent you to Washington in the first place.

Political partisanship offends most Americans because the partisans have forgotten that ours is a representative democracy. To many voters—and even more nonvoters—parties today are suspected of being decidedly unrepresentative. At worst they appear as little more than conduits for special interest money. Our parties will never regain confidence of the voters until they look beyond the consultants and the tracking polls. At the end of the day no leader worth his salt will take comfort in the polls he conducted or the tactical victories he may have racked up. Anyone can take a poll. Only a leader can move a nation. All his life Mel has been that kind of leader.

In the words of the *Reader's Digest*—the magazine Mel has served for more than three decades now—I count Mel Laird among the "most unforgettable characters" anyone could ever have the privilege of meeting. He remains today what he has always been: a model public servant, a can-do conservative who went into politics because he liked people, a man who reflects honor upon Washington and the people who sent him there, a patriot before a partisan. This thoroughly researched biography by Dale Van Atta bringing to life the lessons of Mel's life and service couldn't come at a better time. The reader who peruses these pages of history will soon come to understand how those of us who have known him are so much better for it, as is this country.

Gerald R. Ford Jr.

THE LAIRD LEGACY

Prologue
Dancing with Lepers

❦

BEHIND A TOWERING LEVEE holding back the Mississippi River, on a spit of oak-shaded land at Carville, Louisiana, lived an isolated colony of lepers. In November 1968 they had a rare visit from a U.S. congressman. For almost eight decades, this had been the place where America had banished her untouchables. Early Americans had quarantined the infected behind the closed doors of rundown "pest houses." But in 1894 a crusading seventeen year old cub reporter for the New Orleans *Picayune* pushed for the creation of a clean and safe state home. An abandoned sugar plantation at Carville was leased for five years under a false pretext—the development of an ostrich farm. The first seven lepers arrived from New Orleans secretly by night on a coal barge. They were whisked off at Iberville Parish and hustled to their new quarters, the plantation's crumbling slave cabins.

Some went to Carville voluntarily, but many were seized in their homes and taken against their will in sealed railroad cars or hearses. Though they had committed no crime, they often arrived at the "leprosarium" in shackles and handcuffs. Armed guards at the gate and barbed wire atop the fences assured no one would leave. A small jail on the property awaited those who attempted to escape. Most lepers changed their names to protect their families from embarrassment or worse. When one community discovered that a twelve-year-old girl had been torn from her weeping parents and taken to the faraway leprosarium, the neighbors burned her house down, believing it would prevent the scourge from spreading. Even dead, they were outcasts. The public would not allow burial in public cemeteries, so they were interred in a small graveyard on the Carville property, either under their aliases or an identifying registration number. Outgoing mail and any cash handled by the residents were fumigated. "This place has seen many a tear," observed one patient. "Rivers of tears. It has robbed many of us of life's joys."[1]

Things began to change when the U.S. Public Health Service took over the state leprosarium in 1923 and converted it into a national center. In the mid-1940s, one of Carville's doctors discovered that sulfone drugs were an effective treatment, and patients were allowed to leave Carville without fear they would infect others. By 1957 living at Carville was optional, yet more than two hundred chose to stay at what had become home.

Few were more delighted at the progress than the two U.S. congressmen most responsible for appropriating federal funds for Carville: John Fogarty, a Rhode Island Democrat, and Melvin R. Laird, a Wisconsin Republican, respectively the chairman and ranking member of the House Health Appropriations Subcommittee. For sixteen years, this pair had abandoned party differences to massively build and expand America's health and research facilities. As part of that work, a list of hospitals needing improvement was drawn up, divided in half, and assigned to one or the other of them for inspection visits. After Fogarty unexpectedly died in early 1967, Laird was determined to complete the list on his own. In 1968 Laird helped his friend Richard Nixon win election as president. Two weeks after the election, Laird sneaked off to Carville.

Some of Nixon's aides found Laird's departure inconvenient. Nixon was seeking Laird's advice almost daily on Cabinet appointments and strategy for the new administration. Laird was expected to spend every spare minute at Nixon's headquarters in the Pierre Hotel in New York City. But the congressman had a promise to fulfill to a departed friend.

Jack Mills readily accepted Laird's invitation to go to New Orleans for a couple of days. Mills had first come from Wisconsin to Washington with Laird to work for the Republican Congressional Campaign Committee. The gifted golfer and raconteur was promised a good time, but Mills wasn't exactly exuberant when Laird asked him to join in an inspection tour of one of the country's two leper colonies (the other being in Hawaii). "Jack, I have to go there because no one visits this place. They tell me it's run down, looks like hell, and needs money. Besides, I told Fogarty I'd go down and check it out. You gotta come down with me."

Reluctantly, for the sake of friendship Mills agreed to go. They flew to New Orleans on November 20, checked into the Roosevelt Hotel, and made the rounds of Bourbon Street that first night. The next morning they set out for Carville. As they approached along River Road, Laird and Mills were impressed with the natural beauty of the 330-acre complex bounded on three sides by the Mississippi River levee. The barbed wire was gone, and everywhere they looked were majestic oak trees, as well as magnolia and pecan. Three miles of covered walkways broke up the lush green grass of the Carville campus, bypassing vegetable and flowering gardens tended by the patients and an order of nuns that had been a presence there for decades. A friendly priest, who was to be their guide, greeted Laird and Mills and began the tour with a round of golf on the facility's nine-hole course.

When he later reflected on the visit, Mills called it "one of the most beautiful" of his life, because of the hopeful courage the lepers evidenced. Still, Mills had personal safety concerns and asked the priest for rubber gloves as they entered the Carville hospital. The priest tried to reassure him that there was no danger of infection. "But all I knew about leprosy was that it was contagious," Mills recalled. So he made sure at first to wash his hands repeatedly when he couldn't avoid shaking hands. "I've never seen anybody wash their hands as often as Millsy did," Laird laughed. "He was pretty frightened."

As the sun set, the guests were invited to join the patients for their weekly dance in the old mansion ballroom. With many of the patients hailing from tropical regions south of the United States, the record player began blaring a Caribbean beat. Mills hung back as the patients stepped to the music with gusto, many of them disfigured, missing fingers, toes, or feet, or with faces eaten away by the disease. Laird had visited plenty of medical and mental hospitals, so the scene didn't faze him. In fact, he didn't wait to be asked. He walked up to one woman and graciously requested a dance, the first of many with the patients. "I will never forget the sight of Mel Laird dancing that day," said Mills. "I mean, these people were very deformed, and there he was, smiling as he danced with the lepers. He is that kind of a guy."[2]

That night, the two friends had a game of gin rummy in Laird's room, though only after Mills had taken a bath or two. Laird was amused by his chain-smoking friend's fear of leprosy, since the cigarettes Mills was smoking were much more likely to kill him than his brief visit to the leprosarium. (At the time, Mills was chief lobbyist for the Tobacco Institute.) About 8 P.M., as Laird was on his way to winning $38 from his chum, the game was interrupted by a call from New York City.

"Dick Nixon," the caller identified himself.

Nixon said he had been thinking about his reform plans for programs of the Health, Education, and Welfare Department, and how much trouble the Democratic majority on Capitol Hill was likely to give him. He needed an HEW secretary who was strong, knew Congress, was respected by the members, and could talk them into supporting his plans. Nixon had concluded that Laird was the best man for the job. "I'd like you to be the new HEW secretary."

"Absolutely not, Dick," Laird immediately retorted. "Not under any circumstances! I do not want to go over there, and I will not go over there." As ranking Republican on the committee that oversaw that department, Laird felt that he was already running HEW. He was also a senior member on the Defense Appropriations Subcommittee, which, combined with the Health Subcommittee, gave him significant influence over two-thirds of the federal budget. On top of that, he was chairman of the House Republicans, on the fast track (just behind Jerry Ford) to becoming speaker of the House, if the Republicans ever gained control of the House again.

Nixon was not surprised, because Laird had already told him after the election that he didn't want to give up his seat or his seniority for *any* Cabinet position. When Laird hung up the phone, he told Mills what Nixon had offered. His lobbyist friend was peeved. "Damn it, Mel," he said. "If you'd accepted that job I would have been a great hero over at the Tobacco Institute! I'd have gotten a big promotion and a raise." Both men laughed. The thought of an HEW secretary being tight with the fast-talking mouthpiece for Big Tobacco was almost too preposterous even for these two Washington veterans.

A couple of days after his return from Louisiana, Laird sat down with Nixon in New York to continue conferring over Cabinet appointments. At least six of those who served in a later Cabinet were originally suggested for the positions by Laird in these sessions: George Shultz (Labor), David Kennedy (Treasury), George Romney (Housing and Urban Development), Walter Hickel (Interior), John Volpe (Transportation), and William Rogers (State). But the most important man Laird suggested, and Nixon accepted, was not a Cabinet officer. His name was Henry Kissinger. Laird had worked closely with the Harvard professor during the 1964 Republican platform committee deliberations and was impressed with his foreign policy expertise. Laird pegged him as a perfect candidate for national security advisor. When Nixon protested because he had never even met the man, Laird arranged a meeting, Nixon made the offer, and Kissinger accepted.[3]

Laird also offered the names of several Democrats as potential Cabinet or sub-Cabinet choices, knowing it was Nixon's intention to appoint at least one man from the opposite party. Laird suggested former Peace Corps director Sargent Shriver, a John F. Kennedy brother-in-law, as the U.S. ambassador to the United Nations. Nixon extended the offer to Shriver, who was then ambassador to France, but Shriver, after consultation with his Kennedy in-laws, turned it down. Instead of himself for HEW secretary, Laird advised that Daniel Patrick Moynihan was a good pick. Moynihan had been an assistant secretary of labor for both Kennedy and Lyndon Johnson. But Nixon instead tendered the HEW job to his California friend Robert Finch.

⚜

One important post was left—secretary of defense. Nixon paid close attention to Laird's advice on this, since the Wisconsin congressman was considered the reigning Republican expert in the House on defense matters. At first, Laird suggested he keep Lyndon Johnson's defense secretary Clark Clifford, since he had been in the post for only ten months after Defense Secretary Robert McNamara had resigned. Nixon didn't like the idea of keeping any of Johnson's men and asked Laird to come up with another name. The president-elect favored a Democrat in the post, remembering the kudos Kennedy had received when he had appointed McNamara, a Republican.

Laird came up with the ideal man: Senator Henry "Scoop" Jackson of Washington. Though a Democrat, he was a hawkish advocate of strong military power, as well as conservative about national security. Laird thought Jackson could bring the Democrats along with a new Nixon program in Vietnam.

Nixon readily gave permission for Laird and Bryce Harlow, a former high-level Eisenhower aide then advising Nixon, to approach Jackson with the possible appointment.

An ambitious man, Jackson wanted the Pentagon job, Laird discovered. "Scoop Jackson was dying to go over to the Pentagon under Nixon," columnist Robert Novak also recalled.[4] But Jackson raised a ticklish condition; he wanted a guarantee that Republican Governor Dan Evans of Washington would appoint a Democrat to replace Jackson in the Senate. His fellow Democrats would never forgive him if he crossed over to the Nixon administration *and* left his Senate seat to a Republican. Because Nixon had greatly warmed to the idea of Jackson as defense secretary, he agreed to the condition. Laird and Harlow were designated to bring the bad news to Governor Evans and find out if he was agreeable. They succeeded, but it wasn't over yet. Jackson went to Hawaii for a Democratic retreat and told some of his friends, including Senator Edward Kennedy, of his plans. Kennedy tore into him for even considering working for Nixon. Kennedy and the others wanted a free hand to thrash the Republican prosecution of the Vietnam War. Having one of their own in the Pentagon was unthinkable. If Jackson took the job, the gloves would come off, regardless of their friendship with Jackson. They laid it on, practically calling him "Uncle Tom" to his face. The final warning from Kennedy et al., to the ambitious Jackson: Do this and it will be the political kiss of death. You'll never be president yourself.

Jackson phoned Nixon from Hawaii with his deepest regrets for going back on his word and refusing the post. It was December, Nixon's carefully crafted Cabinet package had come unraveled just days before the planned announcement of all his appointees, and he was furious. He turned his wrath on Laird. "The president-elect thought I had led him down a blind alley," Laird ruefully recalled. It was not so much a request then, but a command that Laird join Nixon on a trip to the Republican Governors Association meeting at Palm Springs, California. It was up to Laird to make it right. "You got me into this mess. You're going to damn well *fix it!*"[5]

⌖

The annual winter soiree of Republican governors was always a swank affair held at a major resort. With California governor Ronald Reagan as host, Palm Springs, was a natural choice. The airport was festooned with state flags; governors were chauffeured to luxury suites along Palm Canyon Drive in new Cadillacs driven by uniformed highway patrolmen. The real cause for celebration was the election of a new Republican president, showing just how far the party had come in the five years since the creation of the Republican Governors Conference. Only sixteen states had Republican governors in 1963 when the association was founded. At the start of 1969 there would be thirty-one, and the party would have its first president in eight years. The governors had not been particularly supportive of Nixon, instead favoring two of their own in the primaries, Michigan governor George Romney and New York governor Nelson Rockefeller. But Nixon had overcome most of their opposition, and not a few governors planned to use Palm Springs as an opportunity to angle for positions in the new administration.[6] Nixon flew to Los Angeles in an Air Force One backup jet on Thursday, December 5, where he spoke at a dinner honoring the city's Roman Catholic archbishop. Knowing his Cabinet considerations were the hot topic of the time, he pointedly referred to Lieutenant Governor Robert Finch, who was seated on the dais, as "Secretary Finch."

There was no good humor the next morning, though, when Nixon summoned Laird to join him aboard the plane for the short hop from Los Angeles to Palm Springs. Nixon groused that the Jackson snafu was Laird's fault, and his inclination was now to name Laird himself as secretary of defense. Laird protested and scrambled to propose more names, Clark Clifford and Nelson Rockefeller among them, but Nixon wasn't biting. Following Nixon off the plane in Palm Springs, Laird knew he was firmly planted in the proverbial hot seat, and it had nothing to do with the desert weather. His first call was to his wife, Barbara, who asked him not to accept the job under any circumstances. He had the same inclination. He loved Congress and everything about it—every back slap, every debate, every marbled hall, every painting and sculpture of legendary representatives who had served before him.

Meanwhile, the president-elect was holding court at the private 233-acre estate of Walter Annenberg, millionaire Philadelphia publisher and owner of TV and radio stations. Officially, Vice President–elect Spiro Agnew, still governor of Maryland, was Nixon's representative at the conference. Nixon was there only as a guest for a Friday dinner. For five hours that Friday afternoon, lounging on his terrace with a view overlooking the beautiful Tamarisk Country Club golf course, Nixon counseled with various Republican governors, calling them away from their conference business.

His most important meeting was with Rockefeller, with whom he had been jousting for Republican Party leadership since 1960. Rockefeller had let it be known he would favorably consider being secretary of defense or state. Exactly what was said between the two of them is not known, but Rockefeller didn't ask for a job and Nixon didn't offer one. It's likely that Rockefeller was too proud to ask, and Nixon was unwilling to tender an offer to his longtime nemesis, who probably wouldn't be a Nixon team player anyway.

One other man might have been in a position to save Mel Laird from what he viewed as a terrible fate: retiring Governor John Connally of Texas, a Democrat. In his memoirs, Connally reported that, after Scoop Jackson refused the defense job, Nixon had asked an unusual political intermediary, the Reverend Billy Graham, to call Connally and gauge his interest in the post. Connally answered that he was already committed to private life.[7] (Two years later, Nixon's quest for a Democrat in his Cabinet would finally be realized when Connally signed on as treasury secretary.)

At the cocktail party before the dinner Friday evening, Laird was not himself. He tried to stay out of sight, since he had told Wisconsin reporters he would be at home in Marshfield, Wisconsin, that week. One of them spotted Laird and asked him to step outside the hotel suite for a word. After Laird joked about the ill-fitting dinner jacket he had rented since he hadn't had time to pack, the reporter asked him how Nixon's Cabinet was shaping up. "I can't talk to you," Laird replied with uncharacteristic discomfort. "I'm sorry, I've talked too much already."[8]

<hr>

Saturday, December 7, was one Pearl Harbor Day anniversary Laird would never forget. He decided golf would clear his head, and as he played he formed a plan to parry Nixon's unwelcome plans for him. Laird would have to come up with a condition to acceptance that was plausible yet so odious that Nixon would never accept it. Halfway through the eighteen holes, Laird's game was interrupted by a call from the House Republican leader, Gerald Ford, a close friend. Ford reported that he had just come from a private luncheon hosted for Nixon by Walter Annenberg. The president-elect had announced to the small group that he would appoint Annenberg as ambassador to Great Britain—and he would likely name Melvin Laird as his choice for defense secretary.

"It came as a little bit of a shock to Jerry," Laird recalled. There was no question that Laird was qualified, and Ford knew it. The two had worked closely for years on the Defense Appropriations Subcommittee where Ford had been ranking member and Laird just behind him. "He was one of the best-informed members of the House or the Senate on defense matters," Ford said. "Then there was his uncommon common sense and his sound political judgment and leadership ability. I knew Nixon would be lucky to get him." But Ford didn't want Laird to leave Congress, and he told Laird so.[9]

Laird was in the greatest quandary of his life as he boarded Nixon's jet for the return trip to Washington, D.C. Ford joined him, as did Bryce Harlow, whom Nixon had named as his legislative affairs liaison. Harlow had joined Laird in lobbying for Jackson for defense secretary, which had blown up in both their faces. Nixon's opening blast was directed at both Laird and Harlow. "You sons of bitches!" Nixon sputtered. "You talked me into this thing with Scoop and now he's backed out." Then he turned on Laird. "There's only one way to fix this—I'm going to announce YOU for defense secretary!"

"The hell you are!" Laird countered. "I'm not going to leave Congress." Laird had been prepared for the assault, and as Nixon's anger diminished, he took more than an hour detailing a list of eighteen reasons why it was better for Nixon if he had Laird as a House leader, with influence over two-thirds of the federal budget, than as a mere secretary of defense. He pointed out that he was not the executive type. Laird had sixteen years of congressional seniority and might be needed as the House's Republican leader if anything happened to Ford. "I would like to be House speaker someday, Dick," Laird revealed. "I love being a legislator. I am not an administrator."

They settled in for an extended, though intermittent, debate on the cross-country flight. "I made the hard sell—even though a friend was involved," Nixon later recalled in a letter to Laird. "I know this was a terribly difficult decision for you to make, but you were the indispensable man—the right man for the right place, at the right time."[10] Less than an hour away from Andrews Air Force Base outside Washington, Laird, mellowed by a manhattan or two, appeared to give in, but it was only an illusion. He had waited to reveal his trump card, the one condition to which Nixon would never agree. "Well now, I'll tell you," Laird wound up, "if you give me a firm, positive commitment that no one in your administration, or you, will ever interfere with any appointment, military or civilian, that is made in the Department of Defense while I serve as secretary, I might consider doing it."

Laird was smug in his belief that no president would surrender that power to a Cabinet secretary. He was so sure of himself that he promised conclusively: "If you give me that kind of commitment, you can count on my doing it."

Nixon thought for a moment, and then replied, "Mel, you have my word on it."

Laird had been outfoxed. In a last grasp for clemency, Laird asked Nixon to put it in writing on a cocktail napkin. Nixon did, and signed the napkin.

The Defense Department had almost five million employees and was the nation's largest employer. Its annual budget was $80 billion, more than the total government expenditures of every nation in the world except the Soviet Union. At the top of this center of power were more than one thousand prized political appointments, including the Joint Chiefs of Staff, the deputy secretary of defense, the assistant secretaries of defense, the individual service secretaries, and the generals and admirals who would control sensitive military intelligence. Those coveted spots were traditionally saved to repay presidential political debts, reward friends, and install a cadre loyal to the president. For this reason, no president before had made such a deal as this one. "He agreed!" Laird recalled. "I didn't think he ever would."

While Laird had been surprised, the demand had been more than a gambit to scare Nixon out of making Laird take the job. If a genie had given the new defense secretary three wishes, Laird later said, complete control of his appointments would still have been first, second, and third on the list. Laird knew Richard Nixon well, and he was beginning to get an inkling of the kind of manipulative staffers the new president would employ as his palace guard.

If Laird was going to run the Defense Department his way, he needed to be surrounded by his own people. He had already decided that he would deal directly with no one at the new White House other than Nixon and Kissinger. The rest of the schemers and sycophants who tried to engage the Pentagon from 1600 Pennsylvania Avenue would be directed to a single staffer in Laird's office whose job it would be keep them off his back.

The cross-country flight had been excruciating, but landing brought another anticipation of agony; he had to tell his wife and his mother.

On Sunday, the day after Laird and Nixon arrived back in Washington, the phone at the Laird home began ringing incessantly. The news of his pending appointment had leaked to nationally syndicated columnists Rowland Evans and Robert Novak. The two journalists were old friends of Laird's. Evans's wife was from Wisconsin, and Novak had befriended Laird while covering the Midwest for the *Wall Street Journal.* It was a mutually satisfactory relationship. Evans and Novak mined Congressman Laird for news tips, and he used them to leak stories that fit his agenda. This time, however, the leak had not come from Laird. Contrary to the presidential practice of announcing Cabinet nominees one by one as they are chosen, Nixon wanted to trot out his entire Cabinet at a press conference. Sensitive to Nixon's sense of public drama, Laird would never have stolen that kind of moment from the president, and he wanted some time to alert his colleagues in the House and Senate before the story leaked.

"The biggest scoop I ever got about Mel was when he became secretary of defense—and he didn't give it to me," Novak recalled. He had attended the governors' conference in Palm Springs and then gone to Las Vegas Saturday night when an "A-grade source" called him from Palm Springs with the tip. Without warning Laird, Novak published the news in his column on Sunday. "Mel called me up, and it was the first time he was really mad at me. He said his mother had heard it on the radio from my column, before he'd had a chance to tell her. She almost had a heart attack, he said. But his anger passed over soon."[11]

Helen Connor Laird was more than just Laird's mother; she was his oldest political confidant, and she was not happy about the appointment. "She thought it was a very bad time to inherit a war that had been going on for seven years," he recalled. "My mother was a pacifist in many ways. She was very much opposed to Vietnam. She thought it was terrible for me to go over to the Pentagon, even when I told her I was going over there to try to bring it to an end." Laird's wife, Barbara, didn't like the idea either. She shunned the limelight for herself and her three children, and now it was likely to get much brighter. Her response to the calls was to take her phone off the hook. Barbara harbored a prescient distrust of Nixon and, like Caesar's wife, cautioned Laird about getting too close.

Laird is not a complex man. He knew he was stepping into the quagmire of Vietnam, but he was also confident that he could end the draft and the war, even if Nixon proved reluctant to do either. There were many other good things he could do as a Cabinet member. Laird's sense of honor and duty to country drove him to finally accept the onerous position.

During his Senate confirmation hearing, he called the decision "one of the most painful of my entire political life, for I will be leaving the institution which I love deeply and in which I had hoped and planned to serve the rest of my productive life." In his first official statement he said, "My decision to accept the post ... was the most difficult decision of my political life. I did not seek the post of Secretary of Defense. I did everything I could to promote other individuals for that office, [but when] the final decision had to be made, I could not tell the President-elect of the United States that I would not serve my country in this most important post."[12]

It was also destiny by default, Laird said. "Nixon couldn't find anybody else who wanted the damn job."

1

The Man from Marshfield

It was the first bright and sunny day after two weeks of dark squalls and heaving seas, but still the crew of the USS Maddox *didn't see the kamikaze until it was too late.*

The 2,200-ton American destroyer was part of Admiral "Bull" Halsey's Third Fleet in early 1945. Her complement of 359 men was exhausted. Along with the other ships of Task Force 38, the Maddox *had just completed a daring eleven-day, 3,800-mile mission in the South China Sea, running a gauntlet through Japanese-occupied positions.*

Under cover of darkness, the task force had slipped into the sea on January 10 through the Bashi Channel, south of Formosa, catching the Japanese unaware with the Allies' first foray into those waters. Bombing raids on Japanese land bases from the aircraft carriers alerted the enemy to their presence and vulnerability. On the sixteenth, Japanese propagandist "Tokyo Rose" had taunted the task force: "We know where you are and know how you got in the China Sea, but how are you going to get out? We'll be waiting."

Fortunately for the force, their high-speed run was never pinpointed, and ten days after entering the South China Sea, they steamed out, unscathed. The Maddox *took up a new position, within sight of the Japanese-held island of Formosa. This time they were thirty-five miles from the center of the task force, assigned to rescue pilots who had splashed down and direct airborne pilots back to their home ships. These planes were supposed to circle the* Maddox *for inspection before being allowed to pass. Wily Japanese airmen had learned that American planes had blind spots below and behind them, so the Zeros had been slipping undetected into friendly aircraft formations and tagging along, back to the most valuable navy target of the war—the enemy's aircraft carriers.*

Sunday morning, January 21, the men on the Maddox *seemed cheerful as they mustered to their stations at 8 A.M., a rainbow embellishing the morning off the port beam. Nothing untoward was suspected until, at 1 P.M., several on deck noticed smoke rising from the USS* Ticonderoga, *a carrier about twelve miles to the east. The ship's executive officer decided to go below and discuss it with the captain.*

No one seemed alarmed. One of the destroyer's key guns was depressed—not ready to fire—because the crew was cleaning it. In the wardroom, several junior officers were just sitting down to second mess. Among them, the supply officer, nicknamed "Pay," sat in his usual post at the end of the table, a few feet from the starboard bulkhead, eating a sandwich.

At 1:10 P.M. a dozen returning Hellcats (F6Fs) headed for inspection over the Maddox. The first group of three arrived and began to circle the Maddox at 1,500 feet, when the middle plane dropped out of formation. Too late, several men on deck identified it as a deadly black Japanese Zero, which was now steeply diving toward the ship, machine guns blazing. The kamikaze leveled off just aft of the radio antennae, which clipped the left wing, driving the plane into a 40-millimeter gun turret. It then crashed through the top deck of the ship, releasing a 132-kilogram bomb that exploded just behind the wardroom's starboard bulkhead. "Pay"—Ensign Melvin Laird—was closest to the blast, taking the brunt of the shrapnel that pierced the air of the wardroom.

In the next few seconds of terror, noise, and pain, when life hung in the balance, Laird was seared with the thought of how far he was from his home in Marshfield, Wisconsin; far from the smell of fresh lumber and fermented brewery hops, far from movies at the Adler Theater, far from his mother, who taught him to love reading, and far from his father, who introduced him to God—all half a world away, and possibly a whole lifetime ago . . . [1]

⟆⟅

"A TERRESTRIAL PARADISE," seventeenth-century French explorer Pierre Esprit Radisson declared about Wee-kan-san, the land of the "gathering of the waters" in Indian tongue. "So pleasant, so beautifull and fruitfull." Eight-year-old William Duncan Connor had to agree when, two centuries later, he first traveled through that still-pristine region. William, son of a Scotsman, Robert, was journeying with his parents from Stratford, Canada, in 1872 to establish an Indian trading post somewhere in the middle of America's thirtieth state, which was still part of the frontier. Mitten-shaped Wisconsin lay between two Great Lakes and the Mississippi River, full of dense forests and wildlife, bejeweled with thousands of lakes, but inviting only to the most hardy, determined, and independent-minded pioneers. The Connors qualified.

Two of William's uncles had arrived ahead of his family, and together the family cleared the land, constructed a sawmill, built a store and post office, and started a school. William, known as W. D., grew up in the town the Connors founded, Auburndale, and worked at the sawmill in between his schooling. Then he took over the reins of the R. Connor Company. William quickly expanded the company, which became a significant banking, farming, and retail empire. The Connor Company and only two other enterprises owned most of the state's hardwood forests by 1895, and that year W. D. decided to move his home and company headquarters to a fast-growing city that impressed him: Marshfield.

In one sense, the founding of Marshfield was the result of a nineteenth-century anxiety that gripped American leaders about the "vulnerable" northern states—a post–Civil War fear of invasion and occupation by Canada. The solution was two-fold: build a defensive "highway" of railroad links, and settle the areas with immigrants as soon as feasible. Marshfield followed soon after the railroad. In only a decade, the bustling city grew to two thousand citizens, not all of whom were welcome. Near the railroad depot a slew of saloons and bawdyhouses grew into what was dubbed "Rotten Row," catering to restless residents and crews from lumber camps. But in 1887, an "act of God" eliminated Rotten Row for good, along with the rest of the town. After several weeks without rain that summer Marshfield was a powder keg. Huge piles of sawdust and discarded wood, seventeen million board feet of lumber, and various chemicals used or derived from the lumbering process were set ablaze by a spark from a passing train. The fire grew so quickly that boards and debris were soon exploding high into the air, and some thought "the end of the world was coming," according to accounts of the day. Not even dynamiting a portion of Marshfield as a firebreak could save the business district and many homes from destruction.

Amid the smoldering embers the next day, Mayor William Upham, a prosperous lumberman and the town's principal employer, made the decision that changed the town's future: he would stay. In less than a year the town was a phoenix, risen from the ashes, its Rotten Row gone, and new brick buildings in place of the previous wooden ones. These were the kind of people W. D. Connor wanted to be among.[2]

At the turn of the century, like a siren song, politics called W. D. Connor. He served on the city council and the Wood County Board for twenty years, but that was not enough for a visionary of Connor's scale. The state's motto is "Forward," and that's where Connor wanted to be. Wisconsin's new Republican governor in 1900, Robert La Follette, became Connor's standard-bearer. La Follette used his six years as governor to launch the Progressive Movement, a natural outgrowth of the predominant German-American constituency of Wisconsin, who were following progressive ideas similar to those of Germanic peoples of Europe. La Follette revamped government programs, started the country's first workers' compensation system, and instituted a state income tax to pay for new government programs to help average citizens.

Connor served as state Republican Party chairman during this time. He represented Wisconsin at the national Republican Convention in 1904 and became friends with Presidents Theodore Roosevelt and William Howard Taft. La Follette became a U.S. senator in 1907, and W. D. Connor at the same time became lieutenant governor.

Marshfield's First Presbyterian Church needed a new minister in 1911 and settled on a young man then preaching to the Presbyterian congregation in Prairie du Sac, Melvin Robert Laird. Reverend Laird was born in 1878 and raised on a farm in Griggsville, Illinois. He worked his way through Illinois College, after which he taught school and became principal of a high school. Then it was to Princeton University divinity school for his master's degree and then an Illinois university to become doctor of divinity. The four years at Prairie du Sac was his first Presbytery, and he was ready to serve the larger congregation in Marshfield.

The new bachelor reverend quickly fell in love and married Connor's oldest daughter, Helen, after she graduated from the University of Wisconsin in 1912. Reverend Laird married into wealth and power but still wanted to make his own way, which he could only do by leaving Marshfield. He left with his new wife in 1913 after accepting a pastorate at Lincoln, Illinois, where he was later promoted to be president of Lincoln College, a Presbyterian institution. Also in Lincoln, two sons were born to the Lairds—William Connor and Richard, known as Connor and Dick.

World War I interrupted Reverend Laird's career, and he enlisted in the army as a chaplain. For more than a year he served with the 335th Regiment in France while his wife and two boys waited at the Connor family home in Marshfield. After the war Reverend Laird moved his family to another pastorate, this time the Westminster Presbyterian Church in Omaha, Nebraska, where his third son and namesake, Melvin Robert Laird Jr., was born on September 1, 1922. "My parents had saved the best name for me, because there's no better thing that a father can leave a son," Laird later said. "The greatest inheritance I ever had was this fine, honorable name."[3]

⌇

After four years of raising three boys and tending to the duties of a minister's wife far from her Connor family home, Helen was drained, physically and emotionally. Reverend Laird set aside his career to take his wife home to Marshfield for recuperation. There was no full-time ministerial assignment there, so he accepted his father-in-law's offer to become secretary-treasurer of Connor Lumber Company. W. D. had a house at 208 South Cherry Street, right across the street from his own. If it was a bitter pill for Reverend Laird to swallow he never voiced it. It certainly changed young Melvin Jr.'s life for the better. All the values and interests he later demonstrated in life were culled from that town and its people. He bragged so often about the Wisconsin town that presidents from Dwight D. Eisenhower to William Jefferson Clinton knew he was "the man from Marshfield." Senator John Chafee, of Rhode Island, said, "We all knew that Mel Laird had roots in this little town of Marshfield, Wisconsin. And he brought friends and people from there along with him in his career. I always thought of Mel from a little town up there, out there in the Midwest—you know, he was, sort of AMERICA. The man from Marshfield."[4]

The childhood Laird describes was Norman Rockwellian. Home was safe and solid with oak—the hardwood floors on two levels, the baseboards, the french doors opening out to the porch. Most meals were eaten at home, and Sunday night supper was served on a tea cart near the fireplace in the living room, where the family laughed and talked into the night. His mother made *stollen* at Christmas, a sweet German bread with nuts and raisins. And there was a baby brother, David, to fuss over—the fourth and last child.

In young Laird's view, he had the perfect parents—a loving mother and a father who, he declared, was "the most respected man in town." His father would hold court every morning at the Coffee Cup Restaurant, planning important town affairs or discussing Greek mythology with Greek immigrants. Melvin Sr. was elected to the Wood County Board, serving for a dozen years, the last two as chairman. And nearly every Sunday there were requests from towns far and near to fill in for their absent Presbyterian pastors. No matter how busy he was he always made time to be home each day at noon to have lunch with Mel.

In those days family and close friends called Melvin Jr. by a nickname that stuck—"Bom." His aunt Marion Connor was an opera singer who went to Italy for training. In one letter home she had asked, "How is our little bambino doing?" The family took to calling Mel "bambino" and then shortened it to "Bom." He was popular in school and as rambunctious as the next boy. He accumulated friends such as Bob Froehlke, who became a lifelong confidante. Bom's second grade teacher gave him an F in conduct, and his sixth grade teacher cracked him with a rubber hose to instill obedience. He was quite a businessman, operating his own door-to-door vegetable business, soft drink stand, and fireworks booth.

Marshfield was full of wonders for a young boy. Brilliant electric lights each night turned Central Avenue, an eighteen-foot-wide boulevard, into the Great White Way featured on postcards. There was the beginning of a zoo, and the World's Largest Round Barn, built by Grandfather Connor on the fairgrounds. It was 150 feet in diameter, 70 feet high to the top of the cupola, and could fit 250 head of cattle in its stalls. The ice man made his rounds, stocking the Kelvinators through alley doors, which meant homemade popsicles now and again. The vendors of the two popcorn wagons downtown would give free kernels, the "old maids," if one asked nicely. The Pickle Pond was good for ice skating in the winter, and there was a new city pool for swimming in the summer.

When Bom was young, there were as many horses as cars in Marshfield. But that began to change after the first concrete road came through town and became part of the Yellowstone Trail, a tourist route to the national park. Sometimes a famous fellow or two would come through—like Baby Face Nelson, who bought a getaway car in Marshfield while he was on the lam after killing a federal agent and slipping through a police dragnet. Little Bom's fascination with autos and the folks who drove them came to cost him dearly. When he was eight a car ran over his left knee, breaking his kneecap. He confessed that he hadn't seen the car because he and a young girlfriend were busy stealing fresh peas off a passing wagon. That single accident prevented him from excelling at sports, hard as he would try.

Laird's family was part of the town's elite, but they didn't display their wealth. If Bom wanted spending money for the "Dime Dinger" of Westerns and serials at the Adler Theater, he had to earn it himself. At a time when the local newspaper was decrying an outbreak of "peddler nuisance," which it called "a natural consequence of the depression," Bom was a peddler par excellence. He started at about six years old selling can openers door-to-door with his brother Connor and then went into business for himself. For several years in grade school he was a middleman for farmers, selling corn, potatoes, and tomatoes to a list of regulars.

At the age of ten, Bom decided what he wanted to be most of all was a U.S. Navy officer. Or at least wear the uniform. The dream was born on a sunny morning in 1932, when he rounded a corner downtown and came face to face with the first navy officer he had ever seen in land-locked Marshfield. The navy commander in brilliant dress whites with gold trimmings was visiting an uncle who owned a dry goods store in Marshfield, and the officer's name was John ("Slew") McCain Sr. The boy trailed the man for most of the day, pestering him with questions about the navy and basking in the reflected glow of that bright white uniform twinkling with brass buttons.

Not too many years later, during World War II, the boy and the man would share a beer on an island in the South Pacific, where the admiral was the commanding officer of a naval task force and the boy was a lowly ensign in that command. A decade or so later, Congressman Laird would work closely with that admiral's son, Navy Commander John S. McCain Jr., who would be liaison between the navy and Congress. Another decade later, McCain Jr., commander of the Pacific Fleet during the Vietnam war, would be reporting to Secretary of Defense Melvin Laird. They would work together to free Navy Commander John S. McCain III from a prisoner of war camp—not guessing then that he would become a respected U.S. senator and presidential candidate.[5]

⌇

There were dark shadows in Laird's Rockwell painting. In a dispute over water rights, one Marshfield farmer sent a surprisingly well-crafted letter bomb to an opponent, which blew off his right hand and killed his wife. There was a violent milk strike, during which Marshfield's police were deployed at the edge of town to turn back a parade of angry farmers. The "Hobo Jungle" by the tracks got more crowded and dangerous every day, prompting the police to shoot the vagrants' stew pans full of holes as a way of encouraging them to move on. And several Marshfield businesses failed, including two of the town's three banks—forced into bankruptcy when townspeople overran the banks all on the same day in 1932.

As Laird grew into his teenage years, he became aware of ethnic, racial, and religious divisions. Marshfield had been built and financed by Protestant

Yankee settlers, and the labor had come from immigrants, mostly from Germany and Austria, who were Catholic or Lutheran. The Presbyterians and the Episcopalians were at the top of the pecking order; the Methodists, Baptists, and Lutherans floated around the middle; and the Catholics were toward the bottom of the economic scale. It was as much a rich-versus-poor as it was a religious debate, and it simmered for decades, occasionally breaking out in "gang wars," as *Marshfield News-Herald* accounts called them.

Laird himself was never involved in the fisticuffs, but the many issues of the day—from union organizing to a Ku Klux Klan rally in Marshfield—were fodder for active discussion and debate at the Laird home. The family took pains in the late 1930s to help German Jewish refugees, Dr. Stephan Epstein and his wife, Elsbeth, learn English by reading with them night after night, occasionally stopping to hear Epstein's account of the growing threat of Adolf Hitler. Epstein took a special interest in Bom and greatly influenced his future course.

Throughout Bom's school years all the Lairds were voracious readers. In that era, the president of the University of Chicago, Dr. Robert Hutchins, and a colleague, Dr. Mortimer Adler, had come up with a list of one hundred recommended "Great Books" that all students should read. The Lairds modified the list for their own challenge. Mother Helen had learned in her father's house and at the university to value intelligent opinions well expressed. "Knowledge Is Power" was one of W. D.'s favorite maxims. His $2,500 gift made possible the Marshfield Public Library. Helen followed in his interests, becoming president of the city library board. She invited educators and religious and political leaders to Sunday teas, hosting the meek and the mighty, from a second grade teacher to presidential candidate Wendell Willkie.

But in those early years, Bom seemed to value discussions with his father the most. No subject was forbidden, not even questioning Reverend Laird's core belief in God. "You make up your own mind on that, Bom." he would say. "I think it's fine for you to question. Always question. You've got to come to your own conclusions on this thing, but here's what I believe."

The first time Bom drank beer, at a tavern called Strikey's when he was about sixteen, guilt took him to his teetotaling father's confessional the next day. Reverend Laird said the decision whether to drink or abstain was up to Bom, but father would prefer that son didn't imbibe. Bom was careful after that to drink only in moderation.

Marshfield's dilapidated McKinley High School burned down when Bom was still in junior high school, so he spent his early high school years in temporary quarters until the new Marshfield Senior High opened in 1940, just in time for him to join its first graduating class. He was the a leader on the winning debate team and editor of the yearbook but admitted that he never let school stand in the way of a good time. Once when school was dismissed for a pep rally, Bom and some friends went duck hunting instead. Their absence was noted, and the acting principal called them on the carpet: "You are the cream of the crop, and you are making a mistake competing with our average students. You are the kind of people who will excel best by competing only with yourselves."

Bom was at his entrepreneurial peak during his senior year. He had many enterprises, one of them as the booking agent for "Earl Ostrander and His Musical Mutineers—That Ten Piece Band from the Dairyland," getting them prom gigs in surrounding towns. In another venture, he talked several class-mates into signing a thirty-day note for a $100 loan from a bank to put on a dance. The dance did well but he had to do some quick borrowing elsewhere when the bank's cashier breathlessly pulled him out of class, insisting on pay-ment two weeks ahead of time because a bank examiner on their premises was not likely to favor loans to teenagers.

The coup de grace for foresight and chutzpah occurred at the state basket-ball championships. As it happened, that year Marshfield had a dream team of sorts. They lacked height and experience; only one of the "Invincible Five" (which included Laird's good friend Bob Froehlke) had played the year before. But they pulled off a basketball Cinderella story. There were game-winning long shots in the last seconds, one of them in double overtime. The team went all the way to the state championships, where they lost in the final showdown by only one point. Somehow Laird foresaw the team's success early and booked a room at a Madison hotel with two beds. As the Marshfield team got nearer to the regional finals, desperate local fans couldn't find a room in Madison for any price. So Laird and his buddy Jack McDonald slept for free in the beds while five classmates slept on the floor and paid the hotel bill.

Laird graduated thirtieth out of a class of 165. The graduation speaker was his father, who gave a rousing address on "Eternal Verities," being faith, hope, and charity. Reverend Laird's eternal optimism worked its magic on his son. Despite ominous war clouds over Europe that spring of 1940, he left the gradu-ation ceremony convinced he could make his own way in the world.

~~~

A coin toss brought Mel Laird to Carleton College, in Northfield, Minnesota, in the fall of 1940. The previous June, he and friend Bill Copps had locked themselves in a room with six bottles of Coke, a can of popcorn, and five col-lege catalogues. After two hours they flipped a coin. Copps went to the Univer-sity of Wisconsin and Bom went to Carleton.[6] He arrived on campus without a plan. His career preferences were teacher, engineer, minister, or journalist, but a Carleton professor, Larry Gould, turned him to science. Gould had been the number two in command with Admiral Richard E. Byrd on his Antarctic ex-peditions from 1929 to 1930. Laird found a universality in science and focused on organic chemistry.

But college classes never received his full attention. As in high school, there were extracurricular, entrepreneurial, and social activities that commanded his interest. He ran a laundry service for students—not doing the dirty work himself but franchising it out to other students and taking 20 percent off the top. He also jumped quickly into a new "co-operative social" program at Carleton which provided entertainment and dances for members only. Laird's favorite duty for the co-op was traveling to Chicago to book bands through the William Morris Agency, including Cab Calloway of "Hi-De-Ho" and "Minnie the Moocher" fame. Laird also dabbled in politics. He was elected president of the freshman class, and at the first freshman mixer he met a bright, pretty girl from Indianapolis, Barbara Masters. They hit it off immediately and dated no one else during their freshman year.[7]

On December 7, 1941, in the first semester of Laird's sophomore year, the Japanese attacked Pearl Harbor, and every young man had a choice to make. Laird was anxious to join the navy immediately, but a college dean persuaded him to wait several months. During that time it was hard to concentrate on his studies so he decided to join the Carleton equivalent of a fraternity, the Phillo Society. Initiation was a scavenger hunt, sending Laird and fellow pledges scurrying around Northfield and beyond for items on a list. One of them was a standing ashtray from the Nicolett Hotel, where the pledges were spotted by the police, nabbed, and taken to the local precinct for questioning. No record was kept by police of the theft, but the college dean, Lindsey Blayney, gave an account of it, at Laird's insistence, to the U.S. Navy recruiting office in early spring 1943, when Laird was ready to enlist. The dean wrote, "It speaks well for young Laird, I think, that he told me he was going to make a frank statement to you about the matter.... Laird is a very fine young man in every way."

With Dean Blayney's recommendation, and others, Laird was called into the Naval Reserves office for a physical. Although he was honest about his scrape with the law, like many other young men who were anxious to serve their country, he fudged the truth about other things that could have disqualified him—his bad knee and a weak right eye. He managed to hide the knee difficulty, but dissembling about his eyesight required a clever deception.

"Put your hand up to your right eye and read the chart," the optometrist commanded. Laird put his left hand up to his right eye, and read it flawlessly.

"Alright, let's try the other eye."

Laird dropped his left hand, and put his right hand over the same eye. And he read it perfectly again. The sleight of hand was good enough to win him admission into the U.S. Naval Reserves Officers Training Program. Ever since admiring Commander McCain a decade before, Laird would think of joining no other service, particularly since the sea was already the service of choice for his two older brothers during World War II.[8]

By December 1942 the terrible machinery of war had chewed up boys who were close to Laird. Marshfield's contingent attached to the famous "Red Arrow" 32nd Division—Company C, 128th Infantry Regiment—got into the thick of things during the battle of Papua, New Guinea. The 32nd's losses in that terrible land battle were very high, and Marshfield boys were among the slain. A more terrible reality came soon enough for Laird—the loss of his oldest brother, Connor.

Connor had learned of the Pearl Harbor attack when he was in Chicago with his friend Walter Kohler, a future three-term governor of Wisconsin, and the son of the bathroom fixtures company founder. The pair went to the navy recruiting office first thing the next day, December 8, and signed up. By early 1943, Ensign Connor Laird was one of twenty-nine men assigned to a minesweeper, *YMS-133*, operating out of Coos Bay, Oregon. *YMS-133* was one of dozens of such U.S. Navy minesweepers assigned to the Pacific Ocean, from the California coast to the western Pacific. Almost as dangerous as the mines was a hidden sand bar in the bay, formed where the Coos River empties into the ocean. In good weather, crossing the bar is tricky, and in bad weather, it is deadly—as dozens of shipwrecks attest. On February 20, 1943, the inexperienced skipper of the *YMS-133* was no match for the sand bar in the high seas and turbulent weather. The captain tried to turn the ship around to head out to sea, in the process putting it broadside to the swells. A twenty-five-foot wave washed over it and rolled the ship twice, filling it with water and sand. Eight men including Ensign Connor Laird died in minutes. Two boats braving the rough seas picked up twenty-one survivors but five of them later died. Connor's body was later recovered.[9]

With the news of his brother's death, Laird knew the time of dreams was past. He put off marriage to Barbara and pushed the navy to give him orders for active duty. In August 1943 he reported to St. Mary's College in Winona, Minnesota, for the navy's V-12 training courses. In December Laird was transferred to Harvard for specialized classes in supply, disbursing, and paymaster practices.[10] But Harvard had run out of room for the Supply Corps school. So Laird and more than two hundred other midshipmen were assigned to two dormitories and Supply Corps classes at the all-female Wellesley College. (Thus Laird became one of the few men in America then who could say he attended Wellesley.) Laird was appointed morale officer—the easiest job he would ever have in the navy, given that there were more than two thousand women at the school.

The courses ran from December until the following April 1944. At Laird's request Carleton College accepted credits from St. Mary's and Wellesley, and he earned his diploma. Before he was to report to a new destroyer being built in Bath, Maine, Laird was given a short leave. Instead of attending his college graduation he asked Barbara to meet him in Marshfield. There he proposed engagement, using a ring his mother gave him from her grandmother. Barbara accepted. Laird was willing to be engaged, but not to risk marriage yet, in case he did not return.

To inlander Melvin Laird the USS *Maddox* was impressive at first sight. The latest of the new Sumner class 2,200-ton destroyers, she had been built at the Bath Iron Works in less than six months. Sleek and ready for action in her camouflage paint, the two-stack, twin-screw, 376-foot-long destroyer rode easily upon the gentle waters of the Boston Navy Yard on June 2, 1944. At 3 P.M., during a brief ceremony attended by Ensign Laird, the *Maddox*—third ship to be named after a distinguished marines captain of the 1800s—was commissioned.[11] Her captain, James S. Willis, was a quiet man not given to levity. He had under him a crew of 338, with twenty officers.[12] Ensign Laird was designated the ship's supply and disbursing officer. He was responsible for all the ship's stores including pay, food, ammunition, oil, and parts. After sea trials out of Boston, Laird supervised the loading of a staggering amount of ammunition, which was stored in every nook and cranny throughout the ship, including racks in sleeping quarters.

The *Maddox* left port on July 6 for a thirty-seven-day shakedown cruise to Bermuda and back. The ship's doctor, Malcolm Burris, recalled that, in preparation for an admiral's inspection, Laird mustered his men for a preliminary dress inspection. He spotted one pair of scuffed-up shoes on sailor William Grubbs, who explained he didn't have a nicer pair. Laird gave him special leave to "requisition" a new pair at the Naval Yard. In the next inspection with the admiral on his way, Laird was visibly upset to spot, amid the spit-and-polish black footwear, the same old pair of scruffy shoes on the sailor.

"Grubbs, where in the hell are those new shoes I sent you for?"

"Well, sir, I'm saving them for a special occasion!"

Laird barely suppressed his laughter at this naïve seaman, who was probably saving them for a date back in Boston instead of the most important special occasion he would have on the ship—the admiral's inspection. With Grubbs re-shod, the *Maddox* passed the inspection, as it had the other tests, with flying colors.[13]

Ensign Laird was quietly reflective Sunday, August 27, 1944, when the *Maddox* sailed past the Boston light for the last time on the way to the war zone. Many other sailors cheered. They had been grousing ever since the Normandy invasion in June that it was taking too long to get into the war. With all the patriotic naïveté of the uninitiated, the men were anxious to be off to war before it was over. The veterans knew better, and so did Laird. Having already lost a brother, he was anxious to do his duty but would have no complaints about "missing the war" if peace were declared before he got there.

The *Maddox* stopped at the Norfolk, Virginia, naval station to join two other destroyers to escort a new aircraft carrier, the USS *Ticonderoga*, to the Pacific Theater. The crew settled down to the sobering task ahead of them. They crossed through the Panama Canal and, on September 24, entered Pearl

Harbor and passed the remains of the USS *Arizona,* a sobering reminder of the Japanese attack three years earlier.[14]

The officers and crew had already learned that it paid to be on Ensign "Pay's" ship. The boy who had cut his teeth on a vegetable stand in Marshfield and a laundry franchise in college was a supply officer of the first order, with commendable scavenging skills that allowed the *Maddox* to be better supplied than most other destroyers. Others on the crew were equally enterprising. One group took a large truck to pick up twenty gallons of paint from the Pearl Harbor supply depot. While the officer on duty was getting the paint, the *Maddox* men liberated hammers, blocks, and coil lines behind his back. The launch back to the ship was so heavy with the booty that Coxswain William Boynton ran it aground. When this "raiding" party finally made it back to the *Maddox,* recalled one participant: "I noted with interest that Mr. Laird gratefully accepted all the gifts that the supply depot had provided without any questions."[15]

On October 6, as the *Maddox* sailed from Pearl Harbor, the men did not suspect it would be a full year before they would return. And not all of them would come back.

When the *Maddox* arrived at these western Caroline Islands, the atoll of Ulithi was the anchorage for the largest naval armada ever assembled—before or since. In late summer, the Third Fleet commander, Admiral William "Bull" Halsey, had selected the atoll as the ideal strategic naval base for the invasion of the Philippines and the final push against Japan's home islands. Ulithi's deep lagoon could accommodate more than seven hundred naval vessels, and the surrounding ring of islets would support an airfield, a hospital, repair structures, and a recreational island. When the *Maddox* arrived at the Ulithi lagoon on October 21, most of the fleet was out, fully engaged in the second battle of the Philippines. The day before, General Douglas MacArthur had waded ashore at Leyte and famously declared, "I have returned," urging Filipinos to rise up and strike their Japanese occupiers as the American invasion moved forward. When the triumphant fleet returned to Ulithi, the armada was a breathtaking sight for the men of the *Maddox.* Within a day hundreds of ships dropped anchor in the vast lagoon, forming neat "Murderers' Rows," as they were called, including formidable lines of battleships, aircraft carriers, cruisers, and destroyers.

The *Maddox* was assigned to Task Force 38, the Third Fleet's renowned "fast carrier task force." Halsey named an old sea dog to head the task force, the irascible Vice Admiral John "Slew" McCain, now sixty, and the same man who had left such an indelible impression on Laird when he was a youngster. (During beers shared at Ulithi, McCain provided details from his own memory to several members of the *Maddox* crew of the pesky boy who shadowed him that day.)

On November 4, the *Maddox* began its first high-speed run toward the

Philippines, more than thirty miles ahead of its task group in "Strike Picket #1 station." To end Japanese air superiority over Leyte, Halsey had ordered two days of strikes on Japanese airfields on Luzon, the largest Philippine island. Operation Pulverize destroyed 439 enemy aircraft and lost 25 of its own planes. The pilot of one of those planes had to ditch in the ocean near the Luzon coast. The *Maddox* was closest for the dangerous rescue in rough seas. One of the *Maddox* sailors dove in the water to help the exhausted aviator to the cargo net and up to the deck. Later that day, the *Maddox* made sonar contact with three Japanese submarines in the area.

After the strikes, the task groups would retreat to refuel and reprovision, before returning for more strikes. This cycle became the routine during the next month for Laird and his shipmates. During one of the fleet's returns, Halsey reconfigured the task force to face its newest and most deadly naval threat yet—the kamikaze. These young, often inexperienced pilots flying older Japanese planes would be escorted by more valued Japanese aviators into the fleet's operating area, where the expendable young pilots would dive-bomb American ships in the face of withering antiaircraft fire. A desperate new tactical measure, kamikazes made their startling first appearance on October 25 during the Battle of Leyte Gulf. It quickly became apparent they could do more damage to the American fleet than enemy ships or nonsuicidal fliers. Almost one in every four found a target and did some damage, and one in thirty-three sank a ship.

To combat this swiftly growing threat, Admiral Halsey radically changed the mixture of aircraft on board the large carriers. And he required all returning aircraft to make a full circle around the outlying destroyers, such as the *Maddox,* for inspection.. This made every destroyer in these new positions the most likely target for kamikazes, and thus the most dangerous post of the entire task force. The *Maddox* drew the tense forward assignment as a radar picket ship for every sortie because it was one of the few destroyers that had been equipped with the newest YE/ZB homing gear that made it easier for returning U.S. aircraft to find the ship.[16]

As the American fleet pushed its way across the Pacific, island by island, battle by battle, its victory seemed inevitable—except to the Japanese. The national Shinto religion implied that Japan was fated to rule the world; defeat was impossible. Emperor Hirohito was the Son of Heaven, and the forces of nature themselves would be harnessed, if necessary, to defeat the invading infidels. After all, it had happened before. In 1281, a large Mongol fleet sent by the great Kublai Khan was bearing down on a far smaller Japanese naval force. Another victory for the Mongols seemed unavoidable, followed by the invasion of Japan and annihilation of her people. At a propitious moment, heaven intervened and sent the legendary Kamikaze—"Divine Wind"—against the Mongols. This monstrous typhoon destroyed the Khan's fleet. Later, when Japan's suicide air corps pilots needed a name, they became the modern kamikazes, a new Divine

Wind that would save the empire from the largest fleet assembled in the history of mankind.

By mid-December 1944 Admiral Halsey had been fully apprised of the destructive force the kamikaze pilots could cause his Third Fleet in the last year of the war. He made alterations to his battle strategy and armament to meet the threat. But Halsey failed to adequately prepare for nature's kamikaze—a monster typhoon. His fleet had already sailed through severe Pacific storms, and one significant typhoon in November, so he paid little attention as another storm descended on his fleet. It cost him, and America, dearly. On December 18, before the storm was finished with the Third Fleet, 3 destroyers sank, 146 airplanes washed off carriers, and 778 men were lost.

For Melvin Laird and the *Maddox,* the ordeal began four days earlier with a series of pilot rescue attempts that had depleted the ship's fuel supply. Escorting a carrier task force was a fuel-intensive business, so on December 16, Admiral Halsey instructed all 132 vessels of Task Force 38 to meet at a rearward replenishment rendezvous the following morning. He was unaware that a furious storm was blanketing an area of eight thousand square miles and headed for the same rendezvous point.[17]

The Pacific Fleet's weather service was always on the watch for such storms, but its monitoring equipment was inadequate to catch and report in real time the fast-moving, deadly compact cyclone that became Typhoon Cobra. There was no satellite imagery, and search planes that gathered meteorological data had orders to avoid bad weather fronts. Land stations never saw Cobra coiling. Even if they had, weather reports transmitted to the fleet were always at least twelve hours old. Halsey was intent on getting the fleet refueled and back to the coast of Luzon for more strikes on December 19. A typhoon forecast would require him to let the fleet scatter, allowing each ship to find the safest course in the storm.

At 5 A.M. on Sunday, December 17, the storm conditions in the Philippine Sea reached the right pitch to become the full-fledged Typhoon Cobra. Five hours later, the first of the task force's ninety-seven ships began arriving at the refueling point through heavy seas and rain. The thirsty *Maddox* pulled alongside the battleship *Wisconsin* for refueling but was hampered by the storm and zero visibility from getting hoses from one ship to the other.

In the afternoon Vice Admiral McCain relayed Halsey's orders to discontinue fueling and head for a calmer fueling rendezvous the next morning. The *Maddox* was one of only three ships ordered to stay put and keep trying to refuel. McCain recognized the desperate need of these three destroyers to fuel immediately. The *Maddox* maneuvered alongside the tanker *Manatee,* and for an hour Ensign Laird watched from the bridge as the fueling crew on the heaving deck managed to get three hoses over from the tanker. But all of the hoses snapped. A fourth hose was manhandled into the fuel tanks and the *Maddox* and was able to fuel for seven minutes. Then a huge wave surged between the ships, causing the *Maddox* to veer sharply to port, ripping the hose beyond its limit. The men on deck covered their eyes and mouths as oil sprayed over them. A second wave tossed the two ships so close that the sailors could almost reach out and touch the tanker. One man with an axe hastily chopped the tow line to separate the ships. With no more hoses, the *Maddox* and the *Manatee* parted company.

At 3 P.M. on Sunday, Halsey ordered the task force to still another rendezvous point, putting it on a course parallel to the typhoon's track. The tankers, battleships, aircraft carriers, and other "heavies," as the sailors called them, were ready to ride out the typhoon because of their weight and size. But the top-heavy destroyers needed more help. Orders went out to the *Maddox, Spence,* and *Hickox*—the three destroyers already light on oil—to pump saltwater into their fuel tanks as ballast. Captain Willis, a veteran seaman, had already been doing that, and the *Hickox,* too, began flooding its tanks. The *Spence* never did. Her captain kept his tanks free of saltwater, still hoping to refuel.

Before midnight Admiral Halsey canceled the third fueling rendezvous coordinates and set new ones for the next morning, farther to the northwest. Captain Willis felt instinctively that it was the wrong course and would take his ship into the center of the typhoon, but he followed orders. Naval historian Samuel Eliot Morison observed with understatement that the new course Halsey had ordered "was unfortunate, as it took many ships straight into the path of the advancing typhoon."[18]

Few on the *Maddox* could sleep that night. When the ship made headway it would impale itself on each wave, forcing the twin screws out of the water, where they would spin and shake the ship with tremendous force. Other waves rolled the ship perilously. Pipe hand-holds on the bridge gave Ensign Laird something to hang on to as his feet swung out from under him with each roll and the *Maddox* leaned on its side. Down below he crouched between walls or clung to pipes during the rolls. In sick bay Doctor Burris used a how-to manual to perform his first emergency appendectomy on a sailor. With the help of two pharmacists mates holding the small intestine during the rolls, the procedure, which should have taken thirty minutes, went on for several hours. "Operating in a typhoon is like threading a needle while trotting on a horse," Burris recalled.[19]

By dawn on Monday, December 18, the waves were thought to be reaching heights of eighty feet. At 7:10 A.M. Task Force 38 was ordered to change course a sixth time. "For more than an hour," a court of inquiry later found, this heading "brought the fleet closer to the storm and contributed to the disaster."[20] Fleet meteorologist Commander George Kosco testified that by 8 A.M. he had determined the storm was a typhoon, but he offered no explanation as to why he did not send out a message to the fleet until five hours later.[21]

Finally, a little after 8 A.M., Admiral Halsey sent a message to General MacArthur, saying the fleet could not support strikes on Luzon on the nineteenth.

It had been a costly delay. By this time, the smaller ships, including the *Maddox,* acting under orders and setting aside standard rules of seamanship, had been led by their commander toward the center of the typhoon. The fleet was ordered to make the seventh course change, each of which had taxed the fuel of the small ships on the rim.

A light aircraft carrier, the *Monterey,* was in serious distress. Airplanes tied down on her hangar deck had broken loose, slammed against each other, and exploded into flames. The crew was able to put out the fire in half an hour and save the ship, but two men were washed overboard and lost. A third man on his way to help put out the fire was saved when his slide overboard was stopped by a thin ridge on deck. It was a touch of destiny for which Melvin Laird was later grateful. He didn't yet know the lucky officer, Lieutenant Gerald Ford, but the two men would one day become best friends.

As the *Maddox* and sister ships were sucked closer to the center of the storm, the winds increased to 150 miles per hour. At 11:23 A.M. the destroyer *Spence* sank. Without seawater ballasting, she was at the mercy of the waves. Belatedly Halsey directed the task force ships to scatter, with each captain allowed to take the safest course for his own ship. At noon the destroyer *Monaghan* sank, followed to the bottom within seconds by the destroyer *Hull.* Admiral Halsey didn't learn of the losses for twelve hours.

By 3 P.M. the peak of Typhoon Cobra had passed, but it took hours for the winds to abate. The search for survivors began in earnest early Tuesday, and the *Maddox* participated after first receiving 137,578 gallons of fuel. The last of only ninety-eight survivors was rescued at 11:40 A.M. on Thursday, December 21. The naval court of inquiry was conducted on the fleet's return to Ulithi. The court concluded that Admiral Halsey was solely responsible for the loss of life and damage to the ships, but that his "errors in judgment [stemmed] from a commendable desire to meet military requirements."[22]

After its minimal typhoon damage was repaired, the *Maddox* was judged fit to sail out of Ulithi with Task Force 38 on December 30. The *Maddox* was equipped with formidable armament. Whenever the claxon rang for general quarters, officers and crew assumed their battle stations. For Ensign Laird, that was the starboard aft set of 40-millimeter cannons, where one round could knock out an enemy plane.

Late on the evening of January 9 the Third Fleet began its unprecedented foray into the South China Sea. It was an excursion Admiral Halsey had been anxious to make for months, but he had been held back to support MacArthur in the Philippines. More than one hundred warships, including the *Maddox,* made this daring raid. The mission was spectacularly successful for Halsey's fleet. They launched a series of deadly strikes against Camranh Bay, Saigon, Cape San Jacques, Hong Kong, and Formosa.[23]

On Sunday, January 21, the task force was treated to the first nice weather and relatively smooth seas in almost two weeks—but that made them more vulnerable to Japanese air attack. The *Maddox* was about fifty miles east of the southern coast of Formosa, screening the "heavies" from Japanese submarines and inspecting flights of returning friendly bombers. At noon, the watches changed. Officers and crew went below for first mess. Ensign Laird was assigned to second mess, which he liked because it was less formal than the first sitting, at which Captain Willis ate. So he was at his starboard 40 millimeter a little after noon when the *Ticonderoga,* about ten miles off the port side, was dive-bombed by two kamikazes.

Those topside on the *Maddox* could see the smoke rising from the carrier, but there was no hurry to get to general quarters. Captain Willis asked the executive officer, Lieutenant Commander Fred Bush, to go down to the combat information center to listen to the radio and check the radar for bogeys. At the various gun mounts around the ship, some of the men had left their more-protected stations to eyeball the burning *Ticonderoga.* Gunner's Mate Mervin Clark went for a cleaning towel as his fellow crewman, Harlan Laws, depressed the barrels below zero in preparation for the sprucing up. Bill Jordan, manning one of the aft quad 40-millimeter guns, felt the left pocket of his dungaree shirt for a cigarette and, discovering it empty, scurried to his sleeping quarters to get a pack of smokes before general quarters would surely be called. (He says today that "smoking saved my life.")

Ensign Laird was beginning second mess with other junior officers, all friends. He was seated at the end of the table in a seat reserved for the mess treasurer at the first mess and for Laird at the second mess because he was responsible for the cooks and stewards. In the combat information center, Lieutenant Commander Bush saw on the radar screen a dozen friendly planes coming for the *Maddox,* giving off their "friend or foe" identification signals. Then he heard a garbled transmission. He couldn't make out the words, but something about the tone of the pilot's voice made him suspicious. He called the bridge and suggested Captain Willis put the men on alert, general quarters. "Hardly had I gotten the words out of my mouth when we were hit."

Only a few sailors and officers saw the black Zero, hiding between two friendly Hellcats, drop out and dive on the *Maddox,* machine guns blazing, ripping up canvas, steel, and men. The plane drove through the upper deck; its 132-kilogram bomb exploded with such force the 2,200-ton destroyer was lifted several feet out of the water. The explosion sent thousands of shards of metal in all directions on the starboard side.

Ensign Laird and his friends in the wardroom felt the explosion before they heard it. One second they were chatting easily, eating their sandwiches, and the next second every one was thrown out of the chairs. Laird had been the closest to the explosion because it came through the starboard bulkhead behind him, which disintegrated into shrapnel.

Doc Burris rushed to the wardroom—the designated prime medical station during battle. He saw blood on the white wardroom hatch before he stepped into the conflagration. As terrible as some of their injuries were, not one of the officers was screaming or crying, which surprised Burris. Ensign Laird was on the deck at the foot of the table, bleeding in many places. After a quick once-over of all the wounded, Burris was relieved that none had been hit in the head or the chest by shrapnel. Laird had been particularly lucky because the steel back of his chair had shielded him. He had been hit in dozens of places along his left side, down his thigh and leg, and in his lower back and buttocks. The two officers to his right and the two to his left were more seriously injured. Burris quickly patched up the most serious wounds, spending most of his precious minutes on Ensign Donald Campbell, who had been to Laird's immediate left, and whose right thigh was bleeding profusely. The doctor stopped the bleeding, checked his vital signs, which were good, and rushed off to attend to the rest of his shipmates. What Burris didn't know was that a piece of shrapnel had lodged deeply in Campbell's groin area. Laird's friend from Ohio, "Soupy" Campbell, died just inches from where Laird lay on the deck. Laird was not given to talking much about that day. Was he afraid? "Oh yeah. You're *always* afraid. There's nothing wrong with being afraid." What was he thinking about? "I thought we might sink."[24]

At least five men had died within minutes of the explosion. Gunners Mate Clark lived long enough to be transferred to the battleship *Wisconsin*. Clark calmly smoked a cigarette while awaiting transfer and told his friends not to worry. In the last mail call he had received a "Dear John" from his girlfriend, who was marrying someone else. Clark had been making her a necklace in the shape of a torpedo from a stainless steel knife. After Clark died aboard the *Wisconsin*, a friend sent the necklace to Clark's mother.

It took two hours for seventeen injured men, including Ensign Laird, to be transferred in stretcher baskets by a line strung from the *Maddox* to the *Wisconsin*. The doctors on the battleship, named after Laird's home state, carved thirty-eight pieces of shrapnel out of his rear end, legs, and stomach. "They couldn't get them all without cutting me up pretty badly," Laird said. More than a dozen pieces were left in his body—some of which worked their way out through the skin over the next six decades. While aboard the *Wisconsin* he wrote his mother that he was injured but in "great shape." He didn't want her to hear a more alarming account from anyone else. Laird knew he had been lucky on this deadly day of the kamikaze. The *Maddox* had suffered eight dead and thirty-two wounded. (All the injured men, including Laird, received a Purple Heart.) The total figure for the day's kamikaze strikes on several ships was 205 sailors killed and hundreds more wounded. The following morning the *Maddox* buried her dead at sea, each wrapped in a mattress cover and weighted with five-inch projectiles.

The damage to the *Maddox* did not hamper her movement and was considered relatively moderate. The ship was ordered to return to Ulithi in company with two light cruisers and two destroyers, all assigned to escort the damaged carrier *Ticonderoga*. For the men of the *Maddox*, it was ironic that the two ships that had come across the world in tandem should be struck by kamikazes on the same day. Because the *Ticonderoga*'s captain was seriously wounded, Captain Willis was the senior officer in the task unit. So the *Maddox* took command of the six ships until they entered the Ulithi lagoon three days after the battle.

By early February 1945 Laird had recovered from his more serious wounds and was released for duty aboard the *Maddox*. The men heartily welcomed him back because the paymaster was both loved and respected. He wasn't a by-the-book man, which boosted morale. Laird knew that men were hiding cases of food and trading them at night—a can of tuna for a can of fruit cocktail. Laird, at twenty-two, understood that hard-working sailors in their late teens and early twenties had prodigious appetites. He both winked at this "requisitioning" and compensated for it. Once Laird was called on the carpet by a supply ship officer for ordering 20 percent more food than allotted. Over the TBS (talk between ships), the captain of the *Maddox* was buttonholed on the discrepancy. Ensign Laird was ordered to the bridge and put on the TBS.

"What was your question, sir?" Laird asked politely.

"Your allotment is 20 percent over what a destroyer should take on. Do you have an explanation for it?"

"Yes, sir. Just watch those guys going down the deck." And soon enough a crew member who was at that moment unloading boxes passed one to a buddy for hiding. "The allotment I've requested is what is needed," Ensign Laird said bluntly.

Finally, after a minute's consideration, the supply ship officer responded: "I understand. We're going to fill your order." The exchange was heard over the ship's loudspeaker, and everyone knew that "Pay" had managed to up the rations by 20 percent.[25]

In off-hours, Ensign Laird played cribbage or cards, smoked, and traded stories with the other officers in the wardroom. Those from Ivy League colleges would kid him about coming from small Carleton College. Lieutenant (j.g.) Paul Arbo said the real sport came after the evening meal, when the officers tried to prove who was the smartest. Laird was a tough competitor particularly on politics or almanac trivia. Ensign Gayer Bellamy, a music major from Yale, challenged Laird to hum classical tunes, and he performed ably. One night Arbo gave him a game-winning multiple-choice question: "How many counties in the state of Louisiana?" The correct answer, which Laird knew, was zero. Louisiana has parishes instead of counties. If there was a loud argument or a lively conversation, Laird was bound to be in the middle of it.[26]

While the *Maddox* was undergoing repairs at Ulithi, Captain Willis was promoted to destroyer division commander, and the *Maddox* got a new commander, Captain Selby Santmyers. The ship underwent repairs for seven weeks at Ulithi, missing the recapture of Manila and Corregidor and the February 19 amphibious landing on an eight-square-mile volcanic island called Iwo Jima. By mid-March, the fleet had a new commander, Admiral R.A. Spruance, and was renamed the Fifth Fleet, to reflect the change of command. Task force commander Vice Admiral McCain also was replaced with Vice Admiral Marc A. Mitscher, and the force was renamed Task Force 58. The fleet had 617 ships in anchorage at Ulithi, readying for the invasion of Okinawa.

When the army and marines began their assault on the island on Easter Sunday, April 1, 1945, the Japanese swung wide the gates of kamikaze hell. Instead of singles and pairs of kamikazes they created mass attacks that they dubbed *kikusui* ("floating chrysanthemum") operations. During the Okinawa campaign, the Japanese initiated ten of these massive *kikusui* attacks. The destroyers that were on outlying radar picket duty, as the *Maddox* often was, took the brunt of the assaults. Three destroyers were sunk, and many men died, among them Captain James S. Willis and ninety-three other officers on the destroyer *Bush*.[27]

As tragic as the loss of their former commander was, the men of the *Maddox* were even more grief-stricken a week later at the loss of their commander-in-chief, President Franklin D. Roosevelt, who died of a cerebral hemorrhage at his cottage in Warm Springs, Georgia. It was a black Friday the thirteenth, and Ensign Laird cried when he heard the news. "When you're a young guy out there in the Pacific in a war and you've been there a while, you wonder what's going to happen if your commander-in-chief passes away. We didn't know Truman too well, and now he was going to take over. Those things *do* have a profound effect on a young man." But the men of the *Maddox* couldn't grieve for long. News of FDR's death came in the thick of the second massive kamikaze attack.[28]

On the day designated for memorial services, Sunday the fifteenth, the *Maddox* had time for only five minutes of silent prayer. A kamikaze attack of 165 planes was already underway by then and continued by the eerie light of flares into the night. Because of the flawless antiaircraft work of ships such as the *Maddox* and naval fighter pilots not one of the kamikazes scored a hit. They were all shot down or fled the battle.

After a record forty-eight days at sea the *Maddox* got a brief respite at Ulithi. Soon enough it was back to the work of war. In one seven-hour period, before dawn on May 14, "Madplay" as the *Maddox* was known by its code name, was attacked by nine Japanese planes, including a torpedo bomber. All nine of the attacking planes were chased off under heavy fire from the *Maddox*'s guns. A few days later, the commander of the task group messaged the ships that it had been a hectic week and the next day they could probably take it easy. One of the destroyer captains responded to the admiral, "Thanks. But for the 'small boys,' see Hebrews 13:8." The executive officer on the *Maddox* looked up the biblical passage and read it aloud: "Jesus Christ (!), the same yesterday, today and forever."[29] The quote became a constant refrain between Laird and his shipmates.

On June 22 the eighty-eight-day battle for Okinawa ended. It had been the bloodiest land conflict of the Pacific war. The Japanese had lost about 110,000, and 10,755 were taken prisoner. Americans had paid for the victory with 7,613 dead or missing army soldiers and marines. Another 31,807 were wounded. The navy had paid a dear price as well. Nearly five thousand navy officers and men had been killed, and a similar number wounded. Thirty-two ships had been sunk and another 368 had been damaged—mostly by kamikazes. During the campaign an estimated 1,900 suicide sorties had been flown against the fleet, and there were many hundreds of attacks more by conventional dive bombers and torpedo planes.

The *Maddox* had earned a rest, and it put in at San Pedro Bay in the Philippines at the end of June. On July 1 Task Force 38 sailed out of San Pedro Bay for the final showdown with Japan. From here on the *Maddox* would operate only in Japanese waters. Though B-29s flying from the Marianas Islands had been systematically hammering the Japanese islands, the enemy was caught totally by surprise on July 10 when one thousand fighters and bombers from Task Force 38 attacked the capital city of Tokyo itself. For the next two weeks, the *Maddox* participated in numerous air strikes and a shore bombardment as far north as northern Honshu and Hokkaido—targets that had been outside the range of the B-29s. But the most memorable foray for the *Maddox* was a daring raid into Tokyo Bay itself in the last weeks of the war.

On July 20, Captain Santmyers received new and unusual operational orders: Destroyer Squadron 61 (DesRon61), made up of the *Maddox* and eight other destroyers, was to conduct nighttime antishipping raids in Sagami Gulf, which was in the outer reaches of Tokyo Bay. While American submarines had slipped farther into the bay, no surface ships had yet penetrated that far.

Their instructions were to fire upon enemy shipping and to shell shore facilities. This was a curious mission, Santmyers knew, since bombardment by planes would be both safer and more effective. Among other things there was the sure danger of mines. They were easy to spot in the daylight, but the idea of a high-speed run into Tokyo Bay at night seemed foolhardy, even a suicide mission. Halsey was trying to protect the more precious "heavies" of his fleet, so the smaller ships were ordered to go ahead to stir up any kamikaze boats or mines waiting in the harbor.

At 6 A.M. on July 22 the nine destroyers detached themselves from Task Force 38 "to conduct anti-shipping sweep," according to the *Maddox* War Diary. The men were on edge. The ships lined up single file to minimize damage from the mines, in the same way the first soldier through a minefield finds a safe way for others to follow in his footsteps. Shortly after 11 P.M. they came upon the first Japanese ships. The destroyers opened fire with torpedoes and guns. The four enemy ships mistakenly thought they were being fired on by planes so they sent an antiaircraft barrage upward. Soon the torpedoes and five-inch rounds of the destroyers found their marks. Though DesRon 61 didn't stick around until daylight to find out, it was believed they had sunk two, possibly three Japanese merchant ships carrying supplies to troops, and damaged the Japanese naval escort that was protecting them. The *Maddox* and its sister destroyers had approached a cornered giant, tweaked his nose, and got away without being crushed. In less than fifteen minutes, the final surface engagement of the Pacific war had begun and ended.[30]

On August 6 the United States dropped the first atomic bomb in history on the southern Honshu city of Hiroshima. The official estimate of dead—before radiation effects were known—was eighty thousand. The second bomb, on August 9, decimated Nagasaki and by official estimate killed sixty thousand. Japanese army and navy chiefs implored Emperor Hirohito to continue with the war. He overruled them, probably because he was convinced by the combination of firebombing and atomic bombs that the Allies would, if necessary, kill every Japanese citizen in order to achieve "unconditional surrender."

V-J Day (Victory in Japan) was August 15, 1945. At 1 P.M. Admiral Halsey broadcast to the whole fleet that Japan had surrendered. A shout went up on the *Maddox* and was echoed in a wave from ship to ship. The *Maddox* continued in a protective screen position outside Tokyo Bay for two weeks. On August 30 they had the proud task of escorting nine American submarines into Tokyo Bay to witness the official surrender. As the peace papers were signed aboard the USS *Missouri* on September 2, the *Maddox* was assigned as a communications link ship patrolling the entrance to Tokyo Bay.

At noon on September 20 the *Maddox* began sailing for home. Past Tokyo Bay, past scattered mines still located as much as a hundred miles out, finally, they felt safe. On the three-week sail home there was plenty of time to reflect on the future. The men, like Laird, knew they weren't the bravest to ship out to war and maybe not the most skillful, but they were definitely among the luckiest. And it was time to plan for the rest of their lives. One day the junior officers were doing just that. "We were philosophizing about what we were going to do after we got out," remembered Ensign Dorsey Thomas.[31] Tony Kane said he was going back into law enforcement. Frank Feeney planned to go to college on the GI Bill, while Tom Thorstensen was intent on earning his Ph.D. Zeke Monsell was going back to work as a manager for Atlantic Richfield Oil Company. It was Laird's turn last. Speaking plainly and directly, he said, "I'm going back to Wisconsin and be a politician."

The men were a little stunned, since they didn't hold the profession in particularly high regard. "Why that?" they chorused.

"Because, goddamn it, I think I can do some good!"

2

On Wisconsin

❧

THE SAN FRANCISCO GOLDEN GATE BRIDGE was a welcome sight
for Lieutenant (j.g.) Melvin Laird and his fellow sailors aboard the battle-worn
USS *Maddox* as they sailed under it on the crisp morning of October 5, 1945.
There were cheers and then long moments of silence as each man pondered the
next step. For Laird it was to fulfill a promise suspended by the war—to marry
Barbara Masters. Within the next six months Laird would experience one of
the most joyful moments of his life, and one of the most tragic.

Barbara had passed the war writing letters to her fiancé, earning a graduate
degree in education from Northwestern University, and becoming a teacher. She
had frequently visited her future in-laws in Wisconsin, and they had decided she
was a good match for their son. Laird's family was among Wisconsin's finest;
hers, among Indiana's best. Her father, Dr. Robert Masters, was head of Indiana
University's ophthalmology department and author of several textbooks on the
eye. Mel and Barbara decided the engagement had been long enough. Ten days
after he landed in San Francisco they were married at the Fourth Presbyterian
Church in Indianapolis. None of Laird's brothers could make the wedding, nor
any of his Marshfield friends including Bob Froehlke because many of them
were still in the service. Melvin Laird Sr. stood with his son as best man. The
newlyweds honeymooned in northern Wisconsin amidst the fall color.

Laird still had a few months to serve in the navy and was assigned as disbursing officer in the family allowance division of the navy's National Bureau
of Supplies and Accounts headquartered in Cleveland. The couple rented a
room in Shaker Heights, and Barbara landed a teaching job. Laird was assigned
the job of managing the war bond distribution and family allowance disbursing programs for the entire navy.

In early March 1946 Laird's parents went to the Mayo Clinic in Rochester, Minnesota, for their annual physicals. The doctors found colon cancer in
sixty-eight-year-old Melvin Laird Sr. and recommended immediate surgery.
Both parents decided not to alarm their children until they knew whether the
surgery was successful. Eight days after what was deemed to be a "successful"
operation Laird senior died of a pulmonary embolism. Helen Laird's call to
inform her three surviving sons of their father's death came as a bolt out of
the blue. Lieutenant Laird rushed to Marshfield. His older brother Richard
was in British Columbia and could not come home, so at twenty-three Melvin
shouldered the burden. Within hours after hearing of his father's death, Laird
decided he would move to Marshfield immediately to take care of his mother,

who was also still mourning the death of her son Connor. Laird's request for a hardship discharge was granted.[1]

At the time of his death Laird Sr. was a Wisconsin state senator and was the only clergyman in the Senate. His colleagues respected him, and his name had been whispered for a possible run for governor.[2] At least one of Laird's uncles and several friends urged him to run for his father's State Senate seat, and finish the two years left on his term. There were both poignant and practical aspects to this proposal. When Laird senior had first run for the seat in 1940, his most ardent campaigner had been his son Mel. As the *Marshfield News-Herald* later reported, "When the contest was won and the elder Laird became Wood County's first state senator in twenty years, he told friends that he was more pleased for 'Bom's' sake than for any other reason, because the boy had worked so hard."[3] Besides, Froehlke recalled with a smile, "He already had the posters he needed: 'Elect Melvin R. Laird.'"[4]

Laird didn't dawdle over the decision. Once Barbara had agreed he threw his hat into the ring less than two weeks after the funeral. The real battle was the Republican primary in August. Whoever won that was usually victorious in the November general election. Laird's opponent was a friend—an older, far more experienced State Assemblyman Walter Cook. But that didn't cow Laird. (Froehlke, who helped on the campaign, recalled how wily his friend could be. At the end of one speech in Neillsville campaigning for his father before the war, Laird had looked at his watch and said: "I'm very sorry that I can't stay. I would like to stay and greet all of you, but there's a vitally important meeting in Port Edwards that I must just rush off and attend this evening." As they left, presumably for the town on the opposite end of the district, Froehlke was puzzled: "Gee, Mel, I didn't know we're going to Port Edwards." "Just wait" was all Laird said, with a smile. After driving only a mile or so Laird pulled the car off the road, turned off the lights, and waited. Within minutes the opponent barreled past them on a wild goose chase to Port Edwards.[5])

Laird was not mustered out of the military until mid-May so much of his campaigning was done in uniform, which his opponent unwisely criticized. Each time Cook brought up the subject of the uniform, Laird responded that, being fresh from the war, he hadn't had time to buy civilian clothes. It was a regular excuse for Laird to bring up his service record. Laird won the primary handily. Cook carried his own county by a margin of only thirty-two votes, but Laird's huge numbers in his more populous Wood County cinched the primary. (The following November, with no Democratic opposition, Laird thrashed his Socialist opponent 22,374 to 821.) Laird remembered the primary as a tough campaign, and acknowledged, "I was elected on my father's reputation and good name."

At twenty-four he was the youngest man ever to serve in the Wisconsin State Senate.[6] Though Laird's win was noteworthy at the time, there was another Wisconsin Republican primary race involving another World War II veteran that captured national attention, the result of which would have a seismic effect on America in less than four years. Highly revered U.S. Senator Robert La Follette Jr. was being challenged by a brash former circuit court judge and marines officer, Joe McCarthy. The historical background that led to that critical primary is important in understanding Laird's political background and the unique Wisconsin brand of Republicanism.

Many historians believe the Republican Party was born in a little white schoolhouse in central Wisconsin when fifty-four of the town of Ripon's one hundred registered voters gathered in March 1854 to fight slavery. Alvan Bovay, an ardent abolitionist, called the meeting to protest attempts by the Democratic majority in Washington, D.C., to spread slavery into the Kansas and Nebraska territories.[7] Disaffected Whigs came to the meeting, tired of their own party's compromises on the issue. They wanted a party that would stand up to the Democrats—whom some dubbed "slavocrats"—and on that night they decided to form their own party, the Republicans. Also at the Ripon meeting was a political activist, Carl Schurz, a close friend of Illinois lawyer Abraham Lincoln. Schurz would be a key voice in pushing Lincoln to run as the Republican Party's first presidential candidate in 1860.[8]

A year after the Republican Party was formed in Ripon, a baby named Robert Marion La Follette was born in the small town of Primrose, southeast of Ripon. He would change both Wisconsin and national politics. By 1885 lawyer La Follette was a U.S. congressman on his way to bigger things. By the turn of the century he had become alarmed at the stranglehold wealthy industrialists had on the Republican Party and the state and determinedly wrested the party from them under the banner of "Progressive Republicanism." He ran a victorious 1900 campaign for governor of Wisconsin, supported in a critical way by Laird's grandfather W. D. Connor who was then the chairman of the state Republican Party.

As governor and then as a U.S. senator, La Follette and his Progressive leadership, assisted by Connor and many other able Wisconsinites, transformed American politics and social policy. What was often dubbed "the Wisconsin Idea" soon became Washington policy. For example, it was the Progressive Republicans who revolted against having political machines select candidates. Instead, in 1904 Wisconsin instituted America's first mandatory primary elections. The Progressive Republicans were also important advocates of the direct election of U.S. senators. Until 1913 senators were chosen by governors or state legislatures. Under Progressive Republicans social services in Wisconsin expanded rapidly, including America's first unemployment and workers' compensation benefit laws. A University of Wisconsin economics professor, Edwin Witte, is sometimes called the "father of Social Security" for his role in crafting that program. In 1920 Wisconsin became the first state to ratify the Nineteenth Amendment for women's suffrage. A year later Wisconsin became the first to eliminate all legal discrimination against women. State historians refer to the

Progressive Republican Wisconsin era, which continued up to World War II, as the Golden Age.

Progress was not without a price. La Follette became known as "Fighting Bob" because he split the Republican Party between "old guard" and Progressives. W. D. Connor broke with La Follette in 1912 when the senator would not support Teddy Roosevelt's presidential candidacy. La Follette had been instrumental in creating a national Progressive Party, presuming he would be its first presidential nominee. He thought he had Roosevelt's pledge of support. Instead Roosevelt himself became the Progressive Party's first presidential nominee. La Follette could not bring himself to fully endorse Roosevelt's run, which disappointed Laird's grandfather. Roosevelt was wildly popular in Wisconsin where, through a near-tragedy, he received his greatest campaign boost. As he was departing from his hotel for an October speech in Milwaukee, a would-be assassin shot him in the chest. The hero of San Juan Hill first insisted on continuing to the speech and delivering it. "I will make this speech or die," he said. "It is one thing or the other." His bravado won him renewed adulation, and he ran second in the election to Woodrow Wilson. The incumbent President Taft came in third.

A dozen years later, in 1924, Senator La Follette formally broke with the Republican Party and ran as the Progressive Party candidate for president. He had the most impressive third-party showing to date, with almost five million votes, but it was not enough. Within a year, "Fighting Bob" died. His son Robert Jr., also known as "Young Bob," held a Senate seat for more than two decades, a good portion of it as a member of the Wisconsin Progressive Party. But that party became moribund after World War II, and Young Bob formally dissolved it in March 1946, urging its members to return to the Republican fold. That meant La Follette could run for reelection as a Republican. Party bosses, however, put their support behind a young opportunist, Joe McCarthy, who had been a Democrat himself until he realized that Democrats didn't get elected in Wisconsin, so he switched to the Republican Party.[9]

Laird, who considered McCarthy an unprincipled man, could not in good conscience support his candidacy, so he actively campaigned for La Follette. But La Follette had too long neglected his Wisconsin constituent base, and he also had a drinking problem. More than once in that primary campaign, Laird, a Republican candidate himself for State Senate, covered for La Follette. "He got to the point where he couldn't appear, and I appeared for him. The problem with Bob La Follette—and I did not know it at the time—was that you just couldn't count on him because he was drinking too much," Laird said. The official explanation for La Follette's virtual absence from the state during the primary was that he was too busy with important matters in Washington.

McCarthy was a hard-working, highly attractive candidate; he portrayed himself as a war hero who was seriously injured in combat (sometimes displaying a limp), as a tail gunner on an aerial reconnaissance missions, and the winner of a Distinguished Flying Cross. He was also adept at smearing the opposition with unsubstantiated charges—a talent he would hone later in the Senate in his witch hunt for Communists in government service. The triumph of the unknown McCarthy over La Follette was not only an upset, but also the passing of an era. It was the first time in more than forty years that no La Follette family member held prominent office in Wisconsin. (Six years after he left the Senate, in March 1953, Robert La Follette shot himself to death.) More than fifty years later, Donna Shalala, secretary of Health and Human Services during the Bill Clinton administration, paid tribute to the role Wisconsin professors and politicians had played in the social services and environmental movements. "Most of the ideas that came out of Wisconsin," she said, "are in fact programs that defined this century and what kind of country we wanted to be."[10]

The Wisconsin State Senate had thirty three members, compared to the assembly's one hundred. Both legislative houses were dominated by Republicans, so twenty-four-year-old Laird began in a good starting position. He loved the legislature from the first; he felt born to it. A typical session was six months, for which legislators earned about $2,000 and a room and board stipend. To make ends meet, the Lairds shared a house in Madison with Bob and Nancy Froehlke.

Senator Laird was assigned to three committees: education, veterans, and labor. He immersed himself in the work and honed his debating skills. Testifying to his quick rise was a laudatory column only six months into his first term by a self-described "unreconstructed Socialist," Aldric Revell of the *Madison Capital Times,* the capital's liberal newspaper. Revell criticized "the mass of Republican legislators—who are unintelligent, and more to be condemned, uninterested in the public welfare." But Laird was different. In "many hours" of discussion with Laird, Revell found him to be "innately conservative" but more liberal than his father. The "strapping, handsome youngster . . . displays a maturity of judgment, a sense of humor, and a deep-seated anxiety to legislate in the public interest one expects only from mature persons."[11]

Contemporary observations such as Revell's help explain how a man in his twenties so quickly gained power in his state. One measure of that power came in 1948 when State Senator Laird twice faced down U.S. Senator Joe McCarthy and beat him both times. In the first case it was in Laird's capacity as the chairman of the state Young Republicans, during their convention at Portage, near Madison. Behind the scenes there was a struggle over who would be elected at the convention as state chairman. The party and McCarthy backed Jack Mills, the Milwaukee County Young Republicans chair. Laird had never met Mills but already favored a different young man, so he summoned Mills to come to his hotel suite to hear the bad news.

Mills was put off from the introduction—first at being summoned, and then at Laird's pashalike appearance in the room, seated in a high-backed chair on a dais, smoking a cigar. "He looked like a king or something," Mills said. After minor pleasantries, Laird came out with it: "I don't want you to run for chairman this year. I will support you in two years."

"You're kidding, right?" Mills blurted out.

"No, I'm not kidding."

Mills was a self-described "cocky little kid," and he couldn't imagine the one-term state senator had the votes against him, considering Mills had McCarthy and party bosses in his corner. And Mills certainly wasn't going to let Laird stop him on his own drive to become governor. So he threw down the gauntlet: "Senator, with Milwaukee County alone, I've got 42 percent of the votes. I'm going to carry it completely. All I need is one other county. And you're asking *me* not to run this time? I'll tell you what: I'll support *your* candidate next time."

Laird was miffed. A splotch of red started at his forehead, and crept across his whole pate. He shook a finger at Mills: "Mills, let me tell *you* something. You can't get elected with just Milwaukee and McCarthy. If you run, you're going to lose!" Mills recalled later, "I ran and I lost. I didn't get one other county. And that was the end of Jack Mills, as far as progressing in the party. I hated him. The bastard! I hated him."[12] (The two later became friends for life.)

On the national scene in 1948 a friend of the Laird family, Harold Stassen, the young governor of Minnesota, decided to make a run for the Republican presidential nomination at the age of forty. Stassen had signed up for the navy with Laird's older brother Connor, and Walter Kohler, the day after the Pearl Harbor attack. The April 6 Wisconsin primary was considered pivotal for presidential primary candidates, and the race was wide open. General Douglas MacArthur, a native of Wisconsin, ran for the nomination, though he didn't bother to come home from Tokyo to campaign. California Governor Earl Warren was also a candidate, and he sent an earnest emissary to Wisconsin to try to win over Senator Laird and other delegates. The emissary was Richard Nixon, and Laird was suitably impressed with him at their first meeting, but not enough to switch his support from Stassen, who won the Wisconsin Republican presidential primary. (New York Governor Thomas Dewey eventually won the Republican nomination and was then defeated by Harry Truman.)

The next vote among the Republican leadership in the state was for chairman of the Wisconsin delegation. McCarthy should have been a shoo-in, according to his biographer Thomas Reeves. But two of the Stassen delegates, Laird and his mother, stood in his way. Mel disliked McCarthy, and Helen didn't trust him. So they successfully backed their friend Walter Kohler Jr. in a humiliating loss for McCarthy. Kohler, the son of a popular former Wisconsin governor, was the Lairds' pick for Wisconsin's next governor.

The 1948 State Senate campaign was an easy one for Laird. He was unopposed in the Republican primary and had no Democratic opponent in the general election, which made for an easy win over a Socialist candidate. So he had time to stump for Governor Dewey. One of the most interesting and heartfelt reasons for Laird to praise Dewey was how genuinely honorable the governor was. In 1944 when he had run unsuccessfully for president against Franklin Roosevelt, Dewey had information that could have ruined FDR; he knew that the United States had broken the Japanese code prior to Pearl Harbor and had advance notice of the attack. "He never made use of this information even though many people agreed it would have elected him president that year," Laird said. Dewey chose not to use the intelligence against FDR because it would have undermined the commander-in-chief in the middle of the war. Laird extolled him as "a man of principle."[13]

Most of Laird's campaign speeches in 1948 centered on principled politics. He had been disheartened, he told one Rotary Club audience, that a recent Gallup poll found nine out of ten parents "do not want their children to go into politics because they regard it as a messy, crooked business with no future."[14] That was not the way he saw it or practiced it, and, he said in another speech, that attitude could lead the nation into "serious trouble." Politics "is the art and science of government; politics is what men and women make it; *we the people* are the government."[15]

Laird's work in the State Senate was wide ranging and reflected broad interests. He was instrumental in making much-needed improvements to Wisconsin's education system, as well as its mental health and general health institutions. He sponsored legislation allowing medical groups to practice on a corporate basis. At the time doctors' salaries were low, and they had no retirement and few other benefits. Laird thought it was vital to allow facilities like his hometown's Marshfield Clinic to operate in a more businesslike manner and attract quality doctors, as well as encourage young people to go into the medical profession.

Senator Laird did not equivocate when his political or moral principles were being violated. For example, he didn't like government handouts of any kind, not even for his fellow World War II veterans, because he knew that hardworking taxpayers would have to foot the bill. As in other states, Wisconsin politicians tried to outdo themselves with emotional votes for special veterans' benefits, wrongly believing that veterans voted en bloc at election time. Laird's record in this regard shows careful discernment. He favored rehabilitation funds and grants to those vets most in need, but he opposed across-the-board bonuses to the state's three hundred thousand vets, viewing them as budget-breaking measures. In the case of home loans for veterans, he crafted a low-interest loan that was balanced by an increase in liquor taxes, so the state didn't lose money.

Senator Laird also became a prominent state tax authority, chairing the legislative council committee on taxation. He pushed forward Wisconsin's pioneering "revenue-sharing" approach to taxation—another "Wisconsin idea" that became federal policy when Laird later persuaded President Nixon to adopt the concept. On a federal level, it meant returning some of the federal income tax to the states to use as they saw fit. On the state level, when Laird was a legislator in Wisconsin, it meant sharing state income tax funds with local and county governments, believing that those who live in the community know better how to use tax funds locally.

One of the most contentious issues during Laird's six years as state senator involved privacy of income tax records. At one point, Laird gamely went into the lion's den—before the annual convention of the Wisconsin Press Association—to debate a Democratic colleague, State Senator Gaylord A. Nelson, on the issue. One of the editors who witnessed the debate wrote in his column, "Some of the foreign journalists studying in this country, who were present, couldn't figure out how two men could get up and literally go after one another with hammer and tongs, verbally, and then sit down side by side and be physically at peace. They fully expected them to start rolling up their sleeves and begin punching each other in the nose."[16] Nelson, who went on to be a popular Wisconsin governor and then U.S. senator, said that from his first day in the State Senate in 1949 he and Laird were great friends. "Fraternizing between Republicans and Democrats in those days was not seen as a treasonable offense. A sense of good will seemed to anoint most political discourse. The political playing field was more user-friendly than it is today."

When Nelson became minority leader in the State Senate, the Republicans had twenty-eight votes and "I was backed up by a mighty strike force of four votes, including my own. Under the rules, a motion for a roll call required the seconds of five members. We only had four. Mel would always graciously raise his hand to assure that we would get a recorded vote. I was grateful for his statesmanlike generosity. However, it finally dawned on me that this wasn't a one-way street. After all, there was something in it for Mel, too—he simply delighted in beating the hell out of us Democrats in public!"

Nelson fondly recalled that less partisan time: "I did most of the debating on the Democratic side, and Mel was the best debater on their side—maybe the best debater in the State Senate. He would contest things vigorously, but he was always civil. He had strong convictions and great integrity, decency, compassion. We would debate all day long, and argue on the floor, and then at sundown sensibly move to the nearest pub to continue our friendly disputations into the night. Every so often Mel would come home with me for dinner, or we'd go to DiSalvo's Spaghetti House. It was more civilized in those days."[17]

~⚓~

By 1951, after only four years as a state senator, Melvin Laird was clearly a star headed for a higher calling. Besides his own native skills and maturity, he had also backed the right horse for governor, Walter Kohler Jr. Kohler outlined an ambitious program in early 1951, and he counted on Laird, despite his youth, as his key man in the State Senate. The *Madison Capital Times*, the voice of the liberal wing of the Democratic Party, was unhappy with Laird's fast rise. In late summer, editor William Evjue published a scathing editorial: "Sen. Laird, who plays politics like the spoiled rich boy who takes his bat and ball and goes home when he can't get his way, has been throwing his weight around at meetings of the Legislative Council. [The] bullying...suits Sen. Laird's character. He is a young man for whom things have come easy. He inherited his political position and his economic security from his parents.... He sees no need for improving anything except his own political position."[18] The paper was right about one thing. An ambitious Laird *was* interested in "improving" his own political position, though primarily as a way, as he had told his shipmates on the *Maddox*, to improve the lives of others.

The previous March, Laird had taken a sentimental journey with Governor Kohler as a member of a small state delegation to Portsmouth, Virginia, for the recommissioning of the USS *Wisconsin*. It was the very ship on which Laird had recuperated from severe shrapnel wounds.[19] After the ceremonies were over, Laird and others decided to come home by way of Washington, D.C. It was Laird's first visit to the capital, and he felt washed with patriotism. The monuments, particularly the Lincoln Memorial, were awe-inspiring. He recalled that he felt much like the Jimmy Stewart character in Frank Capra's *Mr. Smith Goes to Washington*.

But for Laird, more important than the monuments were the people. He made an appointment with friends and mentors, Wisconsin Republican Congressmen John Byrnes and Glenn Davis. Before their meeting he wanted to see Davis in action on the floor of the House of Representatives. After he took a gallery seat, he was pleased to observe Davis in the middle of a debate supporting a colleague, Republican Congressman Gerald Ford from Michigan, who was only in his third year of Congress. Ford was arguing against an appropriations bill that was loaded with expensive goodies for the districts of congressmen on the Appropriations Committee. Laird watched as Davis and Ford courageously and publicly opposed parochial waste. "He and Glenn were making an all-out effort to eliminate the pork in that bill, and doing a splendid job even though they were in the minority party," Laird recalled. "It was the first time I saw Jerry Ford operate on the floor of the House of Representatives, and he did a hell of a job on that debate." The four went to dinner afterward, and Laird soaked it all in.

What impressed him most was that here were three idealistic men for whom their conscience was their primary constituent. Washington would be a great place to be, especially in the company of such men.

3

Mr. Laird Goes to Washington

THE U.S. CONGRESSMAN for the Seventh District of Wisconsin, Reid Murray, was a tall, imposing man. His campaign in 1938 to defeat an incumbent Progressive who had held the seat for eight years was the stuff of state legend. Murray, an agriculture agent who also had been a professor of animal husbandry, knew the district's dairy farmers were rightly upset about closed world markets for their products. So he campaigned for free trade, taking with him everywhere an impressive Holstein cow he named "Reciprocity" to emphasize the issue. Murray and Reciprocity won handily.[1]

Murray had proved a popular congressman in his district, but in the summer of 1951 he became ill, and the buzz in newspapers and at the statehouse was that he would drop out, and fast-rising State Senator Melvin Laird Jr. would run for his seat. While in the hospital recovering from cataract surgery in mid-April 1952 the sixty-four-year-old Murray announced he would run again. Two weeks later he was dead.

For a second time the death of a man Laird respected would advance his career. Laird was playing cards with friends, including journalists and legislators, at a Madison club when the phone call came telling him of Murray's passing. He was silent for nearly an hour and then broke his silence with a resolute pronouncement: "I'm going to run."[2] Out of respect for Murray's family, Laird waited two weeks to announce his candidacy. But he wasted no time in setting the campaign in motion. He asked Bob Froehlke, who was then an attorney with Hardware Mutuals (later Sentry Insurance) in Stevens Point, Wisconsin, to take a leave of absence and manage the campaign.

Another man toying with the idea of national office that spring was war hero General Dwight Eisenhower. Laird liked Ike for president, but the general couldn't be persuaded to declare his candidacy before the Wisconsin primary of April 1, 1952. Laird had accompanied Wisconsin Governor Walter Kohler for a lobbying visit to Eisenhower in early 1951, where the two Wisconsinites had tried to persuade the general to enter the Wisconsin primary. A candidate's name could only be on the ballot if he or she gave permission, and Wisconsin did not allow write-ins. But Eisenhower told them, "I'm not going to be a candidate." At the time Eisenhower wasn't even firmly in the Republican camp; President Truman was urging him to run as a Democrat. While Eisenhower was reckoned a near-sure bet to win the presidency if he decided to run, no one was absolutely sure which party he would join. Conservative Republican critics who were suspicious of him acerbically called him "General Eisenhowever."

Laird expected to be a statewide delegate-at-large to the Republican National Convention, and he had to pledge his support to someone for president, so he settled on Ohio Senator Robert Taft. As the Senate minority leader, Taft was the titular head of the Republican Party. The son of former president William H. Taft, the highly respected senator was often referred to in Washington and the media as "Mr. Republican." When Ike finally indicated in early 1952 that he would run as a Republican, it was too late to register for the Wisconsin primary. But his campaign manager, Senator Henry Cabot Lodge Jr., wrote Laird in April trying to get him to renege on is pledge to Taft and swing to Ike. Under Wisconsin law, delegates were required to support the person to whom they were pledged unless the candidate released the delegate or the candidate failed to poll 5 percent of the total vote. However, there was no penalty for violating the law, so theoretically the delegate could switch. Laird wrote back to Lodge that he had given his word. Ike wouldn't want him to break his word, would he? Lodge replied, "I understand your position perfectly and can also assure you that General Eisenhower is not the kind of man who would ever play the part of a short sport."[3]

When the Republicans gathered in Chicago in July for their twenty-fifth national convention—the first ever to be nationally televised—Wisconsin's delegates, including Laird, dutifully stuck with Taft. But Eisenhower won the party's nomination. Laird could not have wished for a better outcome for two key reasons. First, like most Americans, Laird genuinely admired Ike and knew the popular, charismatic general had a greater chance to win against a Democratic candidate than the dour, conservative Taft. Second, the Taft delegates had ensured that the platform from which Eisenhower would govern, if elected, was full of Taft policies. (Taft's unexpected death from cancer the following summer meant that even if he had won the nomination and election, he would have been president for less than a year.)[4]

Laird was primarily responsible for ensuring that Eisenhower would change positions on a labor issue to favor Taft's most famous contribution, the Taft-Hartley Act—a switch that helped elect Ike. The act, passed in 1947, had ended the domination labor unions had enjoyed over employers during Roosevelt's New Deal. Taft-Hartley outlawed "closed shops" where only union workers could be hired. And it allowed the president to halt a strike that threatened national interests. The law also held unions accountable if they violated workers' rights.

President Truman did the politically expedient thing by vetoing Taft-Hartley in 1947, knowing he could not win reelection the following year without the support of labor unions. But the Republican majorities in the House and Senate overrode his veto within three days. By 1952 the Republican Party was full of those favoring a national "right-to-work" law that could cripple union organizing and bargaining power. By comparison, Taft-Hartley looked harmless. Among influential fans of right-to-work was the junior senator from California,

Richard Nixon. Also, of no small matter, Eisenhower had sided with the right-to-work champions, partly as a successful effort to win over the Texas delegation from Taft.

Then Laird was picked to help write the labor, education, and welfare plank of the national Republican platform before the election. While some rejected party platforms as window dressing, Laird took them very seriously and promoted them as the party's promise for future action. With the other platform representatives, Laird arrived a week early for hearings and platform writing, and he met with top labor leaders. Though they were not pleased that he was a fervent Taft-Hartley supporter, they warmed to Laird because he opposed something they hated more—right-to-work provisions. And he promised he would write language recognizing unions—a first for a Republican platform.

Laird kept his promise, writing a relatively prolabor plank for the platform recognizing union shops. He called the language a "Labor Bill of Rights," and labor union criticism of the Eisenhower candidacy was subsequently more muted. Eisenhower accepted the platform and promoted Laird's Labor Bill of Rights. And he thanked Laird privately for giving him a labor position that was tenable. Unlike many candidates who ignore the written platform statement once the convention is over, Eisenhower was a political petri dish of still-forming views. "He needed that platform," Laird observed. "He had not had a lot of political experience, and he wanted a declaration of policy and principle on behalf of his party. So he took that platform as his declaration of what he was going to do for the next four years in office and he followed it religiously—100 percent." Historical accounts verify this pronouncement, as does Eisenhower himself in his autobiography. Eisenhower wrote: "I accepted my party's platform pledges as binding on me, and took action accordingly."[5]

⟨❦⟩

Two men opposed Laird in his first run for Congress that year in the all-important September Republican primary; it was a serious competition. Leonard Kopitzke was prominent in the state dairy industry and had been president of the Wisconsin Cheese Makers Association for thirteen years. Malcolm Rosholt was an accomplished lecturer and writer whose flashy foreign travel experience included leading a camel expedition across the Gobi Desert in central Asia. To excite public interest in his campaign, Rosholt decided to conduct it from horseback. Over a five-week period he visited seven hundred farms, averaging fifteen miles a day on the horse, which he bedded down at the last farm each day before being driven home to spend the night in his own bed.

But their opponent Laird was a popular, accomplished state senator who had the support of every daily paper in the district and almost every weekly paper. Within days of the vote, his campaign manager, Froehlke, released a letter from Governor Kohler to Laird stating: "I know no one who is better qualified to serve in Congress, nor anyone in whom I would place greater trust as a representative in Congress." The letter, which Kohler may not have intended for public release, cinched the primary election. Laird collected more votes than his two opponents put together in the Republican primary.

Another Wisconsin Republican sailing to a fairly easy primary win, despite intense in-state and out-of-state opposition, was incumbent Senator Joe McCarthy. Two years into his malicious anti-Communism campaign, McCarthy had developed some serious enemies who had uncovered some uncomfortable facts about the senator—particularly the way he had inflated his war record. His true military service was commendable but had not been flashy enough for the egotist, so he embellished broadly. As part of his first campaign for the Senate he had faked a limp and spoke of a serious leg wound, giving various causes. One was that he had been injured when a marines bomber crashed and burned near him, another that he had been hit by exploding Japanese shrapnel. As it turned out, he had slipped off a ship ladder during some horseplay as part of a crossing-the-equator initiation (called a "shellback ceremony"). The medical officer put a cast on his broken foot and later, when taking the cast off, accidentally burned McCarthy with acid, leaving a scar on his leg.

More disturbing than the faked wound was McCarthy's inflation of his flying record, which led to him being awarded medals he had not earned. That was a slap in the face to vets such as Laird, who really carried Japanese shrapnel in his leg, though he seldom spoke about it. But somehow, when McCarthy's lies were exposed, one by one, the truth did not do much to dent his home-state popularity. Republicans, including Laird, Kohler, and Eisenhower, muted their criticism of McCarthy during the 1952 campaign. For the first time in twenty years, they had a real chance to put a Republican in the White House and that could not be done if the party itself was torn apart internally. Though McCarthy was reckless, he served as an effective pit bull, weakening the Truman administration and the Democrat-controlled Congress during a critical election year. On top of that, most Republicans agreed with McCarthy that the Truman administration had not been diligent in rooting out America's main enemies, Communists, from within its bureaucratic ranks.

The conflicting currents swirling around McCarthy came to a painful head for Eisenhower in Milwaukee in early October, when circumstances conspired to produce one of the worst moments of the general's life. It prompted Truman publicly to call Ike a coward because he had not come to the defense of his friend and mentor General George Marshall when McCarthy, on the floor of the Senate, implied that Marshall's views in his new job as secretary of state favored Communism. Reports of the McCarthy speech deeply disturbed Eisenhower, but he was not anxious to take on the senator. He told associates, if "I should oppose him on the ground that he is morally unfit for office, I would be indirectly accusing the Republican electorate of stupidity, at the least, and of immorality, at the most."[6]

Laird was in the same quandary, but it was more personal because his neighbors and friends (as well as prospective voters for his own campaign) were the ones who had elected McCarthy. The best he could do was to not criticize McCarthy, but avoid appearing in public with him. In one roundtable discussion in August with other candidates, Laird was pressed for his view of the senator. Laird's circumlocution was awkward. "I'm running on the Republican ticket," he allowed, and "the leaders of our party, including Governor Kohler, have come out for him. I don't have to agree with everything he has done. My wife doesn't agree with everything I do, and I don't always agree with what she does, but we still care and have faith in each other."[7] And that's the most he said on the subject.

Eisenhower tried to avoid the issue by avoiding Wisconsin, but unbeknownst to him, his staff put him on a whistle-stop train tour through the state.[8] As the date neared, Governor Kohler, who didn't like McCarthy any more than Laird did, cautioned Eisenhower not to slight the senator during the Wisconsin stops. The day before Eisenhower was to arrive in Wisconsin, Kohler and McCarthy met the entourage in Peoria, Illinois, to confer with the general about the delicate matter. By that time Ike had personally written a paragraph praising George Marshall, which he added to his standard stump speech scheduled for Milwaukee. McCarthy, in a private meeting, asked Eisenhower not to use the paragraph, and Ike unloaded on the senator, saying how much he despised McCarthy's irresponsible methods. McCarthy was unruffled, probably because he was inebriated. He described the meeting to waiting reporters as "very, very pleasant."

The next day, on October 3, the Eisenhower train entered Wisconsin, and McCarthy boarded the train along with other Wisconsin Republicans including Laird. For Laird, it was unforgettable as he witnessed rare Eisenhower anger: "Ike didn't like McCarthy, and it was much to his displeasure that McCarthy was even on the train," Laird recalled. As the train rolled forward, an ongoing debate over a series of McCarthy issues ensued; the steam whistle's sound seemed to punctuate the hot tempers. Laird listened, occasionally participating. One of the contentious issues was whether McCarthy and Eisenhower would appear on the train platform together at each stop. Eisenhower refused until they got to Appleton, McCarthy's hometown, where the senator begged for one moment together on the platform. Eisenhower relented and allowed McCarthy to make a short introduction, but insisted that Governor Kohler stand between them on the platform.[9]

The final debate, which Laird witnessed, was over whether Eisenhower would praise Marshall in a speech when the train stopped in Milwaukee. Eisenhower finally agreed not to mention Marshall. That speech ended up to be ironically McCarthy-like in tone—the most inflammatory red-baiting speech of Eisenhower's career. Before a crowd of 8,500 at the Milwaukee Arena, Eisenhower dramatically launched into "a terrifying picture of Communist inroads in our own government," the *Milwaukee Sentinel* reported, and then "went out of his way to urge McCarthy's re-election," saying he needed McCarthy "in this crusade for better government."[10] The support of McCarthy, combined with leaks about the "missing paragraph" from his speech supporting Marshall, dominated the national press coverage. "He has met the enemy, and he is theirs," the *New York Post* headline blared. Eisenhower later regretted the speech and said so in his memoirs.

Despite the personal pain it caused Eisenhower, the Milwaukee speech controversy did not, ultimately, have a significant impact on his campaign against Democratic challenger Adlai Stevenson, a former senator from Illinois. With domestic and foreign issues of much greater import on the voters' minds, the extent to which Eisenhower embraced McCarthy receded in the four weeks of campaigning that followed.

Thrilled at the possibility, Republicans old and young aimed at an electoral sweep of state, congressional, and presidential elections. Among the young Republicans was thirteen-year-old David Obey, who would later represent Wisconsin in Congress as an ardent liberal Democrat. Four decades after his time "as a wayward teenager," Obey sheepishly displayed his "Laird for Congress" button, and acknowledged that in 1952 he had enthusiastically "circulated the literature to one-third of the households in the city of Wausau for Mel, and for Ike, and for Nixon, and for Joe McCarthy."[11]

The Republicans achieved a sweeping victory in November—control of the Senate, House, and White House. Dwight Eisenhower, with Richard Nixon as his vice president, won with 55 percent of the vote. Laird won his first election for Congress with a record-setting 95,049 votes, the largest vote ever cast for a candidate in the Seventh District. It was 72.3 percent of the vote, and a resounding defeat of his Democratic opponent Ernest Kluck. Laird quickly put together a home office staff to serve constituents in Wisconsin (run variously by Bob Dunkel, Pat Trierweiler, and Lois Heide-Browe). Then, at thirty, Melvin Robert Laird Jr. headed to Washington as the youngest Wisconsin man ever elected to Congress.

Burning Tree Club in suburban Bethesda, Maryland, has long been a siren song to the powerful men of Washington, D.C. It was an eighteen-hole enclave of camaraderie in early 1953 when a powerful foursome arrived to play a round of golf. An hour before tee time a call came from the White House to the club's pro, Max Elbin. The Secret Service soon followed to establish a command post in the clubhouse. The buzz started at the "nineteenth hole," the club bar, where members and guests nursed drinks and played cards. The new president of the United States arrived that Wednesday afternoon under a slightly overcast sky, with the two men he knew best from Capitol Hill—the new House Majority

Leader Charles Halleck and Senator Robert A. Taft, whom Ike had beaten for the GOP presidential nomination.[12] To their mutual surprise, less than six months after engaging in intense battle, Taft and Eisenhower had become good friends. The sixty-three-year-old Taft, who was the Senate majority leader, was chipper enough as he played that day, not knowing that he was already in the early stages of a cancer that would claim his life by summer.

The president had chosen Halleck for his golf partner that day and let Taft choose a fourth golfer. Taft's first choice had been the new congressman from Wisconsin, Melvin Laird, but Laird had a sprained ankle, so he suggested that Taft instead invite Jack Westland, another freshman congressman, from Washington State, who had spent his boyhood in Laird's congressional district in Wisconsin. (Westland had recently won the National U.S. Amateur Golf Championship.) Laird went along as the scorekeeper. That afternoon both newcomers were introduced to the members relaxing in the stately Tudor clubhouse. On the fast track to leadership, Laird had already been given an almost unprecedented appointment for a freshman congressman—a seat on the most powerful committee in Congress, House Appropriations. And now he was golfing with the president. Although Eisenhower lost the game that day, he was impressed with his affable young companions.

The importance of golf as a lever of influence during the Eisenhower era cannot be overstated. While fishing and bridge were also favorite presidential pastimes, golf was his first love. A rough calculation shows that he played about eight hundred rounds of golf during his two terms; that is almost twice a week. Few were invited more than one time to play with the president, unless Eisenhower enjoyed their friendship and golfing prowess, as he did Laird's. The congressman became one of Eisenhower's friends and was later invited to Augusta National Golf Club by Eisenhower and the club's founder, Cliff Roberts.

For Laird, one success built upon another from his first days in Congress. The president's and Taft's friendship provided Laird with rare informal access and, more important, influence by association. Congressional friends who admired him had promoted him to the most important committee, which naturally had many senior members seeking to befriend him. He was thus in a good position to help drive the issues of the Eisenhower era, which dramatically began in Laird's first term with the end of the Korean War, the end of McCarthy, and gunfire in the chamber of the House of Representatives.

⌇

Descended from a family of coffee laborers, Lolita Lebron was an attractive woman who easily won a beauty contest in her hometown of Lares, Puerto Rico, prior to immigrating to New York City at age twenty-two. Twelve years later, after marriage and divorce, two children, and a string of jobs, she became an intense Puerto Rican nationalist who believed the United States, which had won the Puerto Rican islands as booty in the Spanish-American War, had no right to rule her native home. She belonged to a wing of the Puerto Rican Nationalist Party, two of whose members tried to assassinate President Truman in 1950. Four years later, on March 1, 1954, Lolita Lebron led three men on a similar "patriotic" mission. They traveled on one-way train tickets from New York, not expecting to be alive to return home. Lolita carried a purse that contained lipstick, Bromo Seltzer tablets, a loaded German Luger, and a note that read: "I take responsible [sic] for all."

They entered the Capitol as tourists, passing a guard who asked if they had any cameras, which were not allowed when the House of Representatives was in session. A guide seated them in a balcony visitors' gallery around 2:30 P.M., as a dull debate on a Mexican immigrant labor bill droned on. Laird might have passed the foursome in the hall as they were arriving. He had visited with a constituent from Wausau in that very visitor's section only moments before they were seated. He reentered the House Chamber to record his vote on the pending bill but was called off the floor by his secretary to greet a U.S. Air Force captain from Marshfield. Within seconds of stepping outside the chamber he heard a sound like "a bunch of chairs falling down some steps." Seconds later, Laird saw a friend, Congressman Ben Jensen, of Iowa, fall across the threshold of the door to the Speaker's Lobby. Blood from his neck drained onto the marble floor.

Simultaneously Laird heard a member yell, "My God, they're in here too! They're in the corridor!" While others tended to Jensen, Laird rushed into the Chamber as James E. Van Zandt, a Republican member from Pennsylvania and decorated navy veteran of both world wars, wrestled with one of the assailants in the balcony. (Three of the four, including Lebron, were captured in the Capitol; the fourth was later arrested at the Washington bus terminal.[13])

What Laird saw horrified him: the historic House Chamber, citadel of democracy, desecrated by a hail of bullets that shattered wooden furniture, tore up the ceiling and wounded five House members including Jensen and Alvin M. Bentley of Michigan, who was hit the worst.[14] Bentley was a close friend of Laird's; only the previous evening the Lairds had had dinner at the Bentleys' home. (Mrs. Bentley was from Laird's congressional district.) Laird found his friend prostrate on the floor, his body shattered by a bullet that ripped through his right lung and diaphragm before decimating his liver. Bentley, bleeding profusely, was already being given first aid by Representative Walter Judd of Minnesota, a physician. There was nothing Laird could do but offer encouragement. He did not expect Bentley to live.[15]

In the evening, Laird visited Bentley at the hospital where he remained in critical condition for several days before recovering. Bentley and Laird were founders of the SOS Club, fifteen freshmen Republicans who had banded together informally to speak with a larger voice. It was an alliance of men who were supposed to drop everything and come to the aid of a fellow member when he needed help in a committee or on the House floor. The night of the attack, the SOS Club arrived at the hospital as one to donate blood.[16]

In his newsletter after the terrorist attack, Laird did not want to give undue attention to the event. He simply offered a one-paragraph personal account as a "sidelight" at the end of his report. He was right to downplay it. Other events far more important to the republic and her citizens were even then occurring, including the explosive army-McCarthy hearings in the Senate.

⌇

Joe McCarthy reached the zenith of his influence during the first two years of the Eisenhower administration—and also plummeted to his exile from power. With Republicans in the majority, he could have become chairman of the powerful Senate Appropriations Committee. Instead he chose to chair the Committee on Government Operations, a watchdog investigative committee, which was likely to garner him more publicity. He named himself chairman of the Permanent Subcommittee on Investigations, which became a platform for his infamous Communist witch hunts.

While it was expected that Senator McCarthy would continue to ride herd on State Department bureaucrats who were suspected subversives, it came as something of a surprise to loyal Republican leaders that he took on his own party's White House appointees. That set Eisenhower's teeth against McCarthy, but, as during the election campaign, he refused to publicly criticize the senator, believing that McCarthy fed on publicity.[17]

Laird was of the same mind. "I understood what a phony he was, and a lot of people didn't. A lot of people in Wisconsin didn't. A lot of conservative people didn't," he recalled. Even in Laird's hometown, McCarthy was a hero. In May 1951 about eight hundred residents had packed the local armory to have dinner with McCarthy and hear his "Report from Washington" speech.[18] Laird, as a state senator, was one of the thirty-one guests on a dais, but he made sure that he was at least five chairs removed from McCarthy at the table. "Hell, I always wanted to stay as far away from him as possible; he was a guy I didn't want to be around too much," Laird added. One of the reasons was that by Laird's observation, McCarthy was frequently drunk. "I would be with him sometimes when he would order a malted milk for breakfast and he'd pour half of it out and put almost half a pint of booze in it. I never admired that."

Wisconsin political operator Jack Mills confirmed this McCarthy predilection. Mills frequently traveled with McCarthy and became such a close friend and admirer that he asked the senator to be godfather to his son. The priest at the ceremony objected because he didn't like McCarthy, but Mills said he changed his tune after McCarthy slipped him a $200 donation. "He was a good senator for about three years," Mills observed, but in Mills's opinion, incipient alcoholism changed McCarthy for the worse. "I know, because I helped him hit the booze. Whenever we traveled, he would have several bottles of BPR, Baltimore Pure Rye, with him. He was a real alcoholic....[A]s time went on I sensed the booze thing was doing him in more than anything else, and he became unbalanced."[19]

It was the vindictive, unbalanced McCarthy who elevated to national notoriety his two most subservient aides—the venal chief counsel to the subcommittee, Roy Cohn, and Gerard David Schine, a dreamy-eyed millionaire's son, heir to great hotels and theaters, night club habitué, and escort of Hollywood starlets. The "Katzenjammer Kids," as they were derisively called behind their backs, took a rampaging trip throughout Europe in 1953. There they denounced as subversive the Voice of America and the U.S. overseas information program, causing libraries to be closed and books to be burned in their fearful wake.

Their next target was the U.S. Army. Schine had been drafted into the service, which occasionally didn't treat him as he felt he deserved, so the young pair declared war on the army. With McCarthy as the assault leader, this unlikely cabal had the army on the run for a while. The televised army-McCarthy hearings hearings ran from April 22 to June 15, 1954, and captured the nation's attention. In a May 5 letter to his constituents, Laird called it a "three-ring circus," and lamented the fact that it "diverted attention ... from many important decisions and activities taking place in our Capital."[20] Two days later, Laird repeated the complaint in a speech at a two-day Marathon County, Wisconsin, Republican rally. He noted that only "four or five reporters were present the other day" during action on a $73 billion defense appropriations bill, while "there were more than two hundred over in the Senate office building [covering the] three-ring circus."[21] McCarthy also appeared at the rally, which gave the *Wausau Daily Record-Herald* a chance to contrast the senator and congressman: "Wisconsin's junior senator is one of the most controversial figures in the nation, both among members of his own party as well as among the Democratic opposition. Most people are either strongly for him or just as strongly against him, with few sitting on the fence.... Unlike Sen. McCarthy, Rep. Laird is not passionately hailed either as a great hero or a villain. But he does evoke universal esteem and high respect for his deep sincerity, integrity, devotion to duty and level-headedness whether or not one agrees with his views on any particular issue."[22]

The nadir of the hearings, the veritable tolling of the bell for McCarthy, came on June 9 when the grand inquisitor finally met his match in Joseph Welch, the army's special counsel. When McCarthy viciously maligned a junior partner in Welch's law firm, Welch scarcely raised his voice in response. "Until this moment, Senator," he began sadly, "I think I never really gauged your cruelty or your recklessness.... If it were in my power to forgive you for your reckless cruelty, I would do so. I like to think that I am a gentleman, but your forgiveness will have to come from someone other than me."

It was as if the nation collectively paused in a hush, as did the Senate hearing room. Stung, McCarthy began sputtering out another attack but Welch silenced him: "Senator. You have done enough. Have you no sense of decency, sir, at long last? Have you left no sense of decency?" The Senate caucus room audience of seven hundred spontaneously erupted into applause, and the hearing was thrown into recess.[23]

Still, it took the rest of the year for McCarthy's demise to play out. Less than a week after the hearing, McCarthy received overwhelming support at the state Republican convention, which was chaired by an unhappy Laird. He knew that many anti-McCarthy delegates, expecting a fanatic show of home state support from his fans, sat out the convention. So it was that only one delegate, Polk County Republican Chairman Harold Michael, dared to speak out against a resolution praising McCarthy. Laird gave him time to make his case, but Michael's words could barely be heard over the roar of boos, catcalls, and shouted insults like: "Sit down!" "Throw the Communist out!" "Shut the microphone off!" "Go back to Russia!" Laird tried without success to gavel them to silence.

The convention was watched closely by the U.S. Senate, whose majority hoped that Wisconsin would punish its own man. When that didn't happen, it was up to the Senate to act. On December 2, 1954, the Senate voted sixty-seven to twenty-two to condemn McCarthy for conduct unbecoming a U.S. senator—labeling his behavior "contemptuous, contumacious and denunciatory." A faint effort was made by his friends to press the Wisconsin congressional delegation, including Laird, into sponsoring a House resolution condemning the Senate's action, but there were no takers.

McCarthy died in May of 1957. He had been hospitalized previously for alcoholism and probably succumbed to cirrhosis of the liver. The Senate allowed a funeral service in the Senate Chamber at the request of his widow. His body was flown to Wisconsin, where thirty thousand Wisconsinites filed through an Appleton church to view the open casket. One of those present for the service was Laird. Until that day he had lived up to his pledge of never missing a roll call vote, even requiring him once to leave a dinner in his honor in Madison, drive to Chicago, and catch a midnight plane to Washington, arriving at dawn.[24] The need to express sympathy to McCarthy's family and Wisconsin friends was important enough to break the pledge. He attended the memorial service and missed his first roll call vote in five years.[25]

Jerry Ford later said that Laird had taken an appropriate arms-length attitude toward McCarthy (as did Ford himself). It had been no small thing, Ford observed years after the event, that neither Laird, nor the more senior Wisconsin Congressmen Glenn Davis and Johnny Byrnes, ever supported McCarthy's anti-Communist campaign. McCarthy knew where they stood, and that it was not with him. "The three of them, Mel, Glenn, and John were just privately embarrassed by McCarthy's demagoguery and his conduct generally," Ford said. "Now, they had a very narrow path to follow, because McCarthy was popular in Wisconsin. Those three House members had to be cautious about any public criticism of McCarthy. I think Mel handled the McCarthy problem very skill-fully. He stayed outside of the McCarthy envelope, so to speak."[26]

Laird maintained that McCarthy and McCarthyism were overblown by his-torians. "It's sad if people think that he had a great influence, because he never did. He had nothing to do with Truman's position on the cold war, or Ike's position—he had *no* influence on Eisenhower. You're just taking away from Eisenhower and Truman if you think he significantly influenced their presi-dential decisions." Nor does Laird believe that McCarthy had any influence on the hundreds of critical legislative bills Congress passed that affected America's history and people a thousandfold more than McCarthyism.

Laird saw it as the bright era of Eisenhower, not the dark one of McCarthy. "When I was with Eisenhower I knew I was in the presence of a great man. There was something about being in the presence of somebody like that," he recalled. "He always focused on you. He listened to you. Those eyes of his fo-cused on everything that you said. If he agreed with you, a big smile would break out on his face and you'd feel great."

If all the milk produced in Wisconsin for a year were packaged in one-quart cartons and stacked side by side, it could form a highway twenty-eight rows wide from New York to San Francisco. The state's license plate logo, "America's Dairyland," is no idle boast: Wisconsin is a leading producer of milk, cheese, and butter. By the mid-twentieth century, when Laird went to Washington, more than half of Wisconsin's land area was farmland, and at least a third of the state's labor force was involved in the production or marketing of farm products. The young congressman was acutely aware that his district was the largest milk- and cheese-producing district in the entire country, and it was not necessarily a good time to be representing those interests.

In January 1953 the country's farmers were in a fix. American agriculture was still recovering from the ravages of the World War II loss of male labor, and the effects of the Depression before that. Middlemen were grabbing more and more of the dairy dollar, and farmers were being squeezed out of their land because of low prices for their products. In recognition of that, Congress had passed the Agricultural Act of 1949, which mandated payments by the Commodity Credit Corporation for surplus products based on "parity" prices. Parity was the price the government declared by law to be fair based on what a farmer must pay for farm and consumer products. Using a base period of the relatively prosperous 1910–1914 years, the government calculated what price it would take in the 1950s to equal that purchasing power. If the sale of one hun-dred gallons of milk bought so many Sunday neckties back then, parity would be the price one hundred gallons would need to sell for in order to buy the same number of ties in the 1950s. However, the government could not afford to pay a 100 percent parity price to the farmer for his surplus. So a maximum of 90 percent was authorized.

During the 1952 campaign, candidate Eisenhower supported 90 percent parity and won the farm vote. But his Secretary of Agriculture Ezra Taft Benson believed that federal aid to farmers was socialism and made that clear in straight-talking speeches. Laird was no fan of a subsidized economy either, so his first speech on the floor of the House was a carefully crafted defense of Benson.[27] He said, Wisconsin's farmers "are not anxious to be dependent on government for largesse, or to accept the measure of government regulation which inevitably accompanies such largesse."[28]

In early 1954 Laird began to get indications that Benson might drop the parity rate to the legal minimum of 75 percent. He had private meetings with Benson and felt he had been assured that any change would happen gradually. Then came the February 15 announcement that meant an uncounted number of dairy farmers would go bankrupt that year. Beginning April 1 the price would be 75 percent of parity. Laird felt personally betrayed. He had defended Benson before and would have defended a drop in the parity price to the mid-80 percent range, which he thought Benson had privately promised. Benson's action was unnecessarily discriminatory because only the dairy industry was subject to "flexible price supports." The parity price for so-called basic commodities—wheat, corn, cotton, rice, peanuts, and tobacco—would continue by law at 90 percent, because those products were grown in states with a larger representation in Congress. Benson had chosen to test out his new program on the political weak spot.

After failing to change Benson's mind or stop him with legislation, Laird pulled rank. He secretly applied to President Eisenhower, using the White House's congressional liaison General Wilton B. Persons. Persons reported back to Laird that the Ike-promised parity would only drop to 82.5 percent—a compromise Laird could live with. But before he could publicly crow about this, another call came; Benson had informed the president that if he insisted on a compromise he would have to find a new agriculture secretary. Eisenhower capitulated.[29] Disheartened, Laird faced a storm of criticism in his first reelection year, having been undercut by his own party's administration. Out of his nine successful campaigns for Congress, the 1954 campaign was Laird's toughest. But dairy ire was not enough to overcome Laird's solid reputation. He won with 59.1 percent of the vote.

In early 1954 an unusual visitor, who would soon become a friend, dropped by Laird's home for an animated discussion—seventy-year-old Roger Baldwin, founder and national chairman of the American Civil Liberties Union. The amiable, aristocratic Bostonian had begun the ACLU in 1920 after being jailed for a year as a conscientious objector to the draft during World War I. Among the ACLU's cofounders were Helen Keller, civil rights lawyer Clarence Darrow, conservative legal brain and future Supreme Court justice Felix Frankfurter, and American Socialist leader Norman Thomas. Its most famous case in the early years was the "Scopes Monkey Trial"—the ACLU's 1925 defense (through lawyer Darrow) of John Scopes, who was being prosecuted by religious fundamentalist and presidential candidate William Jennings Bryan in Tennessee for teaching evolution in a public school. Baldwin was determined to keep the ACLU nonpartisan, so he never joined a political party. Still, the ACLU inevitably took on a liberal tincture from the hue of most of its clients and was considered an enemy of the Republican Party.[30]

As was often the case, Congressman Laird, from progressive Wisconsin, did not have the same view. This friend of labor union leaders felt he could benefit from discourse and friendship with an ardent advocate of the Bill of Rights. So when Baldwin heard through his niece, who was Laird's next-door neighbor, that he would be welcome, the amiable aristocrat in his usual rumpled suit knocked on Laird's door one evening. He came to discuss an "urgent matter": Laird's sponsorship of a bill to add the words "under God" to the Pledge of Allegiance.

The original pledge was written in 1892 by Baptist minister Francis Bellamy, a self-described Christian Socialist. It was only twenty-three words: "I pledge allegiance to my Flag and to the Republic for which it stands; one nation indivisible, with liberty and justice for all."[31] In the 1920s, feeling more specificity was needed, the pledge was changed twice, replacing "my Flag" to "the flag of the United States of America." By the mid-1930s, the pledge was compulsory for most American school children and often done with a straight-arm salute that subsequently went out of favor when the same gesture was used to salute Hitler.

One religious group, the Jehovah's Witnesses, refused to allow their children to say the pledge, believing it meant pledging allegiance to a "graven image." With the help of Baldwin and the ACLU, the Witnesses took the issue to the Supreme Court and lost. The case unleashed a wave of violence against the Witnesses. The ACLU documented violent incidents in more than 350 communities in forty-four states—including the castration of a Witness by a Nebraska mob; the assault on a group of sixty Witnesses by almost all the adults in Litchfield, Connecticut; and an incident in Richwood, Virginia, where members of the American Legion and sheriff's department forced seven Witnesses to drink large amounts of castor oil, after which they were paraded through town. In two years, more than two thousand children of Jehovah's Witnesses were expelled from schools across the country for refusing to say the pledge. The Supreme Court reversed the decision in 1943.

Meanwhile, in 1942 Congress officially recognized the pledge on its fiftieth birthday and added it to the Flag Code of the United States. No change could be made to it without legislation, which is why Laird needed a bill in 1954 to amend the pledge to read, "one nation under God." In their first evening together Baldwin pleaded with Laird to see the danger of adding "under God" to the pledge. Baldwin argued courteously but heatedly with Laird that his resolution violated the First Amendment separation of church and state. Though Baldwin was eloquent, Laird, the son of a Presbyterian minister, was unswayed. While Laird wouldn't drop the bill, Baldwin found him affable and open on civil rights issues dear to Baldwin, so they continued as friends. Laird treasured the wide-ranging, intellectually invigorating debates he had with Baldwin over the next several decades.

"The Pledge of Allegiance is a country pledge and I believed then that it was important to show our majority belief in a supreme deity as well," Laird recalled his rationale to amend the pledge. He was not alone in that belief. Representative Oliver Bolton of Ohio was also outspoken about the urgent need for the "under God" addition. In those days, the House did not allow more than one sponsor's name on a bill, so the only way to cosponsor legislation was to offer identical bills under individual names. Hence, not only was there a Laird resolution, but a Bolton one, as well as at least thirteen others, including one by Democrat Louis Rabaut of Michigan, who the year before had been the first to introduce the idea legislatively in Congress.[32]

Laird appeared before the House Judiciary Committee on May 6 and testified that it was a long-overdue change.[33] He noted that in the constitutions of forty-seven of the states, the authority of God is recognized and declared. Every poll taken at the time showed that as many as 97 percent of all Americans believed in a supreme being, as did the Founding Fathers. Though God was not mentioned in the Constitution, the Declaration of Independence referenced God or the Creator four times. And, Laird dramatically concluded, what better time than on Lincoln's 145th birthday to follow the lead of the president who had uttered in the concluding words of the Gettysburg Address: "that we here highly resolve that these [Civil War] dead shall not have died in vain; that this nation, *under God,* shall have a new birth of freedom; and that government of the people, by the people, for the people, shall not perish from the earth" (emphasis added).

Fifteen days after Laird's testimony, at a Boston meeting of the Unitarian Ministers Association, a resolution was passed opposing the legislation. But supporters were far more numerous, including the leaders of the other Protestant faiths, the Catholic and Jewish faiths, veterans groups, civic clubs, patriotic organizations, fraternal clubs, labor unions, trade associations, newspaper editorialists, and radio commentators. The *New York Times* reported that as a result of a countrywide grassroots effort, "Congress is being flooded with mail...on a subject far removed from the [concurrent] McCarthy-Army hearings that hold the headlines. The letter writers by the thousands daily are demanding Congress amend the pledge."[34] The Senate passed the bill, and the House was ready to do the same, but pride of authorship sparked a lengthy debate. Congressman Rabaut fought to have the House pass his bill instead of the Senate's, which would mean the Senate would have to swallow its pride and vote again on the identical House bill. Republican Floor Leader Charlie Halleck begged Rabaut to back off so the legislation could be signed a few days later on National Flag Day. But Rabaut refused, so the House, including Laird and other cosponsors passed the Rabaut resolution by voice vote on Thursday, June 7. The following day, the Senate obligingly signed off on the House bill. On Saturday, June 12, Laird, as chair of the Republican State Convention in Wisconsin, led the delegates in saying the new pledge. Laird was so pleased that he passed out small cards to children in his district that reelection year with the new pledge printed on them, and a small note that Laird was the cosponsor of the new pledge.[35]

At that time of religious revival in America, when parents worried almost as much about materialistic consumerism as they did about the godless Communists, Laird did not stop with the pledge reform alone. He pushed successful legislation that directed the architect of the Capitol to designate a prayer-and-meditation room in the building, where members of Congress could come to spiritually consider their work.[36]

Laird also was instrumental in making "In God We Trust" the national motto. Its original author was Lincoln's Secretary of the Treasury Salmon P. Chase, who first put the words on coins in 1864. Nine decades later, in 1956, Laird helped steer passage of the bill through the House and the Senate, making the motto official. The following year, the new national motto appeared for the first time on paper money, the one-dollar silver certificate.[37]

More deeply than golf and bridge interests, more profound in some ways than their mutual Republican principles, Laird's shared Presbyterian faith with Eisenhower encouraged a closeness that might not otherwise have existed. During his second year in office, President Eisenhower began an annual practice of inviting Congress, before that year's session began, to join him and his Cabinet for special services at the National Presbyterian Church. As an elder in the church, Laird always participated by passing communion to White House officials and his congressional colleagues.[38] Laird's deep respect for Eisenhower was evident throughout his writings of the time. Once, while in the White House dining room with Ike, Laird memorized the words of John Adams inscribed on the fireplace: "I pray heaven to bestow the best of blessings on this house and on all that shall hereafter inhabit it. May none but honest and wise men ever rule under this roof." After sharing the quote in his newsletter to constituents, Laird wrote that America had been "fortunate indeed" to have Eisenhower as president in that house, "a man of integrity and character, with dedicated loyalty to his country's welfare and a real desire to maintain a just peace."[39] Being so in sync with Eisenhower on core moral issues, Laird became a favorite of the president, who alternately served as a mentor and father figure of sorts for the young congressman.

Some of Laird's speeches in the Eisenhower era reveal the religious touchstone that drove both men—the place of a Christian in politics: "Only those people with the highest altruistic motives [should] have any business in politics. There ought not to be any room for other folks. They ought to be crowded out by the people who believe in the highest ideals, and who work for the best interests of all men." Laird postulated: "If Providence has placed self-government in the hands of the people, the better people had better take over, lest the reins of administration fall into the hands of the improvident." So, "when people ask me, 'Ought a Christian go into politics?' my answer has been, 'How can a Christian stay out?'"[40]

4

Of Chowder and Cheese

RICHARD NIXON WAS A VICE PRESIDENT who never quite came in from the cold of the Eisenhower Oval Office. Eisenhower preferred a different type of man. He had a Cabinet full of millionaires, and Nixon was a professional politician, not a self-made businessman. Eisenhower had many friends among the high-ranking military and their aides with whom he had served, and Nixon, with his lackluster war record, did not qualify in that category either. The president also favored amiable, game-loving raconteurs; if Nixon ever tried to be the life of a party, the strain was evident.

Eisenhower had wanted someone else as his vice president, and that desire accelerated after he suffered his first heart attack in Denver in September 1955. It brought into relief the very real possibility of Nixon becoming president by default. The thought made Eisenhower uncomfortable so, awkwardly, he made a move the day after Christmas to replace Nixon. In an Oval Office discussion the president made the case to Nixon that his presidential prospects would be better if he were in the Cabinet—preferably secretary of defense. Ike noted that Nixon's popularity had not improved in three years and that he probably needed administrative experience in another position. Not knowing the president's ulterior motive, Nixon initially took the suggestion to be a "friendly and sincere one." But at the same time, he suspected Ike's friends had "been sowing doubts on his mind . . . that I might be a drag on the ticket."[1]

Word that Nixon needed a public boost quietly went out to his closest friends, including Laird, who were all members of an exclusive Republican group called the Chowder and Marching Club. The society, which had nothing to do with soup or Sousa, was a fraternity of only fifteen Republican members begun in March 1949 to oppose a multibillion-dollar veterans bonus bill. Many Republicans, then in the minority, opposed the handout to every veteran regardless of need. Among them were Wisconsin Representative Glenn Davis and California Representative Don Jackson, who decided to enlist thirteen other younger members in their cause. Among the charter members were Nixon and Jerry Ford.[2] The fifteen Republican upstarts, most of whom were veterans themselves (including one congressman who had lost both legs in the war[3]), unanimously opposed the Democratic giveaway and managed to successfully kill the bill.

In the process Chowder and Marching became an incubator for future presidents. Some psychohistorians have suggested that Nixon's political genius created the group to use as a kind of secret Opus Dei to promote his presidential ambitions.[4] The facts belie such theories. As Nixon once mused, C&M (as the members called it) was "the most ill-organized, disorderly organization I know."[5] Davis and Jackson were the de facto leaders, but the club was never formally organized and had no officers, rules, or even a clubhouse. The group met every Wednesday at the congressional offices of the members in alphabetical rotation. The club's name is something of a mystery even to members: "We never ate chowder and we never marched," Ford recalled.[6] Jackson had whimsically put the name on the notice for C&M's second meeting, and it's possible it came from a 1933 Cary Grant movie in which one C&M charter member, John Lodge, who had been the first movie actor elected to high political office, played a bit part. At one point in the movie, a banner is held up which says: "The O'Brien Chowder and Marching Club."[7]

While he was a state senator, Laird first heard tales of the group from Davis and Johnny Byrnes, and he watched its workings from afar. When Nixon came under fire from the media for a slush fund of contributions from California businessmen, C&M members rushed to his defense, with Davis helping Nixon to write the televised speech that would save his reputation. That became known as the "Checkers speech" in reference to the "donation" of a dog by that name to his six-year-old daughter, Tricia. Nixon declared with watering eyes that he would not return Checkers to the campaign donor.[8]

Davis and Byrnes pushed to put Laird in C&M as soon as he came to Congress, but there was no opening for him until a year later in 1954. By secret ballot C&M-ers usually voted on a prospective member based on his personality, early indications that he was a "comer," and because he was assigned to a committee not already represented in the club. At every Wednesday meeting each active C&M-er gave a brief report on what had occurred in the executive sessions of his committee. "This reporting was all off the record, just for our knowledge," Laird explained. "It was a way we could get information in a hurry that we couldn't get in the newspapers or anyplace else." Information is power in Washington, and C&M became a unique repository of politically valuable insight.

With the elevation of C&M-er Nixon to vice president, and others who were appointed to the Eisenhower administration, the club grew to mythological stature. Though small in number they were able to lure Cabinet members, the Joint Chiefs of Staff, civilian service chiefs, and federal judges to give them private briefings at Wednesday morning breakfasts. The CIA chief invited them to Langley headquarters for an unprecedented intelligence briefing, and Eisenhower invited the club to the White House for a special off-the-record breakfast. No one turned down an invitation from C&M.[9]

Just as they had in 1952 when Eisenhower had considered dropping Nixon from the ticket, the Chowder and Marching Club, to a man, rallied to Nixon's defense against a similar prospect in 1956. They planned a highly visible show of support in the guise of a January 9 birthday party for the vice president.

Laird took the lead in planning the costly soiree. He leaned on gifted national fund-raisers Jack Mills and Victor Johnson, both friends from Wisconsin, to come up with the more than $10,000 in private contributions for the event at the National Press Club.[10] More than five hundred attended, including most of the Republican luminaries of the day. As hosts, Laird and fellow C&M-ers donned chef's hats and striped butcher's aprons as they brought out the large birthday cake.

Nixon was visibly moved. Three days later he wrote to Laird, "It was [a] superb party." The highlight was when, "I saw members of our group wheel out that beautiful cake with its 43 candles. [It] will never be exceeded as a mountain-top experience." He counted Laird and all "my fellow members of the Chowder and Marching Club my closest political and personal friends in this world."[11] Nixon knew the subtext of the birthday party was a powerful statement to the president that he could ill afford to "fire" a man with such friends; Eisenhower was a general-come-lately to the Republican Party, and Nixon was one of its inner circle.

But the president still waffled on the Nixon question through early spring. In late January he pressed Nixon again to consider a Cabinet post.[12] At a late February press conference, when Ike finally announced that he would run for reelection, the first question was whether Nixon would be his running mate. He demurred that he would wait for the national convention that summer. Laird immediately sent Nixon a telegram emphatically reaffirming his view that he was vitally needed on the ticket. "Your wire was appreciated more than I can tell you," a downcast Nixon wrote back.[13] A few days later, on March 7, Eisenhower told the press it was up to Nixon "to chart his own course and tell me what he would like to do."[14]

Eisenhower didn't want to give Nixon the inside track for the 1960 election, but it wasn't until he had weighed all other options that he finally pledged publicly in April that he would keep Nixon.[15] The agony of Ike's ambiguity toward him was reawakened on July 23 when the popular Eisenhower administration disarmament chief and former presidential candidate Harold Stassen announced he would lead a movement to promote Massachusetts Governor Christian Herter for vice president. When Eisenhower appeared to listen to Stassen, Laird leaped to Nixon's aid. He and nineteen other Republicans sent a telegram to Stassen saying they were "amazed and shocked" by his action. On July 27 Laird addressed the House, urging a unified endorsement of Nixon. After his impassioned speech 180 of the 203 House Republicans voted to endorse Nixon. Eisenhower could hardly miss the significance. The dump-Nixon campaign withered quickly; at the subsequent convention in San Francisco, Stassen himself seconded the nomination of Nixon.

For the Republican National Convention, Laird was again named a member of the platform committee, which was chaired by Senator Prescott Bush, father and grandfather of future presidents.[16] The platform for Eisenhower's reelection sparked little controversy and passed without dissent. Laird had time to relax, including playing the first of many rounds of golf with Senator Bush. He also had time to chat with one of the Bush sons, George H. W., who hustled around with messages and platform drafts as a page for the committee. After the convention Laird traveled with Eisenhower and Nixon to a couple of campaign stops and otherwise acted as an energetic member of Ike's "truth squads." These were senators and representatives assigned to dog key Democratic speakers—especially the Democrats' repeat presidential candidate Adlai Stevenson—and hold alternative press conferences to debunk Democrats' assertions about the national Republican ticket.

On the home front Laird also faced a repeat opponent, who unexpectedly died a few days before the Democratic primary. The man's widow then became one of only twenty-seven women in the United States running for Congress that year, taking up the campaign for the office her husband had twice sought.[17] But she had little chance against Laird. One newspaper noted that Laird had "boom[ed] around the countryside," averaging more than a speech a day, covering every community in the ten-county district twice and eating at as many as three church picnics in a single afternoon. "Despite his great energy, Laird appears older than his years," the reporter added, pointing out a bullet-head pate that would be the delight of future editorial cartoonists: "Partly bald and his remaining hair cropped, he has a deacon-like fringe over his dome." The voters didn't hold his hair loss against Laird; his victory margin was two to one.[18]

The Eisenhower-Nixon ticket also swept to a landslide victory, but with coattails so short that a Democratic House and Senate were returned to Washington. It was only the second time in American history up to that point that the majority had voted for a president of one party and given control of Congress to the opposition. In 1848, Zachary Taylor won the presidency while his party lost the House and Senate.[19]

⚶

During the Eisenhower era Laird's primary base of power came from what was then the most powerful and hardest-working committee in Congress: House Appropriations. No government project can become a reality without money to meet its cost, and no dollar can be spent unless the House Appropriations Committee appropriates it. Laird won the prestigious appointment as a freshman because Wisconsin Representatives Byrnes and Davis had pitched his name to the chairman. "It was quite unusual for a freshman to go on Appropriations," according to former Representative Elford Cederberg, of Michigan, who won the honor at the same time as Laird. They drew straws for seniority between the two and Laird won. Both were bumped off Appropriations in 1955, after the House went to the Democrats. Laird was the first to come back, in 1957, and he stayed on the committee until he left Congress.

The business of appropriations was delicate. Legislative committees and their members won popularity by passing exorbitant authorization bills, well beyond the federal budget available to pay for them. Some legislators even secretly hoped the Appropriations Committee would turn them down after they had taken credit with their constituents for trying. Laird had to deal with that and still win elections every two years, so he would occasionally remind his constituents that the committee had to be the Grinch. Another thing about the committee work that made reelection for its members more difficult was that, by long-standing tradition, no single committee member was allowed to sponsor an appropriations bill. All bills were issued in the name of the committee. That eliminated grandstanding, but it also meant less credit back home for a committee member who was responsible for an appropriation. The campaign opponent of a committee member once disingenuously criticized the incumbent "because he served on the House Appropriations Committee for ten years *without a single bill being reported in his name*," Laird remembered.[20]

No other committee in Congress came close to the number of hours that the House Appropriations Committee spent in session. Laird's load on Appropriations was among the heaviest. At one point he was assigned to four different subcommittees: health, defense, military construction, and commerce. When asked by another congressman why Laird was "assigned to more subcommittee work than any other member of the committee," ranking member John Taber replied: "Mel Laird likes hard work."[21]

The general public was unaware of this service because all appropriations hearings were held in closed session. "You make no headlines as all your work is behind closed doors," Congressman Laird once lamented. What made the lack of attention even harder to swallow for Laird was that, after all his toil and sweat, the Senate Appropriations Committee, building on the House's initial work and tough choices, held "window dressing" public hearings and always added money to the House's appropriations bill—acting, more or less, as a generous appeal body. In one typical Eisenhower year Laird and his colleagues conducted all-day hearings for five and a half weeks on a House Foreign Affairs authorization bill, and finally cut it in half. The Senate Appropriations Committee then held public hearings for just five half-days and added $1 billion onto the bill. "Some people refer to the Senate as 'the upper house.' Could it be because of their record of always 'upping' appropriations?" Laird quipped.[22]

Despite his lack of seniority Laird soon became influential within the committee itself because of his ability to absorb large amounts of information, analyze it, and then use it to buttress a Republican argument or buttonhole a witness; these abilities grew over the years and came into high relief when he was secretary of defense. Laird rarely received public credit for saving the taxpayers billions of dollars in unnecessary federal spending. The work was too mundane for the notice of journalists, and Laird seemed averse to blowing his own horn about the committee work. One of the few times he launched a harangue against a colleague it was to denounce a headline-hunting senator who portrayed himself as the taxpayer's best friend, using a bogus claim that he planned to save them $4 billion with an important bill he had introduced in July 1958. This was Wisconsin Senator William Proxmire, the Democrat who had won McCarthy's seat in a special election. There were two problems with Proxmire's claim, Laird pointed out: An identical bill had already been passed two months before Proxmire became a senator; and the bill would not save a dime, let alone $4 billion. Laird had detected in his nascent stage a seeker of the limelight who would later become famous precisely for tilting against the government waste with "Golden Fleece Awards." Proxmire also would become the most persistent critic of Defense Department spending and would heap criticism upon the future secretary of defense.

Alarmed about the $267 billion national debt when he came into office, Laird was a serious and bona fide budget-slasher. He made it a practice to vote for every reduction that came through his committee and found himself in the minority on some of those votes.[23] Laird found the historical contrast between Democrat and Republican attitudes about deficits and debt to be fairly sharp. He noted one survey which found that the net total of deficits for the Democrats' forty years in the White House from James Buchanan to Harry Truman was $261.7 billion, while the Republicans' sixty-one years in the presidency had accumulated net deficits of only $1.5 billion.[24] With a Republican-controlled Congress and White House, Laird and House Appropriations efficiently turned the tide of government spending in the first year. They slashed by 20 percent the budget left them by Truman, which enabled them to reduce individual income tax 11 percent.[25] Laird energetically and consistently pushed that same agenda every year. With the significant help of Laird and House Appropriations, the Eisenhower era was highlighted at one point with three consecutive years of balanced budget and one year in which surplus money was actually used to pay down the national debt. Though there were two years of recession, overall the eight-year Eisenhower period saw the gross national product rise by almost 50 percent, to more than $500 billion. This golden era was the birth of America's affluent society,[26] though it certainly left some folks behind—such as the farmers.

❧

Agricultural discontent in Wisconsin was the primary reason William Proxmire won McCarthy's seat in a special election in August 1957, after McCarthy's death. Proxmire was a relatively unknown Democratic politician whose opponent was the popular Republican Governor Walter Kohler. In twenty-five years no Democrat had won a U.S. Senate seat in Wisconsin. If Kohler had won, the Senate would have been evenly split, 48 to 48,[27] and Vice President Nixon would have had the tie-breaking vote, automatically reverting the Senate to Republican control. That change would have greatly diminished the chances of the ambitious Senate Majority Leader Lyndon Johnson from becoming a national politician. But so great was the rancor toward Ezra Taft Benson in Laird's home state that Proxmire won the upset election primarily by hammering on the secretary of agriculture, instead of his opponent, Kohler.[28]

When, in the fall of 1957 Secretary Benson took off for a six-week trip to survey "foreign food distribution" abroad, Laird was finally fed up with him. Many congressional leaders in the previous four years, including Republicans, had called for Benson's resignation. Finally, with reluctance, Laird added his voice to the chorus in an October 1957 letter to President Eisenhower: "It is impossible to even talk about the agriculture program without running into tremendous criticism of the Secretary of Agriculture. He has become the issue, not the program he stands for."[29]

After Laird's defection, and increasing calls for the secretary's resignation, Benson pugnaciously held an early December press conference and announced his decision to remain. Behind the scenes, according to Benson's memoirs, he had offered his resignation to Ike, but the president had asked him to stay.[30] In the 1958 election, an analysis of the anti-Benson vote by *Congressional Quarterly* concluded that Benson had cost "one-third of his Republican supporters representing Midwest farm districts"; their seats went to Democratic challengers.[31] Laird's Democratic opponent that year, Kenneth Traeger, had tried to repeat Proxmire's tactics of the year before by tarring Laird with the Benson brush, but Laird took 60.5 percent of the vote.

Supporters back home dubbed Laird "Dairyland's Best Friend." It was more than campaign rhetoric because Laird did much more than fight against precipitous parity price drops. For example, he crafted a far-sighted dairy measure called the "Laird Self-help Dairy Stabilization Bill,"[32] offering it in nearly every term he served, beginning in 1953. "Farmers themselves should be given the opportunity to decide on a program," Laird espoused. The bill called for a nationwide referendum of milk producers before proposals in it became effective. But the bill was regularly blocked, primarily due to the fractious farm organizations themselves.

Laird was, however, fairly successful in limiting the import of cheaper but substandard dairy products. In his first year he prompted President Eisenhower to invoke a section of the 1949 Agriculture Act to cut imports of cheese. The first one-on-one meeting between Ike and Laird in the Oval Office had been a "victory" meeting, at which a beaming Ike was photographed receiving a ten-pound piece of prime Wisconsin longhorn cheese.[33] The battle against foreign imports continued into the Kennedy and Johnson administrations, and Laird was unflagging. He was most incensed when the United States allowed Communist Bulgaria to flood the American market with "Colby Cheese," named after the Wisconsin town in his district where it had been invented.[34]

At the same time, Laird decried a frustrating set of trade barriers that

existed between American states. Intent on protecting their own farmers' products, states with limited dairy production set up a series of fake inspections,
out-of-state taxes, and bogus shipping requirements that effectively prevented
delivery of cheaper milk from states with a surplus. Wisconsin produced 85
percent more milk than was consumed in the state, so its farmers were greatly
hurt by the interstate barriers. Laird spearheaded "free flow of milk" legislation
aimed at setting up a uniform national standard for milk. He was only moderately successful in this effort, which continually foundered on the shoals of
"states' rights."

None of this was enough to get farmers out of the vicious cycle of declining prices and increased production. No matter what Laird or Congress
did they could not repeal the basic economic law of supply and demand. So,
Laird reckoned, people simply had to drink more milk and eat more butter and
cheese. First he scored several victories in the never-ending conflict between
butter and margarine producers. The growth of the oleo margarine industry
was stymied by a 10-cent-a-pound federal excise tax until it was finally lifted
by Congress in 1950. Then in two short years per capita consumption of "butter substitutes" was nearly neck and neck with dairy butter. The armed forces
joined the initial consumer rush to cheaper margarine. On behalf of his constituents Laird was incensed. He mounted a patriotic-sounding campaign to
allow America's servicemen and veterans to have the best—butter—when they
asked for it. And he had an irrefutable bit of logic on his side: why should the
military and Veterans' Administration pay for the lesser margarine when they
could draw from the huge butter surpluses the federal taxpayer had already
purchased? The common-sense approach won the day for dairy and resulted
in major contracts signed by the Commodity Credit Corporation with the
Veterans Administration and Defense Department.[35]

Laird also preserved butter's place in the U.S. Navy. Of all military personnel, only sailors had to be served butter instead of a substitute, because of a law
passed at the turn of the century. The Navy Ration Act of 1902 said that sailors
must get 1.6 ounces of butter for table use, restricting the use of margarine
except for cooking. Margarine moguls repeatedly tried to amend this act and
nearly succeeded in 1958 with a drive made by the pugnacious Representative
Mendel Rivers of the House Armed Services Committee. But he had never
come up against Laird before. Rivers's bill, which would have permitted the
navy to use margarine a third of the time at its tables, made it to the floor of the
House. There Laird offered an amendment that passed, 207 to 161. It said that
the navy *could* use margarine, but only if surplus butter was not available. The
amendment crippled the bill since surplus butter was usually available.[36]

Laird was an indefatigable promoter of milk as well, encouraging packagers
to put milk in small cartons that could be dispensed in vending machines. Also,
he learned that if chocolate milk were available consumers would buy that
without cutting back on white. So Laird promoted chocolate and the inception

of the Chocolate Milk Research Foundation.[37] He placed Washington's first milk dispensers prominently in the Republican and Democrat cloak rooms of the House. Laird presided at the "christening ceremony," for the vending machines, and encouraged every member of Congress to "drink an extra glass of milk a day."[38]

But he was not done. Long before more modern advertising campaigns—"Got milk?"—Laird frequently expounded upon the nutritional value of milk. Where better to do this than with America's children? He realized that the best use of the surplus milk would be to offer it at low or no cost in the School Lunch Program. The School Milk Program was created by legislation Laird cosponsored in 1954.[39] The federal program quickly grew, delivering enormous amounts of milk to public and parochial schools, nonprofit nursery schools, child-care centers, and summer camps.

Laird's dairy work was a sometimes rewarding, often frustrating venture for the congressman. Doing his best was not always enough. At the end of his first year in office he reflected with wry wit to a *Milwaukee Journal* reporter that when he came to Washington "after my six years in the state legislature, I had the notion that dairy products were of top importance in our agricultural economy. Now, I still think those products are of absolutely primary importance, but I found out that there weren't many members that agreed with me. Wheat, cotton and tobacco districts send far more members to Congress than dairy districts do. There are only 38 Congressional Districts out of the 435 that are predominantly dairy districts. Even peanuts have more representatives fighting for them!"[40]

～

Laird's introduction to defense issues in Congress was inauspicious. The first time the future secretary of defense went to the Pentagon for a military briefing he got lost. "I was escorted by a colonel, who I thought could bring me safely to my destination. After traveling what seemed like miles of corridors, and breaking into untold numbers of conference rooms, my guide finally admitted he was lost," he related with amusement to his constituents in early 1953. "Perhaps the story of the Western Union boy who went in the Pentagon to deliver a message and came out a full colonel is not too far-fetched![41]

That Laird would merit this personal escort and briefing by top military brass in only his sixth week as a congressman is evidence of his early specialty with defense appropriations work, and the recognition of his clout. In those early months it was Laird's vote that decided America would build a third "super" aircraft carrier. The Truman administration had planned to build twelve but had earmarked funds for only two, the *Forrestal* and *Saratoga*. With a change in administrations, carrier critics saw an opening to halt the costly program. Appropriations Committee members from both parties lobbied Laird heavily to cancel the carriers and they assumed that as a newcomer Laird would acquiesce. The committee chairman, John Taber, hinted that the president himself was against building the third carrier, but Laird didn't believe it, so he asked Eisenhower directly. The president said he favored the program. When the Appropriations Committee voted, the carrier money passed by one vote, Laird's, and the third carrier (USS *Ranger*) was finished in 1957. Laird never regretted the expenditure. The *Ranger* would earn thirteen battle stars during the Vietnam War and later serve in the first Gulf War before being decommissioned in 1993.[42]

Eisenhower came to office with a zeal for cutting the military budget. The former top general knew that the services' requests for funds were too extravagant and ordered the Joint Chiefs of Staff to take a "new look" at all of it. The "New Look Program" frowned upon large standing armies of American soldiers stationed around the world. Instead its emphasis was on atomic weapons and guided missiles.[43] Early in his first term Laird worked with Eisenhower to cut $5 billion from the U.S. Air Force budget by reducing the number of combat wings. That change set the tone for tough choices on defense in the following years. As time went on Laird turned out to be even more parsimonious than Eisenhower, refusing to approve money for some defense programs and taking heat from the Republican Party and voters back home. He told his constituents that too many members of Congress gave the president whatever he asked for: "No matter how high a regard you may have for the President of the United States, be he Democrat or Republican, you should not blindly give him everything he asks for in the budget. The job of controlling appropriations is vested in the Congress, and it rightfully belongs there."[44]

Laird felt that "the malignant effects of inter-service rivalry" were costing Americans billions in unnecessary duplication.[45] He fought hard, but not always successfully, for the consolidation of bases. And he butted heads with other members of Congress when he tried to eliminate or move military operations to places that made the most sense—not necessarily the places that pleased the most voters.

Laird initially voted against the construction of the Air Force Academy. He agreed in principle with the need, but the bill to authorize the academy in 1954 was passed before any design or site had been selected. Laird saw that as a blank check to the air force. He watched for four years as the project ballooned in size and expense along stunning Colorado foothills real estate. Laird suspected that President Eisenhower himself chose the Colorado site because he loved to vacation and golf in the state where his mother-in-law lived.

Laird won more often than he lost in appropriations subcommittee battles. In one case, he stopped the army from building a new cold storage facility in Hawaii when there was a perfectly good navy facility operating at only 50 percent capacity. More than a million dollars was saved when Laird got the army and navy to grudgingly agree to share the navy facility. Laird discovered a $5.7 million "phantom" U.S. Air Force hospital in Evreux, France, that was overgrown with weeds. The vacant five-hundred-bed facility, guarded by a few airmen in a Jeep, had never housed a patient. Laird argued for turning it over to the French for good will and minor reimbursement.[46]

Jerry Ford and Mel Laird first bonded as friends on the Defense Appropriations Subcommittee. Ford was nine years older and had been in Congress two terms before Laird was elected. The Laird and Ford children grew up together and the two families often vacationed together. The two men shared an almost fanatical interest in golf and were partnered at many tournaments at Burning Tree Country Club. Ford's friendship with Richard Nixon was older, and he calculated that he was about "as close [to Nixon] as anybody got. But there was never the complete intimacy that I have, for example, with Mel Laird." (The Fords referred to Laird as their "adopted" child after a July 4 weekend getaway at the Tides Inn on the Chesapeake Bay with the Chowder and Marching Club. Barbara Laird was in Wisconsin, and the Inn was full, so Jerry and Betty Ford put up Laird in a little "nursery" room in their hotel suite.)

"Even though we were on the same side politically, we also had some differences on that defense subcommittee," Ford recalled. "But the differences were always very straightforward. There was never any hangover." Ford treated Laird as the "idea man," and chief lieutenant. This explains why the Eisenhower White House quickly learned to negotiate the House defense budget with the Democrat leadership and with the Ford-Laird team.

One thing on which Laird and Ford agreed was that a serious push should be made in construction of submarines equipped with nuclear missiles. When Eisenhower first learned in early 1955 that it might be possible to fire a ballistic missile from a submerged submarine, he ordered the project undertaken at once, and the Ford-Laird team backed the costs. The two knew that the United States would need more than forty such Polaris submarines so that at any one time, thirty could be at sea with their missiles aimed at the Soviet Union. They thought Ike was not moving rapidly enough in his budget requests. When it was clear to the president that Laird and Ford would try to almost double his budget request for Polaris subs in early 1960, he invited them for a breakfast lobbying session to talk them out of it. When he found the two were adamant, he submitted an increased budget request for fully funding three Polaris subs—in addition to the nine already completed or under construction. But that was still not fast enough, so Laird and Ford increased the appropriations for five more.[47] Little more than two years later, during the October 1962 Cuban missile crisis, President Kennedy was grateful that Laird and Ford had speeded up the Polaris program by eighteen to twenty-four months.[48]

Laird was often the one the House sent over to the Senate to argue for the House version of defense bills. His command of facts and figures and his common sense cut through the dross and won the many interhouse debates. It was in those sessions that Laird had animated discussions with Lyndon Johnson, a

member of the Senate Armed Services Committee who, in only one term, had
become Senate majority leader. "I had many occasions to work with him as a
legislator, and I had great respect and admiration for his ability as a legislator," Laird told interviewer David Frost.[49] He had chosen his words carefully,
because Laird did not consider Johnson a man of integrity, which meant they
could never be close friends.

For Laird, one telltale sign of Johnson's integrity was his golf game. Burning Tree golf pro Max Elbin said Johnson was the poorest player of all the
presidents: "He couldn't hit a bull in the ass with a bass fiddle."[50] But that was
not the reason for Laird's disdain. Johnson had a tendency to cheat; if he didn't
like where he had hit a ball, he would drop another one and try again, or place
it where he would have liked the first ball to land. Regarding this kind of cheating, the Burning Tree club history was characteristically gracious, noting that
Johnson played "with an abandon that was almost literally carefree [and was]
perhaps the only golfer who never suffered on the course."

A more serious tip-off to Laird that Johnson would not be a worthy friend
was his penchant for using his position to make money. A Democrat whom
Laird truly respected, House Speaker Sam Rayburn, had said: "I have been
unable to save much money in my life. I have been in politics, and in politics
an honest man does not get rich." At the time of his death Rayburn's savings
were only $15,000. But during Johnson's time in the House and Senate he be-
came the multimillionaire owner of a galaxy of radio and TV stations. It was
only possible because he used his political influence to strong-arm the Federal
Communications Commission into giving him favorable licenses, permits, and
rulings. Following Johnson's signals, many lobbyists knew the way to buy political influence with him was not through the outright campaign contributions,
but by paying high rates for advertising on his stations. Laird knew this because
the Wisconsinite he had promoted to become an Eisenhower FCC commissioner and later chairman, John Doerfler, had uncovered the evidence in FCC
files and shared it with Laird.[51] Armed with that, though not referring directly
to the documentation, Laird, in a speech on the House floor, courteously but
pointedly questioned Senator Johnson's improper use of congressional influence. Laird's speech didn't get much attention, but Johnson noticed, and Laird
felt it tainted their relationship. He didn't care because in his mind Johnson
was the kind of man who gave politicians a bad name. He was the kind of man
who could destroy the most important civil rights bill of the century (a Laird-
supported 1957 Republican effort), get credit for passing it in an emasculated
form, and then be hailed eight years later for passage of virtually the same civil
rights act he should have helped pass in 1957.

⚡

Laird was four square behind civil rights legislation, even though there was
little direct need for it in his own district. He had one of the lowest percent-

ages of African-Americans of any congressional district. Of the half million people in his Wisconsin district, he had only two black constituents and he knew both of them. Nevertheless, as a congressman he felt it was vital to pass legislation that would give the federal government a way to enforce voting rights for blacks. The time was overripe in the 1950s for passage of civil rights legislation, especially after an activist Supreme Court in 1954 issued a landmark ruling desegregating American schools. The Republican platforms of 1952 and 1956, in which Laird had played a leading role, called for civil rights reform. Eisenhower's Attorney General Herbert Brownell and his staff obliged. They drafted a wide-ranging bill in 1956 that made it illegal to segregate public places such as schools, swimming pools, bathrooms, and restaurants; created a six-member federal Civil Rights Commission; mandated an additional assistant attorney general in charge of a Justice Department Civil Rights Division; and granted federal courts more authority to enforce constitutionally guaranteed civil rights for all Americans. The Brownell bill passed in the House in July, then went to the Senate, where southern Democrats had killed all civil rights bills since 1875.[52]

The method they used to kill the Brownell bill in 1956 was to bottle it up in a committee where southerners held a disproportionate share of seats—a fact that Laird made sure his constituents were aware of after the civil rights bill was defeated. The Brownell bill was easily thwarted by the Senate Judiciary Committee, whose chairman, Mississippi Democrat James Eastland, bragged that he had "special pockets in my pants, and for three years I carried these bills around in my pockets."[53] Democrats were surprised in November when the defeat of the bill cost them in the national election. A large number of African-Americans voted Republican for the first time. They had been firmly Republican from the time of Lincoln's Emancipation Proclamation to Roosevelt's New Deal, when they were wooed en masse into the Democratic fold.

Vice President Nixon engaged in animated sessions with Chowder and Marching Club members about civil rights bills and how to get them past the southern Democrats. So it was proposed in secret C&M meetings that on the Senate's first day in the 1957 session Nixon would stage manage a change in the rules. Rule 22 in the Senate said that the only way to break a filibuster was through a "cloture" vote of two-thirds of the Senate. Nixon, in collusion with liberal Democratic senators as well as the Republican senators, plotted to revise Rule 22 to require only a simple majority. That would mean the Senate majority could force a civil rights bill out of committee and finally pass it in the full Senate.

By prearranged plan, Nixon gaveled the 1957 session into order and called on Senator Clinton Anderson, a New Mexico Democrat, who made a motion to have the Senate adopt rules for the current session. By prerogative only one senator could stop the vote—the majority leader, who was Lyndon Johnson. He frequently used racial epithets such as "nigger" in private and depended on prosegregation southern senators to keep his elected position. So, having been forewarned about the attempt to change Rule 22, Johnson was quickly on his feet and Nixon had to call on him. His motion to table Anderson's motion took precedence. Using a carrot-and-stick approach, Johnson, over several days, secured a majority vote for his tabling motion. The reformers had to throw in the towel.

In those opening seconds of the session, American history had been changed measurably. Nixon had lined up all forty-seven Republican senators to support the rule change. With the added votes of liberal Democrats, a new Rule 22 would certainly have been adopted. Then the House, with a majority of civil rights proponents such as Laird, would have sent the Senate a bill upon which to vote. The Senate would not be able to bury it in a committee; a vote would be called and the Republicans would have been hailed as civil rights heroes.[54]

The House passed the Brownell bill again in June. As in 1956, Republicans such as Laird proved much stronger in support of civil rights than did Democrats.[55] Johnson biographer Robert Caro detailed how Senator Johnson, knowing he needed to have a civil rights bill to his credit to be considered a serious presidential candidate, emasculated the House bill in the Senate through amendments and secured passage of the first civil rights legislation since 1875. Johnson was praised for the accomplishment by the media of the day.[56]

The new law had no desegregation provision for "public accommodations." It also effectively allowed anyone accused of violating African-American voting rights to get a jury trial. In the South of that time a jury was likely to side with any white person accused of violating an African-American's rights. One of the most emotional moments during the Senate debate came when Laird's friend and fellow C&M-er Senator Charles Potter argued against the jury trial amendment. Shaking from emotion as he leaned on his crutches (having lost both legs in World War II), and, tremulous with moral indignation, Potter said, "I fought beside Negroes in the war. I saw them die for us. For the Senate of the United States to repay these valiant men ... by a watered-down version of this legislation would make a mockery of the democratic concept we hold so dear."[57] The day the jury trial amendment passed in the Senate, Nixon told reporters outside the chamber: "This is one of the saddest days in the history of the Senate."

The primary benefits of the original Republican bill, which Johnson himself had caused to be removed by compromise and amendment, later became the heart of the his administration's 1964 Civil Rights and 1965 Voting Rights acts, for which he has been hailed by historians. But the true heroes of civil rights were the liberal Democrats of the era, Laird and many of his Republican colleagues, and Richard Nixon.[58]

Only twice in the twentieth century did the younger members of a U.S. political party rise up against their party leader in Congress and mount a successful coup. In both cases Laird was a leader of the "Young Turks." It first occurred following the 1958 election when "the Republicans took a terrible licking," as Ford put it.[59] The Democrats won forty-seven more seats in the House, and thirteen more in the Senate—an increase that gave the Democrats close to a two-thirds majority in both chambers.

Vice President Nixon tried to be upbeat in a pep talk letter to Laird: "While we have suffered a major loss, nationally I think the Republican Party came out of this campaign stronger than when it went in because of the very fact that we went down fighting." That was nonsense, and Laird knew it. The Republican elephant's trunk was dragging, and his body was sagging. An emergency transfusion of new blood was needed at the party's leadership level.

The pragmatic Laird did not set out at first to replace House Minority Leader Joe Martin of Massachusetts. No speaker or minority leader had ever been deposed in the twentieth century because the risk of mounting such an effort was great; instigators would be punished with poor committee assignments and loss of many other perks. So Laird set his sights lower. He thought that if his friend Johnny Byrnes of Wisconsin became chairman of the Republican Policy Committee—a job Martin also held—new ideas and a new image for the party might be possible from that perch. On Pearl Harbor Day in 1958 the ball began rolling when Laird asked Representative James Auchincloss of New Jersey, a Martin ally, to persuade him to appoint Byrnes as Republican Policy Committee chair and Ford as assistant floor leader. Considering the proposal impudent, Martin sent word back through Auchincloss the same day: *absolutely not!* Three days later a five-man strategy committee was formed from the C&M ranks and the SOS group. They sent a second message to Martin reminding him that they were *not* asking him to step down as minority leader but simply asking to add Byrnes and Ford to the leadership mix. Again the idea was rebuffed.[60]

The upstarts decided that there was no other choice then; Martin had to go. He had been the Republican House leader for twenty years. Seventy-four and limping because of a blood clot in his right leg, he projected an image of a tired Republican Party. The next step was taken by Laird, who asked Representative Glenard Lipscomb of California to help him. They took two surveys among the House Republicans. The first found a majority would back a coup, and the second poll showed support for three names: Byrnes, Ford, and Charlie Halleck, who was Martin's number two. (In deference to these three more senior Republicans, Laird did not add his own name to the poll.)

Byrnes proved the most popular choice. But Halleck had the support of the president, so Laird and his fellow Young Turks had no choice but to back

Halleck. The Republican caucus met January 6. Laird had counted heads beforehand and was confident that Halleck would beat Martin by four or five votes. On the first secret ballot, Halleck won by only one vote, 73 to 72. "I learned that there are a lot of liars when it comes to secret ballots," Laird ruefully observed. "People give you a commitment and you can't really count on it. You always want a few extra votes in your pocket." An objection was made to the first tally because there was one uncounted vote that had been illegible. In a second ballot Halleck won by four.

Laird crowed a little in public about what he foresaw as the positive results of this historic revolt. Instead of a reputation as naysayers to popular government programs, Republicans would be seen as the "party of fiscal responsibility," which would support programs only when the money was there to pay for them. In the back of Laird's mind remained the thought that Halleck had not been his first choice, and, in a few short years, Halleck's leadership would prove increasingly inept, prompting Laird and friends to rise again in revolt.

∽∾

Though he considered Eisenhower a mentor and friend, Laird did not vote for all of the president's programs. On average, Laird voted for Eisenhower's proposals about two-thirds of the time, according to a calculation of the relevant eight Eisenhower years by *Congressional Quarterly*.[61] Laird favored Ike's domestic programs more than his foreign programs; he voted against half of Eisenhower's foreign policy-related legislation. And no administration effort earned Laird's disapprobation more consistently than foreign aid, which came under the rubric of the "Mutual Security Program." Eisenhower had inherited the effort from the Truman administration and was convinced it was vital to U.S. national security. He also knew it would be tough going to persuade Americans that foreign aid was really a defense issue. Laird supported mutual security in principle, but not in price.

Laird had joined the Congress believing foreign aid was excessive, and his first congressional trip abroad confirmed it. In late 1953 he was one of a five-man fact-finding committee that traveled through Europe. When he returned Laird pronounced emphatically that the time had come to wean Europe. The Marshall Plan, which Laird had favored because it aimed at building Europe to prewar levels, had done such a good job that by 1953 European nations were economically *better off* than before the war. Yet they were still eager to receive American aid at a time when the U.S. national debt of $273 billion was far in excess of the combined indebtedness of all the countries the United States was helping. "To keep on," Laird said, "is to cut our own throats. We have already destroyed our own foreign markets for some agricultural products. The same thing is true industrially. We must remember that we can destroy ourselves if we do not keep ourselves economically strong. Other countries are now balancing their budgets through economic assistance from us."[62] As he laconically observed in a later report, "there has been little or no mutuality to the Mutual Security Program."[63] He firmly believed that the defense burden in particular should be shared with America's allies, and later, as secretary of defense, he instituted that as a bedrock of the "Nixon Doctrine."

Congressman Laird also objected to specific expenditures within the program. For example, he consistently voted against aid to Yugoslavia, a Communist country controlled by a military dictator, Marshall Tito. Laird wrote, "It is folly for us to believe that Yugoslavia would side with our nation should their help ever be needed." In 1956 Laird told his constituents that for the prior three years he had voted against the Foreign Aid Appropriations Act because "it was impossible for me to justify aid to Dictator Tito. I used my vote to 'Veto Tito.'"[64]

A review of all Laird's votes reveals that he never once voted for an Eisenhower mutual security appropriation unless it had been substantially cut, as in 1956 when the House cut foreign aid by $1.1 billion. Those votes were one of the few areas of disagreement between Laird and Ford. "Jerry was much more liberal than I in the foreign aid area," Laird said. Part of Ford's support was parochial—he had served on the Foreign Operations Appropriations Subcommittee, which recommended the expenditures. On that subcommittee Ford was also part of the subgroup that reviewed the CIA's cloak-and-dagger activities—many of which mesmerized the committee but turned out to be foreign policy disasters.[65]

One of the foreign trouble spots that received Laird's scrutiny was the Middle East. In 1953 he had visited most of the Middle Eastern countries including Jordan, Turkey, Lebanon, Iraq, and Egypt, whose King Farouk had been deposed in a coup led by Gamel Abdel Nasser the year before.[66] In Jordan, Laird had an audience with its new regent of five months, eighteen-year-old King Hussein. He was appalled at the condition of the Arabs living near Israel. Some nine hundred thousand Arab refugees, driven out of Palestine, were subsisting on meager rations in United Nations refugee camps. But they were better off than those living in their own villages near the Israeli border and not eligible for UN aid; Laird saw some of them eating grass. Meanwhile, Israel was flouting conditions under which it was created as a state, which included failing to compensate Arabs for their homes or permitting them to return. Yet American assistance paid for two-thirds of Israel's budget, allowing it to finance a well-equipped army while the Arab nations had substandard military strength.

At a Tel Aviv dinner with then–prime minister Moshe Sharett, Laird raised some of these points with Sharett, who unapologetically agreed, "Yes, we have great support in the United States." That might not always be the case, if Israel's course diverged from American foreign policy interest, Laird cautioned him. "There's one thing that I don't want you to underestimate—my Jewish friends are certainly loyal to Israel, but they're loyal to our country first," he added.

"Young man," Sharett smiled, patronizingly, "I think you've got a lot to learn."

In a speech to a service club when he got back home, Laird recounted his observations and the Sharett conversation and lamented the disproportionate amount of foreign aid going to Israel instead of its Arab neighbors. During the question-and-answer period, a Stevens Point businessman, who was Jewish, stood up and said, "You know, that story you just told is the most anti-Semitic story I've ever heard."

"I'm just repeating what happened," Laird replied. "I'm not trying to be anti-Semitic or anti-Jewish or anything else. I really feel that the Jewish citizens of America do owe their loyalty here first, and Israel second." After the meeting, Bob Froehlke took him aside: "Mel, you just lost every Jewish vote and dollar in the Seventh Congressional District. You may have picked up a few Arab votes, but the bad news is that there isn't one Arab in your district and there are a lot of Jews." Years later Froehlke remembered the evening well. "He made it very clear in his speech that he thought the Israelis were being way too hard on the Palestinians, violating their human rights. I was proud of him because that was the way he saw it at the time, and it didn't matter that it would cost him votes."[67] That day was also the first time Froehlke heard Laird utter a maxim that he would repeat regularly in his career: "Bob, I have to live with my conscience longer than my constituents."

❧

Eisenhower declared in one interview after his presidency: "The United States never lost a soldier or a foot of ground in my administration. We kept the peace. People asked how it happened—by God, it didn't just happen, I'll tell you that."[68] Eisenhower sidestepped U.S. intervention in several regional skirmishes, which suited Laird just fine. He preferred diplomacy over shooting. The greatest temptation for American military combat intervention came from a country on the Indochina peninsula called Vietnam.

The French had been trying to hold onto their colony by force of arms against a Communist insurgency led by Ho Chi Minh. On the condition that the French would eventually grant Vietnam its independence, Presidents Roosevelt, Truman, and Eisenhower all financially supported the French military. After an increase by Ike of $60 million in aid in mid-1953, the United States was funding three-quarters of the French war effort, but they wanted more—including ground forces. Eisenhower talked with British Prime Minister Winston Churchill who said that his people hadn't supported a military effort to hold onto their own India colony, so they weren't about to back a military effort on behalf of a French colony. Besides, Churchill added, sending Western ground troops after guerrillas in a tropical jungle would be like going into the water to fight a shark. Unable to secure an international, U.N.-related force, Eisenhower proved extremely reluctant to send American troops to Asia so soon after securing an armistice in Korea. It was a position that Laird enthusiastically supported.

One of the strongest statements Eisenhower made at the time was at a meeting of the National Security Council on January 8, 1954. The declassified minutes say,

> For himself, said the President with great force, he simply could not imagine the United States putting ground forces anywhere in Southeast Asia, except possibly in Malaya, which we would have to defend as a bulwark to our offshore island chain. But to do this anywhere else was simply beyond his contemplation. Indeed, the key to winning this war was to get the Vietnamese to fight. There was just no sense in even talking about United States forces replacing the French in Indochina. If we did so, the Vietnamese could be expected to transfer their hatred of the French to us. I cannot tell you, said the President with vehemence, how bitterly opposed I am to such a course of action. This war in Indochina would absorb our troops by divisions![69]

Several weeks later, as the French were building up a jungle fortress at Dien Bien Phu, 170 miles west of Hanoi (in what would later be called North Vietnam), Eisenhower *did* send ten bomber aircraft along with mechanics who became the first American soldiers to assist the French. When Republican leaders pressed him about the commitment on February 8 at the White House, Eisenhower said he was "frightened about getting ground forces tied up in Indochina" and pledged the mechanics would be pulled out by June 15, which they were.[70]

The Viet Minh forces of more than one hundred thousand men began a massive attack and siege of the sixteen thousand French soldiers at Dien Bien Phu on March 14, 1954. For fifty-five days, there was terrible loss of life on both sides. As the French began losing the battle, the pressure for U.S. ground troops to save the French was great. At one point Admiral Arthur Radford, chairman of the Joint Chiefs of Staff, put together a joint U.S.-French plan called "Operation Vulture," which involved a U.S. B-29 bomber force and the use of three tactical nuclear bombs to save the besieged and badly outnumbered French forces.[71] But Eisenhower would not approve the American involvement without other countries, too.

At an April 7 news conference Eisenhower made his most famous speech about his concerns for Indochina, which became known thereafter as "the domino theory." Asked about the strategic importance of Indochina, the president said there were "broader considerations that might follow what you would call the 'falling domino' principle." If the United States abandoned Southeast Asia, the dominolike "sequence of events" could mean the loss to Communist forces of all Indochina, then Burma, Thailand, Malaya, and Indonesia—and probably the additional loss of Japan, Formosa (Taiwan), and the Philippines, at which point Australia and New Zealand would be threatened.

With such real concerns on Ike's mind if the United States did not intervene, he was more susceptible at that time to pressure from military leaders and right-wing politicians to send in the American military. While Laird was opposed to such a move, his Chowder and Marching buddy, Vice President Nixon, was hawkish. On April 16 before the American Society of Newspaper Editors, Nixon said that if sending American forces was the only way to avoid further Communist expansion in Asia, "I believe that the Executive Branch of the government has to take the politically unpopular position of facing up to it and doing it, and I personally would support such a decision." He appeared to be enunciating a new administration policy contrary to what Eisenhower had ever said, and the statement made headlines around the globe.

Dien Bien Phu finally fell to Ho Chi Minh's forces (under General Nguyen Giap) on May 7—the same day Laird declared pointedly in Athens, Wisconsin, "Indochina is no place for American soldiers to fight."[72] Twelve days later, on May 19, Laird was heartened to hear the president express the same view. The occasion was a White House breakfast for the Chowder and Marching Club. At one point Eisenhower said, "America should never get involved with a land war in Asia." Laird never forgot and frequently quoted Eisenhower's words over the years. Laird also remembered that Nixon had a distinctly different viewpoint, and that Eisenhower "took him to the woodshed" regarding his more hawkish remarks. Evidence of this came in a subsequent breakfast Eisenhower had with the SOS group on June 17. Once again Laird heard Ike's position on Indochina, similar to his own, but this time Eisenhower confided that he had had a disagreement or two with Nixon about it. Though the breakfast was supposed to be off the record, someone (not Laird) leaked a story from the gathering about Eisenhower's differences with Nixon over Indochina. It made only minor headlines since the bigger news was the nearly complete Geneva negotiations that would partition Vietnam at the seventeenth parallel.

Almost seven years later, when Eisenhower completed his term as president, he had held the line against American troop involvement in Vietnam. A total of only 773 military advisors were then in South Vietnam, according to Laird.[73] The number was so infinitesimal when looking at the total number of U.S. forces, and larger involvement in dozens of places around the world, that Eisenhower supporters could boast about his Republican administration, as did Laird: "He got us out of Korea and he kept us out of Vietnam."

5

Hectic and *Healthy* Turmoil

⤬

H. R. HALDEMAN STEPPED OFF THE PLANE on a chilly November Sunday in central Wisconsin, fashionably warmed by a cashmere coat with velvet collar. The Beverly Hills–raised advance man for Vice President Richard Nixon made an unforgettable first impression on Bob Froehlke, who met him at the airport. Froehlke's friend Melvin Laird had asked him to host Haldeman in his home for the evening. Haldeman was in town to pave the way for Nixon's appearance at a party honoring Laird—an occasion that became the Great Kennedy–Nixon Cranberry Debate of 1959.

After six years in Congress, Laird's popularity was such that his friends and supporters had independently planned a formal affair for him—the "Melvin R. Laird Appreciation Night" on November 12. Telegrams were sent to Washington with invitations and requests for testimonials, which arrived by the dozens from Republicans and Democrats. "I have felt fortunate to call him one of my closest personal friends," Vice President Nixon said when he accepted the invitation to serve as keynote speaker for the testimonial.[1] Privately Nixon insisted his appearance be nonpartisan—not a run-up to the presidential campaign—so no local politicos would be invited to sit on the stand with him to boost their own campaigns.

Still Nixon could not ignore the fact that Wisconsin would be a crucial presidential primary state only a few months later. And he was also fully cognizant that his potential opponent, Senator John F. Kennedy, was scheduled to speak in Marshfield on the same night, just thirty-two miles from the Laird dinner in Wisconsin Rapids. This would make it the first Nixon-Kennedy "debate" of sorts, at least as reported in the following morning's newspaper accounts of both speeches. For these reasons, Nixon felt his appearance needed to be well advanced, so Haldeman was sent four days ahead.

As a rising insurance executive, Froehlke was frequently away from home. So the deal he made with his wife, Nancy, was that Sunday evening socializing had to include their young children, which usually meant roasting wieners on a stick in the fireplace. Haldeman's presence and mannerisms gave the Froehlkes pause about continuing that tradition with their California guest. "But I couldn't violate my promise to my wife and kids," Froehlke said. When informed of the evening menu, Haldeman brusquely asked: "Do you always cook hot dogs in your fireplace?" He then agreed to join the family tradition. "So I did entertain Bob Haldeman with his cashmere velvet-collar coat cooking wieners in my fireplace," Froehlke laughed.[2] The square-jawed Haldeman,

79

who was described later as having "a gaze that would freeze Medusa," seemed to enjoy himself.

But the bucolic beginning for the quasi-campaign event did not extend past Monday morning when Health, Education, and Welfare Secretary Arthur S. Fleming started America's first big food scare. The San Francisco office of the Food and Drug Administration (part of HEW) had discovered that a batch of Oregon cranberries was contaminated with the weed killer aminotriazole, which was potentially toxic for humans.[3] At a press conference in Washington, Fleming announced that 9 percent of the Oregon and Washington crops might be contaminated, but that the majority of cranberries, which were grown primarily in Wisconsin and Massachusetts, had shown no contamination. A reporter pressed him: Can a "housewife" feel safe in buying *any* cranberries at the supermarket? "To be on the safe side," Fleming said, "she doesn't buy."[4]

Only two weeks before Thanksgiving, Fleming was the grim reaper. Cranberries disappeared from supermarket shelves across the country and from the menus of many restaurants. Officials in three states banned cranberry sales, while other states asked for voluntary suspension of sales. In Chicago one nightclub instituted a one-to-a-customer limit on cranberry cocktails.

Laird quickly jumped into the fray. His great-grandfather had been the first man to grow the fruit in Wood County, and the crop had taken off to the point that nearly one-third of all cranberries in America were grown in Laird's district.[5] The economic impact of Fleming's "red scare" would be devastating for local growers. Within hours of Fleming's press conference, Laird called FDA Administrator George Larrick and demanded quick action to clear innocent Wisconsin cranberries. As the ranking member of the HEW appropriations subcommittee, Laird held the purse strings and Larrick knew it. "If there is any way of getting clean berries to the public in time for Thanksgiving, we will certainly do it," he promised.

"Fleming was nuts to outlaw that crop and destroy it," Laird recalled. "You'd have to eat a barrel of cranberries for anything to happen to you." Actually, not even a barrel would be enough. The scare had been prompted because rats fed aminotriazole in concentrations of one hundred parts per million had developed thyroid cancer. To duplicate that consumption, a human being would have to have digested 15,000 pounds of contaminated cranberries every day for a number of years.[6] But it was too late to calm the public with such facts. The best Laird could get was an immediate dispatch of one hundred inspectors and sixty chemists to cranberry-producing areas to examine and quickly pronounce the majority of the crop clean. Laird told reporters that the shadow cast on cranberries was "reprehensible" given the low risk and the relatively minuscule contamination found.[7]

By the time Nixon and Kennedy arrived in Wood County, Wisconsin, for their speeches, the crimson crisis was Topic A. Senator Kennedy, from the cranberry-producing state of Massachusetts, ceremoniously drank two glasses of cranberry juice as he spoke to 1,500 Democrats assembled at Columbus High School in Laird's hometown of Marshfield. As he sipped, Kennedy denounced the Eisenhower administration—and by association, Nixon—for "moving swiftly and so recklessly" against the cranberry "menace," but showing "no comparable zeal" in preventing nuclear fallout, which was a "far greater threat to the health of the American people."

With all the cameras pointed at the vice president during the two-thousand-person Laird banquet, the largest dinner ever held in central Wisconsin, Laird whispered to Nixon that he damn well better eat all his cranberries, and ask for seconds. "I'm going to watch you eat them first," Nixon smiled back at Laird. "Then I will." So Laird downed a man-sized portion, and then Nixon started on his cranberry sauce, eventually consuming four helpings. "My mother and my wife both fed cranberries to him," Laird laughed. "We had him eating cranberries until they came out of his ears." (For many years after, Nixon told Laird, he couldn't eat a cranberry without thinking about the Wisconsin Rapids banquet and how they were stuffing them down his throat just like he was a turkey.) The diners adjourned to the Lincoln Field House where Nixon, before an unusually large crowd of 5,400 central Wisconsinites, declared that he would be eating cranberries at both Thanksgiving and Christmas.[8]

Nixon aide Herb Klein remembers the cranberry competition between Nixon and Kennedy as "the first debate."[9] If consumption was the measure, Nixon certainly out-ate Kennedy. But the pro-Kennedy *Madison Capital Times* declared the "cranberry duel" a "dead heat." Yes, "Nixon ate the most cranberries," they pronounced, but "Kennedy got in the best licks"—rhetorically.[10] Laird saw the episode as a harbinger of things to come: his earnest, hard-working candidate Nixon bested by a more charismatic Kennedy, heavily favored by the press traveling with him.

As for the cranberry growers, crusading Congressman Laird sponsored and passed a bill that mandated the federal government indemnify them for the cranberries the government had unnecessarily destroyed. The 1959 cranberry scare became the granddaddy of America's tainted food panics. It laid the groundwork for scares yet to come, such as those concerning cyclamates (1969), DES in beef (1972), nitrites (1972), red dye number 2 (1976), saccharin (1977), coffee and pancreatic cancer (1981), Alar in apples (1989), benzene in Perrier (1990), and so on, according to the American Council on Science and Health in a 1997 booklet, *Facts versus Fears: A Review of the Greatest Unfounded Health Scares of Recent Times.*

⚜

Conventional Washington wisdom in January 1960 was that none of the senators running for the Democratic presidential nomination—Jack Kennedy, Hubert Humphrey, Lyndon Johnson, Stuart Symington, and others—was likely to win. Laird prognosticated to his constituents that it looked like a race was shaping up between Nixon and Adlai Stevenson, the former senator who had twice before been the Democratic presidential nominee against Eisenhower. "We're in for a hectic, healthy, turmoil," Laird wrote.[11]

Laird liked Kennedy, a fellow navy and World War II veteran and a fellow "young Turk" on the other side of the aisle. Their first meeting had been in the White House on a memorable occasion. A Polish pilot, Lieutenant Franciszek Jarecki, had defected on March 5, 1953, flying his plane into Denmark. It was the first time the West had a chance to look at a high-performance Soviet MiG. The CIA had promised the pilot cash and American citizenship; Kennedy and Laird (with Ford) were responsible for pushing a bill through their two houses "For the Relief of Franciszek Jarecki." Eisenhower invited Jarecki, Kennedy, Laird, Ford, and several others to the White House on July 29 for the ceremonial signing.[12] Laird chatted with Kennedy, congratulating him on his engagement only a month before to Jacqueline Bouvier. (Privately, he wondered if the marriage would settle Kennedy down. By then, as Laird later recalled, Kennedy had a reputation as a ladies' man.)

But the first substantive conversation between Kennedy and Laird occurred at an unusual private Democratic dinner during which Laird defended Kennedy to the senator's own party leadership. Laird had been invited to the dinner by Democrat John Fogarty, with whom he'd become close while working on the Health Appropriations Subcommittee. What Laird most remembered was that Kennedy was the butt of criticism for the small gathering of senior Democrats. "They were giving him the needle a little bit about his ambition. These guys had been around a long time, and—well, let's just say that I treated him with more respect than they did." Kennedy's upstart campaign for the Democratic presidential nomination in 1960 was not generally supported by the party leadership. Even after Kennedy won some primaries, Eleanor Roosevelt said that perhaps he should be the vice presidential candidate on a Stevenson ticket.

For a man with few disappointments in his political life up to that point, Laird's selection by Nixon as the *vice* chairman of the 1960 Republican Platform Committee was a small setback—but one that, because of the political vagaries that year, allowed him to shine more brightly than had he been chairman. Beginning in January, Laird's congressional friends from the Chowder and Marching Club leaned on Nixon to choose Laird for the chairmanship. Rumors in the press that Laird would be passed over caused Johnny Byrnes to buttonhole Nixon, who wrote back in mid-April denying the rumors.[13] A month later, on May 11, Nixon passed over Laird and announced as platform chair an Illinois business *wunderkind*, Charles Percy, a fund-raiser for Republican candidates and causes.[14]

After the 1958 midterm election debacle for Republicans, President Eisenhower, prompted by a suggestion from his brother Milton, had decided Republican philosophy needed rethinking and redefining "to put life back into the Republican Party." He and Nixon thought a nonpolitical, charismatic outsider such as Percy was just the man to chair a "Republican Committee on Program and Progress."[15] Percy held hearings. Laird recalled flying to the University of Chicago several weekends to help with the committee's final report, which was published as a book in February 1960, *Decisions for a Better America.* Ike liked the results and Percy's capability, so he heartily encouraged Nixon to make Percy platform chair.

Nixon offered no public explanation for why he made Percy the chairman and his friend, Laird, vice chairman. The press speculated that Nixon had wanted someone more liberal than himself, more handsome, younger, and photogenic. (At thirty-seven Laird was actually three years younger than Percy, but his balding pate versus Percy's fulsome blond mane gave a different impression.) Laird publicly said he was "highly honored" to be appointed vice chairman.[16] He later learned that Nixon passed him over in an attempt to curry favor with Nelson Rockefeller.

In 1960, if America had a royal family, it was the Rockefellers. Their business and philanthropic enterprises affected every facet of American life. Nelson Rockefeller was the first to break the family taboo against politics. Having served in various posts in the Roosevelt, Truman, and Eisenhower administrations, he ran for governor of New York in 1958 and won. Quickly becoming the standard-bearer for the more liberal wing of the Republican Party, Rockefeller was a force that Nixon had to co-opt if he wanted to be president. Charles Percy moved in Rockefeller's circles, so Nixon passed over Laird and tapped a man he thought might help bring Rockefeller to the table. But it was a miscalculation. Around the time of the platform announcement, it was becoming evident that, even though he had not campaigned in the primaries, Rockefeller hoped the Republican delegates would draft him as their presidential nominee at the July convention.

What imbued Rockefeller with such new quixotic obstinacy was his conviction that America had fallen behind in the nuclear missile race. He was not alone. One of his protégés, Harvard professor Henry Kissinger, had written a book that presumed the Soviets were ahead in that race. Senator Kennedy had expressed alarm about the "missile gap" in August 1958, and it was clear that he would make it a major charge against the Eisenhower-Nixon administration in the campaign. For four months Rockefeller felt he had to mute his own criticism so as not to impact an upcoming summit in June between Eisenhower and Soviet leader Nikita Khrushchev. But when Khrushchev abruptly walked out of the Big Four summit in Paris and canceled the Moscow meet, all bets were off for Rockefeller, and Nixon knew it.

"Nixon knew and felt that if he was going to beat Kennedy, he had to have the more liberal eastern Republican establishment with him," Laird recalled, and that required Rockefeller's endorsement. So Nixon sent a rapid series of offers to Rockefeller: Would he like to be the vice presidential nominee? No! Would he chair the Republican National Convention? No. Would he please give the keynote address? No—he might not even attend. On May 25, 1960 Rockefeller announced he was making himself available for presidential "draft." On June 8 he had breakfast with President Eisenhower at the White House, ensuring maximum coverage afterward for a pronouncement on the Rockefeller view of all matters foreign and domestic—a view that was unfavorable to the Nixon-Eisenhower position.

Nixon was still hoping to mollify Rockefeller through emissaries, and he saw Percy as his best hope. Percy met with Rockefeller for three hours in New York on July 6 and was given a nearly six-thousand-word memorandum of what should be included in the Republican platform, which he promptly released to the press.[17] During the week before the convention, when the Percy-Laird platform committee met, Rockefeller minions were lobbying hard for their man's views. In spite of the fuss over him, Rockefeller sensed the platform was not going his way. So on Friday, July 22, his press secretary said Rockefeller was deeply dissatisfied with the platform drafts, implying he might be forced to lead a floor fight.[18]

Nixon "panicked," in Laird's view. The vice president secretly rushed by plane from Washington to meet with Rockefeller around 7:30 P.M. in his penthouse apartment at 810 Fifth Avenue. After a lamb chop dinner, Nixon once again pressed the governor to be his vice presidential candidate; Rockefeller wasn't interested. But he *was* intent on fighting Nixon in the field of ideas—the Republican platform. Though the platform had already been drafted, Rockefeller produced a lengthy list of changes he wanted made. To the governor's surprise, Nixon was willing to compromise on almost every point. What Rockefeller didn't know, and Laird did, was that Nixon did not view the platform as holy writ. In almost every meeting Laird had with Eisenhower on policy issues, the president would confer with the language of the last platform, on which he believed he had been elected, and adjust his view to match it. Nixon didn't think the platform was sacred, so he was willing to compromise with Rockefeller, who held platforms in higher regard.

At 10:30 P.M., after Nixon and Rockefeller had been negotiating for a couple of hours, a five-way telephone conversation between New York and Chicago was arranged to bring other key players into the process. Rockefeller used the phone in his bedroom; Nixon used one in the governor's study. In Chicago, from their rooms in the Sheraton Blackstone Hotel, Laird and Percy came on the line. Roswell Perkins, a Rockefeller deputy, at another hotel, also came on. Broken only by an accidental twenty-minute disconnection by the operator, the five spoke on this "party line" for more than three hours. Though Laird was able to mask it somewhat, he was the primary dissenter. Rockefeller was getting what he wanted; Nixon was getting what he most wanted, which was Rockefeller's support; and Percy was getting what he wanted: a compromise between his friend (Rockefeller) and the likely presidential nominee (Nixon). But Laird didn't like it because he knew what a furor the amended platform would prompt from several quarters that Nixon could ill afford to anger. At one point, he presciently cautioned the four other parties: "There is one person missing in this conversation: the president."

After the call ended at 2 A.M., Nixon stayed another hour and a half, finalizing the press release about the agreement on "specific and basic positions" that would be issued in Rockefeller's name, and then flew back to Washington at 3:30 A.M. The statement, which outlined seven points each on domestic and foreign/national security policy, was promptly dubbed by journalists, who received it after dawn, the "Fourteen-Point Compact of Fifth Avenue." The nocturnal negotiations lit a fuse that, as Laird instinctively knew, would inevitably detonate a series of blasts.[19]

Republican conservatives and moderates were furious, believing Nixon had sold them out. An embittered Senator Barry Goldwater called Nixon's supplication and concessions to Rockefeller a "surrender" that would guarantee "a Republican defeat in November."[20] Many of the 104 platform committee delegates were up in arms as well. They had worked hard during the previous week, and some for months prior to that, and had already produced a platform draft of which they were proud. It was insulting that Rockefeller been allowed to dictate a rewrite. Percy tried to talk them down from their anger but was ineffective. His private view was that the Fifth Avenue Compact represented "a sizable surrender by Nixon to Rockefeller." But, confirming Laird's assessment, Percy noted that "to Nixon, the platform was of secondary importance, that it meant nothing without someone to implement it, and the only way to implement it was to get elected." And he needed the support of the Rockefeller wing to do that.[21]

After the conservatives, platform delegates, and Nixon aides had vented, there was a fourth quarter that erupted with volcanic anger: President Eisenhower. On Saturday morning, at his Newport, Rhode Island, vacation spot, after learning of the accord Eisenhower chose to take out his anger on Laird. The president did not want to confront Nixon directly. The language in the Rockefeller platform about needed domestic and national security changes might be construed as criticizing Eisenhower administration policies. Logically, the president should have called the chairman, Percy, to complain, but instead he went straight to Laird. "Ike was fed up with Percy because he thought Percy was kissing Rockefeller's behind and not protecting his [Ike's] presidency," Laird recalled. Eisenhower had correctly discerned that, behind the scenes, it was Laird who was really running the platform committee. Percy was out of his depth and could not compete with Laird's political savvy.

There was no small talk in the call from Eisenhower to Laird. "He was madder than hell," Laird said. The compact was a personal affront to him. "Mel, that Park Avenue Accord that Dick Nixon has agreed to with Rockefeller is a load of rubbish," Eisenhower began. (The president mixed up the avenues, always referring to it as the *Park* rather than *Fifth* Avenue compact.) What made Ike seethe most were the words about national defense, which implied that it had been insufficient under his watch. "Mel, I know more about the Defense Department than Nixon and Rockefeller will ever know," the president sputtered. "I personally reviewed the defense budget, and I stand by it as 100 percent adequate. It doesn't need another $3.5 billion like Rockefeller says. Just because Kennedy is out there talking about a missile gap doesn't mean there is one."

Laird sincerely agreed and added some facts of his own to buttress the president's argument. The president concluded the call with instructions to Laird. "I want you to go see Dick and tell him I consider this a *personal* thing. They are questioning my leadership. That accord is not in the best interests of the Republican Party, nor of the country. If some of those words get in the platform, especially in the defense section, I cannot support the platform or the candidate." He reiterated this point: "Tell Dick he has to back off, or else I cannot support him. He's got to decide whether he wants my support or Rockefeller's!"[22]

As promised to the president, Laird met privately with Nixon shortly after he arrived in Chicago and delivered the tough message. "He was shocked a little bit," Laird recalled. Nixon had thought that he had cut out the language that might offend his president. Now he was hearing it was not enough. So he leaned on Laird to fix it. "Mel, do what you have to do," Nixon said. "*You* handle it. Take over the committee and run it." But both of them knew Nixon couldn't publicly back away from Rockefeller, having made the Fifth Avenue compact in good faith. So he was depending on Laird to block enough of the language from getting into the final platform that Eisenhower would be mollified.[23]

It was a tricky task, but Laird was as ready for it as Percy was not. Percy had been the first platform chair who had not been an otherwise experienced politician. "He got all fouled up because he didn't know the Rules of Order and other things; he had lost control of the committee, which was in revolt," Laird remembered. For four days, from Saturday to Tuesday night, Laird got little sleep. Percy was willingly dispatched to work on a film about the Eisenhower administration and the platform, which would be aired during the nationally televised convention.[24]

The last drama came over the civil rights wording in the platform. In an effort to placate southern Republicans and avoid a bitter battle at the convention, the original draft of the civil rights section had been lukewarm. Nixon had agreed with Rockefeller to strengthen it. In this instance, Nixon really wanted the language to be more liberal, as did Laird—especially since it was the one hundredth anniversary of the 1860 nomination of Republican Party icon Abraham Lincoln.[25] So both fought hard, calling in IOUs and making trades. Laird

was confident it could be done but it took an all-night session and all his parliamentary skills to thwart the revolt of southern committee members and
other conservatives against the new wording. The civil rights redraft won by
a vote of 56 to 28, as Laird knew it would. "Politics is mathematics. Add and
subtract. You have to be able to count. That's how you get votes. You count,"
explained Laird.

The final 12,485-word platform, which passed on a convention voice vote
July 27, had a generally moderate political tone, having been adroitly mas-
saged by Laird so the three primary players—Nixon, Rockefeller, and Eisenhower—would sign off on it without rancor. Contemporary press accounts
suggested that the Fifth Avenue compact had skewed the platform into Rockefeller's corner, but a close analysis suggests that, in substance, there was little
change from the precompact platform draft.

Laird received praise for pulling a rabbit out of the hat, considering the
many directions from which the Fifth Avenue compact had received fire.[26]
Percy, whose own future political career Laird had saved, later praised Laird
for getting him through "the first real battle that I had—my introduction into
the infighting of national politics." During the convention Nixon also gave
Laird kudos in a talk, calling his work "perfectly superb." But, for Percy's sake,
the vice president could not publicly acknowledge Laird had been de facto
platform chair.[27] Four years later, when Laird was finally picked as the platform
chairman, profiles of him fully acknowledged his "save" of the 1960 platform.

Nixon won the Republican nomination on the first ballot with 1,321 of 1,331
votes. He was the first vice president to be nominated for president since Martin Van Buren, 124 years before. Among the few men Nixon considered for
the vice presidential nomination—after Rockefeller's refusal—was Ford. But
Nixon chose, instead, to go with Massachusetts Republican, ambassador to
the United Nations, and former senator, Henry Cabot Lodge, who could bring
along the eastern intellectual wing of the party.

Laird was fairly secure in his district. (He would win in November with
two-thirds of the vote.) So he devoted substantial energy and time, when Congress was not in session, to campaigning for his friend Nixon. Laird was one
of the leaders of the Republican "Truth Squad," which stalked the Kennedy-
Johnson ticket. During the campaign, the rumor was rife that if Nixon won he
would tap Laird as his secretary of defense. When questioned about it, Laird
expressed his sincere disinterest.[28]

Not so energetic in the Nixon campaign was President Eisenhower. Privately, he regretted that in 1951 his own party, reacting to Roosevelt's four terms,
had helped push the Twenty-second Amendment, limiting a president to two
terms. If not for that—and even though he turned seventy in October, which

made him the oldest president to date—Eisenhower would have run for a third term and defeated Kennedy. Instead, he watched an underling, with whom he was not close and about whom he was ambivalent, run for his Oval Office. Eisenhower made only four major appearances for Nixon, and any good that he did unraveled with the constant quoting of a press conference statement Eisenhower made. When asked to name a major idea Nixon had contributed to the Eisenhower administration, Ike had snapped: "If you give me a week, I might think of one. I don't remember."

Even so, the Kennedy-Nixon race was very close. Kennedy received 49.72 percent of the vote, while Nixon garnered 49.55 percent. Out of 68.8 million votes cast, Nixon lost by only 114,673.

Still, Laird and many other Republicans believe that Kennedy stole the election through massive voter fraud in a half dozen states, particularly Texas and Illinois. In Lyndon Johnson's home state of Texas, ballot stuffing probably gave Kennedy a lead of 46,000 votes out of 2.3 million. For example, in one county that went three to one for Kennedy, 6,138 votes were counted when there were just 4,895 voters on the rolls. In another Texas county, the contrast of two adjoining precincts was telling. In one that favored Nixon, 182 ballots were declared void at the "discretion of the judges," while in the next-door precinct, which went for Kennedy, not a single ballot was declared void.[29]

The most obvious theft of victory was in Illinois, where Kennedy was declared the winner with a margin of fewer than 9,000 votes out of five million. "If we'd have carried Illinois, we would have won," Laird said. "Mayor Daley delivered those final votes that put Kennedy over the top. Every time they needed a few more votes, the damn count in Cook County would come in with another 500 or so for Kennedy."[30] Most historians and political observers agree that Mayor Richard Daley's Chicago machine probably manufactured votes for Kennedy and stole the Illinois election.

Laird wanted Nixon to demand a recount, but Nixon conceded. He feared that after a recount Kennedy might still achieve victory and Nixon would go down in history as a "sore loser." In Laird's conversations with Nixon, the vice president had been fatalistic about a recount. "I remember he felt very strongly about it—that regardless of what happened in the long run, he just couldn't win because they'd keep finding more votes for Kennedy. They'd manufacture more." To punctuate his decision at the time, Nixon flew to Miami and had a meeting with Kennedy to show his support for an orderly transition. (Forty years later, this controversy was recalled during the coverage of the 2000 presidential election when Vice President Al Gore demanded a recount in Florida after his narrow loss to Governor George W. Bush.)

Nixon got belated credit for his statesmanlike concession. But in 1960, it was a bitter pill for him and his close friends. Not given to pessimism, Laird looked for positive signs in the Republican net gain of twenty-one House and two Senate seats. With the Republican standard-bearer Eisenhower soon gone from the White House, and Nixon without an elected position and relegated to inactive Republican leadership status, there was room for new blood at the top of the party. Laird, having acquitted himself with distinction during the convention and campaign, was destined to hold a prominent place in the post-Eisenhower party.

John F. Kennedy came to the presidency shining with charisma, glowing with the promise of youth, and imbued with an errant sense that his lucky star would continue twinkling in the heavens. But there was a rub; the "New Frontier" did not have any magic solutions. The cold war was growing so much colder that before the year was out, backyard bomb shelters were a booming industry. The Republican minority, with Laird as one of its emerging leaders, felt it was critical to provide modified or alternative solutions, as well as balance. As a counterpoint to the new Democrats, Laird deftly began defining himself as a "creative conservative." He had always deplored the idea of being against something just because the other party suggested it. (For example, he thought Kennedy's Peace Corps program was inspired, and supported it.) He preferred to tell the public what he or his party proposed, and not just what they opposed. As a sort of mission statement, Laird's enunciation of his creative conservatism in a January 1961 speech seems timeless (and was a forerunner of "compassionate conservatism" four decades later):

> In the past, the trouble with some conservatives has been just this: They are so busy talking about being conservative that they never ask themselves what they are trying to conserve. Trying to conserve the status quo, good or evil, is a foolish creed...
>
> Some conservatives merely oppose change.... [T]he man who fails to obey the law of change, the man who fails to apply the wisdom of the past to the motions of the future, is not a conservative. He is a reactionary. And a reactive society is doomed.
>
> The creative conservative does not live in a vacuum, ignoring human problems....
>
> The creative conservative is selective. In America today we want to see changed—not to see 'conserved'—depressed areas, social injustices, inadequate medical care, low school standards, and growing bureaucracy.
>
> But the creative conservative wants solutions which will remedy, NOT compound the problems. He shuns methods which set up a new agency, a new subsidy. Agencies and subsidies are controlled by men. Men can be corrupt. Men in Washington miles away from the local problem can make bad mistakes....
>
> [T]he creative conservative would endorse President Kennedy's

statement: "Ask not what your country can do for you—ask what you can do for your country."[31]

As Laird was tentatively testing the waters as loyal opposition spokes-man during the JFK presidential honeymoon, one man was noticeably si-lent—Nixon. He had been devastated by the election loss, though he tried to mask it for his friends. Nevertheless, even during the festive farewell bash he gave for his Chowder and Marching pals, Nixon seemed down-hearted.[32] After he left the vice presidency, Nixon remained silent about the new Kennedy ad-ministration. "In view of my position as the opposing candidate I should allow a reasonable time to pass before saying anything that could be interpreted as critical of my successful opponent," he explained to Laird in an April 11 letter. Since candidate Kennedy had ambitiously promised to do much in his first ninety days, which he hadn't accomplished, Nixon felt that "I should break this self-imposed silence" with a May speaking tour. He asked Laird for speech ideas.[33]

Laird responded: "Somehow or other, we must find a means of dramatizing to the American public the difficulty which the new President has in making big decisions and in standing by these decisions once they have been made. This, I believe, characterizes the new Administration in the foreign policy area.... His public pronouncements sound very good but somehow or other the decisions that are necessary to be made to back them up are never actually consummated."[34]

There could be no better case in point than the Kennedy fiasco that cost dozens of men their lives at a place in Cuba called the Bay of Pigs. Kennedy had authorized a CIA effort to overthrow Fidel Castro using Cuban exiles who would "invade" the island. When they were ambushed, Kennedy refused to send air support, fearing to awaken a Soviet response. More than one hundred of the Cuban exiles were killed and 1,113 were dragged off to prison. In the immediate wake of the disaster, President Kennedy asked Republican leaders to hold their tongues and present a united front. He sent a military aircraft to pick up Laird in Wisconsin so he could participate in the White House brief-ing on the Bay of Pigs.[35] The Republicans agreed to a temporary moratorium on finger-pointing in the interests of national unity, but they could not keep silent for long.

Two months after the invasion, with the gloves finally off, Laird observed, "The invasion fiasco was caused by the failure of our Commander-in-Chief to carry out the original plans [which] included military air support."[36] In the end, Laird felt it came down to a lack of will. In a private letter to Laird, Eisen-hower agreed. "I particularly like your insistence that the greatest single factor in the kind of struggle in which we are now engaged [against Communism] is the maintenance of will and determination to do whatever is necessary to defend ourselves and preserve our rights. Without this will, spirit and understanding, the United States in the long run would be defenseless even though we should double our expenditures for weapons of war."[37]

☙

Laird's suspicions about Kennedy's timidity spilled over into the tug-of-war with the Soviet Union over Berlin. At the end of World War II, diplomatic and military agreements left Berlin one hundred miles inside Soviet-controlled East Germany, and without guarantees for Western access to the city. The city had been split in half, with free West Berlin an island in a sea of Communism. The Russians wanted all of the city and had tested the resolve of both Truman and Eisenhower. Kennedy became the third U.S. president be so tested. He and Khrushchev met in Vienna in June for talks on Berlin, Laos, a test ban treaty, and other subjects. On June 4, after other issues had been discussed at the summit, Khrushchev announced that the Soviet Union would sign a peace treaty with East Germany at year's end, and all of Berlin would become part of East Germany and the Communist bloc. If the United States dared to insist on occupation rights, force would be met with force. "I want peace," he said, "but if you want war, that is your problem."[38]

Laird was briefed on the thrust of the Vienna talks and was convinced that Khrushchev felt he was dealing with a faint-hearted president. Several weeks after the Vienna talks, in an effort to fortify Kennedy's resolve on Berlin, Laird weighed in on a joint statement with Representative John Rhodes, which said: "It should be apparent to any rational man that the Communist belligerence in Berlin is the direct result of our weakness in dealing with the Communist conquest of Cuba. This, plus our lack of decisiveness in Laos and our 'off-again-on-again' China policies, gave Khrushchev the notion that the United States could be pushed around at will."[39]

Once again, as with the Bay of Pigs, some Kennedy administration lackeys tried to blame Eisenhower, for the problem. The State Department issued a document, *Background Berlin—1961,* which stated flatly that toward the end of World War II "the Western armies could have captured Berlin or at least joined in capturing it. But the Supreme Allied Commander, General Eisenhower, believed they could be more usefully employed against the major German forces elsewhere. As a result, the Soviets captured Berlin." An alert Laird caught "this flagrant fabrication" and quickly demanded in a telegram to Secretary of State Dean Rusk that it be withdrawn until the "complete and deliberate misrepresentation of the facts" was corrected.[40] As a result of Laird's telegram and simultaneous House speech, Rusk called Eisenhower and apologized and reprinted the pamphlet with new wording. But Rusk found that the old general was indeed stirred up and would not be silenced easily on the matter.

Five days after Laird blew the whistle, Eisenhower gratefully wrote Laird that he was anxious to clarify World War II decisions after the State Depart-

ment pamphlet had "confuse[d] history," and propagated "erroneous implications and inferences." Ike then highlighted six points that Laird made public.
Eisenhower emphatically stated that it didn't matter politically if the United
States had taken Berlin because "the political leaders of the day determined
long before the closing campaign of the war to divide Germany, for occupational purposes. They decided upon this course despite contrary military advice. I urged a different solution for Berlin than was agreed upon in London,
and which I have always understood was finally approved by the Heads of
Government at Yalta."[41]

The Democrats had been responsible for partitioning Berlin in the first
place, and Laird gave credit to a Republican, Senator Margaret Chase Smith of
Maine, for emboldening Kennedy to finally pledge that he would use nuclear
weapons, if necessary, to defend Berlin in 1961. President Eisenhower had used
the nuclear threat (usually through back channels) several times successfully
to head off Communist Chinese and Soviet probes. In a 1962 book, Laird wrote
that, in addition to the hesitance shown during the Bay of Pigs, Kennedy had
also "invited the Soviets' Berlin probe of his intentions," since during the election campaign "he had been critical of the nuclear strategy of deterrence which
alone could secure continuation of peace." Laird believed the Berlin crisis "grew
dangerously hot because the president had not made it clear that, in response
to a conventional attack on West Berlin or Europe, we . . . would escalate or enlarge the struggle to a nuclear level." Only when Senator Smith made a speech
to that effect on the floor of the Senate was Kennedy prompted to state publicly
that he would use nuclear weapons in defense of Berlin. "The turning point in
the crisis came in the period following this statement. If such a warning had
been issued earlier, when President Kennedy left the Vienna conference, the
Berlin crisis would never have become so serious," Laird asserted.[42]

When Kennedy finally announced he would meet force with force in Berlin,
the East Germans closed the East-West Berlin border with troops, police, and
barbed wire barricades to stop the flow of panicked Berliners into the West. It
was the beginning of the twenty-seven-mile-long Berlin Wall. With the embarrassing refugee flood blocked, Khrushchev publicly dropped his plan to sign an
East German peace treaty, and the crisis cooled down to a low simmer.

6

A House Divided

EVEN IN RETIREMENT, DWIGHT D. EISENHOWER was the closest thing the Republican Party had to a leader in the early 1960s, but the grand old man of the Grand Old Party was not a font of new ideas for Republicans. Presidential candidates and others who sought him out for a passing of the torch came away disappointed. Somehow Eisenhower's popularity never transferred to other Republicans, as the party's congressional losses of 1954, 1956, and 1958 proved. But fresh ideas *were* Congressman Laird's forte. So the era provided fertile ground for him to flourish. "Mel is sort of a maverick of intellect," Gerald Ford later reflected. "He is one of the brightest political people that I ever knew. He had exceptional political perceptions as to issues, candidates, conflicts."[1]

Some Republicans felt that Richard Nixon was the party's future. He had lost the White House to Kennedy by a nose but, in the process, had helped Republicans gain congressional seats in the 1960 election. On leaving office, Nixon sent Laird a vice presidential ash tray as a souvenir, with a note promising to let Laird know "where I will be and what I will be doing [as] soon as I make a final decision with regard to my plans for the future."[2]

It didn't take him long to decide. In mid-1961 Nixon met with his Chowder and Marching Club friends to ask their opinion about his running for governor of California in 1962. "We *all* recommended that he not do it—almost unanimously," Laird recalled. "I didn't think he could win. And if he ever wanted to come back and run again for president, I thought it would be a mistake to get defeated in California." In a few weeks Nixon announced he was going to run anyway, rejecting the considerable wisdom of the C&M and offending the members in the process. "We all thought, 'Why the hell did he come out here and ask for our opinions?' We were all down on him after that." (Laird never let Nixon forget. Years later, on a couple of occasions when President Nixon asked Defense Secretary Laird for advice—and Laird was convinced Nixon had already made up his mind—Laird would say, "Well, I remember when you asked for advice on running for governor." Nixon would laugh and say, "Oh, you son of a bitch!")

With Nixon in the doghouse and Eisenhower fresh out of ideas, Laird decided to follow through on a suggestion made in the early 1950s by the American Political Science Association. The group had proposed that each party draft a declaration of policy in the off-presidential-election years to update the party platforms. Laird started working behind the scenes to form a committee to do just that. In early March 1962, a Republican committee of twelve senators and representatives came together to draft a "declaration of principles" that would guide the GOP through that year's congressional and state elections. Laird was the chairman, and he wanted unanimous consent from all top national Republicans on the document. So all sixteen Republican governors were consulted, as were Nixon and other potential 1964 Republican presidential candidates. Eisenhower and Laird met for breakfast in Gettysburg, Pennsylvania, on May 21 to go over the 3,200-word draft. The committee subsequently incorporated most of Eisenhower's suggestions. The final 2,400-word document from the "1962 Joint Committee on Republican Principles" was read into the record by Laird during a House floor speech on June 7.[3] The statement of principles was approved by both the House and the Senate Republican conferences.

The document began with the enunciation of the "basic beliefs" of all Republicans, which still have currency today—limited government, and an emphasis on individual rights. The statement then reviewed what it called the Kennedy administration's general failure in the cause of freedom at home and abroad. The Democratic domestic program was flawed by the thinking that "government must protect individuals from foolish spending by taking their money and spending it for them." The strongest condemnation dealt with Kennedy's foreign policy: "Despite this Nation's position as the most powerful on earth, the bankruptcy of its leadership was shown at critical times in the past year. It was shown in Berlin and Cuba. It has demonstrated neither the wit nor the will to meet effectively the assault of international communism on freedom."

The verbiage of the Republican principles document was not half as notable as the near-unanimous party approval that Laird obtained for it. He challenged the Democrats to be as united in drafting their own statement of principle, but no one took him up on it. The Democratic Party, from the southern segregationists to the eastern liberals, was more fractured than the Republican Party, whose extremes, from the conservative Barry Goldwater to the liberal Nelson Rockefeller, were less pronounced and visceral.

⌒

No single foreign policy action irked Laird more than Kennedy's dealings and missteps over Laos. The congressman made sure that, when the Republican Principles document was being drafted, one of the strongest sentences— offered as one example of Kennedy's "bankruptcy of leadership"—derided Kennedy's "bluster followed by whimpering in respect to Laos."

The 1954 Geneva Accords, which primarily dealt with Vietnam, had also guaranteed Laotian neutrality. During the next six years, however, an off-and-on civil war caused three factions to vie for power. All of the factional leaders were part of the Lao royal family. On the left was Prince Souphanouvong, who

led the Communist Pathet Lao ("Land of the Lao") forces, which were supported by the Soviets and the neighboring North Vietnamese. His half-brother,
Prince Souvanna Phouma, led a neutralist faction, whose military forces in
mid-1960 were headed by a charismatic general, Kong Le. On the right was
Prince Boun Oum, whose government and royal Lao forces, led by General
Phoumi Nosavan, were supported by the Eisenhower administration. For a
heavy price—upward of $300 million by the end of 1960, which was the high-
est per capita American foreign aid offered to any country—Ike had ensured
that Phoumi's rightist military forces would dominate.

But in late 1960 the Pathet Lao forces, joined by Kong Le and the neutralist army, began pushing Phoumi back. A decision had to be made by the new
president on whether to commit U.S. troops to back the pro-West forces. At
a dramatic March 23, 1961, press conference, flanked by three maps of Laos
that demonstrated the Communist drive, President Kennedy made a statement
that Laird and many others cheered. He squarely blamed the Soviet Union
for priming the crisis and swore to protect Laos and the region from a fall to
Communism.

Some troops in the Pacific area were then moved around to give the impression that military muscle would back the president's rhetoric, but it was all
bluff. Soured by the CIA and military advice on the Bay of Pigs, Kennedy cared
little for their plans of American troop support to fortify the fading pro-West
forces. He was secretly determined to push for a coalition Lao government that
would include the Communists. Khrushchev, who wasn't interested in Laos
at the time, readily agreed at the June 1961 Vienna summit (during which the
Berlin crisis began) to decrease military aid and to pressure the Pathet Lao to
participate in a coalition.

For his part, Kennedy was so determined to achieve a coalition that in
early 1962 he strong-armed America's Laotian allies into an agreement sharing
power with the Communists and neutralists. When General Phoumi proved
reluctant, "an incredible thing happened," Laird recounted to his constituents.
"The U.S. Government, which had somehow got the idea that this [coalition]
arrangement was a good one, withdrew U.S. aid from the pro-western government. . . . Deprived of its main source of income the Royal Laotian government
soon found itself unable to pay its troops. And so, as is inevitable with many
Asian armies, the troops stopped fighting."[4] U.S. withdrawal of financial support so weakened Phoumi and Boun Oum that they finally had no choice but
to go along with a troika government including Communists.

On July 23, 1962, the United States was one of fourteen signatories to the
Declaration and Protocol on Neutrality in Laos. Laird was incredulous. He felt
that Kennedy's failure to keep his promise to get the Communists out of Laos
had "gravely weakened" the president's credibility and respect in the region.
Laird warned that the Communist Pathet Lao would never live up to the agreement. Nor would the North Vietnamese, whose forces did not withdraw from

Laos, although they had promised to do so in signing the agreement. Laird observed that the Kennedy administration had engineered "an arrangement whereby the communists [are] enabled to take over Laos through political means rather than military means."[5]

As Laird had predicted on numerous occasions, by 1964 the agreement on Laos was a cruel charade. The Pathet Lao pulled out of the coalition and continued the civil war for territory in Laos, aided by the North Vietnamese and Soviets, all brazenly violating the 1962 agreement. Meanwhile, Kennedy obligingly withdrew American military advisors and decreased financial support. Later his successor, Lyndon Johnson, would take the battle underground to avoid the appearance of violating the neutrality pact. The CIA and State and Defense departments prosecuted what came to be called "the secret war in Laos" to keep the Communists in check.

Laird—not suspecting then how the story of Southeast Asia would become his own political history in a few short years—strongly believed in the value of military alliances and felt "neutralism" in certain countries was an open invitation for a Communist takeover. He maintained that more should be done to mobilize the countries of the Southeast Asian Treaty Organization, formed by Eisenhower, to militarily secure Laos as an independent country. Several weeks before the final Lao declaration, Laird was pressed during a television interview on whether he thought American troops should be involved. He said, "We are in a real struggle with international Communism, but if we are going to hang back in this fight [and] always take a back seat, I believe that we're headed for serious trouble. It certainly seems to me that it's much better to fight in a place like Laos than in Milwaukee, Chicago, or Washington. . . . I believe that we have to be willing to stand up, and when we have stood up, we have always been successful.[6]

As for Communism *in* the United States, though Laird had distanced himself from Joe McCarthy–style, witch hunts, he believed there was a Communist subversive threat. He did not see Communists under every bureaucrat's desk, as McCarthy had, but Laird was wary of Soviet Communist efforts to make inroads among America's intellectual and governing elite. So when efforts intensified to abolish the House Un-American Activities Committee in the late 1950s, he supported the committee, in part because a Chowder and Marching buddy vouched for its continuing work.

Only once in Laird's sixteen-year congressional career did he publicly call for the investigation of an official because of possible Communist connections. That man was Paul Corbin, a Canadian who had changed his name from Kobrinsky before emigrating to Wisconsin, where he went into public relations. At different times, the politically androgynous Corbin had been chummy with the state's Communist labor union leaders. During the 1960 presidential primaries, Bobby Kennedy became Corbin's patron when Corbin proved himself to be a tireless, if unprincipled, worker in the Kennedy cause. At Corbin's death in 1990, *The New Republic* would eulogize him as "a political operative who single-handedly gave the term a sinister ring.... [W]here Corbin went, havoc was sure to follow."[7]

Laird did not initially view Corbin as a serious player in the national arena but was offended because he gave an unsavory aroma to the profession of politics. The opening for Laird's public criticism of Corbin came in August 1961, when questions about Corbin's background were raised in a *Milwaukee Journal* article that implied he had consorted with Communists in Wisconsin.[8] At a breakfast with top FBI official Cartha "Deke" DeLoach, Laird asked what the FBI knew about Corbin. DeLoach confided that the FBI file on Corbin was so damning, not even Attorney General Robert Kennedy could override it to appoint Corbin to a top post in the Justice Department.

Laird dispatched a telegram to Bobby Kennedy calling for an investigation. Kennedy quickly responded in an August 31 telegram that he had referred the matter to Democratic National Committee Chairman John Bailey. At the time, Corbin was Bailey's special assistant. Bailey promised Laird he would thoroughly examine the matter, but the investigation went nowhere. Bobby Kennedy's patronage of Corbin was too strong for Bailey to buck. He wrote to Laird saying that Corbin had been "a very controversial figure in many of his undertakings," but he had not been a Communist. As proof, Bailey hooked Corbin to a lie detector and determined he was truthful during the test when he denied any past affiliation with the Communist Party.[9]

Laird decided not to pursue the matter; to do so would suggest partisan animosity. Conveniently, the cause had been taken up by a Democrat—Laird's friend and fellow member of the Wisconsin delegation, Congressman Clement Zablocki. Despising Corbin for besmirching the party's honor, Zablocki started a full-fledged House Un-American Activities Committee investigation of Corbin.[10] The committee held seven days of hearings from September 1961 to July 1962. Fifteen witnesses, including Corbin, testified. Several reported that Corbin bragged about his Communist Party affiliation and urged them to join the party. One of those witnesses was Milwaukee labor leader John Dominick Giacomo, who summarized that Corbin was "a pathological liar [and] just about everything a fine, upstanding citizen would not want to be." Corbin denied all accusations and aspersions, and the hearings ended with no formal finding.[11] Corbin kept his party job and continued to roil Washington politics off and on for two more decades in both parties.

Communism gave Laird the fodder for his first book, published in 1962. The genesis of the volume had come from a course—"How to Be a Communist"—Laird had taken from Notre Dame professor Gerhard Niemeyer, who also lectured on the subject at the National War College. Laird was stimulated by the classes held in Washington and Chicago, where he became acquainted with George Shultz, later a Nixon administration budget official and Ronald Reagan's secretary of state. Laird recalled that the class would "lock ourselves up in the Drake Hotel and spend two days discussing various issues like how to meet the Soviet Communist threat." Laird's first book was heavily influenced by those brainstorming sessions.

Laird's special assistant Bill Baroody Jr. and his friend Karl Hess, working with Laird for a year, produced the book, *A House Divided*. The title signified a world that was then, as America had been during the Civil War, half slave (under the Communist thumb) and half free. Subtitled "America's Strategy Gap," the volume dissected Kennedy's foreign policy as an "underdog strategy" that seemed to pursue peace at any price and claimed victory any time a nuclear war did not result. The administration had failed to understand the Communist will, its disinterest in true negotiation, or the evil nature of its leader, Nikita Khrushchev. "Many men have reasoned that Khrushchev is different, that he doesn't want war, that he truly believes in 'peaceful competition and co-existence,' " Laird wrote. But this was the very man who, for Stalin, "directed the mass extermination by execution and planned starvation [in Ukraine] of a population which the most modest estimates place at ten million persons."[12]

As his book implied, Laird felt freedom was the most important issue of the 1962 campaign. Nowhere was that more urgent, he thought, than in Cuba, which by late summer was transforming into a bristling outpost of the Soviet Union. Intelligence briefings Laird received in the Defense Appropriations Subcommittee hearings estimated that an average of 120 anti-Castro and other Cubans were being executed in Cuba each week, and Castro was brutally thwarting his people's attempts to flee the country. The Cuban militia had about 350,000 men, and "arms received [by Cuba] were enough to equip 600,000 men—which meant that the extra arms were intended to ... promote the growth of Communism in other Central or South American countries," according to Laird's assessments of U.S. intelligence reports.[13]

In late August, Laird called on President Kennedy to blockade Cuba. "Communist arms being shipped to Cuba include the most modern jet fighter planes, tanks and rocket equipment—in numbers far beyond what might be needed for the defense of Cuba," Laird publicly charged.[14] Laird knew that if the president imposed such a blockade, the Soviet Union would rattle some serious sabers, but the proper response would be to ignore them. In *House Divided*, written before the Cuban Missile Crisis, Laird had prognosticated that "the most dangerous situation conceivable would be to leave all questions to the hour of crisis, when a group of presidential advisors ... would hover around the President, and seek to influence him. Only doctrine—firm and carefully reasoned in advance—can prevent such an eventuality." Laird feared that because of Kennedy's withdrawal of air support during the Bay of Pigs invasion, "the Communists—instructed by observing our confusion—will create future crises in which our leaders will be forced to make sudden decisions."[15]

The October 1962 Cuban Missile Crisis unfolded in a similar manner. Publicly announcing the existence of nuclear missile sites under construction in Cuba, and proving it with reconnaissance photos, President Kennedy vowed they would not be completed. He instituted a U.S. Navy blockade of Cuba, and for a tense week the world stood on the brink of nuclear war. Khrushchev "blinked" when it became clear Kennedy was willing to go as far as he needed, even with nuclear weapons. After an October 28 agreement, the Russians dismantled the missile bases in return for U.S. pledges not to invade Cuba, to end the blockade, and to remove U.S. nuclear missiles from Turkey, which was already planned..

While it is true that too often the party not in power professes to know how best to run things, in this case the record shows that Laird had suggested all the correct moves seven weeks before President Kennedy, backed into a corner, actually followed through with them. "It is too bad that this nation did not listen to Congressman Laird several months ago," one Wisconsin newspaper editorialized in the direct aftermath of the crisis. "If [Laird's] advice on a 'peace blockade' had been followed, Mr. Khrushchev would have backed down from his Cuban plans long before he reached the dangerous situation of aiming nuclear missiles at U.S. cities." The editorialist added, "[H]ad it not been for an amendment sponsored by Cong. Laird several years ago, only two nuclear submarines would be on duty now." Instead, "today there are six Polaris submarines, each equipped with sixteen nuclear missiles roaming the seas. They could be no small reason why Mr. Khrushchev backed down on his Cuban adventure."[16]

One thing Kennedy did gain by delaying strong action toward Cuba was a rally-round-the-flag reaction from American voters in time for the midterm 1962 elections. Instead of expected Republican gains, both parties maintained the status quo. "The biggest issue—whether the President was doing enough in Cuba—evaporated before election day," one respected publication wrote in review. "The Cuban crisis, developing only a few days before the elections, might have solidified support behind the President, canceled out a central Republican campaign issue and thus minimized Republican gains that might otherwise have occurred." Congressman Laird and many other Republicans felt that way. The Republican Congressional Committee chair charged that his party's chances for big gains had been "Cubanized."[17]

One man who believed he was terribly hurt by Kennedy's strong handling of the crisis so close to election day was Richard Nixon, who lost the California governor's race. He was privately convinced that Kennedy had manipulated the crisis for the benefit of the Democratic Party. An early hint of this classic Nixon paranoia can be read between the lines of a postelection letter from Nixon to Laird: "While the overall results in California were disappointing, the Republican showing generally in the nation was most encouraging, particularly in view of the fact that the Cuban blockade took place just when our campaign was beginning to reach its peak."[18]

Laird easily won his sixth term in Congress, racking up a two-to-one vote margin against his Democratic opponent. This occurred, as before, because Democrats not only voted for him but also campaigned for him. Kennedy's own Secretary of Health, Education, and Welfare John Gardner came to Wisconsin to help drum up the vote for Laird. Years later Laird's congressional successor, liberal Democrat David Obey, offered something of a confession that testified to Laird's 1960s crossover appeal. "In 1962, I was on the ballot running [as a Democrat] for the [Wisconsin] legislature. And I have to be honest about it; we had a turkey on our ticket running against Mel for Congress. I have to admit I voted for Mel."[19]

Getting along with Democrats, and receiving some of their support, did not obligate Laird to support the majority of the Kennedy administration's initiatives. A *Congressional Quarterly* study of key 1961–63 Kennedy-issue roll call votes shows that Laird voted with the president only 28 percent of the time—more often on domestic issues than foreign ones.[20] The *CQ* reports looked at only a small number of critical floor votes. When Laird added up his committee votes, he reported to his constituents that he had supported Kennedy two-thirds of the time—almost as much as he had Eisenhower.[21] Laird's most intense deliberations came in the Appropriations Committee, where he often found himself in agreement with Kennedy in his two specialty areas, health and defense.

The Eisenhower administration and Congress had held the line on post–Korean War defense spending. News commentators would suggest, as each year's federal budget broke a new record, that defense spending was the cause. Laird frequently proved statistically that was not the case.[22] One of the difficulties Eisenhower and the Republicans had keeping defense spending relatively stable was the growing armaments industry lobby. Eisenhower's famous TV and radio farewell address spelled out the problem. He said the arms makers in search of profits, the military services in search of 100 percent security, and colluding congressmen anxious to keep defense jobs in their districts had set up a powerful advocacy group. Eisenhower gave the lobby a name, "the military-industrial complex."[23]

Laird agreed wholeheartedly with Eisenhower that the fight against Communism called for vigilance, but not necessarily inflated spending.[24] He and Ike both felt strongly that Kennedy's campaign charge of a missile gap between the United States and the Soviets was overstated. The missile gap issue was a ruse that helped elect Kennedy. In classified briefings while a candidate, JFK was given the facts and figures that clearly demonstrated there was no gap. Kennedy got away with the rhetoric partly, Laird explained, because he used estimates suggesting there *might* be a gap in the future if the Soviets increased their budget exponentially, and if the United States did not increase its research and development efforts. But when Kennedy took office, he knew that no gap existed, and some of his officials admitted it. Only three weeks after the inauguration, new Defense Secretary Robert S. McNamara acknowledged to reporters that he had found no missile gap.[25] In fact, as Laird knew from the highly classified briefings he had received in 1961 and 1962, the United States had at least a four-to-one and maybe a five-to-one advantage over the Soviets.[26]

The most significant part of the advantage was the Polaris submarine and missile system, which Laird continued to push heavily as "the most nearly invulnerable weapon in the history of warfare."[27] Kennedy agreed and increased the Polaris program funding by 50 percent in his first year—part of a $5.9 billion increase over the Eisenhower budget. While JFK, after learning incontrovertibly there was no missile gap, had not intended to hike the defense budget so much, the Berlin crisis changed that. Both Laird and Eisenhower, who had fought Rockefeller's belief the previous year that a $3 billion increase was needed, concurred that almost double that amount was necessary now for defense spending.

Besides Polaris, there were other defense issues in which Laird found himself immersed. He became the foremost congressional expert and sponsor of the navy's antisubmarine warfare program.[28] He also supported the X-20, an early, manned military space glider dubbed Project Dyna-Soar (for dynamic soaring). In 1961 when the Kennedy administration asked for $100 million for the project, Laird tacked on another $85 million and wrote into the appropriations bill that the whole $185 million could be spent only on Dyna-Soar. The next year he did it again, adding $42 million to the $115 million the administration requested. "The Dyna-Soar Program," Laird wrote in 1962, will "prove just as important as the Polaris Missile Firing Submarine and the Anti-Submarine Warfare Amendments are to our security today."[29]

The X-20 was to be a winged vehicle that could fly at Mach 20 into space and arrive anywhere around the globe in less than an hour. If nuclear-armed it would have been the most invulnerable nuclear delivery system of its day, as well as more accurate and flexible (with a pilot at the controls) than the early 1960s intercontinental ballistic missiles. The six-year-long project employed nearly eight thousand people, including some of the luminaries of the space program such as future moon-walker Neil Armstrong and Mercury astronauts Wally Schirra and Gus Grissom.

But the X-20 was so far ahead of its time that McNamara could not see the technological advantage and extraordinary utility it would give the United States. In December 1963, after $400 million had been spent, McNamara canceled the project.[30] Several days after McNamara's press briefing, Laird was needled on that decision by a television talk show host, Ann Corrick, who began, "Secretary McNamara has been in combat with Congress over a number of things [such as] the cancellation of the Dyna Soar...how would you assess him as a Secretary of Defense?"

With some congressional courtesy, Laird answered that, so far, McNamara had been "a good Secretary of Defense. I don't believe, however, that the Secretary of Defense can be the *sole judge of every decision* that must be made in the Pentagon. And I think that...Secretary of Defense McNamara has...spread himself rather thin on many of the decisions that needed to be made in the Department of Defense."[31]

In a comprehensive book, *Dyna-Soar: Hypersonic Strategic Weapons System,* author Robert Godwin observed that the $400 million had been well spent. "The spin-offs in experience, materials science and technology were enormous and are still paying dividends today," he said. Thirty-six of the sixty-six subprojects supporting the X-20 survived, advancing a variety of air force and NASA programs. The space shuttle program was indebted to Dyna-Soar, and Goodwin concluded that if Dyna-Soar had been allowed to continue, the United States would have had a space shuttle before reaching the Moon.[32]

⚶

Just as the Peace Corps and space exploration are considered two of the most positive legacies of Kennedy's presidency, so also then must American military involvement in Vietnam be counted as that presidency's darkest legacy. As one of the men most responsible for ending America's disastrous military involvement there a decade later, Laird blamed Kennedy for entering the maelstrom.

As a senator, Kennedy had approved all of Eisenhower's decisions regarding Vietnam. Laird was impressed with the leadership of South Vietnam's president Ngo Dinh Diem who had adroitly knitted together his population into a viable nation and, with about $250 million in annual U.S. economic aid, brought social and economic stability. At the end of 1960, South Vietnam still controlled more than 80 percent of its own land area, and the indigenous Viet Cong guerrillas answering to Hanoi numbered fewer than 6,000. The American military mission numbered around 773, and none had been killed in combat. But after Kennedy's election, North Vietnam—possibly to test the mettle of the new president—increased its Viet Cong numbers and activities to the point that Diem declared in October 1961: "[This is] no longer a guerrilla war but a real war waged by an enemy who attacks us with regular units."

The first Kennedy step toward the American quagmire came at the end of April 1961 when he decided to increase the number of American military advisors to more than the ceiling set by the 1954 Geneva accords. Even though the United States had not been a signatory, American leaders had pledged to abide by the accords. Kennedy's executive decision to abrogate the agreement was done in secret; neither congressional leadership nor American allies were informed. The second step came after the return of an October fact-finding mission led by General Maxwell Taylor, who recommended that eight thousand U.S. combat troops could be slipped in under the guise of flood assistance and quietly stay on afterward as military advisors.[33] Kennedy did not sign off on the subterfuge and was reluctant to authorize such a large hike in military advisors; nevertheless he sent in more. By the end of 1961 there were 1,364 of them, and the first American advisor/soldier had been killed in Vietnam combat. The advisors regularly traveled and fought with South Vietnamese units. Though the men were clearly engaging in battle, Kennedy refused to confirm that reality. In a January 1962 press conference, when pointedly asked if U.S. soldiers were fighting in Vietnam, he gave a one-word answer: "No!" That was a lie.

It soon became apparent to newsmen and the more astute military advisors accompanying South Vietnamese troop units that the Viet Cong had the upper hand, despite official U.S. pronouncements to the contrary. After a trip to Vietnam in May 1962, Defense Secretary McNamara, a former corporate executive who believed numbers told the story, reported that "every quantitative measurement . . . shows that we are winning the war." Two months later McNamara again effused: "Our military assistance in Vietnam is paying off. I continue to be encouraged. There are many signs indicating progress."

At the same time the more wizened Congressman Laird had a far less rosy view. He wrote in *A House Divided,* that the "counter-measures to defeat the Communist attack on South Vietnam will not be easy nor will they produce quick results," especially if the enemy was allowed to slip back into the sanctuaries of North Vietnam and Cambodia. "The prime means of penetrating an active sanctuary is to launch counter-offensives behind enemy lines, recognizing no borders." In other words, unless the war was taken into North Vietnam, it would not end.[34]

Diem welcomed American dollars and military arms, but he was never anxious to have increased U.S. troop involvement, foreseeing that its propaganda value alone for the Communists would become North Vietnam's most useful soldier-recruitment tool. Always an ardent nationalist, Diem refused to be dictated to by the Americans. He ignored their behind-the-scenes protestations that the secret police tactics employed by his brother, Ngo Dinh Nhu, were too repressive. No doubt in his ears still rang the sycophantic words of Vice President Johnson, who compared Diem to George Washington, Woodrow Wilson, Franklin D. Roosevelt, and Winston Churchill. Diem seemed to believe that the Americans might privately complain, but publicly they would stand by him as the only dependable game in town.

The tough Diem was always an authoritarian leader, using iron-hand techniques such as torture and imprisonment of political enemies to stay in power. Kennedy stomached those reports until 1963 when South Vietnam's Buddhists and students started rebelling, beginning with a ritual and followed by acts of self-immolation by priests, which Diem's sister-in-law, Madame Nhu, ridiculed as "barbecues." Diem's troops raided Buddhist pagodas in response to antigovernment demonstrations, and Kennedy publicly denounced this reaction as a human rights violation. Privately, he told Diem that the Nhus had to go.

Diem could not agree to sack his most loyal brother, whose control over the secret police was pivotal to Diem's continued rule. When Diem's intransigence was clear, President Kennedy, gave the green light for South Vietnamese generals to plot a coup. When the CIA-assisted coup ended in the assassination of Diem and Nhu, Kennedy was said to be "shocked" by the news. It was a shabby end for an American ally of eight years. Less than a month later, Kennedy himself was killed by an assassin's bullet.

A tale told by Kennedy aide Kenny O'Donnell and Senate Majority Leader Mike Mansfield maintains that the president had told them in the spring of 1963 that he fully intended to completely withdraw all U.S. troops after the 1964 election. In a subsequent conversation with O'Donnell, Kennedy reportedly added that if he did it before the election, there would be a "wild conservative outcry" against his reelection. Even if he pulled out the troops after a presumed victory, he predicted to O'Donnell: "I'll become one of the most unpopular Presidents in history. I'll be damned everywhere as a Communist appeaser. But I don't care. If I tried to pull out completely now [1963] from Vietnam, we would have another Joe McCarthy Red scare on our hands, but I can do it after I'm re-elected. So we had better make damned sure that I *am* re-elected."[35]

Whatever Kennedy's supposed intentions, the fact is that he and Defense Secretary McNamara deployed a total of 16,575 troops to South Vietnam by the end of 1963—a more than 2,000 percent increase over the Eisenhower administration's complement. And the coup, carried out with Kennedy's complicity, created such chaos in South Vietnam, along with commensurate Viet Cong gains, that new President Lyndon Johnson felt even more U.S. troops were needed there in short order.

And so began the tragedy that Melvin Laird would later feel morally and politically compelled to end.

7

Laird Rising

THE BUSY WEEK WAS WINDING DOWN, and Mel Laird looked forward to the weekend. At the Rotunda Restaurant on Capitol Hill he had lunch that Friday, November 23, 1963, with a close Democrat friend, Congressman John Fogarty of Rhode Island. The laughter and consultation ebbed as they checked their watches about 1:45 P.M. and then headed back to an Appropriations Committee meeting. As they walked between the Cannon and Longworth congressional office buildings, the news rippled through the crowds on the street: "Kennedy has been shot!" The two swiftly reached the committee hearing room, and Fogarty announced the session was canceled. Both men returned to their offices to field phone calls. Laird issued a short public statement. He decried the "dastardly blow at the very heart of our Republic."[1]

Though Laird liked Kennedy personally, he had been mystified, as was his mentor Eisenhower, about the nation's adoration of this president while he was in office. They both considered him to be a man who epitomized the triumph of style over substance. Laird had been asked to make some satirical remarks about Kennedy a month hence on December 23 at a Gridiron Club Dinner. The club was organized by Washington journalists in 1885 to host politicians and roast them with good humor. As a top Republican leader, Laird was scheduled to speak before press spokesman Pierre Salinger. "We really have to admire the job that Pierre's doing," he had planned to say. "Imagine trying to keep the press interested in a guy with a $90 billion budget, a beautiful wife, a pair of cute kids, and a whole bathtub full of aircraft carriers." He had also planned to acknowledge Arthur Krock of the *New York Times* who was celebrating his fiftieth year with the Gridiron, and then add: "You know it kind of makes me think—a little wistfully perhaps—when we remember that Art was first elected to this fine club some three years before the second coming. You know, before Jack was born."[2]

Only one week after the Kennedy assassination, President Lyndon Johnson appointed Supreme Court Chief Justice Earl Warren to head a special commission to investigate the assassination. Johnson then called a reluctant Jerry Ford and asked him to be one of the commission's seven members. One of Ford's first phone calls was to Laird, who commiserated with him about the potentially onerous task. After ten months, the Warren Commission produced an 888-page report that "found no evidence that [the assassin Lee Harvey Oswald] was part of any conspiracy.... On the basis of evidence before the Commission it concludes that Oswald acted alone."[3]

Next to the assassination itself, Laird was perhaps most alarmed about self-flagellating commentary condemning America for creating a climate in which such a horrible crime could occur. Eleven days after the assassination, Laird took pains to point out that Oswald espoused "the doctrines of an alien philosophy, the Marxist-Communist philosophy."[4] Anxious to amplify the Communist-based origins of Oswald's dementia, Laird issued a statement as chairman of the Republican Policy Committee on December 6, which read in part: "We are told that hate was the assassin that struck down our President. If it was hatred that moved the assassin, that hatred was bred by the teachings of Communism.... Efforts to make Americans generally feel guilty of the crime now are obscuring the nature of the crime.... There is guilt. But it is not American guilt. It is the guilt of the murderer. There is hatred, fanaticism, and bigotry in the world but America is not its source or loyal Americans its practitioners."[5]

⚶

As early as 1963, Laird was promoted as presidential material by no less than Dwight D. Eisenhower. The former general had been in Europe in August filming a special for CBS, "D-Day Plus Twenty Years." On his return voyage aboard the luxury liner SS *United States,* he spoke with journalists about the Republicans best qualified to be president. Two congressman were on his list of eleven names—Laird and Ford. "We had gotten to be quite friendly," Laird recalled. "I always could deliver pretty well for Eisenhower when he got into problems in the Congress. He may have felt he owed me that or something, so he put me on the list." Richard Nixon was not on the list.[6]

More than once in subsequent private meetings with Eisenhower, the former president "kept bringing up the presidential thing, but I never encouraged that at all," Laird remembered. Laird's son, David, who had the opportunity to probe his father for regrets in later years, confirmed this: "I can definitely say that being president was not on his mind. He truly loved the House back then—not only the way Republicans and Democrats dealt with each other, but the whole committee makeup, seniority—everything about the whole institution itself. Staying in the Congress and hopefully becoming speaker of the House was his ambition."[7]

Laird achieved party leadership by multiple, patient, and persistent steps. The pivotal one was spearheading the "Young Turk" movement that replaced the Republican House leader Joe Martin with Charlie Halleck in 1959, followed by his vice chairmanship of the 1960 platform committee, and then leadership of the 1962 joint House-Senate committee producing an interim platform statement. Early in 1963 another move was made that advanced his influence. In that instance it involved pushing Ford, his senior both in age and congressional service, into an important party position first.

After the poor Republican showing in the 1962 elections, Laird pressed Ford, then forty-nine, to make a bid at the beginning of the next Congress to replace sixty-seven-year-old Charles Hoeven of Iowa as chairman of their caucus, called the House Republican Conference. It was the view of younger members of Congress that Hoeven's leadership was lackluster and that the conference, which rarely met, was in need of rejuvenation. Once again Laird worked in concert with younger Republican members of the House to oust an old guard leader.

Laird's three primary congressional cohorts were Charlie Goodell of New York, Robert Griffin of Michigan, and future defense secretary Donald Rumsfeld of Illinois, all in their thirties. A number of those polled told Laird that he should be conference chair instead of Ford. Out of respect and friendship for Ford, as well as political calculation, Laird declined. "It wasn't as though everybody was wildly enthusiastic about Jerry," Goodell recalled to a Ford biographer. "It was just that most Republicans liked and respected him—he didn't have enemies."[8] There was good reason for that, according to another Ford biographer, Clark Mollenhoff: "Gerald Ford has learned thoroughly over the years the doctrine of 'plausible deniability' and to use other people to do the unpleasant political jobs often referred to as 'dirty work.' Thus, Representative Melvin Laird and others took the heat and made the enemies by ousting Joe Martin, but it was Gerald Ford who moved up the House leadership ladder."[9]

The quartet of Young Turks went about so efficiently and quietly collecting votes for Ford that the coup was not publicly known until the day before the January 8 vote. Ford became the third-ranking House Republican on an 87 to 78 secret vote, and the younger members also increased their representation on the Republican Policy Committee chaired by Johnny Byrnes. Hoeven privately warned party leader Charlie Halleck to watch his back because he might be next.[10]

That Laird would mount such a campaign to promote someone less qualified ahead of himself probably stood the Wisconsinite in good stead. As events demonstrated, Laird was more intellectually and otherwise suited to be conference chair than was Ford, for whom the position was merely a stepping stone on the way to becoming party leader. Ford called only one conference meeting in two years, according to one account, whereas Laird later used the conference to set the Republican Party afire with forward movement. Canny congressional observers could read the tea leaves even then. Laird was winning points for humility while positioning himself for advancement.

⌖

As 1964 dawned the Republican leadership had a problem. The two front-running Republican presidential candidates, Nelson Rockefeller and Barry Goldwater, appeared to be poles apart, which threatened to split the party.

While Rockefeller gave due obeisance to the Republican old guard, Goldwater had no talent for reaching out to moderate and liberal Republicans. Though it was possible in early 1964 that Goldwater might win the nomination, he could never win the presidency unless he had all Republicans and a fair share of disaffected Democrats pulling for him. Therefore, an acrimonious convention battle over the platform could only further hurt Republican presidential prospects.

The party needed a platform that would bridge the gap between Rockefeller liberals and Goldwater conservatives, and who better to write it than the man who had negotiated the treacherous shoals of the 1960 Republican platform? In January Laird was tapped as the platform chair for the convention. Almost a year earlier, in March 1963, when Rockefeller had been the front-runner, Laird had indicated support for him in a Wisconsin campaign swing.[11] But the Rockefeller campaign had stumbled badly in May when the governor, having divorced his wife of thirty-one years, married a younger woman, herself divorced. While Americans had voted for candidates who were divorced, the new marriage of the two divorcées was a count against Rockefeller. From what had been an overwhelming lead over Goldwater, Rockefeller fell behind in the polls.

Taking due note of this, Laird hatched and executed a plan for the Wisconsin primary aimed at keeping both himself and the two Republican candidates out of a bloodbath there. Though Wisconsin was an important primary test state, Laird was able to persuade both Rockefeller and Goldwater that waging political battle there would be bitter, costly, and not a true test of their relative strengths. In Wisconsin, crossover votes were allowed, and many Democrats, given only a choice of incumbent President Johnson in their own primary, would undoubtedly vote in the Republican primary and skew the results. Once Laird had agreements from Rockefeller and Goldwater not to enter the Wisconsin primary, he talked a reluctant Byrnes into running himself as a "favorite son" candidate. The plan allowed the state delegation maximum flexibility to throw their support behind another candidate at the convention, once Byrnes released their votes. Laird's successful political maneuver also allowed him, as a Wisconsin delegate, to remain "impartial" as the platform chair.[12]

Meanwhile Eisenhower was decidedly unhappy with the way things were going for the Republican presidential nomination. Seeking a signal from him, Republican leaders found he was unwilling, early on, to endorse either Rockefeller or Goldwater. Instead Eisenhower pushed hard for others to run—first Henry Cabot Lodge and then Pennsylvania Governor William Scranton. At the time, Laird thought Rockefeller was the man who had the best chance of defeating Johnson, but not a good one. "This was a campaign in which a Republican didn't have a chance of getting elected because the country had just gone through the death of Kennedy and they wanted to give Lyndon Johnson a chance," he recalled. "It was a very difficult campaign for a Republican," and especially for Barry Goldwater, who "was a hip-shooter, bound to exaggerate somewhat and be misunderstood."

Out of Goldwater's mouth came statements that Republican primary challengers and Democratic opponents could twist to their benefit. Frustrated by the liberal eastern Republicans and Democrats, the conservative Arizonan had once said, "It would be a good thing to saw off the eastern seaboard and let it float out into the Atlantic."[13] Convinced that Social Security was not being effectively funded, Goldwater talked about retooling the system, which opponents twisted into a plan to end Social Security altogether. In various statements about nuclear weapons, he discussed them sometimes bellicosely as a usable option in parts of the world, such as low-yield ones for defoliating forests in the Vietnam combat area—though he never actually advocated their use on any occasion. But this was distorted into an image of Goldwater as a warmonger with an itchy nuclear trigger finger. Goldwater also hurt his chances when he voted against the Civil Rights Act of 1964.

In 1964 there were only sixty-two Negroes—as they were then called—in Laird's district.[14] As he advocated for civil rights, southern congressmen would chide "that it was easy for me to vote for that kind of legislation—that maybe I didn't understand the problems it created in their states." Laird would quietly respond that, adhering firmly to the Presbyterian faith, he believed "all men were created equal. Now that doesn't mean that they all have equal abilities; some are different than others—but it has nothing to do with race or color. I voted for civil rights on the basis of my beliefs." And since it was his most firm tenet of political faith that he had to live with his conscience longer than his constituents, he supported civil rights no matter what percentage of his constituents were Negroes.

From this basis of quiet advocacy in 1963, Laird took President Kennedy to task for delaying two and a half years to propose significant civil rights legislation. Republicans in Congress, who voted in higher percentages for civil rights than did the Democrats, could do little to move along a new civil rights act. Congress did act on its own in 1962 to pass a constitutional amendment (the twenty-fourth) outlawing poll taxes, onerous devices used in the South to deny poor Negroes the right to vote. But without an initiative from President Kennedy, there was no chance for a broader civil rights act.

Kennedy finally sent a civil rights bill to Congress in February 1963, but it was so thin that liberal Democrats and pro–civil rights Republicans refused to fight for it. Kennedy tried again and, on June 19, finally offered a more sweeping civil rights measure akin to what Eisenhower had unsuccessfully tried to get past Senator Lyndon Johnson in 1957. Three days later, Kennedy met with civil rights leaders, including Martin Luther King, in the Oval Office to talk them out of a planned civil rights march to Washington, which was timed to coincide with the one-hundredth anniversary of Lincoln's Emancipation Proclamation. But King and the others could not be dissuaded. They felt the time was right. On August 28, nearly a quarter of a million people joined the "March on Washington for Jobs and Freedom," and were thrilled at its conclusion to hear King's "I Have a Dream" speech at the Lincoln Memorial.

King's words failed to move Kennedy's legislation past leaders of his own party who cynically blocked it using procedural maneuvers throughout 1963. After Kennedy's assassination, it appeared that passage of the bill might be possible in part as a way to honor the late president. The vote came up first in February 1964 in the House of Representatives. Laird informed his constituents that he intended to vote for the bill, even though it was not as strong as he would like—nor as strong as their state's own antidiscrimination laws.[15] Laird also predicted that a higher percentage of Republicans than Democrats would vote for the bill in the House, and he was right. The bill passed February 10 on a 290 to 130 roll call vote; 78 percent of the Republican House members, including Laird, voted in favor, while only 59 percent of the Democrats voted to support civil rights.[16]

The bill then moved to the Senate where intense debate continued for four months. As the bill moved toward certain Senate passage on June 19, one presidential candidate, Goldwater, was in a fix.[17] He couldn't vote for the bill because he firmly believed part of it was unconstitutional, and because he didn't like the proposed expansion of federal over state authority. He drove to meet Eisenhower at his Gettysburg farm the day before the vote to discuss his dilemma. If he were in the Senate, Ike said, he would vote for the bill because it was important to show support for civil rights. But Eisenhower promised he would not publicly chastise Goldwater if he voted against the bill.[18]

Some called Goldwater's "no" vote courageous since it was not to his political advantage. Laird defended Goldwater for voting his convictions; he knew the senator was no bigot. With a Jewish father and heritage, Goldwater had known discrimination personally and abhorred all vestiges of it. (One of his famous quips was made when a country club employee, pointing to the "Gentiles Only" clubhouse sign, asked him to leave the golf course. "That's all right," he reportedly replied. "My mother was an Episcopalian, so I'll only play nine holes.")

Because of Goldwater's uncompromising position, Eisenhower, who had promised to say nothing publicly, privately called his new favorite contender, Governor William Scranton, and urged him to step up his opposition to Goldwater at the Republican Convention. He publicly "welcomed the entry of Governor Scranton, whom I have long admired, into the contest."[19] Coming on the eve of the convention, the fallout from Goldwater's vote made Laird's job as platform chair much more difficult. Laird had begun preparations for the job many months before he was even named chairman of the committee. He had tapped great minds of the day—a promising Harvard professor, Henry Kissinger, and thirteen other educators, scientists, and economists—to contribute to a book of essays to be called *The Conservative Papers*. One purpose of the book was to serve as a riposte to *The Liberal Papers*, a 1962 book of essays gathered by a group of House Democrats. On the day the Democrats' book was published, Laird took issue with it on the House floor, saying it was riddled with left-leaning notions about the Cold War world. Even the Kennedy White House felt forced to repudiate the book's views, and many Democrats disowned it. Thus, Laird was appalled to discover that it had become required reading in political science courses at several colleges he visited. When he protested, the professors responded that they would also gladly teach from a conservative collection, but there was none. Laird promised to correct that.

Recalling the times, columnist Bob Novak said Laird was intent on "trying to revive a moribund party. He was trying to provide some intellectual fervor for the Republicans, an intellectual revival."[20] Laird asked eight other representatives, including Ford, to join him on an ad hoc committee to gather scholarly papers.[21] During the editing process, Laird told a *Los Angeles Times* reporter that "so far, the Republican Party really hasn't done the basic research that is needed to crystallize conservative political thought." The book's aim would be to fill what he saw as "the gap in articulation of the conservative philosophy."[22]

Published in March 1964, *The Conservative Papers* had heft. Besides Kissinger, contributors on subjects from nuclear energy to foreign policy to food issues included Edward Teller, University of California physicist and "father of the H bomb"; Harvard economist Gottfried Haberler; University of Chicago economist Milton Friedman; former president of the U.N. General Assembly and Security Council Charles Malik of Lebanon; and Karl Brandt of the Stanford Food Research Institute.

Reviewers across the political spectrum praised the book. Not only did it sell well, but it was included in college curricula across the country. It also provided some of the timely groundwork for the 1964 platform, as Laird had intended.

After being named the Republican Platform Committee chair on January 9, Laird's first important consultation was with Eisenhower.[23] The two enthusiastically chewed over an idea for a series of "town meetings" around the nation. The plan was for the Republican Party to discuss subjects of importance to the voters and thus glean ideas for a platform for positive change. The side benefit would be reshaping of the Republican image as a "party of the people." With Laird's agreement, Ike formally proposed the plan on January 29 at a Republican dinner that was carried by closed-circuit TV to other simultaneous Republican meetings across the nation. "We might call this plan 'United Statesmanship.'" Eisenhower said.[24] The meat of this Party-to-People Program, as it was called, was in six meetings held around the nation, each highlighting a different domestic and foreign policy topic. Eisenhower and Laird each moderated or appeared at several of the meetings, which attracted the desired news media attention. A final report on what had been learned through the town meetings was presented during the July platform hearings.[25]

But the essays of *The Conservative Papers* and the results of the Party-to-People Program were not the only sources of information for the platform. Laird himself was a human vacuum cleaner of policy issues. Columnist Mary McGrory reported from the San Francisco Cow Palace as Laird prepared to convene the platform committee: "A bulky, round-faced, balding 42-year-old who looks older, he is an old hand with the gavel and he has a mania for the stuff of platforms. He devours position papers, he reads the fine print, he loves documents, disputes and policy discussions. He has dispatched crates of material that would bore anybody else to San Francisco, and he has read every word of it."[26]

The platform work was the place where Laird gained an early respect for Henry Kissinger, and thus began a relationship which is of no small historical moment. Later it would be Laird whose urging would get President-elect Nixon to name Kissinger as his national security advisor—even though Nixon had not previously met the professor. But in 1964 Kissinger was still on the learning curve when it came to politics, and Laird would prove to be one of his more important teachers. After Kissinger's work on *The Conservative Papers* in 1963, Laird borrowed Kissinger from his mentor Rockefeller to work on the 1964 platform. Others in Laird's brain trust that year were Dr. William Prendergast and William Baroody Jr. (Both would later serve as speech writers for Laird when he was secretary of defense.) Bryce Harlow, former Eisenhower aide and Laird friend, also frequently holed up in Laird's suite to help with the writing. Officially, the chief assistants were two congressmen who always joined Laird in political and policy-oriented activities, Glen Lipscomb of California and Charles Goodell of New York, focusing, respectively, on the national security and domestic portions of the platform.

A platform chairman is pulled in many directions, particularly when the presumptive nominee (Goldwater) and the convention challenger (Scranton) are at different ends of the party spectrum. Laird didn't aim to please either one of them. He had four rules: don't tarnish the reputation of America or its people; don't dodge the tough issues; don't equivocate; and don't make promises that the party can't keep.[27]

Scranton, who had said that a Goldwater nomination would be a disaster, goaded the committee by reminding them of the low regard Goldwater had expressed for platforms. Goldwater himself assured the committee that he trusted them to produce a platform that he could support. Goldwater was interrupted forty-one times by cheers and applause when he appeared before the committee, which was stacked with avid, sometimes rabid, Goldwater delegates. "We had a lot of very, very conservative delegates on that platform committee, so the committee was not representative of the party as a whole," Laird recalled. Thus public bickering over the platform was unavoidable. The Scranton forces came to the convention primed for opposition, and Laird's platform committee was their venue.

As it evolved at the convention, the most heated platform disagreement between pro- and anti-Goldwater delegates focused on three issues: civil rights, control of nuclear weapons, and extremism.[28]

From the beginning, Laird planned to include a firm endorsement of the civil rights act in the platform—though Goldwater thought it would be redundant. Laird maintained his position, believing along with Eisenhower that it was pivotal to remove any doubt about where the party stood. Anti-Goldwater delegates wanted a plank that not only endorsed the act but also declared that it was constitutional, something Goldwater did not believe. Laird responded quickly: "I don't think the Platform Committee should be passing on the constitutionality of laws. Only the Supreme Court can do that." He blocked any language about the constitutionality of the new law, and the final platform wording promised "full implementation and faithful execution" of the Civil Rights Act. (The following December, the U.S. Supreme Court ruled that the civil rights act *was* constitutional.)[29]

The second assault on the platform by anti-Goldwaterites was their insistence that it include a statement that only the president or someone he designated could decide to use nuclear weapons. Goldwater, who never could sidestep tough questions, had already said he thought the U.S. commander of NATO should be able to decide to push the button if necessary.[30] Eisenhower secretly called Laird up to his hotel suite to tell him that no wording of any kind should appear in the platform about delegating nuclear authority. Both men knew what few others did—a highly classified fact that made the whole issue a moot point but couldn't be publicly acknowledged. Laird knew from briefings for the Defense Appropriations Subcommittee that the NATO commander *already* had been given nuclear "predelegation authority" during the Eisenhower administration. Eisenhower firmly told Laird the secret could not even be hinted at. "Military command plans have no business being part of a platform fight," he hammered home to Laird. "These are matters we want to keep from our potential enemies." (The secret was declassified four decades later.)

The last nettlesome issue was extremism. In 1964 the term "extremist groups" in the media generally referred to one on the left, Communists, and two on the right, the Ku Klux Klan and the John Birch Society. It was the "Birchers" that caused contentious debate at the Republican convention.

They were natural supporters of Goldwater, though he neither joined nor favored them. But many Republicans were concerned about the growing Birch influence within the party and wanted to take a stand. Scranton demanded the Republican platform repudiate political extremism, in general, and name names.[31] Laird successfully opposed the amendment. "I didn't mind a para-graph taking a position against extremism, but I wasn't prepared to name groups and defend what groups would be named," he said.

"The most important thing about a platform is you gotta have guidelines," Laird had written in a short satire for the Gridiron Club. "The first principle [is that] the platform must be short—no more than 50 words. The second guideline is that the platform must deal with principles, not programs—[such as] motherhood and sin." A third principle is that it "must spell out what a party is *against*." Therefore, the title of his "ideal platform" was "Building a better America under the auspices of the Republican Party because history has demonstrated that Democrats lack spunk, leadership, direction, understand-ing, and rural support." That chewed up twenty-five words. The platform itself was "Mother love and love of mother presents us with a challenge and chal-lenges us with the present. Republicans denounce sin and Democratic rule; elect Republicans."[32]

Though he wrote it as a spoof in late 1963, Laird essentially followed those guidelines for the real platform months later. The 1964 Republican platform, titled "For the People," did concentrate more on principles than programs. One of its four sections denounced the Democratic Party and presidencies (though not by name) for what it called their domestic and foreign policy fail-ures.[33] And while it was not 50 words, the platform was, as Laird had pledged in advance, not even half as long—at about 8,500 words—as the Democratic platform that year, which tipped the scale at 22,000 words.[34]

When the platform was finished on Sunday, July 12, an angry Scranton, whose amendments had not been accepted, charged that it was a "Goldwater platform." That charge would stick in the media.[35] A ninety-year-old great-aunt of Laird's, listening to the TV commentators at the convention, called him from Wisconsin and delivered a tongue-lashing. "How can you chair a committee coming up with a right-wing platform like that? That's not our position at all!"[36]

Laird lamented in a speech: "As one who, in an apparent minority, has read the document and as one who was intimately involved in its evolution, I would be forced to conclude that the [critical] references were to some other docu-ment in some other period of history. The fact is that this was one of the most widely misrepresented and least read documents in political party history." Laird believed that a careful, objective reading of the document would prove that it was "the soundest, most progressive, the hardest-hitting Republican platform in years." He never tired of quoting from it and measuring it against its Democratic counterpart.[37]

On the Tuesday evening of the convention, July 14, Laird took the podium at 6:58 P.M., and, as a *New York Times* columnist recounted, "He astounded the thousands and sent a groan across the nation when he announced that members of the committee were so proud of their work that they would read it [entirely] for the enlightenment of mankind. Tradition holds that platforms are written not to be read, and when Mr. Laird started, the delegates at last began doing the things that delegates do at less revolutionary conventions. This included milling in the aisles, stretching, scratching, yawning, waving at cameras and at other delegates and sneaking out for beer and hot dogs. . . . The platform reading ended at 8:47 P.M., one hour and forty-one minutes after it had started."[38]

Some commentators thought this was a shrewd move by Laird to delay acrimonious debate until after prime time TV audiences went to bed. A much smaller viewing audience saw the later spectacle of an erudite Rockefeller trying to offer an amendment while repeatedly being interrupted by boos and catcalls from the galleries. All amendments were rejected. Laird later lamented that the platform itself was essentially sidelined during the campaign by Goldwater's book-length manifesto, *Conscience of a Conservative*. "If our national ticket had run on the platform instead of on the *Conscience of a Conservative*, it would have done much better," Laird opined two years after the event. Most commentators familiar with the election would agree. Successful nominees from either Democratic or Republican conventions have always moved more to the center to win elections. But Goldwater could not be anything but himself, with ample political foot-in-mouth disease. During his nomination acceptance speech, he uttered his most famous proposition: "Extremism in the defense of liberty is no vice . . . moderation in the pursuit of justice is no virtue." Exclaimed one reporter at once to his colleagues: "My God! He's going to run as Barry Goldwater!"

Lyndon Johnson had the advantage of incumbency and the sentiment of the Kennedy legacy making his victory a sure thing. Yet he seemed driven to pile up the most enormous margin of presidential victory ever achieved—perhaps as a way for the insecure Texan to step out of the Kennedy shadow. His most effective tactic was to paint Goldwater as too eager to use nuclear weapons, and the hallmark of that tactic was the infamous "daisy girl" commercial. It aired only once and didn't even mention Goldwater by name. It shows a little girl picking daisies in a field. As she counts them, a man's voice picks up the count and turns it into a countdown to a nuclear explosion on the screen. The voice of Johnson concludes: "These are the stakes—to make a world in which all of God's children can live, or to go into the dark. We must either love each other, or we must die." An announcer adds, "Vote for President Johnson on November 3. The stakes are too high for you to stay home."

Johnson beat Goldwater with 61 percent of the vote, the largest popular vote margin in American history. The "Goldwater drag" cost the Republicans more than three hundred seats in state legislatures, two seats in the Senate and thirty-eight seats in the House of Representatives. It was the lowest point for Republicans in Congress in twenty-eight years. When the House convened in 1965, Republicans had only 140 of the 435 seats. Wisconsin was among the states in the pro-LBJ column, giving him 62.1 percent of the vote. Yet, Laird, aided in part by canny campaigning and careful cultivation of the Democratic voters, was reelected with 61.8 percent of the votes in his district.

⨎

Laird, as one of the strong Republicans left standing after the devastating election, was anxious to rebuild the party. He could not see that happening if the eastern liberals in the party continued to carp about conservatives having driven the GOP to its doom. "They thought that would be a way of coming back in '68," Laird recalled. "They took an I-told-you-so attitude so they would be able to run their candidate in four years." But Laird saw it mainly as a self-destructive ploy that the crippled party could ill afford. "The Republican Party can survive the 1964 election. If it fails to survive, history's verdict will be that it committed suicide," Laird said at the time. "It would be ... suicidal to engage in a bitter factional conflict to secure or to keep sole control over the party. The winner of such a conflict is likely to find himself the sole custodian of a corpse."[39]

Laird was on the move and everyone knew it. He successfully got the party leadership to create a Republican National Leadership Council—a collective of the party's best minds—to rejuvenate it. Then he focused his sights on Republican House Minority Leader Charlie Halleck of Indiana. Laird and other Young Turks had put Halleck in six years before, and now it was time to take him out. The coup was not an ideological one. It had more to do with age and style. At sixty-four, Halleck was tired, not forceful, and not bold. "The Republican Party was comatose in the late 1950s and early 1960s," remembered columnist Bob Novak. "It just didn't look like it was going anywhere. The great Democratic landslides of 1958 and 1964 broke open the congressional majorities for them. The problem was that you had Charlie Halleck–type Republicans who really didn't stand for anything much."[40]

There was a hidden issue, also; Halleck was an alcoholic. Though it was not discussed publicly at the time, it was a prime topic of private Republican conversation. It pained Laird to talk about this aspect of Halleck, whom he considered a "dear guy and a fine, capable person." In early 1964, after an obviously inebriated Halleck came to the House floor, Laird had been appointed by a group of embarrassed Republicans to take the leader aside and deliver an ultimatum. "Charlie," Laird began emphatically, "if you ever come to the floor like this again, I've been commissioned by my colleagues to tell you that we won't reelect you at the start of the next Congress." Halleck ignored the warning and appeared in the House Chamber at least one more time "not in the best of shape," Laird recalled. He felt morally and politically justified in mounting a coup.

The question—reeking of implications for the future—was: Who should challenge Halleck as minority leader? The *New York Times* answered the question after the November election: "The potential challengers are Mr. Ford and Mr. Laird....Each has publicly disclaimed his candidacy but has privately indicated that he would be available if a majority of his colleagues wanted him."[41] Some suggested that Laird's occasional "abrasiveness" and his links to Goldwater made him less electable than Ford. In reality, some of the young conservatives who finally went for Ford would have preferred the more aggressive Laird, if he had just given them the green light.[42] Bill Baroody Jr., one of the Republican leadership's vote counters, said Laird could have won, but his friendship with Ford held him back.[43]

Once Ford confirmed that he was interested in the move up the Republican ladder, Laird stepped aside. They knew that if both of them ran, they would split the anti-Halleck vote and Halleck would win. Ford later portrayed himself as a reluctant candidate, but he was not. It is probable he expected to be tapped as Goldwater's vice presidential running mate, and the disappointment reawakened his longtime ambition to be speaker of the House. Being party leader of the minority was a critical next step. But Ford knew his friend Laird wanted it, too, and that Laird might well win it. At that point either he persuaded himself, or was persuaded by some of the Young Turks including Don Rumsfeld, that he had a slightly better chance to beat Halleck than Laird had. "Mel is able," Ford recounted later. "But as good a man as he is, Mel does irritate people occasionally. So I think the group looked at Mel and said the only person that could win could be Jerry Ford."[44]

As he had in 1959, Ford told the Young Turks he intended to stay above the fray and let them do the campaigning for him. He took three vacations between Thanksgiving and New Year's—enjoying the sun in Puerto Rico, golfing in Palm Springs, and skiing in Michigan. He was not disinterested, but had been assured (particularly by Rumsfeld) that others could handle the campaign. As it began to appear it would be a close vote, the young Republicans asked him to cut short his family Christmas vacation in Michigan and come back to make calls and visits; Ford did so.

After that effort, Rumsfeld predicted a walk-away triumph. But Laird, who was in charge of the vote count, was dubious. "Sometimes Rummy is too optimistic," Laird laughed in recollection. Laird knew that with a secret ballot, one had to line up extra votes. "I sent Rummy back. I said, 'You need at least seven or eight votes more than you get commitments for. If you don't have those votes, you'll lose.'" Laird had learned his lesson with the 1959 secret ballot when some unknown Republicans who had committed to vote for Halleck did not, according to the final count.

On January 4, 1965, all 140 Republicans met on the House floor in their caucus, known as the House Republican Conference. As prescribed, the first order of business was to vote for that session's conference chair (Ford's old post) and after that, to elect its minority leader. Laird won the job of conference chair on a 75 to 62 secret ballot. Ford was then elected minority leader by 73 to 67 votes. "Ford will tell you that he wouldn't have been elected if I hadn't run that campaign for him," Laird said. Ford confirmed it: "Mel urged me to run, and thanks in no small part to his efforts, I won that election by the *landslide* margin of [six votes]."[45]

Charlie Halleck was a gentleman in defeat. He unreservedly congratulated Ford, moved for a unanimous ballot in support of him, and then led a standing ovation. Halleck served two more terms in Congress. Several years after he retired, he was on a fishing trip in Montana with his wife, Blanche, when she fell out of the boat (possibly because of a heart attack) and drowned. Distraught, Halleck reached his friend Laird, then the secretary of defense, through the Pentagon Command Center at 3:30 in the morning. "I'm out here in the wilderness," he wept over the phone. "I have to get Blanche home to Rensselaer [Indiana]. Can you help me?"

"Of course, Charlie. I'll help you anytime." Laird send an airplane to fly Halleck and the body of his wife back to Indiana the next morning. Halleck never really recovered from the loss of his wife; he died in 1986.

8
Cloud Riders

DURING MEL LAIRD'S LIFE of public service, he always had a clear view of what was most important to him, and it was not in the defense arena for which he would become best known. Laird liked to quote American philosopher William James who said: "The great use of life is to spend it for something that will outlast it." For all the money he earmarked to the Defense Department, the military hardware would rust and become outdated, and the best use of nuclear missiles was no use at all. The deep-seated idealism at the core of the Wisconsin pragmatist inevitably drove Laird toward work that would save lives by attacking a host of human diseases.

His seat of power to effect change was as the ranking member of the Health, Education, and Welfare Appropriations Subcommittee for more than a decade. Working through three administrations—Eisenhower, Kennedy, and Johnson—he often forced substantially larger health budgets than the presidents had in mind. With so many demands on the taxpayer dollar, not the least of which was the arms race, could America afford to earmark large amounts for medical research that promised no guarantees? Laird postulated that the question needed to be reversed: How could America afford *not* to spend whatever was needed to speed up medical research? Though he fancied himself a pragmatist, on matters of extending life and improving health, Laird was, in the words of a fellow legislator, a "cloud rider."

When most of America was enthralled with the space race, Laird pounded the podium in the House for more health funds with these words: "I, for one, would rather see this nation first in health, than first on the Moon."[1] The result of his zealotry was multifold, including the transformation of the National Institutes of Health into the world's foremost medical research entity, and the establishment of the Centers for Disease Control and Prevention. One man familiar with Laird's role, Dick Cheney, lauded his "amazing achievements in the field of medical research and improvements in the health and welfare of military and civilian citizens alike."[2] And a president from the opposite political party, Jimmy Carter, pronounced in tribute: "I don't know of anyone who has done more in his service in the Congress, and even subsequently, to promote the strength of the National Institutes of Health, the Centers for Disease Control, and to spread America's technical and scientific knowledge of health processes around the world."[3]

The driving force behind Laird's efforts can be traced to his childhood, his hometown, and an institution that has always been at the epicenter of his pride, the Marshfield Clinic. It was the place where doctors watched over Laird from infant to octogenarian. It was founded by six general practitioners in the horse-and-buggy days of 1916 when medicine was not far removed from its frontier. Group medical practices were then a new notion, and not highly regarded by the American Medical Association, which referred to them, as late as 1937, as "medical soviets."[4] Under Laird's guardianship, the Marshfield Clinic grew into one of the largest private, not-for-profit, multispecialty, group practices in the United States—one that has given the Mayo Clinic in neighboring Minnesota a run for its reputation.

In 1923 one of the early patients of the group practice over a downtown retail store on Central Avenue was little "Melvie," an infant with an earache. Laird's family was visiting from Nebraska, but they soon returned to live in Marshfield, and the clinic's doctors became an integral part of their lives. "These young doctors became my friends," Laird recalled. The most influential of them was Dr. Stephan Epstein. The son of a prominent German dermatologist, Epstein was himself advancing up the medical ladder in Breslau when the Nazi regime came to power. Epstein saw the handwriting on the wall for Jews and sailed to America. Through referrals, he arrived in Marshfield in the winter of 1935, where he intensively studied English so he could pass the state medical boards and work for the Marshfield Clinic. He spent many hours with the Lairds, including high school freshman Melvin, who read English aloud with him. Young Laird found in Epstein a fine mentor, whose importance in his life increased exponentially with the death of Laird's father in 1946.[5]

Their discussions were far-ranging. It was Epstein who first educated the future secretary of defense on the importance of the nuclear deterrent in maintaining peace, as well as the necessity to control nuclear weaponry through negotiation. And he pressed on Laird the preeminence of good health care. He preached to Laird that an individual politician could do more good than any single doctor. That appealed to Laird. As a Wisconsin state senator, he sponsored legislation, opposed by the state's medical society and others, that legalized the corporate practice of medicine in the state. It allowed the Marshfield Clinic and others to attract and retain doctors through the promise of higher salaries and retirement programs. When Laird headed off to Washington, Dr. Epstein "told me that I should get on the HEW Appropriations Committee because he thought health was going to be so very important," Laird recalled.

The freshman congressman followed this advice. When he was assigned to the Appropriations Committee in 1953 by its Republican chairman John Taber, he was allowed to focus on health issues. He was in on the 1953 creation of the Cabinet Department of Health, Education, and Welfare. In 1957 Taber assigned himself and Laird to the HEW-Labor Subcommittee and told the young congressman to act as its ranking member. "You serve here for a little while, and then I'm going to step down," Taber told him. In 1959, as promised, Taber left the subcommittee, making Laird "ranking" for the minority side, or officially the subcommittee's second-most important member. He immersed himself wholeheartedly into the subcommittee's work, remarking at one point that he had spent so much time with doctors and on medical issues that he began "to feel that the M.C. [Member of Congress] behind my name should be changed to M.D."[6] By 1968 he had outlived or out-served all his early committee colleagues. "There is no one else left on the HEW committee in either the Senate or the House that has served ever since the department was created," he said a bit whimsically that November. "This makes me sound like a very old man, but I really consider myself still very young [and] I'm not ready to leave this job yet."[7] Within weeks, not out of his own personal choice, he was named defense secretary by President-elect Nixon.

Laird never forgot his roots in the Marshfield Clinic. His old friend Dr. Epstein became one of the most influential directors of the clinic, and the chief architect of its conversion from a group of general practitioners to specialists, including a burgeoning medical research department enhanced with federal grants delivered by Laird from his appropriations perch. Laird also pressured the clinic to develop an advanced finance program, the Security Health Plan, which was one of the first health maintenance organizations available in the country—and the first to get HEW approval.

Laird's attention to the clinic was minuscule compared to the overall picture of medical history he influenced through funding. But he did not do that alone. Like Laird, John Edward Fogarty was a "boy wonder" who made a big mark on Congress—but there the similarities ended. Fogarty was a New Englander, a Democrat, and an ardent unionist without a college education. He was a bricklayer, like his father and older brother, and was only twenty-three when he was elected president of Bricklayers Union No. 1 of Rhode Island. With little political experience, he was first elected to Congress in 1940 at the age of twenty-seven.[8]

Fogarty knew that to help his home state he needed to go where the money was, the Appropriations Committee. So after two years of hard pressure, he finally netted the cherished assignment in 1947. With the Republican takeover of the House that year, however, he did not get the military subcommittee he wanted. To his great disappointment, Fogarty was assigned to the Subcommittee on Labor and Federal Security Agency (the HEW predecessor). While the labor portion of subcommittee work intrigued Fogarty, the health segment bored him. At one point, as he perused a newspaper during a hearing, subcommittee Chairman Frank Keefe banged his gavel and admonished, "Mr. Fogarty, this is important business we're considering here; you ought to pay attention and maybe you'll learn something!"[9]

Exactly when Fogarty finally started paying ardent attention is unclear. But Laird thinks it was a battle over the cost of streptomycin that made Fogarty a convert. The new drug was introduced to the market in 1947 as an effective treatment for tuberculosis, but it cost $250 a gram. Chairman Keefe, who had taken Fogarty under his wing, enlisted him in a successful fight to appropriate $3 million for the manufacture of synthetic streptomycin so it could be sold for $10 a gram. When the Democrats took back the House in 1949, Fogarty became the new Labor-HEW Appropriations chair. And when Laird joined the subcommittee several years later, there was an immediate bond between the two men.

"There was nothing artificial about this man," Laird said. "He was so open; everything was on the table with him, so we hit it off very well." Laird came to love almost everything about Fogarty, large and small—his robust handshake; his love of bricks, and steak cooked in his brick fireplace at home in Harmony, Rhode Island; his joy in a good joke, but self-consciousness about telling any himself; his unhurried approach that sometimes caused him to miss airplane connections; the way he made it difficult for anyone else to pick up the check at a restaurant; his complete loyalty to and trust in his friends; and his great pride in anything Irish. (He wore a bright green tie as if it were a coat of arms.)[10]

Laird didn't need conversion to the cause of medical research, as Fogarty had. From the first, he signed on to stand strong with Fogarty on appropriations. While Fogarty was often credited with funding that led to major medical advances of the period, because he was the subcommittee chair, the advances were possible only because the minority leader on the subcommittee, Laird, was his energetic partner. "My father was a very quiet, unassuming man," said Mary Fogarty McAndrew. "He never gave the impression he did it alone. Having someone from the other side—Mel—right there with him, and being able to work so closely with him, was a huge advantage."[11]

One man who witnessed their work up close was Representative Hugh Carey, later the Democratic governor of New York. By the time Carey came to the House in 1961, Fogarty and Laird were already inseparable on appropriations. Carey, as a fellow New Englander, Irish Catholic, and Democrat, was quickly brought into Fogarty's fold, and he proved companionable enough to join Fogarty and Laird for 5 P.M. drinks in Fogarty's first-floor office. Fogarty would frequently complain when Carey arrived a couple of drinks behind schedule. "I can't help it, John," he'd mumble. "I'm on the top floor; you're down here in a prime office on the first floor. It takes me longer to get here than Mel." In short order, Carey found himself in an office next to Fogarty, a favor to the latter from the speaker of the House. "[Fogarty] had me moved so I wouldn't be late for drinking hour with him and Mel."[12]

Carey watched with wonder as Fogarty and Laird took on fellow subcommittee members, full committee members, the House, the Senate, and three successive presidents to ram through hefty annual increases in medical research appropriations. The two men manipulated their subcommittee hearings like master puppeteers. The most effective technique was to press HEW officials to admit that they could use more money than the president's Bureau of the Budget had told them they could request. It infuriated Eisenhower, Kennedy, and Johnson, in succession, but the pair were unrelenting. During the Eisenhower era, Laird would be called to the White House for tongue-lashings but wouldn't budge. During the Kennedy and Johnson administrations, Fogarty similarly was denigrated by his party's presidents, but he also refused to cut the HEW budget.

Fogarty-Laird committee hearings were a carefully choreographed steamroller. Expert witnesses were recruited because they would vouch for what the two congressmen already wanted. And the professionals were picked only if they could drop the medical jargon and speak passionately. Fogarty and Laird were so prodigiously knowledgeable about the subjects, having immersed themselves in medical minutiae, that no bureaucrat or politician of either party could best them in debate. When their bills went to the full House, the pair were a bulwark that could not be broken. Not once did they accept an amendment to an HEW appropriations bill; every challenge was beaten back.

In the Senate their ally was the courtly Democrat from Alabama Lister Hill. His father had been a pioneering heart surgeon, and the story goes that young Lister couldn't follow in his father's surgical boots because he couldn't stand the sight of blood. Though he became a lawyer, it was medicine that was closest to his heart. As chairman of the Labor-HEW Appropriations Subcommittee and the Labor and Welfare Committee in the Senate, he had responsibility for all substantive health legislation. The tactics he employed mimicked the Fogarty-Laird techniques, only with a southern tinge. In a familiar routine, he would lean over the table and ask an administration witness courteously: "Are you shuah, Doctuh, that you're asking for enuff for these wunnnderful programs?"[13]

Fogarty and Laird couldn't afford to lose each other, so that meant campaigning for one another across party lines. For example, in September 1964 Fogarty was the featured speaker at a Marshfield Clinic Foundation party in Laird's hometown. He told the crowd he had met only five Democrats in his visit "and they are all going to vote for Mel Laird." Then he added, in a remark that brought down the house: "I would too, if I lived here.... [I]f you want good health and better educational opportunities for your children, I would hope you will vote for Mel Laird in November."[14]

Laird soon returned the favor. Fogarty had built a small library behind his house—of brick, naturally—and he added a fancy brick outhouse, complete with the traditional half-moon cutout in the door. The Bricklayers Union sponsored a dedication of the outhouse as a fund-raiser, with tickets selling at $250 apiece. Laird was featured on the invitation as the dedicatory speaker. Republican Governor John Chafee of Rhode Island was furious when he received the invitation. "Why are you coming up here giving Fogarty all this publicity and campaign help?" Chafee demanded to know.

"Well, John, I would do anything for Fogarty if he asked me to do it— almost anything. I wouldn't cheat, or rob or kill, but when he asks me for a favor like this, I will certainly do it. We have a relationship that goes far beyond partisan politics. And, John, you had to get a lot of Democratic votes to get elected governor. The smartest thing you could do is attend this dedication and show you're above partisan politics, too." Chafee confirmed the exchange and said he took Laird's advice and attended the dedication "of what Mel liked to call the John Fogarty Brick Shithouse—which was actually quite artistically done."[15] Laird's favorite part of the dedication: Fogarty had rigged each toilet seat so that when you sat down, a voice would boom from below: "Please move over; I'm still painting down here."

Though Chafee came to accept the Fogarty-Laird mutual admiration society, others in Laird's party of fiscal conservatives had ongoing concerns about his collusion with a big-spending Democrat. Gerald Ford "thought I went further than I should have gone on health problems—because I raised the Eisenhower and Kennedy-Johnson budgets by millions of dollars each of those years," Laird recalled. "As a matter of fact, if you add it all up, it was in the *billions* of dollars." For the sake of his conservative reputation, the record shows that Laird occasionally appeared to oppose Fogarty on the floor, only to quietly capitulate later as part of their ongoing choreographed dance.

⟶∿⟵

Perhaps their finest monument is the National Institutes of Health in Bethesda, Maryland. In Hebrew, Bethesda means "house of mercy" or "house of grace," and few more apt applications of the term could be used than as a description of the NIH, where medical miracles have been abundant since its antecedent began with a single doctor in a one-room laboratory at Staten Island, New York. In 1887, that doctor, Joseph Kinyoun, was given a $300 grant from the predecessor of the Public Health Service to establish a small Laboratory of Hygiene. With the money, he found the bacterial cause of cholera. In 1930 his lab was moved to Washington and renamed the National Institute of Health. (The name was changed to National *Institutes* in 1948 when the National Heart Institute was created and joined the already-existing National Cancer Institute as part of the organization.) As it expanded, the NIH moved to Bethesda. The institution grew at a progressive pace until 1955, a year that almost threatened to bury its good works, but instead transformed the organization.

In postwar America, there were few more dread diseases than poliomyelitis, and leading the fight against it was the National Foundation for Infantile Paralysis, sponsor of the original March of Dimes. By 1953 Dr. Jonas Salk had discovered his miraculous polio vaccine and had begun testing. With thousands of children contracting the disease every year, the vaccine was pressed into service in April 1955. The first sign of trouble was a call to the NIH two weeks later; a vaccinated Chicago baby had contracted polio. The next day, another call came, this one from Napa Valley, California, reporting that a four-year old vaccinated child had contracted polio. As more cases poured in, the

Public Health Service identified the culprit as Cutter Laboratories in Berkeley, California. Safe vaccine was produced when the live polio virus was inactivated by a process using formaldehyde. Cutter employees failed to adhere to the right procedure, sending out active polio virus in its vaccine. The Cutter lab was shut down on May 7, but by then almost eighty vaccinated children had been infected, and they had spread the polio to another 120 playmates and relatives. Eleven would die, and three-quarters of the group were paralyzed.[16]

When the non-Cutter vaccine was determined to be safe, the public clamored for universal distribution. Until then the federal government had distanced itself from the vaccine's distribution—letting the polio foundation purchase and distribute it. When members of Congress, including Laird, pushed for a federal purchase, HEW Secretary Oveta Culp Hobby resisted. Such a program could lead to "socialized medicine by the back door," she countered. Congress ignored her and enacted a $34 million federal purchase program for massive vaccination of all infants and children through the second grade. Within one year, polio deaths were cut by 50 percent, and, in time, the disease was almost totally eradicated.

The horror of the Cutter fiasco, and then the federal foot-dragging over distribution, meant heads had to roll if the Public Health Service and NIH were to recover quickly. Oveta Hobby resigned, as did others, including the NIH director. The new director, Dr. James A. Shannon, became the founding father of the modern NIH, with his vision to create a peerless, world-class health research institution. In Shannon, the triumvirate in Congress—Congressmen Fogarty and Laird and Senator Hill—finally had a director who shared their vision, and who could spend whatever they sent his way. In hearings Shannon was their best witness. Fogarty and Laird would secretly script how much money Shannon would "reluctantly" agree to settle for. Then in a good show, they would appear to be tough with him in the public hearings. "It was all part of a strategy," remembered Dr. Carl Baker, former National Cancer Institute director.[17] "It looked like they were clobbering Shannon but it was all arranged ahead of time."

The result of their collaboration was evident in Shannon's first year as director, when Fogarty, Laird, and Hill more than doubled his annual budget, from $98 to $213 million. So began a sustained pattern of consistently large annual increases for the NIH, as fast as Shannon could justifiably spend the money. During the 1953–69 period, when the Fogarty-Laird-Hill triumvirate was in operation, NIH's budget increased some twenty-eight-fold. More than a dozen buildings were constructed or begun, some of them brick, at Fogarty's insistence. The most important, in Laird's view, was the $7.3 million National Library of Medicine. To the NIH's already-existing seven institutes, another three were added: the National Institute of Child Health and Human Development (1962); General Medical Sciences (1962); and National Eye Institute (1968). (By 2004, the number of NIH institutes had reached twenty.)[18]

Laird's support of dental research and fluoridation, at a time when some thought fluoridation was a Communist conspiracy to poison Americans, earned him an honorary doctor of dentistry degree. His brother, Dr. David Laird, a former English department chairman at California State University (Los Angeles), needled Mel at one point, expressing amazement at "the range and diversity of the robes and honors," but the dental one was the most curious. "Are we to suppose that it is in recognition of Mel's unquestionable skill in the art of oral implantation—the art, that is, of putting words in other people's mouths?"[19]

The National Mental Health Association named Laird its Man of the Year in 1960, out of gratitude for the tens of millions of dollars he had earmarked for mental health research and the construction of community mental health facilities. He was also intent on the swift production and broad distribution of kidney dialysis machines. He fast-tracked research on the development of artificial heart and heart-related devices by appropriating special money to the NIH for that purpose, over the objections of Dr. Shannon, who thought it was moving too fast. In 1966 Laird reported with justifiable pride to his constituents that he had closely followed the story of a thirty-seven-year-old woman who walked out of a Houston, Texas, hospital and flew home to Mexico—as the first person in medical history whose life was saved with a man-made heart pump. "The Texas story was of particular interest to me because the heart pump, which was developed and used by Dr. William DeBakey, had been made possible by federal funds."[20]

Before the Environmental Protection Agency was created, most federal ecology programs were in HEW, whose purse strings Fogarty and Laird held.[21] Seeing more links between pollution and disease, Laird pushed NIH to create the Environmental Health Sciences Center. The effort was held up all three years of the Kennedy administration because the president insisted it be located in the Washington, D.C., area. Laird was convinced that federal science would benefit from geographical distance from Washington politics. The first step was finally achieved in 1964 when Laird, in conference with the Senate, agreed to appropriate money for the center only on condition "the facility would not be located within 50 miles of the District of Columbia."[22] While Laird might have preferred a Wisconsin site, he did not oppose a proposal to locate the center in North Carolina.[23] Today it is called the National Institute of Environmental Health Sciences. Its studies on cancer-causing agents, lead poisoning, asbestos exposure, dust mite infestation, and the like have formed the basis for government regulatory policy.

Four years after Laird left Congress, reflecting on his large-scale NIH empire-building era with Fogarty, he concluded in a 1973 speech before a group of surgeons: "John Fogarty and I worked as a team, as partners in progress. Together we delivered the rationale and the votes that raised the NIH from a shoestring operation to one of the most preeminent biomedical research complexes on earth. That is the way to make progress, I believe—by focusing on partnership rather than partisanship."[24]

Surgeon General Luther Terry lit up a cigarette in the chauffeured government car taking him to a packed State Department auditorium on January 11, 1964. He was to stand before more than two hundred reporters and deliver the first-ever Surgeon General's Report. Terry had been in the post less than three years but had somehow summoned up the courage to defy the weight of American tobacco manufacturers to produce a damning 387-page antitobacco report, unassumingly titled *Smoking and Health: Report of the Advisory Committee to the Surgeon General of the United States*. Dr. Terry's aide, along for the ride, delicately observed that the first question reporters would ask him would be: "Do you smoke?" No, they won't ask, Terry countered; reporters would be interested in the weighty scientific conclusions, not his personal habits.

As Terry delivered the conclusions of the report to the journalists, the atmosphere was electrifying. His report stated flatly that "cigarette smoking is causally related to lung cancer in men; the magnitude of the effect of cigarette smoking outweighs all other factors." Not only that, but cigarette smoking was "the most important cause" of chronic bronchitis and probably was a significant contributor to heart disease. At the time he said this, 46 percent of American adults smoked. The link between smoking and both cancer and heart disease had been apparent to scientists for decades. Now the Surgeon General had finally declared it an undeniable fact. The air was heavy with the weight of the moment in the smoke-filled room as newsmen, government officials, and tobacco industry lobbyists puffed self-consciously on their cigarettes. Soon enough, a reporter who knew Terry baited him with the question:

"Do you smoke, Dr. Terry?"

Terry turned to the inquisitor, smiled with resolve, and responded simply: "No."

"Dr. Terry, when did you quit?"

"About thirty minutes ago," he said. Terry never smoked again.

Melvin Laird was also a cigarette smoker, and Terry had badgered him to quit smoking during the previous year as Terry became alarmed over mounting scientific evidence of its danger. It was a gutsy move since Terry was still then a smoker himself and was also trying to curry favor for his budget at Fogarty-Laird subcommittee hearings. One night in late 1963, after a grueling hearing over cancer funding and more pestering from Terry, Laird announced to his family at the dinner table that he wasn't going to smoke cigarettes any more; it was bad for his health. Though he remained an intermittent cigar smoker for years, Laird succeeded in quitting cigarettes cold turkey. (His wife of more than forty-five years, Barbara, was unable to quit and died of cancer in 1992.)[25]

The Surgeon General's report advised that "cigarette smoking is a health hazard of sufficient importance ... to warrant appropriate remedial action," so Laird and a majority of Congress soon responded with a law that, beginning in 1966, put warning labels on cigarette packages. Then, when he joined the Health Appropriations Subcommittee, Laird became committed to funding research to cure cancer. He was a consistent supporter of the National Cancer Institute, the primary agency through which the government supported cancer research. Again, there were opponents, one of whom suggested in a hearing that NCI researchers should slow down and "proceed a little more cautiously." A witness at the hearing, Dr. Harry Weaver of the American Cancer Society, was quick to respond, "I know of no single disease ... that was ever controlled by proceeding cautiously."[26] Laird knew how to pick his witnesses, like one doctor who employed Laird's comparison of space research spending over medical research: "If I had a choice between a Moon walk and the life of a child with leukemia, I would never glance upward."[27]

One of the institutions seeking a large NCI grant was in Laird's back yard, the McArdle Laboratory for Cancer Research on the Madison campus of the University of Wisconsin. Bursting at the seams in a small building, the facility needed more space fully dedicated to cancer research. The university couldn't come up with the matching funds that NCI required, so McArdle's director, Dr. Harold Rusch, asked if Laird could help. Rusch went to Washington and met with John Fogarty as well. The two hit it off because Rusch had been an apprentice bricklayer.[28] As a "mate" in masonry, Fogarty was more receptive to Rusch's plea for federal construction funds without the required matching money—especially when he found it was a national problem. Rusch wrote to thirteen other university cancer research centers and discovered they were in the same fix—their affiliated universities weren't able to help them with expansions. So when Laird offered an appropriations amendment in 1960 providing $30 million in start-up construction funds for fourteen regional cancer research centers, Fogarty backed his play. During the full Appropriations Committee, a friend and Wisconsin colleague of Laird's, Representative Glenn Davis, strenuously objected. He was appalled at the huge price tag for the NCI-affiliated regional centers. Laird recalled that Fogarty came to the defense of the bill. "He said, 'I can't understand the gentleman from Wisconsin [Davis] raising Cain with these regional cancer centers.... [T]hose are the ideas of your colleague from Wisconsin. THESE ARE *LAIRD-ETTES!*'" The name stuck and the bill passed.

An envelope arrived at the Capitol Hill office of Senator Tom Daschle in October 2001 with a white substance inside. Within days, four postal workers employed at the Washington, D.C., Postal Processing and Distribution Center who had likely handled the envelope were hospitalized with breathing difficulties; two died. Coming shortly after the 9/11 attack on the World Trade Center, bioterrorism was suspected. The Centers for Disease Control closed down the mail center and identified the powder as anthrax—the first reported outbreak caused by occupational exposure since 1957.[29]

The quick containment and identification of the anthrax was due in large part to the CDC. One of its patron saints who got a thank-you note after the incident was Mel Laird. Vice President Dick Cheney wrote the note to thank Laird for his "long list" of "legislative successes"—in particular, for "helping to establish the Centers for Disease Control."[30]

Legionnaires disease, AIDS, Lassa fever, Hanta virus, Ebola virus, and smallpox are on the short list of epidemics and maladies tackled by the CDC, which owes its existence in large part to Laird and Fogarty. The CDC, based in Atlanta, has its roots in military efforts to control malaria during World War II. By the early 1950s, the CDC's future was uncertain because of competition from other agencies and inadequate funding.[31] That was when the Fogarty-Laird team began operating with muscle, ensuring CDC's permanence and expanding it through funding, just as they did for NIH. CDC historian Dr. Elizabeth Etheridge said that the Fogarty-Laird era is still "looked on nostalgically as the 'good old days' insofar as getting money out of Washington was concerned."[32] Between 1953 and 1969, Fogarty and Laird escalated CDC appropriations more than 1,000 percent, from an annual $5.9 million budget to $62.1 million.[33]

Besides rapidly escalating the CDC's funding, they also shrewdly pressured the Public Health Service to start shifting some of its larger divisions close to Atlanta—venereal disease, tuberculosis, immunization, and other functions. Throughout the 1950s, despite the growth in duties and prestige, the CDC had remained in ramshackle buildings scattered in several cities. Its various offices were a health hazard unto themselves—labs without germ-proof walls, no air conditioning in the summer or inadequate heat in the winter, dilapidated fire-trap buildings that leaked from room to room where diseases were being investigated, and animal facilities that were impossible to secure. (One routine duty of the officer-of-the-day was escaped-monkey retrieval.)[34] The CDC desperately needed a modern headquarters, which only came into being because of the three congressional archangels of the era, Fogarty, Laird, and Hill. In 1947 the Atlanta-based Coca-Cola Company gave the CDC fifteen acres of land next to Emory University to build a headquarters. But the $13 million-plus complex of headquarters buildings didn't get built until Fogarty and Laird made it a funding priority. The six-floor main building spread out to five interconnected buildings with just what the doctors had ordered: offices, labs, and secure animal rooms in abundance. (Also, at the insistence of Senator Hill, who was a segregationist, it had separate restrooms for blacks and whites. But shortly after the 1960 dedication, with a quiet okay from Fogarty and Laird, the CDC took down the "Colored Only" signs, and converted the surplus bathrooms to labs.)

The decade of the 1960s, when Fogarty and Laird wielded the magic wand, turned the CDC into a first-class agency. The CDC's involvement in eradicating smallpox is a prime example. A vaccine for small pox was discovered in the late 1700s but required vaccination of any possible human host to rid the planet of the disease. Only when the CDC joined the effort in 1966 did the vaccination campaign sponsored by the World Health Organization escalate rapidly. Not the least of the problems was that in many of the areas where the disease was most virulent, people suspected it was their gods' way of punishing sinners. In Latin America, for example, the smallpox god was Obaluaye. When the Cuban-born husband of Lucille Ball, Desi Arnaz, recorded the 1950s hit song, "Baba Luaye," he was singing about the god of smallpox. Through careful education, and often after persuading tribal leaders to set the example by receiving the first inoculation, the CDC methodically overcame resistance.[35] The CDC also developed more effective vaccine delivery systems, which brought about the total eradication of the disease.

As Congressman Laird monitored and encouraged the CDC's smallpox work, he met opposition from others in Congress who questioned the expenditure of millions of American dollars abroad, since by the time CDC joined the effort, smallpox was nonexistent in the United States. Laird countered their concern by pointing out a central fact of the modern era: "A disease such as smallpox in this age of fast travel can be spread to countries half a world away in just a few hours."[36] Laird firmly believed that one should never quibble over such things when it came to saving lives. That was his guiding philosophy in nurturing the CDC's rapid growth.

❧

Late Monday afternoon, January 9, 1967, Laird was laying it on thick with Fogarty. They had shared many good times as traveling companions from America to Europe, where they had together visited Pope John XXIII in Rome and attended four different World Health Assemblies in Geneva. Laird was proposing one more trip. "Let's skip the congressional opening ceremony tomorrow and go to Los Angeles and see the Green Bay Packers play in the Super Bowl on Sunday. We'll sign the [congressional] oath of office in L.A." Fogarty felt it was important to take the oath in the House, so he persuaded Laird to postpone their trip for a day. Fogarty never made the ceremony. The next day,

January 10, the fifty-three-year-old congressman suffered a heart attack and died at his desk.[37]

The eulogies multiplied swiftly and eloquently. Dr. Howard Rusk wrote in the *New York Times*, "With his bright green tie and his Irish accent, he was a circuit rider for health, a teacher, a preacher, a fearless foe to any challenger who stood in the way of his crusade. He died on the field of battle. His friends from the scientist to the sick mourn his loss and call him blessed."[38]

Laird, using his influence as ranking member on the Defense Appropriations Subcommittee, secured a Pentagon plane to take any colleagues who wanted to attend, Republican or Democrat, to Fogarty's Rhode Island funeral. Laird, choking with emotion, delivered one of the eulogies: "I have spent more time with John Fogarty than with any other man in public life [so] when I speak of John Fogarty, I am speaking of a man whom I not only loved and admired as much as any man I have ever known, but I am also speaking of a man I knew as well as any man on this earth.... I [will] never forget his great sympathy for anyone, especially children and old people, with a mental or physical disability; his love of God and faith in the Catholic religion that was simple and pure, and completely free from ostentation."[39]

Fogarty, the reluctant convert to health issues, had taken the work with Laird so seriously that he had passed up opportunities to become the governor of his state, or senator, or even secretary of Health, Education, and Welfare—a job President-elect Kennedy had offered him. The attendant respect that fellow Democrats gave him had naturally flowed to his Republican partner, Laird. Early in Laird's congressional career, House Speaker John McCormack, a Democrat, decided to mentor the young Republican. He spent hours tutoring Laird in the ways of the House, partly out of gratitude for the nonpartisan spirit Laird demonstrated in his partnership with Fogarty. After one speech of Laird's in support of a health science bill, McCormack complimented him: "That was a terrific speech today. You're coming along fine." Then, arm around Laird, McCormack ushered him to a little room just off the members' dining room on the House side of the Capitol building.

"I want you to have this room. It's your own private dining room or meeting room for whatever you need to do."

Laird beamed. Capitol rooms were scarce, and this was a very rare assignment of exclusive space from the House Democratic Party leader to a Republican. "The most coveted status symbol in Congress [is] the Capitol hideaway," the *New York Times* noted. There are only about fifty such secret offices possible in the Capitol itself, and "such refuges are more scarce in the House. Party leaders have them, but not many others." When word of Laird's plum leaked, howls were heard from more senior members of McCormick's party. But the speaker stood fast, and Laird kept the private dining room throughout his government service, even using it when he was secretary of defense.[40]

Another unusual by-product of the Fogarty partnership with Laird was an invaluable memento from a Democratic White House. John F. Kennedy suffered from chronic back pains for years, but finally in 1955 he found a physician, Dr. Janet G. Travell, who relieved his pain with a series of prescription medications. Also, in Dr. Travell's New York office, Senator Kennedy discovered a perfect chair for his back, a custom-designed rocking chair. He subsequently ordered one from the small North Carolina company that made it. When he became president, Kennedy appointed Travell as his physician, and she made sure the "Kennedy rocker" was available wherever he might land—in the Oval Office, on Air Force One, on vacation, and so on.

Kennedy also gave away some of the rocking chairs to friends, including Fogarty and Laird. The president had been particularly grateful for Laird's work with Fogarty on mental retardation—an issue dear to Kennedy, whose sister struggled with the condition.[41]

Laird undoubtedly would have traded the rare rocker, the private dining room, and other "perks" to work with Fogarty just a little longer. His death in early 1967 left a large hole in the HEW appropriations subcommittee that could not be entirely filled by successor Daniel Flood, of Pennsylvania. And when Laird was named defense secretary–designate in December 1968, it meant that the last of the big four was gone. Senator Hill had declined to run for reelection in 1968, and Dr. Shannon had retired from the NIH.

On the occasion of Laird's appointment to the Nixon Cabinet, *Washington Star* columnist Judith Randal observed a political irony: "By a strange quirk of politics, Nixon's choice of Laird as Secretary of Defense may have wider repercussions on the medical front than his selection of Robert H. Finch for the HEW Cabinet post. In fact, some observers of the health research scene see in Laird's departure from Capitol Hill a situation that is little short of disaster."[42]

9

The Patron Saint of Football

THE LIFE OF MEMBER OF CONGRESS is not all budgets and bureaucracy; occasionally there comes the opportunity to branch out. For Laird, it was his chance to become a patron saint of many causes, including idealistic youngsters, local governments, Native Americans, and the Green Bay Packers.

Among Laird's neighbors in the Washington suburb of Chevy Chase was an inquisitive teenager named David who loved to argue politics. Though David was the son of a Democratic former congressman from Oklahoma, he would castigate Laird for being "too liberal" and otherwise make a nuisance of himself (including accidentally walking through Laird's glass door). Nevertheless, Laird spent many hours mentoring the teenager. After David studied at Oxford University on a Rhodes Scholarship, he visited Laird to get counsel regarding his future. Laird advised him to return to his father's home county, register as a Democrat, and in good time run for state office, just as Laird had. David Boren followed his mentor's advice, eventually becoming governor of Oklahoma and then a U.S. senator. Boren recalled Laird's tutelage with appreciation and when asked at different times what his political identity was, he would proudly call himself "a Laird Democrat."[1]

Laird's interest in young Boren was not just because he might make a good politician, but because he had the potential to become a leader in any field he chose. Laird made a side vocation of seeking out young people who buzzed with the kind of promise he had felt at their age. In 1965 he invited major national and state leaders to Wisconsin State University (later the University of Wisconsin) at Stevens Point for a day-long discussion with top juniors and seniors from the sixty-four high schools in his district. This was no ordinary high school field trip. As the ranking member of the appropriations subcommittee that controlled the federal education budget, Laird could command the best speakers in the field. Commissioner of Education Francis Keppel was the keynote speaker at that first of many such gatherings, and the workshop subjects included the Vietnam War, civil rights, and morality in a changing society. Using resources from the Library of Congress, Laird sent the high school delegates advance material so the exchange of ideas would be more productive. "These young people came in loaded for bear," Laird recalled later. Keppel effusively told Laird that it was the best discussion he'd had with students since becoming commissioner three years before.[2]

Laird Youth Leadership Day took on a life of its own. Over the ensuing three decades, Laird induced nearly every education commissioner and education secretary (after it became a Cabinet department) to visit the Stevens Point campus, along with many other national and state luminaries.[3] One repeat guest, *Washington Post* columnist David Broder, participated in part because he was likely to meet talented "comers" among the speakers there, such as Elizabeth Hanford. Later she married Bob Dole and was selected in 1983 as Ronald Reagan's transportation secretary. Broder noted in his column that he knew Liddy Dole was a talent destined for big things since he had "met her at a [1971] Wisconsin high school forum arranged by Melvin R. Laird," when she was merely a consumer advisor in the Nixon White House.[4]

Laird knew that many of these students, from low- or middle-income families, could not afford to attend even a state university. Beginning in 1957, he dispensed college scholarships through the Laird Youth Leadership Foundation, funded in its early days with honorariums from his speeches. More than 375 high school graduates in his district received scholarships from the foundation in the ensuing years. Laird's scholarship program was founded because of his basic Wisconsin-bred belief that it shouldn't be just the rich who have access to education. This belief drove his support of a Johnson-era program, Head Start.

In his first State of the Union message, Lyndon Johnson declared "war" on poverty and shortly after named the Peace Corps Director Sargent Shriver to head up the Office of Economic Opportunity. One of Shriver's early aims was to break the cycle of poverty for its youngest victims. Through a steering committee of pediatricians and other specialists, and with Lady Bird Johnson's help, Shriver started a drumbeat for a comprehensive preschool education and nutrition program that would help children from the most impoverished families get a "head start" on their schooling. Laird and John Fogarty embraced the idea so quickly that they appropriated money even before it was requested by the administration. A successful eight-week test run during the summer of 1965 justified Laird's early faith in the idea. Today Head Start is considered the most successful antipoverty program from the Johnson era and routinely wins bipartisan support on Capitol Hill.

Laird was the first to introduce a bill the late 1950s to permit taxpayers to deduct college tuition on their tax returns. While Head Start and other programs helped the poor, Laird felt it was important to provide the middle class with education incentives, too. The broad-based bill, which did not pass, would have covered credits for both private primary school tuition, as well as college costs. Before Democrat Hugh Carey was elected to Congress, he had done some research into freedom of choice in education, and "I discovered some congressman from Wisconsin had put the first bill in to give some support to children in non-public schools. I said, 'I've got to find out who this man is because he has great ideas.' And I did and became great friends with Mel Laird."[5]

Laird never gave up on the idea; he reintroduced the Laird Tax Credit Bill every year and lobbied for it. The far-sighted legislative position was both the genesis of and also decades ahead of the current college tuition federal tax credit, as well as the private school "voucher" movement.

※

Letting taxpayers keep their own money for education was a smaller piece of Laird's growing opinion that states and cities should be able to keep their money, too. One day he looked up the heading, "United States Government," in the Milwaukee telephone book and counted 240 entries. A quick check of the state government directory revealed only 166. Could the same be true for smaller cities and towns in his own district? He found his Wausau phone book and quickly toted up twenty-four federal listings, and only eleven state listings.[6] Long before Ronald Reagan coined the phrase "let's get the government off the backs of the people," Laird developed the same resolution. He decided to do something about it, and his inventive revenue-sharing proposal became one of the most far-reaching federal spending reforms of the twentieth century.

The more Laird investigated, the more sure he became that the monster middleman of federal relations with local governments was the "categorical grant" program. It didn't make sense to him that local taxpayers would send their money to Washington, only to have it sent back to programs in their towns with strings attached. The roots of the program went back to the Great Depression of the 1930s, when Americans had looked to Washington for relief, and Franklin D. Roosevelt had obliged. During an eleven-year period, FDR spearheaded a 650 percent increase in federal grants to state and local governments. The grants, which most often went to public works projects that employed or gave financial relief to out-of-work Americans (such as the Civilian Conservation Corps), had consumed $945 million by 1940. That was a lot of money in 1940 dollars, but it was only the beginning. After the Depression ended, the grant program spiraled out of control. The tab for federal grants-in-aid was $2.9 billion in 1953, the first year Laird became a congressman, and $8.6 billion when Kennedy was in the White House. By 1967 taxpayers were funding federal grants to the tune of $21.9 billion a year.[7]

United States senators and representatives had become hooked on the programs, considering them vital for reelection. They fought for a portion of the grant money so they could prove to their constituents that they could bring home federal dollars—in reality the citizen's own taxes coming back to them, minus the federal administrative cut. Laird was not immune to the exercise, but he soured on it early. One federal grant for improvement of an airport in central Wisconsin, which Laird worked to get, had the ironic effect of turning him into a zealous reformer. It was 1958 and Washington had a $30 million pot for local airports. Congressmen, including Laird, scrambled for some of the dollars for the folks back home. But when he snagged $230,000 for his district's airport, he began receiving irate letters from constituents who thought the money could be better spent on something else. Why should their money be spent on an airport just because the federal government controlled the amounts and categories of spending? At the time there were fifty-three federal aid programs on the books recycling money back to the states. The more Laird thought about it, the more committed he became to changing the system.

As a state senator, he had helped develop a formula to give state income tax money directly into the towns and counties where the taxpayers lived. Under the innovative Wisconsin tax-sharing program, state tax dollars were divided so fifty cents of each dollar went back to the city or town where the taxes had been raised, ten cents to the county, and the remaining forty cents to the state. Wisconsin didn't tell the local governments how to spend their money. The logic of Washington returning a flat percentage of the tax dollars each state had sent to the capital seemed so sound that Laird didn't feel it could be refuted. The plan would use the federal government's talent for doing what it did best—raising revenue—and then pass that back to the states and cities to do what they did best—providing services. Other members of Congress were not immediately persuaded by his arguments. To them it looked like Laird was trying to take away one of the gauges they used to measure their own success. If their congressional districts got flat amounts of money automatically, how could the representatives take credit for delivering that money? But Laird was undeterred. As with tuition tax credits, he reintroduced a Laird bill on revenue sharing every year, and every year he was turned down.

It was during the Johnson era that Laird came the closest to winning passage for his bill. Johnson had inflated federal categorical grants to an all-time high; it was federal paternalism gone awry. Laird ridiculed the illogical approach for reaching Johnson's dream of a Great Society. What Johnson clearly wanted, Laird would often say, was a Great *Planned* Society, one where Washington dictated what was best for every community. Johnson's concept of a Great Society was only great if you were a federal bureaucrat.

While most Johnson aides were not interested in sending tax dollars back to the states without a set of instructions attached, one influential official was. In 1960, two years after Laird floated his first revenue-sharing bill, a University of Minnesota economics professor, Walter Heller, gave a speech urging that rising federal revenues be distributed back to the states with fewer strings; he was a Democrat. Kennedy tapped him to be chairman of his Council of Economic Advisors, and Heller continued in the same post for Johnson. In 1964, he began pushing revenue sharing so hard that it was labeled the Heller Plan, even though Laird had begun the idea.[8] At Heller's prodding, Johnson appointed a special task force headed by Brookings expert Dr. Joseph Pechman. By late 1964, according to several accounts, Johnson had decided to adopt the Heller Plan, announcing it in his 1965 State of the Union address. But an early draft of the task force report leaked, and Johnson suspected Heller was floating a trial balloon. The president dropped his support for revenue sharing in a fit of pique.[9]

Laird was not unhappy when the Heller Plan died because it had differed from his own in one key respect. Heller saw revenue sharing as a supplement to the existing grants programs, rather than a replacement for them. Laird never believed federal taxes should support both categorical grant and revenue-sharing programs. The death of the less-desirable Democratic variation of his plan did not dampen Laird's enthusiasm. By the time he left Congress, he had delivered more than 350 speeches on the subject to a wide variety of groups, but he never got a bill passed.[10] There had been only a partial victory during the Johnson administration when Laird and his fellow Republicans were able to change several categorical grant-in-aid programs into the more effective bloc grants with fewer strings attached.

Just because Laird had to resign from his congressional seat in 1969 to become secretary of defense did not mean his lobbying for revenue sharing, or other pet projects for that matter, was over. Indeed, as he joined the administration, political commentators prognosticated that his influence would be far broader than military policy—in particular on HEW matters and instituting a pioneer program of revenue sharing. In President Nixon, Laird finally found his most receptive listener. During the 1968 campaign, candidate Nixon had clearly condemned categorical grants and seemed to favor revenue sharing as an alternative. Laird also had key allies in the Nixon administration nudging the president down the same road—White House aide Daniel Patrick Moynihan, whom Laird had recruited to write a pro-revenue-sharing essay in *The Republican Papers;* Domestic Counselor John Ehrlichman; HEW Secretary Caspar Weinberger; Office of Management and Budget Director George Shultz; and Paul M. W. McCracken, chairman of the Council of Economic Advisors. Even the addition in late 1970 of Treasury Secretary John Connally, who had favored revenue sharing when he was governor of Texas, was not enough to tip the scales.

It was the same old problem Laird had faced for years; members of Congress enjoyed playing Santa Claus in their districts. The specific roadblock was the House Ways and Means Committee, where both Chairman Wilbur Mills, of Arkansas, and John Byrnes of Wisconsin, a Democrat and Republican respectively, were adamantly opposed to revenue sharing.[11] It took sixteen months to wear them down and required the critical help of two men—Governor Nelson Rockefeller and Defense Secretary Laird. A review of the Oval Office tapes shows that in almost every discussion of revenue sharing, Laird was either in the room or his involvement and help were referenced by the participants.

While Rockefeller rallied the nation's governors and whittled down Congressman Mills, Laird worked on his friend Byrnes. The offensive worked, and Laird's fourteen-year-long dream of a revenue-sharing revolution was finally signed into law in October 1972. "It was a long, tough, hard job selling that idea," Laird remarked a few weeks later.[12] But it was well worth the struggle. Nixon aide William Safire called revenue sharing "the most important legislative achievement of the Nixon administration in terms of [his] New Federal philosophy,"[13] and many commentators agreed. Nixon felt, too, that it was his most vital first-term victory. He wrote later in his memoirs: "On a practical level, revenue sharing was a way of revitalizing local government and local responsibility. On a philosophical level, it was the first change in the direction of federal growth in forty years—no less than the New American Revolution we called it."[14]

From 1972 to 1986, federal revenue sharing dispensed $85 billion back to the states, cities, and communities. President Reagan ended it because he was running hefty federal deficits, and he wanted to end anything that smacked of grant give-backs to the states. But by the time Reagan shut it down, Laird's brainchild had a subtle but powerful side effect of restructuring and rebuilding the Republican Party. By "sending some of the power back to states and localities in the form of money and responsibility," columnist Tom Wicker wrote, revenue sharing "helped build the modern Republican Party." Before revenue sharing, states in the South were so consistent about voting for Democratic candidates that the region was referred to as the Solid South. After revenue sharing, the trend went in the other direction—so popular was the program in small towns and municipalities that had seldom seen anything good come out of Washington.[15]

With his concept of revenue sharing, Laird was instrumental in changing more than federal expenditures and the Republican Party voter base. He used it to resurrect and transform the game of football.

⁓

If any sports team and its fans exemplify the independent, rugged American spirit, it is the Green Bay Packers, the only nonprofit, publicly owned team in professional sports. While the team is based in the smallest city of any National Football League team, the Packers have conversely won more championships than any other NFL team. Though the team did well on the field, its financial underpinnings were precarious in the early years. The Packers were bailed out through various local business loans, playing intrasquad games for the extra admission receipts, and even passing the hat during half time. But the biggest bailout came in 1950, when fans rescued the bankrupt team by selling $25 shares of stock in the team door-to-door and raising $118,000. The primary provisions of the unique sale were that the shares would never earn dividends, could never increase in value, and, if the team was ever sold, the proceeds would be used to build a war memorial at the local American Legion whose members march in to "present the colors" before each Packer game.[16]

The "cheeseheads" had saved the team, but more was needed at the beginning of the television age. As the various NFL franchises negotiated local and national TV contracts with newly interested broadcast executives, it became apparent that the bigger cities, which could command larger viewing audiences, would soon outpace the smaller ones in TV revenue, and their ability to attract competitive players would be greater. At this point, two of the Packers' greatest fans and patrons, Congressmen Melvin Laird and Johnny Byrnes, went to work on the problem. They wound up saving the Packers and the NFL.

The first step was convincing the new NFL commissioner, Pete Rozelle, that he should get an agreement from the owners that the NFL would negotiate with television networks as one and share the revenue equally among the teams. "Pete saw the advantages of revenue sharing," Laird remembered. "He realized the NFL would be better, more competitive, if the money was shared. Pete became a big leader in this thing, because he went along with us." With equal foresight, the owners went along with Rozelle's plan. In early 1961 CBS signed a single-package deal with the NFL, paying $4.65 million for exclusive 1961 season broadcast rights; each of the NFL's fourteen teams was to receive an equal share of the total.[17] Within months, a U.S. district judge in Philadelphia ruled that the agreement "eliminated competition" and was a violation of federal antitrust laws.[18] Laird, Byrnes, and Rozelle had anticipated the ruling and, that summer, worked hard for a congressional antitrust exemption for the NFL. While their combined leadership on both the House Appropriations and Ways and Means committees made Laird and Byrnes formidable, they needed to woo a Democratic majority, so House Judiciary Chairman Emanuel Celler of New York took a visible lead, sponsoring the bill.[19]

For a time in the fall, it appeared that the quartet had hit an insurmountable roadblock. Colleges and high schools opposed the merger, fearing pro football would substantially cut into their Friday and Saturday fan base and their TV revenues. So the professional teams agreed not to play on Friday or Saturday, thus creating Monday night football and clearing the way for final passage of the bill overriding the federal court antitrust decision. It was a watershed victory for the NFL collectively and for the Green Bay Packers especially. "If it hadn't been approved, the Packers' dynasty would not have occurred, because the previous season CBS paid [the Packers] $35,000 for its TV rights and the New York Giants $500,000," *Sporting News* later reflected. The "dynasty" referenced was that begun when a coach named Vince Lombardi was hired by the Packers in 1959. His reign corresponded with the period of continued antitrust lobbying Laird and Byrnes had to do for their team.[20]

With a winning coach fueling Wisconsin's pride, Laird and Byrnes were more determined than ever to protect the Packers. Their second major opportunity at the scrimmage line of football history came in 1966 when, after secret negotiations between the NFL and the fledgling American Football League, a merger was signed, ending a costly bidding war between the two rivals. From the judicial branch came the same accusation of monopoly. But Laird and others were again working to exempt the NFL from antitrust laws. Laird discovered a way to end the resistance that was holding up the legislation allowing a merger. Senator Russell Long, a Louisiana Democrat, was the most formidable opponent. At one point in the stalemate, Senator Long revealed what was really bothering him: "You know, Mel, I've been trying to get a team in New Orleans for a long time. I haven't made any progress and I can't get Pete Rozelle to listen to me on how important it is."

Laird said cannily, "Well, I'll tell you what, Russell. If we get it worked out so that we can get you a team in New Orleans, will you get that bill out and be a promoter of it on the floor?" Long agreed and the deal was struck. Almost immediately after the meeting, Laird called Rozelle and said "you better goddamned give him his team if you want this to pass." Rozelle hustled up to Capitol Hill and made the promise on behalf of the NFL.[21]

The same dance worked for another Louisiana Democrat, Representative Hale Boggs; all he wanted was a Louisiana team, too. Boggs and Rozelle met an hour before the final House vote on the AFL-NFL merger bill. When Boggs asked if the promise of a New Orleans team was firm, Rozelle equivocated: "It still has to be approved by the owners. I can't make any promises on my own." Boggs mused, and then told Rozelle he would hold up the vote until Rozelle had checked with all the owners. "That's all right, Hale," Rozelle corrected himself. "You can count on their approval."[22] Several weeks after Congress approved the AFL-NFL merger, Rozelle, with Long and Boggs at his side, announced with some fanfare the formation of a sixteenth NFL franchise, the New Orleans Saints. Rozelle said that New Orleans had beaten out six other cities competing for an expansion team. Only a few people knew the backroom deal that led to its creation.[23]

The 1961 and 1966 antitrust waivers engineered by Laird "may have been the two most important things that happened in pro football," observed Joe Horrigan, vice president of the Pro Football Hall of Fame. Football historian C. Robert Barnett agreed that it was a sport-saving move when NFL team owners "legislated themselves into parity."[24]

At the same time he was lobbying for pro football, Laird had tried to get baseball and other sports organizations to do the same thing—revenue sharing. He promised antitrust waivers for them, too, but none ever took him up on the offer. (However, baseball officials were so impressed with the congressman that Los Angeles Dodgers owner Walter O'Malley was authorized in 1968 to offer Laird the job of baseball commissioner, which he declined. Bowie Kuhn accepted and was commissioner from 1969 to 1984.)

The only sad note for Laird as he reflected back on the successes of his football intercession was the death of his friend Vince Lombardi. When the coach retired in 1969, the new Secretary of Defense Laird, congressional patron saint of the Packers—hosted a luncheon in Lombardi's honor at the Pentagon. The coach seemed robust, but he was in the first stages of a cancer that would fell him in 1970.

The Menominee Indians of Wisconsin believe humankind was created when a great copper-tailed bear rose up from the banks of a river in north-central Wisconsin and was changed by the Great Spirit into a Menominee, the first human being. As the bear explored his surroundings, he saw an eagle, beaver, sturgeon, elk, crane, wolf, dog, and deer. These were likewise transformed into humans and thus was born the Menominee tribe.[25]

Things got progressively more complicated for the tribe after that, as Menominee artist James Frechette Jr. could personally attest. After years of struggle with the white man, this tribe confronted one of its most formidable challenges yet. Prominent voices in Congress in 1954 were calling for the "termination" of federal support for the Menominee tribe. Frechette's father was one of several tribal leaders who sought congressional guidance, and the man he most trusted was the young freshman Congressman Laird, in whose district the reservation lay. "My father had a lot of respect for Laird," remembered Frechette Jr., "because he's the only Republican who consistently won [the majority of] votes" on the reservation."[26] That kind of trust was not easily earned from the Menominees, who had a history of playing an artful game with Washington, and winning.

While most Native Americans were being forced off or bought off their land, the Menominee held steadfastly to their ancestral claim on northern Wisconsin. In the 1800s, U.S. efforts to force the Menominee west of the Mississippi River were met with fierce opposition. Realizing they were outnumbered and outgunned by the government, the Menominee chose peace talks over war. Chief Oshkosh successfully negotiated several treaties with Washington. In exchange for much of their land, the Menominee were allowed to stay in Wisconsin and were given the promise of eternal government protection.

The 1954 Termination Act was a pilot project aimed at eventually weaning all Indian tribes off federal stewardship. A few select tribes, deemed fit for self-government, were chosen for the experiment. Of these tribes, the three-thousand-member Menominee was by far the largest. The Termination Act was to repeal the Menominee's reservation status, making them, among other things, subject to state and federal taxes. Utah Senator Arthur Watkins, a staunchly conservative Republican, introduced and spearheaded the bill. He believed the Menominee could be self-sustaining based on the lucrative timber holdings on their 234,000-acre reservation. Watkins was simply "wrong on the 'Indian problem,'" Laird said. "He was so conservative that he felt that they all should be just put on their own, and we should not have any responsibility for them."

Laird warned the Menominee about the Termination Act. Nevertheless the tribe agreed to support the act after Senator Watkins visited the reservation. During an informal meeting, Watkins essentially gave the Menominee an ultimatum: they had to either accept termination or lose their claim to a multi-million dollar settlement over government mishandling of tribal lands. Armed with a dubious mandate from the tribe, Watkins went back and steamrollered Congress. Laird resisted until the Menominee asked him to withdraw his opposition and support the legislation on their behalf. Eisenhower signed the Termination Act in June of 1954.

The intervening years saw Congressman Laird continually postponing the actual date of termination, since the majority of tribal members came to believe they had been snookered. The Native Americans learned they could depend on Laird and respect him. "It was just his manner, his way of doing things," Frechette remembered. "He didn't have any hidden agenda and wasn't pulling any strings you couldn't see. The people in the tribe were so used to dealing with bureaucrats that they could spot that kind of crap." Laird was adopted into the tribe as an honorary chief and given a new name which means "Chief Lawmaker." The grateful tribe also observed an annual Melvin R. Laird Day powwow to honor his work on their behalf.

As the years wore on, there remained the quiet, ominous drumbeat of an impending termination date that Laird could not postpone forever. In 1961, after seven years of stalling tactics on the tribe's behalf, the bill finally took effect. Menominee County was officially born, the eleventh county in Laird's district.[27] On the eve of its "emancipation" from federal control, Menominee County was considered the poorest in Wisconsin. It was immediately declared a "depressed area" to qualify it for federal aid. The county welfare director described one house in which twenty-two people were living on one income.[28] The Menominee forest land, expected to be a wellspring of revenue, proved to be a millstone around the tribe's neck. In a few short years, the Menominee treasury went bust, unemployment soared, and upward of 70 percent of the population fell below the poverty level. In a desperate attempt to raise money, the Menominee leaders began selling off lakefront vacation property.

Laird did everything he could to get aid for the foundering tribe. Over the course of several years he secured millions of dollars in federal support, but the tribe continued its downward trajectory. Though the Menominee remained doggedly optimistic—even putting up a sign at the entrance to the reservation that read, "We Will Make It"—their prospects were grim. Ultimately, the U.S. government abandoned its designs for an across-the-board termination policy, and in the early 1970s President Nixon promised continued federal protection to all tribes as then constituted. The Menominee, however, were no longer a tribe because they had already agreed to termination.

When Laird had visited at the Menominee reservation for a ceremony in 1953, by his side had been a young Menominee girl, Ada Deer. Daughter of a white mother and a Menominee father, she grew up in Keshena, the village heart of Menominee country. In 1958 she was one of five Native American girls chosen to take part in a Columbia motion picture. It was the first step that would take Deer on a path to winning international recognition and a host of accolades, including appointment as director of the Bureau of Indian Affairs during the Clinton administration.

In the 1960s, Deer became the first woman in her tribe to earn a college degree when she graduated from the University of Wisconsin. She went on to earn a master's degree in social work from Columbia University and was en route to a law degree when the aftereffects of the Menominee "termination" finally boiled over. Deer was appalled at how her tribe was being forced to sell off land to increase its tax base. It was like "burning down your house to keep warm in a blizzard," Deer said. "Indians look upon land with a sense of spirituality—the mother earth. There's one bumper sticker that says, HOW COULD YOU SELL YOUR MOTHER?"[29]

Inspired to action, Deer dropped out of law school and went to Washington to lobby for her tribe, advocating the passage of a Restoration Act, to undo what the Termination Act had done; it would allow the Menominee tribe to regain its unique autonomy as a reservation while once again exempting it from state and federal taxes. Deer worked to build a coalition of support within the Nixon administration, which was tough going since she was a very vocal Democrat. The man who helped bridge the difference was the former congressman for the Menominee. By that time, in 1973, Laird had resigned as defense secretary but had returned to Washington politics as domestic counselor for Nixon.

"I called Mr. Laird's office," Deer said. "That was the only call I ever made to him—that was all that was needed."[30] Menominee expert and author Nicholas Peroff reported in his 1982 book, *Menominee DRUMS*, "Laird's role was confirmed by a senior BIA official, who commented that the former Wisconsin congressman 'was the mover behind the scenes who formed the White House position on restoration.' Former Congressman Laird's contacts both in the administration and with his former congressional colleagues opened many doors for Ada Deer and other restoration lobbyists."[31] In June 1999, with a nudge from Laird in retirement, the Senate passed a bill giving $32 million to the Menominee tribe as compensation for mishandling their tribal funds in the 1960s.[32] More than twenty years removed from public life, Laird was still looking out for his constituents.

Until the 1960s, conservatives were regarded as the low ideology on the intellectual totem pole. Ralph Waldo Emerson was one of the first to disparage the very idea of innovative conservative thought. "Men are conservatives when they are least vigorous or when they are most luxurious," he said. "They are conservatives after dinner." Emerson continued in his 1842 work, *The Conservative,* saying that this repugnant political view was primarily the province of thoughtless Napoleons: "There is always a certain meanness in the argument of conservatism, joined with a certain superiority in its fact."

Laird was one of the first conservatives of the twentieth century to understand this stereotyping and to find a solution for it. Through several approaches, he mounted a successful assault on the liberal ivory tower. The post-Nixon success of Ronald Reagan, the Bushes—and even Bill Clinton, who expropriated conservative ideas in his move to the populist center—is attributable, in part, to the behind-the-scenes work of Laird.[33] "Mel recognized early on the importance of ideas—that intellectuals could be very helpful to the Republican Party and to their cause, his cause, *the* cause. I would say he recognized the value of this more than many of his colleagues on the Hill, and made more of an effort to outreach and identify these kinds of people who could buttress the conservative ideology with responsible arguments and empirical data," observed Dr. John Bibby, former University of Wisconsin political science professor who was an occasional researcher for Congressman Laird. "You have to remember this was at a time when it seemed most intellectuals were Democrats."[34]

Laird found three places to launch this Republican Renaissance. He transformed the Republican Conference into a more academic center, producing weighty policy studies; he enlisted prominent academics to do policy papers for the Republican Coordinating Committee; and he wrote or edited thoughtful books such as *House Divided* (1962) and *The Conservative Papers* (1962). While these three efforts were evident on the surface, there was a fourth, far-reaching Laird initiative, the ultimate effect of which took decades to unfold in the closed-door world of think tanks.

The term *think tank* was military jargon for the secure, usually windowless rooms used as strategy centers during World War II and was first applied after the war to describe organizations such as the RAND Corporation, which were set up to act as outside advisors on defense strategy. The liberal Brookings Institution was the dominant example, providing the blueprints for most of Kennedy's New Frontier, and Johnson's Great Society. The think tank is an American phenomenon that had Laird as one of its foremost proponents from the 1950s on. Laird was arguably the midwife to the birth or rejuvenation of the four top conservative think tanks of the twentieth century: the American Enterprise Institute for Public Policy Research; the Hoover Institution on War, Revolution, and Peace; the Center for Strategic and International Studies; and the Heritage Foundation.

The story of his backstage role begins in 1953 with Laird's first connection to the American Enterprise Institute—originally called the American Enterprise Association (AEA). Its founding purpose was to be a conservative counterweight to the Brookings Institution, but it was dismissed by many as another megaphone for business interests. One of those men who thought it had greater possibilities was Carl Jacobs, president of Wisconsin-based Hardware Mutual Casualty (later Sentry Insurance), where Laird's childhood friend

Bob Froehlke worked. Jacobs had been a significant supporter in all of Laird's campaigns for State Senate.

At a Washington dinner party just a few days before Eisenhower's inauguration, a core group of conspirators aiming to change the AEA met for the first time. Jacobs had brought along Laird, and others present included economists Paul McCracken and Murray Weidenbaum. Most important, Jacobs had asked a bright, young U.S. Chamber of Commerce staff economist, William J. Baroody, to join them. Laird took to Baroody immediately. He instinctively recognized a can-do kindred spirit who could transform the faltering AEA, but Baroody didn't want to leave his job then. In 1954 Laird hosted a luncheon on Capitol Hill to impress Baroody. He invited the A-list of Republicans, including Gerald Ford. Laird said he "complained to Bill that there were too many very liberal academicians from Harvard, Yale, and elsewhere, all over the Hill testifying and writing papers for congressional committee staffers. Whenever we wanted some good witnesses, we couldn't find them. So we needed a think tank that could develop a whole reservoir of talented, more conservatively oriented university and college professors. We needed research that was not like Brookings, which seemed to be constantly justifying the idea of bigger government and more federal programs." Laird and his peers proved persuasive, and Baroody finally agreed to try it.

Baroody was hired as executive vice president and paid from grant money Laird helped obtain. It took eight years for Baroody to transform the association's reputation by courting nationally known economists who steered AEA away from rabid right-wing screeds to more solid works of scholarship. By 1962 Baroody was the heart and soul of the organization and was made its president. He changed the name to the American Enterprise Institute and became the pioneer of a new kind of intellectual entrepreneurship. Baroody's son, Bill Jr., worked for Laird at the House Republican Conference and regularly cross-fertilized projects between AEI and Congress. He would later succeed his father as AEI president.

Having set the mold, AEI began to encourage like initiatives. The first to benefit was Stanford University's Hoover Institution. It was the oldest of conservative think tanks, but in the early 1960s it had little influence on day-to-day debate in Washington. So it raided AEI, hiring away a research director and putting Baroody on its executive board. Laird became a backstage advisor and Washington patron. The moribund institution soon established itself on the public policy front, with a stable of Laird's favorite experts, such as economist Milton Friedman, nuclear physicist Edward Teller, and political scientist Seymour Martin Lipset. California Governor Ronald Reagan developed a symbiotic relationship with the think tank, which obligingly also fueled his presidential campaigns with strategists and loaned him dozens of top officials for his presidency.[35]

Meanwhile, the Georgetown University Center for Strategic and International Studies (CSIS) was a direct step-child of AEI.[36] Laird would sometimes complain to Baroody that while AEI was producing great economic and domestic policy material for Congress, there was a need for a conservative foreign policy think tank. He and Baroody agreed that the man for the job was a decorated Korean combat veteran AEI had hired only a year before on Laird's recommendation, David Abshire. In 1962, when it appeared it was better for Abshire to found his own institute, independent of AEI, Laird was instrumental in lining up retired Admiral Arleigh Burke, the longest-serving chief of naval operations and a World War II legend, as cofounder with Abshire of CSIS. As was so often the case, Laird didn't leave fingerprints when he influenced events from behind the curtain, but evidence of Laird's involvement is substantive in his private files.

As for the Heritage Foundation, its most important and visionary cofounder in 1973, Edwin Feulner Jr., was a Laird protégé. Feulner's career also was an example of the kind of cross-pollination among the think tanks encouraged by Baroody out front, and by Laird with a more hidden hand. Feulner went to work at Abshire's CSIS for a year and then was given his choice in 1966, under a Hoover Institution grant, to work for Senator Everett Dirksen, up-and-coming Congressman Donald Rumsfeld, or Laird. As Feulner recounted it, the choice was obvious. For Dirksen, he would probably "lick postage stamps"; for Rumsfeld, he would probably have to study the congressman's pet topic, Latin America, which was boring to Feulner. But Laird had a reputation for mentoring bright, young scholars and giving them great latitude to affect legislative policy.

Laird lived up to the advance billing. "The neat thing about Mel Laird—and in some ways, it was kind of prelude to my lifetime career at Heritage—was that he always understood the relationship between ideas and politics," said Feulner. "He was not a heavy intellectual, but he understood how ideas were fundamental to the whole political process." Feulner followed Laird to the Defense Department for another year, before returning to Capitol Hill, and it was then that he saw a desperate need for a think tank that could quickly produce salient analyses before Congress voted on an issue. The other think tanks could not move fast enough for rough-and-tumble congressional debate. With money from conservative Colorado brewer Joseph Coors, Heritage became that cutting-edge advocacy institute that leaped to prominence during the Reagan era.[37] While Laird had little to do with Heritage after it was founded, the foundation was a descendant of the intellectual fire he had kindled.

10

Presidential Plea: "Muzzle Laird"

꧁꧂

AT 3:40 A.M. SUNDAY, AUGUST 2, 1964, the klaxon sounded "general quarters" aboard the USS *Maddox*. Mel Laird's old World War II destroyer was under surprise attack, this time twenty-five miles off the coast of North Vietnam, in the Gulf of Tonkin. The *Maddox* had been patrolling international waters in a conflict that was not yet officially an American war but was about to become one.

Three North Vietnamese torpedo boats moved toward the *Maddox* at high speed, spraying the destroyer with machine gun fire and launching torpedoes. There was no running away from the fight. The small boats could travel nearly twice as fast as the bulky destroyer. The *Maddox* dodged two torpedoes and sank one of the Soviet-built patrol boats. The other two sped away. *Maddox* Captain Herbert L. Ogier radioed the Seventh Fleet, reporting the attack. It lasted about thirty minutes and was the first direct combat between the United States and North Vietnam—the true beginning of the ten-year conflict known as the Vietnam War.

A sailor picked up some enemy shell fragments off the deck of the *Maddox*. Those souvenirs, and a tiny hole in the *Maddox*'s aft gun-sighting platform would later provide needed proof to Washington that the attack had really happened. At the Pentagon, the top brass were puzzled. What had prompted North Vietnam to go on the offensive against an American ship in international waters? Was it a mistake, or was it an act of war by Hanoi that demanded retaliation? President Lyndon Johnson huddled with his advisors, and they decided to let the attack pass. Johnson had an election to worry about and it was no time to start a war; he ordered the *Maddox* to pull farther out to sea. Another destroyer, the *Turner Joy,* was dispatched to pair up with the *Maddox,* and an aircraft carrier, the *Ticonderoga,* was alerted to provide air cover for the two destroyers should they need it.

What happened two days later remains one of the great mysteries of American warfare.

At 7:40 P.M. on August 4, the *Maddox* radioed that it was again under attack, or at least the radar operators on the destroyer thought it was. On a pitch-black night, with zero visibility, they picked up radar signatures from North Vietnamese patrol boats and radar spotting of more than twenty torpedo launches against the *Maddox* and the *Turner Joy* over a four-hour period. In the middle of the confusion, the *Maddox,* received an intelligence intercept from electronic eavesdroppers at the National Security Agency. North Vietnamese radio chatter had hinted that an attack on both destroyers was "imminent."

The destroyers began zig-zagging through the dark seas trying to dodge the unseen torpedoes. The *Turner Joy* locked its guns on what it thought was a patrol boat radar signature and fired. Someone aboard the destroyer reported seeing a column of smoke in the direction of the target. The *Ticonderoga* dispatched two F-8E Crusaders and two A-4 Skyhawks. Within fifty minutes, the four planes were circling the two destroyers, the pilots trying to sort out the frantic radio messages from spotters on the ships. The pilots peppered the water with rockets but never saw an enemy ship.[1] By midnight, officers on the *Maddox* were beginning to doubt whether there had been any torpedoes in the first place, and sent a message to that effect to direct superiors in Hawaii.[2]

The remaining mystery was the intercepted enemy message threatening an attack. It would be several years before investigators figured out that the message probably referred to the first attack on the *Maddox* two days earlier. But on that August day in 1964, in Washington, D.C., alarm bells were going off in the White House and the Pentagon. One attack could be written off as a rash act. But two was too many for President Johnson to ignore. He needed to know if it was one or two, and he needed to know fast.

Defense Secretary Robert McNamara cobbled together spotty reports of sightings from the destroyers, and, with the recommendation of Admiral U.S. Grant Sharp (the area commander in the Pacific, or CINCPAC), McNamara reported to the president that there had probably been two attacks. Twelve hours after the bizarre, and probably one-sided "battle" in the Gulf of Tonkin, Johnson ordered pilots from the carriers *Ticonderoga* and *Constellation* to begin retaliatory bombing runs over North Vietnam. In four hours, the navy planes flew sixty-four missions, blowing up naval bases, oil depots, and patrol boats. One navy pilot, Lieutenant Richard Sather, was killed, the first in Vietnam; another, Lieutenant Everett Alvarez, was shot down and became the first American POW in Vietnam. It would be eight and a half years before he was released.

The war between North and South Vietnam had been joined by the United States in a haphazard manner. Nearly five years later when Laird occupied the office once held by McNamara, he reviewed the reports of the Gulf of Tonkin affair and judged it to be "a phony operation." Not that the evidence of a second attack had been trumped up. Laird eventually came to believe it was badly mishandled and that the details were hyped when reported to him and other members of Congress. But in 1964, based on this faulty information, Laird was full of the same chest-thumping outrage against the North Vietnamese enemy as the rest of Congress.

Johnson went on national television at 11:37 P.M. August 4 to announce the American bombing of North Vietnam. The next morning McNamara took a resolution to the Senate asking congressional authority "to take all necessary steps, including the use of armed force" to protect South Vietnam from its enemies. It was the closest thing to a declaration of war the Vietnam conflict would ever get, and it would stand until Congress repealed it in 1971. (In 1973, Congress passed the War Powers Act to make sure that history would not repeat itself. The act limited the power of the president to make war.)

With reports of the audacious attacks in the headlines, the Tonkin Gulf Resolution eased through Congress. "I rise in support of this resolution," Laird said August 7 on the House floor. "I am confident it will be passed with overwhelming, if not unanimous support." The resolution passed the House with a 414 to 0 vote. In the Senate, the count was 88 to 2, with two Democrats, Wayne Morse of Oregon and Ernest Gruening of Alaska, voting "no."[3] In his speech, Laird cautioned that the resolution did not amount to a policy. America still had to decide whether to dally in Southeast Asia or take "whatever steps are necessary to win the war in that beleaguered area within a reasonable period of time.... We must develop and announce to our friends as well as to the Communists what our policy in Southeast Asia is as we face the future."[4] Talking to reporters, Laird said the United States had to adopt a "winning policy in Vietnam, or get out."[5] For the next five years, there would be no winning policy, just an alarming escalation of American troop numbers until Laird became secretary of defense and pulled the plug.

In retrospect, Laird felt he and others had been strong-armed on the Tonkin Gulf Resolution. "Congress was misled badly," he concluded. He reserved his most bitter criticism for McNamara. In fact, Laird, who regularly defended Washington politics as a largely honest and well-intentioned institution, said he had been outright lied to only twice in his political career. Once was when Richard Nixon claimed he had nothing to do with the Watergate cover-up. "The only other one that ever lied to me like that, I think, was probably McNamara. Because I asked him specifically if there was a second attack on the *Turner Joy* and the *Maddox* and he said there was. I got over to the Pentagon and found out there wasn't." Laird later modified his condemnation of McNamara to say that it was Laird's House committee which had been lied to, not him specifically. But his anger at reading the secret reports when he was defense secretary still simmered four decades after the Gulf of Tonkin incident.

In Laird's mind, McNamara was either a dissembler or a fool on that subject; a dissembler for twisting the inconclusive reports into an excuse for war, or a fool if he believed those same reports. By the time Laird himself was in McNamara's shoes, he had developed a firm policy about military intelligence reports on any given incident: never believe the first report, be skeptical about the second, and less skeptical after the third.

⌇⌇

As memories of the Cold War grow dim, so fades the reason the United States intervened in Southeast Asia in the first place—the "domino theory." The area had long been overrun by one world power after another, including China in the first millennium A.D., France in the 1800s, and Japan during World War II. After that war, a Vietnamese Communist, Ho Chi Minh, had moved into the vacuum of leadership to consolidate North Vietnam under a Communist-style rule. France tried to reestablish a foothold in South Vietnam, supporting a non-Communist regime there. The result was the Indochina War, which ended with the fall of the French garrison at Dien Bien Phu in May 1954. The French made a last-minute appeal to the United States to intervene with a massive air strike against North Vietnamese forces around Dien Bien Phu, but the United States refused. France was out of Indochina, and the specter of a Communist takeover of South Vietnam, and perhaps all of Indochina, loomed large. President Eisenhower likened the region to a "row of dominoes" ripe for a fall to Communism.

Representatives of nine nations, including the United States, were meeting in Geneva that spring of 1954 when the French were run out of Vietnam. The Geneva delegates, including those from Vietnam, "temporarily" divided Vietnam into two nations, north and south, with a timetable set for elections in 1956 to join the two under one government. Those elections never happened, and civil war gradually escalated between the two Vietnams; the United States eased into the role of protector of the South. At first, there were just a few hundred U.S. military "advisors" and CIA operatives working behind the scenes. President Kennedy introduced American military helicopters to carry South Vietnamese troops, and he upped the number of U.S. advisors in the country from 1,300 to 11,000 in 1962. The next year, 1963, brought another turning point for the United States and Vietnam—Kennedy's support of the military coup that overthrew and assassinated Ngo Dinh Diem.

Laird's public pronouncements in 1964 on the Vietnam buildup, before the Gulf of Tonkin incident, were driven by the Johnson-Goldwater presidential election battle. While being careful not to inflame the reputation Goldwater already had for being trigger happy, Laird tried to steer the Republican agenda toward a winning policy in Southeast Asia. At a dinner for Republicans in rural Wisconsin in March, Laird said the United States had three choices: continue the half-hearted and creeping escalation by the Johnson administration; leave Vietnam and support neutrality by outsiders, which he personally believed would open the door to Communists; or, his favored option, "step up the war effort. This would include accepting troops from nations willing to contribute troops to the operations and making greater contribution of our own materials and supplies." Laird warned that Americans should be willing to fight by the same rules that the North was using—specifically meaning to cross into North Vietnam and to blockade its marine resupply routes, which implicitly meant mining Haiphong harbor.[6] A week later, in a similar speech, he predicted that unless this was done, the Vietnam War might "drag on for ten years."[7]

In May Laird stepped up pressure on the Johnson administration to adopt a winning strategy. When McNamara appeared before the Defense Appropriations Subcommittee in executive session on May 21, Laird hammered him with Vietnam questions and arguments; Jerry Ford also joined in. After noon, an exhausted McNamara was quizzed about the morning session by President Johnson, one of many conversations LBJ secretly taped.

"I had Ford and Laird...all trying to make hay out of [our Vietnam policy]," McNamara recounted.

"What are they poking at you about?" the president queried.

"Oh, a 'no win' policy," McNamara responded. He went on to summarize the litany of criticism from the subcommittee that felt Johnson wasn't fighting to win.

"Who tried to do it?" the President pressed. "Laird?"

McNamara told him it was mainly Laird, Ford, and two others. Asked by the president whether they could hurt the administration, McNamara assessed: "Jerry Ford and Laird are dangerous."[8]

Evidence of that came ten days later when Laird trapped LBJ. It was vintage Laird, and the early use of a technique he would employ four years later to help elect Nixon president. The essence of it was to put Johnson in the public position of having to deny that he had a plan to end or win the war. In this case, Laird wanted Johnson and McNamara to deny that they were about to make a move that Laird thought should be made: an attack into North Vietnam. His opening gambit came during a May 31 appearance on a national radio program.

"The administration's position is to move north [allow U.S. troops to cross into North Vietnam] and we are now preparing to move north. This is a preparation which has been going on for several months," Laird announced, adding that his Defense Appropriations Subcommittee in the House was gearing up to support the move with money. "We feel that we should be prepared to move into North Vietnam. I have felt this for some time and I am happy to say that the administration takes the same position."[9]

Johnson was later cornered about Laird's statement at a press conference and tried to quip his way out of it: "I know of no plans that have been made to that effect," he said. "I would say that Mr. Laird is not as yet speaking for the administration. He might next year some time," referring to the upcoming November presidential election.

Laird launched into a speech of umbrage on the House floor after Johnson's press conference. Johnson was trivializing a serious issue, he said. "Today the President at his news conference, I believe, misled the American people," Laird charged. He went on to explain that Secretary of State Dean Rusk himself had told Laird it was U.S. policy to "take whatever steps may be necessary to protect Southeast Asia from a communist takeover. I was further informed that all contingency plans are being made to carry out this policy decision of the administration. The contingency planning includes the preparation of plans to go north into North Vietnam to hit at the heart of the problem."

Feigning surprise at Johnson's denial of invasion plans, Laird concluded that he was in favor of such a move: "I was supporting the Johnson administration in my comments on [the Sunday radio program]." Laird said the president had made a serious tactical mistake in saying that there was no contingency plan. "We *have* contingency plans in this particular area, and we should not advise the potential enemy in advance that we have no such plans. This is very bad national strategy as far as the United States of America is concerned.... Our potential enemy should not underestimate the will and determination of our country."

Johnson continued to steam about it that day, June 2, and raised the matter in two phone calls late in the afternoon to McGeorge Bundy, his national security advisor, and Secretary of State Rusk. Both were with McNamara and the rest of the LBJ national security team in Hawaii conferencing about Vietnam policy.

"Laird is saying that McNamara has [a] plan for invasion of the north," Johnson reported to Bundy. "Well, all I said was that I knew of no such plan. I don't mean that we haven't got plans for any contingency, but I approved no plan to invade anything."

Bundy tried to calm the president down and advised that the best thing was just to ignore Laird this time. "I'd just leave it alone. I wouldn't get in an argument with Laird—he's too small."

Rusk offered a similar view on Laird. "This is a phony issue he's raised."[10]

In June 1964 Congressman Melvin Laird was probably neither "too small" as Bundy suggested, nor as "dangerous" as McNamara characterized him. But only eight months later—after the Gulf of Tonkin incident and Johnson's landslide reelection—Laird could not continue to be ignored. In January 1965 he led a back-stage Republican coup that installed Ford as House minority leader and himself as the number two. Johnson had effectively co-opted opposition in the Senate by winning Senate Minority Leader Everett Dirksen's compliance on the president's Vietnam policies. But now the president could neither control nor afford to ignore the Ford-Laird tag team opposition.

The House Republican Conference was made up of all Republicans elected to serve in the House of Representatives—only 140 members in 1965. As the new chairman, Laird called almost-weekly meetings, which quickly seemed to revive the moribund party. Laird also instituted monthly breakfasts for the conference with Republican luminaries (such as Eisenhower, Nixon, and Rockefeller) and experts in various fields (such as nuclear scientist Dr. Edward Teller and economist Dr. Arthur Burns). Another popular Laird invention was periodic Republican retreats to Airlie House in Warrenton, Virginia.[11]

While technically Laird was number three in the House Republican leadership—after Minority Leader Ford and Minority Whip Les Arends—that was not the reality. He was de facto number two in power and authority. Sometimes he even seemed to take the lead position, as when he gave major policy speeches. One of his speeches, a nine-thousand-word opus decrying federal power-grabbing under Johnson, was quickly dubbed "The Republican State of the Union Message" by some members. Journalists openly questioned why it was not Ford but Laird, an "ambitious, adroit comer in the Republican power structure," who delivered the address.[12]

Laird deliberately fuzzed the line of authority by telling constituents and others that he was "chair of the House Republicans" which, however factual, suggested to the uninitiated that he was number one. To journalists, Laird's energy, forcefulness, and organizational ability suggested more momentum than Ford seemed to show. That earned him both the respect and attention his Republican revitalization plans needed. Conference chairman "can be an empty honor or a position of some importance depending on the energies of the holder," the *Washington Post* observed later. "Laird worked hard at it, calling frequent meetings to discuss issues, creating task forces to prepare position papers and hiring a research staff."[13]

From his 1965 installation as chairman, Laird directed that the primary goal of the House Republican Conference was to come up with constructive alternatives to Johnson legislation, when necessary, instead of just carping about the administration. That was Laird's strategy in a nutshell. The previous year Eisenhower had told Laird that the Republicans must move away from appearing as negativists. Evangelist Billy Graham "is against the devil, but he preaches the Savior to us," Ike pointed out.

The strategy got off to a rocky start with Medicare. For twenty years, proponents, including Johnson, had tried to add medical and hospital coverage to the Social Security safety net. The Senate passed bills, but they got bogged down in the House. The politically astute realized that the 1964 Johnson landslide should change that because sixty-seven of the seventy-one incoming Democratic freshman owed enough to Johnson and his coattails to vote for his most important initiatives.

Laird and many other Republicans opposed the Johnson Medicare bill because it would pay the hospital portion with a regressive payroll tax. Laird didn't feel that low- and middle-income taxpayers should have to bear the medical costs of the aged if some other way could be found. He predicted that the inevitable "increased costs of hospital services in future years will mean periodic increases in the payroll tax until it becomes too great a burden on the working man."[14] Better to finance it through general tax revenues and premium payments by retirees, he reasoned. So the Republicans floated their own bill, and Ford, by minority leader fiat, told the party to stand firm and vote against the Democrats' bill, even if it incorporated some of what the Republicans wanted. The Republican bill was defeated, and enough of the party ignored Ford and sided with the Democrats to pass Johnson's historic Medicare bill. Laird, as a Republican leader, had no choice but to reluctantly follow Ford's ill-advised strategy. It was a fiasco, as Laird had known it would be. In a series of interviews conducted by historian Robert Peabody less than a week after the Medicare vote, Laird was fuming about how he and other Republicans had been forced to vote against the final Medicare bill. "Off the record, he felt that the policy had been played wrong," Peabody's notes reflected.

Peabody asked if this made Ford look bad, particularly since almost half of his Republicans broke ranks and voted for the bill. "Well, sure, that presented some problems," Laird said. "Part of being a leader is making yourself look good. You've got to pick your issues." It was apparent he didn't think Ford had picked this issue well. Peabody wrote in a note to himself, "Laird is clearly ambivalent on Ford's leadership. [H]e is torn [about] helping him and building him up."[15] There were, indeed, some rough edges to the Ford-Laird partnership in the first year, but their mutual opposition to the Johnson administration policy regarding American involvement in the Vietnam War was destined to turn them into the Republican Party's most important and effective team of their day.

⚓

Johnson won the 1964 presidential election by painting Barry Goldwater as a warmonger who would expand U.S. involvement in Vietnam. It was a duplicitous game cynically played against the American voters. In September 1964 White House strategy sessions reached a consensus that air attacks against North Vietnam would probably have to be launched. But it was not advisable to do so until after the election. On September 25, portraying himself as more peaceful than Goldwater, Johnson said, "There are those that say you ought to go north and drop bombs, to try to wipe out the supply lines, and they think that would escalate the war. We don't want our American boys to do the fighting for Asian boys. We don't want to ... get tied down in a land war in Asia." Three days later he said in another talk: "Some of our people [such as] Mr. Goldwater—have all, at some time or other, suggested the possible wisdom of going north in Vietnam.... We are not going north ... we are going to continue to try to get them [South Vietnamese] to save their own freedom with their own men." On October 21 in Akron, Ohio, Johnson made an even more emphatic campaign pledge: "We are not about to send American boys nine or ten thousand miles away from home to do what Asian boys ought to be doing for themselves."[16]

On Sunday, November 1, 1964, two days before the election, the Vietcong shelled a U.S.-supported air base at Bien Hoa, destroying six B-57s and killing five Americans. This was a more serious challenge to the United States than the Gulf of Tonkin provocation, in which no Americans were killed or armament damaged. But this time, Johnson did nothing. He was shaping his new peacemaker persona, possibly with a slim hope that his inaction over Bien Hoa would be a signal to the North Vietnamese of his willingness to negotiate peace.

After the election, unsure of his footing, Johnson turned to Eisenhower. In a December 14 phone call, he started with his trademark flattery and faux humility. "He hoped the President [Ike] would give him [LBJ] the benefit of his advice, counsel, etcetera, but did not want to make a nuisance of himself," noted Ike's secretary, Rusty Brown, who listened on an extension and took notes. "LBJ said, of course, if he got his 'tail in a crack' he would come running to [Eisenhower] on foreign affairs."[17] Thus began Johnson's practice of reporting to Ike, asking his counsel, but going ahead with whatever he planned to do in the first place, and then using the Eisenhower name to try to silence critics such as Ford and Laird. Those were the two Republican leaders who worried Johnson. The president had effectively co-opted the more prominent Senate Minority Leader Everett Dirksen, who held the view that, once the United States was in a war, the commander-in-chief must be supported in his efforts.[18]

By Dirksen's default and their design, Laird and Ford became the Republican Party's only formidable stalking horses on Vietnam. Laird distinguished himself as an exceptional prognosticator of Johnson's Vietnam War moves. Just as Laird had predicted during the 1964 election, Johnson took the war into North Vietnam with an order to begin sustained bombing in late February 1965. The campaign, called Operation Rolling Thunder, continued for three and a half years and became the vehicle for Johnson and McNamara to notoriously micromanage the war—poring over maps, choosing largely insignificant targets, putting key strategic targets off limits, and overriding the wisdom of their military commanders at the Pentagon and on the scene half a world away. While Johnson waged a gradual and limited war, aimed at coaxing the North Vietnamese into peace talks, the military men chafed at the restrictions that kept them from victory. Laird knew this because of his Defense Appropriations Subcommittee work, and from his sources at the Pentagon, not from the White House briefings for Republican leadership, which he quickly found to be a sham.

As a Republican House leader, Laird had dutifully attended the first briefing, held with fanfare the day after Johnson's inauguration. "The briefing lasted for about two and a half hours with no real opportunity for the Congressional leadership to ask questions or to contribute their comments to what the President had in mind," Laird told his constituents at the end of March. "At the conclusion of this briefing, photographers were called in and the impression was created that the President had developed his policies in consultation with the Congressional leaders of both parties."[19] Laird stormed home that night and told his family he wasn't going to be photo fodder for the president anymore.[20] He soon issued an ultimatum to Defense Secretary McNamara in a secret subcommittee hearing that unless the president allowed Republicans to offer their ideas on the Vietnam War in future foreign policy briefings, he would no longer attend. Johnson didn't change the format, and Laird stayed home. At the same time, the White House boasted that there had already been twenty-one hours of "give-and-take" between the president and members of Congress in White House briefings and receptions.[21]

March 8, 1965, marked the day the first American ground troops were officially sent to Vietnam. Two marines battalions landed on the beach at Da Nang, greeted by a welcome sign, flashbulb-popping photographers, and bikini-clad South Vietnamese sunbathers. President Johnson insisted they weren't there for combat, but only to defend the air base. In a speech at the time, Laird complained, "In Southeast Asia, we continue a policy that has caused thousands of South Vietnamese and American casualties, with no effective plan in sight to end this conflict. We continue the fiction that it is a South Vietnam war, that we are only there as advisors."[22]

Laird knew better because his friends at the Pentagon had shared some of Johnson's Vietnam secrets. So while the American public did not know for some time that Johnson had made the decision on April 1 to use American ground troops for offensive action, Laird learned as much within a week. Laird found that Pentagon officials and the U.S. commander in Vietnam, General William Westmoreland, were pushing for tens of thousands more troops. Johnson hadn't determined a number, but he decided he wanted a very public show of support from Congress for whatever his Vietnam policy would be. He asked for a $700 million supplemental appropriation in May. Members of Congress who might have questioned his policy felt forced to vote in favor of the funds needed to support already-deployed "advisors" in Vietnam, as Johnson described them. Laird voted in favor of the appropriation, along with 407 other representatives; only 7 voted against. The Senate ratio was 83 to 3. The three Democrats were Wayne Morse of Oregon and Ernest Gruening of Alaska (the two who had voted against the Tonkin Gulf Resolution the previous year), and Laird's friend and fellow Wisconsinite Gaylord Nelson.[23]

In June and July of 1965 the strain of the war began to show on Johnson. General Westmoreland insisted he was going to need substantially more troops before long, and the president had to make a decision that could portend disaster for his presidency and the country. If he decided to deploy many more ground troops, he knew America would soon be in the Vietnam quicksand up to its neck. Still, he continued to maintain the fiction that the United States was not in combat in Vietnam.

Laird was livid that Johnson was not telling the truth to the American people. "We may be dangerously close to ending Republican support of our present Vietnam policy, " he vented in a statement on June 14. "This possibility exists because the American people do not know how far the administration is prepared to go with large-scale use of ground forces in order to save face in

Vietnam." Laird urged Johnson to allow the bombing of more strategic targets and blockade North Vietnam's Haiphong harbor to stop shipment of war supplies. "To continue to allow the unhindered flow of war materials in and out of that area only insures greater American casualties." Escalating the ground war would only cost American lives, Laird predicted. Johnson was underutilizing American sea and air power, while entangling men in a guerrilla war on the ground.[24]

Coming, as the statement was, from "one of the most influential Republicans in the House," the *New York Times* called it the "first significant sign of potential Republican opposition to the Administration's Vietnam policies." But for the moment, Laird appeared to be the only prominent Republican willing to challenge Johnson. Senate Minority Leader Dirksen immediately kowtowed. "We are going to uphold the President's hand [in the Senate]. What else can you do in a situation like this?" he said.[25] Ford was unaccountably silent, and President Johnson must have sensed a schism with Laird, which meant he might be able to isolate him. In an evening phone call three days later, Johnson probed Ford on that, as well as on the extent of Republican support for his Vietnam policy.

Johnson first waved Eisenhower's approval in Ford's face. "General Eisenhower ... felt we ought to approve Westmoreland's request for these troops too to protect his bases."

Ford wasn't taken in. "How much are we going to use the ground forces?" he asked, fairly bluntly.

"Only when and if and as necessary to protect our national interest," Johnson ambiguously responded, before allowing that they would inevitably be involved in some combat. "This is no Sunday School picnic. . . . I can't tell a commander on the ground that he's got to let his people get wiped out or let his allies get wiped out. That's why we're out there."

"I fully agree," Ford responded. "The only thing, if we're going to do more offensively on the ground, then I think we all ought to sit down and talk about it."

"I'll be glad to do that," Johnson obliged, "if it can stay out of the papers."

LBJ launched into a tirade about recent press reports, and Ford told him not to "worry about that kind of thing."

"I'm not worrying," Johnson said. "I'm explaining to you so that you're on this team. It's your country. And a good many of these boys, I'm told, are *Republicans.* . . . [T]hey're out there fighting, and I think you ought to know the facts."

Ford assured him, "As I have done in the past, you know I sit shoulder to shoulder with you."

Relieved, the president moved onto his final point, testing whether Laird was speaking for himself or for a wider opposition that might include Ford.

"I think you ought to get a muzzle on Laird," Johnson said bluntly. "Make him quit telling me that I can't have ground troops I need to protect my airplanes, because I can't bomb like he wants to if the goddamned Vietcong are destroying my airplanes on the ground."

Ford failed to take the bait and criticize his partner, so a nervous Johnson decided to end the call with a joke suggesting there was at least one person who irritated him more than Laird at the moment.

"Would you consider letting me trade [Democratic antiwar Senator] Morse to you for Laird?" Johnson proposed.

Ford laughed, but said nothing. "I'm sorry to bother you, Jerry," Johnson closed.[26]

✤

At this time Johnson's aerial bombing campaign, Rolling Thunder, and his Vietnam policy were popular, according to the polls. So Laird had to explain to his constituents in a late June letter why he was beginning to speak strongly about a growing need to alter that policy. The president had said his goal was a negotiated settlement with North Vietnam, not a military victory, and had even hinted that Communist elements might be allowed to stay in South Vietnam as part of any truce, Laird explained. Was that something Americans should die for? "Republicans in Congress have supported the President's recent actions but his decision to enlarge the ground war and commit as many as 100,000 or more American ground troops is causing us to raise certain questions about our future role in that war-torn country. . . . It is my view that if a negotiated settlement is our goal, we should not endanger large numbers of American troops," he told his constituents.[27]

But Laird's drumbeat on Vietnam, presuming to speak for his party, prompted some Republicans to suggest that he was trying to usurp Ford. "For whatever reasons, he has, more and more, taken stage center with his Republican colleagues," a June 23 newsletter by some House Republicans noted. "There is more than a slight suspicion that Mr. Laird is the unofficial leader of the House Republicans today." Not so, objected Laird. "This is another splinter group trying to drive a wedge between Jerry and myself. We're not going to let them do it."[28]

Ford turned up the volume on his own rhetoric, matching Laird's, at a July 1 press conference and an appearance on a Sunday television talk show two weeks later. He wasn't Jerry-come-lately, having already held similar views as Laird. Ford had come to believe that it was time to speak out.

Later that day, Ford went public with the warning that, if the "rumors" were true that Johnson was about to commit major ground forces, including a call-up of reserves, he ought to get a congressional endorsement for that.

The next day Eisenhower phoned LBJ to echo that sentiment, advising Johnson that he ought to consult with the House and Senate leadership before making a big move. But Johnson wasn't about to do that. Instead, he said, "I'll tell Dirksen [to tell] Mel Laird and Jerry just not to get excited." Eisenhower said he, too, hoped "to calm these people down by telling them I talked to you."[29] Neither Dirksen nor Eisenhower, however, could silence Laird and Ford. The issue was too important, and the moment too pivotal. Five days later, on the evening of July 27, 1965, Johnson called congressional leaders of both parties to the White House for a heads up about the Vietnam speech he would deliver the next day. Laird did not attend, in keeping with his no-briefing policy; Ford was there.

For Laird and Ford, the decision Johnson announced there was a terrible mistake. And it was a policy that would reverberate down through the history of American warfare. He would be using the draft, not the Reserves and National Guard to continue the buildup of troops in Vietnam. The next day Johnson announced as much at a press conference; the troop complement in Vietnam would be raised to 125,000 by doubling the draft numbers. What it meant was that draft boards could pluck reluctant warriors out of the American heartland one at a time to send them without fanfare to Vietnam, instead of sending Reserve units that had trained together and would leave together. There would be no mass tearful farewells at airports to draw attention to the escalating numbers. At this time, Johnson had already secretly approved another one hundred thousand troops by year's end, and another hundred thousand in 1966.[30]

The next day at Laird's regular weekly luncheon with a half-dozen reporters, Ford joined him for an off-the-record briefing. The journalists reported afterward that unnamed "congressional sources" had spilled the story about what really had happened in the briefing at the White House—that Johnson had planned an emergency call-up of the Reserves and a request for $5 billion to expand the war, but that he had changed his mind at the last minute; and that Senate Majority Leader Mike Mansfield had interrupted Johnson's carefully choreographed meeting by reading a three-page statement warning LBJ of a public backlash if the Reserves were called up.[31]

By the time the news of Johnson's private meeting hit the headlines, he was on vacation at his Texas ranch. He boiled over at the breach of confidence about his meeting with the congressmen, and the implication that he had made his decision about the draft based solely on political advantage. The reports that Democratic congressmen had talked him off a ledge on the issue of troop deployment were "untrue and perhaps malicious," Johnson said. Someone had "broken" his confidence and "distorted" his intent. When he referred to "a backgrounder by one of the prominent members of another party," he was clearly blasting Ford as he said, "Once in a while an inexperienced man, or a new one, or a bitter partisan has to play a little politics. I think they keep it to a minimum, generally speaking, but one or two of them will do it. And boys will be boys." This time Johnson was adding Laird to his mix of calumny. On its own, the leak from the White House briefing should not have riled the president, but this was the last straw laid on his back by Ford and Laird as they tried to force him to change his Vietnam policies.[32] In a news analysis, the *Los Angeles Times* opined that while some assumed the president blamed Ford, "in reality, however, the President's greatest animosity is aimed at Rep. Melvin Laird of Wisconsin."[33]

Jerry Ford knew it was time for Republicans in the House to stand strong together, particularly since the Senate Republicans, under Dirksen, had failed to step up to the plate. Thus was born the party's first "white paper" on Vietnam—a collection of facts and charts showing in stark terms the buildup of American troops, and implying that Johnson's tepid approach to the war had misled the enemy regarding America's resolve. As chairman of the Republican Conference, Laird commissioned the report. The Conference Research Director Bill Prendergast and Dr. John Bibby of the University of Wisconsin wrote the first draft of six thousand words, which was hustled up to Gettysburg, Pennsylvania, for Eisenhower's approval. But Ike was in a box. Alerted about the upcoming Republican white paper, Johnson had ordered a competitive report, *Why Vietnam?* and had sent it to Eisenhower for approval first.

Ike's dilemma was apparent in an August 24 morning conference call with former aide Bryce Harlow, Laird, Ford, and Representative Charles Goodell. Harlow complained that Johnson was deliberately trying to torpedo the Republican report by releasing his first and calling for a press conference at the same time they had scheduled theirs. Ford and Laird "think the President just trumped their ace," Harlow noted.

"That's true," Laird chimed in. He then appealed to the former president's sense of history, telling him that Johnson was trying to blame Eisenhower's administration for the initial entanglement in Vietnam.

Ford added that it would be nice to say Eisenhower had read the GOP white paper and supported its conclusions. But Eisenhower balked, saying he had not read either paper and was reluctant to weigh in during a time of crisis on another president's watch. Ford then expressed hope that, at the very least, Eisenhower wouldn't say anything to undermine the GOP report. In general, he said, according to notes of the conversation, "[W]hile he is not always happy about all the things [Johnson is doing on Vietnam], he has always made it his business to keep still while we are in a condition of crisis." So Ike decided to compromise and issue a public statement of "no dispute" regarding the facts in the GOP white paper, but "no comment" on the report's conclusions.[34]

The next morning, the report, entitled *Vietnam: Some Neglected Aspects of the Historical Record,* was unveiled by Goodell at the House Republican Conference meeting.[35] It was then issued under Ford's signature. During a subsequent presidential press conference, LBJ was tossed a softball question: had the House Republicans "injected undue partisanship into the Vietnam situation?"

"I don't want to get into any personalities in the matter," Johnson said, having regretted his remarks against Ford and Laird a month before. But "the boys that are fighting the war are not divided between Republicans and Democrats," his own Defense Secretary McNamara was a Republican—and, he pointedly added with the subtlety of a sledgehammer, "President Eisenhower has been a tower of strength to me."[36]

Three hours later, Ford, Laird, and Goodell had a press conference to respond and detail more of what was in their paper. Laird pointed out that Republicans—more so than Democrats—had consistently supported Johnson and the soldiers in Vietnam with favorable appropriations and other votes. But there should be "a difference between support of the President's actions and enthusiastic approval of policy decisions that led up to these actions." They said they should be free to debate that policy openly as it was unfolding.

"We shouldn't be muzzled," Ford maintained, using the same word that Johnson had used in asking him to silence Laird a month before. Indeed, the phone call had the opposite effect of what Johnson had intended. Instead of dividing the two friends, it had brought Ford firmly to Laird's dissenting side. So here Ford was, throwing it back at the president: "We shouldn't be smothered. We shouldn't be muted."[37]

One of Laird's purposes in promoting the white paper was to gain support for his own view that the president was wasting American lives to buy time in Vietnam until the enemy agreed to come to the negotiating table. Those lives were being lost on the ground, where U.S. forces were fighting a guerrilla war for which they had little training. This was unthinkable to Laird when the United States had superior air and sea power. It was also unthinkable to the military men who tried to advise Johnson. While Laird and others lobbied publicly for a powerful air war over North Vietnam, the Joint Chiefs of Staff tried to lobby the president privately for precisely the same thing.

They were finally allowed to meet with Johnson on the subject in November 1965. It was an extraordinary meeting, revealing the extent of Johnson's intractability and intemperance over Vietnam, even with his own military leadership. The substance was revealed years later by retired Lieutenant General Charles G. Cooper in an essay for the Naval Institute titled, "The Day It Became the Longest War." At the time of the meeting, Cooper was a marines major and aide to Admiral David McDonald, chief of naval operations. Cooper's job was to carry the maps for the briefing, which was a rare opportunity for the Joint Chiefs to present their best military advice on Vietnam. The first indication it was going to go badly, Cooper recalled, was that Johnson made his visitors stand, signaling that the meeting would be brief.

General Earle Wheeler, the new chairman of the Joint Chiefs, got to the point. "The essence of General Wheeler's presentation," Cooper wrote, "was that we had come to an early moment of truth in our ever-increasing Vietnam involvement. We had to begin using our principal strengths—air and naval power—to punish the North Vietnamese, or we would risk becoming involved in another protracted Asian ground war with no definitive solution. Speaking for the chiefs, General Wheeler offered a bold course of action designed to avoid the threat of protracted land warfare. He proposed isolating the major port of Haiphong through naval mining, blockading the rest of the North Vietnamese coastline, and simultaneously beginning a B-52 bombing offensive on Hanoi."

Johnson asked all the chiefs if they agreed, and they did.

"Seemingly deep in thought, President Johnson turned his back on them for a minute or so, then suddenly, losing the calm, patient demeanor he had maintained throughout the meeting, he whirled to face them and exploded," Cooper recalled. The president shouted obscenities, called the top brass insulting names, and ridiculed them for trying to use a military solution to a political and diplomatic problem, and said they had no idea of what it was like to be in his position. "He told them he was disgusted with their naive approach toward him, that he was not going to let some military idiots talk him into World War III. . . . It ended when he ordered them to 'get the hell out of my office!' "

In the car on the way back to the Pentagon, Admiral McDonald told his young aide, "[T]his day has got to be the worst experience I can ever imagine."[38]

Laird heard about the meeting within a week from Admiral Hyman Rickover and later had the details confirmed by General Wheeler. In public, Laird had been saying the same thing to the president as the Joint Chiefs had tried to say in private—blockade the coast, mine the harbor, and bomb the most vital strategic targets. Ironically, Johnson hoped his "limited warfare" approach would bring the enemy to the negotiating table. But it was not until 1972, when Laird was defense secretary and Nixon was president, that the plan of blockading and bombing became the tool that finally forced Hanoi to agree to a truce.

11

At the Credibility Gap

THE DAY AFTER LYNDON JOHNSON announced that he would feed the Vietnam War by scooping up young men through the draft, four hundred demonstrators in New York City marched from City Hall Park to the local army induction center. There, several of them became the first anti-Vietnam protestors to burn their draft cards. They were not, however, the first to protest with fire. Norman Morrison, a thirty-one-year-old Quaker, had carried his one-year-old daughter Emily to the lawn of the Pentagon on November 2, 1965. He doused himself with kerosene, struck a match on his shoe and burned himself to death. In the last instant before flames engulfed him, he tossed Emily to safety in the direction of a crowd of stunned onlookers. A twelve-foot-high pillar of fire could be seen from the office of the Secretary of Defense Robert McNamara, whose window was forty feet away. Morrison had left a letter with his wife explaining that he had to do something to protest napalm bombings of villagers in Vietnam.

The first significant protests against American involvement in the war began after the late February 1965 launch of the Rolling Thunder bombing campaign. As the bombing continued throughout the spring, the "teach-in" was born. College campuses canceled classes for a day or more (or students would just boycott them), and students would attend seminars debating and protesting the war. The first major national antiwar demonstration was planned by the Students for a Democratic Society for April 17 in Washington, D.C., and drew twenty thousand marchers.

The demonstrations disturbed Congressman Laird because he feared they would encourage the enemy to doubt American resolve. At the time, Laird could be described accurately as a "hawk" about the war, as was the vast majority of Congress. But Laird was a very specific type of hawk—he thought the United States should quickly and massively pound the enemy into submission by air and sea power, not by the use of ground troops. Laird postulated to journalists in a speech on November 20, 1965, in Fresno, California, that perhaps it was time for President Johnson to ask Congress to formally declare war. One reason to support a declaration of war, he said, would be because the enemy could then be compelled to treat POWs humanely under the Geneva Convention. "That's the only reason why I would support it," he concluded, but "I don't think we in Congress should push [the White House] into it."[1] A few days later, he told *New York Times* reporter David Broder: "The fact is sinking in that we are actually in a war there, without one ever being declared.... [T]he

President should have the courage to come to Congress and ask for authorization to fight a war if that is what this is."[2]

Laird knew a declaration of war had many disadvantages. For one thing, who would war be declared against? The United States did not recognize North Vietnam and could not likely declare war against the nameless peasants who made up the Viet Cong then occupying pockets in South Vietnam. Another disadvantage was that it would compel American treaty partners to join the battle. While some proved willing to do that, Laird felt it was better if they did it voluntarily and not by treaty mandate. Yet another downside, and a big one for Laird, was that if America was at war, Johnson could arrogate to himself extraordinary martial law–like powers, such as control over the economy. Already concerned about Johnson's power, backed up by the Democratic majority in the House and Senate, Laird was not anxious to give the president more.

The purpose behind many of Laird's political moves was not always evident from the opening gambit but was usually unveiled over time. Laird knew there was no chance Johnson would ask for a declaration of war. Laird's rhetorical probes were aimed at producing something close, but importantly different. He did not believe the United States was yet involved in an "illegal war" that required a formal declaration. But he also did not think that the Tonkin Gulf Resolution should be a blank check for Johnson. In early 1966 Laird argued that there was a need for a new debate on a second resolution—not formally a war declaration—that would either give the president the war-making powers he had already taken, or limit his use of the military in Vietnam.

In January of 1966 Laird issued a news release proclaiming the time had come for a debate in Congress on the continuation of the war.[3] It was already apparent to Laird that the Johnson administration was lying about Vietnam, which Laird diplomatically called a "credibility gap." The term had been coined by correspondent David Wise in the New York Herald-Tribune, and it gained currency as a definition for the disparity between the facts and the rosy McNamara and Johnson view of the war.

In Laird's mind, there were several options that made more sense than the Johnson strategy. For example, Laird had been calling for trade restrictions and a naval blockade against North Vietnam since March of 1964. In 1965 Laird began pushing a blockade plan with repetitive urgency. Ford wholeheartedly agreed with Laird on this point, and together they managed to persuade the Republican Coordinating Committee—made up of Republican legislators, governors, presidential candidates, and Eisenhower—that it was the right policy for their party to support. On December 13, 1965, several weeks after Johnson had secretly tossed the Joint Chiefs out of the White House for speaking their mind about the need for increased air and sea power, the GOP committee came out with a strong unanimous statement urging the same thing—"maximum use" of American air power against all "significant military targets" in North Vietnam, and an immediate naval quarantine against the enemy.

Broder wrote in the *New York Times* that Laird and Ford were behind the document, and that it represented "the Republicans' sharpest break so far from Johnson administration policy" on an issue that Laird and Ford believed might dominate the 1966 midterm election.[4]

As one of the nation's top defense appropriations experts, Laird was furious about the duplicitous way Johnson was financing the war. Reasonable people could and did differ on tactics for prosecuting the war, but Laird felt that the funding should be a matter of hard numbers in an open book. In 1965 Laird began hammering the president for the accounting sleight of hand that left the public in the dark about how much the war was costing. Johnson and McNamara established a pattern of submitting an annual defense budget that grossly underestimated the actual cost of the war. The administration would then come back to Congress with supplemental requests to pay for the war. The effect was to obscure the bottom line. Laird called it a "fight now, pay later" policy that financed the war "on the installment plan."

The defense budget Johnson submitted in early 1965 didn't include a single dollar for increased American activities in Vietnam. Instead Johnson financed it first with two supplemental appropriations—$700 million in May and an "emergency" $1.7 billion in September added as a late part of the 1966 fiscal year budget. Having included money for his Great Society programs, Johnson was anxious to have his total 1966 budget stay under the $100 billion ceiling. On the floor of the House, Laird called it a "fraud" to suggest that, even with the extra $1.7 billion, the war was fully funded. He predicted Johnson would come back in January and ask for billions more to cover the cost of the fifty-thousand-plus extra troops deployed to Vietnam. Just as Laird had said, in January 1966, the Johnson administration asked for a whopping $13.1 billion supplemental, which was approved in March.

By logical calculation, then, the president and Defense Secretary McNamara had seriously underestimated the Vietnam War cost for fiscal year 1966 by almost $15 billion. Concurrently, they submitted a 1967 budget that Laird knew deliberately underestimated the cost of the war for the next fiscal year, undoubtedly with an eye to the 1966 midterm election. If the war didn't appear to cost as much as it really did, Johnson's party might not lose House and Senate seats. Through 1966 Laird continually publicized what he viewed as Johnson's cynical charade regarding Vietnam War costs.

In October Laird predicted the White House would approach Congress after the election and request an emergency supplemental war appropriation somewhere between $12 and $16 billion.[5] About that time Defense Secretary McNamara denounced Laird, saying that the budget already appropriated would cover all war expenses through the 1967 fiscal year. "Laird doesn't know what he's talking about," McNamara told the press. But three months later, McNamara was back, securing a $12.2 billion supplemental appropriation for the war. Though he'd had it right, Laird didn't crow about it. "I'd rather have been wrong, but I have been proved right," he wearily told a reporter, even as he voted for the supplemental appropriation.[6]

The Johnson method of war financing—trying to feed the Great Society social programs and fight a war—was wrong on every count. "No nation has ever been able to finance a large war and expand domestic services without seriously injuring its own economy," Laird said. "This fact must be remembered by those who insist on 'business as usual' here at home while the war effort continues abroad."[7] The president was trying to get both "guns and butter," and that wasn't possible—though Laird, as a representative from a dairy district, generally avoided using that nineteenth-century expression for nations at war that had to choose between the two. (He occasionally said it was a "guns and oleo" issue.)[8] Even though Laird knew how Johnson was fudging on the budget, he could not bring himself to vote against any Vietnam budget request. "For me not to support the funding of the troops that our President has committed to Vietnam would be irresponsible, and, for me, unthinkable. . . . [W]hen the American flag has been committed in a military action, it is the duty of the Congress to see that the American men who are sent into battle will have all the support our nation can provide to do an effective job with a minimum of casualties," Laird wrote in a newspaper column.[9]

Laird was also accurate in predicting the manpower needs for Vietnam, over and above McNamara's lowball figures. Each time the president raised the troop complement, Laird accurately predicted a higher number would be deployed. In 1966 he began using his own numbers—which included those men Johnson admitted were on the ground in South Vietnam, and those the president didn't mention on ships and on American air bases in other Asian nations, all supporting the war. When Johnson raised the ground troop numbers to 300,000 in August 1966, Laird said the number was really 385,000. (When Laird took over as defense secretary in 1969, Johnson was claiming there were 540,000 troops in the war. In reality, Laird said, the number including the sailors and airmen was nearly one million.)

In 1966 it appeared Laird might have a tougher reelection race than usual. He was running against an incumbent legislator for the first time, Assemblyman Norman Myhra. Myhra was a double-amputee (his hands) World War II veteran with a zeal for campaigning. It was clear he hoped to win the election for Congress, or get appointed as the postmaster in Stevens Point, whichever came first. Word was out that the Democrats had promised him the postmaster job if he would run as their "sacrificial lamb" against Laird. To run, Myhra had to give up his assembly office, so he decided to give it his all. Senator Gaylord Nelson remembered driving with Myhra during the campaign and having to listen to Myhra's vituperative rhetorical attacks on Laird. Nelson had agreed to campaign for a day and lend his coattails to a fellow Democrat, but it was a day that he wanted to forget. "I guess he [Myhra] thought the nastier you were, the better your chances," Nelson recalled. "His attacks on Mel were absolutely embarrassing to me. It was dumb politics, and inaccurate. It was mean-spirited. It is an embarrassment to me now. He got the hell beat out of him."

Taking the higher road, Laird won handily, with 65 percent of the vote. It was then that Nelson says Laird demonstrated the strength of his character. Instead of seeking political revenge for Myhra's bitter campaign, Laird called Nelson and told him that if Myhra was nominated to be Stevens Point postmaster, Laird would not stand in the way. "Anybody that got the treatment Mel did generally wouldn't bother to affirmatively call. Most people would say, 'To hell with him,'" Nelson related. Instead, he was offering to help in overcoming any objections to Myhra for the appointment. Setting the tone of the campaign aside, Laird argued that Myhra had served honorably in World War II and as an assemblyman. "He's paid his dues," Laird concluded to Nelson, who was reluctant to support Myhra after his personal experience. But Laird persuaded him, and Myhra was made postmaster.[10]

Laird's campaign was also aided by the fact that his electorate viewed him in precisely the same way he wanted Republicans viewed—as a party that wasn't always tearing the opposition down, but was offering new ideas and constructive alternatives on the key issues of the day. For example, his positions on assistance for the aging were not typically Republican. He was asked to speak at the 1966 biennial convention of the American Association of Retired Persons and was a hit.[11] This was an organization that was later described by President Nixon's aides in a memorandum as notoriously "uncooperative" to Republicans because of its Democratic slant.[12] Nevertheless, Ethel Percy Andrus, AARP's founder and gifted leader, felt Laird was something of a kindred spirit and nurtured their friendship. No one was surprised, then, when it was Laird who was asked to deliver a eulogy at the Washington, D.C., memorial service for Andrus when she died in 1967.

Part of the reason that Andrus took to Laird was that he had become the leading pioneer of landmark legislation that would change Social Security, hedging it against inflation through a device now known as a COLA, or the cost of living allowance. (In Laird's advocacy for Social Security, there was a trace of a hometown pride, since the man sometimes called the "father of Social Security" was University of Wisconsin economics professor Edwin Witte.) The Social Security program was a major political football, and it was difficult to get past the partisan one-upmanship and pass a compromise bill. Laird thought there ought to be a way to take the politicians out of the equation. "I just got sick and tired of the Congress always debating what they should do each year to raise Social Security," Laird recalled. "I felt that it should be an automatic thing." In 1966 he authored an amendment to tie Social Security payments to the cost of living, but it failed because of Democratic opposition in the House. Undaunted, he reintroduced the bill each successive year.[13]

When Laird left Congress in 1969 to become defense secretary, his interest in Social Security did not wane. In July, he directed the Defense Department to start using Social Security numbers instead of military service numbers to identify military personnel. He then lobbied hard—but behind the scenes—to get the House Ways and Means Committee to send a COLA bill to the full House. Once it cleared the committee that had blocked it, the bill was swiftly passed in both houses, and President Nixon signed it into law in 1972.

⌘

Laird picked up a new prodigy on the political playing field in the summer of 1966. Dick Cheney had been raised in Casper, Wyoming, and got bachelor's and master's degrees in political science from the University of Wyoming. He had spent the summer of 1965 interning for the GOP-controlled Wyoming State Senate, having declared himself to be a Republican. Cheney's parents were dyed-in-the-wool Democrats and had always boasted that their baby boy had been born on FDR's birthday. They weren't particularly happy about his party choice but knew it was a pragmatic decision for their son who lived in a Republican state. Cheney intended to be a professor, as did his wife, Lynne. So they enrolled in doctoral programs at the University of Wisconsin in the fall of 1966.

Before school started, Cheney snagged a summer job as an aide to Wisconsin Governor Warren Knowles, who was running for reelection. Knowles had been friends with Laird since they were seat mates in the State Senate, so they campaigned together that summer, with twenty-five-year-old Dick Cheney in tow. Knowles borrowed a popular Laird campaign technique—taking a Polaroid picture of himself with voters and giving it to them; Cheney was the governor's designated photographer.[14] Laird saw Cheney as a true comer—bright, anxious to learn, and a good listener. He spent time on the campaign trail teaching the young student the political ropes. Lynne Cheney once told a reporter that her husband learned more about politics from Laird that summer than from most of the rest of the politicians he met, put together. ("All my political life, I've tried to emulate you," Vice President Cheney later told Laird.[15]) More than a mentor, however, Laird became Cheney's first important patron in Washington.

What Cheney remembered most from that summer of campaigning was a long conversation about Vietnam on a late-night trip on a small plane between northern Wisconsin and Chicago. Cheney said, "This was before there was a lot of opposition to the war—especially in political circles. But I can remember on that plane ride that night Mel raising serious questions about the judgments and decisions that had been made during the Johnson Administration in terms of getting into Vietnam. I remember him cautioning the governor to be careful about what he said about Vietnam—that all was not right with the policy there."[16]

While the University of Wisconsin campus would later become a hotbed of dissent over Vietnam, it was not so in the fall of 1966 when the Cheneys arrived. In fact, the whole year was a relatively quiet one for the antiwar movement. The nation's electorate was fracturing during that congressional election year, but Laird sensed that it had more to do with Johnson's leadership and inflation than the American involvement in the war. Indeed, the country was still largely supportive of the commitment of troops.

That fall the House Republican leadership issued a second white paper on Vietnam, this one more scathing than the one the previous year. The document's main theme was that LBJ had made the United States a "full-fledged combatant" in a conflict that was becoming "bigger than the Korean War."[17] While the administration policy had prevented Communist conquest of South Vietnam, the Republican leadership argued that its goals for the war were being "watered down" from the "absolute victory" Johnson had once espoused in late 1963. And despite the U.S. involvement, the amount of territory controlled by the Saigon government in South Vietnam was "far less" than it had been three years before.

A significant new theme in the white paper was the administration's lack of candor about casualties, both allied and enemy losses. In mid-1965 the chairman of the Joint Chiefs had said in a speech that the South Vietnamese had suffered some fifty thousand dead and wounded since 1960. A month later, Secretary of State Rusk gave a number 50 percent higher—seventy-five thousand. "It is hard to believe that casualties in one month in 1965 increased so dramatically," the white paper noted. As for the enemy casualties, the numbers were clearly a figment of someone's imagination. In May 1966, knowing the "body count" given by U.S. and South Vietnamese commanders had to be inflated, the Pentagon secretly briefed the House Armed Services Committee. It was reported that the old figure of 365,000 enemy wounded would be replaced by 182,000. No special genius was needed to extrapolate that, had the body count been accurate as reported, the enemy army would cease to exist entirely in the next year or two. The white paper argued that Johnson was a deceiver with no clear idea of how to get out of Vietnam and without the courage to tell the American people the truth.[18]

The white paper added to other Republican campaign themes as outlined by Laird to the Republican Coordinating Committee in early October. He carefully laid out the most salient issues and then summarized them: "Peace, today dominated by the situation in Vietnam; prosperity, today jeopardized by government-caused inflation; the maintenance of the two-party system, today threatened by a gross imbalance of power; and the future of the federal system, today stifled by an overbearing federal government."[19] Laird had found that the most effective campaign oratory tapped into a national discomfort that Johnson and the Democrats were heavy-handedly dictating domestic and foreign policies, without listening to some wise voices of dissent urging more centrist policies.

The Republican victories of the 1966 midterm election were a testament to the effectiveness of the new Ford-Laird House Republican leadership, which had been the driving force behind national Republican policy. With financial and political support, they targeted up to one hundred House seats held by Democrats who appeared most vulnerable. If they secured seventy-eight, Republicans would be the majority party in the House. Laird estimated Republicans would gain anywhere from thirty-one to sixty seats in the November election.[20] When the votes were tallied, they had a net gain of forty-seven. The gains were "a victory for all Americans because two-party government was restored to our nation's capitol," Laird declared.[21]

The victory might have been slightly sweeter for the Republicans had Johnson not pulled a fast one on the eve of the election, to the benefit of his own party. The president concocted a "summit" in Manila in late October with six allies—South Vietnam, Thailand, South Korea, the Philippines, Australia, and New Zealand. From abroad, he issued a unilateral peace offering, promising the allies would withdraw their forces from Vietnam within six months after Hanoi withdrew its own "and the level of violence subsides."[22] Though the resolution was vague and badly flawed, it gave Johnson and his party an eleventh-hour appearance of being peacemakers, which helped stem Democrat losses a bit in the 1966 congressional election.

<hr>

Laird had played such a prominent role in the Republican electoral victories in 1966 that it was inevitable in early 1967 that the media would speculate about him displacing Ford as minority leader. "A searing row has developed among House Republicans," one columnist opined. There were Laird supporters who were pushing for a coup because they viewed Laird as "a tougher, smarter political operative than Ford, and what the party needs in the House for the next two years is not a good-looking but ineffectual guy." The columnist admitted, however, that "the Laird-Ford ruckus has yet to surface."[23]

"Some of the people who were against the Republican Party's rise always tried to make out that Jerry and I were at each other's throats, which was not true," Laird said. "It was not a bad relationship—ever." Ford later told his autobiographical collaborator, Trevor Armbrister, that "despite the news stories, our relationship was good, has always been good, and is good today. Now, there were lots of rumors to the effect that Mel Laird was going to do the same thing to me that I had done to [House Minority Leader Charlie] Halleck. I never believed those. Mel always denied it. I saw no evidence of it."[24]

Despite news reports that sometimes referred to Laird as "the most power-ful Republican in the House," Ford refused to get ruffled. He had a great need for the idea-a-minute Laird as the party's chief strategist. Former Ford aide and biographer James Cannon observed: "In style, Laird combined some of the best qualities of Talleyrand and a medieval alchemist. He excelled in intricate political maneuver; none exceeded him in turning dross into political gold."[25] Because insiders knew just how pivotal and savvy Laird was behind the scenes, some Republicans bragged that he was "our Lyndon Johnson."[26] Other com-parisons were made, such as one by a *Los Angeles Times* political journalist who said that Laird, the man "widely viewed as the gray eminence of Congressional Republicans," had established "a role now likened to that of the French monk Francois le Clerc du Tremblay who, with Cardinal Richelieu, was the power behind the throne of Louis XIII."[27] But the most frequently used appellation to describe Laird was "Midwest Machiavelli," a man of "subtlety and cunning."[28]

Ford himself sometimes used the word "schemer" to describe his friend and partner. "He's the greatest schemer, and he knows that we all know that he does it. That's his nature; he's always got to be scheming. He doesn't scheme for any sinister reason; he just likes to keep the pot boiling. I never got mad at it [because] Mel Laird is one of the brightest political people that I ever knew. He had exceptional political perceptions as to issues, candidates, conflicts. He was, in my judgment, one of the shrewdest political operatives ever—and I say that in the right sense, not as a critical comment. He loved politics, and he absorbed himself in politics."[29] Former Republican National Committee chair Dean Burch added: "Mel is a schemer *and* a planner; they just overlap."[30]

Laird felt Ford had two primary liabilities. One was that he didn't "catch on as rapidly as he should to the political significance of an event or an issue. Once he understands it, there's no problem—but it does take him time." The second was that he was a laid-back leader. "You had to kick him in the ass usually to get him to do something," Laird said. Ford appreciated Laird's goading. "He's a pusher, and I respond to that kind of challenge. So it was a good combination; we worked together very well."

One of the things Laird did for Ford (portrayed as a Machiavellian move by one Ford biographer): "was to relieve the minority leader of the 'burden' of hiring and directing minority staff. Ford went along with that, and Laird, with control of the staff, was well on the way to leading the minority leader."[31] Laird demurred over that view, saying that was not his intention. Ford trusted Laird to bring on the best people and find a way to fit them in the budget. "I picked most of Jerry's staff and put them in place," Laird recalled. His most impor-tant find for Ford was Robert Hartmann, an award-winning *Los Angeles Times* journalist, hired in 1966 to be senior press counselor to Ford. "He was one of the few journalists that was actually a Republican," Laird laughed. Though Hartmann could be brusque and disagreeable, he quickly became invaluable to Ford as his most trusted legislative assistant and speech writer. He went on to become Vice President Ford's chief of staff and President Ford's senior counselor with Cabinet rank. It was wordsmith Hartmann who penned the resonant words Ford uttered at his swearing-in after Nixon's resignation: "Our long national nightmare is over."[32]

From conferring on strategy to hiring staff to making political deals, Laird and Ford were generally in sync, but they did not see eye to eye on everything. One example was Laird's unusual support of Johnson's attempted tax increase in 1967 via a 10 percent surcharge on personal and corporate income tax returns. A leader in Johnson's own party, Representative Wilbur Mills, wouldn't let the bill out of the Ways and Means Committee. When Laird made it clear to Ford that he hoped Johnson would try again in 1968, and they should both back the tax increase, Ford couldn't believe it. What Republican could ever be *for* a tax increase—especially when it was wildly unpopular among Laird's own constituency? Laird explained carefully that if taxes weren't increased by Johnson, then they would inevitably have to rise under the next president, and he could be a Republican. It was better to let Johnson take the heat. Laird helped craft the 10 percent tax surcharge bill that passed in 1968, by joining others in tacking on a requirement that Johnson had to cut $6 billion from the federal budget at the same time the taxes went up.

The one aspect of the Ford-Laird partnership that Laird most disliked was that he necessarily had to be cast as the heavy. They both knew that somebody had to crack the whip and keep Republicans in line with the leadership, and "Jerry was suited to be the nice guy, so I had to be tougher on people than Jerry was." The older Ford gave off a more vigorous physical appearance than the balding Laird. "Even Laird admirers fear that his overbearing manner and devilish look—eyes gleaming, cigar waving—may keep him from attaining any higher elected party post," the *Wall Street Journal* suggested.[33]

For many reasons, the Laird-Ford partnership withstood erosion from external forces. They were close friends and confidants. As members of several social groups, such as the Chowder and Marching Club, they partied together. Laird and Ford shared a great love for golf, which put them on the links often. Their families celebrated birthdays and holidays together. And there was one more key reason for their unbreakable bond that outsiders did not know: Laird and Ford prayed together every week.

The gathering every Wednesday in a little room on the House side of the Capitol was begun by Representative Al Quie, later the governor of Minnesota. A Lutheran anxious to make a spiritual connection with selected House members, Quie said he pondered whom he should approach. He thoughtfully considered the New Testament story of the divine selection of Saul, a Jew who was also a Roman citizen well versed in Greek philosophy. Wanting to follow that example, he asked himself, Who is the best politician in Congress?

"The answer was obvious: Mel Laird was the best politician," he recounted. "So I thought, I've gotta talk to him—but I never got around to it." Quie was afraid of being rebuffed on the prayer invitation. But at one point, when he was seated in the front row of the House chamber, and Laird sat behind him, Quie prayed for the strength to raise the delicate issue. Twice he tried to speak, but could not. "God, I can't do this," he prayed. "You're going to have to get someone else to do it; I just can't."

At that moment, as another member droned on with a speech, Laird leaned forward and said, "Al, I've been thinking we ought to get together some time for prayer and invite some of our friends to pray with us." Quie said that "from that moment on, I never doubted the power of the Holy Spirit." Repairing to the Speaker's Lobby, Laird and Quie worked out the details. The group needed to be small, they agreed, so each of them would invite one friend only. Laird said he would invite Ford; Quie wanted to approach their mutual friend Charlie Goodell. By the next night, when they found each other at a Chamber of Commerce gathering, the excitement was still palpable. Ford and Goodell had agreed. "This has to be of God," Laird said.

From that point on—whenever it was possible on Wednesday around noon—the four met for vocal prayer and reflection. In a weekly rotation, one would say the first prayer, and each of the three others would follow. They would close saying the Lord's Prayer in unison. Certainly it might have been viewed by outsiders as a Republican "power group," since Ford was the minority leader, Laird the Republican Conference chair, and both Goodell and Quie key committee leaders for the conference. But they did not view it that way. "We never made a big thing about it," Laird noted. "We didn't wear our religion on our sleeve, so we didn't talk about it with others. It was informal, comfortable and a very private thing for all of us."

When Goodell was appointed to the Senate in 1968 to replace the assassinated Senator Bobby Kennedy, John Rhodes of Arizona took his place in the small group. The Wednesday prayer group continued through to the end of Ford's presidency in 1977. Throughout that time Laird was defense secretary, White House domestic counselor, and then a senior counselor for *Reader's Digest*. But if he was in town on Wednesday, Laird would find his way back to the small House prayer room and enjoy the spiritual repast once more with his old friends.[34]

12

Into the Quagmire

WASHINGTON LOVES A GOOD FEUD, so when the evenly matched Congressman Laird and Secretary of Defense McNamara locked horns, it was juicy fodder for cocktail parties and political columnists. There were few public exchanges—most of their clashes occurred behind closed doors during Defense Appropriations Subcommittee hearings—but the news frequently leaked out. At first Laird had considered McNamara to be a brilliant defense secretary who had established necessary civilian control at the Pentagon in his first years there. But Laird came to believe that McNamara had outlived his usefulness after one term. And when Laird became convinced that McNamara had not told the whole truth about the Tonkin Gulf incident, the gloves came off. The media took note, frequently describing Laird as McNamara's toughest critic. As one writer for the Scripps-Howard newspapers put it, Laird took on McNamara while most of Washington still believed he was "the greatest thing to hit town since standup drinking."[1]

Laird's most effective tactic was to turn McNamara's own words against him. In a 1966 essay recounting some of his personal favorites from among McNamara's pronouncements, Laird wrote: "Secretary McNamara's best known prediction on Vietnam was his statement of October 2, 1963, reporting his 'judgment' that the 'major part of the U.S. military task can be completed by the end of 1965, although there may be a continuing requirement for a limited number of U.S. training personnel.'"[2]

The most memorable dustup between the two men came during closed-door budget hearings in early 1966 when McNamara was forced to admit he was wrong. His previous Vietnam budget estimate had been short, he acknowledged, and he would need $13 billion more, just as Laird had predicted he would. Laird began pressing McNamara on how he could have so grossly underestimated the budget request. McNamara got testy, and Laird continued to press. By that time, Laird was convinced that McNamara was predisposed to substitute sophistry for candor, and the congressman wanted none of it. "I think the secretary is tired and overworked," Laird said, with a hint of sarcasm. "He has engaged in short-tempered outbursts recently. I think he needs a good rest—at least a week or two away from the desk."

A furious McNamara exploded with a profane remark, jumped up, and appeared ready to lunge across the table at Laird. Representative George Mahon interceded with a quick rebuke to McNamara for his words and body language: "Mr. Secretary, we don't use that kind of language in this room, and we don't have that kind of reaction to questions asked by a member of this committee. Mr. Laird has the perfect right to suggest that maybe you're tired and worn out."[3]

The contretemps was over, but Laird refused to retreat, even though some members of Congress on both sides of the aisle and also White House aides asked him to back off. The following March 1967, when McNamara was back asking for another $12 billion-plus supplemental, Laird got under the defense secretary's skin again, demanding to know how he had made yet another multibillion-dollar error. "Okay, you've got the knife in me," McNamara reportedly protested at one stage. "Just don't twist it."[4] Laird was convinced that McNamara was coming unglued, that he was a broken man, barely hiding his injured psyche under a veneer of bravado. At the same time as Laird was grilling McNamara over the supplemental appropriation, McNamara was reeling from a secret request from General William Westmoreland.

March 18, 1967, could arguably go down in history as the day that broke the will of the Johnson administration concerning Vietnam. The precipitating act happened entirely behind the scenes when Westmoreland, the commander of U.S. forces in Vietnam, insisted that he needed another 200,000 American men, which would raise the total number of ground troops to 670,000. The general also wanted to expand the war into Cambodia and Laos, increase the bombing of North Vietnam, and invade from the sea and through the demilitarized zone. The price tag would have been $10 billion more a year for a war that was already costing $25 billion annually.

Johnson and McNamara were stunned. The Westmoreland memo sat like dead weight on the president's desk and was never answered. It marked a turning point for McNamara. He urged the president to reject the escalation, and then two months later wrote his own memo, which would prove to be the beginning of his end as defense secretary. In that memo McNamara advised Johnson that the approach they were taking was all wrong: Expecting the North Vietnamese to come to the bargaining table was a pipe dream; Hanoi would bide its time hoping that the 1968 election would unseat Johnson; Westmoreland's request for more troops would throw Congress and the American people into a "bitter" debate. "The picture of the world's greatest superpower killing or seriously injuring 1000 noncombatants a week, while trying to pound a tiny backward nation into submission on an issue whose merits are hotly disputed is not a pretty one," McNamara wrote.[5]

A second memo from McNamara to Johnson six months later sealed the defense secretary's fate. On November 1, 1967, responding to more pressure from the Joint Chiefs to escalate the war and seek military victory, McNamara advised Johnson to halt the bombing of North Vietnam and begin turning the war over to the South Vietnamese. "Continuation of our present course of action in Southeast Asia would be dangerous, costly in lives, and unsatisfactory to the American people," McNamara wrote.[6] The president had a military establishment urging him to pull out all the stops, and a defense secretary telling him to pull back. He was not willing to do either. By the end of November Johnson had arranged a new job for McNamara as president of the World Bank. Three months later Clark Clifford moved into McNamara's office.

Looking back on that time, McNamara insisted there was no feud with Laird. He "was a terrific congressman, an extraordinary congressman," and the Defense Appropriations Subcommittee was "one of the best committees in Congress. I testified before him and Jerry Ford for years and years and years. They were Republicans and I was in Democratic administrations under Kennedy and Johnson." When asked if he thought Laird was tough on him, McNamara said, "Well, you know, he was tough in the sense that he was so well informed that you had to be on your toes when you went up there, and keep your hands in your pockets!" He chuckled, remembering. "But he was damn, damn good. I admired and respected him."[7]

In hindsight, Laird also downplayed the notion of a feud. McNamara was one of the first people Laird called on after being nominated as secretary of defense. At a press conference as secretary-designate Laird said, "I did disagree with him on his estimates as far as Vietnam War costs. Only the disagreements seem to make news [but] I was in agreement with him more often than I was in disagreement with him."[8] Laird was referring to all aspects of the defense budget, including manpower policies, weapons procurement, and the vast array of Pentagon issues that went beyond Vietnam.

Though he still regarded McNamara with respect, Laird was critical of McNamara's 1995 memoir, *In Retrospect,* in which McNamara finally admitted mistakes that Laird had pointed out as they occurred in the 1960s. In the book "McNamara never really pays tribute to the men and women who gave so much to their country, died for it." Laird said. "You cannot just turn your back on those young men and women who went out there. You owe them a lot. Right or wrong, you owe them a lot." He said in a later interview, "McNamara was a brilliant man in many, many respects; he was really a whiz kid; there's no question about that. But I don't think he had the feeling or concern for people that you need if you're going to be secretary of defense."

⚒

Jim Albertson was no soldier, but he died in Vietnam while undertaking a mission Congressman Laird had urged upon him. Dr. Albertson was an educator, and a good one. He became the eighth president of Wisconsin State College (later University of Wisconsin) at Stevens Point in 1962. In less than five years, he had tripled the enrollment from about two thousand to six thousand students. To accommodate the growing student population, new campus buildings went up, and, with Laird's string-pulling, Stevens Point was considered for the site of a new federal water pollution laboratory and other projects.

Not content to improve Stevens Point only, Albertson led a successful fight to establish Wisconsin's first community college system—two-year institutions offering both academic and technical training. Albertson was a comer. The only question was how long he would stay at Stevens Point before being lured to head a more prestigious university. When Laird learned the Agency for International Development (AID) was putting together a team to study higher education in South Vietnam to prepare the country for a peaceful future, he thought Albertson was just the man for the job. Albertson himself was not so easily convinced when he was offered the contract. After lengthy consideration, he finally agreed.

The team flew to Vietnam in January 1967 to begin a study of the three public universities of Saigon, Can Tho, and Hue. It took some courage for these educators, since all of South Vietnam was effectively a war zone. But the forty-one-year-old Albertson, a World War II veteran who served two years in the Pacific, shrugged it off. He liked the mission and developed a zeal for it. During a brief return visit to Wisconsin in February, he said—in what was to be his last interview—that it would be "a great tragedy if we won the military war in Vietnam and pulled out. We have a moral commitment to remain and help the country in other areas, as education." On March 23 the Air America twin-engine plane ferrying Albertson and his team around Vietnam landed at an airfield north of Da Nang to wait out a tropical storm. Anxious to get them to their next stop, the pilot decided the weather had cleared up enough to fly. But after take-off the plane slammed into the side of a mountain. Dr. Albertson, the pilot, an AID official, and seven educators from Harvard, the University of Illinois, and colleges in Wisconsin and Minnesota were killed.[9]

Laird was devastated when he heard the news. He struggled to console Albertson's widow and five children. After returning from speaking at Albertson's funeral and thinking it over for weeks, Laird offered heart-felt words in the House Chamber about the loss of the selfless volunteers: "These men with Jim Albertson as their leader were front-line soldiers in the long-range war of ideas. Their weapons were books instead of bullets. Their objective was to help develop universities in which young people of Southeast Asia could seek truth to guide them in deciding their own destiny."

Perhaps Laird felt a special pain because, unlike the many soldiers drafted into the war by Johnson and McNamara, he had been the one to send Albertson to Vietnam. Nevertheless, after praising Albertson in the House, he moved on to the larger tragedy of the Americans who never returned from the war. "The war in Vietnam has brought tragedy and loss to thousands of American families from coast to coast," he mourned. "For hundreds of these boys, we will never know what contribution they might have made to their communities and their nation had their lives not been cut short by the cruel and indifferent consequences of war."[10]

A few weeks after that speech, the name of one of those "boys" appeared on the June 23 roster of the dead—someone Laird knew intimately from back home in Marshfield. Second Lieutenant Charles Leo Johnson was killed in action in Chu Chi while simultaneously directing his men in an attack and trying to drag his wounded radio operator to safety. He had been in Vietnam only six weeks and was in the lead armored personnel carrier returning from a search-and-destroy mission. The lieutenant, who was awarded a posthumous Silver Star for his gallantry, was one of eleven children of Herbert and Adele Johnson, a family that lived behind the Laird home for many years.

"At the time, we were getting casualties regularly in my congressional district and, of course, I got in touch with all the parents immediately," Laird recalled, and that was rough enough. But calling on grieving families at their homes, as he did with the Johnsons, "was a *very* tough experience. I would say that Herb Johnson's son's death came very close to where I lived." Thirty years later, a published Marshfield history reported that the Johnson family believed Charley's death in mid-1967 helped transform Laird from a hawk to a dove on the Vietnam War. As painful as it was to lose someone from home, Laird responded: "I was never a great hawk on Vietnam."[11]

The buzzwords of "hawk" and "dove" were too simplistic to describe Laird and most of his generation. They had fought and won a world war and had paid a dear price for victory. They were not afraid to stand up against tyranny, but experience had taught them that the end had to justify the sacrifice. In Vietnam Laird was pretty sure the American public didn't know what the "end" was supposed to look like, and he strongly suspected the president didn't know either.

In a letter to Johnson in February 1967, Laird pleaded for clarification. The president had recited lofty goals about security and freedom for South Vietnam but was dropping hints of compromise in negotiations with the enemy. "Our country is a great country and our people a great people," Laird wrote. "They are willing to make whatever sacrifices are necessary in time of war to insure honorable success for their country's cause. I pray that you, as our nation's leader, will take them into your confidence and lay before them a full and detailed report on the foreign policy of the United States. I sincerely believe that no greater responsibility faces the President of the United States than that of uniting the American people behind a foreign policy they can understand and support."[12]

An internal White House memo called the Laird letter "a thoughtful piece of work.... [H]e is right in saying that the matters he has raised are among those things which do trouble a number of our people." An LBJ aide said that, as Laird had suggested, the president should make it the subject of a major message, and the aide was fully prepared to work on the first draft.[13] (Laird knew only that the White House sent him a standard-issue reply assuring him that his letter was receiving the "most serious consideration.")

Among issues Laird addressed in his letter to the president was the failure to restrict trade to North Vietnam, as Laird had so often urged. "I have been asked many times why our country refuses to use trade as a weapon or tool of war. Many Americans cannot understand our country's stated intention to increase trade with the Soviet Union and its East European satellites. They cannot reconcile this intention with the known fact that 80% of the strategic war materials now being provided the Communists in Vietnam come from these countries. I must confess that I, too, am perplexed by our past reluctance to escalate with the more humane weapon of trade before escalating by means of bombing."

This time Laird was prepared to make a full-court press on the trade issue. A few days before Johnson got Laird's letter, the president received a heads-up memo from a White House aide who had discussed the issue with Laird at a dinner the night before. "He thinks that the Administration is not facing up to the fact that in Vietnam it is not the Communist Chinese [but the Soviets] who are providing the support that permits North Vietnam to continue the war. He believes that continued bombing under the present limitations is useless and is costing the life of one out of every four of our pilots."[14]

On March 23 Laird introduced a resolution declaring to be "the sense of Congress" that future expansion of trade with the Soviet Bloc be contingent upon "demonstrable evidence that their actions and policies with regard to Vietnam have been redirected toward peace and an honorable settlement."

At a press conference Laird charged that the Johnson administration had deliberately misinformed Americans by suggesting that the Chinese were the main suppliers to North Vietnam when it was, in fact, the Soviets. That fact was admitted by the administration in highly classified briefings not available to the American public. Laird reported that he knew from his Defense Appropriations Subcommittee work that the Soviet Union was the "key to peace in Vietnam" because the Eastern bloc was "now providing more than 80 percent of the strategic war materials furnished to North Vietnam"—and fully $1 billion annual aid to Vietnam.[15]

Two months later, the rest of the Republican leadership finally caught up with Laird. At a meeting on May 25, the top Republican Senate and House leaders agreed it was time to back Laird's position since its logic was irrefutable. After the meeting, speaking for the Senate Republican leadership, Everett Dirksen began his statement with a question: "Have you heard of a single Russian who was reported as a casualty in Vietnam? You haven't and you won't. [Today] the U.S. Command reported that total American casualties were in excess of 70,000 [including] 10,253 dead.... How were they killed? For the most part by Red Russian weapons and Red Chinese weapons in the hands of the Red Viet Cong [and] there are more weapons to come.... These are the people with whom we are asked to turn the cheek of compassion and embark on a policy of East-West trade. Is trade so sweet and profits so desirable as to be purchased at the price we now pay in death and agony?"

Speaking for House Republicans, Minority Leader Ford's statement read: "Russian guns, Russian bullets, Russian surface-to-air missiles, Russian MiGs, Communist machine guns and Communist mortars continue to kill and maim American fighting men and innocent civilians by the thousands in Vietnam.... There may be some who find it wholly consistent that Americans should fight for freedom and survival against Communist aggression on the one hand, while trading and dealing for Communist enrichment on the other. We do not."[16]

Laird was glad to have his fellow Republicans on board, but it was already too late for reasonable success in Vietnam. In March he laconically told a Chamber of Commerce breakfast meeting in his hometown that he saw "no real chance for a U.S. military victory in Vietnam."[17] In a news column about that time, Laird—who had advocated an embargo and blockade three years before—concluded: "Had we used trade as one of the most effective weapons of war at the outset, I am convinced that the agonizing losses both in men and material would not have been as large and the duration of the war would have been materially shortened."[18]

The freshman Republican class of the ninetieth Congress was a large one, with fifty-nine newly elected Republican members of the House beginning their first terms in 1967. They looked to the leadership for guidance, and Laird became a mentor to many of them, as he had to others before them. The new class included George Herbert Walker Bush, whom Laird had first met in 1956 when Bush was a page at the Republican Convention. Bush was able to gain early promotion as a freshman primarily because he was such an impressive rarity—a Republican representative from Texas. He was also ambitious. Shortly after the election, he wrote Minority Leader Ford to make a "strong plea" for a coveted seat on the Appropriations Committee, which he acknowledged was a "grandiose request." Laird himself was one of the few ever to win a seat on the powerful committee in his freshman term. Ford advised Bush that the man to see about the request was Laird.

"I don't want you or any others in the leadership to feel that I expect any special consideration, but [Ford] said to go ahead," Bush wrote Laird.[19] Laird thought Bush had merit, but there was no Appropriations seat available. So he conferred with his Republican colleague from Wisconsin, Johnny Byrnes, who, as ranking member of the equally powerful Ways and Means Committee, agreed to give Bush a coveted seat there. "I tried to help George along as much as I could," Laird recalled. "He'd established his credentials in Texas alright and was a very fine person with all the right thoughts. I can't say enough about his character and his intelligence." While the two were "not intimates," Bush said he respected Laird as well and was "grateful" for Laird's role in getting him on the Ways and Means Committee. The fact that Laird "reached out" to the freshman from Texas was important since "we had such a huge freshman class in those days."[20]

Also, Bush added in his 1987 autobiography, Laird and Ford, as well as the Democratic leadership of the House then, taught him what he called the four fundamentals of "leadership in a free legislative body:"

1. No matter how hard-fought the issue, never get personal. Don't say or do anything that may come back to haunt you on another issue, another day.
2. Do your homework. You can't lead without knowing what you're talking about.
3. The American legislative process is one of give and take. Use your power as a leader to persuade, not intimidate.
4. Be considerate of the needs of your colleagues, even if they're at the bottom of the totem pole.[21]

While Bush was particularly appreciative that Laird embraced rule 4, having "sponsored" Bush's rise from "the bottom of the totem pole," he suggested that sometimes Laird would bend rule 3—that is, he would *strongly* lean on Bush and others in the freshman class to vote with the Republican leadership. "He was always very pleasant to me," Bush laughed, "but Mel was kind of a disciplinarian, a strict guy."[22]

In 1967, as a House leader, Laird was anxious to get the cooperation of the fifty-nine Republican representatives in slowing down Johnson's Great Society spending and forcing a better Vietnam strategy. He knew that, if the Republicans held together, they could out-vote the Democratic majority whenever conservative Southern Democrats sided with them. "The only trouble with George Bush was that he had a hard time voting yes or no on some bills," Laird said. "Bills often have a lot of good things in them as well as a lot of bad things. When the roll is called, you've got to be willing to make a decision. It is 'yes' or 'no.' It isn't '52 percent yes' and '48 percent no.' George really had trouble on that." Laird felt that well-intentioned indecisiveness continued to plague Bush through two terms in Congress and in his other positions and was not licked until shortly into his presidency.

Another in that freshman class was one of Laird's Wisconsin protégés, William (Billy) Steiger, who, at twenty-eight, was even younger than Laird had been when he first began to serve in Congress. Dick Cheney was looking for a job in Washington, and Laird asked Steiger to put Cheney on his staff as a congressional fellow. (Laird would have preferred to take Cheney under his own wing but had no openings at the House Republican Conference.)[23] Another in their circle was Representative Donald Rumsfeld. Later during the Nixon administration, Rumsfeld headed the Office of Economic Opportunity, and Cheney became his key aide. In the Ford administration, Rumsfeld was tapped as chief of staff and asked Cheney to work for him again. Then Cheney succeeded Rumsfeld as Ford's chief of staff. Always behind the scenes was Laird, steering Cheney to the next move. Two years after President Ford was defeated for reelection, Laird encouraged Cheney to run for Wyoming's single House seat, which Cheney won in 1978. Within a few years, following Laird's example, Cheney engineered a fast rise up the House Republican leadership ladder. "You were Chairman of the House Republican Conference, so I strove for that same goal," Cheney later reflected to Laird. "When struggling with the obstacles and frustrations of trying to get anything done while in the minority, I would wonder to myself, 'Now, how would Mel have handled this can of worms?' "[24]

⌇

One recurrent "can of worms" with which any Congress deals is corruption. Congress is empowered to conduct hearings up to and including impeachment proceedings against judges and both the president and vice president. For a minority party, it becomes a matter of sensitive strategy just how much to press the issue of corruption, particularly when the president himself is involved.

Lyndon Johnson was not a man afflicted with an overworked moral compass. Beginning in 1948, when he bought votes and rigged the ballot counting to win a seat in the Senate, Johnson seemed to justify his ethical lapses as necessary steps to reach the presidency and engineer his vision of a Great Society. One of Johnson's most flagrant abuses as a public servant was to "make a fortune by owning, while in government, government-regulated television," recalled George H.W. Bush. "But almost nobody back in those days said it was wrong." Laird was a legitimate exception in a day when political ethics were fairly elastic. In Bush's view, Laird had the moral high ground to raise questions about LBJ's fortune built on finagled Federal Communications Commission variances—and other questionable dealings. "There was never any question about Laird's integrity," Bush said. "Laird was tested by fire. He had plenty of chances to go awry as a congressman. Plenty of people would love to have bought influence with him by giving him illegal money, but he didn't operate that way."[25]

Johnson, by contrast, operated in shades of gray. For one thing, he was a womanizer who carried on affairs even in the White House. Laird knew about it because FBI Director J. Edgar Hoover loved to gossip about it in private breakfast meetings with Representative Glenard Lipscomb, the ranking member of the subcommittee that handled the FBI's budget. Laird, who counted Lipscomb among his closest friends in Congress, was often invited to those breakfasts. Hoover apparently felt he could curry favor with Lipscomb by offering details first on President Kennedy's sexual affairs, and then Johnson's. Since neither Laird nor Lipscomb encouraged the talk, the director didn't go into salacious details. But he loved to paint the Kennedy and Johnson White Houses as, if not morally bankrupt, at least overdrawn. "Try to warn people not to be too loose around here," Hoover would admonish Laird and Lipscomb when reporting presidential sexcapades. "You need to run a tighter ship than the White House is doing. Get to your colleagues and tell them to be careful."

As a leader of the opposition party, Laird declined to use Johnson's bedroom as a relevant subject for public debate. But other issues that Hoover raised in the breakfast briefings—the Billie Sol Estes and Bobby Baker investigations—were a different matter. Laird had to consider long and hard whether to make political hay out of Johnson's obvious connections to men who illegally built fortunes with his apparent help.

Estes was an entrepreneur from Pecos, Texas, who swindled the government and investors to amass a fortune that approached nearly $400 million. Senator Lyndon Johnson was Estes's key federal patron, and a significant beneficiary. By Estes's own account, he siphoned hundreds of thousands of dollars to Johnson for political campaign expenditures and personal use.[26] Estes was convicted in 1963 of four mail fraud counts and one conspiracy count and sentenced to fifteen years in prison. During the 1964 presidential election, Goldwater naturally thought it was legitimate campaign fodder. But considering the Johnson landslide, the scandal had little effect—which is what Laird had suspected would be the case. He cautioned fellow Republicans about making too much of the issue because it was apparent that such things didn't stick to Johnson in the wake of the Kennedy assassination trauma.

Bobby Baker was Johnson's "go-fer" in the Senate and made headlines as the era's top "influence peddler." Somehow, on a salary that never reached $20,000 a year, he toted up a net worth of $2 million. When some of Baker's investments went awry, the FBI, encouraged by Attorney General Bobby Kennedy, took a close look. Other than a stereo and a life insurance commission kicked back for advertising on an LBJ television station, the FBI had trouble proving Johnson was involved or was a significant beneficiary of Baker's financial shenanigans. Still, Vice President Johnson pretended he couldn't even remember his protégé's last name during the investigation.[27] In early 1967 Baker was found guilty of seven counts of theft, fraud, and income tax evasion. Once again Laird passed up the opportunity to score political points against Johnson. In an interview after Baker's conviction, Laird suggested that both Republicans and Democrats should avoid making personal attacks on LBJ in part because it "seriously undermined the President's prestige at home and abroad." He added: I'm not for making the Bobby Baker thing a big expose on the President at this time. [We] have to be very careful to stick to issues instead of getting into personal things."[28]

Laird did feel he ought to be able to take a close look at the special White

House perks that were paid for by the Pentagon, which made President Johnson angry. He stonewalled, lied, and otherwise hid his costly use of the presidential yachts, helicopters, and airplanes from Laird, the inquiring ranking member of the Defense Appropriations Subcommittee. In February 1966 columnists Rowland Evans and Robert Novak approached Laird because they had heard one of Johnson's three presidential yachts, the *Honey Fitz*, was being remodeled at a cost of nearly $1 million. Laird made an inquiry, and, since the information was not classified, he reported back to Evans that the cost was actually $100,000—still a hefty price for such a taxpayer-supported luxury item. After the columnists printed the figure, a furious Johnson personally ordered a clampdown on such information, and a full investigation of Laird. Tipped off to this, Laird wrote Johnson's press secretary Bill Moyers that "things have come to a sorry pass indeed if a Member of Congress cannot be furnished public information from individuals in our Defense Department without fear of reprisal by the White House." He laid out his role and said that when such information was not openly provided to the taxpayers, there is a great "disservice to the Congress as well as to the Executive Branch. I have never been a 'nit-picker' on any White House spending requests funded by our Defense Appropriations Subcommittee."[29]

The president called Defense Secretary McNamara and asked him to make Laird back off the perks issues. According to McNamara's return memo to Johnson, he had called Laird and told him on several occasions that Johnson had issued instructions eliminating "all unnecessary frills or luxuries" on the yachts and aircraft, and that all data relating to them was public record.[30] The wily Laird decided to test the president's word on this. He had the General Accounting Office inquire about renovations to one of the presidential aircraft. Bill Gulley, who would serve in the White House Military Office for eleven years, including as its chief, said that the GAO inquiry for Laird was one of the first congressional requests he handled after joining the staff. "When we told Johnson what they wanted, he said, 'Tell the bastards no!' "[31]

Detecting this LBJ sore spot, Laird made it a point to regularly inquire about various aspects of Pentagon perks for the president. Gulley wrote in his memoirs that Johnson was quite distracted by Laird's probing on these small matters. For example, he wanted to know exactly how many helicopters the taxpayers were funding for the president. "Tell 'em I have one helicopter," Johnson finally grunted to Gulley. "I can only ride one helicopter at a time, so tell the bastards one's all I've got."

"So we only had one helicopter, one pilot and two crewmen," Gulley said. "Of course, we really had 13 helicopters, with a crew of three for each and an additional one hundred ground crew to maintain them, but Johnson never let us report more than one helicopter and three crew."[32]

The Johnson administration frequently used "national security" to put a better spin on Vietnam War policy. Most of the Defense Appropriations Subcommittee hearings were classified sessions. A much-vetted public transcript was released weeks or months after the hearings were held—and only after a Pentagon security team had crossed out sensitive topics. In the spring of 1964 Laird began observing "excessive use of the Pentagon's censorship," much of it done to make McNamara and the administration appear more capable than had been shown during the intense scrutiny of the actual hearings held behind closed doors. "At one point in the hearings, I questioned Secretary McNamara for the better part of several days," Laird reported then. "In reading the unclassified version of this testimony, one is completely misled regarding the purpose of some of my questions." His conclusion was that too many Pentagon deletions from the transcript "were for self security rather than national security."[33]

During the next three years, Pentagon censorship of the hearing transcripts went from bad to worse, especially as McNamara tried to cover up the tragically failing U.S. military effort in Vietnam. To one reporter, Laird provided a telling example of the Pentagon's overprotective red pen. Feeling that the White House was overriding the field commanders, General Earle Wheeler, chairman of the Joint Chiefs of Staff, ruefully observed in one closed-door hearing: "The war will not be lost in Vietnam. This war, if it is lost, will be lost here in Washington." When the transcript was printed, his remark was cut to read simply, "The war will not be lost in Vietnam."[34]

At another closed-door hearing, in March 1967, Laird spoke to the assembled military witnesses criticizing the ability of the South Vietnamese to govern themselves. "I just don't think it's possible," he said. It was a shorthand assessment of his concerns about America taking over the war and not allowing the South Vietnamese to step up to the plate. After the Pentagon's editing, the transcript was released in May and Laird's remark was suspiciously absent. He demanded an accounting from McNamara about the censorship during an open hearing in May.

McNamara explained that the basic role of the censors was to remove passages that might "reveal information to our potential enemies." Laird's statement "may adversely affect negotiations," so it was cut out. McNamara agreed with his subordinate's censorship: "I think it is a mistake to tell the people of South Vietnam today that you lack confidence in their ability to learn how to govern themselves. I do not see how this can possibly improve the relations of our nation with theirs."[35]

Laird let the drama play out in the press without much comment. The media universally sided with him.[36] McNamara was roundly criticized in newspaper editorials for setting himself up as a judge of what Americans had the right to hear. McNamara's "defense is indefensible" and "indicates a Pentagon attitude of superior authority over Congress," the *Milwaukee Sentinel* editorialized. "If McNamara wants to make such judgments, let him resign as Secretary of Defense and then run for Congress. He can, if elected, then help to shape policy instead of, as he is supposed to be doing now, merely carrying it out."[37]

As 1967 wore on, Laird was approaching his threshold of tolerance for Johnson's Vietnam War policy, whether Ford or other Republicans agreed with him or not. Vietnam had become the third-largest war in American history, having surpassed Korea. Its costs were ranging from $2.4 to $2.7 billion a month, and that ignored a figure-fudging technique used by McNamara and Johnson: they stripped American troops in NATO countries and elsewhere of machinery and ordnance, which allowed them to understate the cost of American military matériel expended in Vietnam. Laird highlighted this under-the-table supply shifting in what he called his "$10 Billion Speech" at conventions and other venues in 1967: "McNamara and Johnson robbed NATO of arms and ammunition to feed the forces in Vietnam. Preparedness in NATO was going down the drain, as was morale."

In July Laird traveled to Chicago to address the Lions International Convention with a hard-hitting speech that became his treatise on Vietnam. The event was all the more significant when put in context—a Republican congressman protesting the war to a conservative, middle-aged audience from middle America. "I consider myself neither a 'hawk' nor a 'dove,' but a pessimist," he said. Johnson and McNamara had "Americanized" the war. "American casualties have now mounted to such an extent that they are out-running South Vietnamese casualties by roughly two to one.... Precisely what is the end result we are striving to attain? What is the shooting all about? What is it in Southeast Asia that justifies a kill rate of 10,000 Americans annually and possibly 50,000 wounded?"

The president had said that the goal was freedom, and the GOP had supported him. But Johnson was in danger of losing that support, Laird warned, in large part because of the October 1966 Manila pronouncement in which Johnson made vague promises of withdrawal. "It is my own deep conviction [that] the President's commitment in Manila, if carried out, would ultimately lead to a takeover of South Vietnam by the Communists. If this remains the ultimate prospect of our sacrifices in Vietnam, no American in good conscience would want to support anything more than an immediate unilateral withdrawal of American troops before another drop of American blood is needlessly spilled."[38] With that speech, Laird was allying himself with the moderate-to-left wing of his party.

A month later columnists Evans and Novak trumpeted "a dramatic change of attitude on the war in Vietnam" that was swirling around Laird who was "moving toward an end-the-war stance" because Johnson refused to abandon his Manila declaration that promised a pullout of U.S. forces six months after Hanoi "withdraws" and military activity "subsides" in the South. Such a strategy was something Laird believed would lead to an eventual Communist takeover.[39]

By September 1967 Laird was ready for a major move on the issue of Vietnam. He chose to do it in an address to the American Mining Convention in Denver on September 11. In a lengthy discourse, Laird made a point-by-point assessment of how he had come to the unusual decision as a conservative Republican in the middle of an undeclared war to withdraw support from the White House for its Vietnam policy. One statement summed up the anguish that led to Laird's break: "If the choice is between turning South Vietnam over to the Communists in 1969 or right now in 1967, we might as well do it now and prevent further American casualties." Political commentators called Laird's remarks the beginning of a "strategic retreat from [the Republican Party's] long bipartisan approach to the war in Vietnam." The *Christian Science Monitor*'s Joseph C. Harsch opined that Laird's positioning was a harbinger of Republican tactics for the 1968 presidential election. Laird had "an unusual sensitiveness to the winds of political change.... [W]hen Mr. Laird puts his GOP helm up or down, even by a fraction of a notch, it is because he senses an important change in the LBJ course." The *Denver Post* called it a simple matter of trying to transform the GOP into the "party of peace" as the 1968 election approached.[40]

But, it was more than just a political strategy. Laird, the strident anti-Communist, had mellowed with six years of U.S. involvement in Vietnam. Johnson had "Americanized" a war that never should have been America's burden. The United States had eased in to help an ally and had all but completely pushed that ally aside, assuming full responsibility for the outcome. It was time for Laird to stand up and be counted, no matter how unpopular the stand might be in his party. To his constituents, he offered some thoughts about the necessity of visionary leaders standing up and being counted when wisdom mandated it, no matter the political consequences:

> In Washington, we have a constant tug of war between the long term and the short term. The old aphorism, "A politician thinks only of the next election; a statesman thinks of the next generation," expresses this conflict. The short term is easy, quick, simple, popular and usually wrong in the larger sense. The longer term requires salesmanship, planning and understanding and some sacrifice. Pressure always pushes us toward the short term, while reason draws us toward the long term.[41]

Mel Laird had seen into the future of Vietnam. If Lyndon Johnson pursued his Manila policy, it was time to get out sooner rather than later.

⁂

One Republican who didn't like Laird's disaffection with Johnson's Vietnam policies was Senate Minority Leader Dirksen. He was a man of iron will and old values who was absolutely committed to supporting the president in time of war. His old world view was bound to clash with the new world view of the House leadership, and it did in early December at a showdown with Laird and Ford in Dirksen's office. The patrician Senator began dictating to his House juniors. He demanded that a strong resolution on Vietnam, putting the party wholly behind Johnson's conduct of the war, must be proposed and passed at the December 11 meeting of the Republican Coordinating Committee. Ford and Laird didn't mince words in their strong opposition. The presidential election was less than a year away, Ford argued, and the Republican Party should be developing its own position on Vietnam instead of blindly following Johnson. Laird echoed Ford's position, but added that Johnson's conduct of the war was wrong for the reasons he had consistently and publicly stated. If Dirksen dared propose such a resolution, the Republican Coordinating Committee would split, because Ford and Laird would not sign off on it.[42] Dirksen finally surrendered.

At the same time, the antiwar movement of the younger generation was picking up steam, and it was not wholeheartedly welcomed by Laird. He may have shared their frustration but didn't always admire their style. For example, Laird was disgusted with the American flag burning that was beginning to occur at demonstrations. So, in a 385 to 15 vote, Laird sided with the majority to pass a bill in June 1967 that made it a federal crime to desecrate the American flag. Some Constitutionalists argued that it violated the free speech guarantee. "My own very deep feeling is that our Constitution's freedom of speech provisions were never intended to allow Americans to burn, trample, and insult our flag," Laird countered.[43]

The Pentagon had also become a target as the peace movement became more radical. On October 21, 1967, some fifty thousand antiwar activists, most of them university students, gathered at the Lincoln Memorial for a series of antiwar speeches. About thirty-five thousand of them marched across the Arlington bridge to gather in a Pentagon parking lot. Facing them were hundreds of army troops and federal marshals, determined that they should not enter the building. Several thousand made attempts to breach the human barricade, but were pushed back by tear gas and clubs. Nearly seven hundred were arrested, the most up until that time during an antiwar protest. The confrontation at the five-sided citadel of war, as the activists saw it, energized the movement.

Laird's own transformation into a kind of "closet dove" was evolving at the same time. Another sign of that was a January 1968 statement in which he said that it would be better to negotiate with the Viet Cong, who at least generally lived in South Vietnam, than to talk to Hanoi. Laird had quietly postulated since 1966 that it might be better to give the Viet Cong's political arm, the National Liberation Front, a place in an elected coalition government of South Vietnam than to accept Johnson's 1966 Manila solution, which Laird felt would hand the country over lock, stock, and barrel to the Communists. He hit the issue hard in early 1968, and it was a significant departure for a Republican leader. News reports said that in becoming the first member of his party's congressional leadership to suggest a coalition South Vietnamese government, Laird was "breaking ranks" with other members of the Republican leadership, most notably Ford.[44] As chairman of the House Republican Conference, Laird was tacking his party's ship to get control of the war debate.

The North Vietnamese had an agenda of their own for the 1968 election, and thus the machinations of the war were inseparably connected with the political scene in Washington. Since the spring of 1967, Hanoi had been putting together a plan for a massive offensive it called General Offensive, General Uprising. The "uprising" was what Hanoi expected would happen as the South Vietnamese welcomed their brothers from the north and threw off the shackles of American occupation. It would eventually be known to history as the Tet offensive, for the Vietnamese new year's holiday on which it began, January 30, 1968. Over the course of a few weeks, 84,000 enemy troops attacked more than one hundred towns in South Vietnam, including Saigon, where sappers penetrated the grounds of the U.S. embassy. In the end the offensive failed and the uprising never materialized, but the cost in dead on both sides was high. An estimated 45,000 of the enemy—more than half of the invading force—were killed, while the South Vietnamese military had 2,300 fatalities and the United States suffered 1,100 dead. Though the allies had been taken by surprise, Tet eventually ended in a military victory for the United States and South Vietnam.[45]

Back home the public was shocked. Johnson's "credibility gap" yawned wide, having too often claimed that the United States was near victory. The unexpected, massive, and coordinated attack by the enemy inside South Vietnam seriously eroded American support for the war and the president. By March Johnson's approval rating had sunk to 24 percent, and he nearly lost the New Hampshire primary to an antiwar candidate, Senator Eugene McCarthy. Exhausted, demoralized, and out of steam, Johnson announced on March 31, 1968 that he would not seek reelection. With the incumbent president out of the election picture, the Republicans were looking at a whole new ball game, and master Republican strategist Melvin Laird was primed to play.

13

The Resurrection
of Richard Nixon

CONGRESSMAN JOHN CULVER, of Ohio, spotted Mel Laird at Chicago's O'Hare Airport in early 1968 and stopped for a chat about the upcoming presidential primary elections. Though the two men were of opposite parties, they were friends, and Culver wanted Laird's opinion.

"Well, Mel, who's it going to be for your party? Nixon?"

Laird grimaced. "Nixon? We would never give you Nixon!"

"What do you mean?" Culver asked.

"We'd lose our ace in the hole in the campaign—the fact that no one trusts Johnson," Laird explained. "The trouble is nobody trusts Nixon, either, so why would we give that advantage away?"

While Culver remembered the conversation vividly, Laird did not—though it rang true to his sentiment at the time.[1] Lyndon Johnson had not yet dropped out of the race at that point, and Nixon had the lingering odor of damaged goods. He had lost one presidential election already, in 1960, and he had been warned by his friends in the Chowder and Marching Club not to run for governor of California in 1962—a race he lost by a humiliating three hundred thousand votes. In what was supposed to be his swan song, Nixon told reporters, "As I leave you, I want you to know—just think how much you're going to be missing. You won't have Nixon to kick around anymore, because, gentlemen, this is my last press conference."

A few days later, Nixon wrote in a letter to Laird, "As I leave the political arena, I am greatly heartened by the fact that you will be in there fighting for our cause."[2] Nixon moved as far as he could from California and began practicing law in New York City. In 1964, while some cronies urged him to run for president again, he wisely declined. Instead he gamely campaigned for Republican nominee Barry Goldwater, a man whose political positions were sometimes at serious variance with Nixon's own. In 1966 he picked a few congressional districts that looked like winners and campaigned (and raised money) for Republican candidates. In the process he pocketed a string of gold-plated IOUs.

The political grave opened to permit a Nixon resurrection during an LBJ press conference on, November 4, 1966, at which the president lost his temper. That morning on its front page, the *New York Times* had printed the full text of a seven-point Nixon criticism of Johnson's Manila communiqué on

Vietnam, which Nixon essentially described as an act of capitulation to the enemy. At a press conference that day, Johnson attacked Nixon by name, calling him a "chronic campaigner," a man who "never realized what was going on even when he had an official office," and so on. Nixon realized immediately that Johnson had handed him a great gift; he was suddenly in media demand again, this time as the victim, and he knew how to use it. "I was never one that could be arm-twisted by anyone and frightened even by the towering temper of Lyndon Johnson," Nixon said during a half-hour Sunday TV appearance paid for by the Republican Congressional Campaign Committee. "The speech was a success," Nixon later recalled. "[I]t renewed my credentials as a national spokesman and a fighting campaigner."[3]

And so it was that Nixon began quietly planning for his second presidential bid in 1968. He did it at first without the support of many political friends—including Laird who had to live up to a pledge he had made to support Michigan Governor George Romney. A popular Republican in a state ruled by Democrats, Romney had survived the anti-Goldwater drubbing in 1964. When Romney was reelected again by a half-million-vote margin in 1966, Laird began to see him as a presidential prospect for 1968. Nixon could be a long shot against Johnson and would not likely help the other Republicans on the ticket. Romney was a better pick for that kind of draw, and so Laird began to publicly speak well of him in 1967. Romney announced his candidacy for president, and Laird continued his warm support even after Romney's infamous September gaffe when he said U.S. officials in Saigon had "brainwashed" him into supporting the war. Romney had returned from a 1965 visit to Vietnam with glowing praise for the war effort. He then used the "brainwashing" as the reason for changing his mind and opposing the war in 1967 as a presidential candidate.

The comment caused the Republican Governors Association to cool their support of Romney. Laird called the governors to task for that at a closed door meeting of the Republican Coordinating Council in December of 1967. And when he emerged from the meeting, he groused to a reporter that the governors were letting their man go down the drain. Romney nevertheless forged on honorably toward the New Hampshire primary—until a fellow governor, Nelson Rockefeller, betrayed him publicly. A few days before the primary, Rockefeller, who had solemnly pledged his support for Romney, announced that he himself was available to be drafted as a candidate. After a poor primary showing, Romney withdrew.

Laird's plan had been to help elect a Republican majority in the House, with Gerald Ford as the new speaker. Laird was convinced that either Romney or Rockefeller had coattails that could ensure a Republican sweep, while Nixon did not.[4] With Romney out, Laird let it slip on national television that Nixon would probably be the party's candidate, but Rockefeller would be a better choice.[5] In private, however, it was a different story. Laird invited Rockefeller to lunch at the congressman's special hideaway dining room on Capitol Hill.

He advised Rockefeller not to mistake his publicly encouraging words. He was going to go for Nixon because Rockefeller did not have a reasonable chance to win the Republican nomination without entering primaries for which he was already too late to register, including Wisconsin. Laird would be committed to vote with the Wisconsin delegation after Nixon likely emerged as the state's primary victor. From that time on, Laird repeatedly advised Rockefeller that he should get out of Nixon's way.[6]

There may have been a hint of animus against Rockefeller. Laird still resented the fact that he had sat on his hands instead of working for Goldwater's election in 1964. While Laird knew Goldwater didn't have a chance at the White House that year, he was the party's nominee and, for Laird, that was enough to support him 100 percent. "We knew we were going to lose," Laird later recalled, "but at the same time there was no reason to take a powder. Rockefeller had broken faith with a lot of Republicans over that."

There was another strike against Rockefeller that was no less onerous to Laird. Not only did Rockefeller *not* support Goldwater's campaign, but he also punished a close friend of Laird's who did, Republican Congressman Steve Derounian of New York. In the first years both served in Congress, they were roommates in a Chevy Chase house while their families stayed in their home districts. Derounian counted Laird "my close friend in Washington, D.C., a true patriot, always on the square."

As to the offense, Derounian had backed Goldwater instead of lining up behind Rockefeller, the governor of his state. Derounian had toured the nation with Laird on the "Paul Revere Panels," taking on Johnson and touting Goldwater to whomever would listen. They had been quite the pair, the bombastic Laird introducing the Bulgarian-born immigrant Derounian as "the only man in the United States Congress born behind the Iron Curtain!"[7] Out of spite against Derounian, Rockefeller used his weight as the state's party leader to pit a primary candidate against him in his reelection bid to Congress that year. The candidate was William Casey, who didn't have a chance once Laird and Ford went to New York to personally campaign for Derounian. (Casey recovered neatly, later becoming securities and exchange commissioner in the Nixon administration and CIA director under Ronald Reagan.) Having been weakened by Rockefeller during the primary, Derounian lost the general election, and Laird never forgot Rockefeller's disloyalty.

In 1968 Laird avoided publicly endorsing any candidate until after his state primary on April 2. Rockefeller made it easier for him when, on March 21, the governor telegraphed Laird with the news that he would not run for president after all. Apparently there were no hard feelings. "I value your friendship and deeply appreciate your understanding," Rockefeller wrote in his telegram acceding to Laird's wishes.[8]

In the Wisconsin primary, a Republican selection committee could place anyone's name on the ballot, even undeclared candidates. The only thing that could prevent it was if the person asked not to be listed. As a matter of principle, Laird was opposed to any unannounced candidate being on the state ballot. California Governor Ronald Reagan fell in that category, even though he was unofficially angling to be considered. After a private meeting with Reagan in which Laird thought the governor had promised to sign an affidavit to remove himself from the Wisconsin primary ballot, Laird was miffed when Reagan's aides said he would do no such thing. Though he later wrote it off as a misunderstanding, Laird was not about to encourage Reagan's unofficial presidential bid.[9] The state went overwhelmingly for Nixon—80 percent, compared to Reagan's second-place standing at 10 percent—and from that moment on, the party loyalist Laird was a Nixon man all the way.

Rockefeller continued to be a source of frustration to Laird's hopes for party unity. Ten days after Rockefeller dropped out of the race, a worn-out Lyndon Johnson announced on March 31 that he would not seek reelection. That made antiwar candidate Senator Eugene McCarthy the Democratic frontrunner, with Senator Robert Kennedy and Vice President Hubert Humphrey as formidable competitors. Less than a week after that, the picture changed yet again, becoming darker. The Reverend Martin Luther King was assassinated on April 4, 1968, in Memphis. (Senator Kennedy also was assassinated two months later.) With others, Laird called for "national mourning" and a rededication to the principles of removing racial hatred through nonviolent methods.[10] But African-Americans erupted in America's cities with grief and riotous rage. Parts of Washington, D.C., were soon in flames.

As violence escalated, Rockefeller rose again, believing the country needed him, and announced his presidential candidacy a second time on April 30. The man Eisenhower privately called "on-again off-again on-again Finnegan" was true to form, frustrating Laird, who feared he would once again be a spoiler, wrecking Nixon's chances just as he had Goldwater's four years before. Faintly echoing his mentor Ike's private phrasing, Laird declared of Rockefeller in a TV interview: "I believe the off-again, on-again sort of campaign that he conducted has hurt him and made it impossible for him to secure the nomination in Miami."[11]

⚬

As the Republicans pushed toward their August nominating convention in Miami Beach, Laird eschewed his traditional role as chairman of the committee that would write the party platform. "I'm through with it," he groused when the laurel was proffered again.[12] "I've gotten all the bumps and bruises and nothing else." Letting someone else take a turn getting bloodied was his oft-stated reason for staying off the 1968 Platform Committee. But one Laird in the wings was worth two of any other person on center stage, and savvy Republicans such as Goldwater knew it. "I would like to know what is jumping around in your brilliant mind," Goldwater inquired in a private letter three months before the convention. "No matter who may be sitting in the front office, I know that you are going to be the chief composer of the Platform this year." Laird wrote back: "I have decided to step aside for an older man and sit this one out."[13] The job went to seventy-two-year-old Everett Dirksen. Laird was never one to go through the front door when a side door would do, and that door was the House Republican Conference. He got the conference staff a hotel suite in Miami and began ghostwriting the platform for Dirksen.

A month before the convention, Laird had published a new book, a sequel to his 1964 *Conservative Papers.* This one, called *The Republican Papers,* was edited by a more pragmatic Laird who intended to use it to make his party proactive rather than reactive. Among the twenty-eight essay contributors was a constellation of academic stars such as the University of Chicago's Milton Friedman, Harvard's Gottfried Haberler, and Washington University's Murray Weidenbaum—as well as other Ivy Leaguers. Daniel P. Moynihan, who had served in the Kennedy and Johnson administrations, added a liberal essay. He used Laird's book to reason with his fellow Democrats: "We liberals must inquire into the sources of our own failure, for surely we have not succeeded in bringing the nation along with us. It is not only useless and tasteless to get into a name-calling contest with our presumed opponents; it is also a sure way to avoid facing the possibility that we have some explaining to do about the sources of the present crisis."[14]

The five-hundred-page book was a hit. It was a particularly hot seller on American campuses where conservative students, starved for academic discourse, snapped it up. Radical students also bought it to differ with its authors point by point at forums, teach-ins, and demonstrations. Some colleges and universities made it required reading for political science courses, which also boosted sales. All proceeds were earmarked to pay salaries and boost the staff work of the House Republican Conference.

At the July 3 press conference at which *The Republican Papers* was released, Laird cautioned that it should not be regarded as a "platform document." Yet, several of the people who contributed to the book were members of the Platform Committee, and each committee member was provided an advance copy for "consideration" in their work. By the time Laird appeared as a witness before the Platform Committee on its first day of hearings, he had dropped all pretense. Holding up the book, he said, "These positive proposals, Mr. Chairman, *must* be included in the 1968 Republican Platform document."[15]

Aside from funding the House Republican Conference and providing a template for the platform, *The Republican Papers* also enhanced Laird's image, revealing a more centrist Republican than many had before realized him to be. But image is not political advancement, and there were a few people working closely with him at the time who wondered when Laird would finally make a move himself and run for president. As the book was being compiled, one of

its contributors, Dr. Paul McCracken, met once with Laird and had a memorable conversation. The distinguished economist tried to fill Laird's head with
a higher ambition. Later, after Nixon had been reelected in 1972 and Laird had
announced plans to leave public life, McCracken wrote to him. "I still hope to
walk into the ballot booth in some quadrennial year and find your name at the
top of the list."[16] Thirty years later McCracken summoned up a memory of the
event: "I recall thinking, 'There's a guy who could walk into the Oval Office and
start conducting business.' Of course, I still think so. On the other hand, I don't
doubt that he's had more fun in life not doing it."[17]

During the week of the Republican convention in Miami, 173 more men were
killed in Vietnam. Nearly 20,000 Americans had died in the war, and another
150,000 were wounded. Every twenty minutes, the United States was spending
a million dollars on the war.[18] It was naturally the most important item on the
Platform Committee's foreign policy agenda, and potentially the most divisive.
Laird's appearance on the first day of platform hearings, July 29, a week before
the official convention began, was much anticipated. He was expected to set
the tone. Regarding Vietnam, he told the assembled 106-member Resolutions
Committee in the La Ronde Room of the Fontainebleau Hotel that the platform should first establish that it was Democrats who had gotten the United
States into the war.[19] Mindful of the contentious 1964 platform debate that
had hobbled their candidate coming out of the starting gate, all wings of the
Republican Party compromised on the Vietnam plank, seasoning the platform
with words of war-time resolve and future peace. Once the full week of platform hearings was complete, and the convention begun, all disagreements on
every platform issue had been settled. In a rare show of Republican unity, there
was no convention debate over the platform, and not a single dissenting vote
was recorded when the 11,500-word document was accepted by the delegates.

As to the contest for the nomination itself, Nixon had won it before the
convention began. Both Laird and Nixon were pleased that it was Laird's home
state of Wisconsin that finally put him over the top shortly before 2 A.M. on
August 8. Laird was glad to be one of the thirty Wisconsin delegates who voted
for Nixon, but he was not happy about the nationally televised practical joke
played on him just before the Wisconsin vote was announced.[20] A friend, Representative Glenn R. Davis, standing on a chair, had hollered for silence at the
convention and then solemnly read a supposed newly arrived telegram from
Laird. "Please do your best to nominate Governor Rockefeller," the false wire
said. The convention erupted in knowing laughter at Laird's expense, being
familiar with his strenuous efforts to persuade Nixon to pick Rockefeller as his
vice presidential nominee.[21]

With his usual prescience, Laird had concentrated months before the convention on who would be the vice presidential pick. Since Laird believed Nixon would be the presidential nominee, and the platform would be moderate in Laird's mold, it made sense that he would campaign for a strong vice presidential candidate who would enlarge the party's coattails to include Republican House and Senate candidates. Besides Ford, who had told Laird he didn't want to be Nixon's vice president, Laird had two favorites for the post. The first was John Gardner, a brilliant Republican scholar who had served in the Johnson Cabinet. Nixon took Laird's suggestion and asked Gardner to visit with him in New York City to sound him out, but Gardner told Nixon he was not interested.

Laird's second preference was Rockefeller. No one left could give the national ticket as many votes in areas where Nixon was weak.[22] But Nixon had his own theory about running mates; Laird believed Nixon was looking for a yes-man. So it was that Nixon selected the man his counselors were least enthusiastic about, the man who was the least objectionable candidate among those discussed—and was acceptable to the Southerners who had stuck with Nixon when Reagan tried to raid his convention delegates.[23]

Spiro Theodore "Ted" Agnew, the governor of Maryland, was considered a progressive Republican. Nixon had had several meetings with him and was particularly impressed with the way Agnew had handled the Baltimore riots after the Martin Luther King assassination. Agnew had called a conference of about one hundred black leaders. When they arrived, imagining they would work together to develop a program to quell the discontent, Agnew lashed out at them and blamed them for the riots—accusing them of "circuit-riding, Hanoi-visiting, . . . caterwauling, riot-inciting, burn-America-down type of leadership." Nixon liked that kind of bravado.[24] When Nixon announced Agnew as his running mate, the Republican Party, including Laird, was in a state of shock, which quickly turned to resistance. But Laird forcefully argued that they should vote for Nixon's choice on grounds of party unity, which they did. However, Laird could not bring himself to personally vote for the lackluster Agnew, so he left his convention seat to an alternate-at-large, who voted for Romney.[25] The revolt was short-lived, and Agnew was nominated.

Laird was uncomfortable with Agnew as a man and would soon understand what his instincts were telling him. None of the Republicans at the convention, including Nixon, had any idea that they had nominated a governor and former county executive who was secretly taking 5 percent in kickbacks on county and state construction projects—thousands of dollars in cash bribes in little white envelopes, first delivered to Agnew in Maryland and then later to the White House when he was vice president.[26]

⌇

Among the many Republicans instinctively upset at the choice of the relatively unknown Agnew was a young woman with Coke-bottle glasses named Hillary

Rodham, who had gone to the convention to work for Rockefeller while she was an intern on Laird's payroll. She had come from the affluent conservative suburb of Park Ridge near Chicago's O'Hare Airport, and throughout her high school years her politics had been her father's—bedrock Republican. In 1964 she was a sash-wearing "Goldwater Girl," like many in her neighborhood.[27] Hillary's horizons began to expand when she went to Wellesley College in 1965. She established herself quickly and became president of the Young Republicans Club during her freshman year. Several months into that year she wrote a confessional letter to her Methodist minister back home saying she found herself "leaning left." Her political metamorphosis was hastened by the assassination of Dr. King, just as she was preparing to intern for Laird and the House Republican Conference.

Each summer, the Wellesley College Internship Program sent ten women to Washington as interns. Rodham's political science professor, Dr. Alan Schechter, was responsible for finding the interns a good assignment. He knew she was by then only a nominal Republican but thought one of the best places for independent-minded Hillary was with the quasi-academic atmosphere of Laird's Republican Conference.[28] Laird's first memory of the spunky Hillary was that he joked with her about the fact that he had been one of the first men to attend Wellesley (during World War II), and she laughed heartily. Then she moved the talk to the Vietnam War and her opposition to it. He found her to be unusually outspoken for a college junior. When it came time for Laird to put together a House floor speech that was critical of Johnson's fight-now, pay-later conduct of the war, he asked Hillary to help out.

Of her work for Laird, Rodham-Clinton recalled, "I was very happy because they treated us interns well. Mr. Laird gave us all different research assignments to work on, took us to various locations like field trips, and introduced us to a lot of well-known Republicans."[29] One picture she prized was taken of her with Laird and Ford. She sent it to her father and said it made him "very happy. He had it hanging in his bedroom when he died."[30] Her strongest memory of Laird that summer came from an intern group discussion on Vietnam, at which she spoke up. They debated a little, with Laird politely challenging some of her more naive observations. But he treated her as an equal, she remembered. "He was without pretense. He was down to earth. He was a very powerful member of the Congress who was willing to engage in a back-and-forth with a kid who was only moderately well informed, I'm sure he thought. But at least he took me seriously."[31]

Rodham-Clinton was not chosen to go to the convention with the Republican Conference, but she was invited by Rockefeller's staff. Her disappointment that Nixon, not Rockefeller, was nominated, drove her further from the party of her father. Later, when she became more radically antiwar on her return to Wellesley, she had no hesitance in contacting Laird, the defense secretary. At one point, she told a student protestor from Biafra that she knew Laird and thought he would be glad to hear the student's concerns about that African civil war. A meeting was set up without any difficulty.

When she officially switched parties and became an ardent Democrat, she said Laird would still talk with her. "I would see him from time to time; he always remembered me." Some people say they are bipartisan, she added, but Laird has often been truly so.[32] Laird's Pentagon military assistant, General Robert Pursley, suggested a reason for that bipartisanship. "One of the things that sets Mel Laird apart from anybody I've ever known is his ability to keep contact with people in his expanding universe of relationships. He could have easily dropped Hillary Rodham, a mere intern, out of that universe and forgotten her. But he maintains all those relationships and the universe just keeps on expanding. And nobody *ever* drops out that I can tell."[33] Republicans were wont to rib Laird when they learned that he was partly responsible for the political ascent of Hillary Rodham. For himself, Laird joked that his more moderate Republican influence was still working with her until she got a boyfriend at Yale named Bill Clinton.

The Democratic National Convention had been scheduled in Chicago by President Johnson before he had decided not to run for reelection. The city that had hosted conventions nominating Abraham Lincoln, Franklin D. Roosevelt, and Dwight Eisenhower, hadn't hosted a Democratic convention in twelve years, and Democratic Mayor Richard Daley wanted one badly. LBJ promised his political crony that he would have it. The date at the end of August was set by Johnson to coincide with his sixtieth birthday on August 27. Humphrey, by then the front-runner, wanted to convene earlier in Miami, but Johnson wouldn't budge on the place or the date, and Humphrey dared not cross him.

Various antiwar organizations called for one hundred thousand demonstrators to descend on the city, and Mayor Daley felt a need to brace for the onslaught of the unknown. He did it as if he were expecting an invasion from an armed foreign military. Daley deployed 11,900 Chicago police on exhausting twelve-hour shifts. Some 7,500 Illinois national guardsmen were called out, and another 7,500 U.S. Army regulars were bivouacked nearby. More than one thousand FBI and Secret Service agents supplemented the security.

Daley denied the protestors permits to march, corralled them in city parks, and imposed a curfew. Night after night, with increasing force, the police tried to keep the protestors under control using battle tactics, billy clubs, and so much tear gas that it got into the air conditioning systems of nearby buildings and caused Hubert Humphrey to weep in his twenty-fifth-floor Hilton suite. Police, feeling taunted and maligned, clubbed indiscriminately as they waded into crowds with near-reckless abandon. Reporters, photographers, clergymen, women, children, and delegates were bludgeoned—all on national television.

The picture inside the convention center was not pretty either. Laird, the inveterate political prognosticator, had predicted ten days before the convention began, "You are going to see one of the bitterest Democratic Conventions in the history of politics."[34] Over Humphrey's objections, the president forced adoption of a Vietnam War plank that took a harder line than the Republican plank and was a slap at the large Democratic antiwar forces led by Senator Eugene McCarthy. In an unprecedented move for Democratic conventions, a minority plank was presented by McCarthy—partnered with South Dakota Senator George McGovern and Massachusetts Senator Edward Kennedy—and openly debated. Their peace plank barely lost in the voting.

The worst night was Wednesday, August 28, which should have been Humphrey's evening of triumph. Television images of the police beatings flooded the nation shortly before Senator Abraham Ribicoff of Connecticut rose to nominate his "peace" candidate, McGovern. At one point, seeing some of the bloody scenes on TV monitors, Ribicoff turned to Mayor Daley and said: "With George McGovern, we wouldn't have Gestapo tactics on the streets of Chicago." Daley erupted, and the convention was in pandemonium as the mayor shouted obscenities that the TV audience couldn't hear, although they could read his lips. The convention never fully settled down again. After Humphrey won the first ballot, the traditional call from the dais was made to make it unanimous. Then Democratic convention managers declared it to be unanimous even as hundreds of delegates could be heard by the press and TV viewers shouting, "No!"

Laird could not enjoy the specter of the opposing party in chaos. "The events in Chicago . . . shocked and grieved all Americans," he wrote. "No American is proud of what has happened in our country in recent months and years. Three national leaders have been assassinated and hundreds of citizens have been innocent victims of unjustified violence in our streets. Let us all resolve that such a climate shall not endure in the land of the free."[35]

Laird was not surprised when he got an unhappy letter after the convention from one of its attendees, his second cousin Tom Graham. Graham, thirty-four, was a devoted Democrat, but he had come away from Chicago shaken to the core. "I was so horrified," he recalled. "I was a McCarthy-ite and I was so disgusted at the way McCarthy was treated at the convention. It was not so much the violence as the anti-Democratic manner in which the Johnson forces refused to give McCarthy a decent hearing on the floor." He asked for a job in the Nixon campaign, and Laird found him one. Graham, after working for Laird in the Pentagon, later served as an arms control official and on several treaty delegations, from the Carter through Clinton administrations. Graham said that, after the 1968 Chicago disappointment, he didn't vote for a Democrat again, until 1992 for Bill Clinton, who subsequently appointed him acting chief of the Arms Control and Disarmament Agency.[36]

Hobbled as he was coming out of the convention, Humphrey still had a good chance if he declared independence from the president's policy on Vietnam. Humphrey's first opportunity arose in Philadelphia on September 9, 1968. In a question-and-answer session with college students, Humphrey dropped a headline-making statement: "I would think, negotiations or no negotiations, we could start to remove some of the American forces [from Vietnam] in early 1969 or late 1968."

Laird, always a gatherer of behind-the-scenes information, had learned that this was the opening salvo of an even more definitive Humphrey speech. The tip came from a friend inside the Defense Department who was thrilled that one of the two candidates seemed to favor withdrawals. The source, oblivious to the political implications of the leak, shared the good news with Laird, who took two weeks to figure out just what to do with the morsel.

Meanwhile, President Johnson was meeting with congressional leaders when he first read his vice president's prediction off the news ticker. His famous temper boiled over, and to the congressional leaders who happened to be present, Johnson sarcastically stated that he fully intended to be commander in chief until January 20. The next day, September 10, Johnson went out of his way during a speech at an American Legion convention in New Orleans to say: "We yearn for the day when our men can come home, but no man can predict when that day will come." It silenced Humphrey for several critical campaign weeks. "If he would have stuck to his guns after Philadelphia talking about a withdrawal of troops in Vietnam instead of an escalation, Humphrey would have won that election," Laird said.[37]

As Humphrey was ramping up his campaign, Laird was personally advising Nixon on his own campaign. In the fall, Republican wise men felt Nixon needed some veteran campaigners to counsel him and boost his spirits. Laird volunteered, as did Bryce Harlow. The tag-team plan was to alternate weeks with Nixon on the campaign plane. (Both felt that too much time spent on airplanes with the candidate would make them lose touch with what was going on in Middle America.)

Laird continued to worry that Humphrey would wise up and veer away from Johnson to win the election, so he needed to find a way to check any Humphrey movement in that direction. He was pulling plane duty on September 24 when, in Bismarck, North Dakota, he had a brainstorm that he shared with Nixon. He was going to switch to the press plane for the next leg of the trip to Boise, Idaho, and give the reporters an earful about LBJ's "secret plan" to begin withdrawing troops from Vietnam.

As a member of the Defense Appropriations Subcommittee, Laird knew Congress had been briefed on such a contingency plan for the eventuality of a withdrawal. It was a secret timetable Laird had seen for orderly withdrawal should a peace agreement be signed—with an activation date that Johnson's people called "T-Day" for "termination" of the hostilities. But Laird, the wily politico, was going to gloss over the part about a peace treaty being a prerequisite. Nixon warmed to the idea immediately. "Mel, get back on the press plane and go," he ordered, smiling with new cheer in the middle of an exhausting campaign.

Laird did his job adroitly on the press plane from Bismarck to Boise, and the media, weary of Nixon's stock speeches, swallowed it whole. In fact, by the time the plane touched down in Boise, the headlines had already been made. Laird said Humphrey would announce a planned cutback of up to ninety thousand ground troops in the first six months of 1969. He indicated his belief that Humphrey would be announcing such a program the next week. One stop later, in Seattle, Laird held a press conference to repeat his predictions, and now the news was rebounding through the Johnson administration. Their response couldn't have been better had Laird scripted it himself.[38]

"I've never heard of it," said the White House press secretary.

"I know of no plan which has been developed within the Department of Defense nor submitted to the Department of Defense which would reduce the troop ceiling in South Vietnam beneath the previously announced figure of 549,500," said the Pentagon spokesman.[39]

Laird relished the reports he heard that privately Johnson had told Humphrey if he wanted the support of the current president, he had better shut up about any planned withdrawals from Vietnam. Johnson called his Defense Secretary Clark Clifford and told him to go on record saying there was no withdrawal plan. Reluctantly, Clifford, who wanted to begin a withdrawal as badly as Humphrey did, issued a statement the next day saying that he was still "building toward" a troop level of 549,500 and was about 15,000 men short of that. "We have no intention of lowering that level, either by next June or at any time in the foreseeable future," he said.[40]

Clifford later confided to Laird that Johnson was still fuming and then had "bullwhipped Clifford into going on TV and making an even stronger statement," which Clifford did on Meet the Press the following Sunday, September 29: "I believe it is important that the American people not be misinformed about our plans. The Defense Department has no plans at this time for the return of any troops. The level of combat is such that we are building up our troops, not cutting them down."[41]

Few politicians could work the smoke-and-mirror magic of which Laird was capable. Now the Republican strategist had the Democrats where he wanted them—denying that they had any plans for bringing American soldiers home from the fetid jungles of Vietnam. "I wanted them to deny it, and they did deny it. If Humphrey would have gone along with some withdrawal plan, he would have been elected president of the United States," Laird said.

Ironically, too, the shrewd Laird was able to pull this off without Nixon ever having to define his own plans for ending the war.

One of the greatest myths of the presidential campaign of 1968 is that candidate Nixon once said, "I have a secret plan to end the war." He made no such statement. The roots of the false quote trace to a remark Nixon made in Nashua, New Hampshire, while campaigning on March 5: "I pledge to you the new leadership [speaking of himself] will end the war and win the peace in the Pacific." Reporters pestered him with questions about how he would do that. When he refused to elaborate, journalists began talking about his "secret plan." The *New York Times* subheadline for the March 11 issue said: "Nixon Withholds His Peace Ideas; Says to Tell Details of Plan Would Sap His Bargaining Strength if He's Elected."[42]

Nixon began to think the myth of his "secret plan" wasn't a bad one. His strategy was to make no reference to such a plan, nor to correct reports that alluded to it. When he was pressed on October 7 for more details, he pointed out that Eisenhower "did not indicate exactly . . . how he would end the [Korean] war," before the election, but successfully negotiated a peace after he was president, which his predecessor, Harry Truman, hadn't been able to accomplish. Nixon left the journalists with the assumption that he had a winning formula in mind. "I always knew he didn't have a plan. There was no plan," Laird recalled. On the day Nixon nominated Laird for secretary of defense, Laird pointedly asked Nixon if he had a plan to share, but Nixon did not. He asked Laird to come up with one. "So it turned out that *I was the secret plan!*" Laird laughed. And he had a good idea of what he wanted to do, based on the Vietnam plank he coauthored for the Republican platform—to "de-Americanize" the war as quickly as possible and bring the troops home.[43]

Even if Nixon did not have a secret plan to end the war, some Johnson administration officials became convinced that Nixon had a secret plan to stymie the peace talks before the election. Failure of those talks would not have helped Humphrey. During the fall campaign, the on-again, off-again Paris peace talks provided endless fodder for the Washington gossip mill, speculating whether either or both candidates, and even the North and South Vietnamese governments, were manipulating the talks to influence the election. One persistent rumor circulated around Anna Chennault and the possibility that she had persuaded South Vietnamese President Nguyen Van Thieu to boycott the talks until Nixon was president. The Chinese-born woman was the widow of an American general, Claire Chennault, who commanded the Flying Tigers in China and Burma during World War II.

A friend and fund-raiser for Nixon, Mrs. Chennault also maintained friendships in South Vietnam and was a source of inside information for Nixon regarding the Paris talks. Whether she persuaded Thieu to be stubborn about the talks—and stubborn he was as the 1968 election neared—remains a mystery. Clifford's memoir, citing secret intelligence reports, alleges that Chennault did conspire with her friend South Vietnamese Ambassador to the United States

Bui Diem to funnel information to Nixon. The conduit allegedly was Nixon's law partner and his future attorney general, John Mitchell. Clifford always suspected that the channel also worked in reverse, with Nixon using the connection to encourage Thieu to drag his feet in the Paris peace talks lest an agreement be reached before the election and be credited to the Democrats.[44]

Close to Nixon on the campaign trail, Laird saw no evidence of such finagling and thought Chennault just liked to cultivate the illusion of intrigue around her. "Mrs. Chennault was always anxious to talk to somebody," Laird said, "and Nixon always put her off on Mitchell." Those two may have had some veiled conversations, "but I'm sure the president was not involved," Laird said. "Anna was always full of it." Had Laird suspected any such shenanigans, he would have objected loudly. He never thought Thieu needed Chennault or anyone else to tell him that if he slowed down the peace talks, it would help Nixon, who in turn might be the better presidential choice as far as Vietnam was concerned.

During a visit to Saigon as secretary of defense, Laird specifically pressed President Thieu about the rumors and received an emphatic denial. Ruefully, Thieu added in retrospect that he probably would have been better off had Nixon lost to Humphrey that year. At least the Democrats had always given him what he asked for, which Nixon would not.

A turning point for Hubert Humphrey's electoral fortunes came with his nationally televised speech from Salt Lake City on September 30. That morning, he had met with Utah Democrats and said, "If the elections were held today, we wouldn't have a prayer. You know it and I know it." It was time for him to stand on his own, to step out from the drag of LBJ's Vietnam policy. When he spoke on TV that day, no vice presidential seal was evident, and he was introduced not as vice president but as the Democratic Party's candidate for president. He then offered a three-point Vietnam plan that included a unilateral bombing halt as a way to see if the North Vietnamese would seriously negotiate. It was only slightly different from Johnson administration policy, but he made it sound like a major departure.[45]

Humphrey had found his footing, and Laird was alarmed that if he continued on that course, Nixon might lose. Partly to stir the Johnson pot, hoping LBJ would slap Humphrey down again, Laird called the White House at 9 P.M. that Monday night and spoke with congressional liaison Harold Barefoot Sanders. "He asked if the Humphrey speech represented the new administration policy on Vietnam," Sanders reported in a memo to President Johnson. "I told Mel I was not advised about this—I was just not going to say one way or another."[46]

The most important point for Humphrey, however, was a gift Johnson handed him close to election eve—an apparent breakthrough in the peace talks. On October 31, a scant six days before the election, Johnson announced that he was halting the bombing of North Vietnam as a boost to the Paris peace talks. The expected bump in the polls for Humphrey was more muted when Saigon made it clear that they would not be a party to the talks. Besides Saigon's quick repudiation of the peace talks, there was a suspicion among many voters that Johnson had cynically produced the rabbit out of the hat just to thwart Nixon's election. Laird was one of those doubters. In a memorandum to Johnson from the Pentagon, defense official Paul Nitze reported that Laird supported LBJ's peace initiative. "Hoped things would work out," the cable read. But Laird was "concerned by the time. Said people on the street were upset: attributed this to political considerations." Nitze recounted that he had responded that "the timing was governed by actions of the other side [North Vietnam]. They may have made concessions when they did [because] of the election."[47]

Laird might rightly suspect Johnson's electoral eve political motivations, but even he could not predict what a curse Johnson's bombing halt would prove to Laird personally and to Nixon. It became an albatross that LBJ hung around Nixon's neck. Once halted, the bombing would prove to be a political nightmare to resume. For the next four years Nixon and Laird would have to live with what came to be called the "understandings" with North Vietnam over the bombing. In reality there was misunderstanding and backpedaling instead. Johnson agreed to stop bombing North Vietnam if the North would stop shelling South Vietnamese cities and would not increase their movement of weapons and men through the demilitarized zone. The United States also said it would retain the right to fly armed reconnaissance missions over the north. But nothing was put into writing. Hanoi violated the unwritten pact repeatedly and began to see the U.S. reconnaissance flights as thinly disguised bombing missions.

While the agreement was not put on paper, it was cast in stone in American public perception, and resumption of the bombing became a political impossibility. That was inevitable for a deal that was cut for political reasons. While Laird, as a congressman, supported the bombing halt, he later said that he never believed it had any practical benefit for the Paris talks, as Johnson claimed it would.

For four years Nixon would hold back from resumption of wholesale bombing in the North. Instead, Laird would order isolated strikes, retaliation for attacks on the reconnaissance planes, and occasional diversionary attacks over the North, which he referred to as "protective reaction." "I had to be creative," he said. Not until late 1972 was Nixon able to set aside the "understandings" completely and launch an all out air war over the North that would bring Hanoi back to the bargaining table and bring an end to the U.S. combat role in the war.

Nixon, a two-time electoral loser, won the presidency in 1968 with less than half a million votes and a total of 43.3 percent. His once-strong lead had been systematically whittled down by Humphrey's Salt Lake City speech, the bombing halt, and the strength of third-party candidate, former Alabama Governor George Wallace. Both Nixon and Humphrey saw Wallace as a spoiler for each of them. While debate over what would have happened if Wallace had not been in the race has received little historical attention, another "what if" has garnered greater comment: If Hubert Humphrey had won, could he have gotten America out of Vietnam sooner than the four years it took the Nixon administration? Donald Rumsfeld, who considered Laird a mentor, was outraged by the notion that Humphrey might have been the better peace candidate. "That kind of comment is off the wall; it's made by someone who has both feet firmly planted in midair," he fulminated more than three decades after the Nixon election. "It's a hell of a lot easier to opine on what one would do if they're not there doing it. Now, Hubert Humphrey was a good friend of mine. But I never heard anything out of his mouth that suggested he had a magic formula that would have done better than Mel and Nixon did."[48]

Congressman Laird had his own reelection race to run in 1968, but, as in past contests, his opponent—that year a Wisconsin farmer—never had a chance. Laird was reelected with 64 percent of the vote. He served only sixteen days of that ninth term because his old friend Richard Nixon succeeded in doing what Democrats had been unable to do for sixteen years: remove Melvin Robert Laird from his beloved Wisconsin Seventh District.

14

Cabinet Making

❧

RICHARD NIXON STAGED the first ever en masse rollout of a new Cabinet on coast-to-coast television December 11, 1968; he was the only speaker and he used no notes. Acting as master of ceremonies, he stood on a raised platform behind a simple podium, backed by bright blue curtains in the ornate Palladian Room of Washington's Shoreham Hotel. Facing him, seated in white chairs on a red carpet—for a red-white-and-blue motif—were the twelve Cabinet designees and their wives. As he named each of them, the camera panned to their faces.[1] Though Melvin Laird was well known in Washington and Wisconsin, the only one of the twelve who had national name recognition was George Romney, soon to be Secretary of Housing and Urban Development.

Laird was named third, after Secretary of State William Rogers and Treasury Secretary David Kennedy. Nixon maintained that he had chosen a Cabinet not of specialists but of generalists, and each man had the ability and experience to fill more than one position in his Cabinet. As an example he pointed to Laird—"the Secretary of Defense could be the Secretary of H.E.W.; he's an expert in that field." It was an inside joke; few knew Laird had been offered that post and rejected it.

As the first defense secretary recruited from Capitol Hill, Laird was seen as a powerful antidote to the McNamara years when the Pentagon was run on a corporate model. Laird's Pentagon would be run on a political model. The day of the announcement, the *Washington Post* editorialized that the national security triumvirate (Laird, Rogers, and National Security Advisor Henry Kissinger) were each "able, vigorous, dedicated moderate men." Regarding Laird specifically, the editorial concluded: "Smart is the word one hears most often about Mr. Laird.... [W]hat he lacks almost completely in the way of administrative experience, which is thought to be vital at the Pentagon, may be more than offset by his political skill, a natural touch for the levers of power, an eye for detail."[2] The newspapers were quick to point out that Laird had a Purple Heart and still carried the shrapnel from a Japanese kamikaze attack. As McNamara's biggest adversary in Congress, Laird could signal a potent turnaround on Vietnam policy. Above all, it would be a mistake to underestimate Laird. A journalist who knew him well said: "He looks as bland as Wisconsin cheese, but he is as sharp as Vermont cheddar."[3]

Laird had been forced into assuming the post at the worst possible time and had no illusions about just how tough the job would be. The first secretary of defense, James Forrestal, tormented by critics and weighed down after only two years on the job, had leaped to his death from a tower room in Bethesda Naval Hospital within months of resigning. Knowing the dangerous shoals ahead, Laird sought counsel from the man he respected most.

Since mid-May 1968 Dwight Eisenhower had been a full-time resident of Ward Eight of Walter Reed Army Hospital in Washington, the victim of seven heart attacks. He stayed in the "presidential suite" with an adjoining room for his wife, Mamie. Ike held on against the odds, celebrating Nixon's victory in November. (He lived another three and a half months; it would be Secretary of Defense Laird who would oversee his request for a low-key military funeral including, at Ike's insistence, the standard-issue $80 GI steel coffin.[4])

Though he was frail, Eisenhower agreed to see Laird on Friday, December 13, to offer congratulations and counsel. Laird cheerily greeted his mentor, but he had to hide his alarm at the sight of the old general fading away. Emaciated, pale, and nearly immobilized by hook-ups to an array of hospital equipment, Eisenhower managed to rouse for opening pleasantries, even faintly flashing a shadow of his famous grin. Laird was not expecting much, and he certainly hadn't anticipated so quickly angering Ike that the patient would rally for an hour-long advisory session.

"Mel, have you been down to see President Johnson?" Eisenhower asked within the first few minutes.

"No, Mr. President," Laird responded. "I haven't been down there. You know, Dick just nominated me the other night." Eisenhower nearly came out of the bed, wires and all.

" 'Dick?' " he said with disgust. "Mel, what do you mean by calling him 'Dick?' He's 'Mr. President' to me, and he's certainly 'Mr. President' to you! I never want to hear you referring to him as 'Dick' again."

Laird was speechless. "I took the hit, and it was a good one. I was impressed by his feeling of respect for the office of the presidency, that he didn't want me referring to our old friend by his first name even before his inauguration." While Laird was regaining his composure, the newly animated Eisenhower picked up his bedside Signal Corps phone and asked for the Oval Office. "Mr. President," Eisenhower respectfully addressed Lyndon Johnson. "I've got Mel Laird here and he tells me he hasn't arranged to see you. I think you ought to have a visit with him. I was surprised that he hadn't called you."

Laird could not hear how LBJ responded, but Ike was soon lecturing Johnson: "I know you've got a history with Mel on those conference committees over appropriations. Sure, you've been on different sides of many issues, but he's taken on a big job and responsibility and I want him to come down there and talk to you—get briefed by you so he's fully up to date on what's going on with Vietnam and all."

A pregnant pause followed, as Eisenhower nodded on the phone in agreement. "Well, when do you want him down there?" An appointment was made.

It hadn't occurred to Laird to seek an audience with LBJ, but Eisenhower set him straight. "Mel, you should have gone to see the president first. You should be down there at the White House right now. He is the commander-in-chief of our forces now, and you're the designated secretary of defense, soon the second man in command. You should be getting a full briefing from President Johnson."

With that settled, Eisenhower offered his own counsel. "As you know, Mel, I don't think we should have ever been on the ground in Vietnam to the extent we find ourselves. It's going to be your job to extricate us, but you must disengage us honorably. If you don't do it honorably, the trust and credibility of the United States will not be worth a red cent anywhere in the world."

The two also discussed other defense matters, particularly manpower problems. Eisenhower advised Laird always to show compassion for the families of men and women in the military, something McNamara had not openly done. Laird must be sure to do as much listening as he did talking with the troops. "The problem over in Defense in the last few years is that we haven't had anyone listening," Eisenhower said. "You can learn a lot from these military men and women. You don't have to accept their advice, but at least let them sense that you are listening to them."[5]

Laird's visit with Eisenhower lifted Ike's spirits, as did a similar talk at the hospital that day with Secretary of State Rogers, who had served in the Eisenhower administration as attorney general. When the family saw that counseling incoming Cabinet members was palliative for Ike, they agreed to a request from Nixon that *all* of the incoming Cabinet members be allowed an audience. "To the best of my knowledge, the Boss interviewed and advised each future member of the Nixon Cabinet, somewhat to everyone's amusement," his son, John S. D. Eisenhower, wrote.[6]

On the same day he visited Eisenhower, Laird paid an afternoon call on the outgoing Secretary of Defense Clark Clifford. The day before, Clifford had dispatched a letter to Laird offering his full support during the transition process, including "an office in the Secretary's suite [which] has been set aside for your use."[7] Laird and Clifford already had a "bipartisan" friendship and mutual respect, having known each other for years, including multiple appearances by Clifford before Laird's Defense Appropriations subcommittee. Still, Clifford later admitted "an initial wariness" when he sat down with Laird. Part of that wariness came from Johnson's blustering denunciation of Laird at lunch with Clifford the day before. "He [Johnson] spent much of the time analyzing Nixon's new Cabinet," Clifford recalled. "He was disappointed by the choice of Laird, he told me, whom he considered 'one of the ablest' but also one of the 'meanest and most partisan' Republicans in the House." Clifford took the assessment with a grain of salt, coming as it was from a Democrat who many Republicans regarded as the "meanest and most partisan" Democratic president with whom they'd ever worked. Clifford's first meeting alone with Laird turned out to be comfortable. In Clifford's words, "I did not find him 'mean,' but rather an intelligent, likable ... and astute politician." Laird likewise respected Clifford's acumen, advice, and whole-hearted assistance in the transition process.[8]

In office a scant ten months under a president who wouldn't hear of withdrawal from Vietnam, Clifford confessed to Laird that he would have liked to stay another year or two under a fresh administration; Laird had advised Nixon to keep Clifford, but to no avail. "He [Clifford] made it clear to me that he hated to go out of office before putting in place a plan to withdraw from Vietnam," Laird recalled. "He told me, 'The sooner you start a withdrawal plan, the better off you will be.'" But Clifford was preaching to the choir. That two-hour meeting was the first of many between Clifford and Laird. "I was convinced from our first meeting that Laird would be far tougher than Rogers, and I was particularly pleased to discover that he saw as his major task finding a way out of the Vietnam morass," Clifford recalled in his memoirs.[9]

Mel Laird's event-filled Friday the 13th ended with a press conference. Clifford had arranged it, and Nixon's director of communications, Herbert Klein, hosted it. The second-floor Pentagon conference room was crowded with defense correspondents taking a close look at the new man. Laird reportedly "appeared relaxed and confident" and "handled all questions with good humor." Laird recalled of the event that his main purpose was not to upstage the sitting secretary or announce future policies. (He also politely declined Clifford's offer of a Pentagon office during the transition, determined not to loom too large before his term officially began.)

The reporters lobbed a few softball questions at him, and then, inevitably, someone dusted off a copy of his 1962 book, *A House Divided*. Since the election, demand had been so great for the book that the publisher, Henry Regnery Company, had asked for a new preface to rush out a second printing of ten thousand copies.[10] Laird aide Edwin Feulner had reread the book thoroughly and authored a memo advising Laird on what questions he could expect and how to respond: "When comments on specific points in the book are demanded, explain that these were the views of 1962, which MRL still stands by in the context of the time, but that the situation has changed drastically in seven years, and so perhaps has MRL."[11]

In the book, written before the Cuban Missile Crisis, Laird had advocated making the first nuclear strike if the Soviet Union threatened "the peace of the world." He also supported "limited nuclear reprisals" against Soviet incursions around the world. The unspoken question was: Would Laird be a trigger-happy secretary of defense? At the press conference Laird deftly acknowledged the more aggressive language of the book and relegated it to history. It was written "in a period of confrontation," he said. "We are now in a period of negotiations." But he was not about to let go of the notion of "nuclear superiority" over the Soviets. "Do you believe in it?" one reporter asked.

"I believe that the United States should maintain a superior position as far as its defensive forces are concerned."

His most-quoted remark was almost off-hand, when he expressed a hope that the war in Vietnam would be over before he had to put together the first Nixon administration defense budget, by 1970. There was also some talk of staffing. He expressed "no lack of confidence" about his ability to run the largest military establishment in the world but would look to a talented deputy for assistance.

"Sir, would you favor the appointment of a Democrat as your deputy?"

"Well, I favored the appointment of a Democrat as secretary of defense," Laird smiled. The remark brought down the house. (All the journalists were aware of Laird's behind-the-scenes maneuvers to persuade Nixon to choose either Clifford or Senator Henry "Scoop" Jackson.)[12]

⚬⚭⚬

Johnson did not want to meet with the next administration's secretary of defense; the much-feared Texas tornado was somewhat afraid of Laird. Laird had been a pugnacious partisan adversary to the president, which earned him respect from Johnson. Laird was a fiscal conservative who railed against the waste of taxpayer money, which made him an enemy of Johnson's profligate Great Society and his open-ended Vietnam War. But worst of all, Laird had a more finely honed sense of ethics and morality than did Johnson, which caused Johnson to deal with Laird warily.

Laird had earlier criticized Johnson's accumulation of a media-related fortune via backroom government favors but had said little about his links to the Bobby Baker and Billie Sol Estes scandals. Yet Johnson could never be quite sure whether Laird might launch a major campaign to tar him with those brushes. What Laird *did* do was occasionally raise questions about the president's spending on White House perks such as the presidential yacht, and that infuriated Johnson. Mostly, though, Johnson had been fearful that Laird's snooping might uncover a large amount—$3.7 million—that the president had secretly siphoned out of the military budget to improve his Texas ranch. Unlike the yacht, which would be inherited by the next president, the largesse at the ranch benefited only the Johnson family. A man who watched this interplay closely, Bill Gulley, disclosed some of the details in a memoir of his years as head of the White House Military Office. Laird was "a real antagonist" to Johnson, Gulley recalled, in part because he "was always chasing after LBJ, especially about excesses."

Gulley also offered an insider's account of Johnson's reaction to the selection of Laird as the defense secretary. Johnson was in his bedroom perusing the front page of the *Washington Post* when he read the first report that Laird might be nominated. "Melvin Laird—goddamn it!" the president reportedly cursed. "That son of a bitch'll lock us all up. We're all going to jail now." Gulley knew immediately that Johnson "was thinking about all the military hardware he had down at the ranch."[13]

With that background, Johnson was obviously not anxious to meet with someone he viewed as an ethical nitpicker. But Johnson had promised Eisenhower that he would do so, and he had told Nixon the previous day that he would counsel with some of the Cabinet nominees.[14] He would start, as protocol demanded, with Rogers, and then Laird was unavoidable. So, on Monday, December 23, Johnson met first with Rogers, and then, at 5:37 P.M., Laird was ushered into the Oval Office.[15] Not knowing what was on the president's mind, Laird anticipated a full briefing on Vietnam and discussion of other vital national security matters, including the control of nuclear weapons. The visit turned out to be neither as Eisenhower had billed it, nor what Laird had hoped for.

"Well, Mel," the outgoing president drawled, smiling and clapping Laird on the back as they greeted each other. "I know we've had a lot of disagreements, and we've had some agreements over the years on the Appropriations Committee. But now there are a few things that we've got to have an understanding about."

"If you have any advice, I'd appreciate it," Laird, said, ready to be handed the keys to the Pentagon, the secrets in the presidential safe, the real story behind the Vietnam War.

Then Johnson began with the important business at hand. "I've got this valet—"

Was Laird hearing this right? Was he talking about a valet?

"—who's assigned to me from the Department of Defense. I also have a cook—"

Men were dying in Vietnam, and now the president's talking about his *cook,* as if that should be the first order of business?

"—who's assigned to me from the Department of Defense that's been very good."

Laird respectfully nodded, a bit puzzled.

"I want both of them assigned to me down at the ranch."

That wasn't the end of the presidential laundry list. "I'm having a problem, too, with that heliport down there. I want to get that improved and I've got to get some communication and some good radar in there. Can you handle that?"

"Well," Laird stalled, rolling it over as if he were seriously and fully considering the requests, while he was really trying to recover his composure. He was new at this Cabinet secretary business, but he was pretty sure it wasn't the Pentagon's job to give an ex-president a GI valet-for-life or assign some army cook permanent KP duty at the LBJ spread in Texas. The heliport and communications improvements sounded much more doable in the name of presidential security.

"I'll look into it," Laird promised.

Johnson said he was "surprised" that Laird had been nominated to be secretary of defense since he had been such an archcritic of defense appropriations.

"I have never been a critic of defense, only of certain things the Defense Department has done," Laird protested.

Laird could not know what Johnson's closest aides already did—that his hidden agenda was to secure some hint of absolution should Laird discover down the road the assets LBJ had squirreled away at the ranch using Pentagon money. So he sought to put Laird on the defensive by implying he had been a military critic of sorts. Only after the president's prime concern about his perks was addressed did he turn the conversation to affairs of state. But it was another letdown for Laird, since the president offered no insights or information that Laird didn't already know.

The president complained about how the press had painted the 1968 Tet offensive as a huge defeat for the United States. Johnson was right about this; the enemy took the biggest losses in that offensive. In fact, Tet was a huge military defeat for the North Vietnamese and Viet Cong, but the press had turned it into a more important psychological victory for the enemy. If anything, it was the credibility gap caused by the consistently rosy Johnson and McNamara pronouncements about Vietnam that had caused the press to question the administration when it characterized Tet.

Referring to the recent presidential campaign, Johnson tweaked Laird for implying that the administration had a withdrawal plan for Vietnam. "You got a little out there, Mel, during the campaign," he said.

Laird mostly listened. He reflected later that he didn't see any point in arguing. "Johnson felt that I was wrong, that they had no plans to withdraw and that I had misled the press. I said, 'Well, you'll find that there is a plan over there. I just don't think you can wait around for the Paris peace agreement.' That's about where I left it," Laird recalled of the conversation.

There was one piece of advice that Laird took to heart, because he had seen the evidence himself. Johnson told him that various people would try to drive a wedge between the Defense and State Departments. LBJ advised that the best way to prevent such divisiveness was for Laird to cultivate his own friendship with Rogers, maybe playing golf with him once a week. Laird agreed. (The two friends ended up playing frequently at Burning Tree.)[16]

With historical hindsight, the real possibility exists that Johnson wasted this opportunity with Laird not only because he was afraid Laird might criticize his secret spending, but also because he did not think Laird would be much of a player. Johnson thought Rogers, who was closer to Nixon, would be the strongman in the new administration. Clifford wrote that Johnson confided as much to him. That would partially explain why Johnson had given a substantive briefing on the war to Rogers before he met with Laird. Clifford later recounted to friends, and partially in his memoirs, that Johnson and others of the outgoing administration seriously underestimated the influence Laird and Kissinger would have. And they "seriously overestimated the role Rogers would play as Secretary of State," he wrote.[17]

The curious presidential "briefing" ended at 6:37 P.M. "To be perfectly frank with you, I spent most of that meeting listening," Laird remembered. "I saw no reason to get into any arguments, and I didn't make any commitments on anything." He was cautious with Johnson because Laird knew the conversation probably was being secretly taped.[18] Johnson had microphones everywhere. They were in the Oval Office, in his bedroom, in the situation room, at Camp David, and at his ranch in Texas.[19] There were eight microphones alone hidden under the Cabinet table, which he could activate by using a switch among the buttons marked Coffee, Tea, and Fresca. When Bobby Kennedy visited with President Johnson for a tense, private meeting in early 1968 to discuss Kennedy's possible entry into the presidential race, he was wary that Johnson was taping him. When the tape was later played back, an aide recalled, the only thing on it was a "bzzzzett;" Kennedy had carried a jamming device in his briefcase. "That son of a bitch!" was all Johnson could say when he found out Bobby had foiled him.[20]

Laird doesn't recall exactly when he learned that military officers were the ones running the White House taping system under the auspices of the White House Communications Agency. But he certainly knew before his December 1968 meeting with Johnson. Ever the obsequious informant, FBI Director J. Edgar Hoover had scurried to see Nixon shortly after the election and warned him not to use the White House switchboard during the transition period because Johnson was probably recording every incoming and outgoing call. (It turned out he wasn't, though the system had the capability.) Before Nixon moved into the White House, Johnson himself, with typical braggadocio, showed his successor the cleverly concealed equipment in the Oval Office and the White House bedroom, advising Nixon to employ the same devices for history's sake.

Nixon at first found the idea of secret taping ill advised and wrong. He confided to his aide Robert Finch that tearing out the system would be one of his first acts as president. Laird also found it repugnant when he learned of it. He told Nixon he would not allow the military to be involved in the surreptitious practice, whatever Nixon decided after he moved in. Laird did remove all the equipment and military signal corps operators by mid-February 1969, with Nixon's concurrence. When Nixon later changed his mind in early 1971, he knew better than to ask Laird to bring back the signal corps men. He didn't even want Laird to know the taping system was up and running again, because

he knew his friend would protest that it was unethical. So he had the Secret
Service set up the system and keep it secret.

⚓

Laird had thirty-seven days to fill the top staff positions for the 4.8 million-
member Defense Department. Operating from a suite at the Carlton Hotel,
Laird decided to diagram the task. His chart covered all four military services,
the National Security Agency, and twelve intelligence agencies. An early appointee in the public affairs office, Richard Capen, described the diagram:
"One entire wall was filled with this organization chart. It was huge; it must
have been twenty feet across. It was so terrifying to look at that thing. I couldn't
imagine how this congressman who had been running less than two dozen
people in his Capitol Hill office was now going to manage five million."[21]

Laird spent twelve to fourteen hours every day, including the Christmas
holidays, filling in that chart. He might have been overwhelmed were it not
for the fact that, from his many years on the Defense Appropriations Subcommittee, he knew most of the top players at the Pentagon, and the hopefuls who
wanted jobs there. He appointed his friend in Congress Glenard Lipscomb as
his transition chief. Both men were adept at reading people, so no applicant
was able to steamroller either of them into making a Pentagon appointment
they might regret.

What made Laird's appointments singular—like no other secretary of defense before or since—was that his civilian and military choices could not
be vetoed by the president, unless Nixon were to break the promise made on
the cocktail napkin. In 1968 the Defense Department had thirty-one "statutory" positions requiring appointment by the president and confirmation by
the Senate. Only the State Department, with its large number of ambassadors,
had more positions requiring Senate confirmation. Both Defense and State
were the primary departments that some presidents had used for hundreds
of "patronage" appointments—rewards for the party faithful. But Nixon had
promised Laird he would not do that at the Pentagon.

Those who assisted Laird in the selection process—including Robert
Froehlke and congressional aides Bill Baroody, John Dressendorfer, and Ed
Feulner—all recalled there was great pressure from people Nixon had chosen
to be his White House staff. They had engaged in a much-publicized effort to
write letters to some eighty thousand persons listed in *Who's Who* and other
source books, inviting nominees for government jobs. As a result Laird was
sent boxes full of resumes that filled multiple filing cabinets. Dressendorfer
said, "We had *thousands* of files of people. We got calls all the time from [the
Nixon transition team] trying to place people."[22] Laird's most trusted backstop
against patronage appointments was Carl Wallace, his congressional administrative assistant who followed him to the Pentagon. Wallace or Froehlke would

agree to look at applications and conduct interviews, but that was no guarantee of a job. Future Senator John Warner, who was on the Nixon transition team, said he couldn't "think of a single person who was ever foisted on Mel Laird."[23]

From the beginning, the Pentagon was going to be a place apart, ruled solely by Laird. When White House officials below the president would later try to interfere, Laird would remind them that he had a deal with Nixon. A few times he had to produce the handwritten Nixon napkin and remind them of the promise. Since political patronage was off the table, Laird was free to concentrate on merit. This infuriated some Nixon aides who placed loyalty to Nixon during the campaign as the most vital prerequisite for appointment. As the staffing process continued into the first months of the administration, peeved Nixon aides frequently called Laird's staffers over to the White House for a dressing down. Feulner said he was often asked to explain why Laird had appointed someone "who was right on defense" but had irritated almost "everyone else in the administration."

One early indication that the Defense Department might be peppered with Democrats was Laird's friendship with Paul Warnke, who was one of Clifford's closest colleagues and also head of the Pentagon's foreign policy department, International Security Affairs. "I'd say Paul Warnke was the Democrat who was the foremost pariah [to Nixon's people] in the LBJ Pentagon," recalled General Robert Pursley, Laird's military assistant. Because he appreciated Warnke's expertise, Laird asked him to stay on for a few months to help the new secretary prepare for trips to Vietnam and NATO meetings, and to assist in the opening of arms control talks with Moscow.[24] Nixon's team and top military brass were stunned. In fact, immediately after Laird was named to be defense secretary, a private memorandum had been sent urgently to Laird conveying the "advice" of Air Force Chief of Staff General John McConnell, who was "speaking for [all] the Joint Chiefs," that, above all, "Paul C. Warnke & his *entire staff*...ALL ABSOLUTELY *MUST* GO."[25]

In retrospect, former Ambassador Richard Holbrooke, who coauthored Clifford's memoirs, thought the fact that Laird kept Warnke was highly significant. "It was remarkable to me that Warnke, who was almost the symbol of what hard-line Republicans considered left-wing policies, did not disappear on the first day of the Nixon administration." No less remarkable was Laird's firm friendship with Clifford. Both Nixon and Kissinger soon went out of their way to make Clifford a whipping boy for Johnson's failures. Yet Laird still sought out Clifford's counsel. Aware of how shrew Laird could be, Holbrooke suggested that maybe some of that friendship had to do with Laird using Clifford as "a counterweight" to the Nixon-Kissinger alliance.[26]

Laird also respected Clifford's Deputy Secretary of Defense Paul Nitze. Laird wanted the ardent Democrat to replace Warnke at International Security Affairs, but he found out that Senator Barry Goldwater would block Nitze's confirmation. "Barry held Paul Nitze responsible for putting out all that material in 1964 suggesting Goldwater was a warmonger," Laird said. "I didn't think it was right for him to blame Paul solely for those Johnson commercials about the little girl and the daisies being blown apart, but Barry did and said he found Nitze so personally obnoxious that he would never permit his confirmation." So Laird asked Nitze to serve in a position that didn't need confirmation—as a consultant and a representative to the strategic arms limitation talks. Nitze played a pivotal role in the negotiations of SALT I and II until he resigned in 1974. (Goldwater later told Laird he had changed his mind on Nitze.)

Both Warnke and Nitze were men Laird had known from his congressional work. But there were others from the Clifford regime whom he wanted to get to know, too. He was pleased on the first weekend after his appointment to be invited to the Cliffords' home for a dinner party. It was a chance to size up some of the people who had been running the Pentagon. General Earle "Bus" Wheeler, the chairman of the Joint Chiefs of Staff, was there. There were still a few months left in Wheeler's term, and Laird had to decide whether to reappoint him or go with someone else.

At one point, in the vestibule of the home, Laird bumped into Robert Pursley, then a young Air Force colonel who had been the military assistant to both McNamara and Clifford. Mistaking Pursley for someone else, Laird said, "I'm sorry you're leaving," and after some small talk walked away. "Well, that takes care of that," Pursley said to himself, assuming he had just been fired. But once Laird figured out who Pursley was, and spent some time with him, he asked the colonel to stay on as his closest military advisor—a man who would become so close to Laird that Kissinger would later tap Pursley's phones to keep track of what Laird and Pursley were up to.

Laird also kept two Johnson administration men—Dan Henkin and Jack Stempler—to head his public affairs and legislative affairs divisions, respectively. Henkin, a Democrat, had a long history with the Pentagon. Stempler, who called himself an Independent, nevertheless was surprised to keep his job. (He would later serve in the same position for the Carter administration.) That Laird would tap his chief liaisons with the media and Capitol Hill from LBJ holdovers was quite unusual.

John Warner, who would later serve as chairman of the Senate Armed Services Committee, would witness many Pentagon personnel shifts over four decades. He recalled, "I've been through so many political elections where the new administration says, 'We'll clean the bastards out. Throw them out.' But Mel didn't do that. He had the wisdom to keep good people. Dr. Johnny Foster was one of those—a man who is one of the most brilliant scientists and technology people in the United States." Foster was McNamara's pick for director of Defense Research and Engineering in 1965, and Laird asked him to continue in the post, which he did for Laird's full term. Another example was Robert Moot, Clifford's Pentagon comptroller. Moot was a Democrat, having both

voted and worked for Kennedy and Johnson. But Laird appreciated his credible testimony during subcommittee hearings and asked him to continue in the
post. Moot became one of the people Laird counted on most for running the
Pentagon on a day-to-day basis.[27] Laird felt Barry Shillito was underutilized by
Clifford as logistics chief for the navy. So Laird promoted him to head logistics for the whole Defense Department. Shillito, an ardent Democrat, was as
surprised as the others. He had already made plans to go into private business
but agreed to stay.

Laird's appointments for service secretaries were no different. For secretary
of the air force he wanted MIT professor and deputy administrator of NASA,
Robert Seamans, but Seamans said he couldn't come until he finished the semester at MIT, so Harold Brown (later, President Carter's secretary of defense)
agreed to stay on in the position until Seamans was available.[28] As for secretary
of the army, Nixon had promised the position to two different men—William
Cascy and former representative Howard "Bo" Callaway. But Laird wanted neither of them. He wanted Froehlke but knew he first needed his friend as assistant secretary for administration for at least a year. So he asked Stan Resor,
who had been army secretary since 1965, to stay on. "It never entered my head
him asking me to stay on," Resor recalled. He was even more grateful when
Laird helped him resist pressure from Nixon's circle to name William Casey
as his undersecretary.[29] Laird felt that his top appointees should have much of
the same latitude he had secured from Nixon; they should, after discussion, be
allowed to pick their own assistants and staff.

The position of secretary of the navy was the most coveted Department of
Defense post among Nixon supporters. According to Laird, "there were at least
three people who felt they were going to be secretary of the navy—that Nixon
had made a commitment to them." Two of them were William Mittendorf, a
Republican Party finance chairman, and Jim Copley, head of the Copley newspaper chain. And there were many more applications for the position; Warner,
a Republican loyalist, was one of them. Toiling away on the Nixon transition
team, Warner had decided it was time to throw his own name in the hopper
for a permanent job. "I'd always had a hankering to go over to the Department
of Defense," he recalled. "I had two tours of active duty and ten years in the
reserves of the Marines. So I thought I might as well be head of the navy." Once
he settled on that plan, Warner confessed, he actively worked against almost
every other applicant for the job: "I actually secreted a number of the applications for secretary of the navy." Laird was aware of Warner's keen interest, due
in no small measure to the lobbying efforts of Warner's father-in-law, billionaire Republican contributor Paul Mellon. But Laird finally told Warner the job
was going to John Chafee, and Warner would be his undersecretary.

"Nixon hates him!" Warner protested. "He's a Rockefeller man. Don't you
understand that? He's a Rockefeller liberal! You can't have that guy in there! I'm
the guy that worked with Nixon for eight years!" Warner was about to learn,

as the whole country would soon figure out, that Laird had no objection to a liberal service secretary because Laird himself had "a liberal streak up his back," as Warner affectionately put it.

"Now listen, Warner," Laird told him. "You're only forty-two years old. Chafee is five years older, and he has had more military experience than you. You'll make a great team. Not only will you learn to like this guy, you'll learn to love him." And Warner did.[30]

Nixon was not happy about Laird's bipartisan hiring, but he couldn't do anything about it except cajole. During an all-day briefing with his appointees on December 12, Nixon said one of Eisenhower's greatest mistakes was not Republicanizing the Cabinet departments after twenty years of uninterrupted Democratic power. "I urged the new Cabinet members to move quickly to replace holdover bureaucrats with people who believed in what we were trying to do," he wrote in his memoirs. "'We can't depend on people who believe in another philosophy of government to give us their undivided loyalty or their best work,' I concluded. 'If we don't get rid of those people, they will either sabotage us from within, or they'll just sit back on their well-paid asses and wait for the next election to bring back their old bosses.'"[31]

Eight months into his new administration, President Nixon continued pushing to oust Democrats from the federal departments—Defense, in particular. The White House requested that Froehlke send over a list identifying the party affiliation of the Pentagon's top sixty-eight positions. It was a humorous and painful survey for some of Laird's staff to take. Navy Assistant Secretary Robert Frosch remembered Chafee calling him one day. "Bob, I'm gonna ask you a question, but it embarrasses me a little to ask you. Are you enrolled as a Democrat or a Republican?"

"John," Frosch laughed, "you know I'm a congenital Democrat."

"Yeah, I knew that," Chafee said. "Shit! You're the third one today."[32]

The final tally showed that of the sixty-eight top positions that had been filled at the Pentagon, a little more than half (thirty-six) were Republicans. Fifteen were Democrats, nine described themselves as "Independents" and the political affiliation of eight was "unknown," with no further explanation.[33]

⚓

No appointment for the secretary of defense is more important than that of deputy secretary, yet rarely do nominated secretaries get to make that choice. Because of his napkin deal with Nixon, Laird had a free hand to pick his own person. In his search for the right one, Laird consulted three former secretaries of defense, dozens of university presidents, and civic and business leaders. The name that kept coming up was David Packard, cofounder of Silicon Valley's premier electronics firm, Hewlett-Packard. Laird had met Packard once, in 1959, when the latter was president of the board of trustees of Stanford University. The presidents of Stanford, Harvard, Yale, and other universities had put their most persuasive trustees, including Packard, on a committee that had successfully lobbied Congress—specifically Laird and John Fogarty—for more money for university medical research. Laird had been impressed with Packard's political acumen and business savvy.[34]

Packard was precisely what Laird was looking for in a deputy secretary. In 1939, he had started Hewlett Packard with Bill Hewlett in a Palo Alto, California, garage—later designated a California Historical Landmark as "the birthplace of Silicon Valley."[35] In the year prior to Nixon's election, the company had done $100.7 million in business with the federal government, including the Pentagon. It was a huge conflict-of-interest hurdle that should have prevented Laird from asking Packard to serve, but Laird was intent on having him as deputy secretary. Laird called Packard on the pretext of soliciting his recommendations for Pentagon appointments. Packard wrote in his short memoir that he agreed to meet with Laird at the Carlton Hotel. "After a few hours of discussion, he said he wanted me to join him as his deputy secretary. This sounded intriguing, but the conflict-of-interest requirements were very strict."[36]

Essentially, no Pentagon official was allowed to have more than $10,000 worth of stock in a company that did business with the military. At the time, Packard owned more than $300 million in Hewlett Packard stock. McNamara and Charles Wilson, Eisenhower's secretary of defense, had had to sell all their stock in Ford ($1.5 million) and General Motors ($2.5 million), respectively. Since it was only a small percentage of the outstanding stock of those companies, the sale did not throw those companies into financial crises. But Packard owned a third of his company's shares; a forced sale would severely depress the stock price. So, while he said he would think about it, Packard flew home fairly convinced that he would not be able to serve as Laird's deputy.

But Laird didn't give up. The day after Christmas, at Laird's request, Packard flew east again to meet with Laird. That meeting would be a full-court press. Laird asked former HEW Secretary John Gardner, a close friend of both Laird and Packard (they had been Stanford chums), to join them for breakfast at the Carlton. Gardner arrived first, and Laird buttonholed him. "John, this breakfast is all about one thing, to persuade David to be my deputy. You've got to help me do that." Gardner argued it couldn't be done because the Senate would never confirm Packard unless he sold the stock, which Packard could not do.[37] Laird was undaunted. "John, my approach is going to be that he owes it to the country. I'll work out the details."

"Mel, you'll never be able to work out the details."

Packard joined them at the table and Laird made his pitch. "This country's been awfully good to you and it is payback time," he said.

"I understand what you're saying, but you know I can't do it," said Packard. "I could agree to sell my other stocks and pay the capital gains, which would be millions of dollars. I'll do that because I want to help the country. But I cannot sell the Hewlett Packard stock."

Laird had a plan, though. He told Packard he could persuade Congress to grant an exception—to allow him to keep the stock if Packard put all the dividends and appreciation into charities while he was a public employee. The loss to Packard might be in the millions of dollars, but it was doable. And once again, Laird stressed, Packard owed it to his country.

Gardner chimed in then: "Dave, you can tell him 'yes.' Mel can never work that out." So Packard gave a qualified "yes."

Laird hastened to Capitol Hill and explained his plan to Senator Richard Russell of Georgia, the Democratic chairman of the Senate Armed Services Committee, which would have to approve Packard's nomination. "Mel, no one's that important to you," Russell laughed.

"Yes, Dave Packard is that important to me."

Russell picked up the phone and summoned four other committee members: Democrats Stuart Symington and John Stennis, and Republicans Margaret Chase-Smith and Milton Young. In less than an hour, they had assembled in Russell's office where he spelled out the problem and the solution: Packard's defense-related stock would be put into a blind trust, with all income from it to be distributed among various charities. Incredibly, they all agreed to Laird's terms and said they could deliver the votes of the rest of the committee.[38]

"Congratulations," Laird reported back to Packard. "You're the new deputy secretary of defense. You told me 'yes' at breakfast, and today I have delivered the package."

—◆—

Word soon leaked of Laird's choice of Packard as his deputy, and an irritated Nixon called Laird from his vacation home in Key Biscayne, Florida. Nixon acknowledged that he and Laird had a deal—that Laird would have full power over appointments—but said he at least expected to be told about appointments before he read about them in the newspapers. Laird apologized profusely and said he and Packard would be on the first military plane they could round up. By 4:30 P.M. they were in Key Biscayne. Though Nixon and Packard had briefly met at a cocktail reception in California, this was the first time the two really talked.[39] Laird introduced them and then faded out onto a porch to chat with Pat Nixon while Packard and Nixon got acquainted. After about forty-five minutes Laird stuck his head in the room. "Listen, we've got to go back to Washington. I just wanted you to get to know Dave, but we have to leave." At that time, the two men were so engrossed in a mutual appreciation society, that Nixon asked everyone to stay for dinner, but Laird and Packard begged off, having work to do in Washington. On the way to the door, Nixon took Laird aside and remarked, "I understand entirely why you wanted him as a deputy. He's a big man in every way." (Packard was six-feet seven-inches tall.)

Laird and Packard returned to Washington on Friday evening. Laird had to go back to Key Biscayne the next day for an important national security conference with Nixon, so the announcement was put off until Monday, December 30, when he called a press conference. After Laird introduced him to the media, the fifty-six-year-old Packard began, with evident chagrin, "I must tell you that my friend, Mel Laird, here, is a very clever man. [H]e used a lot of salesmanship on me in the last few days." Packard said he had agreed to make the sacrifice to become deputy secretary because he thought "it was about time that I [did] something in return for my country." Then he outlined his income, which amounted to $1 million a year, much of which he would have to forgo if the Senate signed off on Laird's proposal.

"Mr. Packard," one reporter asked, "what will your salary be in your new job?"

"I don't know," Packard asked. "I didn't ask that."

After the laughter had subsided, Laird informed his new appointee and the press: "His salary will be $30,000."

"It is safe to assume, then, that you are taking a cut?" a reporter asked, to continued laughter.

Packard, also chuckling responded, "Yes, I am taking a helluva cut!"[40]

Packard never seemed to regret his decision to serve in the Pentagon. He mentioned his financial loss only once, that Laird recalled, and that was in a congressional hearing. Texas Congressman Jack Brooks took Packard to task over the expense of a kitchen and caterer in the Pentagon where Packard would lunch with dignitaries. "Tell me, Secretary Packard, what did your lunch cost yesterday?"

Without missing a beat Packard replied, "I'll tell you, Chairman Brooks. As near as I can calculate in my mind right now, that lunch cost me $325,000."

Gerald Ford said in retrospect about the Packard appointment, "Mel recognized he needed somebody from industry who would manage the industrial side of the Pentagon, so he made this very smart move to get this outstanding American industrialist."[41] The symbiotic Laird-Packard team was to become legendary at the Pentagon, and subsequent efforts by defense secretaries to duplicate its success have fallen short.

Laird's inventive solution for the conflict-of-interest issue with Packard wound up greatly benefiting diverse American charities. The accumulated dividends and increase in stock value over his three years of service amounted to $18.8 million, which Packard gave to universities, hospitals, and several predominantly black colleges. In Washington, the Kennedy Center and Wolf Trap Center for the Performing Arts were significant beneficiaries. This trust metamorphosed into one of America's largest, dispensing hundreds of millions of dollars to worthy causes.

ॐ

The conference Nixon called at the Key Biscayne Hotel on December 28 was historically notable as the debut of Nixon's national security apparatus.

He invited those who would, by statute, be members of or advisors to his National Security Council—Laird, Rogers, Agnew, and Kissinger. Other participants included Packard; Bryce Harlow, who was Nixon's pick for congressional relations liaison; former ambassador Robert Murphy, who was the chief Nixon transition representative at the State Department; and General Andrew J. Goodpaster, former national security advisor in the Eisenhower administration, who was acting as Nixon's principal transition expert on national security.[42]

The agenda for the meeting had been set a month earlier when Nixon met Kissinger at the Pierre Hotel in New York and offered him the job of assistant to the president for national security. At that meeting, the two men realized they had something in common—a vision of the way U.S. foreign policy should work. They privately believed it should be run out of the White House by the National Security Council instead of the State Department.

Key to Kissinger's plan was the creation of a revised NSC system, including the National Security Study Memorandum (NSSM) and National Security Decision Memorandum (NSDM) process, which would be the marching orders issuing forth from his new and improved NSC. Study memos would order departments to look into something in which the president was interested; decision memos would be the president's instructions, through Kissinger, to take action. Within days of his own appointment, Kissinger had the first three NSDMs drafted, all of which shifted power to the NSC and to himself.

Before the Key Biscayne meeting, Kissinger had drafted a plan for revamping the NSC to subtly slide the power away from the Cabinet secretaries and into the White House staff. It wasn't subtle enough for Laird and Rogers, who recognized a coup when they saw one. In his memoirs Kissinger relates that Nixon had already approved his plan before the December 28 meeting—but set up the agenda to make it appear as though there would be a healthy give-and-take to get everyone's opinion on the changes before they were approved.

There wasn't much give-and-take. Nixon quickly gave up the charade and declared the Kissinger plan a fait accompli. Disagreement was discouraged as much by Nixon's emphatic support of the plan as by the setting in the screened porch of his Florida villa, where the Saturday breezes off Biscayne Bay gave the illusion of tranquility. So Laird and Rogers kept silent at the meeting, waiting to make their objections to Kissinger on their return to Washington.

Kissinger's critics have often portrayed this first bold step as a calculated grab for power. "This is what they always say," Kissinger protested in an interview. "But the reorganization of the NSC was actually not my idea. That was Eisenhower's and Goodpaster's. I was a bystander on that one....He and I called on Eisenhower [who] had absolutely stern views that the State Department [should] not chair interdepartmental machinery, and that's why we put everything into the NSC. This was not my idea."[43] In the same interview, Kissinger portrayed himself as an early innocent with few or no friends in Washington. He believed the media sided with and promoted him early in the Nixon administration because "I was the press's alibi for their hatred for Nixon. So they kept building me up: every good thing was mine, and every bad thing was Nixon's. That was not my doing."

Kissinger only had one client: Nixon. All Kissinger's power flowed from that one man, whom he aimed to please. "You have to remember that I came in as a Rockefeller man.... [Nixon] didn't know me from Adam." To have gone against Nixon's wishes, or persuade the president to do something he would later regret, would have been self-destructive. "I would be losing my only constituency," he emphasized. Nixon wanted to bring foreign policy power back to the White House through the NSC, and he needed no persuading from Kissinger. "It was what Nixon wanted," confirmed Lawrence Eagleburger, who worked as an aide to Kissinger during the transition. But Kissinger wanted it, too, Eagleburger said. "I love Henry Kissinger; he's my dearest friend. But let us not necessarily believe that Henry was pushed any more than he did the pushing. There was method in his madness, shall we say."[44]

Laird had not objected at Key Biscayne to the new NSC power because he had known Nixon long enough to see when his mind was made up. But Laird knew he could change some of the details in one of Kissinger's proposed National Security Decision Memoranda before it was signed. In his memoirs, Kissinger recalled: "The first to be heard from was Laird, who in the process initiated me to his patented technique of bureaucratic warfare: to throw up a smoke screen of major objections in which he was not really interested but which reduced the item that really concerned him to such minor proportions that to refuse him would appear positively indecent."[45]

The two had dinner together and worked out their differences, mostly in Laird's favor. Kissinger had written the CIA director out of the NSC, but, at Laird's insistence, the CIA was brought back in. Laird didn't like the implication in NSDM #2 that only the NSC could initiate policy and strategic studies; Laird felt that the Defense and State departments ought to be able to propose studies, and Kissinger agreed. Laird lost on one important issue. He unsuccessfully proposed that Nixon shut down the liaison office between the Joint Chiefs and the NSC. Pursley had warned Laird that keeping the position was just asking for trouble. It could be used improperly as a way for the Joint Chiefs to circumvent the secretary of defense or, in the reverse, for the president to work around the secretary and deal directly with the Joint Chiefs. Both Pursley and Laird were right to worry; by 1971 the new chairman of the Joint Chiefs, Admiral Thomas Moorer, would manipulate the liaison office to spy on the president, using a military aide to surreptitiously photocopy and steal White House national security documents.[46]

Laird could hardly complain about Kissinger's first bureaucratic moves. Laird had been the primary advocate for putting Kissinger in as national security advisor, yet he had no illusions about him. John Warner remembered

Laird taking him aside early on and saying with a smile: "Watch out. Henry is gonna try to run it all."

After the Key Biscayne meeting, Laird observed to Kissinger that "he was reaching out for too much authority, and too much power," Laird recalled. "It didn't bother me so much in Defense, but I thought he was just writing the State Department out of everything." Rogers recognized the problem, too, and made similar objections, but not strenuously or effectively. The problem, Laird said, was that Rogers "just never wanted to get in a real confrontation," so it put him at a severe disadvantage with Kissinger. "I *loved* to confront Kissinger, but it was always a friendly sort of thing. We talked almost every day, and he'd be on the phone raising hell with me for something, and then I'd raise hell with him over something else." The two were worthy adversaries. Despite the full backing of the president for much of what he did in the early years, Kissinger knew he had to be very careful with Laird, a man with powerful friends on the Hill and in the media.

Imbued with self-confidence, and understanding Kissinger's strengths and weaknesses, Laird cared little during or after the Key Biscayne meeting about how Kissinger *thought* he would run the show, because Laird intended to run his own Defense Department show, no matter what. Besides, Vietnam was to him a far more pressing issue than bureaucratic infighting.

⌖

When Laird flew to the Key Biscayne meeting, he had a primary goal in mind: to plant the seed of "de-Americanizing" the war in Vietnam. With each man there so concerned about his own agenda, it is not surprising that neither Kissinger nor Laird mentioned the other's agenda when they recalled the fateful meeting. Kissinger's memoirs dwell heavily on how he was able to finesse his NSC memo. Laird remembered the meeting as an amicable one, focused on how the new administration would approach Vietnam. "They decided that I'd go to Vietnam as soon as possible after the inauguration, and that I would come back and report to the president with a program," recalled Laird. "I think the State Department was a little concerned that I had been given the responsibility for developing the program, but I assured Rogers that I was going to talk it over with his people."

At that time Laird didn't know the details, but he already knew what the "program" would be—he was going to pull American troops out of Vietnam as fast as he safely could. In keeping with his back-door style, he didn't say it in so many words at the meeting. "I brought up the fact that in order to maintain the defense budget and maintain any degree of support in the Congress, we're going to have to de-Americanize that situation over there and turn over more responsibility to the South Vietnamese. I reminded them that this was called for in the Republican platform."

Not yet wise to Laird's shrewd footwork, the others at the meeting were nevertheless suspicious. Withdrawing troops could be seen as a sign of U.S. weakness at the Paris peace talks, but Laird didn't have much patience left for those endless talks. "The State Department and Kissinger, and I think the president, wanted to go a little slow until they found out where they were," Laird recalled from the meeting. "Kissinger said that with all these Paris negotiations, don't sell out too soon." Laird countered that the U.S. military was being strangled by the war. "We've got other problems all over the world. We can't let this Vietnam be our downfall," he remembered telling the others.

Laird believed passionately that Nixon had won the election because of the Vietnam War. The American people were fed up with it, and unless Nixon started pulling American soldiers out of Vietnam quickly, he would not be reelected four years hence. Thus the new defense secretary girded himself for the loneliest political battle of his life, one that would pit him against the Joint Chiefs, Kissinger, and, at times, President Nixon himself.

15

Looking for an Exit

⚓

THE MAN WHO TOOK OVER RESPONSIBILITY for the Vietnam War on January 20, 1969, might have tripped the metal detector, if there had been one, when he walked through the door of his new office. Mel Laird's body still carried shrapnel from the Japanese kamikaze attack on the USS *Maddox* during an earlier, different war. He bore the metal fragments proudly and considered them only a minor annoyance when they occasionally worked their way through to the skin and had to be surgically removed. It was the small price a serviceman paid for a big victory.

Now his primary mission for his country was getting it out of another war, probably without victory—and possibly without honor. He had no illusions about the job. The slippery slope on which the United States slid into the Vietnam War would prove to be a treacherous incline when it came time for an orderly exit. When Laird inherited the war in 1969, there were more than half a million American troops in South Vietnam and another half a million supporting the war from U.S. Navy ships and air bases in nearby allied countries. Americans were dying at a rate of two hundred a week. The United States had lost thirty-one thousand men and women; South Vietnam had lost three times that many. The enemy's dead were harder to count, but it was a safe bet that the 1968 Tet offensive and other campaigns that year alone cost North Vietnam 289,000 men.[1]

Putting the horror of casualties aside, at $24 billion a year—one-third of the total military budget—the U.S. Treasury could ill afford the war, which was draining money from domestic programs and diverting U.S. military assets from other hot spots around the world. American soldiers had proudly joined up to fight the Japanese and Germans less than a generation earlier and had come home to tickertape and glory. Now, men were reluctantly drafted to serve in Vietnam and spat upon when they returned.

Laird sized up his office suite that first day. He had been in it several times before as a congressman, but as he stepped off the elevator—the only private one in the Pentagon—he inhaled the fact that it was now his. On one side, two secretaries, Laurie Hawley and Thelma Stubbs, guarded the gate and screened visitors, mindful of the light on the door that indicated if someone was with him or if he was open to visitors. On another side was a private dining room and just beyond it the office of the deputy secretary. Nearby was a bed Laird would use for spending the night during crises.

Laird's private office itself was cavernous, filled with chairs and couches for holding meetings and welcoming VIPs. One magazine called it "Laird's Little Acre." The centerpiece was the imposing glass-topped desk, which had once belonged to General John "Black Jack" Pershing and had the dimensions of a conference table. Three in-and-out boxes attempted to hold the flow of documents requiring his review and signature. In front of the desk was an expensive oriental rug that had been added by Clark Clifford's wife and marred by burns from ashes flying out of Deputy Secretary Paul Nitze's pipe. Clifford had eventually covered it with Plexiglas. Directly across from the desk, on stands framing a space for photo-taking, were two flags—the American flag and the secretary of defense's own ensign: a red, white, and blue flag with an American eagle, wings outstretched, four crossed arrows, and five stars.

Behind the desk hung a portrait of James Forrestal, the first defense secretary, a man who was driven to suicide by the job. McNamara had hung the painting in this place of honor, and Laird decided to keep it. (The Forrestal painting would remain through several more secretaries but was removed by Caspar Weinberger at the beginning of the Reagan administration in 1981.) Near the painting in Laird's day was a ship's bell that chimed the hours, and below the painting was a credenza with a bank of telephones—hotlines to President Nixon, Packard, the Joint Chiefs of Staff, and the commanders in Saigon and Hawaii.[2]

The secretary's suite also had a large walk-in vault, which was full of classified documents including, as Laird knew before he arrived, the request from General William Westmoreland for 205,179 more troops—many of them reservists—to raise the U.S. contingent in Vietnam to more than 700,000. Westmoreland, as commander of U.S. forces in Vietnam, wanted to exploit North Vietnam when it was at its weakest point, after the 1968 Tet offensive. It made tactical sense to a military commander who wanted to win, but at a time when the Johnson administration was trying to soft-pedal Tet as a huge defeat for the enemy, the troop request had a look of panic about it, as if the allies had been tromped by Tet and needed to call in the Reserves.[3]

The request had been in Clifford's office since February 1968, when Westmoreland had submitted it through General Earle Wheeler, chairman of the Joint Chiefs. Laird believed Westmoreland was oblivious to the fact that the American public no longer cared about winning the war, and the general was disdainful of any political pandering to that public opinion. But the facts behind the troop request were more subtle than that. It was General Wheeler who had seen Tet as a turning point that could be capitalized on, and he had needled Westmoreland to ask for enough reinforcements to trigger the calling up of reservists, something President Johnson had been unwilling to do. Westmoreland had gone along, even settling on the exact figure that Wheeler had suggested. Then Wheeler had taken the case to the president and Clifford.

Clifford had been appalled. Johnson had said he would think it over. When he did, he realized it was time for Westmoreland to come home from Saigon.

His replacement was General Creighton Abrams, a gruff World War II tank commander with a much dimmer view of the prospects in Vietnam. Abrams had been Westmoreland's second in command in Saigon, but his skirts were unsullied by the troop request because, inexplicably, no one had told him about it. In a meeting with Johnson while the president was considering the request, Abrams had been asked if he needed more men in Vietnam. No, the current number is plenty, was Abrams's reply.[4] Abrams felt blindsided when he later learned what was behind the question.

The administration lived in fear that the troop request would be leaked to the press. Two days before the 1968 New Hampshire primary, the *New York Times* spilled the story on the front page, blaming Westmoreland, who then felt he had been ambushed. The White House parried the news with a half-truth: that the request had never reached the president's desk. Yet a year later when Laird entered office, the request had not yet been rejected officially because to do so would have set America on a path Johnson was not ready to take—the road that would bring American soldiers home before a peace treaty was signed.

Now Laird, a master at reading and heeding public opinion, was secretary of defense, and Westmoreland was the new army chief of staff. As one of Laird's first acts in office, he formally killed the old troop request, although he would raise it frequently in conversations with Clifford over the next four years, especially when Clifford roiled the waters by publicly calling for faster troop withdrawals from Vietnam. "You left me a request for two hundred thousand more troops for Vietnam and you didn't have the guts to turn it down. Why the hell did you leave that work for me?" Laird would rail. According to him, Clifford would respond, "Well, Mel, you have to understand that the president didn't want me to get involved with anything like that."

The 1964 selection of Wheeler as the sixth chairman of the Joint Chiefs marked a distinct break with the past; some called it the "end of the age of heroes." In the previous seventeen years, the five men who held the post—General Omar Bradley, Admiral Arthur Radford, General Nathan Twining, General Lyman Lemnitzer, and General Maxwell Taylor—had been famous combat commanders in World War II and Korea. Wheeler was not a household name, and he had never served as a combat commander.[5] Johnson picked him for the military's top man in uniform because he was politically adept and an honest broker between the military and civilian leadership. He was careful to express his own strong personal opinion only when asked by the president or secretary of defense and, otherwise, confined his views to the meetings of the Joint Chiefs. Only after McNamara had thoroughly abused Wheeler and the chiefs did Wheeler change his modest approach.[6]

For years, McNamara's reliance on his "whiz kids" in the Pentagon's Office of Systems Analysis had grated on the Joint Chiefs. The job of the systems analysts was to crunch numbers and challenge time-honored military assumptions; they had a monopoly on McNamara's attention, and he did little to hide how much more he respected them than he did his military advisers. Time and again, the young brains led by Alain Enthoven ran roughshod over the career military. The Joint Chiefs took it in seething silence until August 1967 when Wheeler led a revolt.

The service chiefs had come to believe that victory would not be possible without a change in strategy. In late summer they laid out their point of view during a hearing of the Senate Armed Services Committee. They said the war as it was being fought was not winnable. McNamara himself was in the middle of a subtle turnaround, questioning the possibility of victory in Vietnam. He testified before the same Senate committee on August 25, but the Joint Chiefs were not satisfied that he was being realistic enough. Within hours after McNamara's testimony, they met secretly at the Pentagon without aides or stenographers. They all took a pledge never to speak of the meeting's particulars. Wheeler recommended that they all resign in protest the following day, Saturday, after a press conference at which they would spell out their profound disagreement with the civilian leadership. After three hours of intense debate, they unanimously agreed on that course.

But when Wheeler returned to his quarters at Fort Myer in Washington, D.C., he was greatly troubled. He called another meeting, immediately. At 8:30 P.M., the chiefs met again under the same rules, and Wheeler warned that a mass resignation would be "mutiny." This second meeting was more contentious than the first. One of the chiefs argued that they should still resign; Johnson and McNamara weren't listening to them anyway, and American men were dying. But Wheeler persuaded them that they could do more good by staying.

While details of the meeting did not leak until the mid-1980s, Congressman Laird picked up the rumblings and knew a change was occurring. As Laird began to piece together the details from his widespread intelligence network, which included top Joint Chiefs staffers in whom the chiefs had confided, his admiration for Wheeler grew. Laird felt Wheeler had made the honorable choice, based on respect for the chain of command, and could continue to use his position to make a difference. Laird concluded that the longer Wheeler managed the Joint Chiefs, the better off the country would be.[7]

Battling the civilian leadership and keeping the Joint Chiefs together during the Johnson administration wore down Wheeler, who already had a bad heart. He had at least one heart attack in 1967, which was kept secret, and possibly a second. The weariness was painfully evident to Colonel Robert Pursley. He recalled that once on a visit to Saigon, "General Wheeler put his head down on the table in the first briefing and just took a nap."[8] Yet he would end up serving six years as chairman, longer than anyone before or since. By law the chairman of the Joint Chiefs was allowed to serve a maximum of four years, which for Wheeler should have ended in the summer of 1968. But Johnson wanted Wheeler to finish out the administration and provide a stable transition for the next president. Wheeler reluctantly agreed, and an act of Congress made it legal.[9]

Laird was determined to keep Wheeler on for a sixth year, but Nixon didn't agree. He suggested that Marine Corps Commandant General Leonard Chapman be the new chairman. Laird knew that the only reason Nixon urged that promotion was so he could appoint as the new marines commandant a general who had been his military aide when he was vice president, and whom he considered a close friend. Laird said no, and invoked the cocktail-napkin promise. He respected Wheeler as a loyal officer who knew the territory and would carry out orders, even if Wheeler didn't agree with them. Those orders, as far as Laird was concerned, would be to begin taking Americans out of Vietnam as quickly as possible. Conversely, Nixon didn't protest the Wheeler extension primarily because the president thought Wheeler was one general who had not lost hope of victory in Vietnam, and Nixon liked that can-do spirit.

Wheeler had no inkling of these behind-the-scenes discussions. Instead, when he was asked to meet with Nixon in the Oval Office on January 21, he hoped the president would accept his request for retirement quickly. While Laird waited outside, Wheeler began his prepared speech by saying it was important for the president to have his own man as chairman, so he was ready to step aside. Nixon appeared surprised and asked the sixty-one-year-old Wheeler to stay on. Wheeler hadn't expected that and began forcefully making a case about his desperate need for a rest. Nixon wouldn't hear of it. He painted Wheeler as the one man who had wanted to win the war, but victory had been thwarted by McNamara and Clifford. It would be different under the new president, Nixon implied. Wheeler understood Nixon to say that, if he stayed, he would be free to pursue a military victory in Vietnam. Still Wheeler was not persuaded, but he said he would stay if the president made it an order, so Nixon did. As Wheeler left the meeting for a photo with Laird and others, he obligingly tacked on a smile, but the inner warmth was absent. He had been surprised by Nixon's insistence and didn't realize then that it was actually Laird's idea.[10]

The terms of the other chiefs were fixed, and Laird did not tamper with them. He kept the conservative and cunning Admiral Thomas Moorer as chief of Naval Operations. Laird was happy to have General Chapman stay on as commandant of the Marine Corps, and considered him to be "probably the most brilliant of the four-star generals that were in the military at that particular time." He did not feel the same about Westmoreland, who had been army chief of staff for only seven months, but Laird chose to live with him. Westmoreland later complained in his memoirs that Laird never listened to him as a member of the Joint Chiefs. That wasn't true, Laird said; he listened, but he rarely agreed. Westmoreland's views about aggressively prosecuting the war were not always shared by the other chiefs, and he had lost his influence in Congress. "He had worn out his welcome," Laird said, "because each time he came back to testify [from his command in Saigon to congressional hearings] he had a great story to tell, for four years, a great, optimistic story to tell. The Congress had grown weary with the long war."

Westmoreland was not thrilled to have a politician for a boss. Laird frequently had to lecture him on politics. "Politics is not a bad thing, Westy," Laird would say. "That's the art and science of government. We have to make our government work. You have to have support of people. People are important in this country." As was typical of Laird, he still respected the man with whom he differed. Their sons were friends at prep school, and the two men amicably crossed paths at school events. Laird often said the striking Westmoreland looked more like a soldier than any military man he had ever met. "When he'd get dressed up in his uniform, I always felt like saluting."

The man who had been air force chief of staff for four years, General John McConnell, also stayed on but was already a psychological casualty of the Vietnam War. A World War II combat pilot (China-India-Burma theater), McConnell had become brigadier general at the age of thirty-six. He was a fast-rising star who could not conceive of fighting a war in which victory was not the goal. Consequently, the Johnson-McNamara manipulation of the military destroyed him. As his air force pilots bravely flew over North Vietnam, dodging surface-to-air missiles and antiaircraft flak, McConnell was furious that they were not allowed to bomb the best targets. When the Joint Chiefs secretly discussed resigning, McConnell was the most outspoken advocate for doing it. "I can tell you how I feel," McConnell said. "I'm so sick of it. I have never been so goddamn frustrated by it all. I'm so sick of it." But still he stayed at his post, stubbornly keeping a sign on his door: "Our job is to fight and win. Don't you forget it."[11]

To a man, the chiefs were wary of Laird. Though they had known him to be generally supportive of the military in Congress, that experience could not predict how he would act as their boss. He had always voted for the military budget, but only after he held their feet to the fire in attempts to hunt out waste and urge the military to economize where it could. And what would he do with Vietnam? During the transition period, Clifford had "leaked" the substance of his private conversations with Laird to the Joint Chiefs. Clifford warned that Laird wanted out of Vietnam, as soon as honorably feasible. Laird did not see that victory was possible, so it was time to get out, Clifford told the chiefs. For the hawks among them, that was unwelcome news.

Laird's first meeting with the chiefs, on January 22, 1969, was on their turf, in the "Tank." The nickname came from a time when the chiefs met near the boilers in the bowels of the old Army Munitions Building. When the Pentagon was built, the old name for their conference room stuck. Windowless, guarded, sound-proofed, shielded from eavesdropping, and restricted to a very small group, the Tank was the inner sanctum for the thrice-weekly meetings of the military service chiefs. No briefcases, tape recorders, or other devices were allowed. Note-taking was often forbidden. By tradition, the secretary of defense would come once a week, but the obstreperous McNamara had often intruded on their meetings uninvited, which infuriated the chiefs. Adding insult to injury were the orders he dispensed in those meetings without regard to objections by the uniformed military leaders.[12]

As the chiefs convened at 2 P.M., they could not help but feel history about to unfold. The familiar surroundings—the thick gold carpet and gold drapes (an alternate nickname was the "Gold Room"), the neatly placed papers in front of them, the sharpened pencils, and small bowls filled with hard candy—gave them some sense of comfort. They were also reassured when General Wheeler informed them that they "will have to put up with me for another year." Wheeler gave an account of his meeting with the new president and then informed them that the new defense secretary had requested to meet with them. Laird entered and circled the room, shaking hands all around. Then he sat at the head of the table in silence, appearing to wait for permission to speak. When Wheeler nodded to him, Laird began with an apology. "I want to thank you for inviting me here today, and I'm sorry to take this time to interrupt your work."

Laird recalled his cooperative relationship with them when he was in Congress and expressed confidence "that we can cooperate now." Opening the lone folder in front of him, Laird then offered a thirty-minute review of where the new administration stood on most things military. Without showing all his cards on Vietnam, Laird let them know that he knew the issues but welcomed a healthy give-and-take between the chiefs and himself. Then he shook everyone's hand again and walked out of the room. Author Mark Perry's definitive book on the history of the Joint Chiefs, *Four Stars,* recounts what happened next:

> Following the predictable stunned silence, there was an almost palpable sense of relief around the table as well as a chilling realization that an enormously self-confident and adept politician was in control. Laird had accomplished in a few minutes what most officers believed would take years to gain: he had won the trust of a disenchanted high command that was more than willing to mistrust any Defense Secretary, regardless of his policies.
>
> It was no less than a revolution in civilian-military relations, a commentary on what officers prize above all else. In the history of the JCS,

the Laird introduction of January 22, 1969, stands out as the primary example of just how a civilian leader can both dampen military mistrust and gain military allegiance for controversial foreign policy initiatives that run counter to traditional military beliefs....

[O]f all the secretaries who have served at the Pentagon, Laird remains among the most respected, not because he agreed with military programs and policies (he very often didn't), but because he was willing to compromise on JCS positions and accord the chiefs the respect they thought they deserved. Perhaps Laird, with eight terms in Congress under his belt, could not have acted any other way; nevertheless, his intuition to treat members of the JCS as intelligent political equals rather than warmongering subordinates worked wonders in transforming the Pentagon from a battlefield to a demilitarized zone.[13]

On the power scale, Laird and Kissinger were evenly matched in the first years of the Nixon administration. "Henry always told me I was more Machiavellian than he was," Laird said. "I'd say, 'No, I'll give you that award.'" A title more frequently applied to Laird was the "cheese country Richelieu," after the crafty seventeenth-century French cardinal. Laird had an ability to manipulate Congress that mesmerized Kissinger, and Kissinger held similar sway over the president. Each used the skills of the other to strengthen their combined position. Laird knew from the beginning it would be a mistake to alienate the man closest to the president. "You have to get along with people like that," Laird said. "The national security advisor to the president is in a very unusual position. He has almost hourly access to the president. The secretary of defense is not even in the same building. You want him on your team, or you want to be on his team."

The NSC was Kissinger's power base and the place where he and Nixon chose to centralize their control over the State and Defense departments. Laird couldn't stop Kissinger and Nixon from reorganizing the NSC, but he could avoid entangling himself in the machinations, to preserve what he called his "freedom of movement." He rarely went to NSC meetings unless the president was going to be there. Under the Johnson administration, the NSC had a reputation for not paying much attention to the military. But Laird knew Kissinger and Nixon would be different. Knowing Nixon's nature, and suspecting Kissinger's, Laird correctly predicted both would try to establish a separate channel to the Joint Chiefs that bypassed him. By law, the chain of command went from the president to the secretary of defense, and from him to what were then known as the commanders-in-chief (CINCs) of the various commands around the world. For the prosecution of the Vietnam War, the command chain went from Nixon to Laird to the commander-in-chief of the Pacific forces (CINCPAC) in Hawaii, Admiral John McCain. He was an aggressive can-do commander who occasionally had to be cooled down by his superiors. (Even as Laird was taking office and preparing to withdraw U.S. troops from Vietnam, McCain was being quoted in an interview with *Reader's Digest* as saying, after the 1968 Tet offensive, "We have the enemy licked now. He is beaten. The enemy cannot achieve a military victory; he cannot even mount another major offensive.") From McCain, the command chain went to General Abrams in Saigon, the commander of the Military Assistance Command Vietnam (MACV), or "MacVee" as it was called in Pentagon shorthand. He was gaining a reputation as the realist who would not doctor the grim news about the war.

That chain of command did not include the Joint Chiefs, not even the chairman. In theory, they were there to advise the president, but that was not the practice. Since the chairman was in charge of the National Military Command Center (NMCC), from which operational military orders flowed, he acted as if he were part of that chain, just beneath the secretary of defense. The NMCC was also the place into which all information on what was going on around the world was funneled. From the beginning, because NMCC staffers reported to the chairman, Laird was concerned that the command center could become a black hole in a crisis. If, for example, a North Korean fighter jet shot down a U.S. spy plane—as would happen just three months later—the deputy for operations in the command center was supposed to inform Wheeler. Over in the White House Situation Room, aides to the president would get the same intelligence. Dozens of people could learn of the incident and rally a response before anyone remembered to tell the secretary of defense.

Given the personalities of the Nixon players, Laird couldn't let that happen. He insisted that he interview and approve all deputy directors assigned to run the NMCC. "I wanted them to know that *I'd* placed them there," he explained. In addition, Laird and Pursley would frequently drop in on the command center, befriending the senior officers and otherwise inserting themselves into the NMCC command chain that otherwise could have left Laird out.

During Laird's four years as secretary of defense, both Nixon and Kissinger would actively work to sideline Laird, who was not always in agreement with their agenda. The pair energetically tried to co-opt the chiefs, as well as General Abrams. They cultivated "back channels" behind Laird, to glean military advice and scuttlebutt, as well as to convey secret orders. The myth grew up around Laird that he had been bypassed several times by Nixon and Kissinger on critical Vietnam decisions, including bombing targets. The truth, however, was that even if Laird was not a party to an order, he knew about it within hours after it was given and usually before it was carried out. Since he had earned the chiefs' loyalty, and also proved he could protect them and most of their pet programs from Congress, the chiefs and Abrams kept Laird fully informed.

In fact, Laird encouraged the chiefs to meet with Kissinger and the president, as long as they reported back to him. The chiefs could be valuable lobby-ists for defense programs at the White House, Laird felt. They also became Laird's eyes and ears, along with David Packard, on the various NSC com-mittees Kissinger established in his attempt to control the national security and foreign policy apparatus. When one of the chiefs neglected to report on a meeting at the White House, Laird always learned about it from someone else, and then there was hell to pay. In his memoirs, Admiral Elmo Zumwalt, who in 1970 became chief of Naval Operations, reported at length on Kissinger's attempts to turn him into an NSC courtier. At first Zumwalt was flattered. But then Laird became "infuriated" when he learned from another source about an unreported meeting between Zumwalt and Kissinger. "Laird insisted that as a Constitutional official and a critical link in the chain of command he was the conduit through which all dealings with his subordinates must pass, and that he could not tolerate those subordinates being given orders outside the chain of command or engaging in activities that he knew nothing about. That of course was the school I had been brought up in as a military man," Zumwalt wrote.

So when Kissinger next saw Zumwalt on a military matter, the admiral said he was obliged to report back to Laird. Kissinger suggested they could call their appointments "nonmeetings," and he would take responsibility for what happened there; Laird wouldn't have to know. "Nevertheless I soon con-cluded, "Zumwalt wrote, "that professional ethics compelled me to pass along the substance of our conversations to Laird." Within weeks, it became more than a matter of ethics for Zumwalt, who came to view Kissinger as duplici-tous, intellectually arrogant, and dangerously elitist. Conversely, he saw Laird as a straight shooter who deserved Zumwalt's loyalty.[14]

The same was true for the rest of the chiefs. While they valued separate time with Kissinger (and more so with the president), they trusted Laird. Pursley said this discernment on their part saved the careers and reputation of those men. "Normally, the chiefs, when they hear the president say something, are almost immediately going to click their heels, 'Yes sir,' and go try to implement it," Pursley said. "If that had happened during the Nixon administration, Lord help us. It would have been a wild and crazy world. President Nixon was keen on issuing orders that were impetuous, petulant—and a number of other ad-jectives—which weren't really intended to be implemented. . . . Mel Laird pro-tected the chiefs and Abrams from those kinds of things."[15]

⌖

The day after the inauguration, Nixon convened the first meeting of the Na-tional Security Council, which by the grand design of Nixon and Kissinger was to supplant the State Department as the preeminent base of foreign policy power. At the brief meeting everyone was handed a homework assignment from Kissinger. During the previous two months, he and his staff had been energetically pulling together a Vietnam options paper. At Kissinger's request, the president and two experts of the Rand Corporation, a government-affiliated think tank, had flown to New York City to meet with Kissinger at the Pierre Hotel on Christmas Day 1968 to help outline the options. Kissinger was quite impressed with one of them, Daniel Ellsberg. One anecdote Ellsberg conveyed to Kissinger stuck with him. The young consultant mentioned that when McNamara became defense secretary, he had tied the Defense Department bureaucracy in knots by asking them, on paper, to answer ninety-six penetrating questions. Not only did it establish fairly quickly who was in charge, but it unearthed for the record the differences between the military and competing civilian agencies on key issues. Kissinger seized on the idea, which became the genesis of National Security Study Memorandum 1 (NSSM 1) or "Nissum One" in NSC jargon.

With the help of Ellsberg and others, Kissinger produced a paper for the first NSC meeting that asked seventy-eight questions about Vietnam. As the new officials of the Nixon administration began scanning through the six-page, single-spaced assignment, Kissinger explained that the president wanted each agency (Defense, State, CIA, Joint Chiefs, etc.) to answer the questions and send them back separately to the NSC. Aside from the bureaucratic (and autocratic) designs of Kissinger, NSSM 1 was, nevertheless, a valuable questionnaire that would inevitably give a freeze-frame picture of the war from the view of each agency. The parties at that first meeting, including Laird, accepted the marching orders without remonstration. There was little talk that would reveal where they stood, with each keeping his opinion close to the vest until Kissinger's questionnaires were returned.[16]

There was certainly plenty of blame to go around in January 1969 for the way the war had turned out. The American public, which will rally for a crisis but often ignores creeping problems, had paid scant attention to the incremental buildup in Vietnam. America slid into the war with little thought for how it might end. First, the United States sought to defend French colonial rights in the region against rising nationalism. By the time colonialism became politically incorrect, a new reason to make a stand in Vietnam had come to the fore: "hegemony," the possibility that the Soviet Union and China might combine their Communist agendas to take over the world. Under that theory, Vietnam was a domino that, if allowed to fall, would knock over the entire region. Never mind that the Chinese and the Vietnamese despised each other, and that China barely lifted a finger to help its neighbor North Vietnam and would have been safer with a divided Vietnam than a border nation united in Communism and allied with the Soviet Union. Never mind that the war was almost entirely funded by the Soviets. Never mind that Chinese and Soviet Communism were a twain that would never meet.

Laird, as common man, was disdainful of the Ivy League buzzwords Kissinger tossed around such as "hegemony" and "détente." Laird saw things in simpler terms: stay or go, win or lose, in or out. When hegemony began tarnishing as an excuse for American troops to be in Vietnam, there was nothing left but the noble goal of self-determination for South Vietnam, if indeed that was what the South Vietnamese wanted. By 1969 even that wasn't clear. South Vietnamese politics were in upheaval, its economy was built on sand, and its fighting force was uneven. The Communist cause had caught the fancy of an indigenous army of South Vietnamese guerrillas, the Viet Cong, who were the largest permanent "enemy" presence in the South. North Vietnamese troops fought hit-and-run style in cross-border raids from Cambodia, Laos, and North Vietnam.

America's allies, who occasionally joined her in Vietnam, at America's expense, began souring on the war and limiting their support. Even Japan was starting to complain about the use of Okinawa as a base for the B-52s that pummeled North Vietnam. By 1969 it was too late to make an alliance with the North's Ho Chi Minh and try to soften his brand of Communism in the North. The United States had the equivalent of eleven combat divisions, nine tactical air wings, and seven divisions of "advisors" arrayed against Ho Chi Minh, telling the natives of South Vietnam how to fight their war.

Laird's razor-sharp political instincts told him what Americans wanted to hear: if South Vietnam wanted independence from the North, then it was their battle to fight. And if they didn't have the will to fight and win, then so be it. The United States had, bit by bit, "Americanized" the war, crippling the South by treating it as the grunt on the battlefield, suited to take orders but not to command. "We weren't preparing them to do anything," Laird said. "They were in a position where they couldn't govern themselves because we had made it that way. For eight years we had been putting in more and more troops, matériel, wealth. There hadn't a month gone by for eight years that we hadn't Americanized that operation. I wanted to change the Americanization of Southeast Asia to one where we gave responsibility to the Vietnamese. As Ike said, we shouldn't have been involved there in the first place."

Aside from war-weariness, Laird had another reason for wanting to get out of Vietnam as quickly as possible. The war was destroying the U.S. military. While in Congress Laird had begun to harp on McNamara, accusing him of robbing Peter to pay Paul—underestimating the cost of the war to get Congress to go along with his budget, and then taking money from other defense programs, such as NATO, to pay for the shortfall in Vietnam. Meanwhile, the drain was allowing the Soviet Union to narrow the gap between U.S. and Soviet weaponry.

Johnson had chosen not to call up reservists to do the jobs for which they were trained—but used the draft instead to ship hastily trained, often unwilling soldiers to the front. The readiness of the Reserves suffered dearly for Johnson's choice. Not only were they deprived of the chance to use their training and hone their skills in real combat, but their resources were siphoned off by the war. Meanwhile, the draftees, who made up a third of those who were deployed to Vietnam, were demoralized by jungle warfare, dissipated by readily available drugs, torn by racism on the job, and scorned by their countrymen when they came home. Laird's mission was no less than the salvation of the U.S. military.

16

Off the Menu

MEL LAIRD APPEARED BEFORE the Senate Armed Services Committee for a scant two hours before he was confirmed as secretary of defense—a remarkably brief showing for a Cabinet nominee. It was a carefully choreographed love fest, and, as was typical with Laird, he had already counted the votes. The chairman of the committee was his good friend Richard Russell. Laird brought along Senator William Proxmire to vouch for him. Proxmire was a Democrat and a loud opponent of the war in Vietnam. Like Laird, Proxmire was from Wisconsin, and it was traditional for members of Congress to support their native sons in such hearings, even if they differed in philosophy. But Proxmire was not there just out of courtesy. He was the personification of Laird's ability to attract a loyal following across party and philosophical lines. Proxmire told the senators that Laird understood the military and would not be intimidated by it; that he would be completely honest with Congress, and that no one in politics or the military could "bully or browbeat" him. Vietnam did not come up in the questioning, and Laird did not raise it. "You don't want to stir things up when you know you have a 100 percent vote," said Laird.

The pot Laird had to stir was over at the White House, where Nixon and Kissinger were polling the administration about Vietnam. Kissinger's National Security Study Memorandum 1 had worker bees in the State and Defense departments and the CIA scrambling to persuade the president to follow their divergent leads. NSSM 1 posed more than fifty questions in twenty-eight categories. The day after Kissinger distributed the questions, he issued another memo with "Vietnam Policy Alternatives." There were seven of them, ranging from an all-out military assault until the victory was won, to an immediate unilateral withdrawal of U.S. troops. When the answers to NSSM 1 rolled in, the divisions on the Nixon team were glaring. The Joint Chiefs, Admiral John McCain, and the U.S. Embassy in Saigon waxed enthusiastic about the war and the potential for victory. The CIA and the new defense secretary were dubious. There were a few things everyone agreed on: North Vietnam had enough men in reserve to outlast any loss of troops; the enemy was calling all the shots as to where and when the fighting would occur and, thus, controlled the casualty numbers for both sides; and even though decimated by the Tet offensive, the North Vietnamese regular army could still mount major offensives.

At the Defense Department, the most pessimistic voice was that of Paul Warnke, assistant secretary for International Security Affairs. Once all the answers to NSSM 1 were in, Warnke wrote Laird a grim analysis. Hanoi had not come to the bargaining table in Paris because it wanted to negotiate peace, Warnke wrote. The Communists were in Paris because they had figured out it would take too long to wear out their enemies on the battlefield alone, and they hoped to wear them out at the negotiating table, too. The enemy's pool of men was seemingly bottomless. In 1968 alone, 291,000 North Vietnamese soldiers had either died, deserted, or been so badly wounded that they were put out of commission. Yet all of those losses had been made up by 1969. General Abrams had estimated in his response to NSSM 1 that North Vietnam could enlist three hundred thousand new soldiers every year. At that rate the allies would have to kill twenty-five thousand of them a month to stem the tide—something Abrams said the allies could do if called upon. The key point, Warnke concluded, was that the North Vietnamese were able and willing to suffer casualties at unexpectedly high and sustained levels and could still do substantial damage.

Upgrading the South Vietnamese army and then turning the war over to them was Laird's exit plan, and Warnke did not hedge about the enormity of that task. He reminded Laird of a CIA assessment only a month old that said without the help of the Americans, the South Vietnamese army "would rapidly disintegrate under a heavy and sustained communist offensive." The CIA was doubtful that the South could make a better showing "any time soon." This was not consistent with General Abrams's vision, but it was a sobering thought.[1]

Warnke's caution about the folly of trying to pursue a military victory over North Vietnam was a position he had held for some time. His memo to Laird was a warmed-over version of one he and Colonel Pursley had written for Clark Clifford nearly a year earlier. Clifford had given them these instructions: "I want to impress upon the President [Johnson] that our posture is basically so impossible that we have got to find some way out.... We should come up with a memo that makes the case for a disengagement on our part as a matter of transcendent importance for this country."[2] Warnke and Pursley had produced such a memo, and Clifford had agreed heartily with their conclusions, but the memo ended up being for his eyes only because Johnson was not interested in the news it bore. In Laird's hand, the same information reinforced what he already believed about the war, and, unlike Clifford, Laird had the power to do something about it.

~

Even before Nixon took office, General Abrams, seeing the writing on the wall, had delicately approached South Vietnamese President Nguyen Van Thieu with the possibility that the United States would begin a process of withdrawing U.S. forces. On January 17, 1969 Abrams and U.S. Ambassador Ellsworth Bunker went to Thieu's palace in Saigon and told him they were going to recommend that the 9th Infantry Division be sent home from the Mekong Delta. It was a logical place to begin; there were no North Vietnamese units there, only Viet

Cong, and the South Vietnamese army could handle them. Abrams reported back to the new administration that Thieu wanted to know if a withdrawal of some troops would be "well received" in the United States, indicating he knew withdrawals were calculated to please the American public.[3]

Now it was Laird's turn to go to Saigon and be more blunt with Thieu. Laird had promised a trip as soon as he had settled into his office. On March 5 he had breakfast with Nixon and then headed to Andrews Air Force Base to board a plane for Saigon. Laird was not given to introspection, nor was he one to overanalyze what the trip was all about. In his mind it was simple. He needed to know how long it would take to whip the South Vietnamese army into shape so they could take over the war themselves, and he needed to know how quickly he could withdraw U.S. troops while that was happening.

"I never was a great supporter of the war," Laird recalled. "I was a great supporter of getting the hell out of there." The media knew this about Laird. The previous December, before Nixon took office, *Business Week* predicted that Laird would "rapidly 'de-Americanize' the fighting" while the *Wall Street Journal* observed that Laird was "eager to liquidate the U.S. effort there on any seemingly honorable terms."[4]

Laird was aware that others who had made the pilgrimage to Saigon before him had come back optimistic about the war. Being in the presence of the military brass in Saigon had that effect on visitors. When he was vice president, Johnson had gone to Vietnam and had come back convinced the war was noble and winnable. George Romney, while a presidential candidate, made the trip and afterward declared the war was "morally right and necessary." When confronted with political reality, he later said he had been "brainwashed." For Laird such tales were more like hogwash. "I think they were there to listen to how much more U.S. support they needed. I was there to listen to how much more they could get along without. I was looking at a different strategy—one that substituted South Vietnamese capability for that of the U.S. and, in the process, reduced U.S. military presence."

Laird had urgent problems to mull over on the trip. North Vietnam, in a blatant slap in the face to Nixon and the nascent peace talks, had launched another Tet-season offensive in February, shelling South Vietnamese cities. It was a violation of the unwritten "understandings" tacitly agreed to when Johnson had halted the bombing of the North just three months earlier. In the first week of the new offensive, 453 Americans were killed—the worst losses in ten months. General Abrams had initially pushed for a resumption of the bombing in retaliation for the attacks. But Nixon was stuck with those "understandings." Abrams's second option was to hit the North in a place that would hurt almost as much—Cambodia.

North Vietnamese troops had virtually taken over a swath of Cambodia along the South Vietnamese border, kicking out the Cambodians and establishing "sanctuaries" from which to launch cross-border attacks. Logic would dictate that those nests should be wiped out. But there was a roadblock: the United States officially recognized Cambodia as neutral in the war, and any attacks over the border would bring antiwar rioters into the streets of America protesting the expansion of a war that Nixon had promised to shrink.

On February 9 Abrams cabled General Wheeler to share fresh intelligence about the location of the North Vietnam headquarters in Cambodia, called the Central Office for South Vietnam, or COSVN. Abrams said it could be taken out with an hour of B-52 strikes, and the likelihood of hitting any Cambodians was nil, since they had all fled the area. Abrams sent two colonels to Washington to brief Laird, Kissinger, and Rogers on the plan on February 18. Since the group met in Laird's office the first thing in the morning, the operation was given the code name Operation Breakfast.

As usual Laird immediately saw the political downside. He understood the logic of going after the enemy in his lair, but Laird knew instinctively there was no way of selling that logic to the American public or the Democratic Congress. But Nixon was itching to retaliate against the North for the new Tet offensive, and he warmed immediately to the idea of bombing a North Vietnamese headquarters, even if it was in Cambodia. His solution to the public relations problem was simple—don't tell anyone. Laird found the notion of secrecy to be naive to the point of stupidity. Nixon was leaving to make the diplomatic rounds in Europe and was talked out of making any decision on Cambodia until he returned, if for no other reason than it would look cavalier for the United States to be bombing Cambodia while the president was globe trotting.

Then, on the plane to Brussels, Nixon changed his mind. Angry over increased attacks on cities in South Vietnam, he ordered the immediate bombing of the sanctuaries in what was called the Fish Hook region of Cambodia. Kissinger and his military assistant, Colonel Alexander Haig, flew to Brussels to work out the details of how to keep the bombing a secret. Back in Washington, Laird stewed about the deception and cabled Kissinger that it was a bad idea. Once again Nixon canceled the order. Then Nixon capped the confusion by sending two cables to Saigon—one to Ambassador Bunker telling him to inform Abrams that the Cambodia bombing was off, and a second to Abrams telling him to ignore the cable to Bunker and go ahead with the planning. Bunker's boss, Secretary of State Rogers, was opposed to the bombing, fearing the effect it might have on the peace negotiations. Nixon found it easier to keep his old friend Rogers out of the loop instead of telling him the truth. This dissembling became a pattern for Nixon. Although he was the most powerful man in the world, he hated to cross other powerful men and would avoid them and walk on eggs rather than give a direct order.

❧

It was in this charged atmosphere that Laird arrived in Saigon for the first time. With him were General Wheeler, Froehlke, Pentagon press chief Dan Henkin,

Warnke, and Pursley. To greet Laird, the North Vietnamese peppered Saigon with rockets. No sooner had he gotten off the airplane than the press contingent waiting at the airfield asked what he was going to do about this obvious violation of the 1968 "understandings." Would the United States resume the bombing of the North? "I do not want to issue warnings nor make any threats," Laird responded. "I do want, however, to state unequivocally that if these attacks continue unabated, an appropriate response will be made." He wouldn't say what he had in mind.

Laird's first stop was Abrams's headquarters. After some preliminaries, Laird set out his position. This is how he recalled it: "Now Abe, I don't want to hear anything about increases. I just want to talk about our withdrawal program and when we're going to start. How good are the South Vietnamese forces? How quickly can they improve? How soon can they assume larger and more important combat roles?" He didn't get any argument from Abrams; only Wheeler tried to broach the idea of U.S. troop increases. "I would not listen to that," said Laird.

He spent much of the time briefing Abrams on the state of affairs in Washington. "I had to explain to him what the situation was in the United States, what our support situation was in Congress and with the American people, and how we had to try to save as much of the defense budget as possible. We had to get into a position where we could negotiate strategic arms limitations with the Soviet Union, and we couldn't do it if we were in a position of weakness and all of our assets were being dissipated."

Abrams was not offended by the tough talk; he had confidence in the South Vietnamese. That day marked the beginning of a mutual respect between the two men.

Laird spent part of his first night in Saigon in an underground bomb shelter in the backyard of the U.S. embassy while the enemy fired with small arms into a cemetery next door. Laird, Bunker, and Pursley had retreated to the shelter after dinner when the firing came too close for comfort. Unruffled, they talked business for two hours until it was deemed safe for them to resurface. Laird and Bunker came to call each other friends over the ensuing four years, but they didn't always agree on Vietnam policy. As a full-time resident of Saigon, Bunker was close to President Thieu and would frequently take his side in debates about the pace of U.S. troop withdrawals. Although Bunker never spoke up in meetings between Laird and Thieu, he would make his case later to Laird and then cable his bosses at the State Department, complaining that Laird was being too rough on Thieu. Their response would be to send someone to Saigon to hold Thieu's hand and occasionally give him false hope. Then Laird would have to send another emissary to get Thieu back on track.

On day two in Saigon, Laird headed for the presidential palace to deliver his first round of bad news to President Thieu. Laird gave Thieu the courtesy of a home court advantage because the message would be a hard one to swallow.

Amidst the pomp and honor guards, Laird got down to business, unhampered by the subtlety that others might use in a diplomatic setting. "I told him what would take place and he'd better get going on his program. He needed to get going on the modernization of his troops. They had to realize that they were going to take a more responsible role, and it wasn't going to be Americanized any longer." Thieu protested with a hint of authority in his voice that this was not what he had been promised by McNamara and Johnson. That prompted Laird to give him a "civics lesson." "I made sure he understood that we had a new administration and a new president."

While in Saigon, Laird secretly dispatched Froehlke to Thailand to warn its leadership about a possible bombing campaign in Cambodia. Normally that was a diplomatic job that would have been left to the ambassador, but Laird didn't trust that channel. "We had several important air bases in Thailand, and I didn't want them to be threatened in any way. I couldn't rely on the State Department to do it. I thought they would make too much of a deal out of it and it would be all over the papers," Laird recalled.

As would become his habit on successive trips to Vietnam, once the business in Saigon was done, Laird went out into the field, visiting various army corps headquarters and dining with the troops. Consistent with his mission, he gave them little hope that they would stay for a military victory. At a stop in Danang, the press called on him to account for headlines in the *New York Times,* claiming that marines were that very day fighting for control of a slip of land, the A Shau Valley in Laos, supposedly a neutral country. In fact, that campaign in Laos, called Operation Dewey Canyon had been going on since the day after Nixon's inauguration, costing 125 American and 1,600 enemy lives. The command in Saigon had earlier announced the operation, but only the part of it carried out on the South Vietnamese side of the border in the Quang Tri province. No mention had been made when the action spilled over into Laos. And it wasn't the first time U.S. troops had violated Laotian neutrality by crossing the border to harass the enemy supply lines along the Ho Chi Minh Trail. The Johnson administration had authorized such incursions in February of 1968, "in emergency situations . . . in exercise of the right of self-defense against enemy attacks."[5]

There were also two U.S. air campaigns ongoing in Laos at the time of Laird's first visit to Saigon. One code-named "Barrel Roll" used fighters for isolated attacks on communist Pathet Lao rebels. The second and more crucial, "Steel Tiger," used B-52s to bomb North Vietnamese supply lines running through Laos.

While in Danang, Laird dodged the questions about Laos, but the next day in Saigon, while boarding his plane to leave, he had more to say. In what sounded like an off-hand response to a reporter's question about Cambodia and Laos, Laird said American troops were allowed to cross the border to protect themselves, and he made it sound as if that had always been the policy. In reality, Laird had just given that order to Abrams. Laird called it "protective re-action"—as opposed to "hot pursuit," which was not allowed—and it opened wide the door for ground and air attacks into Laos, Cambodia, and North Vietnam on the smallest provocation from an enemy stronghold there. Back in Washington, the State Department recognized Laird's veiled statements for what they were—new policy.[6]

"Protective reaction" was the one bit of good news that the military got from Laird's visit. As the brass bid him farewell in Saigon that day, they knew that he was not going to help them win the war.[7] He was only going to keep as many Americans alive as he could while he worked to bring them all home.

Laird's party made a two-day stop in Hawaii, where they could find seclusion to write a report to Nixon about their findings. Laird also had another mission there—to rein in the commander of the Pacific forces, Admiral John McCain. The February issue of *Reader's Digest* included an upbeat interview with McCain, who was an unregenerate optimist about the war and never lost an opportunity to say so. His briefing charts for visiting dignitaries in Hawaii were the stuff of legend—maps of Vietnam with the Russian bear brooding over the whole of Southeast Asia, its fangs dripping blood over the region. "You'd think the Soviet Union was taking over all that area of the world and the end was soon to come," Laird said. His staff came to call these theatrical sessions the "big red arrow briefings." The diminutive admiral would pace back and forth waving a cigar at the blood and the arrows, describing troop movements and aggressive strategies that would stop the advance of the big bear. Laird privately believed that McNamara had encouraged such talk by his own rose-colored reports to Congress in the early years of the war.

When subjected to a McCain briefing, Laird learned to listen respectfully and then say what he had come to say. This time, in a four-hour meeting with the admiral, he told McCain to tone down his public gushing. This was the son of the first navy officer that Laird had ever seen, decked out smashingly in his white uniform that day more than thirty years earlier in Marshfield. Laird had great respect for the McCain military tradition, from the grandfather down to the grandson, Commander John McCain, who was at that moment a prisoner of war in Hanoi. But he couldn't have Admiral McCain spouting off about the winnability of the war. "I told him that we cannot put out optimistic reports unless we're sure of our facts and figures. I explained to him what we were going to be doing; we were going to start withdrawing and that he had to get with the process," Laird said. McCain's response was a loyal recognition of the chain of command: "Aye, aye, sir."

Holed up at a military beach compound on Oahu, Laird, Warnke, Henkin, and Pursley spent eighteen hours crafting a report to Nixon. It would form the foundation of the new administration's Vietnam policy. Laird told the president several things in that report:

- The combined U.S. and South Vietnamese forces were enough to keep the North from a military victory, and Abrams did not need any more men. But, that did not mean that a military victory over the enemy was anywhere in sight.
- The most recent Tet offensive could be a political ploy instead of a military strategy—Hanoi's way of saying that it was not bound by any "understandings" from Johnson's 1968 bombing halt.
- Resuming the bombing of the North would get the United States nowhere. The United States had already dropped 2.8 million tons of bombs in the war (compared to 2.6 million tons for World War II and the Korean War combined), and the result was still a stalemate.
- Laird said nothing about bombing Cambodia but recommended that the rules limiting cross-border raids should be eased up (something he had already taken the liberty of doing).
- South Vietnam was making surprisingly slow progress toward assuming more responsibility for the war, and the U.S. military had no satisfactory program to hurry that up. In fact, the military assumed that the South Vietnamese army could never be beefed up enough to stand alone. If the generals were right, that meant the United States would stay in Vietnam indefinitely until a peace agreement was reached by diplomats working at a snail's pace in Paris.
- No one at Saigon headquarters was asking for any more men, "but at the same time," Laird wrote, "no one has furnished me with any detailed analysis of the necessity for the continued presence of over 549,000 Americans in South Vietnam and Thailand."
- The United States should withdraw fifty thousand to seventy thousand troops from Vietnam before the end of 1969. This last recommendation was Laird's first card placed on the table, his opening of negotiations with the president, Kissinger, and the Joint Chiefs about the pace of withdrawal, the beginning of the end.

While Laird was away, the president had been stewing over the new enemy offensive taking place on the other side of the Pacific. Nixon issued another order to bomb Cambodia, this one to take effect on March 9. But Rogers protested, and, with Laird still in Vietnam, Nixon backed down again. Finally, on Saturday, March 15, after another brutal shelling of Saigon, Nixon called Kissinger and said he was ready to hit back, but that Rogers was not to be told until it was too late to call the bombers back. With the bright light of the new day,

Sunday, March 16, Nixon had calmed down enough to summon Laird, Rogers, Kissinger, and Wheeler to the Oval Office, ostensibly to discuss the pros and cons of hitting Cambodia. At least two people in the room, Laird and Kissinger, understood how Nixon's mind worked and knew the meeting was a charade. Nixon had already made up his mind, but he could not bring himself to be direct with Laird or Rogers, who opposed the plan for different reasons. So he wanted to make them think he was still open to their suggestions.

Rogers was worried about damaging the peace talks and offending Cambodian ruler Norodom Sihanouk, who could protest the bombing of his country. Sihanouk had already privately hinted to American diplomats that he would welcome any help they could give him in wresting part of his country back from the occupying North Vietnamese. But publicly, if the bombing came to light, he would have to protest and demand an apology. Thus Rogers conceded if the bombing was inevitable, it must be kept a secret.

Laird wanted to support the Joint Chiefs in this first test of their authority under his administration, even though he didn't share their enthusiasm for bombing campaigns in general. He wanted this bombing because the chiefs wanted it, and because it made some sense as a tactic. Plus, the chiefs would then owe him one when he asked for their support of his troop withdrawal plan. But Laird still objected to the secrecy, as did Wheeler. "Secrecy is the worst thing you can do," Laird said, "particularly as it applies to Vietnam." He believed that the minimal benefit gained from the Cambodia bombing would be a waste of what little public support there was left for the war when the secret was discovered. Why not admit the truth, face the criticism, and move on?

At each meeting on Operation Breakfast, the Cambodia bombing, Laird would turn to Wheeler and say, "How many people will know about this?" Wheeler would promptly supply the answer that Laird wanted, "At least twelve thousand." That was the number of military men and women it would take to mount the offensive, from the ground crews that gassed up the B-52s in Guam to the lowly message senders in the Pentagon and Saigon. But, after a couple of hours of debate that Sunday, Nixon said he had decided to go ahead anyway. Fine, said Laird, but he would absolutely not order those B-52 pilots to lie on their flight logs. "I told them I wouldn't send the message." Wheeler left the White House and went back to the Pentagon to cable the bombing orders to Abrams. Kissinger also sent a top-secret cable to the embassy in Saigon with orders for the military to lie. The deception that Laird refused to be a part of involved sending two sets of targets to the pilots. Their instructions on takeoff were to hit targets in South Vietnam near the Cambodian border. But once the planes were in the air, new orders were sent diverting them to Cambodia. Some diversionary hits were made in South Vietnam, but the majority of the pilots flew on to Cambodia. When they returned, the pilots were ordered to file false reports of their targets.

The military public relations machine in Saigon and Washington was prepared with a cover story should reporters get wind of action in Cambodia: sometimes routine strikes come close to the border, and that will be investigated. End of story.[8] As Laird had warned, it was a pretty flimsy plan. The secret would be exposed, but not in the way he had expected.

⎯ ⛯ ⎯

Operation Breakfast was launched March 18, 1969, initially to take out the North Vietnamese command in Cambodia—COSVN—in one strike. As Laird had suspected, the "headquarters" of the enemy was not a sitting duck. COSVN was an elusive, mobile collection of people and equipment that no single bombing run could wipe out. But the door had been kicked open to Cambodia and would not be easily closed. Operation Breakfast was soon renamed Operation Menu, with successive raids, each being given a different meal as a code name: lunch, dinner, supper, dessert, snack, and so on. In the next fourteen months, 3,600 B-52 sorties dropped one hundred thousand tons of bombs on Cambodia. The North Vietnamese said nothing, because to do so would be to admit that they were in Cambodia in violation of that country's neutrality. The Cambodians said nothing because none of their people were left in the region to get hit. Despite his objections, Laird kept his lips sealed, except to tell a few select members of Congress. Still a politician at heart, he felt strongly that the Senate and House leadership on the defense committees had a right to know what was going on. Plus, Laird assumed they would find out eventually, and he wanted his own skirts to be clean.

It took seven weeks before the secret bombing campaign was a secret no more, but the public reaction was so muffled and the news media so restrained in its reporting that the incident remains one of the public relations puzzles of the war. Laird had predicted a huge public outcry once the bombing was exposed. That outcry was years in the unfolding. The immediate explosion was internal—at the White House.

On May 9, New York Times reporter William Beecher, in a front-page story, announced that B-52s were pounding North Vietnamese supply caches in Cambodia. Beecher said the news had been confirmed by "Nixon administration sources." Suspicion fell immediately on the man most opposed to the secrecy, Laird. He was enjoying a round of golf with his friend Jack Mills and Congressmen Jerry Ford and Bob Michel at Burning Tree Country Club when he was summoned to the clubhouse to take a phone call from Kissinger. "I just want you to know you'd better get in touch with the president," Laird recalled Kissinger telling him. "He's mad as hell that you leaked that story to the New York Times." Laird told Kissinger to "go to hell," hung up on him, and went back to the golf game. It was not the first time, and it would not be the last time, that Kissinger and Nixon suspected Laird had spilled secrets to the press. Laird sometimes was guilty as charged, but not this time.

As events unfolded, it was never a mystery to Laird how Beecher got his story. A week earlier, a reporter from the *London Times* had flown over Cambodia in a small plane and had noticed huge pot holes in the ground below. A small story was buried in the London paper and got no attention. Though Laird wasn't sure if Beecher had another source, he knew that Beecher had called Dan Henkin and confronted him with the information. Henkin's response had been that the story was "speculative" and that he couldn't confirm or deny it.[9] As one of the twelve thousand people who knew about the bombing, Henkin did not lie to Beecher.

One of those not among the twelve thousand was Air Force Secretary Robert Seamans. He was in Southeast Asia when the bombing orders were given, so Laird informed Seamans's deputy, John McLucas, who inexplicably never told the boss. When the news broke, Seamans was steamed and complained privately to a few reporters. Incredibly, although several took a stab at the secret-bombing story, none of them hit real pay dirt, and it dropped from the headlines within a few days.

That did not, however, assuage the anger of Nixon and Kissinger. Determined to find the leaker, the president and Attorney General John Mitchell took their problem to a master—FBI Director J. Edgar Hoover. He fell back on his old standby, wiretapping. Nixon, with Kissinger's knowledge, authorized tapping the telephones of seventeen news reporters and administration officials, including some National Security Council staffers whose loyalty Kissinger doubted. They didn't have the nerve to tap Laird's phones, which he would have discovered quickly, as he ordered regular "sweeps" of his phones for bugs. Instead, they tapped the home phone of the man Laird was most likely to talk to after hours—his military assistant Pursley. The tap was kept on his phone for a month, then reinstated a year later—on both Pursley's home and office phones—and kept for almost a year after that. Neither Laird nor Pursley found out about the taps for nearly four years.

There were various excuses for listening in on Pursley's conversations: suspicions that he was leaking advance notice of troop withdrawals or spilling news about an allied invasion of Cambodia in 1970, and the outside chance that Nixon and Kissinger could glean some intelligence on what Laird was up to. But thousands of hours of tapes produced nothing, except complaints from Pursley's wife and children that there was something chronically wrong with their phones.

Pursley had few connections in the media. And if the eavesdroppers expected to get something out of Laird's after-hours conversations with Pursley on the two men's home phones, they were mistaken. Laird and Pursley spent so much time together each work day, that there was little left for them to say on the phone for the few hours that they were apart. The tapes revealed mundane details about schedules for the next day. There was brief speculation by those listening in on the conversations that Laird was having an affair with someone named Kay Graham. (They did not recognize the name of *Washington Post* publisher Katharine Graham when Laird told Pursley that he was going to her house for dinner.) And the eavesdroppers couldn't figure out who the "David" (Laird's son) was who often answered the phone at the Laird home.

~~~

The bombing of Cambodia continued with little media attention until April 1970 when it became just part of the backdrop of a U.S. ground invasion into Cambodia, which was not a secret. It was that invasion that finally triggered a public outcry about expansion of the war into a "neutral" country, the most tragic result of which was the shooting of student protestors at Kent State University.

In the spring of 1969, when the bombing was still a secret, Laird did what he could to prepare Congress for the reality of extending the war into the enemy's sanctuaries in Cambodia and Laos. In mid-March, in a hearing to ask the Senate Armed Services Committee for more money to upgrade the South Vietnamese army, Laird mentioned in passing that Laos and Cambodia were becoming increasingly more troublesome as enemy bases. Laird reminded the senators that Nixon had threatened some form of retaliation should the attacks on South Vietnamese cities continue. Most of the committee members already knew what Laird was talking about, but the American public did not.

At the same hearing, Laird asked for more money for Vietnam operations, and he was careful to tell the senators that the funds were not for exit operations, since that would signal a need for less money. "I do not wish to mislead this committee on what I am talking about here. I am not talking about the withdrawal of American troops at the present time," Laird said.[10] His reluctance to be more forthcoming visibly annoyed the senators who tried without success to pry more information out of him. While Laird may not have been talking about withdrawals openly in the Senate, withdrawal planning was taking up the bulk of his time behind closed doors.

"The good news had to be announced by the president," Laird recalled of his little fabrication in the Senate. "I always said to the president, 'You can announce all the good news and I'll take the bad news. That's my job.'" The announcement of the first troop withdrawals was already planned for a meeting between Nixon and Thieu on Midway Island in June. But before then there was plenty of dickering to be done over specific numbers. Laird's dodge was not just a courtesy to the president, however. It was part of a carefully calculated strategy to make sure he came out on top in that dickering.

The Sunday after Laird's appearance on Capitol Hill, he was a guest on NBC's *Meet the Press*. He continued to sidestep the specifics of a troop withdrawal, but for the first time he put a name to his program for ending the war: "I believe we can move toward *Vietnamizing* the war by the program that I outlined to the Armed Services Committee," Laird said. From that moment on, "Vietnamization" was the buzzword that would define Laird's four years in office.

The next morning, when Kissinger, Nixon, and the Joint Chiefs picked up the *Washington Post*, they got a little lesson in Laird-style politicking. Buried on page 25 was a column by Laird's friends Rowland Evans and Robert Novak announcing his strategy. They wrote that Laird was not satisfied with the old plan to train the South Vietnamese to take on just the homegrown Viet Cong rebels. He had in mind a second phase of training to make them capable of fighting the North Vietnamese army, too, "thus creating the proper psychological climate for the start of U.S. troop withdrawal."

The Evans and Novak column sent Kissinger "up the wall," according to Laird, who admitted years later that he was the source of the leak to the columnists. As was Laird's habit when he was the leaker, he called Kissinger to shift the blame. "I called Henry immediately and told him, 'Damn it, Henry, quit leaking this stuff.'" Kissinger was neither appeased nor fooled, but the leak accomplished its purposes for Laird. It put the public on notice as to his plan, and it let his critics in Congress know that he really was planning a withdrawal, even if he couldn't announce it yet himself. Laird could live with the repercussions over at the White House because he felt he had done the right thing. "I'm always a team player," he explained. "That was in the best interests of the team. But they may not have known it at the time."

Nixon indirectly alluded to his initial resistance to Vietnamization in his memoirs, writing: "Mel Laird had long felt that the United States could 'Vietnamize' the war—that we could train, equip, and inspire the South Vietnamese to fill the gaps left by departing American forces. It was largely on the basis of Laird's enthusiastic advocacy that we undertook the policy of Vietnamization."[11]

Kissinger was wary of Vietnamization as well. In a private memo to Nixon, he complained that Laird's troop withdrawal program would become like "salted peanuts to the American public: The more U.S. troops come home, the more will be demanded." This would add up to unilateral withdrawal, and he was "deeply concerned" about that prospect. "I don't know when Henry ever would have been prepared to see withdrawals start," recalled Lawrence Eagleburger, one of Kissinger's aides and a future secretary of state. To Kissinger, every American boot taken off the ground weakened his negotiating position with the North Vietnamese.[12]

"Nixon and Kissinger were in an entirely different frame of mind," according to Robert Pursley, Laird's military assistant. "They thought: 'We'll win this war. We'll hang the coonskin on the wall. Military victory—U.S.' But Laird was pushing withdrawal. It was clear that Laird's strategy was the logical one to pursue, but it was damned hard for a president and a guy like Kissinger to swallow."[13]

Nixon actually may have been more realistic than Kissinger, the political novice, about Laird's behind-the-scenes balancing act. At a meeting of the National Security Council two days after the Evans and Novak column had announced Laird's strategy, Nixon passed Laird a handwritten note: "Mel, you've done a great job up there [presumably a reference to Capitol Hill] and in your press appearances. RN"

Two days later, March 28, at the next meeting of the National Security Council, Johnson's 1966 Manila accord was all but thrown out. Nixon listened to all the parties present and then issued National Security Decision Memorandum 9. It said there would be no winding down of the war, but that the United States "should be prepared to withdraw all combat forces from South Vietnam if Hanoi meets specific conditions of a mutual withdrawal agreement." The major condition was withdrawal of enemy troops from Laos, Cambodia, and South Vietnam. Nixon alluded to the terms of the Manila accord when he said, "There will be no public repudiation of the former U.S. position that we would complete our withdrawal within six months of the completion of Hanoi's withdrawal." But he added the timing was no longer the driving issue. "The key point will not be the timetable but rather getting Hanoi to comply with the conditions for withdrawal."

In retrospect, Laird explained the secrecy about abandoning the Manila accord. It was President Thieu's last hope of hanging on to U.S. troops indefinitely. "He was attached to it because it promised him no withdrawals until a peace agreement was reached," Laird explained. Until the president could speak face to face with Thieu at the upcoming Midway Island summit, he didn't want Thieu to panic.

As it turned out, the demands for mutual withdrawal spelled out by Nixon at that March 28 National Security Council meeting were just words on paper. Three days later, Laird wrote a memo to the Joint Chiefs telling them how they should interpret the meeting: "There must be alternatives to mutual withdrawal. The principal alternative to be planned for is Vietnamizing the effort."[14] The American troops would come home even if there was no corresponding withdrawal by Hanoi.

And almost before the ink was dry on Nixon's order that there would be no deescalation of the war, on April 1 Laird ordered the number of B-52 bombing raids cut by 10 percent, for "budgetary reasons." Laird was a skeptic when it came to the capabilities of air power as it was being used in Southeast Asia. He neither asked nor told the president about the cutback until after he had ordered it. Nixon's directive at the March 28 meeting had been ignored.

As Laird, Nixon, and Kissinger had walked out of that meeting, the White House physician Dr. Walter Tkach had approached them and said, "Mr. President, President Eisenhower just died."[15] The man who had warned against any U.S. entanglement in an Asian war, the mentor whom Laird had counted on to advise him through the tough times ahead was gone. "I loved Eisenhower,"

Laird recalled. "He always said, 'You've got to make up your own mind on these things, Mel. You're no longer just running for Congress. You can't be running for Congress from that job.' He was always afraid that I would get a little bit too political. I really don't think that he felt the political situation was as bad as it was in the United States on Vietnam. I always reminded him of how he got elected. People got fed up with Korea." That lesson was not lost on Laird. People were fed up with another war, and if his party was to retain the White House he would have to end that war.

17

Template for a Crisis

THE PHONE BESIDE LAIRD'S BED rang before dawn on Tuesday, April 15, 1969. It was Colonel Pursley, who had been up since 1:45 A.M. gathering enough information to justify waking the boss. The news Pursley delivered was Laird's first bona fide national security crisis. Two North Korean MiG fighter jets had shot down an American military spy plane apparently on a routine mission over international waters Monday night. The plane, an EC-121, and its thirty-one crew members were missing in the Sea of Japan. Nixon was getting the news about the same time from Kissinger, who had also delayed waking his boss until the alarming story was fleshed out. The way Laird and Nixon responded to the crisis over the next two weeks would illustrate differences in leadership style and, ultimately, how national security operations would play out. The president was about to find out just how shrewd and sure-footed his defense secretary could be.

The EC-121 was an unarmed propeller plane bristling with six tons of electronic listening equipment. It had taken off from the Naval Air Station at Atsugi, Japan, the evening before with instructions to collect data over the Sea of Japan and land at an air base in South Korea. It was to come no closer than fifty miles to North Korea, well clear of the twelve-mile limit that North Korea claimed as its territorial waters. When the plane disappeared off the radar at 11:50 P.M., the word was quickly passed to the White House Situation Room and from there to Kissinger's military assistant, Colonel Alexander Haig, who made a courtesy call to Pursley. Thus was avoided one of Pursley's worst nightmares: that the defense secretary would be the last to know about a crisis because of the convoluted chain of command.

Pursley shared Laird's steady philosophy when it came to absorbing rapid-fire information coming in during a crisis. As Laird put it: "I wouldn't believe the first report, I might believe part of the second report, but I could start believing more of the third and subsequent reports." One part of the first report was clear: the plane had indeed vanished. The second report was enough for Pursley to awaken Laird: at 2:17 A.M., the official North Korean radio station, Radio Pyongyang, announced that MiGs had shot down an American spy plane because it crossed into North Korean air space. As day broke over the Sea of Japan, the third report came in; an American patrol plane had spotted debris from the EC-121 floating about one hundred miles off the coast of North Korea. The patrol plane radioed two Soviet destroyers that were the closest ships in the area and asked them to begin the search for bodies.

Back at the White House, Nixon had a point to prove. A year earlier, when North Korea had hijacked a U.S. spy ship, the *Pueblo*, then–presidential candidate Nixon had railed at Johnson for his tepid response and had called for military retaliation. The Communists had kept the *Pueblo* crew for more than a year, releasing them only a few days after Nixon took office. In Congress at the time, Laird's reaction to the *Pueblo* incident was more circumspect. He was less concerned about getting even—especially when the adversary was as mercurial as North Korea—and more concerned about why the spy ship had been trolling for intelligence off the waters of North Korea alone and unarmed without any protection from the air.

So, while Nixon stewed about whether to shoot back at the North Koreans for the EC-121 downing, Laird looked both behind and ahead. He wanted to know details of the EC-121 mission. Additionally, he immediately ordered all U.S. reconnaissance flights to stand down from missions near China, Cuba, and the Soviet Union and over the Mediterranean Sea until the Pentagon could figure out if those flights were critical, and, if so, whether armed escorts were needed as part of their routine. The action made so much sense to Laird that he didn't think it necessary to ask the president, or even inform him in any detail.

Haig quickly passed the word through Pursley that Kissinger wanted some options for retaliation. Kissinger also wanted to know how to keep the North Koreans from plucking any survivors out of the water and taking them prisoner. Pursley's quick memo back to Kissinger shows that the Defense Department and the White House were not approaching the crisis from the same mind set. "Mr. Laird has serious reservations . . . about whether we would want to prevent anyone from picking up the survivors," Pursley wrote, tactfully telling Kissinger that since the water temperature was about forty degrees, the Pentagon could be none too picky about who came to the rescue.[1] As it turned out, there were no survivors, and only two bodies were ever recovered.

The National Security Council met on Wednesday to look over a horrific set of retaliatory options drawn up quickly by the Pentagon at Nixon's request: shoot down a North Korean plane over the ocean; bomb the airfield where the offending MiGs were based; bombard the coast of North Korea from U.S. ships; invade North Korea across the demilitarized zone; use American submarines to attack North Korean ships; blockade North Korean ports; mine North Korean waters; seize North Korean assets abroad.[2] By that time Laird knew from other intelligence sources, and had told Nixon, that the decision to shoot down the EC-121 was probably made by a jittery pilot who had not sought approval up the chain of command. Laird also had learned the EC-121 mission had value but was not critical. That tempered Laird's enthusiasm for retaliation, but not Nixon's.

In reality, Laird saw little real value, but major substantial risks, in payback, but he wasn't about to say so to the president who was itching for a way to look tough. Laird enlisted the help of General Wheeler, who was as reluctant as Laird to start a fight with North Korea. In a good-cop/bad-cop ploy, Laird urged restraint while Wheeler appeared to back the president's desire for action. But, Wheeler advised, a military response would take time to mount. It was the time Laird needed to let tempers cool.[3] "I was trying to get Wheeler to stall for me," Laird recalled. "Take time, because everything passes with time."

Nixon was steamed that the options presented were so dire, and he complained that he wasn't given enough alternatives. "We gave him plenty of options," Laird recalled. "He was upset with my position. I had my hands full already in Vietnam and I didn't think we should start up another activity at that time. I felt that this incident was not of such grave concern that we should immediately risk an all-out conflict with North Korea, because I felt that it could readily mean that. We had sixty-eight thousand troops in South Korea at that time and that would not have been sufficient if the North Koreans had come across the border."

In retrospect, Pursley said that having Laird's cooler head prevail "set the tone for the way the national security apparatus was going to work for a long time." Nixon and Kissinger wanted to look tough on that first outing, but Laird stymied them. As Pursley saw it, "The last thing they wanted to hear from Mel Laird was that the better part of wisdom was just to back off and not do anything in terms of retaliation. Instead, he thought it was time to reassess our intelligence-gathering operations, authorize only those of substantial potential value, and protect vigorously those that had such value."

Kissinger recorded in his memoirs that Nixon decided at that moment never to trust Laird again, or Rogers who had sided with Laird: "He would get rid of Rogers and Laird at the earliest opportunity; he would never consult them again in a crisis."[4]

Author Mark Perry, in *Four Stars,* his history of the Joint Chiefs, hinted at how that new distrust may have manifested itself. Within a few days of the EC-121 crisis, Kissinger "reportedly approached Wheeler with a suggestion that the NSC and the JCS cooperate in sharing foreign policy and military information outside the government's usual lines of communication." The implication was that Nixon did not trust Laird, but he did trust the chiefs. "For Wheeler, the President's unaccountable concern could mean only one thing: the White House wanted the JCS to issue orders without Laird's knowledge, in the apparent belief that the secretary was soft on Vietnam and therefore could not be trusted." Perry wrote that Wheeler never took the bait.[5]

Three days after the EC-121 went down, the frustrated Nixon ordered the toughest response he could, given the constraints—the EC-121s would henceforth fly with armed escorts. Except that there were no EC-121s flying over the Sea of Japan, or anywhere in the world, because Laird had grounded them. And he didn't want them flying again until he was finished with his safety review. Kissinger and Nixon hounded Laird for weeks to resume the flights. Using his old standby excuse—these things take time—Laird delayed the resumption of flights until May 8, when he had finished his review.

As for the issue of whether the EC-121 had violated North Korean air space, Laird remained tight lipped, even three decades later. While the incident was ancient history in the United States, it remained a powerful propaganda weapon in the quiver of the North Koreans. "Our government has said they were in international waters. That's the position we continue to take," Laird said. He acknowledged that there had been times when similar reconnaissance flights had strayed "a little closer than they should have been." Of the flight that was shot down, Laird would only say, "They were not over territorial waters of the Koreans—the twelve miles—at the time they were shot down. I can guarantee you that." Laird reported to a closed-door session of the House Armed Services Committee within hours of the incident that the North Koreans had shot down the plane ninety miles from their coastline.

Nixon was so eager to prove the United States right in the episode that he spilled a closely guarded secret and sent the National Security Agency (NSA) into apoplexy. At an April 18 press conference defending the mission of the EC-121, Nixon announced that he knew the plane had not been shot down over North Korean air space, and he knew that the North Koreans knew it too. As proof, Nixon boasted that the NSA had been reading the North Korean radar even as it was tracking the EC-121. And, Nixon elaborated, the United States could do the same with Soviet radar. Until then that tracking ability had been top secret. "I don't think most people in the country realized how significant that [breach of security] was," said Laird. "It was not made a big deal except at NSA and within the confines of the Defense Department. They were upset, there's no question about it." It was the same technology that allowed the Defense Department to track every test missile firing in the Soviet Union and China, and it clued Laird in when the Soviets began putting multiple warheads on their missiles. Oddly enough, although there were ways for the Soviets to quickly scramble their telemetry so it could not be tracked, they were slow to do that even after Nixon's slip of the tongue.

American spying wizardry had given Laird another heads up in the EC-121 case. The communications from the attacking MiGs were monitored and showed that the pilots apparently acted impulsively without seeking the order to fire from their superiors. In Laird's mind, that made the difference between a deliberate act of war and pilot error. Nixon knew that, too, but was determined to retaliate anyway. "Nixon's philosophy was that he wanted to show what some labeled the 'madman' theory. He wanted people to think he might do anything," Laird explained. It was an image that Nixon had told both Laird and Kissinger he wanted to project to America's enemies, to keep them off balance.

In this case, Laird stopped the so-called madman by using delaying tactics and thus passed his first national security crisis with flying colors. If others saw his actions as disrespectful of the president's authority, then they didn't understand Laird's mission. "A secretary of defense has other responsibilities in that set of circumstances," he explained. "You have to look at your priorities. The number one priority of mine was to get Americans out of Vietnam where we shouldn't have been in the first place. So opening up a second front [in Korea] would have been a disaster, an absolute disaster."

When asked years later if he handled the EC-121 incident properly, Laird responded, "No question about that." But Kissinger considered the whole experience a fiasco. He determined to batten down the hatches at the National Security Council. From the framework of the team that had worked on the crisis, he created the Washington Special Actions Group within the NSC to handle future international crises. Laird appointed his deputy David Packard to serve on this group.

Meanwhile Nixon took a military action that he did have some control over. In frustration over the lack of retaliation against North Korea, he ordered another Operation Menu bombing of Cambodia. Although the president had been stymied in his desire to blow up something North Korean, he continued to press his point, and for nearly a year the Defense Department produced reports for Kissinger of how the United States might react should North Korea pull another stunt like the EC-121 shoot down. At one point, the Pentagon turned over to the White House a thirty-eight-page list of targets in North Korea and methods for taking them out should the need arise.[6]

With the crisis fading from the president's agenda, it was time for Laird to get back to Vietnamizing the war. On April 10, 1969, Nixon, through Kissinger, issued National Security Study Memorandum 36, asking for a timetable for turning the war over to the South Vietnamese. The president wanted options to accomplish the plan in one to four years. The next day columnists Evans and Novak published a report that Nixon was planning a "massive reduction" of two hundred thousand troops from Vietnam in an effort to persuade the North Vietnamese to do the same. If the North did not respond, the column said Nixon planned to keep the rest of the U.S. contingent in Vietnam "indefinitely."

Laird said he was not the source of that leak, which was off the mark on at least two points. According to Laird, Nixon never really believed the North would respond to a U.S. troop withdrawal by scaling down its own forces. And the plan was not to withdraw just two hundred thousand men, but all of them, five hundred thousand plus. Laird later told Evans and Novak, "We had to go ahead with withdrawal regardless of what North Vietnam did in response, because we did not have domestic support." That was Laird's mantra for the next four years, that the U.S. participation in the war was doomed because the folks at home were fed up with it. Kissinger, scornful of politics, never agreed. Nixon would come around only as the 1972 election drew closer. Until the president saw the light, Laird had to fight tooth and nail for each soldier he brought home.

The fight began with the plans for the first troop withdrawal, which was to be announced in grand fashion. First Nixon had to get President Thieu on the bandwagon. Although Thieu had been told by Laird in Saigon that troop cutbacks were inevitable, he was still grasping at straws, specifically the commitments the Johnson administration had given him in Manila in 1966, that U.S. troops would not leave until six months after North Vietnam's army had withdrawn. Although the National Security Council had been instructed by Nixon on March 28 to forget Manila, Thieu had not been officially told. Secretary of State Rogers burst Thieu's bubble at a press conference on April 12, when he was asked if the administration still supported the Manila terms. "I don't want to discuss the Manila formula in any detail because there is some ambiguity in the Manila communiqué," Rogers hedged. "In any event, we have our own program."

The administration kept up the dodge for a month until Nixon went on national television on May 14 to announce an eight-point peace program that left no room for the old Manila promise. He offered cease-fire terms, said the United States was willing to accept an election in South Vietnam even if it meant some Communists might be elected, and said the Viet Cong (officially the National Liberation Front) could be part of the political mix. And Nixon said he would present a timetable for U.S. withdrawal. Laird had spent the intervening weeks discussing the timetable with the Joint Chiefs and Abrams, planning just how many soldiers would be brought home in the first wave. "I was at fifty thousand and some of the others were at zero," Laird said. "Abrams had told me he could do fifty thousand."

Ten days before the Midway meeting, the Joint Chiefs delivered their formal recommendation—withdraw 50,000 troops by the end of 1969 and a total of 244,000 troops in three and a half years, leaving more than 300,000 Americans behind indefinitely as advisors and support to the new and improved South Vietnamese army.[7] Laird passed along the memo to Nixon, agreeing with the fifty thousand figure for 1969, but remaining deliberately vague about the rest of the plan. He hadn't told the chiefs yet, but he had no intention of having any American combat troops still in Vietnam by his last day in office. He was keeping that plan a secret from the Joint Chiefs so as not to alienate them early on. Far from being discouraged by the chiefs' initial figures, Laird respected the commanders for taking one baby step away from the war in which they had so much invested. "I thought they'd come a long way in two weeks," he said.

Wheeler eventually signed off on the fifty thousand figure but argued against the number until the eleventh hour—the weekend before the Midway Island summit meeting between Nixon and Thieu where the first withdrawal number was to be announced, ostensibly in a show of harmony between the two presidents. That weekend, Wheeler made a trip to the presidential retreat at Camp David, where Laird was vacationing with his family. (Laird was always quick to educate the uninformed about Camp David—that it was a Defense Department facility that was loaned on demand to the president, not the other way around.) Wheeler's trip was for naught because Laird's mind was made up. His political instincts told him that if he could just get that first contingent of troops out, it would be impossible for Kissinger or Nixon or the commanders to stop the momentum. Additionally, it would impress upon the South Vietnamese the need to increase their military capability. And, finally, it would alert the enemy that South Vietnamese capability was being built up incrementally as the United States scaled down.

Kissinger saw little value in troop withdrawals as a way to end the war; he put his hopes in the peace talks. One of his early tactics was to link U.S.-Soviet relations to a settlement of the war, since the Soviet Union was bankrolling the enemy. Using the State Department to deliver the message, Kissinger let Soviet Ambassador Anatoly Dobrynin know that U.S.-Soviet talks about the arms race and other bones of contention might go more smoothly if the Soviets put pressure on Hanoi to cooperate in any peace talks. Laird nearly spilled the beans about this approach at a Senate hearing in mid-March. When pressed to come up with some progress on the Vietnam front, Laird didn't want to talk about his withdrawal plans, so instead he offered up Kissinger's plans for secret talks in the making. As always with Laird, it was not an accidental slip of the tongue, but a deliberate attempt to put pressure on the Soviets to respond to the overtures. They never did—more evidence to Laird that the solution would not be found through diplomacy.

⨳

While Washington battled over the numbers for the first withdrawal of troops, the business of war went on in South Vietnam. The bureaucrats and generals did not know it at the time, but a bloody campaign to take a place called Hamburger Hill during ten days in May would turn out to be the last major U.S. ground battle of the war fought on Vietnamese soil. The reaction at home was a loud message to the Nixon administration that the American public would never again tolerate another battle like it in Vietnam.

Less than two miles from the Laotian border, the hill the locals called Dong Ap Bia overlooked the Ashau Valley, a funnel the North Vietnamese used to carry supplies into the South from the Ho Chi Minh Trail in Laos. In January American reconnaissance planes had spotted about one thousand enemy trucks a day along that portion of the Ho Chi Minh Trail. In the spring an enemy regiment dug in on top of Ap Bia, threatening the American and South Vietnamese troops trying to maintain control of the valley below. On May 10

Abrams sent in the 101st Airborne to take back what they labeled Hill 937, for its height in meters. The appellation of Hamburger Hill (borrowed from a notorious Korean War battle) was added by either GIs or journalists during the ten days that ensued when the hill became a human meat grinder for both allies and enemies. Code named Apache Snow, the operation cost 56 American lives, 5 South Vietnamese, and an estimated 630 enemy soldiers.

In a tropical downpour that turned the hill to a mudslide, the North Vietnamese division was finally ousted by a combination of rockets, bombs, artillery, and napalm. In the confusion, American helicopter gun ships at one point tried to mow down two battalions from the 101st Airborne Division. The American soldiers who threw themselves against the heavily fortified hill for ten days began to complain to the reporters arriving on the scene that the battle was a pointless suicide mission. The criticism back home intensified when, after holding the hill for a little more than a week, American troops abandoned it. Major General Melvin Zais, commander of the 101st, took the unusual step of holding a press conference in Saigon to defend the strategy. It wasn't about taking Hill 937, he said. It was about wiping out the enemy troops dug in there overseeing their deadly supply lines and picking off the allies in the valley below. Indeed, the Vietnam War was rarely about taking and keeping territory. It was about punishing the enemy enough to persuade him to go home.[8]

Within a month after the battle for Hamburger Hill, the enemy had once again reoccupied it with about a thousand men, though with their fortifications destroyed, the hill apparently was not deemed to be enough of a threat for the Americans to fight for it again. More blood had been shed on other battlefields in Vietnam, and less ink had been spilled reporting them. Generals had made worse calls and led more futile assaults, but this one was different. Coming so early in the administration of a president who had promised he would end the war, who was at that very moment planning a summit conference to announce the first homecoming of troops, the battle for Hamburger Hill struck the folks back home as incomprehensible.

The Midway Island conference on June 8—three days after Hamburger Hill was abandoned—was publicly billed as a meeting where two presidents, Nixon and Thieu, would debate the first troop withdrawal number and reach a compromise. But in truth Thieu's opinion was irrelevant, and the number was decided by Nixon the day before in Hawaii. Nixon had stopped in Honolulu en route to Midway to refuel and break the news to General Abrams and Admiral McCain. On the flight over, Laird was still unsure what number Nixon would accept. "I didn't know whether he'd go along with any withdrawal, to tell you the truth," Laird recalled. "He questioned me quite severely about my recommendation on the way over." In response, Laird fell back on his old standby argument that would appeal to Nixon; the political situation in the United States was such that Nixon couldn't afford *not* to withdraw some troops.

At the briefing in Hawaii were Laird, William Rogers, Kissinger, Wheeler, Ambassador Bunker, and Henry Cabot Lodge, the chief peace negotiator in Paris. There were as many opinions as there were men, but Nixon took Laird's advice. The first phase would bring home twenty-five thousand troops in the summer, with another twenty-five thousand withdrawn by the end of the year. When Laird briefed Nixon in Hawaii, he made it clear that Vietnamization might get messy. His preparatory notes for the briefing say, "These forces [the South Vietnamese army] are improving slowly, and with the right kind of help from us, continuing improvement can be expected. However, even with additional equipment and significantly increased combat support provided by our forces, they are not likely to be able to stand alone against the current North Vietnamese and VC [Viet Cong] threat. Any withdrawal of US forces from South Vietnam must take this into account. Yet improvement in the South Vietnamese forces is also related to morale, commitment and motivation. In this regard, US troop reduction, if carefully balanced, can have a positive effect by making the South Vietnamese realize they must do more." In other words, if America didn't back off, the South Vietnamese would never take the initiative to fight their own war.

The next day, Sunday, June 8, the Nixon party continued on to Midway Island, arriving a few minutes after Thieu's plane landed, contrary to the protocol that Thieu had insisted on. He had wanted to arrive second and cement the impression that it was Nixon's party and Nixon's agenda, not his own. While Nixon headed off to the meeting with Thieu at the home of the American commander of the military facility on the tiny atoll, Laird indulged himself in some politicking. He shook hands with every dignitary and underling at the airfield. Pursley recalled, "If they'd had an election on who was running the whole thing ten minutes after the president arrived, Mel would have won hands down. He knew everybody there and they knew him. It was typical Mel Laird."

Over at the commander's house, things were delayed a moment while Thieu traded the small chair assigned to him for one that was as big as Nixon's. The meeting lasted about four hours, half of that time witnessed by Laird and the others in the American delegation, and half a private meeting between the two presidents, witnessed only by Kissinger and an aide to Thieu. Thieu used the time to present his wish list for more American money and military support. As proof that the Midway "negotiations" were really window dressing, Nixon and Thieu had to take a break from their meeting before they were finished talking to make an announcement to the press waiting outside. There were impatient editors back home in different time zones with deadlines to meet. Nixon made it sound as if the withdrawal had been the idea of two men who wanted it least: "As a consequence of the recommendation by the President

[Thieu] and the assessment of our own commander in the field [Abrams], I have decided to order the immediate redeployment from Vietnam of a division equivalent of approximately 25,000 men." Nixon also perpetuated the fiction that the criteria for continued withdrawals remained in place: progress in training the South Vietnamese army, progress at the Paris peace talks, and a reduced level of enemy activity on the battlefield.[9]

With the formal announcement made, Laird was impatient for the show to end. His daughter Alison was graduating from high school in Washington the next morning, and he was the commencement speaker. A KC-135 tanker airplane was waiting for him on the runway. Air Force One would take Nixon home by way of Hawaii and California because it would need to refuel, but the tanker could take Laird nonstop to Washington. As the summit dragged on, Laird did everything he politely could to get the president to wrap things up. "The thing was dragging on and I couldn't leave until we got Thieu out of there," Laird recalled. With Nixon and Thieu still standing on the tarmac going through the formalities of parting, Laird sat in the KC-135 on the runway checking his watch. Finally he ordered the pilot to get the plane in the air. "I understand when my plane took off it made a little bit of noise and created a delay in the press conference, but I didn't care about that," said Laird. "I had to leave."

The plane deposited Laird at Andrews Air Force Base at 7:30 the next morning, where he hastily told the waiting reporters that Nixon had made a historic decision at Midway. Then, begging off more questions, Laird said he had something important to do and drove on to the high school, arriving with ten minutes to spare. The *Time* magazine photo of proud father and graduating daughter still graced Laird's desk three decades later with the caption summing up the day: "What happiness is."

⤮

Back at the Pentagon that afternoon, Laird held a longer press conference and began putting the public face on the beginning of the end in Vietnam. This wasn't a "unilateral withdrawal," he said. It was a "replacement" of U.S. troops with South Vietnamese troops. The next day, in a closed budget hearing before the Senate Appropriations Subcommittee, Laird could afford to be more candid on the subject of mutual withdrawal: "I want to make it clear that this reduction was not based upon success in Paris. This was based on the improvement of the South Vietnamese forces. Mutual troop withdrawal is an entirely different subject. Although I am not optimistic as far as an agreement on mutual troop withdrawal is concerned, I do not believe that that is any reason to hold up on the Vietnamization program."[10]

The public reaction to the announcement of the first withdrawal was less than ebullient. Clark Clifford—whom Laird was fond of describing as the defense secretary who never took one soldier out of Vietnam—criticized the withdrawal plan as too slow. In an article in *Foreign Affairs* in mid-June, Clifford called for the removal of all American ground combat forces within eighteen months. Peeved by this armchair quarterbacking from the Johnson gang, Nixon went on television to remind Americans of just how many men had *not* come home during their watch. Clifford's meddling secretly pleased Laird. "I had lunch with him the week before and he told me he was writing the article," Laird recalled. "I didn't think it hurt me at all. I knew the program he suggested was impossible, but I still felt that having someone over on that side strengthened my hand rather than weakened it. He knew that the figure he was using was not realistic, but he wanted to get it out in the open. He thought he was helping me."

Clifford continued to use the power of the pen to needle the Nixon administration. "It just drove the president up the wall, and Kissinger was rabid on it," Laird recalled. "They didn't like him suggesting a faster withdrawal than the track we were on." It was a personal affront to Nixon and pressure on him to go faster—as fast as Laird would have liked him to go. Kissinger's main objection to the speed of withdrawals, and Clifford's drumbeat of criticism on the subject, was that it soured the peace talks in Paris. But that was neither here nor there to Laird. "I didn't have the responsibility for the negotiating track in Paris. That was Kissinger's responsibility, and the State Department. They always felt that withdrawals hurt negotiations. I felt they did not hurt negotiations because there were political factors involved. If you didn't keep moving, you would never get support for the program in the long run. Moreover, the last thing the North Vietnamese would want was a South Vietnamese military willing and able to sustain operations against the North Vietnamese indefinitely."

Not content with sliding out of Vietnam the way America had slid in, Laird wanted a concrete change in the Military Assistance Command Vietnam mission statement for the war, in addition to a firm plan for troop withdrawals. On July 7 he went aboard the presidential yacht *Sequoia* to meet with Nixon and Kissinger. There he announced to the surprise of the other two men that he had changed the wording of the mission statement from applying "maximum pressure" against the enemy to pledging "maximum assistance" to the South Vietnamese army.

Nixon, who hated face-to-face confrontations, agreed initially while on the *Sequoia*. Later he changed his mind but still was not willing to order a change back to the old mission statement. That was fine with Laird, who thought it was the defense secretary's call anyway. "Kissinger was upset because I went ahead and ordered it," Laird said. "I was under the impression that it was my responsibility. I didn't think that was Kissinger's responsibility. And as long as the president didn't tell me to change it back, I didn't."

Three days after the meeting on the *Sequoia*, the first of the twenty-five thousand homebound troops arrived in Seattle. The plan was to have each wave of soldiers parade through the streets of the towns where their units were based, hopefully to the welcoming applause of the grateful home crowd. An official army history of the first returning unit tells the upshot of that public relations debacle. Leaving Saigon, one soldier raised his fist in a "black power" salute. Another complained that the ceremony was just for show, and still others worried aloud to reporters that they were being sent home ignominiously without winning the war. Antiwar demonstrators greeted the plane in Seattle. A *New York Times* article noted that on the day the 814 men arrived home, another thousand men had been sent over. It would be the first and last formal welcome-home ceremony for the returning troops.[11]

18

Going Public

WHY DID IT TAKE FOUR YEARS to evacuate about half a million American ground troops from Vietnam? The same number of soldiers, sailors, and airmen were pulled out of Saudi Arabia, Kuwait, and Iraq at the end of the 1991 Persian Gulf War in less than six months. In that case, the objective was independence for Kuwait. With that accomplished, all that remained were logistics—the ratio of departing troops and matériel to available transports. In the minds of many Americans in 1969, particularly those in Congress who wanted to best Richard Nixon in the political arena, the Vietnam War formula was just that simple—order as many planes and ships as needed and bid good riddance through the rearview mirror.

But even after Laird set the military on a homeward bound course, there was no quick exit strategy. Nixon was determined to end U.S. involvement in the war, but he vowed not to go down in history as the first American president to lose a war. Laird and Kissinger were keenly aware of the dishonor that came in international diplomatic circles to a nation that reneged on its commitments and walked away from its allies in their darkest hours. Pragmatically, too, the upgrading of South Vietnamese forces could not be instantaneous. Vietnamization was going to take time; the missteps of the past could not be corrected overnight.

But among the myriad Vietnamization issues was one unique problem. There were estimates of about 1,500 American soldiers, sailors, and airmen missing in action or known to be prisoners of the enemy. They could not be left behind when the last unit boarded the plane for home, no matter how successful Vietnamization had become. Laird had little faith in the negotiation process in Paris as a way to end the U.S. involvement in Vietnam, but when it came to the POWs, negotiations could be a key element in freeing them. The peace negotiations were under the control of the State Department, and the same was true of the POW issue until Laird came along. For liaison with POW families, the Defense Department had maintained a small staff reporting to the assistant secretary for international security affairs. Laird bolstered that staff, brought in an energetic staffer, Roger Shields, and made the issue a personal priority.

With the State Department in charge of policy, the POWs had become the unmentionables in the Paris negotiations. The U.S. diplomats were afraid that by demanding release of the prisoners, or even insisting on better conditions for them, America would signal its desperate concern for those men and thus increase their value as a bargaining chip for Hanoi. Even the families of the POWs had been under strict instructions to keep their silence, lest the North Vietnamese figure out just how much those men were worth back home. Laird had no patience with such timidity. Hanoi already knew how much Americans valued the life of each soldier, sailor, and airman, and the Communists had no intention of letting their hostages go. Credible reports were accumulating in the Pentagon of torture, starvation, disease, and death in the POW camps. Laird quickly realized that the 1,500 MIAs and POWs constituted a powerful tool that the United States could use to shame Hanoi around the world and, in the process, possibly save the lives of the prisoners. Laird saw the aggrieved families as vital partners in that campaign. The wives and mothers of the POWs were tired of stifling their opinions. If they were going to explode, Laird wanted them on his side.

He also felt strongly that the POWs were the Pentagon's responsibility, not to be defaulted to the State Department. From the beginning, Laird would go through the motions of consulting and informing the State Department on POW policy, but he would not wait for their permission to shake up the status quo. The roster of POWs captured in the North dated from August 5, 1964, when the first navy pilot was shot down—Lieutenant Everett Alvarez Jr. By the time Laird took office, the POWs in the North were thought to number about five hundred still living, although without acknowledgment from the enemy it was impossible to have an exact count. Prior to 1969 Hanoi had released only six prisoners, and none of those had been known to be alive until they were released.

The prisoners held in the North were, for the most part, air force and navy pilots and crewmen shot down in bombing raids. They were kept in established camps where camaraderie with other prisoners and their military training and patriotic bent helped them to resist and endure. As bad as conditions were in North Vietnam for American prisoners, the picture in the South was worse. The Viet Cong took their first prisoner in the South, Army Specialist George Fryett, on December 26, 1961. He was released six months later, but more were captured in the South. Those captives tended to be young, immature enlistees captured in ground combat with the Viet Cong or taken when they ventured too far from their units. They were forced to travel with the Viet Cong, like nomads, carried in bamboo cages or dragged from camp to camp, without the company of other prisoners. Many died from the complications of untreated wounds, exposure, starvation, and disease.

One of the prisoners captured in the South by the Viet Cong, Army Captain Floyd Thompson, was the longest held of all the American POWs in the war. He was shot down near the demilitarized zone on March 26, 1964, eventually was transferred to a prison in North Vietnam, and was not released until the peace pact was signed with Hanoi in 1973. Among the prisoners, Thompson was known as the "Old Man of the South." Everett Alvarez was the "Old Man of the North."

∽✲∾

POWs weren't part of Richard Capen's job description when he departed the California-based Copley newspaper organization at Laird's urging. Though Capen was busy as an assistant in the Public Affairs section at the Pentagon, Laird and press chief Dan Henkin talked to him about taking over new responsibilities. Laird instructed Capen to mine all the military intelligence agencies and the CIA to find out as much as he could about the POWs. Laird was ripe for all POW-related suggestions. In Congress he had been a magnet for POW families who found in him a sympathetic ear. Even before he was sworn in as defense secretary, Laird had talked to Colonel Pursley and Bob Froehlke about heightening awareness about the POWs.

In February 1969 Averell Harriman called on Laird at his Pentagon office after hearing rumors of Laird's plan to be more outspoken on the POW-MIA issue. Ambassador Harriman, former Vietnam peace negotiator in Paris, urged Laird not to go forward with his plans. Laird soon assigned Capen to review the current intelligence and report back on May 3 at a Defense Department staff weekend retreat at Airlie House, a conference facility in Virginia. When he heard Capen's findings at the conference, Laird bellowed, "By God, we're going to go public." Thus on that weekend was born what officially became known as the "Go Public Campaign." No more would the POWs get the silent treatment from their own government. "We were going to show photos and we were going to show facts to illustrate that the men were being tortured, that they were being denied medical treatment, that they were not being identified, and that they were not allowed to get mail, in violation of the Geneva Conventions," said Capen.

The civilians at the Pentagon quickly got on board, but the military officers were more reluctant, fearing that by humiliating North Vietnam publicly over the POW issue, Laird might further endanger the lives of the prisoners. Capen took his case to one among the military hierarchy who had the most to lose should that happen, Admiral John McCain, whose son had been a prisoner in North Vietnam since October 26, 1967. "Whatever you feel is right, do it," the admiral told Capen. "Don't let me influence you." It was typical of the tack the admiral would take in the future whenever Laird visited CINCPAC (Pacific commander-in-chief) headquarters in Hawaii and inquired about the young pilot. The admiral would show appreciation for Laird's concern and then quickly change the subject lest it appear he wanted any special consideration for his son.

Kissinger was not enthused about the plan to go public, fearing it would complicate the peace talks. The State Department, from Secretary Rogers down to the negotiators in Paris, thought it was a gamble. Nixon was noncommittal. But Laird pressed ahead. Capen and his staff scheduled a press conference for May 19, 1969, and carefully prepared and rehearsed their presentation on inhumane treatment of the POWs. Reporters, expecting little more than a dog-and-pony show without any news, stirred when Laird himself walked into the briefing room.

"The North Vietnamese have claimed that they are treating our men humanely. I am distressed by the fact that there is clear evidence that this is not the case," Laird began. He detailed the known offenses—failure to release prisoner lists, refusal to deliver prisoner mail, use of the prisoners in propaganda films. Then Laird turned the press conference over to Capen who distributed a packet of forty-six photos (most of them circulated on the black market in North Vietnam) that showed injured American prisoners, some with limbs atrophied from untreated wounds, some in solitary confinement. Capen put the lie to North Vietnamese claims that the prisoners were receiving their mail regularly. One propaganda film purported to show prisoners reading Christmas cards in December 1968. The mail turned out to be Easter cards that were more than eight months old.

Laird's call for the "prompt release of all American prisoners" got a small splash in the next day's headlines. But the reverberations were bigger in the arena that mattered. On May 20 the North Vietnamese delegate to the Paris peace talks blustered that his government had no intention of releasing even a list of prisoner names, let alone prisoners themselves, until the United States took its troops out of Vietnam. Within two weeks, Radio Hanoi began a series of broadcasts in which speakers who claimed to be American POWs waxed grateful about their humane treatment at the hands of the enemy. In one such radio broadcast on June 5, a man claiming to be Lieutenant Commander McCain admitted that he had bombed civilian targets before his capture, and praised the North Vietnamese for "good medical treatment" that had enabled him to walk again. At the time McCain had been beaten and tortured to the point that he attempted suicide to resist his captors' demands that he sign a confession of war crimes. The broken arm that the radio broadcast claimed his captors had so skillfully healed had in reality been rebroken by his torturers.

The day after that broadcast, Laird publicly accused North Vietnam of staging the series of prisoner interviews. "Hanoi has chosen to respond to our plea for humane treatment of our prisoners of war with a series of contrived broadcasts. These broadcasts, like others before them, are a feeble gesture and no substitute for the humanitarian guarantees that we are seeking," Laird said. "These brave men and their families shall not be forgotten."

The next step for Hanoi, on July 3, was to announce the release of three POWs in honor of American Independence Day. It took thirty-two days before the three were actually released and allowed to celebrate their independence—time that their captors spent trying to persuade them that the price of their freedom was to tell the folks back home about the humane treatment they had received. The chosen three were Air Force Captain Wesley Rumble, Navy Lieutenant Robert Frishman, both pilots, and Navy Seaman Douglas Hegdahl, who had been swept off his ship during a storm and picked up by the North Vietnamese. Each of the three had lost from twenty to sixty pounds while in captivity. Rumble, suffering from a back injury, had to be helped off the plane in New York, and reporters were told that he could not speak. He was immediately put on another plane to an air force hospital in California.

Frishman and Hegdahl were taken to Bethesda Naval Hospital outside Washington, D.C., where Laird met with them and learned that they were not about to be used by Hanoi as poster boys for a propaganda campaign. Frishman had memorized in alphabetical order the names of hundreds of POWs, and refused in his debriefing to answer any questions until he could verbally download the list. "Imagine," said Capen, "this was the first time in five years some of these families ever knew, had any indication that their husbands or sons were alive." For Capen, that list alone made the Go Public Campaign a success.

Frishman and Hegdahl agreed to hold a press conference and expose the abuse of POWs. Their captors, they said, had told them to speak highly of the camps, with the reminder that they still had friends there. But their fellow prisoners had urged them to tell the truth, no matter what the consequences. "Hanoi says the best proof of their treatment to American prisoners will come from those they have released," Frishman said. "I am here today to tell of the type treatment that I and other American prisoners of war have received."

Describing the horrors he had seen, Frishman said, "My intentions are not to scare wives and families, but Hanoi has given false impressions that all is wine and roses, and it isn't so. All I'm interested in is for Hanoi to live up to their claims of humane and lenient treatment of prisoners of war. I don't think solitary confinement, forced statements, living in a cage for three years, being put in straps, not being allowed to sleep or eat, removal of finger nails, being hung from a ceiling, having an infected arm which was almost lost, not receiving medical care, being dragged along the ground with a broken leg, or not allowing an exchange of mail to prisoners of war are humane." In response to reporters' questions about morale among the prisoners, Frishman gave poignant insight into how the POWs were affected by changes in American military strategy in Vietnam. "I think the morale is still high, but when the bombing [of the North] stopped and we still remained up there, it was hard on them."

Despite the graphic accounts from the released prisoners, support from the White House for the Go Public Campaign remained lukewarm. Only one unexpected ally emerged. Vice President Agnew was incensed by the way Hanoi had handled the release of the three—in particular the fact that the POWs were turned over to high-profile American antiwar activists who escorted them home. One of those escorts, Rennard Davis, held a press conference in Laos while en route to Hanoi. There he praised North Vietnam for its "humanitarian" policy toward POWs and said, "Our fight is not against the North Vietnamese. Our fight is against the Pentagon, which carries on this policy of aggression and imperialism. Nixon's troop withdrawal is a sham and a token effort to deflate anti-war sentiment in the United States."[1]

Agnew sent a top-secret memo to Laird speculating on the negative effect that selective POW releases into the hands of the "far left wing" could have on the remaining prisoners. The whole affair flew in the face of the prisoners' code of conduct, which said that prisoners would not cooperate with their captors and would not accept release ahead of those who had been there longer or were more in need of medical attention. Agnew feared that those left behind would assume that the freed POWs had capitulated. "[D]o we not strike most directly at the morale of those who have been strongest in their refusal to violate the code of conduct?" Agnew wrote.

At the time Agnew jumped in, Laird was using every angle he could think of to integrate the release of the three POWs into his Go Public Campaign, including drafting an eight-page statement he hoped U.S. negotiator Henry Cabot Lodge would deliver in Paris excoriating Hanoi for failure to live up to the 1949 Geneva Convention Relative to the Treatment of Prisoners of War. Laird delicately let Agnew know that he wasn't getting maximum cooperation from the State Department.

A month later Laird followed his hunch that Agnew might be a strong ally in the White House. He wrote to Kissinger to suggest that, given the differences of opinion between the State and Defense departments, Agnew be designated as "the principal authority on all issues of policy" concerning POWs.[2] It took Kissinger two months to respond that Nixon had vetoed the Agnew idea. "He would prefer to leave the present arrangements in effect for the time being," Kissinger wrote.[3]

Laird was not surprised. "The State Department and the NSC did not want a big thing made out of the POWs," he recalled. "That would put Agnew above the State Department and the NSC as my ally on this thing. I think Kissinger and the State Department thought he would be uncontrollable like I was on POWs." Laird didn't give up on Agnew and continued to draft the vice president into the cause whenever he could. When Agnew made a tour of several nations in December 1969, Laird asked him to insert the POW issue into the conversation with any head of state who would listen.

Still convinced that the POWs needed a high-profile advocate, Laird proposed to Nixon on December 20 that he appoint a "special presidential emissary" to tour world capitals and pound on doors looking for leaders to join the cause. The hope was that a repeated drumbeat of international criticism at the highest levels would embarrass Hanoi into living up to its Geneva treaty commitments. Meanwhile, Laird's special POW Task Force went fishing in the private sector for help. At its urging, in October 1969 the American Red Cross started a "Write Hanoi" campaign, and in November *Reader's Digest* published a story about the treatment of POWs and inserted a detachable postcard for readers to send as part of the Red Cross effort. Laird used his personal connections at the magazine to secure that article. He had cultivated a friendship with owner DeWitt Wallace, who occasionally tried to lure Laird away from politics with offers of a position in the magazine's executive ranks. (Laird would eventually accept Wallace's offer upon resignation from the Nixon administration in 1973.) More than 679,000 *Reader's Digest* postcards filled the mail bags that were sent to Hanoi.

When Laird's POW Task Force enlisted the help of H. Ross Perot, it found the sharpest burr to put in the saddle of Hanoi. The indomitable Texas millionaire had not yet made his reputation in politics, but in the millionaires club he was known as one who would hang on to a cause like a bulldog on an ankle bone. Perot had made substantial contributions to Nixon's election campaign, so Laird figured that gave him some access. Laird talked Perot into calling Nixon personally and asking him to make more noise about the POWs. Perot also pestered Nixon's aides H. R. Haldeman and John Ehrlichman. Perot formed a POW support committee, United We Stand, Inc., and the group bought ads in newspapers and on radio and TV stations around the country. They produced a TV documentary and distributed ten million postcards for people to send to Hanoi.

Then Capen came up with the idea of having Perot fund a shipment of Christmas gift boxes to the POWs. Volunteers packed thirty tons of food, clothing, and medical supplies and loaded them on a plane called Peace on Earth. At the same time, a second Perot airplane was waiting to carry a contingent of POW wives and children to Paris for a Christmas day vigil in front of the Hanoi delegation's offices there. Perot had asked permission to land with his packages in North Vietnam, but he didn't wait for that approval before giving the order for Peace on Earth to take off. With a flurry of publicity at each refueling stop along the way, the plane finally arrived in Vientiane, Laos, where Perot got word that Hanoi had turned him down. Any Christmas packages, they said, would have to be sent through Moscow by regular mail, within ten days, in small boxes weighing no more than 6.6 pounds each.

If the North Vietnamese thought that would deter Perot, they didn't understand the American entrepreneurial spirit. Perot ordered the plane to Anchorage, Alaska, where volunteers were assembled in short order to break down the crates of supplies into smaller boxes, each addressed to the Hanoi post office, via Moscow. Peace on Earth got as far as Copenhagen before the Soviets refused permission for the plane to land in Moscow. In all, the plane carried its cargo more than thirty-five thousand miles, irritating the North Vietnamese at every stop. The second plane carrying POW families to Paris met with little more success. Of the 152 wives and children, only three were given an audience with four North Vietnamese officials who spent thirty minutes on Christmas day haranguing the women about American imperialism.[4]

Perot, keenly aware of the publicity value of his attempts to tweak Hanoi, continued the barrage in 1970 with an offer to buy the POWs' freedom for $100 million in food and medicine for the North Vietnamese people. Hanoi did not take Perot up on the offer. Then he collected a planeload of reporters and took them to South Vietnam for a tour of prison camps where captured North Vietnamese soldiers were held. Perot filmed the enemy prisoners and collected letters for their families, then petitioned Hanoi for permission to fly there to deliver the missives. Again Hanoi refused. Undaunted, Perot continued to find ways to keep the POWs in the public eye. He testified before Congress, built replicas of POW cells and put them on display in the Capitol rotunda, paid for public opinion polls to track awareness of the issue, and repeatedly financed POW advocates in travel to foreign countries to make a case for the prisoners.

⌖

Without much cooperation from the White House, Laird doggedly pressed for his "special presidential emissary." Kissinger suggested a subcommittee under the NSC staff to oversee the POW campaign, but Laird would have none of that. He saw it as a ploy to shuffle the POWs off to the netherworld of the federal bureaucracy. Laird had bigger plans, including asking the Reverend Billy Graham to be the special emissary. Laird would have loved to see Graham go head-to-head with the double-talking North Vietnamese delegates in Paris. "I think it would have been very interesting," Laird said. But he didn't have a chance to find out because the White House quashed the idea.

After a few other nominees turned Laird down for personal reasons, he hit upon former astronaut Frank Borman, commander of Apollo 8 on a lunar orbit mission. By 1970, when Laird was looking him over, Borman was working at Eastern Airlines—not the high-profile celebrity Laird had hoped for, but a respected businessman and a big name in the space program. With Nixon's approval, Borman was given the assignment and took off on an around-the-world mission to buttonhole twelve heads of state. When he returned, he testified before Congress in an attempt to stir them and the public to show more concern for the POWs. Borman's mission was not a huge success, but Laird was grateful for every small step in the Go Public Campaign. There was never another special emissary appointed.

Although in retrospect Laird spoke fondly of Nixon's support for the Go Public Campaign, in reality the president remained mostly detached from the POW issue, in part because of Kissinger's worries about the peace talks. Nixon, with his dislike for confrontation, didn't want to antagonize Kissinger or the delegates to the peace talks. Laird did not hold that against Nixon, seeing the POWs as the Defense Department's responsibility to worry about, not the president's. But Laird also did not ease the pressure on Nixon. He hounded the president in memos to include the POWs in presidential speeches and remarks at press conferences. Something as simple as having the president meet with aggrieved POW wives required weeks of negotiations between Laird and the White House. When that meeting finally came off, on December 12, 1969, it produced the first public speech, however short, Nixon had made in office specifically about the POWs. In six paragraphs, Nixon praised the wives and reproved the North Vietnamese: "Insofar as the treatment of prisoners is concerned, it would probably not be inaccurate to say that the record in this war is one of the most unconscionable in the history of warfare."[5]

The visible elements of the Go Public Campaign must have seemed like baby steps to those who didn't understand the delicate dance going on between Laird and the White House. Recognition of long-suffering wives, attempts to send Christmas packages, public relations tours by POW advocates, an occasional good word from the president, tactful calls for enforcement of the Geneva conventions—all of these seem like the least a government should do for its captured men. Gradually more prisoner lists were released, more mail was allowed, and a few prisoners were let go. But it was not until all the POWs came home in 1973 that Laird knew the full effect of the Go Public Campaign. The men spoke and wrote of a change that came about slowly, beginning in mid-1969, when their treatment improved, torture lessened, and, most importantly, they were grouped together in common cells more often than in solitary confinement. While some speculated that the death of Ho Chi Minh in 1969 changed the rules, Laird was convinced the improved treatment was due in large part to his insistence that the POW issue be brought out of the shadows and into the glare of worldwide public scrutiny.

Laird and the Joint Chiefs shared a passion for getting the POWs out, but they did not always agree on how U.S. policy in the war would accomplish that. The chiefs consistently dragged their feet when it came to troop withdrawals in Laird's Vietnamization program. And at one point Joint Chiefs Chairman Admiral Tom Moorer used the POWs as a pretense to try to stop troop withdrawals altogether. In September of 1971, when Laird had pulled out more than a quarter million U.S. troops from Vietnam, Moorer wrote to him on September 10, 1971, suggesting that further withdrawals would jeopardize any bargaining position the United States might have to get the POWs back.

Rear Admiral Daniel Murphy, one of Laird's military assistants, looked over Moorer's advice and briefed Laird on the logic behind it, which he called "specious." "We have already withdrawn more [troops] than we have left, and the enemy did not give back any POWs," Murphy wrote. "If we stop withdrawals, the enemy could be more inclined to keep our POWs." It made more sense, Murphy said, to withdraw totally and then demand return of the POWs, since the U.S. involvement in the war would be over.[6] Laird later acknowledged that he did not know what he would have done if it had come down to taking the last U.S. soldier out of Vietnam with the prisoners still in captivity. But he had no intention of stopping the troop withdrawal, so he ignored Moorer's suggestion, just as he ignored other attempts by the Joint Chiefs to stop the withdrawal program.

One gambit that Laird tried without success was to offer up North Vietnamese prisoners in trade for U.S. POWs, but the North seemed to find the concept to be incomprehensible. And South Vietnamese President Thieu didn't warm to the idea, even when it meant ridding himself of the expense and headache of maintaining the North Vietnamese POWs in prison camps in the South. At one of Laird's staff meetings on November 18, 1970, Ambassador Bunker tried to explain the mentality at work. Both the North and South Vietnamese considered their imprisoned men to be lost until the war was over. They didn't expect to see them again, Bunker said. Hanoi likely didn't want its prisoners back, according to the ambassador. "They probably had instructed their men in the prison camps in the south to stay there and cause as much trouble as they could," Bunker said. North Vietnamese prisoners who accepted repatriation were looked upon with suspicion; it was assumed they had agreed to spy for the South, or they would not have been released.

So it was with naive hope of success that the U.S. delegation to the Paris peace talks announced on April 29, 1971, that Thieu was preparing 570 sick and wounded North Vietnamese prisoners to be shipped home as a unilateral gesture of good will. The figure had been arrived at through frustrating negotiations with Thieu. Unfortunately no one had thought to ask the prisoners if they wanted to go. The International Red Cross spent days in private interviews with a pool of 660 prisoners. Only thirteen of them—all amputees or otherwise permanently disabled—agreed to go home. And the Geneva conventions prohibited the return of any prisoner against his will. Hanoi then called the whole thing a sham and said it would refuse to accept even the thirteen. They were nevertheless carried by a converted American cruise ship/troop transport to the shores of North Vietnam and deposited on June 3. The North offered no American POWs in trade.

In retrospect, Laird blamed Thieu, not the United States, for the debacle. There was speculation in the press that Thieu had deliberately botched the return of the POWs to make his point that such exchanges were useless. Laird said General Abrams shared that view, but Laird preferred to think Thieu had just been careless in announcing the plan before polling the prisoners. There were other mistakes in South Vietnam that hurt Laird's campaign to free the POWs. The International Red Cross complained, occasionally justifiably, about conditions in the POW camps run by the South. Laird continuously pressed Thieu for better treatment of the prisoners, but it was not a priority in the South Vietnamese budget, and the United States could do little to change that.

It rankled Laird that the International Red Cross, when it inspected camps in the South, would complain about conditions there but didn't raise a protest when Hanoi would not even allow inspections of the camps in the North.

So passionate was Laird about the American POWs that, in late 1970, he gave the go-ahead for a gallant rescue attempt that was at once a spectacular success and a staggering failure. The target was a prison camp called Son Tay deep in North Vietnam, just twenty-three miles west of Hanoi. Since May of 1968 American POWs had been held at Son Tay under harsh conditions of torture and deprivation. Hoping that U.S. reconnaissance planes might overfly the camp occasionally, the prisoners methodically spelled out a coded appeal for a rescue in the arrangement of rock piles and ditches they worked on around the camp. They even hung their laundry in patterns that would call attention from a bird's eye view. Their coded message was that fifty-five men were housed at Son Tay and they wanted someone to come and get them. Laird said the Son Tay prisoners got their appeal out using another method also, which is still classified.

Their plea was decoded at the Pentagon in the spring of 1970, and Laird authorized planning to begin for a rescue raid on the camp. Search and rescue operations for downed pilots were common within hours after crashes, but never had U.S. soldiers crossed into North Vietnam to shoot up a POW camp and take the prisoners home. In South Vietnam there had been just under one hundred attempted raids on Viet Cong camps to rescue U.S. and allied prisoners, but they had netted only one American soldier, and he died two weeks later of wounds sustained from enemy gunfire during the rescue.

The secrecy around the Son Tay raid would be so tight that not even the president would be told until four months into the planning. Laird and Admiral Moorer, along with Colonel Pursley, were the only ones in the top tier at the Pentagon who knew. Moorer did not tell the rest of the chiefs. The details were known only in the highest ranks of the CIA and the Defense Intelligence Agency because those spy agencies needed to supply the intelligence on Son Tay and any possible threat from the surrounding countryside. Even the fifty-nine men who pulled off the raid trained for three months and were not told the nature of their mission until the day before they took off in helicopters bound for Son Tay. Their leaders were Air Force Brigadier General Leroy Manor, who would command the overall operation, and Army Colonel Arthur "Bull" Simons, who would lead the search and rescue team.

At Eglin Air Force Base in Florida, engineers who didn't know what they were building erected a mock-up of Son Tay based on aerial reconnaissance photography. Laird followed the progress of the training closely and was tempted to visit Eglin on a routine trip to Florida that fall but feared he might draw too much attention to the secret site.

On September 24, 1970, General Manor told Laird that the team might be ready as early as October 20. It was time for Laird to tell the president. In the last week of September, Nixon and Laird were on a trip to Europe and had concluded an audience with Pope Paul VI at the Vatican when they retired for the night to an aircraft carrier, the *Saratoga,* in the Mediterranean. It was there that Laird took Nixon aside and explained the plans for the Son Tay raid. In typical Laird fashion, he did not directly ask permission. "I told [Nixon] that unless he had strong objections to my doing it, I was going ahead," Laird said. Nixon's reply, as Laird remembered it, was, "I think it's just fine. Go ahead."

When the timetable was moved back, Laird again briefed the president. On November 6 the two men met alone in the Oval Office. In a "memo for the record" Laird put down the events of that meeting: "I indicated frankly that, while I would take full and complete responsibility for the promulgation of the action and particularly any adverse outcomes, I wanted the President to have knowledge of the plan and the opportunity to veto my proposed actions. I outlined both the positive and the negative results which I could foresee from the plan. . . . I indicated further that on balance, the potential positive results justified the obvious and substantial risks involved. The President did not choose to alter the plans I outlined."[7]

In the end, Laird decided he needed a firm "yes" or "no" from Nixon. On November 18, with the Son Tay raiders already on their way to Southeast Asia, Admiral Moorer came to the Oval Office with his briefing charts and faced Nixon, Kissinger, Laird, Rogers, and CIA Director Richard Helms. After Moorer presented the military aspects of the raid, Laird briefed Nixon on what was known about the conditions the POWs endured. Nixon asked a few questions and said he had to think about it. The next day, at a meeting of the National Security Council in a room full of people who knew nothing about the raid, Nixon passed a note to Laird telling him to go ahead with the mission. "Mel, as I told Moorer after our meeting yesterday regardless of results, the men on this project have my complete backing and there will be no second guessing if the plan fails. It is worth the risk and the planning is superb. I will be at Camp David Saturday. I would like for you to call me as soon as you have anything to report." The note was unsigned.

⚬

The outcome of the Son Tay raid had already been determined, but no one in Washington knew it. The prisoners had been moved out of the camp in July because of a flood on a nearby river. Reconnaissance flights over the camp had shown fewer people moving around the compound during the day, but that could not be taken as proof of no prisoners, especially when the POWs were usually confined to their cells. The day before the raid, the Defense Intelligence Agency got word from a sometimes-reliable agent in North Vietnam that the prisoners had indeed been moved, but that information was countered by the most recent reconnaissance flights over the camp, which showed a resurgence of activity at Son Tay. Laird weighed the new information and informed Nixon. Together they decided the risk was worth it. The raid would go ahead. Laird had always told Simons and Manor that there was at best a fifty-fifty chance that POWs were in the camp, and the two military men said that was enough for them to go ahead.

Three hours before the raid began, the Defense Intelligence Agency dispatched a navy captain to see Laird and make sure he knew that the camp could be empty. The captain wanted to know if the mission was a "go." "The order is 'go' and it won't be changed," Laird told the captain. Laird had already ordered absolute radio silence between the raiders and ground commanders during the operation. "I didn't want anybody countermanding my 'go,'" he recalled.

The helicopters carrying the Son Tay raiders took off from Thailand at 11:25 P.M., November 19, for the three hour flight over Laos and into North Vietnam. Simultaneously, in what would be a more controversial play than the raid itself, navy jets from aircraft carriers in the Gulf of Tonkin took off for the first large-scale bombing raid over North Vietnam since Johnson had halted such bombing two years before. The jets that buzzed Hanoi carried only flares, but planes that flew farther south dropped live bombs. It was a diversion to draw attention away from the helicopters coming into North Vietnam from the west.

Laird had stewed over the idea of a diversionary bombing for weeks, knowing that it would violate the 1968 "understandings" with Hanoi. There had been smaller, isolated bombing raids since 1968, but always on an excuse, however flimsy, that the United States was retaliating against an attack on one of its own reconnaissance planes. On November 13 Hanoi had given Laird just such an excuse, shooting down an Air Force RF-4C reconnaissance plane. On that day Laird warned publicly that retaliation was an option, but he waited until the Son Tay raiders were in the air nearly seven days later. The diversion worked. The arrival of the American helicopters at Son Tay at 2 A.M. was a complete surprise to the soldiers guarding the compound. One helicopter was deliberately crash landed into the center of the camp so the raiders could clear away the first resistance from inside. Then the other helicopters landed outside the fence, and the American forces stormed in, mowing down their stunned enemy. It took just over twenty minutes for the raiders to search the camp, determine that there were no POWs, and leave the way they came.

A message, "negative POWs," was flashed to General Manor, waiting at a command post in South Vietnam, and from there relayed to the Pentagon's National Military Command Center. Laird had been waiting in his office one floor above the command center, along with CIA Director Helms. A squawk box in the office picked up communications from downstairs, and when the first message came through that the raiders were all coming out alive, Laird and Helms hurried to the command center to learn more. When they arrived, they were told there were no prisoners. Stone faced, Laird called Nixon at Camp David and reported the outcome.

As Laird walked back to his office, his stoic demeanor belied the strategy already roiling in his head. He had to get on top of the public reaction and turn the perception from failure to the heroic and compassionate effort he genuinely believed the mission had been. As far as he was concerned, the raid had been a success. The raiders had done their job perfectly, and with no casualties. The fact that there were no POWs at Son Tay was of only secondary interest to Laird at that moment. "I was absolutely relieved," he later recalled. "I had thought [the raiders] might all be shot up."

Laird never thought of Son Tay as a public relations disaster. Even thirty years later, as he prepared for a reunion with the Son Tay raiders, he bristled at the idea that the outcome of the raid might have been tough to spin. "I didn't have any problem with explaining it to the public. I'd have gone any place to talk about what those men did. It really threw the North off base that we could come in that close without being detected. I loved that. As long as those people got out safe, I just loved it." Of the raiders, Laird said emotionally, "They're my boys."

While Laird's enthusiasm may have been the minority view in Washington in November 1970, he learned later that it was echoed in POW camps across North Vietnam. "To the POWs that were in country, it meant a great deal," Laird said. "[The POWs] knew about this within twenty-four hours."

The same twenty-four hours were busy for Laird. He called Bull Simons back to Washington, where Simons advised him to lift the veil of secrecy on the raid. Laird agreed wholeheartedly. Not only was he proud of what the men had done; he knew it would be impossible to keep it a secret. More importantly, the press and the antiwar agitators in Congress were berating Nixon for the surprise bombing raids over the North, and Laird wanted to defend that publicly.

Bull Simons was joined by General Manor in Washington, and the two reluctant soldiers were escorted by Laird into the Pentagon press room. They stood by with squared shoulders and grim faces while Laird dropped the bomb. "On Friday, November 20th . . . about 2 A.M. in North Vietnam, a small rescue team successfully landed by helicopter at a reported prisoner-of-war compound at Son Tay, approximately 20 nautical miles west of Hanoi." Laird continued with more details, all stressing that everything went precisely according to plan. A full twelve paragraphs into his statement, Laird noted, "Regrettably the rescue team discovered that the camp had recently been vacated. No prisoners were located."

The reporters deluged Simons and Manor with questions, many of which were answered gruffly with, "I can't answer that." Laird had brought them to the press to showcase their heroism, but the two were having none of it. They were paid to keep secrets and weren't about to discuss the raid in any detail, nor did they appreciate the attention, especially when they had no POWs to show for their effort. The fearsome looking and aptly nicknamed "Bull" Simons by his mere appearance discouraged the questioning. After a few minutes of watching the officers growl, "Yes," "No," and "I can't answer that," Laird stepped in to give the reporters some complete sentences and paragraphs they could quote.

A tense moment came when Laird was asked if the bombing raids on the North that day were a diversion for the Son Tay mission. "No, they were not," he responded. As a man who always prided himself on telling at least most of the truth to the press, Laird went on to explain. The planes that dropped only flares to create panic and confusion over Hanoi were part of the diversion, but the live bombing raids below North Vietnam's nineteenth parallel—140 miles south of Hanoi—were a "protective reaction" to the shooting down of the reconnaissance plane. After the press conference Laird marched back to his office in a rage and threw out some choice expletives when the reporters couldn't hear. "I thought the press didn't consider the heroism that was involved," he said later. "They were kind of cynical about the whole thing."

⚜

There was more cynicism brewing across the Potomac on Capitol Hill. Laird's antiwar nemesis on the Senate Foreign Relations Committee, William Fulbright, called the next morning. "He wanted to raise hell about Son Tay and wanted to schedule a big formal hearing the next week," Laird recalled. Unwilling to let a week go by in which the surprise in Congress would foment into rage, Laird said, "I'm available now."

"I can't do it now," Fulbright responded.

"Well, I can't come up next week," Laird said. "I'm just going to tell the press that I offered to come up today to be before your committee and you refused."

Fulbright capitulated and Laird hurried up to the Senate for one of the more caustic confrontations he would have with Fulbright during his four years as defense secretary. Laird's opening statement stressed the necessity of the rescue mission, given the mounting evidence of mistreatment and even death among the POW ranks.

With uncharacteristic passion, Laird said, "As it became clear to me that Hanoi, week after week, month after month, and year after year, was rebuffing our efforts at Paris . . . I could not ignore the fact that our men were dying in captivity. Mr. Chairman, I want this committee to know that I have not faced a more challenging decision since I have been Secretary of Defense. I concluded that there was no other acceptable alternative than to recommend that the volunteer force...should be authorized to make a valiant attempt to save their fellow Americans. I have said and I want to repeat today, that it is my firm belief that if there had been prisoners of war at Son Tay, they would be free men today."

After a verbal bow in the direction of the heroes, Fulbright berated Laird for allowing the raid of an empty POW camp, and blamed faulty intelligence for the outcome. The intelligence was just fine, Laird came back. The raiders knew the location of the camp, the layout of the buildings, the location of surface-to-air missiles nearby, the closest military installations, and the capability of the enemy's radar. "The intelligence for this mission was excellent, except for our not having a camera that would see through the rooftop of buildings," Laird said. He would repeat the quip many times in the next few days whenever he was challenged about the quality of the intelligence. Fulbright didn't want to hear Laird's recitation of intelligence successes. "I do not think this is relevant," he said. "There weren't any prisoners there. What difference does it make?..."

"What we have done here has shown all of these prisoners in North Vietnam that America does care," Laird replied.

Fulbright bristled. "Was there any doubt that America cares about them? I did not know that there was any doubt."

"Yes, there was a doubt," said Laird.

Later Fulbright called the raid "provocative," and another committee member, Senator Edmund Muskie, said that even a successful rescue operation "would have been a failure for hundreds of other persons" because it would be a setback to the negotiations in Paris. Fulbright pointedly accused Laird of having given up on the negotiations as a route to peace, as evidenced by his willingness to bomb the North again. That was true, but Laird would not say it outright. "As far as the negotiations are concerned, there has not been improvement in Paris during the past few months," he said.

Laird was battered for weeks over the raid by the press and opponents on Capitol Hill, and for a time he seemed to stand alone in his support of the raid. Even the CIA, which had been in on the planning from the beginning, floated the story that it had not been informed, thus brushing off the blame for faulty intelligence about the camp. But Laird stuck to his story that he had a duty to the POWs. As he told Fulbright, "If this country is willing to abandon its military men to death and captivity, we will have truly lost our national morality and our humanity.... I have no regrets about [the raid] being recommended. My only regret is that we did not bring out any prisoners."

Thirty years later, when asked again whether he had any regrets about the Son Tay raid, Laird raised an old hurt; the military bureaucracy had refused to promote Colonel Simons to general. Laird had requested a promotion for Simons, but the gruff colonel's unconventional career path had focused on small-unit operations and was deemed too narrow to qualify him to be a general. "He was the kind of guy who volunteered for the tough jobs," Laird said of Simons, who had agreed to head the Son Tay raid even before he had been told what it was about. "He wasn't a big West Point man or trained in all of the fancy schools of the Army, but he had the guts and the courage and he was a leader of people. I asked the Army to promote him.... I asked Westmoreland to intercede, but he did not."

Son Tay was the first and last POW camp in the North to be raided in such bold fashion. Laird did not attempt it again, although there had been and would be other escape attempts by the prisoners. After Son Tay, when the prisoners were gathered in from rural camps and concentrated in the "Hanoi Hilton," it was easier for them to plot escape because they had the group to help and encourage. But it was also harder to pull off the plans because the POWs were smack in the middle of the enemy stronghold—white men who would have to disappear into a city teeming with Asians.

Operation Thunderhead in 1972 was one such aborted escape planned simultaneously in Washington and Hanoi. Using a means of coded communication, which Laird would not reveal even thirty years later, prisoners in the Hanoi Hilton managed to get word to the Pentagon that they were ready to break out of the prison, slip into the nearby Red River, and float out into the Gulf of Tonkin. Could the navy be there to pluck them out of the water? Laird reluctantly approved the plan, wary of the risks but unwilling to close any door on the POWs.

The accepted signal that the navy would be waiting was a flyover above Hanoi by two SR-71 spy planes that would create two sonic booms within fifteen seconds of one another. That happened on May 1, 1972, and the two prisoners who wanted most to make the escape were prepared to break out the first week in June, as prearranged through the coded communications. But at the last minute, the senior American officers in the POW hierarchy at the Hanoi Hilton told them the risks were too great for the two men and for those who would be left behind to suffer at the hands of angry prison guards. In two prior escape attempts from the Hanoi Hilton, the four POWs involved had all been recaptured, and one had been beaten to death by the guards.

Unaware that the POW leaders had canceled the escape, a navy submarine and search and rescue helicopters combed the Gulf of Tonkin for the first two weeks of June 1972. The seas were so treacherous that one of the Navy SEALs was killed in an accident. So, unlike the Son Tay raid, there was an American fatality in the Thunderhead operation. But there was no public relations ripple in the United States because Thunderhead remained a secret until long after the war, when historians began looking into the records.

On June 19, 1972, Admiral Moorer sent a memo to Laird. The search operation had been called off. "It must be assumed that the escape attempt...was either not attempted or was unsuccessful," Moorer wrote. He also cabled Admiral McCain in Hawaii to call back the search teams. "Unfortunately, the real purpose of Thunderhead cannot be divulged to most of the personnel who participated in the operation," Moorer wrote. "However, please convey my personal thanks and appreciation for a job well done in this vital humanitarian task."[8]

At the same time Thunderhead was being planned in mid-1972, the Joint Chiefs were plotting the one outrageous rescue that Laird wouldn't condone—a last-ditch rescue effort for every prisoner held in and around Hanoi. Given the precarious state of Kissinger's secret peace negotiations at the time, and the pending reelection of Richard Nixon, this final POW raid amounted to little more than a fantasy in the minds of the Joint Chiefs. They envisioned invading the North with more than three divisions—57,500 men whose insertion into the war at that point would have nearly doubled the number of American troops left in Vietnam then. That raid never got off the drawing board. In retrospect, Laird called the plan "ridiculous" because it would have cost more men than the number of POWs rescued. He never bothered to forward the plan to the White House for review.

In the end, the POWs were "rescued" by the means that Laird had the least faith in—a peace agreement in Paris that ended the U.S. involvement in the war.

19

Slowing the Arms Race

✦

THE CLOSEST CONGRESSIONAL VOTE on a defense issue in 1969 was not over the Vietnam War. It was the decision about whether the United States should build and deploy an antiballistic missile (ABM) defense system to block a Soviet or Chinese nuclear attack. The ABM debate dominated the headlines in the first seven months of the Nixon administration. "Stop the ABM" became a frenzied incantation against the Pentagon—a back door punishment for miscalculation in Vietnam and squandering billions of dollars on wasteful defense programs. Laird had looked down the road and felt sure that the United States would not prevail in arms reduction talks with Moscow unless, like the Soviets, the Americans had an active ABM system to put on the negotiating table. So he worked with prodigious energy to fund a defensive system that he fully intended would be bargained away in return for a Soviet agreement to limit nuclear weapons.

The possibility of a shield against nuclear missiles was first considered in the 1940s and remained controversial into the twenty-first century. In the closing months of World War II, a project was begun to develop antiaircraft missiles to shoot down bombers. Within a decade it had grown into something larger—the Nike family of radar-guided missiles with the potential to shoot down not just planes but eventually incoming nuclear missiles also. As with offensive missiles, there was a body of U.S. security experts who argued for defensive systems. The Russians outstripped U.S. missile development somewhat when, in 1957, one of their rockets boosted into space the world's first orbital satellite, Sputnik. If the Russians could launch a satellite into space, they could launch a nuclear payload as well. Thus was born the race to field an ICBM, an intercontinental ballistic missile that is fired into space on a trajectory that takes it to a target on the other side of the globe. Congress, including Representative Laird, had responded with increased funding for America's missile programs—the offensive ICBM and defensive ABM programs.

Johnson and McNamara had opposed an American ABM system because they felt it was too costly and would never be adequate to protect the United States. They further argued that offensive weapons would always outpace the defense, and at less cost. But the pressure from Congress was intense to focus on a defensive system. Johnson had smelled a 1968 presidential election issue that could work against him. He sensed the Republicans were ready to do to him as Kennedy had done to them in 1960—scare the voters about a "missile gap" with the Soviet Union, this time in both ICBM and ABM missiles. Thus, Johnson decided to deploy a scaled-down ABM system, and he ordered a re-

luctant McNamara to do it. McNamara never concealed his disdain for this
sacrifice of principle for political expediency.

The ABM plan which Laird inherited when he became secretary of defense was called Sentinel—a proposed system of radar and missiles to detect
and shoot down incoming nuclear missiles. After the inauguration, Laird told
Nixon he needed a little breathing room to consider the ABM options, so, on
February 6, 1969, Laird ordered a halt to all construction work on ABM sites. It
had been one thing for Laird to criticize the ABM from his place in Congress. It
was quite another to decide as defense secretary exactly what he was in favor of.
Nixon wanted some kind of ABM program, but he was ambivalent about what
it should be, so the decision was left to the defense secretary. Laird examined
his own deepest thoughts on the matter, and one thing was abundantly clear
to him. Despite the legislative battle it would spark, the Nixon administration
needed to have an active ABM system to use as a bargaining chip in arms talks
with the Russians.

The first chance the Senate had to question Laird about the ABM was during his confirmation hearing before the Armed Services Committee. One senator said he was gratified that news articles suggested Laird had "doubts" about
the Sentinel system.[1] Laird responded, "I see as my primary responsibility as
Secretary of Defense in the new administration, that this nation will never
permit itself to fall into a position where we negotiate from weakness."[2] In case
anyone missed that signal, Laird drove it home during his first defense secretary press conference two weeks later, on January 30: "Now, as far as the ABM
is concerned, we have an opportunity, I think, within the not too distant future
to move into talks with the Soviet Union on offensive and defensive missile
systems. And I do not want to be in a position when we go into those talks, if
we do, with one hand tied behind our back. I think it's most important, as we
go into those talks, to have defensive as well as offensive missile systems up for
discussion, and debate and negotiations."

Meanwhile, the forces against any ABM system were growing. It was shaping up to be an evenly matched debate in Congress, and the press promoted
the upcoming legislative fisticuffs. After he appeared on *Face the Nation* on
February 9, Laird told his staff, "I tried to shift the subject away from Sentinel
four times," but the journalists wouldn't let go.[3]

On March 1 Secretary Laird transmitted his secret recommendation to
President Nixon—that they go ahead with a modified Sentinel program to
defend only America's nuclear weapons cache instead of its cities.[4] Laird had
never liked the idea of defending cities with any ABM system. No ABM system
could be perfect, and millions of Americans could potentially be killed even
with a defense system in place. Instead, Laird thought it was better to defend
probable targets—such as the ICBM silos in the northern United States. If the
ABM system could protect enough retaliatory, second-strike nuclear weapons,
then the Soviets might not be tempted to try a first strike.

When Nixon announced Laird's new plan, he used the word "safeguard" repeatedly, so the press began calling it the Safeguard system to distinguish it from LBJ's Sentinel program.[5] But for the legion of bitter critics, an ABM system by another name stunk just as much. "It's now named after a soap instead of a soldier," columnist Mary McGrory wrote, "but it's the same ABM system that Johnson went for to defend himself when Richard Nixon began to hint at a 'security gap' in 1967."[6]

⋈

What loomed large in Laird's mind during the 1969 ABM debate was more than one hundred feet tall—the Soviet SS-9 missile, which was first deployed in 1967. At first, American intelligence experts presumed it was an incremental advance for Russian strategic forces, which were still technologically behind the United States. But then intelligence reports that did not become clear until early 1969 caused alarm among the few people "cleared" to read the highly classified documents, including the new secretary of defense. The SS-9 was significantly more accurate than previous Soviet missiles. The CIA deduced that it could hit within a half mile of a target on the American continent. It was also estimated that in a second modification of this two-stage behemoth, the Russians had placed a warhead with a yield of up to twenty-five megatons, which was more than 150 times the destructive power of the Hiroshima bomb.

In one of many consultations with Nixon over the ABM program, Laird convinced the president that some of the highly classified reports on the SS-9 should be made public to buttress the case for the ABM. Nixon authorized Laird to declassify whatever he felt was necessary for his first public ABM testimony before the Senate Armed Services Committee in mid-March. But when Laird shared the data with the Senate and the TV viewing audience watching the hearing, Senator William Fulbright accused him of scare-mongering. He refused to ask Laird any questions, saying that the wily Laird would use questions as an opener to filibuster. Senator Albert Gore (father of the future Vice President) offered a hypothetical scenario: "Say a watchman from a farm in Montana calls up the President and says, 'Four and a half minutes ago three missiles were picked up on radar ... which buttons do I push?'"

"The panic button!" Senator Fulbright interjected, and the gallery erupted in laughter.

"This is not a laughing matter," Laird chided. "It is a deadly serious question, and it gets right down to the heart of the discussion here today. I can tell you that if I were ... President I would like to have an ABM to launch—and not have to press the button for the [retaliatory] strike."[7]

It was a telling comeback, and a favorite for replay on TV network news programs. Journalists began referring to the ABM system as *the second button*—an opportunity to save the United States without killing millions of Russians in retaliation.

Another secret driving Laird's support for the ABM was something he could only hint at during the Senate hearings. Intelligence intercepted at a National Security Agency listening post in northwest Turkey had confirmed that the Soviets were testing multiple warheads ("multiple independently targetable reentry vehicle" or MIRV) on their nuclear missiles. That meant that instead of using a single warhead to target a population center in the United States, the Soviets could deploy multiple warheads to take out smaller military targets, such as U.S. missile silos. Laird immediately understood that the MIRVs gave the Soviets a "first strike capability," meaning they could launch an unprovoked attack on multiple U.S. missile silos and take them out without huge loss of life. There would be less risk of raising world anger over such an attack, and the U.S. ability to retaliate would be crippled.

When Laird used veiled terms to describe this new "first strike capability" during the hearings on the ABM, Senator Fulbright demanded to know more. All the other accepted intelligence estimates of the day from the CIA and Defense Intelligence Agency had concluded that the Soviets were not contemplating a first strike, and Fulbright suspected Laird was stretching the truth to suit his stance on ABM. But Laird could not reveal all he knew from the secret National Security Agency intercept out of Turkey. (It carried the highest "code word" level of classification.) Eventually when Laird shared the NSA secrets with the CIA, the intelligence estimates were updated. But for a time Laird stood alone, even taking flak from some parts of the intelligence community, for claiming that the Soviets might be developing a first-strike capability.[8]

After the Fulbright-Gore hearing, Laird's mother called him from Wisconsin, where she had been watching the proceedings on TV, and she complained about his testimony. She hated hearing her son elaborate on the terrible destructive weapons. "It is not the most pleasant subject to talk about," she scolded. "You're scaring everybody!"[9] She was right to be concerned about her boy because it soon became clear that Laird, as the primary ABM spokesman, was the lightning rod for ABM critics—more so than Nixon or Secretary of State Rogers. Commentary on Laird painted him as a hard-liner whose provocative ABM hard sell was out of step with the president's conciliatory language toward the Soviet Union. Behind the scenes, the president was not wholly supportive of Laird's tough stand in the Senate. Nixon sent Laird a copy of his inaugural address with this passage underlined: "We cannot learn from one another until we stop shouting at one another."

⌐∞⌐

Representative Charlie Goodell of New York was one of Laird's oldest friends, having been in the trenches with him on the Republican side of the House. When Laird was House Republican Conference chairman, Goodell was a key member of his brain trust. They were in the Chowder and Marching Club together and the Wednesday prayer group. So Laird was pleased in 1968 when

New York Governor Nelson Rockefeller chose Goodell to fill the unexpired term of assassinated Senator Robert Kennedy. But Laird was soon to regret the choice.

In a few short months, Goodell underwent a profound change. "He became venturesome in a lot of ways, socially and otherwise," recalled former Democratic New York Governor Hugh Carey. Goodell fell for a pretty socialite and divorced his wife. At the same time, he radically changed his political views. "When he was picked to take Kennedy's seat, Charlie metamorphosed completely into a flagrant liberal," Carey added.[10] Laird generally accepted the change and remained friends, but he felt badly abused by Goodell when the new senator proved his new liberal stripes by joining Democrats to kill the Safeguard ABM system. In that cause, Goodell used Laird for a press stunt.

On April 3, 1969, Goodell planned to fly to Ohio, where he would make a statement against the ABM at an air force museum, using as a prop the prototype of a costly air force bomber that was never deployed. At National Airport in Washington, before leaving on his trip, Goodell called Laird from a pay phone in full view of the media entourage. Laird took the call from his friend, and Goodell engaged him in a debate over the ABM. When the phone call was over, Goodell boasted to the journalists that Laird had tried and failed to talk him out of his ABM opposition.[11] At Laird's next staff meeting, he used the incident as a cautionary tale. "In retrospect, I should have refused the call," Laird said, though he couldn't have suspected that Goodell would make it a media event. "In the future, we need to watch with care that we are not used in this manner," he continued, "and we shouldn't let Defense aircraft be used as backdrops for press conferences!"[12]

While Laird was arguably the best lobbyist for the ABM system, the president himself was one of the worst. Laird realized that Nixon had a habit of making members of Congress feel that he thought he was smarter than they were. "You can't get a vote if you start appealing to people from that kind of a pedestal," Laird said. It was not unusual for aides to hear Nixon grousing angrily about senators, saying that "they are just a bunch of pygmies down there—a bunch of god-damned pygmies!" And while Nixon could fume and spout threats when he was alone with aides, he was too often without spine or force in one-on-one efforts to lobby legislators. On the ABM issue, Laird said, "You couldn't count on Nixon for help to get a vote through the Congress. He just didn't think it was as important as I did. More than once, I'd have to remind him: 'By God, we have to win on this thing or you're not going to have any bargaining chips as far as strategic arms limitations are concerned.'" To contemporary observers, it was evident that Laird had been left to "carr[y] the Administration load in the ABM controversy," as the *Washington Post* characterized it.[13]

The full Senate took up the military authorization bill—including the ABM funding—on July 8, 1969. The debate lasted twenty-nine days and was the longest in the Senate concerning a military matter since World War II.[14] In late July, with the opposition claiming at least fifty-one votes against ABM, it looked like Laird and the Nixon administration were going to lose. But Laird was a master vote counter, and his tally said the outcome would be fifty-fifty. He needed another vote for the ABM. So he set out to secure a pledge from the Senate's lone woman, Margaret Chase Smith, of Maine, because he knew it was in his power to do something nice for someone she cared about, her executive assistant, William Chesley Lewis Jr.

The Republican senator and her assistant had a long working relationship that had blossomed into a friendship, and possibly a romantic relationship, although neither admitted to that. Partly due to Smith's patronage, Lewis had advanced to the rank of brigadier general in the air force reserves. When Laird became secretary of defense, he found General Lewis was fulfilling his annual training requirement in the secretary's Legislative Affairs office, which was something of a conflict of interest. That office was responsible for lobbying members of Congress on defense matters. So, several weeks each year Lewis was a lobbyist, and the rest of the time he was the one being lobbied, as a member of Senator Smith's staff. Besides, Laird's legislative team was not fond of Lewis, in part because he had advanced so far in the reserves without having served in combat or commanded men. "He'd never really been on active duty, but he *loved* to wear his uniform," Laird's legislative chief Dick Capen recalled. "But it bothered him that he didn't have many medals." Another legislative aide, Brigadier General James Lawrence, said that Senator Smith would quietly buttonhole him and urge: "You know, it'd be nice if Bill got another ribbon or something."[15]

In the summer of 1969 Laird floated a rumor intended to reach Smith's ears to the effect that he was thinking of changing Lewis's training post to somewhere less convenient. Then, at the right moment in late July, Laird arranged a meeting with the senator to talk to her about her anti-ABM vote: "Isn't there something I can do or say to you to change your mind?" he cajoled.

"No," she responded. "There is nothing."

"Well, I'm sorry, Margaret, I just thought there might be something that you really needed. This is a very important vote, because if we stop the ABM, I think arms reduction and arms control will go down the drain."

She understood his point and added, almost incongruously, that there was one beef she had against Laird when he was in the House. He had not supported Lewis's promotion to brigadier general. Laird had his opening. He reminded her that he currently had some control over General Lewis's military career. "There must be SOMETHING I can do for you now about that, Margaret."

There was a long pause. "Well, Mel," she finally began, "maybe there is. I'm a little worried about Bill. He wants to keep his reserve mobilization assignment with your legislative office."

"Consider it done," Laird said. "And maybe he needs another medal?"

"That would be nice," she smiled.

The historic vote on the ABM funding took place on August 6, 1969. Two days before, at Laird's staff meeting, a legislative aide noted that the opposition claimed to have fifty-one votes. "They are wrong," Laird interrupted. "*We* have fifty-one *pro*-ABM votes."[16] As the debate began at 11 a.m, Senator Fulbright intoned: "I have been in the Senate 25 years.... I do not believe [any] Senator can cite a single case in which a serious challenge has been made on the floor of the Senate to any military program, since World War II, over $1 trillion. I have never heard a serious debate take place on it. This is the first time."[17]

In a series of amendments crafted by her wily aide General Lewis, Smith was able to give Laird the vote he needed to secure funding, while at the same time maintaining her public opposition to the ABM. Her vote provoked a gasp across the Senate floor and caused speculation in the press for weeks, but Laird kept the backstory a secret for decades. And he made good on his promise to her. Lewis remained with the legislative affairs division when doing his reserve duty. And he received a Meritorious Service Medal in 1969, then a Joint Services Commendation Medal in 1971 from Secretary Laird, and a Meritorious Service Medal from Army Secretary Froehlke. In photos when the medals were awarded, Senator Smith stands beaming at the general's side.

Laird's instinct proved correct—that the only way to slow down Soviet missile production was by treaty, and the only way to get a treaty was by having a viable American ABM system to offer up. Nixon and Kissinger agreed in retrospect. "I am absolutely convinced that had we lost the ABM battle in the Senate, we would not have been able to negotiate the first nuclear arms control agreement in Moscow in 1972," Nixon wrote in his memoirs.[18] The man who negotiated that agreement, Kissinger, confirmed the judgment in his own memoirs: "When the SALT [Strategic Arms Limitation] talks started in November [1969], contrary to the dire predictions of arms controllers, the Soviets proved eager to negotiate on ABM.... The trade-off of Soviet willingness to limit offensive forces in exchange for our willingness to limit ABMs was the essential balance of incentives that produced the first SALT agreements three years later."[19]

❧

During the five hundred days of the 1969–72 SALT talks, President Nixon was fairly removed from the process, except to make the major decisions, which, more often than not, Kissinger had already formulated for the president's approval. Within the administration, points of view tended to form on two sides—those reluctant to give away any weapons advantage (the Pentagon), and those more willing to compromise in the quest for peace (the State Department and the Arms Control and Disarmament Agency). While all had input and were crucial to the process, the Pentagon held the power Nixon worried about.

"If the Pentagon refused to support a SALT agreement," Nixon wrote in his memoirs, "the domestic political consequences would be devastating"; in fact, ratification by the Senate would have been unlikely.[20] In Laird, Nixon had someone who could bring the Joint Chiefs in line on major issues and sell the notion of arms control on Capitol Hill. Thus, the U.S. position during the negotiations was primarily the result of compromise between Kissinger and Laird. Kissinger recalled how that give and take worked: "You can read stories that I would go off and, on my own, negotiate these agreements. And I pulled these [arms] numbers out of the air in excesses of megalomania—which are not unknown [for me]," he recalled with a smile. "But I can tell you what really happened: I would go to Mel Laird and I'd say, 'I have to do this. We're going to negotiate it. Tell me what you can *really* live with in the Defense Department. *You* give me the numbers.' And *those* are the numbers I worked from."[21]

Laird had promised Nixon he would deliver a fully supportive Pentagon for the arms talks. The costly Vietnam war had taken away money from U.S. strategic weapons programs at the same time as the Soviet Union was engaged in a massive buildup—producing up to 250 land-based and 128 submarine-based nuclear missiles a year.[22] "Nothing concentrated the minds of American leaders on the advantages of SALT as much as the clear and present danger of one-sided arms control in the form of congressional cuts in U.S. defense budgets," Gerard Smith, who headed the U.S. SALT delegation, wrote in his memoir. "The changing popular and congressional mood about strategic arms was not lost on such an astute politician as Secretary of Defense Melvin Laird."[23]

Laird's military assistant, General Pursley, observed: "There weren't many other [former] defense secretaries who were as knowledgeable or even as interested in arms control as Mel was. It was unusual to have a politically-based secretary who was that incisive about what the arms control issues were, and his influence on the talks was seminal."[24]

From his first days in office, Laird intuitively knew four things about arms control: first, it was vital to get a congressional vote supporting America's ABM program; second, the Soviets feared the ABM and that fear might bring them to the negotiating table; third, Laird had to have his own loyalist as part of the U.S. delegation; and fourth, that person needed to be more knowledgeable and better at negotiating than any other player at the table. That is why Laird asked Paul Nitze to become his arms control representative on June 26, 1969, six weeks before the ABM vote was held and four months before the Soviets even agreed to begin the SALT talks.

It was a major coup for Laird, but not an easy one. Nitze was a longtime Democrat who had served as deputy secretary of defense and secretary of the navy during the Kennedy and Johnson administrations. When Laird wanted Nitze to serve in a high-level post on the Laird-Packard team, Senator Barry Goldwater vowed he would block the confirmation. Goldwater believed Nitze had been the brains behind Johnson's successful caricature of Goldwater as a warmonger during the 1964 presidential election. Laird also knew that Nixon would be suspicious of a man who had been such a close advisor to President Kennedy. So Laird appointed Nitze as his personal representative for arms control, which did not require confirmation, and ensconced him in an office down the hall from the secretary's office.

Nitze, known as the "silver fox" for his white hair and shrewdness, was sixty-eight at the time. An East Coast aristocrat, he had abandoned investment banking for government service beginning with the Roosevelt administration. He was a key member of the team President Truman sent to survey the effects of the atomic bomb on the people and geography of Hiroshima and Nagasaki. He was an instrumental player behind the creation of the Marshall Plan which resurrected Europe, and the North Atlantic Treaty Organization, which defended it. Nitze was also the principal author of NSC 68, the 1950 Truman policy document that outlined the U.S. cold war policy of "containment" of the Soviet Union. In it Nitze declared: "The Soviet Union . . . is animated by a new fanatic faith, antithetical to our own, and seeks to impose its absolute authority over the rest of the world."[25]

When the SALT talks officially began on November 17, 1969, in Helsinki, Gerard Smith was chairman of the U.S. delegation. The four other principal delegates were Nitze representing Laird; Llewelyn Thompson representing the State Department; Major General Royal B. Allison representing the Joint Chiefs; and a civilian scientist, Harold Brown, a former secretary of the air force who was then president of Cal Tech.

Both Laird and Kissinger were wary of Gerard Smith, a staunch advocate for arms control to the point of going on record as supporting a ban on ABMs and a moratorium on MIRVs. Neither was a useful position because the Soviets would never agree to them, nor would Laird and the Pentagon. Kissinger wrote that Smith "was agile in drafting instructions for himself that permitted his nominal superiors [Nixon and Secretary of State Rogers] only a minimum of influence over his discretionary powers."[26]

Laird viewed Smith as a fundamentally decent and honorable man who, nevertheless, needed to be reined in. In June of 1970 Laird complained in letters to Secretary Rogers that Smith was treating directions as "suggestions," and that he was "misleading" the Soviets about the will of the United States. Laird registered the same complaints in a memo to Nixon. The complaints had the desired result, and Laird came to an accommodation of sorts with Smith, letting him know that Laird and Kissinger would be calling the shots.[27] Delegate Harold Brown, who would later be President Jimmy Carter's secretary of defense, watched this bureaucratic battle with intense interest. His conclusion was that the real debate on U.S. positions was between Laird and Kissinger. Kissinger spoke for Nixon, Laird for the military. "Laird and Kissinger had differences, but because there was agreement between them in the end, SALT I was signed," Brown said.[28]

The most important issue on which Laird would not budge was that the United States should never agree to sign only an accord dealing with *defensive* strategic weapons, or ABMs. A freeze on *offensive* arms must be in place at the same time. Soviet pressure for an ABM-only treaty was intense. More than any other issue, this stand-off slowed the talks from 1969 until spring 1971. At different points, nearly everyone involved except Laird flirted with capitulation. In July 1970, anxious about the upcoming congressional elections, Nixon told Kissinger that he was willing to have a summit on ABMs only and deal with offensive arms later. Nixon knew that voters would support this position, because they were anxious for some progress in reducing the number of nuclear weapons in the world. But Laird was adamant, and Kissinger knew it would be a fatal mistake to go ahead without Laird's approval.

By the spring of 1971 Nixon was persuaded that offensive and defensive weapons were part of a package, and he directed Kissinger to secure an agreement that committed the Soviets to negotiate on both. Kissinger did, and it was this breakthrough that set the stage for the Moscow summit and signing the agreement the following spring.[29] But Kissinger had mistakenly told the Soviets that the submarine-launched ballistic missiles did not need to be part of SALT agreement. Neither Nitze nor Laird could believe he had made so haphazard a trade-off. A chagrined Kissinger tried to recant this oversight with the Soviets, who continued to avoid real negotiations on offensive weapons systems. In a series of private eyes-only memos to Kissinger, Laird complained mightily about the situation, which he called "intolerable." Laird reminded Kissinger that the ABM program was his biggest bargaining chip with the Soviets.[30]

The submarine missile issue became the last major SALT I obstacle, and it was Laird who came up with what Kissinger called an "ingenious solution" to end the stalemate. In a January 18, 1972, memorandum to Nixon, Laird urged that it was time to speed up the negotiations, and he was prepared to let the Soviets continue building their submarine missiles, but at a slower rate. Also, the Soviets must dismantle either an older submarine or a land-based missile once a certain number of new submarine missiles had been reached. Nixon directed Kissinger to float this idea through his "back channel" to Soviet Ambassador Anatoly Dobrynin. Dobrynin didn't respond directly, but during a secret meeting with Soviet leader Leonid Brezhnev on April 22, Brezhnev handed Kissinger a paper accepting Laird's idea.

Laird was also pivotal in setting the duration of the SALT I agreement. To Laird, it was vital that the Soviet offensive program be frozen at the agreed-upon numbers for five years. The Russians initially would only agree to eighteen months and then suggested a compromise of three years. But Laird refused to budge from five years, and Kissinger backed him, so Brezhnev finally agreed.[31]

Alone among Cabinet officials, Laird had an inside track on the secret negotiating sessions between Kissinger and Brezhnev. One of his best sources was Nitze. Nixon had already asked Nitze in 1969 to spy on the rest of the U.S. delegation for the White House. According to Nitze's memoirs, Nixon told him: "I have no confidence in [Bill] Rogers nor do I have complete confidence in Gerry [Gerard] Smith. I don't think they understand the arms control problem. So I want you to report anything you disapprove of directly to me." Nixon offered to let Nitze communicate with him through the same back-channel network the president used to bypass Laird to get to the Joint Chiefs, but Nitze didn't like it. "I told Mr. Nixon that I could not do what he was asking."[32] Despite his disdain for skulduggery, Nitze was the one man Nixon and Kissinger most respected on the delegation, so Kissinger kept Nitze privately informed of his secret SALT talks with the Soviets. And since Nitze was Laird's man, he dutifully reported all this to the secretary of defense.

During the 1972 Moscow summit, which featured the first visit of a U.S. president to Moscow, Nixon and Brezhnev signed both the SALT I and ABM treaties. Together they were the landmark first step in halting and ultimately reversing the nuclear arms race, and they were viewed as significant achievements boosting Nixon's reelection chances and his historical standing. However, praise for the progress should be shared by Kissinger, Laird, and Nixon.

If Laird had not been such a polished manipulator, it is likely the accords would have been more to the Soviet's advantage. Both Smith and Kissinger found Laird's skills and hard-line position to be useful in getting concessions from the Soviets. It was axiomatic with Laird that the United States must never negotiate with the Soviet Union except from a position of strength. That was the main reason he secured White House and congressional approval for an accelerated Trident strategic submarine program, a system that was part of what Laird promised the Joint Chiefs in return for their support of the accords.[33]

Laird had "provided crucial leadership by presenting the President with constructive proposals and realistic assessments of potential [SALT] agreements, and by keeping in perspective the goals of security and stability rather than ease of negotiation or popularity," wrote Gardiner Tucker, Laird's systems analysis chief, in a January 1973 overview memorandum. "We have been influential because we have been realistic rather than extreme, and because we have been able to pull the Department of Defense together on the essential issues." Without Laird's leadership, "unwise agreements might well have been reached."[34]

In the end, the SALT I agreement and ABM treaty were imperfect documents.[35] Nevertheless, the two accords were vital forerunners of the many agreements that followed, which would truly limit and reduce the nuclear arsenals of each nation. The ABM treaty itself was in force for thirty years, until President George W. Bush withdrew the United States from it in 2002.[36]

Kissinger deserved the credit he received for his pivotal role in these negotiations, and it could not have been accomplished if Nixon had not seen the wisdom of arms control. But Laird was the third leg of this stool upon which arms control success rested. "SALT I and the ABM Treaty, which could not have happened without Mel's leadership, were incredibly important steps in the progression of arms control within the national security fabric of this country," summarized Robert Pursley. "And it is one of the brightest stars in Mel's crown."[37]

20

Dueling Machiavellis

❦

IN ANY POLITICAL ADMINISTRATION, the question of who gets credit and who takes blame looms large. Absolute power is often maintained through illusion and manipulation. During the Nixon years the masters of the game were the equally matched Laird and Kissinger. In the first year, they quickly became each other's favorite sparring partner. Theirs was a vigorous competition for turf and just plain one-upmanship. "Laird acted on the assumption that he had a Constitutional right to seek to outsmart and outmaneuver anyone with whom his office brought him into contact," Kissinger later wrote. "This was partly a game and partly the effort of a seasoned politician to protect his options." The highly adroit national security advisor observed that Laird's "maneuvers . . . were conducted with all the artistry of a Kabuki play, with an admixture of the Florentine court politics of the fifteenth century."[1]

Kissinger once told a gathering honoring Laird in Wisconsin,

> [N]o one man can handle Mel Laird. So I always had some deputy who had to do the preliminary skirmishing so that I might find out at least where the battlefield was. And there were a number of guidelines I gave to my associates:
>
> Guideline One: Mel Laird is extremely smart.
> Guideline Two: he *knows* he's extremely smart.
> Guideline Three: he will let *you* know he's extremely smart.
> Guideline Four: it is much less painful to do what he wants than to
>   refuse what he wants.[2]

What Laird wanted was quite often the same as what Kissinger wanted, but four major exceptions became evident in the first year. Laird wanted sizable and swift American troop withdrawals from Vietnam, national acknowledgment of the POWs and international pressure for more humane treatment, unhesitating movement from the draft to an all-volunteer force, and a commitment to open government that fully informs the public on all important matters. That Laird won on the first three goals was the more historically significant because it was not only Kissinger but Nixon who opposed him. Laird's loss on the issue of "open government" became a painful one. The paranoid penchant for secrecy that led Nixon and Kissinger to lie about the bombing of Cambodia and other actions redounded to the administration's discredit and later made Nixon's resignation inevitable.

The battle lines were effectively drawn when Kissinger moved to strengthen the National Security Council as the engine of national security policy. Though he said it was not his intention at first, every subsequent move by Kissinger was an attempt to make him the majordomo of national security. By tradition and portfolio, the secretary of state is supposed to be the president's chief foreign policy advisor, and the secretary of defense his chief military policy advisor. As the administration began, political observers reckoned that Laird would become the dominant advisor. "You've got to get up awful early in the morning to outmaneuver him," observed a Democratic opponent in the *New York Times*. "You'd better have a strong Secretary of State to balance him."[3] But no prognosticator had yet divined the talent, brilliance, and design for power that the little-known Henry Kissinger would so effectively employ. As it turned out, it was Secretary of State Rogers who became the casualty.

"Henry was very smart, but Mel was smarter," observed George Shultz, who was a chief budget official in the Nixon administration and later President Ronald Reagan's secretary of state. "Mel enjoyed the bureaucratic in-fighting and was a match for Henry."[4] James Schlesinger was another eyewitness to Kissinger-Laird debates because he was the White House budget official who specialized in national security and would later serve Nixon as CIA director and then secretary of defense. "Henry was just totally frustrated by Mel because Henry could manipulate almost everybody—but when he got to Mel, Mel outsmarted him as frequently as Henry was able to work with him," Schlesinger observed. "Henry—what shall I say—*handled* Bill Rogers over at State very effectively and had him handcuffed. But Mel was too damn slippery to be handcuffed. He worked the back rooms too well. They were frustrated that, hard as they worked on Mel, they couldn't control him. He would just countermand them [Kissinger and Nixon] by slipping over to the Hill and talking to [House Appropriations Committee Chair] George Mahon or some such thing. There was nobody else in the Nixon Administration who could or would do that."[5]

Kissinger became so unsettled with his inability to "handle" Laird that he frequently lost his temper over it. "The guys on the White House staff used to think that Laird's first name was 'Son of a Bitch!' because [with Kissinger] it was 'Son of a bitch Laird did this!' or 'Son of a bitch Laird did that!'" recalled one administration official.[6] "Kissinger would walk around the West Wing ranting and raging and raising his voice," remembered another.[7]

White House Chief of Staff H. R. Haldeman's diary entries are replete with references to an unnerved Kissinger spouting oaths and imprecations about Laird. On one day in October 1969, Nixon confided to Haldeman that he was quite concerned "about K's [Kissinger's] attitude and wants to be sure we keep him upbeat. Can't let him overreact to each little aberration [from] Laird. K argues that you have to maintain tight discipline on the little things or you can't control the big ones. P [president] feels you should lose the ones that don't matter and save your strength and equity for the big battles that really count." Four days later Nixon told Haldeman that the problem was becoming untenable. Kissinger was no longer able to effectively deal with Laird, and this "has become an issue. Wants me to make all this clear to K. Hard to do. [Kissinger] injects himself too much into everything, between P and Cabinet officers, and they just won't buy it. So he becomes ineffective even at getting them to do what they already were ready to do." Months after those entries, Nixon was still fretting over Kissinger's unnecessarily ham-handed way of dealing with Laird. "Poor K," observed Haldeman. "P went into this whole problem especially about K's horrible way of . . . giving all the feeling that they have no part except to follow his orders. P worried about how to overcome this and concludes he has to meet privately with Laird instead of through K, but this will get K up all the tighter, so!?"[8]

Laird acknowledged that things got heated between himself and Kissinger, particularly during the first two years as they parried on policy positions. "Sometimes the voices were very loud at our breakfast meetings at the Pentagon partly because he was so very paranoid about things." Laird's friend Jack Mills, who often traveled with him, recalled Kissinger's frequent telephonic interruptions of their golf games and other outings. "Mel and Kissinger always argued on the telephone. I could only hear one side, but it would go something like this: 'Henrrry. HENry. Now wait a minute, Henry. Don't give me that crap, Henry. You don't have to worry about that, Henry. You're acting like a child, Henry. Don't worry about it! Goddamn it, Henry, I said don't worry about that!'"[9]

⚑

Some of Kissinger's favorite appellations for Laird were "Machiavellian" and "devious." Nixon speech writer William Safire recalled with amusement hearing such "a private assessment of Laird by Kissinger. . . . When Kissinger called Melvin Laird 'a devious man, but when cornered, a patriot,' he was describing himself and the President too—lions and foxes all, as political scientists from Niccolo Machiavelli to James MacGregor Burns have said leaders must be."[10] Laird recalled: "Henry always said that I was more Machiavellian than he was. I'd say, 'No, I'll give you that award.' I always threw it back at him because he was the master Machiavelli."

Kissinger wasn't alone in using such terms about Laird. In his memoirs Nixon quoted Eisenhower telling Nixon in 1967, that of all the Republicans on the national scene, Laird was "the smartest of the lot, but he is too devious."[11] A "sneak" was the worst term Nixon aide John Ehrlichman remembered the president applying to Laird.[12]

"Mel enjoyed being devious," said former defense secretary Caspar Weinberger, a White House budget official during the Nixon administration, who was repeatedly outmaneuvered by Laird on defense budget issues. "If there were two ways to go to a particular destination, and one path was straight and the other went around many curves, Mel always picked the one that went around many curves."[13] Helmut Schmidt, the former Chancellor of West Germany who was a friend to both Kissinger and Laird, said, "Henry is not right in calling Mel Laird 'Machiavellian.' Mel is a shrewd person, but he is a trustworthy human being."[14]

Kissinger was eventually won over by Laird and they became friends. "Mel was Midwestern; he was forthright. I mean, he could be a wily politician but, nevertheless, he was an up-front guy," noted David Abshire, a government official who knew both men.[15] "And Mel had the quality of humor, which became very important in dealing with Kissinger. In Washington if one has a humorous twist, they can say things that are tough without infuriating people as much. If you're dead-square and come in like a ton of bricks, it's more difficult. He could humor Kissinger, and that whole White House circle." Kissinger aide Alexander Haig, who was himself often an antagonist of Laird's, concurred: "Mel was a delight to be around. He had a great sense of humor; he was a *pixie* in many respects; having a *pixie* sense of humor. He and Henry basically got along quite well kidding one another."[16]

That is also Kissinger's view. At one gathering to honor Laird, Kissinger showered him with praise and concluded with a laugh line: "I think of him with *enormous* affection, only slightly tinged with exasperation." In an insightful description of Laird in his memoirs, Kissinger wrote: "[W]hile Laird's maneuvers were often as Byzantine in their complexity or indirection as those of Nixon, he accomplished with verve and surprising goodwill what Nixon performed with grim determination and inward resentment. Laird liked to win, but unlike Nixon, derived no great pleasure from seeing someone else lose. There was about him a buoyancy and a rascally good humor that made working with him as satisfying as it could on occasion be maddening."[17]

Laird confessed he deliberately goaded Kissinger—in part, because it was so much fun, and in part because he didn't think it was healthy for Kissinger to take himself so seriously. "I loved to confront Henry," Laird said. "I tried to stymie him on some things, so he'd be on the phone raising hell and I'd be raising hell with him. It was all with good sportsmanship, and it was friendly."

From his corner of the ring, Kissinger summarized the sparring in this way: "Provided he was allowed some reasonable range for saving face by maneuvering to a new position without embarrassment, Laird accepted bureaucratic setbacks without rancor. But he insisted on his day in court. In working with him, intellectual arguments were only marginally useful and direct orders were suicidal. I eventually learned that it was safest to begin a battle with Laird by closing off insofar as possible all his bureaucratic or Congressional escape routes, provided I could figure them out, which was not always easy. Only then would I broach substance. But even with such tactics I lost as often as I won."[18]

In one attempt to get Kissinger's goat, Laird and his military assistant Pursley had a stamp made which spelled in big letters, "BULLSHIT." Both had noticed that when Kissinger came for breakfast meetings at the Pentagon, he would rubberneck trying to read Laird's private notes. So they stamped several memoranda Kissinger had sent Laird with the bright red "BULLSHIT" and then strategically placed the papers among others in Laird's notebook for the next breakfast meeting. "We thought Henry would see it and say, 'What is that?' And Mel was going to say, 'Why, we stamp all your stuff that way!' We thought that would be kind of funny," noted Pursley. "Sure enough, when Mel turned to the first page, Henry saw it but didn't say a word. Not one word. Mel went over to the next one and so on, another Kissinger memo stamped 'BULLSHIT.'"[19] Kissinger didn't smile; and he was clearly not amused. Larry Eagleburger, who was a longtime friend to both men, said, "That [story] is part of the whole Laird character that I like so much—namely, he could be serious, but he also had a playful streak that could, on occasion, lessen the tension."[20]

When Kissinger finally realized that Laird bore him no ill will, but was periodically mischievous, the national security advisor began to loosen up and finally enjoy a warm friendship with Laird. In a subsequent private letter, Kissinger told Laird he counted it a special privilege to have worked with Laird. "No one who served with you in those years will ever forget your delight in outmaneuvering someone, especially me," Kissinger wrote. Laird's loyalty to the administration, along with his strength and his courage, made him an admirable colleague, he added. But those human qualities were especially amplified by his opponent's "irrepressible good humor and complete lack of rancor—uncommon enough in life but virtually unheard of in high office." Kissinger concluded that, having met many an impressive individual in his life, Laird for him "occupied a special place in the pantheon."[21]

There is one more attribute of Laird's that bedeviled Kissinger: a certain obtuseness. "When Laird employed one of his favorite phrases, 'See what I mean?' there was no possible way of penetrating his meaning," Kissinger recounted. In fact, it became the fifth guideline to his staffers for dealing with the defense secretary: "Guideline Five is, when Mel Laird says to you, 'You know what I mean?' there is no conceivable way you can possibly know what he means." He added, "Laird would think nothing of coming to a White House meeting with the Joint Chiefs of Staff, supporting their position, then indicating his reservations privately to the President and me, only to work out a third approach later with his [congressional] friend Chairman Mahon."[22]

Many who worked with Laird remembered his "you-know-what-I-mean" patter. Assistant Secretary of Defense Barry Shillito suggested, in retrospect, that Laird himself didn't always know why he made one point over another. "He always says, 'You know what I mean? You know what I mean? You know what I mean?' Nine times out of 10 you may not have a clue as to what the hell he means," Shillito chuckled. "And often, I'm not sure he knows what he means either, but he's trying to get it out of you."[23]

Laird's canniness and his solid friendships made him one man in the

administration who could not be fired, no matter how much he might circumvent the White House on issues. "Henry was particularly taken—almost
mesmerized—by the power that Mel had with the Congress," Pursley said.
"It was something that Henry couldn't dream of having, and the president
himself didn't have. But Mel had it in spades, not only because Mel came from
Congress, but because he continued to cultivate it on both sides of the aisle."[24]
Ehrlichman, who was no friend of Laird's, underscored this point in his memoirs: "From time to time Henry Kissinger complained bitterly to Nixon, Haldeman and me about Laird's unscrupulous tactics. But Henry didn't demand
Laird's firing, as he did Secretary of State William Rogers's. Laird was so effective with his old Congressional cronies...that everyone realized he was
irreplaceable."[25]

Indeed, Laird's influence in the Nixon administration was stronger in 1969
than was Kissinger's, as shown in the response to the North Korean shoot-
down of the EC-121, the first troop withdrawals from Vietnam, the beginning
of the end of the draft, the maintenance of U.S. military strength, the critical victory in the Senate for the ABM, and so on. For all Kissinger's vaunted
foreign policy expertise, it was Laird who was the more likely author of the
defining foreign policy doctrine of his administration, the so-called Nixon
Doctrine, which was unveiled at a presidential press conference in the South
Pacific on July 25, 1969.

That July two Americans had landed on the moon. Though it had been John
F. Kennedy who precipitated the race to the moon, and Lyndon Johnson and
NASA who made it happen, Nixon fully intended to bask in the glory of it
as president. He wanted to witness the splashdown and greet the astronauts
on their return to Earth, so he met them on the aircraft carrier USS *Hornet*,
950 miles southwest of Hawaii. For Nixon, it was the first stop of a twelve-
day 24,500-mile round-the-world tour. The next stop was the island of Guam,
where Nixon held a "background" press conference on July 25. In an expansive
mood, Nixon told reporters that, in order to ensure "no more Vietnams," the
United States would reorder its foreign policy in Asia. America would keep all
treaty commitments but would no longer furnish arms and men to friends
who were fending off aggressors unless those friends provided their own manpower to defend themselves. The only exception was if that ally was attacked
with nuclear weapons, then the United States would respond with nuclear
weapons.

The announcement, which reporters dubbed the "Guam Doctrine," caught
Kissinger by complete surprise. He and Nixon had discussed Asia strategies
in preparation for a speech, but Kissinger was not the author of the Guam
Doctrine, as some historians have suggested.[26] Laird was neither surprised nor

upset when he got news of Nixon's unilateral announcement of a new Asia policy, because it was a policy he had been urging upon Nixon since 1967. The principles Nixon espoused in the Guam Doctrine were an outgrowth of the Vietnamization policy Laird had first called "de-Americanization" when he had it inserted in the 1968 Republican Party platform. Laird himself said he promoted the basis of the doctrine in memoranda to Nixon prior to the pronouncement in Guam.[27]

When the first news of Nixon's unexpected pronouncement reached Washington, Laird seized upon it to promote his Vietnamization program. He had his public affairs aides hold a press conference and firmly pin the Guam Doctrine on the president by renaming it the Nixon Doctrine. They further fleshed out the doctrine with three "pillars" that Nixon had not precisely uttered—strength, partnership, and a willingness to negotiate. The Nixon Doctrine, as polished by Laird's staff, meant the United States was committed to strengthening its own defense, helping its allies only if they were willing to help themselves, and negotiating a way out of combat whenever possible.

The Nixon Doctrine might well have been called the Laird Doctrine for its author and most dogged sponsor. He drove it home, almost ad nauseam, at his Monday meetings with the Joint Chiefs and top staff. Laird also pounded the pulpit for the Nixon Doctrine whenever he was asked to make a speech. And when he forgot to mention it, his staff would remind him. If Laird told staffers that he was at a loss for words at any particular speaking engagement, they would enthusiastically reply, "Give them the Pillar Speech!" Laird recalled he could go on for twenty minutes about the three pillars. "Then I'd conclude: 'We must always have a willingness to negotiate. Of course, we can't negotiate without strength! And we can't negotiate without that other pillar, of partnerships!' I had that speech down pretty good." So good, that he endured a lot of ribbing about it from Pentagon staff, who once ordered him a two-layer birthday cake with three pillars holding up the top layer.

Laird pointed out in speeches that the Nixon Doctrine meant that the era of interventionism that President Truman had begun had been replaced by a new, pragmatic era of limits. "America will no longer try to play policeman to the world," he would say. "Instead, we will expect other nations to provide more cops on the beat in their own neighborhoods."[28] Since the United States would not have a cop on every beat, he elaborated at a press conference, it was up to America's allies "to do more of the patrolling in their own areas of the world."[29]

One of Laird's practical initiatives to further that goal was a program to "lend" ships to poorer allies such as Turkey, Greece, and the Republic of China (Taiwan). After the loan of three submarines and other American ships, Taiwan willingly took over the job Americans had been doing of patrolling of the straits between Taiwan and mainland China. One of those ships was the destroyer USS *Maddox*. Laird learned that the *Maddox* was to be decommissioned in 1972, so, instead of having it "scrapped for razor blades," he transferred it to Taiwan as a strong personal and political symbol of his commitment to the new Nixon Doctrine. (Renamed the *Po Yang*, the storied destroyer patrolled the Straits of Taiwan until 1985.)[30]

⚜

When Nixon returned from his round-the-world trip where he had uttered the makings of the Nixon Doctrine, Laird sent him formal notice of the change in America's mission statement for Vietnam—the change that Laird had surprised Nixon and Kissinger with when they met on the presidential yacht a month earlier. Laird's cover letter to the president said that the Defense Department was not going to make a public announcement of the changes, but the word had already leaked to the press and Laird had been artfully dodging questions about it.

As written by Laird, the new mission statement for the war was a direct reflection of the hands-off Nixon Doctrine, whether the president liked it or not. The old mission statement said: "Make as difficult and costly as possible the continued support of the Viet Cong by North Vietnam," "[d]efeat the Viet Cong and North Vietnamese Armed Forces in South Vietnam," and "[e]xtend Government of South Vietnam dominion, direction and control over all of South Vietnam." The new marching orders spelled out how with "maximum assistance" the United States would help South Vietnam shape up its army to fight its own battles: "The objective is to allow the people of the Republic of Vietnam to determine their future without outside interference."

Looking beyond Vietnam, Laird opened negotiations with Japan, Germany, and South Korea to force each of them to take more responsibility for their own defense, too. But lest the United States be perceived as abandoning its allies and withdrawing completely from the world scene, Laird began to shape another doctrine, "realistic deterrence." And this one he called "the most difficult and challenging national security effort we have ever undertaken in this country."

In a nutshell, realistic deterrence meant that the United States would defend itself and continue in its role as protector of the weak, within the bounds of what was politically and economically acceptable to Congress and the American people. That was the "realistic" part of the equation. The "deterrent" part was focused primarily on the Soviet Union. In the 1960s and 1970s the U.S.S.R. was spending from 13 to 16 percent of its gross national product in the arms race with the United States. Given the more prosperous American economy at the time, that would have been the equivalent of the United States spending 36 percent of its GNP on the military. Instead, the military budget was closer to 9 percent of GNP in the United States when Nixon took office. Laird wanted to aim for 7 percent after he disentangled U.S. troops from Vietnam.

Laird fretted that the Communists were sacrificing greatly to keep up the arms race, while in America each dollar had to be wrestled from Congress and begrudging taxpayers who were increasingly suspicious of the kind of military mentality that had led to Vietnam. "We were at a point in the history of our country when the Defense Department was not thought of as the greatest department of government," Laird said in hindsight. "People were fed up with the military. You cannot let that get to the point where it destroys the preparedness and the military and economic strength of our country. That's why I think it was a great challenge to have a realistic deterrent. If we would not have been able to do that, we could have lost the Cold War. The Cold War was won because we faced it realistically and stood down the Soviet Union."

⬥

In 1969, as Laird prepared the Pentagon budget for the coming fiscal year, he had to update the five-year plan for allocating all of the military's assets. Here his goal of realistic deterrence against the spread of Communism had to mesh with the Nixon Doctrine of staying out of the global policing business. That meant scaling down some expectations for the military while still keeping up with the Soviets in the arms race. Laird's solution was to change a standard that had stood since the end of World War II, the standard that said the U.S. military would be ready at all times to fight two and a half wars—major wars on two fronts with an added regional skirmish all at the same time. Instead Laird said it was realistic to be geared up for only one and a half wars.

Given the potential enemies around the world at the time, the new position was a risky one, debated for nine months in the Pentagon in 1969 and finally enacted over the protest of the Joint Chiefs. America had commitments to protect its NATO partners in Europe against a threat from the U.S.S.R. China's expansionist agenda was an unknown factor in the equation. The United States was committed to protecting South Korea from invasion by North Korea. Instability in Africa and the Middle East could flare into a regional war at any moment. Yet Laird looked at the budget and the increasing antimilitary sentiment at home and decided that America could prepare itself to fight a war either in Europe or in Asia, but not in both places at once.

David Packard spelled out the new plans in a memo to the major military departments on November 1, 1969. The Pentagon would maintain the capability to provide, simultaneously, "an initial defense of NATO Europe; assistance to our allies against non-Chinese threats in Asia; and the forces needed to maintain a minor contingency elsewhere. The strategy also calls for the capability to assist our allies against a Chinese attack in either Korea or Southeast Asia, provided that we are not fighting a war in Europe. Our primary objective in Asia will be to help our Asian allies develop the capability to defend themselves, at least against attacks which to do not directly involve Chinese forces."

Although China was aiding North Vietnam by allowing shipment of supplies from the Soviet Union across China, the Vietnam War was never considered a war with China.

Packard's memo added two other bits of realism to the Laird doctrine of realistic deterrence: "[w]e should not plan for U.S. force involvement of the recent level in Vietnam without diversion of forces oriented to NATO or creation of new forces," and "[a]lthough we should be able to meet one minor contingency while simultaneously fighting a major war in Europe or Asia, it is not necessary that we be able to do so without mobilizing some inactive forces, using strategic reserve forces, or temporarily reducing our capability to reinforce Asia." In other words, you could cut the pie only in so many slices, and if more allies wanted to feed from it, then more pies would have to be baked. Laird was not willing to make commitments around the world if Congress was not willing to give him more men and money. And Laird would call up the Reserves, something Lyndon Johnson had refused to do in the unpopular Vietnam War.[31]

Kissinger's stock in trade was the secret deal, which meant keeping even Cabinet secretaries in the dark. The first of the "back channels" Kissinger opened in international negotiations came under the cover provided by Nixon's round-the-world trip in that summer of 1969. After stops in the Pacific area, India, Pakistan, and Romania, Kissinger split off from the president and went to Paris, where he secretly sat down on August 4 with Hanoi's representative, Xuan Thuy, in a private apartment using the multilingual military attaché at the embassy, General Vernon Walters, as his interpreter. Walters's boss, the secretary of defense, was not to be told.

The pattern of attempting to hide some key diplomatic and military maneuvers from Laird, as was so easily done with Rogers, had begun. But the fact that Nixon and Kissinger deliberately kept Laird out of the loop did not mean he was not "in the know." Unlike Rogers, Laird had an extensive circle of friends throughout the administration. He also tended to inspire loyalty for his square dealings. Neither Kissinger nor Nixon could make a significant national security move without involving a military asset or an individual who was likely to report back to Laird.

A month after Kissinger's Paris meeting, the extent of Laird's reach became apparent to Nixon and Kissinger. On September 12, after dinner at Camp David, Nixon had a free-ranging discussion with some White House staffers on what to do about an incident in Vietnam where some Green Berets were charged with murdering a purported North Vietnamese spy. Haldeman recorded in his diary: "Tried to call Admiral McCain to get his view, and Laird found out, and called K, very upset that we hadn't gone to him instead." Haldeman later added to his diary: "The fact that Laird apparently knew immediately of our attempt to call McCain from Camp David gave us something new to worry about. Were the Camp David phones tapped for the Defense Department?"[32]

Ehrlichman elaborated on the spasm of paranoia that gripped Nixon and Kissinger:

> The Camp David operators were all Army enlisted men and their supervisors were Army officers. The only question was: how closely did Mel Laird monitor the President and the rest of us at Camp David when we called someone on his Army telephone system? Did he just keep track of whom we called, or did he also know what was said? Before long, Bob Haldeman arranged for some of the civilian telephone operators to be brought to Camp David to operate the switchboard whenever the President was there. But the White House Communications Agency, the group which handled the President's telephone communications whenever he traveled and which transmitted most of the cable traffic into and out of the White House, continued to be operated by Mel Laird's military.[33]

While Laird does not remember how he learned of the attempted contact with McCain, it was not because he had the Camp David phone system bugged. He never wiretapped anyone—unlike Kissinger, who not only wiretapped his own aides but one of Laird's, too.

～

Not long after he had ferried Nixon around the world in the summer of 1969, Colonel Ralph Albertazzie, the pilot of Air Force One, got an interesting call from Colonel James D. (Don) Hughes, chief of the White House Military Office. "Wander down here to the White House," Hughes advised his subordinate. "Act like you're just visiting people. Don't let anybody know that you're on any particular mission. But eventually show up in the Roosevelt Room about 2 o'clock." Albertazzie followed the instructions and seated himself at the mahogany table in the room near the Oval Office. Hughes was already there, as was Alexander Haig. When Kissinger arrived, it was evident he had called the meeting. He revealed that he was in the process of secretly negotiating peace with the North Vietnamese. For future talks, he needed Albertazzie to clandestinely fly him to Europe in Air Force One or its backup plane.

"The president does not want the secretary of defense or the Joint Chiefs to know about these trips or talks," Kissinger said, his eyes boring into the military pilot. Nor was the secretary of state or the CIA director to be informed. It was up to Albertazzie and Hughes to figure out how that could be accomplished, Kissinger challenged, before leaving the room. Albertazzie didn't question the orders he had received from his commander-in-chief via Kissinger. But how to accomplish the task was something else altogether. "Well, Ralph, all you have to do is concoct the perfect alibi for the world's best known airplane," Hughes smiled as they walked to the door. "It better be good."

Albertazzie soon came up with the answer. The Johnson administration had installed a $25 million voice-scrambler system aboard Air Force One that needed substantial testing before the president could rely upon it. "If the president called the secretary of defense about some emergency, I wanted the secretary to be able to know whether the message was '*start* the bombing' or '*stop* the bombing,'" Albertazzie recalled. "That's a pretty important difference." So the cover story became that the trips to Europe were training missions to test the long-distance capability of the voice-scrambler.

Starting in February 1970, Albertazzie flew Kissinger in the presidential planes to France, Germany, and England on thirteen clandestine missions.[34] While both Albertazzie and Hughes have insisted they did not tell Laird about the flights, Laird himself said he knew about every one of them because he had more than one "source" who informed him about how his military planes—the presidential planes were part of the Defense Department—were being used.

Far more interesting is that Laird not only knew about every one of Kissinger's flights, but precisely what he and the North Vietnamese said in each secret meeting. The revelation of this knowledge to Kissinger in a 2001 interview produced surprises for both Kissinger and Laird. Laird's ace in the hole was the National Security Agency, a huge Department of Defense communications espionage agency headquartered at Fort Meade, Maryland. The NSA routinely intercepted messages sent from North Vietnam's Paris offices to Hanoi. What few knew—even in the highest levels of government—was that the NSA's geniuses had cracked the North Vietnamese code and could read everything transmitted by Hanoi's representatives at peace talks with Kissinger. Because it needed to be a closely held secret, Laird ordered Admiral Noel Gayler, the head of NSA, to send a man to Laird's office with every such decoded intercept as soon as it was ready.

Each time Kissinger clandestinely spoke or communicated with the North Vietnamese, they would dutifully report what had occurred back to their superiors in Hanoi. When Kissinger was informed of this by the author in early 2001, he was astonished. He never knew the NSA had decrypted intercepts of his talks, so he had never seen the transcripts. Trying to keep his composure, Kissinger pointedly asked, "It raises the interesting question: Why did he [Laird] never send those reports over to the White House?"

Kissinger later called Laird to complain. "I thought you always shared with me, Mel." Laird responded that it was not his responsibility to provide NSA intelligence to Kissinger. After he had read the transcripts, Laird had regularly sent the NSA courier to the Oval Office to wait while the president personally read the intercepts. So it was Nixon who had not shared the critical intelligence with his national security advisor. "Goddamn that Nixon!" Kissinger half sputtered and half laughed. "That son of a bitch just wanted to have these so he could check up on me!"

Laird was semiapologetic. "Henry, I probably should have shared those with you. But on these kinds of intercepts that were so sensitive, I had them delivered separately to the president."

"Of course you'd route things that way," Kissinger said. "I understand, Mel. I'm not holding that against you. It's that goddamn Nixon."

Pursley, who had been wiretapped by Kissinger, was amused at Kissinger's astonishment. "Henry would have always assumed that anything like that would fall into his hands one way or another. And usually, it would then be up to Henry to decide on distribution of the classified material. It would never even remotely occur to Henry that Mel would have something like that that Henry didn't have. It was the furthest thing from Henry's mind. Henry is so Machiavellian, and he's just so sure of himself in those kinds of circumstances."

Laird, Kissinger, and Pursley seemed to agree that the primary reason Nixon withheld the NSA intercepts from his national security advisor was so he could make sure from a separate channel that Kissinger was properly acting for the president in the peace talks and correctly debriefing Nixon on what had occurred. As a side benefit, it may have been a way for Nixon to appear to be more brilliant to his intellectual aide. In those same NSA intercepts back and forth were revelations of the positions the North Vietnamese might be prepared to take in the next round of talks. Nixon never shared that information with Kissinger but gave what must have seemed like fairly prescient instructions as the president's chief negotiator prepared for the next talks.[35]

The tale of the NSA intercepts adds to evidence that two of the three pillars of the administration's leadership—Nixon and Kissinger—could never significantly ignore the third pillar—Laird—even though he might sometimes oppose their maneuvers. And any expectation that they could keep him in the dark was folly.

21

Bridging the Generation Gap

BY THE TIME LAIRD became secretary of defense in 1969, the majority of America's young people were against the war. At the end of his first year, in November 1969, a commission formed to examine causes of riots and civil disturbance in America drew that conclusion. Chaired by Milton Eisenhower, the former president's brother, the commission said in a twelve-page report, "Challenge to Youth," that 75 to 80 percent of young Americans opposed the war, though only a minority demonstrated civil disobedience. For those working in the Pentagon, the impact of this generation gap and their personal connection to the prosecution of the war could be severely divisive at home.

"The strain on the families of those serving both in uniform and in a civilian capacity in those days was quite considerable," remembered Senator John Warner, who served as undersecretary and then secretary of the navy for Laird. Warner was married to one of America's youth, a woman ten years his junior. She was "very much involved in the anti-war situation," Warner said, and their home life became difficult. "I don't fault her with this. It was a very stressful existence to be my wife during the Pentagon years." Though she stayed with him until he left the Pentagon, they later divorced.[1] David Packard's children were all opposed to the war and even thirty years later declined to discuss their father's work at the Pentagon, however laudable in others' eyes.

Navy Secretary John Chafee painfully remembered "letters from nephews and nieces sometimes upbraiding me for being part of an organization that was fighting the war in Vietnam. But those of us who worked for Mel felt that what we were doing was the right thing. I felt I was in an honorable occupation because, among other things, we were trying to terminate that war."[2] Army Secretary Bob Froehlke's children "didn't like it one bit" when he agreed to serve in the Pentagon. "None of the kids agreed with Vietnam," he said. But they respected his decision and, in later years, came to view his participation as a worthy endeavor.[3]

The five children of Air Force Secretary Robert Seamans "were all unalterably opposed to Southeast Asia and what was going on there." He discussed the job with them before accepting, and, to his surprise, they encouraged him to take it. "In their words, they said at least there would be one responsible person they had confidence in," he recalled. In April 1969 Seaman's son Joe, a Harvard student, was drawn by curiosity to enter Harvard's University Hall after it had been seized by about three hundred militant students. When four hundred policemen rushed the building to end the seventeen-hour occupation, Joe panicked and jumped out of an upper window. Then, as he stayed to help other jumpers as they landed, a *Boston Globe* photographer captured the moment and Joe was featured on the newspaper's front page as the protesting son of the air force secretary.[4]

None of Laird's children were happy about his acceptance of the job of secretary of defense. "I think you're taking the worst job in the world," oldest son John told him on the phone, when his dad informed him. Attending Wisconsin University in Eau Claire, John was already active in the local antiwar movement.[5] Daughter Alison, in her senior year of high school, was feeling the first stirrings of activism against the war. Characteristically, their father had encouraged the children to follow their consciences. British interviewer David Frost asked Laird in late 1970 what he would be doing if he were twenty, like his son John, and opposed to the war. "I would speak out," Laird unhesitatingly responded. "I told my son that I expected him to speak out on the way he felt about the various issues of the day. This is something that we have discussed in our family on many occasions. We have heated discussions."[6]

Alison recalled, "One of the most important things he taught us was to believe in yourself and do what you believe. Speak out. You can't sit there and tell everybody that you think everything is terrible that's happening if you're not going to do something about it. He made you very much an activist and a volunteer." Just as Melvin Laird Sr. had encouraged Melvin Jr. to go his own way, so Laird, in Alison's memory, "was always eager for us to be involved, whether it was pro or con him."

At her chosen schools, Virginia Intermount in Bristol, Virginia, and then the University of Tennessee, her name cost her friendships, despite her own protest of the war. The war "was very unpopular around the college campus, and it got personal. There were friends and people that came to me and were angry because their brothers or boyfriends ... had died in Vietnam." So they blamed her father, and her by extension. But she always defended her father, at the same time as she opposed the war. Her greatest fear, one shared by her brother John, was "that people would consider us [to be] opposing our father. . . . We loved our Dad, you know. We never stopped talking to him, never got angry with him, understood what he was saying, could defend his point of view even among very radical people."

Laird's youngest child, David, was not silent either. *Avante-Garde* magazine asked high school newspaper editors in Washington to query thirty children of prominent Nixon administration policy makers to ask their opinion. Twenty declined to comment; only one of the ten who did comment—the son of Laird's Assistant Secretary for International Security Affairs Warren Nutter—favored the war. The magazine's editor held a press conference on the lawn of the Laird home, handing out copies of the survey entitled, "The Sins of Their Fathers." Among the ten who offered an opinion was David Laird, who said: "I'm against the war in Vietnam. I think the United States has learned that it shouldn't get into another war like this ever again."[7]

As his family and closest friends knew, Melvin Laird had a genuine love for America's youth, however outspoken, and that allowed him to understand and even sympathize with the youthful antiwar movement. It was an affection and respect that would be shown time and again in his years at the Pentagon. Of the triumvirate running the Vietnam war—Nixon, Kissinger, Laird—the secretary of defense was the only one to bridge the generation gap. "I happen to believe that the generation gap is a vastly over-rated phenomenon," Laird said in an April 1971 speech. "Most young people do not reject the values that our nation has proclaimed since the beginning of its history. Rather, they complain that our actions too often violate these principles—or that we are moving too slowly to realize them.... Most young people ... understand the difference between dissent and disruption. They know the difference between reasoned argument and unreasoning violence."[8]

From the beginning, massive security precautions shielded the Nixon administration from antiwar protestors. The National Mobilization Committee to End the War in Vietnam—called the "Mobe" by its demonstrators—had voted after the November election to give Nixon no honeymoon. Six thousand youth called out by the Mobe and Students for a Democratic Society (SDS) gathered in Washington for a three-day counterinaugural demonstration, the centerpiece of which was a January 19 march from the White House to the Capitol, a reverse of the traditional inaugural route, waving banners, chanting slogans, and demanding peace in Vietnam. Separately, the Youth International Party (Yippies) "inhogurated" their presidential candidate, a pig.

On Nixon's first inauguration day, January 20, despite attempts by the national leaders of the Mobe and SDS to keep the protests civil, a militant splinter group of three to four hundred antiwar demonstrators hurled rocks, bottles, and obscenities at Nixon's limousine along the parade route. Undeterred in his long-awaited moment of triumph, Nixon took the thirty-five-word inaugural oath with his left hand on two family Bibles opened to Isaiah 2:4: "[N]ations ... shall beat their swords into plowshares, and their spears into pruning hooks; nation shall not lift up sword against nation, neither shall they learn war any more." In his address, Nixon never mentioned the name Vietnam, but in general terms he addressed the war, whose promised end had secured his election. "The greatest honor history can bestow is the title of peacemaker," he intoned. "We are caught in a war, wanting peace;" after "endur[ing] a long night of the American spirit," it was time to "gather the light."

In the early weeks of his presidency, Nixon instructed Laird to be prepared with federal troops for anticipated violent protests. Until 1967 use of federal troops in American cities was not an issue of concern. But five days of unprecedented racial violence—including looting, arson and sniper firing—in Detroit in July 1967 prompted Michigan Governor George Romney to request federal troops. Thousands were dispatched, linking up with newly federalized national guardsmen who then waged battle in Detroit neighborhoods from their and armored personnel carriers. When it ended, forty people had been killed and two thousand injured. Nearly 1,500 fires had been set during the rioting, and some five thousand people were arrested. Then, in April 1968, violence erupted in at least 125 cities during the three days following Martin Luther King's assassination, leaving forty-six dead and 2,600 injured. Federal troops were dispatched simultaneously to the three hardest-hit cities—Baltimore, Chicago, and Washington, D.C. In the nation's capital, it took 13,600 federal troops to finally end the rampage of burning and looting.

Then–Secretary of Defense Clark Clifford set up a new entity, the Directorate for Civil Disturbance Planning and Operations, run by the army, to act as a command center for the domestic use of federal troops. The directorate grew rapidly, and there were nearly a dozen secret requests for federal troops.[9] (For example, they were prepositioned to protect candidates at the Chicago Democratic convention.[10]) In 1969 Laird looked into the Pentagon's capability for putting down domestic violence. It was a timely matter as the first anniversary of King assassination approached.

On March 19, he buttonholed Attorney General John Mitchell after a Cabinet meeting, and both agreed that coordination over the use of federal troops on U.S. soil was an urgent matter. Their representatives would meet to draw up a detailed game plan. (Laird and Mitchell later signed a memorandum that made the attorney general the lead Cabinet officer to recommend to the president the use of federal troops, but only after consultation with the secretary of defense.)[11]

The next Monday, March 24, Laird directed that a good portion of the top-level staff meeting be taken up with "planning for civil disturbance operations."[12] Army General Counsel Richard E. Jordan raised a sensitive issue: the gathering of intelligence on the opposition. Local law enforcement and the FBI had been "too slow and weak in the analysis of raw information, so we've been doing most of this on our own," Jordan said. What he failed to mention was that the army operation had far exceeded simple "analysis" of available information. Army agents were systematically spying on American citizens, which would erupt into a major scandal a year later. Still, Laird's well-honed political antenna was piqued by this part of the briefing, and his concern was evident. Jordan sought to reassure him that the army had been very restrained. "The Army view is, to the extent possible, we ought not to get military intelligence organizations deeply involved in terms of civil concern," he explained. "Actually, it has been necessary for Army intelligence command to get into this matter more deeply than we would wish." As to the troops themselves, Jordan announced that the civil disturbance directorate, under a plan code-named "Garden Plot," had secretly assigned contingency missions to more than a quarter million federal troops for twenty-five cities. Jordan had added a hopeful note: the Pentagon had no intelligence that any specific disorders were planned soon.

The Pentagon's intelligence was on the mark; thousands demonstrated on the anniversary of Martin Luther King's murder, but what minor violence erupted was quickly put down without federal troops. In the meantime, the antiwar movement was in a period of relative calm. A Gallup poll in March showed that three out of five people polled approved of the conduct of the war. The same month, William Beecher, the Pentagon correspondent for the *New York Times,* reported that "public pressure over the war has almost disappeared," leaving the Nixon administration "in something of a quandary." The politically attuned Laird knew this was a temporary lull.

At least some of the personal security concerns of the secretary of defense were somewhat allayed during this time. Alison and David Laird attended private schools while their father was secretary of defense—in part, Alison believed, because "Dad was a little concerned or leery about our safety in public schools." As a regular recipient of death threats once he became secretary of defense, Laird had reason for greater security concerns about his family.

At the Pentagon and when Laird traveled, the man in charge of his security, Lieutenant Colonel Joe Zaice, remembered the first half of 1969 as fairly safe. Zaice, who served nine secretaries of defense, said, "The first time my life was threatened was when I went out to Marshfield with Secretary Laird and he drove."[13] Laird had gone home for Mother's Day, and Zaice and advance man Julian Levine attended Presbyterian services with the Lairds. ("Being a nice Jewish boy, and Joe Zaice a nice Catholic boy, we used to enjoy going to the Presbyterian church in Marshfield," Levine remembered with a laugh.[14]) After the services, Laird insisted on driving home. "I offered to drive, but he wouldn't let me," Zaice recalled. "It was a macho thing. We got in the car, and he ran through three stop signs without ever seeing them. That was an exciting time. I was in the back with Mrs. [Helen] Laird, who was a lovely woman, a delight and a card. But she was screaming and yelling at him. I just kept my mouth shut. Yes, that was the first time my life was ever threatened."

That spring of 1969 there was one truly life-threatening incident. It also had to do with transportation, not a demonstration. The occasion was an April 26 speech at small Saint Leo College near Dade City, Florida. As a favor to an old congressional friend, Bill Cramer, in whose district the college was located, Laird had agreed to deliver a commencement address. Laird enjoyed going to colleges and "mixing it up" with students. Unlike some in the Nixon administration, he was unafraid of interchanges with dissenting youth. At the Saint Leo commencement, after actor Lee Marvin received an honorary degree, Laird opened his speech with an icebreaker. He conceded that it had always seemed to him "cruel and unusual punishment to inflict one more lecture on those who have just sat through four years of lectures. " He continued, "My credentials, when I talk about youth, might be challenged. Obviously, I do not belong to the long-haired generation." He brushed his bald pate. Then he detailed the need for a better education system and the six ways in which the Defense Department was helping to resolve domestic problems.[15]

At a short press conference after the speech, he refused to criticize the several hundred demonstrators who were there protesting the Pentagon's antiballistic missile program. While the president and vice president chose to routinely lambaste demonstrators with strident rhetoric, Laird generally offered a handshake and a listening ear. One newsman asked him that Saturday evening, "Do you see any possibility that opposition to the ABM could become as vocal and violent as opposition to the Vietnam War?"

"I think there has been a great deal of frustration over the length of the war, and over the conduct of the war in Vietnam," Laird answered. "I think that this frustration . . . is a sincere protest that they have."[16]

Shortly after 8 P.M., an army Huey helicopter lifted off the campus with the secretary and his party—a half-dozen passengers including two congressmen and high-level military officials. About twenty miles north of Tampa, Zaice saw and thought he smelled smoke. As a precautionary measure, the crew set the helicopter down on the median strip of a busy interstate, I-75, near the Zephyrhills exit. They couldn't locate the trouble, which was later determined to be a short circuit.[17] At the time, the crew and passengers concluded that Zaice had mistakenly cried "fire" when it was only smoke from a passenger's pipe.

Within minutes, they were in a very dangerous situation as the helicopter lifted off. Laird and Zaice recalled an explosion, and sparks shooting through the inside of the helicopter, lighting up the dark night air as the helicopter rotors struck some power lines. The Huey lurched sideways and nearly flipped over before the crew was able to bounce it to the ground near a ditch. At that point, the passengers unceremoniously bolted off the crippled craft, order of military rank be damned. Nearby, an escort helicopter landed to take them to safety, with everyone concerned that the first copter might explode.

"We were all running, to be perfectly honest with you," Zaice said. A fairly fit Laird somehow got in the lead, and Zaice wasn't sure the secretary could see he was about to run into the blades of the second chopper. "I yelled to him, but nobody could hear me. The blades on both choppers were running. So I just ran after him and tackled him." A dazed Laird got up and carefully walked around the blades, boarded the helicopter and continued safely to MacDill Air Force Base for the plane ride back to Washington.[18] Zaice was convinced Laird would have been beheaded if he had not acted.

⚒

It was time for America's second "Summer of Love." The first, in 1967, had sprung out of the Haight-Ashbury district of San Francisco, festooned with flowers, fueled by hallucinogens, preaching of hope and love, and riding radio waves that sent the musical revolution of Jefferson Airplane, the Doors, the Grateful Dead, and others around the globe and back. But that hopeful naïveté had been buried during the summer of 1968. It had been an ugly time, at turns tragically marred by the assassinations of heroes, riots, the Chicago Democratic convention melee, and too many deaths in Vietnam. The voters had turned to a Republican for new hope.

Flower Power came back for one last reprise in summer 1969. A half-million youthful sybarites were drawn to the dairy farm of Max Yasgur, about seventy miles northwest of New York City, in the Catskill Mountains. The three-day festival held the weekend of August 16 was named the Woodstock Music and Art Fair and Aquarian Exposition and quickly became the stuff of legend. While participants openly used illegal drugs, two dozen rock and roll groups entertained them. They were subjected to frequent downpours, traffic jams, and serious shortages of food, water, and medical and sanitary facilities. Yet almost no incidents of violence were reported, and townspeople acknowledged that, stoned or otherwise, the young people were courteous and well behaved toward them.

John Osborne Laird was no flower child, but he and his family well remember their own love story of that summer. The twenty-one-year-old student had fallen for Nancy Huset, who agreed to marry him. John asked his father to be his best man. The nuptials were set for Saturday, June 14, on northwestern Wisconsin's Lake Chetek, where the bride's family lived. It was to be a private family affair. But when the media heard the secretary of defense would be visiting that weekend, they camped out, paparazzi-like, even renting boats from which they could photograph the wedding. Late Friday, Pentagon advance man Julian Levine was surprised back in Washington to get a call from Laird. "Can you get out here real quick?" Levine arrived Saturday morning and arranged photo opportunities and a press conference to satisfy the curiosity of the gawkers.[19]

However peaceful that summer was, the hiatus was temporary for Laird. He knew that the antiwar forces were probably gearing up for their own fall offensive. The genesis for what would become the largest protest against government policy in American history—the Vietnam Moratorium Days of 1969—came not from a long-haired youth but from a businessman just as bald and six years older than Laird himself. At a modern-day Boston tea party of sorts, Jerome Grossman, fifty-two, an envelope manufacturer and founder of one of the oldest regional peace groups, MassPax, rose to address the group in his suburban Boston home on April 20, 1969. He had a simple idea—a nationwide general strike from work, school, and shopping. The strike would be a single day in October, then two days in November, three in December, and so on until the war was over.[20]

The small group liked the idea, and Grossman, ever the entrepreneur, proceeded to do a "market survey," shopping the idea among different friends before the next MassPax meeting in May. One of them was Sam Brown, twenty-five-year-old former youth coordinator for the 1968 Eugene McCarthy campaign, who was then a fellow at nearby Harvard's Kennedy Institute of Politics. He called up David Hawk, a friend who, like him, had been a divinity student turned McCarthy campaigner. On April 29, Hawk had shepherded a small group of draft protestors through press conferences and a rare White House meeting with Kissinger and Ehrlichman in the basement Situation Room. Kissinger was the good cop, listening and then offering a tutorial as to why America couldn't precipitously disengage from Vietnam. Then bad cop Ehrlichman told them their refusal to be drafted would not be tolerated by the White House. "If you continue to think that you can break laws just because you don't agree with them, you're going to force us to up the ante to the point where we have to give out death sentences for traffic violations," he said, according to one account.

Kissinger, speaking specifically about the campus leaders, told *Look* magazine a few months later that he could "understand the anguish of the younger generation." But, he added, "conscientious objection is destructive of society" and "must be reserved only for the greatest moral issues, and Vietnam is not of this magnitude." The *Look* interviewer wrote: "That [Kissinger] considers several hundred thousand dead and maimed in Vietnam of less than the greatest moral magnitude obviously sets . . . Kissinger and the Nixon Administration apart from the demonstrating generation."[21]

At the same time as Hawk and the student leaders were in the White House, Nixon was speaking before the U.S. Chamber of Commerce, painting dissenters as gun-wielding, knife-carrying terrorists who, "in the name of dissent and in the name of change, terrorize other students and faculty members."

After the White House meeting, Hawk joined with Grossman and MassPax in planning the "strike," which, at Hawk's suggestion, was renamed a "moratorium" to avoid any negative connection with labor unions. On June 30 Hawk opened a Washington office of the Vietnam Moratorium Committee and put the first Moratorium Day on the calendar for October 15, to be followed by a march in Washington on November 15. They announced their plan in September and immediately began to gather even mainstream support from some members of Congress.

Senator Charles Goodell proposed legislation requiring withdrawal of all U.S. troops from Vietnam by the end of 1970—an idea met by skepticism even from those who supported withdrawal. New York Governor Nelson Rockefeller, who had appointed Goodell to the Senate, called the idea "ill-advised." Clark Clifford said it was "both unrealistic and impractical" and would result in an American and South Vietnamese "bloodbath."[22] Laird, who privately told mutual friends he thought Goodell had become "flaky," did not attack him personally in public. At the conclusion of a speech at the National Press Club, Laird, responding to a reporter's question, carefully said it would be "a grave error" to "project figures and set dates that we might not be able to deliver on."[23]

President Nixon held a news conference, in part, to disparage Goodell's quixotic idea. And he took a swipe at the upcoming moratorium: "Now, I understand that there has been and continues to be opposition to the war in Vietnam on the campuses and also in the nation. As far as this kind of activity is concerned, we expect it. However, under no circumstances will I be affected whatever by it." The moratorium organizers seized the moment and called a press conference to criticize Nixon's dismissive attitude. And thus they rode a wave of publicity that no amount of student doorbell-ringing could have accomplished.

Attempting to slow the momentum of the moratorium, which he had unwittingly boosted, Nixon held a series of Vietnam strategy sessions with Washington leaders for the next two weeks. On September 29, after a session with the president, Republican congressional leaders came out to the White House lawn and called for a sixty-day "moratorium" on dissent and criticism of Nixon's Vietnamization plan, a notion that died in the birthing. Late the next evening Nixon met again with Senate Minority Leader Hugh Scott and confided that, as for any "bug-out" from Vietnam, he did not intend to be "the first president to preside over an American defeat."

On October 7 Laird became the first secretary of defense ever to address a national convention of the AFL-CIO. He had a two-decade relationship with its chief, George Meany, and thus had been invited to speak at the convention in Atlantic City, New Jersey. While he did not criticize the upcoming moratorium specifically, Laird expressed strong concern about the antiwar movement being misread in Hanoi, whose "leaders ... expect to achieve victory by waiting for us to abandon the conflict as a result of anti-war protest in this country. From their experience with the French and from their reading of events in the United States last year, they are encouraged to believe that they can get all they want if they merely wait long enough."[24]

He told the assembled labor leaders that the country could not afford to precipitously abandon Vietnam. During Vietnamization, "we cannot at any stage of this process subject the American troops left in Vietnam to the danger of being overwhelmed by an enemy force." (The secretary knew from intelligence reports, not only would a swift retreat risk the lives of thousands of American soldiers, but at least 1.5 million South Vietnamese were expected to be slaughtered if America quickly disengaged. When Hue city in South Vietnam was lost for two weeks during the Johnson administration, the North Vietnamese had massacred 3,500 old men, women, and children before the city could be retaken.)

"I cannot promise a miraculous end to the war," Laird told the labor leaders. "I cannot tell you how or when the war in Vietnam will end. It has been my policy in office not to make optimistic forecasts—there have been too many of those." When he finished, he was given a standing ovation. Then the convention's one thousand delegates, representing thirteen million AFL-CIO members, passed a resolution supporting the Laird-Nixon plan of Vietnamization and diplomatic negotiation to end the war. Only one delegate voted against it. After the speech Meany remarked to his friend Laird, a bit wryly, that this was the one group in America that understood the necessity of negotiating from strength.[25] (The next day, Laird received a thank-you note from Nixon for "the strong and exceptionally effective explanation of our Vietnam policy you gave to the AFL/CIO," which he felt was "right on the mark."[26])

Two days later, on October 9, Vice President Agnew lambasted the moratorium as "ironic and absurd." The same day Laird held a press conference at the Pentagon and was asked what he thought of the planned protest. "We recognize the right to dissent in a responsible and legal fashion," he said. "We only hope that those who dissent from the policy will also be well informed about what that policy is." The protestors should at least realize, he continued, that the Defense Department had "changed a good many things" since he had come to the helm. "[W]e've started reducing troops and the troop commitment in Vietnam. Instead of the troop commitment going up and up and up each month, the troop commitment each month is going down as far as American young people are concerned."[27]

The work of the moratorium was being done by thousands of volunteers who were inspiring involvement in hundreds of communities across the country, including Eau Claire, Wisconsin, where one of the student leaders, John Laird, got more attention than he wanted. With sensitivity for his father's position, he had originally intended to keep a low profile. But then a political science professor alerted the local press that the secretary of defense's own son would march against the war on October 15. John Laird told a local newspaper, "I think everybody should be against the war." Did his father know he'd be marching? Yes, and he hadn't objected. What about his father's position? John said his Dad was "doing the best job I think he possibly can. He thinks we're under a commitment [to South Vietnam] and he is trying to fulfill that commitment as well as he can."[28]

There were a few last-minute skirmishes between moratorium adherents and opponents on Tuesday, October 14. The new premier of North Vietnam, Pham Van Dong, broadcast his personal support of his "dear American friends," the antiwar protestors, praising their efforts to end the war. "May your fall offensive succeed splendidly." In the House of Representatives, twenty-three members, all but one a Democrat, were granted unanimous consent to speak on behalf of the moratorium for an hour each. Their plan was to keep the House open all night on October 14 so that the first demonstration of support for Moratorium Day on the fifteenth would in the Capitol itself. Only two speakers, however, got their say before the House voted 112 to 110 to adjourn at 11:15 P.M. Although truncated, that three-hour floor debate was the most extensive the full House had conducted since United States joined the war.

Moratorium Day was a spectacular success for the organizers, marred only by a general lack of live TV coverage. The coast-to-coast event was declared the largest public protest against the war to date. "Possibly millions were involved," noted the *New York Times,* but there was no way to count all the children out of school, employees who chose not to work, businesses closed, hundreds of thousands of demonstrators marching, Americans wearing black arm bands or flying the flag at half mast. In Washington, Coretta Scott King led about 45,000 people from the Washington Monument to the White House. In Boston, 20,000 marched from Cambridge to the Boston Common, where a crowd that grew to 100,000 heard from senators and former supreme court justice Arthur Goldberg.

And in Eau Claire, John Laird marched with thousands of fellow students and townspeople, a *Newsweek* reporter in step behind him. "He thought he was going to get this great big story," John said, but young Laird kept it low key. On Moratorium Day, the *Washington Post* ran a feature story on John's dissent. The newspaper acknowledged that he had been "reluctant to even talk" to the press because he had been "hounded by television, newspaper and magazine reporters" trying to find a "big generation gap, father-son conflict" that didn't exist. One of John's quotes should have been quite revealing about the closet dove in the Nixon administration: "I don't see any conflict with my father. We're not that much opposite on anything."[29] After Moratorium Day, John Laird turned down offers for as much as $2,000 from colleges to speak. He routinely told them that if they wanted a war protestor to speak, they could ask students on their own campuses.

Melvin Laird says he was never offended by his children's antiwar activities. "I got demonstrated against. I got blood thrown at me. But not by my kids. I think John was very responsible in his objection to certain parts of the war. I understood that. Besides, they always defended the old man. They've always been very supportive." John Laird learned something from his brief celebrity status: "I have friends that really haven't talked to their parents since the late 1960s, early 1970s. The Vietnam War divided their family so much that they still really haven't talked to each other." Not so with his father. "My Dad's been my best friend pretty much all my life. He still is."

Nixon was intent on making it appear that his administration was not cowed but was conducting business as usual on Moratorium Day. He held a National Security Council meeting at 10 A.M. and then asked the secretaries of defense and state to stay behind. The president was privately concerned about their "softness," though he did not voice that to them. According to H. R. Haldeman's notes, Nixon's intent after the meeting was "to try to get them in line about Vietnam and [the] November 3 speech." (Nixon had previously announced that he would give a major policy speech about the war on that date.) Both Nixon and Kissinger, though, knowing John Laird would be marching against the war that day, made the mistake of needling the defense secretary about his inability to muzzle his own son.[30] "I told them it was none of their business," Laird recalled. "I said that's the way John felt and I supported him. They never brought it up again."

That evening Laird got away from the office early enough for dinner with his wife. The protestors happened to plan their first Moratorium Day on his wedding anniversary, and Laird wasn't about to let a national demonstration get in the way of celebrating twenty-four years of marriage.

The distance between the Nixon-Kissinger-Agnew condemnatory axis and the Laird-Rogers conciliatory mind-set was starkly evident on October 19 and 20, 1969. At a New Orleans Republican fund-raising dinner on the nineteenth, Agnew charged that the moratorium had been "encouraged by an effete corps of impudent snobs who characterize themselves as intellectuals." He warned that the next one in November would be "wilder [and] more violent" because of the "hard-core dissidents and professional anarchists" within the antiwar movement. On twentieth, at an awards dinner, Secretary Rogers praised many of those who participated, who "wished principally to register dramatic but dignified expression of their deep concern for peace in Vietnam."

⌇

In late October 1969 Laird took his Vietnamization show on the road to his biennial Laird Youth Leadership Conference for high school students, meeting at Wisconsin State University at Stevens Point. So wide was the gap between the Nixon administration and the nation's colleges, that the *Washington Star* declared in advance "it will be the first time a high official closely connected with the Nixon administration's Vietnam war policy has exposed himself to such a forum."[31] Added the *Wall Street Journal*, "[T]he stage was set . . . for a unique showdown between young critics and old politician Laird . . . a rare opportunity for tomorrow's leaders to take pot shots at today's."[32]

As Laird entered the university field house on October 27, he smiled and nodded a greeting to the three dozen antiwar protestors sporting homemade signs such as "Nixon-Laird, Blood Brothers." His mother, who was with him, was upset that "they were calling her son a murderer," Laird recalled. If anything, Laird was energized by the protestors. In his opening remarks, he explained that he looked forward to the youth meetings because "they give me an insight into what young people are thinking, what is bothering them, and what they think we in government might do about it."[33]

As expected, the dominant subject of the hour-long question-and-answer period with the 250 top high school students was Vietnam. The students were prepared with earnest, often well-informed questions and criticisms. Laird reminded them that as their congressman, he had opposed large-scale U.S. involvement in Vietnam. "I want you to know that I will judge whether I have been a success as Secretary of Defense on the basis of whether this war is ended and whether these sacrifices and these deaths can be stopped."[34]

Three days later, October 30, Laird was part of a unique brainstorming session at the White House. The president wanted help on his upcoming speech, so he summoned Laird, Rogers, and Attorney General Mitchell, picking their brains for two hours. One of Laird's main points was that Nixon should focus on the positive aspects of Vietnamization and peace talks in Paris. The televised address, which Nixon personally wrote and fretted over for weeks, became known as the "silent majority" speech.[35] In Nixon's view, it was a raging success. Knowing that polls had consistently shown the majority of Americans favored his Vietnam War policies, Nixon offered no new proposals. Instead, he issued a direct plea to "the great silent majority of my fellow Americans" for support. They responded, flooding the White House with eighty thousand telegrams, calls, and letters of support. A Gallup poll taken among those who watched the speech found 77 percent supported Nixon's view.[36]

But the president had earned this response by deliberately alienating America's youth in one of the most divisive addresses any president has ever made. He depicted the antiwar demonstrators as the enemy who must be silenced. "North Vietnam cannot defeat or humiliate the United States. Only Americans can do that," the president said, and there was no mystery as to what Americans he was talking about. To the silent majority, he pledged not "to be dictated [to] by the minority who hold that point of view and who try to impose it on the nation by mounting demonstrations in the street." If he allowed "a vocal minority, however fervent its cause, [to] prevail over reason and the will of the majority, this nation has no future as a free society."

At his Monday, November 10, 1969, staff meeting, Laird made sure everyone knew civilians would be in charge of keeping order during the march on Washington that week, even though military troops would be prepositioned and ready if needed.[37] "We need to make sure all our command lines work well, and there are no misunderstandings," Laird told his staff at the meeting. "Requests for troops are to go to the Military Commander and not directly to the troops. Civilians are in charge."

The "March against Death" began on Thursday and lasted for forty hours over two nights, leading up to Moratorium Day on Saturday, November 15. From Arlington National Cemetery to the Capitol, the march was solemn and impressive in the freezing rain. Six drummers beat out a funereal cadence as the march began across the Arlington Memorial Bridge, some 1,200 passing over the bridge every hour. Each of the 45,000 participants carried a placard with the name of one American who had died in Vietnam. As the placard carriers passed the White House, each stopped and, often emotionally, called out the name of the fallen soldier. Participants ended their four-mile procession at the Capitol, where each placard was placed in one of forty black coffins.

The big event was Saturday, but just how big it was became a matter of dispute. Laird got dragged into the controversy in late December when his office released reconnaissance photos taken by an Air Force RF-101 photo plane twenty thousand feet over the event. Air force analysts had determined, in the same way they would systematically analyze a spy photo of a May Day parade in Moscow, that there were 119,000 people at the rally, plus or minus 15 percent. The figure was laughably low; it appeared as if the Pentagon was trying to downplay the moratorium. Laird smelled a big mistake and ordered a quick review and correction, if necessary. The Pentagon came clean a week later after finding the photos had been taken possibly as late as 4 P.M., after most of the participants had left.[38]

The organizers estimated the size of the rally at about 800,000. Washington's chief of police estimated 250,000, but he admitted that was conservative. Even at that low number, it exceeded the previous record holder, the 1963 civil rights march highlighted by Martin Luther King's "I Have a Dream" speech, which peaked at 200,000 marchers. Most likely, there were about 600,000 participants at the moratorium rally, which makes it a record holder as the largest antigovernment rally ever held in the United States. That figure comes from the National Park Service, in charge of the Washington Mall, and is officially accepted today.

⚓

Laird was at his desk in the Pentagon that Saturday when he had an idea. He was concerned that too many of the military officials and the civilian leaders at the Pentagon were disdainful of Vietnamization and the need to end the war. They assumed that the "great, silent majority" would continue supporting them year after year, and that the antiwar movement was a flash in the pan. Typical of this attitude was General Earle Wheeler, chairman of the Joint Chiefs, who loved to lampoon demonstrators in his speeches. On the day of the October moratorium, during a speech to the Association of the U.S. Army, he referred caustically to the peaceful protestors as "groups of interminably vocal youngsters, strangers alike to soap and reason."

The secretary of defense thought there was a pair working in the Pentagon on November 15 who would benefit by rubbing shoulders with the protestors—Navy Secretary John Chafee and Navy Undersecretary John Warner. Before noon, he called them to his office. "You guys go down to the Mall and give me a report on what's going on," Laird barked at them. He couldn't go himself because he would be recognized by the crowd, but Chafee and Warner could go incognito. The blue-suited pair changed into some old T-shirts they used in the Pentagon gym, khaki slacks, and sneakers. Their chauffeur-driven limousines wouldn't do, so they borrowed a subordinate's old clunker and drove downtown.

Warner recalled: "It was a scene that's emblazoned on my mind. Here were hundreds of thousands of young men and young women, in a peaceful sort of way, singing and chanting and holding arms. Yes, we could smell the pot here and there. And occasionally some guy would strip down and dive into the Reflecting Pool....After an hour, we just looked at each other and said, 'Unbelievable.'" To the songs of Pete Seeger, John Denver, Peter, Paul, and Mary, and various casts of the musical *Hair,* punctuated by occasional speeches, it was a love fest—Woodstock in Washington. While Chafee and Warner were on the mall, Laird spent part of the day with demonstrators, too. He had heard that his niece Jessica Laird and her friend (and future husband) Jim Doyle, both fresh from two years with the Peace Corps in Tunisia, would be among the demonstrators that day, so he got word to them to come to his office and bring a dozen friends to talk about the war. "I didn't want people who were professionals"—those who made a profession out of protesting the war and organizing rallies—Laird said of his choice of company that day. "I wanted people who had a very sincere feeling about the American involvement in Southeast Asia." (Jim Doyle later became the Democratic attorney general and then governor of Wisconsin.)

As for his Mall scouts, Laird had told them he wanted them to judge the mood of the crowd, but his real intent was for Chafee and Warner to get the shine knocked off any lingering pro-war sentiments they might be harboring. "I didn't want these people to get too gung ho," Laird said of his military and civilian staff. "They were being pressed by people in the Navy that we were in the right place at the right time." Laird wanted Chafee and Warner to spend some time with hundreds of thousands of sincere Americans who thought Vietnam was the wrong place. The assignment had the desired effect.

After Chafee died in 1999, Warner emotionally remembered that experience with his Senate colleague as a high point in their long friendship: "I could see John was so terribly upset because it brought back the carnage he had seen in his previous military experience [World War II and Korea] when the whole nation, every American, was solidly behind every person in uniform." In the car on the way back to the Pentagon, Warner remembered Chafee saying to him: "Boy, just put yourself in the shoes of somebody in Nam today, going through all the hell of combat, and the country's not with him. I remember in World War II you knew that everybody in America was just foursquare behind you, and when you faced the dangers that we faced, it wasn't any question in your mind."

Back in Laird's office, when the two men tried to convey what they had felt, the defense secretary was moved. "We've got to figure some way to get our men out of this thing," Laird agreed with them. "Do it with dignity and do it so that the gains and sacrifices aren't lost."

"From that moment on," Warner said, "John Chafee became a very special counselor to the secretary of defense and, indeed, to the president on the need to bring that conflict somehow to a termination."[39]

Laird remembered the day well, too. "They were a little shaken because I don't think they realized the extent of some of the feelings of those young people. That's what I was trying to get them to understand. But I couldn't get the White House to understand that." Indeed, the contrasting Nixon image of the day is unforgettable. He made no attempt to meet with any of the six hundred thousand in Washington for a political rally. The White House was encircled by a protective barricade of fifty-seven city buses parked end to end. Sharp-shooting soldiers were stationed behind the balustrade of a tall building nearby, and another three hundred soldiers were stationed in the basement of the White House itself and the Executive Office Building next door. The president of the United States, by his own choice, was holed up in Fortress White House watching a college football game on television.

22

Crossing the Line

~∞~

THERE WERE TWO WORDS that had been made the equivalent of expletives in South Vietnam by the end of 1969: *Vietnamization* and *withdrawals.*
South Vietnamese President Thieu outlawed the use of both words in the domestic press. He justified the ban by complaining that to use either suggested
that "this war has been directed by the Americans and is just turned over to the
Vietnamese people's care."[1] For all its promise and for all the money thrown at
it, the biggest concern about Vietnamization was that it could only be as good
as the support it got from the Vietnamese people. General Creighton Abrams,
summed it up: "Sooner or later the Vietnamese themselves have got to settle
this thing. We can only help, and we can only help so much."[2]

As the man who saw South Vietnam's flaws close up through the magni-
fying glass of daily disappointment, Abrams had reason to be pessimistic. Out
of duty and loyalty to Laird, Abrams gave Vietnamization his best effort, but
he was always honest with Laird in assessing how the program was faring.
Abrams's reports to Laird were peppered with frustration about the South
Vietnamese military, which abided corruption at the highest levels. Thieu filled
top positions in his army with political cronies, some of whom Abrams considered grossly incompetent. Laird commiserated with Abrams, but there was
little either man could do to force Thieu to fire those commanders. Incompe-
tence and indifference were among the many speed bumps on the road that
American troops would take to get home. Another was weaning South Vietnam from the dependence on American help, a dependence that the United
States had fostered.

Those who saw Laird's Vietnamization as a fraud, a delaying tactic, or a
cover for a graceful exit from a hopeless cause did not understand the complexities of disengagement. General Bruce Palmer, formerly second in command of
U.S. Army in Vietnam, wrote years later about possible alternative U.S. strategies. He concluded that the United States should have focused earlier on developing a strong South Vietnam. To that end, the U.S. military should have been
training and supporting the South Vietnamese military, rather than fighting
the war for them. General Palmer's conclusion was that, given appropriate time
and support, such a strategy could have succeeded, but it would have taken
time and perseverance by the American people.[3] General Abrams knew that.
Unfortunately, by the time Nixon came to office, time was not an ally, and U.S.
perseverance was a scarce resource.

Training the South Vietnamese to take over their own war was the only way to avert chaos, as well as American loss of credibility among its allies. The U.S. forces could not simply leave South Vietnam overnight, despite demands from the doves in Congress to do just that. To disengage with the haste demanded by those who had lost patience with the war would have caused instant collapse of the South Vietnamese government and economy and would have meant certain death for thousands of American supporters as the country was over-run by the North Vietnamese army. There was the matter of American POWs who could not be left behind, and the issue of defending the last of the sup-port troops when the majority of the combat units were gone. Not the least of Laird's problems were a president who didn't want to be labeled a quitter, and parts of the U.S. military that didn't want to cede authority to the South Vietnamese.

On August 12, 1969, General Earle Wheeler wrote to warn Laird to go slow on the second phase of troop withdrawals. The first had been announced at the Midway conference in June. Nixon was due to announce the second wave in September. Wheeler cited the "serious lack of qualified leaders" in the South Vietnamese army as a drag on Vietnamization. "Neither the assessment of the military situation nor the [South Vietnamese] capabilities justifies a Phase 2 redeployment of more than about 25,000," Wheeler wrote.[4]

With more than half a million American troops still in Vietnam, removing twenty-five thousand wasn't enough in Laird's mind to show the public that he and Nixon were serious about Vietnamization. On September 4 Laird sent Nixon a memo laying out an update of his big picture for bringing home the troops. He attached the Joint Chiefs' recommendation, which said the troop withdrawal should be spaced out over three and a half years—not coinciden-tally, the amount of time left in Nixon's term. Laird gave a bow in the direction of the chiefs' wisdom but told the president that two years was his preference as a point to aim for on the horizon. As for the chiefs' opinion that Vietnamiza-tion would require giving the South as much artillery, airplanes, and logistical support as the American troops typically used, Laird demurred in his memo to Nixon: "While we should provide the Vietnamese with the assistance they need, we should not necessarily endeavor to create [the army of South Viet-nam] as a mirror image of U.S. forces."[5]

Still unaware of Laird's ultimate goal for complete withdrawal, the chiefs had also advised that as long as the enemy was still in South Vietnam, at least 267,500 U.S. troops should be left there indefinitely. Laird coyly wrote to the president, "I see no need to make any firm decision on the size of the residual force at this time." It wasn't until November 10 that Laird revealed to the chiefs his real intent. He ordered them to come up with a Vietnamization schedule that would have all U.S. troops, save a small advisory mission, out of the war by July 1973. There was to be no residual force of any size.[6]

On September 16 Nixon announced a second round of troop withdraw-als—thirty-five thousand men in the next three months despite Wheeler's plea for no more than twenty-five thousand. The announcement was a piece of broader Nixon strategy that fall to put pressure on Hanoi. In Nixon's mind, as recorded in his memoirs, it was a calculated series of moves to back the enemy into a corner: he sent a letter to Ho Chi Minh with the tone of an ultimatum; he announced that he would give a major policy speech on Vietnam on November 3; and he fixed on November 1, the anniversary of Lyndon Johnson's bombing halt, as the deadline for Hanoi to show some sign of flexibility in the peace talks, or else.

But those closest to the president weren't impressed with the saber rattling. Kissinger wrote in his memoirs, "On [Nixon's] world trip he dropped less than subtle hints that his patience was running out and that if no progress had been made in Paris by November 1, he would take strong action. So far as I could tell, Nixon had only the vaguest idea of what he had in mind."[7] Laird proceeded with business as usual, having little faith in the peace talks and seeing salvation in Vietnamization.

Nixon's struggle with the November 1 ultimatum shaped up to be purely in his own mind. Rumors flew that Nixon planned to announce a cease-fire in his November 3 speech. Counterrumors said that General Abrams was threatening to resign if that happened. A unilateral cease-fire was an option, Laird recalled, but Nixon "was never for doing that." And Laird said the loyal Abrams never threatened to resign over any issue. He suspected those rumors came from the U.S. ambassador in Saigon, Ellsworth Bunker, who himself was passionately devoted to the cause of a free South Vietnam and was always the first to object when a cease-fire was discussed.

Nixon also planted another rumor with some Republican members of Congress, knowing they would leak the story. As expected, columnists Rowland Evans and Robert Novak—normally one of Laird's avenues for leaks—wrote that the president had plans to blockade North Vietnam's Haiphong harbor and possibly even invade the north.[8]

Nixon's tactic to appeal directly to Ho Chi Minh by letter fizzled. Ho responded to Nixon's letter with the usual posturing and demands that the only way to end the war was for the United States to get out of it. Nixon received the reply August 30, and three days later Ho died. Hoping to capitalize on the shakeup in Hanoi, Nixon ordered a three-day halt to a B-52 bombing campaign against suspected North Vietnamese strongholds in the South. Ostensibly a courtesy for Ho's funeral, the bombing halt was supposed to signal to Hanoi that everything was negotiable with the new regime, but the signal was an uncertain one.[9] Ho's funeral was an on-again, off-again proposition for a few days. President Thieu said he would not agree to any cease-fire for Ho's funeral. "Would Hanoi lay down its guns for 72 hours if I died?" Thieu protested to General Abrams.[10]

Laird halted the bombing for twenty-four hours and then ordered it resumed when the funeral didn't materialize. General Abrams and Admiral

McCain agreed, both thinking that Ho's death should not make any difference in the day-to-day fighting. Then, Laird recalled, "all of a sudden the president calls me on the phone and says the State Department and Ambassador Bunker would like to withhold [bombing] for 24 hours. It was off and on twice." It didn't really matter to Laird one way or the other. "The bombing wasn't doing a hell of a lot of good," he said.

The death of Ho Chi Minh further diluted Nixon's plans for a November 1 ultimatum and his promised dire consequences. But in reality there never were any consequences. Independent of Nixon's ultimatum, Kissinger had already asked the Pentagon to come up with a plan for a massive invasion of North Vietnam should all negotiating options fail. The Pentagon dusted off one of a dozen such invasion plans that it had on the shelf, this one code-named "Duck Hook." According to Laird, Kissinger "fell in love" with Duck Hook and sold the president on the invasion. But their affection for the plan quickly waned. It initially was timed to begin on November 1, but Kissinger recommended that it be put on hold until the enemy's strength could be reassessed, and Nixon did not object.

Laird called Duck Hook a "crazy idea." With Vietnamization only in its infancy, invading North Vietnam was the worst possible strategy, in Laird's mind. Some historians, such as Walter Isaacson, have written that Laird threatened to resign if Nixon went ahead with Duck Hook, but Laird denied that. "I never threatened to resign at any time," he said. But when it came to invading the North, "I told Nixon I was very much against it and that it would interfere with the whole Vietnamization program, and that if he wanted to see casualties go up rapidly, I could assure him that would happen, and it would be on his hands, not mine. But I never threatened to resign." Nor was it true, as others have reported, that the Joint Chiefs planned Duck Hook behind Laird's back because they knew he would never sign off on an invasion of the North.[11] Laird said he knew about Duck Hook months before the chiefs presented it to Kissinger as an option.

Nixon's carrot-and-stick approach had failed. Hanoi didn't go for the carrot and Nixon had no stick. From his bundle of strategies, he was left with just the speech to give on November 3, and in his mind it became a watershed event in his presidency. He closeted himself at Camp David to write the speech, frequently consulting others, including Laird, who pressed him to emphasize Vietnamization as the cure. In this same speech, where the president called on the silent majority to speak up, he also disclosed his letter to Ho Chi Minh and said the response showed the North's true intent to block any peaceful settlement of the conflict. He also validated rumors about the revised U.S. military mission statement, which Laird had issued four months earlier.

But there were none of the promised new initiatives and no talk of carrying out threats. Nevertheless, the speech struck home to the silent majority. The cables and letters that flowed in to the White House warmed Nixon's heart, even though many of them were churned out by the president's own very effective public relations machine. Even Kissinger recorded that some of the enthusiasm was generated by Haldeman's "indefatigable operatives who had called political supporters all over the country to send in telegrams."[12] Haldeman recorded in his diary that Nixon called him fifteen or twenty times after the speech, checking on the kind of response it was getting and insisting that Laird and Rogers be advised of the volume of mail to "shore them up." As a final plea, Haldeman said, Nixon told him to arrange "100 vicious dirty calls to *New York Times* and *Washington Post* about their editorials," even though, as Haldeman noted, the president did not yet know how those papers would editorialize about his speech the next day. He just assumed the worst.[13]

✺

The Nixon administration's best efforts to peddle its good intentions in Vietnam were frequently undermined by stories from the front—the battle for Hamburger Hill, the secret bombing of Cambodia, the growing problems of morale, racial unrest, and drug use among the soldiers. None of those tarnished the reputation of the American military as badly as the horrific stories of GIs run amok. In 1969 Laird coped with the two most damaging of those stories.

The first came to his attention in a phone call from Abrams some time in July. "He was fit to be tied," Laird recalled. "He was wild, even on the secure phone." A South Vietnamese spy on the U.S. payroll, suspected of being a double agent for the North, had been executed by American Green Berets—shot in the head and dropped in the South China Sea. Abrams wanted to court-martial the Green Berets commander, Colonel Robert Rheault, on murder charges. Abrams knew it would be no easy task, because Rheault was a man of no small reputation. He was a highly decorated Korean and Vietnam veteran, from a prominent Boston family, and a well-connected West Point graduate with a master's degree from George Washington University. He had also done a tour as assistant for special operations to the Joint Chiefs. So when Abrams relieved him of command in July, before he was formally charged, it was quite natural that among the three thousand Special Forces troops serving him, many assumed Rheault was just being moved to a general's slot in the army somewhere, and a promotion would be announced any day.

Rheault and Abrams were not fated to get along, in part because Abrams was naturally suspicious of Special Forces and their unconventional tactics—and the fact that, time and again, Abrams's infantry had to rescue them at great cost from precarious positions into which they shouldn't have ventured. Rheault believed that evidence of Abrams's prejudice against the Special Forces showed in the fact that Special Forces units were targeted to be sent home first when the troop withdrawals began. The logic—one which predated Abrams—was that the smaller and scattered Special Forces groups needed the protection of larger combat units, and thus it would not be safe for the Green Berets to be the last ones in the country.[14] Hindsight has forgotten that even in this, the most unpopular of wars, there were many dedicated career soldiers who did not want to go home and felt their duty was at the front. For those men, an order to be among the first units to disengage was demoralizing.

Seven people under Rheault's command were implicated in the death of the suspected double agent. Two of them claimed that when proof was gathered against the spy, Thai Khac Chuyen, they consulted the CIA and were told that assassination would be the best option, although not one that the government could sanction. The CIA would later deny that assassination was suggested and claim that the Green Berets were specifically told *not* to get rid of the spy. An investigation by Army Secretary Stan Resor put the pieces of the story together. Rheault had ordered the killing, according to his underlings. So on June 20, 1969, three of them took the spy out on a boat, injected him with morphine, shot him twice in the head, filled a canvas bag with tire rims, tied the weight to his body, and threw him overboard in 150 feet of shark-infested water. After the killing, a junior member of Rheault's team, feeling uneasy about what had happened, reported it to the CIA. Rheault initially concocted a cover story, which he tried to float past Abrams, that the man was merely missing while on a dangerous solo mission. But once the facts were out, Rheault admitted he had ordered the assassination but claimed it was with the approval of the CIA.

In a war where body counts were the measure of success or failure, this was just one body. But the alleged double agent had not been killed in battle, nor had he been given the benefit of a trial. He had been interrogated, deemed guilty, and eliminated. And instead of following the canons of military justice, the Green Berets were saying they had acted on advice from the CIA to simply get rid of the problem. As a soldier, Abrams had seen plenty of killing, but this was more than he could stomach. On top of that, the colonel had added to his guilt by lying to his commanding officer. Abrams ordered all eight Green Berets put in solitary confinement in the American military prison at Long Binh.

At home where many already thought the war to be immoral, the Green Beret affair was shaping up as a farce—eight soldiers accused of murder because they killed an enemy agent in wartime. The involvement of the CIA made the whole affair even more odious. But Abrams appreciated that a fine line had been crossed, and it galled him. The final authority on how to proceed was Army Secretary Resor, and he went to Laird for advice. First, Laird said, get the arrested soldiers, who had to be presumed innocent, out of the punitive small cells at Long Binh. Resor ordered that move in less than twenty-four hours. Then Laird challenged Resor to think things through. "What's your game plan here?" Resor offered a few ideas, and together they worked out a strategy. Resor would meet personally with Abrams and go over the evidence and reasons behind the general's decision to court-martial, and come back and report.

Resor flew to Saigon and met Abrams. Years later he recalled that Abrams had showed him signed confessions from each Green Beret: "It was quite clear what they had done, and quite clear that it was a violation of Army regulations."[15] Resor reported back to Laird that he agreed with Abrams—someone deserved to be charged. But the matter of CIA involvement would have to be raised in the trial. "The CIA had told them to treat these people [double agents] with extreme prejudice, a code word for getting rid of them," Resor recalled. The defense would naturally want to call CIA officers to buttress their case. At Resor's direction, Army General Counsel Robert Jordan had already checked with the CIA's general counsel and gotten assurances that the CIA would provide the required witnesses, which would ensure a fair trial.

Laird didn't feel that was enough. With Resor sitting in his office, Laird placed a call to CIA Director Richard Helms, with whom he had a seasoned relationship of trust. Helms personally assured Laird that the CIA would cooperate. Somebody had second thoughts over the next week. Most likely, it was both Nixon and the CIA coming to the same conclusion independently that the agency would not cooperate. The chairman of the House Armed Services Committee, Mendel Rivers, claimed one of the accused men as a constituent. So he warned the president, via presidential aide Bryce Harlow, that if the court-martial proceeded, Rivers would hold open hearings on the matter and give at least three of the Green Berets the chance to rebut the charges. Rivers also reminded Harlow that the administration needed his vote on the ABM authorization bill and other defense expenditures.[16]

For its part, the CIA saw danger in the person of Rheault's lawyer, Edward Bennett Williams.[17] Williams was at the early stages of honing intimidation into an artful defense. It was a tactic he used in high-profile cases involving classified intelligence. The prosecution would be scared into retreat after Williams threatened to put unseemly covert operations on public trial. Laird well knew this scared the CIA. "The CIA did not want a trial because they thought it would expose other things that would not be in their best interest," said Laird. "There were some things there that the CIA wouldn't have been proud of. . . . I was advised, rightly or wrongly, that without the CIA's testimony, there was no case."

In late September Resor was informed that the CIA had reversed itself and was now refusing to provide the witnesses; he had no choice but to drop the case. Laird backed Resor's decision, which attracted suspicion that either he or Nixon or both were the ones who had caved in and forced Resor to drop the charges. Nixon could have ordered the CIA to cooperate but did not, so the outcome was something the president clearly desired. But that was resolution by inaction. At a press conference, when reporters cornered Nixon's spokesman Ron Ziegler about why Nixon didn't order the CIA to testify, Ziegler replied, "I won't take your question."[18]

In theory, even though he had no statutory authority in the case, Laird could have pressured Resor to go ahead, but this was not a battle Laird thought was worth the potential end result. For one thing, why make an enemy of Rivers, who was taking the case so personally? For another, Laird was reluctant to get between the CIA and the army, even if Abrams was passionate about pursuing the case. "I did have respect for the CIA and their people," Laird said. "I can't tell you that they did not influence me; they did. It was a difficult decision."

As a former military man who had seen American sailors taking potshots at shipwrecked Japanese sailors floating in the ocean, Laird had witnessed firsthand, as he called it, "men that wanted to kill when people didn't have to be killed." He understood that lines blurred in times of war. "That's why I tried to support these guys. They were in an operation where they felt this guy [the double agent] had seriously jeopardized and almost got them killed. They felt he was out to execute them."[19]

⚜

As the Green Beret murder case was making headlines, Laird was dreading the day when a far more horrific case would finally become public. With this case, Laird was insistent on putting the full weight of military justice against those responsible. It was the massacre of hundreds of civilians, including women and children, by a company of American soldiers from the Americal Division. It happened on March 16, 1968—during the Johnson administration—in a little South Vietnamese village called My Lai.

Remarkably, for nearly a year, the massacre had remained a secret, except for rumors that circulated among soldiers in Vietnam. Finally in March of 1969, one man who heard the rumors during his tour in South Vietnam, Ronald Ridenhour, wrote letters (after mustering out) to several members of Congress and to General Westmoreland, who was then army chief of staff, asking for an investigation. It took until about April 1, 1969, for one of the letters to land on Laird's desk. He ordered a quiet investigation, and it wasn't until September that the twenty-six-year-old platoon leader, Lieutenant William Calley, was arrested, four days before he was due to get out of the army. More arrests among Calley's company quickly followed. Laird braced himself for the expected press onslaught, but it was surprisingly slow in coming. At the defense secretary's top-level staff meeting on September 15, Resor warned those present that "[t]he My Lai atrocity case may break soon."[20] But it didn't—at least not right away.

The news was kept under wraps until two months later, on November 13, as Washington was filling with protestors for the Moratorium Day. The horror of the My Lai massacre was then exposed by Seymour Hersh of the Dispatch News Service. His reports, which earned him a Pulitzer Prize, precipitated a deluge of front-page stories across the country and extensive TV coverage. "All our fear about this story is proving to be well-founded," public affairs chief Dan Henkin wrote to Laird on November 18.[21] So many of Calley's company were going public that Henkin, a few days later, wrote with alarm to Laird:

"We have an incredible situation here where former Army men are indicting themselves for murder under prodding from CBS and others."[22]

Lieutenant Calley's company had been on a search and destroy mission against the Viet Cong in a small hamlet the GIs had nicknamed "Pinkville." Because of the reputation the village had as a stronghold for the Viet Cong, no one was above suspicion. The attack began with an artillery barrage on the hamlet, then Calley's company moved in, ordered all of the villagers out of their homes, and began setting fire to the wooden structures and setting off dynamite charges in the brick buildings. The villagers, including women and children, were herded into groups and gunned down on Calley's orders. One soldier claimed that when someone balked at obeying the order, Calley did the shooting himself. The number who died that day remains a secret in the army's files. Initial reports were as high as 567, based not on a body count, but on the number of survivors left in the village.[23] Later, the army settled on estimates ranging from two hundred to three hundred but would not be precise, fearing to prejudice any court-martial against the accused killers.

An army combat photographer who was there that day, Ronald Haeberle, had turned over his official photos to the Pentagon, but when his army camera had run out of film, he had used his personal camera to continue taking pictures of the piles of bodies. He kept those photos, and Laird learned at the December 1 staff meeting that Haeberle was asking $100,000 for the pictures. (Haeberle received $40,000 from the Cleveland *Plain Dealer* alone.)[24]

"I remember the first time they brought in those color pictures," Laird said. "I almost threw up." Babies and children were piled next to mothers and teens. Laird was additionally incensed that anyone, particularly someone who had taken these photographs while serving in the army, would be selling them. (He considered, briefly, the filing of civil or criminal charges against Haeberle.) But he also felt that the public needed to see these photos, to understand the full scope of the army's proceedings against Calley and others. Even as Haeberle was busy trying to find a buyer for the photos he had taken with his personal camera, Pentagon lawyers told Laird he shouldn't release the military photos. Finally, two weeks after news of Calley's arrest broke, Laird overruled legal counsel and allowed Resor to take the photos to closed congressional hearings. One congressman had to leave the room, overcome by the graphic pictures. Soon *Life* magazine bought the private photos, and the whole world saw the proof of one company of soldiers gone temporarily berserk. It was ghastly confirmation of the epithet used on some returning Vietnam veterans—"baby killer."

But in one of the ironies of Vietnam War history, the majority of public opinion rallied around the soldiers accused in the massacre. Thousands of letters poured into the White House and the Pentagon arguing that a lowly lieutenant and his men should not take the blame for an immoral war perpetrated by generals and politicians. Even the American Civil Liberties Union sided with Calley, feeling he could not get a fair trial because of the excessive publicity. "It is worth noting that American Legion posts and the ACLU are allies—and that is a strange alliance indeed," one of Laird's aides observed to him.[25] While there may have been public shock and revulsion, there was no sense of surprise. Many folks back home already assumed civilians were being killed indiscriminately, and it looked like the brass had found a scapegoat in Lieutenant Calley.

Laird appointed Lieutenant General William Peers to head up the My Lai investigation. On Capitol Hill Laird's old friend Mendel Rivers decided to do his own investigation, and his sympathies were clearly with Calley as a victim of circumstance. Fearing a surge of public sympathy for Calley that could scuttle the court-martial, Laird went to Rivers and asked him to call off the congressional hearings. Laird told Rivers that as defense secretary he was already walking a fine line, trying not to let public sentiment get in the way of military justice. Laird recalls telling Rivers, "I've not prejudiced this in any way, Mendel, but I feel that it's only fair that just because of the publicity and some photographs that had been released, that we at least wait until the investigation is completed. I think you should keep your powder dry." On the eve of the second hearing, Rivers canceled it out of respect for Laird.

One option for Laird would have been to blame the Johnson administration for the atrocities that happened on its watch and to let the congressional hearings run their course, casting Calley as a martyr in a lost cause. But Laird's preference was to let Calley get due process. For Laird, My Lai was old business that was obstructing the public view of the new agenda, Vietnamization. "I was not trying to go back and find fault with the previous administration. I was trying to look forward to Vietnamization and getting our forces out of there as fast as possible in an honorable way," he said.

Again Laird drew on his World War II experiences with fellow sailors who wanted to kill unarmed Japanese sailors out of vengeance, anger, and fear. "I understood why they wanted to do it, but you had to do everything you could to stop them," he said. "An officer in the United States military has certain responsibilities." Laird believed that what Calley had done was appalling, so he told Resor to press ahead with the court-martial. Laird took flak from many directions over that decision, including a scathing letter in the *New York Times* signed by a young and unknown marines lieutenant named Oliver North, who would later have his own spot of fame in the Iran-Contra scandal of the Ronald Reagan administration. Staffers around Laird urged him to give the insubordinate letter writer his comeuppance in public, but Laird refused, saying he didn't want to give the story more legs.

❦

Although Laird and Resor took full credit for the decision to file criminal charges against Calley, a meeting between Nixon and Laird just before that decision was announced cast suspicion on who was calling the shots. *Time* magazine implied in a report on that meeting that Nixon had insisted on the court-martial. Calley's lawyer was quick to accuse the president of exercising improper "command influence." If the commander-in-chief was meddling in a military court procedure, how could the defendant get due process from soldiers who take orders from the president?

Laird said it never happened. "The president never got directly involved" in the decision to prosecute Calley, Laird said. At the meeting, he said he told Nixon that Abrams and Resor were recommending that Calley be charged with multiple counts of murder, and that he, Laird, agreed. He said Nixon never weighed in, and, in any case, Laird would not have asked the president's opinion. "I wouldn't go to him for advice," Laird said of the court-martial dilemma.

Historical evidence suggests that Nixon, if anything, would have argued with Laird *against* filing criminal charges. In public pronouncements Nixon acted appalled, but privately, with top aides, he expressed sympathy not only for Calley but for the army officials who had covered up the scandal. "It's a pretty cheap shot to allow the generals to be put on the rack for the My Lai business. It was covered up because it was in the interest of the country," he groused to Kissinger in a March 17, 1970, phone call recorded by the White House taping system. "We know why it was done. These boys being killed by women carrying that stuff in their satchels." Kissinger tried to bring the president back to reality. "My first instinct was the same but some of the stories are awful. Four hundred people were killed there and it went on for days.... I don't think the public likes it."

Resor was foursquare for prosecution and conviction of Calley. "Calley was someone who shouldn't have been an officer," he said. "He was a product of the period when we were short of officers and scraped hard to get them." And Resor, even without access to secret White House conversations, instinctively knew Nixon was sympathetic to Calley and the cover-up. He was so convinced, in fact, that it was one of the prime reasons he stayed on as army secretary until mid-1971. "One reason I stayed on as long as I did is that I was afraid Nixon would let him [Calley] off. Nixon had the same view as Mendel Rivers. I think the president didn't want anything that would undermine support for the war, which he wanted to continue."[26]

In 1971 a military court convicted Calley alone of twenty-two counts of premeditated murder. At his sentencing hearing, Calley pinpointed the moral dilemma of the war as he pled for leniency: "I've never known a soldier, nor did I ever myself wantonly kill a human being in my entire life.... When my troops were getting massacred and mauled by an enemy I couldn't see, I couldn't feel and I couldn't touch—but nobody in the military system ever described them as anything other than Communism. They didn't give it a race, they didn't give it a sex, they didn't give it an age, and they never let me believe it was just philosophy in a man's mind that was my enemy out there."[27] The jury sentenced Calley to life in prison at hard labor.

Many Americans felt it was a just punishment, but there were also many who backed Calley, feeling that the lowly lieutenant had unfairly taken the blame for a massacre that thousands of Americans believed to be standard operating procedure in Vietnam. An estimated one hundred thousand telegrams flooded into the White House, ninety-nine of every one hundred of them urging the president to intervene and free Calley. Nixon had courted the silent majority, and many of them now demanded by telegram that he listen to them and not let a soldier in the service of his country—a pawn in a larger game—take the rap himself. Some draft boards quit en masse, and Governor George Wallace of Alabama tried to cancel the draft in his state until Calley was pardoned.

Nixon's bias in the case was clear to Resor when Joint Chiefs Chairman Admiral Thomas Moorer called Resor to report that Calley would be moved from the stockade at Fort Benning, Georgia, to his own quarters while he awaited the results of an appeal. It was Nixon's idea. "The admiral was sort of embarrassed," Resor said. "He said, 'I know this really is an Army matter, but the president has suggested that Calley be transferred to his own quarters while the appeal goes on.'"[28]

Several days later, when Nixon announced he would review the verdict himself, Resor balked. Publicly the Pentagon said it was fitting for the commander-in-chief to review the case after the verdict, but privately Resor's staff wrote a memo to Laird listing reasons why the president should stay out of it. The prosecutors wrote Nixon to protest intervention in a case that had been fairly decided by military officers.[29] Laird did not share their feelings. "It was reasonable for the president to take the action he did, and I supported it."

Calley's appeals continued through military and civilian courts until 1974. Along the way, his sentence was reduced to twenty years, and then ten. At that point Nixon reviewed the case one more time and said he was satisfied with the sentence. Calley finally went to the federal prison in Fort Leavenworth, Kansas, to serve six months before he was paroled. Laird felt justice had been done for a heinous crime. "When you get into a war like that, sometimes people are not as mentally stable as they should be at certain times. I think the highest authority from time to time should take that into consideration. You have to have a penalty or you're not going to be able to maintain the kind of discipline that is needed with your troops. So I refused to stop the court-martial and I instructed the secretary of the army not to interfere with the court-martial. But when it came to penalty, I think the president made the proper decision."

Scandals such as My Lai and the Green Beret murder were side roads that Laird felt detoured the American public from the more important news of Vietnamization. As his first year in office drew to a close, Laird was maneuvering to get as many troops as he could included in Nixon's announcement of the third withdrawal phase. The news release was planned for December 15. Edgy about a possible North Vietnamese offensive during the coming Tet holiday, the Joint Chiefs advised against taking any more men out. The Tet offensive of 1968 had taken the American military command by surprise, and each year as the dry season approached, those commanders vowed never to be surprised again. But Laird was not one to be spooked by the past. Where others saw an alarming buildup of enemy strength, Laird saw only the seasonal flux of troop movements in a country where the monsoons determined the battle plans. And he didn't want that to be used as an excuse to slow down his troop withdrawals. "It would be misleading to interpret this seasonal surge as an escalation," Laird wrote to Kissinger on December 2. "I believe it is of overriding importance to remain flexible."[30] Laird was right that year. The North was still reeling from the high price it paid for the 1968 Tet offensive, and a big escalation was not in the offing.

Still, the Joint Chiefs wanted to move at a more measured pace. If a third round of withdrawal was inevitable, they wanted to send home no more than thirty-five thousand men. And, if North Vietnam did escalate the war, the chiefs said the withdrawals should be canceled and even reversed, sending more men back into the war. And, they said, if there was an escalation on the enemy's part, the United States should respond with a new all-out air war against the North, something that hadn't been used since November 1968.

Laird wrote to Kissinger on December 12 asking for the president to announce a fifty-thousand-man withdrawal. In Laird's mind, Vietnamization would go nowhere without taking a few risks. "Progress in Vietnamization begets further progress," he wrote. As for the chiefs' recommendation that the air war resume over the North, Laird showed his typical skepticism about bombing. "[T]here has been, to my knowledge, no clear relationship demonstrated between a U.S. air/naval campaign against North Vietnam and a reduction in the latter's military capabilities. ... [T]here is no analysis that I have seen which would demonstrate any decisive results from an air/naval campaign against North Vietnam. To the contrary, for marginal gains we could sustain high and perhaps politically decisive costs."[31]

Kissinger couldn't argue with Laird's political instincts; troop withdrawal was the only thing that would satisfy the voting public back home. But Kissinger privately complained about how Laird was juggling the numbers. Sometimes it seemed from the view in the White House that the defense secretary was making unilateral decisions about how many troops were coming home. "Mel Laird is not going to have his own troop withdrawal program," Kissinger reportedly snapped once when looking at the numbers of troops coming home.[32] But Laird passed that off as a problem of bookkeeping. Soldiers came into Vietnam individually for one-year rotations on a regular schedule, but withdrawing troops were taken out in units. It was a balancing act to keep the exact number of authorized troops in the country, and occasionally that number fell below the official ceiling. "That had nothing to do with the troop withdrawal program, although Henry always thought it did," Laird said.

On December 15, 1969, Nixon announced the third round of withdrawals at fifty thousand men by April 15, 1970. It was just the figure Laird had asked for and fifteen thousand more than the Joint Chiefs wanted in their worst-case scenario. That day Kissinger sent Laird a memo to make sure the defense secretary understood the president didn't want him to get ahead of the program, especially going into the Tet season. "In executing the actual troop withdrawal every effort should be made to restrict the withdrawals in January, February and early March to the smallest number manageable, and to concentrate the larger actual withdrawals in the end of the period, i.e., late March/early April," Kissinger wrote.[33] Nevertheless, Laird kept his own pace.

Nixon did not stop the withdrawal plan that Laird had put in motion. In less than six months, Laird had prevailed over the military establishment and talked the president into bringing home 115,500 men.

23

Den of In-equity

WHEN LAIRD TOOK OVER as secretary of defense, he was determined to end one of the most unfair systems the U.S. government had ever devised—the military draft as it then existed. For four years of the Vietnam buildup, the draft had supplied the army infantry with the soldiers who were most likely to be wounded or die. Avoiding the war became a national preoccupation for many young men. The stern finger of Uncle Sam pointing from recruitment posters produced not a dash to the colors but a wild scramble for cover. The threat of military service scared thousands into premature marriages, undesired fatherhood, unscheduled schooling, and self-inflicted physical impairments. The system of deferments, which allowed the sons of the well-to-do to stay safely in college while the sons of the poor and minorities were sent off to war, became a national scandal. As Americans surveyed the backgrounds of the young draftees serving on the front lines, it was hard not to conclude there was a class war of sorts.

The architect of the inequitable draft system and its chief supervisor was a crusty septuagenarian, General Lewis B. Hershey. The former Indiana farm boy joined the National Guard in 1911 and transferred to the regular army in 1920, after World War I, having seen no combat. He was assigned to the Selective Service System in 1936 and was appointed by President Franklin Roosevelt as its director in 1941. By 1969 he had served under five presidents and had become the personification of the selective service. Sporting a military crew cut, Hershey had an autocratic style. And he firmly believed in exemptions from the draft, as long as they followed the lines he had prescribed after World War II. He had been alarmed that the best and the brightest of American youth had been sent to war as cannon fodder, and he was determined to prevent that in future drafts. So, he devised a system that pressured the able and affluent into education, useful occupations, or other desired avenues of service (such as the National Guard or the Reserves), while those without such options were drafted.

Selective service laws were administered by 4,098 local draft boards, which meant 4,098 different sets of standards for induction. In some places young men were being drafted at age nineteen, in other places at age twenty-two. The local board examiners were generally white and veterans of World Wars I and/or II. Fewer than 2 percent were black. In Alabama and Mississippi there was not a single African-American on a draft board. For a time in Louisiana, the chairman of the largest draft board was also the grand dragon of the state's Ku Klux Klan.[1]

Anecdotal evidence suggests that the older, promilitary, white males who dominated these boards used the draft as punishment for those who seemed to show a lack of respect for their elders by manners, dress, or beliefs. One board member, after talking with a long-haired pacifist, growled to a clerk: "He needs a shave, a haircut, and a good scrubbing. Make him 1-A." The clerk dutifully placed the young man in a call-up status. At another board proceeding witnessed by a social scientist, an examiner concluded, "This is the sort of guy you would take down to the latrine and scrub down with a wire brush. Let's make this baby 1-A. We'll fix his trolley."[2]

Such attitudes were subtly encouraged by General Hershey. After a December 1965 protest at the Ann Arbor draft board by thirty-nine University of Michigan students, Hershey advised that the selective service would have a new policy of reclassifying protestors for near-immediate induction into the military. In an interview with the university's campus newspaper, Hershey said, "I'm one of those old-fashioned fathers who never let pity interfere with a spanking." Within weeks, twelve of the protestors lost their student deferments and were reclassified 1-A as "delinquents," which the law had allowed in World War II. Hershey bragged that the threat of induction would end the wave of sit-ins faster than criminal prosecution.

But the military was furious at the punitive reclassification trend. To them, it appeared that Hershey would be loading the army with malcontents. The antiwar ideas of such draftees could not be shorn with a swipe of the hair clippers. In 1968 the reclassification authority was overturned by the U.S. Supreme Court in a case brought by one protestor who had turned in his draft card and had his exemption taken away. During testimony in that case Hershey said, "I'm as popular as a bastard at a family reunion with the military because they don't want to run a correctional institution. But they have the know-how to teach discipline."

Hershey sometimes described the selective service system he designed as "an uncomfortably warm room designed to encourage people who faced the draft to find a door out of that room." It allowed him to tinker with social reform by "channeling" young men into responsible (and deferment-eligible) activities such as education, marriage, and fatherhood, occupations such as medicine or the ministry, and so on.[3] Hershey's vision became an exercise in "survival of the fittest" in which the fittest were deemed useful enough to society not to be sacrificed to war.

With some exceptions, and contrary to previous military policies, the National Guard and Reserves were not called to serve in the Vietnam War. Laird was the defense secretary who changed that for the post-Vietnam military. He established that the Guard and Reserves would be the first called to active duty in the event of major American military action, which occurred in both the 1991 Gulf War and the "War on Terror" in Iraq and Afghanistan. During the Vietnam era, "thousands lined up to join Guard and Reserve units, not in the tradition of volunteer citizen-soldiers but because they sought a safe haven from the draft and the war in Vietnam," recounted Roger Kelley, Laird's manpower and reserve chief.[4] It was such a well-known way to avoid the draft that the National Guard had a waiting list of one hundred thousand.

The first draft exemption for millions of young men was 2-S, for college students. Because the number of 2-S applicants jumped exponentially as the Vietnam War began, steps were taken to tighten up the exemption. Since good grades were mandatory, some sympathetic professors automatically passed every able-bodied draft-age male in their class. For those whose grades slipped along with their ranking in the class, beginning in 1966 they were required to take the Selective Service College Qualification Test, and those who scored poorly lost their 2-S status and were drafted.[5]

By 1967 it had become apparent that thousands of students who were fearful of the Vietnam draft were prolonging their studies with extra postgraduate work until they passed the age of twenty-six. Theoretically they could turn 2-S into a permanent exemption by pursuing more than one postgraduate degree, such as law school followed by engineering school. So, in 1968, the deferment for nonmedical graduate studies was eliminated, which ended an educational pyramid scheme that had greatly fattened postgraduate university enrollment.

Because schooling was always a temporary exemption, only 371,000—or less than 3 percent of those who were disqualified, deferred, or exempted from the draft—were exempted *solely* because they were students. For some of the millions who benefited from the student exemption, the best way to graduate from 2-S was to go on to 3-A—fatherhood. In 1963 President Kennedy exempted married men from military service. Draft boards were soon inundated with prospective inductees showing up with last-minute marriage certificates. An immediate 10 percent rise in marriage rates for twenty- and twenty-one-year-olds was noted. The marriage exemption lasted only two years; beginning in 1966, married men without children could be drafted. Finally, a half-million men were given occupational deferments. These were reserved for ministers or divinity students (4-D), farmers (2-C), or one of several "critical" occupations (2-A), including teachers.

In his early congressional years Laird favored the concept of universal service, which was that all young men would serve their country for a set time whether in the military, as a teacher's aide, a hospital assistant, or so on. But the idea never had strong support in Congress, so by the mid-1960s, Laird was convinced that an all-volunteer military was the way to go. Since that could not be a Defense Appropriations Subcommittee initiative, Laird was not out front on the issue. Instead, he urged friends such as Congressmen Billy Steiger and Donald Rumsfeld, who were legislative pioneers on the subject, to lead the charge.

There were powerful philosophical reasons for Laird to move to an all-volunteer force. He concluded that if presidents did not have a draft to provide any amount of manpower when needed, they might be less likely to involve the United States in dubious ventures like a land war in Asia. Laird also thought it was important to break the military's unhealthy addiction to the draft. "It was too easy for them to get manpower. All they had to do each month was send a requisition over to Selective Service, and they got whatever they needed." General Hershey, in fact, often compared the Selective Service System to a gas station, with the Pentagon (driver) telling Hershey (attendant) the quantity of men (gas) they needed. Laird thought it was more onerous than that, being a system only slightly more sophisticated than the British navy's method of shanghaiing crews from waterfront taverns in the 1700s.

Laird's negative view was fueled by the abysmal treatment of draftees. Their wages were not comparable to private industry and less than voluntary enlistees were paid for doing the same jobs. "The draftees were being paid slave wages; it was really cheap, forced labor that was unacceptable in this country," Laird recalled. The military simply didn't see the need to pay them more because they didn't need to compete with the private sector for the men, and there was a serious question whether Congress would raise the budget to give the draftees parity.

To Congressman Laird, the shameful pay scale represented a burdensome and hidden taxation of the draftees. As Republican economist Milton Friedman explained it: "Conscription is a tax in kind, forced labor from men who serve involuntarily. The amount of the tax is the difference between the sum for which they would voluntarily serve and the sum we pay them. The real cost of manning the armed services now, including this concealed tax, is greater than the cost of running a volunteer force of the same size." Friedman, who was well known for this point of view, recalled that Laird was a behind-the-scenes leader in promoting such arguments against the draft, particularly at meetings at the American Enterprise Institute, on whose advisory board Friedman served.[6]

As a presidential candidate, Nixon had initially seemed set on backing the draft, as he had throughout his political career. The initial catalyst for altering that view was Martin Anderson, a Columbia University professor who joined Nixon's small informal campaign advisory group in January 1967. While Friedman was the intellectual force for change, Anderson was the most active agent within the Nixon campaign. In one of the advisory group's weekly meetings at Nixon's law firm in March 1967, the issue of the draft arose. Anderson had just read an eloquent essay by Friedman urging the formation of an all-volunteer army. He offered to put some ideas on paper for Nixon about how to end the draft and beef up the military at the same time. Soon Nixon, who had not previously spoken out against the draft, was talking publicly about ending it.[7]

The new Nixon view was one that Laird had adopted several years earlier, and, as was his habit when he had an idea, he codified it in the Republican platform as soon as he got the chance. The 1968 platform said, "When military manpower needs can be appreciably reduced, we will place the Selective Service System on standby and substitute a voluntary force obtained through adequate pay and career incentives."

In the weeks leading up to the 1968 election, Nixon gave a series of important radio addresses, one of which focused on the all-volunteer force. Nixon denounced many of the inequities of the draft and said, "[J]ust as soon as our reduced manpower requirements in Vietnam will permit us to do so, we should stop the draft and put our Selective Service structure on stand-by." Some later thought that candidate Nixon had pledged to end the draft early, but he had not. Instead, he had said in the address that he was "proposing that we start toward ending the draft when the war is over.... However we might wish to, we can't stop the draft while we are in a major war."[8]

Laird was pleased with the address, though his attitude would have been much different had he even remotely suspected that in two months he would be pressed by Nixon to become his secretary of defense, the person who would be responsible for implementing the new policy. "Since Nixon had made that campaign commitment, I became the one who had to deliver on it, and I knew it would be one of the toughest damn jobs I could ever have," Laird recalled.

∾

A little more than a week after the inauguration, Nixon ordered Laird to develop a "detailed plan" to end the military draft and create an all-volunteer force. At a February 3, 1969, staff meeting, Laird announced that he would create a Pentagon panel to handle Project Volunteer, a proposed seven-to twelve-month study of compensation, recruitment, and related issues. The president, he said, wanted to create his own independent commission out of the White House to do much the same thing, and Laird told the top-level staff he hoped that would be delayed until the Pentagon's Project Volunteer study was completed.[9]

Both Nixon and Laird were shrewdly gauging the climate in Congress and at the Pentagon. Nixon thought a commission was needed to prepare Congress to pass the legislation required to create an all-volunteer force. Laird knew the opposition among all the military services was strong. The army objected because it heavily depended on the draft to fill its ranks; the navy and air force, because the majority of their enlistments were "draft-induced," meaning most joined these services to avoid being drafted into the army. So Laird realized he needed a year to prepare the services for such a radical change, and the best way to bring them along was to initiate a Pentagon study in which the military could have input.

Nixon congratulated Laird in a February 6 letter for starting so quickly to study the problem but made it clear he felt that a concurrent presidential "outside commission" was needed for the concept to "continue at full speed." He asked Laird for "a list of suggested members for this commission."[10] Laird complied by making sure the presidential commission was weighted civilians who shared his point of view, including Friedman.[11] "That commission had a good cross section of college professors, those who had had military service, businessmen, and African-American leaders whom I suggested," Laird recalled. "I thought it was good to have an outside group like that because we would need it when we went to Congress with our proposal. So I stacked the panel." Laird suggested former secretary of defense Tom Gates as the chairman. Thus the president's Advisory Commission on an All-Volunteer Armed Force became known as the "Gates Commission."[12]

Two weeks after the commission was formally announced, Laird appointed Assistant Secretary of Defense Roger Kelley to chair the parallel study in the Pentagon, called "Project Volunteer."[13] The work of committees is inherently slow—neither would conclude its work until early 1970—so Laird felt it was vital to move ahead on reforming the draft before the two committees finished.

⤜⤛

The Selective Service System is not part of the Defense Department even though it is umbilically tied to that department. Since Laird had no absolute authority over General Hershey, he had to work around him. Hershey reported to the president and the National Security Council, of which Laird was a member. At the first Nixon NSC meeting on January 25, 1969, the president asked Laird to provide him some quick-fix ideas for the draft. A week later Laird privately wrote Nixon that changing the draft to a "random selection" or lottery system was the way to go. Nixon approved but predicted that Congress would never go along with a lottery. Others had tried before and gone down to defeat.[14]

Laird had several reasons for pushing a lottery. Among them was the fairness of random selection instead of choices made by biased draft boards. Also, the existing system drafted the oldest eligible men first. That meant young men were vulnerable to be drafted for seven years, from their nineteenth to their twenty-sixth birthdays, during which time they were unable to plan their futures. They were unsure of continued deferments, unlikely to find good jobs, and unable to commit to careers. Recognizing this, Laird had written into the 1968 Republican platform a promise to "revise" draft policies in part by "reduc[ing] the number of years during which a young man can be considered for the draft, thereby providing some certainty to those liable for military service."

The first roadblock to a lottery was a 1967 law that barred the president from using random selection. In a mid-February press conference, Laird announced that the administration would send new legislation to Congress to override that law.[15] Standing in the way of that change was House Armed Services Committee Chairman Mendel Rivers, who had been opposed to a lottery. Another roadblock was Hershey himself, who considered the lottery idea an affront to his ability to run a fair system. Even the public was not on board. A Harris poll on March 3 indicated that although half the public thought the draft system was unfair, they were two to one against changing to a lottery.

During a memorable phone call with Yale University President Kingman Brewster, Laird was told he was a fool to make a run at a lottery system. Brewster had been a member of a commission that tried to get Congress to approve a lottery during the Johnson administration two years earlier, and he had emerged bloodied and defeated on Capitol Hill. "You can never do that!" he practically shouted at Laird. "You'll NEVER be able to do that!" Brewster bet Laird a steak dinner that he could never get Congress to agree.[16]

Nixon's opening salvo came on May 13, 1969, with a request to Congress to change the order of call from an oldest-first to a youngest-first policy, reduce the period of prime draft vulnerability from seven years to one year, and select those actually drafted through a random lottery system.[17]

Laird always saw Brewster as a key to draft reform. The Yale president was a prominent leader of the American Council on Education, which represented nearly every higher education organization in the country. He had managed to keep relative peace on his own campus by sympathetically conferring with his students without capitulating to unreasonable demands. So Brewster was at the top of the guest list when Laird decided to begin a "Conversational Lunch" series at the Pentagon on August 20, 1969. In addition to Brewster, the guests at that first lunch included labor leader George Meany, Washington Post publisher Katharine Graham, and presidential campaign scribe Theodore H. White. Laird's intent was to use the lunches to gather a sounding board of prominent American thinkers and leaders and then tell them what he was trying to do on a variety of fronts. He wanted the first one to focus on draft reform, so he seated Brewster to his immediate left, which made him the first speaker. "Brewster was not a supporter of Nixon, or a supporter of mine, or a supporter of the Vietnam War," Laird recalled, "but I knew our thinking was the same on the lottery." Brewster performed persuasively but reiterated in front of the others that it was a quixotic, hopeless quest to seek a random draft selection process.

Laird smiled. A few days before, Nixon had privately given him the go-ahead to move into Hershey's turf with vigor.[18] Laird came up with an ultimatum that he outlined to Nixon in an August 29 memorandum. He said the president should warn Congress that if it did not act by January 1970, Nixon would institute a legally allowed but complex and confusing "moving age group" draft system which would come a bit closer to a random selection process.[19]

In a meeting with congressional leaders on September 18, Laird made his request simple. All they had to do was remove a single sentence from the 1967 draft law—the provision that prohibited the president from instituting a random selection system of inductions. The next day, following Laird's plan, Nixon gave a speech in which he proposed the simple one-sentence change in the existing draft law and promised "unilateral action" by the White House if this was not done. Laird met with reporters in the Roosevelt Room after the president's speech and reiterated: "If Congress fails to act, we will take appropriate executive action," which would mean a default to the "moving age group system." He then tried to explain what that meant, prompting one newspaper to call it "so complicated that Mr. Laird could barely unsnarl it for reporters at the press conference."[20]

At first the chief congressional roadblock, Congressman Rivers, appeared unmoved. He had forty-three draft reform bills bottled up in his committee and had said they would stay there until some unspecified date "consistent with existing commitments." After a favorable reaction to the Nixon-Laird proposal from newspaper editorial boards across the country, Rivers agreed to hold subcommittee hearings beginning September 30, with Laird as the first witness. The subcommittee gave Laird a cool reception, and the press began to speculate that the lottery was dead, but they had underestimated Laird. He continued to lobby members of Congress and eventually played the national security card: give the commander-in-chief what he says he needs to make America more secure. To the shock of Capitol Hill pundits, the House Armed Services Committee unanimously approved the draft bill on October 16 and sent it on to the full House, where it passed 382 to 12 on October 30.[21]

As the House was voting, Senate Majority Leader Mike Mansfield announced that the Senate would not take up the president's legislation until the following year. He knew that if the Senate Armed Services Committee considered it, a group of antiwar senators led by Edward Kennedy would debate it to death in an effort to push more sweeping reform, which was not likely to pass. So rather than waste the Senate's time, Mansfield stalled. Once again political prognosticators predicted that draft reform was dead. Once again, they had underestimated Laird. He became a regular on Capitol Hill, buttonholing senators and promising them future reforms. "I told them I'd entertain their amendments the next year and give them full and complete consideration, but we had to get on with this now," Laird recalled.

More important, though, was Kingman Brewster. Laird produced him on November 5 at a hearing of an administrative subcommittee chaired by Kennedy. Brewster strongly argued for a compromise that would allow the lottery bill to pass and that would defer more comprehensive reform until the next year. "It has often been said that the best is the enemy of the good," Brewster noted. "This bright, cynical generation of students is not going to appreciate it if this opportunity for meaningful reform falls by the wayside because of a desire to do more than can realistically be done in this session of Congress." Kennedy openly embraced Brewster's compromise. Draft reform was alive again, and Laird let Brewster off the hook for the steak dinner.[22]

The full Senate passed the lottery bill by voice vote, and it became law on November 26, 1969. During that year, President Nixon had sent several dozen domestic proposals to Congress. None of the major ones had passed. So the single-sentence draft reform bill, which simply repealed a sentence in an existing law, was declared by the *New York Times* to be "the first major piece of new legislation that the Administration has obtained from Congress during 10 months in power."[23]

⚓

Now Lewis Hershey had to go, and Laird knew it. After a little convincing from Laird and White House aides Arthur Burns and Martin Anderson, Nixon knew it too. The president suspected Hershey of actively working behind the scenes against the lottery legislation. Laird considered Hershey a friend, but he had not kept up with the times. "He was a fine man, but the time had come for a younger person in there," Laird recalled. "Most importantly, we needed someone who would get behind the lottery and the all-volunteer force. Hershey didn't think either of them would work. It was at my instigation that he was replaced."

In September Nixon tasked Bryce Harlow with the sensitive assignment of moving the obdurate seventy-six-year-old out of his job. It was a difficult thing for Harlow, who had worked with Hershey since the Eisenhower administration, and he was not happy with his friend Laird, who seemed to have foisted this firing on Harlow. Hershey failed to take the hint that it was time to leave, so Harlow began a series of tough meetings with him to explore how his resignation could be accomplished amicably. The old general was adamant; he would not voluntarily retire. Harlow knew that to many in Congress Hershey was a sacred cow, and an untimely fight would ensue if Hershey did not go quietly.

As the days wore on, though, Hershey saw the handwriting on the wall and decided to cut the best deal possible for himself. Though he might stand down from the Selective Service System, he said he must be given another related job of stature. Harlow proposed that he be presidential advisor on military manpower mobilization, a position created just for him; Hershey agreed. Hershey also insisted that he must be promoted from three-star to four-star general. That was trickier, and Harlow knew the only man who could pull that off was Laird. The army was likely to balk because there were only so many four-star slots in the force. Laird disliked Hershey's terms. Hershey had never served in a combat leadership role and was not on a par with the heroic four-star generals such as Dwight Eisenhower, Omar Bradley, Douglas MacArthur, George Patton, and Lucius Clay. But ever the pragmatist, Laird said if that was what it took to remove the Hershey obstacle, then so be it. Laird was sure he could get the necessary approvals from the army and the Senate.[24]

On October 10, 1969, five days before a national anti-Vietnam protest, Hershey was asked to visit the Oval Office. He figured he was there to seal the promotion and reassignment with Nixon. But during the fifty-minute chat, ever anxious to avoid confrontation, Nixon never raised the subject. Instead, Hershey learned he was getting a new job a few hours later when the White House press office issued a press release announcing his reassignment effective February 16, 1970.[25]

⚬⚬⚬

The first Vietnam-era draft lottery was held December 1, 1969. While both Presidents Wilson and Roosevelt had personally observed the initial draft lottery drawings of World Wars I and II, Nixon declined to be present at the 1969 drawing, which was held in a cramped auditorium of the selective service headquarters. As his final public act, Hershey presided, using the same large glass fish bowl he had used in 1942 at the last drawing. Some had argued that a computer should be used, but he insisted on keeping it simple.

At 8 P.M., with a nation tuned in by radio and TV to the event that affected every American male between the ages of nineteen and twenty-six, the lottery opened with a prayer. Then the ranking Republican on the House Armed Services Draft Subcommittee plunged his hand into the bowl, picked out the first of 366 blue capsules, and twisted it open. He handed it to another official, who called the date: "September 14." During a press conference at the White House the previous week, Laird and a presidential aide had explained how the lottery would work. The first birth date drawn would identify those men who would be called first in the 1970 draft, the second birth date drawn marking those who would be called next, and so on. In the 1969 lottery, the birth date number applied to all men born between 1944 and 1950. (Those with deferments would still keep them.) Laird estimated that those men with numbers in the first one-third drawn (without deferments) would certainly be inducted. The middle third *might* be drafted, and those in the last third would escape the draft. Thus, nearly two-thirds of the 850,000 draft-vulnerable men would have a better idea of their fate.[26]

The ninety-minute lottery broadcast was without theatrics—just solemn, dry pronouncements of dates. Yet, in the history of American television, it was one of the most dramatic shows ever broadcast. Thousands of young men huddled in front of TV sets and radios in their living rooms, pool halls, bars, college dormitories, fraternity houses, and apartments. At Berkeley, the sound of "taps" could be heard in the night air, alternating with repetitive "Happy Birthday" choruses.[27] A Wesleyan University sophomore threw his chair through the TV at his fraternity house when his birthday was called first.[28] A Stanford

University sophomore was astonished that his birth date was number 1 while his roommate's was number 366. A Colorado man recalled that on that life-changing night he had drawn number 258, while his identical twin, who had been born a few minutes before him was number 56. "He was drafted within two weeks and served in the Army, and I stayed home. Our relationship has never been the same," he wrote in a 1998 newspaper column.[29] The only eligible member of Nixon's household—son-in-law David Eisenhower—drew number 30.[30] He enlisted in the navy after his 1970 college graduation and served as a lieutenant (j.g.) aboard the guided missile cruiser USS *Albany*. Laird's son, John, got number 325.[31]

Some of the antiwar youth leaders opined that Laird and Nixon had cleverly decimated their radical ranks. "If the purpose of Nixon's lottery was to divide us, he's won quite a victory," remarked a senior at the University of Pennsylvania. No longer was an entire generation subject to the draft. The two-thirds not likely to go to Vietnam had no personal vested interest in protests, though some of those in the top third likely were radicalized into the antiwar movement. Overall, a Harris poll found three-quarters of Americans approved of the lottery, and three-fifths rated the Nixon-Laird handling of the draft as "good to excellent."[32]

The draft and the lottery would reverberate down through the years for the generation of up-and-coming politicians who were then of draft age. Future vice president Dan Quayle, who was given number 210, stayed in the Indiana National Guard, which was probably a safe bet. Men with numbers as high as 215 were drafted in 1970. In Georgia, undergoing pilot training, was future president George W. Bush, who snagged number 327. He had already signed up with the Texas Air National Guard.

A special case in this group was future president Bill Clinton. He had a student deferment while attending Georgetown University and hoped it would continue after he won a Rhodes Scholarship in early 1968 to attend Oxford University in England. At the same time, however, Johnson had abolished deferments for nonmedical graduate students. Because of that, Clinton was reclassified 1-A in March 1968. His family and an influential friend persuaded the draft board in Hot Springs, Arkansas, that the winner of a Rhodes scholarship deserved to spend at least a year at Oxford. (Other Rhodes Scholars also received exemptions because of the pride of small-town draft boards.) After Clinton's year was up, he got his draft notice, but he hastily joined the Reserve Office Training Corps at the University of Arkansas School of Law in Fayetteville. Even though it was against the rules to sign up for the ROTC after a draft notice had been received, Clinton's connections waived that rule for him, and he signed a six-year ROTC commitment, including two years of active duty in the army. Then he got a dispensation from the university's ROTC chief to return to Oxford for a short time. When he didn't return on schedule, Clinton was reclassified 1-A at the end of October. By that time, having been involved in antiwar activities, Clinton had no desire to fulfill his ROTC obligation, so he gambled on the lottery and won. He got lucky number 311, and, two days after the drawing, Clinton wrote a letter to the Arkansas law school's ROTC director thanking him for "saving me from the draft" and saying that it was better if he did not fulfill his military obligation because he was antiwar and antidraft.[33]

⚔

As 1970 dawned, and one month after the first lottery drawing, Lewis Hershey was still titular head of the Selective Service System. During this lame duck period, he was notably unwilling to lead the charge for Laird's draft reforms. The White House had four months to come up with Hershey's replacement while he still held the position. When Nixon had asked for Laird's advice, the secretary said the new director should be a civilian, a younger person, and one who was prepared to head a declining enterprise. (Laird never called for the complete abolition of the Selective Service System because he always believed standby draft authority should be maintained.) Laird told Nixon he had just the man: Curtis Tarr, the assistant secretary of the air force for manpower. He came from Laird's stable of Wisconsin friends and had been a university president. Laird was somewhat reluctant to lose Tarr from the Pentagon, where he had become a cheerleader for Vietnamization.

Tarr met with a White House aide just before Thanksgiving and said "no thanks" to the new job.[34] He wasn't the only one; over a three-month period, a variety of academicians, politicians, and at least two college football coaches declined to serve as selective service director. There was no one to replace Hershey, and the draft reform was losing its momentum. Meanwhile, Tarr was getting an awful feeling. In mid-February, he was at the White House at Pat Nixon's invitation for the unveiling of Andrew Wyeth paintings in the East Room. He was alarmed that the president, while introducing Tarr to the artist, spontaneously provided details about Tarr's background that sounded like Nixon had been reviewing his resume.[35] On March 2 while getting off a plane in San Francisco, Tarr was passed a slip of paper by a young coast guardsman asking him to call Laird as soon as possible.

"Curtis, I hate to do this to you," Laird began.

"Well then, Mel, don't do it!" Tarr responded.

"I have to; the president made me promise that I would. You know that selective service job you talked with the White House about and you didn't want three months ago?" Laird asked.

"Yes, I still don't want it."

"I know, but will you see the president about it?"

"Of course I will talk with him; I can't refuse to do that. But Mel, isn't there some way you can get me out of this? Can't you tell him that you need me?" Tarr pleaded.

"Well, I have tried to impress upon the president that you are doing a good job where you are, but I think you had better try to convince him yourself."

Tarr probably suspected that, truth be told, Laird viewed it as a win-win situation. Either at his current air force position, or as the new Selective Service System head, Tarr was a big plus for the defense secretary. "I certainly did like the idea of having someone from my own team over there," Laird recalled.[36] Two days later, Tarr was in the Oval Office, hoping he would have the chance to decline gracefully. Instead, Nixon thanked Tarr for taking on the new responsibility, predicting it would be "a feather in your cap."

When Tarr started the job, he found the agency in chaos. With more than four thousand local draft boards and fifty state directors acting independently, there was no rhyme or reason to procedures. In the first state he visited, Mississippi, Tarr met with the governor, in part to discuss putting more African-Americans on the board. Governor John Bell Williams was offended. "There isn't any point in putting niggers on the boards because they just can't do the job," he told Tarr. The reform that had most stymied the boards was the lottery. Their antiquated filing system was built on an oldest-first system, and many could not efficiently manage a change-over to youngest first, by lottery number. "The system was a mess," Tarr recalled. "I didn't even share with Mel at the time how, every month for awhile, I thought that the whole thing might fall apart and we couldn't deliver the manpower. I always thought that the worst possible way to get out of the war in Vietnam would be if we couldn't get any men in the Army."[37] Laird was not clueless about the troubled system. In the first three months of 1970, the selective service had fallen 23 percent short of providing the men the Pentagon had requested.

As he undertook an overhaul, Tarr had to suffer through Hershey's carping from the sidelines. As presidential advisor, Hershey was frustrated that Nixon seldom called on him for draft-related advice. When he failed to win the president's ear, Hershey sent his former legislative liaison chief, Bernard Franck, to meet with members of Congress to urge them to oppose draft reform. Considering what an obstacle Hershey was, Tarr asked two White House aides why they just couldn't get rid of him once and for all. Both said it would be impossible to retire Hershey because he would raise a ruckus. "They agreed that they would continue General Hershey in his position until the Army clamored for the four-star slot that he occupies," Tarr recorded. When the army finally did that in April, 1973, seventy-nine-year-old Hershey still refused to resign, so he was involuntarily retired from the service; the only four-star army general in American history ever to have received that rank without having served in a combat role.[38]

24

Into Cambodia:
Objections Overruled

ᴖᴗᴖ

RICHARD NIXON'S PATH TO WATERGATE was littered with friends, aides, and political cronies who were cast aside one by one when they disappointed him. All that remained in the end was a phalanx of sycophants who were not prescient enough to stop the president when he crossed the line. Laird was among the first of Nixon's old friends to fall from grace, possibly as early as the EC-121 shoot-down in March of 1969. In the immediate aftermath of that event, Laird took steps to forestall Nixon's actions that had the significant possibility of starting a war with North Korea. Secretary of State William Rogers, Nixon's old friend, was the next domino to fall, in large part due to the machinations of Henry Kissinger, who wanted Rogers's job. Kissinger managed to retain the president's confidence much longer.

So by 1970, only one year into the new administration, Laird was already out of the inner circle. And that was his preference. In the spring of 1970, when other Cabinet members were beginning to mumble that the president was withdrawing himself from his advisors and behaving erratically, Laird had no such complaints. As far as he was concerned, the less meddling he had from the White House, the better. "I liked to run the thing without contact," he said. "I never had any problem getting through to [Nixon], but I always told Kissinger that I didn't want to. I wanted to run my operation. I always tried, however, to keep the president informed."

The Nixon-Laird friendship had unusual aspects. Laird respected Nixon, stuck by him through his early rocky political career, and worked harder than most to see him elected president. In the end, Laird was one of the last of the president's men to believe that Nixon had nothing to do with the Watergate break-in. Yet, in spite of that loyalty, Laird knew Nixon had a penchant for skullduggery, and Laird had installed his own safeguards for the moment when he lost favor in Nixon's eyes. It began the day Nixon convinced Laird to be defense secretary and signed a cocktail napkin promising Laird full control over all the appointments in the Defense Department. Surrounded by loyal men of his own choosing, Laird was prepared to circumvent any back-channel maneuvers the president might attempt.

That advance work came to Laird's rescue in 1970 when Nixon retreated into himself and his inner circle to plan his most controversial campaign of the Vietnam War—an American ground-force incursion into Cambodia. It was a move that nearly wiped out the public relations gains Laird had accomplished to that point with his Vietnamization program.

The year had begun optimistically enough with Laird's second trip to Vietnam. He and Joint Chiefs Chairman General Wheeler went to the White House Sunday morning, February 8, 1970, to get marching orders from Nixon for their trip the following day. Wheeler's walk had become markedly slower since the year before, and he showed signs of flagging energy. It would be his last trip with Laird. The president wanted the two men to return with a thoroughly honest assessment of Vietnamization as it moved into its second year.

That Sunday morning the headline on the cover of *Newsweek* magazine echoed what was eating at Nixon: "Vietnamization: Will Nixon's Plan Work?" Laird, as always, was confident it would, but Nixon was more circumspect and beginning to make a dangerous plan of his own—an escalation of the war into Cambodia. *Newsweek* had deftly summarized what was at stake: "Should Vietnamization fail, it will present Mr. Nixon with an agonizing choice: to re-escalate the conflict, thereby reviving the bitter domestic discord over Vietnam, or to become the first President in American history to nakedly lose a war."[1]

One objective of Vietnamization, albeit a political one, had already been accomplished by early 1970: taking the war off the front pages every day. Nixon was about to change that, but in February when Laird and Wheeler traveled to Vietnam, all the signs pointed toward the fact that Vietnamization was helping to satisfy the American public. And that fact was sticking in the craw of the Hanoi government. Laird saw the irritation in the more frequent pronouncements from Hanoi casting doubt on the ability of the South to eventually take on its own defense. Laird capitalized on that in a meeting with the press corps when he arrived in Saigon, a meeting that started as an off-the-record cocktail party but evolved into a press conference when Laird inevitably became quotable. "I think that the program of Vietnamization has caused [the enemy] to reevaluate his present strategy, and I think that it should," Laird said, in a message pointed toward Hanoi.

At a second press conference in Saigon, Laird was asked if the progress of Vietnamization was due only to the fact that the North Vietnamese had been holding back. "My answer is no," Laird barked. When asked to elaborate, Laird would only say, "I have confidence in the Vietnamization program. I have confidence that it will work."

Laird's confidence was not blind optimism. In a three-hour meeting with General Abrams, Laird got what he later called the "most optimistic" report on Vietnamization to date. On the way back to the United States, Laird stopped over in Hawaii and wrote a fifteen-page report to Nixon. In that report Laird called the mood in Saigon "cautious optimism" and added, "[W]e now have and can retain sufficient strength to keep the enemy from achieving any kind of military verdict in South Vietnam."[2] Part of the good news Laird delivered to the president in that report was the fact that only about one-fourth of the total enemy forces were Viet Cong and three-fourths were North Vietnamese regulars. Five years earlier, the ratio had been the reverse. It meant that efforts to neutralize Communist sympathizers in the South were meeting with success. The Tet offensive had also gone hard on the Viet Cong, significantly reducing their numbers and their commitment to the cause.

Laird reported that Vietnamization had put Hanoi between a rock and a hard place. The Communists were not strong enough to mount a major offensive at that point to test whether Vietnamization was working, or whether the waning of U.S. troops in the region had weakened South Vietnam's ability to defend itself. "The best the enemy can hope for, therefore, is some localized and short-term tactical military success," Laird advised Nixon.[3] Laird was optimistic about Vietnamization, but Nixon was about to show his own lack of confidence in the plan.

🙰

Nixon's Cambodia incursion—even decades later Laird bristled at the use of the word "invasion" to describe it—had its roots in 1963 when North Vietnam invaded Laos and at the same time took up residence in several provinces of Cambodia that bordered South Vietnam. The Cambodian chief of state, Prince Norodom Sihanouk, officially ignored their presence, having neither the manpower nor the ideological inclination to rid his country of Communists. The North Vietnamese ran most of the Cambodians out of those regions and established "sanctuaries"—outposts along the Ho Chi Minh Trail supply line from which main forces staged cross-border attacks into South Vietnam.

Covert special forces teams crossed into Cambodia regularly to harass those sanctuaries. On Laird's first visit to Saigon in 1969, he had authorized overt "protective reaction" raids across the border in an attempt to limit the enemy's ability to wage war from an allegedly neutral country that was just a day's march from Saigon. The secret Operation Menu bombing by B-52s begun in 1969 was Nixon's ham-fisted approach to the sanctuaries, an approach Laird never had much use for.

When Sihanouk left Cambodia in January 1970 to spend a few months on the French Riviera and hobnobbing with his friends in Moscow and Peking, the opportunity arose for Nixon to strike the kind of blow he had been longing for. On March 18, following a series of anti-Communist demonstrations across Cambodia, the country's parliament dismissed the absent Sihanouk and installed Prime Minister Lon Nol as the new head of state. The new government closed the port of Sihanoukville to North Vietnamese supply ships and attempted to blockade the Communists' overland supply routes.

Persuaded that the Lon Nol government would not last long on its own, Nixon asked Laird on March 25 to have the Pentagon come up with a plan for attacks against the border sanctuaries. Laird was delighted. The sanctuaries had long been a threat to U.S. troops in South Vietnam, and Laird saw an operation against them as a way to showcase the new and improved South Vietnamese army, which had been beefing up in anticipation of fighting the war without American soldiers at its side. In Laird's mind, the operation could be handled strictly by South Vietnamese troops.

The defense secretary knew, even before Nixon asked, that a South Vietnamese operation wasn't what the president had in mind at all. Nixon did not yet trust the South Vietnamese army to go it alone. The Joint Chiefs fell in line with Nixon. Within a day, they forwarded to Laird a plan for a joint U.S.–South Vietnam operation, complete with a list of the American divisions that would cross over the border. Laird slipped into his delay-by-obfuscation mode. On March 26 he sent a laundry list to the chiefs asking them how much the operation would cost, how it would affect the rest of the Pentagon's budget for Vietnamization, what intelligence they had that an American foray into Cambodia would make any difference, and what the risks were compared with "the marginal benefit which might be derived."[4]

But it was too late for those questions. On the same day, Kissinger sent Laird an order from the president: come up with a proposal for a joint American/ South Vietnamese operation into Cambodia within a week.[5] As was Nixon's habit when he knew Laird would not agree, the president didn't admit that he had already made up his mind to send troops into Cambodia no matter what Laird concluded. In this case, he also had to mask his intentions from Rogers, who was likely to join Laird's camp. Nixon initially issued orders that the State Department wasn't to be told about the planning. Then on March 27 he said the U.S. ambassador in Saigon, Ellsworth Bunker, could be informed, but he was not to tell his boss Rogers.[6]

By this time, behind the scenes, Rogers was already privately colluding with Laird to slow down Nixon's push on Cambodia. In a letter he hoped the president would never see, Rogers wrote Laird on April 1 that he had some ideas of "steps we might take to influence Cambodia developments." He included his March 31 memorandum to Nixon, which he confided to Laird was an effort "to highlight our determination to avoid another major involvement in a Southeast Asian country."[7]

Unlike Rogers, Laird didn't stop with memos. He had learned to stay one step ahead of Nixon. On his trip to Saigon in February, Laird had discussed with General Abrams the possibility of a move into Cambodia. Although the topic took up a fair share of their time together, Laird never breathed a word of it in his formal report to Nixon at the end of the trip. The private discussion would later figure prominently in Laird's futile attempt to talk Nixon out of a U.S. operation in Cambodia. Laird's military assistant, Colonel Pursley, sat in on the meeting with Abrams and remembered that the general was confident the South Vietnamese could handle the operation, possibly with some American artillery support from the Vietnamese side of the border, and rescue units if needed.[8] But Abrams's opinion would not stand up to the pressure Nixon was about to put on him.

Through his politician's eyes, Laird could see nothing but misery coming out of a U.S. incursion into Cambodia. It would make a mockery of his claims that Vietnamization was going well, and it could be seen by the American public as an expansion of a war that Nixon had promised to end. Pursley remembers the tone of Laird's arguments: "You're going to pay a pretty high price for this. You'd better expect phenomenal incremental benefits if you're going to pay what any reasonable person is going to recognize as a huge cost in the U.S . . . in terms of public support." If self-determination for South Vietnam is the goal, Pursley remembered Laird arguing, "then launching these big, new massive U.S. combat operations probably isn't going to get you to that kind of an outcome at all."[9]

Nixon was not oblivious to the possible reaction back home to the reports of U.S. troops invading Cambodia. When South Vietnamese troops began making aggressive forays into Cambodia on their own in late March and early April 1970, the reaction in the press was negative. Nixon ordered Ambassador Bunker to ask President Thieu to keep his powder dry until the big picture could be sorted out. But the South kept up the attacks.[10]

Antiwar activists in the United States perked up their ears, and the resultant increase in criticism rattled Nixon. He canceled a trip to his daughter Julie's college graduation, knowing his presence there could touch off a riot. Also preying on Nixon was the need to decide how many American troops would be withdrawn from Vietnam in the fourth round of redeployments. The Laird plan called for bringing home an average of ten to twenty thousand men every month, but the Joint Chiefs wanted to call off any more withdrawals, especially if Nixon really meant to make a major foray into Cambodia. To further shake the president that month, the Apollo 13 space capsule was crippled in orbit around the Moon, and there was a chance the three astronauts would be stranded in space.

On April 17 Nixon flew to Hawaii on a jubilant mission: to greet the Apollo 13 crew that had managed to limp back to Earth. In Hawaii, Nixon huddled with Admiral John McCain, the Pacific area commander-in-chief (CINCPAC commander) who knew just how to pump the president's aggressive war plans with one of his "big red arrow" briefings. Nixon was so impressed with McCain's take on the Communist menace in Southeast Asia, that he invited the admiral back to the Nixon home in San Clemente, California, to give the briefing to Kissinger.

With Nixon planning an invasion of Cambodia and weighing continued troop withdrawals, the last thing Laird wanted him to hear was a McCain pep talk about how the war could be won. Laird was not invited to San Clemente for the big show. Instead he watched from afar as Nixon went on television in California on April 20 and announced that he would withdraw 150,000 troops from Vietnam over the next year—the number Laird had wanted. Nixon had made up his mind about the number possibly as early as April 9, without telling Laird. Presidential aide H.R. Haldeman recorded in his diary on that day that Nixon had set up a meeting for the following week, ostensibly to get input from Laird and Rogers on the next wave of withdrawals, "[b]ut will not tell them the real plan." According to Haldeman, Nixon wanted to leak the news to the *New York Times* and *Washington Post* that he was withdrawing only 40,000 men, and then he planned to surprise everyone with the real figure of 150,000.

Laird was rarely surprised by anything Nixon did. The 150,000 figure sounded good, but Nixon had a way of making less look like more. He ordered Laird to end-load the program by making few withdrawals in the remainder of 1970 and the majority in early 1971. Laird asked for an audience with the president to appeal the decision as soon as Nixon was back in Washington. On April 21 the two men met, and Laird played a card he hoped would resonate with the president. If Nixon didn't take out at least 60,000 men by the November congressional elections, the Republicans could suffer at the polls.[11] Laird recalls telling Nixon that the withdrawal rate had to be steady, and that Abrams couldn't function with troops leaving in fits and starts. Nixon disingenuously promised to weigh Laird's advice. The next day Laird got a memo from Nixon ordering that no more than 60,000 of the 150,000 would be sent home before the end of 1970. It marked a significant slowing in the pace of withdrawals to only about 7,500 men a month.

Laird was sure that the slowdown, coupled with an expansion of the war into Cambodia, would be seen by the American public as a betrayal of a promise to end the war. He wasn't going to let that happen. In August, with the election pressing, Laird persuaded the president to withdraw ninety thousand troops before voters went to the polls. The move was indicative of how Laird managed to have his way throughout the entire withdrawal program by juggling numbers and using his considerable powers of persuasion with Nixon.

Try as he might, however, Laird could not talk Nixon out of sending American soldiers into Cambodia. On April 22, 1970, as South Vietnamese forays into Cambodia intensified and the new Lon Nol government struggled to maintain a foothold, Nixon summoned the National Security Council to the White House for a meeting. A decision had to be made about how and when to attack two Communist strongholds in Cambodia—a region called the "Parrot's Beak" just thirty-three miles from Saigon, and another area code-named the "Fishhook," which was believed to be the hideout for COSVN, the headquarters of the North Vietnamese army in Cambodia.

Laird was selective about attending NSC committee meetings but always had a representative present, preferring to let his underlings hash out the minutiae at the staff level. But this time, after lunching at the Pentagon with the vice premier of China, he went himself to stand up for his position. It was time to test Vietnamization, and Cambodia was a perfect test, Laird argued. "You've got to give them a test some time, but if you throw in American support, that isn't much of a test," Laird recalled telling Nixon. His strongest argument was his understanding from Abrams two months earlier that the general was willing to do the operation without putting U.S. troops over the border into Cambodia. Nixon waffled in the face of confrontation and announced to the NSC that he would authorize a South Vietnamese incursion in the Parrot's Beak using only American air support, not ground troops.

At the meeting Vice President Agnew rattled Nixon by calling the whole debate "pussyfooting." If the sanctuaries were a threat, then why not wipe out both strongholds using all of the American firepower and manpower that could be mustered?[12] After the meeting Nixon fumed over being blind-sided by his vice president, and Agnew was not invited to future discussions on Cambodia. But the seed of doubt had been planted.

On April 26, a Sunday evening, Nixon called the NSC together again. Since the previous meeting, he had been privately briefed by Admiral Tom Moorer, who was then acting chairman of the Joint Chiefs, and in the running to replace the ailing Wheeler. Moorer had explained in detail how U.S. troops could be used to invade the Fishhook while the South Vietnamese were striking in the Parrot's Beak. Nixon had not told Laird about that briefing from Moorer, but Kissinger had informed Laird on the sly. (In his memoirs, Kissinger said he thought it unseemly in that case that the Joint Chiefs should be briefing the president on military operations behind the defense secretary's back.)[13] It was not Laird's only report about the secret briefing. Unknown to Nixon and Kissinger, the chiefs regularly told Laird about any calls from or meetings they had at the White House. Laird insisted that they obey the National Security Act, which said that the chiefs were to be military advisors to the president. But Laird also encouraged the chiefs to fill him in after the fact.

The NSC gathered that Sunday evening, and Nixon sat as if uncommitted while the rest of them got the same briefing from Moorer. Laird and Rogers repeated their objections to a joint operation, and both of them added another caution. It looked like the president was once again putting too much stock in wiping out a COSVN headquarters. Laird reminded Nixon that technically there was no such facility in Cambodia, only a scattering of commanders and outposts that was constantly on the move. Nixon listened and then adjourned the meeting, confident that he had not shown his cards. Immediately after everyone else left, Nixon told Kissinger to issue the order. U.S. troops would cross into Cambodia.

The next day that order—National Security Decision Memorandum 57—was on Laird's desk, signed and initialed by the president lest anyone question his authority. Not surprised, Laird scanned the order for any way he could salvage his position. He found an alarming note in the last paragraph: "The Washington Special Actions Group is designated as the implementing authority for these steps."[14] WSAG was the committee Kissinger had formed to strengthen his and Nixon's authority after the EC-121 crisis when Laird had taken charge of the military response and circumvented Nixon's impulse to attack North Korea. Laird wasn't about to let an NSC committee run an invasion of Cambodia (although he and Deputy Secretary Packard were members of that committee.) He called Kissinger and politely asked to have the memo reworded. Then Laird said he was on his way over to see Nixon and make one last pitch.

Rogers had the same idea. The two Cabinet officers confronted Nixon for an hour that Monday morning. Laird continued to maintain that Abrams didn't think U.S. troops were necessary. To settle the question, Nixon sent a cable behind Laird's back to Abrams asking him once and for all for the "unvarnished truth" on where he stood on the question of American troops in Cambodia. According to Nixon's memoirs, the response from Abrams was unmistakably gung ho: "It is my independent view that these attacks into the enemy's sanctuaries in Cambodia are the military move to make at this time in support of our mission in South Vietnam both in terms of security of our own forces and for advancement of the Vietnamization program."[15]

Laird tells the story with more shades of gray. Yes, Abrams wanted the sanctuaries cleaned out, but as soon as he got the back-channel cable from Nixon asking for the "unvarnished truth," he called Laird. According to Laird's memory of the conversation, Abrams told him the president had asked for a *100 percent guarantee* that if American troops were not used, the South Vietnamese army could accomplish the mission on its own. Abrams, not a man to offer guarantees, apologized to Laird that he could not make such a promise to the president. "They didn't ask him if he could guarantee success using American troops. He would have said no to that question, too," Laird said. Laird told Abrams he understood.

The next day another memo from Nixon—NSDM 58—arrived in Laird's office. The decision to use U.S. troops was firm. The only change from the prior day's order was in the last paragraph. It now said WSAG would "coordinate," not "implement," the Cambodian incursion.[16] It was only a small victory. Laird was stuck with the operation, but he wasn't stuck with taking the blame. The loyalist in him would carry out the president's orders without any public complaint, and he would never speak ill of a battle when brave men were fighting it. But privately he wanted his opinion put in the record. He sent a seven-page memo to Nixon outlining the downside of a U.S. move into Cambodia. "I do not believe the sum total of potential benefits to be decisive in the conflict in Southeast Asia," Laird wrote. He said he didn't think the attacks on the sanctuaries would bring Hanoi to its knees at the Paris negotiations. In fact, Hanoi might become even more obdurate in Paris if the Cambodia operation triggered "strong U.S. popular and Congressional disapproval."[17] Laird's message was tactfully worded but alarming. Things were about to get messy; Congress would not like it; the American people would not like it; and Hanoi would capitalize on that dissent and become even more pig-headed in Paris. Laird told Nixon he was risking American public support for Vietnamization and warned that the casualty rate could go up dramatically.

Nixon didn't buy any of it. He was already busy drafting a speech to announce to the American public on April 30 that the Vietnam War was taking a detour into Cambodia. On the day of the speech, Nixon sent William Safire, his conservative speech writer who had polished the text, to the Pentagon with a courtesy copy for Laird to review. "I went right through the wall, in Safire's presence, seated across from my desk," Laird recalled. "I had to call the president." Nixon had loaded the speech with references to the COSVN headquarters and how it was the prime target of the American mission. Laird said, "I knew we would never hit it and I proved correct. We never did." Nixon was setting the mission up for failure in the public eye because the primary target, announced before the fact, did not exist.

Another line in the speech caught Laird's eye: "For five years, neither the United States nor South Vietnam has moved against these enemy sanctuaries because we did not wish to violate the territory of a neutral nation." Laird's quick call to Nixon included the tactful reminder that American B-52s had been pounding Cambodia for more than a year, and, even though the pilots were dummying their flight logs, the bombing was not the best-kept secret in Washington. Nixon did not take the line out of his speech.

Sometime during the afternoon, Laird got a note from Haldeman. The defense secretary was disdainful of suggestions from the president's young sycophants, and this one was particularly grating. Haldeman instructed Laird on what kind of spin to put on the Cambodia operation after Nixon announced it in his speech. Among the things Laird was supposed to tell the press was that without the incursion the American troop withdrawal program would have ended. Laird didn't believe that for a minute and never used the line.[18]

At 9 P.M. on April 30, 1970, Nixon went on camera, armed with maps and righteous indignation, and announced that thirty-one thousand U.S. troops were at that moment moving into Cambodia to ferret out the COSVN headquarters. (The original plan was to begin the operation two days earlier, but when Abrams consulted his Vietnamese counterpart about the date he was told that the Vietnamese general's astrologer had advised a delay. Laird agreed to wait until the stars were in a better alignment, but he didn't tell Nixon why. "I just told the White House that the weather and things weren't just right," Laird said.)

❧

The American public reaction to Nixon's announcement was immediate and virulent. No matter how he dressed up the operation, and no matter how threatening the sanctuaries were to the U.S. war effort, the American public saw the operation for what it was: an expansion of a war that Americans just wanted out of. The fact that Nixon made the announcement himself on national television contributed to the feeling of escalation. Laird and his public affairs people had urged Nixon to let General Abrams do the briefing in Saigon with as much of a business-as-usual aura as he could muster under the circumstances. But Kissinger advised Laird that the president wanted to make it clear that he was in charge. Laird recalled his reply: "Okay, Henry, but I'm telling you, it would be a lot better if Abrams announced it."

When Nixon woke up the next morning, he decided to visit the Pentagon to show just how "in charge" he was. Outside the entrance, at 8:30 A.M., he was heckled by hundreds of antiwar activists up since the crack of dawn to protest the news he had delivered the night before. Nixon's memoirs didn't mention that encounter. He wrote instead of the warm greeting he received from Pentagon employees inside the building where he was "mobbed by people cheering and trying to shake my hand. 'God bless you!' 'Right on!' 'We should have done this years ago!' they shouted."[19]

But the president was visibly agitated about the protestors when Laird met him at the entrance. Laird figured that Nixon probably was caught off guard, not knowing that protestors were not barred from the grounds but were allowed to take their demonstrations to the steps of the Pentagon's main entrance. Nixon was first escorted to Laird's office and then to the National Military Command Center, where the Cambodia operation was being monitored. Already things were not going as Nixon had hoped. The expectation of striking at a COSVN headquarters was not materializing, the briefers told Nixon. Laird stifled the urge to say "I told you so." "I might have thought it," he later recalled. "I told him [COSVN] would still be very difficult to locate."

Accounts of what happened next vary widely. One Kissinger biographer, Walter Isaacson, gleaned reports from some who were in the room. By their account, Nixon launched into an "obscenity-punctuated harangue" and ordered more enemy base camps added to the list of targets. "I want to take out all of those sanctuaries," he ordered. "Let's go blow the hell out of them."[20] General Westmoreland, who was present, recorded in his memoirs that Nixon "seemed to be in a hurry," cut the military briefing short, and got up to leave. Westmoreland couldn't let him go on that note. "As he rose to leave, I interrupted. The President's unbridled ebullience and his obvious expectation of spectacular results required some adjustment to reality," Westmoreland wrote. The general tried to temper Nixon's expectations with some warnings that the bad weather and the shortage of troops probably would water down the outcome.[21]

As Laird spoke an aside to Westmoreland, thanking him for his words of caution, Nixon strode with his entourage into the hallway where he was again met by what he called "a friendly, cheering crowd." Connecting with one tearful woman whose husband was in Vietnam, Nixon tried to comfort her with a phrase that made the headlines the next morning. "You see these bums, you know, blowing up the campuses. Listen, the boys that are on the college campuses today are the luckiest people in the world, going to the greatest universities, and here they are burning up the books, storming around about this issue.... Then out there we have kids who are just doing their duty. And I have seen them. They stand tall, and they are proud."[22] Nixon's attempt to praise the soldiers was lost in the outrage from the so-called bums.

Laird, who had witnessed a few Nixonian outbursts in their long friendship, didn't remember anything irrational about the president's performance that day. He recalled no presidential obscenities. "That didn't happen," Laird said. "Nixon did not throw that kind of fit over there at all. If they thought he was agitated, they haven't seen him very often." Pursley, who was at Laird's side for the meeting, agreed. While Nixon "clearly was charged and he was a bit agitated, I don't recall any ranting or raving."[23]

The demonstrators who greeted Nixon that morning were just a taste of what was erupting all over the country in response to the Cambodia operation. The antiwar movement had been somewhat subdued since the Moratorium Day protests of the year before. The progress of Vietnamization, the troop withdrawals, and the general weariness with the war had damped the spirit of the movement. But Cambodia had rekindled it. ROTC buildings were set ablaze on at least five college campuses. The atmosphere on some campuses was so tense that administrators closed them down for a short cooling-off period. A riot at Kent State University on the night of May 1 prompted Ohio Governor James Rhodes to call out the National Guard to patrol the campus. On May 3 guardsmen charged students at a sit-in and stabbed some with bayonets. The next day the unthinkable happened. Jumpy guardsmen fired sixty-one shots into a crowd of students, killing four and wounding nine. It was a bloody and tragic fulfillment of Laird's warning.

Laird also saw it as a manifestation of the condition into which the National Guard had fallen—its budget and training neglected by the Johnson administration, while money flowed into the war. In his view, the Ohio guardsmen had too many inexperienced, exhausted young guardsmen who cracked. "A young man, eighteen or nineteen years old, there on guard duty, they're bound to have reactions like that," Laird said. "Now the National Guard is trained much better than they were at that particular time."

The Kent State killings brought one hundred thousand protestors to the White House on May 8. Holed up inside, his home surrounded by a security ring of buses and soldiers, Nixon endured an evening press conference in the East Room at 10 P.M. Later, unable to sleep, he put on a recording of Rachmaninoff's Second Piano Concerto and brooded about Cambodia and the public reaction. Finally, sometime after 4 A.M. on May 9, Nixon summoned his valet Manolo Sanchez, and the two of them, along with a Secret Service agent, drove to the Lincoln Memorial, where more students were camping for the night in protest. One clutch of students near the monument was stunned when the president of the United States approached them and struck up a conversation about the war, about sports, about politics. Then the president's party moved on to the darkened Capitol building. There Nixon made his valet give an impromptu speech from the podium on the House floor while the president applauded from the chair he had once occupied as a congressman. Alerted to the fact that the president was roaming the city, Haldeman joined the entourage at the Capitol. He later described that morning as "the weirdest day so far."[24]

The day after the Kent State killings, Nixon announced to a contingent of congressmen, without consulting his military commanders, that the Cambodia incursion would be over by June 30 and that the American troops would go no more than nineteen miles into Cambodia. The same day, Abrams, trying his best to juggle the politics back home with the military objectives in Vietnam, got a memo from General Wheeler, who was serving out his last few days as chairman of the Joint Chiefs. "[I]t would be very much to our advantage to be able to announce . . . the withdrawal of some forces back to Vietnam as soon as this is operationally feasible and desirable. . . . I do not wish to imply that we would want you to prematurely terminate an operation or in any way jeopardize it just to gain a press advantage. However, it would be highly desirable for higher authority to be in a position to exploit fully the termination of an operation or withdrawal of at least some of the forces engaged in Cambodia."[25]

Abrams wrote back that with the sluggish pace of the war of late, "it took some doing to get people back into the offensive spirit," and there was no way he wanted to dampen their enthusiasm now by announcing a withdrawal when the operation had just begun.[26]

⌒⋎⌒

On May 6, Nixon opened his *New York Times* to find a story quoting anonymous sources saying Laird and Rogers had "serious misgivings" about the Cambodia incursion. Although Laird was dutifully defending the operation at press conferences and in testimony before hostile congressional committees, the president angrily assumed his defense secretary leaked the news of his opposition so he could show clean hands, especially after the Kent State tragedy. Laird was adept at leaking, but this one was not his fault, he said later. He would not have provoked the edgy Nixon at that time, nor would he have let news of his doubts leak during the heat of an operation where American lives were at stake. Laird assumed that the leak came from some staffers in Kissinger's office who had resigned from the NSC staff because they could not sanction the Cambodia operation.

Within a week of Nixon's decision to invade, four of Kissinger's closest staffers, William Watts, Roger Morris, Larry Lynn, and Anthony Lake (who would later serve as national security advisor during the Bill Clinton administration) had resigned in protest. While the four did not openly trumpet their resignations, Laird suspected they were the anonymous sources that planted many of the stories critical of the invasion. "The press was very sympathetic to the people that walked out of the White House," Laird said. "There were quite a few people at that time that were doing a lot of briefing of the press. They never used their names, though."

Laird was painted into a corner. He respected the uses that could be made of the press, and so he did not want to ruin his credibility with reporters by lying to them about his misgivings. But he also did not want to be a naysayer at the height of a critical military campaign. So he issued a short statement saying he had always supported operations against the sanctuaries. At a press conference on May 6, Laird tiptoed around his opposition to Americans in Cambodia. "I supported the use of Americans as required to carry out this very important mission," Laird said, without adding that he didn't think Americans were "required" as ground troops in Cambodia. Then he quickly changed the subject to the success of Vietnamization.[27]

Finally on May 14 while speaking to a small group of reporters at the National Press Club, Laird owned up to his opposition, saying that he had initially not wanted to send in U.S. troops, but that he had changed his mind when it looked like the risk to them might be small.[28] It was one of those half-truths that Laird was capable of spinning when he was cornered. Indeed, he had become more comfortable with the U.S. role when he saw the risk would be minimal. But he didn't know that until the operation was in full swing and it became obvious that the bulk of North Vietnamese troops had abandoned the sanctuaries in advance of the invasion. The enemy opposition was so weak that Laird's original point was proved—the South Vietnamese could have indeed handled it on their own. But Laird could not say that publicly without tipping his hand.

The rumors of Laird's opposition lingered into June. He agreed to appear on a *Meet the Press* TV broadcast on June 4 opposite a friend, columnist Robert Novak. A few days before, Laird had made the mistake of trusting Novak with the details of his true feelings. During the broadcast, Novak came at the question every which way he could, first asking Laird, "[I]n retrospect, do you think that the South Vietnamese troops could have handled this exercise, this operation, without any help from American troops?"

"The South Vietnamese forces have done very well," Laird dodged. Then he tried to change the subject.

"[B]ut you didn't answer the question," Novak came back. "Do you think that they could have handled the incursion into Cambodia without the help of U.S. troops?"

"No," Laird said, and then added a qualifier, "the operation could not have been carried out as successfully."[29]

Decades later Laird was still steamed about the exchange. "I always say the Americans can always do the job better, but I did not say the South could not have done it. I was very careful not to say they could not have done it. I was particularly uncomfortable because I'd talked to [Novak] about the situation, and how I thought the South could have done it alone. That damn Novak knew it because I'd visited with him on Friday before *Meet the Press*, which was on Sunday. I gave him hell afterwards. He knew what he was doing. He wanted me to come out with the position that I'd taken prior to the operation. When the operations are still going on, I just couldn't do that."[30]

Just as Laird would not speak ill of the mission while it was happening, he also would not publicly disavow Nixon's reckless claims that the troops would destroy the COSVN headquarters. When it became obvious that there would be no decisive blow at that target, the White House had to find a new spin to put on the incursion to measure success. General Wheeler suggested emphasizing the tons of supplies that were being captured and how long the enemy might be out of commission because of that. Laird ran up a red flag to that idea in a carefully worded memo to Nixon on May 7. He began by reminding the president that in announcing the invasion on April 30, Nixon had painted it as part of the larger goal of self-determination for South Vietnam. In other words, Nixon had justified the invasion on the larger strategic scale of warfare. And now Wheeler was recommending a retreat to smaller tactical gains as a measure of success. That ran the "risk of turning the dialogue on Southeast Asia into one of statistics and numbers rather than policies and long-term solid accomplishments," Laird cautioned.[31] Laird had been working too hard selling Vietnamization to allow the debate on the war to return to a numbers game of body counts, territory held, skirmishes won, and weapons seized.

At a press conference in Detroit on May 11, Laird was grilled about the statistics and tried to point to the big picture. "I think that the important thing though is not to look at the day-to-day tactical successes of this operation which are many. This operation will be judged on the basis of its overall strategic success. The strategic success of the destruction of the Cambodian sanctuaries will be measured some weeks from now on the basis of the troop withdrawals, on the basis of the reduction of American casualties, and on the basis of the progress of the Vietnamization program."[32]

But because Nixon and others did not pick up Laird's tone, the last offensive action for American ground troops in the Vietnam War was judged not by ideology or strategy, but by statistics. Nixon's own memoirs proudly reported the take: enough weapons to equip seventy-four infantry battalions; a four-month supply of rice for all the Communist troops in the sanctuaries; fourteen months worth of rockets, mortars, and bullets; 11,688 bunkers and military facilities destroyed.[33]

For Laird, the statistics meant only that the enemy had been dealt a temporary setback. "To tell you the truth, I don't see how it affected Vietnam that much," he said in retrospect. "I think it helped to get rid of those supplies. It would have helped more had we used just South Vietnamese forces." Pursley agreed that for all the controversy and negative reaction, the benefits of the invasion were "exceedingly small. The North Vietnamese would have the capability to come back another day from other areas and keep you there almost interminably." On the home front, the operation "agitated and exacerbated contentions between the White House and the Defense Department," Pursley said. "It certainly left a lot of bruises and bad feelings."[34] Some of the fallout landed on Pursley himself. Because of the news leaks that Laird had opposed the operation, Kissinger and Nixon reinstated the wire tap on Pursley's home phone and kept it on for another year, hoping to snare him or Laird in an act of disloyalty to the president.

One enduring impression from the Cambodia operation was that Nixon was so angered by Laird's opposition that he tried to cut Laird out of the planning for the invasion. A Defense Department blue ribbon panel headed by Gilbert Fitzhugh concluded in July 1970 that the Joint Chiefs bypassed Laird and took some of their recommendations directly to Nixon, knowing he would be more sympathetic. But Laird insisted that never happened. Because he opposed the use of American troops, the word spread that Laird was never told about the plan to use them. "That's absolutely false," Laird said. "There was a disagreement and my recommendation was not followed. I was given every opportunity to make my case. The president made his decision after looking over both operational plans, and he insisted on using Americans after I'd had my day in court. I went along. I sent the orders."

The same blue ribbon panel accused the Defense Intelligence Agency of feeding Nixon bad information implying that the COSVN headquarters *could* be located and destroyed. Laird thought that, after the fact, Nixon and Kissinger had tried to blame that DIA report for giving the president enough confidence to announce in his April 30 speech that the COSVN headquarters would be destroyed. "They blamed the DIA," Laird said, "but they had plenty of notice that they should have left that out of that speech." In Nixon's next speech, on June 3, he praised the successes of the ongoing Cambodia operation, saying, "[A]ll our military objectives have been achieved." There was no mention of the COSVN headquarters.

Among the voices raised in protest of the Cambodia invasion was that of Laird's predecessor, Clark Clifford. He called the operation "reckless" and "foolhardy." In an article published in *Life* magazine during the heat of the invasion, Clifford accused Nixon of "leading us more deeply into Vietnam rather than taking us out." He correctly predicted that the operation would "achieve little" but would be praised in "glowing reports" from the administration. Clifford wrote that Nixon should pull American troops out of Vietnam "no later than the end of 1971" and that the faster the United States moved, the more willing the Communists would be to negotiate a peace. As usual Laird could not let Clifford's public posturing go by without speaking to him privately. "I appreciated him keeping the pressure on for the withdrawal of forces," Laird recalled, "but I told him, 'You are very naive if you think a unilateral withdrawal will help us in Paris.'"

As the president had promised, the last American troops were out of Cambodia by the June 30 deadline, one day ahead of a vote by the Senate to ban funding for any future American ground combat forces in Cambodia. The law did not faze Laird. He had already done what he could to make sure there would be no more Cambodian incursions. Two weeks before the operation was over, Laird had his staff draw up rules for future Cambodia operations. "These operations are to be conducted on the ground in Cambodia by indigenous personnel only," the policy said.[35]

General Abrams stewed about the impact that the new rules, including those passed by the Senate, would have on his ability to spy on the sanctuaries. He tried to get Laird to consider an exception to the rules to allow U.S. ground troops to go into Cambodia secretly as "advisors" to South Vietnamese units for the purpose of gathering intelligence about Communist movements in the sanctuaries. Laird refused to budge, saying the president had promised the American people that no more American ground troops would cross into Cambodia.[36]

Laird also refused when the Joint Chiefs asked for blanket authority to continue bombing the Cambodian sanctuaries. "I didn't want unlimited air support without having targets approved by me, but in fact, I never turned down a target request from the Joint Staff or Abrams," he said. Later in the year the Pentagon was accused of continuing to use the bombing for something other than hitting at the Communists as they reopened their supply lines. Some of the air raids looked more like a blatant attempt to provide air support to prop up the Lon Nol government in its own private war to overthrow Communist invaders. Laird insisted that the success or failure of the Lon Nol government was never his concern, even though others in the administration would have widened the war to keep the Cambodian domino from falling to the Communists. "I debated that with Kissinger and with Tom Moorer [soon to be the chairman of the Joint Chiefs]," Laird said. "Everything I did, the basis on which I approved the targets, was, 'How does this affect the Vietnamization program and our withdrawal program and our training program of the South Vietnamese?' I was not involved in other issues. I did not want to get involved in a large operation in Cambodia. I was only interested as it affected Vietnamization. I kept repeating that over and over."

In counterpoint to Laird, the president pushed for more defense of Cambodia. Hamstrung by public opinion and by the Senate's refusal to fund ground operations in Cambodia, Nixon nevertheless held out hope that the United States could save Cambodia from Communism. Kissinger's WSAG committee met on June 15, about two weeks before the end of the Cambodia operation. Nixon showed up to lecture the group on his views and then instructed Kissinger to summarize those views and distribute them in a memo to the Pentagon, the CIA, and the State Department. "We have already accomplished a great deal in Cambodia with our attacks on the Communist sanctuaries and supplies; we now have to ask what more Cambodia is worth to us," the memo said. "Together with other countries we must shore up Cambodia psychologically and militarily; we must take whatever heat is necessary rather than being passive and fail through not trying."[37]

With and later without American help, Cambodia eventually fell into Communist hands in 1975 and endured four years of genocide resulting in the deaths of three million Cambodians. By then Nixon had resigned in dishonor, and Congress had pulled the rug out from under Laird's Vietnamization plan.

Laird congressional
re-election poster

Postcard from Laird's re-election to Congress
campaign—the back featured a recipe for
Wisconsin Cranberry Cake with Hot Wisconsin
Butter Sauce.

Members of the HEW House Appropriations Committee with President John F. Kennedy to present an HEW budget. From left, Rep. George Mahon, (D-TX), President Kennedy, Rep. Robert Sikes (D-FL), Rep. Jamie Whitten (D-MS), Laird, Vice President Lyndon Johnson, Rep. William Natcher (D-KY).

Republican Papers press conference and unveiling of "The Republican Papers," written by Melvin R. Laird.

House Republican Conference summer interns with Congressman Laird on the steps of the Capitol, 1968. The fourth woman from right is Hillary Clinton.

Reception for Secretary of Defense Laird by Admiral McCain in Honolulu.

"Just call me Mel" with Jack Benny and former Miss America, Vonda Van Dyke. Ms. Van Dyke, also a ventriloquist. used Laird as her "dummy" and had no idea he was the Secretary of Defense. *(Reprinted with permission of the National Association of Chain Drug Stores)*

Laird poses in his office in a "Kennedy rocker."

Laird with his assistants, Laurie Hawley (left) and Kathy Weaver, in his Washington *Reader's Digest* office (1988).

Laird arrives in Marshfield on the "Laird Express," a special rail tour from Waukesha to Marshfield, for the 1997 groundbreaking ceremony for the Laird Center.

Sharing a moment on the "Laird Express" with lifelong friend, Robert (Bob) Froehlke, 1997.

Henry A. Kissinger, former President Gerald Ford, and Laird celebrate after the ribbon cutting for the Laird Center, 1997.

Henry A. Kissinger, former President Gerald Ford, and Louis Sullivan with Laird at the Laird Center Dedication, 1997.

Laird in his office at the Laird Center at Marshfield Clinic.

Laird speaking in the Froehlke Auditorium in the Laird Center at Marshfield Clinic.

U.S. Navy Ensign Melvin R. Laird, c. 1945.

The USS *Maddox*, on which Laird served in World War II. The *Maddox*, along with the USS *Turner Joy*, later played a central role in the August 1964 Gulf of Tonkin incident that led to the escalation of the Vietnam War.

Newly elected to the U.S. House
of Representatives, Laird presents
President Dwight D. Eisenhower
with a sample of Wisconsin
cheese and an early invitation to
return to Minoqua, Wisconsin,
for another fishing trip, 1953.

Campaigning for re-election to Congress in 1954.

With his children John,
David, and Alison, 1957.

Laird with his wife, Barbara,
at Laird's home office, prior
to raising a new flag from
the Capitol, 1959.

Vice President Richard M. Nixon passes a dish of Wisconsin cranberries to Laird after the great "cranberry scare" in 1959. This first nationwide food panic was triggered by the anouncement that domestic cranberry products contained trace elements of a weed killer known to cause cancer when fed to laboratory animals in massive amounts.

With Carl Wallace, Leon Parma, and Jack Mills at a gathering of the Chowder and Marching Club, 1956.

With Congessman John E. Fogarty (D-RI), right, at the World Health Organization in 1959. During the 1950s and '60s, Laird and Fogarty worked in a bipartisan manner on a number of initiatives in the field of medical research and education, including the National Institutes of Health, the Centers for Disease Control, twelve regional cancer centers, and the National Library of Medicine.

Viewing a model of the McArdle Cancer Research Center at the University of Wisconsin–Madison, one of twelve regional cancer centers initiated with Laird's active support. Pictured with Laird, from left to right: McArdle director Harold Rusch; Dr. Kenneth Endicott, director of the NIH Cancer Institute; and University of Wisconsin president Fred Harvey Harrington, 1962.

Laird on a canoe trip with his daughter, Alison, along the Wolf River on the Menominee Indian Reservation in Wisconsin, 1968.

Laird fields questions from high school students on Laird Youth Leadership Day at the University of Wisconsin–Stevens Point. Laird began the program in 1958 to promote leadership among young people from central and northern Wisconsin. In addition, Laird endowed the Helen C. Laird Theater at the University of Wisconsin–Marshfield.

Upon becoming secretary of defense in January 1969, Laird became a popular subject for political cartoonists, who often depicted his head in the shape of a missile. *(Right: A 1969 Herblock Cartoon, © 1969 by the Herb Block Foundation, reproduced with permission. Below: © 1969 by Bill Mauldin, reproduced with permission of the Mauldin Estate.)*

Responding to questions at a press conference, June 1969.

Secretary of Defense Laird with President Nixon during Vietnam discussions in the White House Cabinet Room, September 1969. U.S. Ambassador to Vietnam Ellsworth Bunker and Secretary William Rogers are seated on Nixon's right.

Laird with newly appointed Deputy Secretary of Defense David Packard, 1969.

Laird with then
Air Force Colonel
Robert Pursley, who
served as Laird's
military assistant
from January 1969
to early 1972. Pursley
was later promoted
to lieutenant general.

Laird threw himself behind the Go Public Campaign, launched in March 1969 to pressure North Vietnam into treating prisoners of war humanely. At this June 1969 press conference, he is joined by the wives of POWs in an effort to raise the American public's awareness of the extent of the prisoners' mistreatment.

In May 1969, cartoonist Bob Stevens depicted Laird's efforts as a ray of hope to prisoners of war. The results of the Go Public Campaign became clear only several years later, when returning POWs reported an improvement in their treatment in mid-1969. *(Reprinted with permission of Bob Stevens and Copley Newspapers.)*

Laird with South Vietnamese General Ngo Quang Truong, February 1970. Distinguishing himself in South Vietnam's response to the Tet Offensive in 1968, and playing the leading role in the defense against the Easter Offensive of 1972, Truong earned widespread respect among U.S. military leadership. General H. Norman Schwarzkopf, a Vietnam veteran, would later call Truong "the most brilliant tactical commander I'd ever known."

Laird with Army General Creighton Abrams, commander of U.S. forces in Vietnam, February 1970.

Nixon, Laird, and Packard at the Pentagon, May 1, 1970.

Laird lunching with troops aboard the USS *Little Rock*, 1970.

Laird with his mother, Helen Connor Laird, on the occasion of the dedication of the Central Wisconsin Regional Airport, May 1970. Wisconsin Governor Warren P. Knowles descends the steps behind them.

Japanese Defense Minister Yasuhiro Nakasone meets with Laird at the Pentagon in September 1970. This meeting and immediate friendship led to the first-ever visit to Japan by a U.S. secretary of defense the following summer, when Laird and Nakasone agreed to a new burden-sharing arrangement. Nakasone became prime minister in 1982.

Laird, Air Force General Daniel "Chappie" James Jr., and Hal Short, owner of the Washington Senators, look on as Army Master Sergeant Daniel L. Pitzer, who spent four years as a POW, throws out the first ball of the 1971 baseball season at Kennedy Stadium in Washington, D.C.

Laird, with his friend German Defense Minister Helmut Schmidt, reviews the honor guard at the Pentagon's River Entrance, July 1971. Schmidt became chancellor in 1974.

Laird and fellow Congressmen Gerald R. Ford (R-MI) and Bob Michel (R-IL) at Burning Tree Club in Bethesda, Maryland, discussing their favorite subject—politics—prior to a Saturday afternoon tee-off, November 1971.

Morning staff meeting in Secretary Laird's office, June 1972.

Laird with General Omar Bradley at the dedication of the Pentagon corridor named in Bradley's honor, June 1972.

Laird illustrating final Vietnam troop withdrawals at a press conference, October 1972.

Laird at the last of the regularly scheduled breakfasts with National Security Advisor Henry A. Kissinger, January 1973.

Laird with women who made flag rank (general or admiral) during his tenure as secretary of defense, 1973. Prior to Laird's new initiative on women in the military, women had never been promoted to flag rank.

During the energy crisis of 1973–74, in his role as counselor for domestic affairs, Laird urged Americans to turn down their thermostats and start wearing sweaters—advice that was promptly spoofed in this *New York Times* cartoon. *(Reproduced with permission of Zenowij Onyshkewyeh.)*

Laird with Henry Kissinger (right) and Gerald Ford (below) at the dedication of the Melvin R. Laird Center for Medical Research at Wisconsin's Marshfield Clinic, September 1997.

"DON'T THINK IT WASN'T GREAT WORKING FOR YOU, DICK"

TO MEL LAIRD — GOOD LUCK AND BEST WISHES ON YOUR NEW ADVENTURES — GENE BASSET

Laird resigned from his position in the Nixon White House in February 1974. At the press conference where he made his announcement, he encouraged the House Judiciary Committee to undertake its constitutional obligation to consider impeaching the president. *(Reprinted with permission of Scripps Howard News Service.)*

Laird with Kissinger, Ford, and wife Carole Laird at the Laird Center dedication.

Laird informally advised Secretary of Defense Donald H. Rumsfeld throughout his six-year tenure in the George W. Bush administration. Meeting with Rumsfeld in February 2001, Laird reminded his friend that "it's a helluva lot easier to get into a war than it is to get out of one." In this meeting they were joined by author Dale Van Atta, at left.

The Laird family in front of the Marshfield, Wisconsin, home where Melvin Laird spent his childhood.

Governor Warren Knowles of Wisconsin and Secretary of Defense Laird, 1969.

Laird at his confirmation hearing for Secretary of Defense, 1969. Deputy Secretary of Defense David Packer is seated to his left.

Laird receives the Presidential Medal of Freedom from President Nixon, 1974.

Laird with then Governor of California Ronald Reagan, 1960.

25

Sea Changes

ON A SWELTERING MORNING, July 2, 1970, Laird stood in a hangar at Andrews Air Force Base, surrounded by the crème de la crème of the U.S. military. The whine of a Strategic Air Command tanker jet outside on the tarmac threatened to drown out Laird's words as he rose and approached a microphone to address the crowd. Front and center was General Earle Wheeler, retiring that day after thirty-eight years in the army and six years as the chairman of the Joint Chiefs of Staff.

Wheeler had heart trouble. He should not have stayed on the job as long as he did and had expected Laird would let him retire soon after Nixon took office. But Laird had recognized in Wheeler a loyal and honorable soldier, an innovator, and a team player. "For the last eighteen months," Laird told the assembled brass, "he has been among my closest associates, among the most trusted advisors, and the warmest of friends.... I shall miss him very much."

Seated near Wheeler was his replacement, Admiral Thomas Moorer, whom Nixon had announced two months earlier would be bumped up from chief of naval operations to the center seat in the Joint Chiefs' circle. As cunning as he was distinguished, as political as he was military, Moorer would require watching. He would try repeatedly to circumvent Laird's wishes and cut the defense secretary out of the chain of command to the president. Eventually he would preside over the most bizarre story of intrigue in the history of the Joint Chiefs—a plot to spy on the White House staff and steal secret documents from Henry Kissinger.

Laird had taken a gamble on Moorer. Although no formal rotation among the services was required in the chairman's seat, the navy's turn was past due. Of seven chairmen since the position was created in 1947, only one had been air force and one navy. The rest had been army generals—a source of some irritation to the other services. Laird could have picked any military officer he liked. His top military assistant, Colonel Pursley, was shocked to learn Laird was considering Moorer. "The Navy was very keen on Tom Moorer," Pursley recalled, but he wasn't. He had seen Moorer try to circumvent Laird's predecessor Robert McNamara on a procurement issue. Pursley concluded that Moorer "was insubordinate—that's about the only word you could use, and that may be too kind." A military assistant to three defense secretaries in succession, Pursley didn't mince words about Moorer's unsuitability for the job. "He was, quite frankly, a devious kind of guy. He was not to be trusted."[1] Pursley told Laird as much during the selection process.

Moorer ended up with the job because of choices Laird later said he regretted. Laird had preferred Marine Corps Commandant General Leonard F. Chapman Jr., and choosing a marine for chairman would have been a bold move. At the time, the marines service chief was not even a formal voting member of the Joint Chiefs. But Laird didn't pick the marine because that was exactly what Nixon wanted him to do. The president had a close friend, Marine General Robert E. Cushman Jr., who had been Nixon's military aide when he was vice president. If Laird promoted Chapman to be chairman, then the way would be opened for Cushman to be the new commandant of the Marine Corps. "But I didn't do it. I shouldn't say this," Laird laughed sheepishly, "but if Nixon wouldn't have suggested it, I might have made Chapman the chairman. In retrospect, maybe I should have followed Nixon's suggestion. But he had an ulterior motive for it, and I didn't like that."[2]

If Nixon had an ulterior motive, so did Laird. He wanted Moorer out of the chief of naval operations slot so he could fill it with a relatively young navy admiral, Elmo "Bud" Zumwalt Jr. Choosing a marine to be chairman would have shaken up some generals, but promoting Zumwalt was an equal jolt to the admirals in the navy. Zumwalt was one of the navy's fastest-rising, most savvy admirals, and his meteoric ascension had ruffled feathers, including those of Admiral Moorer. In late 1968 Moorer had promoted him to three-star admiral and put him in charge of the riverine forces in South Vietnam, the so-called brown-water navy. Moorer reckoned that it was a job at which the upstart was doomed to fail. Zumwalt later confirmed, "Moorer's way of getting rid of me: *Promote the son of a bitch and nobody will ever hear from him again.*"[3]

But Zumwalt had performed well in the job and, more importantly, had embraced and carried out Laird's Vietnamization program. Zumwalt privately believed that American ground troops should never have been committed to South Vietnam, so he became such an enthusiastic fan of Vietnamization that he managed to turn 80 percent of all U.S. brown-water combat vessels over to the South Vietnamese by mid-1970. He moved so fast that, by year's end, the U.S. inland naval forces could be totally withdrawn.

Abrams had been the first to plant the seed with Laird to consider Zumwalt for chief of naval operations. In early 1970 Laird instructed Navy Secretary John Chafee to make sure he included Zumwalt among the three names to be considered as the next CNO.

"But Bud's never had a fleet," Chafee noted. All the former navy chiefs had commanded at least one of the navy's four fleets; Moorer had commanded two.

"That's a bunch of bullshit!" Laird responded quickly.

Chafee later chuckled when recalling the dress-down. "That was Mel's reaction, and it was Mel all over. It was, 'What the hell difference does it make?'"[4]

There were many other obstacles to the Zumwalt selection. The navy chiefs traditionally had been aviators or submariners. And there were more than thirty admirals who would have to be passed over to reach down to Zumwalt's rank and seniority. Also, Zumwalt had said some things that indicated he would shake up the navy. He had freely spoken about the need to root out racism, overhaul disciplinary practices, promote minority and female officers, and otherwise overturn centuries of tradition. All of that was music to Laird's ears, but there was serious opposition at the White House. Military assistants to Kissinger, including Alexander Haig, were grumbling about Zumwalt, whom they suspected of being a peacenik. When Laird got wind of the developing opposition, he called Kissinger and said, "Henry, you understand this is going to be the man, and it would be a great mistake to test my appointive power on this issue." Kissinger promised and delivered his support.

No one was more surprised at the choice of Zumwalt than Moorer. He "damn near went nuts," Laird recalled. "He spent a lot of time in my office, for two days, concerned that Zumwalt wasn't qualified. He felt that his personality wasn't right to assume command. He had serious questions about Zumwalt's ability." When Moorer finally realized that pleading with Laird wasn't going to change the boss's mind, he walked back into his office, shut the door, and soundly kicked a trash can across the room.[5] Zumwalt was the price Moorer would have to pay if he wanted the highest uniformed job in the military. Thus began a contentious relationship between Laird and Moorer that ranged from simple cat-and-mouse games to outright spying by Moorer as each tried to stay one step ahead of the other.

⌇

As Vietnamization picked up steam, Laird could see even more clearly the biggest stumbling block in the way of total success: the "piaster problem." The South Vietnamese economy was completely propped up by the United States, from the cost of the war to the stabilizing of the currency—the piaster. Laird had reminded Nixon of that in his report after the second trip to Saigon in February. Like a lenient parent with an open wallet, the United States had created a dependent child. "As part of the war effort, designed to attract popular support to the cause, we have followed a policy of raising the standard of living for the populace rather than imposing a regime of austerity," Laird wrote the president.[6] With $3.6 billion in U.S. nonmilitary aid to South Vietnam already spent over the course of the war, above and beyond the $105 billion cost to the United States of fighting the war to that point, Congress was tired of doling out money.[7] And Saigon was getting comfortable with its unrealistic view of what the United States could continue to do. "This is a matter to which we and the South Vietnamese must devote immediate and concerted attention," Laird warned in his memo to Nixon.

It didn't happen, and Laird became a chorus of one on the subject of the South Vietnamese economy over the next three years. On April 4, 1970, Laird wrote again to Nixon warning, "[T]he Vietnamese economy is a major uncertainty and perhaps the weakest link in the Vietnamization program. Neither our mission in Saigon nor we in Washington have given the issue adequate attention."[8] South Vietnam was in danger of not meeting its own military payroll that year, dissatisfaction was rampant among its soldiers because of their low pay, and desertion was a constant threat. If Saigon couldn't hold its own army together because of its budget problems, then U.S. troops could be called back to take over the battle again.[9]

On May 15 Laird gave Kissinger a report with more dire warnings and a recommendation to focus on building up the Vietnamese private-sector economy. "Current U.S. strategy on the economic front is primarily designed to prop up the war-torn Vietnamese economy while momentum is gained on the military and political fronts," the report concluded. "Unless a sound and expanding economic system can be established in [South Vietnam], as in Korea and Taiwan, the South Vietnamese may not be able to shoulder the major share of their own defense responsibilities for at least a decade to come."[10]

In another memo sent on August 11, Laird reminded Kissinger of "the serious concern I expressed to you about implications of the economic situation in South Vietnam for Vietnamization."

Two days later Kissinger issued National Security Decision Memorandum 80, titled "Vietnam Economic Policy."[11] It pledged a $750 million ceiling of foreign exchange support, with Defense Department assistance, and tepidly offered generalized goals such as attempting to tweak sales of imported American rice in South Vietnam. Laird knew the policy was no more effective than spitting in the wind.

He continued to harp on the economic aspects of Vietnamization because he felt the South Vietnamese economy was a bigger threat to success than the enemy was. Failing to get much response from the White House, Laird began the touchy job of persuading the Saigon government to cut the fat out of its own military budget by reducing the size of its army. In a memo to the Joint Chiefs on June 5, Laird requested that General Abrams begin a review of the South Vietnamese army to see how many soldiers could be sent back to civilian life. With that army flush from a credible performance in the Cambodia invasion, Laird felt it was time to make the first cut of one hundred thousand troops to bring it down to one million men.[12]

It took the chiefs six months to respond to Laird's suggestion, and the answer was "no." "[T]here is no indication that reductions below the 1.1 million level will be feasible in the near future," the chiefs wrote back on December 1.[13] Laird was learning that withdrawing U.S. troops was a cakewalk compared to downsizing the South Vietnamese army. Admiral Moorer and the Joint Chiefs were not about to encourage any cutbacks, even in the face of an economic meltdown in Saigon.

The economy at home was almost as worrisome to Laird as the picture in Saigon. Scaling down the U.S. operations in Vietnam meant that the Defense Department had to show some sort of "peace dividend"—a budget reduction as the war wound down. Yet Laird needed to hold onto as much money as he could to resuscitate U.S. defense operations elsewhere that had suffered from the drag of the war. A frequent target of Laird's budget scissors was the air war in Vietnam—a money-sucking operation that Laird felt yielded too little to justify it.

At one of their regular breakfast meetings in early June 1970, Laird and Kissinger talked about the failings of tactical air operations. On June 5 Laird followed up with a memo hoping to get Kissinger to see the light, and perhaps to influence Nixon, who was a big fan of the bombing campaign. Bombing of North Vietnam was not allowed, but bombing of the enemy supply lines through Laos, Cambodia, and South Vietnam had become big business. "Despite the intensity of this interdiction bombing, we have apparently not been able to reduce logistics flows to the point that enemy activity levels in South Vietnam are significantly curtailed," Laird wrote to Kissinger. In the prior year, the Defense Department had spent $3.5 billion on aerial bombing—about one-fourth of the cost of the war. Yet the enemy rebuilt and resupplied seemingly overnight. If anything was slowing the enemy, it was the loss of men in battle, not the loss of trucks and supplies along the Ho Chi Minh Trail, Laird said.[14]

Laird sent the memo and headed off for NATO meetings in Europe. But his deputy, David Packard, kept up the drumbeat while Laird was gone. Packard wrote to Kissinger on June 18 urging a cutback in the bombing budget. "The magnitude of our air operations is unprecedented," Packard said. "Since 1965, we have dropped over 4.5 million tons of bombs on Southeast Asia, which is more than twice the tonnage we dropped in all theaters during World War II and seven times that dropped in the Korean War."[15]

At the same time Admiral Moorer, still acting chairman of the Joint Chiefs and two weeks away from taking over officially, was lobbying for more use of air power. When Laird asked the chiefs in June to come up with other ideas for cutting off the enemy's supply lines, Moorer responded with the status quo. "The Joint Chiefs of Staff have reviewed the current interdiction strategy and consider the present concept sound," Moorer wrote in a top secret memo to Laird on June 15, the same day Packard was giving Kissinger an earful on the poor results of the air campaign. Moorer added that increased cross-border air raids would help, and he couldn't resist the opportunity to get a dig in about the ban against bombing North Vietnam itself. "The most effective strategy ... would be to attack the system ... from the ports of entry in North Vietnam to the individual enemy soldier in the field," Moorer wrote. In this war, he added, no bombing is allowed until the supplies cross into Laos.[16]

Once again Laird was a chorus of one, bucking the president and the Joint Chiefs. Yet he kept singing the same song: building up the South Vietnamese army, not dumping more bombs, was the long-term solution. Laird's personal files on the war are littered with requests from Moorer for permission to bomb more targets—called "strike authorities"—in North Vietnam and to pick up the pace of bombing in Laos and Cambodia. The targets in North Vietnam were frequently surface-to-air missile (SAM) launchers that threatened American reconnaissance planes flying over the North. The SAMs also harassed bombers working over Laos and in the demilitarized zone between North and South Vietnam. Moorer pushed for blanket authority to bomb the SAM sites, while Laird was only willing to approve authority for one-time strikes, as long as the bomber pilots had some proof that a SAM site was actively being used against U.S. reconnaissance flights. Those flights had been allowed to continue after President Johnson had stopped bombing runs over the North in 1968. By 1970 they were the chicken and the egg—an invitation to an attack from the SAMs that then gave the B-52s an excuse to retaliate with more bombs.

᠆᠊᠆

The fall of 1970 gave Laird plenty of justification for his argument that Vietnam was sapping the resources of the Defense Department and could leave the United States vulnerable when there were other fires to be put out around the world. What would come to be called "Black September" in the Middle East began as all Mideast conflagrations begin—in ancient history. The immediate precedent was the Israeli victory in the 1967 Six Day War, in which the Jewish state won territory, including Jerusalem and the west bank of the Jordan River. Palestinians fled east in such numbers that, when added to the exodus from previous conflicts going back to 1948, they soon outnumbered the residents of their host country, Jordan.

Jordan's King Hussein, an Arab moderate, was struggling to keep armed raiders from Yasser Arafat's Palestine Liberation Organization from crossing the border from Jordan into Israel to wreak havoc. And Hussein had nineteen thousand Iraqi soldiers camped in his country; they had come to fight the Israelis in the Six Day War and never left. Sporadic armed battles between the Palestinian guerrillas, known as the *fedayeen,* and the king's troops continued throughout the summer of 1970, particularly after the Palestinians tried twice to assassinate Hussein. The *fedayeen* had become increasingly arrogant and lawless, assuming the dimensions of an independent armed power within Jordan. With the country on the edge of all-out civil war, Hussein hesitated to act.

The crisis was gravely escalated on September 6 when hijackers from one of the most extreme groups of the *fedayeen,* the semi-Marxist Popular Front for the Liberation of Palestine (PFLP), hijacked one Swiss and two U.S. airliners in Europe.[17] One of the American planes was diverted to Cairo, where it was blown up after the passengers had disembarked. The other two were forced to land at a remote desert airstrip in Jordan. Palestinian commandos surrounded the planes on the dirt field and wired them with explosives. The PFLP announced that the passengers would be released only if PFLP terrorists jailed throughout Europe and Israel were released within seventy-two hours. If the demand was not met, the 306 passengers—many of them Americans—would be blown up along with the planes.

Laird quickly began deploying American military resources to the area. The buildup in the next two weeks would eventually include twenty-thousand American troops and three aircraft carriers. When Laird convened his weekly staff meeting on September 8, there was only one piece of good news: the *fedayeen* had released 127 passengers, all the women and children. At that meeting Admiral Moorer revealed that two Pentagon officials and a military enlisted man were among the passengers.[18]

That afternoon Laird engaged in a lengthy discussion about the crisis with Nixon, Kissinger, Secretary of State Rogers, Attorney General John Mitchell, and FBI Director J. Edgar Hoover at the White House. During that meeting the only order the president gave Laird was to take the "lead responsibility" in putting armed guards on American airliners and electronic security devices at airports to prevent future hijackings. Otherwise he listened laconically to Laird's assessment that no successful rescue attempt could likely be made. Laird remembers that during the meeting when the talk got tough, "I was trying to keep people cool about it." Unbeknownst to Laird, Nixon had earlier told Kissinger that he wanted to use the hijacking as a pretext to strike back against the Palestinian terrorists in Jordan, but the president said nothing about that at the meeting.[19] Laird had known him long enough to discern suppressed rage, dangerously fed by a feeling of impotence.

So Laird was not altogether surprised when he got a call from the president giving him an order so controversial that neither Nixon nor Kissinger decided to include it in their memoirs.[20] The president apparently had had a few drinks, and he ordered Laird to "bomb the bastards."[21] He wanted navy planes from the aircraft carrier *Independence* in the Mediterranean to bomb at or near the airfield where the hijacked planes were being held, and possibly other *fedayeen* encampments. Laird didn't know what Nixon expected to accomplish. "He wanted to drop a few bombs to get their attention," Laird surmised. Also, he knew the president was obsessed with stemming the tide of Soviet influence in the region, that he suspected the Russians were somehow behind the hijackings, and that he liked to make them think he was a bit crazy and unpredictable. So Nixon "probably wanted to show the Russians that, by God, they couldn't tell what he might do."

But Laird knew it would be the height of folly to "bomb the bastards." Laird's staff had already weighed various options that day, according to a classified after-action report, "but direct U.S. military action was ruled out primarily because of the virtual certainty that the introduction of U.S. military forces into Jordan would result in the death of the hostages." Additionally, "such overt U.S. action would increase the risk of a direct U.S.-Soviet confrontation and almost certainly destroy the U.S. Middle East peace initiative."[22]

Laird chose not to dispute the commander-in-chief's instructions directly. "I didn't fight with him over the telephone," Laird recalled. "I told him we would do the best we could. I didn't have a big argument about it; I just didn't do it." Fearing Nixon's next call would be to the Joint Chiefs, Laird immediately called Moorer. "If you get a call tonight," Laird warned, "just let him know that the weather is bad, because we're not going to make any strike on that airfield in Jordan." The weather remained "bad" for forty-eight hours, until Nixon changed his mind about the bombing.

Was it Laird's place to ignore orders from the president of the United States? "It's something I don't like to talk about," Laird said carefully in recalling that incident and other times when he felt Nixon was being rash. "Nixon liked to do things at night. He would call sometimes at very peculiar hours, and you knew probably he was having a couple of snorts with [friend] Bebe Rebozo or someone like that. I was always very careful about that."

Kissinger's memoirs are replete with stories of rapid-fire phone calls from the president in the middle of the night, often with orders that Kissinger would put aside to be examined in the sober light of day. In this instance Kissinger not only knew about the order, but buttonholed Laird at least once over the next two days to find out why the bombing had not occurred. On other occasions when Kissinger anticipated what the president was likely to do when in a particular mood, he would forewarn Laird. "He would call me and say, 'Mel, the president's up at Camp David this evening. If you get a call, don't get too excited about it.'" Kissinger would swap tales with other staffers about those calls, but Laird was not comfortable with that kind of talk. Thirty years later, with Nixon dead and the facts relegated to history, Laird still didn't want to say that Nixon had a drinking problem. "I want to allude to the fact that sometimes orders that came at night were not good orders to follow," he demurred.

The night of September 15, 1970, was supposed to have been a pleasant respite for Laird. During a black tie dinner at the Airlie House conference center in Warrenton, Virginia, he was being honored with the Statesman in Medicine award for his work in Congress on health issues. But with Washington in a dither over the Mideast crisis, many at the event were distracted. The president phoned his congratulations from the White House. Kissinger was at the dinner but kept taking urgent phone calls until, after consultation with Laird, he returned to the White House. So, midway through the banquet, Kissinger, Admiral Moorer, and CIA Director Richard Helms left the estate by helicopter and convened an emergency meeting of the Washington Special Action Group at the White House, still elegantly dressed in their dinner jackets.

During the week following Nixon's order to bomb Jordan, Laird's level-headed response was vindicated. The PFLP hijacked a fourth plane, a British airliner, on September 9 and took another 115 hostages. Three days later they blew up the empty planes. Eventually all the hostages were released unharmed, and Nixon began to focus on the emerging threat to Jordan. King Hussein could not allow the belligerent *fedayeen* to challenge him further without re-sponse. While the Washington elite had been at Laird's award dinner, Hussein had secretly informed the U.S. embassy in Jordan that the following day he would disband his civilian government and declare martial law. The *fedayeen* openly defied the new government, unified themselves under Arafat's PLO banner, and launched a countrywide insurrection on September 17. With the large-scale outbreak of civil war throughout Jordan, Laird ordered the attack aircraft carrier *Saratoga* to join the *Independence* one hundred miles off the coast of Israel. He directed four more destroyers and two attack submarines to the area and alerted army units in Europe and the 82nd Airborne Division at Fort Bragg to prepare for battle.

On September 19, when it appeared King Hussein was winning without foreign assistance, elements of the Syrian army, crudely disguised as *fedayeen*, crossed Jordan's northern border to join the *fedayeen*. Estimates of the number of tanks that rolled into Jordan over the next two days ranged from several dozen to more than three hundred. King Hussein asked for aerial reconnais-sance at one point, and Nixon turned to the Israelis for overflights. But they wanted to do more than just take pictures. On September 22 the Israeli em-bassy in Washington sent a message to the White House saying they wanted to strike from the air, and possibly send in ground troops.

Laird didn't like the Israeli proposal one bit. He thought King Hussein could hold on by himself because Laird rightly assumed that the first intel-ligence reports on the size of the Syrian intervention were grossly inflated. His fear was that the Israeli involvement would tip the delicate Mideast balance into a full-fledged conflagration, involving all the other Arab states. Nixon and Kissinger had similar concerns, but, in the heat of the crisis, they made costly pledges to the Israelis that threatened to backfire in the future. Within a day, the need for Israeli intervention was moot. On September 23 the Syrians with-drew. The civil war was all but over except for the formal signing of a fourteen-point accord between King Hussein and Arafat on September 27.

～

Laird did not let up on his oversight and interest in the Mideast in the months that followed. He believed the war could be won and the peace still lost. The White House was in a mood to give the Israelis whatever they wanted, without full regard for their already dominant military superiority. During the previous summer Laird had been almost a lone voice for withholding America's most advanced military technology in the face of increasing demands from the Israelis. At the time, Nixon was trying to induce the Israelis to sign a cease-fire with the Egyptians over disputed Suez Canal territory and troop placements. On June 5, in a top-secret memorandum to Nixon, Laird concluded that Israel's request for more F-4 fighters was counterproductive. "Israel, which already has a very substantial bombing superiority over its combined Arab foes, has no immediate need for such aircraft: against the Arabs they are unnecessary, and against the Soviets they would be insufficient," he wrote. "We must not permit ourselves to be pressured into actions which will weaken our [peace] initiatives. We are looking for long-term solutions, and sleight of hand maneuvers to meet short-term Israeli aircraft requests pose too great a risk to be acceptable."[23] Nixon agreed, for the time being.

In early July the Israelis had urgently reported that the situation along the Suez had worsened. The Soviets had assisted the Egyptians in quickly setting up advanced surface-to-air missile batteries, which threatened Israeli air dominance. Laird repeatedly cautioned the Israelis that there was no surefire protection against the SAMs, as the United States had learned in Vietnam. Israeli planes would be shot down, and, in a war of attrition in which the Soviets supplied Arab countries, the Israelis would inevitably lose. The only viable long-term solution was peace.

The Israelis backed off their demands briefly, until an accord was signed with the Egyptians on August 7. After that, their requests increased by quantum leaps. The Pentagon had a program to evaluate the Israeli "orders," and wryly named it Project Binge. At one point Warren Nutter, head of International Security Affairs at the Pentagon, wrote Laird with alarm, "the list of Israel's 'wants' is limited only by their knowledge, which is extensive, of our latest and most advanced weapons."[24]

After the Jordanian crisis, Laird could hardly hold back the flow of Israeli arms requests because an ecstatic Nixon, flush with victory, wanted to show his gratitude to the brave Israelis. In an October 3 memo to the president, Laird recommended against providing the most-advanced equipment Israel had asked for, some of which did not even exist "except in the research and development stage." Supplying Israel, "given present Israeli intentions and in the absence of peace talks, carries with it certain serious risks.... [T]here is a grave danger here that the Soviets would respond by further escalating the conflict, thus placing Israel in jeopardy and bringing the U.S. closer to a direct confrontation with the Soviets."[25]

At Laird's insistence, Nixon denied the Israelis several specific military items, but otherwise the president pledged a $500 million arms package—most of it coming out of the Pentagon's budget. ("There is a tendency by some to feel we can finance almost anything in the Department of Defense," Laird groused in one of his staff meetings.[26]) In December, as Israel's Minister of Defense Moshe

Dayan visited the United States, Laird implored Nixon in an exceptionally tough memo to resist a rush of arms to Israel. Catering to Israel meant "deferring what I consider to be higher-priority U.S. needs" such as NATO and Vietnam, and "it would further increase Israel's already very considerable advantage in attack aircraft.... I am disturbed that what may be our best chance for real peace in the Middle East will be let slip by an Israeli leadership which is too concerned for immediate security advantages to take a reasonable risk for peace."[27]

After the Dayan talks, Laird reported in his staff meeting that the defense minister had indeed been "demanding" and wanted "more goods before Israelis will enter into talks." While Laird told the assembled Pentagon senior officials that "we are working on a sort of acceptable compromise," he opined that the Israelis would likely get more than he wanted them to have. (Nixon soon approved an accelerated delivery of the F-4s to the Israelis.) "The Israelis are smart negotiators," Laird offered in grudging admiration. "We could take lessons from them."[28]

Less than forty-eight hours after the end of the Syrian invasion of Jordan in September, the United States was frighteningly close to another confrontation—not with a minor Mideast power but with a nuclear superpower, the Soviet Union. It was a possibility that Laird had warned about and predicted more than seven years earlier. In February 1963, after the Cuban Missile Crisis, Congressman Laird had told the Associated Press that the real goal of Russian operations in Cuba was establishment of a submarine base there, and that would be more serious than a few missiles.[29] By 1969 the Soviets were intent on demonstrating to the United States that they had a right to sail in any international waters—including America's back yard. In July 1969 a flotilla of six surface ships became the first Soviet task force to show their flag in the Caribbean, as they sailed to Havana to celebrate Fidel Castro's tenth anniversary in power. Their arrival coincided with what U.S. intelligence determined was the largest deployment of the Soviet navy out of port ever, with thirty Russian combat ships in the Mediterranean alone that summer.[30]

Then in May 1970, a second Soviet naval task force sailed into the Caribbean, coming within forty nautical miles of Louisiana. This time they put in at a deep-water harbor in the Bay of Cienfuegos, on Cuba's southern coast, for a ceremonial welcome. When two of the ships subsequently sailed to Havana, they were given a twenty-one-gun salute as they entered the port. What concerned Laird and the Joint Chiefs was that lurking in the Cienfuegos waters was a Soviet Echo-class nuclear-powered submarine with nuclear missiles.[31] An August 26 U-2 over flight of Cienfuegos Bay raised Laird's level of concern. There was new construction on the island of Cayo Alcatraz suggesting the beginnings of a Soviet naval base. When that information was combined with intelligence reports of a third Soviet naval flotilla steaming for Cuba, Laird decided to go public. He chose a morning coffee klatch with reporters in the Secretary's Dining Room on September 2. "I have a little rundown here on the naval task force of the Soviet Union ... that has been moving from its usual operating area in the Barents Sea on course toward the Caribbean. I think it should be made public," he said, calling it a "significant development." While the size and nature of the force would be unprecedented for the Russians in the Caribbean, he calmly said, "I do not see a crisis."[32]

A week later, the Soviet flotilla reached Cienfuegos and Laird ordered U-2 flights on September 14 and 18. The reconnaissance showed the makings of a major submarine refueling base well on its way to completion at Cienfuegos. Nixon's first impulse was to sit tight—at least until after his upcoming European trip and the midterm elections two months off. He didn't want a situation as tense as Kennedy's Cuban Missile Crisis.

On September 23, at a National Security Council meeting, Laird made a case for a measured showdown with the Russians before they completed the base. Kissinger, who was of the same mind, wrote that he was "extremely uneasy" about Nixon's go-slow approach during that meeting. "He ordered a very low-key public posture, confined simply to noting that we were aware of what was happening and were watching. Mel Laird pointed out that this would never work; too many people knew what was going on; the story [about the base] would leak."[33] As usual, Laird thought silence would be futile, and, as usual, he was right. Kissinger sent press guidance to both the Pentagon and State Department restricting comments about the Cienfuegos facility. But two days later, Laird blew the cover off the quiet approach.

New York Times columnist Cyrus L. Sulzberger, in a September 25 editorial titled "Ugly Clouds in the South," warned that the Soviets were building a possible submarine base at Cienfuegos. Laird's deputy press secretary, Jerry Friedheim, knew he would get questions about it that morning. The Pentagon press corps had been asking him daily about the movements and location of the Soviet flotilla and the trailing submarines. Rather than suggest that the Pentagon didn't know where those hostile forces were, Laird opted for public disclosure. "Jerry talked to me in the morning about the briefing and I told him to go ahead with details about Cienfuegos," Laird recalled.

Friedheim was asked about Cienfuegos by reporters and spelled out in detail what was known about the ongoing construction of a Russian submarine base in Cuba. The Associated Press sent out an immediate alert about the new crisis, and it was inevitably front-page news. Kissinger hurriedly gave a background briefing to reporters in which he took a hard-line approach that, if it was a base, it would be a violation of the informal Kennedy-Khrushchev 1962 understanding that the Soviets would not deploy such "offensive weapons" to Cuba. He delivered a similar message to Soviet Ambassador Anatoly Dobrynin that afternoon.

Laird apologized to Kissinger that day—not for disclosing the information, but for failing to tell Kissinger in advance. He needn't have. The columnist Sulzberger revealed in his memoirs that it was Kissinger himself who had leaked the story to him. CIA Director Helms had filled in more details for Sulzberger, and by the time the columnist had met with Laird to pump him for more information, Laird knew Sulzberger already had the story. And he wasn't the only one. Before Nixon had given the order to be low key about the submarine base, Kissinger had already leaked the details to other journalists and members of Congress.

Instead of the public showdown Kennedy chose in his missile crisis, Nixon eventually elected for secret diplomacy, giving the Soviets a graceful exit. That approach also depended on silence from administration officials, and this time Laird wholeheartedly agreed. He knew that if the administration provided the Russians with a way out of Cuba, they might take it, so Laird maintained a tight hold on information about the negotiations with Moscow. He even had to bite his tongue when his antiwar nemesis, Senator William Fulbright, taunted him in a Senate hearing, accusing Laird of "hoodwinking" Congress about an alleged base to scare up a bigger defense budget.[34] Laird kept his own counsel, even having his Pentagon briefers imply that the United States was no longer sure that the Soviets had ever intended to bring submarines to Cienfuegos. "That was after we got assurance that they wouldn't," Laird explained later. "We had to quiet the situation down after Dobrynin assured the president through Kissinger that the plans had been negated. We never said we were wrong. We were just cooling off." It worked. Nixon, in his memoirs, said he was pleased that Laird and others had kept "the secret so well that ... several prominent political leaders and journalists dismissed Cienfuegos as a trumped-up crisis.... I did nothing to discourage such mistaken opinions."[35] The Soviet ships sailed home, and construction was stopped within a month of public disclosure.

With the crises on the wane, Laird accompanied Nixon to Rome for the start of the president's nine-day, five-nation tour of Europe. Laird was deeply religious, and though his upbringing was Presbyterian, he was looking forward to meeting Pope Paul VI when the pontiff gave Nixon an audience. But the U.S. representative to the Vatican, Henry Cabot Lodge, had advised Kissinger that Laird's presence might steer conversation toward the controversial war in Vietnam, and nobody wanted to open that discussion at the Vatican. (Ironically, Lodge himself was a key architect of the war in Vietnam, having served as U.S. ambassador in Saigon during the Johnson administration.)

Since the president was showing off the U.S. commitment in the Mediterranean, he was to spend the night after the papal audience on the aircraft carrier *Saratoga*.[36] Laird was asked to bring a military helicopter to St. Peter's Square to pick up the president after his visit and transport him to the carrier. Laird arrived on time, but the president was not yet at the Vatican. His handlers had ordered his arrival via motorcade through the streets of Rome to set up photo opportunities that would put the European tour in a grander context. But the motorcade was caught in traffic, and so the helicopter that was to take him to the *Saratoga* arrived at the Vatican one hour before the president.

"The pope's aides came out as I was landing in the helicopter and told me the president was running late, and the pope would like to see me," Laird recalled. "So I went in alone to see the pope." He insists that it was papal aides who pressed him into the meeting, and he didn't want to be rude. "He wanted to visit with me. You don't turn that down. You don't say, 'No, I won't go in.' So I went in and had a good visit. I spent about thirty minutes with him. We discussed what was going on in Vietnam and I explained Vietnamization to him. We even got into a little discussion of NATO. He was very knowledgeable."

Thus it was that when Nixon and his entourage, including Kissinger, finally swept into St. Peter's Basilica, they found Laird already ensconced in a papal audience. Kissinger was livid that Laird had violated protocol. "They were shocked to see me sitting there next to the pope," Laird laughed, "but I moved over, you know, so that there would be room for these dignitaries." One of Kissinger's aides, Lawrence Eagleburger, laughed as he recalled the moment, but he said Kissinger was humorless. "Henry was convinced that when Mel was told they didn't want the defense secretary with the pope, that Mel did this helicopter exercise purely and simply so he could get Henry. This was an aspect of sort of acute competition between them."[37]

That night on the *Saratoga*, Laird was still flush from his coup over Kissinger and the advance men. At a dinner for Nixon in the officers' wardroom, Laird regaled the assembled dignitaries with details of his papal encounter. The invitation to enter had caught him by surprise, and he claimed that he had to tuck his lit cigar into his suit coat pocket. Then, while he was surrounded by papal functionaries, his pocket had begun to smoke. Laird said he slapped it so hard that others in the company began politely applauding, thinking the pope had said something profound. The smoke led some to speculate that the College of Cardinals was electing a new pontiff, Laird related in his after-dinner entertainment for the president and guests.

It was a side-slapping story, literally and figuratively, as Nixon and the others at dinner roared with laughter. But it was not true. "I was just blowing a little smoke that night as we were having a few cigars after dinner out on the carrier." Laird swore that he couched the whole thing as a joke, but he did not know he had been taken literally until Kissinger published his memoirs in 1979 and passed the story off as true. In fact, Kissinger's account suggests he was an eyewitness to the event that never happened—even to the point of claiming he had wisely "urged Laird at least to do away with the cigar while we were in the papal presence."[38]

The revelry on the *Saratoga* was quickly dampened that night with the news that Egypt's President Gamal Abdel Nasser had died. Laird had scheduled a firepower demonstration by the Sixth Fleet for Nixon the next day but had to scale it down in deference to the mourners. Kissinger wanted the whole thing canceled, but Nixon's heart was set on it, so Laird authorized some takeoffs and landings from the carrier. "We had some mock things without firepower so the president could see how we operated," said Laird. The next day Laird and Nixon parted company, with Nixon going on to Yugoslavia, and Laird, along with admirals Moorer and Zumwalt, making visits to Turkey, Greece, and Malta on NATO business. The visits were billed as an extension of Nixon's itinerary, since the two nations were disappointed the president himself was not coming.

Between Greece and Turkey, Greece was, at that juncture, the more symbolically important visit. Greece was ruled by a military junta that had wrested power from the elected government three years earlier. It had become known as the Coup of the Colonels. The primary plotter, Colonel Georgios Papadopoulos, became prime minister and also was acting as defense minister at the time of Laird's visit. Attempting to influence the repressive regime, the Johnson administration had instituted a selective arms embargo until the Greeks showed democratic improvement. About a week before Laird arrived in Athens, the arms embargo had been lifted, and $56 million worth of U.S. aircraft, tanks, helicopters, and other equipment was scheduled to be delivered after his visit. As a crucial member of the southern flank of NATO, Greece had become a friend to openly embrace once again.

Not all Greeks welcomed the embrace. On October 3, after laying a wreath at the Tomb of the Unknown Soldier, Laird, accompanied by heavy Greek security, went to the premier's office for a meeting. Shortly after they sat down, both were rocked by an explosion about sixty yards away in the national gardens. It was the work of an antigovernment agitator who wanted to assassinate both men. The explosion was heard throughout Athens, whose residents could also see a pall of smoke rising from among the trees of the park, but neither Papadopoulos nor Laird was hurt.[39]

Laird shrugged off the incident at the time, and when he recounted it later. He felt he was in greater danger that afternoon when a reckless-driving Papadopoulos "kidnapped" him for an afternoon respite at an out-of-town resort. "He wanted to get the heck out of town and said, 'You come with me. Forget about this security business,'" Laird said. "So I got into some hopped-up car with him, and he drove eighty or ninety miles an hour to some resort he had stashed away in the mountains. Our security people didn't know where the hell I was!"

❧

There was another terrorist bomb that went off during that period that did, in a sense, injure Laird more than the Greek dissident's attempt—even though in this case he was nearly a thousand miles away, safe and secure at Camp David, when it exploded. The University of Wisconsin at Madison was close to Laird's heart. His mother was on the university's board of regents, and he had arranged congressional appropriations to fund several research buildings on campus. On the morning of August 24, 1970, Laird woke up at Camp David to the news that the Army Mathematics Research Center at the UW had been bombed, killing one student and injuring four others.

Laird took it very personally. "I had been responsible for the math center. In the 1950s, I had put in the congressional appropriation for the advanced mathematics facility, one of the first in the country to use computers," he explained. "They thought they were getting even with me now that I was secretary of defense. It was intended to raise hell with me, a sort of retribution. And they killed that young man."

In general, 1970 was a searing year when Laird was made to feel the antiwar protest up close and personal. During the week of the May 4 Kent State shootings, Laird was headed home one evening in Bob Froehlke's chauffeur-driven car; the two men were neighbors and sometimes shared the ride. As the car approached a congested traffic circle near American University in Washington, they could see hundreds of students milling in the circle, reacting to the fresh wound of Kent State. Someone in the crowd spotted Laird and students surrounded the car, shouting and shoving. "Get the hell out of here!" Laird ordered the driver, but they could only inch through the gridlock of people and traffic. Thirty years later Froehlke could laugh at the memory of the frustrated defense secretary ordering his helpless driver to do the impossible. But that day, Froehlke was shaken and feeling lucky that they had emerged unscathed.[40] Laird was philosophical then and years later about the incident. "I can understand that during the war people felt that the only way of stopping things was to lay down in front of a car or demonstrate in the streets," he said. "These students didn't do much. They just rocked it a little bit when we were standing still. I waved to them."

Speeches by the defense secretary were also a magnet for protestors. Two weeks after the American University incident, on May 23, Laird was invited to the Pick-Congress Hotel in Chicago to speak to the General Assembly of the United Presbyterian Church. He brought along Air Force General Daniel "Chappie" James, a Pentagon aide for public affairs and POW issues. Imposing in size and military decorations and noteworthy as one of the air force's few black generals, James drew attention when he traveled with Laird. A few among the onlookers that day got unexpectedly rowdy, shouting epithets at Laird. Confident that he was safe among fellow Presbyterians, and aware that General James was a practicing Christian with a deep baritone singing voice, Laird cranked up the volume on the microphone and announced, "Ladies and gentlemen, we will now be singing some hymns. And they will be led by General Chappie James."[41]

James went along with the pacification ploy, which worked. "He could sing hymns like no one else I've ever heard," Laird recalled. "He was beautiful to watch." So beautiful was he that when the two men went across the street to the Conrad Hilton Hotel for a press conference after the speech, Laird prevailed on James to sing a hymn for the jaded reporters, too.

When Laird left Chicago, leaving General James behind, he flew directly to dedicate the Central Wisconsin Airport in Mosinee, in his former congressional district. He was greeted by, among others, more than one hundred demonstrators protesting the Cambodia invasion—and by his mother, who was very unsettled by the hostility toward her son. Laird refused to take personal umbrage at the demonstrators; he ended his talk with, "The chance to hear the viewpoint of young people has always been valuable to me."[42]

That valued exchange of views was frequently denied to Laird by event planners. For instance, the annual Madison, Wisconsin, service clubs dinner held at the University of Wisconsin campus uninvited Laird as its September 1970 speaker, fearing disruption by campus dissenters. The *Milwaukee Journal* decried the decision in an editorial, calling it censorship of one of the highest officials in the land. "In a democracy, every point of view should be given a hearing. Yet there are those who, contending that they represent freedom, refuse to listen to those with whom they disagree and, much worse, would prevent anyone else from listening. This is repression, and by a minority which imposes its views by its ability to cause trouble and disorder."[43]

No similar rejection caused Laird more hurt than one from his own alma mater, Carleton College. As Laird recounted it, in the midst of the countrywide protests against the Cambodia invasion, a letter from a Carleton faculty official arrived at the defense secretary's office and was brought to him by his aide Carl Wallace. An incensed Laird read that the faculty was pressuring the administration to withdraw his bachelor's degree to punish him for the Vietnam War. Though the letter has been lost, Laird remembered that it was not from Carleton's president, antiwar Quaker John Nason, or from the students. "It was from the faculty. They had some radical faculty members, one of whom was later U.S. Senator Paul Wellstone." Laird dashed off a response, asking for a visit and discourse with the faculty to explain Vietnamization. He was summarily turned down. "They refused to let me appear. It was wrong. Academic freedom should at least give you the opportunity to present your views. I felt rather strongly about the way that was handled, and I washed my hands of Carleton's faculty support for academic freedom."

For their part, the college later made attempts at reconciliation, which led to an easing of tensions.[44] But research uncovered that Laird also had been passed over for an honorary degree from Carleton in the 1980s because he was still considered too controversial. (The college bestowed an honorary degree on President Bill Clinton in June 2000 on the heels of the Monica Lewinsky affair and perjury charges, lauding him as someone the graduates should emulate because his "personal commitments ... are highly congruent with Carleton's values."[45])

While the defense secretary was a reluctant warrior, he was an avid lifesaver. Laird's first love was his work in the health field, and he found ways to express that passion. A significant moment came in mid-1970 when he implemented an idea he had had as a congressman. "One of the brighter spots of our experience in Vietnam has been the effectiveness of helicopter evacuation of the wounded from the front lines," he observed at a national medical conference on trauma in 1968. The previous year, more Americans had died from "the carnage on our highways" than were killed in Korea and Vietnam combined. Many could be saved if helicopters and trained paramedics were available to provide swift treatment and transportation, and the military bases across the country had both in abundance.

As defense secretary, Laird sold Transportation Secretary John Volpe on the idea. In July 1970 they jointly announced the Military Assistance to Safety and Traffic (MAST) pilot program to be conducted in five western states, using military helicopters to respond to civilian medical emergencies. In the first fifteen months, the air force and army flew 681 humanitarian missions. Two-thirds of the missions took patients from small hospitals to better-equipped facilities. The pilot program proved to be such a success that Laird soon approved MAST's expansion to fourteen more states.[46]

As secretary, Laird also dispatched U.S. military relief missions abroad, such as to the Biafrans in Nigeria in 1970, and to Nicaragua when a 1972 earthquake leveled Managua. At home, Laird dispatched military helicopters to help in search and rescue efforts during several hurricanes, notably Hurricane Agnes in 1972, at that time the most damaging hurricane ever recorded. When the Susquehanna River flooded over its banks, during Agnes, Laird quickly sent his own Pentagon helicopter and forty more to rescue thousands of citizens from roofs and hilltops. The Army Corps of Engineers, 1,500 servicemen, and Laird's wife, Barbara, vice chairman of the national Red Cross, joined the battle against the flood waters and saved lives, holding the death toll at 129.[47]

In two famous but failed efforts, Laird's military searchers could not locate the bodies of Pittsburgh Pirates right fielder Roberto Clemente or House Majority Leader Hale Boggs, who died in separate aviation accidents. Clemente was flying on a mercy relief mission to Managua when his plane crashed off the coast of Isla Verde, Puerto Rico. Boggs was flying with another congressman and two others when his plane disappeared over a remote section of Alaska's southern coast. More heartening was the successful rescue of famed aviator Charles Lindbergh and forty-seven others on a conservation mission to a remote, densely forested area of the southern Philippines in 1972.[48]

In addition to adding regular search and rescue jobs to the Defense Department's list of duties, Laird also took on one more duty that no other secretary has had to—he became America's postmaster general for a brief time. In March 1970 U.S. postal workers walked out in the first strike of the office's history. Nixon directed Laird to call up forty-thousand reservists who were then trained for postal work. As acting postmaster general, Laird set up a command postal center in the Pentagon and had the Reserves moving the mail smoothly by the second day. His longtime friend, labor leader George Meany, was furious with him. "Mel, what the hell are you doing?" he demanded on the phone.

"We gotta get the mail through, George, but we'll be real careful," Laird replied. Then he reminded Meany that it was a felony for a federal worker to go on strike. The use of the Reserves spurred a settlement with the postal unions in less than a week.

Nineteen seventy had been a tumultuous year for Laird on so many fronts, but he ended it well—with the dedication of a room in the Pentagon that filled a personal need for him and, he was sure, for others—a Meditation Room. Not many were aware of the deeply religious side of the secretary, because he did not wear it on his sleeve. One who knew was the Reverend Billy Graham. "I had the privilege of being with him on a number of occasions, both at social events and as his guest at the Pentagon," Graham recalled.[49] Laird feted Graham in February 1970 at a Pentagon luncheon attended by the Joint Chiefs of Staff and a half-dozen congressional leaders, followed by a meeting with some of the military's top chaplains. Affirmed Graham: "Mel Laird was not only deeply religious, but he used his great influence to further the Kingdom of God in unique ways."

The cigar-chewing, political animal had started a prayer circle in Congress. And then the dovish defense secretary decided that the people at the Pentagon also needed some place to petition God. At a dedication ceremony for the Meditation Room in the A-Ring of the Pentagon on December 15, 1970, Laird carefully shared his spiritual side. He told the assembled crowd that the Pentagon had plenty of shops and restaurants to "satisfy the needs of the body." Now it would have a corner to cater to the needs of the spirit, a place where "the needs of the inner man can find satisfaction. It is a place where men and women can reflect and pray and find guidance and inspiration. . . . This small room is an affirmation that, though we cling to the principle that church and state should be separate, we do not propose to separate man from God. For without Him, who is the source of our being, our wisdom, and our strength, we can do nothing."[50]

26

Just Call Me Mel

VONDA VAN DYKE WAS NERVOUS. Miss America 1965 was an accomplished singer and a confident entertainer on the convention circuit, but the engagement before the National Association of Chain Drug Stores in Palm Beach, Florida, was different. Legendary comedian Jack Benny had let her know he might want her to tour with him, but only after she "tried out" as his opening act at the Florida convention; he would watch from backstage to see if she "had it."

Her opening set went well. The older crowd responded warmly to her medley of songs from their youth. But then came the high-risk segment of her show—the ventriloquist act. Since passing her crown to her successor six years earlier, she had tired of carrying a heavy dummy on the road as she pursued her entertainment career, so during shows she would select a human "dummy" from the audience instead. She favored balding men. "Generally speaking, I had found that they were more at ease, more comfortable with themselves," she recalled. "If I got someone who was balding, the audience immediately loved them, and they were always more receptive to me."

Among the several men she sang to at this Breakers Hotel gig that night, the audience responded best when she crooned to one man of shiny pate: "You Must Have Been a Beautiful Baby." Vonda did not know she was serenading the secretary of defense, who was there to be the keynote speaker for the convention. "I bet you drove the little girls wild," she flirted with the smiling gentleman. "You must have been a beautiful baby, 'cause baby look at you now!" When she was done, his friendliness persuaded her that he was the perfect dummy to join her on stage. As Laird rose to follow her to the stage, half a dozen security men stood up as well and hovered near him, much to Vonda's confusion. Laird dutifully sat on the stool beside her.

"Now, what's your name?" she asked.

"Just call me 'Mel,'" he answered, and the audience roared.

She whispered to him that each time she squeezed the back of his neck, he was to open his mouth as if he were talking. "Are you having a good time?" she asked him. "Oh, my, yes!" he appeared to answer in the Betty Boop–like voice. More laughter.

After some back-and-forth, with Vonda "throwing" her voice, she asked Laird if he would sing a song with her. Laird, who was no singer, declined, so she said she would do "The Alphabet Song" for both of them—"A, you're ador-able, B, you're so beautiful, C, you're a cutie full of charms." Appearing to come from Laird's mouth, the falsetto voice was hilarious, and the audience was on its feet, clapping and cheering. "I didn't usually get a standing ovation in the middle of the act," Vonda recalled. As she was finishing her "duet" with Laird, Jack Benny came out on stage and interrupted the act. In his patented droll manner he mock-pleaded: "You've got to stop this. Honey, don't you know who this is?"

"Yes," she said, meekly. "It's Mel."

"That's the secretary of defense," Benny lectured. "You've got to get him off the stage here, because you're ruining my whole act. I cannot follow this!"[1] The performance won Vonda the spot as Benny's new opening act. Those who watched that night got a taste of what it was like to be near "Mel," also known around the Pentagon by a tongue-in-cheek moniker of his own choosing, CINCMINC, "Commander-in-Chief, Military-Industrial Complex."[2]

When Laird was defense secretary—and until skyscrapers exceeded one hun-dred floors—the Pentagon was the world's largest office building, boasting 6.5 million square feet, three times the floor space of the Empire State Build-ing. Each of its five floors is arranged into offices along five concentric rings, from the "A" ring, which encloses the center grassy five-acre court, to the more prestigious outer "E" ring with views of Washington, D.C., and Virginia. Ten spokelike halls connect the five rings. Altogether, there are 17.5 miles of cor-ridors, and yet it is said that the design makes it the most efficient building of its size, allowing one to walk between any two offices in the building in less than ten minutes.[3]

Laird did a lot of walking in the Pentagon. He believed that the more he was seen by the nearly thirty thousand workers in the building, the greater his success as a manager would be. "Management by walking around" was a much-heralded technique used by David Packard at the Hewlett-Packard company. But no secretary before Laird had used it at the Pentagon. Generally they holed up in their E-ring office suite and summoned subordinates to them. Not so with Laird who, as the first professional politician to become secretary, found that walking around suited him perfectly.

"He liked to walk the halls," said Laird's public affairs spokesman, Jerry Friedheim. "He liked to visit other people in their offices, always stopping to chat with the secretaries and enlisted personnel in the outer offices. Sometimes he'd go to the cafeteria and eat with employees. Somehow, he remembered most of the names of people after meeting them once and would acknowledge them when he saw them again. It was very much hands-on management. He just had the innate political sense that it was good to let the people see you and for you to see the people."[4]

"He'd always say, 'I'm Mel Laird,'" recalled secretary Thelma Stubbs. "Once, [Admiral] Dan Murphy went on a trip with the secretary and would say, 'I'm Admiral Murphy.' By the time he got back from the trip, it was 'I'm Dan Murphy' because of Mr. Laird's example."[5] In that era, this unpretentiousness was unusual for someone in such a prestigious position. One of his longest-serving executive assistants, Kathy Weaver, noted that before she worked for Laird, her boss was a construction company executive who had hired her after a white-glove, high-heeled, hair-in-a-French-twist job interview. She was required to be similarly "proper" and subservient on the job, "waiting on my boss hand and foot. It was my place to get his coffee and know how he drank it." But on her first day working for Laird, "he came out of his office and asked, 'Can I get you a cup of coffee?' It bowled me over!"[6]

Authors Richard Stubbing and Richard Mendel, in a book about the Defense Department, contrasted several defense secretaries and concluded: "Laird understood the value of the personal touch. This was particularly beneficial within the Pentagon, which during the McNamara years had become a figurative free-fire zone."[7] The best evidence of the camaraderie Laird engendered is that—alone of all the secretary-deputy secretary pairs that served at the Pentagon—the "Laird-Packard Team" had well-attended periodic reunions into the 1990s (until the mortality rate significantly diminished their numbers).

Midway through Laird's term, the *Armed Forces Journal* recognized that the Defense Department's first politician-in-chief had become "a good manager—the principle proof of which is that he persuaded another good manager, Deputy Secretary of Defense Packard, to join the team as number two man and then unloaded much of the day-to-day management burden on *him*. This has freed Laird himself for the more important policy-making, Congressional fence-mending and public relations duties which he handles so well."[8] The list of responsibilities that Laird gave to Packard was substantial. With Packard's acknowledged industrial and engineering expertise, he was assigned to take the lead on the Pentagon's weapons technology, from research and development to testing to procurement, with some of the budget process also. In addition, Packard helped oversee the intelligence agencies and the Systems Analysis and Manpower offices and was Laird's point man on certain strategic nuclear policy and arms control issues. Explained in shorthand, Packard was "Mr. Inside" and Laird was "Mr. Outside."

With the rugged frame of a former Stanford football player, Packard had a commanding personality to match. "When he came down the Pentagon halls, he made them seem narrow," Senator John Warner recalled. "When he walked around the building, everybody scattered practically, because it wasn't just a lope—he was really *moving*. And if he came in unannounced through your door, you knew you were in big trouble. But we really learned to love him."[9]

Among many qualities, Packard was appreciated for his decisiveness and candor. A favorite memento kept by one of his former military assistants, Lieutenant General Ray Furlong, was a "buck slip" that, in Packard's handwriting, read: "Tell the S.O.B. no!" It typified his boss's straight-forward, no-nonsense approach. Sometimes Packard's blunt remarks bordered on naïveté. At his first press conference, after he acknowledged he was taking "a helluva cut" to a $30,000-a-year salary, Packard blurted out: "But I don't intend to *live* on $30,000." The press corps, most of whom lived on less than that, nevertheless roared with laughter. They found his lack of pretentiousness refreshing, as did Congress. When the Nixon administration espoused a new nuclear doctrine called "strategic sufficiency"—essentially meaning they could not seek nuclear superiority over the Soviets anymore—someone asked Packard, after congressional testimony on the subject, what "sufficiency" really meant. Packard peered down on the inquirer and said: "It means that it's a good word to use in a speech. Beyond that, it doesn't mean a damned thing."[10]

With all its Byzantine regulations and internecine bureaucratic battles, government work frustrated Packard. He understood the temperature of the hot seat he occupied and was not reluctant to tackle problems. But in business he had made the final decisions. In government Packard found his decisions could be overruled in any number of overt and covert ways—through inaction by subordinates, legislation by Congress, or intrigue at the White House. "He became utterly disgusted with Washington, with the way power was distributed," said James Schlesinger, who served then as assistant director at the Bureau of the Budget on national security matters and, later, as secretary of defense. "Dave would give a command at the Pentagon, like tell the Air Force to do X, and then he'd come back seven months later and the Air Force had not done X. He really did not understand a system in which the chief executive officer of a company, the man put in charge of operations, which was David's responsibility, would give an order and nothing might happen. But that was the distribution of power within the Pentagon. You have to chase down everything."[11]

Ironically, it was Schlesinger himself who seemed to bedevil Packard most. As they negotiated over the defense portion of the Nixon budget to be presented to Congress each year, Packard frequently lost patience with Schlesinger's insistence on seemingly capricious White House cuts of the defense budget. At one point Packard was so mad at Schlesinger that he walked out of the White House budget meeting and told Laird he was quitting. Laird calmed him down with the promise that he (Laird) would handle the budget meetings until Packard regained his stomach for it. When Laird subsequently met with Schlesinger, he explained Packard's absence with a sly remark: "You know, Jim, Dave Packard is wonderful, but he thinks that the shortest distance between two points is a straight line." Schlesinger knew there was a new "player" in the room who just might out-fox him. He also decided he was better off negotiating with Packard than Laird. "That story tells you a great deal about David Packard, but it also tells you a hell of a lot more about Mel Laird," Schlesinger laughed.[12]

Each day Packard served during his thirty-five months on the job, he missed his home state of California. In Washington he and his wife, Lucile, bought a $300,000 California-style home that had been built for the last pre-Castro Cuban ambassador. It was nothing like their quiet West Coast home among acres of apricot trees. Asked once how Mrs. Packard was faring, he replied with a grinning good-news-bad-news answer: "She gets up in the morning and reads the *Washington Post,* and that spoils her breakfast. She sees me on early morning TV, and that spoils her lunch. I come home and tell her my problems, and that spoils her dinner. So she lost 20 pounds the first month we were here." Partly as a way to rejuvenate himself, Packard invited the Joint Chiefs to an annual deer hunt on his San Felipe ranch south of San Jose. But these visits home could not assuage the daily frustration of dealing with the Washington bureaucracy, which, Packard explained once, was like "trying to *push* on one end of a 40-foot-rope to get the other end to do what you want."[13]

Packard required regular pep talks to keep him from quitting. He consistently praised the support he got from Laird, who never undercut Packard's authority or overruled his decisions. Since the two had never worked together before, nor had they been close friends, many expected there would be major differences between them. Much in the way children "test" their parents individually to exploit differences, so too did the military services and Joint Chiefs try to discern Laird-Packard differences to use to their advantage. One of Packard's military assistants, General James Boatner, said the chiefs viewed Packard as "more of a hawk," so as soon as Laird left town they would come to the deputy's office for approval of more aggressive Vietnam bombing campaigns or other initiatives. Boatner and Ray Furlong, the other military assistant, used to "joke about it. We'd be sitting there and we'd say, 'Well, Mr. Laird's airplane is about to take off from Andrews. We ought to see the JCS up here shortly." The ploy never worked, he added. Furlong concurred, adding that the pair was so complementary that it seemed as if "Dave Packard and Mel Laird had been born for one another." Their compatibility was even a surprise to Packard who, at the end of his tour of duty, confided at the secretary's Monday staff meeting that he could not recall a single instance in which he and Laird had disagreed on a key decision.[14]

Norman Augustine, who was working in the research and engineering portion of the Pentagon at the time, and who later became a defense industry CEO, said Laird's ability to "augment his own talents with people around him that complemented him, like Dave Packard, was exceptional. And the team of

Laird and Packard was a classic—the best example of a team. There have been other good ones at the Defense Department, but they were the best."[15]

Later efforts to match the Laird-Packard magic were less successful. When Dick Cheney was appointed secretary of defense by George H.W. Bush in 1989, Cheney looked to his predecessors for advice. "What I always remember about Mel is that he showed up with David Packard. The two of them. They'd been a great team, so I tried to re-create it." Emulating Laird, Cheney the politician would be "Mr. Outside," and Donald Atwood, former General Motors vice chairman, would be "Mr. Inside." Cheney conceded their pairing never quite rose to the Laird-Packard standard.[16]

In 1993 when former Congressman Les Aspin—a Wisconsin protégé of Laird's—was appointed defense secretary by President Clinton, Aspin chose technology-oriented William Perry as his deputy. Perry recalled: "When he invited me to be his deputy, he wanted me to do for him what Packard did for Laird. It didn't work out that way, just as it hadn't for Cheney and Atwood. In fact, the Laird-Packard image is so instilled in people's minds that many teams have tried to emulate it. Their explicit goal has been to achieve the same success the Laird-Packard team did." (Clinton forced Aspin to resign after only a year on the job. Perry replaced him as secretary and served from 1994 to 1997.)[17]

Anyone trying to manage the Defense Department, even in the best of times, can get drawn into a quagmire of competing interests. Not only do the services compete amongst themselves for every dollar and program, but there are dozens of ongoing battles within each service for the allocation of money and manpower. Naive CEOs have advised, "Just run it like a business." But what business has to report to a 535-person board of directors like the U.S. Congress? "It is *very* difficult to run it in a businesslike way," said Harold Brown, a former defense secretary. "Congress, the defense contractors, the media, the public, they all have a lot to say and a lot of influence they want to exert on the department. But then, the framers [of the Constitution] didn't set up the U.S. government to be the most efficient. That wasn't their goal."[18]

To handle the job, Laird embraced a new operating philosophy called "participatory management." Some had trouble defining and understanding it. "No one seems to know precisely what they mean by the term, partly because the layman's mind boggles and his eyes glaze over whenever an attempt is made to explain how the Pentagon runs," one military correspondent carped in an early 1969 column.[19]

Laird's first deputy for administration, Robert Froehlke, who had first suggested participatory management to Laird, took a crack at describing it to an *Armed Forces Management* editor: "It involves 'channeled conflict' and essentially requires knowledgeable people, who know and respect each other, to enter the arena together, with the senior manager as moderator. It is in this crucible of conflicting analyses that the real issues are crystallized and various facets of the problem stripped of their sometimes misleading veneer."[20]

McNamara had confessed to Laird that one of the greatest mistakes he had made was not truly listening to his employees, particularly the uniformed military men and women: "You can learn a lot from them. You don't have to accept their advice, but at least they need to sense that you're listening to them. The problem I had over my last few years is that we didn't have anyone listening." Laird didn't really need to be told that. "Mel liked to get his information by talking to people rather than reading long memoranda," according to the longest-serving Pentagon administrator, David "Doc" Cooke. "Conversely, Bob McNamara would happily read or go through a fifty- or a hundred-page memorandum, making notes in a rather unintelligible left-handed crawl. McNamara was a paper person; Laird was a people person."[21]

Norman Augustine, who was several layers below Laird on the management food chain, was surprised one day to get a lunch invitation signed "Mel." "This was something that hadn't happened before. Whenever [Laird] had a free lunch or another break, he'd bring a half-dozen people in and talk to them about their concerns as well as give them a vision of what he was trying to accomplish."[22] By letting everyone participate in the development of policy, Laird aimed at a team spirit in which everyone then backed the final decision. "It was made clear that the right to participate had to be earned and that concomitant with the right to a full hearing before a decision was made was the duty to accept and support the decisions reached," Robert Moot, the department's comptroller, explained in an end-of-term review of the success of participatory management.[23]

Laird made it clear he was not going to micromanage. Since he had personally chosen or endorsed all the top-level political appointees for their jobs, he trusted they would perform at a top level. So when he gave an assignment, he let each of them run with it. In his thirty years at the Pentagon, Moot said it was the most successful approach any secretary had ever employed. "There was an atmosphere of confidence, trust, and true participation."[24] Trusting his staff was a matter of self-preservation. At the end of his long days, Laird would often look upon a pile of documents needing his signature. To read them would take twenty-four hours. So, instead, he'd trust that his staff had prepared them well, take a quick drink and sign them all. He called it "5 o'clock roulette."[25]

At one of his final interviews, Laird was asked what he would like to be remembered for. He responded: "I hope I'll be remembered as the person who put the major emphasis on the importance of people in this department, and the importance of having all people, whether they be military or civilians, a part of a participatory system of management.... I think that we have the highest morale in this department of any department in government today."[26]

A big part of being the boss was making the tough calls. Froehlke offered a personal example. When he was an insurance company executive and later secretary of the army, Froehlke's stomach would churn before he took action against someone who wasn't performing. "Mel didn't fret. When he was convinced that someone had to be chewed out, or had to be transferred, demoted, or fired, he did it."[27]

In the spring of 1969, the USS *Guitarro*, a $50 million attack submarine, was moored at Mare Island Naval Shipyard in Vallejo, California, going through its final fittings before an expected commission at the end of the year. Two construction crews worked at cross purposes on both ends of the sub at the same time. Unaware of what was happening with the other crew, each kept filling ballast tanks in an effort to level the submarine. At one point, the forward crew, thinking the *Guitarro* was stable, left for lunch. Meanwhile, the aft crew let water out of the stern tanks, which then caused the nose to go under until 3,500 tons of seawater poured into open hatches and completely submerged the vessel. In less than five minutes, the workmen had caused $25 million in damages.[28]

A week later on the House floor, Congressman George Mahon bemoaned military waste and cited "neglect" and "carelessness" in the *Guitarro* incident. He added, "I am a little afraid that the commander of the Navy yard is not going to be court-martialed. I am afraid he will probably be transferred and promoted."[29] Laird was already on top of it. Both he and a special three-man House investigative panel soon determined that the rear admiral commanding the shipyard was responsible for the "wholly avoidable blunder." Yet the navy was reluctant to penalize the commander until Laird stepped in and told the chief of naval operations: "I don't want any monkey business with this. That commander has to go." He did.[30]

∿

Laird usually awoke about 5 A.M. daily and swam laps in his pool. His Pentagon driver, William Johnson, would arrive with the morning's important paperwork for Laird's perusal at home and on the way to the Pentagon. Johnson became a beloved Laird family member and was a guest on their holiday vacations. Laird's two sons were somewhat in awe of Johnson, who was a crack pistol shot and provided additional security for Laird. On one family fishing trip, a snake came racing across the water toward one of the Laird canoes, and Johnson took out his gun and shot its head off. "It *really* impressed my kids," Laird laughed.[31]

The secretary usually arrived at the office about 7:15 A.M. He would either have breakfast alone at his desk or a working breakfast with guests. Kissinger visited frequently for an eggs-and-toast breakfast. Froehlke was allowed to bring anyone he wanted for breakfast, which naturally included some of their Wisconsin friends. At least every other Friday, Laird convened an "intelligence breakfast," which included CIA Director Helms, as well the heads of all the Defense Department intelligence agencies. Air Force Undersecretary John McLucas also attended because he served as head of the National Reconnaissance Office, the agency that dealt with satellite imagery and was so sensitive that, at that time, even its name and acronym were classified.

Laird's first daily meeting was with the "8:15 Group," which focused on public affairs and legislative issues. This was the meeting Laird used as if he were in an election-year campaign—a way to keep the department "on message," focusing on its primary objectives such as Vietnamization and the all-volunteer force, despite whatever crisis might be temporarily distracting them. At the beginning of his term, Laird also met at 9 A.M. every day with the "Vietnam Task Force," made up of military and intelligence representatives. Their job was to make sure Vietnamization was kept on track. Those meetings became less frequent later in his term as U.S. participation in the war lessened.

Laird met with most of his assistant secretaries and discussed their areas of responsibility at least once every other week. On the military side, he also met with each of the chiefs of staff once a week. On Friday he might have their meeting in "the Tank." The chairman separately met with Laird at least twice each day, including one lunch every week. Laird also made sure he had frequent one-on-one meetings with his two personally appointed and loyal heads of the Defense Intelligence Agency and National Security Agency, General Don Bennett and Admiral Noel Gayler, respectively.

Of all the regular meetings Laird held, none was more important than the weekly staff meeting that convened every Monday morning at 9:30 in his dining room. Seated at the head of the conference table were Laird and Packard, with the service secretaries and Joint Chiefs at the table in order of seniority. Assistant secretaries of defense and other key staff members sat in chairs around the perimeter of the room. Attendance was mandatory unless the official was out of town; then a representative had to be sent. (Packard ran the meeting when Laird was out of town.)

"We have to play this game straight if we are to succeed," Laird cautioned at one staff meeting. Because he encouraged candor, each meeting was filled with talk of the problems besetting the military. "Some of you have commented that this meeting leaves you with a gloomy attitude for the rest of the week," Laird observed at one meeting. "I don't want to make this 'morbid Monday,' but this is just the meeting we [need] to face up to our problems. Maybe I should start out with a few jokes or stories, but that's not going to help. We have a lot of successes here, too, and we discuss them. But I still want everyone here to speak up about their concerns, even if it's negative. It's the only way we can move toward success."[32]

For the most part, Laird praised the hard work of his people each Monday, but at times he showed flashes of anger. He was careful not to harshly dress down the senior officials at the table in front of the others. Instead he would correct the high-profile offender indirectly by addressing "constructive criticism" on the same subject to an underling, who quickly realized he was the sacrificial lamb for the day. The primary exception was if he had discovered someone was dealing with the White House without his knowledge. That was the only time, his staff recalled, that he directly lambasted the guilty party, no matter who it was.[33]

⌇

It is probable that no other defense secretary employed meals as thoroughly as Laird did. He would host small working meals in the dining room attached to his suite, or larger ones in the "Gold Room," which accommodated more than a hundred. Once a week Laird had lunch with the service secretaries. Sometimes "he would go down to the employees' cafeteria and eat with custodial workers, privates, sergeants, or whoever happened to be sitting at the table," noted Jerry Friedheim. When out of town, Laird made a practice of eating with the troops, especially on holidays.[34]

One of his more intriguing ideas was the "conversational lunch," to which an eclectic mix of a half-dozen nongovernment, nonmilitary leaders would be invited for a wide-ranging discussion about the Defense Department. About two hundred people in all enjoyed those mixers during Laird's term. Common Cause founder John Gardner vividly recalled his own "conversational lunch" experience in October 1969. (His fellow guests included TV commentator Shana Alexander, health lobby leader Mary Lasker, columnist Carl Rowan, and Packard.) Gardner had become a Laird friend as HEW secretary during the Johnson administration. Having been a Cabinet member himself, "I had a lot of familiarity with the enormous bureaucratic complexities of making [the Pentagon] function." So he buttonholed Laird at the lunch with a couple of questions: "How do you deal with these acres of desks and tens of thousands of people that make this place go, or fail to make it go? How do you handle just the sheer organizational task of getting your purposes accomplished?"

Gardner recalled that Laird looked over at Packard "rather wryly," smiled, and then finally answered with a laugh: "Well, I'll tell you, John, Dave and I have thought a lot about it, and we have just about concluded that one lifetime is not long enough to get your arms around it."[35]

It was common for young people to be at these lunches, but their participation varied. Susan Williams, later a Los Angeles lawyer, didn't remember saying a word. She had been invited to represent Princeton University, where she was a freshman. "I was a policeman's kid who had gone to public school and was adjusting to Princeton as a freshman, which was tough enough. Then here I was, awfully overwhelmed among all those full-fledged adults with prominent national positions; it was an eye-opener."[36]

Laird's natural way with young people spawned hands-on involvement with the White House Fellows program. President Johnson began the fellowships in 1964. More than a dozen young people at a time were assigned to Cabinet-level and other high offices throughout government, writing reports and speeches, attending conferences, drafting proposed legislation, answering congressional inquiries, conducting briefings, heading projects, and performing other duties. When Laird became secretary of defense, he realized how beneficial the fellow-ships could be for young military officers. He needed to bring up through the ranks people with political savvy and a healthy respect for Congress and the White House. So Laird asked Nixon to make an exemption from the rule that said fellows could not come from within government. Laird was authorized three slots for military officers, all of whom he could personally select.

He spread the word among the services and pressured them to send him applications from the best and the brightest young officers they had. And that is what changed Army Lieutenant Colonel Colin Powell's life. "There may be one moment in our lives we can look back on later and say that, for good or ill, it was the turning point," Powell wrote in his memoirs, *My American Journey.* "For me, that day came in November 1971," when a major sent him an eight-page application for a White House fellowship and told him to fill it out by the weekend. "Secretary of Defense Melvin Laird had been displeased because so few military candidates were applying, and consequently the branch had combed the personnel files looking for prospects. I had been drafted. I filled out the forms, provided the required references, met the deadline, and promptly forgot about the matter. I was one of over 1,500 candidates." Laird picked Powell from the list.

As so often happens in the lives of America's stars, timing is everything. In Powell's case, the fact that he was one of the seventeen White House fellows selected for the class of 1972–73, and then was assigned to the White House's Office of Management and Budget, meant that he was there when OMB Director Caspar Weinberger and Deputy Director Frank Carlucci could mentor him. Both would become secretaries of defense. Powell credits Carlucci's patronage in particular for moving him up the ranks to become chairman of the Joint Chiefs of Staff in 1989, but he owed the opportunity to Laird.[37]

One of the things Laird knew instinctively about creating team loyalty was the need to win the support of spouses and children. So he made an effort to include families at every possible Pentagon event, beginning with the of-ficial oath-of-office ceremony. Laird made a point of personally swearing in every top-level political appointee and scheduled the event only when he was assured the individual's family and friends could be there. No former secre-tary had handled this time-consuming task personally. Many of Laird's ap-pointees recounted independently how moved they were, and how committed they became, during that swearing-in ceremony. Laird always made sure the wives had flowers and the children were noticed. His manpower chief Roger

Kelley recalled that "Mel gave my wide-eyed twelve-year-old, Paul, a personally conducted tour of his suite. When we left, Paul thanked our busy host for the tour and then said: 'Mr. Laird, I have one more question. How is my Dad doing?'"[38]

In his first month as defense secretary, Laird announced at the Monday staff meeting that in March there would be a three-day out-of-town "orientation" conference for staff and spouses. He originally planned to have it at Camp David, but there wasn't enough room, so he settled on busing everyone to a long weekend at the rustic Airlie House conference center in Virginia, forty-five miles southwest of Washington. This first "Laird-Packard Management Conference" in 1969 was a success. Roger Kelley said, "Relationships grew out of it and we began to function as a team."[39] The *Washington Star*'s military correspondent, Orr Kelly, observed in a 1971 article that the Airlie meetings were well worth the $8,000 they cost the taxpayers. "In the sport-shirt and first-names-only informal atmosphere of the conference, many of the officials get to know each other much better in two days than they would in a year at the Pentagon—and will have a chance to seek directly, in face-to-face conversations, some answers that seem so elusive when they get caught in the bureaucratic cobwebs."[40]

Two other military journalists, in a critical examination of the performance of several defense secretaries, observed that the programs were impressive, "but the real agenda was that of team-building. The spouses of his staff members arrived by chartered bus for the last day of the conference, and Laird, who had a prodigious gift for remembering names, made a point of chatting briefly on a first-name basis with each of his staff and their spouses during the weekend. Through these meetings Laird was able to keep morale high."[41]

The success of those conferences during the Laird era prompted a tradition for Pentagon leadership until James Schlesinger was secretary of defense. "My dear friend Jim—whose management style, I often told him, was 'management by intimidation'—didn't think it was worth it," recalled Doc Cooke. Cooke had come to the Pentagon in 1957 as a judge advocate naval officer and subsequently held administrative posts under defense secretaries. Laird made him deputy assistant secretary for administration. Long revered by the nickname, "Mayor of the Pentagon," Cooke died in 2002, at the age of eighty-one, after serving eighteen defense secretaries.

Not long before he died, Cooke recalled with fondness the first Airlie House conference with Laird. "I remember when everybody first gathered for the cocktail party out there that kicked it off. I noticed that the uniformed military was clustering by service in different parts of the room, the civilian staffers in other parts and so on. But by the time we held the fourth [conference], there had been a merger. Mel had succeeded in creating a healthy give-and-take friendship among a diverse team—the 'Laird-Packard Team.'" The Pentagon never again saw its like, Cooke concluded.[42]

27

Finessing Congress

IT WAS A WEDNESDAY EVENING in Washington, July 1971, and the joint was jumpin' at the Army-Navy Club where members of the Piscatorial and Inside Straight Society (PISS for short) were gathered to make some noise. The club of Wisconsinites was started by the dean of the state's political reporters, John Wyngaard, to gather reporters, editors, and politicians who enjoyed fishing and playing cards at lakeside cabins when they were in their home state.[1]

Whenever Melvin Laird convened PISS in Washington, its roster of Wisconsinites always included Supreme Court Chief Justice Warren Burger, as well as two Democrats—prominent lawyer Tommy "The Cork" Corcoran and Senator Gaylord Nelson. On this Wednesday evening Tommy the Cork was on the piano, the chief justice was belting out songs, and Laird was picking a fair tune on the garbolene, a country bass fiddle (sometimes called a "gut bucket") made out of string and a large lard bucket or garbage can.

Some time after midnight, Nelson got into a friendly disagreement with Laird. For years they had been debating one another with healthy mutual respect, since they had served together in the Wisconsin State Senate on different sides of the aisle. (The *Christian Science Monitor*'s Godfrey Sperling said that when he made a trip to Wisconsin in the late 1940s, he was told that "the two smartest men" in the legislature were Laird and Nelson, and he was surprised that for being "from such opposite poles" they got along so well together.[2]) This particular debate at the PISS gathering turned into a wager; for what stakes, no one remembers.

Senator Nelson insisted that the "hotline" between Moscow and Washington was located at the White House. Laird, who ought to know, maintained that it was at the Pentagon. When Nelson wouldn't concede the point, Laird decided to settle it that very night. He loaded Nelson into a chauffeured car and took him to the Pentagon. Probably the combination of the late hour (3 A.M.), the libations at the PISS affair, and the trust Nelson had in Laird overcame any reluctance the senator might have had to enter the Pentagon. Nelson was known as a consistent antiwar vote in the Senate, and his legislative interests leaned toward the environment. To have a tree-hugger and peacenik taken into the bowels of the Pentagon was a rare event.

Nelson recalled, "I got out of Mel's car and he pulled out the longest key I ever saw; it must have been four or five or six inches. As he put it into the [elevator] slot, sparks flew and all that. An elevator came for him and we were whisked up a couple floors, where we were met by a bird colonel or a brigadier general." They were then led into a cavernous room, two stories tall and full of military personnel at work in the middle of the night. It was the National Military Command Center, where Laird settled the bet by triumphantly showing Nelson the hotline, which was similar to a teletype machine and not a telephone. They spent the rest of the night there talking. Laird remembered that there was "quite a little stir with the chairman of the Joint Chiefs and a few other people the next day that I had brought an anti-war senator into the command center. I told them: 'He's my friend,' and that ended the complaints."[3]

Robert Pursley said the incident was typical of Laird, who wooed members of Congress like no other defense secretary before or since. "Steps like taking Senator Nelson in the middle of the night to NMCC were exceedingly helpful. I'm sure Nelson regaled all of his friends over on the Hill about what he'd seen and done. Mel made a lot of money for the Defense Department that way." Laird probably also set a record for the number of federal legislators hosted at the Pentagon in a four-year period. In one year he managed to lure almost all one hundred senators to the Pentagon in groups or individually, often for breakfast or lunch. For many of the lawmakers it was an unexpected and welcome opportunity to explore the inner sanctum. One of the Laird-era service secretaries recalled that, at one luncheon, Democratic Senator John McClellan of Arkansas "was almost in tears as he expressed thanks for being invited into the Pentagon for the first time in eight years."[4]

Not willing to wait for the legislators to come to him, Laird couldn't keep himself away from Capitol Hill. He would wander the halls of Congress several times a week even when he was not scheduled for testimony at any committee hearing. His most common excuse was the haircut gambit. Use of the House barber shop was a perquisite for current and former members of Congress, and Laird haunted the shop regularly, in spite of his lack of hair to cut. The longtime Pentagon administrator Doc Cooke said it was often noticed around the E-ring that Laird would disappear for an hour or more, sometimes more than once a week, to get a haircut. An internal accounting by a Pentagon intern of Laird's hours spent on Capitol Hill showed that the secretary's "haircuts" seemed to take anywhere from forty minutes to three and a half hours. "Mr. Laird must have been especially well-groomed in December [1971], when the record lists three haircuts in one eight-day period," the study reported.[5]

The wily secretary had discovered an ideal neutral setting in which to keep up his contacts with individual members of Congress. "A lot of people would hear I was there and come in and visit with me," Laird laughed. House barber Joe "Q" Quattrone confirmed that. The Italian immigrant began as a House barber in 1970 and had a vivid recollection of Laird holding court while he got a haircut and maybe a manicure or a facial, too. "*Everybody* wanted to visit him when they heard he was here—both sides, Republican or Democrat, it didn't matter," Quattrone said.[6]

Dr. John Foster, the Pentagon research chief, observed that Laird's haircuts

were primarily "an intelligence-gathering operation" and one of the most effective Capitol Hill had ever seen. Laird's legislative affairs chiefs Rady Johnson
and Dick Capen were responsible for keeping track of what was happening in
Congress. "He was always a step ahead of us," recalled Johnson. "He'd go up to
the Hill and get—quote—'a haircut' and see fifteen senators I couldn't have
seen in a week." Capen reckoned that the haircuts were also an escape from the
pressures of the Pentagon, a "chance to go back to the past he had loved." But
the haircuts added to Capen's stress. "I always knew when he went for this ritual because my hotline rang the instant he returned; he was calling just to rattle
my cage with information he had gathered and I had not. 'You certainly should
have known that!' he'd prod. 'What in the hell are you doing?'" As Capen saw it,
the simple fact was that no one in the Pentagon—or the entire Nixon executive
branch, for that matter—could compete with Laird's knowledge and contacts
on Capitol Hill. "Hell, he'd come back after thirty minutes on the Hill in a
barber's chair having learned more than my seven hundred [legislative affairs]
people could learn in a month about what was really going on there."[7]

At one cocktail party, Lieutenant Colonel George Dalferes was asked what
it was like working for Laird in legislative affairs. "It's kind of like being the
pope's religious advisor," he quipped.[8]

⚬

As a group, the men who were probably closest to Laird were the half dozen or
so who met with him at 8:15 every morning. That included his personal staff
(headed by special assistant Carl Wallace, military assistants Pursley and Admiral Dan Murphy, and speech writer Bill Baroody), Deputy Secretary Packard,
General Counsel Fred Buzhardt, and the public and legislative affairs leadership. The previous evening's newscasts and the morning newspapers were
reviewed, as well as any action on Capitol Hill the previous day. There was a review of what was expected to happen in both the media and legislative arenas,
and Laird issued marching orders for the day. (He referred to it as his "public
relations" meeting, but the group never had a name that stuck.)

Laird was more comfortable with this group than at any other personnel
meetings—which, of course, meant he would vent more there. If he walked
into the meeting with storm clouds evident above him, he would point to the
one he was blaming that day for some embarrassment in Congress or in the
media and say, "It's your turn in the barrel."

"We'd take bets on who would be 'in the barrel' that morning because of
some disaster," Capen said. "We dealt with some terrible situations, as well as
some very inspiring situations." After Capen left, he bought a small wine keg
and had a plaque mounted on it: "To Melvin R. Laird: Morning Memorial
Barrel Awarded Daily for Extra-Meritorious Screw Ups. Donated By a Devoted
Laird Admirer and Frequent Barrel Occupant Who Thrived On the Hazards

of the Hill." Laird placed it prominently behind his desk and would award it occasionally to "the biggest foul-up of the day."[9]

Legislative affairs was the only top civilian office that had three chiefs rather than one or two during Laird's four-year term. The first to hold the position as assistant to the secretary for legislative affairs was Jack Stempler, a career government attorney who had served in the job since 1965 for both McNamara and Clifford. The tough ex-marine was a no-nonsense career civil servant valued by Laird when he had been a congressman, which was why Laird kept the Democrat on the job. In 1970 Stempler transferred to a position with the air force secretary. (He later served again as legislative liaison chief during the Carter administration for Defense Secretary Harold Brown.)[10] Stempler was replaced by Capen, who had moved from the public affairs shop to become chief Pentagon lobbyist for a year and a half. He returned to the newspaper business in California in mid-1971. (Capen became a top editor in the Knight-Ridder newspaper chain, noted author, and U.S. ambassador to Spain at the end of the George H.W. Bush administration.)[11] Rady Johnson finished the term with Laird.

All those who worked for Laird could repeat in their sleep his constant reminder to them that Congress is a *co-equal* branch of government. "He always used that term," noted Assistant Secretary for Atomic Energy Carl Walske. "It wasn't good enough that it was just an equal branch; it was CO-equal."[12] All were told to cooperate as fully as possible with any legitimate request from Congress. Part of that cooperation went further than the standard fare of protecting bases, military projects, and defense contractors in the congressional districts. On rare occasions Laird could help a member of Congress by arranging a better posting for a soldier. (He recalled doing a favor for Senator Al Gore Sr. when his son Al Jr. was sent to Vietnam. Laird arranged a desk job at the *Stars and Stripes*. Young Gore never knew what his father had done.) Many requests came from patrons of young men who wanted to avoid the draft, but Laird was unsympathetic. Not once did he keep someone out of the military who didn't otherwise qualify for draft exemption. And only rarely did he hasten a promotion at the request of someone else, as he did with Senator Margaret Chase Smith's chief of staff to win the 1969 ABM vote. A former assistant secretary of the air force, Richard Borda, remembered being heavily pressured by one congressman to promote the son of one of his campaign supporters. Knowing Laird's policy generally forbade such special intercession with promotion boards, "I told the congressman 'No,' and he kicked me out of his office."[13]

Foremost among the favors Laird had at his disposal was the military's transportation fleet—from chauffeured government cars to yachts and jet aircraft. "I kept these under my control," Laird said. "I didn't let any of those goodies get too far away from me." He had no problem, for example, personally authorizing the dispatch of an army officer in a chauffeured department car to transport Senator John Stennis to Walter Reed Army Medical Center for continuing medical treatment after Stennis, who was chairman of the Senate Armed Services Committee, was shot by a burglar.[14]

Since the Defense Department paid for the operation of the three presidential yachts, Laird was free to use them any time the president didn't need them. The smallest was the sixty-four-foot cabin cruiser whose Kennedy name *(Patrick J.)* was changed to *Julie* by Nixon, and there was a larger ninety-foot cabin cruiser whose Kennedy name *(Honey Fitz)* was changed to *Patricia.* Nixon decided to sell both of those navy-operated yachts in 1970, leaving him with the 104-foot *Sequoia,* which never failed to impress his or Laird's guests. Originally built for a prominent Philadelphia family in 1925 out of fir, teak, and mahogany, the *Sequoia* was bought by the Department of Commerce six years later to use on the Mississippi River as a decoy to trap rum-runners. Herbert Hoover commissioned it for his use in 1933, and it served every president until Jimmy Carter sold it. Franklin Roosevelt met with Winston Churchill on the *Sequoia* to discuss D-Day. Harry Truman played many card games on it or entertained guests on the Kimball piano brought aboard. Actress Marilyn Monroe sang a lusty "Happy Birthday" to Kennedy on the yacht. Laird found that a peaceful Potomac River cruise on the *Sequoia* could be just the ticket to persuade recalcitrant members of Congress to give the Defense Department a break.[15]

As for the military's aircraft, Laird didn't want the department to become an air-taxi service for Congress, so he required the House speaker and the Senate president pro tem to sign a document declaring that each flight requested by a member of Congress was in the national interest. Laird had seen massive abuse of military flights during the Johnson administration and was anxious to limit the waste. Even with a cautious clampdown, the department still flew hundreds of legislators on trips home to their district, on "fact-finding missions" around the world, and other errands deemed useful to the government.

In a colorful private paper for a September 1969 presentation to the Cabinet, Nixon's legislative liaison Bryce Harlow acutely described the situation Nixon faced with "that hypersensitive, volatile, infallibly hindsighted, caustic power center known as the Congress": immediately after the election win, "as our adrenaline subsided, it became evident that this sweet nectar of victory held a droplet of hemlock." The returns showed the new Nixon administration "would face a substantial hostile margin in both Senate and House." Republicans were eight votes short of a majority in the Senate and twenty-six short in the House. "All this," Harlow continued, "makes one pucker a bit to realize that not for 120 years had a brand new Administration started out in such adversity on Capitol Hill."

Harlow listed the extraordinary demands made by the Democrats even before Nixon was inaugurated. The "first garlic in the traditional honeymoon" was an ultimatum from a Senate Democrat that unless all pending postmaster nominations were confirmed at once, all of Nixon's Cabinet confirmations would be held up. The chair of the Senate Rules Committee called Harlow during the transition to say that if the federal printer was changed to a Republican nominee, things would go roughly for the administration. "Other Democratic chairmen were similarly discreetly menacing," Harlow reported.[16]

Nixon could count on one finger his miracle worker with Congress—it was Mel Laird. Because of that, Laird was "irreplaceable," wrote former Nixon aide John Ehrlichman in his memoirs. Ehrlichman was present on occasions when Nixon or Kissinger railed about Laird going his own way. "But Henry didn't demand Laird's firing.... Laird was so effective with his old Congressional cronies that everyone realized he was irreplaceable," Ehrlichman wrote.[17]

Nixon tried to get more help with Congress, first approaching the rising Republican star in the House, Robert Michel of Illinois. Early in the Nixon administration and Michel's seventh congressional term, Harlow and Republican leaders pushed Michel to resign and help the White House's struggling legislative liaison efforts. At a key moment, Michel recalled that Laird—who couldn't imagine anyone leaving the House—encouraged him to decline the offer, so he did. "Mel saved my life," Michel later said. The congressman, who counted himself a Laird protégé, went on to become the House minority leader from 1981 to 1995.[18]

One of the reasons Hill leaders liked Laird was because he readily made himself and his people available for testimony or consultation. He sometimes used staff meetings to coach them on how to be model witnesses: Don't hide information just because it looks bad; don't bring too many aides with you because it makes you look like you're not prepared; and *never* get hostile or combative with the legislative inquisitors. Learn how to politely filibuster when time is limited and the questioner seems to be building to a dramatic negative point; you can thus throw him off his game.[19] (The *Washington Post* once wrote that "when Laird was on Capitol Hill testifying, he was at his best.... As a witness, he was clearly better at answering or evading questions than many legislators are at asking them. His ability to make his point, whether it had any relation to the question, was maddening to veteran lawmakers." Senator Fulbright once called him "a genius of semantic confusion."[20])

On more than one occasion, Laird was secretly invited into executive House sessions where defense bills were "marked up" for final submissions. Normally no member of the executive branch is allowed near the door in those sessions. Laird also used to his advantage his unique relationship with the General Accounting Office and Elmer Staats, its comptroller general. The GAO is the investigative arm of Congress, and Laird had used it many times to poke around at the Pentagon when he was a congressman. Aware of the damage the

GAO could do with a good audit, Laird actually assisted the auditors tasked to the Defense Department. Because of the personal relationship he cultivated with Staats, Laird was always forewarned about what an audit contained before Congress got it. Thus, he either corrected the problem before the audit became fodder for a legislator, or he had a plan in place that he could immediately announce as a way of correcting the problem.[21]

There is no better measure of Laird's prodigious legislative success than the fact that, when he was secretary of defense, he never lost a single roll call vote on defense matters in either the House or the Senate. Rady Johnson said the key to Laird's success in Congress was that he "knew how to compromise when compromise made sense." Such a record, by a Republican Cabinet officer dealing with a Democratic Congress full of animosity toward the Defense Department, gave Laird standing to ignore or circumvent Nixon and Kissinger if his keener political sense deemed it necessary. "Nixon kept me on because he needed me—because I was the only one who could get along with Congress on a lot of these issues," Laird flatly stated.

The legislative record confirms that Laird was Nixon's only Cabinet official who never suffered a major defeat in Congress. For example, in 1969 the president sent forty domestic proposals to Congress, including tax reform and bills to control crime, drugs, and pornography—and his premiere effort: welfare reform. Only a handful of minor bills passed the first year.[22] After that year, the three most important legislative victories were defense-related—the ABM vote, the draft lottery bill, and the Vietnamization program, all engineered by Laird.

It was not easy for Laird, despite his congressional prowess. It required careful planning, hard work, and shrewd maneuvering. And it required him, by President Nixon's own insistence, to help the administration on Capitol Hill on many nondefense issues that Laird had originated in Congress when he was ranking member of the HEW Appropriations Committee—which included automatic cost-of-living increases in Social Security payments, the war on cancer, and revenue sharing with the states.

❧

"May the Lord—and President Nixon—give you strength to keep defense spending down," the CBS producer of *Face the Nation* had written to Laird before he arrived at the Pentagon.[23] The tenor of the times was such that almost everyone expected slashed defense budgets, even though the United States was still fully involved in a war. On the other side of he debate was Laird, who firmly believed there was a desperate need to modernize the armed forces, restock all the troops not supporting Vietnam, and speed up research and development to stay ahead of the Soviet Union.

Laird had an innate ability to anticipate an outcome. CBS newsman Bob

Schieffer, who covered the Pentagon in Laird's day, called him "one of those rare guys in Washington who could look at a situation and tell you how it's gonna come out down the road." Pursley explained, "Mel seems to know what people might do or are going to do—being a keen enough student of the human spirit to predict people's views and actions way before they themselves know what they are going to do. He was certainly two to three years ahead of everybody in the administration in knowing where Congress was going to come down on things, shaping policies that would take that into account."[24]

What Laird saw was ominous: Johnson had robbed men, matériel, and money from every other part of the defense budget—including NATO troop support and weapons research—to feed his Vietnam War machine. Money was needed to produce new weaponry to keep ahead of the Soviets. Military pay had to be increased substantially to create an all-volunteer force. The public had to be disabused of any expectation of a "peace dividend," which had been fueled by presidential hopeful Hubert Humphrey in the 1968 campaign.

The man Laird had in the Defense Department on point for this predictably unpopular budget battle was his chief financial officer, Assistant Secretary Robert Moot. He was so respected in Congress that there had been no doubt in Laird's mind that Moot, a Democratic holdover from Clark Clifford's administration, should stay on as comptroller. The decision proved fortuitous. Besides the "selling" of the defense budget to the White House and Congress, Moot also had to figure out a way to run the department for months at a time on the promise of money while Congress dawdled in approving a budget. Laird lamented in one press conference that there never seemed to be a day he was not dealing with Congress to approve the defense budget. "Every day is budget day as far as the Department of Defense is concerned," he said. When he had been a congressman, the defense budget was decided during one week of House hearings and two or three days of Senate hearings, but not so by the time he became defense chief.[25]

Moot said he got through the four years with his sanity intact because of Laird's unswerving support and guidance. Laird's behind-the-scenes lobbying was pivotal in persuading Princeton University to name Moot as one of the prestigious Rockefeller Public Service Award winners in 1971. Laird proudly announced the award at a staff meeting. "It is not often that someone from the Defense Department is a recipient of one of these annual awards," Laird said. "One has to be a strong candidate to win."

"Or have an outstanding and persistent boss," Moot interrupted. And he added in all seriousness, "By the way, we will run out of money today."[26]

⤣

A week before Lyndon Johnson left office, he had delivered a budget to Congress that included about $80 billion for defense. Well knowing the mood of many members of Congress, as well as the public, Laird feared that Congress would gut his first-year budget by as much as $10 billion, or about 12 percent. Given Laird's plans to increase pay, modernize weapons systems, and restock non-Vietnam supplies in Europe and elsewhere, that was totally untenable. To Laird it meant that in trying to keep the Soviet Union "contained" through the Vietnam War, America might easily lose the cold war.

Laird, possessing formidable knowledge about every detail of the defense budget, had hit the ground running. First, he made some quick, cold calculations: what could the department live with and what had to go? When he was done with the review, Laird came up with a bottom-line figure. Defense could stand a $5 billion cut. Once he had the number, Laird sat down separately with the chairmen of the four defense-related congressional committees and told them that the military needed $75 billion to survive and that he was willing to let Congress take credit for any cuts. One of their number, at the right time, could call for $5 billion in cuts, and, for his part, Laird would publicly grouse about it. At the same time, he would progress with a series of moves aimed at meeting the $5 billion figure.

The deal was struck. In March Laird agreed, ostensibly under pressure, that he would abandon his proposal for a $1.2 billion military pay increase on the way to an all-volunteer force. He would wait until 1970. Within weeks he announced that he was canceling the air force's manned military space satellite program, which was a $2 billion-plus program that competed with NASA. At the time, his new Air Force Secretary Robert Seamans, who had come to the Pentagon from NASA, was a strong advocate for the service's Manned Orbital Laboratory (MOL) program. "I asked Mel for a day in court" to save the program, Seamans recounted. "My day arrived on a Saturday afternoon when [the project director] and I met with Laird, Kissinger, and President Nixon in the Oval Office. Kissinger called me on Monday to tell me I had made an excellent presentation, and on Tuesday MOL was canceled."[27]

Laird also deactivated eighteen navy ships, decreased the number of costly B-52 bomber raids in South Vietnam, and took other measures that brought the total in cuts to $3.2 billion in April—a good point to stop. He kept the remaining budget cuts in his pocket until the time was right to announce them. Then in July 1969 the White House budget boss, Robert Mayo, said that he expected "very substantial" cuts in defense spending, more than Laird had already announced. Laird had prepared for that contingency, and while he had told selected members of Congress about his end game, he did not reveal his hand to Mayo and the White House defense budget specialist, James Schlesinger. "I always had two budgets that I presented to different parts of the government," Laird recalled.

"I didn't realize he *ever* confined himself to only *two* budgets," Schlesinger laughed in hindsight. Like a shell game, Laird floated several defense budgets at any given time, only confiding to a trusted few which one he really needed.

Laird said he would give the White House a budget version with cuts in it "that I knew would horrify Nixon. For example, Nixon had more interest in supporting NATO than Vietnam, so I would send over a budget to the White House—or Congress, in some cases—that would show big cuts in NATO. I couldn't have survived without that strategy."

At an August 11, 1969, staff meeting, Laird bemoaned the lack of support in Congress. He said he was doing all he could, but many legislators were being unreasonable. "Mr. Mahon, of course, understands." Two days later Congressman George Mahon, Laird's willing coconspirator in the House, played the role of bad cop and called for serious cuts in the defense budget—"at least $5 billion," he said. Legislators began lining up behind the number, not knowing that Mahon and Laird had already colluded on the figure. A couple of weeks later Laird, true to the plan, came up with a total of $4.1 billion in cuts. Any more than that, he said in a speech, "would be counterproductive." Defense critics calling for larger cuts "are urging a very dangerous course," he said. Then, in collusion with Kissinger, Laird persuaded Nixon that the military had too many international missions that were not being fully financed by Congress and the taxpayers. Yet, since the end of World War II, Congress had approved mutual-defense treaties with forty-two nations. U.S. troops were deployed to more than two thousand spots around the globe; it was simply too much.

The quickest way to make a change, Laird argued, was to get rid of the U.S. military doctrine that dictated America needed "force levels" capable of fighting two-and-a-half wars simultaneously. The military was already stretched thin fighting just one war. Laird and Kissinger persuaded the president to change the force-level goal to one-and-a-half wars. On October 11, 1969, Nixon signed the secret National Security Decision Memorandum 27, changing "the approved United States strategy for general purpose forces." *New York Times* reporter William Beecher got wind of the new strategy and made it public.

At the same time this was happening, Mahon and others in Congress were telling Laird that the pressure from colleagues had become so great they weren't sure they could hold the line at the agreed-upon $5 billion in cuts. So on October 27 Laird announced that he was going to save $609 million a year by downsizing or closing 307 bases—only 27 of them overseas. The 280 domestic bases were spread out over forty-two states, which meant that thousands of jobs would be lost in the districts of eighty-four U.S. senators and a majority of representatives. *Newsweek* dubbed Laird "Mel the Knife." At this point, even the most ardent defense critics in Congress knew they had been outfoxed. So they declared victory...and retreated swiftly back to the safer, compromise $5 billion figure. (After the first-year's budget battle, Laird went on to close more bases than any defense secretary before or since. In four years he closed 400 installations and reduced 1,400 others.)

One more hurdle unexpectedly arose as Nixon was holed up at Camp David over the Christmas holidays to review the budget one more time. Word was soon passed to Laird that the president wanted to cut another $3 billion or more from defense to balance the budget and pay for increases in popular domestic programs. Rather than confront Nixon directly, which the president always avoided anyway, Laird called Mayo and said, simply: "Bob, please tell the president that if he wants more cut than the $5 billion, he'll need to look for a new secretary of defense." It was the only time in four years that Laird threatened to resign; he didn't need to again. Nixon immediately capitulated and never again tried to push Laird further than he was willing to go on the budget.[28]

⚜

Kissinger also made a run at taking the defense budget out of Laird's hands. It was probably the largest grab for power that Kissinger made without success. He regularly and almost effortlessly sidelined the State Department and other elements of government, but the Pentagon was a big piece of the pie that he could not claim—not for lack of trying. He made his first move into defense budget territory ironically in response to changes proposed by Laird.

In midsummer 1969 Laird suggested a new way to review defense budget alternatives by telling the president the economic and political impact of each option. Nixon eagerly accepted the idea and in October 1969 authorized creation of the Defense Program Review Committee (DPRC) as a National Security Council–level committee. As with many of the NSC committees, Kissinger had the option of being chairman, and he jumped at this one as a way to inject himself into Laird's budgeting choices. While the changes were only supposed to give the president and Congress a big picture of defense spending, it was Kissinger's inclination to delve into the nuts and bolts of the defense budget. Thus, what could have been a more productive way to look at spending turned into a debate on decisions that had historically been left to the defense secretary.[29]

Once Laird saw that the DPRC was a Kissinger grab for turf, Laird checkmated Kissinger through a time-honored practice—delay by paperwork. DPRC meetings had to be repeatedly postponed because the Defense Department was "not ready" with a background paper. Laird wasn't subtle about his parrying moves. Kissinger's deputy Alexander Haig once called Pursley to angrily complain about the Defense Department's failure to respond to a DPRC directive from Kissinger. "Why aren't you doing what we are asking you to do?" Haig demanded. Pursley didn't fence: "Mr. Laird ordered that I ignore that directive." Haig hung up on him.[30]

Kissinger's frustration was painfully evident as early as 1970. At one DPRC meeting, Kissinger thought one of his decisions was being criticized, so he got up and walked out in anger.[31] The level of his fury was evident in a column written by Joseph Kraft (after someone in the meeting leaked the story to him).

"Laird has ceased to be a willing accomplice of the DPRC in its effort to contain the defense budget," Kraft wrote in November 1970. "His office has been very slow to forward alternate estimates on service appropriations. In some cases, it recommends spending figures way out of line with the force structure proposed. One high civilian official in attendance at a recent meeting called the Defense Department's position 'surrealistic.'"[32]

While the original DPRC design ultimately withered and died, what Laird had foreseen in 1969 came to pass over the next four years. His plan succeeded—to accept cuts for two years and then turn the budget around for slow growth. The first-year's budget of $75.3 billion dropped in the second year to $68.75 billion, then rose to $73.55 billion, and the final budget submission was $79.6 billion. Laird was able to hold the defense budget—after four years—under LBJ's final proposed budget in 1969.

Part of Laird's foresight included consideration of the defense budget in reference to the gross national product. "I have always thought," he said, "that the American people would not, on a long-term basis, be willing to devote more than 7 percent of the GNP to national security requirements. As a rule of thumb, I always used a figure along that line." So Laird's determined budget-cutting in the first two years and slow growth in the last two brought the defense budget from an LBJ high in 1968 of 9.5 percent of the GNP down to 6.4 percent in late 1972, the lowest percentage in twenty-two years.[33]

More significantly, Laird helped Nixon achieve something Democrats had talked about for decades but had never been able to accomplish: spending more on human resource programs than on defense. The historic turning point came in July 1971, when, for the first time, the budget of the Department of Health, Education, and Welfare exceeded that of the Defense Department. A startling reordering of national priorities occurred in just one Nixon term, which could not have happened without Laird's deft congressional budget gamesmanship. When Laird became secretary of defense, 44 percent of LBJ's last budget had been spent on defense and 33 percent on human resource programs. "We've now [reversed] those priorities so that 33 percent is devoted to national security and defense, and 44 percent to the human resource program of our government," Laird pointed out in 1972.[34]

"When all the smoke had cleared from Laird's tenure, the defense budget had been reduced by almost 30 percent excluding inflation," authors Richard Stubbing and Richard Mendel observed in *The Defense Game*. That "he managed to accomplish this while still retaining the full support of the military services" was something of a miracle, they added. The services seemed to feel all the vital military requirements were being met, including an appropriate force structure and readiness for the new one-and-a-half war strategy. "Perhaps the best evidence in support of Laird is that the military chiefs accepted *without protest* the budgets they received from Congress."[35]

28

Laird on *Dee*fense

WITHIN WEEKS OF BECOMING SECRETARY, Laird lectured his top staff, including the Joint Chiefs, about the need to mingle with the masses on the speakers' circuit. "We need to make an effort to explain the significant contributions that the military makes to this country. The military has been downgraded for too long. We must take the offensive on this matter!"[1] But the order was ignored. So hostile was the American attitude toward the U.S. military that a public speech by any Defense Department representative was likely to be met by obscenities and rotten produce.

At the end of Laird's first year in office he asked for a statistical summary of speeches. The generals and admirals were avoiding the lecture circuit like cats avoiding a bath. When they did venture out, it was to preach to the choir—to soldiers, veterans, retirees, and friendly Rotarians. Grudgingly, the new Joint Chiefs chairman, Admiral Moorer, scheduled a single college speech at Princeton University in March 1972. It was a disaster. As Moorer approached the lectern, about a hundred students in the front row stood up and turned their backs to him. The decorated admiral told them that the first time he came to Princeton was to play a football game in the 1930s, and his team lost 9 to 0. This time, too, "I did not come because I thought it would be an enjoyable experience." In an attempt to quiet the catcalls, he told them that they were the only college audience he was scheduled to speak to in 1972. But the response suggested they didn't consider it a privilege. Noisy heckling, booing, and hissing continued. "I would recommend that all of you, as you grow older, say what you're for and don't spend so much time saying what you are against," the sixty-year-old Moorer counseled. They didn't like that either. He pleaded: "Let's communicate a little bit because you certainly don't get anywhere by making idle noise." Moorer continued to struggle through his thirty-five-minute speech and left despondent, with a memory of one of the large antiwar posters reading: "No Moorer Murder."[2]

General Westmoreland made a foray or two into academia, with a similar lack of enthusiasm or success. He agreed to give a speech, "The Army's role in the Search for Peace," at Yale in April 1972. But when he got to the auditorium, it was an out-and-out melee. Demonstrators were overrunning campus police, who told Westmoreland they couldn't guarantee his safety. On the advice of the Defense Department security men with him, Westmoreland left without delivering his speech on peace.[3]

David Packard was game, but it was disheartening for him to be spurned at his own Stanford campus—his alma mater, to which he had contributed millions of dollars, and a place whose administrators, faculty, and students revered him until he agreed to serve his country by becoming deputy secretary to Laird. Admiral Zumwalt commiserated with Packard at a staff meeting after one of his own talks to students. He couldn't even tell the long-haired boys from the girls anymore. "I was talking with one student, saying 'yes, ma'am,' and I later found out he was a man. Now we have to be careful with these young people when we say 'yes, sir' or 'yes, ma'am' to them."[4]

Anecdotal evidence suggests that by far the most fearless of the brass was General Daniel "Chappie" James, assigned to Laird's public affairs office. Otherwise, the civilian leadership, including Laird, were more willing than the military men to go out on the speakers' circuit. Froehlke accepted more college invitations than most of the top Pentagon staff but could recall only one at which he was not heckled—Brigham Young University in Provo, Utah, where six thousand students listened to him quietly. "I'm not sure they agreed with me at all, but they were polite," he recalled.[5]

These were times when, as new Army Secretary Froehlke discovered in 1971, the rank-and-file army at the Pentagon had to be ordered to wear uniforms at least once a week. "Particularly the enlisted and the lower-ranking officers didn't want to wear their uniforms...because people would spit on them and denigrate them," said Froehlke. "We had to force them once a week. That's how bad it was. A crying shame."

Froehlke understood why Americans were conflicted, and he sympathized to a point. "I want you to know that I'm not sure we're right," he said in his speeches. "I'm doing what I think is right. But there's one group that I know is wrong, and that's the group that's sure it is right." He didn't always get far enough into his speeches to say that, such as during his attempted oration to a crowd of four hundred at Harvard in 1972. "My wife was with me and as I walked in you could see a dozen dirty, disheveled kids right down front. They threw every four-letter word at me," he said. Thinking it would shame the crowd into civility, Froehlke remarked, "I would like you to meet my wife." But they continued to shout, and security guards advised the Froehlkes to leave, which they did.[6]

Laird felt it was key to lead by example. "I went to colleges all over the United States," he recalled. "I got demonstrated against. I got eggs tossed at me. I got animal blood thrown at me. I met with student classes and explained positions. Sometimes there was disagreement, but at least I wasn't afraid to face them." The egg-and-blood sideshows were often more remembered than Laird's speeches, which tended to be dry, even when his tone would intensify on cue to sell the "three pillars" of the Nixon Doctrine. But he could come alive during question-and-answer sessions, or he could be deliberately dull if he chose. His most common way of dodging a question was to launch into a lengthy policy analysis, leaving his listeners yawning. Laird didn't mind boring them as long as they forgot what they had asked him in the first place.

What most upset Laird was not the demonstrations on the campuses, but the defeatist tone the military officers seemed to have in their talks. All speeches were supposed to be cleared five days in advance with the public information office. One reason was to avoid duplication, like the time all three service secretaries agreed to give talks at the same seminar on the same day, which Laird considered a waste of stars that should be scattered all across the American firmament. The clearance process also allowed Laird to detect trends. At one point he said at a staff meeting that they must stop speaking as if the Soviet Union were ahead of the United States in the missile race: "We certainly don't gain a lot by talking as if we are a second rate power."[7]

By 1970 Laird had become "the talkingest Defense Secretary yet," according to *Washington Star* columnist Orr Kelly. The Pentagon kept audio tapes of speeches and congressional testimony by Laird and his predecessors, and Kelly counted the hours. In little over a year Laird had filled eighty hours of tape compared to ninety-two hours for McNamara in his entire seven years, and sixteen hours for Clifford's one year. Kelly factored in Laird's slower, more deliberate pace of speaking—he averaged 100 words a minute, Clifford 130, and McNamara 180. The result was that Laird, in his first sixteen months in office, had spoken 786,000 words on Defense Department business in public. The close-to-the-vest McNamara, on the other hand, over his seven years had spoken 923,000 words.[8] Laird considered public relations a primary part of his job; he practiced what he preached, and he preached what he practiced.

When Laird first came to the Pentagon, he was appalled at how run-down, dreary, and "just lousy-looking it was. It looked like hell," he said. He assigned Froehlke to beautify its halls with commemorative artwork and exhibits. "I believe this building deserves more than a maze of meandering passageways," he declared at one ceremony. "Its history, its importance to American security, and its deeply entwined association with our society and our people deserve more than a coat of paint and occasional sweepings."[9]

Laird's first project was to dedicate the E-ring third-floor hall in front of his office to the late President Eisenhower. Laird always believed in honoring people—holding up heroes and heroines as examples for others to follow as he had done. Because he was a penny pincher, Laird induced the Eisenhower Library to donate most of the materials, and he privately solicited $28,000 from IBM's Tom Watson for a newly commissioned portrait of Ike. Mamie and John Eisenhower, as well as the only remaining five-star general, Omar Bradley, attended the May 1970 dedication.[10]

The next corridor to be named for a defense luminary was in front of the offices of the Joint Chiefs of Staff. General Bradley, the beloved "GI's general," was a natural choice. At almost eighty he was able to attend the dedication in June 1972, along with his wife and his golfing buddy, comedian Bob Hope. Bradley was typically terse in response to the evening's festivities: "I am a soldier, serving my country in peace and in war. Thank God for the privilege, both then and now."[11] Following Laird's example, Donald Rumsfeld on his first tour as secretary of defense in 1976 named a third corridor for the legendary World War II general and statesman George C. Marshall. After that there was a controversial groundswell to memorialize General Douglas MacArthur with a hall. President Carter's defense secretary, Harold Brown, refused to so honor the man whose insubordination to President Truman caused his recall from Korea and retirement in 1951. But when Ronald Reagan became president, he chose as his defense secretary a former aide of MacArthur's, Caspar Weinberger, who promptly memorialized MacArthur with a hall in 1981 in the presence of Reagan and MacArthur's widow.[12]

Laird thought it was a good idea to have a Corridor of the Secretaries along the A-ring, which featured portraits of the nine men who had gone before him. With typical self-deprecating humor—knowing he would "hang" there one day—Laird remarked at the January 1972 dedication that in the "bewildering spider web" that is the Pentagon, "this corridor may never rival the Louvre or the National Gallery of Art in popularity, but I am sure that it will never be without visitors—scholars, military and civilian, the idly curious, and the hopelessly lost."[13]

Some of Laird's beautification efforts focused on the Pentagon grounds. He oversaw the planting of trees, mandated that construction of parking lots be done in such a way as to protect the greenery, and forced the builders of the new Washington subway system to tunnel around some of the older foliage. (He once joked that he hoped to be remembered as "the secretary who saved the trees.")[14]

Another indoor memorial that Laird oversaw was the Hall of Heroes, which recognized every Medal of Honor recipient beginning with the Civil War. At the time, that included more than 3,200 men and one woman, Dr. Mary H. Walker, a Civil War surgeon. Most poignant for Laird was how few of the recipients held a rank higher than sergeant. While Laird was secretary, eighty-one servicemen distinguished themselves with "conspicuous gallantry and intrepidity in action at the risk of life, above and beyond the call of duty" in Vietnam. Twenty-five lived to receive their medals, but fifty-six medals were awarded posthumously. Laird recalled with deep emotion the times the medals were given to grieving family members.[15]

The final dedication of a corridor by Laird occurred just before Thanksgiving 1972: the Corridor of Correspondents—because, Laird firmly believed, "a strong free press and a strong free nation are inseparable." The hall has become a tribute to the men and women of the media who cover the military through war and peace. This section of the Pentagon's second-floor B-ring houses the Pentagon press room and offices of the Public Affairs Division. At one end of the corridor Laird had a memorial built for the thirty-six correspondents who lost their lives in World War II, eight killed in the Korean War and sixteen (up to that point) who had died in Vietnam. A large painting of Ernie Pyle, the legendary Scripps-Howard "GI Joe" chronicler, portrays him at his typewriter in a correspondent's field uniform. On the day of the dedication Laird said, "We have made our mistakes and have apologized for them. Some of those mistakes we catch, some the Congress catches, many of them you correspondents catch—and that, ladies and gentlemen, is exactly as it should be. We need not apologize for the adversary relationship of government and the press. Instead we should praise it and we should preserve it. And, as we go about our Constitutional business of being adversaries, we should avoid becoming antagonists."[16]

The new correspondents' corridor was filled with combat paintings, Pulitzer Prize–winning photographs, art work of news correspondents, photos of every defense secretary meeting with the press, and photos of the Pentagon correspondents who were then on the beat. Laird also thought it important to include the best work of editorial cartoonists "in keeping with our belief in good humor and our belief in honest criticism." This from a man who was one of the all-time favorites of political cartoonists; they loved to depict his bald head in the shape of a missile. "I think I was recognized on the street more from those cartoons than anything else," Laird laughed. His aides repeatedly tried in vain to get him to wear glasses, at least for television appearances, to break up the bomb-head look, but Laird would have none of that.[17]

Finally, in the corridor Laird reserved a special place for two glass-framed documents: a replica of the 1967 Freedom of Information Act, which he had supported as a congressman, and a copy of the Public Information Principles he had first laid out in a March 1969 memorandum. The aim of those principles (which were sent as an order to the entire Defense Department) was to begin a new day in military-press relations by treating the media "in an open manner, consistent with the need for security." The principles Laird laid out include "No information will be classified solely because disclosure might result in criticism of the Department of Defense," and "Propaganda has no place in Department of Defense public information programs."[18]

⌇

The preeminent media scourge of the Nixon administration was syndicated columnist Jack Anderson, who had taken over Drew Pearson's *Washington Merry-Go-Round* column upon the latter's death in 1969. While Nixon put Anderson at the top of his "enemies list," Laird seemed to welcome the attention from the self-described "muckraker." One morning, David Heebner, deputy director of Defense Research and Engineering for Tactical Warfare, found himself named in the Anderson column as billionaire Howard Hughes's "representative in the Pentagon." (Heebner had previously worked at Hughes

Aircraft Company.) He recalled his reaction: "I thought it was awfully outrageous—and untruthful!" So he went to Laird asking what he should do. Laird laughed and said, "Don't worry about it. You've just had your reputation made in this building."[19]

When Anderson nicked Laird for being chauffeured in a Cadillac, with another luxury car at the ready, the secretary admitted it with a complaint that "the emoluments which I had as the ranking congressman were much greater than the emoluments which I enjoy as Secretary of Defense, and the work as Secretary of Defense is much greater."[20] When Anderson revealed that Laird had a "hideaway" in the Pentagon to which he sneaked off to have cocktails with aides at the end of the day, Laird invited the columnist over to have a look. Anderson brought a camera and photographed the room, which amounted to little more than a closet with a refrigerator and space for a few people to stand.[21]

When Anderson grumped about nice boats used to ferry enlisted men and flag officers across the Potomac River from Bolling Air Force Base to the Pentagon, Laird responded at a press conference that it appeared Anderson's main complaint was the fact that the seats were leather. "I'll look into that," he laughed. "I'm not sure that the leather upholstery is too great a sin, [but] I will see to it whether they have been excessive on the use of leather upholstery on the boat."[22]

And when Anderson wrote that Laird, "the Pentagon panjandrum," had had the gall to deliver by government limousine his annual Christmas gift (cheddar cheese from Wisconsin) to friends around Washington, including members of Congress, administration officials, and journalists, Laird responded with a memorable gag. He picked the best-looking female marine sergeant he could find and asked her to take a gift-wrapped box of cheese to the columnist. She was to personally deliver it to Anderson and take him to the window to point out the fine government limousine in which she had come. The attached note read: "Dear Jack, I'm sorry I forgot you last Christmas." He signed it: "The Big Cheese." Anderson laughed uproariously.[23]

Sometimes, however, Laird was alarmed at the poor Pentagon security that allowed reporters to discover military secrets that he was not willing to be so open about. In April 1971 Laird complained at a Monday staff meeting: "We seem to have a bad leak on the Joint Staff. Jack Anderson seems to get back-channel messages sooner than I do!" Henkin agreed that "the recent number of leaks seems to be increasing." At the same time, Laird ordered an investigation into the sources of at least thirty Anderson columns over the previous three months, including one exposing U.S. Air Force cloud-seeding over the Ho Chi Minh Trail to make rain and bog down the North Vietnamese supply lines. According to a memorandum on the investigation, a team of Defense Intelligence Agency investigators spent weeks but failed to find any of Anderson's sources.[24]

Laird's method for dealing with critical press, and Anderson in particular, was in stark contrast to Nixon's reaction. Laird would acknowledge when Anderson had justly criticized him and never let it get under his skin. Nixon would curse, fume, and plot in the Oval Office with his aides. Laird ordered an investigation to try to close off Anderson's sources for classified information at the Pentagon, but not an investigation of Anderson himself. Nixon not only conducted CIA surveillance of Anderson, but also had aides, including G. Gordon Liddy, plot various ways to surreptitiously drug the columnist to embarrass him in public. Liddy even offered to assassinate Anderson.[25]

Laird admitted that, when he was secretary of defense, he did leak stories to select reporters. Having become a practiced planter of unattributed items when he was in Congress, Laird was not about to abandon that useful tool to advance his ambitious goals as secretary. "I leaked a few things from time to time when I wanted to put a little pressure on the president," Laird confessed. "If it was something on which I needed to go around the White House or the president, I felt I had to do a little of that in order to protect our flanks."

Kissinger—himself an able practitioner of the leak—said he had a rule of thumb in dealing with Laird. "If Mel calls you up and complains about a story in today's paper, you know he has put it out." Most of the time, however, Kissinger and the White House were wrong to peg Laird as the source of the story. He probably did not leak a quarter as much as the White House suspected him of leaking. (For example, though he said he was "tempted" to slip the classified McNamara history of the Vietnam War, later known as "The Pentagon Papers," to a trusted reporter, he did not do it.)[26]

Most of the time, Laird—or, at his direction, one of his public affairs aides, speechwriter Bill Baroody, or executive assistant Carl Wallace—provided defense-related information to selected journalists in one-on-one background sessions. "If Mel Laird had not foolishly decided to devote his life to public service, he could have actually made something of himself in my business," joked the *Washington Post*'s David Broder, dean of political reporters. "Instead, Mel became one of the—and I capitalize these next two words—Great Sources in Washington, D.C. He scooped up information. He loved to expose plots. When there wasn't a plot to expose, he would invent one. He was a reliable source on everything from the latest political gossip to the most arcane and important international strategy."[27]

Broder remembered "a running joke back when [Laird] was at the Pentagon, that it was really remarkable that a man with all of those heavy responsibilities that he was carrying could still find time to produce five columns a week under the byline of Evans and Novak." CBS newsman Bob Schieffer recalled using that line in one of his radio commentaries at the time. Nixon used to rib Laird about his close relationship with Evans and Novak. "Even at Cabinet meetings, Nixon would bring that up," said Laird. "He'd say, 'Well, I read Evans and Novak today, and I enjoyed your column.' Or, 'Your column was really bad, Mel. Why the hell did you leak that to them?'"[28]

With Laird's permission, Novak acknowledged that Laird was a key source for him and Evans during Laird's congressional days and as secretary of defense. "We used to have lunch or breakfast with him at the Pentagon, and he would tell us what was going on. He gave us the scoop on Vietnamization for a March 1969 column. We got that straight from Laird. He was very, very accurate; we never got any bum dope from him." One of the ironies of the times was that, by 1970, Kissinger had become a source for Evans. "So we kind of had competing leaks between them," said Novak. Because the views of Kissinger and Laird were sometimes starkly different on issues, Novak said he and Evans had to be "very careful about it" to keep both as sources.[29] President George H. W. Bush recalled with amusement that the "battle of the leaks" between Laird and Kissinger was a source of amusement in Nixon administration inner circles, where midlevel aides kept occasional score sheets on who was winning.[30]

Among the journalists Laird favored with exclusive information were more than a dozen who had earned his respect. If he wanted information spread broadly and fast, timed for use by the TV networks, the best conduit was Fred Hoffman of the Associated Press. If the information could hold, then he would likely give it to Charles Corddry of the *Baltimore Sun*—as an indirect way to get an article in the *New York Times,* which was likely to pick up the story. "If you planted something in the *Sun,* you could be guaranteed good coverage in the *Times,*" Laird remembered. Orr Kelly of the *Washington Star* became a close friend of Laird's. Sometimes Laird tipped Sarah McClendon, the iconoclastic reporter who wrote for several Texas newspapers. (He once gave her a golden whistle to use at White House press conferences when he noticed she was having trouble getting recognized.)[31]

Laird shared information with the Pulitzer Prize–winning investigative reporter Seymour Hersh, who was respected by Laird for being such a hardworking, generally accurate Pentagon critic. Hersh first became friends with Dan Henkin, but that never prompted Hersh to pull any punches on the Pentagon. For example, Hersh mercilessly hammered Laird with questions and opinions in an October 1972 *Face the Nation* appearance. The next day, at the Monday staff meeting, Henkin advised those who had not seen it that a transcript was available. "Don't bother reading it," Laird groused. "It should have been called 'The Seymour Hersh Program.'"[32]

Laird also liked the *Christian Science Monitor*'s venerable, unusually civil Washington bureau chief, Godfrey "Budge" Sperling. In 1966 Sperling spawned the first of a series of news-maker breakfasts that became a Washington institution. Anywhere from twenty-five to forty Washington journalists (usually including at least a half-dozen Pulitzer Prize winners) were invited by Sperling for breakfast at the Sheraton-Carlton Hotel with a top administration official, politician, academic, or economist. Many of the Sperling breakfasts made news. Laird was one of his favorite guests, Sperling recalled, agreeing to more than a dozen breakfasts—and always leaving the press with a good *attributable* story. (Kissinger was the only guest who insisted some of his appearances be "on background.")[33]

The two premiere newspapers, the *New York Times* and *Washington Post,* were hard for Laird to influence, but not for lack of trying. Both were antiwar and heavily critical of the Pentagon on their editorial pages. Dan Henkin confided to Laird in a March 1969 memo: "For some years now, I have been trying to think of ways in which this building could get a fair shake on the *Washington Post* editorial page. I'm still thinking."[34]

As for the *Times,* Laird was puzzled that often the thorough reporting of reporter Bill Beecher would be followed by a distorted view of the facts on the editorial page. In one memo to Laird, Henkin wrote, "The NYT editorial Board continues to wallow around in the Defense area wringing its hands, wailing, but not offering any specific suggestions." In that memo, Henkin said he had told a top *Times* editor at a dinner the previous evening that the *Times*'s editorials on defense were "just plain boring." Laird and Henkin were often surprised by the stories the *Times* chose *not* to cover. For example, after the correspondents' corridor was dedicated, Henkin noted to Laird: "Funny, we don't find anything in the *New York Times* despite the fact that the names of two *New York Times* [reporters] appear on our memorial plaque. Maybe it wasn't fit to print."[35]

During Laird's tenure, the single most controversial press-versus-Pentagon hour of television was the CBS documentary *The Selling of the Pentagon.* Narrated by Roger Mudd, it first aired in February 1971. The thrust of the CBS show was that the military was spending more than $30 million of the taxpayer's money annually to convince those same taxpayers that it was money well spent. To make its case, CBS used deceptive editing practices that are no longer allowed today. Henkin had given an interview to the program, but CBS had selectively edited his answers to make him appear confused and misleading—even using answers he had given to one question as if they were the answers to another.

In a private tirade to Laird, Henkin called the program "one of the most vicious, demagogic, arrogant and misleading pieces of television ever seen anywhere."[36] In public, following Laird's lead, Henkin's remarks were much more temperate. Laird felt the program was unfair, but that it had legitimately raised a number of issues about old training films and other public relations practices that needed to be changed. His public position was that CBS had not been as professional as it should have been. There was little need to say anything else because Representative Eddie Hebert, the Democratic chair of the House Armed Services Committee, was aiming at CBS full bore. Feeling betrayed after having cooperated with the show, the promilitary Hebert publicly denounced it as the "most misleading, damaging attack on our people over there [in Vietnam] I've ever heard of."[37]

In an attempt to mollify critics, CBS re-aired the program with an additional fifteen minutes of edited reactions from Hebert, Vice President Agnew, and Laird. For a time CBS was on the ropes. The chairman of the House Commerce Committee, which had oversight over broadcasting regulations, conducted a full-scale hearing and demanded all the CBS outtakes and memoranda used in the production of the show. CBS refused to comply with what was an overreach for the committee. Henkin was among those publicly opposed to forcing CBS to provide details of its confidential sources and internal editing methods. He publicly stated, "The Pentagon is not for sale, and not for sale either is the right of a free press to criticize the Pentagon."

<hr />

Perhaps Laird's greatest achievement on the public-information front was to make it a habit for the military to follow principles that he had written and framed for the Corridor of Correspondents—to deal with the press and public "in an open manner, consistent with the need for security." His effort to establish trustworthiness won points with the media fairly quickly. By 1970 the *Armed Forces Journal* reported: "Laird has largely erased the Pentagon's credibility gap with Congress and the press."[38] He had two highly capable former newsmen, Henkin and Jerry Friedheim, to help him. Together, they decided that many of the old ways were not working. For one thing, the Pentagon was not well served by infrequent press briefings. Laird suggested daily briefings, and Henkin agreed to try it out.

Neither Laird nor Henkin was sure daily briefings would work. "He [Laird] wanted to have that opportunity to speak every day, on the record," recalled Friedheim. "We told the press that we might not have a big piece of news for them every day, but we'd be there to answer any questions they wanted to ask. We would be *available*." The morning Pentagon briefing quickly became an institution and tripled the number of reporters hanging around the Pentagon. Their editors were afraid the reporters might miss something if they weren't there. Military officers began asking to appear at the briefings, in part because common lore had it that there were two ways to be promoted to general or admiral—by fighting or by briefing.[39]

In a short period of time, as Henkin found it necessary to handle the overall Pentagon public affairs efforts, Friedheim became the department's chief spokesman. He won mixed marks; he was cool under fire and used humor as a disarmament tool, but he could also frustrate the press. The *New York Times* once castigated him for reaching a "new low in obfuscation." Asked about the editorial during the day's briefing, Friedheim responded: "I don't want to quibble with that. I might have chosen 'high' instead of 'low.'" At a briefing shortly after, Friedheim opened his announcement folder to find a red-white-and-blue banner put in there by Laird that urged in large letters: "Eschew Obfuscation."[40]

Laird's most frequent injunction to his press people was, "Make it a plus!"—try to point out anything positive in the news. If a commonly used word in the media wasn't appropriate, Laird told the staff to try to promote a new one. Hence, "body count" was changed to "enemy deaths" or "enemy killed"; U.S. troops were "redeployed" not withdrawn; "cost overrun" became "cost growth." Staffers were told to never make predictions that might unravel, such as when the war would end; never answer hypothetical questions, because they were traps; and never take themselves too seriously.

In four years, Laird himself averaged one news conference a week, for a total of 194. He never got flustered. In his last month as secretary, the pentagon press corps presented him with what became one of his most prized possessions: a football with all their signatures on it. It was inscribed, "Laird 194, Press 0," a recognition that Laird had gone undefeated. Even *Sports Illustrated* was moved to report on the unusual tribute, adding a quip: "Now, that's *dee*fense."[41]

29

Laos: The Elephant under the Handkerchief

⌇⌇⌇

ON NEW YEAR'S DAY 1971 fresh fighting broke out when the North Vietnamese once again broke the holiday truce. One American soldier was killed, earning the tragic distinction of becoming the first casualty in the second decade of the Vietnam War. During the Johnson administration the Vietnam War had already become America's longest war. For the purpose of keeping statistics, the Pentagon dated the U.S. entry into the war at January 1, 1961. A decade later, despite two years of troop withdrawals under Vietnamization, the casualty statistics were grim—44,900 Americans dead and 293,225 wounded. The South Vietnamese had lost 117,900 men. The count of enemy dead was just a guess, but hovered around 690,400 North Vietnamese and Viet Cong.[1]

Laird set out for Saigon the morning of January 5, 1971, for his third official visit there and another chance to take the pulse of Vietnamization. One day earlier, the last of the U.S. Green Beret camps in Vietnam had been turned over to the South Vietnamese government, marking the end of the official Special Forces role in the war.[2] There were still 335,800 Americans in Vietnam, down from more than half a million when Laird took command. President Nixon had tried to put a gag order on any public pronouncements about more withdrawals until Laird returned with a report. Kissinger had forwarded that order in a memo to Laird, Rogers, and CIA Director Helms: "The President has directed that there will be no speculation either on or off the record or in any forum."[3]

"I never felt that applied to me," Laird said, recalling the directive. He went on with business as usual, arriving in Paris on the way to Saigon and telling the press corps there that the U.S. combat role in Vietnam would end by midyear, marking the end of Phase I of Vietnamization. Laird said the United States could then move into Phase II—providing logistics and air support for the South and security for the remaining U.S. support troops.[4] Back in Washington, reporters asked presidential spokesman Ron Ziegler if what Laird said was true, that U.S. combat troops would be out by summer. "[W]e are not prepared to say," Ziegler demurred.[5]

Laird had deliberately overstepped his bounds, publicly committing the administration to a goal that had been his alone. And he did not stop there. In

Saigon Laird used his favorite phrase to describe the pace of troop withdrawals, saying the Pentagon would "*meet or beat* the announced troop authorization strength of 284,000 as of May 1st, just as we have met or beaten every
troop reduction announcement made by the President since re-deployment
started in mid-1969."[6] Each time Laird said he would "meet or beat" the deadlines, he infuriated the Joint Chiefs and the White House, particularly Kissinger, all of whom had to *meet* the deadlines but were not eager to *beat* them.
In Saigon Laird paid lip service to Nixon's original conditions for withdrawal,
repeating that the pace of withdrawal would always be tied to progress at the
Paris peace talks and the strength of the enemy. But then, as always, those
standards were honored more in the breach than in the observance.

Laird was reminded that despite the considerable sway he held with the
press, he did not have exclusive access to the newspapers. While Laird was still
in Saigon, syndicated columnist Joseph Alsop wrote a scathing column accusing
him of "sabotaging" Vietnamization because he wasn't willing to leave behind
enough tanks, helicopters, and airplanes to let the South Vietnamese win the
war on their own.[7] Alsop was a friend of Nixon's and gave the president all the
credit for Vietnamization, calling Laird the "grand saboteur" behind the plan.

Laird read between the lines and saw not the hand of Nixon but of General
Westmoreland, a tireless advocate of giving more weaponry to South Vietnam.
Laird made some discreet inquiries to his friend columnist Rowland Evans,
who said the angle for the column had been shopped around by Westmoreland. Laird's press aide, Dan Henkin, wanted him to take on Alsop in print and
Westmoreland in private, but Laird declined. "If I'd taken it on, it might have
taken some legs," Laird explained. "You have to learn in government and in
politics when to take something on. If you want it to have legs, fine. But if you
don't want it to have legs, keep your mouth shut."

One of Laird's prime objectives in Saigon, in addition to assessing the progress of Vietnamization, was to talk General Creighton Abrams out of leaving.
Abrams, who was fifty-six years old, had been in Saigon for more than four
years, and speculation was rampant in the press that he would be reassigned
and replaced by his deputy, General Frederick Weyand. Abrams's health in the
previous year hadn't been the best. In January he had spent a week in the hospital with pneumonia; in Japan in July he had his gall bladder removed; and
on September 30 he collapsed during the dedication of a stadium at Vung Tau
and was hospitalized for a viral infection.[8]

But it wasn't health, as it turned out, that had Abrams down. It was the
crushing impact of being too long in charge of an unpopular war. Laird knew
that Abrams wanted to return to the United States and get another assignment that would wash the stain of Vietnam out of him before he retired. "He
thought he had made a lifetime out of Vietnam," Laird recalled. "He had a great
background. He was one of General George Patton's greatest young tank commanders in World War II. I think he thought he had gotten bogged down in

Vietnam. There was no question that Abe wasn't delighted to end up his Army career in Vietnam."

But Laird wasn't ready to part with him, and so Laird promised that if Abrams would stay, he would become chief of staff of the army when Westmoreland retired. The top job in the army was appealing to Abrams, but probably more persuasive was Laird's call to duty: "I told him I had great respect for him, and that I really needed him there, and the country needed him there, and if we were going to make this thing work, he had to stick it out another year and a half."

In a day-long briefing with Abrams, Laird got an earful of the general's fears that the South Vietnamese, and particularly President Nguyen Van Thieu, were not taking Vietnamization seriously. The meeting the next day between Thieu and Laird was a cat and mouse game. In part Laird felt he had to play "bad cop" to counteract the "good cop" treatment Thieu regularly got from U.S. Ambassador Ellsworth Bunker, who was inclined to be more accommodating to Thieu's requests. Thieu's government had drawn up a costly shopping list of military equipment that was of "questionable utility," in Laird's words. Specifically, Laird was irked that Thieu wanted the South Vietnamese troops who were fighting in Cambodia to be subsidized by the United States "in the same manner as other third-nation forces," as Laird remembered in his "Memorandum of Conversation" after the meeting.[9] There were U.S. allies, such as South Korea, who were assisting in the war, but Laird was not about to treat South Vietnam as a benevolent third party pitching in to solve Cambodia's problems. He told Thieu that Congress would fund some support operations for South Vietnamese troops in Cambodia, but only as far as it was necessary to preserve the security of South Vietnam and to protect U.S. troops, not to fund a separate war between the Cambodians and Communist infiltrators there. One war in Southeast Asia was already one too many.

Laird also made a mistake in sharing with Thieu some hypothetical numbers for the next withdrawal phase, tentatively due to be announced in April, and Thieu leaked the news to the press in Saigon, angering the touchy Nixon. The president expected Laird to be frank with Thieu about numbers but didn't want their discussion to go beyond the palace walls. Laird recalled telling Thieu, "I did not want that particular thing to leak because it drove them nuts back in Washington."

The tentative number discussed by Laird and Thieu was 150,000 more American troops to be taken out between May 1971 and May 1972. Thieu wanted the number end-loaded after 1971 because he was running for reelection that fall. He also wanted to know just how many American soldiers might still be in South Vietnam at the end of 1972. Laird said possibly fifty to seventy-five thousand American troops might still be around in *mid*-1972, but he reminded Thieu that Nixon had made a campaign promise that the war would be *over* for Americans by the end of his first term, January 1973.

While in Saigon and on visits with the troops in the countryside, Laird saw the natural fallout of downsizing. The morale among the troops was low. The career soldiers were discouraged to be part of a war where their role was being written out of the script. And the draftees, knowing that everyone was going home, just wanted to know when their turn would come. "I tried to pep them up each time I had a chance to talk to them, whether it was in the dining room or out in the bush someplace," said Laird. "I always tried to impress upon them that Vietnamization was going to work and that their responsibilities were even greater then. I assured them always that we could build up the South to take the job."

⌬

Laird's publicly stated reason for going to Saigon in January 1971 was to assess Vietnamization. But his secret agenda was to plan a test of Vietnamization—an invasion of Laos using South Vietnamese troops. In principle, it made sense. In practice it would become as difficult as the U.S. incursion into Cambodia in 1970, and not nearly as successful.

The geography of the small kingdom of Laos, about the size of Idaho, doomed it to a history of conflict. Laos was bordered by six nations, including the People's Republic of China (from which its people primarily migrated in the thirteenth century). Both North and South Vietnam were on its eastern border. Throughout the 1950s Laos strove mightily to resist being drawn into the maelstrom of the Vietnam conflict. Finally the 1962 Geneva Convention guaranteed Laotian neutrality and independence, at least in theory. All signers, including North Vietnam and the United States, agreed to keep their troops out. But the North Vietnamese ignored the agreement after signing it and conducted seasonal wars with the Lao government forces. Each dry season beginning in 1964, the North Vietnamese—with assistance from up to fifty thousand indigenous Communist Pathet Lao forces—had successfully attacked government strongholds. And each wet season that followed, when Communist supply lines slowed down in the mud, the Royal Lao government forces generally retrieved their territory.

The United States could hardly let the Communist incursions go unchallenged. In 1961 the CIA had recruited a Meo tribal leader, Vang Pao, to raise an army sufficient to hold the northern region around the Plaine des Jarres (Plain of Jars), a strategic oval about twenty-five miles wide and thirty-five miles long. With CIA financing, General Vang Pao gathered a twenty-five-thousand-plus army of Meo (also called Hmong) people. It was known locally as the "AC," or the *Armée Clandestine.*

Vang Pao was clever and corrupt in earning the loyalty of his troops, many of whom were forcibly conscripted to join the AC's ranks. The key to Vang Pao's personal power lay with the airborne supply-and-rescue force that the

CIA put at his disposal—"Air America." Ostensibly, the company was contracted to the U.S. Agency for International Development, and it did deliver thousands of tons of rice to the Meo and others in the north.[10] But it was bought and paid for by the CIA and carried as much weaponry as it did rice. Vang Pao controlled the weapons and gave the rice only to those villages that had contributed men to his army.[11] On return flights after delivering food, Vang Pao's army often carried crates of opium from the Golden Triangle area; the profits from drug sales helped keep Vang Pao and his top officers happily in line. Most Air America pilots, especially the Americans, chose not to open the crates and could legitimately maintain they never knew they had transported drugs. The CIA also didn't care to pry too closely into Vang Pao's lucrative side business.

The war in Laos was one over which the Pentagon had little jurisdiction, in spite of the fact that several Green Berets were military advisors to the Laotians. Perhaps the first to become concerned early in the Nixon administration with the CIA's secret war in Laos was Air Force Secretary Seamans. "We weren't supposed to be there, yet we had a clandestine operation going," he recalled. "My own Air Force people walked through a door in Laos and became civilians somehow. If they were killed in action, their families might not know they were there. And the two questions in my mind were: Is it all worthwhile what we're doing? Are we really accomplishing anything? It was highly questionable in my mind so I discussed it with Mel."[12]

Another Laird official with misgivings about Laos in 1969 was a Johnson administration holdover, Acting Assistant Secretary for Systems Analysis Ivan Selin. He had three objections: the cost of air support for Vang Pao; the drug smuggling; and the CIA's exaggerated reports about success in Laos.[13]

In his first year, Secretary Laird had more to worry about with Vietnamization and troop withdrawals than the problems in Laos. He had loosely followed the issue as a congressman, having been briefed on the Defense Department logistical support, which came out of appropriations that his committee had approved. So Laird wasn't particularly alarmed when he got a mid-September 1969 top-secret note from Kissinger passing on Nixon's directive that more M-16s and airplanes be given to the Laotian forces. "If more pay and allowances would make the Lao fight better, this, too, should be provided," Kissinger wrote.[14]

It was no secret to Laird that U.S. military planes regularly bombed the Ho Chi Minh Trail as it ran through Laos. But most Americans—and many in Congress—were unaware that there were hundreds of air strikes being called in to support the Royal Laotian forces and their allies in their civil war against the Pathet Lao. In fact, when bombing of North Vietnam had stopped in November 1968, the Pentagon had simply moved the air war to Laos. From time to time there were more American planes peppering the skies over Laos than over South Vietnam, where the war was supposed to be contained. Losses of American planes over Laos were not publicly acknowledged because the Johnson and then Nixon administrations did not admit to the flights in the first place.

Of course, compared to the fifty thousand North Vietnamese combat soldiers operating in Laos—belying the notion of a purely "civil war"—a few hundred Green Beret advisors on the ground staying carefully out of uniform were a drop in the bucket.

But Laird began to engage fully in the Laos question in October 1969 when a Senate subcommittee held closed hearings on the subject. When details of the classified testimony leaked to the press, Senator William Fulbright obligingly confirmed the story, saying the United States was spending more than $150 million a year to supply, arm, train, and transport a clandestine army of thirty-six thousand men in Laos. Fulbright offered an aw-shucks commentary: "I knew that we were doing a little of this and a little of that in Laos, but I had no idea it was a major operation of this kind."[15]

The White House forced Laird to respond with one hand tied behind his back. Nixon, with the secretive Kissinger urging him on, was adamant: neither Laird nor his people were to confirm CIA and State Department activity in Laos, on or off the record. Jerry Friedheim recalled his boss's palpable anger at not being able to speak out. "Mel wanted to go public on Laos as soon as possible. Department of Defense people were getting killed in Laos. There were more than a hundred military attachés and Special Forces in Laos and they were involved in combat. When they got killed, we couldn't acknowledge it because Henry didn't want to talk about Laos. The [State Department] diplomats who talked to Henry didn't want any acknowledgment that there were Americans in [Laos] engaging in combat. And it was ridiculous after all these years, because everybody knew it, especially the correspondents."[16]

Laird said later that he regretted not raising a greater objection to the untenable position his department had been put in of paying the bills in Laos while the State Department controlled the operation. McNamara had never made an issue of it when Laird was in Congress. "The way he testified, I thought he was involved with all of these operations, but I found out when I got over to the Pentagon that the secretary of defense wasn't too involved," Laird said. Instead, the CIA and the State Department were calling the shots of a covert war with the commander being a diplomat—G. McMurtrie Godley, the U.S. ambassador to Laos, and a man Laird came to call the "field marshal."

Laird wasn't happy with the role of banker to the field marshal without any say-so over how the money was spent. While he didn't personally want to preside over a war in Laos—covert or overt—he did want to exercise enough control to keep operations there from escalating in the hands of CIA spooks and American diplomats. So in the fall of 1969 he had his staff review the way things were being handled. The resultant report, sent to Secretary of State Rogers on December 1, is best read between the lines. It is replete with references to diplomats and CIA agents controlling U.S. air power, picking targets, and directing ground troops. Laird's report suggested more input from the Joint Chiefs, especially on the number of bombing runs, "to prevent unintentional escalation of effort to the point that it would have a political impact."[17]

Meanwhile, by early December 1969 Senator Fulbright and his supporters were in full throttle. The Laos operation, in their view, was perfect evidence that Nixon was expanding instead of contracting the war. (This predated the more widely condemned Cambodia operation of the following spring.) Republican Senator John Sherman Cooper offered an amendment to the defense appropriations bill that would prevent expenditures for the air bombing that was protecting Vang Pao and his army in their mountain redoubts. Fulbright opened debate on the Cooper Amendment in the Senate on December 15 by demanding that the administration openly acknowledge the extent of the activities in Laos. "I have been hornswoggled long enough," he said. "Most of the Senate doesn't know what is being done with the money in this bill in regard to Laos, and they ought to know." (Fulbright acknowledged that a few Senators on the appropriate committees had been regularly briefed about it by the CIA and other intelligence groups, but he felt it was time for *all* Senators to hear the truth.) In response, one senator who did know the highly classified dollar figure blurted out that it was $90 million.

An alarmed Senator John Tower walked quickly to the front of the nearly-empty chamber and asked Senate Democratic leader Mike Mansfield to put a stop to the spilling of national security secrets. These are "sensitive matters" that should only be discussed in closed session, he said. Mansfield agreed and promptly ordered out all spectators in the galleries, including the press. The doors were locked, and the hearing continued in secret—only the fifth such hearing for the full Senate since World War II. Behind closed doors the Senate voted 73 to 17 to order that none of the $69.3 billion in Defense appropriations could be spent "to finance the introduction of American ground combat troops into Laos or Thailand." The compromise was called the Church Amendment, for its sponsor, Senator Frank Church. Under it, ground troops were banned, but the State Department and CIA could still have air cover to continue their secret war.

Some of the debate had been acrimonious, so at least one Washington columnist, Marquis Childs, was heartened to hear that not long after the hearing Laird had gone golfing at Burning Tree with three of his opponents on this issue—Fulbright, Clifford, and Rogers. The latter had fought to keep control of the secret war in the hands of the CIA and his diplomatic corps. "The lion of dissent may not lie down with the lamb of administration orthodoxy, but they do play golf together," Childs opined. "If such a mixed foursome can agree on the explosive issue of golf scores, a consensus on a way out of Vietnam and Laos should not be impossible. And isn't it better, as one of the foursome (Laird) remarked, that, 'We're doing this rather than throwing rocks at each other'? "[18]

～～

In February 1970 the North Vietnamese picked up the pace of fighting in Laos and attempted to re-take the strategic Plain of Jars from Vang Pao. Nixon ordered the financing of two Thai battalions to go to the aid of the Laotians, and he added American B-52s to the mix of fighter bombers and helicopter gun ships already active in Laos. The daily sortie rate was approaching six hundred flights, which was a little too noisy to be a secret. Three western reporters hitchhiked to an air base in Laos and saw Americans, in civilian garb, directing operations there. The newsmen were arrested by a Lao soldier and interrogated by an American before they were sent back to Vientiane on an embassy plane. Without commenting on the presence of American soldiers in Laos, Ambassador Godley reportedly responded to the story by saying, "the American mission has lost any interest in helping out the press whatsoever."[19]

The day after the report appeared, Laird testified before a House Appropriations Subcommittee, saying, "We have no American ground combat forces stationed in Laos. Ground combat activities are carried on by Laotian forces. We have a small military advisory and training group there. We are interdicting supplies on the Ho Chi Minh Trail with B-52s and tactical aircraft."[20]

When the members of Congress pressed Laird for more details, he went off the record, and the official transcript doesn't include his response. "I told them off the record in the classified briefing that it was a CIA operation," Laird recalled of that hearing. When he stepped outside of the hearing, Laird was surrounded by newsmen who wanted to know more. He tried to dampen the story by making it appear as if there was nothing new. "I want to make it clear that there's been no change in the policy as far as Laos is concerned by this Administration. As a member of this same Defense Appropriations Committee, when I was a member of it, I was always fully briefed on the matters of Laos, as well as Vietnam, and there has been no change as far as Vietnam is concerned."[21]

The next day Air Force Secretary Seamans sent Laird a memo suggesting more candor. The secret money to fund the CIA operations in Laos was coming out of Seamans's air force budget, and he was nervous about jeopardizing other funding by trying to maintain that secrecy. "If we are going to continue our air operations in Laos, even at reduced levels, we are going to require substantial funding from the Congress and the underlying support of the American people," Seamans wrote. "Because of the importance of these operations to our overall posture in Southeast Asia, it thus becomes in the national interest to be more candid publicly; otherwise I question how long we can maintain the necessary public support."[22]

Laird was called back to Capitol Hill the day after this memo, this time to explain Laos to the House Armed Services Committee. He told them there were 220 American military people in Laos, and he quibbled with the legislators over what to call them if they were not combat troops. Laird said they were attachés with the embassy, military advisors, and training personnel, but he refused to call them a formal Military Assistance Advisory Group, because such military advisors were banned under the Geneva neutrality treaty regarding Laos. The committee wanted to know why the Americans wore civilian clothes.

"Well, they are often out of uniform," Laird hedged, and then turned to General Earle Wheeler to elaborate.

"I have never been to Laos," Wheeler said, bluntly.

The obfuscation about the U.S. presence in Laos was not fooling anyone. A typical report from the *Wall Street Journal's* Peter Kann said,

> Gen. Vang Pao is a cocky little former sergeant in the French army who now heads a clandestine, U.S.-backed army of mountain tribesmen here. Resplendent in a fancy field uniform and bedecked by so many medals that he almost appears armor-plated, he sits for an interview.
>
> Are U.S. jets bombing in Laos? he is asked. No, he says, though his voice is periodically drowned out by U.S. jets flying overhead.
>
> Are his troops armed with U.S.-made M-16 rifles? he is asked. No, he says, though the very men guarding him are carrying M-16s.
>
> Are U.S. helicopters supporting his war effort? he is asked. No, he says, though he boards a U.S. chopper after concluding the interview.
>
> The interview says much of life in Laos.[23]

An unidentified western diplomat in Vientiane, speaking to a *Newsweek* correspondent, spoke to the absurdity of the situation: "How can you hide all this? It's like trying to hide an elephant under a handkerchief."[24]

Finally Nixon himself decided to make a speech on the Laotian war. Laird tried to coach the president on what to say: Nixon should stress that North Vietnam was the repeat offender when it came to Laotian neutrality; the president should restate that there were no U.S. ground combat troops in Laos, and no plans to send any. Laird included a short list of what Nixon should *not* talk about, including the cost of the Laos operations, the extent of the CIA involvement, and whether the Americans there constituted an official Military Assistance Advisory Group.[25] The return interoffice mail on March 4 brought a draft from Kissinger of the statement Nixon wanted to make. It ignored Laird's cautious approach and, in Nixon's aggressive style, defended the obligation of the United States to do all it could to help Laos in its fight against Communism.[26]

That cut too close to the original rationale for entering the Vietnam War, and Laird wrote back immediately: "[T]his is not the kind of statement the President should make." There was too little about why and what the United States was doing in the present and too many promises about what it could deliver in the future. Nixon made no mention of the B-52s, even though the press was clamoring for an explanation about what they were doing in Laos. "The tone of the statement is alarming," Laird wrote. Nixon used terms such as "massive presence," "blatant moves," and "deliberate and open onslaught" to describe the enemy presence in Laos. And then he promised the United States would do something to stop that enemy. "This appears to be an open-ended commitment rather than minimal activity," Laird warned.[27] He rightly assumed that a magnanimous pledge to protect yet another country in Southeast Asia from the Red Menace would not sit well with the American public.

Nixon paid some heed to Laird's warning, toning down the speech that he delivered from Key Biscayne on March 6, 1969. He promised that no U.S. ground troops were or would be sent to Laos. And then Nixon made a statement that strained credulity. He said: "No American stationed in Laos has ever been killed in ground combat." Laird almost jumped out of his seat when he heard that. From his congressional days, he personally knew of two Americans who had died in ground combat several years before. In fact, in his first memo to Nixon about the speech he specifically listed "casualty data" among the items he "should not discuss." The *Los Angeles Times* was the first to put the lie to the statement. Within hours of the president's speech, they reported that Army Captain Joseph Bush had been killed during a Communist attack at the western edge of the Plain of Jars only a month before; he had even earned a posthumous medal for heroism.

The press was all over it. "Virtually before the ink was dry, the thrust of press attention on the President's Laos statement shifted from the statement itself to stories stating...the President had not told the whole truth," Henkin wrote in an after-action report. "Rather than admit an error, the White House, after lengthy discussions with us Sunday, decided to take the semantic approach. So far, that has only dug a deeper hole."[28] Indeed, the press and public let out a collective guffaw when a deputy presidential press secretary insisted that Captain Bush had not technically died from a "ground combat operation" as such, but had been killed by "hostile action" he had not initiated.[29] This was too much tip-toeing through semantic tulips to be credible.

While the White House confirmed the death of Captain Bush and 26 American civilians in a similar fashion from "hostile action," Nixon had failed to mention the 200 Americans dead and 183 missing in air operations, which the press was also quick to point out. The fudging of those numbers, and the failure of Nixon to say anything about the B-52s in Laos, continued to raise more questions than answers. The president's attempt to explain the Laos operations wound up looking more like a cover-up.

And there were fourteen air force deaths in Laos that remained a secret even after the fallout from the president's speech. Laird told Kissinger about those belatedly in a top-secret memo on March 13.[30] Those deaths occurred in 1967 and 1968, and the airmen were voluntarily working undercover as civilians at the time. The Pentagon needed to install radar sites in Laos, and the best people to do it were air force personnel. "Since overt military presence was determined to be politically unacceptable at that time, the only alternative for operation of the site was to man it with civilian personnel," Laird explained to Kissinger. So the men were mustered out of the air force and put on the Lockheed corporate payroll as contractors.

Fourteen of them were killed in two separate raids on radar sites. Thirteen[31] were posthumously reinstated in the air force so their widows could get their military benefits, and that made them military ground combat casualties; one of them, Chief Master Sergeant Richard L. Etchberger, had even been awarded the Air Force Cross for heroism.[32] Since it hadn't happened on Nixon's watch, Laird recommended that the names not be released so long after the fact. The widows themselves had been sworn to secrecy. Then Laird added a caution: "I am unable to state categorically that these are the only casualties related to these or similar operations in Laos."

All of the attention to Laos in early 1970 made the State Department uneasy. It was their own joint operation with the CIA that came closest to violating the Church Amendment—the Senate ban on funding ground operations in Laos. But the diplomats privately pointed the finger at what they said was a bigger offender, Operation Prairie Fire. That was the code name for shallow cross-border raids by South Vietnamese soldiers taking place about forty times a month with the help of American air cover and directed by the U.S. Army. Those raids, controlled by the Defense Department, were to gather intelligence and to harass the flow of enemy supplies along the Ho Chi Minh Trail.

On May 29, 1970, Undersecretary of State Elliot Richardson sent a top-secret memo to David Packard, saying that Prairie Fire constituted American ground combat in Laos, no doubt about it. "We therefore consider that the language of the Church Amendment and the President's statement require us to terminate U.S. involvement in this type of operation," Richardson wrote. "In addition, we are concerned about the possible political cost should these operations become generally known."[33]

Packard asked the Joint Chiefs to rethink the need for Operation Prairie Fire. "I am convinced that there is sufficient uncertainty now with respect to the Congressional attitude toward this type of program to see if less politically sensitive alternatives are feasible," Packard told the chiefs in his written order.[34]

On July 17 the State Department sent Packard the written opinion of its legal advisor—that Prairie Fire was a violation of the Church Amendment and that the American soldiers who accompanied South Vietnamese raids into Laos did not comport with Nixon's promise on March 6: "There are no American ground combat troops in Laos."[35] Undersecretary of State for Political Affairs U. Alexis Johnson added his own opinion to that of the lawyer: "It has been almost four months since the President's statement on Laos in which he stated categorically that 'there are no American ground troops in Laos' and that the Administration 'had no plans for introducing ground combat forces in Laos.' In light of these strong statements from the President, I believe it would be extremely embarrassing for us to have to explain an apparent failure to comply with the President's stated policy."[36]

The president himself was not pressing the Pentagon to live up to his "stated policy." In fact, he was caught in the middle of the debate between Laird and the State Department. In Laird's mind the president had simply misspoken. As far as Laird was concerned, the small Prairie Fire missions did not add up to all-out ground combat and did not violate the Church Amendment. "I don't think the Senate intended in any way to ban volunteer missions to go in and blow up things on the Ho Chi Minh Trail," Laird explained in retrospect. "They were really doing an important job. They would do a better job in many respects than large bombing raids. I put that in the whole bushel basket which I called 'protective reaction.'"

Laird rightly concluded that the committees he had to answer to in Congress were not bothered about the raids into Laos. But the committee that Rogers reported to, the Senate Foreign Relations Committee and its antiwar chairman, Fulbright, was not so sanguine. "It was their problem, a political risk for them," said Laird. "I wanted to let them know that unless I was ordered by the president, I wasn't going to stop it. I wasn't going to take directions from the State Department." Laird told Alexis Johnson precisely that in a letter on September 2, 1970: "In my opinion, the decision to continue or discontinue ... Prairie Fire should be a political one rather than a legal one, and should consider the military value of these operations. As we both know, the political costs could be quite high, given the current political climate, if these operations were to be made public. However, these same operations contribute significantly to our military interdiction program." Laird included a lengthy analysis of the pros and cons by Assistant Defense Secretary Warren Nutter, who said the legal arguments were "inconclusive."[37] Johnson quickly responded that it was time to take the matter to Nixon himself.[38]

Nixon solved the problem with a compromise. In October 1970 he secretly endorsed the Prairie Fire operations for a ninety-day period (back-dated to September 18) to give the Pentagon time to come up with a way to replace the American soldiers with South Vietnamese troops.[39] "We did everything we could to encourage the South Vietnamese to carry on those operations," Laird said. But did he meet the president's deadline? "If you're asking me if there were some Americans that went across with the South Vietnamese in some of those operations after the ninety days, I would have to tell you that there probably were, and I did not object to it." The ninety-day order expired in mid-December and Laird formally asked Nixon for a sixty-day extension.[40] He never received a response. After that, there was no more word from Nixon on the matter and Laird stopped asking for permission.

30

The Ho Chi Minh Trail

AT 10 A.M. ON FEBRUARY 8, 1971, the First Armored Brigade of the South Vietnamese Army (ARVN) rolled across the border into Laos. They went alone; not a single American soldier or advisor accompanied their advance. American troops were not allowed across the border, a fact pointedly made by a sign erected just short of the border, which read:

"WARNING, NO U.S. PERSONNEL BEYOND THIS POINT."

On the reverse side, a GI had defiantly added another message:

"NO NORTH VIETNAMESE TROOPS PERMITTED BEYOND THIS POINT."[1]

A little more than two years before, President-elect Nixon had asked Laird to come up with a plan to get out of Vietnam. Laird had already inserted into the 1968 Republican National Platform the plan to de-Americanize the war in Vietnam. As secretary of defense, Laird had come up with Vietnamization, and now the rubber, and boots, had hit the road, Route 9, headed for the Ho Chi Minh Trail. If there was a day and an hour when Vietnamization came into its own, this was it.

For American military planners, their prime target of opportunity to foil the enemy was not even in North or South Vietnam. It was a stretch of the Ho Chi Minh Trail that ran through two allegedly noncombatant countries: Laos and Cambodia. In the 1960s Ho Chi Minh had piggybacked on the ancient trade routes between Southeast Asian capitals to build a network of trails over which his soldiers could transport supplies to within shooting distance of South Vietnam. The earliest plotters of the trail battled insects, leeches, malaria, and monsoons. With Chinese and Russian help, they turned the trail into a supply superhighway, when the weather cooperated. The main north-south trail, dubbed "Route 92" by the U.S. military, traveled through Laos, parallel to its border with South Vietnam, and down through Cambodia. In some places it was as narrow as a footpath, and some places as wide as thirty miles. And all along it were trails branching off east and west. It was, as one U.S. military officer described it, "a spider web on top of a spider web on top of a spider web."[2] The U.S. military eventually mapped 3,500 miles of the trail and its many tributaries, but this may have been less than half of the system.[3]

Down this road came hundreds of thousands of tons of food and supplies on the backs of men, on bicycles, in oxcarts, and, where the trail was widened, in trucks. Supply depots, rest areas, truck parks, and telephone lines needed constant tending, and as many as fifty thousand boys and women worked on the road repair gangs, called the "Youth Shock Brigades against the Americans for National Salvation."[4] U.S. military intelligence estimated that for every sixty combat soldiers there had to be forty "support troops" to handle the supplies and logistics necessary to move large caravans through the rugged terrain.[5] During the dry season, usually from November to March, the trail teemed with tens of thousands of Viet Cong guerrillas, North Vietnamese regulars, and their support forces—all hidden under a jungle canopy.

Beginning in 1965, as part of President Johnson's Operation Rolling Thunder, U.S. aircraft pummeled the Ho Chi Minh Trail. But McNamara came to realize by early 1966 that the trail traffic could not be stopped by bombs alone. For one thing, U.S. intelligence had determined that the North needed only to deliver sixty tons of supplies a day to the South—an estimated twenty truckloads—to meet the needs of their troops. And the enemy routinely factored in the losses and started twice that amount down the trail from the northern end each day of the dry season. More surgical targeting was needed, and it came about as a side effect of a quixotic plan known as the "McNamara Line." It was a barrier of barbed wire fences, land mines, electronic sensors, artillery emplacements, and mobile troops, supported by aircraft, along the sixty-mile DMZ and the upper South Vietnam border with Laos—the busiest part of the trail.[6] As a congressman, Laird had approved the $1 billion McNamara Line. The idea eventually failed because Laos objected to a cross-border barrier, and military commanders realized in short order that neither the United States nor the South Vietnamese could afford the troops to defend a Maginot Line in the jungle.

But one part of the project bore fruit: the movement sensors (seismic intrusion devices, or SIDs) along the trail, which became precursors to anti-terrorism technology of the twenty-first century. First as a congressman and then as defense secretary, Laird was an enthusiastic supporter of the top-secret $1.63 billion sensor project. When placed around military bases the sensors could save lives. And along the Ho Chi Minh Trail they denied the enemy the traditional cloaks of bad weather, jungle, and darkness. The trail was seeded with hundreds of thousands of air-dropped SIDs, some designed to catch in the trees and some that pierced the ground or sat on the surface disguised as plants. (Ones that looked like animal droppings were nicknamed "turd SIDs.") They detected the vibrations of trucks, oxcarts, and even footsteps. One picked up the conversation of enemy soldiers trying to dismantle it; another carried back the sound of an enemy soldier urinating on it.

Using the sensors, U.S. commanders could target their bombs in what became known as the "truck war." Laird agreed with General Abrams that the war of attrition could be better won by destroying supplies instead of soldiers. Laird deplored a "body count" mentality but embraced the "truck kill" statistics, which he thought suggested real progress against the enemy. Beginning in mid-October 1970 Laird directed an unprecedented bombing campaign against the trail and its trucks when it had become the last route available to North Vietnam to infiltrate troops into South Vietnam. Earlier in the year, the Cambodia campaign and the overthrow of Prince Sihanouk had closed the port of Kompong Som (formerly Sihanoukville) to the enemy. Nor could they send supplies and infiltrators across the DMZ, for fear of sparking another bombing campaign against North Vietnam itself. So the trail was the last line of supply and troop infiltration. In late fall, when the sensors and intelligence reports pointed to a huge amount of tonnage being started on the trail in preparation for a 1971 offensive, the bombing campaign began in earnest. The air force claimed that twenty-five thousand trucks were destroyed between October 1970 and May 1971. Sometimes as many as five hundred bombing sorties were flown in a single day. From 1965 to 1971, more bomb tonnage was dropped over the Ho Chi Minh Trail than was used in all theaters in all of World War II.[7] But it was not enough; supplies and men were still making it down the trail. There was only one more thing to try: soldiers on the ground.

Laird had one major combat operation in mind in late 1970 as he began withdrawing U.S. ground forces: tying a tourniquet across the Ho Chi Minh Trail. As the dry season in late fall approached, Laird knew the enemy would be engaged in the largest overland supply effort of the Vietnam War. In less than half a year, they had to bring enough to feed and arm four hundred thousand soldiers for a full year. Laird also determined from intelligence reports that the enemy was planning to greatly increase its shipments down the trail in preparation for a 1971 offensive to disrupt South Vietnamese elections and stockpile for a major offensive to discredit Nixon before the U.S. presidential election in 1972. At Laird's request, plans were prepared by the Joint Chiefs for a ground operation against the trail. Laird was appalled at the chiefs' first suggestion: to use American ground forces, along with South Vietnamese troops, in direct violation of the Church Amendment. Laird quickly discerned that Westmoreland and Haig were behind the idea to use American soldiers.

Whether Nixon would have considered such a plan if Laird had proposed it will never be known. Laird presented the option at one point to the president, almost with a laugh, and said that it would never be approved. Nixon agreed. So Laird, using presidential authority, sent word to Abrams to devise a preemptive plan against the trail using only South Vietnamese soldiers backed by U.S. air power. Abrams suggested a three-month cross-border operation into the Tchepone area of the trail in the Laotian panhandle. Two days before Christmas 1970 Nixon convened a meeting to discuss the plan. All present—Laird, Moorer, Kissinger and Haig—agreed to it in principle.[8]

The president authorized Laird to discuss the plan further during his January 1971 trip to Saigon. The South Vietnamese leadership needed no convincing, although, according to Laird's memorandum of conversation, Thieu was concerned about "political repercussions." Laird reported, "Some would say we had widened the war. [Thieu] suggested our reply should be that we are widening the peace. It was quite clear to him that military movement into the Laos panhandle would shorten the war," and that they "could and would succeed."[9]

Shortly after Laird returned to Washington, Nixon convened a meeting in the Oval Office on January 18, 1971, on the Laos invasion. All the principals from the December meeting were there, with two significant additions, Secretary of State Rogers and CIA Director Helms. Laird and Nixon both knew Rogers would be hesitant, so Laird laid the plan on thick during the lengthy briefing. "I stood up there with a pointer, and maps, and went through the whole damn thing. He finally went along. He had no objection at that time."

Rogers waffled after returning to his office, and obstructionist amendments to the plan began emanating from the State Department. "Some people in the State Department—like 'Field Marshal' Godley—thought they were running the war up in Laos and they didn't like to have any interference," Laird said. The State Department insisted that Laotian Prime Minister Souvanna Phouma should have to sign off on the invasion of his country, which would be tantamount to political suicide for him. Nevertheless, Kissinger won over the prime minister. In an "exclusively eyes only" memo Kissinger sent Rogers and Laird, he warned that while Souvanna was on board, he might publicly "denounce operation."[10]

On January 27 Nixon signed off on Phase 1 of the Laotian invasion and it commenced three days later.[11] The South Vietnamese had the choice of what to call the invasion, since they would be running the show. They dubbed it Lam Son 719, after an ancient Vietnamese victory over the Chinese in 1427.[12] They named the three key helicopter landing zones for the operation "Liz," "Sophia," and "Lolo," after three Western movie stars: Elizabeth Taylor, Sophia Loren, and Gina Lollobrigida.

⚜

The plan was for the South Vietnamese solders, with air and cross-border artillery support from the Americans, to move into Laos on Route 9 toward the village of Tchepone on the Ho Chi Minh Trail. Flanking fire-bases to protect the infantry movement would be set up via helicopter lifts. In the first week, the South Vietnamese located and destroyed huge caches of enemy food, ammunition, and supplies. American air support demolished additional caches and enemy troop concentrations. When White House briefers explained the operation to the public, they strayed from the cautionary script Laird had provided and implied that the final objective was Tchepone and that the operation would last a couple of months—neither of which was true. The objective was to destroy the caches all along the way to Tchepone, and there was no time limit. Laird laid down the law as gently as he could at a Cabinet meeting on February 16. He didn't point the finger at the White House, but he said some of the announcements to the press had been "like announcing how far you will walk on the moon and then not making it as far."[13]

Laird himself waxed enthusiastic only once, telling a group of Pentagon reporters that the battle, carried out by the South Vietnamese, would show a "very, very dramatic change" in their military capabilities. Abrams immediately protested from Saigon that Laird was setting up unrealistic expectations about the South Vietnamese Army and did not give enough credit to American air support and advisors.[14]

Laird and U.S. commanders were both surprised and unhappy when the South Vietnamese halted their advance about ten miles short of Tchepone on February 12, in the face of only light opposition. A month later American commanders heard reports that the field commanders had halted on secret orders from President Thieu. Unbeknownst to U.S. commanders, Thieu had allegedly ordered his generals to halt the Laos operation once they had sustained three thousand casualties, dead and wounded. Thieu, who was up for reelection that year, was all for invading Laos, as long as it didn't affect his numbers at the polls. He didn't want high casualties to reflect badly on his administration, and he didn't want to sacrifice the best of his soldiers when they might be needed back home to protect him from a coup. Thieu himself denied that he ever gave such an order. And there was no reason for stopping because, at that point, there were few casualties. It was more likely Thieu stopped the advance to better assess what the enemy reaction might be, but it was a serious mistake. It allowed the North Vietnamese to mass the largest force they had ever assembled for a single battle, which had been significantly underestimated in the Lam Son planning. According to a North Vietnamese history of the war, sixty thousand troops were sent into the area.[15]

The press began to smell disaster, pinning their judgment on the idea that the South Vietnamese army was "bogged down," unable to move to Tchepone. The reality was that the pause had allowed the enemy to join the battle in massive numbers and the South Vietnamese found themselves overwhelmed. Still, they inflicted greater casualties (with American air support) than they suffered.

On February 24 Laird thought it was time to hold a press briefing to remind the media what the real objectives of the operation were. He brought with him Lieutenant General John Vogt, head of the Joint Staff. "Tchepone is not a city," Vogt informed them. "Tchepone is not an objective in itself. Tchepone is a deserted village [with] a few bombed-out buildings. It presents, by itself, no worthwhile military objective." Laird added his voice, that Tchepone "has never been an objective [of] this operation."[16] The objective, according to Laird, was "to slow up, to disrupt, the logistics supplies, to cut off and to downgrade the capability of the North Vietnamese to wage any type of warfare in South Vietnam." And to achieve that objective, he warned, "hard fighting lies ahead."[17]

That ninety-minute briefing temporarily marred Laird's record of candor with the press. While both Laird and Vogt had been careful in all their statements, a misleading impression was left regarding a visual aid—a three-foot section of Russian pipe. At one point Laird stepped aside to let Vogt tell about a major achievement of the South Vietnamese two days before in cutting 1,500 feet of a 150-mile gasoline pipeline that began in North Vietnam and was used to supply gas to the trucks all along the Ho Chi Minh Trail. "I would like to show you what that pipeline looks like. I have a segment of that pipeline," Vogt continued, unveiling the example. "This is a four-inch diameter pipe. It's capable of carrying about 350,000 gallons during a 24-hour period, if used to maximum capacity."

The reporters didn't ask and Vogt didn't say when this particular section of the pipe had been cut, and who did the cutting. But the reporters were left with the impression that the pipe had come straight from the battlefield of the Lam Son operation and that it had been cut by South Vietnamese soldiers. Vogt probably felt he could not reveal the true provenance of the piece because it had been retrieved several months before in a cross-border intelligence-gathering raid by South Vietnamese and U.S. Special Forces troops. That news would have sparked a controversy about possible violations of congressional restrictions on American military in Laos.

Whether Laird himself knew the truth about the pipe is in question. In later years he used the story as an example of how important it had been for him to be straight with the press. Laird's memory is that General Abrams called him after the press conference and told him the implication about the pipe was inaccurate. At that point Laird said he immediately called another press conference to clear up the record. But during questioning by Congress in 1971, Laird testified that he *knew* that the pipe had not been collected during the Lam Son operation.[18] His press aide, Jerry Friedheim, believed Laird did not know and did not deliberately mislead the press about the pipe. That Laird would say otherwise during congressional testimony was in keeping with his policy of letting the buck stop with him. "He believed in civilian support, not just civilian control," Friedheim said. "He didn't think the military guy should be left out there to hang on his own."[19] In his congressional testimony Laird said, "I do not hold General Vogt in any way responsible—I support him. It was probably an oversight on my part.... If anything happens in the Department of Defense, I take the heat for it. Don't feel sorry for me in that regard."

The press had a field day with the pipe story. The Washington *News*, under the heading, "Pentagon Pipe Dream," editorialized that "technically, the Laird-Vogt performance was not a lie. But it was deceptive."[20] Humor columnist Art Buchwald wrote an imaginative story in which Laird, "wearing his usual ebullient smile," unveiled rifles from Custer's Last Stand, chickens from a World

War I engagement, sandbags from the battle for Iwo Jima, and Chinese tanks captured at the Korean War battle of Inchon.[21] "It hurts so much when you laugh," press aide Dan Henkin wrote his boss. But "obviously it is time we pipe down."[22]

In the long run the minor flap had the effect of helping Laird's credibility with the press corps because he admitted the mistake. But privately Laird saw it as symptomatic of a much greater problem: intense press frustration with the administration over the Lam Son operation, which would seriously taint their stories about its success. They had bridled at a news embargo during the first few days of the operation and had been prevented by the South Vietnamese from going into Laos and reporting on the battles. Laird explained the serious-ness of this problem at the March 1 staff meeting: "When we are able to get the newsmen into the area, the reports will probably be better. Their news is based on interviews with men coming back from the actions. Usually this is the worst time to talk to these fellows because they always think they have been in the worst action to date, and quite often are scared.... We can't bar this kind of reporting. There are 150 newsmen in the area and they don't have anything better to do."

But the long-term ramification was the risk that the media could turn a true military victory into a defeat, Laird reminded his top Pentagon officials. "We must bear in mind that we don't want to make these operations into either a victory or defeat at the present time. We don't want the psychology in the country to end up like it did after the enemy's Tet offensive of 1968. Here an allied victory was turned into a defeat. The TV and newspaper assessments that Tet was a defeat could never be turned around."[23]

During the initial weeks of the Lam Son operation, Kissinger was on the defen-sive. Laird remembered that Kissinger was smarting from "a lot of heat coming from his friends in Congress." In the wake of the Cambodia invasion the previ-ous spring, and the subsequent restrictive Church Amendment, Kissinger had reassured congressional leaders and media friends that the administration had no plans to go into Laos. "He made a rather broad statement," Laird said. "He led them to believe that it included the use of South Vietnamese troops." Laird remembered it distinctly because he had been careful to testify only that "we would not use American troops. I never told them we'd never use South Viet-namese troops in Laos." So Senators William Fulbright, George McGovern, and others, as well as the *New York Times,* "raised a lot of hell with Henry" because they felt they'd been misled.

Kissinger knew there was nothing like success to silence critics. And to him, only by reaching Tchepone could Lam Son be qualified as a military victory. He demanded explanations and action from Laird. "He was upset about it,"

Laird remembered. "He'd call every day." Laird chose to "needle him a little bit" by responding, "You know, Henry, I'm not the secretary of defense for the South Vietnamese, and President Nixon isn't their commander in chief. It's *their* operation."

At that point, in Laird's view, the operation had already been quite successful. Into the National Military Command Center flowed communications intercepted between enemy troops about the diminishment of supplies.[24] Thus, when pressed about Tchepone by newsmen on March 5, Laird emphasized that Lam Son "is clearly an operation to disrupt the logistics supply routes, the men and material.... [T]o say they would waste their efforts on a desolate town with no people would be the height of military folly."[25] Laird already knew that Kissinger, through Abrams, had pushed Thieu into mounting an offensive against that desolate town. Thieu ordered his troops back into the fray and sent in reinforcements.[26] He decided that if he leap-frogged an airborne assault near the village he could declare victory and depart—a "touching base" maneuver. No one expected him to hold Tchepone, since Lam Son was supposed to be an in-and-out operation.

So on March 6 the U.S. forces at Khe Sanh mounted the largest, longest-ranging helicopter assault of the Vietnam War. Making three round trips that single day, 276 Huey helicopters took two South Vietnamese infantry battalions forty-eight miles to a landing zone next to Tchepone. There they held on long enough to destroy substantial caches of supplies and equipment. Two days after the landing, General Abrams pronounced Lam Son a success. They had seized enough rice to feed 159 battalions for thirty days; enough rifles, small arms, machine guns, mortars, and artillery pieces to equip seventeen infantry battalions; and 714 tons of ammunition.[27]

Four days after arriving in Tchepone, the South Vietnamese began to pull out, against the wishes of Laird and others who had hoped Thieu would capitalize on the success a little longer. But these were Thieu's best troops, and he would need them in the future to protect South Vietnam, particularly as American troops were withdrawing. He ignored American advice and ordered the retreat, which quickly took on the look of a rout. Route 9 was a tangle of disabled tanks and other vehicles that had run out of gas—and not a few corpses. Most of the South Vietnamese troops had to either hike or be helicoptered out. Given the high helicopter losses sustained by the U.S. force from the anti-aircraft artillery along the trail, pilots were ordered to fully pack their choppers with retreating soldiers to cut down on the number of round trips. A small number of panicky soldiers interpreted the situation as a shortage of room and jumped onto the helicopter skids, creating unforgettable photographic images when they landed in Khe Sanh where the American news media waited.

As the South Vietnamese numbers in Laos diminished, the enemy attacked in greater force, and the situation became desperate. Instead of an orderly retreat, the final days left the impression of a desperate scramble to safety inside

South Vietnam. Laird publicly defended the performance of the South Vietnamese soldiers and praised their success. Behind closed doors he expressed
disappointment during the March 29 staff meeting that they had not stayed
longer. But he agreed with Admiral Moorer, who said at that meeting, "[W]e
have no argument with the South Vietnamese. This was their operation, and it
was President Thieu's decision to end it."[28]

While those military leaders were relatively sanguine, Nixon and Kissinger
were not—and the object of their anger was the dutiful soldier Creighton
Abrams. Years later Kissinger recalled, "I thought Abrams screwed up the Laos
operation." But, he added, "The poor guy was sitting out there [under difficult
circumstances]. Every six months, we took more troops away, and we were
expanding his missions to include Laos. So I had sympathy for that."[29]

Nixon was so angry that, according to Haig's memoirs, the president ordered Haig to take over for Abrams: "Go home and pack your bag. Then get on
the first available plane and fly to Saigon. You're taking command." Haig said
he replied, "Good God, Mr. President, you can't do that." The next day Nixon
changed his mind, and Haig was dispatched instead on a fact-finding mission
to Saigon.[30]

Laird is not inclined to believe the story; no one has told it except Haig. By
"cocktail napkin" agreement with Laird, Nixon couldn't have relieved Abrams
without going through the secretary. Still, as the Watergate tapes and other
accounts later showed, Nixon was subject to fits of temper, so it may well have
happened as Haig said. In Nixon's memoirs he said Lam Son was a "military
success but a public relations disaster."[31] Kissinger concluded that the operation
fell short of expectations but had prevented the North from launching an offensive in 1971 and seriously curtailed their 1972 Easter offensive. Abrams died
several years after the war without penning his own memoirs, but author Lewis
Sorley published transcripts of tape recordings Abrams made of his meetings
in Saigon. In August 1971 Abrams had conducted a review of Lam Son, calculat-
ing the damage done to enemy supply lines and the reduced ability of Hanoi to
mount a major offensive that year. "I'm beginning to have a conviction about
Lam Son 719 that that was really a death blow," Abrams is quoted on one tape
as saying.[32]

Laird himself believed similarly: "In hindsight, I would say it was a good
thing to do. It diverted the North for a period of time to reconstruct that portion of the supply route. The South Vietnamese casualty rate was higher than
I expected, but the North Vietnamese position was stronger than I had been
told it would be by our intelligence." An independent review of the operation, including assessment of action reports that came into Laird's office, suggests that Lam Son 719 was a qualified success. U.S. intelligence concluded that
more than thirteen thousand enemy troops were killed, and probably twice
that number wounded, suggesting a casualty rate as high as 70 percent. U.S. air
power was pivotal in achieving that result. Some 1,280 B-52 sorties alone were

flown in support of the operation during the six weeks the South Vietnamese were in Laos. On a daily basis, some six hundred U.S. helicopters were committed to the battle.[33]

Lam Son seriously disrupted the Ho Chi Minh Trail. The CIA's Office of Economic Research sent a report to Laird that spring concluding that "large-scale enemy military operations in South Vietnam for the remainder of 1971 were probably impossible and that Hanoi would have to undertake a major resupply campaign before any offensive could be launched in 1972."[34]

North Vietnam declared a great victory, but Laird knew Hanoi was reeling, because intercepted messages demonstrated that the usually chest-thumping propaganda from the field was more subdued. [35]

And for the first time the North Vietnamese in their radio traffic were talking about their wounded and dead, months after an operation. Admiral Moorer told Laird at the July 12 staff meeting: "[T]here was considerable traffic concerning the large number of wounded during Lam Son 719. The enemy has had to establish temporary places en route to take care of the large number of wounded, and they have also made special provisions for burial grounds."[36]

A final positive point for Laird was the relatively muted student protest over Lam Son—far less in number and intensity than the Cambodia protests of the previous spring. In part, it was because Lam Son occurred during the winter when only the most diehard protesters would have turned out. In larger part, the diminished use of U.S. forces, and concurrent withdrawals, were persuading the public that the United States was pulling out of the war and not expanding it. Still, Laird was the target of protests. For example, he had agreed to deliver a speech at the University of Wisconsin before Lam Son but had to cancel during the ongoing operation. General "Chappie" James went in his place and received an antiwar reprimand from the chancellor and a thirty-name petition protesting the war from the students serving the luncheon. Out in the cold were about two thousand antiwar protesters led by Rennie Davis, who had been convicted in the "Chicago Seven" trial of crossing state lines to incite a riot at the 1968 Democratic National Convention. He shouted to the demonstrators in Wisconsin, "If the government doesn't stop the war, we are going to stop the government." And he chided Laird for not showing up: "Laird is not all fool. If he would have come here today, we would have really kicked some ass!"[37]

On February 10 several hundred students at the University of Illinois in Champaign burned Laird in effigy.[38]

⋙⋘

Lam Son had caused Laird to focus more closely not just on the Ho Chi Minh Trail interdiction, but also on the secret war in Laos, which the Pentagon was required to support. In 1971 he became fed up with standing on the side lines while the CIA and the State Department ran the covert war in Laos, using his budget. He decided he wanted a man he could trust to take a closer look and ride herd over it. The man he chose would eventually become chairman of the Joint Chiefs of Staff during the Reagan administration: General John W. "Jack" Vessey. In late 1971 he was a new brigadier general running support operations out of Thailand for the effort in Laos. Vessey heard rumors that the Laos job might be coming to him, but he didn't believe it would happen. "We weren't supposed to have anybody in Laos," he recalled. "I knew there would be great political consternation back home, with the different agencies involved, in having a military guy, particularly an Army guy, go [to Laos] with control of the budgets and with the direction to put some sense into the strategy."

Laird visited Thailand in person and told Vessey what he wanted. He recalled telling Vessey, "You've gotta get up there to Vientiane, because I don't understand what's going on up there with the State Department and the CIA, and we're going to get tarred with their brush. They keep asking for more and more ammunition—our assets—and I want to make sure we're getting a dollar's worth of bang for the buck we send."

In the time it took to pack his bag, Vessey was in Laos. Following Laird's orders he presented himself at the U.S. embassy in Vientiane to report to Ambassador Godley. Godley's assistant, Monte Sterns, waylaid him and said, "The ambassador is pretty busy today and won't be able to see you. Why don't you get a room and look around and make contact with the other agencies?" Vessey made the rounds of the CIA and the Agency for International Development, which had a role in the war and provided cover for the CIA. In two days Vessey was back at the Embassy. Sterns again came to the waiting room. "Well, the ambassador's still not ready," he said. But Vessey wasn't leaving. "I've been ordered to report to the ambassador. It seems to me I ought to see him."

At that point, having overheard the conversation, Godley stormed out of his office and confronted Vessey. "I didn't ask for you and I don't want you here!" he bellowed.

"Well, Mr. Ambassador, I didn't ask to come here, and I really don't want to be here," Vessey retorted, "but I've been ordered to be here and it seems to me we ought to figure out how to make this work."

Godley calmed down, but he set one ground rule: "The first thing I want to tell you is you can't send any backchannels to your military superiors." Vessey fell back on good military order and said he couldn't cut off any means of communicating with his superiors, but he promised he would never send anything to Washington without showing it to Godley. Then he added, "Maybe we can work out the same arrangement." To his surprise, Godley agreed that the channel of communications would be open on both sides. "We became very fast friends," Vessey recalled, "and eventually worked very well together."

While neither ever conceded that the other was the boss, Vessey was firmly in charge of the purse strings. Godley kept control of the air war, but Vessey found a way to insert his views through his friend and handball partner General Charles Gabriel, who then ran the air wing in Udorn, Thailand, which supported the Laos operations. "We'd play handball sometime between midnight and two in the morning [and] conjure up ways to sneak a little extra support for the war in Laos that made sense," Vessey said of his occasional visits back to Thailand to meet with Gabriel. "It was an operation that would get you an 'F' if you drew it up on an organizational chart and submitted it to the War College, but we made it work."

The constraints imposed by Congress and the Geneva Convention meant that Vessey had to do much of his strategizing on the sly. His own presence in Laos was known only to a few insiders. He kept a low profile, and on the few occasions when he went to social events he wore civilian clothes. "I think the only people who knew I was there were the Russians and the Chinese," he recalled. They would follow him with cameras on his rare public outings.

Vessey was one of the few American soldiers who actually lived in Laos during the war. Because of him, Laird was able to keep congressional committees better informed about the war in Laos, and he had Vessey host congressional visitors in Vientiane—ensuring they would get the Pentagon view during briefings. Still, Vessey managed to keep his presence a secret from the press. Once, in the spring of 1972, as Vessey was working to beef up the Royal Laotian Army, American Green Berets were sent to do the training. They were flown into Laos in the morning and out at night, so it could not be said that they were "stationed" there. But the *Washington Post* reported their presence at one of the training camps, and Vessey got a message through channels from Laird that fairly burned on the paper. As Vessey recalled the word from Laird, "If he ever heard of it happening again, I was toast—well, stronger words than that."

Under his cloak of secrecy, Vessey managed to impose Laird's stamp on the Laos operations. He stayed within the budgetary limits that Congress had set for aid to Laos and forged tight relationships with the CIA and State Department bosses there. "By the time the cease fire came around [in 1973], we had almost all the rice growing land under the control of the [Lao] government. We had about 80 percent of the people [under] control of the government, and it was a relatively successful strategy," Vessey said.[39]

Successful indeed in a nation where the United States never officially fought a war.

31

When the Hawks Have Flown

ON THE BRISK SPRING EVENING of April 5, 1971, the secretary of defense left the Pentagon shortly after 8 P.M. and was driven to the Watergate apartment complex in Georgetown. He looked forward to the private dinner hosted by Senator Jacob Javits in a luxurious penthouse. It would be a catered meal for ten senators and Laird. The secretary expected a companionable evening with a wide-ranging discussion on administration policy. But not long after sitting down to eat, Laird realized that he was to be the main course. The Republican leaders at the table were sick of Laos, sick of Vietnam, and disenchanted with the president's exit plan, and they took it out on Laird.

"The president must think in terms of finality," declared Hugh Scott, the Senate minority leader. Knowing that Nixon was scheduled to make his next major troop withdrawal announcement two nights later, Scott lamented, "We just can't hold the line any longer on [withdrawal] numbers. He must make public some formula that clearly indicates the end of American participation in the war." It was an untenable position to Laird, who knew as well as they should have known that giving a certain date of departure would rob the United States of negotiating power with the North Vietnamese.

But Laird was not surprised at their sentiment. He had watched the mood of Congress, and, just that morning, Dick Capen had reported at the Monday staff meeting that "many long-time supporters of our effort in Vietnam are changing their positions."[1] That was glaringly evident at Javits's dinner table. After adjourning for cognac and cigars in the living room, the senators continued their assessment of the war and its impact on the American people. Senator Marlow Cook asked directly, if the president announced that the war was over tomorrow, how long it would take to get the troops and equipment home. Laird reckoned nine months. Time and again the senators came back to their central theme: they would not be able to hold their party and sympathetic Democrats together on war issues if Nixon did not announce an end date. Absent that, an end-the-war resolution might well win in Congress that year, which would force the president's hand. Driving the point home, Alaska's Ted Stevens told Laird, "I come from the most hawkish state in the union. I ran in '70 as a hawk. I couldn't do it in '72." Scott soberly added: "You don't see any hawks around here. The hawks are all ex-hawks."[2]

After a congressional breakfast the next morning, Laird paid an unusual call on a freshman congressman, Jack Kemp, a boyish-looking former pro football quarterback whom Laird believed was headed for political stardom. For Kemp, a new "back bencher," it was a singular honor, but for Laird it was a chance to shore up some support in his own party.[3] Kemp told Laird to forge ahead with the Vietnamization game plan no matter what the naysayers might throw at him. During Kemp's years with the Buffalo Bills he had learned to take the bad days with equanimity. "When you've been booed by 60,000 fans, politics holds no terrors," Kemp often said.[4]

Laird was not necessarily in need of a pep talk, but it was welcome. The handwriting was on the walls of Congress: time was running out because more Americans were calling for a speeded-up withdrawal. On the day Kemp and Laird met, voters in Madison, Wisconsin, overwhelmingly supported a referendum calling for an immediate cease-fire and withdrawal of all U.S. forces from Vietnam.[5] And in the most conservative county of Laird's old congressional district, the audience surrounded his Democrat successor, Congressman David Obey, after a Rotary Club speech and told him it was time to end the war. "It surprised the hell out of me," Obey told the *Wall Street Journal*. "These people don't want to hear any more talk about getting out—they just want out."[6]

Laird left Capitol Hill that morning and went back to his office to compose a memo to Nixon, whom he was sure would be feeling the lack of patience in the party. Entitled "Tempo of the War," Laird's memo began with heartening words: "The attention given to operations in Laos tends to obscure the fact that U.S. involvement in the war is declining rapidly." Laird reminded Nixon of some of their war-related achievements, which the president could use in his scheduled address to the nation the following night. The enemy had been able to launch only "two large ... attacks" in the previous nine months, compared to eight in the same period the previous year. U.S. troop numbers were 44 percent below their high point. Combat deaths were down 55 percent from the prior year. And the cost of the war had fallen by $4 billion in 1970 and would fall another $5 billion in 1971.[7]

Nixon was cheered by the memo and called Laird at noon the next day to his hideaway office at the Old Executive Office Building to go over the speech. In it, Nixon announced the fifth round of troop withdrawals from Vietnam. As with the prior four, the behind-the-scenes maneuvering had been intense. For example, anticipating the president's announcement, Clark Clifford had once again added his two cents. On April 2 he publicly challenged Nixon to have every American soldier and airman out of Vietnam within six months.[8] Senator George Aiken of Vermont, who had attended the Javits dinner, declared in a radio interview on April 6 that he fully expected Nixon to declare a withdrawal rate of 18,000 men a month—or 5,500 men above the ongoing average.[9] As usual, Nixon was steamed by the meddling. Laird feigned annoyance but privately welcomed the pressure for more speedy withdrawals.

Laird had learned the week before Nixon's speech that the Joint Chiefs and General Abrams were emphatic about slowing down the rate of withdrawal to only 8,500 a month instead of 12,500. President Thieu also preferred the slower rate since he was up for reelection in the fall. It was Laird's duty to convey their views to the president and then offer his own recommendation, which he had done on April 3.[10] Laird was determined to persuade Nixon not to accept the Joint Chiefs' plan and to go for an increased rate of withdrawal instead. He tactfully reminded Nixon that the president had promised publicly in two speeches that the withdrawal would "continue at its present level," so the Joint Chiefs' recommendation was unacceptable for that reason alone. He advised Nixon to consider a faster withdrawal rate for three reasons. First, the president should understand that "congressional and popular U.S. support for our programs in Southeast Asia are now more tenuous than ever."

The second and third reasons Laird raised had to do with the terrible human and financial costs of the war. Even though casualties were far fewer than under the Johnson administration, more than fifteen thousand Americans had died in the war since Nixon took office. Only by increasing the rate of withdrawal would combat deaths continue to come down.

Though rarely mentioned in public up to that time, Laird made a powerful point in his private memo to Nixon about the second great cost of the Vietnam War—that of falling behind the main enemy, the Soviet Union. The impact of the war's financial drain on the defense budget "is one of the major reasons the Soviet Union has been able to make such marked military strides relative to the United States during the past few years," Laird wrote.

Laird had warned the military ahead of time that he would advise Nixon to increase the pace of withdrawal, which prompted General Abrams and Admiral McCain to fly to Washington from Saigon and Hawaii, respectively, to make their case personally to the president to go slower. But Laird had made the more persuasive argument, and Nixon announced in his speech that another 100,000 troops would be withdrawn by December 1, leaving about 184,000 Americans in Vietnam.

Though the president's speech failed to produce any dramatic announcements, newspaper editorial writers found his plan thoughtful. The *Washington Post* called it an "undeniable step in the right direction, which you have to give him credit for, just as he must be credited with the quarter of a million troops already withdrawn [and] with the dramatic decline in American casualties over the past two years."[11] Most congressional leaders were not satisfied, however, including those who had attended the Javits party. Still, as they began to add up the numbers it was undeniable that such a continued withdrawal rate meant that only twenty-five thousand troops would be left in Vietnam when voters went to the polls in November 1972 to reelect or bounce Nixon.

Media prognosticators wondered whether a reelected Nixon would leave that many troops in the war indefinitely as a "residual force." In his speech the president had promised "total withdrawal," provided that peace negotiations were concluded. Journalists tried to set up a disagreement between Nixon and Laird by juxtaposing Nixon's "total withdrawal" with earlier Laird statements about a residual force. With White House approval Laird had testified at a congressional hearing in February 1970 that the final phase of the Vietnamization plan contemplated a military advisory group that would be smaller than the sixty-four thousand men then stationed in South Korea to guarantee the armistice with North Korea. Later, after the raid on the Son Tay prisoner of war camp, Laird suggested that a residual force would stay only until the last American POW had been released—a formula that Nixon fully embraced.

But the president didn't want any mention of "residual forces" after his speech, and he thought that Laird was stoking the issue in the press. Nixon's fury was captured on the secret taping system in his office on April 9 as he conferred with Kissinger. "We don't want a residual force; our goal is total withdrawal!" Nixon insisted. "Why can't Laird shut up?" Kissinger promised to have a talk with Laird at a private Pentagon luncheon the following Tuesday. "I'm going to try to shape him up."[12]

Kissinger left, but Nixon continued to fume. He decided he couldn't wait until Kissinger had a private word with Laird. Instead Nixon issued a highly unusual gag order, classified it "Secret/Eyes Only," and had it delivered to Laird, Rogers, Helms, and the Joint Chiefs: "Until further notice, I want no discussions by Government officials with the media concerning U.S. troop withdrawal plans or U.S. plans for maintaining a residual force in South Vietnam. This applies to discussions with the press, either on or off the record, background briefings and informal speculation."[13]

Laird received copy number one, and he knew it was a slap on the wrist. The order would be easy for the others to keep because they rarely talked, even in background briefings, about Vietnam plans. By default, this made Laird the front man on Capitol Hill and with the media. (Had Laird chosen to leak to the press the presidential order itself, that would have been a larger story than speculation about a residual force.) When Laird could not be informative at a news conference a few days later,[14] the correspondents were frustrated and detected a strain. The Washington Post's experienced Pentagon correspondent George Wilson wrote: "Laird appeared defensive and jumpy—his hands visibly shaking at times. His usual exuberance and confidence seemed to be missing."[15] At the time, Laird was suffering from a double hernia, but his shaky performance probably had less to do with physical pain than the veteran politician's discomfiture at working under a gag order.

One of the subjects raised at that press conference was a new type of antiwar demonstration that was coming the following week—a march by antiwar veterans. Never before had American veterans marched on Washington to protest a war that was still being fought. Worse, the Pentagon and press had been told that many of the disenchanted Vietnam vets planned to return their service medals. The very thought of such a spectacle was unnerving for Laird—the more so for being a World War II veteran himself.

⚓

The witness at the table in the cavernous Senate Foreign Relations Committee room on April 22, 1971, was tall, prepossessing, blessed with a Kennedy-like visage, hair, and even the late president's initials. John Forbes Kerry's testimony was searing. "How do you ask a man to be the last man to die in Vietnam?" he said to the packed hearing room. "How do you ask a man to be the last man to die for a mistake?"

The twenty-seven-year old Kerry was no hippie. He was a decorated veteran who had commanded swift boats in Vietnam and had been awarded three Purple Hearts, a Silver Star, and a Bronze Star. Thirty-three years into the future he would be a senator himself and a presidential candidate. But in 1971 he had joined a small, moribund protest group—the Vietnam Veterans against the War—and was instrumental in inflating its influence beyond its numbers. The group's performance became the opening act of the spring 1971 protest season in the nation's capital.

For several months the Pentagon had geared up for the expected spring demonstrations. The protests were initially planned through loose coordination between antiwar groups in three acts: a massive march on the Capitol April 24; a week of guerrilla theater around Washington; and a shut-down of the city by blocking traffic May 3–5. Late in the planning, a week-long Vietnam Veterans encampment was tacked onto the plans. It was born out of frustration at the minimal media attention given in February to "hearings" by Kerry's group in Detroit, during which dozens of veterans openly confessed to acts of criminal violence they claimed to have committed or witnessed in Vietnam.

From a potential pool of more than two million veterans, about two thousand Vietnam veterans answered the call for a variety of demonstrations beginning on April 19. They called it "Operation Dewey Canyon III, a limited incursion into the country of Congress." The first few days were inauspicious and ad hoc: a demonstration at Arlington Cemetery and the Supreme Court, a day lobbying Congress, and a march of about fifty veterans to the Pentagon to turn themselves in as "war criminals."

By Thursday April 22 the national news media were primed for Kerry's two-hour performance before the Senate Foreign Relations Committee. It was a wide-ranging and rational indictment of the war by one whose service demanded the country's attention. "We wish that a merciful God could wipe away our own memories of [our] service," Kerry said. But since God had not done that, the veterans were unitedly determined "to undertake one last mission—to search out and destroy the last vestige of this barbaric war, to pacify our own hearts, to conquer the hate and the fear that have driven this country these last ten years and more, so when thirty years from now our brothers go down the street without a leg, without an arm, or a face, and small boys ask why, we will be able to say 'Vietnam' and not mean . . . a filthy obscene memory, but mean instead the place where America finally turned and where soldiers like us helped it in the turning."[16]

Kerry's moving testimony was followed the next day by the final scene of the protest, a wrenching return of the medals and honors to the government. Over a wire fence hastily erected in front of the west entrance of the Capitol, about six hundred veterans lobbed ribbons and medals (the highest being a Silver Star), which landed in a pile at the feet of the statue of Chief Justice John Marshall.[17] (Not all discarded their *own* medals. Kerry admitted in 1984, during his first successful run for the senate, that he had tossed someone else's medals for them that day. "I did not want to throw my medals away," he said then, because he was proud of his service.[18] For the same reason, others at the demonstration chose not to toss away specific ribbons or medals given for valor.)

Kerry's public statements rankled many at the Pentagon who found him outlandish, prone to exaggeration, and possibly guilty of conduct unbecoming an officer. (Although no longer on active duty, he was still in the Navy Reserves.) Chief of Naval Operations Admiral Zumwalt and Navy Secretary Chafee urged Laird to agree to court-martial proceedings against Kerry, but Laird turned them down flat. His view then was that Kerry would enjoy a few minutes in the spotlight and never be heard from again.[19]

During the veterans' demonstration Laird refused to criticize them. In private and public he avowed their right to dissent. Laird was questioned by the editors of *U.S. News and World Report* in their Washington office and was asked his opinion about the latest round of demonstrations. He answered, "When you get right to the heart of it, I think the answer is that the American people are tired of war. They are understandably frustrated and concerned over the length of time we have been engaged in a costly war. They want peace."[20]

The veterans' portion of the spring demonstration, Laird knew, had been very effective in reaching a wide swath of America. One man, however, was not only unmoved but angry: President Nixon. According to Haldeman's diary entry of April 23, the day the medals were discarded, Nixon was typically not interested in the message of the protesters but only in how it made him look. "We got into quite a discussion of the media problem; they're really killing us because they run the veterans' demonstration every night [on TV] in great detail, and we have no way to fight back," Haldeman wrote. A quick poll done by the White House showed that the president's approval rating had dropped three points, and there had been "a switch back to disapproval on Vietnam from our previous position of fairly strong approval."[21] Nixon emerged with an animosity toward Kerry sufficient to reportedly keep him up late on the following year's election night to witness Kerry's loss in a run for Congress.[22]

The seventh mass march in Washington against the Vietnam War—and the fourth during Nixon's presidency—occurred on April 24, the day after the veterans tossed their medals. More than double the number of the expected protesters came—two hundred thousand plus—and the group included more older adults than in previous marches. Other marches had headed for the White House or Pentagon. This one went down Pennsylvania Avenue to the Capitol, making it the largest mass rally ever to be held on the West Lawn of the Capitol grounds. When the rally was over, the marchers, mindful of Earth Day, cleaned up after themselves. The *New York Times* called it "less electric in mood" than the previous year's angry protest against the invasion of Cambodia. "The scene was one of Americans who appeared more frustrated than furious, more persistent than volatile."[23] It was the most peaceful antiwar march yet, with not one incident of violence.

The next day the goodwill won by the veterans and peaceful marchers began to erode as about a thousand homeward-bound New England demonstrators stopped their cars on the New Jersey Turnpike and built a bonfire that blocked traffic for four hours and resulted in one hundred arrests. On Monday, April 26, the uninvited "People's Lobby" invaded the old Senate Office Building, including the inner offices of a dozen senators and a meeting of the Senate Foreign Relations Committee. Bands of wailing women in burlap sacks smeared with red paint and with red liquid drooling out of their mouths, ran through the marble halls and into Senate offices screaming such things as, "No! No! Stop it! God have mercy, don't kill my baby!" They were pursued by men in remnants of uniforms, toting toy guns. Several of the demonstrators got into the spectators' gallery of the Senate and shouted curses and epithets before they were cleared by guards. One group made a special trip to Maryland to continue the grotesque guerrilla theater at the home of the secretary of defense.

Laird had some forewarning, and a small security force was there in civilian clothes. Laird's children were at school, and he was at the Pentagon. His security man, Joe Zaice, was inside the house with Barbara Laird. Zaice and his men simply watched as a dozen or so demonstrators in "costume" conducted a mock battle on Laird's lawn, spilling a red liquid, shouting oaths, and hanging a Viet Cong flag from his front porch.[24] The antics were featured on national television and were a prime topic of conversation the next morning in an Oval Office meeting between Nixon, Agnew, and Haldeman. Nixon was outraged by the demonstration in the Senate and blamed his former opponent, Senator Hubert Humphrey, who was presiding and had not cleared the galleries in time to stop the fracas. Agnew added that as president of the Senate, he had previously asked that the gallery be surrounded by soundproof glass so the spectators could not be heard. "The gallery, as you know, act disgracefully all the time," Nixon added.[25]

Then Haldeman recounted: "They went out to Mel Laird's house, ya know, and staged a guerrilla theater business on Mel Laird's front lawn. They all ran around killing gooks and dying and piling up in his driveway, and all this. And there were about seven neighbors there who viewed it with some disgust. But the TV cameras were there and managed to get it on the networks last night."

"I don't think that's gonna help," the president observed, speaking of the antiwar cause.

"That doesn't help 'em," Agnew agreed.

Haldeman said he was a little worried about what the Laird "home invasion" portended for the future. "It's gonna stimulate more of them to go to more people's homes and start, ya know, to go out [to that] busy residential neighborhood in Bethesda and start scaring people."

The president ended the conversation, as he needed to go to the 8 A.M. Cabinet meeting, where several others ribbed Laird about the antics on his lawn. Laird himself appeared nonplused about it at his 11 A.M. press conference in the Secretary's Dining Room at the Pentagon.

"Were you or your family home yesterday, Mr. Secretary, when you had the visitation?" a reporter asked.

"We've had visitations, of course, before," Laird responded with a dismissive smile. "My wife was home, but I'm sure people know where I am most of the time. I was here trying to do my job."

In an ebullient mood, Laird told the assembled correspondents that he had called the press conference in part to report that he had a "not very grave problem" and would check into Walter Reed Army Hospital the next day to take care of his double hernia. "After that press conference of a week ago, George [Wilson] reported that I was shaking and not my old self, I thought I'd better let you look me over. . . . I'm getting it taken care of so I'll be around."

For how long? a reporter asked.

"I'll be around until the change of the guard [in 1973]," Laird said. "I've always said that Secretary McNamara served too long. I think that four years is long enough to serve in this particular job. So when you ask me how long, it'll be that long and no longer." With that, Laird publicly restated his initial one-term pledge, making him the first member of the Nixon Cabinet to state unequivocally that he was leaving.

The correspondents asked if he would consider going back to Congress, to which Laird responded, "I don't think I want to go back and start all over again." He did confirm that he believed the Republican Party would return his seniority to him if he were elected to the Congress again.[26] The remarks prompted a flurry of speculation on his political future. *Time* magazine concluded that Laird had presidential ambitions and might run for the Senate from Wisconsin as a step to the White House.[27] Laird quickly put that rumor to rest. But other theories circulated that he would take a different Cabinet post or that Nixon would dump Agnew and choose Laird as his running mate in

1972. No one could believe that the career politician would simply walk away from it all at the top of his game.

⌐◦⌐

Within a few hours of his successful hernia surgery on April 29, Laird was on the phone from his hospital bed ordering the deployment of federal troops into Washington.[28] For several weeks the radical antiwar May Day Tribe, whose stated purpose was to "create the specter of social chaos," had been calling for thousands of demonstrators to help them shut down Washington, D.C., on May 3. Besides marching on the Pentagon, they would block twenty-one intersections during morning rush hour to prevent government workers from reaching their offices.

In an earlier staff meeting with Laird, General Westmoreland had urged him to get the president's permission to bring in a lightly armed army helicopter assault force that could be "skillfully used for a number of purposes—like picking up automobiles blocking highways."[29] Laird declined. Ultimately, though, it wasn't his call—it was the president's, and Nixon had declared that on Monday, May 3, Washington would be an "open city." The lines were drawn; no protesters would be allowed to shut down the city. In an effective preemptive move, Washington police ordered fifteen thousand protesters out of their camp site in West Potomac Park before dawn on Sunday, dispersing the organizers and fouling up some of the plans. During the same time, at the request of the Justice Department, Laird placed some four thousand federal troops around the area on alert. By late Sunday afternoon, another six thousand (including paratroopers) were flown in by C-130s to Andrews Air Force Base, where they would wait to be called in if needed.[30]

When Monday morning dawned, at more than a dozen intersections and bridges around Washington, pitched battles erupted between demonstrators throwing projectiles of various kinds and police lobbing tear gas and making unnecessarily rough arrests. The march to the Pentagon was blocked; only a handful of protesters made it to the building, where they flung paper bags full of chicken excrement onto the steps, saying it was "for the chicken colonels."[31] Traffic was disrupted, but only temporarily, and it appeared to be a "win" for the authorities—at least until the numbers of those arrested began to mount. By the end of the day D.C. police had made more than seven thousand arrests, an all-time record for a civil disturbance.[32] (A total of twelve thousand were arrested by the third day of the May Day "activities.")

The police were unprepared for the numbers and held thousands without basic facilities in a fenced practice field of the Washington Redskins football team near the Robert F. Kennedy Memorial Stadium. The sweep of arrests was so broad that innocents were scooped up as well. As their numbers bulged at the football field, a large black limousine drove up to the front gates, and

Senator Ted Kennedy emerged, requesting to speak to the prisoners. The guards turned him away as the protestors booed him for leaving. Next came gutsy Congresswoman Bella Abzug. With her trademark hat flapping in the wind she barged past the guards into the enclosure, asking if there was anyone who didn't belong there. A few began shouting about the fascist state, and Abzug told them to shut up. She had no sympathy for those who came to be arrested to make their point. But who among them was in the wrong place at the wrong time? A terrified middle-aged woman in a fur coat, clutching her small dog, emerged from the crowd and Abzug whisked her out past the guards as the crowd cheered.[33]

Although the arrests gave the authorities a minor black eye—and later a successful class action suit by the demonstrators—the American public generally sided with the police. The good will that had been garnered by the antiwar veterans had been undone by the guerrilla theater antics and more violent demonstrations at the end of the eighteen days of sustained protest. Nixon knew that, which prompted his thank-you notes and congratulatory calls to agency heads. Laird got his call Wednesday morning. "The one, really, that was effective against us was the veterans' one," Nixon observed to Laird. "But since then, *this* group—God, that's a horrible-looking bunch of people. On television they just look so bad that people are gonna just throw up their hands."[34]

A few days later at the Monday staff meeting, Laird led a discussion about "the recent civil disturbances and demonstrations." He was pleased that his troops had made no arrests and never used tear gas and that they generally had "avoided confrontation with citizens." He also was proud that, unnoticed by the press, the Defense Department had provided thousands of blankets and fifteen thousand meals for the demonstrators. Make no mistake about it, he told the staff, though there were "other issues involved in these demonstrations, the Vietnam War is the catalyst." The most effective way to silence the demonstrators was to end the war.

32

Defending the Pentagon

⌦

MEL LAIRD HAD A TICKING TIME BOMB in the walk-in safe of his office. Sitting on a shelf there among other top-secret documents during the summer of 1971 was a seven-thousand-page history of how the United States had stumbled its way into the Vietnam War. The existence of the forty-seven-volume set was known to few in or out of government; only fifteen copies had ever been distributed. The public revelation of portions of the study, which became known as the "Pentagon Papers," would prompt one of the most dramatic confrontations between the press and government in American history. From that conflict would emerge a more emboldened, cynical, and hostile press, as well as a more paranoid president determined to protect his Oval Office by any means necessary, legal or illegal.

The Vietnam War history project was conceived quietly and conducted on a need-to-know basis by Robert McNamara. When finished, the weight of its research analyses inevitably proved the Johnson administration's tragic Americanization of the war. The study also uncovered the deception that Johnson and McNamara knowingly or unknowingly engaged in to justify the war.

One of the few individuals with insight into the project's genesis was the man who began it at Secretary McNamara's request, Colonel Robert E. Pursley. As military assistant to McNamara, Pursley was taken aside by his boss in May 1967 and given the assignment. According to a 1971 FBI interview with Pursley, McNamara "wanted this study done so that he could read in depth on the subject and better equip himself to answer questions."[1]

Pursley took notes of McNamara's verbal instructions, but those notes ended up in a classified file at the Pentagon, and officials repeatedly denied him access to them, even after the controversy died down.[2] But he remembered that McNamara never intended for the study to be published. "The term the secretary used for the study was an *encyclopedia*. He wanted for himself and Deputy Secretary Cy Vance an encyclopedia that they could refer to, to really try to understand how in the world we got to where we were in 1967 regarding the Vietnam War."[3]

Pursley conferred with the chief of the Pentagon's International Security Affairs (ISA) section, John McNaughton, and they settled on one of his "whiz kids," Leslie H. Gelb, to head up the Vietnam History Task Force. (Gelb would later become a top State Department official, *New York Times* reporter, and then head of the influential Council on Foreign Relations.) He assembled an all-star team of nearly forty people for the project.[4] After the most important documents were assembled, sections of the study were apportioned out to at least thirty-six men who wrote analyses to introduce the documents. Few of these authors or the additional consultants who were called in, such as Harvard professor Henry Kissinger, knew of the big picture. Fewer still were ever cleared to read the study, other than their own portions.

The project was so comprehensive that it was not completed until after Mc-Namara resigned as defense secretary, and only five days before his successor Clark Clifford left office as well. The final study was not distributed to its select audience until June 1969—five months into Laird's term.[5] The study, entitled "History of U.S. Decision-Making Process on Vietnam Policy,"[6] comprised 2.5 million words broken up into four thousand pages of documents accompanied by three thousand pages of analysis. As one of many later analyses summarized, it was an explosive study that, among other things, conclusively demonstrated that the Kennedy and Johnson administrations "had systematically lied, not only to the public but also to Congress, about a subject of transcendent national interest and significance."[7]

Laird put his copy on the top shelf of his large vault without reading it. "I don't recall any of us ever going back to dig into it much," said Pursley. Laird said he referred to the books "from time to time because they were background information." But he never had time to read all seven thousand pages.

Seven copies of the report, including Laird's, were kept at the Pentagon. Two more were in State Department safes among the private papers of two former State Department officials. McNamara and Clifford each had a copy. Two more were given to the National Archives for the Kennedy and Johnson presidential libraries. One set was assigned to one of the project's leaders, Morton Halperin. The team leader, Gelb, also was allotted a copy. Gelb and Halperin, who both resigned from the Nixon administration to work at the Brookings Institution, decided to put their copies in the vaults of another private think tank, the RAND Corporation.[8]

RAND's success had been built on a series of lucrative defense contracts under McNamara, who considered RAND's analysts worth ten times what he paid them. One of those analysts was Dr. Daniel Ellsberg, a former marine who took a civilian assignment in Vietnam to work on the CIA's "pacification" program to neutralize the Viet Cong. He came back from Vietnam with his prowar opinions tempered. When he was assigned by RAND to work on a portion of the Pentagon Papers, Ellsberg soon evolved into a full-blown antiwar convert, though he kept his conversion a secret in Washington. Had Kissinger known of the depth of Ellsberg's disenchantment in late 1968, he likely would not have hired Ellsberg to draft the first Nixon National Security Council options paper on Vietnam policy.

Ellsberg's first leak of a portion of the Pentagon Papers occurred on November 6, 1969, when he met with Senator William Fulbright and several staffers for the Senate Foreign Relations Committee. Ellsberg gave them a section of the study that proved the Gulf of Tonkin incident was deliberately overblown so President Johnson could escalate U.S. involvement in Vietnam. Fulbright decided the only way he could credibly expose the deception was to get the administration to give him a copy of the entire Pentagon Papers. So the senator made the request of Laird two days after meeting with Ellsberg.[9] Laird took six weeks to turn Fulbright down. His denial of the request in a December 20, 1969, letter marked the first official confirmation to Congress that the study existed.

Laird wrote to Fulbright that the history was "an accumulation of data of the most delicate sensitivity.... As intended from the start, access to and use of this document has been extremely limited. It would clearly be contrary to the national interest to disseminate it more widely." Meanwhile, in February 1970, Ellsberg secretly delivered another three thousand photocopied pages of the study to Fulbright's staff. So when Fulbright wrote Laird again in April, the senator was already in possession of about half the documents he was requesting from Laird.

Since release of the Vietnam War history could presumably hurt only the Kennedy and Johnson administrations, why wasn't Laird anxious to provide them to Fulbright? Laird recalled, "At that particular time I had enough on my hands that I didn't want to take on a frontal attack of McNamara." Also, Laird was mindful that Democrats controlled the Congress. If Fulbright had a copy, it would inevitably leak to the press and then Laird would be blamed for manipulating his office to blacken the reputations of McNamara, Johnson, and Kennedy. His greatest fear, however, was that the documents would focus too much attention on how the United States got into the war and might distract from his plan to get out. Finally there was a point of protocol. As chairman of the Senate Foreign Relations Committee, Fulbright rightly should have taken his request to the State Department (which had two copies). If leaders of any of the defense committees in Congress had asked Laird for the study, he said he would have produced it.

So Laird stonewalled Fulbright, turning down the senator's fourth and final request on July 21, 1970. After six months of fruitless attempts, Fulbright took to the Senate floor on August 7 and denounced Laird's decision. "The Executive Branch—in what has become a reflex action—has again slammed the door on Congress," the senator intoned. But, he warned Laird with a rhetorical wink, "as the old saw goes, 'Nothing is secret for long in Washington.' I hope that the first enterprising reporter who obtains a copy of this history will share it with the Committee." Ellsberg got the message. By late March 1971 he had found just such an "enterprising reporter": Neil Sheehan of the *New York Times*.

❧

Early on Saturday afternoon, June 12, 1971, Laird was enjoying a round of golf at the Burning Tree Country Club. The game wasn't as leisurely as he usually liked because he had an appointment at 4 P.M.—the White House Rose Garden wedding of the president's oldest daughter, Tricia, to Harvard University law student Edward Cox. Laird was on the sixteenth hole when a club employee came rushing out to him in a golf cart to tell him Kissinger was calling, urgently. Laird told the messenger he would be along soon. "He called me at Burning Tree many times," Laird laughed. "Henry wasn't doing anything on Saturdays, so he called me." Never before had a Kissinger call to Burning Tree actually been urgent, or of national security import, so Laird saw no need to interrupt his game.

So many top Nixon officials enjoyed playing on Burning Tree's links that a secure phone to the White House had been installed in the clubhouse. Laird used it to call Kissinger after the game. "Henry started right out raising hell—telling me the president of the United States was very upset with me for leaking the papers" to the *Times*, Laird recalled. It was a repeat of Kissinger's call to Laird a year before accusing him of leaking the Cambodia bombing to the *Times*. So Laird had little patience for yet another false accusation, and, when he could get a word in, he responded angrily: "Henry, this is *absolute bullshit!*" Then he hung up the phone.

The next morning, Sunday, the *New York Times* landed on doorsteps across America. In the top left-hand corner under the headline "Tricia Nixon Takes Vows," was a picture of the bride and her proud father standing in the Rose Garden. Next to the picture was another headline, "Vietnam Archive: Pentagon Study Traces 3 Decades of Growing U.S. Involvement." The front-page story continued inside the paper on six full pages of mind-numbing detail from the secret study that, likely, only the editors themselves would read from start to finish. But alarm bells went off all across Washington on the doorsteps of those who knew what they were holding in their hands that morning.

Laird was scheduled to appear on the CBS talk show *Face the Nation* that morning. To prepare, he met top aides—Dan Henkin, Bill Prendergast, Bill Baroody, Dan Murphy, and Bob Pursley—for a major "DQ" (dirty question) session over breakfast at the Mayflower Hotel. "I wanted the dirtiest questions that I could get. Whether they'd be asked or not, I wanted them to prepare me for the hardest, toughest questions that I could be asked," Laird recalled. "We thought the *New York Times* story would be the big issue on that morning talk show." Thus loaded for bear, Laird walked over to the CBS studio at 2020 M Street five minutes before the program began.

"I was all set to discuss the Pentagon Papers and that great Washington press corps never asked me one question about them." Neither Laird nor his aides could believe their luck. One of the newsmen on the CBS panel, Pentagon correspondent Bob Schieffer, explained, "Number one, we didn't understand the significance of it. And number two, we thought, he was the wrong secretary of defense to ask about it. Anyway, we didn't ask about it nor was it even mentioned. I remember our boss, Bill Smart, ripped our asses off!"[10] The CBS panelists weren't alone in initially missing the significance of the story. Senator Hubert Humphrey, who had been vice president during the period covered by the study, wasn't asked about it either when he appeared on ABC's talk show *Issues and Answers* that morning.

In retrospect, Laird later wished he had raised the topic himself on the air that Sunday morning. He believed if he had, history might have been different—that "Watergate" would have been just the name of a building, not a national scandal that brought down the president. Laird blamed himself for not taking the opportunity to talk freely and in dismissive terms about the Pentagon Papers, emphasizing how little of the collection was really newsworthy, and characterizing it as a Johnson administration problem. And, he would have stressed that there were few if any real secrets worth hiding in the papers. "I had decided to say, if asked, that 'I'm not going to support printing classified information, but I do support the information being made public that's in the papers, because I think that very little of it is really classified.' I could have set the tone for the whole administration that day. That would have been before Nixon went a little berserk on it and before Kissinger, particularly, went nuts. If I had been able to do it that day, we wouldn't have had such a stir over it." And without such a "stir," Laird speculated that Nixon might never have gone so far as to condone multiple burglaries to get to the source of the leak.

Nixon, indeed, was immediately unnerved by the story. In public he waved the flag of national security concerns, but in private, as the White House tapes indicate, he was personally affronted. What should have been one of the happiest days in his life, his daughter's wedding day, had been ruined by the liberal Eastern media establishment using purloined state secrets.

Nixon let Attorney General John Mitchell know on Sunday that he wanted action, strong and quick—prosecute the leakers to the full extent of the law and shut down further publication of the documents. Appearing to be obliging in a phone call the same day with Mitchell, Laird formally requested that the Justice Department investigate the breach of national security. While he supported the pursuit of leakers, Laird did not favor a Nixon court challenge of the *Times'* right to publish the information. The Constitution's guarantee against prior restraint of the press was likely unassailable in Laird's view. Besides, Laird believed that if the issue were kept out of the courts, the story was likely to die quickly of its own voluminous, scholarly weight. He privately told his general counsel, J. Fred Buzhardt, to cooperate fully on the leak investigation but to "go easy" on the press challenge.

The next morning, Monday, June 14, Laird had a good laugh. As was often the case, it occurred because of Kissinger, who tried so hard to distance himself from the leak of the McNamara study that he lied outright—and Laird was one of the few who knew it. According to the *Washington Post* that morning, Kissinger had denied ever seeing the study "and had no word of its impending publication until he picked up the Sunday *Times* on his doorstep." Laird's first meeting Monday was with Dan Henkin, who had personally informed Kissinger's staff of the impending publication on the prior Friday, and Kissinger had called Laird at Burning Tree on Saturday. "More likely what we see there is an attempt to dramatize that the White House knew nothing about this thing and that, therefore, the leak could not have come from the White House," Henkin surmised in a memo.[11]

At the White House the president was in no laughing mood. By Monday morning Nixon's furor was in full throttle. His fulminations as he met with Haldeman at 8:49 A.M. were captured on the Oval Office taping system. He vented about his prime suspects—Gelb, Halperin, and the Brookings Institution.[12] Though both men had worked for the Nixon administration, they had been Johnson holdovers and were never fully trusted by the White House. Halperin, while at the National Security Council in 1969, had been the primary target of the wiretaps Kissinger ordered, being the chief suspect in Nixon's eyes of early "national security" leaks.

Laird's determination to defuse the story was evident when, at Laird's appearance that morning before the Senate Foreign Relations Committee, Senator Stuart Symington baited him about the McNamara study. After complaining that the committee had unsuccessfully tried to obtain from Laird the same documents being printed in the New York Times, Symington proposed that the committee would "undertake a full examination of the origins of the war in Vietnam," keying off the McNamara papers. Laird opposed the idea, saying that debating the past "would not serve the interests of the country and would not help us in disengaging from Southeast Asia at this time."[13]

Unfortunately it was already too late to defuse Nixon. He focused his suspicions on a new suspect whom Haig moved near the top of the list, Daniel Ellsberg, who was at that time with the Massachusetts Institute of Technology.[14] Not the least of Nixon's targets was the New York Times. On the president's instructions late Monday, Mitchell sent the editors an "or-else" cable. If they did not voluntarily suspend publication of the Vietnam War history in Tuesday's editions, the government would take legal action. The Times editors refused to stop the presses. Tuesday morning the Times published the third installment of the ten-part series, which by then already totaled eighteen full pages of newsprint.

The Justice Department filed a civil suit in the U.S. District Court in New York, and Judge Murray I. Gurfein issued a temporary injunction against publication while the courts sorted out the constitutional issues. For the first time in America's history, a newspaper had been restrained in advance by a U.S. court from publishing a specific article.

⌇

One of Laird's frustrations with the Pentagon Papers was not being able to give them a better name that would stick. "Mel was a master at giving things a label," remembered former assistant secretary of defense Carl Walske. "He always kicked himself for not putting the right label on the Pentagon Papers soon enough."[15] At the June 21 top-level staff meeting, Laird expressed his "concern about them being called the Pentagon Papers" because it suggested an overlap into the Nixon administration. "I would like you all to refer to them as the 'McNamara Papers,'" Laird told the staff.[16] Press aide Jerry Friedheim tried out the new moniker at a Pentagon press briefing that day, and reporters noticed immediately. Friedheim pointed out, with some of his usual wit, that if Laird had done a similar study, it would have been called "How We Got the U.S. Out of Vietnam."[17]

In truth, Laird was not unhappy that the Pentagon Papers had leaked. They proved what he had been saying for years, that the war had been Americanized. Having anticipated how useful their publication might be for his cause, Laird admitted that he was tempted to leak them himself, more than once. But though he "might have talked to people about some of the information that was in the papers, I never leaked a page of them. It was helpful to me that they were leaked."

Still, he was surprised at the magnitude of interest in the dry history. But it was Nixon who magnified the scoop exponentially by seeking a restraining order against the *Times*. Nixon had transformed a dry tome about the sins of his predecessors into a juicy scoop about how the government was trying to cover up the history of the war. Laird had tried to talk him out of it. He pointed out that the "national security" claims in the lawsuit would not hold up. There wasn't a document in the collection that wasn't at least two and a half years old. That put them beyond the point of secrecy for the sake of security and into the zone of secrecy that protects the government from embarrassment and scrutiny.

Failing to sway Nixon, Laird tried working on Kissinger. "I told Henry that he was making a mistake. They were going to make it into more of a big deal by challenging it," Laird said. His advice went unheeded again. Laird even checked in with former president Johnson, whom Nixon had unsuccessfully hoped to enlist in his crusade. Johnson was upset, but for different reasons than Nixon. In a phone conversation on June 24, Johnson complained to Laird that it was all a Kennedy conspiracy to embarrass him. McNamara was always a Kennedy man, never truly loyal to Johnson, Johnson reasoned. So naturally McNamara had used anti-LBJ analysts who had riddled the study with their biases. Laird couldn't disagree with that evaluation of the tone. "From my own selfish standpoint, the only people embarrassed by the Pentagon Papers were McNamara and the Johnson Administration," Laird recalled.

True to form, Laird didn't stop when he failed to sway Nixon or Kissinger on the *Times* case. In a back-door maneuver not even known to his colleagues at the Pentagon, Laird went to the man who would matter most in the fray—a longtime Sunday morning golfing buddy, U.S. Solicitor General Erwin Griswold,

who would prosecute the government's case against the *Times* if it got as far as
the Supreme Court, which Laird was sure it would. While the *Times* had been
restrained from publishing, Ellsberg gave part of the study to the *Washington
Post,* which published it on June 18 and 19. When the government got a restraining order against the *Post,* Ellsberg gave the papers to the *Boston Globe.* For a
third time, the Justice Department obtained a restraining order. Three days
later, on June 25, the Supreme Court agreed to hear the case.

It was a classic constitutional confrontation that was decided more by Griswold and Laird than historians have hitherto realized. The issue was freedom
of the press versus the government's right to keep its secrets. Griswold, as the
government's lawyer, had to prove further publication would pose grave and
imminent danger to national security. To do that he would be almost wholly
dependent on government security experts familiar with the 2.5 million words
in the papers, which meant vital Pentagon cooperation. The Joint Chiefs, the
heads of all the military intelligence agencies, and Deputy Secretary Packard
were 100 percent in favor of restraining the press from publishing the Pentagon
Papers. But what Packard and others didn't know was that their boss did not
agree and was working at cross purposes to them.

Laird had one of his trusted aides quietly do a thorough review of all the
classified material in the papers that had been leaked. He concluded that there
were only "six or seven paragraphs in the whole thing that were a little dangerous." This material, if understood, might have alerted the enemy that the
United States had broken some of their codes. But by the time the review was
conducted those "thirty-five lines," as Laird counted them, had already been
published. He never shared his findings with the leadership at the Pentagon.
But he did tell Griswold how flimsy the national security claim was. "I know
why you have to take certain actions," Laird said, recognizing that Griswold was
getting heat from Nixon and Mitchell. Nevertheless, Laird made it clear that
he personally would not join in the government's challenge. There would be
no affidavit from the secretary of defense about national security secrets. He
didn't believe in the rightness of the cause.

Armed with Laird's warning, Griswold put the screws to the Pentagon's
security experts, forcing them to whittle down their voluminous list of items in
the Pentagon Papers that were too sensitive to publish. Author Sanford Ungar,
in his book *The Papers and The Papers,* reported that Mitchell "was personally
opposed to any further narrowing down of the government's case but reluctantly relented in the face of Griswold's judgment." Griswold's insistence was
due, in part, to "private reservations about the overkill in the way the government had handled the newspaper cases thus far."[18]

Fred Buzhardt reported at Laird's June 28 staff meeting that the Department of Defense had finalized the list for Griswold of every item in the forty-
seven volumes that "would pose grave and immediate danger to national
security if published." They had determined that only thirty-three fit that de-

scription. Laird's personal view, again shared with Griswold, was that not even those thirty-three would hold up in court, since the most sensitive of them had already been published. No doubt those private conversations emboldened Griswold himself to undercut his own case before the Supreme Court when he disavowed the list as "much too broad." Ungar labeled it "an unusual expression of disgust with his own clients within the government." The U.S. Supreme Court ruled for the press, 6 to 3, on June 30, and the *New York Times, Washington Post, Boston Globe,* and other newspapers began on July 1 to publish the rest of the papers they had been leaked.

Two sets of cardboard boxes labeled in large letters "TOP SECRET, VOLUMES 1–30" and "TOP SECRET, VOLUMES 31–47" were delivered on handcarts from the Pentagon to the leaders of the Senate and the House on June 28, 1971. They contained a full set of the Pentagon Papers for each house. Following Laird's instructions, the "couriers" were top officials of the Defense Department. Several army majors and sergeants were additionally assigned to guard the boxes on their short trip across the Potomac. The arrival was well attended by a mob of press, which photographed the transfer to congressional leaders who were required to sign receipts. Each house promptly locked up its set in a Capitol vault, placing the papers under twenty-four-hour guard.

The relatively swift delivery, ten days after the papers were leaked to the press, was one of a series of deft moves Laird made that stood in sharp contrast to Nixon's reaction to that crisis. Laird felt that the public deserved to know what the papers revealed. Nixon appeared to view the same episode as an assault on the sanctity and prerogatives of the Oval Office. Nixon's reaction was the first lesion of what Watergate coconspirator John Dean would call a "cancer on the American presidency." Before it was over the scandal called Watergate would disgrace and even send to jail officials from different executive branch departments who had been caught by the many tentacles reaching out from the Oval Office. But those tentacles never penetrated the Defense Department.

Laird's natural instincts had already built a formidable barricade around the Pentagon that Nixon and his White House cronies found unassailable. Laird began his term by establishing a strict rule, that there were only one or two approved channels of contact between the White House and the Defense Department. Nixon's coconspirators were unable to establish any back channels that would have enmeshed in the scandal whatever unfortunate defense official assisted them.

Feeling that the public had a right to see for themselves as much of the Pentagon Papers as possible, Laird was intent on swift declassification. On June 22 he announced that the documents would be declassified in ninety days by an interagency team led by Dan Henkin.[19] It took more than one hundred government officials working on the declassification to meet Laird's deadline.[20] The

Government Printing Office rushed out a twelve-volume set of the declassified, expurgated Pentagon Papers, priced at $50 and totaling 7,800 pages. It barely sold out its first and only printing of five hundred copies because Bantam Books beat the government to the presses and issued a paperback based on the *New York Times* stories, selling more than a million copies. The Bantam paperback was $2.25, with all the good parts left in.[21]

To deter future leakers, Laird believed it was important to find and prosecute the person who had spread the Pentagon Papers around. The first government identification of Ellsberg as the likely leaker came from the Pentagon when a close examination of what the *Times* was publishing revealed several of the documents to be unique to a copy Ellsberg had signed out when he was at the RAND Corporation. "The press is not working from the final published documents," Laird confided to his top-level staff. "Someone spent a lot of time taking working papers home and reproducing them."[22] They were demonstrably earlier drafts because they included some documents edited out of the final edition.

Three days after the *Times* first began publishing the purloined papers, other media outlets began speculating that Ellsberg was the leaker. Ellsberg went underground for eleven days, during which time he leaked the documents through intermediaries to the *Post* and the *Globe*. On June 29 Ellsberg turned himself in. He confessed to leaking the documents both to Senator Fulbright in 1969 and to the media in 1971. His "only regret" was that he had not done it sooner—before "two invasions and 9,000 more American deaths," by his calculation.[23] At almost the same time Ellsberg was turning himself in, Laird and his top staff were discussing the first item on their weekly agenda: the "McNamara Papers." The question that most hung in the air that morning came from Admiral Zumwalt: "Will Dr. Ellsberg end up as a national hero or a villain?"[24]

If there was a single day that could be pinpointed as the day the presidency of Richard Nixon began to unravel, it was June 30—the day of the Supreme Court decision and the day after Ellsberg turned himself in. Nixon was embittered that the press had lionized Ellsberg, and the president told his closest associates that everything must be done to demonize Ellsberg instead. The legal process would take too long to paint him as a criminal instead of a patriot. So Nixon decided to do it himself in the court of public opinion. Nixon began peppering all his private conversations with the word "conspiracy," and the conviction grew in him that Ellsberg had not acted alone. He was only the most visible culprit in a broad-based leftist conspiracy against Nixon.

Laird had gone to the White House on the afternoon of June 30 for a National Security Council meeting. While the NSC met, the Supreme Court's 6 to 3 decision against the government was handed down. Directly following

the NSC meeting, Nixon called a brainstorming session in the Oval Office with
Laird, Mitchell, Kissinger, and Haldeman. According to Haldeman's diary, the
conversation turned to the conspiracy theory: "There's a general agreement
that there is very definitely a conspiracy here, on these papers, and Laird alluded to some intelligence they had that he didn't get into detail on." On the
tape of the Oval Office conversation, though somewhat garbled, Laird can be
heard using the word "conspiracy" and saying that he had "several hundred
people" at the Pentagon working on an investigation and declassification.[25]
Having used the word "conspiracy" with Nixon, Laird had unwittingly stoked
the president's growing paranoia. It was a veritable red flag, but Nixon had
misunderstood Laird's meaning.

It became evident to both Pentagon and FBI investigators that there was,
indeed, a limited family-and-friends plot to leak the Pentagon Papers. Ellsberg
had not acted alone. Others were already known to have assisted him in the
voluminous photocopying of the documents. That was the conspiracy Laird
had been speaking about, not the one Nixon was imagining. Nixon believed
that the "unauthorized disclosure" of the Pentagon Papers had been part of a
concerted leftist campaign by former liberal NSC staffers and their cohorts to
end the war. At the time, Nixon's fears of a liberal conspiracy behind Ellsberg's
leak were shared by other conservatives including Packard. "We should recognize the New Left and revolutionaries are behind a lot of this," Packard opined
at a staff meeting during the controversy. "A number of people in the country
are out to raise hell with the military and the Establishment."[26]

By the next morning Nixon was on a tear. The White House taping system recorded the details. Nixon told Haldeman and White House aide Charles
Colson that they needed to prosecute Ellsberg and his coconspirators in the
press because the courts would take too long. "Convict the son of a bitch in
the press! That's the way it's done," he insisted. Nixon said he needed someone
who could "run this," a first-class political operator who didn't mind dirtying
his hands. For that reason, Nixon told his confidants, the attorney general was
out. "John is just too damn good a lawyer," so "it just repels him to do these
horrible things. But they've got to be done. We have to fight this." Among all
the names discussed, Laird was mentioned as someone to whom the appointed
cloak-and-dagger man could go for information. "Laird's got lots [of people
on this]," Nixon observed. And Laird had "said there's a conspiracy." The most
promising prospect to do the president's dirty work was suggested by Colson—it was E. Howard Hunt, who had just left the CIA.[27]

In a meeting the next morning, July 2, with Haldeman and Ehrlichman,
Nixon pointed out a newspaper story in which "Ellsberg says there were a
number of people that worked with him," and Nixon felt something must be
done about that. "I want to go after everyone. I'm not so interested in Ellsberg,
but we have got to go after everybody who's a member of this conspiracy. There
is a conspiracy and I've got to go after it."

Haldeman again pitched Howard Hunt as the man for the job. Nixon knew it would never be enough to have a covert operator like Hunt creating havoc below the radar. Somebody had to spread the story that Nixon was zinging the left-wing conspirators. For a moment, having always been envious of Laird's vast network of connections, Nixon opined about Laird being the best disseminator of a countercampaign: "Now Laird—this is one place where we can take a guy who's a ... sonofabitch—and maybe Laird just might want to make a hero out of himself. I want you two to have a talk with Laird." Ehrlichman knew that would be fruitless. Laird was too canny for him and Haldeman. Besides, he wouldn't even take their calls. So he dismissed the idea, reminding the president that Laird was gone on a foreign trip for three weeks.[28]

Amid the many meetings Nixon had with White House intimates hatching plots that summer of 1971, Laird's name came up once more—as a point of frustration for Nixon. Laird and his general counsel, Buzhardt, had become aware that Nixon had misunderstood Laird, thinking the Pentagon was on the verge of proving a broad-based conspiracy. On July 1 Laird dispatched Buzhardt to the Justice Department for a meeting with Mitchell to douse the conspiracy talk. Mitchell reported that to the president on July 6. In the middle of a lengthy conversation about the Ellsberg investigation, Nixon reminded Mitchell: "Laird sat in here, as you recall, and said he had all this thing—that he thought it was a conspiracy and so forth."

"But I want to tell you, Mr. President," Mitchell finally had to correct, "after Mel Laird said that that day, I asked Buzhardt over the next day—and they weren't even close to it [proving a widespread conspiracy]."

"Is that right?" Nixon asked, surprised. "They [were] just bulling?"

Mitchell didn't respond.

"But they've got a much bigger outfit working on this than Edgar Hoover has," Nixon pressed.

"I know they have," Mitchell conceded, explaining that they weren't finding proof that any of Nixon's suspects were part of a conspiracy.[29]

Laird had started to sense that White House aides, particularly Haldeman and Ehrlichman, were getting a little wild, so it was imperative for him to control the information. J. Edgar Hoover had helped by refusing to bring the FBI in on the hunt for conspirators. That allowed Laird to control the information uncovered by a Pentagon investigation. Buzhardt confirmed that important victory at the July 12 staff meeting: "We are doing this ourselves, rather than having outsiders do it."[30]

―☙―

Laird's final security response to the Pentagon Papers was to clamp down on loose practices at the RAND Corporation, now that it had been confirmed it was RAND copies that were leaked. He ordered air force guards to take over security of all classified documents in RAND's possession—an amazing collection of 173,000 documents, according to an air force survey.[31] The Pentagon Papers scandal rocked RAND, forcing its president, Henry S. Rowen, who had mentored Ellsberg, to resign in November.

In Nixon's mind there was a bigger think tank ripe for a clampdown: the Brookings Institution, where Gelb and Halperin worked. He saw it as a house of enemies. Breaking into the Brookings safe became a Nixon obsession. He remembered having requested in the early days of his administration a Pentagon file of events leading up to Johnson's 1968 decision to halt the bombing of North Vietnam. He was told the only copy was at Brookings. He was, he recounted, "furious and frustrated" that top-secret government reports "were out of reach in the hands of a private think tank largely staffed with anti-war Democrats. It seemed absurd." He wanted it back, "even if it meant having to get it surreptitiously."[32]

The White House tapes confirm these as his earliest insistent orders to aides to conduct an illegal break-in. The first meeting at which the president uttered this thought out loud was the same June 30 evening meeting, which followed the Supreme Court decision and included Laird, Mitchell, Kissinger, Haldeman, and Ehrlichman. While the National Archives log of the White House tapes suggests all five men were all in the room from 5:14 to 6:23 P.M., it is possible some of them filtered in and out of the informal conference. For many minutes both before and after the portions of the tape in which the Brookings break-in is postulated by the president, Laird's voice was not heard. "I wasn't in the room," Laird recalled emphatically. "I know I was not present for anything like that. I was not in that room at that particular time."

The colloquy between Nixon and Haldeman would have been hard to miss:[33]

> President Nixon: They [the Brookings Institution] have lot of material.... I want Brookings—I want them just to break in and take it out. Do you understand?
> Haldeman: Yeah. But you have to have somebody to do it.
> President Nixon: That's what I'm talking about. Don't discuss it here. You talk to [E. Howard] Hunt. I want the break-in. Hell, they [the CIA] do that. You're to break into the place, rifle the files, and bring them in.
> Haldeman: I don't have any problem with breaking in. It's a Defense Department approved security—
> President Nixon: Just go in and take it.

The next morning, meeting with Haldeman and Kissinger, Nixon buttonholed Haldeman in a tirade:[34]

> President Nixon: Now you do it. Wake them up. Get them off their goddamn dead asses.... We're up against an enemy, a conspiracy. They're using any means. We are going to use any means. Is that clear?

Did they get the Brookings Institute raided last night?
No?
Get it *done!* I want it *done.* I want the Brookings Institute safe *cleaned out.* And have it cleaned out in a way that makes somebody else look [guilty].

On July 2, for the third day in a row, the president made sure his inner circle got his message. "I really meant it when I—I want somebody to go in and crack that safe. Walk in and get it. . . . They've got to do it!" From those three days of increasingly insistent presidential orders, the infamous "plumbers unit" was born.

Gerald Ford pondered for many years the reasons Nixon went awry after his promising beginnings. In 1997 Ford concluded, "He made one serious mistake. He put Haldeman, Ehrlichman, and Colson in his inner circle. They were an evil influence on Dick Nixon." But had Laird been part of that White House inner circle at the same time, Ford believes Watergate would never have happened, because Laird would have put a stop to it in its earliest stages—"absolutely! Mel Laird had absolute political integrity."

A tip-off regarding the trio's influence came from Ford's examination of Nixon's White House tapes. When Haldeman, Ehrlichman, or Colson were in the room or on the phone, the president can be heard using rough language that neither Ford nor Laird ever heard him use in their presence. Ford said, "I'll bet you that 90-something percent of the bad language he uses on the tapes is when those three people are there. He appointed them, and they poisoned him."[35] Ford's conclusion was that the trio brought out the worst in Nixon and were willing to serve his darkest desires.

About two weeks after Nixon first said he wanted his men to use "any means" to counter the antiwar "conspirators," Ehrlichman created the "Special Investigative Unit." He appointed for its two codirectors one of his own domestic council staff, lawyer Egil "Bud" Krogh, and David Young, a lawyer from Kissinger's NSC staff. Howard Hunt and former FBI agent G. Gordon Liddy were recruited as the foot soldiers. When Young tried to explain to his mother-in-law what his new job was, he told her he was plugging leaks that infuriated the president. She said that it was nice to have a plumber in the family. Amused by the analogy, Young stuck a sign on the door of Room 16 in the basement of the Old Executive Office Building that read: MR. YOUNG, PLUMBER. The White House Plumbers were open for business and they immediately focused on Ellsberg.

The initial plan was to portray Ellsberg as eccentric and unstable. Nixon asked CIA Director Helms to prepare a psychological profile on Ellsberg. According to later testimony by CIA psychiatrists before a Senate subcommittee, this was the first time the agency had ever done such a profile on an American. The CIA profile was too mild, so the Plumbers concocted a way to please the president. They broke into the Beverly Hills office of Ellsberg's psychiatrist looking for the doctor's notes on Ellsberg but couldn't find them.

In September 1971, the same month the Plumbers broke into the psychiatrist's office, they were unsuccessful in breaching the Pentagon fortress. Sometime shortly after the September foray in Beverly Hills, Gordon Liddy showed up at one of the Pentagon's entrances, flashing his White House pass. Laird had firmly established a rule that White House staffers could not approach the Pentagon in person or by phone without going through his personal assistant, Carl Wallace. So Wallace was called by the Pentagon guards. Liddy said he wanted to look at some files in connection with the ongoing Pentagon Papers investigation. Laird's general counsel, Fred Buzhardt, was alerted, and "Buzhardt and I had him out of the building within fifteen minutes," Laird recalled.

In September Howard Hunt also tried to get some documents from the Pentagon that Nixon wanted to use against the previous Democratic administrations. The president wanted the Plumbers to get as much classified material as possible that would embarrass Johnson over Vietnam, or Kennedy on either the Bay of Pigs fiasco or collusion in the 1963 assassination of South Vietnamese President Ngo Dinh Diem. Over a week's time Hunt made several cursory contacts and at least one visit to the Pentagon looking for assassination-related material. Each time he was stopped short by Laird and Wallace. Hunt was welcomed by the State Department, which allowed him to copy 240 classified diplomatic cables relating to the Vietnam War. But the Plumbers thought the cables were not enough to satisfy Nixon's unquenchable thirst for anti-Kennedy material. So, using those cables as models, Colson ordered Hunt to forge two more cables that would clearly implicate the Kennedy administration in the bloody coup against Diem, according to Hunt's later grand jury testimony.[36]

At about the same time, failing to breach the Pentagon's defenses, the Plumbers tried to go around Laird by asking one of his top intelligence chiefs over to the White House. National Security Agency chief Admiral Noel Gayler dutifully showed up, thinking he was going to an NSC meeting. He found himself in a meeting with Attorney General Mitchell and White House aides later identified with the Plumbers, who asked for any wiretap or other information about anti-administration Americans who hadn't been identified as part of the Pentagon Papers investigation. Knowing Laird would be upset he had even gone to the White House without clearing it first, Gayler made a quick exit without offering any help.

Gayler headed straight to Laird's office. There, Laird said, "I told him if he ever went to a meeting like that again with those guys he was out of a job!" From Gayler's description of the White House "briefing," Laird later characterized it as an attempt to secretly get his top intelligence man signed on as part of the Plumbers group. Laird immediately called Mitchell. "Listen," Laird began, "I'm willing to share some of this NSA or DIA material with Justice and the FBI when there's something criminal involved. But I'm not sharing any of this information EVER on civilians."

⌯⌯

Of all the instructions Laird's subordinates ever received, the "liaison law" was the most repeated and most enforced: "My office deals with the White House; you don't." Wallace handled the White House staff and Pursley dealt with the NSC. Otherwise, only Laird himself and Packard were authorized to talk to anyone at 1600 Pennsylvania Avenue.[37] Senator John Chafee, who was Laird's first secretary of the navy, said that it was literally in the first few days of the Nixon administration that Laird laid down the "liaison law." "We were *not* to respond to any request from the White House.... There was no deviation from this policy. Mel was *adamant* about it."[38]

Assistant Secretary Barry Shillito, who had served in earlier Democratic administrations, said, "We were fortunate that [Laird acted] so quickly and so early in the administration. Mel saw the need and got it under control. He probably got on top of it before people on the White House staff realized that this had all been worked out." Dr. Johnny Foster, who served as director of research and engineering for McNamara and Laird, called it a "very clever move. I don't know any other secretary that has done that.... Hell, if he hadn't done that, I would have been making mistakes which he thus arranged for me to avoid."

Nixon-era scholar and author Stanley I. Kutler thought Laird "wasn't out to protect people. He was out to cement his own power." Certainly keeping others' noses out of his Pentagon business was a real motivation for Laird. "White House staffs back to Eisenhower's days had become harder and harder to handle," explained Shillito. "They'd grown like mad, taken on a power base of their own. And Mel saw that Nixon's White House staff tried to move into his decision-making process almost immediately." Pursley agreed. "Mel didn't want the White House to ever get the feeling that they could somehow manipulate the Pentagon." Former air force secretary John McLucas remembered Laird saying, "If you get a call from the White House, they're just trying to end-run me."[39]

Another reason Laird established the rule was that he knew many Pentagon officials could get themselves into trouble because of the "holy cow" factor. Shillito said outsiders may not "appreciate the impact it can have on a fairly sound-thinking person who comes into government and gets a call from the White House. Even really mature people are overawed by this crap. But it's mostly just crap—some Mr. XYZ, almost a nonentity, asking for a favor. But somehow they get this weird idea that the president is calling them for some kind of a fireside chat." At one staff meeting in 1970, according to the minutes, Laird pointed out that there were some three hundred people working at the White House and "each of these 300 people has a telephone. Many of them think they are speaking for the president, but usually they are not. We have to protect the president himself from these types of requests."[40]

Friedheim said Colson was a prime example. "Chuck was always calling Carl [Wallace] wanting things done that we couldn't do. It got to be so much that Carl nominated me to listen to Chuck Colson about once a day, every day." Colson was exactly the kind of sycophant that Laird knew would get the president in trouble. Friedheim said, "Chuck would hear some comment from the president like, 'Get the bastards!'—and he thought Nixon meant, 'Get the bastards!' But most of the time it meant Nixon was blowing off steam. People who knew Nixon understood that, and would come back with a plan to do some things short of 'getting the bastards.'"[41]

Former air force secretary Seamans made the mistake of complying with a request that came from White House staffers one weekend in the early months of his appointment. He agreed to loan them one of his public affairs officers for a while, so he was surprised to see the man still in the Pentagon on Monday. "I didn't think I was going to see you this morning. I thought you were going over to the White House," Seamans said.

"I never heard anything about that," the staffer responded.

Puzzled, Seamans hurried over to Laird's office for the regular Monday staff meeting. At one point in the meeting, Laird said, "Now, I've told all of you that you're not to communicate with the White House. You're not to respond to any requests from the White House." As Seamans recalled, Laird then "went on to describe what had happened in enough detail that I knew he was talking about me." So Seamans finally identified himself as the guilty party.

"Mel, I guess you're talking about me," he sheepishly owned up.

"I am," Laird said, "and I mean it, and don't do it again."

Seamans called it "a good lesson" that stuck. He never did it again, he said, which "saved me a lot of trouble." For example, a White House functionary called him on behalf of the first lady asking if a tiger could be carried aboard a National Guard training flight. "There's a tiger in the St. Louis Zoo that Mrs. Nixon is very anxious to have mated with a female in the San Diego Zoo. Couldn't they just take that tiger from St. Louis to San Diego?"

Seamans responded, "Well, you know, a decision like that is not really one for me to make. You need to talk to Carl Wallace."

"Oh *shit!*" the White House aide muttered. "I've already talked to him, and he turned me down."[42]

So that there was no misunderstanding, Laird reiterated the "liaison law" each time it was ignored. "I am not exaggerating when I say that he reiterated his rule maybe a hundred times in the four years," Bob Froehlke recalled. This is how the lecture would go: "Don't take a call from the White House. If someone says, 'The White House is calling—,' you say, 'A building can't talk.' If they say, 'The president wants—,' you tell them, 'Whatever the president wants, he will tell Mel Laird.'"

The first time Froehlke heard that script he said, "Geez, Mel, you're being harsh. Those responses are, at least, impolite and maybe impolitic."

Laird replied, "Bob, you have a lot of amateur zealots over there like Bob Haldeman, and they're going to get into trouble."[43]

Until he read about them in the newspapers, Laird had no idea about any of the White House follies that came to fall under the "Watergate" rubric. White House staffers such as Haldeman or Ehrlichman knew better than to approach him with their plots and plans. Even if Laird's character had not prevented the Plumbers from co-opting his people, the liaison rule that he established with the White House was a brick wall they couldn't surmount. The most effective mortar in that wall was a signed commitment Laird had extracted from the president himself that the Pentagon would never have to respond to White House staffers. Pentagon correspondent Orr Kelly of the *Washington Star* wrote in 1973 that the unfolding Watergate scandal failed to touch the Defense Department because "Laird erected a formal paper barricade between the Pentagon and the White House in the form of a letter, signed by the President, requiring all contacts with the department to be made through three men on Laird's personal staff."[44]

A review of the internal defense secretary documents shows that Laird decided he needed formal Nixon approval for his policy, which he sought through discussions in 1970. According to the minutes of the August 31 meeting, "Mr. Laird said he had talked to the President about the situation. He has told the President, and the President has approved that Mr. Laird will not pay any attention to requests from the White House unless the NSC matters come to Mr. Laird or Mr. Packard and other matters through Mr. Wallace. [Nixon military assistant] General [James] Hughes sent out a memorandum on this policy to White House Staff members."[45]

But in the ensuing months White House staffers persisted in trying to breach the Pentagon ramparts. Laird surmised that he needed a presidential memorandum on the subject. Just four months before the birth of the Plumbers unit, Laird had asked Nixon for written confirmation of the verbal agreement about the narrow authorized channels of communication between the White House and Defense Department. Laird reminded Nixon in a March 15, 1971, memorandum that "the intent of this simple and direct channel was to obviate the establishment and proliferation of numerous communications lines which would run the high risk of counter-productive actions." For the first two years of the administration, the procedure had worked fairly well, keeping both the Pentagon and White House out of trouble. But in early 1971 Laird reported in a memo to Nixon an "increased incidence of contacts from many offices among the White House staff to various officials in the Department of Defense. The result of this trend can only result in varying levels of unsatisfactory results for the Administration."

The purpose of the memo, Laird informed the president, was to "be certain my understanding" of the guidelines was "still accurate and valid" so he could "reaffirm [them] strongly" with his own staff. [46] The White House staff tried to block a response. "The staff people over there were furious," Laird recalled. But they could only hold off Nixon's response for three weeks. On April 8, 1971, the president wrote Laird: "Your understanding of my wishes is correct and I would like to strongly reaffirm these liaison procedures." On issues "involving national security or defense policy" Nixon would "communicate either directly to you or through [Kissinger]." On "other matters not involving policy I want all communications to be channeled through my Military Assistant, who will maintain liaison with your Special Assistant, Mr. Carl Wallace."[47]

As for Laird's own top-level staffers, they were uniform in their gratitude for Laird and his liaison policy. "There wasn't anybody who got into any trouble. Nobody was within five gillion miles of Watergate," said Capen. "We would have been sucked into Watergate fourteen ways to Sunday—except for Mel establishing such a large bulwark against that kind of thing," said Pursley. "He kept the Pentagon out of Watergate," agreed Norman Augustine, who was in Pentagon research and development. "He did an awful lot for the Pentagon in the sense of just maintaining its integrity during that whole thing, during that tough time." Former Delaware Governor Pierre "Pete" du Pont was a congressman in the 1970s who watched as agency after agency of the federal government was implicated in the growing Watergate scandal—but not the Pentagon. "The military was absolutely kept out of it, and they thanked the Lord and Laird."[48]

Two men who served Laird as successive navy secretaries, John Chafee and John Warner, understood that Laird's instincts had saved not only them but their families from the Watergate henchmen. Laird preserved their reputations in such a way that both were able to become influential, respected members of the Senate. Two days before Chafee died unexpectedly, he reviewed his personal debt to Laird and became emotional. There was no way to thank his friend Laird enough for what he had done other than to say that, in retrospect, "what made my respect for Mel go up even more" was the prescience of funneling all White House contacts through his own assistant. "I've recommended to every secretary of defense since then that they adopt this, that they use exactly the same system that Mel had." None, he found, took the advice.[49]

Alone among all of the top Pentagon officials, Warner had worked closely with Haldeman, Ehrlichman, and others as part of Nixon's 1960 and 1968 presidential campaigns. Warner recalled that he had been at the Pentagon only a couple of weeks in 1969 as navy undersecretary when Haldeman and Ehrlich-man began calling. Laird heard about it and ordered Warner to come to his office.

"I hear you're seeing your old buddies," Laird began sternly. He got up from his desk, and went over to the window, motioning Warner to follow. "What's that over there?"

Warner didn't know what he was pointing to and made a couple of wrong guesses.

"It's the Potomac River!" Laird finally said, exasperated. "I want you to hear this and remember it well: don't you cross that river and go to the White House! *If I ever see you crossing that river to go to the White House, you'll go home in a taxi and not come back!*" In imitation of Laird, Warner paced around his room, shouting as Laird had. But then Warner laughed softly. The message had been received loud and clear. "So I stiffed old Haldeman and Ehrlichman and everybody else. All of them. I really chopped them off." He paused, and a big smile crossed his face. "If I hadn't done that because of Mel, I might have done something in the whole Watergate thing. And that would have been the end of me."[50]

33

Friends in High Places

❦

HELMUT SCHMIDT WAS ELECTED to the West German parliament, the *Bundestag,* in 1953—the same year that Melvin Laird was elected to Congress. Sixteen years later both men would be selected as defense overseers in the cabinets of their respective countries. And then they would become fast friends through a shared respect for the responsibility that comes with military power.

Schmidt had written two books on defense policy and was an expert on military affairs when he became West German defense minister in October 1969. Yet when he took the job, he discovered a secret: a NATO plan to bury a chain of nuclear weapons along the Iron Curtain from the Baltic Sea to the Alps. Schmidt was aghast. One of the first meetings on his schedule was the NATO Nuclear Planning Group (NPG), to be hosted in November by Laird in Washington, D.C. Schmidt decided he would talk to this American politician privately and see if he was a man who could be reasoned with.[1]

During the cold war the United States secretly manufactured hundreds of small nuclear land mines called "atomic demolition munitions" (ADMs). The smallest of them could be carried in a commando's backpack and had an explosive power of ten tons of TNT. The nuclear wallop of the larger one was a Hiroshima-sized fifteen kilotons, yet it weighed less than four hundred pounds and could be transported easily by boat, helicopter, or jeep. The purpose of ADMs was to blast craters, create landslides, and take out bridges, depots, and dams or underground targets such as pipelines and tunnels. Because friendly troops would be operating in the area of ADM use, the weapons were designed to be as "clean" as possible, giving off minimal (but still deadly) radiation.[2]

The ADMs' best use, in the view of NATO planners, was as nuclear land mines planted along the predictable routes of invasion that Warsaw Pact forces could use to cut through Western European countries. To that end, in 1969, when Schmidt and Laird became the defense chiefs of their respective countries, more than two hundred of the American ADMs were stored in West Germany, awaiting burial in sunken concrete chambers along the borders. The United States and NATO had not given the green light to actually plant the bombs, nor is it clear whether that ever would have happened, given the need to closely guard any nuclear weaponry. But burial sites had been chosen and some holes had already been dug in the anticipation that the strategy formed only on paper might actually be carried out.

Schmidt pulled no punches at the November 13 meeting with Laird. The

German acknowledged the appeal of the smaller-yield ADMs as a defensive weapon but then stated bluntly: prepositioning ADMs in peacetime along the border would not be possible in his country. Schmidt pounded his fist on his knee to punctuate his questions: Who would control them? Who would be allowed to detonate them? How would the Soviets and the East Germans react when they found out the weapons were buried and waiting?

Laird had been silent but appeared to nod in assent. Finally, he said simply: "Don't worry, Helmut. I realize the problem you raise, so I promise you it will not happen—the ADMs will not be put in place."

The classified record shows that Laird kept his word. Few subjects were more discussed than the issue of ADMs at semiannual meetings of the NPG. Between the NPG's founding in the 1960s and a June 1970 gathering of the NATO defense ministers in Venice, Italy, there had been twenty-five reports on the subject. At the Venice meeting defense ministers from Italy, Turkey, the Netherlands, Canada, and the United Kingdom all spoke up in favor of the ADMs. Then Schmidt protested, saying none of the proposals for actually planting the ADMs were acceptable to the West German government. When Laird spoke up, he praised all sides for their work on the issue. Schmidt immediately recognized what Laird had *not* said. He had not expressed his own or his country's opinion on chambering the ADMs. "I knew our agreement was in place," Schmidt recalled. It was vintage Laird; he planned to stall the issue while still giving the appearance of progress.[3]

Five months later, on the day before the group met again in Ottawa, Laird and Schmidt had a one-on-one meeting to reaffirm their understanding. Mindful of note-takers at the meeting, Laird signaled Schmidt that he was working on getting approval from Nixon on what had been "discussed between our two departments on a secret basis," according to the notes.[4] The next day, the eight NATO ministers agreed to give authority for NATO's military commanders to plan for the possible movement of the mines from storage to points closer to where they would be used in the event of war. There was no approval for actually burying of the mines.[5]

During the cold war, no matter how a military planner looked at it, there was no way for Western Europe to win if the Soviet Union decided to invade. Time and again the outcome of the highly classified war games was never rosy. Europe would fall unless the United States stepped in with nuclear weapons. After World War II most Western European nations had downsized their military forces even as the Soviets were building their own and those of the Warsaw Pact countries. By 1967, in an attempt to motivate the European nations to take more responsibility for their own defense, the U.S. plan for responding to a Soviet invasion had been changed. Instead of an immediate nuclear response, the U.S. plan called for a "flexible response," which began with conventional forces and contemplated use of nuclear weapons only as a last resort.

This put the NATO nuclear option temporarily on the back bench, or so it seemed. In reality, the nuclear option still remained at the top of the NATO planning pyramid. Since most of Laird's fellow NATO defense ministers were neophytes on nuclear weapons and strategy, he threw himself into using the NPG for substantive discussion purposes. But Laird worried that even with their limited experience, the NATO partners were getting too heady. For example, smaller European nations were emboldened to push for a U.S. pledge of full consultation with their political leaders if the use of nuclear weapons was imminent. But in a war with the Soviet Union, it was unlikely there would be time, for example, to get Belgium's permission before America reacted.

So Laird's job was to give the smaller, nonnuclear NATO countries the reassurance that they were being consulted on U.S. nuclear policy, without giving them actual control over decisions. He genuinely felt that in peacetime it was well worth the effort to consult with all of NATO's partners, and he argued with top U.S. military officials that it was time to share more information. Toward that end, at the June 1970 NPG meeting in Venice, Laird treated the NATO defense ministers to a highly classified briefing on the U.S.-Soviet strategic balance, using twelve satellite photos of Russian silos, submarine bases, bomber bases, and radar installations. "I must remind you of the extreme sensitivity of this source of intelligence," he began. "Because of the special responsibilities we share in the NPG, President Nixon has agreed with me that you should receive this briefing and see these photographs."[6]

The defense ministers were wowed. And to Laird's surprise, none of them leaked the information.[7] As a result he was willing to share more secrets at the start of each semiannual NPG meeting. Laird's candor carried the risk of revealing more than he planned about the limitations of U.S. intelligence, and inevitably the NATO defense ministers, particularly Schmidt, began pressing him for more details. Laird had to bob and weave at the meetings to appear cooperative while not spilling sensitive information.

⌒⌒⌒

During Laird's term at the Pentagon, Senate Majority Leader Mike Mansfield attempted regularly to cut the number of U.S. troops stationed in Europe. He had begun the effort in 1966 as the Vietnam War caused eroding support for the military and troops abroad. By 1968 it appeared that Mansfield might have enough votes to cut the number of U.S. troops in Western Europe by half—at least until the Soviets invaded Czechoslovakia, which doomed the Mansfield Amendment that time. Though it was little noted then, the U.S. troop level in Europe had already been substantially cut after reaching a peak (during the 1961–62 Berlin crisis) of 434,000 soldiers. When Laird became defense secretary, the number was 28 percent lower at 320,000.[8]

Each time Mansfield tried, Western Europeans and the West Germans in particular reacted vehemently and with some evident fear that the number might be cut. They regarded the level of U.S. troops in Europe as the most important barometer of American concern for the future of NATO and the defense of Western Europe. Having deployed an expensive nuclear deterrent, the United States should have been able to decrease the number of American troops stationed in Europe, since their numbers were not great enough anyway to beat back a Soviet attack on the ground. But NATO allies became apoplectic at any suggestion that a few of the 320,000 U.S. troops might be sent home.[9]

Laird was initially opposed to troop cuts as well. "I always had the feeling that if we really got into a conflict over there, it would be very difficult to be using nuclear weapons in Europe. That's why I felt that you had to have a legitimate conventional force deterrent there." However that also meant to Laird that the NATO allies had to share the burden by beefing up their conventional forces. As Laird outlined in his first memorandum to President Nixon regarding NATO: "The United States has for years urged its Allies to provide better conventional forces. [But] there are some Europeans, of course, who continue to believe that the best defense is the *threat* of an immediate nuclear response to almost any aggression. Having a substantial conventional option makes that threat less credible, in their eyes, and is therefore undesirable."[10]

A critical showdown on this issue occurred as Mansfield once again put forward his amendment in 1971 calling for only 150,000 U.S. troops to be left in Europe by the end of the year. The Nixon administration was alarmed at the apparent support for Mansfield; it was time to roll out the big guns. As the Senate debate tilted toward the cuts, Laird and Nixon secured pledges of opposition from twenty-four high-ranking officials of past administrations, including former presidents Johnson and Truman. As these heavyweights spoke up, Mansfield's supporters suggested compromises, but Mansfield himself refused to budge. When the vote was finally called just before midnight May 19, Mansfield lost again, 36 to 61.[11]

At the same time as the debate was occurring, the Soviets were making noises that, after three years of consideration, they might be willing to sit down and negotiate a mutual and balanced force reduction pact. In one respect, the gambit by Soviet premier Leonid Brezhnev backfired. It bolstered the case of opponents to the Mansfield cuts who argued that it was not the time to make unilateral cuts when reductions could be used as a negotiating chip to get the Soviets to downsize, too. On the other hand the propaganda move was well timed to lull Western European governments into thinking that it was unwise to increase their own military forces when lower levels were likely to be amicably negotiated with the Russians. So when Laird met with Schmidt in West Germany five days after the Mansfield Amendment vote, he discovered a despondent defense minister. According to the account from Laird's military assistant, Rear Admiral Daniel Murphy, Schmidt was discouraged about the antimilitary attitude in West Germany and had no hope that the European members of NATO would do more for the alliance.[12]

The next day Laird sat down with Peter Carrington, Britain's defense minister. The smaller European nations tended to follow the lead of Schmidt and Carrington when it came to defense issues, so Laird was disturbed to find Carrington in similar doldrums. According to Admiral Murphy's account of this second meeting, Carrington said again, "I'm like Helmut; I'm depressed." Laird warned him that NATO must be prepared more than ever before. It was not the time to be discouraged.[13]

When Laird returned to Washington he tackled the problem of a disintegrating NATO alliance with such energy that the situation was turned entirely around by the end of the year. In November 1971 he beat back another challenge from Mansfield, when the senator tried to put a troop-reduction amendment in a budget bill.

The Schmidt-Laird collaboration was an important precursor to the strong cooperation between their two nations when Schmidt served as chancellor of West Germany from 1974 to 1982. Schmidt later explained, "Mel is not too intellectually complicated, but I'm not interested in intellectuals particularly as friends. I'm interested in a dependable human being, and Mel is one of those—a dependable counterpart in international affairs and a dependable friend." Laird had proven that from the moment of their first meeting when he pledged to Schmidt that he could be trusted on the atomic demolition munitions issue.

In retrospect it is apparent that the time Laird invested in shoring up the NATO alliance paid off. According to an internal 1972 Pentagon study, "[t]he visible effect of the Secretary's rapport has been most notable in the cases of some of our largest allies—the United Kingdom, the Federal Republic of Germany [and] France.... In each of these cases, we believe Secretary Laird's personal rapport with the allied Minister of Defense...was in large part responsible for significant improvements in our relations."[14]

That report added a fourth country with which Laird's relationship with one of its defense ministers had made an historical and positive difference: Japan.

※

On March 23, 1945, Lieutenant Laird and the sailors on board the USS *Maddox* had joined the American fleet in a series of relentless preinvasion strikes on the Japanese island of Okinawa while fending off enemy aircraft attacks. On April 2 the first marines and army infantry landed on the island, and for nearly three months they fought to hold it. When it was over on June 22, some 7,700 American troops had died; the enemy had lost more than fourteen times that number. At sea, the U.S. fleet lost more than 4,900 sailors, making it the bloodiest battle in American naval history.[15] The peace treaty with Japan gave the United States full jurisdiction over the Ryukyu island chain, including

Okinawa. The treaty did not oblige America ever to return the islands to Japan, but the United States subsequently recognized Japanese "residual sovereignty" over the islands.

It is not hard to imagine the depth of feeling that Secretary Laird felt when he was confronted with an insistent demand from the Japanese government that Okinawa be returned to Japan. Not only was there a vivid memory of the sacrifice of his fellow World War II veterans, but also for Laird there was the resistance of Pentagon military chiefs who felt Okinawa was too strategic to relinquish. The island is located within a thousand-mile radius of mainland China, most of Japan, the Philippines, Korea, and all of Taiwan. A quarter-century after the war, Okinawa was a vital link in America's Far East security system and a key staging area for the ongoing war in Vietnam.

When Eisaku Sato became the Japanese prime minister in 1964, the return of Okinawa was one of his primary goals. A first step toward reversion occurred in November 1967 during a summit Sato had with President Johnson in Washington, D.C. They agreed to restore the Bonin Islands and Iwo Jima to Japan and stated an "aim of returning administrative rights over [the Ryukyu] islands to Japan." The U.S. ambassador to Japan at the time, career diplomat U. Alexis Johnson, pushed hard for a more substantive promise, and Sato felt he had a private understanding that reversion would take place within two or three years. When Nixon took office Sato was comforted by the knowledge that the advocate of reversion, Alexis Johnson, was promoted to become undersecretary of state for political affairs.

Laird's opposition to the reversion carried great weight at the White House. Aside from his normal clout in the administration, a long-standing executive order had designated the defense secretary the sole civil authority over Okinawa. So when Laird, as the administrator of the Ryukyus, voiced a negative view on reversion, Nixon had to pay attention. Laird discerned early that Undersecretary Johnson was playing heavily on Nixon's desire to have a summit with Sato. Japan was America's most important partner in Asia, and Sato had secretly informed Nixon he would not come to Washington unless the president agreed on a fixed date for reversion. Meanwhile, Alexis Johnson pushed through presidential National Security Decision Memorandum 13 in May of 1969 that chose 1972 as the year for reversion. But before Nixon agreed to the NSDM he promised Laird that if the defense department opposed the negotiations over Okinawa at any point, reversion would not happen in 1972.[16]

Laird discussed the secret presidential decision at the next top-level Pentagon staff meeting, on June 2, and sometime later that day someone leaked NSDM 13 to Hedrick Smith of the *New York Times*. Less than five months into his administration, Nixon reacted furiously to this first major national security leak. He ordered a Justice Department investigation and vowed not to hold another National Security Council meeting. It was over this issue, according to Haldeman's diary, that Kissinger first considered wiretapping his own staff. Nixon suspected either an NSC staffer or a top Pentagon official. He had Haldeman call Laird several times to demand a Pentagon investigation.[17]

At the same time Nixon dispatched a handwritten note by messenger to Laird to punctuate his anger. The single sentence read: "That leak on Okinawa was a real blow—as far as our bargaining position with Japan is concerned." Since Laird was known to have many friends in the press and to be unhappy with the Okinawa reversion idea, it's probable that Nixon suspected him and sent the note as a warning. Alexis Johnson suspected Laird and pressed Secretary of State Rogers to call Laird and ask him point blank if he had done it. Rogers called and Laird assured him that he was not responsible for the leak.

A few weeks after the Okinawa leak Joint Chiefs Chairman General Wheeler unloaded his frustration in a throw-down-the-gauntlet memorandum, which was hand-delivered by messenger to Kissinger at the White House. "Over the years, we have made many concessions to the Japanese," Wheeler began. He included generous trade concessions to Japan that allowed them "to freely market their goods in the U.S." Japan had responded with "restrictions on U.S. trade and capital investment in their country." The United States had gone to enormous lengths and cost to rebuild conquered Japan into a nation of unprecedented prosperity, and its government had responded by erecting trade barriers that froze out American business. Wheeler argued that he saw no good reason to proceed with such "unnecessary haste" to give them the strategic jewel of Okinawa.[18] Unfortunately for Wheeler and Laird, their go-slow position was unexpectedly undercut by an accident on the island that became public that summer of 1969.

A terse message was delivered to Laird on July 8, 1969: "Rabbit dead at Chibana." Laird bit down on his cigar. It seemed like every day at the Pentagon was two steps forward, one step back. If things went well in one area, they were sure to be catastrophic in another, and that Tuesday was no different. He had been looking forward to the day; solely as a result of Laird's planning and pressure on the president, the first 814 soldiers from a group of twenty-five thousand troops were flown out of South Vietnam that day, marking the first-ever withdrawal of U.S. forces from that conflict. Laird felt like celebrating and was in an ebullient mood as he donned his tuxedo for the evening's White House dinner with the Ethiopian Emperor, Haile Selassie. Then came word of the dead rabbit.[19]

It had been caged near some deadly nerve gas stored in fifty-two earth-covered igloos at the secret Chibana Army Ammunition Depot just off the approach pattern to Kadena (U.S.) Air Force Base on Okinawa. Without the chemical agent detectors that are available today, the Chibana chemical corps relied on animals to alert them to chemical leaks, much as coal miners used caged canaries to alert them to methane gas. The Japanese had never been told that President Kennedy had ordered eleven thousand tons of mustard and nerve gas munitions to be stored on Okinawa for possible use in a Pacific conflict. Since the United States still "owned" the island, such a disclosure to the Japanese government was neither required nor politically wise.[20]

One of the many goals Laird set for himself upon taking office was to radically change America's military chemical and biological weapons (CBW) priorities. Laird aimed to persuade Nixon to destroy all U.S. biological weapons and severely reduce the chemical weapons cache. His plan was to destroy most of the World War I mustard gas that made up half of America's total thirty-thousand-ton chemical weapons stockpile. He also planned to detoxify the aging GB and VX nerve gas munitions, which made up the other half of the stockpile, and replace them with a smaller quantity of new and safer-to-store "binary" chemical weapons that become lethal only when two or more chemicals were mixed. A March 1968 VX aerial spraying accident at Utah's Dugway Proving Ground had killed 6,400 sheep and become a major public embarrassment. Laird was determined to move the eleven thousand tons of chemical weapons off of Okinawa before their existence became known. But he instinctively knew when he received the dead rabbit message that secrecy was out the window and there would be hell to pay.

Within hours word came to Laird that the rabbit had been felled by a leak of GB nerve gas. The twenty-three army soldiers and one army civilian employee who had been near the canisters were taken to a military hospital for observation. They were released and returned to duty with a clean bill of health in less than six hours. Normally, Laird followed a full-disclosure policy regarding accidents, but any mishap involving chemical or nuclear weapons was not disclosed because that would betray the location of the weapons. So Laird waited for the other shoe to drop.

On July 17, *Wall Street Journal* reporter Robert Keatley called Laird's press chief Dan Henkin and asked for comment on a story that there had been a nerve gas leak that put soldiers in the hospital on Okinawa. It was a long night for Henkin, as he reported to Laird the following morning. He negotiated through the night with the *Journal*'s editors to "kill publication of this story in the national interest," but to no avail. Laird issued a brief statement saying there had been a minor "mishap" on Okinawa. It was not enough to quench the furor that erupted among Okinawans.[21]

A quick connection was made between the Chibana chemical weapons storage facility and the mysterious skin ailment accompanied by a high fever that 267 elementary school children suffered one day in August 1968 when they were swimming at a beach less than five miles from Chibana. There were also reports of a strange blight in the pine forest around Chibana, as well as tales of mutant frogs, including a ten-legged one that had been found nearby. The Okinawan Legislature quickly passed a resolution that demanded removal of the chemical weapons.[22]

Laird confirmed that the chemical agents were there and also revealed that he had requested a CBW study the previous April, in part because he planned to remove the weapons from the island. He publicly pledged to remove the toxic weapons as soon as it was safely possible and a destination was found. At first the Joint Chiefs resisted Laird's decision to remove the weapons. The chiefs were anxious to have chemical agents at the ready in Asia to deter both the North Koreans and the North Vietnamese from using similar weapons. "But I was secretary of defense, and I *never* planned to authorize chemical weapons use in Vietnam, so I thought it was crazy that this was stuff was in Okinawa," Laird said. "I wanted it moved. Fast." Laird's single vote at the Pentagon was bigger than any other combination of dissenting opinions.[23]

The Joint Chiefs scouted various locations for moving the weapons, and the best option was tiny Johnston Island, seven hundred miles southwest of Hawaii, where storage facilities and America's first full-scale chemical agent detoxification plant would be built, costing tens of millions of dollars. Under the name "Operation Red Hat," the last of the Chibana toxins were shipped to the island in September 1971.[24] (Johnston Island, where nuclear weapons had been tested in the 1950s and 1960s, remained a CBW dump until final cleanup in 2005.)

Meanwhile Laird had moved so fast and hard on the CBW front that he won a historic, unanimous decision from the NSC and the president before his first year in office was over.[25] On November 25, 1969, Nixon announced to the press the multifaceted CBW policy that Laird had crafted. Nixon pledged that the United States would never engage in germ warfare and would destroy any lethal biological weapons stocks. The president renounced all but defensive uses of chemical weapons.[26]

Another historic announcement had been made by Nixon, with Laird's concurrence, four days earlier. Both men had concluded that the only way to win easy approval in Tokyo for the ten-year renewal of the U.S.-Japan Security Treaty in 1970 was to accede to Sato's request for a fixed date on the reversion of Okinawa. At the end of a three-day summit in Washington, Nixon and Sato announced on November 21 that the last major issue of World War II in the Pacific would be resolved when Okinawa was returned to Japan in mid-1972.[27] With the Okinawa issue settled, Laird had an even bigger Japan matter on his plate: weaning the Asian nation from the American military dole.

❧

The ink was barely dry on the postwar Japanese constitution when its authors on General Douglas MacArthur's staff came to regret Article 9, the most famous section of the "peace" constitution. It still reads, in part: "The Japanese people forever renounce war as a sovereign right of the nation.... Land, sea, and air forces, as well as other war potential, will never be maintained." Many countries in the region were happy to keep Japan toothless, but the Nixon administration was not. Laird felt strongly that Japan should beef up its forces and military spending to become a true partner with the United States in maintaining the region's security. It was the primary subject Laird planned to raise with Defense Minister Yasuhiro Nakasone when he arrived for a five-day visit to the United States in September 1970.[28]

The two men could not have been better suited to understand one another. Both had come from families whose livelihood was made in lumber. Each served in his navy as a paymaster. They both had lost brothers in the military—to storms and not combat. Laird's older brother Connor died when his U.S. Navy mine-sweeper sank during a storm. Nakasone's younger brother Ryosuke died when the plane in which he was flying crashed in a blizzard.[29] Both Lieutenants Laird and Nakasone were witnesses from afar of the first atom bomb explosions. Nakasone saw the mushroom cloud over Hiroshima from the nearby Takamatsu naval base. Laird was aboard the *Maddox,* close enough to Nagasaki to hear the atomic explosion there three days after the one at Hiroshima.

Both emerged from the war with the resolve to go into politics. Nakasone won a seat in the Japanese Diet in 1947 at the age of twenty-eight, five years before Laird was elected to Congress. Both had their detractors who envied their shrewd, quick ascent in the leadership of their parties. Laird was decried as a "Midwest Machiavelli" whose manipulative ability in pursuit of his political aims was difficult to parry. Nakasone was nicknamed "Mr. Weathervane" because of the way he switched allegiances among various factions of the Liberal Democratic Party to facilitate his rise to power.[30]

When Laird and Nakasone met in Washington in September 1970, each recognized a kindred spirit; they tackled the tough subjects head on. Laird explained that it was time for a genuine mutual security arrangement between the two countries. It was fine that Japan enjoyed the protection of the American umbrella, but it was time they helped hold that umbrella, which was costing the United States more than $500 million a year. Nakasone agreed that the Japanese would become involved to a greater extent in sharing the burden of U.S. military costs in Japan. It was the first time that Japan acknowledged it had a responsibility for the cost of its own defense. Nakasone promised to push for a major increase in his defense budget. He was anxious that some of the U.S. bases in Japan, particularly near Tokyo, be turned over to the Japanese. Laird agreed and confided that he already planned to reduce the U.S. presence in Japan by ten thousand men, or one-fourth of the force.[31]

Perhaps the most sensitive topic dealt with nuclear weapons. Laird knew from American intelligence sources that Nakasone, who had once advocated that the Japanese acquire small defensive nuclear weapons, had earlier in the year ordered a secret study to determine how much it would cost and how long it would take for Japan to become a nuclear power. The study concluded that it would take $555 million and five years, but that it was impractical because of the absence of suitable land for a nuclear test facility.[32]

Laird pointedly asked Nakasone if he still felt the need for a Japanese defensive nuclear force. No, Nakasone answered. He was coming to the realization that possession of nuclear weapons would bitterly divide the Japanese, who were the only people in the world to have suffered from the use of the atom bomb. Also, as long as the U.S. nuclear deterrent was in place, there was no need for a separate Japanese atomic force. If Nakasone really believed a Japanese nuclear program was impractical, then Laird said the Japanese shouldn't mind making it easier for the United States to protect them with U.S. nuclear weapons. With evident courage and subtlety, Nakasone agreed, telling Laird that the United States could assume that rules about bringing U.S. nuclear weapons into Japanese territory would be more relaxed in the future. The treaty between the two countries allowed temporary storage and transportation of nuclear weapons in and around Japan without consultation in times of "emergency," and Nakasone said he was willing to be flexible in the definition of "emergency."[33]

Considering the agreements fruitful, Nakasone proposed that the two of them conduct annual consultations. It wasn't as easy as it sounded; no U.S. secretary of defense had ever been invited to Tokyo, for fear of massive demonstrations. Nakasone conceded the problem and said he would think on it further.

After the Washington, D.C., conference, both men were as good as their word. A month later, Nakasone issued the Japanese Defense Agency's first-ever white paper. Previous defense ministers had been too afraid to put their military priorities in writing. Several months later Nakasone proposed more than doubling defense spending when he submitted his budget.[34] Also forthcoming was an invitation to Laird to visit Tokyo. The State Department strongly advised against it, but Laird ignored their concerns. He wanted to be the first American secretary of defense to visit Japan.

In the spring of 1971 the president's senior military aide, Brigadier General James "Don" Hughes, contacted the pilot of Air Force One, Colonel Ralph Albertazzie, on a secure phone line and asked him to hurry over to the White House without telling anyone where he was going. Once there the pilot was taken down to the "shelter," a hardened concrete-and-steel bunker intended for temporary use by the first family in the event of an attack on the White House. "We've got an interesting one this time," Hughes began, a big grin spreading across his face. "The Boss [Nixon] is sending Kissinger to China. Secretly. You know a way to smuggle him in? And out?"

"You mean Communist China? Good Lord!" Albertazzie exclaimed. Once he was over the shock, the two brainstormed, then Albertazzie headed back to Andrews Air Force Base to mull over the best way to conduct the covert mission.[35]

Of all the secret discussions Kissinger ever had, those preceding the China opening were regarded by him as the most sensitive. Nixon agreed with Kissinger's request that Laird and Rogers would be kept in the dark until just before the public was informed. But keeping such a secret from Laird was next to impossible, especially when the secret involved military officers, planes, and communications equipment.

The most incontrovertible and detailed information came from the National Security Agency, whose director, Admiral Noel Gayler, was appointed by Laird. Kissinger's communications with the Chinese went through CIA "back channels." The NSA routinely intercepted those international messages, and Gayler personally passed them along to Laird. On May 31, 1971, the Chinese (through Pakistani intermediaries) informed Nixon that they were agreeable to a Nixon visit to Peking, provided Kissinger himself secretly came first to Peking July 9–11 to make the arrangements. In less than a day after the invitation was issued, Laird was informed by Gayler about it. He smiled to himself and thought he would have some fun with the secretive Kissinger. But first he would give Kissinger a chance to brief him on the mission.

On June 4 Kissinger went to the Pentagon for a routine breakfast. In the course of their wide-ranging discussion Laird dropped a few questions about the People's Republic of China to give Kissinger an opening but Kissinger didn't bite. So Laird decided to "throw a hook at Henry," as he put it. Laird was already planning to visit Japan and South Korea in July, which the White House had approved. A few days after his breakfast with Kissinger, Laird sent the White House an updated itinerary that now included a side trip to Taiwan on precisely the days when Kissinger would be in Peking. It was Laird's playful way of saying he knew what the national security advisor was up to. But Kissinger wasn't amused. The prospect of a defense secretary in Taipei talking about the U.S.-Taiwan alliance just as Kissinger was in Peking trying to downplay that very alliance was too much for Kissinger. For two days, without giving Laird a good reason, Kissinger frantically pressed Laird to cancel the Taiwan portion of the trip. When Laird had had his fun—which he called "giving Kissinger the needle because he didn't share his trip with me"—Laird let the national security advisor off the hook and dropped the bogus Taiwan plans.

Kissinger never knew it was a setup. In his memoirs, he wrote that "Mel Laird conceived the idea of inspecting defense installations on Taiwan on just the days when I would be in Peking [but he] was a good soldier. Without inquiring into my reasons for asking, he rearranged his schedule."[36] Thirty years after the fact, when the charade was revealed to him, Kissinger took umbrage. "He shouldn't be proud of that," Kissinger said. "That was not something to jerk my chain on." A friend of Kissinger's and Laird's, former secretary of state Larry Eagleburger, thought it was hilarious and suggested that Kissinger needed to "get over himself. Mel mentioned the whole thing to me as a way of trying to stick it to Henry. I think it's funny under any circumstances."[37]

On the Fourth of July 1971 the first American secretary of defense to visit Japan landed in Tokyo to great fanfare. His Japanese counterpart, Nakasone, had arranged for formal welcome with a military band playing the national anthem. Nakasone laughed in recalling the event later: "The staff of Mr. Laird, who got off the ramp of the special plane dressed casually in bell-bottom trousers, surprised the Japanese managing staff who welcomed them. Then there were two teenagers who also got off the plane. One of them was Mr. Laird's son [David] and the other the son's friend. Both of them were sixteen years old and in high school." The proper Japanese were put off because, at the time, "We would never think of allowing children to fly with an official delegate," Nakasone explained.[38]

The following morning Laird met with Nakasone, who was just minutes from resignation. The week before, Prime Minister Sato had suffered a setback in parliamentary elections, which prompted him to reorganize his cabinet. At Nakasone's request Sato had kept him on the job long enough to host Laird's visit. The outgoing Nakasone told Laird how much he had enjoyed their short association. The controversial issue of returning the island of Okinawa to Japan had been settled. Nakasone also thanked Laird for the planned removal of chemical weapons from Okinawa and the promise that the island would also be free of nuclear weapons when it was given back to Japan a year later (May 15, 1972).[39]

At one point in the Japan trip Laird experienced an awkward moment. Nakasone "was vitally interested in U.S. policy toward the People's Republic of China," Laird wrote in his report to Nixon after the trip. "I told Nakasone we were proceeding cautiously and that, from a military standpoint, I could see no imminent fundamental changes on either side." While that was true, the fact that he could not disclose in confidence to this new friend and ally the visit of Kissinger to Peking four days hence was difficult for Laird. But he also knew that the Japanese government leaked like a sieve, and such a public revelation would cause the Chinese to call the whole thing off. So he kept silent. The meetings with Nakasone had otherwise been very successful. A top Pentagon official later wrote that it was "as a result of these meetings [that] Mr. Nakasone swung from being a critic of the [U.S.-Japan] Security Treaty to the role of an active and staunch supporter." It was this second visit with Nakasone that firmly established the annual consultations between the U.S. and Japanese defense agencies that have been conducted since.[40]

Laird had recognized in the dynamic, charismatic Nakasone a present and future star. "We shall see and hear more of Nakasone over the coming years," Laird predicted in his report to Nixon. On July 7 Nakasone hosted a private dinner for Laird and his group at a Tokyo restaurant. Fueled by saki, the two World War II veterans slipped back into memories of that engagement in which they had fought on opposite sides. Nakasone thought his country's surprise attack on Pearl Harbor, objectively viewed, "was a great military coup, and we should have gone right on to San Francisco and Los Angeles." Laird courteously disagreed and then mentioned that he had with him some "medals" that the Japanese had given him during the Pacific conflict.

"I'd like to see those," the curious Nakasone said.

Laird obligingly pulled up his pant leg and showed Nakasone blue gray splotches on his leg where pieces of embedded shrapnel were working their way out. "This is my great remembrance of Japan. I carry a lot of Japanese *metal* around with me. I think it's fair to say I've got quite a few Japanese *medals* that I've been awarded." Nakasone laughed and then soberly reflected on how far the two nations had come. Laird offered a toast: "To be honest, it will always be difficult for me and many other Americans to forget Pearl Harbor, but this is a new day." Using a Japanese phrase he had learned for the occasion, he then held his glass up to toast the "new start" that he and Nakasone had forged between the military leadership of the two nations. At his departure press conference Laird wryly noted that this visit to Tokyo had been more enjoyable than his last one—as a sailor in 1945.[41]

Laird returned to Washington by way of Hawaii, arriving just after midnight on July 14. It was about this time that Kissinger officially informed Laird on a secure phone line about his trip to China. Laird did not reveal that he already knew about it but did request that he be allowed to tell Nakasone six hours in advance of the July 15 public announcement. Kissinger thought it was an unusual request but acceded, in part because Laird had not complained about being kept in the dark. The Laird-Nakasone friendship continued to benefit both the United States and Nakasone later when Nakasone himself was elected prime minister.

The Japanese government as a whole was not as unflappable as Nakasone had been about the U.S.-China opening. The Japanese were not perturbed about the new relationship itself but were instead very upset that, as America's closest ally in Asia, they had not been consulted. It was the first of several "Nixon shocks" that strained the relationship and subsequently contributed to Sato's loss of his post as prime minister less than a year later.[42]

There was other fallout of a more unusual nature from Kissinger's China trip. As it happened, there was a young navy yeoman aboard the plane who was a spy for the Joint Chiefs, rifling through Kissinger's briefcases and copying documents. But that fact would not be discovered until India and Pakistan went to war at the end of the year.

⚓︎

The 1971 skirmish between India and Pakistan was inevitable given their history. Pakistan was created in 1947 with a partition of India that resulted in two Pakistans—East and West—both under the same government, but with the whole of India in between them. Pakistan (East and West) was a nation of Muslims and some Hindus, under a military dictatorship ruled by Yahya Khan. India, the world's largest democracy, under the leadership of Indira Gandhi, was predominantly Hindu. In 1971 a strong independence movement was brewing in East Pakistan, but Yahya Khan was not about to let it go. He sent in a sixty-thousand-man army from predominantly Muslim West Pakistan and targeted for extermination the Hindus living in East Pakistan. At least five hundred thousand, and possibly as many as three million, were slaughtered by Yahya's soldiers.

Hindus from East Pakistan fled by the millions into neighboring India.[43] Indira Gandhi decided to weigh in on the side of independence for East Pakistan. As superpowers are wont to do, China and Russia took sides, with the Chinese supporting Yahya Khan in his effort to keep East Pakistan under his thumb, and the Soviet Union hinting that it would back India if Gandhi decided to intervene on behalf of East Pakistani independence. On November 23 the Indian Army invaded East Pakistan.

It was inevitable that East Pakistan would and should become an independent country. But Nixon feared Gandhi would use the crisis as a pretext to attack West Pakistan as well. So the president and Kissinger crafted a secret policy tilt toward Pakistan. Publicly, the White House claimed that the United States was neutral. But those in the secret policy councils chaired by Kissinger in late 1971, primarily the Washington Special Action Group, knew better.

At a December 3 WSAG meeting, David Packard and others listened as Kissinger launched into a series of mini tirades. He sputtered at one point: "I am getting hell every half hour from the President that we are not being tough on India. He has just called me again. He does not believe we are carrying out his wishes. *He wants to tilt in favor of Pakistan.*" After the State Department representative outlined some options that would punish both India and Pakistan, Kissinger complained about having to reproach them equally when he wanted to favor one. "It's hard to tilt toward Pakistan when we have to match every Indian step with a Pakistan step."[44]

It was a cynical deception, and Packard was as disgusted as was Laird, who abhorred Kissinger's penchant for secret maneuvering that was at odds with public pronouncements. Besides, at the Pentagon and in other agencies of the government, many felt that the president and his national security advisor were biased toward Pakistan because they were both obsessed with the China opening and China was Pakistan's ally.

Nixon suspected Laird was not in agreement with his tilt toward Pakistan and, on December 6, ordered Kissinger to get the defense secretary "to follow the White House line."[45] That same Monday morning military opposition to the tilt toward Pakistan broke out in Laird's top-level staff meeting. Admiral Elmo Zumwalt, the chief of naval operations, used the meeting to express his doubts. "I am disturbed," he said. "The U.S. will take a lot of lumps siding with the Pakistanis." He said that inevitably East Pakistan would gain its independence, and the United States would look bad while the Soviets picked the winning side. "In the short term, the military balance in the Indian Ocean area will go against us."[46]

That same day India recognized an independent East Pakistan under the new name of "Bangladesh." As the crisis was winding down, however, a leak of the WSAG meeting minutes and other documents to columnist Jack Anderson—proving the Nixon-Kissinger tilt—prompted an investigation that shook the highest levels of government. When the minutes of the heated WSAG meetings on India and Pakistan began appearing in Anderson's column on December 13, the White House scrambled to find out the source of the leak. They found it in the Pentagon. Admiral Robert O. Welander, who was the liaison between the Joint Chiefs and Kissinger, immediately suspected his young stenographer, Navy Yeoman First Class Charles Radford, who frequented the copy machine and had a soft spot for India, where he had once been posted. Radford was hooked to a polygraph machine. Under questioning, his connection to Anderson was left unresolved (and Anderson maintained even until his death in 2006 that Radford was not his source). Radford did confess that he had been stealing Kissinger's documents but that he did it under orders from Admiral Welander, who was then slipping the documents to the chairman of the Joint Chiefs, Admiral Moorer.

Laird's general counsel, Fred Buzhardt, investigated and found a morass of mistrust and spying—the inevitable offspring of Nixon's own secretive and manipulative style, which infected every office from the White House on down. Radford's job was to keep Welander informed about what Kissinger was doing, and Welander's job was to keep Moorer informed. Knowing Kissinger's penchant for secrecy, Radford's best option was to pilfer Kissinger's bags. Buzhardt's investigation concluded that while Welander never asked Radford to steal, the admiral knew how the yeoman was getting the documents. Similarly Moorer never asked Welander to steal, but he also didn't discourage the flow of purloined papers. Buzhardt reported back to Laird that during the investigation, "Admiral Welander acknowledged that he did not believe he would have been given authorized access to much of the materials obtained by Radford on his trips with Dr. Kissinger and General Haig. Admiral Welander stated that he had informed [Moorer] of the method by which Radford obtained the materials."[47]

Zumwalt summed up the bizarre and paranoid environment of the time in his memoir: "Kissinger telling me he distrusted Haig; Haig telling me he and others distrusted Kissinger; Haldeman/Ehrlichman trying to bushwhack Kissinger; Kissinger and the President using Moorer to help them make plans without Laird's knowledge and therefore pretending to keep Moorer fully informed while withholding some information from him, too.... What I find hard to believe is that rational men could think that running things like that could have any other result than 'leaks' and 'spying' and all-around paranoia. Indeed they had created a system in which 'leaks' and 'spying' were everyday and essential elements."[48]

For Laird it was just more justification for his "firewall" between the Pentagon and the White House, and he took steps to reinforce that wall. But he was too sanguine about the atmosphere to be taken by surprise. Kissinger, who had condoned wire-tap spying on the Pentagon, was outraged to be on the other end of espionage. But Laird was as nonplused about the stolen documents as he had been about the wire taps. When Kissinger demanded punishment, Laird told him to back off. Radford was transferred, and Moorer got a slap on the wrist from Laird. "I called Moorer in and told him that it was the greatest personal disappointment that I'd had," said Laird. "But he said it was all for the good of the Pentagon, 'and for your good too, Mr. Secretary.'" Moorer's excuse was that the White House was too tight with its secrets to the point of blocking the necessary flow of information to the Pentagon. "Well," Laird replied. "I just want it to stop." And the admiral was allowed to go back to work. Within a few months, Moorer was back in the good graces of Nixon, who found in him a willing accomplice whenever the president tried to maneuver around Laird.

34
A Friend in Deed

⌁

THE DECISION WAS NOT EASY for Robert Froehlke when his old friend "Bom" asked him to come work at the Pentagon. During their many years together—commiserating over Mel's fifth-grade punishment by Miss Semrau with a rubber hose, debating or shooting hoops in high school, living as duplex neighbors in college with their brides, or campaigning around the Seventh District for nine Congressional elections—neither imagined they would work together at the top of the U.S. military hierarchy. But once he was there, Bom couldn't imagine doing it without Bob.

While Laird was in the Pacific on a destroyer, Froehlke was in Europe rising to the rank of captain in the army. After the war, when Laird went into politics, Froehlke went into law. Within a few days after Laird accepted Nixon's arm-twisting offer to be secretary of defense, he knew he needed his lifelong friend, first as an assistant defense secretary and then as secretary of the army.

Froehlke learned early that the more success he achieved on the job, the more assignments Laird would give him. So it was in May 1969 that he accepted an unusual new task from Laird: to evaluate the performance of the military's various intelligence agencies. Laird had an ingrained distrust of intelligence bureaucracies. In his first days as secretary he moved quickly to grab the reins of the intelligence services. He ordered the ultrasecret National Reconnaissance Office (NRO), run by the air force, to turn over satellite photos to him first. Previously the photos went first to the CIA, which then sent them to the White House and the Defense Intelligence Agency. Then the DIA would forward them to the Joint Chiefs and, maybe, to the defense secretary. Laird changed the pattern so he saw the photos first, but he ordered that his new practice be kept secret. He didn't look at every picture and wasted no time in approving transmission to the CIA, which then, as before, shared them with the White House and the DIA. Laird had been in Washington long enough to know that information is the ultimate power, and getting your own agency's information first was essential to effective control.

Still, he knew that intercepting his own department's intelligence was not enough to control it. The DIA had more than six thousand employees, and the larger National Security Agency, which dealt with electronic intelligence such as communications intercepts, had another ten thousand military and civilian staff members. Many were career employees who had seen defense secretaries come and go and did not readily spill their agency's secrets to someone who was only going to be around for four years. So Laird decided to impose a strong hand. He had several concerns: that the services were exceeding their charters, conducting potentially embarrassing clandestine operations; that they were wasting millions of dollars in duplicative espionage activities; and that they were being limited in their productivity by questionable management processes and organizational structure.

Among Froehlke's first recommendations was that Laird put his own men over the DIA and NSA. So Laird put Froehlke in charge of finding those loyalists. Second, Froehlke advised Laird he needed to take a deeper look. In mid-August 1969 Laird gave Froehlke an additional title: special assistant to the secretary for intelligence. With a fourteen-member staff to assist him over the next two years, he shook up the intelligence community, improved communication between the intelligence services, and eliminated waste by uncovering excessive duplication.

Froehlke's staff also found some espionage abuses by the military agencies and corrected them. But one big problem that Froehlke and Laird thought they had arrested continued to run on, silent and deep, until its exposure became a major controversy in 1970 and1971: spying and massive information collection by the U.S. Army on American civilians who were engaged in perfectly legal political activities.

In early 1965 the Army Intelligence Command had been formed and headquartered at Fort Holabird, Maryland. One of its purposes was to conduct security checks on army personnel and others doing work for the army. But civil unrest and race riots prompted the military to expand its mandate to include dossiers on Americans likely to cause civil disturbances. By 1968 when the CONUS (continental United States) intelligence operation peaked, there were more than a thousand military intelligence agents in three hundred field offices across the nation gathering "intelligence" on as many as eighteen thousand civilians who were thought to be planning potentially violent demonstrations.[1]

By the time Nixon took office in 1969, at least three large army data banks held thousands of dossiers on Americans. When Laird first inquired about the program he was told not to worry, that it was mostly a collection of newspaper articles, not wiretapping or the like. He was informed that among the files were the names of people who had made threats against him. But Laird had a rule when it came to intelligence: never trust the first incident report, or even the second. And he didn't completely trust the assurances he got from army intelligence. So he directed Froehlke to shut down any surveillance of civilians, such as political activists, if they had not threatened him personally or the military in general.[2]

Unknown to either Froehlke or Laird, data continued to be collected and operations continued. The first alarm bell was sounded by a small publication, *Washington Monthly,* in January 1970. In an authoritative article by a former army intelligence officer, the entire operation was laid out factually and critically, using as the source an army captain who had been a part of "CONUS Intelligence."[3] Froehlke went back to the service intelligence officials to make sure there was no misunderstanding, that spying on law-abiding Americans must end. Laird then ordered the army to destroy all "inappropriate" files on civilians.[4]

Senator Sam Ervin took up the crusade and began an investigation, some details of which leaked to the press. Former army lieutenant Joseph Levan, who was attached to the 108th Military Intelligence Group, said his Manhattan field office ordered him to spy on campus activities at the city's colleges and on welfare mothers protesting outside city hall. The unit even paid tuition to register a black agent in college who was then tasked to spy on the black studies program.[5] There was certainly an element of Keystone Kops. In September 1969, when military agencies heard there would be a large antiwar demonstration outside Fort Carson, Colorado, spies were dispatched to pose as demonstrators. One sergeant involved said there were 119 people at the rally, 53 of whom were either army spies or reporters.[6]

A whistle blower from an army intelligence unit in Chicago charged that his group had targeted eight hundred civilians in Illinois, including newspaper reporters, religious leaders, political contributors, and politicians—among them Senator Adlai Stevenson III when he was Illinois state treasurer.[7] Army Secretary Stanley Resor investigated and said the allegation about army spying on Stevenson was "without foundation in fact."[8] But Laird asked Froehlke to take a closer look, and he found the file on Stevenson. Froehlke had to go to Capitol Hill to apologize and confess that there was indeed a file on the senator. But he said it was only a collection of newspaper clippings, and that the army had never done actual surveillance on Stevenson.[9]

On December 23, 1970, given the level of concern on Capitol Hill and his own concern, Laird issued a directive aimed at shaking up the military intelligence services. In it he shifted control of all military intelligence activities from the Joint Chiefs to a civilian, Froehlke. In addition the DIA and the National Security Agency were to report directly to Laird. The news rolled through the Pentagon brass like a shock wave, but Laird not only ignored the outrage of the Joint Chiefs, he included in the memo to them a warning against setting up their own ad hoc intelligence networks to bypass the DIA and NSA.[10]

The more Froehlke dug into the matter, the more he found that the Johnson White House should bear the blame for foisting the spying duties on the military. Though Froehlke mentioned no names, he told Ervin's Senate panel that he found "high civilian authorities" had ordered a "reluctant" military to conduct investigations on civilians.[11] In closed-door testimony at the same time in a House appropriations hearing, Laird echoed Froehlke's account that the trail led to the Johnson Oval Office. "This operation was completely known to the highest authorities within our government," he stated emphatically, providing no names or further details.[12]

The Ervin hearings unearthed little news that had not already been leaked, and it soon became clear that the Pentagon and Froehlke had weathered the storm.

⌲

When Laird became secretary of defense, one of his plans was to make Froehlke the secretary of the army. And he had to overrule Nixon twice to do it. Nixon had promised the job to two wealthy Republicans at the same time—William Casey and Bo Callaway. But Laird refused to nominate either. He knew he couldn't give an outsider such as Froehlke the job right out of the gate, so he asked Army Secretary Stan Resor from the Johnson administration to stay on for a while. Resor ended up serving six years in all, longer than any army secretary since the post had been created in 1947. In early 1971 Laird told Resor he could leave soon, and Resor was relieved that Laird was finally willing to let him go.[13]

By April 1971 Laird had let Nixon know that Resor would be resigning, and he wanted to name Froehlke as the replacement, but Nixon wasn't happy with the choice. He had finally rewarded campaign contributor William Casey two months earlier with a controversial appointment as chairman of the Securities and Exchange Commission. That left Bo Callaway, a former Georgia congressman, as Nixon's top choice for army secretary. A week after Resor's May 21 resignation announcement, Laird was in Brussels for a NATO meeting when aide Carl Wallace tipped him off that the White House was on the verge of naming Callaway. Laird was furious. "Carl said you could hear me all the way across the Atlantic when I got that word!" he said. Laird called Nixon and reminded him of "the deal" written on the cocktail napkin in 1968. Nixon relented, but just to be sure, Laird called Kissinger and sternly told him, "Listen, I don't want any monkey business on this. The nomination papers are there, and I want them sent to the Senate. That's part of my understanding with the president, and I want it carried out." The next day, Laird recalled, the White House sent Froehlke's nomination to the Senate.

While the post was an honor for Froehlke, because of the timing it was a dubious honor. He would be taking over the army at one of its most troubled times. There was the army spy fiasco, which Froehlke had finally wrapped up before Resor resigned. But there were ongoing problems such as drug abuse by soldiers, racial divisions, the repercussions of My Lai, corruption scandals involving military service clubs, and profit-skimming from the massive PX system, as well as an antiwar rebellion across the country, in Congress, and within the army itself.[14] Even the *New York Times* knew it was no brass ring. "Now Mr. Laird has asked his friend to render him the most difficult service he has ever attempted—running an Army that has been racked in recent years by a series of troubles."[15]

Froehlke knew it as well. White House budget aide James Schlesinger, who went to Froehlke's swearing-in at the Pentagon July 1, 1971, remembered that Laird began the program with "this flowery talk about what a marvelous talent Bob Froehlke was." Then it was Froehlke's turn. In the jocular but candid manner he always had with Laird, he told a story about a son who was announced as the heir to take over his father's nearly bankrupt business. After being introduced with a glowing talk by dad, the son, with a hint of subtle sarcasm responded, "Thanks a lot, Pa." Turning to Laird at that point, with a wry smile, Froehlke said: "Thanks a lot, pal!"[16]

Laird had a gift for choosing loyal friends such as Froehlke who could be trusted to follow his lead. Daniel "Chappie" James was one of them. At 6 feet 4 inches and 235 pounds, with a deep, rich voice to match his physical frame, James was a commanding presence. As an air force colonel, he was just the man Mel Laird needed to handle a tense crisis in Libya, during which James faced down Muammar Qaddafi, pistols at the ready. Later James was precisely the person Laird needed at the Pentagon to be the department's compassionate liaison with the wives of POWs and MIAs. He also delivered dozens of flag-waving speeches on the college campuses of the nation, where he spread the word that, despite racial divisions erupting in the armed services, the Defense Department was serious about equal opportunity—that the military was one of the best places for African-Americans like himself to be.

Because he believed what he said and believed in Laird, James earned Laird's gratitude, loyalty, and patronage, which became pivotal on his path to becoming the air force's first black four-star general. As he was growing up in the ghetto section of Pensacola, Florida, James's mother had told him, "Don't stand there banging on the door of opportunity and then when someone opens it, you say, 'Wait a minute, I got to get my bags.' You be prepared with your bags of knowledge, your patriotism, your honor so that when somebody opens that door, you charge in." With World War II raging, James became one of the now-famous "Tuskegee Airmen," an army aviation "experiment" to see if Negroes could learn to fly airplanes. In the late 1960s Colonel James served heroically in Vietnam. With five rows of medals on his chest, his next assignment in 1969 was to the relatively sedate Wheelus Air Base in Libya, where he would become the new commander.[17]

Wheelus, near the Libyan capital of Tripoli, was the largest American air base in the world at the time. On September 1, 1969, while seventy-nine-year-old Libyan King Idris was undergoing medical treatment in Turkey, a group of Libyan army leaders, led by the twenty-seven-year-old Muammar Qaddafi, overthrew the throne and created the Libyan Arab Republic. At first the revolutionaries said the Americans could stay at Wheelus, but by the time Colonel

James assumed command of the base on September 22, Qaddafi's nationalist zealots were making threats about kicking the Americans out. Laird made a series of phone calls to James, telling him that there was an "urgent need" for the United States to hang on to Wheelus. James agreed, but that meant he would have to stand up to Qaddafi.

A defining moment occurred on October 18 when Colonel Qaddafi himself stormed onto the base with a column of halftracks, driving at full speed through the housing area and then out again. Colonel James rushed to put up a barrier at the front gate and faced the menacing Qaddafi and his nationalist firebrands, looking like a scene out of *High Noon*. James relayed an account of the incident excitedly to Laird on the phone that evening: "I met Qaddafi a few yards outside the gate. We were both standing. He had a fancy gun and holster and kept his hand on it. I had my .45 in my belt. I told him to move his hand away. He finally did. If he had pulled that gun, he never would have cleared his holster!"

Qaddafi left and never came back, and he didn't send any more halftracks for a repeat show of force, but James operated the base for weeks in a crisis mode. American oil companies, fearful Qaddafi might nationalize their Libyan operations, had pressured the State Department to mollify him by abandoning the base. To the great disappointment of Laird and James, the diplomats during the last days of the Johnson administration had agreed that America would voluntarily abandon Wheelus by July 1970. But when Qaddafi insisted the United States leave millions of dollars worth of equipment behind, Laird was furious. He issued a direct order to Colonel James: "Take it all out. Fly everything to Germany at night, if you have to. Don't you leave so much as a damned typewriter there!"

It was not an easy order for James to carry out. As the base began packing up, several Libyan "delegations" descended on James to protest. One of the first such groups demanded that the valuable U.S. radar systems must stay. James invited them into his house to talk, but when their driver joined them, resting a submachine gun in his lap, James was furious. "I told the senior officer in charge that I was going to count to three and if that S.O.B. was not out of my living room by that time, I would physically throw him out," James recounted to Laird on the phone that evening. "The man left, and was pretty quick about it."

The final agreement for evacuation was signed in Tripoli on December 23. Over the next few nights, per Laird's instructions, U.S. military cargo jets flew much of the most valuable equipment out under cover of darkness. James managed to remove everything that wasn't nailed down, and a lot of things that were.[18]

As James was winding up his Libya command in 1970, Laird called him back to the Pentagon for a conference. Greatly impressed with James, Laird told the colonel he needed him in the Public Affairs section of the secretary's office. "But you know I'm a fighter pilot," James responded.

"Listen, Chappie," Laird said, "you *were* a fighter pilot. Now you're going to fight different battles on the ground and over the airwaves. Some of them will be tougher than combat. You're going to be promoted to general for this position. . . . I need you."[19] True to his mother's advice, James's bags were packed when the door of opportunity opened.

The new deputy assistant secretary of defense for public affairs was a larger-than-life figure, the kind of person Laird wanted to front for the military on college campuses, so he asked James to join him for several speaking engagements. And when Laird—the son of a minister—learned the general had a fine baritone voice for singing spirituals, he couldn't help but turn some of their appearances into revivals. Laird would sermonize and James would sing.[20]

Often the subject of race came up during the question-and-answer period after James's speeches. A bearded white youth heckled him at one university: "How can a black man like you defend the racist, fascist establishment?" James retorted: "Look friend, I've been black 50 years, which is more than you will ever be, and I know what I believe in."[21]

One of the most emotional moments for him came during a speech at an all-black university where hundreds of students had previously watched as an arsonist burned the ROTC building to the ground. James began his talk quietly, but his anger built as he thought of the arson. He vented to the antimilitary students in the crowd: "You didn't have the right to do that. You didn't have the right to destroy what you didn't build! You didn't build that; I did! I built it with sweat and blood and to prove that black men could be responsible pilots in the United States Air Force, and they deserve ROTC establishments on black campuses to produce these black officers, because that's where most of us came from."

One of the things James was most proud of was the way Laird's Defense Department was leading other government agencies and segments of private business in the equal opportunity arena. At a talk on the topic of "racism in the military" to the Air Command and Staff College in Alabama, the general said he was tired of "wild charges of institutionalized racism in the services." What he had personally seen was a defense secretary who was devoted to solving race problems. "If we catch any practicing bigot, he is dead professionally in [the military]. We do not have any place for a commander who cannot be concerned about racism and have a commitment against it. Mr. Laird has stated there will be no more of that. And if we find them out, they will not command a latrine detail in this service, anymore, anywhere, I can promise you."[22]

꿈

Laird's private actions demonstrated his inner beliefs about racial equality. As a congressman he had joined the Kenwood Golf and Country Club because it was within walking distance of his home and had a swimming pool for his children. But in 1968, when the waiters refused to serve his luncheon guest, Walter Washington, the black mayor of Washington, D.C., Laird was furious. He held his temper, though, and insisted on and got service. Later, the club president took him aside and told him he couldn't do that again. Laird didn't storm out; he did decide that if the policy didn't change, he would resign from the club. Others, led by Senator Frank Church, started a petition drive in late 1968 to force the club to open up to blacks. In 1970, as the petitioners pursued a court case, it was revealed in court documents that two prominent Republicans, Laird and Secretary of State Rogers, had already resigned in protest of the club's discriminatory membership practices.[23]

As the new defense secretary, Laird came out fast and hard for equal opportunity throughout the department. His point man for this initiative was Roger Kelley, the assistant secretary of defense for manpower and reserve affairs. Kelley thought something more than memos and directives was needed, something like a charter. So one was written around a table with Packard, the Joint Chiefs, and all the service secretaries, lest anyone miss the message.[24] The "Human Goals Charter" was issued in August 1969, signed by the department's highest-ranking civilian and military leaders, and said, in part, "We [will] strive . . . [t]o make Military and Civilian service in the Department of Defense a model of equal opportunity for all regardless of race, sex, creed, or national origin."[25]

Laird well knew the lessons of American history regarding race. A high-minded charter was just words unless it was followed up with action, such as promoting more black officers to flag rank. But he had to force the uniformed military to comply, and that meant tabling promotion lists until qualified blacks (and, later, women) were on those lists. When Laird became secretary, only two blacks held the rank of general. By the end of his term the armed services had promoted another thirteen.[26] While the air force and army appointed black generals, the navy was slow to appoint a black admiral. Laird leaned on Navy Secretary John Chafee in early 1969 to make sure the service moved quickly to promote a black captain to admiral. Laird suggested the first candidate, Captain Samuel L. Gravely Jr., a frigate commander who in 1962 had become the first black to command a U.S. warship. So conservative had the navy been that Gravely was the only possible choice for admiral; he was the only one of three black navy captains who had had a sea command. (The other two were a chaplain and a medical doctor.) With the help of Chafee and the innovative Admiral Zumwalt, Laird was able to announce in April 1971 that Gravely would become the first black admiral in American history. "I will not be the last," Gravely said in a radio message from aboard the USS *Jouett* in the Pacific.[27]

While the army had promoted blacks as generals, none had a division command until Laird's tenure at the Pentagon. At that time the army had about two hundred major generals (two-star), but only thirteen divisions, so most of the generals wound up in desk jobs. Major General Frederic Ellis Davison became the first black to command an army division when he was tapped in April 1972 to head the Eighth Infantry Division in Europe.[28]

As for the air force, Laird saw it as a personal mission to push the career of Chappie James, who was then serving as the number three man in the Defense Department's public affairs division. Normally it is difficult for anyone to be promoted in such a noncommand position. But Laird felt James was so valuable to the military that the secretary made sure he was given his second star in 1972 and his third in 1973 (after Laird had resigned, but at his recommendation). Laird's influence on behalf of this protégé continued into the Ford administration, when Laird helped engineer James's appointment to commander of the North American Air Defense Command in Colorado, requiring a fourth star. Upon receiving the honor that made him the first black four-star in American history, James quoted his late mother: "My mother told me a long time ago that there are two Negroes we can do without: That *first* one and the *only* one; the *first* one to do this and the *only* one to do that. She said, 'I'm looking forward to the day when so many black people will be doing so many things that are noteworthy that it will no longer be newsworthy.'"[29]

When it came to insisting that American and foreign businesses deal with minority troops on an equal basis, the primary tool Laird used was the threat to cut them off. For example, an investigation of 4,100 West German establishments during Laird's term found 123 of them had discriminated against U.S. servicemen, 50 of them specifically against black servicemen. Laird declared 35 of the worst offenders—West German hotels, nightclubs, and restaurants—to be "off limits" to all U.S. troops, regardless of color, stationed in or traveling in West Germany.[30]

The problem was not confined to foreign postings. In the same month he was promoted to general, Chappie James was refused service in a bar in his hometown because he was black. (He had returned to Pensacola to accept an award from the Kiwanis Club as the "Man of the Year.") The bar was soon declared off limits to Defense Department personnel, which deprived the club of a major source of its revenue.[31] The same action was taken against apartment buildings that refused to rent to minority servicemen.[32]

Prior to the Nixon administration, a series of equal employment laws imposed nondiscrimination policies on any company that wanted to do business with the federal government. Laird looked for a case to show he was serious about enforcing those rules. He found it in early 1970 with the huge contract award for the air force's F-15 fighter. Notre Dame's president, the Reverend Theodore Hesburgh, was appointed by President Nixon in March 1969 to serve as the chairman of the U.S. Civil Rights Commission, and in January 1970 he learned that the contractor of the multibillion dollar F-15 fighter plane, McDonnell Douglas Corporation, was not following the rules. Father Hesburgh wrote to Laird that the Defense Department compliance office had not yet made the required inspection of McDonnell Douglas employment policies.[33] When Laird found out that Father Hesburgh had been right, he promised quick action.

Laird called Air Force Secretary Robert Seamans's office, but Seamans was at a Strategic Air Command (SAC) conference in Puerto Rico and Undersecretary John McLucas was in charge. Laird let McLucas know that Seamans better get to St. Louis and solve the problem *that very day.*[34] Seamans was enjoying a Caribbean respite at the conference, planning afterward to spend the weekend in the Virgin Islands with his wife and her mother, when he got the phone message. His undersecretary told him that Laird was threatening to re-bid the whole F-15 aircraft contract if the air force didn't handle this satisfactorily and promptly. Seamans ordered McLucas to handle it, but McLucas responded, "Mel insists *you* go to St. Louis *this afternoon.*"

Seamans was shaken. He informed the SAC commanders he had to be in St. Louis "in the shortest possible time." He recalled, "I was soon taken by SAC police, sirens screaming, to the flight line where a tanker was off-loading fuel as we approached." Seamans and aides clambered up a ladder into the nose of the tanker and by midafternoon arrived in St. Louis. Hearing in advance of Seamans's unusual unplanned flight, reporters from Washington had scrambled to St. Louis to meet him. His plane taxied onto the ramp at the McDonnell Douglas plant. Awaiting them were James McDonnell, the CEO of the company, and a bevy of journalists, including TV news crews. "After shaking hands all around, I vented my pique about the lack of an affirmative action plan, in front of the TV, and we then headed for the negotiation table," Seamans remembered. "The contract was appropriately amended in a few hours. Mel Laird was appeased, and I returned to Puerto Rico."[35]

Dramatically overshadowing equal opportunity was the racial tension that existed in the military. In the late 1960s and early 1970s, black and white soldiers jockeyed for position, chafed at integration, and often chose violence as a response. It was the war within the war, and Laird felt responsible to negotiate peace. In Vietnam the treatment of minorities was mixed. Out on patrol, when lives depended on cooperation, black and white soldiers found camaraderie fighting a collective enemy. But as more troops withdrew and the majority of the American force was no longer in combat, latent racial tension and resentment erupted sporadically, sometimes in murders known as "fragging," because of the use of the fragmentation grenade in some of the assaults. In West Germany, where racial tension was also at violent levels, a white noncommissioned officer confided anonymously to a reporter: "*Race* is my problem—not the Russians, not Vietnam, [not] maneuvers. I just worry about keeping my troops—black and white—from getting at one another."[36]

At various times during Laird's term, a variety of groups—his own civil rights experts, teams from the services, NAACP fact finders, and members of the Congressional Black Caucus—took the temperature of the armed forces worldwide and found trouble. For Secretary Laird the battle against racism was as complex and frustrating as it had been for America generally. As General James had pointed out in one speech, Laird made sure that "practicing bigots," especially among the officer corps, were educated or court-martialed out. At least a dozen officers, including an army captain who refused to shake hands with a fellow black officer, were discharged from the services.[37] Yet, for every racial issue Laird solved, two more cropped up to take its place. Laird figured that among the best solutions were increased communication and education. So he encouraged formation of "human relations" or "racial harmony" councils that would bring black activists in contact with white senior officers to air differences. He directed that a crash course in race relations and sensitivity become a standard part of basic training. He applauded "black festivals" put on by black soldiers, such as one at the Air Force Academy that introduced the predominantly white cadet corps to soul food, soul books, soul singers, and soul thought.[38]

And, together with Roger Kelley, Laird created the Defense Race Relations Institute at Patrick Air Force Base, Florida, to which thousands of equal opportunity officers were sent for training. In time, gender sensitivity was added to the training, and the institute became the "Defense Equal Opportunities Management Institute" and is still in operation.[39]

The history of women in the military reads less like a Cinderella story and more like a war of attrition. By posing as men, women first maneuvered their way into military service during the Revolutionary War. They were also present behind the scenes in the Civil War. Women did not officially join the armed forces until the turn of the century. The Army and Navy Nurse Corps were formed in 1901 and 1908 respectively. During World War I the number of women in uniform reached approximately thirty-six thousand. Servicewomen performed such tasks as fingerprinting, administration, and munitions work.[40] The Women's Army Auxiliary Corps was created in 1942 by Congress and President Roosevelt. (Its name was soon shortened to Women's Army Corps, or WAC). Women also served in the Army Air Forces, the forerunner of the U.S. Air Force.

After World War II the 1948 Armed Forces Integration Act granted both regular and reserve status to women in all four services, but with significant restrictions. One was an enlistment cap stipulating that women could make up only 2 percent of the total enlisted strength in each service. There was also a promotions cap at lieutenant colonel for the army and air force and commander for the navy. In 1967 President Johnson lifted many of those restrictions, but his administration paid lip service to the law. Jeanne Holm, a female pioneer in the air force, observed that Secretaries McNamara and Clifford didn't promote the cause of women in the armed forces. "It was almost as if we didn't exist," she said. "Women were then treated kind of as separated categories of people in the military, though that was typical of our society at the time."

That all changed when Laird came along. "I'll never forget the day he walked in as the new secretary of defense at the Pentagon," Holm, then a colonel, recalled. It was January 23, 1969, and many Pentagon civilians and uniformed employees had been invited to the fifth floor Pentagon auditorium to hear a welcoming address from President Nixon. But Holm's memory was of Laird. "Mel Laird came in there like he owned the place and like he just loved every bit of being with us. He was just wallowing in the event." She found this first impression was correct. "He went around the halls and met people, and he always remembered you."[41]

Like Holm, Laird remembered the day Nixon visited the Pentagon in January 1969. The new secretary recalled searching in vain for any women among the honor guards carrying flags and the ceremonial military bands on hand for the auspicious occasion. It was symptomatic of an exclusion of the gender that had to end, not only because it was unfair, but because Laird knew the all-volunteer force could only come into being if a significant number of women were attracted to join. That day would be the first time, but not the last, that Laird would express his disappointment to organizers of such events. Public affairs aide Jerry Friedheim said, "Mel would look around and say at some point during or after the ceremony to the officer in charge, 'You have this really nice-looking honor guard. They're wonderful young men; they're spit-and-polish; they're the very best. But you have some women in the navy, don't you? I didn't see any of them out there today at the ceremony. You know, I think the next time that you have a navy ceremony out here, I think I'm going to come down to the front door and look out, particularly at the honor guard, and if I don't see a woman in there, I may not come out the door. You wouldn't want me to do that, would you?'"[42]

Far more important to Laird than pushing for a smattering of women among the public relations–type units was the need to promote qualified woman to flag rank in the services. That was more difficult to accomplish because each service had its own promotion boards, which prized their independence. Civilians had, in effect, a veto power over promotion lists, which first went to Laird, then Nixon, and then Congress. At any point in the chain of command, the list could be sent back. But in practice that had happened only rarely, which meant the boards had come to believe that promotions were one area where the civilians would not meddle. Laird changed that.

At times, he used the same ploy he had used to advance blacks—refusing to accept a promotion list unless there was a woman on it. The requirement was not put in a memo, nor was it explicitly stated. Laird hoped to get there by implicit persuasion. When Navy Secretary John Warner handed him an all-male promotion list, Laird responded: "John, I'm not going to accept this, and you know why. It is incomplete. You haven't done your homework, so take this damn thing back."

The implicit method didn't always work, so there were times Laird had to issue explicit orders to the services in the form of deadlines to promote a certain number of women to specific ranks. The net result was the first-time promotion of women to flag rank in the three primary services. The first iceberg to move was the army. On June 11, 1970, Anna Mae Hays, director of the Army Nurse Corps, and Elizabeth Hoisington, director of the Women's Army Corps, became America's first female brigadier generals.[43] A year later Jeanne Holm became the first female brigadier general in the air force. Later, just before he left the Pentagon, Laird made sure Holm was promoted to major general, becoming the first female two-star.[44]

The conservative navy was not moving full speed ahead toward eliminating the gender barrier, so in 1972 Laird began applying pressure to John Warner. First, he repeatedly returned Warner's promotion list as incomplete. Then Laird began mentioning in every public speech, starting on March 22, that he fully intended to name the navy's first woman admiral before he left as secretary. Finally the admirals shook off the barnacles and nominated Captain Alene B. Duerk, chief of the Navy Nurse Corps, to rear admiral rank.[45]

The pace of change began to accelerate until the various services were subtly vying for firsts: first woman on a warship, first woman in a combat-ready cockpit, first woman in command of a major unit and so on. In August 1972 the navy announced it would begin sending women to sea on warships, a move many saw as a harbinger to women in combat. The air force answered a few days later with the announcement that it had become the first service to place a woman in command of a major unit composed of both men and women.[46] By the time Laird left office, there were seven female admirals and generals. On one of his last days on the job, Laird invited all of them to his office for a farewell coffee. By way of appreciation, they presented him with a framed group picture, on which was irreverently written: *The women Mel Laird made while he was at the Pentagon.*

⁂

Among Laird's most urgent problems was the rampant drug abuse among U.S. soldiers in Vietnam, who were demoralized by the unpopular war, far away from home, and in a country where drugs were cheap and readily available. The drugs flowed into South Vietnam from Cambodia along a supply line eerily similar to the Ho Chi Minh Trail. Because the drugs were so cheap on the streets, Laird suspected North Vietnam of subsidizing the market to hook American soldiers, and then funneling the money back to the Viet Cong.

Laird also suspected that Nguyen Van Thieu's government didn't care much about the drug problem. Laird knew that Ambassador Bunker had a secret list of Thieu's own government officials who were reputed to be narcotics traffickers.[47] So the frustrated Laird went public with a blunt accusation that Thieu and his government were "not doing enough" to cut off the drug flow into South Vietnam. He was the first senior U.S. official to make the charge.[48] The Thieu administration got the message and began a crackdown, tacitly admitting that drug abuse in Vietnam was no longer solely an American problem.

The American military drug problem reflected the growing civilian drug subculture. The majority of those using drugs in Vietnam had begun that use in the United States.[49] Contrary to popular belief, "the volunteers were twice as likely to abuse drugs as the draftees were, which was counter-intuitive," recalled Dr. Richard Wilbur, the former assistant secretary of defense for health whom Laird assigned to concentrate on the military drug problem. "You would have thought the draftees, having been dragged over there, would use the drugs."

Laird and those addressing the problem at the Pentagon were frustrated by the lack of reliable statistics regarding users in the ranks. After a preliminary congressional inquiry into the problem in early 1970, Senator Thomas Dodd concluded: "We find that up to 80 percent of our service personnel in Vietnam may be abusing drugs to one extent or another."[50] Contemporary press reports seemed to settle on a figure of more than 50 percent. Laird called these estimates "a gross exaggeration." He authorized issuance of a fact sheet disputing the notion that a majority of service men and women in Vietnam were drug abusers. "The unique environment of military life, characterized by close personal association...make[s] it altogether unlikely that any great number of persistent drug or marijuana users would go undetected for any protracted period of time." Nevertheless, "no military establishment, where security is always vitally critical and relies on the team concept, can risk having any member of the team mentally unbalanced, even if only for a moment, through the voluntary use of drugs."[51]

Laird initiated a massive urinalysis testing program for all troops leaving Vietnam, which the soldiers called "Operation Golden Flow." Laird felt that the military had a responsibility to find and treat its drug addicts before they were discharged. The program marked the first wide-scale drug testing ever undertaken by the U.S. government or even a civilian entity.[52] In a private note to President Nixon in May 1972, Laird said the Pentagon's pioneering urinalysis testing offered "hope for success in the civilian sector," also.[53]

The military urinalysis program was quickly expanded to test not just those leaving Vietnam, but all service personnel still there. Next it was moved to the troops in Europe, and then random testing was instituted. Another new aspect of the Laird drug-detection program was to offer amnesty from court-martial to those addicts who voluntarily came forward to accept treatment. The number of drug treatment centers run by the military and the Veterans Administration expanded rapidly. The Nixon administration, which was the first to declare a "war on drugs," is the only one to have authorized more money for education and treatment than for law enforcement.[54]

By mid-1972 the heroin crisis was well under control. "You did an outstanding job last year in responding to the heroin abuse crisis in Vietnam," Nixon told Laird in a May 3 memo. "You can rightly take pride in your success in creating an effective program to deter, detect, and treat military drug abuse."[55] Laird appreciated the note, but he was under no illusions. As he had dryly observed in a staff meeting the year before, the best way to handle the drug problem in Vietnam was to get the troops out of Vietnam.

35

Withdrawal Symptoms

━━◆━━

THE 173RD AIRBORNE BRIGADE, called the "Sky Soldiers," had been the first army line unit deployed to Vietnam. In August 1971 the unit finally packed up its gear and came home. During World War II, under General George S. Patton, this paratrooper unit had fought valiantly in the Battle of the Bulge and the Rhine River crossing. Vietnam action had added fourteen campaign streamers from more than six years of nearly continuous combat. The soldiers who came back alive from Vietnam knew they were not necessarily more skillful, nor more courageous, than their comrades who came home in body bags. They were simply luckier. More than 1,700 of the men of the 173rd died in Vietnam.

The prospect of personally greeting the returning brigade appealed to President Nixon, in part because the previous May, after he honored a marines unit returning from Vietnam, he had been unexpectedly hoisted up on the marines' shoulders before the Secret Service could stop them. CBS White House correspondent Dan Rather noted, "No one in his official entourage could remember the last time that Mr. Nixon was carried away joyously on anybody's shoulders."[1]

Laird thought Nixon should draw attention to other defense issues besides troop arrival ceremonies; Vietnam was winding down and Congress wanted to cut the defense budget. So Nixon went to Fort Bragg to observe a major airborne exercise, and Laird was the one to welcome home the 173rd at Fort Campbell, Kentucky, on September 2. The return en masse of the first army unit to go to Vietnam was major proof that American involvement in the war was ending. There were other signals throughout 1971, both large and small. For example, in a Fort Campbell press conference, Laird noted that when he first came into office, some twenty-seven million cases of soft drinks and "good Wisconsin beer" were being shipped annually to Vietnam, but that had dropped to a yearly rate of seven million cases.[2]

The year also saw the departure from Vietnam of the Fifth Special Forces Group, the First Cavalry Division (Airmobile), the Twenty-fifth Infantry Division, and the American Division. By the end of the year only one full U.S. division—the 101st Airborne—was still operating in Vietnam. All the "Jolly Green Giants" (HH-3 helicopters) had flown home, and the use of herbicides for anything except clearing military outposts of foliage had been terminated. Laird's promise had been that by July 1, 1971, the South Vietnamese would assume "all ground combat responsibilities."

In April Admiral Moorer had balked at the schedule. He thought it might not be possible to meet the deadline and that the changeover itself might be misunderstood. U.S. troops that were still in Vietnam to support the South would have to protect themselves and their equipment, and that meant daily patrols and possible brushes with the enemy. If those soldiers were sent out into the jungle after being told publicly that their "combat" duties were done, "severe leadership and morale problems could arise," Moorer wrote in a memo to Laird. He asked Laird to stop using the phrase "all ground combat responsibilities" and instead say that "primary responsibility for ground offensive combat operations" was passing to the South Vietnamese.[3] Laird readily agreed. The subtle semantics were lost on Americans at home who just wanted to know when their men and women would be out of harm's way.

For Laird the best news from the war in 1971 was that the American casualty rate was declining rapidly, from an average of about fifty a week in the early part of the year to fewer than ten a week by year's end. In one week in late December, only one American was killed[4]—and this compared to as many as five hundred dead in the weeks before Laird became secretary of defense. But in a September press conference Laird reiterated, "As I have always told all of you, I won't be satisfied until we get to zero American combat deaths in Vietnam."[5]

The departure of ground combat troops from Vietnam at the rate of twelve thousand a month in 1971 prompted Admiral Moorer to intensify his requests for more air strikes. On April 6 General Abrams joined Moorer in a request for at least ten thousand tactical air flights, or sorties, and one thousand B-52 sorties each month extending into 1973. "The maintenance of these sortie levels is essential to the progress of Vietnamization and vital to the orderly and secure redeployment of US Forces," Abrams wrote. "Anything less than this proposed sortie level significantly increases the risk in achieving US objectives in [South Vietnam]."[6] Moorer and Abrams found receptive ears at the White House, but not at the office of the secretary of defense.

Laird was not a booster of the air war and in fact had begun to suspect that the air force and navy were flying more missions than necessary just to preserve their funding for the air war and make it appear as though the high numbers were needed.[7] He was also skeptical about the success they claimed for the sorties they had. "I tried to stress with everyone that I was the last person who would shoot a messenger—I wanted the bad as well as the good. But every darn sortie seemed to be a great success." Laird recalled later that, while 60 to 70 percent air-strike effectiveness was being reported to him, a subsequent RAND study found it was less than 40 percent.

As the White House prepared to approve Moorer's request for increased air sorties, Laird weighed in with several critical points that revolved around expected congressional opposition. "As far as Congress is concerned, support for our air operations is the lowest it has ever been," he wrote Kissinger in May. Laird offered an example of why Congress would balk. Two months before, in March, with the B-52s alone, "we dropped more than 23,000 tons of ordnance in a 20 x 30 mile area of South Laos. That equates to more tonnage . . . than the less-than-20 kiloton impact on Hiroshima in 1945."[8] He knew that those kinds of numbers would set Congress off. Indeed, the following November Laird told his staff to "stay away from precise tonnage figures" because "they are large in relative and absolute terms." Then he dropped an incredible, secret statistic: "Probably more than six million tons have been dropped in all of Southeast Asia during this war, which is roughly three times the amount dropped by the U.S. in all theaters during all of World War II."[9] And the war was not over yet.

Laird's objections fell on deaf ears at the White House. Nixon was a big fan of air power, and in early August 1971 he approved the sortie levels Abrams and Moorer wanted.[10] Laird told the military chiefs now that they had gotten what they asked for they were going to have to eat the increased costs from the current budget—which his staff estimated to be as high as $720 million.[11] The cost will have to "come out of your hides," he wrote the Joint Chiefs in a memo.[12]

As 1971 progressed, the chiefs pressed for an expansion of their target list to include North Vietnamese surface-to-air missile sites and MiG fighters striking below the twentieth parallel. Admiral Moorer related in one staff meeting that "the North Vietnamese have deployed the heaviest anti-aircraft defense against us so far in the war."[13] So they pushed Laird hard for authority to hit off-limits targets in North Vietnam itself. Typical of the dance between Laird and Moorer on this subject was an exchange in late February and early March of 1971. Moorer had asked for permission to hit SAM sites in North Vietnam, in the name of "protective reaction"—the term Laird had used in 1969 when authorizing cross-border raids into Cambodia. He didn't do it often, but this time Laird passed the request on to Nixon with this warning: "I feel that there is military value to this proposal. . . . On the other hand, from a political point of view, I believe that this is not the proper time for such action by the U.S. government."[14]

Nixon approved the request, and on March 6 Laird informed Moorer that U.S. planes could make a one-day strike against the SAM sites. Laird's language was testy. He reminded Moorer that in 1969 and 1970 he had approved general operating orders for air strikes in North Vietnam when needed under very limited conditions, and he wanted to know why those orders weren't adequate. Laird tried to give Moorer a lesson in political versus military reality. "If we continue strikes into North Vietnam, particularly on a frequent basis, we encounter certain risks. On the one hand, unless we strike repeatedly and on a sustained basis, we risk not achieving any substantial durable military benefits. . . . On the other hand, if we do strike repeatedly and with enough frequency to have any significant or long-term military value, we will have clearly abrogated the November 1968 bombing-halt understandings. As you appreciate, there are military ramifications to such actions, as well as impacts that transcend the military."[15]

Laird was not willing to nickel-and-dime his way around the bombing ban, nor was he ready to ignore it completely. As much as it was violated, it still had the effect of keeping the North from building up troops in the demilitarized zone. That was the deal Hanoi had made when President Johnson had halted the bombing.

Moorer's response bristled with sarcasm. He expressed "regret" that Laird was under the impression that the old operating orders should be adequate, because they never were. And he said he agreed with Laird that anything less than sustained strikes against the SAM sites could be a waste of time. Had his pilots been given freer rein over the North all along, things would have been different, Moorer said. As it was, they were hamstrung by decisions made in Washington instead of in the field. "[I]t is imperative that this strike authority be held by the field commander rather than requiring him to process a time-consuming request to higher authority," Moorer wrote. It was his oft-repeated refrain, but Laird was not about to grant that authority.[16]

Laird's files are replete with such correspondence between himself and Moorer. Sometimes Laird said yes to the strikes, sometimes he said no. "I just don't understand their request," he puzzled in one Vietnam Task Force meeting in July, 1971. "I don't see why the Joint Chiefs are suggesting increased bombing and use of the B-52s in North Vietnam at this point in time. It's just an impossible thing to do, given the current low level of combat activity, and the political situation here."[17] Laird consistently refused to transfer blanket authority to the field.

In the fall of 1971 North Vietnamese MiGs intensified their harassment of American bombers and fighters headed for missions over Laos. Hanoi was pressing its advantage along the DMZ, sensing that the United States was hobbled by the top-down chain of command for bombing and by the 1968 bombing halt. They were partly right. In late October Moorer asked Laird for permission to blow up a North Vietnamese airfield from which many of the MiGs took off, but Laird turned him down. Three weeks later, Moorer came back with another plan to hit the same airfield, and Laird said no again. Finally, after a near miss between a MiG and a B-52 over Laos on November 30, Moorer asked again,[18] and Laird took a harder look. Moorer's request was ambitious. Instead of a one-time strike against the offending airfield as first proposed, Moorer wanted at least forty-eight hours of sustained strikes against several targets in North Vietnam.

Two days after making the request, while Laird was still considering it, Moorer stormed into Laird's office clutching a cable that he wanted to send to Saigon. A jittery air force general in the field, without consulting Washington, had halted all B-52 raids over Laos in reaction to the MiG attacks. Laird wasn't in the office, but David Packard told Moorer to send the cable immediately, ordering the resumption of bombing. The loss of a B-52 would be terrible, Moorer acknowledged in the cable, "[h]owever, a precipitous termination of B-52 operations in this vital interdiction area also has considerable military and political significance. Consequently, it would have been helpful at the Washington level if the JCS could have had some prior warning that you contemplated such unilateral action."[19]

Moorer's frustration, and that of the pilots, fairly shouts between the lines of memos that made their way around the Pentagon that December as the MiG activity heightened. "Protective reaction" attacks on the MiGs were allowed, but the American pilots who were fired on had to get permission before shooting back, and delays frequently hampered their hot pursuit. On December 3 MiG radar locked on four F-4 fighters escorting B-52s on a bombing raid over Laos. The fighter pilots received permission to defend themselves, but within minutes permission was rescinded because the hot pursuit was taking the F-4s too far into North Vietnam. Chief of Naval Operations Elmo Zumwalt described the on-again-off-again dogfight to Packard in a memo the next day. Packard scribbled a note and clipped it to the memo, apparently reflecting a conversation with Moorer: "Tom Moorer. Why don't we let these fellows shoot?"[20]

Why, indeed? Because Lyndon Johnson had set the rules in November 1968 by ending bombing missions over the North in exchange for certain expectations of good behavior from the enemy. It was a deal that Hanoi never acknowledged but that Washington had tried to honor. On December 9, 1971, Laird decided it was time to bend the rules. On that day he sent a memo to Nixon proposing the first sustained bombing raids over North Vietnam since 1968. Laird offered Moorer's suggestion for a forty-eight-hour campaign, code-named "Proud Deep," against four enemy airfields and other targets. "It would have the best chance among the options available to signal our concern caused by their violating the bombing halt understandings and possibly to deter further MiG aggressiveness," Laird wrote.[21] Nixon agreed, and on December 19, one day after MiGs shot down four U.S. fighter-bombers over Laos, Moorer sent the cable to Admiral McCain in Hawaii authorizing the execution of Proud Deep. It was to begin as soon as possible and end before the already-planned Christmas cease fire.[22]

Bad weather moved in, pushing off the operation until after the Christmas truce (which the enemy violated at least nineteen times in twenty-four hours).[23] Finally, as midnight approached in Washington on December 25, B-52s took off in Southeast Asia to begin the pounding of North Vietnam. The original forty-eight-hour mission was extended until December 30 when, after nearly eight hundred bombing runs over the targets, Moorer cabled McCain to terminate Proud Deep. The mission cost Nixon in heavy criticism at home, most of it from the Democrats who were shaping up to oppose his second run for the presidency. But Nixon saw it as a setback he could overcome before the election. His five-day display of air power that December was designed to show Hanoi that the air war could go on even as American foot soldiers withdrew.

～

Throughout 1971 the prospect of a one-candidate election in South Vietnam threatened the progress of Vietnamization. President Nguyen Van Thieu had taken office in 1967 with the support of only 35 percent of the voters. He wanted a clear mandate for the second election and wasn't above bending the rules to get it. After Laird's trip to Saigon in January, he advised President Nixon that it was in the United States' best interest to have Thieu remain in office. On that trip Laird had met with the only other likely candidates: Vice President Nguyen Cao Ky and General Duong Van Minh (known as "Big Minh"). Laird concluded that Thieu was better qualified to carry out his program of Vietnamization. Laird suggested that the Nixon administration should do all it could, quietly, to support Thieu. "I recommend an explicit but discreet program to support Thieu's re-election," Laird wrote the president, while "assiduously avoiding public or official intervention in the South Vietnamese election process."

That translated to "sensitivity" about election day when choosing the timing and numbers of U.S. troop withdrawals, helping to stabilize the South Vietnamese economy, and putting out the word that the Thieu regime was cooperating in the Paris peace talks. Laird suspected that Thieu himself had little interest in the Paris talks. When Laird visited Paris on the way to Saigon in January, he learned that Thieu's representatives at those talks got little or no guidance from Saigon. "They rely for preparation, mainly on the U.S. team in Paris," Laird reported to Nixon. "When I mentioned to President Thieu that I had met with his representatives in Paris, he showed little interest."[24]

It was pivotal for the American involvement in the war that South Vietnam have a fair, multicandidate election. As early as February Laird personally reminded Thieu that the world needed to see an open and fair process in a country that was supposed to be championing democracy over Communism. In April Laird's nervousness was compounded when some members of Congress began threatening to cut off all funding to Vietnam if it looked like the Nixon administration was trying to pull a fast one in the election.

In retrospect, Thieu's reelection was all but guaranteed five months before the May vote as a result of his wily legal maneuvering and the CIA's substantial political war chest, which was made available to Thieu. The CIA bankrolled him to the tune of millions of dollars, which he carefully dispensed to ensure political support across the spectrum. It assisted him in privately receiving promises of endorsements from the majority in both houses of the South Vietnam National Assembly and from most of the provincial councilmen. Once he had those pledges in his pocket, Thieu shrewdly proposed a new election law saying presidential candidates had to "qualify" to run by obtaining the endorsements of at least forty of the national legislators or one hundred of the provincial chiefs. After some bribery of National Assembly legislators by the CIA, the law was passed in early June.[25]

General Minh could secure enough endorsements to qualify, but he was not a serious threat to Thieu's reelection. Under Thieu's crafty plan, the candidate who was the greatest threat, Vice President Ky, would find it hard to qualify under the new law. "Present estimates are that only President Thieu and Gen. Minh can receive the necessary endorsements," the Pentagon's International Security Affairs chief, Warren Nutter, reported to Laird at an early June staff meeting. "This may mean that Vice President Ky cannot run for President." And since Minh wasn't happy with Thieu's control of the election, he might drop out. "The presidential candidacy may turn out to be a one-man race."[26]

Two weeks later Nutter told Laird that, unexpectedly, Ky had been able to obtain seventy-one of the necessary one hundred provincial councilor endorsements, according to U.S. intelligence. And, in the corrupt South Vietnamese political world, it had only reportedly cost Ky "$3[,000] to $4,000 a head" for the endorsements, Nutter added. By mid-July Nutter was back to tell Laird that Ky had privately confided he had 147 provincial endorsements, which was "considerably more than the 100 required. Some of these endorsements, however, are suspect," Nutter cautioned.[27]

In the midst of this, Kissinger arrived in Saigon. He met with the opposition candidates as well as Thieu on July 5, 1971. What he told Thieu is still in dispute, but it is likely he gave an iron-clad guarantee that Thieu would be reelected with full covert support even though, publicly, American officials might complain about the way Thieu was conducting the elections. "Henry insisted that he did not do that," Laird said. But at the time Laird was suspicious of just what representations the wily Kissinger had made to Thieu. On July 30, at a meeting of his Vietnam Task Force, Laird did everything but call Kissinger a meddler in the election. "Is the Senior Review Group [run by Kissinger]—or anyone—following this political situation carefully?" Laird asked his staff. If American troops were losing their lives to keep South Vietnam free, then fair elections were a linchpin of the American-supported war effort. "We have to make sure we don't have a disastrous one-man race in these elections, as it could have very serious implications for U.S. policy in Southeast Asia."[28]

On August 4, after Vice President Ky had submitted 102 provincial endorsements (two more than he needed to qualify as a candidate), President Thieu pulled the rug out from under Ky. Forty of those names had secretly signed endorsements for Thieu before Ky approached them. In fact, Thieu had bagged 452 of the 500-plus provincial leaders, making it impossible for anyone else to get on the ballot. The South Vietnamese supreme court dutifully disqualified Ky from running in the race.

U.S. Ambassador Ellsworth Bunker was steaming in Saigon; there appeared to be no way to change the perception (and the reality) that the U.S.-backed candidate had fixed the election. Bunker flew back to Washington and visited Laird and his Vietnam Task Force at the Pentagon on August 10 to report on his efforts to influence Thieu. "He made it impossible for Ky to qualify," Bunker confirmed to Laird. "The only possibility now is that Thieu give up enough of his endorsements to allow Ky to use them." Bunker said he had pressed Thieu to do just that, "to let Ky run. But President Thieu won't do it. He feels very strongly about this matter. He is still smarting from only getting 35 percent of the vote in the last election. He wants a clear mandate, a clear majority, this time." Bunker said he had warned Thieu that he was "taking a very great risk" in not letting Ky run, that "if Minh should pull out of the race and it became a one-man race, there is a great danger the U.S. Congress will no longer support the war and provide South Vietnam the resources it needs." Thieu wouldn't budge, according to Bunker, but had reassured the ambassador that Minh would stay in the race.

Laird interrupted his briefing to ask the ambassador, "Is there anything we can do to help keep Minh in the race?"

"We are trying to encourage him, but there is not really much we can do," Bunker lamented.[29] Bunker did not mention then that he might use CIA funds to bribe Minh to stay in the race. After Bunker got back to Saigon, he met with the wavering Minh on August 19 and told him that the United States would financially back his candidacy. Though Bunker later denied that he had proffered the money, one of Minh's aides leaked the "offer" to the South Vietnamese press. A former top CIA official in Saigon, Frank Snepp, disclosed in his memoirs that it had a $3 million price tag, but it wasn't enough.[30] Minh dropped out of the race the next day.

Bunker switched his efforts back to Thieu, pressuring him to let Ky run. Finally confident that he couldn't lose reelection, Thieu pulled some strings and the South Vietnamese supreme court reinstated Ky as a candidate the day after Minh dropped out. Pentagon foreign policy chief Nutter reported to Laird two days after, on August 23, that "pressure now is on Thieu *and* Ky to run for the good of the country. If there are not at least two candidates, the U.S., which has been trying to ensure a representative democracy in South Vietnam, will be placed in a bad position with their continued support of the government."[31] That very day, however, Ky withdrew from the election, leaving Thieu the lone contender, and painfully mimicking the Communist-run Kremlin elections, where every Soviet citizen had a right to vote but only one candidate was on the ballot.

Laird was livid. At the Vietnam Task Force meeting he asked his staff to come up with a paper detailing ways the United States could ensure a multi-candidate, fair election in South Vietnam. Nutter was as chagrined as his boss. There had been "no systematic review of the situation within the U.S. government. I don't understand why there hasn't been a Senior Review Group meeting on a subject as important as this!" Though Kissinger ran that group and determined the subjects, Nutter tactfully did not blame Kissinger in the meeting. Two days later Laird learned that his international experts had come up with options that could delay the election until opponents could be found. But "[a]s far as we can see, we don't have any attractive options."[32]

In September, with less than a month to go before the election, Democratic Senator Henry "Scoop" Jackson, who had once been such a supporter of the Nixon Vietnam policy that he was considered for the post of defense secretary, accused Nixon of trying to sabotage the election. He said Bunker had covertly spread the impression in Saigon that Thieu was the man the United States wanted as president and that the administration had allowed Thieu to chase off the competition. Laird looked into the events that had led to this sorry situation and found Kissinger at the core. Always cautious, Laird barely tipped his hand about this knowledge in a Vietnam Task Force meeting. "[Laird] had read a recent memo that someone had provided him on the political situation indicating that Dr. Kissinger's [July] trip may have contributed to the confusion and Thieu's attitude on the election," according to the minutes.[33]

Thieu won the October 3, 1971, election with 94.3 percent of the vote. The embarrassment of the landslide was compounded by his government's dubious claim that 88 percent of Vietnam's 7.2 million registered voters were civic-minded enough to turn out for an uncontested election.[34] The message to Americans was that they were spilling their own blood to keep the Communists out of a "democratic" nation that couldn't even mount a fair election, and whose leader behaved more like a banana republic dictator.

In public Laird plied the U.S. government line: while he had hoped for a race with more than one candidate, America could not dictate to South Vietnam. The United States cannot be "the political policeman of the world" and cannot force other nations to choose their governments in an American manner.[35] In private, Laird felt the election had been a serious blow to Vietnamization. And there was no way he would sit next to Thieu at his October 31 inauguration. So when the White House tried to push him to represent the administration there, he openly squelched it at a mid-October Cabinet meeting. "I am not going to go," he emphatically stated at the meeting. (Treasury Secretary John Connally went instead.)[36]

As U.S. troops turned the reins over to South Vietnam, Laird became increasingly concerned about the will of the South Vietnamese to fight. He lectured at the June 21 staff meeting: "The North Vietnamese either have to fight or be killed. There is no return for them. The South Vietnamese soldier has a choice of fighting or going home. These two sets of choices make the leadership and motivation of the South Vietnamese very important."[37] Two days later, he wrote

a memo to Moorer ordering a substantive review of South Vietnamese leadership—including a listing of the seventy-five best and seventy-five worst South
Vietnamese commanders. "In many cases, the reason for poor performance
has been poor morale and leadership, not insufficient equipment or [U.S.]
support."[38] The Joint Chiefs and General Abrams responded in November that
"only one senior [South Vietnamese] military commander needs changing."[39]

Dan Henkin carefully tracked the behavior of the Saigon-based U.S. media
and predicted increasingly negative news reports—even as Laird was doing
exactly what the majority of the American public wanted, bringing the boys
home. "Vietnam continues to be of lesser interest" to the better correspondents, Henkin said at a September staff meeting, noting that the number of
correspondents had dropped from 450 to 335 and would continue to decrease
rapidly.[40] Observing the replacement of first-string journalists by second- and
third-stringers, Henkin concluded at a November meeting that, "as far as the
present stories coming out of Vietnam, we have not the best talent assigned to
the area to begin with and it is getting worse."[41]

Another trend Laird detected in 1971 as the war wound down was the increasing number of official visitors who wanted to go to Vietnam. They were
taking up too much of General Abrams's time and taxing his ability to protect
them. When Senator George McGovern arrived in September, he had given
the State Department only two days' notice. He declined any official briefings,
opting to look independent of the Nixon war machine. (At the time he was the
only announced Democratic presidential candidate for the 1972 race.) Once in
Saigon, McGovern also turned down military security, which led to a terrifying
incident. Outside a meeting in a Catholic school with South Vietnamese antiwar leaders, a mob quickly gathered and erupted into violence. McGovern was
trapped for twenty minutes inside as the mob threw firebombs and stones at
the building and burned vehicles. American military police and U.S. embassy
security had to ride to his rescue.[42]

Laird declared after the McGovern mishap that all official visits to Vietnam
must be cleared with the Pentagon's International Security Affairs division. He
remained tough on that point. In an early October Vietnam Task Force meeting, he angrily reported that he had learned via "a back-channel message" that
Westmoreland, still the army chief of staff, was planning a late October visit
just before Laird's own scheduled visit to Saigon. "I thought I made it clear
that I wanted no one to visit Vietnam during the weeks before my visit or
after," Laird reiterated. The ISA lamely noted that they knew nothing about it
because Westmoreland hadn't cleared it with them, so Laird "turned that trip
off myself."[43]

A few days later the State Department approved a Vietnam visit for former
Joint Chiefs chairman General Maxwell Taylor, who had served as ambassador
to South Vietnam for two years. Laird canceled it over the "strong opposition" of the State Department, and he had to talk to President Nixon to do

it. Nixon believed Laird's logic that any other officials visiting Vietnam in the October-November time period would dilute the president's upcoming troop withdrawal and Vietnamization message.[44]

❧

Soon after President Thieu's reelection and inauguration, Laird made his fourth and final trip to Vietnam, leaving on November 2, 1971. Just before boarding his plane at Andrews Air Force Base outside Washington, Laird reminded the press corps of his first visit in March of 1969 when there were more than half a million Americans fighting in Vietnam. Now the number was 196,000 and dropping.

Laird had come directly from the White House where he and the president had discussed how many more troops would be brought out in the tenth withdrawal phase, the details of which Nixon was supposed to announce in mid-November. Laird told Nixon that he would like to speed up the rate of withdrawals to at least eighteen thousand a month, with a goal of having only sixty thousand Americans in Vietnam by June of 1972. In late August he also instructed the reluctant Joint Chiefs to plan on that as the bottom line.[45]

Previously Nixon had agonized over the figures, but this time it was different. He didn't tell Laird before the trip, but the president was aiming for an even higher figure than Laird wanted. Nixon's interest in having more troops on the homebound planes was growing in direct proportion to the proximity of the 1972 presidential election. Laird had expected that would happen. "I knew that from the day I became secretary of defense," he said. "Early on I had to put the pressure on, but the last two years, the president was all for it. The first two years he was a little reluctant because Kissinger was always telling him, 'Don't withdraw until we get an agreement [in the Paris peace talks].' My position was, we'll never get an agreement." Laird thought Kissinger's reluctance about troop withdrawals was fueled in part by his military assistant Al Haig. "Haig had no political feel for anything," said Laird.

The North Vietnamese must have become wary of Laird's trips to Saigon, because those trips usually coincided with increased American bombing. In January 1971 Laird's trip had been a precursor of the South Vietnamese invasion of Laos and the raining of hundreds of thousands of tons of bombs on the Ho Chi Minh Trail. The December trip was no exception. U.S. bombers opened a new campaign against the trail in Laos, but Laird claimed the timing was mere coincidence.

His first job in Saigon was to calm the nervous Thieu, who quizzed him about a recent vote in Congress to kill Nixon's 1972 foreign aid bill, which included $549 million in economic assistance for South Vietnam. Laird assured him it was just politics and that a package would inevitably be approved. Privately Laird thought the foreign aid scare was good medicine for Thieu, who needed to get the message that it was time for his country to become less dependent on U.S. help and more attentive to its own economic growth.[46]

After a morning meeting and lunch at Thieu's Independence Palace, Laird and Thieu each dismissed their entourage and sat down for a private talk. Burned by past news leaks from these meetings, Laird didn't tell Thieu specifically how large the next troop withdrawal might be, but he warned Thieu to expect that no more than sixty thousand American soldiers would remain in Vietnam by mid-1972. Thieu surprised Laird by hypothesizing a withdrawal rate of nineteen thousand a month, "and did not seem bothered by such a prospect," Laird's notes of the conversation recorded. "He seemed either to miss the point that such a U.S. redeployment rate would see all U.S. forces gone in less than ten months or to accept the premise that militarily, such a rate was acceptable."[47]

Laird spent four days in South Vietnam, much of it in the company of General Abrams, who was optimistic about the progress of Vietnamization. "I think actually we may have *hoped* they would step up to the plate the way they have," he told Laird, "but there certainly wasn't anybody that could guarantee it. But I think the truth of the matter is the Vietnamese have stepped to the plate."[48]

Laird left Saigon bound for Honolulu, where he spent the weekend composing his report to Nixon. These Hawaii stopovers had become welcome respites for Laird between the war zone in Vietnam and the political battles back in Washington. This time the memo to Nixon was carefully crafted to keep the president on the fast track to total withdrawal. "The view of U.S. civilian and military leaders in Vietnam and of the [South Vietnamese] leadership is that we now have and can maintain sufficient military strength to preclude the enemy from achieving any kind of military verdict in South Vietnam," Laird wrote. "The United States can continue its force redeployments. In fact, the redeployments can safely be accelerated."

Laird buttressed his optimism with statistics: Nixon had brought home nearly 360,000 troops, American combat deaths were less than 10 percent of what they were in Johnson's last year in office, the Vietnamese economy was more stable, the cost of the war in 1971 dollars had dropped from $25 billion to $8 billion during the Nixon term, and tactical bombing flights were down from thirty-five thousand a month at the height of the Johnson years to six thousand a month. (Acutely aware of Nixon's fondness for air power, Laird noted, "We are maintaining, of course, the capability to fly sorties at higher rates, as you have specified.")

Laird never liked body counts as a way of gauging the success of the war, but he couldn't pass up the chance to tell Nixon that enemy combat deaths were running at about a hundred thousand a year. For a country the size of North Vietnam, that was the equivalent of the United States losing a million men a year. The willingness of Hanoi to sacrifice men in such astounding numbers meant that even though a big enemy offensive was unwise in the coming year, Hanoi might try one anyway, in an attempt to show that Vietnamization was not working. "If Hanoi is willing to pay a frightful price in manpower, there is little that can be done to prevent such an action." Nevertheless, neither Abrams nor Thieu felt Hanoi "can now make a move that is decisive in a military sense," Laird wrote.

Laird's report concluded with three options for the next withdrawal phase: 12,500 a month, which was the Joint Chiefs' preference; 18,000 a month, which was Laird's preference; and 25,000 a month, which neither wanted.[49] On November 12, two days after receiving Laird's options, Nixon announced his own plan, a hybrid of Laird's three. He said 45,000 more Americans would be called home in December and January, a rate of 22,500 a month. Unlike past announcements, which had been made in televised speeches, Nixon made this one without warning at a press conference. Thus Nixon could take credit for a big drawdown without the drum roll and flourishes that gave Hanoi an excuse for grandstanding at the peace talks.

Americans were getting wise to Nixon's reelection agenda, and the following Sunday on NBC's *Meet the Press* Laird was asked to make the connection between the pace of withdrawals and the coming election. First, the reporters on the panel wanted to know what would happen after January 1972, the end of the withdrawal phase announced by Nixon. Laird never allowed himself to be drawn into speculation about the numbers; that would have riled the president. But, he said, "I will make the prediction that the war in Vietnam and America's involvement in that war will not be the big political issue so far as the campaign is concerned in 1972. . . . The issue of peace and the fact that we have been able to bring 450,000 American service personnel out of Asia already will be a great plus for the President in the political campaign." Then Laird quickly added, "This was not done on the basis of politics."

Robert Goralski of NBC saw an opening: "It does strike many as perhaps a remarkable coincidence that perhaps the troop withdrawal timetable will reach a denouement just about the time that Americans are considering who to vote for for President next year. Are you saying that domestic politics have nothing to do with the withdrawal timetable from Vietnam?"

"That is correct," said Laird, for whom domestic politics was reason enough to bring the military home. He went on to explain that the timetable was always based on how prepared the South Vietnamese were to assume the war themselves. It was also true that American politics—the right of the people to govern themselves—was the impetus behind Vietnamization. The American people had said "no more" to the war, and Laird was honoring that choice. The fact that it would take a full four-year presidential cycle to do it had not been Laird's preference.[50]

The next day Laird sent orders to Moorer to keep a tight lid on speculation about any troop withdrawal numbers after January. But for planning purposes, Laird said, "[Y]ou are authorized to look towards a U.S. force goal in the Republic of Vietnam of 60,000 by 30 June 1972." Moorer wanted off the roller coaster of shifting monthly withdrawal mandates from the president. On December 30 he wrote to Laird asking for a bit more flexibility in the next round. General Abrams and Admiral McCain had both complained that the short-term announcements "could generate severe problems in personnel turbulence, logistics, base closures and force structuring." If 60,000 was the bottom line for June, then Moorer hoped the president would announce that and give the chiefs six months to get there at a monthly pace of their own choosing, based on the needs in the field.[51] It was a reminder that getting out of a war of this size was not just a matter of loading up the troops and flying them home, as some in Congress assumed. It was a delicate dance that involved the safety of the remaining troops and the interplay of their various responsibilities for keeping one another alive.

~∞~

The year ended with a touch of sadness for Laird. His right-hand man, David Packard, resigned as expected to go back to his company, Hewlett-Packard. "I cannot convey adequately my appreciation for the job he has done in the last 35 months," Laird told the staff. "His honesty, candor and hard work are legendary. In every area Secretary Packard has touched, his good influence was felt, and he touched just about every area."[52] At the morning press conference that followed the staff meeting, Packard offered a sincere ode to Laird. "I did not really know Mel Laird when I came out here three years ago, but I do know him now." He called him "a great Secretary of Defense with fine administrative ability combined with a great compassion for people. I also know him as one of the great politicians on the contemporary scene. And I know him also as a very good friend." Packard said he could "recall no major issue in which he and I have had a fundamental disagreement. In fact, I guess, Mel, I can think of hardly any minor ones either."[53]

Packard pledged to "do whatever I can to help the President win the election next year." But the Laird-Packard team had already been instrumental in securing Nixon's reelection. Thanks to Laird's persistence, by the time Americans went to the polls one year later, Vietnam was barely a campaign issue for Nixon. Even at the end of 1971 it was slipping from the top of the national priority list. A Gallup poll in mid-December found only 15 percent of Americans felt that the war was the biggest problem facing the nation. Their bigger worry was the economy.[54] But Laird still had 139,000 American soldiers to bring home.

36

Drafting the Volunteer Army

❦

IN EARLY 1971 Felix Edward Hebert of Louisiana was one man standing in the way of Mel Laird's plan to abolish the draft. The chairman of the House Armed Services Committee, Hebert had been an eccentric fixture in Congress for thirty years. His office was the most ornate and garish, including a fountain that one constituent mistook for a urinal. Just off the main office were two private rooms: one he called the "Adult Room," with a bar and pictures of naked ladies; the other he called the "Adultery Room," with a TV and a couch. Hebert (pronounced "a-bear") never left the office without a phalanx of staffers, much like a military general on a march. Some joked that bunching up aides on both sides kept him walking straight, since a boyhood friend had accidentally shot one of his eyes with a .22 caliber rifle and the other eye was clouded by a cataract.

Hebert was notorious for getting his way in his committee. Once, a Laird legislative aide, George Dalferes, made the mistake of asking Hebert if he had secured the support of other committee members for a defense bill. Hebert replied, "I *told* you I'd take care of it, you dumb shit!" Hebert would be "the last of titans" (which he titled his autobiography)—a committee chairman with absolute control of the members.[1]

Laird wasn't overly concerned about Hebert as chairman of the committee. They were friends, and, as fate would have it, the Laird family had spent the Christmas 1970 holiday in New Orleans as a favor to Hebert, who wanted Laird to attend the Sugar Bowl and ride in the parade. In Hebert's view, Laird was a fresh breeze after the stagnant era of Robert McNamara. "Laird will go down as one of the greatest secretaries of defense," Hebert opined in 1972, in part because Laird knew and allowed for the "shortcomings and foibles" of Congress and dealt in a straightforward manner with its members.[2]

But Hebert and Laird had one serious disagreement. Laird was deeply committed to the creation of an all-volunteer military force (AVF). Hebert was a staunch opponent—he thought it was unrealistic and impractical—so he was focused instead on the continuation of presidential draft authority, which was due to expire in mid-1971. Hebert's first Armed Services Committee hearing after becoming chairman was scheduled for February 23, 1971, with Secretary Laird as the first witness on the subject of extending the draft. The night before the hearing, Dan Henkin ran into Hebert at a social affair and later wrote a note to Laird about the encounter. "He told me he has a new line: 'The only way you are going to get an all-volunteer Army in this country is to draft one!' I would guess he can hardly wait to get that one on the public record."[3]

When the hearing opened, Hebert wasted no time getting to his punch line. He read his opening statement, occasionally peering at Laird through the special glass lens over his one good eye: "Members of the Committee are aware that I have publicly stated I have grave reservations about the feasibility of an all-volunteer Army. In our present situation *I think the only way to get an all-volunteer Army is to draft it.*" Hebert paused with a smile as reporters scribbled the quip. The chairman added that, while debate over the all-volunteer force would certainly occur, the point of the hearings was not to create such a force but, instead, to extend the draft, enact some draft reform, and grant the currently serving servicemen and -women a long-overdue pay raise.

Laird had no problem with that because Hebert's stated goals inherently helped Laird's cause. He needed two more years of draft authority to overcome all opponents and obstacles and create the all-volunteer force. He also desperately needed a large military pay raise and other incentives to make the military attractive enough so the volunteers would come. "What you are considering today, Mr. Chairman, is a legislative proposal of the highest importance," Laird testified that day. "People—not arms or equipment, not buildings or computers, not any of the hardware requirements of defense—are the priceless vital asset of our national defense. People are the most important asset in our national security planning."[4]

The great draft debate of 1971 was more than a year overdue. It was supposed to have been argued and settled in 1970 on the heels of the final report of the President's Commission on an All-Volunteer Armed Force, called the "Gates Commission" for its chairman, former defense secretary Thomas Gates. The commission began its work in the spring of 1969, and its tenure was marked by combative hearings. The Joint Chiefs were invited to testify and did so energetically. None of the chiefs was as vigorously pro-AVF as their boss, Defense Secretary Laird. One of them, Westmoreland, was vehemently opposed and did not disguise his disagreement with Laird. At a private commission hearing, which Laird was not invited to attend, Westmoreland declared that he personally would not command an all-volunteer army because the presumably well-paid men would be nothing more than an "army of mercenaries." Commission member Milton Friedman angrily interrupted, "General, are you saying you would rather command an army of slaves?"

Westmoreland took umbrage. "I don't like to hear our patriotic draftees referred to as slaves."

"I don't like to hear our patriotic volunteers referred to as mercenaries," Friedman countered.[5]

It was the last time Westmoreland dared call a future all-volunteer force a "mercenary" one, but the army did not back off its opposition to Laird's proposed all-volunteer force. When he was questioned at a January 1970 commission dinner, Army Secretary Stan Resor admitted that he personally, and the army generally, didn't like the idea of an all-volunteer force. They wanted to keep the draft, partly because they thought it ensured an army drawn from all economic strata of society as opposed to the poor and middle class only. An air force official at the dinner immediately disagreed and pointed out that Resor well knew that sons of affluent families had avoided the draft, so the army was hardly a melting pot.[6]

As Laird had hoped, Friedman became the strongest voice on the committee. After ten months of work, Nixon received a 211-page report from the commission on February 21, 1970. The members had unanimously agreed that "the nation's interests will be better served by an all-volunteer force, supported by an effective standby draft, than by a mixed force of volunteers and conscripts; that steps should be taken promptly to move in this direction; and that the first indispensable step is to remove the present inequity in the pay of men serving their first term in the armed forces."[7]

While applauding the commission's general conclusions, Laird was disturbed that it had called for the draft to end when the current authority expired in mid-1971. He needed at least sixteen more months to create such a force before giving up the draft, and he needed Congress to give him that extension. It was a frustrating time for Laird, who had to praise the overall conclusions of the Gates Commission but take issue with the fine print. The commission's assumption that the way to get a volunteer force was to buy it with pay increases was incomplete, Laird felt. Housing, education, skill training, improving the image of the military, and a host of other initiatives were needed, along with pay increases. These changes would take more time and money than the commission had estimated. Laird spelled out those objections in a memorandum to the president on March 11, and Nixon concurred. After that he followed Laird's recommendations down the line.[8] Pentagon and White House officials together crafted an April 23 presidential message to Congress in which Nixon asked the lawmakers to "move now toward ending the draft" and enact pay raises. And he announced his own initiatives to make the lottery system more equitable in the meantime. Laird had just over one year to figure a way to get Congress to extend the draft one more time when it expired in July 1971.

If Laird had expected to make any progress on that front in 1970, his expectations had been dashed on April 30, when Nixon announced that U.S. troops were being sent into Cambodia, sparking a new wave of antiwar sentiment. By August 1970 Laird told his senior staff that it would be better if the legislation was not voted on that year because "we do not have the votes in the Senate to extend the draft at the present."[9]

The strong antiwar and antimilitary coalition in the Senate, and the opposition of Edward Hebert, were not the only significant hurdles Laird faced. There
were so many strong anti-AVF forces in the 1969–71 time period that Washington insiders thought it would be a miracle if Laird could pull off an all-volunteer force before his self-declared one term in office was over in January 1973.
The most important ally Laird had was the president himself, but it was not a
deeply held view for Nixon that the nation *must* have an all-volunteer force.
Nixon had embraced the goal for political exigency. If the winds of politics
had blown another way, he would have been content to keep the draft. While
Nixon had AVF-zealot Martin Anderson on his staff, who was pushing him in
the right direction, the more influential Kissinger was far less committed.

The strongest opponent Laird had on the subject was the army brass. "The
army was always against it," Laird recalled. "They loved the draft." One army
officer who rose to prominence, Colin Powell, concurred. In 1970 Lieutenant
Colonel Powell was a midlevel Pentagon official working for the army's assistant vice chief of staff. "At the time, those of us who were career professionals
for the most part weren't crazy about it. We were going to have to compete in
the open labor marketplace, something we hadn't done before. Manpower was
a free good in those days because you just drafted more. Then, suddenly, you
would not only have to recruit them but you had to try to keep them, so you
don't have to go out and recruit another one. We would have preferred to see
the draft remain."[10]

So the army, throughout 1969 and 1970, was dragging its heels on the all-
volunteer force, conducting a paper drill to please Laird. Behind closed doors
on Capitol Hill, when pressed by members of Congress whom they knew to be
all-volunteer-force opponents, the army leadership freely expressed their personal opposition. Such testimony undercut Laird's initiative, but he was careful
about rapping their knuckles at first. He knew army leaders were gambling that
they could outlast him. They had seen presidents and Cabinet secretaries come
and go. If they could play a game of delay, they could drop the whole idea when
Laird was out of the picture. So Laird did some heavy soul-searching. As had
been evident with his statements about Vietnam, he was not a man who liked
to commit himself to deadlines or timetables when there might be many factors out of his control that could prevent his success. By mid-1970 he reasoned
that the only way to succeed was to publicly make a deadline pledge, with the
Joint Chiefs lined up behind him.

Since World War II, Congress had traditionally extended draft induction
authority four years at a time. They had last done that in 1967. The Gates
Commission urged Nixon to let the draft expire in 1971, optimistically predicting an all-volunteer force could be in place by that time. Laird's friends
in Congress told him that there was no way he could win a vote for the tradi-

tional four-year extension. The easiest victory would be a one-year extension, but Laird didn't think that was enough. He did not want to be fighting for another extension one year later during a presidential election campaign. So he settled on a two-year extension. In March 1970 he privately recommended that to the president, but Nixon did not sign on immediately. For another year Nixon listened to different advisors who argued for three different timetables: the winnable one-year extension, the tougher two-year, and the traditional four-year authority.

As the internal debate continued, Laird moved ahead on his own. Time and again he had proved that, if he took unilateral action, the momentum would swing the White House and other participants his way. He decided that it would be possible to create an all-volunteer force by mid-1973. By fall 1970 that was the goal he was ready to publicly announce. Only one more step was needed before he did that. Laird would have to confront Westmoreland. "The military was sabotaging us," recalled White House aide Martin Anderson. "They were totally opposed to the All-Volunteer Force, and, at the highest level of the military, they were putting out the word on the Hill and elsewhere, 'Kill this idea!' And it was General Westmoreland who was leading the charge." For almost two years, Laird had allowed Westmoreland to speak his mind in speeches and in congressional testimony, but it was time to shut down the four-star general.

In late September Laird met with Westmoreland and issued an ultimatum. "I told Westy it was time for him to get on board or get out." Though Laird conveyed it in more courteous terms, Westmoreland knew he was being asked to resign as army chief of staff if he could not become an active supporter in the development of an all-volunteer force. He told Laird he wanted to keep his job. Westmoreland did not recount this in his own memoirs, but Martin Anderson was intimately familiar with the confrontation. He related, "My recollection is that [Laird] told Westmoreland, 'You've got two choices. You can either support the all-volunteer force and enjoy being army chief of staff, or you can be someone who's totally opposed to an all-volunteer force, and be an *ex*-member of the Joint Chiefs of Staff.' Shortly after that, General Westmoreland gave the damnedest speech endorsing the all-volunteer force."[11]

Monday, October 12, 1970, was the day Laird set out to announce, with sufficient ceremony, his ambitious mid-1973 time line for the achievement of an all-volunteer force. In a memo to the Joint Chiefs and service secretaries, he informed them that the U.S. military would henceforth be committed to "zero draft calls " by the end of fiscal year 1973. Meanwhile the services had much to do themselves to make military careers more appealing and competitive with private industry. "This matter should receive your urgent personal attention, and action plans should proceed without delay."[12]

That morning, having already distributed the memorandum, Laird convened his weekly Armed Forces Policy Council staff meeting, which included all senior Pentagon and military officials. He announced the new goal and ticked off events to come: his own press conference to announce the deadline, a speech by Westmoreland on Tuesday, and another press conference by Pentagon manpower chief Roger Kelley on Wednesday. General Westmoreland obligingly chimed in, according to the minutes, with terse support: "Army has been studying this matter for many months. We have several ongoing programs and many are being initiated. Army feels that zero draft calls is a feasible objective."[13]

At Laird's press conference that day, with 1970 midterm elections only a few weeks away, one correspondent asked, "[I]s it fair to assume that [setting a deadline for ending the draft is] your bit to help the Republicans?"

"I don't know how you can come to any such conclusion," Laird smiled.[14]

Laird had lunch that day with Admiral Moorer, who opposed the all-volunteer force but, unlike Westmoreland, had not spoken publicly against it. The lunch was a symbolic opportunity to sign Moorer on for the long haul. As a good soldier and, in Laird's eyes, a loyal one (if supervised properly), Moorer agreed to follow the Laird line. Then Laird gathered all the Joint Chiefs for an hour-long meeting at which he made sure none of them had any illusions about standing in his way.

At 6:25 P.M. General Alexander Haig arrived for a private meeting with Laird. It was to be the secretary's last hard sell of the day. As a deputy to Kissinger, Haig had become the most vehement all-volunteer-force critic at 1600 Pennsylvania Avenue and a powerful influence on Kissinger himself. In the meeting with Laird the obdurate army general wouldn't budge, and Laird could not order him to fall in line. Only a month later Haig was actively pushing for a four-year draft extension, which would buy him the time he needed to thwart the all-volunteer force until Laird was gone. Not long after word of Haig's continued opposition got back to Laird, Kissinger found himself required to call Haig on the carpet and direct him to join the all-volunteer team. "I finally got hauled in and told to butt out," Haig recalled. "I was told the president was very unhappy with my opposition." He rightly suspected that it was actually backroom wizard Laird who had outmaneuvered him.[15]

On October 13 Westmoreland dutifully delivered a major address to the annual meeting of the Association of the U.S. Army. "I am announcing today that the Army is committed to an all-out effort in working toward a zero draft—a volunteer force," he said. With this speech, according to one army historian, "the Army's approach to achieving an all-volunteer force changed. Seemingly overnight, the Army shifted from its wait-and-see attitude to an activist posture."[16] By then Westmoreland knew the army did not have to wait for Congress to approve a pay raise to make the army a more attractive line of work for volunteers. One of Westmoreland's brightest commanders, General Bernard W.

Rogers, had already shown the way by radically transforming a dismal western post into one with high morale and performance in little more than a year.

Just south of Colorado Springs, Colorado, lies the sprawling 140,000-acre Fort Carson, named for the legendary frontiersman Brigadier General Christopher "Kit" Carson. The post was created in World War II as both a training facility and a prisoner-of-war camp and then evolved into a major army facility by the late 1960s. As the Vietnam War heated up, it became a year-round training area for units to be deployed to Southeast Asia, prominently including elements of the Fifth Infantry Division (Mechanized), known as the "Red Diamond Division."

By September 1969, when General Rogers arrived as the new commander of Fort Carson's twenty-five thousand men, it was a post in serious trouble, suffering from abysmal morale that came from many sources including racial division, drug-abusing troublemakers, and an overcrowded stockade filled with miscreants, deserters, and those caught AWOL. The division's manpower had a 14 percent turnover every month, which meant that after every seven months Rogers would effectively be commanding a completely new set of soldiers. More than half of those reported to the post directly from Vietnam combat duty, and many were draftees with only a few months left to go on their two-year hitch. Disenchanted, disgruntled, and not seeing the sense in it, they were in a mood to rebel at any effort to keep them combat ready. "There was much work to be done," Rogers recalled. His chief of staff, Colonel David R. Hughes, a much-decorated combat hero, put it more pithily: "I served in three wars: Korea, Vietnam, and Fort Carson."[17]

General Rogers barely had time to get his boots muddy before Laird came for a five-day visit in October 1969 that included inspections of Fort Carson, the nearby Air Force Academy, and the Cheyenne Mountain NORAD (North American Air Defense Command) complex just west of the post. After morning briefings, Rogers took Laird on a tour of the sprawling base in a Huey helicopter. McNamara had slated Fort Carson for closure until a visionary general took a similar helicopter trip and concluded it was a western jewel the army should not give up. Eastern bases such Fort Bragg were already encroached upon by urbanization, but Carson was likely to give the army mechanized maneuver room in perpetuity.

Laird's helicopter set down in a remote location to observe a training exercise of the post's Recondo (Reconnaissance and Commando) School. Rogers invited Laird and two friends he had brought along to walk ahead on a trail in the tranquil woods. Suddenly Laird's friends became alarmed as they heard a chorused shout—"Re-CON-do!"—and saw a half-dozen black-faced, camouflaged soldiers rushing at them through the bushes, guns pointed. An unruffled Laird eyed the patrol leader and quietly said the password for the day, which Rogers had given: "Fort Worth." It was the only time during his tenure that American soldiers pointed weapons at the secretary of defense.[18]

Laird's primary memory of the visit was his excitement about the new commander, General Rogers, an enlightened Rhodes Scholar and decorated combat veteran who had been commandant of the cadet corps at West Point. After Laird heard a number of complaints during his mess hall lunch with the division's enlisted men, Rogers didn't try to make excuses when his men spoke up. "What they need is for someone to give a damn," Rogers said.

"Amen," Laird responded.

He saw in Rogers a kindred spirit. Just two weeks before, Laird had issued a directive that ordered commanders to allow protest within their ranks unless it interfered with morale, discipline, or military "effectiveness." Laird had written: "Dissent in its proper sphere is healthy for the United States [and] the service member's right of expression should be preserved to the maximum extent possible, consistent with good order and discipline and the national security."[19] (During Laird's visit, Rogers thanked him for the directive.) Both Rogers and Laird believed the soldiers deserved a significant say in troop operations and could be trusted to speak up without a loss of discipline. It was the essence of Laird's participatory management style over the Defense Department.

Both Laird and Rogers also had a way of simplifying complicated matters. And both knew that the incoming soldiers were a different breed, and that was not a bad thing. "They want to participate in the policy making of the army," Rogers summarized. "They are interested in 'why' we do certain things in certain ways. Answers based on faith—'just believe me'—or authority—'it's so because I say it's so'—or custom—'we've always done it this way'—were not good enough," Rogers said. "These soldiers were prepared to stand up and be counted, to tell it like it is, and they expected the same to be true of their superiors. Intellectually, they were at a higher level at their age than had been my generation, but the challenge was that they didn't have the experience or discipline to balance that intelligence."[20]

Laird felt that if Rogers succeeded in making the army more attractive and empowering for the men, it would be a test case for the all-volunteer force. When Laird returned to the Pentagon, he advised Westmoreland to watch for good things to come from Rogers and Fort Carson.

Rogers's successes at Fort Carson were due in large part to an "Enlisted Men's Council," with representatives elected from each unit. Rogers also created "Racial Harmony Councils," so black soldiers could air their unique concerns in separate forums. He authorized an on-post coffee house where commanders occasionally dropped in at give-and-take sessions. Rogers's chief of staff, Colonel Hughes, explained, "We let the men get it off their chest. We let them do guerrilla theater in the post theater and brought in controversial speakers. At the coffee house and elsewhere we ordered all the battalion commanders to sit on their butts and keep their mouths shut and listen. If [the men] could get it off their chest in a socially approved forum like the coffee house rap session or 'theater,' we could expect them to salute when they walked out the door. And they did."[21]

As a result, many changes were made. Of more than one hundred serious recommendations received from the enlisted men's councils, about 70 percent of them made sense to Rogers and he implemented them. He got rid of make-work projects, the dreaded Saturday inspections, and early-morning reveille. He remodeled barracks to provide more privacy, added recreational options, and improved the food in the mess halls. Reenlistments increased 45 percent, and the retention rate of junior officers doubled. Two-thirds of the noncareer GIs rated their own morale as "fair to excellent" in one survey. AWOLs radically declined, as did disciplinary problems and incidents requiring investigation by the provost marshal.[22]

Westmoreland kept close watch on Rogers and Fort Carson from the Pentagon, as Laird had advised him to do. He was impressed enough to ask Rogers to come to Washington and brief the army commanders' conference. Some of the commanders openly objected to what Rogers told them. One general groused, "If this is the way the Army's going to be, I'm glad I'm about to retire!"

At that, Westmoreland turned to Rogers and observed: "That's our problem, isn't it, Bernie?"

"Yes sir, that's our problem," Rogers responded. "Old Army folks who won't accept what the future holds for us and what we need to do."[23]

On November 2, 1970, the *New York Times* discovered Rogers and Fort Carson and hailed their achievements in a major article. Laird was thrilled as a media blitz followed portraying Fort Carson as the most progressive troop-oriented base in the American military. (Rogers went on to become army chief of staff and then supreme commander of NATO.)

Not to be outdone, the navy stepped up to the plate. After working on a new directive for almost four months, Chief of Naval Operations Admiral Elmo Zumwalt on November 10, 1970, issued his most famous and controversial directive. (His directives were informally called "Z-grams.") Z-57, originally titled "Mickey Mouse, Elimination Of," ordered liberalization of navy regulations in twelve areas including hair and beard styles, where uniforms had to be worn and where they were not necessary, motorcycle use, and so on. The memo itself said the objective was to eliminate "demeaning and abrasive regulations" in the navy, which were alternately described in the memo as "Mickey Mouse" or "chicken regs." The message was electrifying, and Zumwalt became a hero to the sailors. At a POW prison in North Vietnam, longtime POW Captain Jim Stockdale tapped on the walls of a new POW to elicit news: "What's new?" The answer came back: "Got a new CNO, named Zumwalt. No more Mickey Mouse or chickenshit."[24]

Not to be upstaged, Westmoreland used a commanders' conference on November 30 to issue liberalizing orders that followed Rogers's reforms at Fort Carson almost completely. In one stroke he abolished daily reveille formations, liberalized pass policies, put beer in the barracks and mess halls, encouraged commanders to establish open-door policies to listen to complaining enlisted men, called for a review to end all "irritants" such as make-work projects and meaningless rituals, and allowed longer hair.

Still, Westmoreland was the reluctant reformer, never fully on board with an all-volunteer force, as Laird had anticipated. "Westmoreland believed the Army needed to be both reformed and modernized, [but] he did not want to be the man to do it," one Westmoreland biographer, Samuel Zaffiri, wrote. "He thought of himself as a field soldier [and] found going head-to-head with the Army establishment distasteful."[25] Still, the wily general was willing to go along, gambling that Laird would not eventually accomplish an all-volunteer force. Meanwhile Westmoreland reckoned the army could benefit from all the improvements. He admitted as much in a private meeting in January 1971 with Curtis Tarr, the Selective Service chief. "He is going to use the all-volunteer force as a means by which the Army might be improved in ways that otherwise would not be possible," Tarr wrote in his journal after the conversation. A month later, a *Look* magazine article entitled "The Dump-the-Draft Talk Is Double-Talk" quoted Westmoreland's designated point man on the all-volunteer force, Lieutenant General George Forsythe, as saying, "I don't want to get rid of the draft. Neither does General Westmoreland."[26]

The final draft extension debate began when President Nixon sent Congress a proposal at the end of January 1971. Despite a push by some White House aides, including Haig, for either a four-year or a one-year extension, Nixon sided with Laird and asked Congress for two more years of draft authority. The bill included additional requests for draft reforms, as well as a military pay increase and other measures aimed at laying the groundwork for recruitment of an all-volunteer force. Laird feared all the side issues in the bill would cloud the central need for an extension. He was right to be concerned. The draft bill embroiled the House and Senate in eight months of stormy debate, taking so long that the draft actually came to an end for three months in the summer of 1971 because the president's induction authority had temporarily expired.

The bill was close to passage in June. Laird had mollified Congressman Hebert by minimizing the talk about his end game—the all-volunteer force—and focusing instead on extending the draft, which Hebert wanted. Then Senator Mike Mansfield, the majority leader, added an amendment that declared that it was U.S. policy to withdraw *all* American troops from Southeast Asia within nine months of the passage of the bill. The bill, with the nettlesome amendment, passed the Senate and went on to the House, where Hebert flatly refused to accept the amendment. The president would never have signed a bill with such a mandated withdrawal deadline in it anyway. Mansfield agreed to soften his amendment language to read that the troops would be withdrawn as soon as was practicable. The House agreed to that, but then the Senate balked.[27]

It was time for Laird to pull out all the stops, which he did on September 14. He wiped his schedule clean for the day and summoned the secretaries of the army, navy, and air force, as well as the four (of five) Joint Chiefs who were in town. After their meeting, five Pentagon limousines roared up to the Capitol, and the magnificent seven of the military trooped down the corridors and into the Senate Armed Services Committee room in what one newspaper called "the most glittering display of brass assembled on Capitol Hill" in the post–World War II era. Then they fanned out to visit the offices of senators from both parties.[28] The next morning, Laird appeared on the NBC *Today* show and expressed concern about the Senate's recalcitrance. Failure to pass the draft bill would mean "utter chaos as far as the [military] manpower problems of the United States are concerned," he said. The next day Nixon held a news conference: "I don't like to speculate as to what would happen if the draft bill is defeated, because I think this would be one of the most irresponsible acts on the part of the United States Senate that I could possibly think of." The Senate approved the bill on September 21.[29]

Besides a two-year draft extension, Laird won most of the serious draft reforms he was after. The final bill was also full of newly funded benefits for military servicemen, the most important of which was a 100 percent pay increase for those with less than two years of service. There had been general acknowledgment in government that the pay for new draftees and enlistees was a national shame, just as the draft itself had become. The government hadn't paid them well because it didn't have to; draft labor was cheap labor.

Laird had been headstrong about that pay raise from his first month on the job. "Too many [military] families suffer financial hardships, some of whom are forced to go on welfare to survive," Laird charged in 1969. He ordered a study, and it revealed in early 1970 that more than twelve thousand servicemen were on the nation's welfare rolls. Many more thousands qualified for welfare, but they leaned on family, friends, and their own fiscal restraint to get by without tapping government sources.[30] By the time Laird left office in 1973 he had achieved a salary increase for the "under two" servicemen of more than 300 percent, bringing pay closer to what they might receive in civilian life. "They weren't qualified for food stamps when I left," Laird proclaimed proudly.[31]

That September 1971 Laird felt, after so much planning and lobbying, that he had most of the tools he needed to make it possible to end the draft by mid-1973 or even earlier. But that confidence was not widely shared. Westmoreland's top assistant on the all-volunteer force, General Forsythe, stated publicly at the time that he believed it was impossible to achieve an all-volunteer force by Laird's target date. "Although we're going to try and do our level best, we are not going to make it ... in the time that has been prescribed for us to do this. That's just too short a time.

As always, Laird took naysayers in stride—and in good humor. A short time later one news organization solemnly reported that "the Navy is trying to recruit porpoises as bodyguards for its divers and others who may find themselves threatened by sharks." A poker-faced Laird declared to the Pentagon press corps, "I feel we can safely say that, soon, only volunteer porpie will be sent overseas, and we will meet or beat our goal of an all-volunteer porpoise force by July 1, 1973."[32]

37
Cardinal Virtues

⬦

EVEN IN THE BEST OF TIMES the job of secretary of defense is one of the toughest in America. The huge bureaucracy and its budget far exceed those of any single American corporation or even any other government department. All defense secretaries must deal with rivalry between the services; military officers intent on advancement; intense competition for lucrative weapons contracts; diverse agendas in Congress, which holds the purse strings; dictatorial White House staffers; and a carping media ready to pounce on any mistake. But all those troubles increase during wartime and were multiplied further during America's most unpopular war when the military was viewed with distrust and derision. Former president Gerald Ford observed, "Let me say this, and *I say it with emphasis:* few public servants have been so tested by events as Mel Laird in those days of tumult and challenge."[1]

Laird's direct predecessor, Clifford, held the grueling position for only eleven months. Before him, McNamara was defense secretary for seven years—the longest time any single person had held the position.[2] Antiwar sentiment was relatively slow to build and sporadic until McNamara's last year as secretary. In contrast, Laird was under fire from his first day on the job.

Coming from stoic Wisconsin stock, Laird had an indomitable air that was both tempered and highlighted by his humor and easy manner at the center of every storm that beset the Pentagon. But he was not impervious to pressure. As he began his fourth and final year in the grueling job, the cracks began to show. Though Laird was not one to whine, when he was closely questioned by the press between February and April 1972, he offered brief acknowledgments of the pressure and spoke about looking forward to a long vacation after his resignation. At a Milwaukee press conference in late March, Laird said: "After I have completed this particular term, I hope to take six or seven months off, and then I will consider some very attractive offers which have been made to me. I will not consider them until I have had at least six months off from this job which has required 24 hours a day duty, 365 days a year."[3] In April, at a breakfast with TV correspondents in New York City, one asked him if he "agonized" about the job. Laird conceded, "[I]t should be no surprise, it is rather difficult. I am not overjoyed with being Secretary of Defense."[4]

In what became almost a mantra at that time, Laird noted that seven of the previous nine defense secretaries had averaged less than two years in the position before resigning. As to the prominent exception, McNamara, Laird implied when questioned on one occasion that McNamara had privately admitted it was a mistake for him to stay longer than four years. "I have a great deal of respect and admiration for Secretary McNamara, and we get together quite often [to] discuss some of our problems," Laird began. "But I think that he would be the first to state that he stayed too long in the office of Secretary of Defense."[5] Each time he was asked, Laird emphatically stated, as he did to TV interviewer Hugh Downs: "There's one thing that I am sure of and that is that four years is long enough for any man to serve in this job."[6]

The idea of a man with his level of competency leaving a job no one else wanted was unsettling, even to critics and political opponents in Washington. On February 15, 1972, when Laird appeared before the Senate Armed Services Committee for a budget hearing, senators from both parties pressured him to reconsider his one-term pledge. The normally taciturn chairman from the opposing party, Senator John Stennis, began his plea in a stumbling manner: "I want to make it clear to Secretary Laird that I am not here flattering him; I am not given to flattery—I hope I am not. I think he has done an outstanding job as Secretary of Defense. He has had more than his share of the problems. Whatever limitation you have made that you are planning to leave, I hope you will reconsider and stay with us."[7] As he did with the senators, Laird noted to reporters outside the hearing room that, though flattered, he still planned "to serve out my term" and then leave.

One of Laird's greatest supporters during that time—though also an intermittent scolding critic—was his mother, Helen Connor Laird. A February 1972 news article began, "Every few days, Mrs. Helen Laird, a widow in her 80s, writes to her son Melvin, who works at the Pentagon, and lets him know how well she feels the federal government is serving the people of Marshfield, Wis. A friend who has been permitted to share the Defense Secretary's mail from home testifies that the news is not always good. Indeed, the letters from Marshfield on occasion bring handwritten motherly scoldings, supported by newspaper clippings telling about things that have gone haywire at the Pentagon."[8]

While journalists wrote with humor about Mrs. Laird's letters, what they missed was her fierce support of her son against all comers, and the rock-solid foundation she provided him. "She was the strongest woman I ever knew," Laird recalled. "I was very close to my mother. When I was growing up, I used to say prayers with my mother every night." The two had an undeniable bond; one's unhappiness invariably precipitated sadness in the other. Secretary of Defense Rumsfeld told a favorite story about his friend and mentor, Laird. A news magazine had described Laird as "clever." Rumsfeld said Mrs. Laird called her son: "[S]he was dadburned upset about the fact that her dear, lovable, sweet, warm, fuzzy son, Melvie, had actually been called 'clever.' That is NOT a nice word for someone to call him, she felt. So Mel was ranting and raving and saying to me, 'People should stop using that word.' I remember it as the time I saw Mel the most excited, unhappy, concerned, anguished, and irritated."[9]

Jerry Friedheim remembered a high-level staff meeting that was interrupted by a call from mother Laird. Early in his term Laird had given his mother a private phone line into his office after too many confused temporary receptionists had fumbled calls from an older woman asking for "Bom." That line lit up on his console one morning in the middle of a somber national security discussion with top staff and military leaders. As Friedheim remembers, Laird punched the button, and his mother was on the speaker phone.

"Hi, Bom," they could hear Mrs. Laird say.

"Oh, hi Mom!" the secretary effused.

"I just wanted to tell you that the most beautiful cardinal has just landed on my bird feeder. And it's just lovely. I thought you'd like to know about that."

Friedheim recounted, "He talked to her for about fifteen minutes about the cardinal on the bird feeder. Everybody sat there while he talked to her, and then he said, 'It was very nice talking to you this morning, Mom. I'm glad it's a nice day out there in Marshfield.'" Friedheim said it was a "Lairdism" that helped explain why his staff was so loyal to him. No one could help being won over by a man who would so easily take time for his mother.[10]

Sometimes those moments were too few and far between, especially when vitriolic protests hit home. In personal letters that revealed something about each of the men, President Nixon acknowledged that the stress of those events was much greater on Laird, whose Bethesda neighborhood was occasionally "invaded." Unlike Laird, Nixon closeted himself in the fortress he made of the White House during the protest years, with a phalanx of sycophants to keep the critics at bay. Laird waded among the protesters and took the worst they had to offer, defending their right to speak out unless a law was broken in the process. Still, it inevitably had a deleterious, disheartening effect, which Nixon recognized. He wrote to Laird in late 1972:

> In addition to the ordinary burdens you have had as Secretary of Defense, you and your family [have been] subjected to the brutal brunt of the anti-defense, peace at any price establishment. I had not realized until we spoke, of how personally difficult that must have been for Barbara and for your children, not to mention yourself. After my speech of November 3, 1969, the decision on Cambodia, and May 8, 1972, not to mention Laos and ABM, all of the violent protesters with their obscene words and acts, descended on Washington. But, Pat, Tricia, Julie and I, at least had the haven of the White House. If the air-conditioning were turned up high enough, we could not hear them chanting outside as they marched by the thousands past the gates. On the other hand, you had no such protection. When I heard of some of the things they did right in your front yard, my heart went out to your family and to you. What really matters is that you didn't let it get to you. You continued to do your job with your usual splendid, unruffled spirit.[11]

Laird could look back and laugh about some of the indignities. "There were a few wackos that would come out once in awhile," he said. He recalled the day the famous antiwar poet Allen Ginsberg urinated on the front of his house, with television cameras duly recording the protest.[12] Another protester threw a brick through his den window. "My kids and my wife were pretty good about it," Laird said, proudly. To take the pressure off, sometimes he would take the family for a Camp David retreat when the president was not there.

The greatest difference for the family was that he was much busier than he had been as a congressman, got less sleep, and was wearier. Oldest son John, who lived in Wisconsin during Laird's Pentagon years, said, "He had so many things on his mind that he was just kind of not there sometimes when we were together. When we sat down to watch TV at Christmas time, within five minutes he was sound asleep because he just needed to relax and rest."[13]

With John in Wisconsin and daughter Alison off to college in 1969, that left son David to be most impacted by a more absent father. He did not complain about it, however. His father "had a lot more on his mind," David conceded, "but I was still amazed at his generally easy manner. When I would go to the Pentagon and see him with the people he worked with, he had the ability to conduct himself in a way that everyone understood they had a serious job to do, but they could have some fun as well, even though it was very difficult." A fond and frequent memory was that nearly every time his father would join David and his friends to watch a football game on TV, Dad would be snoring within a few minutes. "Then a huge snore would jostle him up and he'd have five little faces looking at him. 'Great game, eh boys?' And he would know exactly what was going on in the game!" Mostly, David said, they were years when he worried about his father—"not only that something traumatic would happen, but how he was handling it all. I think he handled it fine, but you get concerned because you know it's tough. Even then, he made the majority of my Landon High School basketball and football games. He's somebody you love very much, and you just watch him taking hits at Fulbright's hearings, or taking hits in the newspapers and on TV reports. . . . [H]e always just said, 'Nah, don't worry. That's okay.' It didn't seem to faze him."[14]

But it did, of course. "It is a very difficult job," Laird allowed to journalists at an early 1972 breakfast. "You are up at least three times a night. You start out at 7 o'clock in the morning, and you work long hours. My wife says it is because I am not organized as well as I should be. You *can't* get organized on this job as well as you should be."[15]

<hr />

One thing that made his final year particularly difficult for Laird was the departure of David Packard, who had shouldered a sizable portion of Laird's load. The resignation also created some sticky national security issues. Without a deputy secretary, Laird confided to his senior staff at a mid-December 1971 meeting, the president had asked him not to leave town while Nixon was away. "Since the President will probably be out of town for 72 out of the next 90 days, I will be sticking close to home," he laconically told his staffers.[16]

On January 6, 1972, Laird wrote an "Eyes Only" memo to the president expressing his frustration at finding a suitable replacement for Packard. He had been conducting "an extensive talent search" since the previous spring, personally interviewing thirty people and reviewing the qualifications of another sixty. His greatest disappointment was not finding a single acceptable candidate outside government who wanted the job. He lamented to Nixon that "it seems everyone I talk to from the outside would love to work at the State Department or be an Ambassador to some country, but when it comes down to this building [the Pentagon], the tendency is to run like scared rabbits." Most of the top-drawer candidates demurred by saying that they couldn't take the job for at least a year because it would take them that time to divest themselves of stock that might pose a conflict. Those who didn't use this excuse, Laird added, "invariably turn out to be second-raters whom it would take at least nine or ten months to educate properly."

Privately Laird had one hands-down favorite for the spot: Robert Froehlke. But Laird had agreed with Nixon that Packard's successor needed to be someone who, when Laird left in early 1973, could either continue as deputy secretary for another two years or become secretary. Froehlke did not want to stay at the Pentagon after his friend Laird departed, so he had taken himself out of the running. In the January memo, Laird mentioned four qualified choices: Pentagon Comptroller Robert C. Moot and Assistant Comptroller at the General Accounting Office Thomas D. Morris, both Democrats; and Pentagon General Counsel J. Fred Buzhardt or Air Force Secretary Robert Seamans, both Republicans. Any of those four men would be easily confirmed by Congress, and all could hit the ground running, Laird assured the president.[17]

Nixon sent back word by the next morning that he preferred former Texas governor William Clements.[18] Still armed with the cocktail-napkin promise, Laird knew he could insist Nixon nominate one of his four, but he reckoned this would be impractical pique. If the person was to stay on, or have hope of succeeding Laird, he had to have Nixon's full approval and confidence. So, recouping quickly, less than a day after he had submitted his memo to Nixon, Laird put in an early evening call to Kenneth Rush, the U.S. ambassador to West Germany, asking him to come to the Pentagon at his earliest convenience for a discussion of some urgency.

The courtly, silver-haired sixty-two-year-old had been an assistant law professor at Duke University, where he taught a bright student, Richard Nixon, with whom he had forged a life-long bond. When Rush arrived at Laird's office on January 11, he sat down for a tough two hours of arm-twisting. The two had met on several occasions, even golfed together, and enjoyed each other's company. But Rush did not want to be deputy secretary of defense. "I want to be secretary of state," he kept telling Laird.

"If you want to be secretary of state," Laird argued, "coming over here as deputy will be great preparation—and you might even want to stay here as secretary of defense."

"No, I want to be secretary of state," Rush maintained.

By the end of the session Laird felt he had won, but Rush didn't give him a decision right then. Laird informed Nixon that his old friend had been offered the job, and the president was relatively pleased with the compromise candidate. What Laird didn't know then is that Nixon, through outgoing Attorney General John Mitchell, had secretly promised Rush that if he took the less-desirable job of deputy secretary to Laird, the president would guarantee his ascension to secretary of state in 1973. Rush came aboard in late February. Laird had nothing negative to say about his performance, but Rush was no savvy star like Packard, and his heart was always across the Potomac River at the State Department.

~

On the Vietnam front, early 1972 was the calm before a major storm. The North Vietnamese were planning a multipronged military action that, according to captured enemy documents and other intelligence, appeared to be scheduled around the mid-February lunar Tet holiday. Laird was determined that there would not be a repeat of the 1968 Tet offensive, when the enemy suffered a military loss but won the battle of perception in an American election year. His aim, beginning the previous November, had been to prepare the American public for the expected offensive and to project a win for the South and a sure victory for Vietnamization.

In Laird's view there was no reason to slow the American troop withdrawal, even though the enemy was massing to strike. Neither General Abrams nor Admiral Moorer agreed with him. As Nixon prepared to announce new withdrawal numbers in mid-January, Abrams and Moorer argued that, in view of the looming invasion, the withdrawal rate should be drastically reduced to 15,800 men per month between February and July.

Laird presented the Abrams-Moorer point of view in his memorandum of recommendations to the president on January 11. But he argued that going along with the military on this meant that Nixon would have to go back on his public statement of nine days before that "our withdrawal will continue on schedule, at least at the present rate," which was then averaging 22,500 a month. Laird wrote that Nixon would have to offer a "major explanation to the U.S. public" on why he was reversing himself so quickly when there had been no actual change in the situation. Instead, Laird suggested *increasing* the rate to 24,000 a month.[19] Nixon settled on 23,300 a month for three months. At a joint news conference with Laird two days later, the president announced that 70,000 more Americans would be withdrawn from Vietnam by May 1, 1972, leaving only 69,000 on that date.

After announcing the numbers Nixon turned the microphone over to Laird, who seized the moment to make his points about the coming offensive in the most high-profile forum he had: "On my return from Vietnam in November, I had the opportunity to brief many of you in this room and I made the point at that time that the enemy during the dry period would be able to stage what I referred to as two or three spectaculars with the kinds of force which they had. I had confidence—and General Abrams had confidence—in the capabilities of the South Vietnamese military forces to handle their combat and security responsibilities during this period. That does not mean that the South Vietnamese will win every battle during this period, but I can assure you that the vast majority of the battles will be won by the South Vietnamese forces. They have the capability, they have the equipment, they have the training through this Vietnamization program to do this job."[20]

At the first Monday morning high-level staff meeting of the year, Laird reminded those present that the American military had been given three full years to train the South Vietnamese to take over their own war. While the Pentagon had done its best, and the South Vietnamese appeared ready, "we are not in a position to guarantee the will and desire of any military force anywhere in the world except our own." Laird said, with a verbal nod to the Joint Chiefs, that "there will be some who say we need another 18 months, another two years, another three years" to train the South Vietnamese, but time had run out. "We have done the best we could and we should take pride in the job that has been done, particularly by General Abrams and his people. We are now nearing the cut-off date. We have to be strong."[21]

A week later, in a memo to Kissinger, Laird summarized the situation including his estimation of why the North would launch such a large offensive at that time; Hanoi wanted to discredit Vietnamization in an election year and to demoralize the South Vietnamese. But, Laird added, "I do not believe that the North Vietnamese have it within their power to achieve decisive results in either a political or military sense." He made it clear that he was ready to let the South Vietnamese prove their mettle. "The true test of the coming campaign will be decided by the effect it has on the South Vietnamese willingness to fight for what is theirs."[22]

Intelligence indicators continued to point to a mid-February launch date for the enemy offensive, but the February 15 Tet holiday came and went without incident. Intelligence reports were recalculated to suggest that the offensive would start on or before Nixon arrived in Peking a week later for his historic summit. Still it didn't come. Admiral Moorer reported on March 6 to Laird and assembled Pentagon officials that "it is quite clear the enemy is in a position to attack in South Vietnam. We just don't know why he has not done so, except that he may have been significantly hurt by our air strikes."[23] Later evidence suggests that a combination of the early 1971 Lam Son operation in Laos, bad weather, and other factors had delayed the launch date.[24] As Admiral Moorer surmised at the time, the stepped-up air strikes had only done enough damage to slow down, but not stave off, the offensive.

The president also had a gambit in mind that might blunt the invasion. On January 26 he broke the news that Kissinger had been secretly negotiating with Hanoi in a shadow effort to the formal Paris talks. Nixon's purpose, in part, was to silence critics who said the United States was being intransigent in Paris. At the same time Nixon offered a cease-fire and a complete withdrawal of American troops within six months if Hanoi agreed to his terms. If North Vietnam was going to continue with plans for an invasion, then the president was doing his best to make them look like the warmongers. Hanoi one-upped Nixon a week later by making public its own peace proposal, secretly given to Kissinger seven months earlier, and said that Nixon hadn't taken it seriously.

Behind the window dressing of peace proposals, however, Nixon was preparing to escalate the war. On February 4 National Security Decision Memorandum 149, signed by Kissinger, landed on Laird's desk. The president had ordered that a fourth aircraft carrier be made ready for Vietnam duty and that additional B-52s and fighters be sent to Guam and Thailand to be ready for the offensive. And Kissinger added something Abrams had asked for, but Laird had already turned down: "[Y]ou should authorize air strikes into the northern portion of the DMZ whenever the field commander determines that the enemy is using the area in preparation for attack in the south."[25] That order was short-lived because, after intensified U.S. air attacks on the North in early February, Nixon and Kissinger had Laird suspend the missions entirely for two weeks before and during Nixon's trip to China. "They were getting queasy about it over at the White House," Laird recalled.

On March 9 Moorer sent Laird an "Urgent Request for Air Authorities," which looked to Laird like an all-out resumption of the bombing of the North.[26] Laird passed the request on to Nixon, emphatically stating he didn't agree with Moorer. Laird believed the 150,000 tons of bombs already dropped on key targets in Southeast Asia since January 1 under the "protective reaction" premise had "in no small part...accounted for Hanoi's inability to date to generate the expected major offensive operations." But "there has been no flagrant provocation for renewed air attacks," Laird added, and thus no defensible public reason for abandoning the 1968 bombing halt understandings. He advised the president to wait until the invasion was launched, adding that even when that finally happened, "I do not foresee...the North Vietnamese being able to overwhelm friendly forces to the extent that the progress of Vietnamization is reversed."[27] American generals in Saigon saw the coming invasion as the big problem. But for Laird, Vietnamization was the bottom line. After three years as secretary, he viewed the conflict as South Vietnam's responsibility. When the invasion came it wouldn't be pretty and there would be casualties, but that was not reason enough to escalate American involvement.

For the time being Nixon, who was leery of renewed congressional and public protest in an election year, agreed. He wrote Laird on March 18: "The request for additional air and naval gunfire authorities are not approved at this time. [They] will be reassessed should the anticipated major enemy assault begin." To give it greater chain-of-command authority, the order was signed by Nixon, not by Kissinger, as was the norm.[28]

⚜

A disturbing subtext to the military push for expanded bombing was the discovery by Laird in March that his top air force commander in South Vietnam, General John D. Lavelle, was deliberately defying his commander-in-chief and allowing unauthorized missions. It was the most serious insubordination by a high-level military officer since General Douglas MacArthur had been sacked twenty-one years before for publicly opposing President Truman in his determination to bomb Chinese bases during the Korean War. Lavelle, the commander of the U.S. Seventh Air Force in Vietnam, was a highly respected officer. He had served as a special assistant to Laird himself and was credited with helping develop the "electronic battlefield" sensor system that had been pivotal in slowing down enemy traffic on the Ho Chi Minh Trail.

But by November 1971 Lavelle had become alarmed at an enemy buildup of air defenses north of the demilitarized zone that was threatening his reconnaissance and attack flights with more sophisticated ground control radar and surface-to-air missile sites. It also began to look like the enemy might be putting antiaircraft sites in the DMZ itself and was gearing up to add more MiG fighters to the mix. So when Laird visited Vietnam at that time, Lavelle used his personal friendship to sit down with Laird for a private meeting at Ambassador Ellsworth Bunker's home to plead for more bombing authority. Laird was sympathetic, but his recollection of the meeting was that he told the general to do the best he could under the current rules. (Lavelle would later defend his actions based on that conversation, claiming that Laird had strongly implied that the general had permission to bend the rules.)

The day after Laird left Saigon, Lavelle made a decision to stretch the existing rules of engagement to the breaking point; he sent planes on a mission unauthorized by the president, the secretary of defense, or even the field commander, General Abrams. Under the rules, strikes on various targets had been allowed only if the enemy fired upon American planes. Laird's "protective reaction" permitted a more liberal interpretation, hitting enemy antiaircraft sites if enemy radar was tracking an American plane or had been activated on previous missions to the same area. Lavelle took it one step further, authorizing a policy of "planned protective reaction." The pilots were to assume that they would be fired on for every mission. On November 7 Lavelle told his pilots to interpret it as an attack every time enemy radar was activated while they flew reconnaissance or legitimate strike missions over Laos and southern North Vietnam.

In Lavelle's mind that constituted a potential attack on his planes, which allowed him to shoot back. But he was not sure his bosses would see it that way, so he mandated falsification of the pilot reports to keep Abrams and Laird in the dark. It began the first time one mission came back after dropping bombs on North Vietnam, with the pilot truthfully reporting "no reaction," meaning the enemy had not fired upon them. An angry General Lavelle told his next in command, General Alton Slay, that the pilots should never report "no reaction" when enemy radars had been activated against them. Lavelle later said he never intended to order his pilots to file false reports of enemy fire. But Slay and the pilots took it as an order to report enemy "reaction" no matter what.

Laird's first hint that something was amiss came in December when he noticed an uptick in the number of "reaction" incidents being reported. He sent Admiral Moorer a memo questioning the numbers. Moorer came back to him with a report in January concluding that there was nothing inappropriate about the figures. Laird asked him to keep an eye on the statistics but heard nothing more from him about it. The Lavelle subterfuge went on for three months before the first whistle was blown in late February. Among the dozens of senior and junior air force personnel involved in the charade—possibly more than two hundred men—was a lowly intelligence analyst for a reconnaissance wing stationed at Udorn Air Base in Thailand, who wrote a letter of complaint to his senator, Harold Hughes, a member of the Armed Services Committee. The sergeant, Lonnie Franks, wrote that "we have been reporting that our planes have received hostile actions whether they have or not," and that "we have also been falsifying targets struck and bomb damage assessments." He concluded, "I do not know where the original authorization comes from and this is my major concern."

By a quirk of fate, Senator Hughes received the letter on March 3, just before a lunch appointment with Air Force Chief of Staff General John Ryan. The senator shared the contents of the letter; Ryan was immediately concerned but could not imagine General Lavelle was involved.[29] Ryan hurriedly sent an inspector general team to Southeast Asia to investigate. Lavelle made another serious error by lying to the investigators in a belated attempt to cover up the insubordination. Nevertheless the air force inspectors soon uncovered at least seventeen unauthorized missions and accompanying false reports since the previous December. When Ryan received the initial report, he ordered Lavelle back to Washington and confronted him on the weekend of March 24. The encounter did nothing to persuade Ryan that Lavelle had been in the right. Ryan, who had been keeping Laird in the loop from the beginning, asked the defense secretary for a private meeting early Monday morning, March 27.

Laird was seriously unsettled when Ryan laid it out.[30] While he considered

Lavelle a "fine officer," Laird was not surprised that the general would aggressively stretch and break the rules in the belief he was protecting his men and aircraft. But he was surprised that Lavelle would lie about it when caught. Laird recalled that "sometimes our pilots, on their way back, had extra bombs, which they dropped on targets that weren't authorized for that run. But they came back and reported it in a forthright manner. You'll never find a single pilot that was ever disciplined for that type of activity." Under Lavelle's command "they were falsifying targets and then they lied to Ryan's team. You can't have that. If Lavelle would have told the truth about it, I don't think there would have been as great a problem. I don't expect people to lie, and I didn't expect him to. I think he should have owned up to it."

There were also some larger issues at play, which Robert Pursley put in perspective. He noted that the Lavelle incident came on the heels of the discovery that Yeoman Radford had been spying on the White House for the chairman of the Joint Chiefs. And now a top air force officer had ignored the president's orders and was bombing North Vietnamese targets on his own. "It occurred to me that this could be really wild for any administration to have this much military misfeasance going on right under their nose. Now two instances don't make a pattern, but those are two people in very high positions who were doing things far beyond anything anyone could comprehend. The whole idea of a military gone a little berserk was not something the Nixon administration wanted to have brought up in an election year."[31]

Laird's view was straightforward: Lavelle had to go. "You have to maintain some type of civilian control and authority," he recounted later. "It was basically rebellion," former top Pentagon systems analyst Ivan Selin observed. "Once you can't trust your commanders to report accurately what they tell you, you can't trust anybody. This was some guy who felt he knew better than the secretary and president how to conduct this war."[32]

The day after his meeting with Ryan, Laird wrote a stern memo to Admiral Moorer stating that "the authorized rules of engagement must . . . be adhered to strictly." The secretary wanted an immediate check "throughout the command channels to insure strict compliance with the authorized rules of engagement." The Lavelle incident was not referenced, but it had been the obvious precipitant.[33] Two days later, on March 30, Laird left no doubt in a memo to Moorer that he personally wanted Lavelle relieved of command. "[I]t is in the best interests of the United States and all concerned to remove the incumbent 7th Air Force Commander from his existing post and place him in a different status." This should "be handled on an urgent and discreet basis." Moorer passed the instructions to Ryan, who promptly followed through.[34] In deference to Lavelle's previously distinguished career, Ryan told him he could stay in the air force and receive a lesser assignment, or retire quietly. He chose the latter, retiring on an emphysema disability. The day before it was publicly announced, Laird informed the appropriate senators about it.[35]

On April 7, 1972, it was announced that General Lavelle was retiring for "personal and health reasons." But a tip-off to a greater problem came with notation that the four-star general would be retired at three stars. Veteran journalists raised eyebrows; this was the first time in modern U.S. military history that a four-star general had been demoted upon retirement. The hunt for the facts was on and they could not be kept secret for long. In early May, amid erroneous reports about the reason for Lavelle's departure, Laird confirmed it had occurred because he personally "had lost confidence" in Lavelle's leadership. On May 16 a Laird press aide issued a statement that Lavelle was bounced "because of irregularities in the conduct of his responsibilities."[36]

Both Ryan and Lavelle were called before a closed door hearing of a House Armed Services investigative subcommittee on June 12, where during four hours of testimony the facts were laid out—that Lavelle had allowed at least twenty-eight unauthorized bombing missions involving 147 aircraft between November 7, 1971, and March 9, 1972. "I'm the commander and the buck stops here," Lavelle admitted. But, he added, "I think General Abrams knew what I was doing." That was enough to prompt a three-week inquiry by the Senate Armed Services Committee that ultimately cleared Abrams, who neither knew about nor would have approved the missions. The committee recommended in October that Lavelle be stripped of yet another star. Two months later the House committee actually praised Lavelle, saying his actions were "not only proper, but essential" to protect American servicemen.[37] In fact, most of Lavelle's targets were authorized to be hit once the North Vietnamese invaded the South. "I approved more than half those targets a month or two later," Laird agreed, "but they weren't approved when they were hit."

Whenever Laird got a microphone during that time, such as an appearance on CBS's *Face the Nation,* he would defend the military. "This one incident of wrong-doing...should not be used to judge every man and woman that wears the uniform of our country. I have great respect and admiration [for them]; 99 and 9/10ths percent of those men and women understand orders and follow them."[38] Additionally Laird did something very rare for a government official whose department has been embarrassed by a whistle blower; he publicly praised Sergeant Franks for coming forward, and promoted him.[39]

As for Lavelle, Laird felt betrayed by the general. "I always told him to use the authority granted to him, to use protective reaction. I was giving him a lot of latitude. I believe he was a sincere military officer who thought he was doing the right thing. But he let his judgment interfere with the execution of his orders."

As part of his response to the command problem that the Lavelle incident identified, Laird made two significant changes. In April 1972 he created the Defense Investigative Service as a separate agency over the individual service investigative bodies, answering directly to the secretary of defense. Secondly, he created a large new group of inspectors general "embedded" in every unified command headquarters. As Laird predicted at the time, both moves curbed disobedience by later military commanders in war and peace.[40]

But before these solutions were implemented, and before the Lavelle aberration unraveled publicly from April onward, the immediate upshot in March 1972 was that the veteran air chief in Southeast Asia was relieved, and his command put in some disarray, on the very day that the North Vietnamese finally began their Easter offensive.

38

Easter Offensive

❧

IT WAS RELATIVELY TRANQUIL AT NOON on March 30, 1972, just south of the demilitarized zone—the forty-mile strip that separated North and South Vietnam. The South Vietnamese soldiers in the fire bases in northern Quang Tri Province were getting ready for lunch when the first shell came screaming south across the DMZ. It was followed by an artillery barrage the likes of which few had experienced—a total of twelve thousand rockets and mortars throughout the Easter weekend. On March 31 whole divisions of the North Vietnamese army came out of the DMZ with tanks and new Soviet 130-mm guns, which had a range of eighteen miles. Over the next two days the North Vietnamese also invaded through Laos and Cambodia, attacking the South Vietnamese in the Central Highlands and farther south, headed for Saigon. The invasion force would eventually grow to number about 350,000 men from fourteen of Hanoi's fifteen regular army divisions. Along with hundreds of artillery pieces and armored personnel carriers, nearly four hundred tanks led the soldiers in the multipronged offensive that was intended by the North to be the last battle of the war.

Depleted by the Tet offensive of 1968 and hammered by U.S. and South Vietnamese forays against the Ho Chi Minh Trail, the North Vietnamese took four years to get to the point where they could mount such an attack. This was not stealthy jungle guerrilla warfare; the pacification efforts in the south had all but neutralized the Viet Cong who were the experts at that kind of fighting. This was not hit-and-run skirmishing from the sanctuaries in Laos and Cambodia. This was tank and artillery battering of cities and massive movement of troops taking territory inch by inch the old-fashioned way. It was just the kind of conventional warfare Americans excelled at, but the Americans were essentially gone from the ground war. Only ninety-five thousand U.S. troops remained, and few of them, other than the advisors, were in ground "combat" roles. So by dint of circumstances and timing, this was to be the bloody "acid test" for Melvin Laird's Vietnamization strategy, and it came in the last year of his leadership at the Pentagon. Hanoi named the campaign "Nguyen Hue," after an eighteenth-century Vietnamese emperor who repelled an invading Chinese army. The Americans simply called it the "Easter offensive."

On Good Friday, March 31, Laird advised President Nixon that the artillery barrage and first indications of an invasion force in Quang Tri province were not just another battle but were likely the beginning of *the* battle the allies had been waiting for. South Vietnamese President Nguyen Van Thieu told his people grimly that night in a ten-minute TV speech: "This is the final battle to decide the survival of the people."[1]

President Nixon waited a few days to see how the South Vietnamese would handle the challenge. A debate raged behind the scenes about the use of American air support, with Nixon and Kissinger leaning toward an all-out bombing campaign over the North, and Laird—backing the judgment of General Abrams—wanting to concentrate the bombs on the battlegrounds as direct assistance to the South Vietnamese troops. Laird's vision of Vietnamization had always been to prepare South Vietnam to defend itself on its home turf, not to take the battle across borders. The first air support was tentative. On April 1, the second day of the invasion, Nixon lifted some restrictions to allow bombing enemy military concentrations in the DMZ itself and up to twenty-five miles north of the DMZ, but bad weather muted the attack.

Against the massive North Vietnamese assault on the ground, the South Vietnamese army gave way in less than a week, abandoning seventeen fire bases and falling back behind the Cua Viet River. On Easter Sunday, April 2, after the North Vietnamese had succeeded in overrunning the northern half of Quang Tri Province, President Nixon, against Laird's advice, ordered full-scale bombing of the North, including the use of B-52 bombers stationed at Guam. Before the offensive was over, the number of B-52s involved had increased from 42 to 148, shutting down an entire runway on Guam for use as a parking lot. Four more aircraft carriers were also brought into the seas off Vietnam, along with five cruisers and forty-four destroyers.[2]

At the Monday staff meeting (the day after Easter Sunday), Laird had Admiral Moorer do the main briefing. He reported that the South Vietnamese had held to their predetermined fallback position at the Cua Viet River. Retreat might not have been necessary if not for the bad weather that had hampered U.S. air support. The planes that were able to fly were taking heavy fire from surface-to-air missiles launched from inside the DMZ. Laird urged calm; he knew a crisis mentality would give Hanoi the victory in the public relations war, just as it had in the Tet offensive. "We have never gotten over the 1968 Tet offensive," Laird added. "We lost that battle the first two days in Washington, even though it was a great North Vietnamese defeat."[3]

☞

Laird and Nixon had decided that it was best that the president not speak about the invasion for a while, lest he contribute to an atmosphere of crisis. So Laird himself became the point man. At a Pentagon press conference one week after the invasion was launched, Laird raged against Hanoi's "spectacular disregard for the DMZ" and the South's sovereignty, which abrogated the 1968 bombing halt understanding. "The enemy has scornfully rejected the American people's patience, restraint and desire for peace. Our patience has been met with propaganda, and with provocation. Our restraint has been answered by invasion. Our actions have been to withdraw our forces and to reduce tensions. The enemy has escalated the actions and has committed new forces. He has dared us to abandon our allies and we will not." Laird lambasted the Soviet Union for being a "major contributor to the continuing conflict in Southeast Asia" and having supplied the North with the means to mount this invasion.[4]

It was hard for the combative Nixon to keep a low profile, which relegated him to coaching from the sidelines. On April 15 Nixon sent Laird a three-page memorandum of talking points for use at a scheduled Senate hearing. "Under no circumstances must we show any wavering," he directed Laird. "We must attack the enemy's invasion and his massive violations of all agreements." The like-minded Laird was already planning to do that.[5] As expected, the April 18 hearing before the hostile Senate Foreign Relations Committee and its antiwar chairman, William Fulbright, was full of fireworks. In front of the committee Laird was every bit the president's pit bull, dominating the debate so strongly that at one point Fulbright jumped in to silence him. "If I could say one word or two before you interfere," Fulbright bristled. "This is supposed to be a hearing, not a monologue."

"I would like to testify as to those points," Laird countered, unabashed.

"I would like to make an observation," Fulbright interrupted and then filibustered his views for several minutes.

"You are excellent as a witness," Laird smiled at the senator, with only the barest hint of sarcasm.

"I am not as professional as you are," Fulbright allowed.

When Laird was questioned about the buildup of U.S. naval and air forces while the combat troops were marching out the back door, he acknowledged that navy presence in the seas off Vietnam had nearly doubled. "But this isn't an increase in the number of people in the Navy, it is a change of their operational area for a given period of time, and that is what naval power is all about," Laird said. The B-52s and tactical air squadrons were not technically stationed in Vietnam, Laird went on. And half the air sorties were being flown by South Vietnamese pilots, although Laird stressed that they were not doing the flying in the raids over North Vietnam. "We have not given them the ability to penetrate and attack outside of their country. One part of our program is to give them defensive capability to maintain their own in-country security."

Fulbright tried to shut down Laird's pep talk on the success of Vietnamization: "You have sold us all and I am sure you have sold everybody here on the idea that you are making progress in Vietnamization, but you haven't sold me that that is worth what it is costing the United States.... I am strongly of the view that, granted everything you have said, it is a wrong policy and is not in the interest of the United States to continue this war."[6]

During his spirited public defense of the bombing, Laird was somewhat conflicted. Privately he would have preferred more control from Washington.

"I wanted to know what the targets were," he recalled. "I wasn't giving blanket authority to go in there and hit anything. I'm enthusiastic if you show me a good target. I wanted to make sure the cost in human life was worth the target." Some reporters at the time picked up on Laird's reticence. The *New York Times* reported on the same day Laird was testifying before Fulbright's committee that the defense secretary was "less than enthusiastic about bombing targets in the vicinity of Hanoi and Haiphong." A Pentagon spokesman was quoted as saying "obliquely" about Laird: "He's been on the side of restraint on Vietnam since taking office."[7]

Laird wrote to Kissinger privately a few days later, suggesting it was time to tone down the air support. Laird argued that "the sum total of these additions [the added naval and air forces] to friendly forces exceeds, in my judgment, that which is needed for military purposes. It is doubtful that sending additional elements would have much positive political visibility." Shortly after, Kissinger notified Laird that "the President agrees that for the present we should not proceed with further air or naval augmentation...." But Nixon did not want to curtail the bombing of the North.[8] Laird saw it as unwarranted bloodshed in the North that would not stop or slow the invasion in the South.

At a speech before a Rotary Club in Brooklyn, Laird let his guard down. Until then he had given no hint of any differences between his own position and that of the Nixon-Kissinger White House. But during the question-and-answer period Laird was unusually open: "The question is: Would I support the use of air power and bombing in North Vietnam under the circumstances that exist in Southeast Asia today? I, of course, have recommended the conservative use of air power in Southeast Asia, in North Vietnam. I would continue to use that air power when there are effective military targets that are interfering with the progress of our troop program and that would endanger the lives of service personnel." That was his view in a nutshell. If it didn't save American military lives or assist the South Vietnamese defenders, he saw little point.

Two days later Nixon sent a "flash message" to Laird through Kissinger that synthesized his own philosophy about the bombing of the North and hinted that he knew Laird did not agree. Nixon ordered the " absolute maximum number of sorties must be flown"—around a thousand a day—to have the "maximum psychological effect." He also demanded an immediate report on how his orders were to be carried out, and he closed with, "There are to be no excuses and there is no appeal."[9]

From years of working with Nixon, Laird knew there was always an avenue of appeal using political grounds, especially in an election year as was 1972. That is how he succeeded in persuading Nixon to continue with American troop withdrawals even as the North Vietnamese invasion was peaking. Nixon had publicly announced in January that he would take 22,500 men out of Vietnam every month until May 1. As that date approached the pressure mounted for Nixon to announce the next withdrawal phase. On April 16 Abrams sent a request through channels that the troop withdrawals be stopped until July 1, given the fact that the Easter offensive looked like it would stretch into the summer.[10]

Laird reported the request to Nixon but sent two of his own reports to the president within three days of each other asking that the withdrawals continue, but at a slower pace of about 6,700 a month with the long-range goal of having only 15,000 men in Vietnam by December 31. The first memo to Nixon spelled out Laird's rationale, but four days later he had reason to think the president might not pay attention to him. General Haig had made a fact-finding trip to Vietnam, and Laird feared that Haig's gung-ho attitude about the war might prevail, persuading Nixon to suspend any more withdrawals.

"The denigration of Vietnamization is one of Hanoi's key goals in its current offensive," Laird warned Nixon in writing on April 24. "An announcement of redeployment suspension would lend credibility to Hanoi's charge that Vietnamization is a defunct concept. Of equal importance, an announcement of redeployment suspension would have, in my judgment, a dramatic adverse political impact domestically." To this memorandum General Pursley appended a note for his boss: "Hope this does the job." It did.[11] Nixon not only continued the withdrawals, but announced a higher monthly rate than Laird had recommended, and over a shorter term—sending twenty thousand more men home by the end of June, a rate of ten thousand a month.

Laird felt confident about continuing the troop withdrawal program in part because he was receiving glowing reports from General Abrams (which he forwarded to the president) about the success of Vietnamization in the face of the Easter offensive. "The clear purpose of this invasion is to destroy the Armed Forces of South Vietnam," Abrams began in a cable sent on April 26, the day of Nixon's announcement on new withdrawals. "In this battle so far, U.S. air power and advisory support have been of tremendous value. This invasion could not have been held at this point without U.S. air support. However, ten times the air power could not have done the job if the Armed Forces of South Vietnam had not stood and fought." He added, "as in all combat situations, there has been a mixture of the heroic and not so heroic" by the South Vietnamese servicemen. "But on the whole, the heroic performances stand out as the trademark of this battle to the death."[12]

One of many gratifying aspects for Abrams and Laird was how quickly the previously untested South Vietnamese learned to take out enemy tanks. In late April Laird directed that one of the Pentagon's newest weapons, the wire-guided antitank TOW missile, be rushed to South Vietnam. The new missiles were fired from tubelike launchers mounted on jeeps or in helicopters. The Pentagon acronym stands for "tube-launched, optically tracked, wire-guided missile." Once the missile is launched, two thin trailing wires more than a mile long rapidly unreel. Through the wires the gunner can send last-minute electronic commands to adjust the trajectory. In their first weeks of use in Vietnam most of the TOWs were shot by Americans from Cobra helicopters. General Abrams was reluctant to give them to any South Vietnamese units that might carelessly leave them behind during a retreat. He didn't want the technology falling in the hands of North Vietnam. For a new weapon its performance was impressive. Of the first seventy-three TOW firings, fifty-seven were hits, eleven misses, and five malfunctions; dozens of enemy tanks were falling victim to the TOW.[13]

It was not the only new weapon getting its first workout in Vietnam. The most important of the innovations, which forever changed air-launched missile warfare, was the Vietnam-era development of PGMs—"precision-guided munitions," known better as "smart bombs." The first variant effectively employed during the war (in 1967) was the navy-developed Walleye electro-optical bombs. A TV camera mounted in the front of the bomb allowed an operator in the delivery airplane to guide the missile to its target while the plane was streaking out of danger.

During the years of the bombing halt, the air force had been perfecting its Paveway series of smart bombs. While these laser-guided bombs were used in 1971 against the Ho Chi Minh Trail, the real test came over North Vietnam's heavily defended military areas. After Nixon lifted bombing restrictions during the Easter offensive, the PGMs came into full and frequent use. The F-4 Phantom pilots were thrilled about the new bombs, not only because of their accuracy, but also because they allowed a pilot to drop the bomb and immediately perform evasive maneuvers while still guiding the bomb to its target.

While these new weapons were a major assist to the South Vietnamese defense, they didn't halt the daily, bloody grind of the ground battle on multiple fronts. Throughout April the enemy made headway, despite some reverses and serious matériel losses (such as tanks and artillery pieces). The North Vietnamese still held the northern half of Quang Tri Province. They were close enough to Da Nang to shell it. In the Central Highlands the provincial capitals of Kontum and Pleiku were threatened, while just sixty miles north of Saigon, at An Loc, enemy attacks increased in intensity. At the time, because of the U.S. troop withdrawal program, the only Americans facing the brunt of battle with the South Vietnamese army were about ten thousand heroic advisors—the same job description given to the first men President Kennedy sent to Vietnam in 1961.

In February, before the Easter offensive, General Westmoreland had argued heatedly in Laird's Monday staff meeting that the advisors should not be withdrawn until the last possible moment. "We can't have our withdrawal program be a double psychological blow to the South Vietnamese," he said. "First, the troops leave, and then if we have the advisors leave it would bring the problem of a 'bug out' psychosis. We can avoid this 'decompression' if we slow down the removal of the advisors." Westmoreland had just returned from another trip to Vietnam, where General Abrams had agreed that he would like to keep the advisors with the South Vietnamese army, but he had to begin withdrawing some of them to make the withdrawal quotas. Laird agreed the two generals had a good point and said he would figure out a way to keep the best number of advisors there.[14]

A month after that meeting, the advisors had proved their value during the Easter invasion when, together with American air support, they were credited with saving South Vietnamese soldiers and cities in dozens of battles. One of those advisors, John Paul Vann, was a living legend. He had learned survival at a young age as the illegitimate son of a sometime-prostitute living in the "white trash" section of Norfolk, Virginia, during the Depression. He enlisted in the Army Air Corps, where he served as a B-29 navigator in the latter part of World War II. He first went to Vietnam in 1962 as a senior advisor in the Mekong Delta area. At five feet, eight inches and 150 pounds, Vann was not a large man, yet he displayed courage on a gigantic scale, bordering on the foolhardy. He fought at the front of the South Vietnamese troops he was advising and was in the thick of nearly every firefight. Vann saw earlier than most the futility of fighting a guerrilla enemy with conventional strategies. He carefully documented his assessments and became a primary, authoritative source of disenchantment to the reporters who were sensing the same futility, even that early in the war. The military advisors then were part and parcel of what he called the "bright, shining lies" of U.S. engagement in Vietnam. In 1963 Vann resigned from the military in frustration and left Vietnam to work for a defense contractor. But Vietnam was in his blood and he returned in 1965 and stayed for the next seven years under contract to the State Department and other agencies.

Though he was always officially an "advisor," Vann functioned as a soldier and, often, a de facto commanding cogeneral to the South Vietnamese forces he was "advising." During those years one of his protégés was a former RAND Corporation analyst, Daniel Ellsberg, who gleaned from Vann firsthand an eloquent dissent from the way the Johnson administration was handling the war. But Vann loved Laird's Vietnamization strategy. It was the plan for which he had long waited, as Vann made clear to reporters and anyone else who would listen. Beginning as a congressman, Laird met with him on several occasions and came to appreciate Vann's commitment, bravery, and insight. Thinking that Vann could personalize the argument for Vietnamization, Laird encouraged a meeting between Vann and President Nixon, who often needed pep talks on the topic. Vann and Nixon conferred in the Oval Office in December 1969, and Vann predicted then that when the South Vietnamese army inevitably faced North Vietnamese invaders, the South would prevail.

That was his message to the media in Vietnam as well as Washington when he returned for recuperative trips that included regularly briefing Laird. In

January 1972 the one-time pessimist told an audience in Kentucky, "This program of Vietnamization has gone kind of literally beyond my wildest dreams of success." By that time Vann had become—in position and influence—the third most important American in South Vietnam after Abrams and the U.S. ambassador, Ellsworth Bunker. No other leader had his decade-long Vietnam battle experience.

When the Easter invasion occurred, Vann helped save the besieged Fire Base Delta by repeated resupply and gunnery runs with his own helicopter. He then wrote an upbeat memo to his "friends," including Laird—friends who had come to think Vann was invincible. On June 7 a *Washington Post* reporter, Larry Stern, caught up with Vann for an hour-long interview that was to be his last. Stern described Vann as "the American civilian advisor who is personally directing the air and ground war in the embattled Central Highlands."

Vann told Stern that months before he had personally delivered to Laird the blueprint strategy he was sure the Communists would follow when they invaded, and he had been right. "I expect to defeat—I expect the Vietnamese to defeat the North Vietnamese force," Vann told Stern. "I have predicted success since December." Not many days before, after lunching with two visiting Senate staffers, he called out as they were departing: "Say hello to Dan Ellsberg." It was Vann's way of twitting his former acolyte who had become infamous the year before as the source of the Pentagon Papers.

During the Easter offensive Vann was determined to fly his light helicopter from Pleiku to the besieged Kontum every day. One of his objects was to deliberately draw fire from the enemy to "spot" them for the defenders. Two days after the interview Vann and a less-experienced pilot took off from Pleiku after dark en route to Kontum. Along the way they hit rain and fog that disoriented the pilot, and the helicopter crashed into a stand of tall trees covering a graveyard. Everyone in the chopper died. Though Radio Hanoi exulted the next day that they had finally shot down "one of the most important and most cruel [American] advisors," it was an accident that felled Vann.

Laird was at a loss for words when he heard the news. At the following Monday staff meeting, Laird paid tribute to Vann as "a great fighter, and a person who understood the situation better than anyone else. He will be missed. We will close the meeting in silence by recalling his service to his country."[15] On Friday afternoon Laird was on hand at the Oval Office when President Nixon presented a posthumous Presidential Medal of Freedom for Vann to his family. That morning Laird had attended Vann's funeral at Arlington National Cemetery. Among the official pallbearers were General Westmoreland and William Colby, the future CIA director. Seated behind the Vann family was the indicted Ellsberg, still facing a prison term for the Pentagon Papers leak. The *New York Times* reporter to whom he first gave the papers, Neil Sheehan, was struck by the conglomeration of those who came to the funeral, and the history it represented. That night he drafted a memo to himself, the beginning of a sixteen-year book project that culminated in the 1988 publication of *A Bright Shining Lie: John Paul Vann and America in Vietnam.* At the time he reflected that as Vann's funeral service progressed, "I had the feeling that we were burying more than John Vann—that we were burying an era, the whole era of confidence that Henry Luce had so boastfully called 'the American century.'"[16]

A month before the Easter offensive, Westmoreland had returned from a trip to the Far East and conveyed some of his findings to those attending Laird's Monday staff meeting. He was pleased to report that "the South Vietnamese leadership has steadily improved since I visited there 18 months ago." But the generals over two of the four military regions of South Vietnam were a serious concern. The first was Lieutenant General Ngo Dzu, in command of the Central Highlands. Dzu, a political appointee, was a hack—"possibly the weakest Corps Commander," Westmoreland said. However, he added, the fact that "his U.S. advisor is John Paul Vann helps to make up for General Dzu's weaknesses."[17] (This was four months before Vann was killed.)

The second problematic regional commander was Lieutenant General Hoang Xuan Lam, who was in charge of defending the northernmost provinces, including South Vietnam's third largest city, Quang Tri. "I got the impression that General Lam has become 'war lordish,'" Westmoreland told the staff meeting. Over the previous year Lam had been the subject of several of Laird's meetings with the Vietnam Task Force. At one such meeting a U.S. intelligence report was read that charged that Lam was making a fortune promising the rights to various U.S. bases after they were turned over to the South Vietnamese.[18]

Lam did not inspire leadership or loyalty. Though Quang Tri City withstood punishing artillery assaults for a full month when the offensive began, the lackluster leadership finally spelled its doom, and the provincial capital fell to the North Vietnamese invaders on May 1. Abrams cabled Laird: "This is a battle to the death. The Communists have planned it that way and will not quit until they have been totally exhausted." Abrams met with President Thieu and told him that his commanders were toying with defeat. Then Abrams ordered his field commanders to stop airlifting jittery South Vietnamese commanders out of the heat of battle unless they had orders from higher up.[19] Thieu acted immediately, replacing General Dzu with a more competent commander to work with Vann, and also firing General Lam. His replacement was Lieutenant General Ngo Quang Truong, who had previously defended Hue successfully during the 1968 Tet offensive.

Truong was cut from entirely different cloth than Lam. A rarity among higher-ranking South Vietnamese military leaders, he was honest, incorruptible, lived a Spartan existence, and believed that his place was with the troops in the hottest part of the battle. Truong knew the first thing he had to do was stanch the flow of South Vietnamese soldiers fleeing the front with their families, so he announced that any soldier caught leaving would be shot; he then set up one hundred armored cars equipped with .50-caliber machine guns and orders to carry out his "shoot on sight" directive. On one day, four deserters were shot, and soldiers began returning to their posts.[20]

In the days after Quang Tri City fell, some media critics badgered Laird about the failure of Vietnamization and the imminent collapse of South Vietnam. Laird was nonplussed. Like Vann he had always thought some territory would be lost in the initial stage of an enemy invasion, only to be regained later. The slow pace of the North Vietnamese onslaught was cited by Laird in the early weeks to tamp down the apocalyptic prognostications from inside and outside of the administration. On May 10, for example, even though Quang Tri City had fallen, he declared at a news conference: "I have told you on many occasions that the South Vietnamese will not win every battle, or every encounter, but they will do a very credible job in the vast majority of encounters which they will have."[21]

While the defense secretary was able to allay panic throughout the department and uniformed military, his calming influence was not enough of a tonic for the commander-in-chief. Nixon was at this point a skittish president who feared he might be presiding over America's first war loss at precisely the time he was running for reelection. So, in the fervid milieu of those early May days Nixon made a decision to do something Laird had advocated seven years before but no president had authorized—mining the harbors of North Vietnam.

When he was a congressman in 1965 Laird began strongly and repeatedly urging Lyndon Johnson to mine the harbor at Haiphong as a way of preventing huge shiploads of Soviet military hardware from entering enemy territory.[22] Laird saw mining as a cheap, relatively safe, and extremely threatening way to attack North Vietnam's supply lines. It made more sense to interdict at that point, without risking American servicemen, than to rain bombs on the Ho Chi Minh Trail when supplies were already in the pipeline. He made the same argument as defense secretary, but Nixon and Kissinger didn't initially favor mining. Laird said that Nixon feared a Russian ship might be blown up in the process, and Kissinger feared mining might "queer the negotiations" with Hanoi on the war and Moscow on arms control.

Once the Easter offensive had begun, Laird was inclined to think that it was too late for the mining, since the horse was already out of the barn. In early April, when the Joint Chiefs submitted a plan for mining Haiphong Harbor, Laird sent it along to Kissinger with a recommendation that it be rejected. Laird's note to Kissinger at the end of the typed memo said: "Henry—The political impact of these plans may be what is wanted by the President. The military impact would be minor and the impact on the present battle would be even long. If the Russians want an excuse to stop their present major (80%

supplies) contribution to North Viet Nam, mining might have that political impact—but I would doubt it."[23]

More than a week later Laird was on the hot seat before the Senate Foreign Relations Committee, again, as the chairman, Senator Fulbright, kept him answering questions for almost four and a half hours. What made headlines was Laird's declaration that he absolutely would "not rule out" a future strategy of mining Haiphong Harbor.[24]

The political argument for mining finally won out in May. Kissinger, who was paving the way for Nixon to attend a summit meeting in Moscow, thought he had received some assurances from the Soviets that they could make North Vietnam be more flexible in the peace talks. Kissinger hung his hopes on a negotiating session on May 2 with his North Vietnamese counterpart in Paris, Le Duc Tho. The meeting went nowhere, and it was apparent that the Soviets, the major suppliers of war matériel to North Vietnam, either could not or would not twist arms in Hanoi to bring the war to an end. Kissinger returned to Washington convinced that it was time to take off the gloves with the North Vietnamese. He said as much to Nixon.[25]

The president met with his National Security Council on the morning of May 8 after spending the weekend at Camp David weighing the decision about the harbors. Knowing its importance, Laird had scheduled his Monday staff meeting ninety minutes early so that he could attend the NSC session, which ran from 9 A.M. to 12:20 P.M. Prior to the meeting Kissinger was tasked to find out the views of each principal. The primary foreign policy trio—Laird, Rogers, and Helms—were all opposed, but for different reasons. In his memoirs Kissinger reported that Laird was against the mining because he "thought the battle would be decided in South Vietnam [and] the battlefield impact of mining would come too late to affect the Easter offensive." Kissinger wrote that he agreed, "but I was concerned with Hanoi's actions after the offensive. [Laird] also thought the North Vietnamese would be able to replace seaborne supplies with overland routes."

Kissinger recounted Laird's debating points made during the NSC meeting: "Laird argued that the most critical supplies came in by rail and in any case the North Vietnamese had four to five months of stocks in reserve. He expressed confidence that the South Vietnamese 'can make it. Hue may go but it will not be as bad as 1968.' His conclusion was that the mining and interdiction campaigns were unnecessary. The cheaper solution from the budgetary point of view was to send more equipment to South Vietnam."[26] Laird did not dispute Kissinger's account. "I didn't think the president should be misled that this was going to change the outcome of the offensive that was planned and going forward at that time. It may have an effect a year or so out. Mining was a psychological thing more than anything else."

Nixon asked his Cabinet favorite, Treasury Secretary John Connally, to stay behind after the NSC meeting along with Kissinger. Connally was a zealous war hawk at that point and advised Nixon that "sometimes it's not *what* you decide but *that* you decide." Nixon asked the two if anything they had heard in the NSC meeting had changed their minds about favoring mining. "We both told him that the discussion had *reinforced* our conviction to proceed," Kissinger wrote. With that, Nixon called for the necessary "execute" papers and signed the new orders at 2 P.M.[27]

Nixon arranged for a briefing in the White House's Roosevelt Room for congressional leaders at 8 P.M., an hour before his televised address about the new measures (which included intensified bombing of North Vietnam). The president asked Laird, Rogers, and Admiral Moorer to answer questions from the members of Congress. Nixon began by hinting that the precipitating factor for the mining was the intransigence of Moscow and Hanoi. "In four days in Moscow, Vietnam was not only discussed by the Soviet leaders, they urged us to go back to the conference table, leading us to believe they would play a con-structive role. Whether they did or not is unknown, but the results are clear," Nixon recounted. "The North Vietnamese had the most insulting, intransigent attitude in five years of negotiation." So, he suggested, since "the negotiation path has been closed to us," he had nothing to lose with the escalation. "If you can give me your support, I would appreciate it," Nixon told the members of Congress, as he was rising to leave. "If you cannot, I will understand."

Nixon speech writer (and later *New York Times* columnist) William Safire, who was present and taking notes, thought Senate Majority Leader Mike Mans-field was the most unsettled by the decision. He looked "unusually pale" and made the first objection to Laird, Rogers, and Moorer, who were left behind to explain for the president. "What it means," Mansfield charged, "is that the war is enlarged. It appears to me that we are embarking on a dangerous course. We are courting danger here that could extend the war, increase the number of war prisoners and make peace more difficult to achieve." Laird was the first to respond. "As far as *extension* is concerned, Mike, it was extended by the enemy. It's not fair to charge *us* with that responsibility." Rogers added that the North Vietnamese themselves had used mines during the ongoing war, so they could hardly complain now.[28]

At 9 P.M. President Nixon told the world that he had already ordered the mining of all North Vietnamese harbors. Ships currently in those harbors had seventy-two hours to leave before the mines would be remotely activated. The operation was code-named "Pocket Money" and was part of the overall Opera-tion Linebacker, which included heavy bombing of enemy supply depots and transportation facilities. Planes from the USS *Coral Sea* took only three min-utes on May 9 to drop the first thirty-six mines over the Haiphong shipping channel as diversionary air strikes were conducted by the USS *Kitty Hawk* to protect the mine-laying operation. Over the next two days six other important ports of North Vietnam were seeded with the mines.

Precisely at 9 A.M. on May 12 all of the mines were remotely switched on.

As Laird had been predicting for seven years, it was a "fail safe" operation; no men or planes were lost.[29] There was, however, loss of face in Saigon, where General Abrams was not told about preparatory navy ship movements toward the harbors before the presidential decision. Laird had dispatched Barry Shillito in early May to assess the needs of the South Vietnamese army and convey a strong message of continued U.S. support. At a meeting the first week of May, Abrams complained to Shillito about ongoing navy exercises that he had not known about. He raged that, as usual, the navy was fighting its own war without a word to him about it.

Shillito instantly realized that the exercises were related to the potential mining operation and that Abrams was completely in the dark about the deployment. Abrams had known that the mining was being considered, but the command to move the ships in preparation had gone to Abrams' boss, Admiral John McCain, who had not told Abrams. Shillito cabled the news to Laird, who was embarrassed and angry. He knew that McCain and Abrams were barely on speaking terms at the time. Laird called McCain on the phone and chewed him out. Then Laird cabled an apology to Abrams who took it in stride.[30]

According to the polls, a majority of Americans supported Nixon's mining decision. However the mining and intensified bombing had the effect of rousing the sleeping antiwar movement in the United States—triggering renewed protests, including a particularly explosive one that hit home for the secretary of defense.

39

The View from Maggie's Farm

❧

MAY 19, 1971, WAS HO CHI MINH'S BIRTHDAY, and a radical anti-war group in the United States decided that a bomb in the Pentagon would be the perfect gift. Revolution was the order of the day for these urban guerrillas, who called themselves the "Weathermen" (later the "Weather Underground" or "Weather Bureau") after a line in a Bob Dylan song: "You don't need a weather man / To know which way the wind blows." They were full of antiestablishment fury and antiwar rage, further fueled by a sense of impotence. Cofounders Bernardine Dohrn and Bill Ayers spewed generational venom: "Kill all the rich people. Bring the revolution home. Kill your parents; that's where it's really at." Several-hundred strong at their peak, the Weathermen went underground as they began to plot murder and mayhem in the name of their shifting causes. Living and moving about in "cells," they developed their own "slanguage." The Pentagon was "Maggie's Farm," from another Dylan song with the refrain, "I ain't gonna work on Maggie's farm no more."[1]

In early 1970 three Weathermen had been building a bomb in a Greenwich Village townhouse when they blew themselves up. That bomb had been intended for Fort Dix, New Jersey. On March 1, 1971, the Weathermen had succeeded with a bomb in the "Big Top" (the Capitol). The predawn explosion blew up a men's room across from the Senate barbershop. For the Weathermen the Pentagon was the mother of all targets. In the spring of 1971 a three-person Weather cell set up shop in a cheap apartment near the Pentagon. The Weather woman of the trio dressed in a suit, donned a dark wig and thick glasses, and carried a briefcase into the Pentagon each morning for several days to case the building. After repeatedly entering unchallenged among the throngs of workers, she identified a fairly isolated woman's restroom in an air force section of the building as the best place to hide three pounds of dynamite, under a floor drain.

The bomb exploded at one minute before 1 A.M. on Ho's birthday. The blast on the fourth floor of the Pentagon's E-ring shook that section of the building, including the offices of Air Force Secretary Robert Seamans and Air Force Chief of Staff John Ryan. Windows and a lavatory brick wall were blown out, and thousands of gallons of water poured through a gaping hole in the floor.[2] While security sweeps for other possible bombs began, a trans-Atlantic call was placed to Laird in Copenhagen, where it was after 7 A.M. He was already up, dressing for a morning meeting of the NATO Nuclear Planning Group. Assured that no one had been hurt, Laird ordered Dan Henkin to downplay the incident with the press. He did not want to give the terrorists the satisfaction of extensive attention.[3]

Two of those responsible, Ayers and Dohrn, went on the run for more than a decade. Dohrn made the FBI's "Ten Most Wanted" list, with J. Edgar Hoover labeling her "the most dangerous woman in America." After the pair had their second child together, Ayers and Dohrn gave themselves up to the FBI in 1981. In the end all federal charges were dropped against them because the FBI had engaged in a variety of illegal actions while pursuing them. Dohrn became a professor at Northwestern University and a crusader for juvenile justice re-form, while Ayers became a professor of education at the University of Illinois at Chicago. In 2001 Ayers published an unapologetic memoir, *Fugitive Days*. In a terrible irony the *New York Times* printed a sympathetic profile of Ayers and his new book on September 11, 2001, under the headline: "No Regrets for a Love of Explosives." At the beginning of the story, published on the day the World Trade Center towers fell to terrorists, Ayers was quoted as saying: "I don't regret setting bombs. I feel we didn't do enough."[4]

⌖

With bombings at home and abroad, the 1972 presidential election campaign was off to a volatile start. Inveterate campaigner Laird was loath to sit on the sidelines, but tradition held that a secretary of defense did not become in-volved in the partisan battle. At a press conference in December 1970 Laird had been asked if he would take part in Nixon's reelection campaign. "It's very difficult for me to remain inactive politically," he had responded. "But I have followed the instructions of the commander-in-chief, and I have stayed away from partisan politics ever since I have been in this position."[5]

Laird was constitutionally incapable of keeping such a pledge. It was Nixon's opponents who opened the door that let Laird into the campaign when they began poking a stick at Vietnamization. In January two of Nixon's potential Democratic challengers, Hubert Humphrey and Edmund Muskie, said Nixon was too slow to get out of Vietnam. This was too much for Laird. He could not keep silent while the party that had escalated the war was criticizing the party that was winding it down. Without naming names, Laird said, "Strangely enough, some of those individuals that are going around the country today criticizing programs to withdraw Americans from Vietnam were silent in 1968 and before when we were on the escalator going up and up and up."[6]

As an issue, Vietnam showed no sign of cooling, if Laird's lecture circuit experience was a thermometer. In February 1971 protesters burned Laird in effigy outside a San Diego luncheon at which he appeared. In early March at a Bloomington, Illinois, dinner honoring his friend House Republican leader Les Arends, Laird had to be hustled in a back door because the front door was blocked by three hundred protestors.[7]

The anti-Vietnam sentiment seemed to change some old campaigning truisms, such as the one that mandated that no presidential candidate during a war, even the cold war, could appear to be soft on defense. During Nixon's first run at the presidency, John F. Kennedy had made points by charging that the Eisenhower-Nixon administration had allowed the United States to fall behind the Soviet Union militarily (the bogus "missile gap" issue). This time around, the leading Democratic contender, Senator George McGovern, attacked Nixon for spending *too much* on defense.

McGovern unveiled his "alternative defense posture" on January 19, 1972. He advocated a $30 billion cut in the Pentagon's budget, which he said could be accomplished by cutting the navy's fleet of aircraft carriers from fifteen to six, canceling the F-14 and F-15 fighter projects, withdrawing all forces from Southeast Asia and South Korea, and reducing the American troops supporting NATO in Western Europe from 300,000 to 130,0000. Major newspapers buried stories on his position paper on their inside pages.[8] Laird chose to remain silent at first because he was sure candidates from McGovern's own party would attack the plan if McGovern became the frontrunner during the primary elections. Laird was right. Senator Henry "Scoop" Jackson called McGovern's plan "simplistic thinking." Former vice president Hubert Humphrey said McGovern would "cut into the muscle" of U.S. security and would "make America a second-class power."[9]

As aghast as Laird was over McGovern's alternate defense plan, he might not have found a way to speak out about it if he had not been asked his opinion during congressional hearings. On May 31 Laird's comptroller, Robert Moot, had been asked during an appearance before the Joint Economic Committee of Congress to assess the McGovern plan. He said McGovern had miscalculated by at least $10.1 billion; McGovern's plan would cost that much more than he had figured. (McGovern soon conceded the point.)[10] So the issue was on the table when Laird appeared before a Senate appropriations subcommittee on June 5. Wisconsin Senator William Proxmire, a penny-pinching defense critic, asked Laird to evaluate the McGovern proposal. Laird's answer made the next day's headlines: "I would say that the thing to do if you go the $30 billion reduction route is to direct the Department of Defense to spend at least a billion dollars in white flags so that they could run them up all over because it means surrender." Thereafter Laird continued to refer to McGovern's plan as the "white flag–surrender budget," sometimes amplifying the point by saying that the Pentagon would have to buy out all the white sheets in department stores across the country and hang them out of the windows if McGovern became president.[11] In retrospect, Laird did not think he became too political during the 1972 election. "I only answered the things in which McGovern tried to criticize me and the Defense Department. I didn't want to be political, but I had to answer that budget proposition," Laird demurred.

The McGovern budget percolated as a major campaign issue into the fall, and Laird didn't miss any opportunity to attack it. Nor did he neglect to point out that at the Democratic National Convention the platform committee failed to include their nominee's "alternate defense posture" in the party's policy document.[12]

Decades later, in 2003, McGovern still thought it had been a good idea to propose cutting the defense budget by a third. He laughed about the energetic thrashing he had received from Laird. "It didn't surprise me that Mel got into the campaign somewhat. At least at that stage of his life Mel was a pretty hard-core partisan. My relations with him in recent years have been very congenial, and I think he's mellowed somewhat."[13]

If the 1972 election year is remembered for one thing, it is the Watergate scandal that forced Nixon's resignation two years later. The Watergate break-in was a foolish effort to spy on the Democratic National Committee, presumably to get dirt on McGovern or otherwise thwart his campaign. In those same summer weeks Nixon's dirty-tricks squad *did* successfully pirate Pentagon documents about McGovern that Laird had refused to turn over.

Decades later dozens of Nixon administration officials and legislators from that era still expressed amazement that Laird was instinctively able to keep the Pentagon out of the scandal that eventually tainted the Justice Department, FBI, CIA, IRS, and other government agencies and officials.

Former White House communications director Herb Klein said the simplest answer as to why the Watergate scandal never touched Laird or his people was that "Mel knew how to say 'no.'"[14]

Former president Gerald Ford said that, as a Cabinet member, Laird was "too independent for Dick Nixon to swallow. He wanted 'yes' men; he also wanted people that he could absolutely trust, who he felt would not undercut him, nor compete with him." That is why, "in an era when the White House was tainted by scandal, Mel Laird stood out as a model of personal and political integrity." Former president George H. W. Bush, who was chairman of the Republican National Committee during the scandal, had a similar view. In a July 1974 letter to his sons, Bush lamented that Nixon had "surrounded himself on his personal staff with people unwilling to question the unlovely instincts we all have—and that he [Nixon] has in spades." These men "condon[ed] things [they] should have condemned," were "arrogant to a fault" and "appeal[ed] to the dark side of the Nixon moon." In contrast, Bush said later, concerning Laird, "there was never any question about his integrity."

That integrity, and a healthy dose of suspicion, prompted Laird to deny a peculiar request from the White House in early 1972. Nixon, through an aide, asked Laird for McGovern's World War II military records. (McGovern had been a bomber pilot.) Nixon hoped he might find some dirt. "We had a lot of requests like that from the White House," Laird recalled, "but we never honored them at any time." Laird did not know until years later that White House aide David Young apparently had been successful in smuggling a copy of the McGovern personnel folder out of the Pentagon. Young, a lawyer, was a one-time Kissinger aide who had been recruited by domestic counselor John Ehrlichman and then made codirector of the five-man team that engineered the 1971 break-in at the office of Daniel Ellsberg's psychiatrist. Ehrlichman also assigned Young as the liaison to the Pentagon during the Yeoman Radford investigation, where he got to know some of the Defense Department investigators.

The reference to Young's subsequent heist of McGovern's file came in an August 3, 1972, Oval Office conversation involving Nixon, Haldeman, and Ehrlichman. A transcript of the discussion, which occurred two months after the Watergate break-in, reveals that Nixon was agitated about not being able to get government dossiers on McGovern and other Democrats. Ehrlichman complained: "I sent to the Department of Defense for McGovern's service jacket because I was curious about what his bombing experience [was] and that kind of stuff. And I got it, but Jesus, the grief I took in getting it is unbelievable. Carl Wallace called me from Laird's office [and denied the request]. Finally, the way I got it was that Dave Young went over there and he had his contacts as a result of the Ellsberg case and some other cases, and he went in and got it for me and brought it over here. But guys like Laird ... are just touchy as hell about cooperating with us on this kind of thing."[15]

Nixon must have been disappointed when he was briefed on the contents of the file. McGovern had been a B-24 pilot who flew thirty-five combat missions in Europe and won the Distinguished Flying Cross. There was no evidence of cowardice in the file, but the right-wing John Birch Society charged as much—a charge that backfired when McGovern requested his own file from the army and then released it to the press.[16]

In Laird's mind there was no question about using political pressure during his campaign to end the war. He had played the politics card repeatedly to keep Nixon on track with troop withdrawals. In June of 1972, when the Easter invasion was in its twelfth week and the Joint Chiefs were calling for an end to troop withdrawals, Laird got Nixon to hold to the schedule. Admiral Moorer wrote to Laird on June 21 asking to temper the next round of withdrawals unless "overriding considerations at the national level dictate continued redeployment increments." The overriding consideration, of course, was the reelection of Richard Nixon.[17]

Laird suggested that Nixon announce a withdrawal rate that would put the total number of U.S. troops in Vietnam at fifteen thousand by the end of the year.[18] On June 28 the White House announced that ten thousand more troops would return home before September 1, bringing the total remaining down to thirty-nine thousand. It was a more conservative option than the one Laird recommended, and it slowed the pace of withdrawals, but it was still a surprise to many who thought the United States would halt withdrawals. The biggest news in Nixon's June 28 announcement about the new numbers was that no more draftees would be sent to Vietnam unless they volunteered to go. The president had pushed Laird hard for more than three years to be allowed to make that announcement.

After the 1968 election economist Milton Friedman had written Laird a letter urging that even though it might take time to build an all-volunteer force, in the interim "the new administration could reduce enormously the bitterness, dissension and division arising from the Viet Nam conflict by . . . sending no more draftees to Viet Nam." Friedman had lobbied the idea all over Washington, and conservative columnist William Buckley took an interest. In a February 1969 column, Buckley floated the idea that an announcement should be made of a date certain after which no more draftees would be sent to Vietnam. Nixon tore out the article and scribbled on the margin: "Get Laird's comment on this intriguing idea." Laird was not enthused so Nixon dropped it.[19]

In early 1970 Nixon latched onto the idea again. Laird was warned by a good friend, presidential aide Bryce Harlow, that Nixon planned to make such an announcement as a campaign tidbit in a speech to support some Republican congressional candidates in the midterm election. Laird, the Joint Chiefs, and all the military services were opposed to giving Vietnam service any special draft-free status, fearing the impact on the morale and quality of the troops. "We have had reports that consideration is being given to establishing an all-volunteer force in Vietnam," Laird began cautiously in a February 1970 memo to the president. "I *strongly* urge you not to make a public commitment to this policy at this time." The possibility of no draftees in Vietnam was "too distant a prospect to warrant an announcement now." Besides, "promising a volunteer force in Vietnam at this time would only serve to undo the good will and confidence you have built up as it became clear that the promise could not be fulfilled for some time to come." Nixon took the promise out of that speech.[20]

Six months later, with the midterm election heating up, Nixon was again ready to make the announcement, when Laird sent him another memo with new arguments against it. A premature announcement might cut the number of volunteers, since waiting to be drafted would be the sure way to avoid service in the Vietnam. Thus the draft numbers would have to go up just to staff the military. Also it would "set a dangerous precedent by dividing the Army into those who have to serve in a war zone and those who don't." Once again, Nixon stood down.[21]

During 1971 several senators, including Gaylord Nelson of Wisconsin, tried to take the decision out of the president's hands through amendments that would require him to send no more draftees to Vietnam after a fixed date. Anxious to preempt the possible passage of such an amendment, Nixon pressed Laird again for an opinion in May 1971. Laird, echoing the views of the uniformed military, was still vehemently opposed, so Nixon lamented on June 1 in an aside during a public speech that "the question of whether we could stop sending draftees has been considered, and I find that we are unable to do so at this point."[22]

Nixon revisited the topic again in October 1971, and Laird again objected for the same reasons. So, for the fourth time, Nixon decided not to override Laird. But 1972 was a different year, and Laird knew it. That year it was not just a congressional election on the line, but Nixon's own reelection. When Nixon pressed more than once during the spring, Laird forwarded the army's primary objection: "We believe that the all-volunteers-for-Vietnam concept is quantitatively possible [but] philosophically extremely dangerous. . . . It is a Pandora's box, and would give official sanction to those who contend that a soldier should be allowed to decide when he does or doesn't want to follow his country's policy."[23]

But Laird knew he had pushed Nixon as far as was practical. Even though it would soon be "possible to stop sending draftees to Vietnam," Laird wrote on June 23, he still thought a public statement was a bad idea. However he provided some carefully chosen words to the president "if you wish to make a statement." With that green light from Laird, Nixon finally got to say what he had wanted to for more than three years. "I thought it would be a public relations coup for the president," Laird recalled. As usual, "Nixon was able to announce the good news."[24]

⌇

Even with draftees out of the Vietnam pool, the protest movement found another rallying point when some of North Vietnam's dikes suffered ancillary damage during bombing runs. The system of dikes held back the Red River—both the giver of life, and the destroyer when it flooded.[25] The worst flood in decades had occurred in 1971. Aerial photography and intercepts of North Vietnamese cables sent to its embassies confirmed that the flooding had exceeded normal flood stage by as much as sixty feet in places. Raging water had broken through sections of major dikes, leaving two million people homeless and destroying much of the autumn rice crop. Rail and highway traffic between Hanoi and China was entirely stopped for most of September. Even in November 1971 huge areas of the delta east of Hanoi were still under water. Given the North Vietnamese propensity for hard work, western intelligence analysts were surprised that so many of the dikes still needed repair by the following March 1972. When the Easter offensive started it was evident that

North Vietnam had chosen to siphon much of its manpower into the military invasion instead of dike maintenance.[26]

Given the widespread nature of the dike-and-dam system and the intensified bombing under Operation Linebacker, it was inevitable some of the dikes would be hit. The North Vietnamese realized they had a major propaganda issue, especially in an election year. On May 9 they tentatively tested it by charging over Hanoi Radio that the United States had deliberately hit several dikes. The story was false and did not draw too much attention. But at the same time Nixon was musing about authorizing dike bombing beginning in early May as he was egged on by his new confidant, the hawkish Treasury Secretary John Connally. In a May 4 Oval Office chat Connally goaded Nixon. "Bomb for seriousness, not just as a signal," he said, "and don't worry about killing civilians. Go ahead and kill them.... People think you are now [killing civilians anyway]. So go ahead and give them some."

"That's right," Nixon responded.

"There's pictures on the news of dead bodies every night," Haldeman chimed in. "A dead body is a dead body. Nobody knows whose bodies they are or who killed them."

Nixon added that there was no point in overreacting to civilian-killing charges—or bombing dikes, for that matter. "We need to win the goddamned war [and as for] what that fellow [said] about taking out the goddamned dikes, all right, we'll take out the goddamned dikes.... I am [for that]. I am for the Connally idea." At almost the same time, however, Nixon, during a speech in Texas, ruled out bombing any dikes.

No dike-bombing order was ever given by Nixon, who frequently engaged in boys' club braggadocio with his pals that never went beyond the Oval Office. Also, the Pentagon had looked at the possible military value of dike bombing and decided it wasn't worth it. "The extensive dike system of the Red River delta offers a potential target whose destruction during the wet season would flood some 10,500 square kilometers of the most densely populated area in the country," one Defense Intelligence Agency appraisal summarized for the Joint Chiefs. But "because of the massiveness of the earthen dikes (some of which are 80 to 100 feet at their base), a large expenditure of ordnance would be necessary to breach them." The U.S. Air Force was already stretched thin bombing high-value military targets in North Vietnam, and it simply wasn't worth it—especially considering the potential political fallout of such an action.[27]

In late June the North Vietnamese charged that the United States had deliberately attacked dikes sixty-eight times between mid-April and mid-June. "We have convinced almost everybody that this is just a periodic Hanoi propaganda tactic," Henkin assured his boss. "None of the newsmen take it seriously." But then the enemy's propaganda campaign got a serious boost from a gullible French correspondent and a Swedish diplomat who were given "tours" of the damaged dikes by their Communist hosts. It was a made-to-order issue for the American left, including McGovern supporters, and they ran with it.[28]

On July 6 Laird issued the first authoritative denial during a press conference. He said, extemporaneously, "We have never targeted a dam or a dike in our targeting system as far as North Vietnam is concerned." He added that the enemy sometimes put antiaircraft weapons on dikes and dams, and then they became fair game. But the real damage to the dikes had been done by flooding. "I believe that the North Vietnamese with their people are carrying on this [propaganda] campaign in order [to] relieve themselves from the responsibility with their own people for their failure to adequately repair this system since the major flooding of last year.[29]

Though Laird's explanation was never disproved, that didn't stop antiwar critics in the United States and abroad from believing that the Nixon administration was capable of destroying dikes and thus wiping out North Vietnam's food crops. U.N. Secretary General Kurt Waldheim publicly proclaimed that he had "private and unofficial" evidence of a U.S. dike-bombing campaign, and it should stop. Nixon immediately dispatched America's U.N. ambassador, George H. W. Bush, to sit down with Waldheim and straighten him out. Within minutes of the meeting Waldheim issued a "clarification" that he could not actually verify any of the allegations.[30] Four days later the State Department took the rare step of releasing a CIA report on the subject. The CIA, from photographic evidence, determined that the United States had hit North Vietnamese dikes in twelve places while bombing other targets. The damage was minimal, and the CIA concluded the dikes could have been fixed in a few days.[31]

Still this was not enough to stamp out the charges, which festered into August.[32] Henkin predicted to Laird that the Pentagon would "be blamed for a long time for every leaf that falls in Vietnam, even in the natural process of autumn. In the case of the dikes, as we predicted, this will not go away. We can't expect any help from any fact-finding teams junket[ing] to North Vietnam because one of the prerequisites for letting them [into North Vietnam] will continue to be the fact that the other side has reason to believe they are friends of theirs."[33] The most colorful of those "fact-finding teams" was a lone woman who not only stirred up some of the most widespread publicity for the false cause célèbre, but also garnered animosity for herself from Vietnam veterans and others—bitter feelings that continue to this day.

❧

Actress Jane Fonda became prominent as an antiwar critic by touring U.S. bases and nearby neighborhoods with a counterculture, anti-U.S.O.-type show. She saw the dike issue as tailor-made for an election year. When the North Vietnamese invited her to visit Hanoi in July 1972 and see for herself, she jumped at the chance. As she got off the plane Fonda breathlessly issued an opening statement of support for the enemy: "Your struggle, courage and culture has forced us to recognize certain truths about our country. . . . I come to Vietnam as a comrade."[34]

For two weeks, occasionally ducking U.S. air raids, Fonda was led through museums and outdoor exhibits that purported to illustrate American war crimes, including dike bombings. Absolutely convinced of this, Fonda made at least ten broadcasts over Hanoi Radio, pleading with American pilots to stop their bombing campaign. Those broadcasts earned her the sobriquet "Hanoi Jane," which was a reference to World War II's "Tokyo Rose."[35] On the last day of her visit Fonda, clad in black Viet Cong–type pajama pants, allowed herself to be photographed and filmed giggling in the gunner's seat of an enemy antiaircraft battery being used to shoot down American planes. In her 2005 memoirs *My Life So Far,* Fonda wrote that the pose was a "lapse" of judgment and the only one on the whole Hanoi trip for which she felt belated "regret."[36]

In her final Hanoi press conference Fonda aimed her enmity at Nixon and Laird. "Melvin Laird the other day said that bombing of the dikes may be taking place, but that it is accidental, and it only happens if there is a military target on top of the dikes," she said. "Does he really think the Vietnamese would be foolish enough to put a military installation on top of an earth dike?" At that press conference and another when Fonda stopped in Paris, some reporters hesitantly pointed out that if there hadn't first been an invasion by the North Vietnamese of the South, the Americans would not be bombing. She was unmoved. "Vietnam is one country," she argued. "How can the Vietnamese invade Vietnam?"[37]

Fonda's actions prompted charges of treason on the floor of the House and Senate. When Laird was asked on July 17 by a reporter whether her broadcasts "constitute treason or grounds for prosecution under our laws," he answered "yes" but said it ultimately was for the Justice Department to determine, not the secretary of defense. The primary question was whether her Hanoi Radio broadcasts—which were played repeatedly over North Vietnamese radio stations and into the cells of American prisoners of war—rose to the level of a violation of the law intended to punish anyone who foments "insubordination, disloyalty, mutiny, or refusal of duty by any member of the military or naval forces of the United States." While Fonda never urged the men to defect, the clear intent of the messages to the American pilots and sailors was that they should disobey orders. However, the Justice Department declined to prosecute, a decision Laird supported.[38]

In 1972 Laird's personal inclination—and his direction to the top military leaders—was that they should not speak out against Fonda; they should simply ignore her. "I was not one of those that got up and raised hell with her for being in Hanoi," Laird recalled. "I just said it wasn't helpful." That was what he said publicly, but his private view was stronger: "She was there to demoralize the troops who were in the Hanoi Hilton and South Vietnam, to demoralize all the men and women serving us in that war, and to demoralize public opinion." At the July 31, 1972, staff meeting Laird was quoted in the minutes as saying: "Jane Fonda's visit was worth millions of dollars to Hanoi for propaganda. When Hanoi does this kind of propaganda campaign, and we spend all our time answering, we will lose. A response to Fonda's visit would only increase the momentum of their campaign. We just cannot win on the dikes and dams."

At that point Admiral Zumwalt interjected: "Why wasn't Jane Fonda invited to South Vietnam to view the damage *there?*"

"Well, she was invited to talk to the South Vietnamese representatives in Paris, but she refused," Laird reported. The wanton naïveté was what irked Laird most about Jane Fonda.[39] Where was the outcry, Laird asked at the time, about the killing of civilians by the North Vietnamese in the South? "Let's look at An Loc," Laird said at a May 10 press conference. Into that two-mile-square civilian area the North Vietnamese had fired 35,000 rounds of explosive shells. "Let's move on up to Quang Tri," he continued. "In the four days before [it] fell, the enemy was putting into that civilian population area a total of 3,000 rounds a day. On the last day, they put 4,600 rounds of artillery on that civilian population center. They showed a complete lack of regard for the civilian population. They sprayed artillery into those civilian centers just as if they were using a water hose. I think that this lack of regard for civilian population centers should be called to the attention of the entire world."[40]

Those weren't the only incidents of that type by the North Vietnamese. After occupying the Binh Dinh province of central South Vietnam, the North Vietnamese executed hundreds of Saigon government officials by rifle, bayonet, hanging, and disembowelment. During the siege of An Loc a North Vietnamese tank rolled into a church on the outskirts of the city and slaughtered the one hundred women and children attending services there, according to a U.S. Army captain who witnessed the incident. He added that that night, as wounded civilians and soldiers were moved into a "clearly-marked hospital, the North Vietnamese blew it away with mortar and artillery fire and killed every last one of the people inside." Two American majors witnessed a deliberate attack by the North Vietnamese on refugees fleeing Quang Tri before the city fell. "They literally shredded the refugee column," said one of the Marines. "It was the worst sight I have ever seen. It was a massacre." As many as two thousand civilians were killed in that two-day shelling.[41]

At the time, Laird felt that Jane Fonda and others were both illogical and hypocritical when they remained silent about these war crimes as they eagerly indicted their own country. As for the dike issue, it finally washed away in late August 1972 when it was plainly evident to the world that no flooding occurred as a result of damaged dikes during the normal flood season.

40

"Peace Is at Hand"

⎯⫰⎯

THERE WERE SOME THINGS MELVIN LAIRD didn't like about William Westmoreland, but Laird preferred to focus on the general's positive traits—competence, loyalty to the civilian leadership, and his unique ability to support the careers of promising men such as Generals Bruce Palmer and Creighton Abrams. "Westy wasn't an Abrams or a Palmer," Laird said. "He was, however, one of the best-*looking* generals we've ever had"—the handsome chiseled face, the graying hair, the ramrod spine holding erect the impeccable uniform.

Westmoreland looked as distinguished as ever on the evening of June 30, 1972, when he stood for his last parade in the gymnasium at Fort Myer, Virginia. Rain had forced the retirement ceremony inside, dampening the pomp of the cannons and marching troops to which he was entitled after an honorable thirty-six-year career that spanned three wars.[1] Laird was on hand to praise the departing Westmoreland generously for commanding with "boldness, valor and great professional skill" through his last assignment as chief of staff of the army. The words were heartfelt, but privately Laird was relieved to see the general go. The two men had disagreed fundamentally on the Vietnam War—Westmoreland convinced it could be won with enough U.S. troops, equipment, and money, and Laird equally convinced that it wasn't America's fight any more. Westmoreland's four years on the Joint Chiefs had been frustrating for both men as Laird listened to and then dismissed the general's suggestions for a more aggressive approach to the war.

Westmoreland was disappointed that he was not asked to stay on with the Joint Chiefs another term as General Earle Wheeler had been. He had political ambitions and may well have thought he might run for president in 1976. Instead he ran for governor in his home state of South Carolina and lost. Westmoreland's last battle was with CBS, which he unsuccessfully sued for libel in 1984 after the network embarrassed him in a documentary about fabricated (overly optimistic) intelligence information used during his tenure as commander of U.S. troops in South Vietnam from 1965 to 1968.

Abrams stood in sharp contrast to Westmoreland, being all substance and little style. "Westmoreland was always saying, 'You cannot do it.' Abrams was always saying, 'You *can* do it.' That was the biggest difference—Abrams was a 'can-do' general," Laird explained. Unlike Westmoreland, Abrams regularly mingled with the soldiers in the field. His helicopter could be seen frequently in the countryside, and he did not confine his journeys to safe regions. "When I traveled with him I sometimes wondered if he was testing the courage of his Pentagon boss," Laird laughed.

Abrams loathed ostentation and pomp. When he took over from West-moreland in Saigon in 1968, Abrams ordered the lavishly decorated office to be redone using only standard army-issue equipment. When a visiting politician advised him that surely someone of his rank deserved something better than his metal green desk, Abe shot back: "As long as I've got men fighting and dying out there, I will not sit behind a damn mahogany desk."

In private, however, few enjoyed life's luxuries as much as Abrams. When the occasion allowed, he loved fine wines and gourmet food. He was also a pro-digious cigar smoker, having four to six of them lined up like soldiers next to his dinner plate. He also loved classical music, of which he had an encyclopedic knowledge, and with which he laced his briefings at times. He explained while delivering one battle plan that "a great conductor will rehearse his orchestra until all the members are skilled enough to do a perfect job. That's the way a military operation should be regarded. An air strike or a round of artillery must come at an exact moment, just as in a symphony one stroke of a drum must come at an exact millisecond of time."[2]

Unvarying honesty touched everything Abrams did. He never once predicted stability for Vietnam without the essential qualifiers and stubbornly refused to offer quick assessments of events, even if the president was demanding them. He constantly admonished those around him, "Bad news does not improve with age." Once Laird asked him why he was recommending the severest of penalties for an errant commander. Abrams's face flushed with anger and he growled, "I could have forgiven his mistakes, but I will not tolerate a man who lies." It was often said in Saigon that this general, who had been Patton's favorite tank com-mander in World War II, deserved "a better war" to oversee than Vietnam. Laird always felt that Abrams deserved more recognition than he got. "Because of the turmoil surrounding our final years in Vietnam—and Abe's steadfast refusal to allow others to trumpet his actions to the press—the American people largely missed the style that he brought to his command. It should never be forgotten," Laird wrote in a 1976 Reader's Digest profile.[3]

Abrams deplored the self-deception that had become ingrained in the American bureaucracy in Vietnam. Once, after sitting through a long, rosy briefing about a damaging enemy offensive, he observed bluntly, "Gentlemen, they beat the tail off us," then he stalked from the room. He often admonished groups of officers with the words: "Doesn't anyone out there want to do a good job, with that *alone* as the reward?"

When Laird became defense secretary he gave Abrams the difficult task of Vietnamizing the conflict while simultaneously withdrawing U.S. troops under his command. That Abrams did this with loyalty, equanimity, and a minimum of complaints earned him Laird's highest praise and promotion. In a March

1972 phone call, with two aides listening, Laird called Abrams in Saigon to test his feelings about becoming army chief of staff upon Westmoreland's retirement. "I firmly believe no one else in uniform has done more over the past few years for his country than you," Laird told him. "You have had a task of unparalleled proportion which you have discharged with consummate skill. No one else, in my judgment, could have done what you have done. I have a strong personal loyalty to you and want to offer you another back-breaking task as the chief of staff if you think you're up to it. If you would prefer, you can have the prestigious, but less strenuous, position as commander in Europe." (By this time Abrams had been hospitalized more than once with various viral infections, lung inflammations, pneumonia, and a gall bladder ailment.) Abrams chewed on Laird's words for a moment, just as he did on his cigars.

"Well," the fifty-seven-year-old general finally said, "my goal throughout my career has been to become army chief of staff. I don't believe I'm too old for this." However, he added, he would only be willing to serve for half of the standard four-year term. Laird was pleased, and said so, but cautioned that because some senators were still hot about the Lavelle bombing episode that had occurred on Abrams's watch, confirmation might be difficult. Abrams understood that. As he explained to one of his own aides: "Just remember this, the higher you get up the greasy pole, the more your ass shows."[4]

What Abrams didn't know was that within the administration Laird stood almost alone in his support of Abrams for the post. President Nixon, who had a personal dislike of Abrams, favored Alexander Haig to replace Westmoreland. Even Laird's closest friend, Army Secretary Froehlke, argued that Abrams was not the best choice; Froehlke wanted to appoint a younger four-star or even three-star general to shake up the army as the Zumwalt selection had done for the navy. Laird went ahead anyway, metaphorically waving his cocktail-napkin promise from the president. "I brought Abe in over the objections of Haig, the president, and the secretary of the army," Laird recalled with pride. The *New York Times* reported that "Laird feels obligated to Abrams because Abrams has gone along with Vietnamization even when the Joint Chiefs of Staff objected."[5]

So the only barrier standing in the way was Congress. The Lavelle debacle was still winding its way through congressional investigations, and Laird realized it would be months before Abrams's skirts would be cleared of any involvement. Two weeks before Abrams left Saigon, Laird sent Nixon a memo advising him that Abrams would not be able to assume his new duties for a while. In the meantime, Laird told Nixon, General Bruce Palmer would be acting army chief. To soften the news for Nixon, Laird said he would propose promoting Haig as the new vice chief of staff once Abrams was approved by Congress.[6]

When General Abrams had arrived in Saigon as Westmoreland's deputy five years earlier, the United States had more than half a million troops in

Vietnam. When Abrams left there were only forty-nine thousand Americans (mostly airmen and advisors). Westmoreland's strategies for the war had been upended by Abrams. Under Laird's policy of Vietnamization the general had reversed the roles of the Americans and Vietnamese even in the face of a full-scale North Vietnamese invasion. The *New York Times* summarized the job as "one of the most difficult ever given to a military man—withdrawing his troops from a country continuously engaged in combat with a well-equipped and highly-motivated enemy without allowing a catastrophe to befall them."[7]

Abrams slipped out of Saigon in June without the usual fanfare or the speeches of a formal change-of-command ceremony. There had been a brief meeting with President Thieu at the palace, where Abrams had received a medal to signify the gratitude of the Vietnamese people. Then he got on an airplane, and his deputy, General Fred Weyand, moved into the office as the new commander of diminishing U.S. forces in Vietnam, downgraded to an "advisory group."[8] Laird had not even considered going to Saigon to give Abrams a big send-off. "Abe felt that getting the men and the military bands out and going through all those reviews was kind of a waste of time," he explained. (For his own retirement eight months hence, Laird would take the same low-key approach.)

❧

The change of command in June 1972 coincided with Laird's realization that the enemy's Easter offensive was stalling out. The high-water mark of the North Vietnamese invasion had been the capture of Quang Tri on May 1. On that day Laird had warned his staff not to be unduly alarmed. "The South Vietnamese have stood up well in most cases," he said.[9] A week later Laird's logistics man on the scene sent back gloomy reports about the performance of America's ally at various locations. Too many of its commanders panicked too quickly and called for a helicopter airlift out or unnecessary heavy air support. "One general told me that they tend to call for air support every time they go to the bathroom," Barry Shillito cabled Laird. "It is a physical impossibility for anyone to meet all their demands." He added, "The greatest single problem is unwillingness of some elements to get in the fight."[10]

George McGovern's presidential campaign, as well as antiwar members of Congress, capitalized on the growing media reports that hinted of an impending defeat for South Vietnam. Some within the Nixon administration itself feared the South might not hold. But not Laird. In response to badgering questions and criticism about South Vietnamese losses, he said at a press conference, "The American people always have supported our President when Americans are endangered and the cause of freedom has been threatened. This is no time for quitters or for a lot of talk about instant surrender. I don't think the American people want to clamber aboard some sort of a bug-out shuttle."

By early June Laird's optimism was looking more like realism. After sixty days the enemy had failed to achieve any one of its goals: the collapse of the South Vietnamese army, taking meaningful territory, and generating a popular uprising in the South in favor of the Communists. The legendary enemy general Vo Ngyuen Giap, who had beaten the French in 1954, overextended his supply lines and proved incapable of commanding a three-front offensive. He was not even able to take the old imperial capital of Hue. The southern cities of Kontum and An Loc withstood enemy sieges of two and three months, respectively.

So to the naysayers among the legislators and elsewhere, Laird had a few words to offer during June 5 testimony before the House Defense Appropriations Subcommittee, on which he had once served: there had been some setbacks, but, for all the claims of critics, the enemy had been able to move its forces only twenty-two miles into South Vietnam and had captured only one of forty-four provincial capitals in the South. Laird's words and the reality of the stalled offensive got the message across. A week after his testimony, the *New York Times* summarized: "The initial North Vietnamese successes were shattering and spectacular. They caused some people to rush to a judgment that 'Vietnamization' had clearly failed. The stagnation of recent days has brought suggestions that Vietnamization has been vindicated."[11]

When the South retook Quang Tri in mid-September, the enemy offensive was officially over. South Vietnamese ground forces and U.S. air power had turned the enemy back. General Giap was removed as North Vietnamese defense minister shortly afterward. But Laird knew all this did not mean that the South had won. He rightly expected North Vietnam would try again. Westmoreland had believed that the United States and South Vietnam could prevail through a deadly war of attrition—kill so many North Vietnamese that the enemy could no longer fight. But with half the North Vietnamese population under the age of eighteen, "you just cannot kill them fast enough," one skeptic remarked. And, Hanoi did not seem to care how many of its people died in the campaign of bloody Communist aggression. "Enemy staying power is his most effective battlefield characteristic," General Abrams had summarized in a cable to Laird. "It is based first on his complete disregard for the expenditure of resources, both men and materiel, and second on discipline through fear, intimidation, and brutality. An enemy decision to attack carries an inherent acceptance that the forces involved may be expended totally."

Hanoi had lost seven men for every South Vietnamese soldier killed in the offensive. It sickened Abrams that all General Giap had to do was pull back across the DMZ to end the bloodshed, yet he would not. "What is going on now is just a lot of unnecessary killing," Abrams said to a friend in mid-May. The noted British expert on Vietnam, Sir Robert Thompson, felt similarly. In a private meeting with Laird in early July he said: "I think the North Vietnamese launched this campaign prepared to lose 50,000 men; however, by the end of this month they will have lost 100,000. It is terrible how twelve men on their Politburo can wipe out the youth of their nation."[12]

꘎

By late July Laird felt confident enough about the South Vietnamese military that he publicly stated it would be possible to withdraw even more U.S. troops than already announced. An NBC *Today* show interviewer complained to Laird when he appeared on the show July 20 that the United States was unilaterally withdrawing while the North Vietnamese were doing nothing to decrease their effort. How was that sensible? "We're withdrawing on the basis of the improved strength of our partner," Laird patiently explained. "That's what the Vietnam-ization program is all about."[13]

The last American ground unit in Vietnam—the U.S. Army Third Battalion, Twenty-first Infantry, which guarded the huge U.S. air base at Da Nang—was withdrawn on August 11. A week later at a press conference held at California's McClellan Air Force Base, Laird noted: "It was only three and a half years ago that there were 11 American divisions that had the total and complete ground combat responsibility in South Vietnam. Only one South Vietnamese division was capable of handling a ground combat responsibility. Today, the situation is reversed. There is not a single American division having a ground combat responsibility." Even better, by mid-September the weekly casualty report listed not a single American killed in action, the first time that had happened in seven years.[14]

While the United States continued to bomb North Vietnam, the South Vietnamese took on more and more of the air support responsibilities over their own territory. "We are Vietnamizing the air activities at a much more rapid rate than we had anticipated," Laird reported in late August. That new responsibility for Saigon's forces did not go off without a hitch, however, in-cluding a famous mistake at the village of Trang Bang, about thirty miles north of Saigon. On June 8, in the middle of a battle over the village, a South Viet-namese pilot flying at three hundred miles an hour missed his enemy target and dropped fiery napalm on civilians and South Vietnamese soldiers fleeing the city. One witness, Associated Press photographer Huyn Cong (Nick) Ut, snapped the unforgettable image of a badly burned, naked nine-year-old girl running down the road screaming: "Non'g Qu'a! Non'g Qu'a!" ("Too hot! Too hot!") The photographer doused the young Kim Phuc with water and rushed her to the hospital, where she was not expected to live. She did, after going through seventeen operations.[15]

The Pulitzer Prize–winning photograph was splashed on front pages all over the world and featured at the front of TV newscasts, testifying to the hor-ror of war. The naturally conspiratorial Nixon suspected the photo was staged to incite the antiwar crowd. Four days after it was first shown, he discussed that "napalm thing" with his chief of staff, H. R. Haldeman, in one of his many secretly taped conversations.

"I wonder if that was a fix," the president mused.

"Could have been," Haldeman responded, "because they got that picture of the little girl without any clothes. It made a hell of a bounce out of that one, but it was North Viet—[Haldeman corrected himself]—*South* Vietnamese bombing South Vietnamese by accident. They thought they were hitting the enemy but they got their own refugees, apparently."[16]

Nixon and Kissinger worried about how any misstep or swell of public opinion about the war might damage America's new relationship with the People's Republic of China, an opening the two had carefully crafted to fruition at the summit in February 1972. As a result of that sensitivity Nixon held the line, for the most part, in denying the air force any authority to bomb within twenty-five miles of North Vietnam's border with China. Hanoi took note of this bomb-free sanctuary and began stockpiling huge amounts of war matériel there. In late July Laird put on a full-court press on behalf of the Joint Chiefs to secure limited approval to bomb the region. In a memo to Kissinger, Laird reported that "as much as 25 percent of Hanoi's entire inventory of rolling stock is located within this safe area," as well as up to one thousand trucks ready to roll with war matériel. This was undoing the effect of the harbor mining, since the overland route from China through the no-bomb zone was safer. When Kissinger didn't respond within four days, Laird took it up with the president, who grudgingly granted limited authority for the one-time-only destruction of three rail bridges located between fourteen and sixteen miles from the Chinese border.[17]

For America, the war in Vietnam had become almost entirely an air war—actually four distinct air wars over North and South Vietnam, as well as northern and southern Laos. The South Vietnamese air force did their share in the skies over their own country, flying more than twenty thousand combat sorties as well as airlifting men and supplies during the Easter offensive. But Vietnamization was not crafted to let them engage in an offensive air war over another country, so they were not flying as part of Operation Linebacker over the Hanoi-Haiphong area. That region was defended by the most active air defenses ever assembled in history—850 missile launchers and antiaircraft guns. Aircraft losses became particularly sensitive and expensive.

Throughout 1972 the reelection of Nixon was never far from Laird's mind. Ever the canny politician, Laird offered to address both the Republican and Democratic platform committees before each of the party nominating conventions. In his February annual defense report, he had declared that he "would be pleased . . . to consider favorably an invitation to appear before the platform committees of both of the two major parties, where responsible citizens from all over America will be deliberating on the nonpartisan issue of national security."[18]

The Democrats didn't proffer an invitation, but they did want Laird to send troops to guard the July 10–13 Miami convention site. No one wanted a repeat of the 1968 Chicago Democratic Convention. Laird was reluctant to oblige since he felt that federal troops should not be sent when local and state law enforcement should be able to handle it. "I am not in favor of putting anything into the area for a while," he explained at the June 26 staff meeting. "The problem is that the local Miami police are not carrying out their responsibility, and this lack of commitment will result in a black eye for the military if trouble occurs. We will not have this while I am Secretary of Defense."[19]

The protestors were contained, as Laird had hoped, by local law enforcement. Inside the convention hall McGovern gave his acceptance speech around 3 A.M. July 13, after the prime-time audience had gone to bed. His oratorical theme was "come home, America"—from war, waste, privilege, and prejudice. McGovern blamed the Nixon administration and its three predecessor administrations for charting "a terrible war behind closed doors.... I want those doors opened, and I want that war closed." In a sideswipe at Nixon from the 1968 campaign, he added: "I have no secret plan for peace. I have a public plan. As one whose heart has ached for 10 years over the agony of Vietnam, I will halt the senseless bombing of Indochina on Inauguration Day."[20]

The big news from the Democratic National Convention was the selection of Senator Thomas Eagleton as McGovern's vice presidential running mate. "You're kidding! Before you change your mind, I accept," he reportedly said over the phone. (He was at least the fourth man to receive McGovern's invitation.)[21] Laird sensed an exploitable conflict between McGovern and Eagleton, probably before either of them realized it. McGovern's alternative defense budget included among its serious cuts the cancelation of the Air Force F-15 "Eagle," being manufactured by McDonnell Douglas in St. Louis, Missouri, Eagleton's home state. Laird soon spread the word that Eagleton's acceptance of the vice presidential nomination must have been conditioned on McGovern's secret pledge to save the F-15 contract. As telegrams from constituents fearful of the loss of jobs flooded Eagleton's office, he could only lamely say that he would ask McGovern to "take a second look at it [the F-15] before junking it."[22]

Instead, McGovern took a second look at the senator and junked him. On July 25 Eagleton revealed that he had voluntarily hospitalized himself three times in the past for "nervous exhaustion and fatigue." He withdrew from the ticket on July 31, and McGovern picked R. Sargent Shriver, the first Peace Corps director and U.S. ambassador to France, to be his running mate. For Shriver Laird had only praise.

McGovern's convention speech and campaigning suggested that he expected to win on the war issue. But Laird's persistent push for troop withdrawals and Vietnamization of the war had robbed McGovern of any hope for the high ground. A Harris survey taken several days after the Democratic Convention showed 52 percent of Americans supported the Vietnamization plan for "ending U.S. involvement in Vietnam," while only 33 percent supported McGovern's war-ending proposals. (The "minority" opposing the Nixon-Laird program was still very noisy, however. On July 31 Laird was booed and shouted down by fifty antiwar protestors at Wilmington, Ohio, when he tried to get through a speech. "How many people did your Department kill?" "Out now!" many yelled.[23])

During the week before the Republican National Convention began in Miami in August, Laird was the first administration official to appear before the GOP platform committee. Unlike the Democrats, the Republican leadership had invited him. He urged the platform writers to "reject policies of planned weakness, of white-flag waving, of begging, and of abandonment of the nation's role in helping to maintain peace." They should tout the success the Republican administration has already had, he urged, such as his Vietnamization program, which had withdrawn most of the U.S. troops in Vietnam. "This has been our active program of 'Come Home Americans,' and it is deeds, not words," he said, in a jab at McGovern's "come home" theme.[24]

Laird's "nonpartisan" campaigning was all of his own making. White House Special Counsel Charles Colson, soon to earn Watergate fame and a prison sentence, tried to order Laird and his staff out on the trail, but to no avail. "He was wont to call up and want things done that we couldn't do," Pentagon spokesman Jerry Friedheim recalled. Colson was supposed to go through Laird's established White House channel, Carl Wallace, but "it got to be so much that even Carl didn't want to spend time listening to him, so I got nominated to listen to Chuck Colson call up every day and say all the things he wanted done, like 'Send all the assistant secretaries to speak to the Chambers of Commerce in Texas and California, because we need to carry those states.'" Neither Friedheim nor Laird recalled a single instance in which they did Colson's bidding. Certainly Laird needed no coaching from White House operatives to tell him how to walk the fine line between political campaigner and Cabinet member.[25]

On the road Laird was a formidable noncampaigner for Nixon. "At a Cabinet meeting in July," speech writer William Safire recalled, "when someone referred to McGovern's proposed military cuts, the President turned to Laird, [who] said to some laughter that he intended to make only nonpolitical trips to defense bases telling them what to expect if McGovern won." He did just that, visiting several cities that relied heavily on defense employers and warning how decimated their local economies would be if McGovern got elected and implemented his severe defense cuts. McGovern took to calling Laird the chief "fright-monger" for the Nixon campaign, a "lackey" who was "do[ing] Nixon's dirty work."[26]

Laird grinned when he recalled how indefatigable he was as a non-campaigner. Just before the election, and over David Packard's objections, Laird ordered four new electromagnetic pulse (EMP)–protected 747 planes from Boeing for presidential airborne command posts. The planes were needed for use against the newly identified EMP threat, but not urgently. By ordering early, Laird propped up Boeing and insured Republican support in the Seattle area, where the jobs would go. The same thing was true when he bought trucks in Detroit and toilet paper in Wisconsin, and elsewhere.[27]

As a subtext of the Vietnam War issue, the cause célèbre of the 1972 election season was the POWs and those listed as MIA in Southeast Asia. Private businesses got into the act trying to ransom POWs. A nonprofit company sold more than a million bracelets engraved with the names of POWs. When high school students at Henrietta, Texas, asked the visiting Laird whether the bracelets did any good for the cause, he said that any attention that encouraged the North Vietnamese to treat the POWs humanely was a good thing. Though he himself did not wear a bracelet, Laird said he did not want to discourage anyone else from doing so.[28]

Then began the exploitation of POWs by those with political agendas, stoked by Hanoi. The first to be sucked in was Harvard professor and Nobel Prize–winning biologist Dr. George Wald, who returned from a tour of North Vietnam to report that the North Vietnamese "were ahead of the Geneva Convention in the treatment of POWs." Laird had outlined nine violations of the convention, including refusal to let the prisoners receive or send mail.[29] The facts didn't stop partisans from going to Hanoi for tours of model prisons. Jane Fonda was among the more prominent who went, visiting with seven carefully prepped POWs during a July 1972, trip. She was followed by former U.S. attorney general Ramsey Clark, who declared that Hanoi's treatment of POWs "could not be better." As a matter of fact, the health of the POWs with whom he met was "better than mine, and I am a healthy man," Clark said.

Both Laird and officials of the National League of Families of American Prisoners and Missing in Southeast Asia were furious. They could not imagine how a former high official could broadcast such preposterous statements over the enemy's radio stations.[30]

In March McGovern campaigned with three POW wives at his side, and he chose a POW wife to second his nomination to be the Democratic presidential candidate. On June 28, meeting with South Carolina delegates in advance of the national convention, he was cornered by one delegate who was upset by what appeared to be McGovern's capitulation to Hanoi: "You want us to do all they demand and then beg them to give back our boys?" McGovern replied, "I'll accept that. Begging is better than bombing. I would go to Hanoi and beg if I thought that would release the boys one day earlier." It was a negotiate-from-weakness comment McGovern never lived down. Laird called it a "surrender now, beg later" policy.[31]

Still, McGovern persisted even in the face of Hanoi's active support of his campaign, one of the most counterproductive efforts in which that regime ever engaged. As if they were working in concert with McGovern, officials in Hanoi hinted broadly to visitors and journalists that if McGovern were elected there would be an immediate peace deal favorable to the United States. At the convention McGovern had pledged that "within 90 days of my inauguration . . . every American prisoner will be . . . out of their cells and back home in America where they belong." Laird, who had agonized over the POW issue for nearly four years, responded that McGovern must know something that no one else did. "He evidently has better contacts with the enemy than I do," Laird said at a subsequent press conference.[32]

Laird's outrage about McGovern and the POW issue peaked in September when Hanoi released three American pilots into the hands of an antiwar group, which flew them home via Beijing and Moscow. When U.S. military officials attempted unsuccessfully to get the POWs to go home on a military transport instead, McGovern accused the Nixon administration of delaying the release of the three men and "playing politics" with them. Laird lashed out at McGovern: "Senator McGovern apparently is willing to act as an agent for Hanoi in undermining the rights of American prisoners of war under the Geneva Conventions. It is a despicable act of a presidential candidate to make himself a spokesman for the enemy." One wire service report called it "the harshest rhetoric of the 1972 presidential campaign."[33]

Throughout the year, Kissinger had been feverishly negotiating a peace treaty with Hanoi in hopes of settling the war before voters went to the polls in November to reelect Nixon. His efforts to strike a deal with Hanoi in the Paris peace talks boiled down to three demands: the American POWs would be returned; the South Vietnamese would be allowed to determine their own form of government; and there would be a cease-fire "in place," meaning the enemy troops could hold their positions in South Vietnam.

Thinking this might be a workable deal, both the Soviet Union and the United States began pouring supplies into the field, assuming at some point a peace treaty would require each of them to back away from helping their surrogates and turn the battle into a true civil war between North and South. Hanoi denied its own massive resupply effort and called the American infusion of matériel a warlike act that threatened the peace talks. The American effort at resupply was called "Operation Enhance Plus" and began while Kissinger and General Abrams were in Saigon in October trying to persuade President Thieu to accept the terms of the treaty. Under Laird's direction, nine squadrons of planes were handed over to South Vietnamese pilots along with one hundred thousand tons of equipment.[34]

As a show of support for the peace talks, on October 14 Laird ordered Admiral Moorer to gradually reduce the number of bombing runs over North Vietnam. Kissinger was "very, very upbeat [about the peace talks]," Laird recalled. "We didn't want to be in a position where they could accuse us in any way of spoiling the opportunity." Although Laird was uncomfortable using bombing strategy as a bargaining chip in Paris and not confident that it would make any difference, he bowed to Kissinger's request. "I understood Henry's problem and what he was trying to do. I didn't want to be a fly in the ointment." At the same time, Laird let Kissinger know that, if Hanoi didn't come around quickly, the bombing would be intensified.[35]

Contemporary press accounts hinted that Nixon and Kissinger had taken over direct command of the bombing raids, picking targets and dictating how many raids would be flown, just as Lyndon Johnson had done in his effort to micromanage the war from Washington. Laird said that was never the case. But, he began sending categories of sensitive targets, such as power plants, to the White House for approval as a courtesy to Kissinger. "I didn't want them to read about it in the paper when they were thinking they were getting so close to a solution [in Paris]," said Laird. He recalled sending Nixon and Kissinger a sampling of about seventy-five targets in the few weeks before the November election. The cautious Nixon, mindful of his own reelection campaign and Kissinger's challenge in Paris, approved only about a third of them. And, on October 24, he halted all bombing above the twentieth parallel in North Vietnam, which included the cities of Hanoi and Haiphong.

Meanwhile, after waiting more than three months for confirmation as army chief of staff, Abrams was in the final stretch. He had to undergo four hours of grueling testimony on the Lavelle bombing matter before he was determined to have clean hands. Abrams was sworn in on October 16 and before the end of the day was on an airplane headed to Saigon with Kissinger. The official story in a press release from Laird's office was that Abrams was going along "to make an on-the-scene evaluation of Vietnamization progress." But the truth was that Kissinger needed him as a mediator with the South Vietnamese president.[36]

Kissinger thought he had a deal that America could live with. But the one person who couldn't live with it was President Thieu, and Kissinger felt that Abrams had enough goodwill with Thieu to draw him into agreement, especially if Abrams brought along the list of weaponry that the United States was promising to continue supplying the South Vietnamese. Thieu would have none of it. He publicly denounced the peace proposal, and Kissinger and Abrams returned to Washington. Fairly confident he could override Thieu, Kissinger uttered a phrase at an October 26 press conference that would haunt him: "We believe that peace is at hand."

Nixon was not pleased with the off-the-cuff remark, Laird recalled. It made the president look like he was manipulating the minds of voters two weeks before the election with a promise of peace but with no treaty signed. Laird himself never believed Kissinger was close to a deal with Hanoi at that point. He based his opinion on lukewarm communications that the National Security Agency intercepted between Hanoi and its delegation at the talks in Paris. But Laird also didn't think that Kissinger was playing politics, other than a justifiable attempt to do the president a favor by settling as quickly as possible. "I think Kissinger believed it," Laird said.

Laird was in London on NATO business at the time Kissinger's remark was widely reported, and the defense secretary refused to be drawn into the issue by reporters. "I didn't think we should put out a lot of optimistic statements until we had a bird in the hand," Laird said. And, believing the bird was still at large, Laird ordered B-52s that had been bombing the enemy in Cambodia to instead be sent over North Vietnam, where intelligence reports were seeing another buildup of troops like the one before the Easter offensive.[37]

The November 7 election came and went without a peace treaty. Nixon won 61 percent of the vote—a landslide. And there would be hell to pay for Hanoi. Laird had confided to Sir Robert Thompson that the North Vietnamese had been warned that if they didn't sign off on a peace deal before Nixon won re-election, they would be dealing with an enraged madman afterward. Laird put it a little more diplomatically to Thompson: "As you may know, we are trying to signal to Hanoi that after the elections Mr. Nixon will be virtually irrational."[38] What neither suspected, however, was just how irrational the victorious Richard Nixon would be.

41

The Morning After

❧

THERE WAS NO TIME FOR THE WORKER BEES in the Nixon administration to revel in his 1972 election victory. The president himself made sure of that by firing them all on the morning after the election. For months Nixon had been privately raging to Haldeman and Ehrlichman that he should have made a total purge of Johnson administration bureaucrats after the 1968 election. Nixon had wanted a full slate of Nixonites at the top of every agency, but some of the Cabinet officers—particularly Laird—had resisted. In November 1971 Nixon had demanded a list of the party affiliation of every "Schedule C" (political) appointee. Just in case Democrats tried to pass themselves off as Republicans, they were asked for the state in which they were registered to vote so their answers could be checked. As it turned out, no Cabinet department had more Democrats at its top levels than the Defense Department, but Nixon could do nothing about that; Laird had kept the cocktail napkin.[1]

The pent-up discontent erupted when the president woke up the morning after the election with the realization that his landslide was only the *second* most impressive in American electoral history. (Johnson had beaten Goldwater by a slightly greater margin in 1964.) Nixon called an 11 A.M. White House staff meeting and explained that he was going to shake up the administration. Without sitting down he perfunctorily thanked those present for their work. Then, by Haldeman's account, he let them know that no one's job was secure. "There are no sacred cows," he said. "We are going to tear up the pea patch in this reorganization." He asked for all their resignations immediately and for a list of documents in their possession that should be added to his own papers.[2]

In his memoirs Nixon admitted that a "melancholy" had come over him on election night, perhaps because of the "marring effects of Watergate [or] perhaps it was because this would be my last campaign." Even Laird was surprised by the Nixon he saw at the Cabinet meeting that followed the White House staff meeting. Nixon was thankful for the efforts of his Cabinet members but surprisingly withdrawn, as if so many defeats in the past had been easier to handle than an all-out victory. Laird was not disturbed for himself but for his people who might want to stay on into the second term. Laird had already submitted his resignation letter that morning, noting that all of his goals had been achieved or were within sight. "As we discussed four years ago, I have felt strongly that no individual should serve as Secretary of Defense for more than four years," Laird wrote to Nixon. "Therefore, I respectfully request that you allow me to submit, and that you accept my resignation [effective] January 20, 1973."[3]

That afternoon Carl Wallace received a packet of letters from the White House, individually addressed to each political appointee in the Defense Department. Inside was an unsigned White House memorandum titled "Post-Election Activities," which began: "All Presidential appointees are expected to submit a *pro forma* letter of resignation to become effective at the pleasure of the President.... The purpose of the resignations is to give the President a free hand to strengthen the structure of the government as he begins his second term."[4] Also in the packet were form letters for resignations and a job application to be filled out if an appointee wanted to stay in his or her job or move to another one. Laird was furious at the tactless move; he told Wallace not to deliver the letters and to call a special staff meeting for the next morning, Thursday, November 9, at 10 A.M.

Laird backed into the painful purpose of the meeting with a pep talk about the election victory and goals achieved, which had been possible because of the team's hard work. "No Cabinet officer or the President has received greater loyalty exhibited by the presidential appointees and non-career executives than I have had at this department during the last four years," he declared. But the term was not complete, and Laird needed their continued focus and help. "The next 60 days will be very important to the success or failure of the Vietnamization program," he said. "We are at the make-or-break stage." Laird said he hoped no one saw him "as deserting the ship. I simply feel that this ship will be better run if someone new comes in."

Then to the matter at hand—the packet of letters and job application forms from the White House. Laird said the White House was handling things in an "unfortunate" manner. In fact, he was personally "embarrassed" for the president. Froehlke was asked to read aloud the unsigned White House memorandum they were all receiving. Laughter rolled through the room. Laird said he would refuse to submit any pro forma letters of resignation to the White House. "Your letters will not leave this Department. And there will be no applications and no job descriptions filled out by any of you. We will not handle personnel matters in this way. We will talk with each of you and hope as many as possible will agree to stay. We have a great team, and I apologize for the way the White House has done this. I will speak to the President about it. Otherwise, I advise you to let Carl toss these packets in the trash." (One of the appointees recalled that several of them ceremoniously dropped their unopened packets in Wallace's waste basket.)[5]

The election year had already seen personnel moves of historic importance—among them Westmoreland's retirement and Abrams's promotion to army chief of staff. For the new vice chief, Laird and Froehlke had younger candidates in mind. Both liked the idea of reaching down to the two-star rank to find a bright, young army general who could infuse the new army with new ideas. By June they had narrowed their choices to two names, according to the "Eyes Only" memo Laird sent Nixon. One was Major General Bernard W. Rogers, the outstanding officer who had made many innovations at Fort Carson. The second name was Major General Haig, who had the inside track because Laird had promised Nixon that Haig could have the number two job if Abrams were number one. The promise won out. Haig's elevation to vice chief of staff, the second highest position in the army, was meteoric. He had been a major general for only six months—so short a time that on the day of the announcement of his nomination, the release of an official photograph was delayed because no picture could be found of Haig with more than one star. Vaulting him from two-star to four-star rank also meant that Laird was jumping him over 243 more-senior generals. He was given the high post without ever having commanded a division in the army.[6]

When Nixon first informed Kissinger about Haig's move to the Pentagon, Kissinger groused that he couldn't afford to lose Haig from the National Security Council staff. To ease the transition Laird agreed that Kissinger could have a hot-line phone link to Haig. This was an unusual concession for Laird, who didn't want White House aides pulling the strings at the Pentagon. Although Laird and Haig disagreed on many things, Laird was at ease with the phone line. "Henry asked for that privilege, and I felt that because of their relationship it was alright," Laird recalled.[7]

Haig's replacement at the NSC was Air Force Brigadier General Brent Scowcroft, a talent Laird had spotted when Scowcroft worked for the Joint Chiefs and one of many luminous careers Laird shepherded at critical moments. In late 1971 Laird had urged Nixon to bring Scowcroft to the White House as a military assistant. Laird saw him as one of the star soldier-statesmen (like Colin Powell, later) whom the uniformed services and executive branch needed for the military in the future political age. The move put Scowcroft in a key place that made possible his ascension to national security advisor in the Ford administration when Kissinger was secretary of state. (Kissinger and Scowcroft, among others, later formed a lucrative consulting business together when they left government.)[8]

Meanwhile Laird lived up to the pledge he had made to Vice Admiral Noel Gayler when he had made Gayler the head of the National Security Agency, the largest U.S. intelligence agency. Laird had promised that, if Gayler was loyal, he would be promoted to four stars. Gayler had performed efficiently and, despite numerous Kissinger and White House runs at co-opting him, was loyal to Laird. So when the commander-in-chief of the Pacific forces, Admiral John McCain, retired in September, Laird promoted Gayler to the four-star position.[9]

Probably the second-most serious loss to the Laird team—after the December 1971 resignation of David Packard —was the departure of Laird's right-hand man, Air Force Major General Pursley. For six years Pursley had been putting in sixteen- to eighteen-hour days as the military assistant to three successive secretaries of defense. Clark Clifford called him "one of the most intelligent and broad-gauged military officers I have ever known." But it was grueling work. Laird said of Pursley, "He would not only take on the chief of staff of the air force, but would also take on the chief of staff of every service, and the chairman of the Joint Chiefs on my behalf. He took on Al Haig over at the White House, too, almost every day. And he took them all on tough." It was one of those many encounters that pushed Pursley beyond his limits.

Laird was in Europe at a NATO meeting in May 1972 when Pursley paid a call on Haig at the White House, hoping to talk about ways they might improve relations between their offices. Instead, Haig turned to a credenza behind his desk and produced a large black notebook in which he said he had been collecting a list of grievances against Pursley since early in the Nixon administration. (Pursley didn't know then about the most egregious of Haig's collection techniques, the tapping of Pursley's phones for extended periods.) The black book was the last straw. When Laird returned from NATO Pursley told him that he didn't think he could continue to work for the Nixon administration; he wanted to retire. But Laird could not let him go altogether. "He was too valuable an asset for our country," Laird recalled. So he persuaded Pursley to withhold his resignation and take on a new assignment. In December he became commander of the Fifth Air Force as well as U.S. forces in Japan. A third star came with the assignment, making Pursley the youngest lieutenant general in the air force at the time.

Another major departure in 1972 was Navy Secretary John Chafee. Laird had persuaded him to take the job after Chafee had lost his bid in 1968 for a fourth term as a rare Republican governor in the predominantly Democratic state of Rhode Island. The defense job rejuvenated Chafee to the point that, by early 1972, with Laird's support, he decided he would go back to Rhode Island and run for the Senate. Chafee lost that election because, in a fervently antiwar state where Democrats outnumbered Republicans two to one, he could not overcome his three-year association with the Vietnam War. Four years later, however, Chafee won a Senate seat, which he held until his death in 1999.[10] With Chafee gone from the Pentagon, John Warner finally got the job of navy secretary, for which he had waited three years.

⚜

If ever a man from a family of limited means was born to be a gentleman in manners, demeanor, and appearance, it was John William Warner. He came from a middle-class family but married money—Catherine Mellon, the only daughter of wealthy philanthropist Paul Mellon. As Laird's undersecretary of the navy, Warner had distinguished himself, but the job had cost him his marriage. Long days at the office, his out-of-town trips, and support for Nixon's prosecution of the war distanced him from his wife. When Warner supported U.S. bombing in Vietnam, his wife called him a "warmonger." He called her "a hippie." Though Warner never faulted her with the dissolution of their marriage, it came to an end in early 1972.[11]

The bachelor father of three threw himself even more into the work of the Pentagon. Warner remained navy secretary for more than a year after Laird left. Still, "I always had a restlessness to go into elected office," Warner recounted, and he thought about a 1974 campaign race. But Laird strongly advised against it. "You think you can jump out of the Pentagon and get elected?" Laird lectured Warner. "Do you remember what happened to Chafee? No, after being Navy secretary during this unpopular time, you've got to take a bath." Laird said he knew of just the "bath" for Warner—to be administrator of the American Revolution Bicentennial celebration. Warner saw the wisdom in spending some time as a benign political figure traveling the country drumming up patriotism in every state for bicentennial celebrations. The month of the bicentennial, July 1976, Warner was asked to escort actress Elizabeth Taylor to a British Embassy dinner Queen Elizabeth was hosting in Washington, D.C. He was smitten, and by December Liz Taylor had become his second wife; Warner was her seventh husband.[12]

Two years later, when Warner ran for the Senate from Virginia, Laird enthusiastically campaigned for him. "Dear Boss," Warner wrote that April, "No friend in my lifetime has been more supportive of my career than you." With critical fund-raising assistance from his wife, Warner won a narrow victory.[13] During four reelection campaigns that followed, Laird was active in support of his protégé.

Shortly after Nixon's reelection victory, he retreated to Camp David to cogitate and seek inspiration on second-term appointments. On the afternoon of Friday, November 17, Nixon invited Laird to the presidential retreat in the western Maryland mountains for a bittersweet three-hour chat. The president's first order of business was to determine if Laird would reconsider resigning, or would accept another post such as an ambassadorship or U.S. representative to the United Nations. Laird politely turned Nixon down. He and Barbara needed a long vacation from government service before settling on a new career. "I told him I could not go home that night and even *discuss* such an idea with my wife," Laird recounted during a press conference a week later.[14]

The next matter of business was to ask Laird for his recommendation on his successor. In past visits with Nixon, Laird had pushed three men—New York Governor Nelson Rockefeller, ex–treasury secretary John Connally, and Laird's deputy secretary since February, Kenneth Rush. But by the time of the Camp

David meeting, Nixon had already refused to consider his old rival Rockefeller. And Connally, the president's favorite Democrat, had asked that Nixon not expect him to serve in the Cabinet again. On election night Connally had publicly said that if another Cabinet job were offered him, "I hope I would have the good sense not to take it."[15] That left Rush. But Nixon already had plans to make him undersecretary of state, with the promise that he would move up when Secretary Rogers retired.

After disposing of Laird's recommendations, Nixon asked him what he thought of Elliot Richardson as defense secretary. "I did not object," Laird recalled. He respected Richardson and considered him a friend. Richardson was already in the Cabinet as secretary of Health, Education, and Welfare. Laird's only "knock" on him was that he never seemed to hold a job more than two years. "He seems to always want to move to something else," Laird warned Nixon.

Most of Laird's session with Nixon was warm and nostalgic, as both men realized their service together was ending. Nixon confided that he felt he had won reelection on the very issues that Laird had spearheaded for him, such as Vietnamization, the impending end of the draft, and creation of an all-volunteer force. "He told me I had done a hell of a job," Laird said. That evening, after Laird left, Nixon wrote him a four-page letter expressing a "profound sense of sadness" at losing Laird, the administration's "indispensable man—the right man for the right place, at the right time." Not until their heart-to-heart Camp David talk had Nixon realized the high price Laird's family had paid for his service. So Nixon agreed that a well-deserved "sabbatical from political life" was overdue Laird and his family. Nixon continued:

> Now that you are leaving, I am sure that you will look back to these hard four years and wonder if it was all worth it. I can only say that the Nation will be forever grateful to you for the part you played in winding down the war in Vietnam, and helping to create the conditions which, I pray, will make possible a peaceful settlement in the not too distant future. To have bugged out the day after we got into office would have been easy—and some say—good politics. It would have won us a few good headlines and a great deal of public support in the short run—for a few days, weeks or even months. It would, of course, as we both know have been disastrous for America in the long run, and for the cause of peace and freedom in the world. We saw it through and although our contemporaries may not praise us, historians will record we did the right thing.[16]

Nixon sat down with Richardson three days later at Camp David and offered him the post, which he accepted. But the president refused to give him the rare personnel deal Laird had wrung out of Nixon. Richardson didn't get to select his own deputy. Nixon picked William Clements, a wealthy Texas oil-driller who would go on to be Texas governor. The White House leaked that the president had deliberately picked Clements so his Republican conservatism would balance Richardson's progressive Republicanism.

Laird assured his appointees who wanted to stay during the second term that Richardson would give them a fair hearing, which he did. But the final decisions were not Richardson's to make. In unpublished memoirs, Air Force Undersecretary John McLucas recounted a lunch with Richardson, who complained that he had been blocked from promoting McLucas to secretary of the air force. Richardson said it was because he had not been able to cut the same deal as Laird had with Nixon regarding nominations. All the new service secretaries were to be chosen because of their political loyalties, McLucas said. "Since I was nonpolitical, I was automatically disqualified."[17]

True to Laird's prediction, Richardson would be the shortest-serving defense secretary ever. He lasted only four months on the job before accepting Nixon's request to become attorney general in May 1973.

⚊⚊

During the three months between the election and Laird's resignation, he did not have the luxury of being a lame duck. He had to shepherd the 1973 fiscal year budget and form up the next budget, which Richardson would inherit. Some antidefense members of Congress had been shocked on June 5, 1972, when Laird testified he could not support ratification of the ABM and SALT agreements unless Congress began funding a new ballistic missile submarine, the beginnings of the B-1 bomber, and a far-sighted cruise missile program. All of these systems were allowed by U.S.-Soviet negotiations, and Laird believed they were all necessary for the United States to maintain an effective nuclear deterrent as the SALT II talks got underway.[18] Laird had always been a fan of the submarine because it was less vulnerable to attack than land-based missiles or strategic bombers. Now he was determined to speed up the next phase of sub modernization, the undersea long-range missile system (ULMS).

The need for ULMS was great, Laird felt. The Soviets' accelerated sub-building program meant that, by 1978, they would have about ninety modern nuclear missile submarines, while the United States would have only forty-one aging Polaris and Poseidon subs. The ULMS, with more missiles and each of them with multiple independently targeted warheads, would more than match the Soviet's sub missile power. Because of its higher range, the ULMS submarine did not need foreign bases close to Russia, nor did it need to patrol so close to Soviet naval bases.

In January 1972 Laird had recommended that Nixon immediately request from Congress more than $900 million for the ULMS program, and Nixon complied. Laird's next step was to get the submarine a better name than ULMS. Warner suggested "Trident" and it stuck. Laird understood the value of a name. He had already broken the navy's pattern of naming new cruisers after cities; Laird changed it to states, thus ensuring a larger fan base for the ships. Breaking with a seventy-year navy tradition, Laird also mandated in his first year in office that attack submarines would no longer be named after fish but would be named after prodefense legislators who had died. "I had a bitchy time with Admiral Hyman Rickover when I told him we would quit naming submarines after fish," Laird recalled. Rickover, who headed the nuclear propulsion division at the Pentagon, was a cranky, often-arrogant power in his own right. After a two-hour showdown between the two men over ship names, Laird finally convinced the politically savvy Rickover with three words: "Fish don't vote!" Rickover capitulated. The first new attack submarine was named *William H. Bates* for a Laird friend who had been ranking member of the House Armed Services Committee. Three more followed, named after late friends of the Pentagon in Congress, *L. Mendel Rivers, Richard B. Russell,* and *Glenard P. Lipscomb.*

Shortly after Nixon's reelection, Laird urged him to give the Trident program an official designation as being of the "Highest National Priority," which made it a "crash" program that had first call on the nation's industrial capacity. Nixon concurred in December, but in the post-Laird era his successors had difficulty obtaining continuing funds for the $1 billion per sub program. As a result the first Trident sub, the USS *Ohio,* was not deployed until 1981. Within about twenty years eighteen Trident submarines were deployed in the Atlantic and Pacific fleets, carrying about half of all U.S. strategic nuclear warheads. As much as anyone else, Laird was the father of the Trident.[19]

Laird similarly "fathered" a dozen other key weapons systems still in use today. On that list are the cruise missiles, whose tactical use was formidable in both wars with Iraq and in Afghanistan. Nuclear missiles were first "MIRVed"—given multiple warheads—under Laird. The B-1 strategic bomber program also began during his term. While that expensive bomber was rarely deployed, some of its advanced technology was incorporated into the B-2 stealth bomber. Among other Laird-sponsored stand outs are the air force's F-15 and F-16 fighters, the A-10 close air support aircraft, and the radar-packed E-3 Airborne Warning and Control System (AWACS); the navy's F-14 and F-18 fighters, S-3 carrier-based sub-hunting aircraft, DD-963 class destroyers, SSN-688 *Los Angeles*–class attack submarines, and the strategic Trident; and the army's antitank TOW missile system and main battle tank, the M1.

So great was Laird's respect for Abrams that Laird was determined the M1 tank under development during his tenure would be named after the general. "I always referred to it as 'the Abrams' when I was secretary," Laird said, feeling that it was an appropriate honor for the World War II tank commander. When Abrams died of lung cancer in 1974 Laird turned up his nomenclature lobbying. By the time the first M1 rolled off the assembly line in 1978 it was officially the "M1 Abrams Main Battle Tank (MBT)."

With his resignation letter in the president's hands, Laird still had to put the draft to bed. The fourth and last draft lottery had been held in February 1972. Three months later Laird had announced that no more than fifty thousand men would be called up for military service in 1972—the lowest number since 1949. It was a major achievement for Laird and Nixon; the year before they came into office, draft calls had peaked at nearly three hundred thousand.[20] In a July report to the president, Laird wrote that the "dramatic decline in draft calls" was made possible partly by attracting more voluntary enlistees. "Military leaders have put their shoulders to the wheel and made things happen. Tremendous credit is due them for moving to convert the Armed Forces from 'conscript' to 'volunteer' promptly, aggressively, and with a high degree of success." Laird also reduced the overall size of the active forces by more than a third, from a Vietnam War peak of 3.5 million to 2.3 million, which helped reduce the need for draftees. As a result Nixon and Laird were able to announce in March 1972 that, if Congress passed a pay increase for the military, the draft could officially end on June 30, 1973, when the two-year draft law extension expired.[21]

Creating the all-volunteer army would be "an extraordinary accomplishment" and an unprecedented one, Laird conceded in his July report to Nixon. "Never before has a nation maintained a military force of this size (2.3 million) on a strictly voluntary basis, and we are within reach of that objective." But Laird knew there were still steps to make toward that goal before he left office. The 1971 draft extension bill had not included something Laird thought was needed: enough money to end KP ("kitchen police") and janitorial duties for soldiers. The air force and navy had already contracted those duties to civilians, for the most part. Air Force Chief of Staff John Ryan explained the decision at one of Laird's staff meetings in these words: "It made no sense to us to send a radar mechanic to the mess hall all day."[22] But the army still inflicted the despised chores on its rookies. In trying to end KP, Laird ran into trouble with an old friend in Congress, George Mahon, the House Appropriations Committee chairman, who felt that it was good for a GI to peel potatoes, just as Mahon himself had once done in the service. Besides, contracting out the work would cost $100 million. Nevertheless, Laird won the short-lived KP debate in Congress. Wisconsin Congressman William Steiger persuasively argued that it made as much sense to have trained soldiers do KP as it did to have members of Congress "clean the latrines in the Rayburn Building."[23]

As the draft wound to a close Laird faced a new problem of dwindling medical personnel. Sufficient doctors and nurses had joined the services during the height of the war so they could avoid the draft and get better assignments.[24] The surgeons general of the military services insisted that a doctors-only draft would have to continue indefinitely to supply the fourteen thousand health-care professionals the military needed. Dr. Richard Wilbur, the Pentagon health chief, arranged a meeting with Laird and the surgeons general. The military doctors started explaining to Laird why the all-volunteer concept would not work for the medical people. Dr. Wilbur recalled, "At one point Mel cut short the complaints by slamming his hand on the table so hard that the coffee cups went flying. 'We are going to an all-volunteer force, and that is that!' he said. The conversation changed totally at that moment. I never had any more trouble with them."[25]

Laird eventually solved the medical shortage with more medical school scholarships, higher enlistment bonuses, and pay increases. The most innovative solution was Laird's creation of a special military medical academy, the Uniformed Services University of the Health Sciences (USU). It had long been the dream of Congressman Hebert, who called it a "West Point for doctors." Nixon opposed the idea, but that didn't stop Laird from joining forces with Hebert to persuade Congress to fund the university. Both the Office of Management and Budget and the Department of Health, Education, and Welfare urged Nixon to veto it, but he decided it would be fruitless to take on Laird and Congress over that one issue.[26]

Based in Bethesda, Maryland, USU enrolled its first thirty-two students in 1976. On Laird's recommendation its first president was Dr. Tony Curreri, a noted Wisconsin physician, and its first chairman of the board of regents was David Packard. President Jimmy Carter tried to kill the university by cutting off funding, but Laird mounted a formidable defense. "Mel kept calling me, saying, 'Don't do it!'" recalled Harold Brown, who was Carter's secretary of defense. "Then he went around to his friends in Congress and insisted it be funded—so it was." When the Clinton administration in the late 1990s, as part of Vice President Al Gore's "reinventing government" initiative, attempted to close USU, once again Laird succeeded in rallying opposition to what he felt was a misguided, short-sighted move. In its first three decades USU graduated more than 2,500 physicians. The majority of health professionals in both Gulf Wars were military medical school graduates.[27]

The final piece of Laird's plan to end the draft on schedule was increasing the benefits, training, and missions of the nation's Reserve and the National Guard forces. Almost seven hundred thousand reservists and guardsmen were called up during the Korean War, but the political fallout had been severe. Because most units were filled with men from the same local area of a state, if they suffered high casualties it had a devastating impact on those communities. During the 1961 Berlin crisis President Kennedy called up the Reserves, an action that also had unwelcome political repercussions. So when Lyndon Johnson decided to escalate U.S. participation in Vietnam, he avoided using the Reserves. Johnson found it easier to draft the men he needed, so the Reserves and National Guard actually became a haven from the draft.

Congressman Laird had thought that was all wrong. He felt the primary value of the Reserves and National Guard was to provide adequately trained backup forces to supplement the active forces in time of national emergency or war. So, as secretary of defense, he issued a historic memorandum on August 21, 1970, mandating that the Reserves and National Guard would be called upon *first* in such times. He called it the "total force concept," and it necessarily stipulated beefing up those Reserve forces that had been cannibalized by Johnson to pay for the Vietnam War. When Laird entered office, the Reserves budget was $2.1 billion. By the time he left, it was $4.1 billion to fund much needed new equipment, training, and modernization.[28] Laird's 1970 decision regarding the total force concept became an integral and institutional part of military planning for thirty-five years. Both Presidents Bush used the Reserves and National Guard for both Gulf wars in precisely the way Laird had intended.

For the last draft induction of the Vietnam War, three hundred men were ordered to report to their local induction centers on December 28, 1972. But then former president Harry Truman died and that day was pronounced a national day of mourning. Some potential inductees reported anyway and were sent home to await further instructions that never came. The draft was dead, except for the formal expiration of the law, even though the war in Vietnam was still not over.

Though Laird lacked total faith in the peace negotiations as they dragged on, he nevertheless sent Kissinger a memorandum in mid-November listing negotiating terms Laird felt were essential. The most prominent among his points was the return of the POWs and an accounting of the missing—to include American inspections of crash sites in North Vietnam. A month later and still with no treaty finalized, Laird took his case for the POWs directly to Nixon.[29]

The nation was weary of the yo-yo peace talks and promises of an accord. President Thieu was digging in his heels for more concessions, and the Hanoi government kept changing the terms. While Nixon and Kissinger seemed to aim for an air-tight treaty, Laird's solution was to sign whatever marginally acceptable agreement Hanoi had offered, get the POWs home, and worry about compliance later. The North Vietnamese "appear to be stiffening by reopening issues once considered settled," Laird wrote the president. Kissinger had "encouraged the U.S. people and the rest of the world to believe that peace is at hand and that our POWs would be home momentarily," and congressional leaders "do not understand why we are delaying the signing of the agreement. . . . I am concerned that you are putting in jeopardy your reputation as a world leader and your future effectiveness on the world scene. I believe the far better course of action is to sign the agreement now, get all our POWs home and get an accounting of our MIAs, and then test the sincerity of the North

Vietnamese. If the test proves that the North Vietnamese have deceived us, then is the time to take action to help the [Saigon government]."[30]

Nixon didn't choose the sign-now-pay-later route. He had suspended bombing over North Vietnam on October 22 as a negotiations incentive, but it didn't work. So Nixon leaned toward one last massive bombing campaign by B-52s to bring the enemy swiftly to its knees. At Nixon's request Laird sent him a plan on December 7 for a bombing attack "designed to produce a mass shock effect in a psychological context." Laird submitted a list of thirty-seven targets, from railroad yards and shipping docks to power plants and bridges. They could be taken out in seven days if the weather cooperated. Tangentially he also recommended reseeding the harbors with mines, although he never believed the tactic had much sort-term military impact.[31] According to one analysis for Laird, after the initial mines were planted in May it appeared that Hanoi had only taken three months to reroute its formerly seaborne supplies to road and rail supply lines.[32]

Never a strong advocate of bombing campaigns either, Laird thought that before Nixon went ahead with it he ought to consider increasing pressure on the South Vietnamese. In a memorandum to Kissinger, Laird outlined possible ways to knock some sense into President Thieu and persuade him to agree to peace terms: a "sudden and substantial drop" in bombing runs; withdrawal of U.S. ships, and pulling out all but fifteen thousand American soldiers, essentially leaving the South to its own devices if Thieu would not cooperate in the peace talks.[33]

When Kissinger reported to Nixon on December 16 that the peace talks were at an impasse, Nixon ordered the bombing of North Vietnam to resume again the following day (after a two-month hiatus). Anticipating the president's decision, Laird had already advised the Joint Chiefs to prepare for massive B-52 strikes beginning on the December 17, but it wasn't until the next day that conditions were suitable and the twelve-day campaign began. It was officially known as "Operation Linebacker II," but it came to be called the "Christmas Bombing." It was brutal and costly. By Laird's count 121 American pilots and crewmen were killed or taken prisoner. The United States lost ten B-52s in the first three days. Through private and public signals, Laird made sure Nixon and Kissinger were informed that the campaign had no military value. It was strictly an attempt to bring Hanoi back to the negotiating table. At a press conference at Pearl Harbor on December 29 Laird responded carefully but honestly when asked if Linebacker II was designed to wipe out Hanoi's military might. "No, I don't believe that would be a fair assessment of the situation, because North Vietnam depends largely upon supplies and military equipment that are not produced within the borders of North Vietnam."[34]

Admiral Moorer didn't see the strategic value of the bombing campaign either, and, after it was over, he went so far as to say publicly that no one had consulted him about whether it was militarily necessary. After a dressing down from Laird, Moorer took back his words the next day, saying there had been continuous talks between him and the White House. Laird suspected Moorer was trying to duck accountability for a bombing campaign that he didn't like.[35]

Contemporary press reports played on the perceived reluctance of Laird, Moorer, and even Kissinger to support the bombing campaign. Laird personally felt Kissinger "kind of ran for shelter a little bit" when his friends in the liberal media began criticizing the bombing. "The president was always sore at Kissinger because he felt Kissinger was trying to appeal to the liberal press," Laird said. In the end Laird respected Nixon's right to try the bombing as a tactic to bring Hanoi back to the table. "I'd have to say the president turned out to be right. I'm glad he did. Nixon was in a position then where he was very withdrawn and it was hard to talk to him during that period. But I told him after it was all over that he was right."[36]

After four days of bombing, Nixon cabled North Vietnamese leaders to say that the assault could end if they came back to the bargaining table. Getting no response, Nixon allowed the pilots to take Christmas Day off and then ordered the heaviest bombing attacks of the war, beginning on December 26. More than 1,300 bombing sorties were flown, dumping twenty thousand tons of bombs. In one fifteen-minute raid over Hanoi and Haiphong, ten targets were destroyed by a fleet of twenty bombers. Within a day Hanoi said it was ready to talk, but it took three more days of negotiating the terms of the next meeting before Nixon finally halted the bombing on December 29. In the end there were virtually no more military targets worth hitting in North Vietnam. They had all been destroyed.

While Nixon and Kissinger dickered with Hanoi about restarting the peace talks in January, Laird began cleaning out his desk. He had promised four years earlier that he would leave on inauguration day—January 20, 1973—whoever was president, and he had reserved a taxi for that purpose in advance. In mid-December Laird had hosted a going-away party for his team in the elegant reception rooms of the State Department. David Packard came from California, and retired general Earle Wheeler joined the party to give it the air of a family reunion. It stood out as one of Laird's fondest memories from his four years at the Pentagon. He didn't prepare a speech, but he stood to tell the small group that he was proud of them and proud of their families for what they had sacrificed. He said there would never be another team like them with the loyalty, devotion, and courage they had shown. Froehlke looked over the group of friends and said it was more than a party. "When you look at all these people, you realize there's more than a facade of a party here; it goes deeper.... [I]t shows Mel Laird put together an amazing team. Some day the American public will appreciate what this team did—not today, but some day."[37]

On January 8 Laird testified before the House Armed Services Committee for the last time and declared that Vietnamization was essentially and successfully completed.[38] The South Vietnamese had in hand more than $5.3 billion in equipment provided by the United States in the last year of the war, and they knew how to use it to keep the enemy at bay. When Kissinger reopened the peace talks that same week, he began putting in place the rules for continuing resupply of Saigon by the United States and of Hanoi by the Soviet Union. Each of the superpowers was going to be allowed to keep their surrogates resupplied with replacement parts, but not to escalate the level of aid.

Laird held his last press conference on January 19, and reporters tried to get him to come clean on some of his disagreements with Nixon. How did he *really* feel about the invasions of Cambodia and Laos and the last massive bombing of North Vietnam? Discrete to the end, Laird responded: "I am not going to discuss matters of privileged communications between the President of the United States, the Secretary of Defense . . . and the Joint Chiefs in connection with on-going operations or previous operations. I can only state to you that I supported the actions which we have taken and I have always supported those actions, and I continue to support those actions."

Laird expressed disappointment that the Senate had not yet confirmed Elliot Richardson as his successor, which meant Laird could "not leave this building unattended." He explained, "I left the Congress because I felt I had a duty to serve my country. I did that as a favor to the President, and a duty to my country. You can discount it all you want, but that is the reason that I am here. . . . I have fulfilled my commitment, but you cannot leave this building without a Secretary of Defense."[39]

In the next few days Laird made some phone calls to senators asking them to speed up the process so he could get on with his new life. However, the nine-day postponement of his taxi ride did allow him to leave on a high note. On Monday, January 22, Laird talked with Kissinger before Kissinger left on his final flight to Paris where, both of them knew, he would initial a secretly concluded agreement. "If it hadn't been for your work, I would not be leaving this morning to initial this agreement," Kissinger said emotionally in sincere tribute to Laird. The peace accord was initialed by Kissinger and North Vietnamese negotiator Le Duc Tho in a public Paris ceremony on January 23 and was formally signed four days later by the respective foreign ministers.[40]

For the United States the Vietnam War was over. (Former President Lyndon Johnson died at the age of sixty-four of a heart attack the evening before the treaty was initialed.) The United States and Hanoi both agreed to put no more troops into South Vietnam, the POWs would be returned within sixty days, and the war would continue with each side replacing lost equipment but adding no more to the conflict—all terms proposed by Laird to Kissinger in his previous advisory memoranda. Laird genuinely believed that, under those terms, Vietnamization of the war had been and would continue to be a success.

The United States had agreed to bankroll the war in Vietnam, but not send any more of its young men to die there, as 45,933 of them already had, according to the best estimate at that time.

Before Nixon went on television to address the nation at 10 P.M. on Tuesday, January 23, he held a special Cabinet meeting. During the meeting Nixon confidentially reported on how the agreement was reached and singled out Laird for praise. "Without Vietnamization," he said, "there would have been no settlement and this night would not have been possible." Laird responded that he had an "exhilarating sense of pride" in the accomplishment, as well as great satisfaction that he had helped Nixon "make good on every promise he has made about the war he inherited." This was "the finest hour of the Nixon team upon which I have been privileged to serve."[41] The remaining U.S. troops were soon on their way home, and the POWs would join them within a month.

Four days later Secretary Laird accomplished his final major goal by declaring an end to the draft five months ahead of schedule. In an official order transmitted to the three service secretaries and the Joint Chiefs on January 27, Laird declared: "I wish to inform you that the Armed Forces henceforth will depend exclusively on volunteer soldiers, sailors, airmen and Marines. Use of the draft has ended."[42]

"I don't think at the time the public appreciated the significance [of Laird's order], but in retrospect it was a major accomplishment," reflected former president Ford, who added that Laird deserved to be called the "father" of the modern volunteer armed forces. Many prominent Democrats have agreed. "The volunteer Army was a huge achievement by Laird," noted Clinton administration ambassador Richard Holbrooke, who coauthored Clark Clifford's memoirs. "Ending the draft was one of the most important pieces of social legislation that the United States has had. And it was Laird, who was the only guy in the Nixon administration who understood politics as well as policy, who brought us to an outcome that has served the nation very well."[43]

Among Laird's most treasured memorabilia is a handwritten note dated the same day the draft ended and the Vietnam cease-fire began. "My warmest congratulations on your successful efforts in dealing with the war in South Viet Nam," wrote a White House official named Donald Rumsfeld, who considered himself a Laird protégé. "It has been a privilege to see the intellect, wisdom and courage you and your associates have brought to bear on this thorniest of problems." Without any foreknowledge that he himself would serve as secretary of defense under two future presidents, and oversee the next unpopular war, Rumsfeld concluded: "You are one hell of a guy and my candidate for 'The best Secretary of Defense in history.'"[44]

On February 1, 1973, Laird closed his office door for the last time and left without any fanfare. Eleven days later, on February 12 at 3:20 P.M. Washington time, the first of the American POWs came off an airplane at Clark Air Force Base in the Philippines. Laird watched it on television, as the rest of the nation did, and uncharacteristically shed a few tears. A week later a letter arrived at Laird's home from President Nixon: "As I saw our POWs come off the plane at Clark Field, I was never so proud to be an American.... I just wanted you to know how much I personally appreciate all you have done to help achieve the honorable peace we fought for."[45]

42

Trying a Man's Soul

❦

"MEL AND MOM DO THE TOWN," read the headline of one Wisconsin newspaper a week after Laird resigned as secretary of defense. With his eighty-five-year-old mother, Helen, on his arm, Laird walked the streets of Madison shopping for a coat for her and then taking her for a medical checkup. When Laird stopped at a private club for lunch he was hailed in the lobby by old friends, who called out, "What are your plans now?"

"I'm going to rest for three months," Laird said.[1]

"You deserve a rest and change of environment—God knows you've earned it," an old friend, Interior Secretary Rogers Morton, said in a letter. Morton's missive was one of hundreds of accolades Laird received upon his retirement. They came in newspaper articles and editorials, television and radio commentaries, and private letters. One of those praising him was James Schlesinger, chairman of the Atomic Energy Commission, who wrote: "This has been a difficult period to lead the Department, as you well know, in view of the disenchantment both on the Hill and in the public at large. In these troubled circumstances, I can think of no one who could have handled the problem more skillfully than you have done." (Schlesinger himself would become defense secretary a few months later.)[2]

Laird had promised his wife, Barbara, that he would go to work in private business so they could settle down out of the limelight. Offers poured in, some of them in the six-figure range. At least one major airline company and one large aluminum firm wanted Laird to come aboard as the chief executive officer. While Laird acknowledged that he would like to serve on the boards of several major companies (twenty-two had offered seats), he did not want to be a CEO. He also turned down an invitation to become the $200,000-a-year chairman of the New York Stock Exchange.[3]

Laird was only fifty and at the top of his game. Few could believe that he would abandon politics altogether. *Washington Star* military correspondent Orr Kelly wrote that one clue to Laird's future was the fact that "he is one of this nation's relatively few true professional politicians. He is not one of those successful lawyers, businessmen or labor leaders who turn to politics. He began in politics when he was barely old enough to vote and legislative politics has been his life's work except for the last four years." Though Laird himself had considered the Pentagon a "political graveyard," Kelly observed that "he probably is coming out with a better reputation than he had expected. Since his resignation was announced ... editorials in newspapers throughout the country have been almost uniformly complimentary and some have praised him lavishly." So a political future was not unthinkable.[4]

Many reports quoted friends saying that Laird was being urged by Wisconsin Republicans to consider running for governor, senator, or congressman again from his home state.[5] There was also a spate of stories pushing the proposition that Laird would almost certainly run for the presidency in 1976. "It can be flatly stated that Laird believes Spiro Agnew should not be the next President of the United States after Nixon. Less flatly, it can be said he wants the job," opined the *Chicago Tribune*. David Broder of the *Washington Post* reported that Laird indeed considered himself "and ought to be considered" as a "potential contender" for the presidency. Broder quoted an anonymous Laird "associate" as saying, "Laird may not be well-loved by liberals, but if he goes into the primaries battling Spiro Agnew, it would do wonders for his middle-of-the-road image. And Mel knows the middle of the road is where the payoff is." The *Christian Science Monitor* editorialized that there was no harder job in the federal government than the one Laird had just left, so he would have no trouble being president next. "When Republicans start thinking seriously about their ticket for 1976 they will be thankful for a Melvin Laird in their spectrum." Nixon privately told Ehrlichman that he thought his friend Mel wanted to run for the Senate, having already been in the House.[6] In a November 1972 letter to Laird, Nixon urged him to get back into politics:

> When you told me today that you were "only" 50 years of age I thought back to the fact that I was 50 in 1963 right after I had lost the race for Governor of California and when the odds makers in Las Vegas, not to mention myself, wouldn't have given me a million-to-one shot to come back and be elected President in 1968 and win by an overwhelming landslide in 1972.
>
> You are taking your *sabbatical from political life* at the same age, but you are going out not in defeat but on top. . . .
>
> I wish you the best in whatever you undertake in the future. But as I told you in our meeting today, the Defense Department's gain was politics' loss. You are one of the most astute politicians that America has produced in this century . . . a fact that is recognized by most political observers across the country today.
>
> The Nation needs you. After you and your family have a well-deserved period of relief from the enormous burdens you have carried over these past four years I hope you will re-enter the political arena. Whatever you decide to do you have my best wishes.[7]

Laird would get his short vacation, but no more. He would be working in the White House sooner than any prognosticator had forecast. And while there, Laird would find himself in the unique position of being the only man in history to almost single-handedly choose a president of the United States—the only president who got the job without anyone ever voting for him.

~~~

The day after Laird left the Pentagon he played golf at Burning Tree Club with Jack Mills. On the second green Laird putted to within three feet of the cup. Although it's possible to miss such a short putt, courtesy often induces an opponent to declare it done. But Mills said nothing, so Laird peered up at him. "Is this good?" he asked Mills.

"Would have been good yesterday," Mills said dryly. "Yesterday I would have given you the putt."

"You son of a bitch!" Laird growled as he sank the simple putt.

"Oh, how the mighty hath fallen!" Mills laughed. Courtesy would have demanded he give the defense secretary the putt. "But you don't have to give a three-foot putt to a guy who's not important anymore!"

Mills had not wrung everything he could out of the joke. Back in the clubhouse Laird held up his finger and beckoned Mills, who was talking to other club members. Loudly, so all could hear, Mills said, "Mr. Secretary, let me tell you something. When you lost your private helicopter and your private plane and your limousine, you lost all your personality. As far as I'm concerned, I don't want to see you put that finger up again and order me around. You are nobody now."[8]

Laird loved it. He was getting back to the life he once had, and beginning to enjoy being home without crisis phone calls at all hours of the day and night. In March the Lairds spent two weeks together on a beach in Mexico. Barbara had prepared a list of 150 books she knew Laird would enjoy now that he had time to read for pleasure. He got a good start on the list in Mexico. By the time he returned to Wisconsin in late March for a meeting of the Laird Youth Leadership Foundation in Stevens Point, he was tanned, rested, and ready—but for what? Local reporters asked about his political future and he artfully dodged the question. He was also pointedly silent about the news of Watergate that had percolated in his absence. He had been out of touch in Mexico, he demurred.[9]

It is unlikely that Laird, the political animal, had missed much, even while tanning on that Mexican beach. The scandal called Watergate had begun in June of 1972 with the break-in at the Democratic National Committee headquarters in the Washington, D.C., Watergate Hotel. Seven men were arrested in the act of planting bugs in the office, apparently at the behest of Nixon's Committee to Reelect the President. The news dribbled out at such a slow pace that by election time in November, only the seven hired burglars and their immediate handlers were implicated, leaving the president and the upper echelons of his campaign organization clear of any charges of wrong-doing. It was not a significant campaign issue.

In January 1973, as Nixon prepared for his second inauguration, five of the seven pleaded guilty to burglary and wire-tapping charges. Then the culpability began to spread like a blood stain. The Justice Department charged that Nixon's reelection committee was playing fast and loose with its money, some of which had gotten into the hands of G. Gordon Liddy, one of the remaining defendants, who was also the lawyer for Nixon's election finance committee. There were implications in the press that some of the money went to the burglars, even after they were arrested, as inducements to take the fall for higher-ups in the campaign organization. Liddy and the other remaining burglar, James McCord, were convicted on January 30. But the president's skirts remained apparently clean.

While Laird was shopping with his mother in Madison in early February, the Senate was voting to start its own Watergate investigation, chaired by the irascible Democrat from North Carolina, Sam Ervin. While Laird was vacationing in Mexico, the Watergate mystery crossed paths with the nomination of Patrick Gray to be Nixon's new FBI director. As acting director of the FBI, Gray had been in charge of a Watergate probe and had fed information about the case to White House Counsel John Dean. Gray told the Senate committee voting on his confirmation as FBI director that Dean had probably lied to Watergate investigators, but Gray continued to send Dean confidential FBI reports on the investigation. Then Gray clammed up at his confirmation hearing, saying he was under new orders from Attorney General Richard Kleindienst not to talk to Congress about Watergate anymore.

Within a month Gray's nomination had been withdrawn, then he resigned as acting FBI director when it was reported that he had burned some FBI files related to Watergate because John Dean told him they "should never see the light of day." On April 30 Dean in turn resigned over the blossoming Watergate affair, along with Kleindienst, Haldeman, and Ehrlichman. Laird's replacement at the Pentagon, Elliot Richardson, was quickly pressed into service to be the new attorney general, confirming Laird's complaint that the upwardly mobile Richardson never camped very long in any job.

A few days earlier Laird had been visiting his mother again in Marshfield, still trying to maintain the aura of being on a hiatus as he watched from a distance while the White House crumbled. A local reporter asked him if the rumors were true that Laird would be taking Haldeman's job as chief of staff. "I was drafted four years ago to end our involvement in South Vietnam and to end the draft, and I cannot be drafted again," Laird responded, smiling broadly. "We are now on a basis of all-volunteer service."[10]

Laird had a few more days in late April to pretend Watergate was not his concern. On May 1 he acknowledged that two Cabinet members, Secretary of State Rogers and Treasury Secretary George Shultz, had asked him if he would consider working at the White House to straighten out the havoc Watergate was wreaking on day-to-day business there. But Laird insisted he wasn't interested. And, he added ominously, if it was discovered that Nixon himself was involved in the scandal, it would be better if the country never found out. "From the standpoint of getting into a trial of the presidency, that would be a terrible mistake," Laird said. "I am confident from knowing the President that he just would not be involved in any way in this kind of operation. If he were, it would be very bad for the country."[11]

At the same time Laird said he had no plans to get back into politics. He had already secretly accepted an offer from DeWitt Wallace, publisher of the *Readers' Digest,* to join the magazine as a senior counselor for national and international affairs, which meant retiring from public life.

In the game of musical chairs that was to become the modus operandi for the Nixon administration's second term, Nixon found a new chief of staff in General Haig, who thus served only four months as army vice chief of staff. But Ehrlichman's domestic policy advisor post remained empty, and Laird began hearing alarming reports from his old friends on Capitol Hill that the business of running the country had ground to a halt. The White House was constipated by Watergate, and Nixon had withdrawn into a cocoon. Laird rightly guessed that the president needed help but didn't necessarily want it from someone as strong willed as his old defense secretary, so Laird continued to mind his own business.

He was more distressed by the thoughts of a Pentagon adrift without leadership; Richardson was gone after only eighty-seven days, and Bob Froehlke was going through with his long-planned resignation as secretary of the army. Laird made a call to David Packard to see if he would return as defense secretary. For a few days the offer hung in the balance, then Packard declined, as he did not think it would be possible to work out the same blind trust arrangement that Laird had engineered through the Senate for him in 1968. The president finally settled on CIA Director Schlesinger to take over the Pentagon.[12]

Within days of the April 30 resignations of Haldeman and Ehrlichman, House Minority Leader Gerald Ford and other senior Republicans saw that the White House was floundering. Vital government business was being sidelined as Nixon wallowed in the Watergate morass. Something had to be done, they agreed, as did the Democratic leadership when they were brought into the discussion. They needed to find some old hands whom the bipartisan leadership could trust, and then persuade them to shore up the sinking ship at 1600 Pennsylvania Avenue—*and* persuade Nixon to accept their help. The first name that came to them was Melvin Laird, who "by then was Washington's 'indispensable man,'" Ford recalled. The second name was Bryce Harlow, the presidential counselor who had advised both Eisenhower and Nixon.

The party leaders agreed on a full-court press. Harlow made an appointment for them with Laird at his Bethesda, Maryland, house, and they descended en masse in early May. The group was led by two Democrats, Senate Majority Leader Mike Mansfield and House Speaker Carl Albert, who were backed by Senate Minority Leader Hugh Scott and House Minority Leader Ford. Another dozen legislators of both parties, including future Speaker Tip O'Neill and House Minority Leader Bob Michel, crowded into Laird's basement for the secret conference.

Their message was stark. The president's domestic agenda was in a shambles. No one was putting together the next fiscal year's budget, no legislation was getting through Congress, and the president was incommunicado. Would Laird and Harlow come back to the White House as a team to avert a calamity and get the administration back on track? Ford later remembered, "I made a pitch on a very patriotic level, frankly, that if they didn't do this, it would be a catastrophe for the new administration ... and that it was in the obvious best interests of the United States." Harlow was willing, but "Mel was very reluctant to go. He had all these new connections in the outside, non-political world. He wondered if going down there wouldn't aggravate these new business relationships. He wasn't very happy about going down there and working in 'that jungle,' I think he called it."

Harlow lingered behind after the others left. The two old friends and veterans of many a political battle were both poised on the brink of normal life; Laird had promised Barbara that things were going to be different for them with *Readers' Digest*. Harlow was already settling into a job as government liaison for Procter and Gamble. The two men agreed then that they would go as a team or not at all.[13]

Laird's former aide Bill Baroody and Defense Department General Counsel Fred Buzhardt had gone to work at the White House and were enlisted to lean on their former boss to roll his sleeves up and join them. Vice President Agnew also pressured him to accept. As part of the lobbying effort some friends "even went to my wife," Laird recalled. "My wife was very upset. She thought President Nixon was lying about the Watergate cover-up, that he was involved. She thought I should get the hell out of town for a while." As naive as it sounds, with Watergate and Nixon's undisputed culpability being taught in U.S. history books now, Laird believed in May 1973 that the president was innocent. It wasn't that Laird didn't think Nixon capable of deceit; it was simply that Laird thought he had measured the president enough times to know when he was lying. But he had to know for sure, if only to reassure his wife. So when Nixon summoned him and Harlow to Camp David for a face-to-face job tender, Laird was determined to raise the delicate issue as directly as he could.

At one point in the hours-long discussion Laird approached the question naturally, but indirectly, at first. "I told him how my wife felt, and then I put it to him: 'Mr. President, did you have anything to do with the break-in or the cover-up?'"

"Absolutely not," Nixon replied.[14]

Laird recalled Nixon was "vehement" in his denial—that he "had nothing to do" with Watergate in any way. "I believed him; I really did."

Eventually, and only after Harlow had signed on, Laird let Nixon know he was willing to be the new counselor for domestic affairs. Then he had to tell his wife. Laird met her at Washington National Airport, which he thought was useful as public and neutral ground. Barbara was a Red Cross official heading disaster relief efforts, and she had just flown in from Mississippi where tornadoes, accompanied by heavy rains and flash floods, had killed at least forty-seven people in ten states over the Memorial Day holiday weekend. "I told her I was going over to the White House." Laird said. "She damned near walked away from me; she was really mad. She had loved the Congress, and she never liked Nixon."

Nor was Nixon himself likely any happier that Laird had accepted. He respected Laird enough to run the Pentagon but didn't trust him with White House secrets, and there were secrets aplenty. Nixon had been talked into hiring Laird by the congressional leadership and Haig. At one point the secret White House taping system in Nixon's office recorded an exchange between Nixon and Haig on Laird's appointment:

> Haig: "We made a helluva move and I think Laird's gonna be a big asset around here. We need—"
> Nixon: "Somebody to go out and leak everything."
> Haig: "That's right."
> Nixon: "He loves to do that."
> Haig: "That's right." (Laughter)

Haig then reminded Nixon that Laird was a "tough political in-fighter" who would be a "big asset" with Congress. In a more recent interview Haig remembered lobbying Laird, and the gratitude he felt for Laird's sacrifice in coming to work at the crippled White House. "When I got there it was no-man's land," Haig recalled. "We had 90 vacancies, including Cabinet positions, agency chiefs, independent agency chiefs, assistant secretaries. In all our departments we had 90 vacancies to fill in an America in which it became almost the kiss of death to join the administration. You had to risk your whole life, your reputation and career. I asked five major financial leaders to be secretary of the treasury, and they all turned me down." Although Haig and Laird had butted heads, Haig knew Laird was the man Nixon needed to shepherd his domestic legislative package through Congress. "If Mel was any single thing, he was a mirror of the legislature. Mel Laird knew the body from which he came, and in an incredibly astute way."[15]

White House chronicler John Osborne of *The New Republic* called the day of the announcement of Laird's appointment—as well as Haig's retirement from the army for his civilian White House job—a "weird" one. Without acknowledging the prearranged presence of one hundred reporters and photographers, President Nixon, Laird, and Haig stepped out of the Oval Office and into the Rose Garden, smiling and chatting. As if they weren't being watched and photographed, the trio walked the full length of the garden, wheeled around and walked back into the Oval Office. "On the porch steps, Mr. Nixon reached up and patted General Haig's right shoulder," Osborne wrote in a column. "It was done in total silence. Something about the scene, perhaps nothing more than its staged artificiality, made the watching reporters nervous. One of them said in a shaken tone, 'I guess it's to show that Nixon is up and taking nourishment.'"[16]

In a few moments Laird brought the surreal moment back down to earth when he paid a visit to the White House press room. He was introduced by White House press aide Gerald Warren, who announced that, unlike Ehrlichman whose job Laird was filling, the former defense secretary would hold Cabinet rank and sit in on National Security Council meetings because of his expertise on defense matters. Then for thirty minutes Laird answered questions. Osborne thought he looked "distraught and somehow embarrassed" to be there. But the *New York Times* White House correspondent reported that Laird "in his relaxed and easy manner submitted to questions."[17]

Laird was pressed with Watergate-related queries. He declared that it was important for the Senate and House to continue their investigations, as well as an inquiring press, because the Democratic system cannot work unless "the total and complete truth [is] made available.... The truth will be known, and it should be known." But, he said, he personally had "great confidence in the President of the United States. I have been assured of his noninvolvement, and I accept that." A reporter followed up: "Did you personally ask the President for his assurance that he was not involved?" Laird confirmed that he had received "personal" assurance of Nixon's innocence.

Laird told the reporters he had accepted the counselor position in part because "the government, in some quarters, is at a standstill, and this cannot be allowed to continue." He had been promised twenty-four-hour access to Nixon, but he didn't want the press to get the wrong idea. "I am not much of a night man," he laughed. A reporter asked if he had "any intention of running for office at any future period?" Laird emphatically stated: "No, I do not." But then he paused, realizing the incongruity of an absolute when his very presence belied his previous declaration not to return to any government position for at least a year or longer. Of course, he corrected himself, "I didn't have any intention of coming here," either.[18]

In the darkening days of Watergate's creeping reach throughout the White House, the news media uniformly praised the placement of Laird in the West Wing. But at home, the reaction was not so positive. "Barbara got pretty damn sore about it because she felt that I had agreed to get out of there," Laird recalled. "That was a very tender, tough thing." She made plans to move to North Carolina to be near their daughter in the hope that her husband wouldn't be at the White House more than six months. She didn't believe Nixon was innocent, and she wasn't going to wait any longer for her husband to come to his senses and extricate himself from Nixon's orbit. Laird called the choice to go back to work for Nixon perhaps "the biggest mistake I made. It wasn't good for my relationships with my wife or my family." (The Lairds would eventually enjoy nearly two decades of private life before Barbara died of cancer in 1992.)

⌒

As the incoming secretary of defense in 1969, Laird had known that President Johnson had a system for taping phone calls and meetings in the Oval Office. The system had been operated by the Army Signal Corps from the White House basement, but Laird had ordered all the equipment pulled out. "I didn't think the Department of Defense should be in the business of listening to the president's private conversations," he said. "I just didn't want to be a party to it, and I wasn't."

Laird assumed that Nixon had put in a similar system, without the help of the Defense Department. Toward the end of his term Laird discovered that Nixon had had the Secret Service install and operate the Oval Office system. One reason Laird was never worried about anyone hearing his own voice on the White House tapes that were later released was because, for the four years that he was in the Cabinet, he took it for granted that every conversation he had with President Nixon or a White House official was being recorded and might be leaked. "I always assumed that anything I said in any conversation could possibly appear in the *Washington Post* the next day," he said.

Laird also was pretty sure in 1973 that Ehrlichman had wired his own office in the White House. So before Laird moved in on June 14, 1973, he ordered an electronic sweep. The federal inspectors discovered two concealed microphones—one of them in the ceiling—which were tied to tape recorders hidden in a cabinet behind Ehrlichman's desk. Laird had them all removed before his first day on the job.[19]

About the same time a close personal friend of Laird's, Fred Buzhardt, was listening with increasing horror to some of the secret Oval Office recordings from the time of the June 1972 Watergate break-in to the spring of 1973. As Nixon's lead special counsel, Buzhardt was the only one allowed past the Secret Service guards and into the basement room in the Executive Office Building where the tapes were kept.[20] A former South Carolina lawyer, Buzhardt had spent eight years as a top aide to Senator Strom Thurmond before Laird recruited him to be general counsel for the Defense Department. Laird found Buzhardt to be a man of wisdom, discretion, and loyalty. On his own departure Laird had recommended to his successor that Buzhardt be named as a second deputy secretary of defense (which Congress had authorized). But the new principal deputy, William Clements, wanted to be the only deputy. So Buzhardt was in limbo until May 10 when Nixon named him as the president's special counsel on Watergate. Immersing himself in the defense of the president, Buzhardt had helped persuade Laird to accept the White House position with assurances that Nixon was innocent.[21]

After a month on the job Buzhardt found out by listening to the tapes that his client, the president of the United States, was guilty, at a minimum, of criminal obstruction of justice. Buzhardt agonized over the information that, because of attorney-client privilege, he was bound by professional ethics not to share with anyone. He couldn't tell Haig or any other White House officials who seemed convinced of Nixon's innocence and were actively defending the president. But Buzhardt decided to share the news with the one man he felt he owed more to than the commander-in-chief—his old boss, Melvin Laird. "Buzhardt was loyal to me," Laird recalled. "He also felt he had a responsibility to me because he had urged me to take on the job because he told me Nixon was innocent."

So it was in late June or the first week of July that a distraught Buzhardt appeared at Laird's front door late one evening. They went to the basement for a confidential conference. "I've misled you, Mel," Buzhardt began apologetically. "The president was involved in the cover-up."

"How do you know?" Laird asked.

"I've listened to some of the tapes," Buzhardt responded, "and he was in the cover-up right up to his eyeballs from the beginning."

Laird was dumbstruck. After Buzhardt's visit Laird brooded through the night on what he had to do. When he was a boy he had learned a hard lesson about lying. The house rule was that he couldn't have breakfast until he made his bed. One morning he told his mother he had made his bed when he hadn't. "I really got severely disciplined for lying," he recalled. "It was a good experience." Though he had been in politics most of his life, Laird's presumption regarding those with whom he dealt was that they would tell the truth. "I don't *expect* people to lie," he explained.

But, as a congressman who interrogated witnesses with finesse, Laird had found there were many who would shade the truth to their advantage. While he liked to believe on first meeting that a person would not lie to him, Laird also had a healthy skepticism. In the more than two decades that he had been friends with Nixon, while Nixon may have kept secrets, Laird believed the president had never outright lied to him. The depth of his disappointment with Nixon over the Watergate lie was hard for Laird to discuss, even years later. It was only the second time he felt he had been misled in a major way, the first being Defense Secretary Robert McNamara's account of the August 1964 Gulf of Tonkin incident as a witness before Laird's Defense Appropriations Subcommittee. "Those two lies—Nixon's and McNamara's—were two very big disappointments," Laird said.

The morning after Buzhardt informed Laird of Nixon's guilt, Laird went to the White House determined to confront the president on the matter. He waited all day for the opportune moment. Finally, it came on the walk back to the White House from an early evening meeting with Nixon and others in the president's hideaway office in the Executive Office Building. Laird maneuvered himself into position next to Nixon, out of earshot of others, as they strolled back to the West Wing. "That's when I confronted Nixon," said Laird. "I can remember it as if it was yesterday: I told him that I had been advised that he had not leveled with me on his involvement in the Watergate cover-up, and it was hard for me to stay and work there. I said at the time, 'I would have come here probably anyway, if you'd have told me the truth. I was here to help because my friends on the Hill wanted me to be here to help. But having not been told the truth, it's very hard to help somebody. I just can't stay.'" Nixon was quiet; his silence confirmed his guilt. "He knew that I knew that he lied to me," Laird said. The only response the president finally offered was a single sentence: "Well, I hope you don't leave."

After another night to think it over, Laird notified two friends—Harlow and Buzhardt—that he would be leaving. Buzhardt was "very upset" and Harlow "went through the roof," Laird recalled. Both contacted key members of Congress to warn them that it looked like a despondent Laird was going to jump ship. Laird recalled, "Within a matter of two hours, I had all these guys like Jerry Ford, Les Arends, Carl Albert, and Hugh Scott calling me on the phone telling me that they understood that I was resigning." Without divulging what he knew about the tapes from his confidential source, Laird explained to them generally: "I've got a problem over here, and I told the president it was very difficult for me to work any further for him." Unanimously they told him that he couldn't leave because the country needed his work on the budget and other legislation that Nixon was neglecting. "So I agreed, at their urging, to stay only through the preparation of the next year's budget and then leave."

It wasn't until two weeks or more after the dramatic Buzhardt revelation to Laird and subsequent confrontation with the president that the American people learned of the existence of Nixon's tapes. On July 16 Alexander Butterfield, a former Haldeman aide, testified before the Watergate committee about the extensive taping system Nixon had used since 1971. For the next year the nation would be embroiled in a constitutional crisis as President Nixon resisted congressional and court-ordered demands for access to the tapes. During that time Laird was one of the few individuals who absolutely knew their release would sink the president.

When Froehlke heard about the tapes from Butterfield's televised testimony, he called Laird. "Have you listened to the tapes?" Froehlke asked.

"I wouldn't listen to those tapes if you paid me. I want to have nothing to do with them," Laird responded. Froehlke discerned that Laird expected he might be called to testify before the Senate committee about what the president knew, and he wanted to be able to claim ignorance.[22]

About the same time, Agnew visited Nixon who was in the Bethesda Naval Hospital recovering from viral pneumonia. "Abruptly, Nixon asked me what I thought he should do about the tapes," Agnew recalled in his memoirs. "I advised him to destroy the tapes. I thought then, and believe today, that the tapes should have been burned."[23] That sentiment was shared by Jack Mills, who had lunch with Laird at the Sheraton-Carlton Hotel the same day as the Butterfield testimony. "This is going to be a problem for the president," Laird said, ominously. "What do you think should be done?"

"Burn the tapes," Mills responded, in all seriousness.

"Mills, some day I think you're going to end up in jail," Laird said.[24]

Laird's knowledge of the president's guilt had "poisoned" his relationship with Nixon. Nixon had not apologized for his dishonesty; Laird could not forgive him. "He'd always look at me a little strangely" in the months that followed their confrontation, Laird recalled. A review of Laird's public remarks and press conferences in late July and early August offers hints of what life was like for him as he continued to work for sake of the country but not for the president. "The longer I'm here, the more the President will like Haig and dislike me," Laird bluntly told the *Chicago Daily News* on July 22, in what appeared to be an overt reference to Haig's tendency to kowtow to Nixon.[25] By then Washington was awash with rumors that Laird, after only a month on the job, was leaving. Probably some inkling of the earlier lobbying by congressional leaders had finally leaked. But it also had become clear that Laird was no longer part of the "inner circle," based on an analysis of the time he was spending with the president versus the amount of time Nixon gave Haig and Press Secretary Ron Ziegler. So on July 26 Laird called a press conference primarily to deny he was leaving. "The word 'quit' is a good word for headline writers, but I would like to see the word 'stay' used. I am a 'stayer' and I will be staying as long as I can make a contribution," he declared.[26]

Laird wrestled for weeks with his decision. What constituted the greater good? If he left he could hold his head high, his family would be happy, and he could look forward to less stress with a much larger salary. If he stayed he risked his reputation and his marriage and would add nothing to his future financial security. But he would be performing a public service by expertly steering needed legislation through Congress while others (including the president) were obsessed with Watergate. By August 10 he seemed to have settled the inner conflict. In a Chicago speech before the National Legislative Conference Laird used words that, between the lines, read like a personal resolution of his private dilemma: "I have faith in America. I have faith in Americans. I don't believe that we're going to become a nation of quitters and nay-sayers just because we happen to be living—as in the days of Tom Paine—in 'times that try men's souls.'" In the same talk he was optimistically prescient: "This is the most exciting time imaginable to be alive and to be active in politics in America," he added. "We are on the brink of something very big and very basic. The faith of the Founding Fathers in the ability of free men to govern themselves is going to be vindicated once again."[27]

43
On the Ropes

AS WHITE HOUSE DOMESTIC COUNSELOR, Laird had an office in the West Wing and was a member of the Nixon Cabinet, but that did not make him a member of the president's inner circle. As the besieged Nixon hunkered down in mid-1973, journalists adopted a rule of thumb: those who spent the most time with the president were the most powerful. Yet Laird neither wanted nor needed access to Nixon to become one of the most powerful men in government that fateful year—a man whose influence led to the elevation of three others to positions that changed American history.

One of them, Texan Leon Jaworski, would successfully battle Nixon all the way to the Supreme Court for possession of the White House tapes. The second, Wisconsinite John Doar, would prosecute Nixon in the House of Representatives and lead the House Judiciary Committee to pass three articles of impeachment against him. The actions of both men would lead to the first resignation of a U.S. president. When that happened, the third man whom Laird boosted into office, Gerald Ford, would replace Nixon as America's first president never elected by the people.

During Nixon's first term and into his second it was apparent that he had shown a penchant for operating in a solitary manner. When he reached out it was no further than to a palace guard of political amateurs. Even as Watergate was unraveling, the distrustful Nixon walled himself off behind protective yes-men. In the first term Nixon had an inner phalanx of three—Haldeman, Ehrlichman, and Kissinger—none of whom had professional political experience. After the first two were fired in April 1973, the new trio in the second term became Haig, Kissinger, and spokesman Ron Ziegler—again, none of whom had a professional political background.

Columnists Rowland Evans and Robert Novak wrote in the *Washington Post* that Nixon "shows signs of sticking to old habits in facing this historic crisis of government. He obviously prefers to spend more time with . . . Haig and . . . Ziegler, both new to high national politics, than the seasoned Melvin R. Laird. . . . By steering clear of Laird, Nixon will avoid the kind of blunt advice that has always irritated him."[1]

From late July on, Laird was pestered repeatedly with questions about his "access," or lack of it. "I have no problems as far as access is concerned," he said at one press conference. The more time he spent with the president, the less real work he could get done fashioning and pushing domestic legislation. "I am not going to go to all the social functions in the White House," he added. "The

President has told me that I don't have to go to all of them." That was why, he explained, he had declined a state dinner for the Shah of Iran and was home mowing his lawn instead.[2]

At another point he affirmed that he visited with Nixon "every day that he is in town, and I am in town." The closest any reporter got to what was really happening was when one journalist on the NBC *Today Show* asked Laird: "Do you have the access to the President you would like to have?"

"Yes, I do," Laird answered accurately.[3]

He could see Nixon any time he wanted to, but he simply didn't want to, and for several reasons. One was that the wound of betrayal was too fresh. Another was that "Nixon felt he was forced to take me in the first place," so "it was not the best working relationship I've ever had." And third, Laird quickly found that time spent with the troubled Nixon was time wasted. "I could go in and see him any damn time I wanted," Laird recalled, "but Nixon really had withdrawn from active participation in anything. I didn't really find out until I got over there that the only thing the president was concerned about was Watergate. Otherwise, he was completely withdrawn. He didn't want to make decisions about anything else, so there was no sense in meeting with him."

One promise Laird had won from Nixon before accepting the White House job was that he would not be required to be involved with Watergate-related problems. "I didn't come over here to handle Watergate matters," he said each time reporters asked about the subject. "I personally am not involved with the Watergate past, present or future," he bluntly told one interviewer. Instead, his job was to jump-start stalled domestic projects and legislation, which meant specifically not getting pulled into the Watergate maelstrom. After Laird confronted the president about his culpability and Nixon knew that Laird knew the truth, Nixon was even more determined to keep Laird out of the Watergate loop. Nixon told Haig on July 12 that, regarding participation in any Watergate defense, "you can't get Mel in it at all."[4]

Four days after that Oval Office conversation, on July 16, the world was officially informed via a televised Senate Watergate hearing that Nixon had a collection of secret tapes that might establish his innocence or guilt. Immediately the Senate Watergate committee—officially, the Senate Select Committee on Presidential Campaign Activities—demanded Nixon release tapes from June 1972 and other conversations that might have involved Watergate-related discussions. Even though he knew the action might sink the president, Laird privately but strongly urged Nixon to make the tapes public. Instead Nixon denied the committee's request.

In late July, taking Buzhardt and at least one other White House lawyer with him, Laird conferred with the Republican leadership on Capitol Hill, including his friend, House Minority Leader Gerald Ford. Laird revealed that Nixon had spent ten to twelve hours listening to the tapes before reaching a decision against public release. "This was against my advice," Laird explained.

Nixon had chosen to follow the advice of his lawyers and make a legal stand on grounds of executive privilege. Not long after Laird left that meeting, Ford shared the information with a reporter. Laird's advice to come clean with the tapes became widely known. Months later, asked about it again, he explained: "I have never talked about advice that I have given to the President of the United States after he has made a decision. I have never gone around and tried to second guess afterwards." The only reason it came to light was because Ford went public with it.[5] Laird never revealed at the time that, for him, Nixon's decision was proof that Buzhardt's secret assessment was correct; the tapes would prove the president guilty of criminal activities.

Even as the specter of Watergate hovered over the Capitol, Laird plied his agenda through the halls of Congress as if the credibility of the republic was not on trial around him. He spread his message quickly by meeting in the first two weeks with all the Cabinet secretaries on their own turf. "Some of these guys hadn't made a decision for months; they [had] almost forgotten how," one of Laird's aides said. One contemporary columnist agreed, labeling the Cabinet secretaries "obsequious yes men . . . who were turned into limousine puppets by the Ehrlichman-Haldeman White House."[6]

But with Laird's refreshing visits, there were almost immediate signs of independence, creativity, and a will on the part of the reinvigorated Cabinet officers to get their message to Congress. "The heavy hand of the White House was lifted, and we were able to do very much the kinds of things that we thought we should do with very little direction or dictation from the White House," Caspar Weinberger, who was then secretary of Health, Education, and Welfare, recalled of Laird's direction.[7]

Laird saw it as primarily his responsibility to break the logjam of White House domestic bills on Capitol Hill, and in spite of his attempts to finesse the Cabinet members, he sometimes ruffled their feathers. One of the territorial among the second-term Cabinet members was Treasury Secretary George Shultz. He was happy to have a "real heavyweight, a good person" in the White House, but that didn't mean Shultz enjoyed it when Laird poached upon his territory. Shultz was attending a fall international trade conference in Tokyo when Laird made front-page news with the announcement that Nixon was "considering" tax changes to curb inflation. A Reuter's correspondent caught up with the fuming Shultz, who complained: "He [Laird] always gives press conferences on economic subjects when I'm away. He did this to me when I was in Paris trying to negotiate monetary rearrangements—he sounded off about the exchange values of the dollar. And here I am in Tokyo, and he's sounding off about taxes. I think the President's advisor on domestic affairs can keep his cotton-picking hands off economic policy."

Deputy Treasury Secretary Bill Simon rushed to the White House to head-off reports of internecine domestic policy warfare and to make it clear there was "no disagreement" between his boss and Laird. On the way into the White House Simon borrowed a pair of white cotton gloves from a Marine guard standing outside and presented them ceremoniously to an amused Laird—a reference to his "cotton-picking hands." When Shultz returned from Tokyo and they met, Laird carefully explained to Shultz that he (Laird) had been working on economic tax policy in Wisconsin "before you were even in government," and he would continue to keep his hands on *every* aspect of domestic policy.[8]

At other times Shultz was grateful for Laird's legislative meddling on his behalf, including a time when "he traded a body for a vote," as his former Pentagon legislative aide Rady Johnson recalled the tale. Senator Russell Long asked Laird to help him arrange a burial in Arlington National Cemetery for a friend whose military background didn't meet all the criteria for an Arlington plot. Laird was moved by compassion, and by the fact that Senator Long was pivotal to passing economic and tax legislation that was important to Shultz. Laird got Nixon to sign a waiver allowing the burial.[9]

Laird was also the key player behind a major farm bill that was partly de-signed to bring skyrocketing food prices down. In several public appearances Laird explained that food prices had gone up because Americans were buy-ing cheaper electronics and small cars from Japan and Western Europe. Those countries then used the billions of dollars to buy American food, which drove prices up. Laird thought this was a "good problem," the long-term solution to which would be to stop the subsidies that paid American farmers *not* to plant crops. "We've got to produce more food," Laird argued as he participated in the crafting of an historic farm bill that changed the pattern of government subsidies into a new "production of plenty" philosophy. After the bill passed, Agriculture Secretary Earl Butz thanked Laird in a private note: "I'm grateful for the way you handle agricultural and food matters with those wonderful 'cotton pickin' fingers' of yours."[10]

The Department of Health, Education, and Welfare was also a special inter-est and focus for Laird because of his prior work in Congress. HEW Secretary Weinberger was grateful for Laird's help, especially with the media. One Nixon administration official, Dr. Richard Wilbur, illustrated Laird's facility with the media: At a press conference to explain a new health insurance plan, Wein-berger's dry and clipped style of answering questions prompted an annoyed *Washington Post* reporter to start "hissing" at Weinberger in disapproval. "So Cap [Weinberger] left, to this chorus of disapproval." Laird stepped to the po-dium, and soon, "People were writing like crazy, taking notes and all. And they would totally lose track of the subject that the question had been about, so the follow-up questions would be on whatever Mel was interested in. They were being led around by the nose and they loved it. When he left they applauded. And yet, by my standards, Cap's answers were far more on target than Mel's.

But when it came to handling this group of journalists, Mel was absolutely superb."[11]

In the prior two years Nixon had vetoed three different HEW appropriations bills as being too high. Laird broke that old impasse. He negotiated a compromise that meant, for the first time in three years, HEW could operate on a budget passed by Congress and signed by the president. "This was important," he explained at a press conference, "because they weren't able to program or plan anything in an adequate fashion [before]." Laird engineered a similar compromise for the large Defense Department appropriations bill, whose secretary, James Schlesinger, didn't get along well with Congress. It was easy for Laird to argue for the bill because it was based on the last defense budget he had drafted before leaving the Pentagon.[12]

Among the other major legislation Laird engineered and steered through Congress were a manpower retraining bill, the creation of the first health maintenance organizations, a reorganization of volunteer agencies such as the Peace Corps into a single department, a four-year highway program that allowed localities to use federal funds creatively for developing mass transit systems, and programs needed to meet a growing national energy crisis without resorting to gas rationing.[13]

Laird spent little time discussing these measures with Nixon. In fact, there were some signatures on presidential documents in those days that Laird later admitted came from Nixon's auto-pen. "Nixon was so withdrawn at the time that I had to use the automatic pen regularly in the basement. Seriously." Sometimes, when he was in doubt as to what Nixon might want, Laird asked Vice President Agnew for permission before using the pen. "The only thing Nixon was really talking about during that particular period was Watergate. So I went to Agnew." Not once did Nixon overrule Laird on any of his decisions regarding major domestic legislation.

With his international affairs expertise, the domestic counselor also weighed in heavily on foreign policy issues. It fell to Laird to negotiate a forty-five-day extension for U.S. bombing of Communist forces in Cambodia, who were not party to the Vietnam peace accord. Legislative opposition to *any* continued military operations in Indochina was so substantial that even Republicans in Congress could not stop Democratic initiatives to cut off all funding. On June 18, 1973, Kissinger appealed to Laird for help in delaying the ban on Cambodian operations that was due to go into effect June 30. Kissinger wanted any Cambodian bombing ban pushed off until September 1, and Nixon didn't want any ban at all. Laird was in a no-win situation. With the White House on one side and an angry Congress on the other, the best he could do was to split the difference. He got Congress to push the ban back to August 15.[14]

That summer Kissinger was pressing hard for Nixon to make him secretary of state, according to Laird. Kissinger maintained in his memoirs that he had "not sought Cabinet office," but Laird said that was false modesty. "Henry was always pushing Nixon to become secretary of state. He kept pushing him—pushing him awfully hard." A widespread rumor in July that Secretary Rogers would soon resign brought an angry response from a top "State Department official," according to columnist Joseph Kraft. The official said "the source of the rumors about Rogers stepping down was Dr. Kissinger. [He further] said that Kissinger wanted the State Department job to get out from under Watergate and did not have the guts to ask the President directly."[15]

In his memoirs Kissinger said Laird had advised him the previous spring "that my position as [White House] Assistant would soon become untenable. I would be ground down between Congress and the increasingly assertive bureaucracy. I would have to become Secretary of State or resign." In August Nixon asked Rogers to resign and finally named Kissinger as secretary, a popular move he thought might draw attention away from Watergate. Kissinger would also continue to serve as national security advisor. (Thus Nixon reneged on his promise to promote Kenneth Rush once Rogers left.) Kissinger was confirmed in September 1973, awarded the Nobel Peace Prize in October, and named the "most admired" man in America in December.[16]

With Indochina military issues resolved to a certain extent, the Middle East was shaping up to be the next most likely hot spot for a surrogate U.S.-Soviet military clash. The Arab-Israeli conflict had already spilled over into increasing incidents of terrorism. In one such incident a Syrian-operated spy ring tried to mail letter bombs to Nixon, Laird, and Rogers, but alert Israeli security officials intercepted them. In another case Laird personally conveyed a tip from U.S. intelligence sources that saved Israeli Prime Minister Golda Meir from a planned car bomb.[17]

Arab provocations and tough Israeli reprisals finally culminated in full-scale war on October 6, 1973—Yom Kippur, the holiest day of the Jewish calendar. On that day Egypt and Syria attacked Israel simultaneously on its northeastern and southwestern borders. By the end of the third day Israel had lost hundreds of tanks, dozens of planes, and a thousand people. Israel had so dominated the Arabs in previous wars that it came as a shock to its leaders and its American ally that they desperately needed equipment and ammunition resupply in less than a week. At first Kissinger tried to avoid using a U.S. military airlift for fear of aggravating the Soviets. Laird jumped in to get a military airlift going. He first had to overcome Defense Secretary Schlesinger's foot-dragging. Schlesinger was planning to send only three of the huge new C-5A Galaxy transport planes, but Laird argued for more, saying that there would be as much diplomatic heat for sending three planes as thirty. Nixon seconded that assessment. The Soviets were already airlifting seven hundred tons of war matériel a day to Egypt and Syria, so, Laird argued, it was time the

United States not only matched the Russian resupply but exceeded it. So began a thirty-three-day airlift code-named "Nickel Grass." Golda Meir witnessed the first C-5A land, watched the nose lift up, and then saw two M-60 tanks come out of it. She was so moved that she bent over and kissed the ground as it shook underneath the treads of rolling tanks. It was Laird as defense secretary who had overseen the funding and development of the C-5A to provide that kind of military airlift capability.[18] Kissinger negotiated a cease-fire in the conflict on October 22.

The United States paid a high price for its lone support of Israel. Before the cease-fire was in place, several Arab countries, including Saudi Arabia, instituted a total oil embargo against the United States. As that expanded to include oil from all Arab countries, America found itself in the midst of a full-scale energy crisis. Laird oversaw efforts to combat the shortages, including the appointment of an "energy czar" (former Colorado governor John Love). As November began Laird urged Americans to turn down their thermostats and wear sweaters, which became a rich source of editorial cartoons about Laird, as well as ribbing from all quarters. ("Where's your sweater?" Nixon needled Laird in late November as they posed for photographs prior to a televised presidential address on energy conservation.)[19]

⌇

In the fall of 1973 the White House was the choke point for a series of crises. As if a war in the Middle East and Watergate were not enough to handle, the news broke that Vice President Agnew had accepted cash bribes of thousands of dollars in unmarked envelopes handed to him in his White House office. Agnew never had been a favorite of Nixon's. During the 1972 election Nixon hadn't discouraged "dump Agnew" movements by various politicians. There was no doubt in anyone's mind that the man he wanted as vice president and his future successor was John Connally, but Connally was then a Democrat. The Nixon preference for Connally over Agnew became so widely known that the vice president once joked, when arriving late at a luncheon: "I did my best to hurry, but John Connally had me down at his ranch for a barbecue, and it took me an hour and a half to cut myself down from the spit." By early 1973 Connally had switched parties, after which Nixon hired him as a special White House consultant.

Agnew began to suspect in mid-July that an ongoing secret grand jury investigation into contractor bribes in Baltimore County, Maryland, might be a White House–instigated effort to get rid of him. Attorney General Elliot Richardson also worried the investigation might appear to be a vendetta once it became public. That was why, in late July, Richardson talked with Laird about the seriousness of the evidence being gathered and provided some details about the witnesses and the testimony they were prepared to give at the grand jury.

The two key witnesses were senior partners in two engineering firms, Lester Matz and Allen Green, who admitted that they had been paying kickbacks to Agnew for state contracts he had funneled to their companies when he was Baltimore County's chief executive in the mid-1960s. Green kicked back 1 percent of every contract Agnew had steered his way, and Matz paid 5 percent. Both said they had delivered payments to Vice President Agnew in the White House to settle old debts. Other witnesses made similar allegations of kickbacks and bribes to Agnew.[20]

Richardson shared enough of the evidence to prompt Laird to urge him to vigorously continue the investigation regardless Agnew's high office. Shortly after the meeting with Laird, Richardson sent a letter to Agnew informing him that he was under investigation for possible conspiracy, extortion, bribery, and tax evasion. Agnew told this to Nixon, who then allowed Richardson to tell Buzhardt, who then told Laird, who decided to tell the Republican leadership in Congress. Laird's first opportunity to warn members of Congress came August 4 as he flew to Groton, Connecticut, for the launching of the new nuclear submarine named after Glenard Lipscomb. Like Laird, Gerald Ford had been a close friend of Lipscomb's, so he attended also. Ford and Laird sat next to each other on the ride back to Washington aboard an air force plane. They conversed about Nixon, the White House, Watergate, and the "rumors" of an Agnew investigation.

"You think things are bad now," Laird hinted ominously. "They're going to get worse."

"Tell me about it," Ford pressed him.

Laird said that the Agnew matter was serious and that Ford should be careful about aligning himself with Agnew and should "be prepared for some major changes." Laird meant only that there was no telling what the ramifications of an Agnew indictment would be. Neither man suspected just how prescient Laird's advice would be.[21]

That weekend Buzhardt reported to Nixon that the federal case against Agnew was "one of the most solid cases" he had ever seen. On Monday morning, August 6, Richardson met with Nixon and reinforced what Buzhardt had already said. That night Al Haig and Bryce Harlow met with Agnew and urged him to resign.[22] The following morning the story about the Agnew investigation and allegations finally broke in the Wall Street Journal. When Nixon met Agnew, the president didn't demand a resignation. (He couldn't; Agnew was an elected official, so Nixon could not fire him.) Instead Nixon warmly expressed his friendship and support. With that encouragement Agnew appeared at a press conference the following day and vowed to fight. He called the charges "damned lies."[23]

Meanwhile Laird was calling the Republican leadership to warn them that siding with Agnew would be a political mistake. One of them, House Republican Caucus Chairman John Anderson, tipped off columnists Evans and Novak

to the Laird warning. The call was "new and harsh evidence to party professionals of the depth of the crisis that threatens Mr. Agnew," they reported. "His
[Laird's] message: don't get out on a limb in the Agnew affair, particularly with
an all-out defense of the Vice President. Stay away from the Agnew affair as far
as possible."[24]

Agnew was furious. He had always viewed Laird as "the ultimate professional politician," a man who was "pragmatic, evasive, with ice water in his
veins." But Agnew felt this was beyond the pale, according to his memoir account. Agnew apparently concluded that Nixon had asked Laird "to undermine
me in Congress."[25] At the time, Evans and Novak quoted "Agnew intimates" as
suspecting the whole affair was an attempt to make Connally vice president.
But the columnists concluded (and Laird energetically affirmed later) that his
warnings to Congress were "a flashing signal of caution based not on any desire
to do in Agnew but on a rational and informed judgment that Agnew is a
goner."

Still Agnew fought. At one point he asked the House to begin impeachment
proceedings, reckoning his chances were better before a fraternity of politicians
than in a court of law. But House Speaker Carl Albert privately told him there
would be no immediate impeachment investigation; they would let the Justice
Department act first. At another point Agnew promised a cheering crowd of
Republican partisans that, even if he were indicted, he would not resign.[26]

Laird felt Agnew's resignation would be the best resolution of the crisis.
By mid-September Laird and Harlow were making that case in the strongest
possible manner with Attorney General Elliot Richardson. "Harlow and I expressed to Elliot our very strong feeling that the thing to do here was not to go
through that process [an indictment], but to get his resignation," Laird said.
When Laird and Harlow sent an intermediary, Fred Buzhardt, to Agnew to
urge his resignation, the vice president sent back word that he wanted a guarantee he would not go to jail. "He indicated that if we could get Richardson to
agree not to go forward with the prosecution, he would resign," Laird said. "It
was somewhat difficult to get Elliot to go along with that sort of an arrangement. But over a period of a couple of days, quite rightly, he saw the merit in
the proposal. Some people said it was a mistake not to prosecute him; others
said it was the best way to handle it. I feel it was the best way to handle it."[27]

Agnew finally capitulated, and on October 10, 1973, he became the first vice
president of the United States to resign in disgrace. Minutes after the formal
letter was tendered to Kissinger, Agnew pleaded "no contest" in the U.S. District Court in Baltimore to one count of income tax evasion (failure to pay
taxes on the bribes). He was fined $10,000 and given three years' probation.

44

Crowning Achievements

PRIOR TO 1973 the vice presidential office had been vacant a total of thirty-seven years in American history. Seven vice presidents had died in office and another had resigned. A few, including Harry Truman and Lyndon Johnson, had succeeded to the presidency upon the death of a president. (Truman was president almost a full term with no vice president.) In all those instances the republic survived without vice presidents because the presidents did not die or resign. But practicality compelled Congress in 1967 to ratify the Twenty-fifth Amendment to the Constitution, which provided that the president could appoint a new vice president subject to approval by a majority of both houses of Congress, without a national election.[1]

When the amendment got its first test in October 1973 the choice should have been Nixon's. In reality, because the president was crippled by the Watergate scandal, the decision came down to the most powerful—still functioning—man in the White House, Domestic Counselor Melvin Laird. On the morning after the Agnew resignation, the *Wall Street Journal* placed Laird as the second-strongest vice presidential possibility, after John Connally. On all the TV network newscasts, as well as in the *New York Times, Washington Post,* and other newspapers, Laird was listed in the top three or five candidates. But none of the pundits had talked to Laird himself. He had already decided to mount a campaign to pressure the president to select Gerald Ford.[2] Laird felt, because Connally had changed parties, that his confirmation process would be a partisan bloodbath. More ominously, Laird was looking ahead to possible impeachment and resignation of the president. He felt Ford was the one with enough good will in Congress to ride out the storm, and that he had the trust and integrity the nation needed in a crisis.

Fellow Republican wise man and White House counselor Bryce Harlow was pushing Laird to seek the position himself, as was a congressional group led by John Byrnes. But Laird never varied, despite the flattering blandishments. He thought he was the only one who could talk Nixon out of Connally, and he could not do that if Nixon suspected he was promoting himself. Therefore Ford was the best man for the job. Never before had Laird concentrated so intensely on a task, in part because he knew the time was short. Between the time Agnew resigned on Wednesday, October 10, and when the new vice president was announced late Friday, October 12, Laird talked with Nixon almost a dozen times. In at least two face-to-face meetings, Harlow accompanied Laird to provide extra support. In one of those meetings, on Wednesday morning,

Nixon firmly told them that Connally was going to be his choice. He had already promised the job to him four days earlier.

"Mr. President," Laird said firmly, "we cannot get Connally confirmed. It will be a disaster."

"Well, I disagree with you," the president said. "Connally is the best qualified, and he is my choice."

Laird agreed that Connally was qualified and a capable politician. "I have nothing against him," he added. "But he has antagonized many Democrats by converting to the Republican Party, and many Republicans don't really accept him as a true Republican. They regard him as an opportunist. It would be a long, hard struggle to confirm Connally."

Harlow added a few carefully chosen words, concurring with Laird's dismal assessment of Connally's confirmation prospects. On a different tack, he added: "Why don't you look at it from John Connally's perspective? If he is rejected by Congress in the confirmation process, it would end his political career."

Laird chimed in again: "We cannot help. It is an impossible assignment to get Connally confirmed."

Nixon was taken aback by the strong words, but still adamant. As all around Nixon knew, the president viewed Connally on a pedestal above all other politicians. "He LOVED Connally, who was the kind of guy—flamboyant, extroverted—that Nixon himself wanted to be," Laird said. Nixon admired his stature, his sureness, his authority. "He thought Connally was the greatest politician in America." *Loved* was the same word used by Haig, Kissinger, Agnew, speech writer William Safire, George H. W. Bush, Ford, and a host of others to describe Nixon's regard for Connally.[3]

Laird had one last gambit for use with Nixon that Wednesday morning, and it was a strong one. "Mr. President, would you at least talk to the leaders of the Senate and House—both parties—before you make your decision? We'll get them in here to talk to you." Nixon agreed.[4] Laird and Harlow, as well as others they asked for help, began calling the leaders. (When one of the emissaries caught up with Senator Robert Byrd near the Senate chamber, the partisan Democrat said, "Tell my friend Dick Nixon that if he sends Connally's name to the Senate, blood will be running out from under the Senate door.") The most important two calls were those from Laird to Senate Majority Leader Mike Mansfield and House Speaker Carl Albert. Laird confided to them that, just that morning, the president had told him in no uncertain terms that Connally would be nominated. But the best man for the job, and the one man that Nixon might accept, was Gerald Ford. Mansfield and Albert didn't want Connally either, and concurred with Laird's wisdom on the matter.

The first congressional leaders to call on the president at the White House on the day of Agnew's resignation were the minority leaders of the House and Senate, Ford and Hugh Scott. Nixon told them he was going to ask his staff, the Republican National Committee, and all the Republican members of Congress for their top three choices. At that meeting Ford shared his own preferences: Connally, Laird, Rockefeller, and Reagan, in that order.[5] Less than an hour later Democrats Mansfield and Albert arrived for what was the most important meeting of the three days. Laird walked into the Oval Office with them, partly to make sure by his presence that they would follow through with the game plan to which they had committed. Nixon began as a matter of courtesy by asking Albert—the speaker of the House and the next in legal line of succession—if he was interested in being vice president. Albert said he was not, but offered to suggest the name that would be most easily confirmed.

"Who is it? Jerry Ford?" Nixon asked.

"Yes sir," Albert said."[6] Mansfield quickly agreed.

Nixon then asked them about Connally. His confirmation would be next to impossible, they replied. Many Democrats were furious that Connally, who had so recently deserted their party, would dare aspire to be a Republican vice president. In their view Connally's nomination would also split Republicans into two camps. Laird smiled broadly after they left. Nixon had been swayed by the power of their preference for Ford and promises of a protracted battle if Connally were chosen. Not long after that meeting, Nixon instructed Haig to call Connally and tell him that it was becoming evident that Ford might have to be the choice in the interest of a speedy confirmation. Nixon still had made no final decision, so he was not yet reneging on his commitment, but Connally immediately conceded. It is probable that he saw the prospect of being the "Watergate vice president" as the end to his own presidential prospects.[7]

At about the same time Haig was breaking the news to Connally, Nixon met again with Laird and Harlow to ask a pertinent question: "How do you know Ford would accept?"

"I will sound him out and let you know," Laird responded. "But I am fairly positive he would. I know we can get Ford through both the House and Senate, and, Mr. President, we need to get this over with."[8]

Ford stayed at the House for an evening vote and then attended the National Press Club's annual Congressional Night. He arrived home after 8 P.M. and had a late dinner with his wife, Betty. About 10 P.M., as they were watching the television news, Laird telephoned. He made small talk for a few minutes, a habit that Ford recognized in his old friend as a prelude to something big. Then Laird got to the point: "Jerry, if you were asked, would you accept the vice presidential nomination?"

Ford sensed the seriousness of the question. "I knew Mel well enough to realize that his question hadn't come just like that," Ford said. "*Someone* had told him to call." So Ford asked for some time to talk with his wife before he would call Laird back with an answer.

Jerry had already promised Betty that he would be done with politics in January 1977. Since there was little chance as a Republican that he might achieve his ambition to become speaker of the House, he would not run for congressional reelection in 1976. They debated the pluses and minuses of the vice presidency as opposed to continuing his Republican leadership in the House. In the end both saw the vice presidency as a "splendid cap" to Ford's political career. Ford called Laird back before midnight and said, "We've talked about it and agreed that, if I were asked, I'd accept. But I won't do anything to stimulate a campaign. I'm not promoting myself."

"I understand," Laird responded. "I don't know what's going to happen. I just wanted to check. But if the president does call, don't hedge! Just say, 'Yes.'" Ford agreed.

After the second conversation with Laird, the Fords felt pretty sure that Nixon would *not* choose Jerry. "I was too valuable to him on Capitol Hill. Besides, other Republicans—Connally, Rockefeller, and Reagan—had national reputations and ambitions to match. I thought Nixon would select one of them."

Laird called Nixon to relay Ford's interest but shrewdly emphasized that "Jerry has promised Betty he will get out of politics in January 1977." The point was not lost on Nixon, who now knew he had a vice presidential option who might leave the 1976 Republican field open for Connally.[9]

⚓︎

As Thursday, October 11, dawned, Ford went generally unmentioned in news speculation. Representative Barber Conable, who was policy chair of the House Republican Caucus (and later president of the World Bank), thought Ford was being overlooked. "I was concerned that Nixon liked Connally so much," Conable said. So he called Ford's best friend at the White House, Mel Laird. Unaware of Laird's aggressive campaign, Conable said he wanted to sponsor a congressional resolution backing Ford as the best choice and was sure he could get it passed in the House. Laird was aghast. "Barber, I'd appreciate if you didn't do that," Laird quickly responded. "It would be the worst thing we could do during this difficult period over here at the White House because that kind of resolution will get Nixon's back up. He might harden on a Connally choice instead of Ford."

Conable dropped the idea immediately and asked what he could do instead. Laird told him it might be helpful if he got some Democrats in Congress to write Nixon a letter suggesting Ford—but not too many, or the president would get suspicious. Also, make sure Republicans filling out the president's survey rank Ford as their first choice. "Consider it done," Conable said.[10]

In one of Laird's meetings with the president that Wednesday, Nixon asked if he would be interested in the job himself. "Absolutely not," Laird responded. He had only two recommendations: Ford and Rockefeller in that order. Kissinger and Al Haig both heavily favored Rockefeller but did little to push their candidate. That left Laird as Nixon's most influential advisor to openly push Ford, as well as maneuver other advocates into the president's field of view.[11]

By the end of the day Wednesday Nixon had more than four hundred surveys to consider, and he took them to Camp David. As he tallied the results, according to his memoirs, "Rockefeller and Reagan were in a virtual tie for first choice; Connally was third; Ford was fourth. Ford, however, was first choice among members of Congress, and they were the ones who would have to approve the man I nominated."[12] He reckoned that Rockefeller or Reagan would split the Republican Party. "This left Jerry Ford," he wrote. Ford met all his criteria: qualification to be president, ideological affinity, loyalty, and the ability to be confirmed. The Laird campaign had worked; Nixon had received the message through the various loudspeakers Laird had put in place.[13]

Nixon returned to the White House by helicopter at 8:30 Friday morning. He told Haig he had decided on Ford and asked Haig to contact both Ford and Senator Scott (a possible candidate because he was Senate minority leader) for a meeting. Laird slipped in to see Nixon in the Oval Office before leaving for a West Virginia engagement. He wanted to make sure Nixon was still leaning to Ford; the president confirmed that Ford was his first choice. At 11 A.M. Scott and Ford arrived at the White House, expecting to see the president together, but he asked for Scott first. As a courtesy, Nixon told Scott that he couldn't afford to make him vice president and sacrifice Scott's seat in the Senate because Pennsylvania's Democratic governor would undoubtedly select a Democrat in his place. "Also, we don't want to have a fight in the Senate over the Republican leadership. I'm sure you understand."

Scott said he did, then asked: "Does that leadership reason also apply to Jerry in the House? Is he disqualified for the same reason?"

"Yes, he is," Nixon replied.

Scott never understood why Nixon lied to him when the truth would be out in a matter of hours anyway. It is likely that Nixon knew Scott was gabby with the press. The president didn't want to lose the element of surprise. Upon leaving the Oval Office, Scott told Ford: "Jerry, it's not going to be either of us." Back on Capitol Hill Scott shook his head when reporters asked if it was going to be himself or Ford.[14] After Scott left it was Ford's turn. Nixon surprised him with the news that he wanted him for vice president, but Nixon needed assurances that Ford didn't have any political ambitions beyond that. "In '76 I am going to campaign to nominate John Connally to be President," Nixon told Ford.

"That's no problem for me," Ford replied. He reiterated that he had committed to his wife that he would be out of politics as of January 1977. Ford explained that he had already told Connally that he would probably campaign for him for president. These were the magic words Nixon wanted to hear and confirmed what Laird had already told him. The deal was sealed.[15]

The official announcement, broadcast live across the nation, was made by Nixon at 9 P.M. in the White House before an East Room audience of Cabinet members and congressional and other federal leaders. Nixon reveled in his moment of surprise, holding back the name for effect. As he reached the line—"He is a man who has served for twenty-five years in the House of Representatives," the audience began applauding and looking at Ford. With mock protest Nixon quieted them down. "Ladies and gentlemen, please don't be premature," he said. "There are *several* here who have served twenty-five years in the House." Laughter filled the room. Finally, he named Gerald R. Ford as the fortieth vice president of the United States. The East Room erupted in whoops and whistles as Ford strode to the podium to accept the appointment.

That night Laird was in West Virginia at the Homestead resort attending a Business Council dinner at the request of David Packard. But he was pleased at a distance with the conclusion of his production. At the time only a few insiders were aware of the role Laird had played. Both Haig and Kissinger, as well as George H. W. Bush, cited Laird's involvement as critical. Journalists such as Robert Novak and William Safire also testified to Laird's Richelieu-like role in the event.[16]

In various interviews Laird usually hedged claims of credit for other achievements with extensive qualifiers or a list of others who deserved credit. But, with the single exception of gratitude for Harlow's support as a White House ally, Laird was unequivocal about his historic role in this particular gambit. "I know—as much as I can know anything in politics—that if I had not been in the White House, Jerry Ford would never have been president, because he would never have become vice president first. If I wouldn't have been at the White House, John Connally would have been selected. I *know* that; he [Ford] knows that." Over the years Ford imbibed every account from every witness he could find in the Nixon White House about how he was selected. He wound up concluding that Laird's claim was true; he had been the most responsible. In a 1997 interview Ford said, "I'm sure Mel was the one who convinced Nixon that I should be the nominee; he was the coalescent who saw all the realities and convinced Nixon."[17]

⚜

Throughout the fall of 1973 Nixon resisted legal efforts by Watergate Special Prosecutor Archibald Cox to obtain nine Oval Office tapes. On August 29 U.S. District Judge John Sirica ordered the president to release the tapes to him so he could listen and determine whether the claim of executive privilege should prevent the tapes from becoming public. Nixon appealed to the U.S. Court of Appeals, which, on October 12 (the same day Ford was nominated as vice president), in a 5 to 2 decision upheld Sirica. Instead of an immediate appeal to the Supreme Court, Nixon came up with a compromise. He would allow a Democrat, the respected seventy-two-year-old Senator John Stennis of Mississippi, to listen to the tapes and verify the accuracy of White House summaries that Nixon was willing to release.

With Nixon's concurrence, Attorney General Elliot Richardson had named

Cox, his former law professor at Harvard, to the special prosecutor post the previous May. The two were old friends, but Cox also skewed toward the Democrats, with close ties to the Kennedy family. Reportedly only one of his ten senior staffers at the special prosecutor's office was a Republican. Nixon felt Cox was out to "get" him. If Cox refused to accept the Stennis compromise, the president told Richardson he would have to fire Cox.[18]

On Friday afternoon, October 19, Richardson privately conferred with Laird and told him he was willing to fire Cox only if Cox proved obdurate. Several hours later, however, as Laird was preparing to go to an annual benefit then known as the "Crippled Children's Ball," he was called to the phone and heard an anxious Richardson say that everything had come apart. "When I went back to the Justice Department after I talked with you earlier there was an outright rebellion among my people over this whole thing," Richardson said wearily. "I've changed my mind. Cox has refused the compromise and I just can't fire him. I can't do it. I'll have to resign." The conversation was short and Laird tried to calm Richardson, telling him not to do anything hastily. They would talk tomorrow, Saturday, and Bryce Harlow would be with him. Richardson accepted that and then hung up.

Laird went ahead to the ball, but it was interrupted when he was urgently called by Haig to go back to the White House. Once Laird arrived he found Harlow already there. Haig told them that Nixon was determined to fire Cox, but it would actually be Attorney General Richardson who would do it. Haig asked Laird to call the members of the Cabinet to give them advance warning. Laird was in a quandary. He wasn't going to tell Haig about his conversations with Richardson, but he also thought Nixon was fooling himself if he thought Richardson would fire Cox. "I'll be glad to call them, but I have to know first, are you sure Elliot's on board?" Laird said.

Haig missed the hint that Laird had inside information. Instead, Haig confidently replied that Richardson was ready to follow Nixon's orders.

"Well, you'd better call and make sure," Laird advised. Okay, Haig agreed, and asked Harlow to do it. When Harlow called, Richardson cautiously said, "No, I'm not really on board."

This was news to Haig, who said he would have to talk with the president and they should wait until the next day to warn Cabinet members and others.

Laird went back to the benefit ball. A lot was on his mind, and he decided to confide in a good friend at the table, Fred Vinson, and ask for recommendations to replace Cox. Vinson was a politically connected Washington attorney, a Democrat, and the son of a former chief justice of the Supreme Court. "I could use your help, Freddy," whispered Laird. "We have to have a real good Democrat to appoint as the replacement for Cox. Elliot is refusing to fire him and will probably resign. But *someone* in the Justice Department will fire him then, and we'll have to clean up the mess by finding fast a very good Democrat to be special prosecutor," Vinson asked for time to think.

"You gotta give me one now, Freddy," Laird pressed.

"Okay, here's the best one: Leon Jaworski," Vinson responded. "I know him well. He's a Democrat and he lives in Houston. He was president of the American Bar Association and has an absolutely flawless reputation. If he would take it, he would be the best."

Laird didn't need time to think about it. He knew of Jaworski. (One of Laird's uncles, Dick Modrall, of Albuquerque, New Mexico, was a good friend of Jaworski's.) *He's perfect,* Laird thought.

~~~

The next morning, Saturday, October 20, Laird and Harlow had a private meeting with Richardson, who once again let them know that he would not fire Cox, even if the president ordered it. In the early afternoon Cox held a news conference that deliberately baited Nixon. Cox said he refused to accept Nixon's idea to have Stennis vouch for the content of the tapes and was going to pursue his lawsuit for access to them. Shortly after 2 P.M. Nixon transmitted the order through Haig to Richardson to fire Cox. Richardson refused and told Haig he wanted to see the president so he could tender his resignation. Nixon and Haig met with him at 4:30 P.M., and they could not talk Richardson out of resigning. His deputy, William Ruckelshaus, also refused to fire Cox and resigned instead. The third man in the Justice Department line of authority was Solicitor General Robert Bork. Later a controversial Supreme Court nominee, Bork didn't necessarily agree with Nixon's decision to remove Cox, but he felt the president had the authority to order it. So Bork gave Cox his walking papers, which was announced at 8:30 P.M. A firestorm of criticism erupted and the event was soon dubbed the "Saturday Night Massacre."

On Sunday morning, NBC news producer Lawrence Spivak knew he had scored a coup for his network talk show, *Meet the Press.* Laird was already scheduled for an appearance, and now they had a white-hot subject to grill him about. That morning also marked the first appearance of a nervous young NBC correspondent named Tom Brokaw. Just before the show began, Brokaw recalled that Spivak told him, "Listen this is going to be the most important program all year, and tradition has it that the NBC correspondent gets to ask the first question, so it better damn well be a good question." As the cameras rolled Spivak introduced the distinguished guest, and then said: "We will have the first questions now from Tom Brokaw of NBC News." A little nervous, Brokaw began:

"Mr. Laird, let me briefly summarize all that has happened this weekend. The President has ignored an order from the federal Appeals Court; he has fired the special Watergate prosecutor, Archibald Cox; he has accepted the resignation of Attorney General Elliot Richardson, and he has forced the resignation of Deputy Attorney General William Ruckelshaus. In view of all that, don't you expect now that impeachment proceedings against the President will begin in the House of Representatives?"

Laird was too much of a political pro to be caught by Brokaw's question and immediately deflected it. "First, with all due apologies to you, Tom, I can't accept the premise of your question." He instead repeated Nixon's compromise, which had at its core the respect and trust of Congress for one of its own, the venerable Senator Stennis. But Brokaw didn't let Laird off the hook, challenging his answer by suggesting that the Stennis compromise had nothing to do with the federal Appeals Court ruling ordering release of nine subpoenaed tapes. Laird said he was no lawyer and gamely continued to defend the compromise. "I believe that the compromise that has been worked out should have been accepted by the special prosecutor," he added. Congress might see it that way too and decide not to initiate impeachment action against the president, he suggested.[19]

Over the weekend Nixon had confided to Laird that there would be no more special prosecutors; he would dissolve the office and assign the investigation to Justice Department regulars. But Laird knew that decision could not pass public muster. So, two weeks after his successful "operation" to win Nixon's acceptance of Gerald Ford as vice president, Laird felt it was his duty to mount a new campaign for another candidate that required Nixon's appointment: Leon Jaworski as special prosecutor. Toward that end manna fell from heaven into Laird's lap. He received a call on a Sunday afternoon from a respected Republican congressman from Texas, Bill Archer, one of many Laird congressional protégés.

Archer told Laird there was only one candidate to be the new special prosecutor, a friend of Archer's named Leon Jaworski. Laird didn't let on that Jaworski was already his choice. Instead, he listened as Archer made his case. Jaworski was at the sunset of an illustrious career. He had been a prosecutor at the Nazi war crimes trials in Germany. A Democrat, Jaworski became a respected Texas trial lawyer with influential friends including Lyndon Johnson, who had offered him an appointment as attorney general, or a seat on the Supreme Court, but Jaworski had turned both down. During the 1972 presidential campaign he had headed Texas Democrats for Nixon. In the spring of 1973 Jaworski had been approached by Richardson to be the special prosecutor before Cox was chosen. Jaworski threw cold water on the idea, feeling that there would not be enough independence from the White House to do the job right. The Jaworskis were next-door neighbors to the Archers. "He is the most honorable man I know," Archer averred.

"Then how could we get him to accept that job *now?*" Laird asked.

Archer had already sounded Jaworski out and found that he might be willing to accept it under the right conditions. The two men had been at a party Saturday night, and Archer had appealed to Jaworski's sense of duty. Jaworski had responded, "I think I may be able to be of service to my country, but I would need to be guaranteed total independence."[20] Laird suggested Archer make two calls to White House officials—Haig and fellow Texan Anne Armstrong, who was at the time a counselor to Nixon. Laird cautioned Archer not to mention Laird's name, so the impact would be undiluted. They would be impressed that a conservative Republican congressman was vouching for a Democrat, which hinted that both parties in Congress would respect the appointment.

It was at this point Sunday afternoon that Laird's campaign for Jaworski kicked into high gear. The plan was to funnel Jaworski's name to Haig from as many sources as possible. Haig, who had important military contacts, was a political neophyte with no civilian network to tap. In the White House Haig depended on Laird and Harlow for their political contacts and prodigious Rolodexes.

President Nixon had many political connections, of course, and Laird worked hard to make sure the name he got from them was Jaworski. A great hole card was the knowledge that the one politician Nixon most respected, John Connally, was already an admirer of his fellow Texan Jaworski and would vouch for him to the president.[21] But Laird made numerous other calls to move the Jaworski name forward in the Oval Office, including securing an agreement from the head of the American Enterprise Institute, William Baroody Sr., that he would personally push Jaworski's nomination in his talks with Nixon and other public opinion leaders.

At first Nixon wasn't interested in *anyone* for the office. He tried to stick with his plan of disbanding the special prosecutor's office, but the response to the weekend "massacre" was too withering. In the press and in Congress Nixon was called "reckless," "desperate," "Gestapo," and without "respect for law." By Tuesday there were twenty-one resolutions calling for his impeachment and six formerly pro-Nixon newspapers had called for his resignation.[22] On November 1 acting Attorney General Bork announced Nixon's nomination of Jaworski as the new special prosecutor. To win Jaworski's assent—as well as head off a congressional move to name a special prosecutor themselves—Nixon promised Jaworski that he could not be fired without the approval of at least six of eight designated congressional leaders.[23]

Because of Jaworski's integrity, and because of Nixon's guilt, the Laird-engineered appointment was a serious setback for the president. "Jaworski's political and professional reputation denied the President the chance to portray him as a partisan or ideological enemy. The Texas lawyer had enormous prestige, with currency in a world apart, even alien, from that of Cox," wrote Wisconsin professor Stanley Kutler, a Watergate historian. Jaworski was, professionally, head and shoulders above Cox. Even though Cox has "always remained the hero to most members of the Watergate Special Prosecution Force and to much of the media," Kutler said that it was Jaworski's appointment that "truly was a disaster for Richard Nixon."[24]

Four days before the Saturday Night Massacre, Laird had said something that rocked the capital on its heels. At a breakfast meeting with reporters on October 16 Laird confirmed rumors that he had privately advised Nixon that he would face impeachment if he dared to defy any Supreme Court decision to turn over the White House tapes to the Watergate grand jury. That made Laird the first White House official to publicly utter the word "impeachment." After Agnew's resignation, bumper stickers had appeared around Washington with the ominous message "One down, one to go." And now the *New York Times* reported, "there was talk of impeachment, and from some surprising sources [including] Melvin R. Laird."[25]

Privately Laird was the only White House official who hoped that the House of Representatives would begin impeachment proceedings as soon as possible. He had looked down the road and reasoned that impeachment hearings were inevitable, and the sooner they happened, the better for the country. On the basis of cold analysis by Laird, it was better to force the issue sooner than later, before the 1974 congressional elections. That partly explains why it was Laird from within the White House who pushed the president to turn over the tapes, even though Laird had knowledge that they would likely be very damaging. On October 17 columnists Evans and Novak wrote that Laird was "alone among Nixon's senior advisors [who] urged him to turn over the tapes to special prosecutor Archibald Cox in the first place."[26]

Los Angeles Times columnist Clayton Fritchey pointed out that Connally had temporarily lost influence with Nixon when he suggested openness about Watergate "but was quickly restored to favor when he later publicly upheld Nixon's right to withhold the tapes. Laird could hardly be unaware of that." Therefore, Fritchey continued, it was remarkable that Laird continued to be "consistent" in advising Nixon "to be forthright about Watergate, and [going] so far as to warn his principal that he would be courting impeachment if he did not give up the Watergate tapes." Fritchey rehearsed several other examples of solid Laird advice that Nixon ignored. "The trouble is, the President didn't want to hear most of it. What nearly all Presidents really want to hear, as Mel Laird can now testify, is yes-man advice."[27]

Laird's crystal ball may not have always been appreciated by Nixon, but it was fairly accurate. The pressure for impeachment took a quantum leap following the Saturday Night Massacre. Three days afterward, Nixon publicly vowed to release the nine subpoenaed tapes. Ten days afterward, the House Judiciary Committee, on a party-line vote, gave itself subpoena power. On November 15 the House of Representatives appropriated $1 million for the Judiciary Committee, chaired by Peter Rodino, to begin the process of impeachment. For any special committee investigation the most important person is not so much the congressional chair as the chief counsel who stage manages the investigation.

Rodino began his search in earnest on October 22, the first workday after the Saturday Night Massacre. Over the next two months he screened more than a hundred candidates. Toward the end of that process he got word from Laird that there was an excellent prospect named John Doar. Rodino had already looked at Doar, but Laird's call let him know that Doar would be accepted by Republicans.

Doar was from a solid Wisconsin Republican family; his father was in a law partnership with Warren Knowles, a popular governor. Laird was a good friend of the Knowles and Doar families. In 1960, toward the end of the Eisenhower administration, Congressman Laird's recommendation had placed Doar in the Civil Rights Division of the Justice Department. In 1965 Doar was named head of the division. He was on the front lines in the cause of civil rights. He was on hand for most of the key civil rights marches and events of the first half of the 1960s, whether personally marching at Selma, Alabama, riding buses with the freedom riders, or representing the federal legal position on civil rights in southern courts. Doar was at black student James Meredith's side when Meredith was turned away by the governor at the doors of the University of Mississippi. He was back again in September 1962 when Meredith was finally admitted, which touched off a riot. Doar slept in Meredith's dormitory room that night to give him official protection. In 1963 Doar's presence and reputation prevented a riot in Jackson, Mississippi, after the head of the state's NAACP, Medgar Evers, was assassinated. Five thousand black mourners came to the funeral and were confronted at one point by two solid lines of police. Some in the angry crowd started throwing bottles at the police. Doar stepped between the two camps and shouted: "My name is Doar, D-O-A-R. I'm from the Justice Department and anybody around here knows I stand for what is right." He then circulated through the crowd, single-handedly quelling the threat of violence.

When Doar had left the Justice Department in 1967 Laird had tried to talk him into running for Congress or some state office in Wisconsin. Laird told him that politics needed men of his integrity, whatever party he chose. But, by then, Doar was a committed apostle of civil rights and decided to head up Bobby Kennedy's Brooklyn self-help organization, the Bedford-Stuyvesant Development and Services Corporation. Nobody could accuse the Democrat Rodino of partisanship if his chief counsel was Doar. On December 20 Rodino announced his choice for chief counsel, and Doar was introduced to a national television audience. Rodino pointedly let it be known that Doar had been a Republican most of his life (before registering as an Independent in New York City).

Only one endorsement was read by Rodino from the podium, and it was thus featured prominently in all the news stories. Rodino reported that top White House official Mel Laird had telephoned during the press conference and left a message that Rodino "should be congratulated and commended" on his selection of Doar.[28] After Ford and Jaworski, the third Laird selection was in place to pursue justice and help restore balance to the ship of state.

⌘

When he first agreed to accept the domestic counselor position, Laird had pledged to Nixon that he would stay "six months to a year" and no longer. That disinterest in wielding power imbued Laird with a special authority. But, the longer he stayed, the worse things got at the White House. Around the time Jaworski was chosen as special prosecutor, Buzhardt testified in court that two of the nine subpoenaed tapes did not exist. The tapes had been subpoenaed because notes and logs of Nixon's conversations and meetings indicated that on those dates and times Watergate was a main part of the discussion. However, there were no tape logs. Buzhardt said the two particular conversations had not been recorded, in one case because the recorder had run out of tape.

The "missing tapes" revelation on top of the Saturday Night Massacre prompted the New York Times to editorialize for the first time that Nixon should resign. In its first editorial in fifty years Time magazine also called for Nixon's resignation. Senator Edward Brooke of Massachusetts became the first Republican in Congress to publicly urge Nixon to step down. Then on November 21 Buzhardt disclosed to Judge Sirica that one of the subpoenaed tapes had been partially erased—a tape that recorded conversations three days after the Watergate break-in and on the first workday on which Nixon had the opportunity for discussions with Haldeman, Ehrlichman, and others in the Oval Office.

Buzhardt explained that, as near as could be determined, the president's secretary, Rose Mary Woods, had "accidentally" erased the tape. On the day she was transcribing it she got a phone call and left the recorder running while "accidentally" hitting the "record" button. She testified that the mishap only accounted for "four or five minutes" of the eighteen-and-a-half-minute erasure because she had not been on the phone that long.

Just who caused the infamous "eighteen-and-a-half-minute gap" will probably remain Watergate's lingering mystery. A panel of experts chosen by Jaworski and the White House unanimously concluded it was no accident. It was a deliberate erasure done in at least five, and possibly as many as nine, "separate and contiguous" segments. Watergate investigators tended to believe that either Woods or Nixon himself had done it, though his defenders maintained the president was too mechanically incompetent to erase the tape. Nixon pointed the finger at others, including his own lawyer, Buzhardt.[29]

None of those disclosures helped Laird do his job as domestic counselor. Because he had always been straight with the press, he naturally was pummeled with questions about Watergate when he gave interviews on the defense appropriations bill or other domestic issues. "He *wants* to talk about things like the energy crisis, but he gets asked about the scandals and he seems uncomfortable when he replies," *Newsday*'s Martin Schram wrote. Asking him a question about the scandal risked getting a "filibuster in response." When Laird was asked about a brewing influence-peddling scandal involving the nation's milk producers, his response dwelled "on the modern economic history of cheese producers in Laird's home state, Wisconsin." Sometimes he could duck the question and sometimes he couldn't.[30]

When Laird met with a group of reporters in the White House's Roosevelt Room on the morning of November 29, the first questions were about whether the erased tape had hurt Nixon's public relations efforts with Republican members of Congress. Laird responded directly, "Yes, it has hurt; it has not helped." Has it increased the possibility of impeachment? Laird answered that there was not "great support at this time for impeachment." He explained that he had always been an accurate vote-counter in the House, and, based on his survey the previous day, there would currently be "a substantial vote" *against* impeachment.

But he allowed that his prognostications hadn't always been accurate. For example, Laird continued, he had predicted that Ford would be confirmed within two weeks after the completion of the FBI background check. That had not yet happened. Laird smiled while dropping a little bombshell of his own; as soon as Ford was confirmed, Laird would not stay at the White House much longer. He had always said he would only stay as long as he could make a contribution. Until Ford came along Laird was considered the only White House official with enough influence in Congress to push through the president's legislative agenda and budget. But Ford was almost a match for Laird in that regard.

At the same time as he was being fairly candid with reporters, Laird was heavily lobbying his former colleagues in Congress to speed up the Ford confirmation process. Laird's anxiety had much to do with his knowledge from Buzhardt that release of the tapes would prove Nixon guilty. Well-connected columnist John Osborne got wind of Laird's campaign to get Ford confirmed and summarized it on November 24: "The former Congressman . . . tells Republican and Democrat alike that they've got to confirm Gerald Ford without delay because another Watergate crunch, maybe worse than any yet expected, is coming soon. He is saying that a confirmed Vice President ought to be in place when it does. [He] doesn't quite say in addition that a Republican Vice President has got to be in office, ready to replace Mr. Nixon when and if he resigns or is impeached and removed. But that's the impression he leaves."[31]

No previous nominee to political office was ever more thoroughly investigated than was Gerald Ford. Having missed the bribery in the Agnew background check, the FBI was determined not to be caught falling short again. Some 350 FBI special agents from thirty-three of the bureau's field offices interviewed more than a thousand witnesses, including a former teenage football player who had been tackled by Ford after the whistle blew during a Michigan high school football game.

The Senate finally confirmed Ford on November 27 by a 92 to 3 vote. The House followed on December 6 with a 387 to 35 vote. Laird was invited to be present as Ford was sworn in that same day in the House chamber, the site of so many years of Ford-Laird service as Republican leaders. Some astute commentators observed that the confirmation was a watershed event for Nixon, and not a good one. Columnists Evans and Novak wrote the same day that the "remorseless crumbling erosion of President Nixon's standing where it counts most—in the bosom of his own party—has now moved to a point of maximum danger with the accession [of Ford as his] heir apparent." They noted that some Republicans had taken Laird's announcement that he would leave after the Ford confirmation as a signal that "obligations in the party to defend Richard M. Nixon [can] end."[32] Included in the media's speculation was that, if and when Ford needed his own vice president, it would be his loyal friend Melvin Laird.[33]

⚓

On the same day as Ford was confirmed Laird gave written notice to Nixon that he would be resigning at the end of the year—only three weeks away. At first Nixon refused to accept it. He told Laird he didn't think Ford could do everything that Laird had been doing. Laird maintained that Ford was "eminently qualified," but that Nixon would need to give him extensive authority as vice president to do it; a domestic counselor would not be necessary. Nixon finally agreed, but with one stipulation: Laird must not leave until the end of January after he had helped prepare the 1974 State of the Union message, and the budget. "I will be pleased to postpone my departure from the White House staff for thirty days in order to help," Laird wrote in a formal December 17 letter of resignation that he presented to Nixon in an hour-long Oval Office meeting that afternoon.[34]

Two days later a press conference was held to announce that the president had accepted Laird's resignation effective February 1, 1974, as well as to report Laird's new job as senior counselor for national and international affairs for *Reader's Digest*. After three decades of public service, Laird said to the assembled journalists, "I would like to encourage people that are interested in seeking a very rewarding career to not turn aside from politics." One definition called politics "the art and science of government," Laird continued. He felt that, just as other scientists had done much for "the well-being of people through their work, [so] I think the science of politics is very rewarding." Considering the friends he had made and the good they had done together, "political service has been very rewarding to me," Laird continued. "I have been treated very well as a politician."

What made news from the press conference was Laird's unusual encouragement to the House Judiciary Committee to undertake its constitutional obligation of considering impeachment of the president. But he urged that a House vote on impeachment be taken no later than March 15. "I think a vote would be healthy and I do not believe it would serve this country well to postpone that vote just to have it closer to the 1974 congressional election," he said cautiously. Laird was demonstrating his independence to the end.[35]

At that juncture, however, Nixon wasn't taking offense at anything Laird said or did. The president, who had yanked Laird from a comfortable seat in Congress, who had lied to him about Watergate, who had shut him out of the Oval Office, and who had failed to heed his advice, now sent Laird a kind letter. "More than anything else, I have valued your loyal friendship during this difficult period. It has been a constant source of reassurance to me and words cannot adequately convey how much I appreciated your steadfastness."[36]

The news of Laird's resignation plans was received with editorial lament. For the second time in less than a year newspapers across the country mourned the passing of Melvin Laird from government. Laird himself wasted no time grieving. He had accomplished the domestic agenda he set for himself and had served without compromise under a president he no longer respected. The one thing Laird could not do was to get Nixon to listen to his advice on healing the wounds created by Watergate and reestablishing a relationship with his party and with Congress. But Laird felt confident that he was leaving that job in the capable hands of Gerald Ford.

45
Ending the Nightmare

THE LAST THING LAIRD EXPECTED a year after American soldiers and POWs had come home from Vietnam was an antiwar demonstration. Yet there it was, as he arrived at Providence College on January 27, 1974, a year and a day after the peace agreement had been signed in Paris. When Laird's friend John Fogarty had died in 1967, the family had set up a foundation to honor those who made significant contributions to the field of mental retardation. Laird considered his work on health issues with Fogarty in Congress to be one of his finest contributions as a politician. When Laird was chosen to receive the foundation's 1974 award, Vice President Jerry Ford offered him a ride on Air Force Two to the college in Rhode Island, where Ford would personally present the award. Inside the auditorium seven hundred political luminaries and other guests waited to honor Laird, but outside there was another crowd.

As Ford and Laird stepped out of their limousine, their ears were assaulted with shouts from about 150 protestors rounded up by a radical group that called itself the "Attica Brigade": "Humanitarian we say no, Melvin Laird has to go!" "Melvin Laird, you can't hide, we charge you with genocide!" "Ford, Laird, better start shakin', today's pigs are tomorrow's bacon!" Before the Secret Service or local police could react, the protestors began tossing eggs, tomatoes, oranges, and snowballs at Ford and Laird. Neither was struck, though the police commissioner and a police lieutenant were hit. Then the demonstrators burned an effigy of Laird. One *Providence Journal-Bulletin* reporter said the "rancorous Vietnam War demonstration...appeared almost to have been frozen in 1968 and defrosted" just for Laird.[1] He was unflustered but the irony was apparent. Here was a man who was as much responsible for "peace" in Vietnam as Kissinger. Yet Kissinger received the Nobel Peace Prize, and Laird could not show up to receive a humanitarian award without discord marring the modest event.

What irked Laird most was not lack of credit for helping to achieve "peace," but the propensity of Nixon and Kissinger to characterize the Paris accord as "peace" in any form. Two weeks before the Paris accord was signed, Laird had confided to his senior staff: "I am concerned that many people will be carried away with any agreement and oversell it. The war may quiet down a bit for a few months, but it will resume. The more any accord is sold as a peace agreement, the more difficult it will be to get the U.S. support needed to help the South Vietnamese repel further attacks."[2] Despite the fact that Laird had shared his qualms with Nixon and Kissinger, the two let fly repeated statements about "peace with honor," and the "right kind of peace." Throughout 1973 Nixon and Kissinger had left the American public with the impression that peace had been achieved.

In his last month as presidential counselor, Laird vented some of his frustration with the overblown peace rhetoric. Without naming either the president or Kissinger, he gave several interviews in January 1974 disparaging their persistent pronouncements of peace. The Nixon administration should never have talked about "peace in Vietnam," he told the *Washington Post*. Over the previous year about sixty thousand North and South Vietnamese had been killed during this "peace" (which some called the "cease-fire war"). That was more death in one year than all the Americans killed during the country's decade-long involvement in the conflict. "The war in Southeast Asia has gone on for 30 years and will go on, perhaps, for another 20 years," Laird predicted. When he referred to the Paris Accords, Laird said he "always talked about *United States involvement*. . . . I never thought [it] would bring peace, and I never sold it as a peace program." (The *Post* called this remark "an implied rebuke to the Nixon-Kissinger rhetoric.") All along, Laird maintained, the administration should have emphasized that the Paris treaty ended American military involvement in the war, which would have been enough to legitimately crow about and a more accurate characterization of the achievement.[3]

Private life gave Laird more freedom to speak his mind publicly, and he did so on January 29, 1974, at his last press conference before leaving the White House. The session was a free-wheeling one in which Laird spoke, as one observer put it, "with the frankness of a man retiring from government without obligation to toe the official line." In Laird's mind, he had almost completely made the transition from reported-on to reporter. After making several candid comments about Nixon administration missteps, Laird waved off other probing questions with the remark that he was about to be one of the media, and he needed to save some of his choice editorial observations for publication in *Reader's Digest*, his new employer. When the press conference was over, and a few exclusive interviews had been given to favorite journalists, Laird had effectively unloaded on Nixon for failure to clear up the Watergate mess, on Kissinger for criticizing NATO allies over the Middle East, and on new Defense Secretary Schlesinger for changing the U.S. nuclear weapons strategy. He publicly advised Ford not to get involved with Nixon's Watergate defense. He also spelled out, in stark relief, his differences with Nixon on the subject of amnesty for draft resisters who were in prison or exile.

Nixon was adamantly against amnesty, but, as was often the case, Laird saw shades of gray in the argument. He had told a group of students at the Pentagon in February 1972 that the government could not consider offering amnesty until the war was over and all U.S. prisoners had been released. To do otherwise would deplete the draft authority of the Selective Service System and demoralize soldiers still in harm's way. But he foresaw a "proper time" when a limited amnesty could be offered. He observed that America was a country that strove "to temper justice with mercy." At the same time, Laird had directed Army Secretary Froehlke to secretly work out a postwar amnesty plan.[4]

Nixon did not let Laird's parting criticism at the press conference cloud his view of the personal and political debt he and the country owed Laird. At a White House dinner in Laird's honor on March 26, Nixon presented him with the Medal of Freedom, the nation's highest civilian honor. Any evidence of a rift between the two was put aside as Nixon hosted the gala attended by more than one hundred government and military luminaries, as well as Laird friends and family. "Few men have served America better," Nixon said. "Lawmaker, administrator, theorist and master of the American political process, Melvin Laird has helped preserve a strong, free United States and has left an indelible mark on the history of our times." Laird was effusive in return: "No other president could have given a secretary of defense any stronger support than you gave me."

The event was not all cheery bonhomie, coming as it did while the Watergate investigations inexorably ground on. In the middle of the banquet the wife of General Robert Cushman rose to give an impromptu toast and turned it into a passionate harangue against the press for picking on Nixon. (Cushman, the commandant of the Marine Corps, had been Nixon's aide when Nixon was vice president.) After Mrs. Cushman's first toast, the embarrassed hush that came over the crowd was broken by whispered questions at the tables as guests tried to figure out who she was. Oblivious to the fact that others in the room might not share her fierce loyalty to Nixon, the tipsy Mrs. Cushman rose and tapped her glass for a second toast, but the dinner band continued to play, so she sat down. Then, after scheduled speakers had their say, she rose a third time and called Nixon "one of the greatest presidents in history." When she sat down that time she nervously turned to Al Haig at her table. "Did I do all right?" she asked. "You did just fine, Mrs. Cushman," Haig reassured her. No reporters were allowed at the dinner, but when word leaked out about his wife's speech, the general had no comment. "I'm not sure what he was doing during her tirade," one guest told the *Washington Post.* "He probably was holding on to his four stars and hoping he wouldn't be demoted to PFC."[5]

As the Watergate investigation proceeded, admiration for the president was in short supply, especially in the office of the Watergate prosecutor. Nixon had been led to believe by Laird and Connally that Leon Jaworski would be far more favorable to the president's interests than Archibald Cox had been. Laird's primary belief, however, was that Jaworski was a man of integrity who would impartially weigh the merits of the prosecution. Jaworski had come to the job as a Nixon admirer, but that admiration had evaporated as he listened to the White House tapes. One March 1973 tape caused Jaworski to feel physically sick as he listened to the president—a lawyer—coaching Haldeman on how to hedge the truth without committing perjury. On another tape Nixon discussed with Haldeman and aide John Dean the usefulness of hush money payments to the Watergate burglars. "Listening to him scheme, *knowing* he was President of the United States, I felt as if my heart was shriveling inside of me," Jaworski later wrote. It was impossible for him to conclude anything other than that the president had engaged in criminal activities, including obstruction of justice.[6]

Laird was temporarily spared the heartache over Nixon's fall from grace because he had not yet heard the tapes. He knew from Nixon's lawyer, Buzhardt, that the president was probably criminally culpable in a Watergate cover-up conspiracy. But, not having listened to the tapes, he could still believe that Nixon was a fairly decent man who had made some political mistakes that could be finessed to avoid impeachment. When Laird left the White House, he predicted that impeachment would fail in the 435-member House of Representatives by about a hundred votes. At the same time, he criticized the president for his handling of Watergate.

~~~

During the spring of 1974 Laird was a mixed blessing for the White House. At the same time as he expressed confidence in Nixon's ability to continue as president, he also avowed the utmost confidence in Nixon's nemeses, Jaworski and John Doar. Nixon's palace guard was bent on savaging the two men, but Laird would have none of that. He had deliberately maneuvered these very men into place to judge Nixon fairly, so he could hardly disparage them.

On April 11 Doar secured a 33 to 3 House Judiciary Committee vote to send subpoenas to the White House demanding the tapes and related documents. Never before in American history had the House subpoenaed a president to provide evidence that might lead to his impeachment. Nixon agreed to turn over some heavily edited transcripts, and even those contained explosive revelations. For many Americans the most interesting of those revelations was the president's vulgar vocabulary. (So much of the language was edited out that the transcripts became famous for bringing the words "expletive deleted" into the American lexicon.) Still, without a smoking gun in the transcripts, veteran vote-counter Laird opined that the president could still beat impeachment, but the margin of victory had narrowed to fewer than thirty votes.[7]

The House Committee was not satisfied, nor was Jaworski; both demanded more complete transcripts. By mid-July even the chief of the White House military office, Bill Gulley, could see that the president knew he was doomed. He recorded that three signs of Nixon's imminent downfall were (1) Kissinger was "beginning to speak in the first person," abandoning the "we" form that previously included Nixon; (2) Haig granted more White House perks to Vice President Ford, which indicated that Ford was no longer a stepchild; and (3) Laird was a more frequent visitor to the White House and was telling journalists that Nixon couldn't hold on much longer.[8]

In mid-February Laird began urging Ford to think about who he would want in his own Cabinet. For a month the new vice president demurred, but by late March he was ready to face his possible succession to the presidency. He opened up to John Osborne at *The New Republic* and admitted that he had been thinking about what he would do if he became president. One of his first orders of business would be to try to persuade Laird to come back and help him run the country.[9]

On April 6 the Washington elite, along with Laird, gathered for the annual Gridiron Club dinner—traditionally an occasion to poke fun at the president and the press. When Ford spoke he reminded the guests that he had appeared at the dinner six years before, along with then–vice president Hubert Humphrey, and Ford repeated what he had said at the time: "Let me assure the distinguished Vice President of the United States that I have absolutely no designs on his job." Laughter erupted, with Laird one of the most amused. "I'm not at all interested in the vice presidency," Ford continued. "I love the House of Representatives despite the long, irregular hours. Sometimes, though, when it's late and I'm tired and hungry on that long drive home to Alexandria, as I go past 1600 Pennsylvania Avenue, I do seem to hear a little voice say, 'If you lived here, you'd be home now.'"[10]

Behind the scenes Laird had already become part of an informal group of Ford friends plotting the presidential transition. By July 1974 he was inundated with phone calls from Nixon Cabinet secretaries who wanted to know what Ford thought of them. Laird told each person what he could about what might happen in a transition, but publicly Laird continued to maintain that the House would not impeach Nixon, and Nixon would not resign.

All that changed overnight on July 24 when the Supreme Court unanimously ruled that Nixon must turn over *all* subpoenaed tapes. Nixon knew that on one of those tapes he had incontrovertibly schemed to thwart an FBI investigation by falsely claiming that the CIA had national security concerns. Once Nixon relinquished the tape, he suspected, impeachment in the House of Representatives was a sure thing.[11] The same day as the historic Supreme Court ruling, the House Judiciary Committee began its impeachment hearings. By July 30 it had passed three articles of impeachment regarding obstruction of justice and abuse of power. The articles were forwarded to the full House for a vote. By that time Jaworski had secured a sealed judgment from the Watergate grand jury that Nixon was considered an "unindicted coconspirator" in the various Watergate-related crimes.

Still, Nixon had not released the most damning of the tapes, although he had finally revealed the contents to Haig and his lawyers. Their verdict was unanimous; there was no way out. Nixon would certainly be impeached by the House. And it was likely that he did not have enough Senate support to beat back conviction during a Senate trial on the articles of impeachment. Nixon vacillated, reminding himself that he was always a fighter. His family members pressed him not to resign. But when the tape was finally released, the impact was devastating, costing Nixon many of his remaining supporters in Congress.

☙

At 11:30 A.M. on August 7, 1974, four men bowed their heads in prayer in the office of House Minority Leader John Rhodes. It was the regular Wednesday morning prayer meeting for this group, which had first come together for spiritual fellowship in the 1960s when they all had served in Congress together. Rhodes was there, along with Minnesota Congressman Albert Quie, Vice President Ford, and Laird. As was their habit, they each took a turn saying a prayer and then recited the Lord's Prayer together. They didn't mention the president's troubles. Quie remembered that, toward the end of the prayers, Rhodes's secretary came into the room and said, "I know I'm never supposed to interrupt this meeting, but considering the circumstances I think I should. The White House just called and said Jerry Ford should come down to the White House right away." No one needed to ask why.

Quie had one question for Ford: "Just before you leave, Jerry, you always have said you never wore your religion on your sleeve. But what if, when you have a press conference, somebody should ask you, 'Where were you and what were you doing when you found out that you were going to be the president?'"

"Nobody's going to say that," said Ford over his shoulder as he left the office.

"Well, on the way down there, think about it," Quie called after him. (He was concerned that his prayer group would look like "some big cabal," but Ford was never asked the question, nor did the prayer group ever come under any public criticism.)[12]

Ford hurried to the White House for a meeting with Nixon. Rhodes later joined him along with Republican Senators Hugh Scott and Barry Goldwater. Nixon was fishing for advice about what he should do. Goldwater, who had been pushing behind the scenes to get Nixon to resign, was blunt: "You haven't got more than twelve people who will stand with you in the Senate. I've got to be frank; I don't know whether I would be one of them." Nixon told them he was close to making a decision about his future.

For his part Laird could take satisfaction from having saved the nation from one additional trauma. While Nixon was pondering resignation, John Connally, the man Laird talked Nixon out of choosing as his vice president, became embroiled in a bribery scandal. In August 1974 the nation's largest dairy cooperative pleaded guilty to bribing Connally to increase federal milk supports when he was treasury secretary. Connally himself was indicted on two counts of accepting an illegal payment, one count of conspiracy to commit perjury, and two counts of making a false statement to a grand jury. (He later was found not guilty on the bribery charges and the other counts were dropped.)[13]

On Thursday evening, August 8, Nixon announced over national television at 9 P.M. that on the following day at noon he would resign. He was the first U.S. president ever to do so. During the fifteen-minute speech Nixon was not contrite or apologetic. Instead he suggested that he was only resigning because his congressional support had abandoned him.

At 12:03 P.M. the next day, in the East Room of the White House, with Laird looking on, Ford was sworn in by Chief Justice Warren Burger as the thirty-eighth U.S. president—the only unelected chief executive in American history. Ford acknowledged in his short address the "extraordinary circumstances" that brought him to the position without an election. He asked Americans to pray for him and "for Richard Nixon and for his family" so that the man "who brought peace to millions" would "find it for himself." Most memorably, the new president declared: "Our Constitution works. Our great Republic is a government of laws and not of men. Here, the people rule.... My fellow Americans, our long national nightmare is over."

A few days later Ford, having not yet moved into the White House, threw a small party at his modest home in Alexandria, Virginia. Present were the Fords, their four children, and a few intimate friends, including Mel and Barbara Laird. "Some of us sat on the floor of the small living room and Betty served snacks as we talked," Laird recalled. "Having taken off his coat and tie, Jerry helped in the kitchen and made sure everyone felt at home. He paid as much attention to the opinions of his children as those voiced by his friends. His questions showed me, and them, just how intently he was listening. I had seen Jerry in his shirt sleeves listening to others countless times. Now I realized I was no longer looking at Jerry but at the President." Sitting cross-legged on the floor, Laird smiled and savored the moment.[14]

⁕

The man at the top of Ford's list for vice president was Melvin Laird. The old friends had played a round of golf in the summer of 1974, and Ford confided to Laird that he wanted to name Laird as his vice-presidential successor if Nixon resigned. "That's a terrible idea," Laird laughed. "I'm from Wisconsin and you're from Michigan. We're too close to each other. You'll need someone who's not from the Midwest to balance the ticket in 1976 when you run for reelection."

"Now, Mel," Ford responded, "you know I've promised Betty—and the Congress—that I will not be a presidential candidate in 1976, no matter what happens with President Nixon."

Laird paused at the hole they were playing on the Burning Tree Club course. Then he looked Ford squarely in the eye: "Jerry, if you do become president this year, you *can't* rule out running in 1976. If you do you'll be a lame duck from the minute you take the oath, and you won't be able to get anything done!"

Ford was taken aback by Laird's vehemence, but finally smiled. "Okay, Mel," he said, noncommittally, to end the conversation.

Laird's best defense against a job offer he didn't want was the one he had often used in the past—to come up with another candidate, in this case Nelson Rockefeller. The conservative wing of the Republican Party did not like Rockefeller's "liberalism," but Laird appreciated his breadth and depth of knowledge and ideas. So well known was Laird's affinity for Rocky that it was rumored in early 1974 that Laird would be campaign manager for Rockefeller's 1976 presidential bid. Rockefeller, however, was suspicious of Laird's motives. When word spread among insiders that Laird was thinking about backing Rockefeller for vice president, he and some of his aides were convinced Laird had floated the name to create a firestorm of conservative protest, forcing Ford to reach for the best compromise candidate—Laird himself. "Mel has many friends . . . *all wary*," groused one Rockefeller aide to the *Wall Street Journal,* which added that Laird could be characterized as "a man whose playful deviousness is his most enduring feature . . . a kind of unguided missile within the Washington establishment, leaving intrigues, strategies and inside information in his wake."[15] This time, however, there was no hidden agenda.

After Ford became president he told Congress he would announce his vice-presidential choice in about ten days. Just as Nixon had done he requested that Republican leaders submit suggestions. Then he scheduled meetings with a dozen close friends to hear their advice; first up would be Laird and Bryce Harlow. Before mounting a full-court press for his candidate, Laird had required a firm commitment from Rockefeller, who was notorious for vacillating on political opportunities. Laird reached him on Saturday, August 10, at his summer home in Seal Harbor, Maine. "I have recommended to the president that *you* should be the vice president," Laird informed him.

"No, Mel, *you* are the man who ought to be the one," responded Rockefeller, still wary that he was being set up. "You have been in the White House. You've been in government. You are in touch. You have no problem in Congress."

Laird immediately parried the suggestion with the same points against his own nomination that he had made to Ford more than once, the most important of which was that he really didn't want the job. Then he continued with his pitch: "Now, Rocky, I want to make sure you're on board with this thing because I'm not going to go to a lot of trouble and find out that you're going to play games."

Rockefeller took a breath. At the age of sixty-six, after several failed presidential bids, he was ready and very much willing to become vice president. "Mel, I'm not playing any games. I'll do it; I *want* to do it."

"That's all I want to know," Laird said.[16]

The next day Ford asked Laird once again if he would consider being vice president. And once again Laird declined. (Until the president named his choice, Laird was consistently named high on the "A list" of possibilities. One political cartoonist whimsically assembled the ideal vice president for Ford by cutting out parts of each of the potential candidates; Laird's donation was his brain.) Laird took most of his half-hour in the Oval Office laying it on thick for Rockefeller—first by reporting to Ford the commitment from Rockefeller. Then Laird outlined what he thought were Rockefeller's qualifications: talent, wealth, a circle of influential friends, loyalty, a team player, and a formidable addition to the next presidential ticket. When Ford golfed with Laird at Burning Tree on Sunday, August 18, Laird lobbied for Rockefeller again. There Ford confided that he had already decided on Rockefeller.

President Ford announced his choice on August 20, and the decision was hailed by opinion makers in politics and the media. The following day, the president authorized his spokesperson to announce that Ford would "probably" run for the presidency in 1976.

~

On the day he became president, Ford's immediate choice to head a rapid transition team was Donald Rumsfeld, then the U.S. ambassador to NATO. The team completed its work in two weeks, then Rumsfeld returned to Europe. But in late September he was asked to become Ford's chief of staff—replacing Haig, who was tired and too closely associated with the disgraced Nixon. (Desiring to return to the military, Haig accepted a new post as the supreme commander of NATO.) Rumsfeld quickly drafted as his deputy Richard Cheney, a former subordinate and Laird protégé.

One of Rumsfeld's most insistent suggestions to Ford in his first week on the job was that, since he was going to keep a majority of the Nixon Cabinet in place, there was an overriding need for a group of trusted outsiders to advise him as well. "My conviction was that he kind of climbed into a flying airplane, and the crew was already pre-selected," Rumsfeld said. "So he needed to feel there were these friends who knew him well that would be regularly scheduled to visit with him in the Oval Office." The use of "wise men" from outside government had been a hallmark of the Roosevelt, Truman, Eisenhower, and Kennedy administrations. Rumsfeld explained the advantages: "People are generally reluctant to tell a president what they think. As chief of staff, they'd come to me and say, 'Oh my God, President Ford is messing up this or that. I've gotta see him.' Fine, I'd say, and take him in. As soon as he walks in, the guy kisses the president's ring, slobbers all over his hand, tells him how wonderful he is and then comes out and says: 'Well, I really told him!' So I felt Ford needed guys who knew him so dad-burned well that they would tell him what they thought—with the bark off."[17]

The Ford group came to be known as the "Kitchen Cabinet." While as many as a dozen names were included in various listings of the Kitchen Cabinet, Ford identified in his memoirs a core group of six—Laird, Harlow, former congressman John Byrnes of Wisconsin, David Packard, former Pennsylvania governor William Scranton, and U.S. Steel executive William Whyte. The Kitchen Cabinet met with Ford at least once a month. Rumsfeld and Cheney sat in on the meetings when they were permitted. Sometimes they would leave early so the group could talk candidly with Ford about the White House staff's performance. The Kitchen Cabinet's primary function was to tell Ford the unvarnished truth. Cheney recalled, "It was a very good idea—and Mel was good at it. Mel never had any qualms about telling President Ford what he thought."[18]

Cheney added that Laird was preeminent among the Kitchen Cabinet. "I knew I could just stick him on the president's schedule any time—the president would always see him." Part of Laird's power derived from the fact that he sought no position in the Ford administration. The only official position he ever accepted was as a member of the President's Foreign Intelligence Advisory Board (PFIAB).

Aside from the Kitchen Cabinet, the PFIAB meetings with Ford, and the frequent private meetings and phone calls between the pair, there were many other opportunities for Laird to associate with his political and social friend of two decades. The prayer meetings continued, although not weekly. About once a month the group would gather at the White House to pray with Ford. Laird would often "stay over for another five or ten minutes and just talk to me as sort of a Dutch uncle, trying to tell me what people were thinking on the outside about how we were running the White House," Ford recalled.

Both Ford and Laird kept their membership in the Chowder and Marching Club, too, and in the informality of that setting the new president occasionally took a beating. Former representative Clarence "Bud" Brown of Ohio remembered one session where the society members aired their complaints about Kissinger as secretary of state. "Somebody started in on Kissinger and suggested that Jerry was losing some advantage as president by Kissinger's ego having left the impression that he was determining foreign policy and that Jerry wasn't or that he didn't understand it," Brown said. "Several people picked up on the theme and said, 'Mr. President, you've got to assert yourself.' Literally, the president followed me out and said, 'Bud, you get back and tell those so-and-sos that I *am* the president of the United States, in spite of the way they treated me at this meeting. I *do* make policy.'"[19]

Laird also golfed almost every weekend with President Ford at Burning Tree, something the friends had started doing together in the early 1950s when they were seat mates on the House Defense Appropriations Subcommittee. Two earlier presidents, Nixon and Eisenhower, had moved their lockers upstairs to a special private room that was dubbed "Fairyland" by the members. Not Ford; he kept his regular locker. Jack Mills recalled that Ford was changing clothes there one day when the locker room phone near him rang. "It kept ringing, so President Ford picked it up and said, 'Burning Tree.'" The caller was looking for another club member who was in the card room. "Just a minute," said Ford, who happened to be naked. "He's bare ass, except for a towel around his hips, and he pokes his head in the card room and says, 'You've got a phone call,'" recounted Mills. The man was a lobbyist and the caller was his boss, so excitedly he picked up the phone and said, "Do you know who answered the phone?"

"What the hell's the difference who answered the phone?" the caller barked.

"Well, it happened to be the president of the United States."

Mills concluded: "That's what kind of guy Jerry was. He answered the telephone and went into the card room without any clothes on. Nixon never would have done that."[20]

∽⚓∽

Laird's influence on President Ford was so pervasive that he was profiled as "The Man of the Ear" by *New York* magazine in the fall of 1974. The cover featured a caricature of Laird whispering into the enormous left ear of a befuddled-looking Ford. The article, written by friends of both men, Rowland Evans and Robert Novak, said Laird's prominence as an advisor was a good thing:

> More than any other single power broker in this country, Laird is most qualified to advise a president across the board. . . . In an age of specialization, he is the political Renaissance Man, whose flexibility and adaptability vividly clash with the self-destructive stolidity typifying the Republican party's congressional wing.
>
> What may obstruct Ford from fully partaking of this cornucopia of good sense is the highly unusual manner of doing business, often bordering on the obstreperous or even obnoxious, that has made Laird something less than the most beloved man in Washington. Although an uncommon delight when gossiping about politics over cocktails or lunch, with all the juicy tidbits at his fingertips, Laird is that rare figure who has made his way in this town by force of will and knowledge, not amiability.[21]

The White House staff below the Rumsfeld-Cheney level had less reason to love Laird than to fear him. In early 1974 Laird had advised Vice President Ford that some of his staff was not White House caliber and should be dismissed if he became president. Shortly after Ford moved into the Oval Office Laird further advised that he should make a clean sweep of most of the Nixonites at the top level—including, after a respectable interval, Kissinger. Partly out of self-preservation, some White House staffers carped about Laird within Ford's hearing, implying that he should cut off Laird's access. But Ford ignored them.

While Laird was still in the Nixon White House as domestic counselor, he had talked to Vice President Ford about a conditional amnesty for draft evaders. With Ford as president, Laird was convinced that conditional amnesty would be an ideal program for Ford to announce early in his administration. Prodded by Laird, Ford raised the idea of amnesty with Secretary of Defense Schlesinger, who expressed his approval. Ford chose a speech before the Veterans of Foreign Wars in Chicago on August 19 as the venue to announce his plans for something he called "earned reentry" for draft evaders.

On September 16 Ford made public how his amnesty would work; it was strikingly similar to the plan that Laird had tried to get Nixon to adopt in 1973. It established a Presidential Clemency Board and provided amnesty for draft evaders if they turned themselves in and agreed to perform two years of alternative service to their country. Military deserters would be allowed to return to their branch of service and spend two more years in the military before being granted clemency for their offenses.[22] It was a fair plan that earned praise from most quarters, but the warm feelings Ford earned quickly faded in September with the single act of clemency he granted to a lone exile in California—the ill-timed pardon of Richard Nixon.

If Ford had been a complex man like Nixon, commentators might have thought the pardon reflected a deep-seated desire for self-destruction. But Jerry Ford was not a man full of such deep crosscurrents; he was not a layered thinker. He lacked the strategic political view that Laird had in abundance and simply failed to foresee the folly of issuing a pardon to Nixon so soon. Laird could have provided him with that foresight, but Ford did not ask, nor did he even inform Laird before he made the pardon public on national television. The reasons he did not confide in Laird can be deduced from Ford's autobiography and knowledge of both men. First, Ford was worried that his decision might be leaked in advance of his announcement. It is not unreasonable to surmise that, if Laird had received early warning, he might have instigated a media and congressional backlash to stop Ford. Also the new president knew that his friend was quite capable of talking him out of the precipitous action—and Ford didn't want to be talked out of it.

During the first two weeks of Ford's presidency, Laird had learned that Haig and Kissinger were planning to lobby Ford for a swift pardon of their old boss. Laird never felt that pardoning Nixon was wrong, but in politics timing is everything, and the time for a pardon was months away. So Laird called Phil Buchen, who was then acting as Ford's White House counsel: "Look Phil, I've gotten word that Haig and Kissinger want to talk to Ford about Nixon. Just keep Jerry away from them. Now is not the time for this." Buchen agreed.[23]

During those same two weeks Laird also talked briefly with Ford about the possibility of a pardon, only to find the president wasn't ready or interested in discussing it. Laird advised him that if he did plan to pardon Nixon at some point, it was best if it looked like the idea came from Congress. Laird had already put out some feelers and was convinced that he could line up an impressive coterie of House and Senate leaders to visit with Ford about it. But Ford dismissed the subject quickly because, at the time, it was something he planned to consider only after Nixon was indicted—or even later than that, after a likely conviction. Ford convinced Laird that the prospect of a presidential pardon in the near future was nonexistent. Then Ford underwent an unexpected turnaround on the subject, almost as a knee-jerk reaction to his first press conference on August 28.

When staffers prepared him for the event, Ford assumed that most of the questions would be about issues of governing facing him. Only his longtime aide Bob Hartmann anticipated questions about Nixon, but Ford thought that was unlikely.[24] The first question came from UPI White House correspondent Helen Thomas, who asked if Ford would pardon Nixon. Ford tried to dodge the question, but the reporters pressed him and he acknowledged that he was not "ruling out" the pardon option.[25] Laird watched the press conference closely but had no inkling of just how close the president was to granting a pardon. Laird might have had that inkling if he had seen how furious Ford was as he walked back to the Oval Office from the press conference. In an interview years later Ford recalled what was going through his head. "Goddamn it! I am not going to put up with this. Every press conference from now on [will] degenerate into a Q&A on: 'Am I going to pardon Mr. Nixon?'. . . I had to get the monkey off my back."[26]

Laird was wholly in agreement with Ford's primary reason for granting a pardon: the need to move beyond Watergate as quickly as possible. But Ford's method and timing were all wrong. Laird was a great believer in allies and coalitions. "You have to prepare people just a bit, and I was convinced that I could get thirty of the top people in the Congress to visit with Ford and urge him to pardon Nixon for the good of the country," Laird explained later. There is little reason to doubt that Laird could have accomplished the feat, but only after the November 1974 congressional elections. Before that time both parties would be posturing for maximum political advantage. During the Thanksgiving and Christmas holiday season, after the election, was the ideal time for a pardon.

Those were arguments Ford never fully heard. Instead, though Buchen, Hartmann, and former representative Jack Marsh, who was acting as Ford's congressional liaison, all felt it was too soon for a pardon, they were unable to sway the president. Ten days after the pivotal press conference, on Saturday, September 7, Ford and Laird were partners in a two-day golf tournament at

Burning Tree. Ford was in a good mood and invited Laird to join him at an afternoon crab fest he was hosting for Soviet cosmonauts. Laird declined the invitation. Ford never told Laird that he had more planned for the weekend than a crab fest. He was going to pardon Nixon.

On Sunday morning, before resuming the golf tournament with Ford, Laird gave a speech to an association of women journalists at the Kennedy Center for the Performing Arts. As he was leaving, one of the women approached him with the news: "Ford has pardoned Nixon." He had gone on television that morning and granted a "full, free, and absolute pardon . . . for all offenses against the United States." A stunned Laird managed to express his agreement with the decision to the reporter, then headed for Burning Tree to finish the golf tournament. "I couldn't believe it," Laird recalled of the news. "I could have gotten the Democrats requesting it. That could have been done!"

At Burning Tree, the two golf partners met at the first tee, Laird uncharacteristically quiet. Ford broke the silence, as Laird recalled the conversation: "Mel, I went ahead and did it. I just wanted to get it out of the way. I signed the papers this morning. What did you think of that?"

"Mr. President," said Laird, "we're on the first tee. We can win this tournament. I'm not going to talk to you about the pardon or the manner in which it was handled. We'll talk about that after our golf game, not now." They lost the tournament by two strokes. Afterward Laird gave Ford an earful about what should have been done and just how costly his unilateral decision was going to be. Ford was taken aback. "Mel's reaction was a harbinger of the public outcry that was developing," Ford recalled in his memoirs. Laird pitched in quickly to try to get as many statements of support as he could, but it was too little too late.[27]

Instead of administering a healing balm, Ford had poured salt into the Watergate wounds. His own press secretary, Jerald F. terHorst, resigned in anger within minutes of the announcement. "The mere fact that Ford could throw away the new national mood of trust for the sake of Richard Nixon [and] without getting a signed 'confession'" appalled terHorst. Like many others, terHorst thought the decision gave off the scent of a secret deal between Ford and Nixon. (No such deal was ever proven, and Laird didn't believe any deal existed.)

Many Americans were outraged by what appeared to be a sense of dual justice—Nixon free and his aides facing prison. Others were angered at the hypocrisy of offering draft evaders a "conditional" amnesty while Nixon was forgiven outright. Republican congressional leaders were privately aghast that Ford would expose his own party to criticism just eight weeks before the election in which every House seat and a third of the Senate seats were being contested. (Republicans lost forty House seats and four Senate seats, disproving Ford's rationale that his pardon would make it easier for him to govern.) His popularity dropped twenty-one points overnight. "The President's going to have to be unpopular for a while," Laird flatly told the *New York Times*.[28]

A final irony of Ford's mortal mistake was that if he had waited just a few weeks a pardon would not have been necessary. Very secretly, Watergate Special Prosecutor Leon Jaworski had decided not to indict Richard Nixon for any crime. This was something Jaworski did not admit even in his 1976 best seller, *The Right and the Power*. In the memoir Jaworski details his disgust with Nixon and his belief that Nixon had committed a series of crimes. "I had no doubt but that the grand jury wanted to indict him," Jaworski wrote. "But to be valid, an indictment required the signature of the Special Prosecutor so, in the last analysis, the decision of whether to indict the President was my responsibility." Jaworski never publicly admitted that he was on the verge of giving Nixon a get-out-of-jail-free card when Ford's pardon preempted him.

He did, however, tell the two men most responsible for his appointment as special prosecutor—Laird and Congressman William Archer. In a 2000 interview conducted simultaneously with both men, the secret came out. Discussing how the two had engineered Jaworski's selection, Laird lamented to Archer that Nixon never understood how principled Jaworski was, and how that would benefit Nixon in the end. "I don't ever think that Nixon fully appreciated him," Laird said.

"I don't either," Archer agreed.

"He was going to make a recommendation. . . . He was going to do a great service for our country," Laird continued.

"That's it—the biggest thing that he could have done," Archer said. "You [Laird] are the only other person that knows about this. Jaworski personally talked to me about it; it was never in his book."

Laird explained that Jaworski was going to recommend against indictment. Jaworski confided to the two separately that he was, as his final act, writing "more or less a defense of Nixon," Laird said. Jaworski had personally concluded that while Nixon deserved censure from Congress, he should not have been removed from office either by forced resignation or Senate conviction on articles of impeachment. Jaworski's recommendation was against prosecuting the former president in the criminal courts as well. Why did Laird and Archer feel that would have been a great "service" to the country? Because both felt that, ultimately, the majority of Americans did not want to see a former president go to jail.

Jaworski had told his staff he would end his work and deliver his decision by November. With a Jaworski announcement of no indictment, Ford would not have needed to issue a pardon at all. Any calumny for Nixon's absolution would have fallen on Jaworski instead of Ford and likely enhanced Ford's reelection chances in 1976. As for the implications of what might have been, Laird generally eschewed speculation about whether a little bit of patience would have saved Ford's presidency.[29]

46
Citizen Laird

THE DEEP SENSE OF PERSONAL BETRAYAL Laird felt after the fall of South Vietnam in 1975 continued for decades. For him, Vietnamization was never a cover for retreat or a face-saving "decent interval" before South Vietnam was overrun. It was a plan that Laird firmly believed would have worked if the United States had kept the promises it made at the signing of the Paris Peace Accords.

A congressional vote to cut off funding to South Vietnam in 1975 spelled the end for that nation. But Laird personally blamed three men: Kissinger, who lacked the will and ability to persuade Congress to honor the treaty that had won him the Nobel Prize; Defense Secretary Schlesinger, who was, by personality and intellectual arrogance, incapable of engendering enough good will in Congress to effectively lobby for *any* defense programs; and President Ford, who failed to use the weight of his office to uphold the treaty. "There's *no* president that should be defeated on an issue like this if they choose to really exert full presidential authority and commit to fulfill a firm commitment of our country," Laird said.

At the Paris accord signing in January 1973 the North Vietnamese pledged to respect South Vietnam's right to determine its own political future. They also pledged not to send more troops and arms into South Vietnam. Both pledges were promptly broken. The Russians and Chinese, by continuing to supply North Vietnam with offensive war matériel beyond prescribed limitations, also played a role in sabotaging the treaty. After the cease-fire, the Russians and Chinese poured arms and aid into North Vietnam conservatively valued at $2.5 billion.[1] Throughout the same period, the Nixon and Ford administrations did just the reverse for their ally, progressively reducing the amount of support far below what was allowed by the treaty. When the first major North Vietnamese treaty violations occurred in 1973, Nixon failed to respond with American air support as he had promised. Then in August of 1973 Congress took away Nixon's options for a renewed air war by banning any further U.S. military combat activities in Southeast Asia.

While Congress still allowed some funds to flow to Saigon for the replacement equipment, parts, and ammunition promised in the treaty, that pipeline began to be squeezed in 1974 when Congress cut deeply into the appropriation for South Vietnam. In early 1974 Nixon had requested $1.4 billion for South Vietnamese aid. Schlesinger thought he could get it by playing off the chairmen of the House Armed Services and Appropriations committees against each other. Vice President Ford had to step in to salvage the situation and negotiate a compromise of less than half the appropriation the administration had requested. (Only $158.4 million was ever actually delivered in arms to South Vietnam before it fell.) Ford confided in March to John Osborne of *The New Republic,* that, while Schlesinger was a brilliant intellectual, he was incapable of dealing with Congress. Ford added that, if he became president, one of the first things he would do was fire Schlesinger.[2]

The North Vietnamese had closely watched this American retreat from the Paris agreement and viewed the new President Ford as someone who would be unable to hold the line. Prime Minister Pham Van Dong privately expressed to his comrades his view that Ford was "the weakest president in U.S. history." Hanoi tested Ford by capturing the capital of the Phuoc Long Province of South Vietnam. "When Ford kept American B-52s in their hangars, our leadership decided on a big offensive against South Vietnam," recalled North Vietnamese Colonel Bui Tin.[3] Within weeks the North Vietnamese began pouring a massive force into South Vietnam. By late March 1975 they had captured thirteen more provinces. In the meantime, the Communist guerrillas in Cambodia achieved major victories and surrounded the capital of Phnom Penh, preparing for the kill. Ford requested an emergency $222 million supplemental appropriation for Cambodia, but Congress denied the funds. Schlesinger's lobbying was inadequate, and Kissinger was away on diplomatic junkets. At several stops along one of those trips in March, U.S. and foreign diplomats asked Kissinger if his trip was going to be cut short to return to Washington because of the desperate situation in Cambodia and Vietnam. Kissinger appeared surprised at the questions. "What more can I do?" was his usual response.[4]

In 2006 documents came to light that hinted Kissinger might have given up on a democratic South Vietnam as early as June 1972. George Washington University's National Security Archive made public some of his papers, including notes from his trip to China that month to meet Premier Chou En-lai. At the time, Nixon had ordered resumed bombing of North Vietnam to counter the Easter Offensive, and Kissinger was trying to finesse the situation with Chou. Kissinger indicated then that he was open to the possibility of a Communist takeover of the region, "if, as a result of historical evolution it should happen over a period of time, if we can live with a communist government in China, we ought to be able to accept it in Indochina." He cautioned Chou that if the Communists moved in too soon after the U.S. withdrawal, then Nixon might have to send American troops back in. Appearing to allow for some attempt at a truce followed by renewed fighting, Kissinger told Chou, "If the North Vietnamese, on the other hand, engage in serious negotiation with the South Vietnamese, and if after a longer period it starts again after we were all disengaged, my personal judgment is that it is much less likely that we will go back again, much less likely."

When his words were dredged up in 2006 Kissinger said he was trying to get "Chinese acquiescence in our policy" and cautioned against judging that in hindsight.[5] But for Laird it was further proof that Kissinger was predisposed to take a passive role in 1975, a time when he should have been defending the Paris Accords and demanding ongoing congressional aid to an ally.

On March 25, 1975, President Ford dispatched General Frederick C. Weyand, then army chief of staff, on an urgent mission to Saigon to assess the situation. Weyand reported back to Ford that the South was about to lose because it was running out of ammunition. Ford appeared before a joint session of Congress on April 10 to ask for $722 million in military aid and $250 million for economic and humanitarian assistance. "We cannot . . . abandon our friends while our adversaries support and encourage theirs," he argued. Two freshmen Democrats walked out on Ford, and there was little applause. Congressional leaders told Ford they would take up the request after the Easter recess, but by then it was too late.[6]

On April 17, 1975, Phnom Penh finally fell to the Khmer Rouge forces, who quickly demonstrated the face of monumental evil that was to become their hallmark. The bloodbath that Americans leaders feared would occur if Southeast Asian allies were abandoned unfolded with appalling rapidity. Every resident of the city of nearly three million was ordered to leave immediately. Many Cambodians who were pushed out of the hospitals died in the first hours. In less than a day, everyone who was mobile was on congested roads going out of the city. Those who fell behind on the slow march, including children, were executed on the spot. As many as three hundred thousand were killed by the Khmer Rouge in the first week of forced marches. Pushed into the rural areas that became Pol Pot's infamous "killing fields," as many as three million Cambodians were slaughtered at the hands of the Khmer Rouge over the next four years in horrendous fashion—babies torn apart limb from limb, pregnant women disemboweled, and many victims buried in sand up to their necks to suffer a slow death.[7]

Four days after Phnom Penh fell, South Vietnam's President Thieu resigned and fled the country as Communist forces moved closer to Saigon. In Washington there was an eerie anxiousness to have the end come swiftly. On April 25 Communist forces surrounded Saigon and began the final siege of the city. Four days later American Armed Forces Radio played "White Christmas" and announced: "It's 105 degrees in Saigon and rising." This was the prearranged code for all Americans and key South Vietnamese employees to go to their evacuation locations. The American leadership there had waited too long, however, and the two-day evacuation became a stampede as locals rushed planes and helicopters. Almost lost from media coverage of the frenzy were details of just how heroic and effective were the American military forces once they were finally given the go-ahead to evacuate allies. In eighteen hours, seventy helicopters and 865 U.S. Marines flew 630 round-trips from Saigon. By the time the evacuation was over, all the Americans and 130,000 at-risk South Vietnamese had been taken to safety.[8]

Private citizen Melvin Laird went to the White House to join the Ford staff monitoring, and mourning, the death throes of Saigon on April 30, 1975.

The North Vietnamese Communists were perhaps not as savage in victory as the neighboring Khmer Rouge, or at least not as methodical, but much blood did flow. As many as 250,000 South Vietnamese died in brutal "reeducation" prison camps; another 65,000 were executed outright. Two million became refugees with an unknown number of "boat people" lost at sea. During the war itself, 275,000 South Vietnamese soldiers had been killed in action, while another 365,000 civilians had died during the shelling of cities or were assassinated by terrorist infiltrators. Hanoi had also paid a high price for the war. According to its own estimates, the North counted at least 1.1 million dead and 300,000 missing.[9]

In the years since, many voices have been heard about how South Vietnam was lost—some blaming Congress, others citing South Vietnamese ineptitude. In Laird's view it was lost not because the South Vietnamese people proved unequal to the task but because the Ford administration lacked the will and wherewithal to continue the arms pipeline in the face of Congressional opposition. "I hold Ford, Kissinger, and Schlesinger responsible for not putting on a full-court press to meet our commitment," Laird said. "Kissinger was the one who made those commitments in Paris, yet he didn't spend a day in Congress—*not one day*—in support of the agreement in those last months. I tried to help a little, but there was no support from the State Department, very minimal support from Defense, and hardly any support from the White House. They lost that vote and that broke the back of the Vietnamese."

Laird was convinced that the outcome would have been different had he been walking the halls of Congress lobbying for continued support of South Vietnam. As secretary of defense he never lost a budget battle over aid to Vietnam (or any other defense issue), and it is likely he would have won this battle, too.

⚜

Kissinger's abdication in the fight to stave off the fall of South Vietnam was not the only disappointment Laird had with his former administration sparring partner. There was an ample Laird bill of particulars that began forming almost as soon as Nixon named Kissinger as secretary of state in August 1973. At Kissinger's Senate confirmation hearings, Laird was surprised to learn details of the wiretapping of Colonel Pursley's home phone. Though Laird had defended Kissinger publicly, he was never absolutely sure that Kissinger had not been trying to spy on conversations between Pursley and Laird.[10]

There was also Kissinger's handling of the October 1973 war in the Middle East (the Yom Kippur War) only a month after he'd been sworn in as secretary of state, and while still retaining his role as Nixon's national security advisor.

Laird thought it was gross overreaction by Kissinger to call a worldwide nuclear alert without waking up Nixon to tell him. The Russians were immediately alarmed; the alert was called off after a few hours, but not before it had leaked to the press.

What upset Laird even more were Kissinger's repeated intemperate rebukes of NATO allies for not joining in America's military airlift of arms to the embattled Israelis. NATO had been set up primarily as a European counter to the military threat posed by the Soviet Union and its Warsaw Pact satellites. It was never intended to get involved with Middle East conflicts. The criticism was too much for Laird, who had carefully cultivated the defense secretaries of the NATO countries and understood them well. In his final January 1974 interviews as domestic counselor, Laird had gone out of his way to criticize Kissinger publicly. In what was described by a reporter as "an uncharacteristically loud and angry voice," Laird blasted Kissinger for "damaging" relations with NATO nations. During his four years as defense secretary, Laird observed, NATO foreign ministers had "always" made it clear that each nation would forge its own Middle East policy. "*Anybody that knows anything about NATO knows about that.*"

Kissinger knew Laird was right and privately asked Laird to help him smooth out some of the rough waters. Laird knew precisely what the problem was. Kissinger had never been a politician. He was authoritarian by nature and was more comfortable dealing with Arab strongmen and Communist dictators than the elected leaders of independent democracies.[11]

The sharpest and most consistent disagreement Laird had with Kissinger was the latter's push, under the rubric of détente, to sign agreements with the Soviet Union that, in Laird's view, benefited them more than the United States. Laird's first article for *Reader's Digest*, in February 1974 was as straightforwardly critical on this subject as its title heralded: "Let's Not Fool Ourselves about U.S.-Soviet Detente." He argued that too many had assumed détente meant true cooperation between the two superpowers, when, at best, it was only "a relaxation of tensions between nations." Laird then ticked off the various "disquieting indications that the Soviet Union might look upon *detente* as an opportunity to lull the United States into complacency while gaining strategic global advantages."[12]

As secretary of defense, Laird had been committed to negotiation of the 1972 Anti-Ballistic Missile and SALT I agreements. He wasn't happy with everything in them, but he was supportive, in part because the expert he had appointed in 1969 to represent him and the Pentagon in the talks, Paul Nitze, had reassured him that the agreements were something the U.S. military could back. Nitze had stayed on the job to act as the Pentagon eyes and ears when SALT II negotiations began in November 1972. By late 1973 he had become the only U.S. SALT negotiator who dared to disagree with Kissinger in public about the talks. Nitze's private assessment to Laird was that Kissinger was not a tough negotiator and was too anxious to conclude a SALT II agreement in order to save Nixon from Watergate. That insight from Nitze had been a driving force behind Laird's analysis of détente in his *Reader's Digest* article. Four months after that published analysis, in June 1974, Nitze quit the Nixon administration in disgust.

Laird meanwhile was pushing a new idea tied to détente. Instead of spending so much time negotiating a U.S.-Soviet *strategic* arms agreement, it would be better for the world if the two superpowers and other countries met to reduce *conventional* arms sales and deployments. In a July 1974 interview with *Forbes* magazine, Laird opined: "To me, the most important agreement that can be worked out in the next four or five years is to involve the Soviet Union, the U.S. and all other arms-producing countries to limit the sale and delivery of conventional military equipment into the Middle East, Southeast Asia, Latin America and Africa. Hey, I'm all for *detente,* but *detente* means easing tensions and a reduction in the weapons of war and I have not seen any movement in that area."[13]

Ford ignored Laird's advice on this score because Kissinger was calling the shots on foreign policy and still wanted a strategic arms deal with the Soviets. As a result, in November 1974, an arms accord was signed between Ford and Brezhnev at a summit in Vladivostok. Laird met with Kissinger on his return and hammered his former colleague. "Henry, you're making out like détente is what it isn't. We still have to preserve our own strength at the same time. If you say you're in a détente with the Soviet Union and you don't keep up our military strength and keep up our NATO partnership, it's folly." As Kissinger seemed to bristle, Laird added with a mischievous grin: "Look Henry, if I had your kind of détente with my wife now, I'd say we were close to divorce!"

He didn't stop with Kissinger. Though Laird was gentler with the president, he repeatedly raised his objections about détente with Ford. He also leaned on the man he had recommended as deputy national security advisor, General Brent Scowcroft. "Mel used to call and rant and rave and shout, 'How can we be doing this to the president?' and so on and so forth," Scowcroft recalled. Both he and Kissinger remained friends with Laird because his complaints were only a genuine difference in policy positions. "Mel doesn't do these things personally, you know," Scowcroft added.[14] Laird still respected Kissinger and considered him a friend for decades after the two men butted heads. Laird's motto was, "It's alright to disagree but never to be disagreeable."

Laird continued to use used the pages of *Reader's Digest,* the world's largest-circulation magazine, to make his case against détente. In one article, an interview with his longtime friend West German Chancellor Helmut Schmidt, Laird highlighted Schmidt's pithy disagreement with the Kissinger-Ford version of détente. "While we should persist in our efforts toward *detente,* we cannot afford to delude ourselves about the danger in the continuing Soviet military buildup," Schmidt argued. "It is useless for sheep to pass resolutions in favor of vegetarianism while the wolf remains of a different opinion."[15]

The most important détente article by Laird appeared in the July 1975 issue of *Reader's Digest* under the title, "Is *This* Detente?" The United States had been making "major concessions and numerous gestures of good will to induce the Soviet Union to help defuse world powder kegs that could explode into war," he began. While there was still a hope that the effort would succeed, "it would be dangerously foolish to confuse hope with reality." Laird laid out the "unpleasant facts" about how the Soviets had taken many opportunities to enable aggression by their allies (including Hanoi) and had even cheated on the SALT I and ABM agreements by installing and testing new missile and radar systems.[16]

Ford read the article and ordered a point-by-point analysis from Kissinger, who conceded that Laird had the facts right but saw the interpretation differently.[17] Ford invited both men to lunch on July 23 to watch them go head-to-head before he left for more negotiation with the Soviets at the thirty-five-nation Conference on Security and Cooperation in Europe held in Helsinki, Finland.[18] From that lunch, and subsequent conversations with Ford, Laird saw that détente was on the wane with Ford, as was Kissinger's influence. Laird immediately stopped criticizing the Ford administration about it.

It was certainly not Laird alone who finally hobbled Kissinger over his détente. The other notable opponents were James Schlesinger, Senator Henry "Scoop" Jackson, Ronald Reagan, and leaders of American labor unions.[19] The AFL-CIO set up the most personal embarrassment for Ford over détente when it invited Nobel Prize–winning Russian dissident Alexander Solzhenitsyn to address a Washington banquet on June 30. The capital was rocked when word passed that President Ford had refused to receive the Nobel laureate at the White House. Initially his spokesperson said he was "too busy," and then that Ford "did not like meetings that are symbolic and empty of substance." The real reason, the press soon uncovered, was that Kissinger had advised Ford that it would upset the Soviets too much if he met with their most effective native dissident. The snub reverberated when Laird, Senator Jackson, Schlesinger, and U.N. Ambassador Daniel Patrick Moynihan attended the labor banquet and sat at the head table with Solzhenitsyn. "About the only thing this group has in common is its lack of admiration for Secretary of State Kissinger," *New York Times* reporter Leslie Gelb wrote after the event. As expected, Solzhenitsyn's speech was a towering indictment of the Soviet Union and the dangers of détente with such an untrustworthy partner.

Ford reversed himself right after the dinner, realizing that Kissinger had handed conservative Republicans an issue with which to bludgeon him in the future. In an effort to undo the damage, he issued an open invitation to

Solzhenitsyn to come to the White House, but Solzhenitsyn said he was not interested.[20]

"Détente" had become a bad word at the White House, and Kissinger had to reinvent himself and his own definition of détente. Instead of a being a warm and fuzzy cold war–thawing process, as he had implied in the past, Kissinger started calling détente "a means to regulate a competitive relationship," after Laird's dissent was published in the July *Reader's Digest*. A few months later Kissinger again redefined détente as something that was "designed to prevent Soviet expansion." In a March 1976 speech President Ford declared: "We are going to forget the use of the word *detente*."

～✦～

Citizen Laird also involved himself in counseling Ford on domestic issues such as the sluggish economy and energy situation. In 1975 he played a hidden role in "saving New York City." In May of that year New York City Mayor Abraham Beame and New York Governor Hugh Carey asked for an urgent meeting with President Ford. The city had overspent and undertaxed and needed $1 billion in credit to prevent imminent bankruptcy. The federal government was already subsidizing 25 percent of the city's budget through welfare and other programs, and Ford said he wasn't willing to spend a penny more. His view was in keeping with that of the general public, which felt that New Yorkers had gotten themselves into the mess and there was no reason that taxpayers in Iowa or Alaska or other states should have to bail them out.

Over the summer months Carey and Beame worked on various state plans to forestall a default on bonds and obligations. When it appeared their efforts would not be enough, Carey began lobbying Congress, where he had once served as a representative. But, in an appearance before the National Press Club on October 29, Ford promised to veto any congressional bail-out legislation. Perhaps, he said, it was time for the city to declare bankruptcy and let the reorganization of its government be handled by federal bankruptcy courts. He had been reassured by Federal Reserve Board Chairman Arthur Burns that there would not be a devastating ripple effect on the U.S. banking system if the city defaulted. The next morning's New York *Daily News* headline said, "Ford to City: Drop Dead."

In desperation, Carey turned to Laird for help. This is Carey's memory of how his appeal to Laird went: "I'm getting nowhere with Jerry," Carey said. "I thought I had a good relationship with Jerry. He knows I walked into the middle of this New York City mess when I came in as governor. It's been cold water all around. Can you help me? What should I do?"

"I can't tell you over the phone what you should do," Laird said. "Have you got an airplane?"

"Yeah, I've got an airplane, a state airplane."

"Well, get in the airplane and make believe you're going to New York [City] and turn south and come to Dulles [Airport, outside of Washington] and meet me," said Laird. "Bring your golf clubs and we'll talk this over."

"I haven't got any time to play golf," sputtered Carey.

"If you don't come down, I can't tell you," replied Laird.

"Alright," Carey groused.

"I'll pull up near your airplane. I'll have a long, sleek, silver car. You'll find me in the back and see how I live," Laird said, enjoying every minute of the game he was playing with the governor of New York.

Carey said Laird indeed showed up in a limo with his golf clubs and a fully stocked bar in the back. "This is how I live," Laird smiled.

"So what am I going to do about this?" Carey pressed him.

"No, no, be patient," replied Laird. "You brought your sticks? We're going to Burning Tree. We're going to play eighteen holes of golf and I'm going to play you for money. Then, when we've played the eighteen holes, if you settle up—then, *maybe,* I can give you some help."

They played, and Laird won a $100 wager. He made Carey pay up on the eighteenth fairway in full view of the picture window of the clubhouse. Carey looked up and realized Laird had filled the "gallery" with political cronies to see him skunk the governor at golf. "I looked up at all our colleagues. Everybody I could think of was looking through the window. Mel had advertised he was going to play me, that the governor of New York was going to give him $100 when he beat me in golf," Carey laughed.

Laird took the money. "You've done your part of the bargain," he said, then led Carey to a quiet corner of the clubhouse for a drink.

"I'll tell you what your problem is," Laird said. "Jerry's been told by *some-body* that when New York collapses, the financial center of the United States may move west to Chicago. Your [Democratic] friend [Chicago Mayor Richard] Daley heard that, and that's why you're not getting votes out of Chicago or Illinois."

"Who's doing this?" Carey asked.

Laird paused for a moment, leaned closer, and lowered his voice. "Well, Rummy comes from Illinois," Laird hinted, his eyebrows arching. "Rummy" was Donald Rumsfeld, Ford's chief of staff who had once been a congressman from Illinois. "Rummy is not averse to making friends with Mayor Daley. *Rummy* is your problem for the time being."

Carey was surprised. Was there indeed a conspiracy to use New York City's plight to turn Chicago, America's "second city," into its first city?

"I know Don," Carey responded in slight disbelief. "We weren't enemies. I'll go see him."

"No," said Laird. "You won't change Rummy's mind. He's having some fun with you on this. Go visit with Daley in Chicago instead."

So Carey did, and learned that Daley had indeed been influenced by the siren song of some Chicago bankers who saw golden opportunity in the collapse of New York. Carey appealed to his sense of fair play and turned Daley around.

Laird also followed up with a dizzying array of telephone calls and visits with key players. "First, I took care of Arthur [Burns] and Rummy. I said, 'Rummy, you're making a helluva mistake here. We can't let New York go down the drain!'" Rumsfeld went along. He hadn't been deeply opposed in the first place but had simply seen little benefit for the White House to help out the city—and he had seen the upside for Chicago if New York City belly-flopped into bankruptcy. Laird also bent Vice President Rockefeller's ear. The stumbling block there was both personal and political: Rockefeller didn't like Carey and had no interest in helping either him or Beame, both Democrats. But Laird brought Rockefeller up short. He pointedly reminded Rocky that, as governor of New York from 1959 to 1973, he had personally contributed to the problem that Carey inherited. Rockefeller sheepishly agreed. "Yeah," he laughed, "I drank the champagne and Carey's got the hangover." He said he would set aside party differences and help Democrats Carey and Beame. "He didn't want to be helpful at the start, but he came around," Laird recalled.

Aside from some Laird back-patting on Capitol Hill, there were other touches. As a board member of Metropolitan Life of New York, Laird encouraged its president, Richard Shinn, to step up to the plate. Shinn was named chairman of the city's new management council, and MetLife became a major purchaser of New York City bonds. Laird even asked Helmut Schmidt for help. During a subsequent conversation with President Ford, the West German chancellor found a perfect moment to make an unforgettable statement. While speaking with Schmidt about the European economy, Ford asked, "How's the Bundesbank? How's the mark?"

"Mr. President, never mind the Bundesbank or the mark!" Schmidt responded bluntly. "If you let New York go broke, the dollar is worth shit!"

Having prompted such inventive lines of influence to the Oval Office—and neutralized Rumsfeld, Rockefeller, and Burns—Laird moved in for the coup de grace: an arm-twisting session with Ford himself. Laird complimented the president for holding tough, which had forced Beame and Carey to come up with rigorous fiscal reforms. Laird summarized some of the calls he had made to various New York City financial wisemen and congressional leaders who felt it was time to help the city. "You've got to do this right away before this falls through the cracks," he concluded. "We can't have this happening in New York City when it is being worked out in a way that will satisfy most of the issues."

Ford was impressed and agreed to meet with Governor Carey again. Carey outlined further reforms and pledges New York City and the state were prepared to make in return for federal aid. Ford made the deal immediately. On November 26, in a nationally televised address, the president asked Congress to approve legislation making up to $2.3 billion available to the city annually—which would be repaid at 1 percent higher than the prevailing interest rate. The process had been painful, and the Big Apple had to make do with reduced services, but in the end both the city and state kept up their ends of the bargain. Carey gave substantial credit to the advice and hard work of citizen Laird. "It would never have happened without Mel. He saved New York City."[21]

ᴡᴡ

With all his meddling in the nation's business, Laird had the responsibilities of his "day job" as the senior counselor for national and international affairs with *Reader's Digest*. It was a job for which DeWitt Wallace, the most successful magazine publisher in American history, had courted Laird for nearly two decades. Founded by DeWitt and Lila Wallace in 1922, *Reader's Digest* quickly made its mark with a mixture of stories and anecdotes full of humor and drama, as well as flag-waving patriotism, praise for self-reliance, faith in God and capitalism, and muckraking reports on the evils of Communism and excessive American government spending. Many of those pieces were condensed from stories other magazines had published.

On its thirtieth anniversary in 1952, the same year Laird first ran for Congress, *Reader's Digest* circulation had soared to 9.5 million in the United States and 6 million abroad. Two years later, after the Republicans had taken a bath in the midterm election, the conservative DeWitt Wallace sat down and studied a directory of the Eighty-fourth Congress looking for surviving conservatives he ought to get to know. The biography of Melvin Robert Laird impressed him, not just because of his whiz-kid style or his party affiliation, but also because he was the son of a Presbyterian minister in Wisconsin. Both DeWitt's father and Lila's father had been Presbyterian ministers in the neighboring state of Minnesota. DeWitt invited Laird to New York for lunch and the two hit it off immediately.[22]

During Laird's final days as secretary of defense in late 1972, Wallace made him promise that he would accept no other job offer before *Reader's Digest* was able to put together an attractive employment package. Laird was quickly drawn back into the Nixon administration, and Wallace had to wait. In November 1973 an old friend of Laird's, Joe McConnell, who had headed several large corporations, invited Laird to a round of golf and a game of bridge in Florida so they could talk over job opportunities. Also in the party was Al Cole, the business manager for *Reader's Digest*, who took Laird aside in the afternoon and asked him not to make any decisions until he visited Wallace.

Laird soon found himself and Barbara being wined and dined in unforgettable fashion. They were flown by private plane to the Wallaces' 105-acre wooded estate in Mount Kisko, New York, overlooking Lake Byram. On the walls of the twenty-two-room mansion were some of the most valuable privately held paintings in the world—by van Gogh, Renoir, Degas, Cezanne, Matisse, Modigliani, and Monet. What Laird remembered most from the evening was the gold cup from which Lila Wallace drank. Laird noticed the gold was so pure that Mrs. Wallace was subtly changing its shape as she applied pressure with her fingers. He asked where she had acquired it, and, with an "oh-this-little-thing" expression, she explained that it was a golden chalice from King Tut's tomb. As a sponsor of the traveling Tutankhamen exhibit in the United States, she had "borrowed" the cup for a little while. (Considering that the Wallaces' arts and museum donations went into the hundreds of millions of dollars, no curators were likely to complain.)

Wallace and Cole made Laird an offer he couldn't refuse. He wouldn't have to move to the *Reader's Digest*'s Pleasantville, New York, office. Instead he could have a Washington office, secretarial assistance (longtime secretary Laurie Hawley and newcomer Kathy Weaver), a chauffeured car, and an expense account. Wallace had left two spaces blank on the contract—the amount of Laird's salary and the length of employment. Wallace and Cole told him to write in whatever he wanted. Laird penned in a six-figure salary and an initial ten-year term. The contract required his regular appearances at Reader's Digest Association offices around the world to offer editorial, political, governmental, postal, and trade advice on national and international issues. He was soon sincerely telling friends, "I think I've got the best job in the world. It's just made for me!"[23]

That's how Laird, one of the most powerful politicians of the day, went to work for a magazine. He had not been bluffing all those months when he said he would not run for president or any other office. Laird, the politician who was then only fifty-one, would be Laird the editor, writer, and advisor for nearly twice as long as he had spent in Congress or at the Pentagon. In the next few years, as Laird traveled the world visiting the outposts of *Reader's Digest,* his picture appeared in newspapers around the world, and he used the bully pulpit provided overseas to speak out on politics at home and abroad. He was an international celebrity who never failed to draw the press wherever he went.

One of the more memorable outings occurred during his first swing through the Asian offices of the magazine in September 1975. Laird had invited Jack Mills, then a tobacco lobbyist, along for the tour, which included visits with Japanese Emperor Hirohito and Yasuhiro Nakasone (then secretary-general of the Liberal-Democratic Party), as well as Madame Chiang Kai-shek in Taiwan. Mills remembered that when the two checked into their hotel rooms in Tokyo, Laird's room was full of flowers, candy, and fruit baskets, along with a welcoming card from Tongsun Park, a soon-to-be-notorious South Korean lobbyist. Though Park was not yet embroiled in a bribery scandal with members of Congress, Laird already had pegged him as a suspicious character. In 1970, when he was secretary of defense, Laird had warned the State Department that Park and his Korean lobby were working against Laird's plans to reduce South Korea's dependence on U.S. troops for its defense. At the time Laird had advised the Justice Department to investigate Park's dealings with Congress, but he was ignored.

"Let's have dinner with this guy," Laird told Mills. "I don't trust the guy, but if we have dinner with him, we can get it over with. Let's find the most expensive damn restaurant we can and stick him with the bill." Mills decided to enjoy himself in high fashion, so he ordered the most expensive steak on the menu, a $200 bottle of champagne, and brandy. "I figured out that my bill alone in American money was about $550," said Mills. Laird had warned Mills that Park would try to fix them up with female companionship. Two women approached them and Laird kicked Mills under the table in warning. "Don't worry," Mills laughed. As his final "joke," Laird took Park aside at one point in the evening and said, "You may not know it, but Mills is a very big lobbyist in Washington. This is a big guy, not a small guy. And he was a little hurt when he walked in his room and didn't see any flowers." When Mills got back to his room it was filled with flowers and food. The two Americans arranged to have the bounty moved to a Tokyo hospital when they checked out of the hotel.[24]

There was one man, first and foremost, whom President Ford wanted to oversee his 1976 campaign: Melvin Laird. Ford pressured Laird to accept the challenge during a round of golf at Burning Tree on March 29, 1975. Laird gently declined, saying he could not expect his new employers to loan him to the campaign. However, in typical Laird fashion, he was full of advice.[25] The biggest challenge, Laird said, would come from Ronald Reagan. At the time Laird mistakenly predicted that, when it came down to it, Reagan would not actually run. Knowing Reagan, Laird felt the former governor's loyalty to the party would preclude such a divisive intraparty contest.

Still, there was a growing group of conservatives around Reagan rallying and urging him to run, so Laird thought it prudent to try sidetracking them. Vice President Rockefeller was a lightning rod for the Republican right wing, which could use him as a reason to reject Ford. Laird firmly believed Ford should not dump Rockefeller from the ticket because it would make Ford look disloyal and reactionary. Privately, Laird thought Rockefeller would actually be an asset to Ford in the election. If Ford was forced by the radical right to take more conservative positions during the campaign, Rockefeller would provide balance that would please the centrists in the party. So Laird publicly floated a compromise idea to appease the Republican conservatives: perhaps the 1976 convention should be an "open" convention on the question of a running mate for Ford. Laird hoped that if the Reaganites thought their man had a chance of being nominated vice president at the convention, they might not press as hard for the presidential nomination. And Laird believed Rockefeller would win anyway. The ploy failed because Reagan's acolytes didn't bite. They told journalists their man would never consider second place on the ticket.[26]

It was Ford's first campaign manager, Howard (Bo) Callaway, who was the prime mover to dump Rockefeller. At Ford's request Callaway had resigned as secretary of the army in June 1975 to take the campaign job that Laird had turned down. Laird thought Callaway was a bush-league politician without the credentials to manage a national campaign. Callaway was eventually fired, but not before he had done some serious damage. As soon as he was hired Callaway had wasted no time in sniping at Rockefeller. He named the reelection organization the "President Ford Committee," with no mention of Rockefeller. At campaign headquarters all the photographs were of Ford, with Rockefeller nowhere to be seen. In late July, when goaded by reporters, Callaway said flat out that Rockefeller was Ford's "number one problem."

Laird had persuaded David Packard to be finance chairman for the Ford campaign, but he quit because Callaway was such a poor manager. About the same time, a frustrated Rockefeller was tired of getting mixed signals of support from Ford. So, as a test of sorts, during Rockefeller's weekly meeting with the president on October 28, he offered to remove himself from the 1976 campaign. Ford eagerly accepted.

⌇

On October 16 five charter members of the Kitchen Cabinet met with Ford for what turned out to be a rough session. Bryce Harlow often started the round-table discussions. After acknowledging the good things that Ford had done for the Republican Party, and a compliment about his "vitality," Harlow cited eight criticisms the outside advisors had identified about the Ford White House. The most serious was the appearance of "internal anarchy" and feuding at the top. Laird agreed that something had to be done to get the White House in order, but knew that wholesale firings were not the way to go at that point in the campaign. However, Ford had already been forming a plan to reorganize his administration's leadership, and the Harlow lecture sped up his implementation of that plan.[27]

Ford was particularly unsettled by his relationship with Schlesinger, the man whom Ford, as vice president, had said would be the first to be fired if he became president. Schlesinger routinely butted heads with Ford on defense issues, showing little deference to the office of president. Ford decided he would offer the contentious Schlesinger another job in government and make Donald Rumsfeld the new secretary of defense. Dick Cheney would be promoted to White House chief of staff to replace Rumsfeld. Knowing that the Schlesinger dismissal would anger conservatives, Ford planned to mollify them by removing Kissinger from his second job as national security advisor and promoting his deputy, the conservative Brent Scowcroft, to the post. Ib found out the reorganization, Ford wanted to replace CIA Director William Colby with George H. W. Bush, who was in China serving as America's chief liaison officer. The prickly part of the equation was Schlesinger, who would not go willingly. When, on October 28, Rockefeller unexpectedly offered to announce he would not run for the vice presidency, Ford considered it a political gift that would "appease" Reaganites even more than the Kissinger demotion.

On Halloween, October 31, President Ford called Laird in Paris with Rumsfeld on hand in the Oval Office. Ford wanted to run the plan by Laird. The president informed Laird of Rockefeller's "offer" to bow out and the plan to fire Schlesinger. Unhesitatingly Laird told the president the whole thing was a "stupid" idea. "I can understand that you want to dump Schlesinger tonight. But don't dump Rockefeller—and, if you do, you must *absolutely* not do it at the same time as Schlesinger!" said Laird.

Laird recalled later that he understood why Ford wanted to drop Schlesinger. "Ford was a smart guy, but Schlesinger was always kind of speaking down to him. He had such a superior attitude that Ford just couldn't stand it. After all, Ford knew defense—he knew defense better than Schlesinger. He'd been on the House Defense Appropriations Committee for twenty years while Schlesinger was down there teaching economics at the University of Virginia." It was a budget issue that was Ford's final straw. Schlesinger was balking at Ford's proposed defense budget, refusing to take what the president offered and complaining publicly about the "deep, savage and arbitrary cuts" he was being asked to accept by Congress.

"Schlesinger wouldn't give me a 'yes' or 'no' answer as to whether he'd support the budget. And I can't have a secretary of defense that won't support the budget," Ford raged over the phone to Laird.

"Well, that's true," Laird said, trying to steer the president away from a rash announcement. "But I think we can work that out. This isn't the time, on a budget issue, to get rid of Schlesinger."

"My mind is made up. I just can't get along with him."

Laird gave up on Schlesinger and tried to save Rockefeller. He told Ford that "dumping Rockefeller isn't going to get Reagan to pull out of the convention."

"I tell you," Ford countered, "the Reagan group will crucify me if I don't make that announcement soon."

"Jerry, they're going to oppose you whether you dump Rockefeller or not. This is just ridiculous to do this so far in advance."

Laird argued that Rockefeller, in the last analysis, was likely to help rather than hurt the Ford ticket. Laird's bottom line was that, no matter what Ford decided, he should not blurt out the news without greasing the political machine first. "Can't you wait until I get back there?" Laird pleaded. "We need to talk more about it because this is a very bad political mistake. It's almost as bad as the way you handled the [Nixon] pardon." The two men argued over the phone for more than an hour, but Ford couldn't be influenced much. The president only agreed to think it over again, and perhaps delay the sequence of events.[28]

However the following day, Saturday, Ford learned that *Newsweek* had the scoop on part of his plans and was going to press on Monday with the story. The president wanted to break the news himself, so he sped up the timetable, firing Schlesinger forthwith during a Saturday morning session that was "one of the most disagreeable conversations I have ever had," according to Ford.

On Monday, November 3, Ford announced the sweeping personnel shifts and the fact that Nelson Rockefeller would not be his running mate in 1976. Once again, as with the Nixon pardon, it had the opposite effect of what Ford had intended. "I am not appeased," said Reagan, who formally announced his challenge of Ford for the nomination two weeks later. Opinion makers wrote that the "Halloween Massacre" was reminiscent of Nixon and had demonstrated Ford's weakness. Reagan jumped ahead of Ford in the polls.[29]

In retrospect Laird said, "I always felt that if I hadn't been in Paris, I could have stopped that, or at least gotten it timed properly. Rockefeller had been as loyal as you can get. He was sort of a consensus guy. He would have helped us much more than any other candidate on the ticket. I guarantee you, we could have won that election."

Many suspected at the time that an ambitious Rumsfeld, who had been critical of Rockefeller, was the hidden hand behind the whole imbroglio. While Rumsfeld denied playing any puppet-master role, Laird put some of the responsibility on him. "It was all just terrible and stupid. I love Rummy but I blame him for that a little bit. How could he let Ford do it?"[30] Ford never regretted firing Schlesinger, but the Rockefeller abandonment was an entirely different matter. "It was the biggest political mistake of my life," he later concluded. "And it was one of the few cowardly things I did in my life."[31]

❧

Starting in late 1975 Kissinger became a juicy target for Reaganites and a campaign liability. The secretary offered to resign at one point, but Ford refused to accept. Laird wholeheartedly agreed that Kissinger should stay on through the rest of Ford's term. In 1974 Laird had advised that it would be better for Ford if Kissinger left. But by mid-1975 Laird felt it was too close to the election season to make the change. So, from the summer of 1975 until the election, Laird often defended the secretary against putative "dump Kissinger" movements. Laird was consistently rumored to be Kissinger's replacement, and Kissinger publicly favored that idea, even joking about it. Magazine publisher Malcolm S. Forbes sat down with both men and inquired of Kissinger "how it felt to fall from Deity to Devil." Kissinger laughed and poked Laird, asking: "Mel, why were you in my office the other day with that interior decorator?"[32]

During the 1976 election campaign, however, Laird publicly stated more than once that Kissinger planned to step aside if Ford was elected. "We will have a new Secretary of State in the next Ford Administration," Laird matter of factly told Wisconsin reporters as he campaigned for Ford in that state's April primary. "Henry knows that. He will bow out because he knows he should not serve beyond the present term." Laird explained he had had several discussions with Kissinger about it, advising him not to "pull a McNamara" and stay too long.[33]

Ford narrowly beat back the Reagan challenge at the Republican National Convention held in Kansas City in August. He had more than a little assistance from the gracious Rockefeller, who delivered the New York delegation's votes to Ford. During the convention Laird stumped hard to get Ford to announce he was keeping Rockefeller on the ticket, but the president chose Kansas Senator Robert Dole instead; Rockefeller gamely nominated Dole.[34] Another convention surprise, which was a last-minute addition by Ford himself in his acceptance speech, was a challenge to the Democratic nominee, Georgia Governor Jimmy Carter: "I'm ready and eager to go before the American people and debate the real issues face to face with Jimmy Carter," the president said. "The American people have the right to know first-hand exactly where both of us stand." It had been sixteen years since presidential debates had been held; the last ones had been the 1960 Nixon-Kennedy debates.

At the point Ford issued the challenge he was running thirty-four points behind Carter in the polls, so some aides argued that he had nothing to lose. Laird disagreed. He thought Ford's best chances were to continue to appear presidential, not share the podium with a peanut farmer. Besides, he knew Ford was not a gifted debater. "He doesn't think rapidly on his feet when challenged," Laird said later. On several occasions during debates on the House Floor someone else, such as Congressman Laird, had to step in for Minority Leader Ford if the talk was fast moving and contentious. "Jerry does well if he is prepared and knows what he's going to say, but when there's give-and-take—well, I just thought he wasn't good at that and shouldn't get involved in it."[35]

Ford did better than Laird expected in the first presidential debate. But in the second he made a serious foreign policy gaffe: "There is no Soviet domination of Eastern Europe," he mistakenly stated. It was enough to stall the momentum of his campaign, which had been rapidly closing the gap on Carter's lead. Ford was ultimately defeated by Carter on November 2, 1976, by a mere 2 percent margin. The electoral vote for Carter was the narrowest presidential victory in sixty years. "What if I hadn't pardoned Nixon? How many people had voted against me because of that?" Ford asked himself afterward.

❧

On January 18, 1977, the Fords were preparing to leave the White House, and the president arranged one last gift for his wife. He lured her away from the

White House to a private dinner party, and, while they were gone, the Marine Band slipped into the White House along with some surprise guests. Betty Ford had known the band would be there that night for a photo session, so their presence at the foot of the grand staircase was not unexpected when she and Jerry arrived home.

With the guests in hiding, the president said, "So long as we're here, why don't we have a last dance?" She smiled and asked the band to play "Thanks for the Memories." As the two twirled around the floor, from the hallway emerged other couples gliding onto the floor, including the Lairds, the Harlows, and the Kissingers—more than one hundred friends in all, dancing around the First Couple. Betty Ford gasped in surprise and began crying and hugging and kissing friends as the dance drew to a close. "Seeing her so happy was one of the greatest joys of my life," Ford said later.[36]

It was the end of an era of sorts for Melvin Laird, too. His party was out of power, and he was free to jump completely into private life.

47

Boardroom Dramas

CENTRAL WISCONSIN DAIRY FARMER Meldon Maguire was bone tired as he drove home on a rural Wisconsin road one September night in 1997. The thirty-five-year-old farmer had tended his forty dairy cows, put up hay on his farm, and spent the evening at a meeting of the town board, where he was an elected supervisor. As weary as he was, Maguire kept a lookout for the number-one threat on Highway 153: white-tail deer. As an experienced emergency first-responder, Maguire had seen too many deer versus car encounters along this road. Up ahead in his headlights, Maguire saw the latest casualty—a dead deer on the road and a white stretch limo with its hood up, steam hissing from the radiator. Maguire steered his pickup truck to the shoulder of the road, donned a reflective red vest, and stepped out to help. One of the men from the limo approached and introduced himself as Reed Hall, director of the Marshfield Clinic, along with his wife, Ellie. Then Hall turned to the portly gentleman near him and said, "This is Dr. Henry Kissinger." Maguire chuckled, thinking how interesting it was that a doctor at the Marshfield Clinic had the same name as a former secretary of state.

After determining that no one was seriously hurt, Maguire dragged the deer off the road and agreed to drive the group to Marshfield in his extended-cab truck. He pushed aside some fast-food refuse to make room for the Halls in the back, with Nobel laureate Kissinger riding shotgun. It was only after they were well down the road that it began to occur to Maguire that this was *the* Henry Kissinger. The tip-off was some small talk about Kissinger's attendance just five days earlier at the funeral of Princess Diana, and his anxiousness about keeping President Ford waiting in Marshfield. "I almost asked him a couple times what he did for a living before it dawned on me who he really was," Maguire recalled.[1]

Kissinger and Ford and a host of other luminaries were descending on Marshfield that night for the dedication the next day of the Melvin R. Laird Center for medical research at Marshfield Clinic. Laird wasn't fond of people naming things after themselves. During his time in Congress he had routinely voted against naming projects after living people. Once out of public service Laird had been approached on several occasions to lend his name to an edifice or project, but he declined. Then, in 1994, Bob Froehlke had come to him with a proposition. The Marshfield Clinic was literally bursting at the seams. A new center was needed, and Froehlke, who had become a prodigious fund-raiser in private life, knew there was only one way to do it: talk Laird into letting it be named after him.[2] Laird quickly agreed. In October 1994 Health and Human

Services Secretary Donna Shalala announced the Laird Center project during a dual-site press conference in Washington and Marshfield. Having once been chancellor of the University of Wisconsin at Madison, Shalala was a longtime Laird friend and booster.[3]

Once Laird had agreed to put his name on the center's marquee, raising the needed $12.6 million from Laird's many friends and fans had been a snap for Froehlke. In the first two months two *Reader's Digest* charities pledged $2 million, and David Packard pledged $1 million. Froehlke had visited personally with Packard at his Palo Alto, California, home. After reminiscing about their Pentagon days, Packard asked Froehlke point blank what the real purpose for the meeting was, at which point Froehlke explained the need for a Laird Center for medical education and research in Wisconsin.

"What do you want me to give?" Packard asked.

Froehlke thought for a few seconds and replied: "Dave, I think it would be great if you would contribute $1 million

Packard's reply was: "You got it," and he wrote out the check on the spot. Later he called Laird and said, "Bob let me off the hook too easily; I was prepared to go up to $5 million!"

Laird himself never had to make a single phone call asking for money. A total of 1,370 people made donations, "many of whom didn't know that there was a Marshfield Clinic. But they knew Mel Laird," Froehlke said.[4]

On dedication day, September 12, 1997, Laird sat on a stage surrounded by political movers and shakers. After decades in politics and private life he had returned to his first doctor's office and to the first love that he found in Congress—the promotion of health care. The day was a particularly heartwarming one for Laird as he sat beside his second wife, Carole Howard Laird, whom he married in 1993. Children and grandchildren were there to swap stories—son John and his wife, Nancy, daughter Alison and her husband, Raymond Large, son David and his wife, Felice; grandchildren Raymond Large III, John David Large, Connor Laird, and Harry Laird; and step-daughter Kimberly Dalgleish with her husband, Jim, and daughter, Carly.

The keynote speaker, President Ford, said, "Long before today's talk of a health care crisis in America, Mel Laird was legislating in hopes of averting a crisis." Former colleagues from Congress were there, such as Bob Michel, John Rhodes, and Gaylord Nelson. Representative David Obey and Governor Tommy Thompson, who would later serve President George W. Bush as Health and Human Services secretary, were also on hand. Kissinger praised the man who had frequently been his sparring partner in the White House. He speculated aloud that Laird had probably arranged the encounter with the deer the night before. "He trained the deer for weeks and he had it on the side of the road," Kissinger opined as Laird erupted into laughter. It was a salute from America's Machiavelli to the man from Marshfield, who had been more than his equal in the halls of power.

The two-story, fifty-two-thousand-square-foot Melvin R. Laird Center helped to make the Marshfield Clinic one of the ten largest medical research complexes in the United States. Congressman Laird had secured the clinic's first federal research grant in the 1950s. Within four decades, and with the addition of the Laird Center, the clinic boasted more than 750 scientists and physicians leading five hundred studies involving more than thirty-six thousand patients. These researchers publish hundreds of scientific papers each year in prestigious scientific books and journals, focused on pioneering applications of molecular genetics combined with preventive medicine, as well as rural health and safety research. The Laird Center itself houses the National Farm Medicine Center, the Center for Medical Genetics, and the Marshfield Epidemiology Center.[5] In 2008, the Laird Center more than tripled in size with the addition of a 129,000-square-foot building. Funding for the $40 million wing began with a $10 million federal grant that Obey attached to a House Health Appropriations Subcommittee bill. It secured easy passage because the language included the fact that, in addition to the research the money would fund, it was also a way to honor one of the subcommittee's most distinguished members.

~⚓~

One of the rooms at the Laird Center holds a full-scale replica of Laird's office—not the one in the Pentagon, but the one at his more enduring job, the *Reader's Digest*. Laird and the magazine were born in the same year, 1922. And since the magazine's founders, DeWitt and Lila Wallace, were the Midwest children of Presbyterian ministers, their vision for the magazine and the country was the same as that of another Midwest Presbyterian preacher's kid, Mel Laird. The populist magazine, which promoted flag-waving, God-loving Americanism, was precisely the right fit for a populist politician with identical beliefs. Laird's position at the *Digest* for more than three decades (under the title of "Senior Counselor for National and International Affairs") has been both ubiquitous and invisible. Most of the *Digest*'s staffers had no idea what exactly he did, but no *Digest* CEO or chairman of the board felt the magazine could have been as successful without him. As he had been in his political life, Laird was even more effective behind the scenes than out front.

The first issue of the *Digest,* produced in February 1922, circulated five thousand copies in the United States. Its first foreign office was opened in London in 1938, and two years later in Havana the first foreign-language edition was produced. When Laird joined the magazine in 1974, U.S. circulation had ballooned to eighteen million, while millions of readers around the globe were able to read the magazine in their own language. During Laird's tenure the *Digest* continued to grow, reaching a peak worldwide readership of one hundred million with forty-eight editions in nineteen languages. This made

the "international" portion of Laird's role pivotal. Besides glad-handing and
pep-talking the local *Digest* leadership during on-site visits, Laird also enmeshed himself in solving critical labor, postal, and other issues for those
foreign editions. "I was on the road a lot," Laird recalled. Among the more
challenging foreign assignments were his dealings with the governments of the
Soviet Union, India, and the People's Republic of China to establish a *Digest*
presence in those countries.

At first Laird also wrote two or three articles a year for the magazine, which
often made headlines and had an impact on the policies of the Ford and Carter
administrations. There were also news scoops along the way. For example, in a
1976 article, "Let's Stop Undermining the CIA," Laird reported one of the CIA's
secret successes, that Israel's premier Golda Meir had been targeted for a terrorist attack while visiting New York City on March 4, 1973. Police, following
a tip, found two cars, on a street Meir would pass, with enough Soviet-made
explosives to kill everyone within a one-hundred-yard radius.[6]

To protect intelligence sources and methods, Laird did not reveal in that
article that, when he had been secretary of defense, he had saved the life of this
same fellow Wisconsinite on an earlier date. Meir (born Goldie Mabovitch)
emigrated from Russia to Milwaukee with her family when she was eight years
old and lived there fifteen years. Before she emigrated to Palestine in 1921 she
taught for several years in the Milwaukee public school system. In 1969 Meir
was elected Israel's first female prime minister. The day before Meir attended
her first White House dinner, Secretary Laird bragged at the National Press
Club: "This is Wisconsin Week. . . . The Prime Minister of Israel will be here tomorrow and she's a Milwaukee girl."[7] Not long after that—Laird cannot recall
the precise date—he was given urgent intelligence from the National Security
Agency that indicated a car bomb was set to go off on a Jerusalem street as
Prime Minister Meir was driving by. Laird conveyed the intelligence to Meir
"within minutes," he said. The threat proved real, and a grateful Meir later presented Laird with fourteenth- and seventeenth-century B.C. bronze artifacts
including two arrowheads, a spearhead, a dagger, and a war axe in a framed
case.[8] "This is for saving my life," she explained.

Laird by-lines in the *Digest* began trailing off during the Reagan administration, not only because the magazine's demands on his time were greater in
other areas, but also because, as Laird explained, "it seemed to work more amicably to suggest and review articles and condensations, rather than to compete
with the other talented editors for space in the magazine." For his entire *Digest*
career, Laird reviewed most of the articles two or three months ahead of publication, as DeWitt Wallace initially charged him to do. The frank exchanges he
had with editors included both positive and negative suggestions and advice.

There were notable disagreements, such as the *Digest*'s support of congressional term limitations and a federal constitutional amendment requiring
a balanced budget. The editors didn't always agree with his politics, but they

realized his value as a front man to smooth over disputes with celebrities—as when rock star Bruce Springsteen was misquoted, or when the *Digest* criticized Senator Al Gore's wife, Tipper, for her campaign to police obscenity in record lyrics. Laird's luminous role always provided entree to politicians and foreign leaders. "No *Digester* opened more doors than Mel Laird when editors or writers needed access or an interview with a top U.S. official or foreign leader," said Bill Schulz, former Washington bureau chief for the magazine.

✺

DeWitt "Wally" Wallace wanted to put Laird on the *Reader's Digest* board when he joined the privately held company in 1974. But he recognized that it might not be politic to install Laird as an "inside" director when he had no previous history as a *Digest* employee. After the childless Wallaces died, leaving no heirs, 72 percent of the voting shares reverted to two charitable foundations. In 1990, when the *Digest* went public, Laird went on the board and helped drive up operating earnings from $240 to $353 million in his first three years.[9] The magazine's CEOs figured out early that the best way to use Laird was not on the editorial side but on the business side. Considering both the revenue he raised and the money he saved the company, his financial value for the *Digest* added up to tens of millions of dollars.

One way Laird accomplished that feat was, most simply put, as an ad salesman. He traveled from one end of the country to another as well as abroad at the request of many *Digest* advertising account executives. He attended numerous industry conventions and made community appearances at the request of advertisers. Successive *Digest* publishers called his entertainment of advertisers "legendary." Particularly effective were annual outings with advertisers at exclusive golf clubs to which he belonged. Greg Coleman, a former *Digest* publisher who went on to become president of Yahoo, said that the *Digest* advertising staff "credits Laird with helping to sell more advertising pages than anybody else in the history of the *Digest*."

Laird's work with the *Digest* on postal and regulatory issues began when he was a congressman. At that time Congress had the responsibility for establishing postal rates—an issue of critical interest to the magazine. The *Digest*'s business manager for decades, Al Cole, the man who turned the magazine into an international powerhouse, met Laird at a luncheon at the Wallaces' house and the two men became friends. In time Congressman Laird came to believe in a favorite axiom: "What is good for *Reader's Digest* is good for the country."

When he became an employee of the company, his missionary fervor accelerated. Nobody schmoozed with America's postmasters general like Laird did. His appointment books beginning in 1974 were filled with golf outings, lunches, and dinner meetings with "PMGs." Since *Reader's Digest* mails out millions of pieces of literature every month and is one of the postal service's largest customers, Laird didn't think it uppity when he first asked PMG Bill Bolger (1978–1984) for a monthly meeting to discuss business issues. Bolger agreed, and the PMGs who followed him continued the practice. Laird never lobbied for a favor outright—that was the business of the *Digest*'s registered lobbyist, former postal official and lawyer Tim May. Instead, most of the time Laird asked how he could best help the U.S. Postal Service.

The 1970 Postal Reorganization Act took the responsibility for setting postal rates out of the hands of Congress and gave it to the independent Postal Rate Commission, whose members are appointed to staggered six-year terms by the president. That commission and the U.S. Postal Service are often at odds, and Laird acted as an intermediary. It didn't hurt that he knew all the commissioners. Add to that Laird's influence with former colleagues in Congress, whose ears he would bend on behalf of the Postal Service if he felt their cause was just and in the best interest of the taxpayers. Some of these shrewd behind-the-scenes maneuvers account for the request from PMG Marvin Runyon (1992–1998) that Laird be the dinner speaker at his retirement. On that occasion Runyon remarked that the service had "no greater friend" than Laird in Washington, even if he often gave advice that Runyon did not want to hear.

The fact that Laird was respected and considered a close friend by disparate powers in the postal nexus—the commission, Postal Service, and Congress—paid off in big dollars for *Reader's Digest*. One example is Laird's successful negotiation for a *Digest* discount on the first class rate in late 1977. His reasoning was sound: The *Digest* presorted all its mail before delivering it to the regional postal centers and ought to get credit for saving the Postal Service tens of thousands of man hours. Bill Bolger agreed. Before the first class rate was hiked to 15 cents the following May (1978), the postal service granted a discount that saved the *Digest* $14 million in the first year alone.

Laird became the chief troubleshooter when a random audit by the U.S. Postal Inspection Service found that the *Digest,* over a five-year period, may have miscalculated its rates and shorted the postal service as much as $40 million. An outside postal consultant was hired who determined that the *Digest* may have assumed too broad an interpretation of several technical mailing rules. But it wasn't as bad as the audit suggested. Laird insisted on setting up a new system that invited the Postal Service to review the "format" of major *Digest* mailings so no such technical disagreement would occur in the future. After three years of talks at the regional and national levels, Laird negotiated down the amount owed to less than $10 million.

The hardest thing Laird ever did in his three-plus decades with the *Digest* was getting the Postal Service to issue a stamp honoring DeWitt and Lila Wallace. No *Digest*-related mission was more heartfelt for Laird, whose gratitude for the Wallaces did not diminish with the years. Laird's stamp quest, which was his own idea and wouldn't financially benefit the *Digest,* literally took more than ten years. Not long after DeWitt Wallace died in March 1981 Laird fell into conversation with author James Michener and Wilbur Cohen, LBJ's secretary of Health, Education, and Welfare. All three were admirers of Wallace and lamented his passing. How about a commemorative stamp honoring him? Laird asked. Both Michener and Cohen served on the little-known Citizens' Stamp Advisory Committee, which has sole authority to commission new stamps. They advised Laird of the rule that no one could be featured on a postage stamp until at least ten years after his or her death. (The only exception is deceased presidents, who may get a stamp on the first anniversary of their death.) "So we couldn't do it until 1991," Michener added. "Since we decide about three years in advance of a stamp, you should start pushing it in about 1988."

Laird patiently waited six years and sent his first suggestion to Postmaster General Bob Tisch in December 1987. Tisch felt that Wallace was, indeed, a worthy subject, and he promised to forward the recommendation to the Citizens' Stamp Advisory Committee, an iconoclastic bunch over whom he had little influence.[10] Then, Laird made his appeal to a new PMG, Anthony M. Frank, in 1988. He offered the same arguments as he did to Tisch, along with a handwritten note at the bottom: "Tony—The fact that we are among your top customers over the years should not be held against this request!?!" Frank obligingly recommended it to the committee at meeting after meeting but received a negative response year after year until he left in 1992.[11]

Then came PMG Marvin Runyon, and Laird got more creative. First he enlisted former stamp committee member Michener by reminding him that he owed a great deal to Wallace's tutelage and support when he was a young writer. Michener had no luck with the committee either. So Laird appealed to Runyon in 1994. Runyon had no problem with a Wallace stamp, but the committee saw as many as forty thousand such requests each year and chose only thirty or forty "issues." (An "issue" may have twenty or more different stamps with a common theme.) Laird was getting frustrated. The previous year a rule-breaking stamp had been issued featuring football star O. J. Simpson. Laird wrote to Runyon, "When I see the stamps that have been issued, I cannot help but feel that the contribution of these two people [the Wallaces] far outweighs—in a lasting and continuing sense—some of the individuals who have been recognized. Seriously, Marvin, what do you think I can do to make the Wallace stamp become a reality?"[12]

Finally, in 1996, Runyon called Laird to tell him the committee had decided that both Wallaces would be featured on a 32-cent first class stamp in July 1998. Laird's elation was tempered by the realization that it had been easier for him to make Gerald Ford the president than it had been to get a stamp printed. After the stamp was unveiled, Laird campaigned to make sure it was well used. The Postal Service had printed millions of the stamps, and Laird reckoned the *Digest* should make sure that a respectable number were purchased. The *Digest* used many of the stamps for sweepstakes mailings and other purposes.

But Laird became disappointed that some of the main beneficiaries of Wallace philanthropy weren't using the stamp. Word of Laird's dissatisfaction got around to the beneficiaries, and, in a few short months, eighteen million Wallace stamps were sold, which made it one of the fastest- and highest-selling single-issue stamps honoring an American in postal history.[13] (Elvis Presley is still king. The 1993 stamp featuring him remains the all-time bestseller.)

The path leading from the halls of government to the corporate board room is a well-worn one, and Laird didn't feel he was selling out to follow it. His friend Supreme Court Justice Arthur Goldberg once cautioned him against joining corporate boards, saying that the legal liability far outweighed the compensation or satisfaction of the work. But Laird's experience taught him differently. "Arthur was wrong and not heeding his advice was the correct decision for me," Laird said. "Legal suits against me in government and in the corporate world have been many, but it has been more than worth the inconvenience. Our system needs corporate directors completely independent of management on these corporate boards if our capital markets are to be believed."

A confirmed believer in the capitalist system, DeWitt Wallace strongly encouraged Laird to join boards for the experience and the public service. When Laird left the White House as domestic counselor in 1974 he had invitations from twenty corporate boards looking for the prestige and insider knowledge of the former defense secretary. At first Wallace agreed that Laird could serve on just six boards. The first six board positions Laird accepted were with Northwest Airlines (1974–94), Chicago Pneumatic Tool (1974–86), Metropolitan Life Insurance Company (1974–94), IDS Mutual Funds Group (1974–97), Communications Satellite Corporation (1974–96), and Purolator Inc. (1975–81). Eventually Laird added more corporate boards to his schedule, some of which landed him in the middle of the most infamous hostile takeover bids of the twentieth century.

The decade of rapacious corporate cannibalism began on August 25, 1982, the day the chairman of Bendix Corporation announced his hostile intention to digest—at a bargain price—America's twelfth largest defense contractor, Martin Marietta. The battle *royale* that ensued lasted less than thirty days. On the one side was the brash young gunfighter, Bendix's forty-three-year-old William Agee, and on the other side was Martin Marietta's determined veteran, sixty-year-old Thomas Pownall. Agee and Bendix were backed by a board, one of whose leaders was former Ford administration defense secretary Donald Rumsfeld. Martin Marietta had its own former defense secretary on the board: Melvin Laird.

At the point when Agee attempted his corporate raid, Laird had been on the Martin Marietta board for less than a year. In the 1970s there were no rules to forbid a former Pentagon chief from immediately joining the board of a defense contractor. But Laird thought that doing so was unseemly and unethical. He explained to defense suitors that he would honor at least a five-year waiting period before he could consider joining any of their boards. Martin Marietta was unapologetic about courting former top Pentagon officials. Pownall said the company considered itself nothing less than "an extension of the Defense Department." Between 1979 and 1981 the corporation placed 231 former high-ranking military officers and Defense Department officials on its payroll, which was more than twice as many as any other defense contractor. "Many of the top people at Martin Marietta were my friends and neighbors in Washington and some had worked for me in Defense," Laird recalled. He joined the thirteen-man board in September 1981.[14]

Laird liked the resoluteness he found in Pownall. A favorite story of Laird's had to do with a New Year's Eve arm-wrestling match between Pownall and Congressman Jack Kemp. Kemp, a former quarterback for the Buffalo Bills, bragged that he had never been beaten at arm wrestling. Pownall, who was thirteen years older, thought he had a chance because of the muscles he first developed milking cows. The two locked arms for almost five minutes before Kemp finally won. A few days later Pownall quietly checked into a hospital where it was discovered that he had dislocated his shoulder and torn the ligaments from the shoulder to the elbow.[15]

Pownall's opponent in the corporate battle was no slouch either. In his first five years at Bendix the folksy but wily Agee had doubled the operating profits of the auto-parts, aerospace, and machine-tool manufacturer. But he had dragged Bendix through an embarrassing episode when he swiftly promoted a young assistant, Mary Cunningham, with whom he was rumored to have a romantic relationship. In 1980, board member Rumsfeld was designated to tell Agee that his girlfriend had to go. Cunningham was bounced from the company, and a newly divorced Agee soon married her. But the feeling on Wall Street was that Agee was damaged goods.[16]

Corporate raiders try to keep their intentions hidden as long as possible. But at the point when they have secretly acquired 5 percent of the target's stock, the Securities and Exchange Commission requires them to disclose their take-over plan. From April through July 1982 Bendix bought 1.6 million shares of Martin Marietta, or about 4.5 percent of the company, at about $27 a share. Then Bendix made public a tender offer of $43 a share to gain control—a $1.5 billion bargain bid to take over Martin Marietta, which was then grossing $3.3 billion a year.[17] The day of the announcement Laird was in Sun Valley, Idaho, participating in a charity benefit golf tournament. Pownall called him for advice, and Laird was full of fighting words. Agee was not the kind of person who should be running Martin Marietta, and Bendix's other managers would upset the delicate defense mission of the company and destroy it. Other board members had the same view. Over the next several days they formed what would become famous as their "Pac-Man Defense": Martin Marietta would try to gobble up Bendix first.

Pownall convened the board in New York City on the morning of August 30. Laird set the tone by voicing strong objections to the tender offer, and others agreed. Bendix had a reputation for short-term thinking and drawing attention to itself. Martin Marietta kept a low profile and preferred long-term strategies.[18] The board voted to make an offer to buy Bendix for $1.5 billion (about $60 a share).[19] Agee was shocked when he learned that Martin Marietta had turned the tables on him. His investment bankers called it the "Jonestown Defense" and began distributing Kool-Aid packets to suggest that the Martin Marietta was suicidal, analogous to the followers of the Reverend Jim Jones who had famously swallowed cyanide-laced Kool-Aid in Guyana in 1978.

On September 7 Pownall and the board deployed a powerful secret weapon: a partner. They announced that United Technologies Corporation had made its own offer for Bendix stock. Agee's weaker counterstrike was to raise his tender offer to $48 a share. Six days later Laird and the board pulled out all the stops in a move they called "assured second-strike capability." They removed all legal fail-safe buttons and bound Martin Marietta to buy Bendix shares after midnight on September 22, even if Bendix by then owned a majority of Martin Marietta. Agee, trying to head off what he thought would be the certain demise of both companies, met with Pownall in New York on September 20 for a round of fruitless talks. Agee begged for a chance to present his case to the Martin Marietta board the next day. Though Pownall could not promise an audience, Agee flew to Washington with his wife, Cunningham. As the couple waited outside the Bethesda board room on September 21, Pownall recommended to the board that they hear Agee out.

Laird objected. As far as he was concerned, Agee had fired the first shot, and Martin Marietta should continue the fight until Agee surrendered. As Laird recalled, when Pownall continued to recommend that Agee be allowed in, it was another board member, Griffin Bell, who silenced the chairman. "We just elected you CEO a few months ago," Bell noted. "If you can't handle the board's decision not to meet with Agee right now, we can always elect a new CEO." Pownall showed the Agees the door.

Incredibly, at the time that Agee tried to get in to see the board, he and Bendix already owned Martin Marietta. Four days earlier they had passed the majority mark, having acquired more than 50 percent of the stock. Normally the majority owner can call a special shareholder's meeting to kick out the old board and install a new one. But Martin Marietta was incorporated in Maryland, which required ten days' notice before such a meeting could be held.[20] Desperate, the next day Agee offered to sell Bendix to another company, Allied Corporation. The Bendix board was stunned, and Rumsfeld and three others resigned on the spot.[21] Meanwhile Allied chairman Edward Hennessey met secretly with Pownall and made Martin Marietta an offer they couldn't refuse.

He told them he was only interested in consuming Bendix, and, once he did, Martin Marietta shareholders could buy back all their company stock that Allied would have acquired by taking over Bendix. Agee knew nothing about this deal. Within six months, Allied tore apart Bendix.[22]

Martin Marietta paid a heavy price to keep its independence. The company accumulated a $1.3 billion debt primarily as a result of its takeover defense. To reduce the debt as quickly as possible the board authorized a radical restructuring and, within just one year, had bought back all of its shares from Allied.[23] Pownall wrote in a letter to Laird. "[W]e survived, thanks in considerable measure to the wisdom, advice and guidance that you and Judge (Griffin) Bell, in particular, provided. Seriously, it made a big difference."[24] Laird eventually helped promote a strong successor to Pownall in 1988, Norman Augustine, who had been Laird's deputy director of research and engineering at the Pentagon. Augustine called one side of the Martin Marietta board table "Power Alley," for Laird, Bell, Jack Byrne (chairman of Geico Corporation), and Jack Vessey (former chairman of the Joint Chiefs of Staff).[25]

On March 15, 1995, Martin Marietta merged with Lockheed Corporation, becoming Lockheed Martin. Laird, who was still on the board, traced the successful merger directly back to the response to Agee's takeover attempt. Had Agee succeeded, Laird believed the company likely would have died. Instead Martin Marietta stockholders saw their shares more than triple in value by the time of the merger with Lockheed.

ॐ

Big oil also had come courting Laird as a potential board member during his last days in the White House in 1973, but he was in no hurry to choose. He was inclined toward Oklahoma-based Phillips Petroleum, the country's ninth-largest oil company, but did not join the Phillips board until 1976 when a federal judge ordered him to do so in the wake of a major political slush-fund scandal involving the company.

As part of the investigation of Nixon and his reelection campaign, Watergate Special Prosecutor Archibald Cox found that some American companies had made illegal contributions to Nixon. He offered special plea-bargain deals to those companies whose officers made a full confession. Phillips chairman William W. Keeler admitted that the company—using international couriers, code names, false invoices, and fraudulent bookkeeping—had funneled more than $1 million in foreign earnings through a series of subsidiaries in India, France, and Panama, through a Swiss bank account, and then to the United States to donate in cash to American politicians. In 1968 Keeler had personally handed $100,000 in cash to candidate Nixon in his New York City apartment. Four years later another $100,000 in cash was given to Nixon's reelection committee and $200,000 to Senator Kerr of Oklahoma (chairman of the Democratic Senate Campaign Committee). Hundreds of thousands of dollars kept in a safe at Phillips's headquarters was divvied out to several dozen Republican and Democratic candidates for House and Senate races between 1964 and 1973. Keeler was fined $1,000 and resigned; Phillips was fined $5,000.

Thinking that the company needed fundamental change, a Los Angeles–based nonprofit public interest legal group filed a class action suit seeking that change on behalf of Phillips shareholders. Federal District Judge Jesse Curtis ruled on behalf of the shareholders, ordering a restructuring of the company, whose board had allowed itself to be controlled by company managers. He mandated that six new "outside" directors be added to the eleven-member board, giving independent board members a nine to eight majority. The public interest lawyers and Phillips's lawyers submitted names for the judge to consider. One of them was Laird, who won easy approval. Though there is no record of who first raised his name during the court negotiations, it is likely that it was Clark Clifford, Phillips's top lawyer in Washington.[26]

Laird had always liked Phillips because it was an oil company that had a "family" feel to it. Phillips research had been pivotal in the production of high-octane aviation gasoline and artificial rubber during World War II. In 1951 the company invented polyethylene plastic and, later, the first all-season motor oil. The first to drill for oil in Alaska, Phillips also drilled the first commercial oil well in the North Sea, which led to the discovery of Western Europe's first large oil field. Much of that innovation had occurred under the direction of a Phillips president, K. S. "Boots" Adams. On Adams's sixty-sixth birthday, in 1965, schools closed in the Phillips company town of Bartlesville, Oklahoma, so families could attend a parade. The guest of honor was an Adams' golfing buddy, Dwight D. Eisenhower. Also in the parade was an important Republican House leader, Melvin Laird. "I always liked the idea of going on the Phillips board ever since I was at the parade, which happened in the heaviest downpour I've ever seen in my life," Laird recalled. While Ike stayed dry in his car, the marching bands persisted with their woolen uniforms during the torrential storm. "Old 'Boots' went back and paid for new uniforms for all the bands that marched in the rain," Laird later found out.[27]

Most Phillips board meetings were held in out-of-the-way Bartlesville. Laird would be picked up at his house by Clifford and driven to Dulles Airport, where a Phillips jet would fly them to Oklahoma. Sometimes the board meetings were moved to more interesting locations, but the best "perk" Laird remembered, with fondness, was a Phillips trip he took in 1978 to a North Sea drilling rig with his two sons, John and David. "It took more than an hour by helicopter to get to it, and we had to wear wetsuits on the flight so we wouldn't die in those damned cold waters if the helicopter crashed," he recalled.

Laird felt his primary role from the beginning was to keep the company "cleaner than a hound's tooth." He did that in part by stocking the board with friends, including Carol Laise, the retired director general of the U.S. Foreign

Service. Laise had been U.S. ambassador to Nepal when her husband, Ellsworth Bunker, was U.S. ambassador in Saigon. As a favor when Laird was defense secretary, he recalled, "I'd send a fighter plane to Nepal to pick Carol up once or twice. She'd ride in that little fighter plane all the way down to Saigon so I could surprise Ellsworth with a visit from his wife as a way to improve his work during that war."

In April 1984 Laird brought the chairman of the Equitable Life Assurance Society onto the Phillips board—Bob Froehlke. By December Laird and the others were ready when they faced the biggest corporate war in the history of Phillips. Their opponent was a former employee who became the most famous American raider of them all, T. Boone Pickens. He had left Phillips in 1954 and struck out on his own, founding Mesa Petroleum. He had a gift for business deals and soon became the head of a growing independent oil company. By the early 1980s, when the stock price of most oil companies was depressed, Pickens realized it was cheaper to acquire oil companies along with their oil reserves than it was to drill for new oil. In 1982 he went after Cities Service of Oklahoma, which was twenty times the size of his Mesa Petroleum. Though he failed when Cities Service rushed into the arms of a bigger bidder, Occidental Petroleum, Pickens and his Mesa group made a fast $31.5 million profit. When raiders acquired stock and Wall Street knew an acquisition was "on," the stock price generally went up. Thus even a failed raider could make money by selling his stock to the successful raider. Those who had no intention of actually acquiring the target company were called "greenmailers" because they were out for the quick profit by blackmailing the company into paying them to disappear. Pickens always maintained that he was not one of those—that he truly wanted to run a big oil company. But he profited by failure nevertheless. In a 1983 failed attempt to acquire Gulf Oil, Pickens netted more than $500 million. With Pickens's war chest bursting at the seams, the talk of Wall Street in 1984 was speculation about who would be his next target.[28]

On December 4 he revealed his plan: he wanted Phillips. He had already bought nearly 5 percent of the company and made a tender offer to pay $60 a share for the rest. The total came to $9.3 billion. Phillips chairman William Douce convened the board, which had as one of its assets Laird, a veteran of the Bendix battle of two years before. As he had on the Martin Marietta board, Laird urged Phillips's chairman to fight to the death. Laird was pivotal in directing a public relations strategy that turned Pickens almost overnight from a folk hero to a villain in the mold of TV's J.R. Ewing.

The people of Bartlesville, rightly concerned that Pickens might move the Phillips headquarters to Texas, rallied in impressive fashion. "Boone Buster" logos appeared everywhere on T-shirts, buttons, and coffee cups. Local churches held twenty-four-hour prayer vigils, and a "crisis meeting" was called by the Chamber of Commerce, at which four thousand people belted out a song whose chorus went: "There's gonna be a meeting at the old town hall tonight / And if they try to stop us, there's gonna be a fight. / We're gonna get our company out of this awful fix, / 'Cause we don't want to change our name to Pickens 66."[29]

The TV networks obligingly covered the battle of the small town against the corporate raider. "In the short term, media perception is very important, and this time it was going against us like a tidal wave," Pickens wrote in his autobiography. The only way to explain what happened next is that a newly thin-skinned Pickens lost his will to fight. He cut a deal with Phillips on Christmas Eve that allowed him to walk away with an $89 million profit. Meanwhile, another corporate raider, Carl Icahn, started buying Phillips stock and made a run at the wounded company several weeks later. He also failed.[30]

Phillips, like Martin Marietta before it, paid a heavy price to keep its independence; its debt load doubled to $9 billion. The company tightened its belt, trimmed its bureaucracy, sold off unprofitable assets, and made other shrewd business moves often suggested by Laird and the board. By 1989 its debt was cut in half.[31] By the time Laird left the board in 1994 the share price of Phillips stock had quadrupled from the pre-Pickens days. In 2002 Phillips joined in a friendly merger with Conoco to become one of the largest oil companies in the world.

◆

Laird's first corporate board, Northwest Airlines, gave him his third encounter with corporate raiders. His history with Northwest traced back to his first years in Congress when he helped the airline win the rights to a Hawaii route in a competition with Pan American World Airways. The most notable period of Laird's service at Northwest began in early 1989 when Denver oil billionaire Marvin Davis offered $90 a share in a $2.7 billion bid for the airline. The move prompted a frenzy of bidding for the airline, so the board agreed to an auction.[32] Laird quickly realized that the best deal was being offered by Los Angeles financiers Al Checchi and Gary Wilson. Laird had known them both when they worked for the Maryland-based Marriott Corporation. Unlike Laird's previous business adversaries, Checchi and Wilson actually wanted to run the company and turn it into a more profitable operation, which they did with Laird's help. Laird was the only member of the old Northwest board whom Checchi and Wilson asked to stay on. In part it was because they were trying to lure former vice president Walter Mondale to their new board, and Mondale told them he would join only if they kept Laird as head of the board's audit committee.[33]

On the list of people Laird admired most from his service on boards was Sandy Weill, the president of American Express. Something of a perpetual motion machine, Weill was always on the lookout for the next big deal, and in July 1983 he decided Amex could acquire Minneapolis-based Investors Diversified Services (IDS) for $1 billion. Laird had been on the board of the IDS mutual funds group for almost a decade. He took Weill's measure and liked everything about him, including the merger idea. After Weill made the offer public he was embarrassed when Amex Chairman James D. Robinson overruled him and scaled the purchase price down to $727 million. Weill thought it was bad form, but he obliged and the merger went through. Weill ran the company for a short term and then left to pursue his own ventures.

For his first acquisition, Commercial Credit Company, Weill asked Laird to purchase stock and join the first board of directors. Laird agreed and recruited another member, former president Gerald Ford. In 1988 Commercial Credit bought Primerica Corporation for $1.5 billion, which meant it also owned the brokerage firm Smith Barney Harris Upham. With Laird and Ford still on the board, watching the stock grow by leaps and bounds, Weill renamed the company Primerica Financial Services. In time Weill acquired Travelers Corporation, an insurance company, and merged it with Primerica. Ford agreed to stay with Weill, but Laird chose to leave out of loyalty to his first board, MetLife, a competitor to Travelers.[34] (MetLife later acquired Travelers from Citigroup.)

For Laird, board positions were more than an easy paycheck or the honor of being asked. He could anticipate issues emanating from Washington that might affect the companies. He could be window dressing for a building dedication or a ribbon cutting one day, and the next be a savvy advisor who didn't mince words. Accustomed to having people carry out his orders without delay, Laird had little patience for board meetings that meandered off the topic. He snapped many meetings back on track with pointed humor or a firm course correction. David Heebner, who served with Laird in the Pentagon and later on the board of Science Applications International Corporation (SAIC), recalled a meeting where an executive promotion was being discussed.

"Do you intend for that fellow to report to so-and-so?" Laird asked. And the chairman said, "Yes."

"That'll never work," said Laird.

"Why?"

"Those guys can't stand one another," Laird observed.

"Well, how do you know that?" asked the chairman.

"Look," said Laird, "I come to your preboard dinners, and I watch how your people interact with one another. I make my life understanding how people relate to one another. And let me tell you, I will guarantee that those guys can't get along."

Laird was "right on the money," Heebner recalled.[35]

⚓

The man who originated one of the most commercially valuable ideas of the twentieth century and sold it for $40 was noted British author Arthur C. Clarke. In an article for the October 1945 issue of *Wireless World,* under the title

"Extraterrestrial Relays," he introduced the idea of artificial satellites. Clarke reasoned that if a rocket could reach the speed of five miles a second and could be powered by the sun's energy, it would never fall down but continue to circle the earth, like a second moon. He explained that the most valuable orbit would be at a height of twenty-two thousand miles, because at that elevation it would take precisely a day to revolve around the earth. If it were placed above the equator it would seem fixed in the sky, neither rising nor setting like other heavenly bodies.[36]

Clarke, best known as a science fiction writer, frequently wrote about this topic in the 1950s. When President Kennedy proposed the Communications Satellite Act of 1962 to establish just such a system for the United States, Congressman Laird enthusiastically backed the initiative. The act called for the creation of a new company, half private and half publicly owned, Communications Satellite Corporation (Comsat). One of its first goals was to create what became the International Telecommunications Satellite Consortium (Intelsat), a global group of countries that would participate in the project. Though not a fan of some international organizations, Laird always considered Intelsat to be a neighborly cooperative that shared the skies with all mankind.

Twelve years later, in 1974, citizen Laird was persuaded to join the Comsat board by another board member, labor leader George Meany, a Laird golfing partner. Laird quickly became one of the most influential Comsat board members, according to Joseph H. Charyk, the founding Comsat president. Not only were Laird's ideas useful, but he was willing to expend his considerable political capital on behalf of Comsat and Intelsat. Laird led the fight against an attempt by the Federal Communications Commission in 1984–85 to break the Comsat monopoly and allow private competition.[37]

A high-level Reagan administration interagency group had decided competition was a good idea, but Laird, normally a proponent of a competitive marketplace, didn't think the time was right to fix something that wasn't broken. He wrote a series of letters to Secretary of State George Shultz urging him to get some backbone and stand up for Intelsat.[38] Through additional letters, meetings with National Security Advisor Bud McFarlane and various members of Congress, and an editorial by Laird in the *Washington Post*, the initiative failed.[39]

With that kind of demonstrated loyalty, Charyk gave Laird a lot of leeway, including the prerogative to name new board members—a privilege that prompted an episode that Colin Powell never forgot. When Lieutenant General Powell was national security advisor to President Reagan in early 1988 he was paired at a dinner function with Laird. Powell, a longtime admirer of the former defense secretary who had chosen him more than a decade before for a White House fellowship, made some small talk at the dinner about an article in the *Wall Street Journal* that said black generals were having trouble breaking into the business world when they retired from the military. "That's astonishing!"

Laird said, genuinely surprised by the news. "This is ridiculous—these guys would bring such talents to any board."

Sensing an opportunity Powell offered his prime example. After a distinguished thirty-four-year career, the first black four-star army general, Roscoe Robinson, had been retired for more than two years and hadn't been able to land a seat on a major corporate board. Laird was offended at the news. General Robinson had served him well in Japan during the reversion of Okinawa when a more senior commander had been dragging his feet. Powell recounted, "Before I knew it, Mel had called Roscoe and put him on a board." That appointment was at Comsat in May 1998. "It meant a lot to Roscoe," Powell continued. "Gave him financial security and got him into the business world. And Mel Laird was the sparkplug for that." The following January, Laird got Robinson on the Northwest Airlines board and in 1991 paved the way for appointment to the MetLife board. When Robinson died in 1993 Laird set up a perpetual Comsat scholarship in Robinson's name for black students from Washington, D.C.[40]

Robinson wasn't the only beneficiary of Laird's "placement service." After Lynne Cheney left her post as Reagan's chairman at the National Endowment for Humanities, she found Laird anxious to help the talented wife of his long-time protégé, Dick Cheney.[41] Laird made sure she was appointed to the boards of American Express–IDS, Lockheed Martin, and *Reader's Digest*—a combination that, in 1999 alone, earned her $265,000 in board compensation fees. When Hubert Humphrey died, leaving his wife, Muriel, only a Senate pension, Laird saw to it that she was appointed to the American Express–IDS board also. And when Larry Eagleburger and Oklahoma Senator David Boren retired from public life, Laird got them seats on the Phillips Petroleum board.

When Senator Barry Goldwater retired on his Senate pension, without benefit of a family fortune, Laird saw an opportunity to help him, too, and got President Reagan to appoint Goldwater to the Comsat board. Bill Clinton was president when the ultraconservative Goldwater came up for reappointment at Comsat, and Laird saw a potential problem. But his solution was not long in coming. He learned that Clinton wanted to appoint Peter Knight, a Democrat, to the same board. Knight had managed Al Gore's vice presidential campaign, and the Senate committee that had the power to approve the presidential nominations to Comsat was controlled by Republicans. Laird recounted his solution: "I told them over at the White House that if they would reappoint Barry Goldwater I would see that Peter Knight's appointment was confirmed in the Senate." Laird pulled some strings among old friends in the Senate, and both men were approved. It was no hardship for Laird, who counted Knight among his friends, too.

During Laird's last four years at Comsat, 1992–1996, he served as chairman of the board. It was a colorful era when Comsat CEO Bruce Crockett expanded Comsat's "entertainment" division into professional sports. By Laird's account

Crockett became enamored of owning both the Denver Nuggets basketball team and a Canadian hockey team, the Quebec Nordiques, which he transplanted to Denver and renamed the Colorado Avalanche. It was heady stuff and profitable at first; in their first season (1995–96), the Avalanche won the Stanley Cup. Laird urged Crockett to turn his attention back to the core satellite business. Laird personally involved himself with the Nuggets only once: when Nuggets center Dikembe Mutombo's parents disappeared in 1993 in war-torn Zaire, Laird applied pressure on the State Department to find them.[42]

Typical of his modus operandi, Laird was busy much of the time behind the scenes restructuring Comsat to become an appealing acquisition for a company over which he had some influence: Lockheed Martin. That acquisition was announced two years after Laird resigned and was finally completed in 2000.[43]

⌇

Under his original agreement with DeWitt Wallace, Laird was not limited in the number of nonprofit public service boards he could join. Wallace specifically wanted Laird on the board of the World Rehabilitation Fund, headed by Wallace's friend Dr. Harold Rusk. In short order Laird added public service board memberships with George Washington University; the American Film Institute; Airlie Foundation; Representative John Fogarty's Research Foundation; Senator Henry M. Jackson's Foundation for Medical Research; the Boys Clubs of America; and as chairman of the Wolf Trap Foundation, the celebrated Virginia arts center. Over time Laird served on twenty-seven nonprofit boards.

No nonprofit service carried more financial responsibility than Laird's work with the eight trusts and two foundations that DeWitt and Lila Wallace left in place after their deaths. Both Wallaces felt excessive profit was unseemly, and they gave away tens of millions of dollars during their lifetimes. Laird felt a very personal responsibility in handling the Wallaces' money after their deaths. He served as chairman of the investment committee for their nine different funds, which exceeded $5 billion in value.[44]

Laird found his work on the board of trustees of the John F. Kennedy Center for the Performing Arts nearly as interesting. The five-stage marble box on the Potomac River, which is the only official federal monument to the late president, is intended to be the "nation's theater." The board has forty-five members, thirty of them appointed by the president to ten-year terms, and the other fifteen ex officio from among the House, Senate, and other federal units. Laird was appointed by President Ford in 1975, then reappointed by President Reagan in 1985, and made an emeritus trustee in 1995. For many Kennedy Center trustees it is a reward for good works, an honor that doesn't require them to pitch in and help. So the trustees that were the most valued were the few like Laird, who took an active role in fund raising and management of the facility.

Laird recalled one late night congressional session when only he and longtime Kennedy Center executive Charlotte Woolard were on Capitol Hill trying to save the center's expansion funding. "If it were not for Charlotte and I being on the House side of the Capitol that night, our special legislation would have gone down the drain," Laird wrote in a letter of remonstration to fellow trustee Senator Edward Kennedy. "No other Trustee was present to help."[45]

The volunteer time Mel Laird spent in Washington on nonprofit boards, and personal financial donations he offered, did not usually have as much emotional resonance as the special charities he set up closer to his family roots. For example, Laird made contributions of more than $454,000 to the "Laird Endowment for the Arts," which funds programs in the Helen C. Laird Fine Arts Building and Theater of the University of Wisconsin–Wood County. The building was dedicated in 1984 in tribute to his mother, who was committed to education and the arts. Laird additionally designated the fine arts program as the beneficiary of one of his $500,000 life insurance policies. He also directed a $100,000 Lila Wallace grant to support the arts programs, for a total of more than $1 million.[46]

"My greatest *personal* pride and joy with the nonprofit work is with the Laird Youth Leadership Foundation (LYLF)," Laird said. He established it when he was serving in Congress to honor his father. The funding first came from honorariums he received while in Congress and expanded through Laird's personal donations after he left government. Beginning in 1954 the foundation awarded scholarships to students, ranging from $1,000 to $5,000. LYLF, chaired by Laird's son John, continues to support the Laird Youth Leadership Day on the campus of the University of Wisconsin–Stevens Point.

While making a list of the boards and other Laird activities for a journalist, Laird's executive secretary, Kathy Weaver, was amazed. She went to work for Laird when she was twenty-nine and was Laird's sole administrative assistant beginning in early 1996, when longtime assistant Laurie Hawley retired. "There were so many days that I was swamped just trying to keep up with him, but I've truly enjoyed it. I've always gone home with a proud sense of accomplishment in my association with such a distinguished American. If there is one thing I have always had for Mel Laird, it is the utmost, highest respect. I love working for him, and I respect him with all my might. How could I work these past twenty-seven years for someone I *didn't* respect?"[47]

48

War and Peace

⌇⌇⌇

THE APACHE HELICOPTERS of the 101st Aviation Brigade crossed the border into Iraq on a clear night, with a new moon giving advantage to their night vision capability. They had been chosen to spearhead the biggest air assault in world history, and to fire the first shots of Operation Desert Storm on January 17, 1991. Many miles to the south, in Riyadh, Saudi Arabia, General Norman Schwarzkopf assembled his staff in the war room and asked a chaplain to pray for the troops. But the United States had more than a prayer going for it because of the groundwork Melvin Laird had laid two decades before. Most of the equipment at Schwarzkopf's disposal, and even the nature of the U.S. fighting force, was directly traceable to the Laird era.

Shortly after Saddam Hussein's army invaded Kuwait on August 2, 1990, the massive C-5As and other cargo planes built during the Laird administration began lifting American personnel and equipment to bases in Saudi Arabia, beginning an operation to free Kuwait. On August 22, when President George H. W. Bush called up forty thousand reserve troops, his ability to do so had come because of Laird's "total force" concept. Twenty years earlier, to the month, Laird had ordered that the Reserves, rather than the draft, would provide manpower for future troop buildups.

During the four decades between World War II and Desert Storm, the Reserves had been called up eleven times—for the Korean War, the Berlin airlift, the Cuban Missile Crisis; after the Tet offensive; and for various civil disturbances at home. President Nixon used the Reserves once—to handle mail during the postal strike in March 1970. Both Nixon and Johnson had been loathe to use the Reserves and National Guard for the Vietnam War, so those outfits had become a haven for young men who wanted to avoid combat. The derisive term "weekend warriors" came into the lexicon, and these units were considered second- or third-string until Laird mandated the total force policy at the end of his term. During the next twenty years the army, navy, and air force became dependent on the Reserves. Roughly 70 percent of the army's combat support functions, such as those performed by medical and logistical units, were being filled by the Reserves by the dawn of Desert Storm. They comprised two-thirds of the water supply units and half the ammunition and fuel-handling units. Reserves accounted for 93 percent of the navy's cargo-handling units and 59 percent of the air force's tactical airlift capability.[1] Schwarzkopf eventually tapped more than two hundred thousand reservists during the conflict for a wide variety of needs, including combat; seventy-one of them lost their lives in that first Gulf War. There was no more snickering about "summer soldiers."

While the Apache helicopters were striking Iraqi antiaircraft missile batteries in the early hours of Desert Storm, the navy was firing its first shots, primarily from the battleship USS *Wisconsin,* marking the first use of Tomahawk cruise missiles in battle. Laird had started the cruise missile program over the objections of the air force and navy. Those forces were pilot oriented, and a weapon like the cruise missile could be seen as making pilots obsolete. Laird's successors also had to overcome fierce opposition to keep the missiles in the defense budget.

The subsonic missiles rocketed away from the *Wisconsin* at speeds up to 550 miles per hour, hugging the ground at altitudes as low as fifty feet (well below radar range) through the use of preprogrammed photographic terrain data. Fired from more than eight hundred miles away, the Tomahawks were able to strike targets within a few feet of the bull's-eye. Some of them easily penetrated concrete-reinforced Iraqi bunkers by bursting through doors. More than 85 percent of the first 150 Tomahawks launched in the war struck their intended targets. As praise was heaped upon him during Desert Storm, the missile's designer, Robert Lynch, publicly affirmed that "the only thing that kept cruise missiles alive was the determination of Defense Secretaries [beginning with] Melvin Laird."[2]

When Secretary Laird took over in 1969, the military procurement situation was a colossal mess. "Many major weapons systems were in serious trouble," Pentagon Comptroller Robert Moot wrote in a 1972 summary report. The reasons were varied: daily demands of the Vietnam War, inflation, procurement procedures instituted by McNamara, and some questionable weapons choices. "Whatever the causes," Moot wrote, "the Department had a great amount of expensive dirty linen to wash at a particularly inopportune time"—just as Laird was taking the job.[3]

Laird felt the best way to tackle the problem was to identify just how bad things had become on his predecessors' watches, then candidly hang out that "dirty linen" in front of the Congress. The first time Laird appeared before a congressional committee on the defense budget he delivered the bad news all at once. In a review of current defense contracts he had found a total of $16.2 billion in cost overruns on thirty-four major defense weapons systems. He told the committee it was important "to set forth all of the overruns which we uncovered when we took over this new watch.... The only reason these reports haven't been put in the record before is that they contain classified information on these weapons systems." Laird declared he wasn't going to hide behind the secrecy stamp as other secretaries had done. He pledged to disclose even the most embarrassing facts about weapons procurement as he learned of them.[4]

Laird explained at a press conference, "In the weapons acquisition area,

[it] is far easier to identify the troubles in a timely fashion than it is to devise practical, immediately-effective solutions," especially when that included serious interservice rivalries competing for dollars.[5] One of the most nettlesome interservice procurement issues that Laird inherited was the bitter "close sir support" debate. Three aircraft—the air force's A-X, the army's Cheyenne helicopter, and the marines' Harrier—were all being developed for roughly the same mission: supporting American ground forces in a battle by knocking out enemy tanks, guns, and troops from the air. Altogether the services were trying to buy about a thousand aircraft at a cost of $4 to $5 billion. Laird, who had monitored the requests when he was in Congress, immediately put David Packard to work on a compromise.[6]

Within weeks Packard knew what the solution was: the trouble-plagued Cheyenne helicopter program needed to be canceled; purchase of the Harriers from the British had to be scaled back; and the air force should get the go-ahead for the A-X. As sharp and deft as Packard was, however, it took him three years to get the feuding services to come to the same conclusion. It was an emotional issue, particularly for the army, which didn't feel that the air force in wartime supported army troops as willingly as they performed other more glamorous air force missions. The army didn't want to have to rely on the air force to come to the rescue in a timely manner with the A-X, when an army Cheyenne could do the same job, with the added bonus of always being dependably on call.

Packard's first move in May 1969 was to cancel the production contract for the Cheyenne, declaring Lockheed was in "default" for having failed to solve serious rotor stability problems. Next, in January 1970, Packard ordered the army and the air force to come up with "a unified Department of Defense position."[7] The result two months later was a document so rare that the Pentagon didn't have stationery to accommodate it. "Departments of the Army and Air Force" had to be typed in at the top of the joint memorandum signed by Army Secretary Stan Resor and Air Force Secretary Robert Seamans. Between the lines was the mutual opinion of the civilian secretaries that the A-X should move to production while the Cheyenne would be stopped at the prototype stage.[8]

Seamans wrote in his memoirs that the uniformed military was uniformly furious. Air Force Chief of Staff General John Ryan berated his service secretary, Seamans, for allowing continued work on the Cheyenne in any form. Army Chief of Staff Westmoreland similarly pounded on his secretary, Resor, for "giving away the store." Resor later remarked: "Bob [Seamans] and I must have done something right. Both of our staffs told us that we sold them down the river."[9]

Packard wasn't finished. Common sense said that the Cheyenne helicopter should be terminated, but the army was not ready to give it up. After more than a year of additional contentious meetings, David Heebner, a Pentagon research and development official who worked on the issue, privately approached

Packard with a draft of an order to kill the Cheyenne, which he urged Packard to sign.

"Have you ever herded cattle?" Packard, the working ranch owner, asked Heebner.

"No," Heebner answered, wondering where Packard was going.

"When you herd cattle, you spend a lot of time going over the range rounding them up. After a lot of work, you get them alongside the corral fence. Then, acting real cool, you have somebody open the gate kind of slowly. Pretty soon, one of those doggies walks into the corral, and then the rest of 'em follow in. And you're done. But, sure as hell, if you try to push them they'll scatter all over the range and you have to do it again. I think we have them alongside the corral fence. Just wait a little longer."[10]

Sure enough, Heebner recalled, within a few weeks the army brass told Packard they were ready to *consider* giving up on the Cheyenne. The program was finally killed in August 1972, having cost $400 million. (The research was not completely wasted, however; years later, the research for the Cheyenne was rolled into the army's Apache attack helicopter.) Meanwhile the marines were limited to purchasing 60 Harriers from the British instead of the 112 they wanted.[11]

The A-X became the Fairchild-Hiller A-10; more than seven hundred of these awkward-looking aircraft (nicknamed "Warthogs") were produced. Though air force commanders were never fond of the ungainly plane, the army was grateful they had been built. The A-10s and their air force pilots performed heroically and with efficiency during the 1991 Gulf War. The A-10 carried Maverick missiles, five-hundred-pound bombs, and antiarmor cluster bombs, but its chief armament was a 30-mm, seven-barrel Gatling gun the size of a Volkswagen, which fired dense depleted-uranium ammunition at 4,200 rounds a minute. Besides supporting ground troops, the Warthogs in that war also knocked out Scud missile sites, artillery supply points, radar installations, and surface-to-air missile sites. One even rescued a downed navy pilot, while another won a dogfight with an Iraqi helicopter. Not one of the Warthogs was downed by antiaircraft fire. One that was hit had a gaping hole in its right wing, a destroyed landing gear pod, and one of its hydraulic systems taken out, but the plane made it back to its base and flew again.[12]

~ꞷ~

In the run-up to the first Gulf War, Laird was not one of those who were anxious to see his procurement and manpower decisions ratified in the heat of real battle and loss of life. In October 1990, three months before the first shots were fired, Laird met with President George H. W. Bush for a Sunday brainstorming session in the upstairs White House sitting room. He urged continued caution, including the imperative that war, if it came, should be a U.N. operation, just as Korea had been. "This is a test, not only for the charter and purpose of the United Nations, but also a test even for the *name* United Nations," he explained that month to a Marshfield audience. "We cannot go it alone."[13]

President Bush successfully pushed for U.N. support and, on November 29, won U.N. Resolution 678, which authorized the use of force against Iraq if it did not withdraw its forces from Kuwait by January 15, 1991. It marked only the second time in the United Nations' forty-five-year history that it had affirmatively provided authority for member states to wage war against another country. (The first was in 1950, at the outset of the Korean War.)

The day after the U.N. resolution Laird and six other former defense secretaries were gathered in Atlanta for a PBS forum sponsored by the Southern Center for International Studies. The seven were in agreement that Bush should pursue a peaceful end to the Kuwait crisis, counseling patience to give economic sanctions more time to work. Laird added, however, that it would be a mistake to send a signal to Saddam Hussein that the United States would be unlikely to use force. "The important thing here is that we have until the fifteenth of January to get down to some very serious business with Saddam Hussein," he added. "It would be a very grave error to send a direct message about what we will or will not do." Laird qualified his own view with the observation that the United States only has "one Secretary of Defense at a time," and he would support Secretary Dick Cheney in upcoming Senate testimony.

Only one of the former defense secretaries was singled out by the press as being particularly hawkish. Donald Rumsfeld "stressed the merits of an attack on Iraq," the *New York Times* summarized. He said American superiority could be used to destroy Iraqi weapons of mass destruction, ending Western and Saudi concerns about them. "I am not the slightest bit uncomfortable with military action, particularly if it goes to degrade the unconventional weapon capability of Saddam Hussein." Rumsfeld additionally observed that Saddam "is not going to be persuaded by diplomatic niceties. He [only] understands force."[14]

In the end Saddam would not capitulate, which prompted forty days and forty nights of war. The final test of the war came for the ground-combat component of Laird's most important legacy, the All-Volunteer Force. At 4 A.M. on Saturday, February 24, Armed Forces Radio played Elton John's "Saturday Night's Alright (for Fighting)," and the ground war was on. One hundred hours later, it was over. Iraqi forces were evicted from Kuwait and thoroughly routed. The All-Volunteer Force had proved its mettle and wisdom at every level. While reflecting on the All-Volunteer Force six years after the war, former President George H. W. Bush noted, "Desert Storm was clearly the first major, all-out war since the volunteer army began. I'm a strong supporter of that. Anybody who saw the dedication and the commitment of these forces would agree that this was the finest fighting force the U.S. had ever put together. Everybody was there because they wanted to be   To the degree that it was an all-volunteer effort, it vindicated Mel Laird's commitment to having that kind of force. We *did* call up the Reserves and the National Guard. But still they were there because they wanted to be there."[15]

Colin Powell felt the same when he later served as President George W. Bush's secretary of state. Powell said Laird was owed a debt of gratitude for the All-Volunteer Force—which Powell and many other senior military officers had opposed when Laird pushed it. "But over time, we all became the greatest champions of the All-Volunteer Force, especially after President Reagan came in and funded it properly," Powell recounted. He added, with emphasis: "You won't find anybody in active duty—well, you might find one, but I doubt it—who, at a senior level, would want to go back to a draftee force. I would never again serve with people who didn't want to be in the service."[16]

～⚔～

Laird both publicly and privately advised every administration, whether Democratic or Republican, over the three decades after he retired from government. President Carter considered his association with Laird to be a fond one, despite the difference in their political parties. His respect for Laird increased when Laird supported Carter's attempt to withdraw all U.S. ground troops from South Korea. The controversy erupted in May 1977 when Carter announced—without careful political preparation of his own military and allies—that he was going to pull U.S. troops out. The chief of staff of the American military command in Seoul, Major General Jack Singlaub, was quoted by a reporter as criticizing his commander-in-chief and was promptly ordered home and fired by the president.

Carter tried to regain the initiative, in part by personally asking Laird for a supportive statement that Carter could use at a May 26 press conference. Laird was more than willing to oblige since his own plan when he was secretary had been to remove those ground troops. He had begun the first phase by removing twenty thousand U.S. troops from Korea. Just as he had with Vietnamization, it was Laird's plan to Koreanize Korea—providing enough funds and training so Korea could defend itself in ground combat. In his statement to support Carter, Laird said, "I have always questioned . . . a ground combat role for our forces in Asia" when the allies in question can provide it themselves. "Our Asian allies should rely primarily on air and sea support from the United States and must accept under these mutual defense treaties the primary responsibility in providing the ground combat deterrent. This was my position during the Eisenhower, Kennedy, Johnson, Nixon, Ford and Carter Administrations. It has not changed."

President Carter used the statement to some effect at his press conference, but the opposition to his plan was already too strong in Congress. Laird said he would have helped more if Carter had included *all* of Laird's plan—which had as its key element a seven-year modernization program of Republic of Korea ground, air, and sea forces, funded by the United States. "Carter forgot that part of the plan so his effort failed," Laird concluded.[17]

Carter enlisted Laird again regarding the Panama Canal treaty. A return of the canal to Panama was an implicit promise by a number of administrations. Panamanian President Omar Torrijos was insistent that the time had come to finalize a treaty. Carter asked Jerry Ford and Laird to round up moderate Republicans to come out in support of a treaty. The conservative Republican opposition, led by Ronald Reagan, was intense and emotional in the counterattack, charging a "giveaway" of the canal. In the end Carter and Torrijos signed treaties providing for the return of the canal to Panama twenty-three years hence, on January 1, 2000. The bitter politics of that battle so tainted Carter that, as he explained in an interview twenty years later, "in my own life, I kind of divide people into two parts—the ones who helped me with the Panama Canal treaties, and the other ones who tried to stab me in the back....And Melvin Laird was one of those who knew the importance of keeping the canal open, and he was a good supporter of those treaties, which I really appreciated."[18]

On occasion Laird had some fun with the earnest and intense Carter. In 1978, while Laird was on a Phillips Petroleum trip with his two sons, John and David, he included a stopover in Hamburg to visit his old friend West German Chancellor Helmut Schmidt. Schmidt had just completed a four-day summit with Soviet Premier Leonid Brezhnev and had tried to call Carter to personally brief him on the talks, but Carter was teaching his Sunday school class and wouldn't take a phone call unless it was an emergency. Laird and his sons arrived soon after, at 5 P.M. that Sunday. "Let's have a drink," Schmidt pronounced, unwinding after the four-day summit. Then Schmidt asked Laird why Carter wouldn't come out of church to talk with the chancellor. Laird understood Carter's priorities and did his best to explain. Carter finally returned the call while Schmidt was drinking and chatting with Laird.

Schmidt and Carter talked for about twenty minutes about the summit and other issues, arguing heatedly at least once. More than a little irritated with Carter, and just for fun, Schmidt finally said, "I have a good friend who's here with me, and I'm going to let him talk to you."

"So I get on the phone," Laird recalled. "Carter didn't know who I was so I said, 'This is Mel Laird,' which drove Carter a little nuts because he thought I was there somehow for the Brezhnev meeting."

After a short exchange between Laird and Carter, Schmidt came back on the phone and ended the conversation. As soon as Schmidt hung up, he groused to Laird: "That SOB. I was doing something nice to call him at all, and he started arguing with me...raising hell about the things I *didn't* talk with Brezhnev about!" Schmidt was never a fan of Carter, who waffled on three important occasions when Schmidt took an unpopular stand on behalf of Carter (including support of the neutron bomb), only to have Carter reverse his position. "Carter was always asking his moral conscience, 'Is it right what I said yesterday? Is it right what I decided yesterday?'" Schmidt explained in a 2001 interview. "And then, under the influence of his wife, Rosalyn, he would come to another conclusion the next morning. But I had relied on his decision yesterday, and taken action on the basis of that decision. Then, a couple of days later, he comes up with a new insight. This happened several times."[19]

The morning after drinks with Schmidt Laird got a frantic call from the CIA's top man in Berlin, George Carver. Laird knew Carver well since Carver had been one of his CIA briefers on Vietnam when Laird was defense secretary. "I have to see you right away," Carver urged.

"The boys and I are not going to be in Berlin until Tuesday or Wednesday," Laird responded.

"I *have* to see you," Carver reiterated. "The president is all upset with us that we didn't know what you were up to regarding Schmidt and Brezhnev."

Laird's son John remembered that his father responded, "I'm here with my two boys, so we'll have to go out to dinner when we get to Berlin. What's the best restaurant in town?" Carver grudgingly agreed to pick up the tab, only to find that Laird had been on a harmless visit with an old friend instead of being part of some massive right-wing conspiracy with Schmidt to undercut Carter's initiatives with the Soviets.[20]

Perhaps Laird's biggest impact on the Carter administration was his role as a burr in Carter's saddle on the SALT II strategic arms limitation talks. Laird was a proponent of arms control, but only if the United States kept up its strategic strength with robust defense spending. In August 1977, after the Russians rejected a radical arms-reduction proposal by Carter, Laird offered a plan to get the talks moving again. But that plan meant Carter would have to promise to increase defense spending, which was a commitment he would not make at the time. In December Laird used the *Reader's Digest* to air his opinion in a story titled: "Arms Control: The Russians Are Cheating!" Laird deplored the fact that even as the Soviets were increasing their own defense spending, the United States was decreasing its budgets.[21] After the article appeared, Defense Secretary Harold Brown began consulting more regularly with Laird, anxious to enlist him on the side of SALT II. But Laird continued to express displeasure with some of the cruise missile limitations being proposed, as well as other issues.

Carter and Brezhnev signed the SALT II agreement in Vienna on June 18, 1979. Three months later Laird published a *Reader's Digest* article that questioned the value of the treaty. Though Laird was disparaging about aspects of the treaty, he did not come right out and oppose Senate ratification. Brown said that was the result of a deal he had made with Laird. "In return for an increase in defense spending, Mel agreed to at least keep quiet about it—*not* oppose it."[22] It was the Soviets who killed any possibility of ratification when they invaded Afghanistan in December 1979. Though it remained unratified, both sides generally abided by the signed accord for seven years.

Laird and Carter never became bosom buddies, but they shared a healthy mutual respect. At a minimum Carter respected Laird's network of friends. When the former president ran into a zoning problem regarding an access road to his presidential library in Atlanta, Laird called a childhood friend from Marshfield who was a city councilwoman in Atlanta. He prevailed upon her to rule in Carter's favor. One thing Carter never knew: Laird wrote a private letter in the mid-1990s to the Nobel Prize committee arguing as a Republican that the Democratic ex-president was deserving of the prize. When Carter was finally awarded the coveted honor, Laird heartily congratulated him without mentioning the letter.

～～

The intellectual foundation of what became the "Reagan Revolution" was laid most prominently by the American Enterprise Institute for Public Policy Research (AEI). Congressman Laird was one of its original founders and kept his hand in it. After he resigned as defense secretary, Laird became more intimately involved in buttressing and growing AEI. The failure of Gerald Ford to win his first election for the presidency in 1976 proved a particular boon to AEI, which became a virtual Republican government-in-exile during the Carter years as nearly two dozen former top Ford and Nixon officials collaborated with the organization. By 1977 AEI's budget had ballooned to $10 million, and the following year Laird spearheaded a three-year campaign to raise a $60 million endowment. Laird used AEI as a launch pad for some of his strongest ideas during the Carter administration, particularly on military matters. Laird co-authored a study on military personnel costs with former Pentagon official Lawrence Korb and was credited with framing the debate on that subject and getting the military a much-needed pay raise. (On Laird's recommendation, Korb was later made assistant secretary of defense for manpower in the Reagan administration.) In 1978 Laird's former assistant Bill Baroody Jr. was named to succeed his father as president of AEI.

Presidential aspirant Ronald Reagan and his advisors kept in close touch with AEI to utilize its expertise while preparing his presidential run.[23] Meanwhile, to Laird's surprise, Jerry Ford was showing signs that he might like to try for the presidency again in 1980. "Jerry is bitten with running again," Laird told the *Washington Post* in September 1978. "I think it's a mistake, and I've told him that. But he thinks lightning can strike twice." In March 1980 Ford voiced his thoughts about possibly running, and there was Laird, acting in the role of an honest friend, dousing the sparks again. While it would be "very easy" to find Republicans eager to have Ford run, Laird told the *Post*'s David Broder, it would require every one of Reagan's opponents, including George H. W. Bush, to drop their races and back Ford to wrest the nomination from Reagan. "I don't want to see Jerry hurt," Laird told another reporter. "I just don't think the numbers are there now," and he was right.[24]

After Reagan won the nomination, Ford angled for the vice presidency. Reagan aides and Ford's emissary, Kissinger, determined that what Ford really wanted was power that would make him a copresident of sorts. Laird did nothing to help. Instead he quietly advised Reagan in the strongest terms that there was only one possible choice as his vice presidential nominee—George H. W. Bush. "I thought that would be the best way to bring the party together. As a moderate, George was the best candidate and could do more for Reagan than any other candidate." Though he had not been forceful publicly about it, Laird had actually been pro-Bush, not Reagan, during the presidential primary cycle—in part, out of loyalty to Ford. "Jerry was never really able to recover from Reagan's challenge in 1976, and I always held Reagan responsible for that loss," Laird explained. "Maybe I should forgive and forget, but I am blessed or cursed with a long memory."

When Reagan won the nomination, Laird put those feelings aside and jumped into the campaign on Reagan's behalf. He authored editorials, made speeches, and otherwise stumped for the Reagan-Bush ticket.[25] It was enough to earn him a seat at the table when Reagan began choosing his Cabinet. Laird flew to California and gave a hard pitch to make George Shultz secretary of state. Laird had promoted Shultz's career, suggesting him for Nixon's first secretary of labor, then later secretary of the treasury. Working against Shultz was Caspar Weinberger, a longtime rival. Shultz was president of Bechtel Corporation, and Weinberger was vice president. Weinberger whispered in Reagan's ear that Shultz didn't want to leave Bechtel. Laird learned that it wasn't true but couldn't warn Shultz in time. Meanwhile, Weinberger and Reagan advisors were pushing hard for Alexander Haig as secretary of state. Laird's take on Haig was "Hell, you can appoint him, but you'll be sorry because he has no feel for the political situation. You have to have someone in the State Department who has some good political instincts." He said as much to Reagan's advisors, but they overrode him. Haig was appointed secretary of state and Weinberger became defense secretary.[26] Nine months later Laird was at a White House reception when an exasperated President Reagan took him aside: "Mel, you sure were right. I wished I'd have followed your advice in the first place." Haig lasted only eighteen months on the job before he was replaced by Shultz.

Laird despaired of Weinberger's long reign at the Pentagon. Weinberger had been called "Cap the Knife" when he was chief of Nixon's Office of Management and Budget, regularly trying to slash Laird's defense budgets. But once he became secretary himself, Cap the Knife became Cap the Ladle, pouring out money and capitulating to the services. In a November 1980 *Washington Post* essay Laird had warned the incoming Reagan administration of the course Weinberger would take: "The worst thing that can happen is to go on a defense spending binge that will create economic havoc at home and confusion abroad and that cannot be dealt with wisely by the Pentagon." He urged a moderate buildup, not a binge, now that the defense-minded Reagan was in control. What disturbed Laird the most—other than the record deficits that began to accrue with increased defense spending—was *what* Weinberger was choosing to spend it on: nuclear weapons. In two *Washington Post* essays in 1982 and 1983 Laird urged the administration to focus on quality manpower, not the bells and whistles of costly new hardware.[27]

By the second Reagan administration, with Weinberger still in place and pushing the expensive strategic defense initiative (SDI, or "Star Wars"), Laird raised the volume of his criticism. Not only was the complicated technology not workable, but it was also burning up money that would be better spent on the men and women of the military. While not abandoning his pursuit of nuclear missilery, Weinberger did lobby successfully for better funding for personnel. "The volunteer system was breaking down, and they always kept asking me *when* we were going to start the draft again. Not *whether*," Weinberger recalled. With Laird's help, he acknowledged, "we ultimately turned the whole thing around. By the time I left, we had waiting lists of people who wanted to get in the military. We didn't have enough slots for them."[28]

꧁

During the Reagan administration, Laird was continually plied with requests to serve in government again. He rejected some entreaties but accepted others. The first came from President-elect Reagan who asked him to serve as chairman of the President's Foreign Intelligence Advisory Board. The *Reader's Digest* considered it a conflict of interest, so Laird turned it down.

In early 1982 Laird accepted a cochair position (along with former senator Adlai Stevenson) on the Commission on the Presidential Nominating Process under the auspices of the White Burkett Miller Center for Public Affairs at the University of Virginia. The ten-member bipartisan panel concluded something that Laird already knew before the commission was formed—that the presidential primary system was a mess. But the panelists put it more politely in their final report, saying the whole process had become "cumbersome, complex, and confusing."

In the 1960s most delegates to party conventions were chosen in state party caucuses and could exercise an independent choice about their party's nominee. Presidential primaries played an important but secondary role, with many of the delegates still retaining the right at the convention to choose the candidate they wanted, no matter who had won the state primary. By 1980, however, some thirty-seven states held primaries and nearly three-quarters of the delegates were bound in their convention to follow the popular vote. The problem was that the early primaries knocked out some candidates, leaving voters in the later primaries without a full slate of choices.

The Laird-Stevenson panel recommended a reduction in the number of primaries to no more than sixteen, which proved impossible to achieve. Among other recommendations, they urged that more ex officio delegates—drawn from among members of Congress, governors, and high party officials—be included in the nominating conventions because they would not be bound by the results of state delegate selection contests. The Democratic National Committee, which was already considering changes, adopted several of the reforms, including the participation of a specified number of elected officials at their national conventions.[29]

The following October, in the wake of a terrorist bombing that killed 241 marines in their Beirut, Lebanon, barracks, Reagan and Shultz leaned on Laird to take over for Robert McFarlane as the administration's roving Middle East envoy. (McFarlane had been appointed the new national security advisor.) "My nonacceptance was not easy to communicate to these two friends," recalled Laird, who felt he was too busy at the *Digest* and on corporate boards fending off raiders to accept such a no-win assignment. Columnists Evans and Novak noted that Laird had long been frustrated that the Reagan administration, and others preceding, had put the United States in the role of "playing 'Israel's attorney' and thus alienating the Arabs." That one-sidedness invited future disaster, he warned. Reagan and Shultz went to their second choice, Donald Rumsfeld, who agreed to take on the difficult task.[30]

That same year John McCloy invited Laird to a luncheon at the River Club in New York. Among other things, McCloy had been undersecretary of war in World War II, high commissioner to Germany following the war, and chairman of Chase Manhattan Bank. McCloy explained that he would soon be stepping down as chairman of the Public Oversight Board and wanted Laird to take his seat as a member. The autonomous body of five members was established in 1977 by the American Institute of Certified Public Accountants to oversee the self-regulation of accounting firms. Laird accepted and served from 1984 to 2001.[31]

In February 1985 the Center for Strategic and International Studies at Georgetown University announced that Laird had agreed to cochair the forty-one-member Commission on National Elections with former Democratic Party chairman Robert Strauss. The commission heard from thirty-seven witnesses at five public hearings before issuing its report on November 26, 1985. Its chief contribution was the creation of the Commission on Presidential Debates to institutionalize quadrennial debates. Prior to that time, the League of Women Voters had sponsored the debates. The two-party commission has run the presidential and vice presidential debates for the last two decades, while the League has continued to sponsor presidential primary debates.

As interesting as some of the panels and commissions were, none of them could hold a candle for sheer intrigue to the outfit President Reagan got Laird to chair in 1987—a panel to assess serious problems at the old and new U.S. embassy buildings in Moscow. Since 1952 the U.S. mission had been housed "temporarily" at an old apartment building on Tchaikovsky Street in Moscow. During those years the Soviets had managed to bug it in every possible manner. In 1987 American electronics experts discovered a tiny microphone in the middle of a hand-carved replica of the Great Seal of the United States, which had been presented as a gift from the Russians and had likely heard every conversation near it since 1945. From 1953 on, the Russians bombarded the embassy with microwaves in an attempt to pick up emanations from other bugs in the embassy. In May 1964 Americans found fifty-two microphones that had been cleverly hidden in bamboo tubes built into the embassy walls. In one of the more infamous episodes, from 1976 to 1984 the Russians managed to place bugs in thirteen electric typewriters used at the embassy. The bugs transmitted the movements of the rotational typing element to nearby listening devices, allowing the Russians to re-create the secret memos, reports, and correspondence typed on those machines.[32]

Two embarrassments finally caused Reagan to convene the Laird panel in April 1987. Marines had been arrested in sensational espionage cases that portrayed them as having been compromised by KGB-controlled Russian girlfriends. And the new U.S. embassy chancery under construction in Moscow had been found to be so infested with electronic bugs that many thought it should be torn down and reconstructed under tighter security measures. It was an intelligence disaster, and Laird felt a patriotic call to arms to correct the problem. He chose as his fellow panelists General John Vessey, former chairman of the Joint Chiefs of Staff; Richard Helms, former CIA director and ambassador to Iran; and Diego Asencio, former ambassador to Brazil and Colombia. General Robert Pursley, by then retired from the air force, served as special assistant.[33]

In June the panel traveled to Moscow, where the Russians accommodated them in a thoroughly bugged guest house. General Vessey's room had twin beds, while two women—counterintelligence experts assigned to the panel—had to share a double bed in an otherwise similar room. One day when Laird and Vessey were walking down a Moscow street near the U.S. embassy, the general suggested he switch rooms with the women. By the time they got back to the guest house, their belongings had already been moved to the new rooms. Somehow the conversation between Laird and Vessey had been picked up on the street by the KGB and orders had been given to make the move.[34]

The Moscow Assessment Review Panel's final report was classified and never publicly released. The panel made fifty-three recommendations, the majority of which were enacted, according to a subsequent (also classified) State Department report.[35] Laird placed ultimate blame for lax security on U.S. Ambassador Arthur Hartman, although he was not named in the report. "The Ambassador, as the senior official present, is responsible for all that the Embassy staff does or fails to do.... He employed a management style that remained aloof until a specific event occurred that required his attention. This was clearly inadequate," the report said. Hartman once ordered a metal detector removed from a marines post because he found it inconvenient. He also advocated continued use of Russians in clerical positions even though he knew many of them were KGB agents. His attitude about counterintelligence needs left the building and its American employees wide open to Soviet surveillance.[36]

Laird's report urged a clearer policy regarding embassy personnel and fraternization with the Russians, as well as a downsizing of personnel while vital repairs were made to the old embassy, which the report described as "seedy" and "disgraceful."[37] In the wake of the report, President Reagan made the decision to tear down the new unoccupied embassy and rebuild it from scratch with only U.S. workers and materials. The George H.W. Bush administration agreed with the decision, but experts during the Clinton administration felt it could be saved as long as they put a four story "top hat" of secure offices on the top of the building. In 1976 the new embassy had been projected to cost from $75 to $100 million. After construction, deconstruction, and reconstruction, when the new building finally opened in May 2000, it had cost $370 million, making it the most expensive diplomatic building project in U.S. history.[38]

Bill Clinton and Mel Laird were never pals. "I attended briefings at the White House, some receptions, and a couple of lunches," Laird recalled. "But I don't have a great personal relationship. I'm not his greatest admirer." Nevertheless successive Clinton defense secretaries consulted with Laird, just as their predecessors had done. The first was a close friend of Laird's, former Wisconsin representative Les Aspin. His tenure was short, and he was replaced by William Perry, a longtime Laird fan who listened carefully to what Laird had to say. A key reason for that respect was Laird's "Founding Father" role for the All-Volunteer Force. Perry said, "To qualify my view, I'd say I was somewhere between skeptical and negative about instituting the volunteer army, when it began. I knew Mel had quite a lot of resistance from other sources on that, but he bulled it through anyway. By the time I became deputy secretary [in 1993], I came to believe that it was one of the great successes in reorganization of defense in decades. It's a magnificent success story now, and Mel doesn't get full credit for it. He gets the credit for instituting it, though it took a lot of other people after him to actually implement it."[39]

While Laird was fond of Perry, he was less enamored of his successor, former Maine senator William Cohen. Laird got so frustrated with Cohen's inability to manage the Pentagon and hold off the White House's demands that in 1998 he wrote a letter of complaint to Senator John Warner, chairman of the Senate Armed Services Committee. "Over the past several months, I have continued to get reports that the Administration is using the Defense Department as a dumping ground for non-performers in other parts of government," Laird wrote. A former Clinton White House deputy chief of staff had related: "We use the Pentagon to take our under-performers from the White House." Having learned by his own experience, as Warner well knew, Laird asked Warner to remind his former Senate colleague to resist such manipulation by the White House. "I have failed to get this message to our friend Cohen. He is headed for real trouble if he does not get the message."[40]

Perhaps the most intriguing aspect of Laird and the Clinton era was his relationship with his former intern, Hillary Rodham Clinton. She considered him an important mentor, and the friendship endured, mostly carried on behind the scenes through a mutual friend, Health and Human Services Secretary Donna Shalala. Once chancellor of the University of Wisconsin, which brought her into Laird's circle of friends, Shalala secured his help for her confirmation process. "He's my favorite wiseman," she said. "He just knew more than anybody how to survive in Washington." Early in 1998 Laird correctly predicted to Shalala and other friends that Hillary Clinton would run and be elected to the Senate from New York.[41]

But Laird could never bring himself to admire her husband. When a disgraced President Clinton, post–impeachment hearings, was invited in 2000 to speak and receive an honorary degree at Laird's alma mater, Carleton College, Laird was not pleased. He said of Clinton, "This is the greatest actor we've ever had in the White House; he could give acting lessons to Ronald Reagan." Laird was "at a loss to understand why Bill Clinton is so admired and respected."

Laird considered George W. Bush's electoral victory over Al Gore in November 2000 prima facie evidence that "Bush is the luckiest presidential candidate in my lifetime—because everything was against him. Gore had everything going for him, and he just lost the election. Gore was a little too polished, and he made everybody think he was brighter than them. What you want to do is make people always feel that they're brighter than you." The *second best* piece of advice Laird gave Bush during the campaign was to debate Gore. "Bush didn't want to debate, and his father agreed with him. His father didn't like debating in the House or as a candidate, so that colored his thinking. So I leaned real hard on (George W.) Bush to debate." Laird solicited Bob Strauss, his partner in establishing the Presidential Debate Commission, to urge Bush's participation in the debate. Laird was confident that Bush would come across as more approachable than the stiff Gore.

Laird maintained that the *best* advice he gave candidate Bush was to select

Dick Cheney as his running mate. Once the election was won, Laird regularly called and visited Cheney during the transition. "I made certain recommendations, among them that Rummy [Rumsfeld] be secretary of defense. I went through all kinds of hell doing that. But that's another story," and one Laird was not willing to detail. Cheney leaned toward Paul Wolfowitz for defense but finally recommended that Rumsfeld would be secretary and Wolfowitz would be deputy secretary.

Laird's advice, while never totally predictable, was always interesting. When former president Reagan died in June 2004, Laird was recovering from knee replacement surgery and could not travel to Washington for the funeral. But he rallied to stop a move by Senate Majority Leader Bill Frist to name the Pentagon after Reagan. He called Senator Warner and recounted how, in the emotional aftermath of Eisenhower's death, Senators Barry Goldwater and John Tower and others had called on Secretary Laird to support naming the Pentagon after Ike. The late five-star general was a soldier-hero of the first order, yet Laird thought it was a mistake to name the Pentagon after anyone. Warner agreed and opposed renaming the Pentagon. The Senate was appeased by naming National Airport after Reagan. "Mel, my valued advisor: Your input on this naming issue was critical," Senator Warner wrote by hand after the debate. "The 'Pentagon' will, I am confident, remain!"[42]

49

Another Vietnam?

~~✦~~

AMERICA'S TENTH SECRETARY OF DEFENSE arrived at the Pentagon for a wide-ranging private conference with the newly installed twenty-first secretary of defense on a brisk February afternoon in 2001. The escort whom Secretary Donald Rumsfeld had sent to meet his friend Mel Laird at the River Entrance offered to give him the standard VIP tour. Sure, Laird said with a smile. But soon he took over the tour himself, providing the escort with a firsthand view of history.

As they walked through the General Omar Bradley Corridor, Laird explained: "These corridors used to be stinking, lousy-looking corridors. They were run-down and looked like hell." But in his day Laird thought there was no reason for the Pentagon's seventeen and a half miles of hallways to be so dreary, so he had them spruced them up—decorating, naming, and dedicating some of the halls. The tour continued to the A-ring "Corridor of Secretaries," where the walls were hung with framed portraits of all past secretaries of defense.

Laird drew his escort's attention to the air force wing where antiwar radicals in his day had set off a bomb. There was the Meditation Room, which he had established as a place of solace for those who guard the nation. At the end of the "Corridor of Correspondents" that he had dedicated, Laird had also created a memorial to war correspondents who had been killed on the job. And down another corridor was the "Hall of Heroes," displaying the names of every Medal of Honor recipient. Laird had personally presented some of those medals.

Laird and his escort arrived at the defense secretary's complex in the Eisenhower Corridor, which Laird had dedicated for the World War II hero who had been his mentor and friend. Rumsfeld emerged and greeted Laird warmly. It was a fine time for the military, they agreed. The eight-year era of Bill Clinton's strained relationship with the military was over. Rumsfeld, a navy veteran, was spearheading a transformation of the Pentagon that had already created an upbeat mood. Rumsfeld thanked Laird for the all-volunteer force he had "fathered," and which Rumsfeld had implemented when he became the thirteenth secretary of defense under President Ford in 1975.

One of the most important things for the new secretary, as well as the new President Bush, was not to closet themselves with a small group of yes-men, Laird advised. Don't worry, Rumsfeld said, you're preaching to the choir. Rumsfeld rehearsed how he, as White House chief of staff, had been the one to advise President Ford of the same thing. Knowing one of Nixon's fatal flaws had been to create a phalanx of sycophants, Rumsfeld had encouraged the notion of a "Kitchen Cabinet" for Ford, of which Laird became a prominent member.

The two discussed some of the key lessons from Vietnam and Laird's program of Vietnamization, which Rumsfeld praised. The plan to transfer all military operations to the South Vietnamese had worked well, both agreed. The South Vietnamese had defended their nation for more than two years on their own. Laird reminded Rumsfeld that Saigon had fallen in April 1975, when he was Ford's chief of staff, primarily because a weak White House lobbying effort had failed to prevent Congress from cutting off military supplies and financial aid. Rumsfeld took the veiled criticism well, and the conversation continued to other topics.

The most memorable moment came as Laird was leaving. The two were standing in the hall, looking at some of Rumsfeld's photos and talking about past wars that had left thousands of U.S. troops still stationed around the world in a protective capacity—Germany, Japan, South Korea, and elsewhere. Laird got up close to his old friend and pointedly said: "Remember this, Rummy: *it's a helluva lot easier to get into a war than it is to get out of one!*" "I will, I will," an amused Rumsfeld agreed, happy that he had inherited a first-class volunteer military that was not engaged in any war.[1]

A few weeks before that meeting, on January 26, 2001, Laird had gone to the Pentagon for Rumsfeld's welcoming ceremony. A half-hour before it began Rumsfeld held a press conference and invited Laird to observe and critique his performance. "Before I start," Rumsfeld told the waiting correspondents, "I want to introduce Mel Laird in the back." After Laird stood up to applause, Rumsfeld continued: "Mel and I served in Congress together, and he's a longtime friend, and I'm delighted he's able to be here today."

Rumsfeld delivered a short speech about his goals, including a desire to preside over "years of peace" as Pentagon chief. The first question he took buttonholed him on a subject of special interest to Laird: "During your confirmation hearings, you described the ABM treaty...as ancient history. Are you...ready to scrap that treaty?"

Laird winced. Candidate Bush had vowed to explore various missile defense options, and abandon the treaty, so Rumsfeld had no choice but to offer a qualified yes.[2] After the short press conference, Laird walked with Rumsfeld to the official ceremony. Laird complimented him on his performance with the press but noted that he would like to revisit the ABM topic with Rumsfeld another day. Laird understood that Bush and Rumsfeld wanted to build a small-scale missile defense against a possible future nuclear missile launched by a rogue nation or terrorists. But he felt that could be done by *amending* the ABM treaty and said so in a *Washington Post* editorial on August 23. The treaty, which he had been instrumental in achieving, had worked for thirty years and was "key to maintaining stability" between the United States and Russia.[3]

At a press briefing the same day, Rumsfeld was asked about Laird's article. "Mel is a smart man," he averred, before noting that no decision had yet been made to withdraw from the ABM treaty.[4]

Several editorials of the day supported Laird's position. The *St. Louis Post-Dispatch* headline read, "Listen to Mr. Laird," and the newspaper opined that it was "odd" to find that a former defense secretary whose conservative politics and bald head had once been caricatured as "a human nuclear bomb" would now find himself "to the left of a Republican president on the issue of arms control."[5]

September 11 terrorist attacks on the United States came less than three weeks later, changing the world and wiping out any chance for cooler heads to prevail. In mid-December Bush notified the Russians that the United States would withdraw from the ABM treaty the following June.

During the first days of the Bush administration, Laird had also tried to push for ratification of the Comprehensive Test Ban Treaty (CTBT). Retired General John M. Shalikashvili had been recruited by President Clinton to study what would be needed to secure approval of the CTBT. Laird was one of the "wisemen" Shalikashvili had consulted. Laird offered sixteen recommendations, all of which the former Joint Chiefs chairman incorporated into his final report delivered on January 5, 2001, in the last days of the Clinton administration.

Laird joined former defense secretaries Harold Brown and William Perry in authoring a column published in the *New York Times*, which endorsed CTBT ratification. The trio noted that the first President Bush had unilaterally suspended nuclear tests in 1992, a policy that was likely to "remain in place for many years to come." They considered the treaty "an important element of the global nonproliferation regime, and crucial to American leadership of those efforts."[6] Any hope for the CTBT was swallowed up in the focus on the subsequent war on terror.

❧

On most defense issues in 2001 Laird was foursquare behind Rumsfeld, who privately enlisted him time and again for help on difficult problems, such as Rumsfeld's ambitious plan to close many unnecessary military bases. Rumsfeld turned to Laird for help because he knew that the wily ex-pol had successfully closed more bases than any defense secretary before or since. While closing all U.S. bases in South Vietnam had helped boost Laird's numbers, the majority of the bases he closed were in the United States and elsewhere, besides Vietnam. In four years Laird closed 400 installations and downsized 1,400 others, saving billions of dollars. By December 1972 he had finished another round that would close or cut back 274 more military bases.

But since Laird's time at the Pentagon, base closures had become so politically impossible to achieve that a congressionally supervised entity was created: the Base Closure and Realignment Commission (BRAC). In four different rounds between 1988 and 1995 these earnest cost cutters were able to accomplish only ninety-seven major closures. Nothing had happened between 1995 and 2001, so Rumsfeld was anxious to get BRAC working again. He turned to Laird for help.[7]

As Laird consulted with Rumsfeld's experts, it became clear that while the active duty military had shrunk by half after the cold war, commensurate base closings had not followed. Some 425 installations were identified for closure, a number that represented 20 percent of the military's infrastructure and would save as much as $3 billion a year. Laird quickly signed on to a letter of support but suggested waiting until as many former defense secretaries as possible could be added to the letter to give it more weight. Seven others signed, and it was dispatched in mid-October to key members of Congress. The premise of the letter was that money spent on unneeded bases was money not available for the war on terror.[8]

It was not enough to dislodge the pork barrel bases, but Laird kept tilting at this windmill. In a February 2002 MSNBC interview he complained, "We have many more bases than we need. We're 33 percent overbased as far as our military is concerned, and we should be cutting back. But it's ridiculous what [Rumsfeld] has had to go through to get approval. I hope that he keeps his guns blazing."[9]

⌇

Laird's first reaction to the tragic events of September 11, 2001, was similar to that of other Americans—profound shock and deep sorrow. But like many veterans of battle, Laird's thoughts quickly moved on to the next step—how to respond. It was the kind of training ingrained into the young Ensign Laird and other navy men in the Pacific in 1945 as they fended off kamikaze attacks by the Japanese. Memories of those kamikaze attacks had not faded, and the day before 9/11, some of the men of the *Maddox* had coincidentally been sharing those memories. It was an eerie backdrop for Laird and the men as they watched suicide pilots of another ilk crash planes into the World Trade Center and Pentagon. "Today's events are shockers—even for vets," said a shaken *Maddox* shipmate of Laird's, Mel Cunningham.[10]

Many opinions were offered by retired defense experts and officers on television and radio shows, in magazine and newspaper columns. They were full of advice for President Bush and Secretary Rumsfeld about how to respond, but Laird was not among them. The *Washingtonian* magazine rushed out an article identifying the "71 People the President Should Listen To," and Laird was prominent on the list.[11]

Three weeks after 9/11 a confidant pressed Laird on why he wasn't in the thick of it. "What makes you think I'm not?" he responded.

Laird had learned that the best advice is given privately and is most useful when the advisor doesn't seek public credit for it. Rumsfeld had called him soon after 9/11, but Laird had declined to join the host of meddlers and second-guessers. Early on he went to the Pentagon several times, at Rumsfeld's request, to review the intelligence and offer ideas, but chose not to go public with any advice.

The only public connection Laird had to the 9/11 aftermath was a tender one. In 2002 he was asked by Rumsfeld to serve on an eleven-member committee determining the appropriate memorial for the 184 service personnel and civilians who died when American Airlines Flight 77 struck the Pentagon on 9/11. Laird and others on the committee pored over almost 2,500 design entries and consulted the families of victims. The winning design, "Light Benches," features 184 illuminated aluminum benches, each engraved with the name of a victim. The memorial, which includes clusters of shade trees, stands on two acres of Pentagon lawn, within three hundred feet of the crash site.[12]

Privately Laird lamented the disparity between financial reparations given to the 9/11 families and the neglect of the families of military men and women killed in action. He vented a little bit about that in a letter to former Joint Chiefs chairman John Vessey. "When we compare the million dollar award to some of the families who suffered in the attacks in Washington and New York, with the losses of the families of our men and women on active duty every day, it does cause some of *these* families—if not our troops—to wonder. *All* these losses are truly mourned."[13]

⌖

In the run-up to the March 2003 invasion of Iraq, behind the scenes Laird was firmly opposed to the timing and necessity of the action. Only an occasional hint of his feelings showed in public. For instance, almost a year before, at the fourteenth annual Conference of the Secretaries of Defense, Laird had opined that the key issue with Iraq was not whether a war could be won. "The question is what we do afterwards," Laird said. Frank Carlucci chimed in with agreement. "If we thought [nation-building in] Afghanistan was tough, try Iraq!" Added Harold Brown: "If you put American troops in an urban setting where there are terrorists, the Americans are going to end up being the target."[14]

Perhaps most distressing to Laird in early 2003 was that the top officials of the Bush administration did not seem to want to listen to anyone who was not bent on war. Laird and his friends Brent Scowcroft and Larry Eagleburger (who served, respectively, as national security advisor and secretary of state to the first President Bush) spoke about this frustration among themselves. Only the usually cautious Scowcroft had gone public with his opposition. His authorship of an August 2002 *Wall Street Journal* column criticizing Bush's

Iraq policy had made him persona non grata at the White House. Each of the three men polled his sources within the Bush administration and got reports of an inflexible determination to bring down Saddam Hussein. President Bush and Vice President Cheney had become absolutely committed to the course. Scowcroft was surprised to discover that his own protégé, National Security Advisor Condoleezza Rice, was just as evangelical as Bush and Cheney about changing the face of the Middle East.

Rumsfeld was "gung ho" on the idea of a challenge in Iraq and was being stoked by Deputy Secretary Paul Wolfowitz and close Pentagon advisor Richard Perle. Laird wanted to wait for more reliable intelligence reports about weapons of mass destruction in Iraq. He reminded Rumsfeld of the intelligence failure that launched the Vietnam war—a nonexistent "attack" on two American destroyers in the Gulf of Tonkin.

Both Eagleburger and Laird made inquiries at the State Department and found more of a propensity for restraint and patience. Laird pinned his hopes on Secretary of State Colin Powell—the man whose illustrious career Laird had helped launch by sending him over to the White House as a young officer. (Laird had also propelled Scowcroft on his path by insisting to Nixon that Scowcroft be the general ready to replace Alexander Haig as Nixon's military assistant.)

"A war cannot be fought by this country without the support of both the State Department and the Department of Defense—any president knows that would be folly," Laird said. "But Colin did not question the intelligence in a more adequate and firm way, so he acquiesced when I believe he shouldn't have."

The unusual trio of "antiwar" conspirators had one last move: Scowcroft would ask his friend former president George H.W. Bush to get Scowcroft and a few others into the Oval Office for a confidential sit-down. Laird had learned from a friend that the younger Bush's mind was made up, and "he wasn't listening to the old man." "The president's circle of friends had become very small. He just didn't want to talk to anyone who cautioned patience, who suggested he should wait a few weeks more to build up support," Laird said. The backstage lobbying efforts of the trio failed, and once the invasion was on, all three publicly supported America's new war effort.[15]

A month after the U.S. invasion of Iraq, the chairman of the Senate Armed Services Committee, Senator John Warner, met with 350 high school students in Laird's old congressional district. He was a guest speaker at the nineteenth biennial Laird Youth Leadership Day. The invading U.S. soldiers had found no weapons of mass destruction in Iraq, and disgruntlement was building. Warner told the group that Laird's opinion was still highly valued in Washington. Knowing of Laird's doubts, Warner obliquely noted: "I will eventually do an analysis on what went right and what went wrong in the war on Iraq, and I will call on this man for his opinion."[16]

Rumsfeld would occasionally ask Laird for his opinion, too, and get it in spades. With Laird's candor, the distance between them grew. Laird visited the Pentagon for occasional briefings on the war, which are generally offered to former defense secretaries to keep them up to date. But he tired of it and walked out in the middle of one of the briefings. Rumsfeld heard about it and was miffed. They didn't talk for awhile.

In early February 2004, as the presidential election began heating up, Rumsfeld reached out again and asked for Laird's opinion. "You asked me to be frank on how things are going," Laird began in a February 11 note. "You were somewhat upset with me for walking out of the briefing last year on the Middle East situation. I hope you have gotten over it. The briefing was so formalized there was no opportunity to raise questions or make suggestions, only listen. No one is required to follow anything we old timers say, but sometimes it doesn't hurt to listen." Laird reminded Rumsfeld of Laird's own policy about intelligence: never believe the first and second reports. Similarly he said. "As I told you in your first week in office, you can believe the third assessment report on any operation if they concur with the first two—and even then you can be disappointed." The administration was making a serious mistake in thinking that stabilizing Iraq would be "a cakewalk."

The four-page letter covered a variety of subjects. Laird urged Rumsfeld to release Bush's entire National Guard record because of the controversy then swirling around whether Bush had avoided Vietnam service. "His record, which ended in an Honorable Discharge, should be officially disclosed. Public disclosure and transparency are the best policy. Bush certainly did not desert; he did not go to Canada; but rather, he volunteered, served, and then requested an early out to attend graduate school."

The same advice about openness held for their mutual friend Vice President Cheney. "Cheney's unwillingness to divulge the names of individuals meeting with him on energy policy continues to be a mistake. Because of his background after leaving government, transparency and full disclosure should have been his number one concern," Laird wrote.

"Anyway, Rummy, I have rambled around in this note—[but] you asked for it," he concluded. "Tear it up after you have read it, but remember I do love you and Joyce. Your plate is full, but by putting on an extra full-court press, we may be saved and win in November."[17]

The temporary rift was repaired. Rumsfeld found the recommendations useful and prescriptive, following up on all of them. "I just once again reread your February 11th memo and found it helpful," he wrote back on June 6. "If you have other thoughts and suggestions as we go along, please do let me have them. Thanks, my friend."[18]

In early May 2004 the first photos and reports were published of the American torture of Iraqi prisoners at Abu Ghraib prison, twenty miles west of Baghdad. The notorious prison that was the center of Saddam Hussein's torture of dissidents and innocents was being used by American interrogators to extract information from alleged insurgents. At the forefront of the reporting was Seymour Hersh, the same reporter who had exposed the My Lai massacre in Vietnam in 1968. Hersh revealed the army's own damning fifty-three-page investigation of Abu Ghraib in *The New Yorker* magazine. The practices were abhorrent to Laird, who had spoken up so often and eloquently during the Vietnam War against the North Vietnamese torture of American prisoners of war.

In an unrelated event on May 26 the National Archives released twenty thousand pages of private Kissinger documents, a move that Kissinger had unsuccessfully contested. Reporters quickly found many tantalizing tidbits, especially in the notes of telephone conversations taken by Kissinger's secretary. Laird had seen some of the notes before and had considered the source to be questionable. He knew Kissinger had a habit of doctoring the notes to make himself look better.

Among the conversations reporters latched on to was a November 21, 1969, discussion between Kissinger and Laird about the unfolding My Lai scandal, which had happened during the Johnson administration:

"K[issinger] was calling about the atrocity case," the secretary's notes began. "The President wants to make sure L[aird] [has] got a game plan. K said it was going to be a terrible mess." Laird asked if Kissinger wanted to see the photos which were "pretty terrible," but Kissinger wasn't interested. "L said about a game plan, he'd like to sweep the whole thing under the rug, but you can't do that." He planned to confirm the story, and release the results of an investigation he had begun the previous March.

When the notes were released, Laird was surprised to see the language, "sweep the whole thing under the rug." He remembered telling Kissinger that the government investigative report on My Lai would have to be released as soon as military lawyers assured Laird that the release would not harm their prosecution. Still, the transcript made headlines in 2004. "News had just broken of a terrible wrongdoing committed by American soldiers, and the secretary of defense and the national security advisor debated whether there was any way to stop newspapers and television news programs from showing graphic photographs of the victims," the *New York Times* began its story on page one. The incident had "uncanny echoes of the Iraq war and the abuses at Abu Ghraib prison, at least in the fact of the photographs, if not in the severity of wrongdoing." National Public Radio's senior analyst Daniel Schorr, a veteran Vietnam war reporter, similarly concluded: "Interesting how the present echoes the past. My Lai then, Abu Ghraib now, and both times, Seymour Hersh to break through the official silence."[19]

It was only a temporary distraction for Laird, who had bigger matters on his plate. He was gradually considering going public with some of his criticisms about the war, which was not his nature as an *ex*–government official.

⟆⟇

The Iraq war had become a "quagmire" of sorts, and commentators and politicians began making more frequent comparisons to Vietnam, resurrecting old recriminations about the war. It roiled Laird's sense of pride about Vietnamization and renewed his old resentments about how Ford, Kissinger, and Congress had abandoned South Vietnam in 1975, throwing away the work of Vietnamization.

He wrote Kissinger a private letter in January 2002 after reading an incomplete account by the former secretary of state about the fall of Vietnam. Laird felt Kissinger was distancing himself from the Paris Accords, which "under your skillful leadership" had been negotiated. "I sold Vietnamization to the President, you, the Congress, Abrams, Bunker, and the Joint Chiefs in 1969, clearly stating that our personnel withdrawals would be based on our longer-term military aid to the South until the South and North could themselves negotiate a settlement," Laird wrote to Kissinger. "We welshed on our promises as a nation, thus assuring that no peaceful agreement between the North and South would ever be reached. We invited by our actions the complete takeover by the North."

A few paragraphs later, he placed the blame on the Ford administration. "I never lost a vote on Vietnamization and the support of military aid to the South Vietnamese forces upon our withdrawal," he wrote. But after Laird left office, "the ball was dropped . . . by the White House, Defense and State [a reference to Kissinger himself] in marshaling the support for the promises of the Paris Agreement and the Vietnamization program. . . . It takes hard work to get the right numbers to obtain a majority vote, but any Secretary of Defense or State who can't get that vote, just hasn't tried hard enough."

Laird cheerily ended the recitation "with best wishes" and averred that none of this temporary dispute about history lessened his "respect and admiration" for Kissinger."[20]

While Kissinger took more care about his public pronouncements on the subject after the correspondence with Laird, others were not so precise about Iraq-Vietnam comparisons. Throughout 2004 and into 2005 talk escalated in Congress and around the nation about how the United States should get out of Iraq before it became "another Vietnam." The octogenarian Laird had finally had enough.

In the thirty years since the end of the Vietnam War, Americans had come to accept the explanation that the United States had "lost" that war. In an effort to set the record straight Laird wrote a lengthy analytical cover article for the November 2005 issue of the influential *Foreign Affairs* magazine, published by the Council on Foreign Relations. Entitled "Iraq: Learning the Lessons of Vietnam," Laird wrote that he feared a shorthand version of history had left America "timorous about war, deeply averse to intervening in even a just cause, and dubious of its ability to get out of a war once it is in one." The article compared and contrasted the Vietnam and Iraq wars and said that the only way the Iraq War could become "another Vietnam" would be if the United States ignored the lessons of history and pulled out of Iraq precipitously. Echoing his early advice to Rumsfeld, he added in a much-quoted sentence: "Getting out of a war is still dicier than getting into one, as President George W. Bush can attest."

The lesson of Vietnamization was that the Bush administration "must adhere to a standard of competence for the Iraqi security forces, and when that standard is met, U.S. troops should be withdrawn in corresponding numbers." It had worked in Vietnam, and similarly in Iraq, "the United States should not let too many more weeks pass before it shows its confidence in the training of the Iraqi armed forces by withdrawing a few thousands U.S. troops from the country. We owe it to the restive people back home to let them know there is an exit strategy, and, more important, we owe it to the Iraqi people. The readiness of the Iraqi forces need not be 100 percent, nor must the new democracy be perfect before we begin our withdrawal."

As to the prisoner abuse scandals, there was no excuse. "To stop abuses and mistakes by the rank and file, whether in the prisons or on the streets, heads must roll at much higher levels than they have thus far," Laird wrote. "For me, the alleged prison scandals reported to have occurred in Iraq, in Afghanistan, and at Guantanamo Bay have been a disturbing reminder of the mistreatment of our own POWs by North Vietnam. The conditions in our current prison camps are nowhere near as horrific as they were at the 'Hanoi Hilton,' but that is no reason to pat ourselves on the back. The minute we begin to deport prisoners to other nations where they can legally be tortured, when we hold people without charges or trial, when we move prisoners around to avoid the prying inspections of the Red Cross, when prisoners die inexplicably on our watch, we are on a slippery slope toward the inhumanity that we deplore."

Regarding Secretary Rumsfeld, Laird's friend of more than forty years whose appointment he had personally urged on President Bush, it was time for a make-over. "[H]is overconfident and self-assured style on every issue, while initially endearing him to the media, did not play well with Congress during his first term." It was also a mistake to think he had to appear "much smarter than the elected officials" to whom he reports on the Hill. Laird said he had been heartened that Rumsfeld seemed to be modifying his style to become "more collegial."

Laird implied that Bush had become the Great Uncommunicator. "His west Texas cowboy approach—shoot first and answer questions later, or do the job first and let the results speak for themselves—is not working." Laird publicly advised the president to more forcefully and candidly market the mission in Iraq. "When troops are dying, the commander-in-chief cannot be coy, vague or secretive. We learned that in Vietnam, too."[21]

The opus, with equal parts criticism and support, attracted national attention. The *New York Times* said the piece had been " heavily read." Senators John Kerry and Russell Feingold quoted from it as they grilled Secretary of State Condoleeza Rice at an October 19, 2005, hearing of the Senate Foreign Relations Committee. Even former West German Chancellor Helmut Schmidt wrote from Hamburg that he had read it "with the greatest of interest. You are still as clear-cut and outspoken as ever before." Schmidt added that it would be "much more difficult" to find a solution for "the Iraq quagmire [because] it will require much deeper understanding of the different civilizations of the Kurdish people, the Shiite Arabs and the Sunni Arabs. This understanding presently seems to be absent in the White House."[22]

Laird made sure copies of the *Foreign Affairs* article were delivered in advance to both Rumsfeld and Bush. The president soon began a series of prime-time television speeches to educate the public on the Iraq mission. On January 5, 2006, Bush convened a bipartisan meeting of thirteen former secretaries of defense and state and then turned it into a dog-and-pony show with military briefers on video feed from Iraq monopolizing the time. Only Laird and former secretary of state Madeline Albright forcefully spoke their minds. As the group stood for a photo opportunity, Bush told reporters that "not everybody around this table agreed with my decision to go into Iraq, and I fully understand that. And I am most grateful for the suggestions that have been given. We take to heart the advice."

The *New York Times* called it singular that Bush "had waited more than 1,000 days into the war in Iraq—and after many mistakes had been made—to gather together the men and one woman who once held their own skull sessions in that [Roosevelt] room, and who once used the West Wing as a backdrop for arguments over Vietnam and Somalia, the Balkans and the 1991 Gulf War." *Times* columnist Maureen Dowd found it "disturbing ... that with several hundreds of years' worth of foreign policy at his elbows, and a bloody, thorny mess in Iraq, Mr. Bush would devote mere moments to letting some fresh air into his House of Pain."[23]

Privately Laird felt similarly; less than fifteen minutes had been allotted for any or all of the thirteen to speak. But he was heartened in the following days to see Bush personally escalate his public relations campaign about the war and Rumsfeld become a bit more respectful of Congress. Then on May 12 Laird returned to the White House with nine of the other secretaries for a second meeting at which Bush acknowledged there had been little time for them to talk during the first round. "This time he really did want to listen, and it was a much better meeting," Laird said.[24]

The war on terror also gave Laird cause to come to the defense of his "total force" concept. In an essay for the *Washington Post* on February 6 Laird praised the work of the National Guard and Reserves during the war and criticized moves by the Bush administration to downsize the Guard and to be stingy with its equipment needs.[25]

Laird had not been timid about tutoring or criticizing Rumsfeld, but he was equally quick to defend "Rummy" against what Laird saw as unwarranted criticism. In the spring of 2006 several retired generals went public with their complaints about how Rumsfeld was handling the war, accusing him of sidelining those in the military who disagreed with him. Laird took up his pen again, this time with former military assistant Robert Pursley as coauthor, on another *Washington Post* essay. The two men wrote that the carping generals had passed up plenty of chances to speak when they were on active duty. The subsequent armchair quarterbacking was divisive and would be perceived by the enemy as a sign of weakness. Laird valued and defended civilian control of the military. "Rumsfeld respects the delicate balance between military and civilian control, but in the end, the decisions are his to make," Laird and Pursley wrote.[26]

Laird gave no quarter to increasing calls for Rumsfeld's resignation. But in June, at the annual former defense secretaries conference, Laird repeated his belief that no defense secretary should serve more than one term. "I told that to Rummy—that he should stay only four years," Laird said. "But he didn't pay any attention to me." In September Laird again noted to a *USA Today* reporter that "I've cautioned everybody that four years is enough in that particular job. You kind of wear yourself out."[27]

Rumsfeld, who had been both the youngest and oldest man to serve in the post, resigned of his own accord in December 2006, only a few days short of being the longest-serving secretary; Robert McNamara is still that title holder.

⚬

"Let's face it, the war was the top issue," Laird bluntly told the *Los Angeles Times* as the reason for the Republican loss of Congress to the Democrats in November 2006. "It's easy to get into a war, but it's hard to get out—that's what voters are telling the president and Congress, and now they have to get it right."[28] But Bush did not seem to get the message. Without reelection of his own to worry about, the president became increasingly intractable, and his approval numbers plunged. The openness and public dialogue that Laird saw as key to public support for the war on terror fell victim to Bush's determination to justify his agenda in Iraq. Congress saw an opportunity to excoriate Bush and piled it on.

Without actually defending Bush's performance or leadership, Laird instead argued in early 2007 that this was no time for Congress to cut off funding for the war. In Vietnam, "it would have been devastating if Congress had cut the purse strings before our troops were withdrawn and before the South Vietnamese had learned to stand on their own," Laird wrote in the *Washington Post*.[29] "Democrats are positioned to offer a plan for Iraq, but cutting off funding is not a plan." He urged an increase in the defense budget to assure better pay and equipment—essentials for the all-volunteer army to thrive.

Parenthetically he praised his former intern, Senator Hillary Clinton, as a model of probity in thoughtfully addressing the issue. He called her "the best hope for leadership" from the Democratic majority and said other presidential candidates "would do well to follow her example." Though Senator Clinton's views on the war evolved after Laird wrote that in January 2007, Laird's point was valid when he said, "In 1972, the Democratic presidential nominee, George McGovern, carried only two states because he had no plan for the war; he only criticized the Vietnamization withdrawal plan." Any presidential candidate in 2008 who simply slammed Bush without proposing his or her own well-reasoned exit strategy for Iraq was not likely to win, in Laird's view.

The "lessons learned" from Vietnam continued to percolate in Laird's thinking. Following a Kissinger essay in the *Washington Post*, Laird wrote in the *Post* again on June 29, 2007, recalling his tough talk with the South Vietnamese leadership in early 1969. "The South Vietnamese finally realized that they had the ball in their court: There would be no more 'surges' in American military personnel—only reductions.... The schedule of withdrawal should never be telegraphed to the enemy, nor should the ebb and flow of the enemy attacks dictate the pace of withdrawal. That pace should be based on the improvement of the Iraqi defense forces. But Iraq might need some straight talk and threats to make those improvements, just as Saigon needed to see the first American combat units walking out the door."

He concluded: "The same kind of well-devised plan for withdrawal over time is needed for Iraq as it takes over the military security job that belongs to the Iraqi government." The United States cannot simply, "walk away from their responsibilities and promises as they did in 1975. We have an obligation to carry through in Iraq. Many Americans did not agree on the reasons for going to Iraq in the first place, but the Middle East, with its political, economic, social and cultural issues, is of greater long-term interest to our national security than was Vietnam. Wars are very easy to start but very hard to get out of, as we are finding today in Iraq."[30]

In August 2007 President Bush began making his own comparisons between Iraq and Vietnam. "Three decades later, there is legitimate debate about how we got into the Vietnam war and how we left," Bush said in a speech before the Veterans of Foreign Wars convention in Kansas City, Missouri. "Whatever your position is on that debate, one unmistakable legacy of Vietnam is that the price of America's withdrawal was paid by millions of innocent citizens whose agonies would add to our vocabulary new terms like 'boat people' [and] 're-education camps,'" and the United States must not similarly "abandon" Iraqis struggling to build a democracy.[31]

At the time of the president's speech, U.S. troops had been in Iraq for more than four years, and the taxpayers had spent more than $600 billion on the war on terror, roughly equal to the inflation-adjusted $614 billion spent on the Vietnam War, according to the nonpartisan Congressional Research Service. During that time, more than 3,700 U.S. soldiers and possibly as many as 600,000 Iraqis had died.[32]

Finally, in September 2007, Bush accepted a recommendation from his commander in Iraq, General David Petraeus, and announced plans to begin bringing home a few U.S. troops. For Laird, Petraeus's recommendations were an echo of reports from General Creighton Abrams in Vietnam. "Training the Iraqi troops is a difficult job indeed, but it can be done if the Iraqi government really wants security," Laird said. His own assessment was an echo of his Vietnam drumbeat—that if the people of South Vietnam really wanted their democracy, they were capable of taking over the war to win that democracy.

Melvin Laird turned eighty-five in September 2007. He had two knee-replacement surgeries in 2004, which limited his air travel. But age did not dull his political or military instincts. Powerful friends in and out of government continued to give him a bully pulpit when he had something to say. As long as his mind was clear, his pen sharp, and his phones and computer in good working order, quitting was not an option. "I plan to be active until the day I die," he said. For a man who was involved in public service, one way or another, for more than sixty years, the reason is the same as the one young Ensign Laird proffered to his shipmates coming home from World War II: he felt there was some good he could do, and there is no end to such an imperative.

Epilogue

⌣

POLITICIANS LIKE MELVIN LAIRD don't come along often. In his second life, the one after politics, he did not have to remake himself. He moved through the years with the confidence of one who did not feel the need to make excuses for himself. To observe him is a lesson in how politics ought to work—with civility and integrity, across party lines, compromising for the greater good, and keeping a close ear to the rumble of public opinion and the sound of democracy. Reading the speeches made about him at the dedication of the Laird Center for Medical Research in 1997 is like hearing a clarion call for what is needed in politics today. Former president Ford asked:

> Wouldn't it be great if our politics today could also reflect Mel's blend of principle and pragmatism? To many voters, and even more non-voters, parties today are suspected of being decidedly unrepresentative. At worst they appear as little more than conduits for huge amounts of special interest money. But fund-raising abuses are by no means the only cancer eating away at our democracy. Today we look with horror upon the smoke-filled rooms of legend. Over the years, I've sat in more than my share of smoke-filled rooms. So has Mel. I think it's sort of fair to say, both of us, we've even inhaled from time to time. I ask you, who is more accountable to the voters? Those in the smoke-filled room whose jobs depended on keeping their word and who gave us Lincoln, both Roosevelts, Truman and Eisenhower? Or the professional hired guns of today, whose services are for sale, whose convictions are located in focus groups, and whose loyalty may not outlast election day?[1]

For Laird, the nation as a whole was the only focus group that counted, and politics was the art of answering to the focus group with a rare and successful blend of integrity and pragmatism. It wasn't always just about doing good, but about having fun as well. David Broder, who was also on hand at the Laird Center dedication, punctuated that point in a short speech. He cited three reasons why Laird got along so well with journalists, when so many politicians don't:

> Mel Laird was a great source for us in Washington because he scooped up information from his network of pals. He was a reliable source on everything from the latest political gossip to the most arcane and important international strategy.

The second thing that made him [unique] was that he loved to expose plots. And when there wasn't a plot to expose, he would invent one. And sometimes, as when he maneuvered President Ford into the Oval Office, those plots actually worked. And he usually got someone else to carry them out.

Most beguilingly for me and many others, Mel Laird always did his business with that twinkle in his eye that told you that he knew, as well as you did, that politics was really the only game that was worth a grownup's time.[2]

NOTES

PROLOGUE

1. Sister Francis Louviere, Daughters of Charity of St. Vincent de Paul, Carville, La., interview, 5/8/03; Betsy Bensen, Iberville Parish Library, interview, 5/12/03. "The National Leprosarium in the United States," *International Surgery*, 10/69; "Carville Hospital Celebrates 40th Anniversary," *Advocate* (Baton Rouge, La.), 2/6/71; "Carville: A Century's Worth of Miracles," *Louisiana Life*, Winter 1993; "100 Years in the Fight against Fear," *Advocate*, 11/20/94; "Key Dates in the History of Hansen's Disease Center at Carville," *Advocate*, 7/21/96; "The Only World They Know," *Newsweek*, 3/29/99; "Twilight at a Leprosy Center," ABC News, 3/30/99; "Last Days at the Leprosarium," *Life*, 4/99. Julia Elwood, quoted in *Life*, 4/99.

2. Jack Mills, interviews 11/12/99, 6/2/00, and 10/4/00. After he returned to Washington, Laird put through an emergency appropriation for much-needed maintenance work at Carville. In 1994, when the hospital campus celebrated its centennial, the keynote speaker was President Bill Clinton's chief political strategist, James Carville, whose family gave the town its name. As a child, Carville had spent evenings at the facility watching movies in the hospital theater. One of his father's best friends was a patient there. ("James Carville Will Be Speaker at Celebration," *Advocate* (Baton Rouge, La.), 11/20/94.)

In 1999, the facility was transferred to the Louisiana National Guard and has been partially used as a boot camp for high school dropouts who want to earn a diploma. About fifty residents were allowed to continue living in their long-time homes at Carville, driving for treatment elsewhere. ("Leprosy Hospital's Closure Means New Start for Patients," CNN, 4/24/98; "Leprosy Victims Protest; Patients Fight Ouster from U.S. Facility," *Washington Post*, 3/12/99; "Carville Patients Adjusting to New Lives," *Advocate*, 7/3/00.)

3. Kissinger said it was "very possible" that Laird was, indeed, the key man who promoted his candidacy, but "I have no idea." (Henry A. Kissinger, interview, 1/10/01.) Occasional news reports suggested Laird's behind-the-scenes role. *Los Angeles Times* reporter Rudy Abramson wrote in early 1972 that "it is widely believed that Laird . . . is largely responsible for bringing Henry A. Kissinger into the administration as the President's national security affairs adviser." (Abramson, "Even Pentagon Fails to Ruin Laird's Career," *Los Angeles Times*, 2/20/72)

Laird would occasionally drop hints that his relationship with Kissinger predated that of the president. For example, in a March 1972 interview when he was secretary of defense and was asked about his relationship with Kissinger, Laird told a defense correspondent in his Pentagon office: "Henry and I sat right at that table this morning and had breakfast. I've known Henry longer than the President has." (Orr Kelley, "Laird May Aid Nixon Drive," *Washington Star*, 3/4/72.)

4. Robert Novak, interview, 10/2/00.

5. Laurie Hawley, Laird's long-time executive assistant, interview, 8/12/99; Sen. John Warner, interview, 11/10/99; Richard Capen, former assistant secretary of defense (Legislative Affairs), interview, 8/8/00; Rady Johnson, former assistant secretary of defense (Legislative Affairs), interview, 8/22/00; Herb Klein, former White House director of communications, interview, 7/30/01.

6. James Marshall, former chief of public affairs, Republican Governors Association, interview, 4/18/02.

7. John Connally with Mickey Herskowitz, *In History's Shadow: An American Odyssey* (Hyperion, 1993), 231.

8. "Energetic Laird's Success No Surprise to Followers," *La Crosse Leader-Tribune*, 12/12/68.

9. Pres. Gerald Ford, interviews, 8/28/97, 9/12/97, and 10/24/01.

10. Pres. Richard M. Nixon, letter to MRL, 11/17/72.

11. Robert Novak, interview, 10/2/00. Laird believed that Jerry Ford had leaked the story to their mutual friend, Novak, but Ford denied this.

12. MRL, statement, distributed by Carl S. Wallace, administrative assistant, 12/11/68.

1 / THE MAN FROM MARSHFIELD

1. World War II veterans of the *Maddox:* Joseph Fanelli, interview, 7/1/01; Marshall (Zeke) A. Monsell Jr., interview, 8/14/01; Mel Cunningham, interview, 8/30/01; Bill Haldane, interview, 9/8/01; Dr. Malcolm Burris, interview, 8/30/01. J. P. Truesdell, Lieutenant, USNR, Deck Log, log book of the USS *Maddox* (DD731) entry for 1/21/45; James S. Willis, Commander, U.S. Navy, Commanding USS *Maddox,* War Diary, USS *Maddox* (DD731), entry for 1/21/45; *War Damage Report,* "Report of damage from suicide plane crash aboard at 1310 (I) 21 January 1945 while on picket duty in Task Group 38.1 during air strike on Formosa," 1/28/45; (*Maddox*) War Communique No. 2, March 1945; Samuel Eliot Morison, *The Liberation of the Philippines: Luzon, Mindanao, the Visayas, 1944–45,* History of United States Naval Operations in World War II, Volume XIII, U.S. Naval Institute (1989), 180–1; MRL, "Interview with David Frost," *David Frost Show,* 12/2/70; Capt. Paul Arbo (Ret.), *Howgoesit, Maddox* veterans newsletter, 3/94; Harlan Laws, GM3/c, notes from the personal diary of Harlan Laws 1944/45, *Howgoesit,* 5/95; Bill Jordan, *Howgoesit,* 9/96; Mel Cunningham, *Howgoesit,* 11/98.

2. Wisconsin Gov. Tommy Thompson, interview, 9/11/97; Marshfield History Project, *The Marshfield Story, 1872–1997: Piecing Together Our Past* (1997), 3–8, 95, 158.

3. Robert F. Froehlke, former secretary of the army, interview, 9/10/97; Ambassador Tom Graham, former acting director of Arms Control and Disarmament Agency, interview, 10/26/99; Jeff Kleiman, Marshfield historian, interview, 9/27/01. MRL, "Certificate of Registration of Birth," Omaha, Neb., 9/1/22; *Marshfield News-Herald,* 3/19/46; Program, "Melvin Laird Appreciation Night," 11/12/59; *Marshfield News-Herald,* 12/9/68; *Marshfield Story,* 8–9, 12–16, 22–3, 31, 118, 184, 190, 361–3.

4. John Chafee, interview, 10/22/99.

5. Robert Froehlke, interview, 9/10/97. MRL, "Sidelight," *Your Washington Office Report,* 4/26/61; MRL appearance on "Interview with David Frost," *David Frost Show,* 12/2/70; Sen. Gaylord Nelson, speech, 9/12/97; *Marshfield Story,* 20, 23–4, 27–32, 34, 36–7, 42, 51–4, 72, 167, 188–9, 229, 237, 360–3, 421–2.

6. MRL, "Why I Chose a Liberal Arts College," ca. 1941.

7. MRL appearance on "Interview with David Frost," *David Frost Show,* 12/2/70.

8. David Laird, MRL's son, interview, 2/27/01; Jack McDonald, interview, 9/29/01.

9. James A. Gibbs, author and shipwreck expert, interview, 9/28/01. Coast Guard cables on relevant dates; John L. Reynolds, Commander, USN, Director, Welfare Division, memorandum for the director of special activities, 2/27/43; James A. Gibbs, *Shipwrecks of the Pacific Coast,* Binford & Mort Publishing (1957), 155–6; Don Marshall, *Oregon Shipwrecks,* Binford & Mort Publishing (1984); "Oregon Coast Proves a Veritable Graveyard for Ships," *The Oregonian,* 2/14/99.

10. MRL transcript, St. Mary's College, Winona, Minn., 11/11/43.

11. The ship was named after William A. T. Maddox who, at the age of twenty-two, commanded a company of volunteers in the Creek and Seminole wars of 1836. He was appointed a second lieutenant in the Marine Corps a year later. During the Mexican War, he served as commandant of the Middle District of California and was promoted to captain for "gallant and meritorious conduct" during the Mexican uprising at Monterey and at the battle of Santa Clara in January 1847.

The first *Maddox* was launched in October 1918 and served with the U.S. Navy until 1941, when it was transferred to the British Royal Navy under the lend-lease program. The second *Maddox* (DD 622) was launched in February 1942 and served with the Atlantic and Mediterranean fleets before being sunk July 10, 1943, by a German dive bomber. Her captain, seven other officers, and 203 crew perished that day.

12. The number and names of all those aboard the *Maddox* are in the ship's Deck Log for Friday, June 2, 1944. All the Deck Logs, the War Diary and the Action Reports cited in this chapter have been preserved by the National Archives.

13. Dr. Malcolm Burris, interview, 8/30/01; William Haldane, interview, 9/8/01; War Diary, USS *Maddox* (DD731) from 2 to 30 June 1944, and 1 to 31 July 1944; Deck Logs, June and July 1944; Burris, *Howgoesit,* 1/93.

14. Capt. Arbo, *Howgoesit,* 3/94 and 5/96; Capt. Cunningham, *Howgoesit,* 9/96.

15. Joseph Fanelli, interview, 7/1/01; Zeke Monsell, interview, 8/14/01; Mel Cunningham, interview, 8/30/01; Malcolm Burris, interview, 8/30/01; William Haldane, interview, 9/8/01; Lt. Warren Olsom, USN (Ret.), *Howgoesit,* 6/99.

16. Joseph Fanelli, interview, 7/1/01; War Diaries and Deck Logs, relevant dates, Morison, Liz [sic]

June 1944 to January 1945, History of United States Naval Operations in World War II, Volume XII, 48–50, 101 and 166; Edwin P. Hoyt, *Japan's War: The Great Pacific Conflict, 1853 to 1952*, McGraw-Hill Book Company (1986), 373–4; Arnold S. Lott, LCDR (USN Ret.), *Brave Ship, Brave Men*, United States Naval Institute (1986), 127–8.

17. Capt. C. Raymond Calhoun, USN (Ret.), interview, 8/24/01; Mel Cunningham, interview, 8/30/01; Raymond Calhoun, *Typhoon: The Other Enemy; The Third Fleet and the Pacific Storm of December 1944*, United States Naval Institute (1981), 29; Cunningham, *Howgoesit*, 6/97.

18. *Maddox* War Diary and Deck Logs for relevant time period; Calhoun, *Typhoon*, 20, 32–38; Morison, *The Liberation*, Volume XIII, 63–5; Arbo, *Howgoesit*, 3/94 and 5/96; Cunningham, *Howgoesit*, 6/ and 12/97.

19. Joseph Fanelli, interview, 7/1/01; Burris, *Howgoesit*, 1/93 and 12/97; Cunningham, *Howgoesit*, 12/95 and 12/97.

20. Calhoun, *Typhoon*, 161–2.

21. The Court of Inquiry found that "Adm. Halsey was at fault in not broadcasting warnings to all vessels early in the morning of the 18th. The aerological talent assisting (him) was inadequate" (Calhoun, *Typhoon*, 161).

22. Morison, *The Liberation*, 82–7; Hans Christian Adamson and George Francis Kosco, *Halsey's Typhoons*, Crown Publishers (1967).

23. *Maddox* War Diary and Deck Logs for relevant dates; *Maddox*, "War Communique No. 2," 3/45; Morison, *The Liberation*, 91–2, 157–8, 164–75; Lott, *Brave Ship, Brave Men*, 65–6; Arbo, *Howgoesit*, 3/94 and 5/96; Harlan Laws, GM3/c, "Notes from the personal diary of Harlan Laws 1944/45," *Howgoesit*, 5/95; Cunningham, *Howgoesit*, 11/98.

24. Interviews with Joseph Fanelli, 7/1/01; Zeke Monsell, 8/14/01; Mel Cunningham, 8/30/01; William Haldane, 9/8/01; Malcolm Burris, 8/30/01.

J.P. Truesdell, Lieutenant, USNR, Deck Log, log book of the *Maddox* (DD731) entry for 1/21/45; James S. Willis, Commander, U.S. Navy, Commanding *Maddox*, War Diary, *Maddox* (DD731), entry for 1/21/45; *War Damage Report*, "Report of damage from suicide plane crash aboard at 1310 (I) 21 January 1945 while on picket duty in Task Group 38.1 during air strike on Formosa," 1/28/45; (*Maddox*) War Communique No. 2, March 1945; Morison, *The Liberation*, 179–181; MRL, "Interview with David Frost," *David Frost Show*, 12/2/70; Arbo (Ret.), *Howgoesit*, 3/94; Laws, *Howgoesit*, 5/95; Bill Jordan, *Howgoesit*, 9/96; Cunningham, *Howgoesit*, 11/98; Fred Bush, *Howgoesit*, 6/99.

25. Joseph Fanelli, interview, 7/1/01.

26. Arbo, *Howgoesit*, 3/94; Malcolm Burris, interview, 8/30/01.

27. Selby Santmyers, interview, 7/5/01. USS *Maddox* War Diary and Deck Logs on relevant dates; Morison, *Victory in the Pacific*, 186–91, 199–209, 234–5 and 239; Adamson and Kosco, *Halsey's Typhoons*, 164–5; Arbo, *Howgoesit*, 5/96; Cunningham, *Howgoesit*, 6/99.

28. Morison, *Victory in the Pacific*, 230–232; Adamson and Kosco, *Halsey's Typhoons*, 165–6.

29. Arbo, *Howgoesit*, 5/96.

30. The men of Destroyer Squadron 61 never received the commendation they should have for this mission, but some veterans of the operation are attempting to secure appropriate recognition. Author Owen Gault, with the key help of *Maddox* shipmate Joseph Fanelli, wrote a detailed article on the raid, which appeared in the April 1996 issue of *Sea Classics* magazine.

Interviews with Joseph Fanelli, 7/1/01; Selby Santmyers, 7/5/01; Zeke Monsell, 8/14/01; William Haldane, 9/8/01; Mel Cunningham, 9/11, 10/3, and 10/4/01; War Diary and Deck Logs on relevant dates; Morison, *Victory in the Pacific*, 330–1; Cunningham, *Howgoesit*, 12/92; Arbo, *Howgoesit*, 6/94; Monsell, *Howgoesit*, 12/95; Arbo, *Howgoesit*, 5/96; Burris, *Howgoesit*, 1/93.

31. Dorsey O. Thomas Jr., letter to MRL, 1/3/73.

2 / ON WISCONSIN *pages 33–41*

1. MRL, "Release to inactive duty—request for/by Melvin R. Laird, Lieut. (j.g.), (SC), USNR, 331064," letter to Chief of Naval Personnel via Chief of Field Branch, Bureau of Supplies and Accounts, 3/19/46.

2. John Wyngaard's June 1943 column suggesting Laird Sr. for governor was published in the *Marshfield News-Herald* and was quoted in a profile of Melvin Robert Laird Sr. in the *News-Herald*, 12/9/68, on the occasion of Laird Jr.'s selection as secretary of defense.

3. *Marshfield News-Herald*, 11/6/46.

4. Robert Froehlke, interview, 9/10/97.

5. Robert Froehlke, interview, 9/10/97.

6. Laird's record was broken in 1963 when Martin Schreiber was elected at the age of twenty-three. Since Laird's birthday was September 1, he had turned twenty-four by the time of the general election.

7. A smaller group met with Bovay a month before, on February 28, for the same purpose but adjourned without forming a new party. The meeting in March is considered the "birth" of the Republican Party by many because the fifty-four present did form a new party. AP, "GOP Birthplace Needs New Owner," *Chicago Tribune*, 3/31/87; "Ripon Traces GOP's Roots to a Schoolhouse," *Chicago Tribune*, 4/14/88; "Ripon's Grand Old Party ties; Town claims mantle as site of meeting that led to creation of Republican Party," *Milwaukee Journal-Sentinel*, 7/2/98.

8. The National Register of Historic Sites designated the Ripon schoolhouse, which still stands, as the birthplace of the Republican Party, as has the Republican National Committee. But there are several dozen other claimants to this title. During that same time period many similar meetings were held by northerners in a variety of cities, though only a few used the term "Republican" at their anti-Democrat gatherings. For example, Iowans believe the Republican Party started at Crawfordsville during a February 23, 1854, meeting at the Seceder Church. The former governor of New Hampshire, Hugh Gregg, has campaigned to have Exeter, New Hampshire, designated the birthplace. A meeting of anti-Democrat political leaders held by Congressman Amos Tuck at the Blake Hotel there on October 12, 1853, not only preceded by months the Ripon meeting, but also heard a suggestion by Tuck to use "Republican" as the name for their new party. Michigan Republicans say the first Republican *statewide* convention held in Jackson, Michigan, on July 6, 1854, was the birthplace. But those in Pittsburgh say the real beginning was in their city when the Republican Association, forerunner to the Republican National Committee, held its fist meeting there in February 1856. Philadelphians say the real birth of Republicans was in their city at the first national Republican convention in 1856.

"Paternity Disputes over Birth of a Party," *Washington Post*, 11/30/86; Frank Baker, "Former Gov. Says GOP Started in New Hampshire, Not Wisconsin," AP, 10/14/93; "Grand Old Dispute: Where Were the Republicans Born?", *Chicago Tribune*, 10/19/93; AP, "Candidates Ignore Crawfordsville, Republican Birthplace Claims," *Telegraph Herald* (Dubuque, Iowa), 1/28/96; "Exeter Is Birthplace of Republican Party, Britannica Says," *Union Leader* (Manchester, N.H.), 10/9/97; AP, "N.H. Historians not Relinquishing Claims Exeter Was Birthplace of GOP," 8/10/99.

9. Quoted by Thomas Reeves, *The Life and Times of Joe McCarthy*, Stein and Day (1982), 71.

10. From Craig Gilbert's comprehensive articles on Wisconsin political history in the 8/8/99 edition of the *Milwaukee Journal-Sentinel*. Shalala was once chancellor of the University of Wisconsin–Madison.

11. Aldric Revell, *Madison Capital Times* as published in the *Marshfield News-Herald*, with the headline, "Laird Gets 'Let Up' From Madison Political Writer," 6/9/47.

12. Jack Mills, interviews, 11/12/99 and 6/2/00.

13. Untitled campaign speech dated 10/20/48.

14. "Senator Laird Speaks to Rotary," *Greenwood Gleaner*, 4/22/48.

15. Untitled speech among Laird documents, University of Wisconsin collection, circa 1948.

16. "Coffee Time by the Editor," *Deerfield Independent*, 4/12/51.

17. Senator Nelson's quotes are from an interview of 2/7/01 and a 9/12/97 speech he gave at the dedication of the Laird Center in Marshfield, Wisconsin.

18. "Sen. Laird Fashions a Gag for Mr. Keliher," *Madison Capital Times*, 8/29/51.

19. "Kohler to Attend Recommissioning of USS *Wisconsin*," *Wisconsin State Journal*, 2/19/51; "Weather Nearly Torpedoes States Battleship Delegation," *Milwaukee Journal*, 3/4/51.

3 / MR. LAIRD GOES TO WASHINGTON

1. "Holstein Helped to Elect Pol to Congress," *Madison Capital Times*, 5/29/98. The author recalled that "a replica of 'Reciprocity' was on display both in Washington, D.C., and in several locations in Wisconsin throughout Murray's term in office."

2. "Energetic Laird's Success No Surprise to Followers," *La Crosse Leader-Tribune*, 12/12/68; John Wyngaard, "A Letter to Mel Laird's Mother," *Wisconsin State Journal*, 12/19/68.

3. Henry Cabot Lodge Jr., letter to MRL, 5/10/52.

4. Taft himself acknowledged Laird's strategy in an 8/8/52 letter of appreciation to Laird, noting his role in "fighting for a cause" successfully that would keep the Republican Party "free of New Deal influences" and ensure that the nominee would "conduct a government based on sound Republican principles."

5. Dwight D. Eisenhower, *White House Years: Waging Peace, 1956–1961,* Doubleday & Company (1965), 323.

6. Stephen E. Ambrose, *Eisenhower: The President,* Simon and Schuster (1984), 1:561–2.

7. *Wausau Daily Record-Herald,* 8/20/52; Laird also said that "I think McCarthy has done a useful service in dramatizing the issue" of the Communist threat in America.

8. All Eisenhower memoir quotes regarding his campaign stops in Wisconsin are from, Dwight D. Eisenhower, *Mandate for Change, 1956–1961,* Doubleday & Company (1963), 316–319.

9. Reeves, *The Life and Times of Joe McCarthy,* 437–440.

10. "Ike Gives Hottest Speech Here; Hits Treason in U.S.; Declares He Needs M'Carthy on 'Team,'" *Milwaukee Sentinel,* 10/4/52.

11. Rep. David Obey, speech at Laird Center dedication, 9/12/97.

12. Eisenhower, *Mandate,* 194.

13. The three men—Rafael Cancel Miranda, twenty-five; Irvin Flores Rodriguez, twenty-seven; Andres Figueroa Cordero, twenty-nine—were convicted of multiple counts of assault with intent to kill, as well as assault with a dangerous weapon. Lolita Lebron was acquitted of the "intent to kill" counts, convincing the jury that she only shot at the ceiling, but was convicted on the "dangerous weapon" counts. At the June 1954 trial, three of the victims, including Bentley, testified.

In 1979, responding to international and domestic pressure, President Carter granted clemency to Lebron, Cancel Miranda and Flores Rodriguez, who had all served twenty-five years in prison. (Figueroa Cordero had been released two years earlier by Carter in a grant of clemency.)

"Carter Frees 4 Puerto Ricans Who Attacked U.S. Politicians," *Washington Post,* 9/7/79; "Puerto Rican Terrorists Retain Nationalist Zeal After 25 Years in Prison," *Washington Post,* 9/11/79; "Puerto Rican Nationalists Don't Rule Out Violence," *Washington Post,* 9/12/79; "Terrorists Given Heroes' Welcome In Puerto Rico," *Washington Post,* 9/13/79; *Newsweek,* "Clemency Granted," 9/17/79; *U.S. News & World Report,* "Freedom for 4—And a Debate about Clemency," 9/17/79; *U.S. News & World Report,* "Truman-Era Terrorists Now 'Heroes,'" 9/24/79; AP, "Irvin Flores, 69, Dies; Wounded 5 in Congress," *New York Times,* 3/21/94; "Shots That Haunted 3 Generations; A Family's Struggles in the Aftermath of an Attack on Congress," *New York Times,* 5/26/98.

14. Also wounded were Rep. Kenneth Roberts, shot in the left leg; Rep. George H. Fallon, shot in the hip; and Rep. Clifford Davis, shot through the calf of his leg.

15. "Rep Laird Called from Chamber Just before Shooting," *Marshfield News-Herald,* 3/2/54, noted: "Laird had just walked through the 'danger zone' where two of his best Congressional friends were to be shot down, when yesterday's history-making assault on the House membership was made."

Also, AP, "Badgers Tell Vivid Tale of Shootings," *Sheboygan Press,* 3/2/54; and, a brief account in Laird's *Your Washington Office Report,* 3/10/54.

16. "Inside Washington," a report on the SOS Club in *Look,* 7/54.

17. Eisenhower, letter to Harry Bullis, 1953, OF 99-R, Eisenhower Papers at the Kansas presidential library.

18. *Marshfield Story,* 75–6.

19. Jack Mills, interview, 10/4/00.

20. MRL, "Communists in Government," *Your Washington Office Report,* 5/5/54.

21. "Laird Terms Row Hearing 3-Ring Circus," *Wisconsin Rapids Tribune,* 5/8/54.

In his 5/19/54 newsletter, under the heading, "Trip to the District," Laird explained his view further:

"Last week, while I was home in the District, I . . . pointed out that during the important debate of the Defense Department Appropriations bill for fiscal year 1955, there were only a handful of the members of the working press here in Washington covering the important general debate on this legislation.

"The Defense Appropriations bill contained $28.5 billion in new spending authorizations and affects the future economic and military security of this nation for a good many years to come. I pointed out that at the same time this bill was being considered in the House, the 'sideshow' was taking place in the Senate Office Building which was being covered by over two hundred members of the working press. Here in Washington, the working press includes TV, radio and news reporters.

"One of the newspaper men in our District for whom I have the greatest respect stated that the criticism which I made was not proper. He felt it was the duty and responsibility of the news reporters to cover those events in Washington which the people back home wanted to hear about and that a fight always had the greatest news appeal.

"My criticism was not directed at the news media in our District but at the situation as it exists in Washington. There are many measures which are being considered in this session of Congress which are of great importance to our future. The working press here is so involved with this Senate circus that the attention of our entire nation has been diverted from many important problems and decisions. *I do have to personally admit that this is one of the greatest disappointments which I have encountered in my political life*" (emphasis added).

22. "Laird and McCarthy . . . ," *Wausau Daily Record-Herald,* 5/11/54.

23. "McCarthy Assailed as 'Cruel, Reckless' in Attack by Welch," *Washington Post,* 6/10/54.

24. "Time Never Lags for Congressman: Representative Laird Likes Job Although It Pays No Overtime and Lacks Security," *Milwaukee Journal,* 12/6/53.

25. Laird recorded under the "Sidelights" section of his 5/15/57, newsletter: "This past week I missed the first roll call in the House of Representatives while attending the funeral ceremonies of the late Senator Joseph R. McCarthy. I have been proud of my record in answering every roll call but it certainly was necessary that I be in Wisconsin."

On the other hand, Laird missed the birth of his third and last child, son David, on July 16, 1954, because, unlike Congressional votes, births are not as well scheduled. In an article entitled, "Stork Doesn't Wait, Laird Gets Home Late," the July 20 *Stevens Point Daily Journal* had some fun with Laird over David's early arrival and his dad's tardiness:

"Congressmen are supposed to know what's going on in their districts, and Laird usually does, but sometimes things happen a little before they are expected.

"That was the case Friday when a new constituent arrived in (Laird's) district. Laird had planned to be on hand when the newcomer arrived, but the exact time of arrival was an uncertainty.

"So Mr. Laird hastened to board a plane at Washington and, although he took 'the high road' instead of 'the low road' (an auto), David Malcolm Laird was in Marshfield before him."

26. Gerald Ford, interview, 8/28/97.

27. AP, "Laird Defends Benson In His First Speech," *Stevens Point Daily Journal,* 2/19/53.

28. "Laird Speaks Up," *Marshfield News-Herald,* 2/19/53.

29. "Claim Benson Killed Dairy Setup Ike OK'd," *Sheboygan Press,* 3/31/54.

30. Samuel Walker, *In Defense of American Liberties: A History of the ACLU,* Southern Illinois University Press (1990); "ACLU Celebrates Its Veterans," *Washington Post,* 11/17/78; "Founder of the A.C.L.U. Reflects on His 97 Years," *New York Times,* 1/22/81; "Roger Baldwin, 97, Is Dead; Crusader for Civil Rights Founded the A.C.L.U.," *New York Times,* 8/27/81; "Roger Baldwin, a Founder of ACLU, Dies," *Washington Post,* 8/27/81; "Roger Baldwin," *Washington Post,* 8/28/81; "Roger Baldwin's Feisty Legacy," *Legal Times,* 5/7/90.

31. "Socialist Wrote Pledge of Allegiance," AP, 10/17/88; " 'I Pledge Allegiance . . . ' Nears Century Mark," AP, 9/2/92; Harry Wessel, "Pledge of allegiance rolls into 2nd century," *Orlando Sentinel,* 10/21/92; Arthur Schlesinger Jr., "When Patriotism Wasn't Religious," *New York Times,* 7/7/02.

32. In a contemporary *New York Times* article, a reporter noted there were at least fifteen House bills by mid-May: "Over on the House side where fifteen such resolutions have been introduced, it was Rep. Louis C. Rabaut, Democrat of Michigan, who offered the granddaddy of them all. On April 20, 1953, he dropped his resolution in the hopper at the suggestion of H. Joseph Mahoney of Brooklyn, N.Y. In a postscript on a letter to Mr. Rabaut, Mr. Mahoney wrote: 'Why don't you recommend the addition to the pledge of allegiance of the words *under God.*'" ("Big Issue in D.C.: The Oath of Allegiance," *New York Times,* 5/23/54).

33. "Include God in Pledge, Lawmakers to Be Urged (by Laird)," *Milwaukee Sentinel,* 5/5/54; MRL, press release, 5/6/54; "Laird Asks Flag Pledge Revision," *Wisconsin Rapids Tribune,* 5/6/54; "God in Pledge of Allegiance," *Two Rivers (Wis.) Reporter,* 5/6/54; "God in Pledge of Allegiance," *Chippewa Falls (Wis.) Herald,* 5/10/54; "Congressman Laird Sponsors Change in Pledge to Flag," *Adams (Wis.) Times,* 5/13/54.

34. MRL, "Religious Note," *Your Washington Office Report,* 5/19/54; MRL, "Supreme Court and Constitution," *Your Washington Office Report,* 7/25/62; MRL, "Sidelight," *Your Washington Office Report,* 7/10/63.

35. "Both Candidates Claim Sure Victory in Seventh," *Milwaukee Journal,* 27/54.

36. MRL, "Religious Note," *Your Washington Office Report,* 5/19/54.

37. "Motto on Coins Remains at Odds with Ruling against Pledge," *Dallas Morning News*, 7/6/02; Schlesinger, *New York Times*.

38. When the service was first instituted, the *Washington Post* noted that at that time there were thirteen Presbyterian senators and forty-one Presbyterian Representatives. ("Congress Will Pray at Ike's Church," *Washington Post*, 1/3/54.)

39. MRL, "The Presidency," *Your Washington Office Report*, 8/12/59.

40. MRL, Speech, "A Christian's Place in Politics," 2/19/58.

4 / OF CHOWDER AND CHEESE

1. Richard M. Nixon, *Memoirs*, Grosset & Dunlap (1978), 167; Ambrose, *Eisenhower: The President*, 285.

2. Gerald Ford, interview, 8/28/97. Also, three unpublished manuscript histories distributed to C&M members: "The Chowder and Marching Club, 1949–1955," 1955; "The History," part of the program and menu for twentieth anniversary celebration of the Chowder and Marching Club, 3/20/69; "A History of the Chowder and Marching Club," 1/84.

3. This was Charles E. Potter of Michigan, who was later elected a senator. Besides Jackson, Davis, Nixon, Ford, and Potter, the other ten original charter members of C&M were Johnny Byrnes, (Wis.), John J. Allen Jr. (Cal.), Caleb Boggs (Del.), Norris Cotton (N.H.), Kenneth Keating (N.Y.), John Lodge (Conn.), Harold O. Lovre (S.D.), Thruston B. Morton (Ky.), Charles P. Nelson (Me.), and Walter Norblad (Ore.).

4. Fawn Brodie, *Richard Nixon: The Shaping of His Character*, book jacket and 190; Vamik Volkan, Norman Itzkowitz, and Andrew Dod, *Richard Nixon: A Psychobiography*, Columbia University Press (1997), 53; Irwin G. Gellman, *The Contender: Richard Nixon, The Congress Years: 1946–1952*, Free Press (1999), 268.

5. "G.O.P. Success Recipe Often Includes Chowder," *New York Times*, 3/15/82.

6. Gerald Ford, interview, 8/28/97.

7. "A Speedy Turnaround," *Washington Post*, 7/29/96.

8. Laird talked with Davis about his involvement and maintains that Davis was coauthor of the Checkers speech. While it is likely Davis offered Nixon specific suggestions regarding the speech's content, it is less likely he was on the scene with Nixon in Los Angeles helping him write the draft. Nixon does not mention Davis's role in his early memoir, *Six Crises*, nor his later postpresidential memoir. In a book commissioned by the Glenn Davis Charitable Foundation, author Kevin B. Smith tried but was unable to confirm Laird's account that Davis was on-site in California. ("Davis, Co-author of 'Checkers' Speech, Dies at 73," *Milwaukee Sentinel*, 9/22/88; Kevin B. Smith, *The Iron Man: The Life and Times of Congressman Glenn R. Davis*, University Press of America (1994), 135–7; Richard Nixon, *Six Crises*, Doubleday & Company (1962), 73–129; Nixon, *Memoirs*, 92–110.)

9. Manuscript history of Chowder and Marching Club, 1955; John Wyngaard, "Rep. Laird Member of Exclusive 'Chowder and Marching Society,'" *Marshfield News Herald*, 4/17/54; *Appleton Post-Crescent*, 5/19/54; "Rep. Davis Guest (at) Breakfast Meet at White House," *Beaver Dam Citizen*, 5/22/54.

10. Jack Mills estimated the money they raised for this one-night affair to be anywhere from $5,000 to $20,000. (Mills, interviews, 11/12/99 and 6/2/00.) Laird thought the cost was roughly $30 a head—which, with five hundred attendees, put the total at about $15,000, a healthy sum for a party in 1956.

11. Vice President Nixon, letter to MRL, 1/12/56.

12. Nixon, *Memoirs*, 167–8.

13. Vice President Nixon, letter to MRL, 3/2/56.

14. Nixon, *Memoirs*, 170.

15. In his comprehensive biography, *Eisenhower: The President*, Stephen Ambrose detailed the history behind this decision on pages 320–21.

16. MRL, "National Convention," *Your Washington Office Report*, 8/1/56.

17. Kenneth Anderson died of a heart attack at the age of forty-seven, just five days before the Wisconsin Democratic primary. His widow, Margaret, was drafted to run. "Democrat Files for Congress," *Wausau Record-Herald*, 7/14/56; "Mrs. Anderson Would Accept Nominee Post," *Stevens Point Daily Journal*, 9/24/56.

18. "Contest in 7th District like Script for Movie," *Milwaukee Journal*, 10/27/56. Margaret Anderson received 49,422 votes, or 38.2 percent, to Laird's 61.9 percent, or 80,143 votes.

19. *1956 Congressional Quarterly Almanac*, 752; Joe Martin, as told to Robert J. Donovan, *My First Fifty Years in Politics*, McGraw-Hill Book Company (1960), 222.

20. MRL, letter to Wisconsin journalist John Wyngaard, 3/3/58.

21. MRL, letter to John Wyngaard, 3/3/58.

22. Laird used this example and the quip in the letter to Wyngaard, 3/3/58. In his 3/4/53 newsletter, he attributed the "upper house" remark to then–House speaker Joe Martin. It was Laird's annual wish that "the Senators will be willing to give up their claim" to upper housemanship because of inflating every House Appropriations bill.

23. AP, "Laird Reveals One of His Disappointments," *Stevens Point Daily Journal*, 3/27/53.

24. MRL, "National Debt," *Your Washington Office Report*, 7/3/57.

25. *1953 CQ Almanac*, 131; MRL, "Tax Reduction," *Your Washington Office Report*, 7/22/53.

26. Phrase "birth of affluent society" from Piers Brendon, *Ike: His Life and Times*, Harper & Row (1986), 261.

27. Since neither Alaska nor Hawaii was yet a state, the Senate had ninety-six senators.

28. See Robert A. Caro's account of the potential Senate even split in *The Years of Lyndon Johnson: Master of the Senate*, Alfred A. Knopf (2002), 955, 1000–1.

29. MRL, letter to Pres. Eisenhower, 10/22/57; "McDowell in Benson Post Urged," *Milwaukee Sentinel*, 10/24/57.

30. Ezra Taft Benson, *Cross Fire: The Eight Years with Eisenhower*, Doubleday & Company (1962), 359–375.

31. Of the thirty-five midwestern Republicans from farm districts who voted with Benson, ten had been defeated by Democrats. One who retired and one who died had both been replaced by Democrats. "On Farm Voting: Benson Loses Midwest Farm Support in House," Fact Sheet, *CQ Almanac*, 1958, 737–8.

32. It was written with the acknowledged help of W. D. Knox of *Hoard's Dairyman Magazine*.

33. Laird also presented the president with a leather-bound state tourism book, *This Is Wisconsin*, which included pictures of Ike fishing in Wisconsin after a postwar European tour. MRL, *Your Washington Office Report*, 6/24/53; "Laird Chats with Eisenhower; Gives Him State Cheese," *Green Bay Press-Gazette*, 6/26/53; "Laird Fishes for a Wisconsin Vacationer," *Wisconsin State Journal*, 6/26/58.

34. MRL, "Dairy Imports Create Emergency Situation," Weekly Newspaper Column, 9/25/68; MRL, "Emergency Restriction on Dairy Imports Welcome," Weekly Newspaper Column, 10/2/68.

35. MRL, *Your Washington Office Report*, 3/4/53; AP, "Rep. Laird in Tussle with VA over Butter, Oleo," Wausau *Daily Record Herald*, 7/16/53; "Congressman Wins Battle to Have Butter Served by VA," Appleton *Post-Crescent*, 1/20/54; "New Contract Will Give Vets Butter," Clintonville *Tribune-Gazette*, 1/21/54; *1954 CQ Almanac*, 101.

36. *CQ's Congress and the Nation: 1945–1964; A Review of Government and Politics in the Postwar Years*, 736.

37. MRL, "Promote Milk Consumption," press release, 2/17/56.

38. MRL, press release, 3/5/55.

39. Laird's cosponsor, Rep. August Andresen, R-Minn., was his senior, but Andresen's death in 1958 left it to Laird to carry the milk pail for the program into the last Eisenhower years and successor Democratic administrations.

40. "Time Never Lags for Congressman: Representative Laird Likes Job although It Pays No Overtime and Lacks Security," *Milwaukee Journal*, 12/6/53.

41. MRL, "Sidelights," *Your Washington Office Report*, 2/18/53.

42. Information from two books published by the Naval Historical Center, *Dictionary of American Fighting Ships* and *United States Naval Aviation, 1910–1995*.

43. MRL, "Defense Department," *Your Washington Office Report*, 2/10/54.

44. MRL, "Defense Items," *Your Washington Office Report*, 3/20/57.

45. "Laird Charges Duplication Wasting Funds; Defense Department Policies Blasted by Badger Lawmaker," Appleton *Post-Crescent*, 8/10/59.

46. MRL, address, 5/17/58; Wilton B. Persons, Assistant to the President, White House, list of letters referred to Department of Defense, 6/26/59; " 'Ghost Hospital,' " *Wausau Record-Herald*, 7/9/59; "Mention Laird's Name . . . ," *Green Bay Press-Gazette*, ibid., 9/7/60.

47. In Eisenhower's appointments schedule for the relevant date, an "off-the-record" breakfast

for the president is listed with Representatives Ford and Laird, with White House aides Wilton B. Persons and Bryce Harlow also present.

Both the Eisenhower and Laird-Ford budget numbers actually included twelve subs. Eisenhower proposed fully funding three and partially funding nine, while Laird-Ford called for five fully funded subs, and seven partially funded. (*1960 CQ Almanac,* 70–1, 373, 376.) A total of forty-one Polaris subs were eventually constructed, the last one in 1967. Credit must go to Rear Admiral William F. Raborn and his special projects team, which outdid the legendary Admiral Hyman Rickover. In *Rickover,* Simon and Schuster (1982), 552, authors Norman Polmar and Thomas B. Allen acknowledged: "Special Projects—through hundreds of contractors—delivered the Polaris submarines and missiles several years ahead of the initial schedules. Rickover's nuclear-propulsion program could not claim such a record. Indeed, one could probably argue that, except for the Polaris submarines, no nuclear-powered ship was ever delivered earlier than scheduled, and most were delivered later."

48. On the 1/30/72 *Issues and Answers* TV program, Secretary of Defense Laird recounted: "You'll remember very well, I am sure, how important those 18 to 24 months' speed-up in the Polaris program were—to have those Polaris submarines out after the Congress took action at the time President Kennedy had his confrontation with the Soviet Union on the Cuban missile crisis. That action of the Congress was important then." ("Laird Grabbed Gavel to Close Platform Rifts," *Milwaukee Journal,* 7/27/60; MRL, press release, "Remarks on the Floor of the House," 1/25/61; Editorial, "Melvin R. Laird—Man of Judgment ... ," *Wausau Record-Herald,* 11/1/62; "Rep. Laird: Bright G.O.P. Star," *Chicago Tribune,* 6/23/63; MRL, letter to Vice Adm. H.G. Rickover, 10/28/63.)

49. MRL, "Interview with David Frost," *David Frost Show,* 12/2/70.

50. Max Elbin, interview, 1/11/02.

51. For a more thorough recitation of Johnson's accumulation of wealth see Robert Caro, *The Years of Lyndon Johnson: Means of Ascent,* Alfred A. Knopf (1990), 80–118. The Rayburn quote is taken from that chapter's precede.

52 Caro, *Master of the Senate,* 852.

53. Caro, *Master of the Senate,* 783.

54. Philip A. Klinkner, professor at Hamilton College and author of *The Unsteady March: The Rise and Decline of Racial Equality in America,* holds the view that had the Republicans succeeded, African-American support for the party would have helped elect Nixon president in 1960 instead of Kennedy. In a review of Caro's *Master of the Senate,* Klinkner, in *The Nation* (5/20/02), wrote:

If ever one needs evidence of the contingency of history, imagine, if you will, those seven votes going the other way. Jim Crow would have died in the late 1950s, avoiding much of the tumult of the 1960s. The Republicans, led by Richard Nixon, would have been the party of civil rights, not the Democrats and Lyndon Johnson. From there, one can spin off any number of plausible scenarios that result in a very different history of the past forty years.

But none of these scenarios were acceptable to the Lyndon Johnson of 1957, since they would have conflicted with his ambition; and at that point, despite Caro's claim, his ambition was still more important than his compassion. Switching sides on Rule 22 would have destroyed his Southern support and with it any chance he had of becoming President. Johnson's compassion would eventually shine through, and as a result, civil rights would eventually come to black America. But they would not come until Lyndon Johnson's ambition would allow them to come.

55. In its vote analysis, the *1957 CQ Almanac* (559), concluded: Republicans in the House in 1956 and 1957 gave stronger support to civil rights legislation than Democrats. The breakdown on passage of the bill in 1956: Republicans, 168 to 24; Democrats, 111 to 102. In 1957 on passage: Republicans, 168 to 19; Democrats, 118 to 107.

56. Caro, *Master of the Senate,* 711–16, 761–800, 848–1012.

57. Caro, *Master of the Senate,* 946.

58. Though President Eisenhower backed the Brownell measure, his private view was more sympathetic to the white Southerners of the time. That watered down the support he expressed in public for his administration's own initiative.

59. Ford, *A Time to Heal,* 72.

60. Laird gave a play-by-play account to an Associated Press reporter within days of the insurgency. ("Badgers in Wisconsin: Tell Laird, Byrnes Role in Defeat of Rep. Martin," AP, 1/16/59.)

61. MRL, "Not Needed," *Your Washington Office Report,* 9/12/62; MRL, press release, "Rubber Stamp Congress Not Needed," Mel Laird Testimonial Dinner, Shawano, Wis., 10/10/62.

62. "Rep. Laird to Tour," *Antigo Journal*, 8/1/53; AP, "Laird Sails Today for Europe, Asia Inspection," *Wisconsin Rapids Tribune*, 9/3/53; "3 Senators 5 in House Off on Tour," *New York Herald-Tribune*, 9/5/53; "Laird Tells Audience: Europe Now Capable of Maintaining Itself," unidentified Wisconsin newspaper, 11/3/53; "Laird Reviews Overseas Trip; Tells Businessmen of Waste, Competition," *Marshfield News-Herald*, 11/7/53.

63. MRL, "Foreign Aid," *Your Washington Office Report*, 5/21/58.

64. MRL, "Aid to Tito," *Your Washington Office Report*, 9/19/56; MRL, "Foreign Aid Program," *Your Washington Office Report*, 6/20/56.

65. Ford, *A Time to Heal*, 71; James Cannon, *Time and Chance: Gerald Ford's Appointment with History*, Harper Collins (1994), 65.

66. "Two American Representatives Will Arrive to Cairo Tomorrow," *Al Ahram*, 10/8/53; AP, "Laird Arrives in Cairo Today," *Antigo Daily Journal*, 10/9/53; "An American Representative in Cairo," *Al Sadaka*, 10/15/53.

67. Robert Froehlke, interview, 9/10/97.

68. Peter Lyon, *Eisenhower: Portrait of the Hero*, Little, Brown and Company (1974), 851.

69. Minutes of the 179th Meeting of the National Security Council, 1/8/54.

70. Ambrose, *Eisenhower: The President*, 175.

71. Ambrose, *Eisenhower: The President*, 177–9; Nixon, *Memoirs*, 150.

72. "Competition, Restrictions, Top Threats to Dairymen, Laird Asserts at Athens," *Milwaukee Journal*, 5/8/54.

73. In interviews, Laird has used various figures for the number of men in Vietnam at the end of the Eisenhower administration—178 people, in one interview, 350 in another. But the figure 773 is believed to be accurate because it was the figure he used in statements contemporary to the event, and it was close to the number used in a Congressional hearing.

In a statement Rep. Laird released on June 14, 1965, he said: "The Eisenhower-Dulles policy scrupulously avoided a large-scale use of conventional ground forces in Southeast Asia. As a matter of fact, at the time President Eisenhower left office, there were only 773 members of the U.S. Military Mission in Vietnam."

On February 17, 1966, during Hearings before the Senate Committee on Foreign Relations concerning Supplemental Foreign Assistance bill, Part I, pg. 450, the exchange is recorded:

Senator Hickenlooper: Now, up until the end of the Eisenhower administration, we had only about 750 military personnel in South Vietnam, did we not?

General (Maxwell) Taylor: It was very small, something like that.

Senator Hickenlooper: I think that is within 25 or 30 of the number, either way, and they were entirely devoted to giving technical advice on training to the South Vietnamese troops.

General Taylor: That is correct.

Senator Hickenlooper: To your knowledge, did we have any commitment or agreement with the South Vietnamese up to that time that we would put in active field military forces to conduct a war along with them?

General Taylor: No, sir. Very clearly we made no such commitment. We didn't want such a commitment. This was the last thing we had in mind.

Senator Hickenlooper: When was the commitment made for us to actively participate in the military operations of the war as American personnel?

General Taylor: . . . Insofar as the use of our combat ground forces are concerned, that took place, of course, only in the spring of 1965.

5 / HECTIC AND *HEALTHY* TURMOIL

1. "Richard Nixon to Give Talk at Recognition Dinner for Congressman Melvin Laird," *Mosinee Times*, 9/24/59.

2. Robert Froehlke, interview, 9/29/00.

3. The weed-killer was erroneously reported by the press at the time, and occasionally since, as *aminothiazole*, when it was actually *aminotriazole*, known as Amitrol.

4. Adam J. Lieberman and Simona C. Kwon, *Facts versus Fears: A Review of the Greatest Unfounded Health Scares of Recent Times*, American Council on Science and Health (1997), 6–7.

5. Diane L. Burns, *Cranberries: Fruit of the Bogs* (1994), 18, 11, 13

6. Lieberman and Kwon, ACSH study.

7. "Case of Confusion: Work Starts to Clear Innocent State Berry," *Appleton Post-Crescent*, 11/11/59; AP, "FDA Team to Check on State Crop," *Eau Claire Leader*, 11/11/59; "U.S. Widens Taint Check for Cranberries" and "Cranberry Crop Facing Huge Loss," *New York Times*, 11/11/59.

8. "The Fear of Buying; The Challenge of Rebuilding Public Confidence," *Washington Post*, 10/21/82.

9. Herb Klein, interview, 9/29/00.

10. Elliott Maraniss, "Nixon-Kennedy Cranberry Duel Ends in Dead Heat," *Madison Capital Times*, 11/13/59; "Kennedy Tells Throng of Communist Danger," *Milwaukee Journal*, 11/13/59; Nixon photo caption, "Yes, He Likes Cranberries," *Wisconsin Rapids Tribune*, 11/13/59.

11. MRL, "The 1960 Contest," *Your Washington Office Report*, 1/20/60.

12. President's Appointments Log, 7/29/53. According to *Newsweek* ("Update; Polish Defector: Making It Big," 11/5/79), Jarecki, who changed his first name to Frank, married an American woman, had four children, and became a millionaire by making precision valves through his own Jarecki Industries in Erie, Pa. His only regret was that his mother, who had no prior knowledge of his intentions, was imprisoned by Polish Communist authorities for three years.

13. Vice Pres. Nixon, letter to Rep. John Byrnes, 4/15/60.

14. Sen. Charles Percy, interview, 4/18/01. Alan Otten, *Wall Street Journal*, "*Playboy* Interview: Charles Percy," *Playboy*, 4/68; "Charles Percy: Balancing Act in the Senate," *Washington Star*, 6/21/86.

15. Eisenhower, *Waging Peace*, 383.

16. "Laird Gets Important GOP Convention Role; 'Highly Honored' with Resolutions Committee Office," *Green Bay Press-Gazette*, 5/12/60.

17. "Governor Meets Platform Chief; Confers 3 Hours with Percy— Discusses Differences with Nixon on Issues," *New York Times*, 7/7/60; "Rockefeller Sets Platform Goals: 6,000-Word Summary Sent to Committee Chairman—Nixon Is Silent," *New York Times*, 7/10/60.

18. "Rockefeller Gains as Well as Nixon," *New York Times*, 7/24/60.

19. Front-page and accompanying stories in the 7/24/60, *New York Times*: "Secret Nixon-Rockefeller Talks Draft a Basic Platform Accord; Rule Out Governor for 2d Place"; "Rockefeller Gains as Well as Nixon"; "Pact Opens Way for Party Amity"; UPI, "One Party Line Failed Nixon and Rockefeller"; "Chicago: The Truce of Fifth Avenue, or Morningside Revisited."

Also, "11th-Hour Encounter," *Newsweek*, 8/1/60; Theodore White, *The Making of the President, 1960*, Atheneum Publishers (1961), 191–198; Nixon, *Six Crises*, 313–16; Nixon, *Memoirs*, 215; CQ, *National Party Conventions, 1831–2000*, CQ Press (2001), 119.

20. "Goldwater Hits Platform Accord; Pledges Fight in Convention on Nixon's 'Surrender' to Rockefeller Ideas," *New York Times*, 7/24/60.

21. Charles Percy, interview, 4/18/01.

22. This account comes from Laird, who recounted the phone call in several interviews. David Abshire, who was in the hotel room when Ike called, and overheard the call, remembered it slightly differently. He recalled Eisenhower as saying, sarcastically: "Tell Dick Nixon he doesn't really need my support in the campaign. He can get along without me."

23. After word leaked out about Ike's mood, his aides denied to journalists that he was angry about the compact or that he had meddled with the platform. For example, a Newport-datelined *New York Times* story quoted White House sources as saying that "the President does not intend to influence in any way the preparation of platform pledges." ("President Shuns Goldwater View; Doesn't Consider Agreement by Rockefeller and Nixon a Republican 'Munich,'" *New York Times*, 7/25/60.)

During his August 10, 1960, press conference, Eisenhower also disingenuously denied expressing displeasure about the Fifth Avenue compact. Chalmers M. Roberts of the *Washington Post* asked: "[On] the Nixon-Rockefeller agreement, it was reported in Chicago at the time of the convention that you were personally upset at what that agreement had to say about defense on the grounds that it was implicitly critical of your Administration. Were you upset and did you try to get the platform language changed at Chicago?" Eisenhower: "No. I don't remember that I was upset.... Now, there were many calls as to what I thought would be a good thing to put in—in the planks of the platform—that had to do with defense, and I conferred by telephone with a good many people and for a good many hours." (Text of press conference, *New York Times*, 8/11/60.)

24. "G.O.P. to Present Its Platform in a $25,000 TV Spectacular," *New York Times*, 7/9/60.

25. "Rockefeller Ready to Fight on Floor for Rights Plank," *New York Times*, 7/25/60; "Nixon Says Rights Plank Must Be Made Stronger," *New York Times*, 7/26/60; White, *The Making, 1960*, 202–4.

26. A later *New York Times* profile put it this way: "In 1960, Mr. Laird, as vice chairman of the GOP platform committee, took command from the chairman, Charles H. Percy, a businessman, to break a committee stalemate over civil rights through his grasp of practical politics." ("Professional Politician: Melvin Robert Laird," 7/7/64.)

The *Chicago Tribune* noted: "In 1960, he was made vice-chairman of the platform committee. The policy disputes of that convention were memorable. Insiders said Laird should be credited with the bringing of order out of chaos and the drafting of party principles on which dissident elements could unite." ("Rep. Laird: Bright G.O.P. Star; Chose His Career as Wisconsin Lad of 17," *Chicago Tribune*, 6/23/63.)

And liberal columnist Drew Pearson recounted that "when Nixon and Rockefeller got together . . . and wrote their own GOP platform, there was such a storm of resentment that Laird took over the gavel from the inexperienced Percy, who was more accustomed to quiet board meetings than tumultuous political pow-wows." ("Here's What Makes Platform-Writer Mel Laird Tick," *Madison Capital Times*, 7/10/64.)

But equally telling to these press acknowledgments was the secretarial note of a phone call between Bryce Harlow and former president Eisenhower on September 3, 1963. The first matter discussed was whether Eisenhower should support businessman Charles Percy in a Republican primary bid for the governorship of Illinois. "BNH says no," the note reads. One of the primary reasons he gave Ike for not backing Percy was his lack of political skill as demonstrated when the "1960 convention platform operation of Percy's failed—Laird had to help out."

27. "Laird, Byrnes, Davis Are in Nixon's Club," *Milwaukee Journal*, 7/27/60.

28. "Mention Laird's Name as Defense Secretary," *Green Bay Press-Gazette*, 9/7/60. In August *U.S. News & World Report* had additionally mentioned that Laird was being "talked about" as Nixon's potential secretary of agriculture.

29. Nixon, *Six Crises*, 411–13.

30. One of Nixon's 1960 advance men, John Warner, later secretary of the navy and senator from Virginia, agreed in an 11/10/99 interview with the author: "If Nixon had won in Illinois—if he would have won Chicago, he'd have won the election. It was very close."

31. MRL, Speech before the Women's Forum on National Security, Presidential Ballroom, Statler Hotel, 1/27/61.

32. Cannon, *Time and Chance*, 68.

33. Richard Nixon, letter to MRL, 4/11/61.

34. MRL, letter to Richard Nixon, 5/1/61.

35. In his 4/26/61 *Your Washington Office Report* newsletter, Laird wrote: "This past week I had visits with President Kennedy at the White House, Chancellor Adenauer at lunch, and many other leaders in and out of government." The Kennedy meeting was the Bay of Pigs briefing to seek postdebacle Congressional support.

36. MRL, "Back Door Diplomacy," *Your Washington Office Report*, 6/14/61.

37. Eisenhower, letter to MRL, 7/5/61.

38. Arthur M. Schlesinger Jr., *A Thousand Days: John F. Kennedy in the White House*, Houghton Mifflin Company (1965), 371–4; Theodore C. Sorensen, *Kennedy*, Harper & Row (1965), 584–6.

39. MRL and Rep. John Rhodes, R-Ariz., "Joint Statement on the President's Speech on the Berlin Crisis," 7/26/61.

40. MRL, telegram to Secretary of State Dean Rusk, 9/7/61.

41. Eisenhower's succinct explanation to Laird concluded with the following six "salient points":

1. The political leaders of the day determined long before the closing campaign of the war upon dividing Germany, for occupational purposes. They decided upon this course despite contrary military advice.

2. I urged a different solution for Berlin than was agreed upon in London, and which I have always understood was finally approved by the Heads of Government at Yalta. (The pamphlet gives September 1944 as the date of final approval).

3. In the light of political decisions already reached to dispose of central Germany, it was futile, especially when there were important military tasks to be performed elsewhere, to expend military resources in striving to capture and hold a region which we were obligated, by prior decision of a higher authority, to evacuate once the fighting was over.

4. Being unfettered by political decision as to other areas, I directed troop advances toward Denmark and Austria.

5. The Western Allies front being some 250 or more miles to the west of Berlin when the Soviets, with a bridgehead already established west of the Oder were 35 miles to the east of Berlin, it is indeed a venturesome military critic who would now contend that the Western forces might have taken Berlin before the Soviets could or did.

6. Any inference that military action, taken subsequently to the political decision for occupation, played a significant role in producing the political situation today prevailing in Germany is not correct." (Eisenhower, letter to MRL, 9/12/61.)

42. MRL, *A House Divided: America's Strategy Gap*, Henry Regnery Company (1962), 53–4.

6 / A HOUSE DIVIDED

1. Ford, undated interview with Trevor Armbrister, 1977–79; also Ford, interview with author, 8/28/97.

2. Richard Nixon, letter to MRL, 1/16/61.

3. "12 Republicans Draft Principles; Congress Group Starts Work on Statement for Voters," *New York Times*, 3/1/62; UPI, "G.O.P. Unit Picks Laird: Drafters of Party Principles Will Avoid Philosophic Label," *New York Times*, 3/3/62; Eisenhower, Palm Desert, Calif., letter to MRL, 3/29/62; Eisenhower, letter to MRL, 5/7/62; articles in 5/17 and 5/21/62 issues of *Gettysburg (Pa.) Times*; MRL, speech on House floor, "A Report of the 1962 Joint Committee on Republican Principles," 6/7/62.

4. MRL, "Background on Laos," *Your Washington Office Report*, 6/13/62.

5. MRL, *House Divided*, 64, 117–120.

6. MRL appearance on *Washington Viewpoint*, 6/18/62.

7. "Paul Corbin, R.I.P: Memories of the Legendary Fixer," by Ken Bode, *The New Republic*, 1/29/90.

8. "Many Are Wondering What of Corbin's Past?" *Milwaukee Journal*, 8/24/61.

9. John M. Bailey, Chairman, Democratic National Committee, letter to MRL, 9/7/61; AP, "Bailey Clears Aide of Subversive Ties," *New York Times*, 9/9/61.

10. "Home Town Wants Corbin Ousted," *Janesville Gazette*, 10/11/61; AP, "Corbin's Record Being Checked, Says Zablocki," *Stevens Point Daily Journal*, 11/30/61.

11. Fulton Lewis Jr., columnist, "Somebody Lied at Probe of Dem Leader Corbin," *Antigo Daily Journal*, 10/11/62; "Write-In Efforts Put Kennedy 'Helper' on Shelf," *Washington Star*, 3/18/64.

12. MRL, *House Divided*, 33, 43.

13. MRL quoted in "Laird Asks Americans to 'Back Kennedy,'" *Manawa (Wis.) Advocate*, 10/25/62.

14. MRL, press release, "Laird Renews Call for Peace Blockade of Cuba," 9/25/62.

15. MRL, *House Divided*, 74.

16. "Melvin Laird—Man of Judgment . . .", *Wausau Record-Herald*, 11/1/62.

17. *1962 CQ Almanac*, 63, 1029–30.

18. This was a letter that congratulated Laird on his sixth congressional campaign victory. (Nixon, letter to MRL, 11/16/62.)

19. Rep. David Obey, speech, 9/12/97.

20. Final percentages averaged from the *CQ Almanac*'s three annual reports.

21. MRL, "Not Needed," *Your Washington Office Report*, 9/12/62.

22. MRL, issues of *Your Washington Office Report:* "The Budget," 1/25/62; "The Deficit Grows," 5/23/62; "The Hundred Billion Dollar Budget," 1/30/63.

23. Eisenhower, *Waging Peace*, 614–16.

24. Because commentators focused on only the warning paragraph of Eisenhower's January 17, 1961, Farewell Address, Laird always felt the speech was frequently misinterpreted as a screed against defense spending. "I talked to Ike about that quite a bit," and the former president agreed, Laird said. In the speech itself, Eisenhower stressed the vital need for a strong military posture. (MRL, "Eisenhower Farewell," *Your Washington Office Report*, 1/25/61.)

25. "Missile Gap Issues Fizzles," *1961 CQ Almanac*, CQ Press (1962), 144; MRL appearance on *Washington Viewpoint*, 6/18/62.

26. MRL, *House Divided*, 48. Later, as secretary of defense, Laird, in a November 23, 1971, "Address and Question-Answer Period" at Fort Leavenworth, Kan., recalled: "It should always

be remembered that we had a 5 to 1 superiority in the field of strategic nuclear weapons (when) President Kennedy stood up to the Soviet Union in 1962 during the Cuban missile crisis."

27. MRL, press release, "Remarks on the Floor of the House," 1/25/61; speech before the Women's Forum on National Security, Presidential Ballroom, Statler Hotel, 1/27/61.

28. At the end of his tour of duty in 1963, Admiral George Anderson, chief of naval operations, thanked Laird for his "firm support of the Navy. No less was expected of a Navy man like yourself, but we are all of us none the less extremely grateful." The admiral added, "In particular, your interest in and thorough knowledge of ASW [antisubmarine warfare] operations and your ability and willingness to explain them to those less informed have been of the greatest help to the Navy, as has your advocacy, of a strong Navy, adequate to protect our shores and to keep the seas free, as they were meant to be, for peaceful travelers." (Adm. George Anderson, Chief of Naval Operations, letter to MRL, 7/26/63.)

29. MRL, "Defense Appropriations Committee," *Your Washington Office Report,* 9/26/62.

30. Robert S. McNamara, Secretary of Defense, "DoD News Briefing Cancellation Announcement," 12/10/63.

31. MRL appearance on *Washington Viewpoint,* 12/63.

32. Robert Godwin, *Dyna-Soar: Hypersonic Strategic Weapons System,* Apogee Books (2003), 7–11.

33. Stanley Karnow, *Vietnam: A History,* Viking Press (1983), 252.

34. MRL, *A House Divided,* 111.

35. Kenneth O'Donnell and David Powers, *Johnny, We Hardly Knew Ye,* Little Brown (1972), 16. After an excerpt of the book appeared in *Life* magazine, Senator Mansfield confirmed that Kennedy told him he would pull out the troops after the 1964 election. ("JFK Decided in '63 to Order Viet Pullout after Election," *Washington Post,* 8/1/70.)

7 / LAIRD RISING

1. MRL, statement, "For Immediate Release," 11/22/63.

2. MRL, undated draft of remarks prepared for Gridiron Dinner, which was canceled. In a book on the Gridiron, *From Grover Cleveland to Gerald Ford... The President Speaks Off the Record,* Dow Jones Books (1976), author Harold Brayman wrote: "Probably no President, with the possible exception of Theodore Roosevelt, enjoyed the Gridiron dinners as much as Kennedy did. The cracks at him and his associates didn't bother him, and truly for him the Gridiron 'glowed but did not burn.'... He had the wit, and he exhibited some of the best of it at these dinners, especially when he laughed at himself" (660).

3. *Report of the Warren Commission on the Assassination of President Kennedy,* introduction by Harrison Salisbury, *New York Times* edition (1964), 41–2.

4. "Killing [A] Communist Tool, Rep. Melvin Laird Says," *Appleton Post-Crescent,* 12/4/63; AP, "Laird Makes Comment on Accused Killer," *Marshfield News-Herald,* 12/4/63.

5. The statement was issued in a 12/6/63 press release of a three-member subcommittee of the House Republican Policy Committee—Laird, John J. Rhodes, and Katherine St. George.

6. Eisenhower was often asked to name Republicans who would be good presidential candidates. Prior to the European trip, he named ten: Generals Lucius Clay, Alfred Guenther, and Lauris Norstad; Senators Thruston Morton and Barry Goldwater; Governors Nelson Rockefeller, George Romney, and William Scranton; and two perennial favorites, his brother Dr. Milton Eisenhower and Robert Anderson, the ex-secretary of the treasury. (Eisenhower, "Personal and Confidential," letter to Chauncey Weaver, 6/30/63.)

At a press conference on August 15 in the ship's promenade lounge, Eisenhower gave a more public list of ten names, including only five from his confidential letter's list of six weeks before—Clay, Goldwater, Norstad, Rockefeller and Romney. The new five were Governors John Anderson Jr., Mark O. Hatfield, and John A. Love; Congressman Ford and banker Gabriel Hauge. ("Eisenhower Hints He Backs Treaty," *New York Times,* 8/16/63.)

That Laird was an eleventh name Ike later added to the list aboard the ship was confirmed by an Eisenhower spokesperson in an AP story, and by later accounts in the *New York Times* and other newspapers. For the next six years, when the issue was raised periodically by journalists writing about Laird, Eisenhower never denied that he had named Laird as one of the eleven Republican men "well-qualified" to be president. (AP, "Laird Is Presidential Timber: Ike," *Wausau*

Record-Herald, 8/17/63; "Professional Politician: Melvin Robert Laird," 7/7/64; "After the Pentagon, What?: Melvin Laird Looks Ahead," *Baltimore Sun*, 8/7/72.)

During the ship's press conference, Eisenhower said that Nixon "told me frankly and positively he just cannot be considered."

7. David Laird, interview, 2/27/01.

8. Richard Reeves, *A Ford, Not a Lincoln*, Harcourt Brace Janovich (1975), 5–9.

9. Clark R. Mollenhoff, *The Man Who Pardoned Nixon*, St. Martin's Press (1976), 2.

10. Ford, *A Time to Heal*, 73–4; Cannon, *Time and Chance*, 75.

11. At a 3/9/63 news conference, Laird was one of two Wisconsin Republican congressmen who "indicated...that they favored Rockefeller" ("Rockefeller Displays Charm to State GOP," *Milwaukee Journal*, 3/10/63). Rockefeller soon wrote Laird a letter of thanks for his support, the "warm reception" Laird had given the governor, and the obvious boost from standing beside the young congressman in his home state where he was held "in the highest esteem." (Gov. Nelson A. Rockefeller, letter to MRL, 3/15/63.)

12. AP, "Byrnes Wouldn't Be Favorite Son if Major Candidates Enter Primary," *La Crosse Leader-Tribune*, 8/19/63; "Wisconsin G.O.P. Wary of Primary," *New York Times*, 10/13/63; MRL, "The John Byrnes and John Reynolds Candidacies," *Your Washington Office Report*, 2/5/64.

13. Barry Goldwater, *With No Apologies: The Personal and Political Memoirs of United States Senator Barry Goldwater*, William Morrow and Company (1979), 11.

14. This was the number used by the *New York Times* in a 7/7/64 profile of Laird.

15. MRL, "Civil Rights," *Your Washington Office Report*, 2/5/64.

16. On 12/16/63, Laird had predicted on the *Washington Viewpoint* television show: "You will also find that when final passage comes that you will have a higher percentage of Republicans voting for the bill than you do of Democrats, as the bill goes into final passage."

On the day of the vote, there were two vacancies in the House, and thirteen members (five Republicans and eight Democrats) did not vote. The final tally was 138 Republicans and 152 Democrats for the bill, as 96 Democrats and 34 Republicans voted against it.

17. The Senate vote was 73–27. On July 2, the House voted on the Senate version of the bill and approved it 289–126. President Johnson signed it into law a few hours later.

18. According to Eisenhower's appointment book for 6/18/64, Goldwater asked that morning to come out to visit him, which he did from 2:55 to 3:40 P.M. to discuss "his position on Civil Rights Cloture and Bill." Also, Charles Mohr, "Eisenhower Stand on Bill Reported," *New York Times*, 6/20/64; *Gettysburg Times*, 6/19/64.

19. Lyon, *Eisenhower*, 840–1.

20. Bob Novak, interview, 10/2/00.

21. The eight Congressmen who joined Laird on the project were Gerald R. Ford (Mich.), Thomas B. Curtis (Mo.), Peter Frelinghuysen (N.J.), Charles E. Goodell (N.Y.), Glenard P. Lipscomb (Calif.), Clark MacGregor (Minn.), John J. Rhodes (Ariz.), and Robert Taft Jr. (Ohio).

22. *Los Angeles Times*, 8/30/63.

23. According to Eisenhower's appointment book, the two had lunch on 1/12/64.

24. Eisenhower, speech at a fund-raising dinner sponsored by the National Republican Finance Committee, Cobo Hall, Detroit, 1/29/64.

25. Robert Merriam, Prospectus for "Party-to-People Program," 2/24/64; Transcript of "Party-to-People Forum," Biltmore Bowl, Biltmore Hotel, Los Angeles, 3/31/64; Republican Platform Committee, news release, "Eisenhower, Other Statesmen to Discuss Foreign Policy at Forum Here on June 15," 5/28/64.

26. Mary McGrory, "Melvin Laird Relishes Job as G.O.P. Umpire," *St. Louis Courier-Journal*, 6/30/64.

27. MRL, Chairman of the Republican Platform Committee, "Statement," 6/64.

28. "Surprisingly, there were only three areas in which any criticism to this document was raised," Laird put it in his newsletter. (MRL, "The Republican Platform Committee Chairmanship," *Your Washington Office Report*, 8/12/64; also, MRL, press release, 10/5/64.)

29. UPI, "Romney Asks Plank Backing Rights Bill," *New York Times*, 6/30/64; MRL *Meet the Press* appearance, 7/5/64; AP, "GOP Platform Must Affirm 'Rights' Law: Rockefeller," *Sheboygan Press*, 7/7/64.

30. Lee Edwards, *Goldwater: The Man Who Made a Revolution*, Regnery Publishing (1997), 207, 302.

31. AP, "Platform Should Name John Birch Society, He [Scranton] Says," *Rhinelander News*, 7/7/64; AP, 7/11/64.

32. MRL, draft of remarks for Gridiron Dinner, 11/63.

33. Republican platform 1964, "For the People," presented to the Republican National Convention, San Francisco, 7/14/64.

34. Laird thought the 1960 platforms of his own party (fifteen thousand words) and the Democrats (twenty thousand words) had been "too lengthy." So in January 1964, after he had been named platform chair, he said a prime objective would be to hold the platform to about three thousand words. But by April, it was clear it would be longer, so he revised that by promising that it would be "a shorter document" which "at most" would be half the length of the 1960 Democrat platform of twenty thousand words. He succeeded. (AP, "Laird Says GOP Platform Ready; Objectives to Show Party Differences," *Marshfield News-Herald*, 1/22/64; "Interview with Melvin Laird: The G.O.P.'s Platform Prospects," *Washington Star*, 4/19/64.)

35. For example, from Evans and Novak, "Laird for Romney?" 1/10/66: "Because of the way Laird ramrodded the Goldwater-endorsed platform through the 1964 San Francisco Convention, he is not well loved by moderate Republicans."

Or this from "House Republicans—They're Out to Win," *Wall Street Journal*, 3/14/67: "As formal chairman of the party's 1964 Platform Committee, Mr. Laird rammed through a document intended to maintain traditional GOP commitments—to civil rights, for example—without embarrassing the by-then-certain Presidential candidacy of Barry Goldwater. By bulldozing anti-Goldwater forces, however, he gained their lasting enmity."

36. Ambassador Thomas Graham, former acting director of the Arms Control and Disarmament Agency, recounted the reaction of his grandmother, Elizabeth Graham, Laird's great aunt. Thomas Graham, interview, 10/26/99.

37. MRL, remarks on floor of the House of Representatives, "Republican Opportunity and Responsibility in 89th Congress," 3/1/65. *New York Times*, 7/13/64. MRL, *Today*, NBC, 3/28/66.

38. "Cactus Jacobins Ready for Revolt on Bastille Day," *New York Times*, 7/15/64.

39. MRL, statement, "Laird Calls for Moratorium on Party Bickering," 11/11/64.

40. Robert Novak, interview, 10/2/00.

41. "G.O.P. Caucus Will Test Halleck's House Strength," *New York Times*, 12/14/64.

42. Reeves, *A Ford, Not a Lincoln*, 5–9.

43. Bill Baroody Jr., interviewed by Dr. Robert L. Peabody on 1/29/65.

44. Ford, undated interview with Trevor Armbrister, ca. 1978.

45. Ford, speech at dedication of Melvin R. Laird Center, Marshfield, Wis., 9/12/97.

8 / CLOUD RIDERS

1. MRL, speech on the floor of the House of Representatives, *Congressional Record*, 5/25/67.

2. Vice President Dick Cheney, letter to MRL, 8/15/02.

3. Pres. Jimmy Carter, interview, 10/23/97.

4. "Marshfield Clinic: A Special Place," brochure produced by the Marshfield Clinic, 1989.

5. G. Stanley Custer, M.D., Marshfield Clinic historian, "The making of Stephan Epstein, M.D." and "The Epsteins Come to America," both published in 1991 issues of *Pulse*, the Clinic's staff newsletter.

6. MRL, "Medicine and Politics," speech before State Officers' Conference of the American Academy of General Practice, 4/20/68.

7. MRL, speech, Detroit, 11/12/68.

8. "Representative John Fogarty Dies at 53," *New York Times*, 1/11/67.

9. Stephen P. Strickland, *Politics, Science, and Dread Disease*, Harvard University Press (1972), 80.

10. At one point, Fogarty won passage of an appropriations bill amendment that, while not naming Great Britain, effectively banned foreign aid to them until their partition of Ireland ended. Waking up "the morning after" to Fogarty's clever move, the House reversed itself two days later. He had made his point.

11. Mary Fogarty McAndrew, interview, 9/30/03.

12. Hugh Carey, interview, 10/24/01.

13. Strickland, *Politics*, 91–6; Ed Regis, *Virus Ground Zero: Stalking the Killer Viruses with the Centers for Disease Control*, Pocket Books (1996), 50–2.

14. "Hospital and Foundation," *Marshfield News-Herald*, 9/28/64; MRL, letter to John R. Fogarty, 10/1/64.

15. John Chafee, interview, 10/22/99.

16. Eisenhower, *Mandate*, 494–7; CQ, "Public Health," *Congress and the Nation: 1945–1964*, 1136–7; Brendon, *Ike*, 232, 311; Edward Shorter, *The Health Century*, Doubleday (1987), 64–70; Elizabeth Etheridge, *Sentinel for Health: A History of the Centers for Disease Control*, University of California Press (1992), 71–80.

17. Dr. Carl Baker, interview, 1/16/02.

18. Richard A. Rettig, *Cancer Crusade: The Story of the National Cancer Act of 1971*, Princeton University Press (1977), 25–6. *NIH Almanac 2000*, 254–8; MRL, weekly news column, "Health Needs Deserve High Priority," 4/10/68; MRL, speech before State Officers' Conference of the American Academy of General Practice, "Medicine and Politics," 4/20/68; MRL, press release, 4/26/68; MRL, "Interview with Hugh Downs on Irving Kupcinet Show," Chicago, 3/24/72; MRL, "Remarks and Question-Answer Session at TV Correspondents' Breakfast," Harvard Club, New York City, 4/26/72.

The seven National Institutes that existed when Laird came to office were Cancer (1937), Heart (1948), Dental Research (1948), Microbiological (1948), Mental Health (1949), Arthritis and Metabolic Diseases (1950), and Neurological Diseases and Blindness (1950).

19. Dr. David Laird, remarks at a Wisconsin dinner in his brother's honor, 9/11/97.

20. MRL, *Your Washington Office Report*, 9/28/66.

21. HEW then had the following "ecological" entities: National Air Pollution Control Administration, Bureau of Solid Waste Management, Bureau of Water Hygiene, Bureau of Radiological Health, and the Food and Drug Administration (which restricted pesticide use).

22. *1963 CQ Almanac*, "Labor-H.E.W. Funds," 156–7; *1964 CQ Almanac*, "Labor-H.E.W. Funds," 186; "Public Health," *Congress and the Nation: 1945–1964*, CQ, 1145, 1148–50.

23. "Laird Has a Good Proposal," *Green Bay Press-Gazette*, 5/10/63.

24. MRL, remarks before the Wisconsin Chapter of the American College of Surgeons, Marshfield, Wis., 10/27/73.

25. In "Early Switch," a 1/27/64, Wisconsin newspaper article, reporter Frances McKusick noted that Laird had quit cigarettes "months ago, long before THE REPORT came out." Alison Laird-Large, MRL's daughter, interview, 3/2/01.

26. Strickland, *Politics*, 118–19.

27. Rettig, *Cancer Crusade*, 77.

28. Harold P. Rusch, M.D., *Something Attempted, Something Done: A Personal History of Cancer Research at the University of Wisconsin, 1934–1979*, Wisconsin Medical Alumni Association (1984), 119–122.

29. CDC, "Bioterrorism-Related Anthrax: Inhalational Anthrax Outbreak among Postal Workers, Washington, D.C., 2001," *Emerging Infectious Diseases*, 10/02.

30. Vice President Cheney, letter to MRL, 8/15/02.

31. Etheridge, *Sentinel*, xvii.

32. Dr. Elizabeth Etheridge, 1/12/04; Etheridge, *Sentinel*, 107.

33 Fiscal Year 1953 CDC figure from *The Budget of the United States Government for the Fiscal Year Ending June 30, 1955*; FY 1969 amount from *The Budget of the United States Government, 1971*.

34. Etheridge, *Sentinel*, 104–5; Regis, *Virus Ground Zero*, 49–52.

35. Regis, *Virus Ground Zero*, 62–9.

36. MRL, weekly column, "The 18th World Health Assembly," 5/19/65.

37. Fogarty had suffered his first heart attack in 1953 and used both Eisenhower's heart specialist, Paul Dudley White, and NIH Director Dr. James Shannon in the role of personal doctors. (Dr. James P. Crowley, "Paul Dudley White, MD, and John E. Fogarty," *Rhode Island Medicine*, 12/92.)

38. Howard A. Rusk, M.D., "Mr. Public Health: Death Ends Efforts by Representative Laird to Give United States Freedom from Disease," *New York Times*, 1/15/67.

39. MRL, eulogy, included in the *Congressional Record*, 1/18/67.

40. "Coveted on Capitol Hill: the Hideaway," *New York Times*, 3/7/83.

41. According to Ann Waisbrot, director of New Visions Gallery in Marshfield, Wis., the plaque on the back of Laird's Kennedy rocker reads: "This rocker was designed at the suggestion of President John F. Kennedy's physician, Janet Travell, M.D., by White House carpenter Larry Arata. There were four rockers built—two owned by the Kennedy family, one given to Congressman John Fogarty of Rhode Island, and one given to Melvin Laird. Doctor Travell gave advice to the

Fogarty-Laird HEW Appropriation Committee." (R.I. Lt. Gov. Charles Fogarty, nephew of John Fogarty, 9/16/03; McAndrew, 9/30/03.)

UPI, "President Picks Woman Doctor, First to Serve the White House," *New York Times*, 1/25/61; "Woman in the News: Pioneering Physician—Janet Grame Travell," *New York Times*, 1/27/61; AP, "Kennedy Uses a Rocking Chair to Relax on the Job," *New York Times*, 3/22/61; "The Kennedy Rocker, Still a Favorite," *New York Times*, 8/29/83; "Tiny North Carolina Company Still Making Kennedy Rockers," AP, 3/10/96.

In April 1996, at Sotheby's Jacqueline Kennedy Onassis auction, one of the Kennedy-owned rockers sold for $442,500. ("Kennedy was a man of many rockers," *Boston Globe*, 4/26/96.)

42. *Washington Star*, "Laird's Transfer to Defense Dept. May Be Felt Most on Medical Front," *Janesville (Wis.) Gazette*, 12/19/68.

9 / THE PATRON SAINT OF FOOTBALL

1. David Boren, interview, 5/14/02; Bob Burke and Ralph G. Thompson, *Bryce Harlow: Mr. Integrity* (2000), 75, 139–40.

2. MRL, letter to 64 High School Principals, 10/28/65; MRL, news release, 11/3/65; MRL, weekly column, "Youth Leadership Workshop," 11/24/65; MRL, "Remarks before the Student Body, Wayland Academy," 1/14/66.

3. Lee Dreyfus, who was UWSP Chancellor from 1967 to 1979 (resigning to become Wisconsin governor), also said Laird's program powerfully elevated the quality of UWSP, the only university in Laird's congressional district. "My own belief is that the quality of the university is determined by the quality of the students, not the professors so much. The students will push the professors and make them better," Dreyfus observed. "So here was Mel inviting the top two juniors and seniors of every high school to my campus every other year—a first-class recruiting opportunity for us." (Dreyfus, interview, 1/29/02.)

4. David S. Broder, "Two Good Choices," *Washington Post*, 1/9/83.

5. Hugh Carey, interview, 10/24/01.

6. MRL, speech, "Tax-Sharing with the States—A Way Out," National Conference of State Legislative Leaders, Shoreham Hilton, Washington, D.C., 11/17/66; MRL, House floor speech, "Strengthening the Federal System—The Case for Revenue Sharing," *Congressional Record*, 2/15/67.

7. CQ, "Tax Policy—1967 Chronology," *Congress and the Nation, 1965–1968*, 164.

8. Among the observations regarding Laird's revenue sharing authorship as the Heller Plan was being touted were these:

"[T]he 'Heller Plan' is not really the creature of former Presidential Advisor Walter Heller. That key Republican legislative proposal—federal sharing of tax revenues with the states—is the brainchild of Rep. Melvin Laird, chairman of the Republican Conference Committee." (Vera Glaser, *Washington Star*, "That 'New' Heller Plan Is Really Melvin Laird's," as in *Berkshire Eagle*, 11/23/66.)

"Laird has been pushing this idea since 1958." (*Business Week*, "GOP congressmen get early start on '68," 9/2/67.)

"Although Heller was responsible for generating widespread interest in the proposal, many persons who studied the issue gave Rep. Melvin R. Laird (R-Wis.) the credit for having introduced in 1958 the first bill which embodied many of what later were considered the essential principles of revenue sharing. The Laird bill provided for the automatic return of a portion of federal revenues to the states with relatively few conditions attached." ("Tax Policy—1967 Chronology," *Congress and the Nation, 1965–1968*, 164.)

"He was the first Congressman in either party to introduce revenue sharing legislation." ("Viet picture pleases Laird," *Philadelphia Bulletin*, 11/14/71.)

"He had made his mark in diverse fields: revenue sharing, of which he was a pioneer advocate; medical care, which brought him the Albert Lasker Award in 1964." ("After the Pentagon, What?: Melvin Laird Looks Ahead," *Baltimore Sun*, 8/7/72.)

"The father of modern revenue-sharing is generally acknowledged to be Walter Heller, the economist, yet the concept claims a spectrum of champions. Among them were the former Representative Melvin Laird, who advocated revenue-sharing in 1958; Senator Barry Goldwater, the Republican Presidential nominee in 1964, and two Democratic Presidential candidates, Edmund

S. Muskie and Hubert H. Humphrey. Howard Baker, later Republican majority leader, was first elected to the Senate in 1966 by advocating revenue-sharing." (James A. Cannon, "Federal Revenue-Sharing: Born 1972. Died 1986. R.I.P.," *New York Times*, 10/10/86.)

9. Evans and Novak, "Inside Report: Walter Heller's Boomerang," *Washington Post*, 11/18/66.

10. MRL, question-answer period following remarks to AP editors, Kansas City, Mo., 11/16/72.

11. John Ehrlichman, *Witness to Power: The Nixon Years*, Simon and Schuster (1982), 208–10.

12. MRL, remarks to the Washington Ridder Newspaper Group at the Pentagon, 11/22/72.

13. William Safire, *Before the Fall*, Doubleday (1975), 223.

14. Nixon, *Memoirs*, 767–8; Timothy Conlan, *New Federalism: Intergovernmental Reform from Nixon to Reagan*, Brookings Institution (1988), 19–91; Henry Reuss, *When Government Was Good: Memories of a Life in Politics*, University of Wisconsin Press (1999), 115–16.

15. Conlan, *New Federalism*, 95–237; John A. Ferejohn and Barry W. Weingast, editors, *The New Federalism: Can the States Be Trusted?*, Hoover Institution Press (1997).

16. Bob Harlan, president and CEO, Green Bay Packers, 1/25/02. Denis J. Harrington, *The Pro Football Hall of Fame: Players, Coaches, Team Owners and League Officials, 1963–1991* (1991), 125–7; "America's Small-Town Team: Packers Play for Touchdown Not for Profits," *New York Times*, 1/13/96.

17. "C.B.S. Gets Rights to Pro Football," *New York Times*, 4/27/61.

18. "TV Football Pact Voided By Court; National League–C.B.S. Deal Held Antitrust Violation," *New York Times*, 7/21/61; AP, "National Football League Denied Plea to Delay Voiding TV Pact," *New York Times*, 7/29/61.

19. *The NFL's Official Encyclopedia History of Professional Football*, Macmillan Publishing (1973), 32; David Harris, *The League: The Rise and Decline of the NFL*, Bantam Books (1986), 14–15.

20. AP, "N.F.L. Gains Right to Pool TV Pacts," *New York Times*, 10/1/61. Almost as important as the TV deal was Rozelle's decision to have the NFL take over all team products and share that revenue equally.

21. Tex Schramm, interview, 1/25/02.

22. Harris, *The League*, 17; Robert Mann, *Legacy to Power: Senator Russell Long of Louisiana*, Paragon House (1992), 272–5.

23. Ted Brock and Larry Eldridge Jr., *25 Years: The NFL Since 1960*, Simon and Schuster (1985); Michael L. LaBlanc, Editor, *Professional Sports Team Histories*, Gale Research Inc. (1994) 471–2.

24. C. Robert Barnett, interview, 1/25/02; Joe Horrigan, interview, 1/25/02.

25 James F. Frechette Jr., interview, 12/17/01; Verna Fowler, *The Menominee*, Raintree Steck-Vaughn Publishers (2001), 5–6, 32.

26. Although technically a sovereign nation, the Menominee were located in Laird's 7th Congressional District and were actively seeking his representation in Congress. Moreover, the Menominee were eligible to vote in local and national elections.

27. MRL, statement, "A Plea for Justice for the Menominee Indian People," 5/9/61.

28. Nicholas Peroff, *Menominee DRUMS: Tribal Termination and Restoration 1954–1974*, University of Oklahoma Press (1982), 129; "For 12 Long Years, Reservation Struggled to Make It as a County," *Milwaukee Journal-Sentinel*, 5/21/98; "Income Data Make Poverty Painfully Obvious," *Green Bay Press-Gazette*, 8/15/65.

29. Ada Deer, 1/18/02; Patricia Raymer, "Wisconsin's Menominees: Indians on a Seesaw," *National Geographic*, 247–9, 8/74; *Newsweek*, "The Indian," 7/4/76.

30. Ada Deer, interview, 1/18/02.

31. Peroff, *Menominee DRUMS*, 215–16.

32. "Senate Panel Signs Off on Bill to Pay Menominee Tribe," *Milwaukee Journal-Sentinel*, 6/11/99.

33. Others were pivotal to the growth of the intellectual movement. The most important was probably William F. Buckley Jr., who both edited the *National Review* and authored *God and Man at Yale*. Two other seminal works were Russell Kirk's *The Conservative Mind* and Barry Goldwater's *The Conscience of a Conservative*. Both *Human Events* and *Reader's Digest* promoted conservative thought, though not in as "high-brow" a manner as Buckley's *National Review*.

34. Dr. John Bibby, interview, 4/27/01.

35. "Idea Factories of the Right," *Newsweek*, 12/1/80; "Hoover Institution Gains Entree to White House," *New York Times*, 12/22/80; "Right-of-Center Defense Groups—The Pendulum Has Swung Their Way," *National Journal*, 1/24/81; "The Hoover Reunion," *Washington Post*, 4/29/82; "Conser-

vative Comraderie," *Washington Post,* 1/11/84; James Smith, *The Idea Brokers: Think Tanks and the Rise of the New Policy Elite,* The Free Press (1993), 184–8, 190–1, 287–8.

36. David Abshire, interview, 4/5/01; James Allen Smith, *Strategic Calling: The Center for Strategic and International Studies, 1962–1992,* CSIS (1993); "Abshire to Aid Reagan Team," *Washington Post,* 11/9/80; "Right's New Weapon—Think Tanks," *Christian Science Moniter,* 2/10/81; "Revolving Door to Power Gives GU New Pride," *Washington Star,* 7/5/81; "Thick & Think Tank; David Abshire's CSIS Ponder Policy with Kissinger & Fred Flintstone," *Washington Post,* 9/21/82; "Abshire: 'Pragmatic Republican,'" *Washington Post,* 11/30/86; "For Abshire, New Step in Career as Counselor," *New York Times,* 12/27/86; Smith, *The Idea Brokers,* 4, 13, 208–12.

37. Ed Feulner, interview, 7/30/01; John Dressendorfer, interview, 7/20/00; "Issue-Oriented Heritage Foundation Hitches Its Wagon to Reagan's Star," *National Journal,* 3/20/82; "Heritage Led by a True Believer; Foundation Chief's Resume Impeccably Conservative," *Washington Post,* 9/24/85; Smith, *The Idea Brokers,* 194–202; Lee Edwards, *The Power of Ideas: The Heritage Foundation at 25 Years,* Jameson Books (1997), 3–11, 23, 41–49, 185–191.

10 / PRESIDENTIAL PLEA: "MUZZLE LAIRD"

1. Robert Pursley, interview, 7/17, 10/3, 11/6, and 11/28/00; Alexander Haig, interview, 1/21/02; "Interview with Melvin Laird," *David Frost Show,* 12/2/70; "Gulf of Tonkin 'Attack' Doubted by Many," *Christian Science Monitor,* 6/28/71; "Ellsberg Says Tonkin Tapes Show Congress Was Misled," *Washington Post,* 7/10/71; Orr Kelly, "A Book for Today: Tonkin Gulf Incident Recalled," *Washington Star,* 9/28/71; *U.S. News and World Report,* 7/23/84; "Debris From the Tonkin Resolution," *New York Times,* 8/5/84; "The Tonkin Chronology," *Los Angeles Times,* 4/29/85; J. Norville Jones, former Senate Foreign Relations Committee staffer, 1964–77, letter to the editor, "Robert McNamara's Bad Information," *Washington Post,* 11/23/95.

2. *U.S. News and World Report,* 7/23/84; Robert S. McNamara, *In Retrospect,* Vintage Books (1995), 133.

3. Public Law 88-408, 88th Congress, H. J. Res. 1145, 8/10/64; *1964 CQ Almanac,* "Viet Nam Resolution," 331–2.

4. MRL, House floor speech, *Congressional Record,* 8/7/64; "Laird Reminds House Viet War 'Still Goes On,'" *Appleton Post-Crescent,* 8/8/64.

5. AP, "Congressmen Say Attacks Deliberate," *Stevens Point Daily Journal,* 8/5/64.

6. AP, "Grim Viet Decision Ahead, Laird Warns," *La Crosse Leader-Tribune,* 3/3/64.

7. AP, "Laird Denies Congress at Fault for Viet Nam," *La Crosse Leader-Tribune,* 3/9/64.

8. White House tape, 5/21/64, section beginning at 12:42 P.M., Lyndon Baines Johnson Library, Austin, Tex.

9. Radio Press International, "From the People," 5/31/64; AP, "U.S. Preparations for Blow at North Vietnam Reported," *New York Times,* 6/1/64.

10. Tape transcripts by Michael R. Beschloss, *Taking Charge: The Johnson White House Tapes, 1963–1964,* Simon & Schuster (1997), 379–83.

11. "Program for Airlie House Conference, Warrenton, Va.," January 4–5, 1966; William B. Prendergast, "The Indoctrination Session for New Republican Members of the House," memorandum to MRL and Charles E. Goodell, 11/14/66; MRL, "Fifty-Eight New Congressmen Begin Work," weekly column, 1/4/67; Laird appearance on *Meet the Press,* 1/8/67.

12. MRL, "Republican Opportunity and Responsibility in the Eighty-Ninth Congress," Remarks on the floor of the House (23 pages), 3/1/65; Tom Wicker, "Laird Challenges Johnson Policies," *New York Times,* 1, 3/2/65; "GOP: Is Great Society Just 'Great Mistake?'", *Detroit News,* 3/1/65; "It's Laird vs. Ford—New House GOP Hassle," *New York Herald-Tribune,* 3/2/65; "Few Republicans on Hand for Laird's House Speech," *Wall Street Journal,* 3/2/65.

13. "House Republicans Squaring Off for Fight to Fill Laird Party Post," *Washington Post,* 12/11/68.

14. MRL, *Your Washington Office Report,* 4/21/65; MRL, "Medicare," *Your Washington Office Report,* 5/18/60; MRL, "Medical Care for the Elderly," *Your Washington Office Report,* 4/18/62; MRL, speech on House floor, "A Report of the 1962 Joint Committee on Republican Principles," 5, 6/7/62; MRL, *Your Washington Office Report,* 1/27/65.

15. MRL, interview by Dr. Robert L. Peabody, 4/13/65.

16. *Public Papers of the Presidents, Lyndon B. Johnson, 1963–64,* Vol. II, 1126, 1164, 1391.

17. Eisenhower appointment book for 12/14/65.

18. Richard L. Strout, "Master Politicians Feud but Remain Friendly," *Christian Science Monitor*, 8/6/65.

19. MRL, weekly news column, "Bipartisan Foreign Policy," 3/31/65.

20. Alison Laird-Large, interview, 3/2/01.

21. "Laird Boycotts Policy Briefings, Says GOP Is Used for Publicity," *Milwaukee Journal*, 4/18/65.

22. MRL, remarks on floor of the House, "Republican Opportunity and Responsibility in the 89th Congress," 3/1/65.

23. Gaylord Nelson, interview, 2/7/01; Lawrence F. O'Brien, Special Assistant to the President, letter to MRL, 5/13/65; "Viet Nam Defense Funds," *1965 CQ Almanac*, 74; Frank E. Vandiver, *Shadows of Vietnam: Lyndon Johnson's Wars*, Texas A&M University Press (1997), 112–14.

24. MRL, statement, 6/14/65.

25. "Portions of 3 U.S. Divisions Reported Going to Vietnam," *New York Times*, 6/15/65.

26. Michael Beschloss, *Reaching For Glory: Lyndon Johnson's Secret White House Tapes, 1964–1965*, Simon & Schuster (2001), 360–2.

27. MRL, *Your Washington Office Report*, 6/30/65.

28. Tom Wicker, "G.O.P. Unity 'War' Escalates Again," *New York Times*, 6/23/65; "Laird Denies Power Rift," *Milwaukee Sentinel*, 6/23/65; "Is Laird Becoming Mr. House Republican?" *La Crosse Leader-Tribune*, 6/27/65.

29. Beschloss, *Reaching for Glory*, 403–5.

30. Clark Clifford with Richard Holbrooke, *Counsel to the President: A Memoir*, Random House (1991), 422.

31. Evans and Novak, "Johnson's Home Front," *Washington Post*, 7/30/65.

32. "President Scores a Leader of G.O.P. For 'Untrue' Talk," *New York Times*, 8/2/65; Tom Wicker, "Misunderstanding, Ford Says in Reply to Johnson Attack," *New York Times*, 8/3/65; "Ford Declines to Argue over LBJ's Charge," *Washington Post*, 8/3/65.

33. "Laird Seen behind Row Between Johnson, Ford," *Los Angeles Times*, 8/8/65.

34. Eisenhower appointment book entry for 8/24/65.

35. Richard H. Poff, Secretary, House Republican Conference, "Minutes of the Conference of the Republican Members of the U.S. House of Representatives," House Chamber, 8/25/65.

36. "News Conference," *New York Times*, 8/26/65.

37. "Viet Critics Brushed Off by Johnson; But GOP Leaders Fire New Rounds at Own News Parley," *Washington Post*, 8/27/65; "GOP on Viet-Nam; Looking Both Ways," *Washington Post*, 8/27/65; "The One-Two Punch," *Time*, 9/3/65.

38. Lt. Gen. Charles G. Cooper, U.S. Marine Corps (Ret.) "The Day It Became the Longest War," *Proceedings of the U.S. Naval Institute*, 5/96, 77–80.

11 / AT THE CREDIBILITY GAP

1. "GOP Leader Urges War Declaration; Idea Not Aimed at Demonstrators, Laird Tells UROC," *Los Angeles Times*, 11/21/65; "Laird Would Support War Declaration," AP, 11/22/65.

2. Broder, "Ford and Laird View Vietnam as Major '66 Issue," *New York Times*, 11/25/65.

3. MRL, news release, "Let's Close the Credibility Gap," 1/30/66.

4. Broder, "G.O.P. Finds Rising Peril of 'Endless' Vietnam War," *New York Times*, 12/14/65.

5. MRL, weekly news column, "The Costs of War," 10/5/66.

6. "Window on Washington: Mel's Prediction Comes True," *Madison Capital Times*, 3/13/67; Laird appearance on "From the Capital," ABC radio news, 7/18/66.

7. MRL, *Your Washington Office Report*, 1/26/66.

8. MRL, weekly column, "Guns or Butter?" 8/11/65; Tom Wicker, " 'Guns or Butter'; Republicans Pressing the Issue," *New York Times*, 8/15/65; " 'Guns or Butter' Haunting Laird," unidentified Wisconsin newspaper clipping, 1/26/66; "It's 'Rifles or Ruffles' to a Butter Booster," *Milwaukee Journal*, 1/26/66.

9. MRL, weekly column, "Memorial Day 1967," 5/24/67.

10. Gaylord Nelson, interview, 2/7/01; "Congress Races Start to Hum," *Madison Capital Times*, 9/26/66; "Laird's Foe Better Bet for Postmaster," *Milwaukee Sentinel*, 10/25/66; "Myhra Runs Hard in Race with Laird," *Milwaukee Journal*, 10/31/66.

11. MRL, "Meeting the needs of older Americans," *Modern Maturity,* October-November 1966; from speech given 9/8/66 at AARP Convention in Salt Lake City, Utah.

12. Fred Malek, "Uncooperative Aging Organizations," White House memorandum to L.J. Evans Jr., "Administratively Confidential," 11/17/72.

13. MRL, weekly news column, "Laird Favors Tying Social Security to Cost of Living," 7/27/66; MRL, *Your Washington Office Report,* 8/3/66; MRL, weekly news column, "Cost-of-Living Social Security Bill Gains Support," 8/17/66; "Rise in Social Security to Match Living Costs Is '67 G.O.P. Goal," *New York Times,* 11/29/66; MRL, *Your Washington Office Report,* 8/9/67, 6/5 and 8/22/68; MRL, "Social Security," *Your Washington Office Report,* 10/16/68.

14. Paul Hassett, former executive secretary to Gov. Knowles, interview, 12/29/01; "Cheney Began Career in Badger State," *Milwaukee Journal-Sentinel,* 7/26/00.

15. The full quote: "All my political life I've tried to emulate you, having observed many years ago your special aptitude for doing great things to benefit many people." (Vice President Cheney, letter to MRL on the occasion of Laird's 80th birthday, 8/15/02.)

16. Vice President Cheney, interview, 2/20/01.

17. Republican Conference of the House of Representatives, MRL, Chairman, "The United States and The War in Vietnam," 19–21, 9/20/66.

18. "G.O.P. Chiefs Say War Is Johnson's; 3 House Leaders Assert He Must Bear Responsibility," *New York Times,* 9/20/66; AP, "G.O.P. Says Johnson Deceives On War," *New York Times,* 9/21/66; Laird appearance on NBC's *Today Show,* 9/22/66.

19. MRL, "The Great Issues of 1966: A Republican View," report to the Republican Coordinating Committee and delivered on the floor of the House, 10/3/66.

20. MRL, press release on Rockton, Ill., speech, 3/5/66.

21. MRL, weekly news column, "The Elections of 1966," 11/23/66. This was the largest Republican House membership in ten years, and the net gain of eight Republican governors meant that their party had chief executive in half the fifty states, including five of the nation's seven largest. ("Republicans Score Net Gain of 47 House Seats" and "Coattail Effects," *1966 CQ Almanac,* 1398.)

22. White House, press release, "Text of the Joint Communiqué Issued at the Manila Summit Conference, Manila, The Philippines," 10/25/66.

23. Ted Lewis, "Ford, Laird Seek Top GOP Spot in House," 1/5/67.

24. Gerald Ford, undated interview with Trevor Armbrister, ca. 1977–79.

25. Cannon, *Time and Chance,* 82.

26. In an interview as defense secretary, Laird was asked by David Frost whether he considered "as a compliment or an attack" the phrase "our Lyndon Johnson," which one Republican had used to describe Laird. "I have heard that term used," Laird smiled, before moving on to the next subject, without characterizing his view. (MRL appearance on "Interview with David Frost," *David Frost Show,* 12/2/70.)

27. John H. Averill, "Both Parties Watching as Laird Stirs Again; GOP's Gray Eminence Steps Up Criticism of Johnson's Policies on Vietnam, Taxes," *Los Angeles Times,* 9/18/67.

28. "Melvin Laird's Platform Caper," *New York Herald-Tribune,* 3/26/66; "Mel Laird: The Complete GOPolitician," *Milwaukee Journal,* 1/21/68.

29. Gerald Ford, interview, 8/28/97.

30. Dean Burch, undated interview with Trevor Armbrister, ca. 1978.

31. Richard Reeves, *A Ford, Not a Lincoln,* Harcourt Brace (1979), 30.

32. Gerald Ford, interview, 8/28/97. Robert T. Hartmann appointment, House Republican Conference press release, 1/5/66; Program, "Commissioning of the USS *Glenard P. Lipscomb* (SSN685)," 12/21/74; Robert T. Hartmann, *Palace Politics: An Inside Account of the Ford Years,* McGraw-Hill Book Company (1980); Cannon, *Time and Chance,* 91–2.

33. "House Republicans," *Wall Street Journal.*

34. Ford, 8/28/97; Rep. Albert H. Quie, R-Minn., 4/5/01; Ford, *A Time to Heal,* 25–7; Cannon, *Time and Chance,* 267, 275; Albert Quie, *Riding the Divide,* Quie Publications (2003), 273–6.

12 / INTO THE QUAGMIRE

1. "Laird Reported to Be Nixon's Pentagon Choice," *Washington Post,* 12/9/68; "Rep. Laird Known Navy; New Defense Boss Served in Destroyer in War," *San Diego Union,* 12/12/68; "Laird Tough McNamara Critic," Scripps-Howard, 12/10/68.

2. MRL, statement, "McNamara, Vietnam and the Credibility Gap," 5/18/66; MRL, *Your Washington Office Report,* 5/30/66.

3. There is no official transcript of this session available. At the time, intemperate remarks were often excised before the final hearing record was published. However, Laird's words to McNamara were later quoted in a contemporary account by a Wisconsin journalist, who placed the incident in March 1966. ("The Vast Empire of U.S. Defense May Get Vaster under Laird," *Milwaukee Journal,* 12/15/68.)

4. "Window on Washington: Mel's Prediction Comes True," *Madison Capital Times,* 3/13/67.

5. McNamara, *In Retrospect,* 269.

6. McNamara, *In Retrospect,* 307.

7. Robert McNamara, interview, 12/13/01.

8. MRL and David Packard, Press Conference, Federal Office Building #7, 12/30/68.

9. Lee Dreyfus, interview 1/29/02; AP, "Report Lists 3 Casualties from State," *Fond du Lac Commonwealth Reporter,* 3/24/67; " 'Couldn't Say No,' Said Albertson of Mission," *Stevens Point Daily Journal,* 3/24/67; Wisconsin State University–Stevens Point, press release, "Dr. James Albertson and Team of Educators Killed in a Plane Crash in Vietnam," 3/24/67.

10. MRL, House floor speech, "The Late James A. Albertson, President, Wisconsin State University, Stevens Point," *Congressional Record,* 5/4/67.

11. Paul Johnson, "Charles Leo Johnson, Native of Marshfield, KIA Vietnam," and "Herb and Adele Johnson," *Marshfield Story,* 403–6.

12. MRL, letter to President Lyndon B. Johnson, 2/9/67; AP, "Laird Calls Goal in Vietnam Vague," *New York Times,* 2/28/67.

13. William J. Jorden, "Memo for Mr. Rostow," White House, 2/17/67.

14. Douglass Cater, White House, memorandum "For the President," 2/1/67. In a February 8 news column, Laird elaborated on his dinner conversation points. "For every dollar the Soviet Union spends in support of North Vietnam, the United States spends $18 to $20. In addition, the impact on their economy is in no way as damaging as the impact of the Vietnam war on our own economy. Most importantly, the loss in life and limb to America is high whereas to the Soviet Union and its satellites, it is minimal." (MRL, weekly news column, "U.S. Trade Policies Prolong Vietnam War," 2/8/67.)

15. MRL, press release, 3/23/67; "Laird Demands Red Trade Ban," *New York Times,* 3/24/67; Richard L. Strout, "U.S. Urged to Apply Soviet Trade Lever," *Christian Science Monitor,* 3/28/67.

16. The Ford and Dirksen statements were part of "Press Release Issued following a Leadership Meeting," the Republican Leadership of Congress, 5/25/67. The press release listed as the leadership then: for the Senate: Everett M. Dirksen of Illinois; Thomas H. Kuchel of California; Bourke B. Hickenlooper of Iowa; Margaret Chase Smith of Maine; George Murphy of California; Milton R. Young of North Dakota; Hugh Scott of Pennsylvania. For the House of Representatives: Gerald R. Ford of Michigan; Leslie C. Arends of Illinois; Melvin R. Laird of Wisconsin; John J. Rhodes of Arizona; R. Allen Smith of California; Bob Wilson of California; Charles E. Goodell of New York; Richard H. Poff of Virginia; William C. Cramer of Florida.

Presiding: National Chairman Ray C. Bliss.

17. "Laird Sees No Hope of Real Vietnam Win," *Marshfield News-Herald,* 3/30/67.

18. MRL, weekly news column, "U.S. Trade Policies Prolong Vietnam War," 2/8/67.

19. George Bush, *All the Best: My Life in Letters and Other Writings,* Scribner (1999), 97–8.

20. President George H.W. Bush, interview, 10/14/97.

21. George Bush with Vic Gold, *Looking Forward,* Doubleday (1987), 94–5.

22. President Bush, interview, 10/14/97.

23. Another key figure moving Cheney along his career path was Maureen Drummy, a Young Republicans leader at the University of Wisconsin who recommended Cheney to Governor Warren Knowles for an internship. Drummy was also close to Billy Steiger and was hired by him as his chief aide. Drummy was very high on bringing Cheney on staff in 1968 on the congressional fellowship, which came from the American Political Science Association. ("Cheney Began Career in Badger State," *Milwaukee Journal-Sentinel,* 7/26/00; Nicholas Lemann, "The Quiet Man: Dick Cheney's Discreet Rise to Unprecedented Power," *New Yorker,* 5/7/01.)

24. Vice President Cheney, letter to MRL, 8/15/02.

25. President Bush, interview, 10/14/97.

26. "Return of Pecos Billie," *Newsweek,* 9/5/77; "Billie Sol Estes: Last One Standing," *Houston Chronicle,* 6/23/96; "Billie Sol Estes May Face New Charges," *Washington Times,* 12/4/97; Robert Dallek, *Flawed Giant: Lyndon B. Johnson and His Times 1960–1973,* Oxford University Press (1998),

38–40; "In a State of Scandal; Texas Has Left a Lasting Mark in the World of Politics," *Dallas Morning News*, 3/4/99; "The King of Con," *Fort Worth Star-Telegram*, 7/20/02.

27. "Bobby Baker," *Newsweek*, 5/30/77; "Excessive Discretion: Bobby Baker's Story," *Business Week*, 6/12/78; "Bobby Baker at 55: Still Wheeling and Dealing, but Broke," AP, 4/16/84; Victor Gold, "Wheeling and Dealing; Bobby Baker Was the Ultimate Senate Insider—but He Tried to Get Too Rich Too Fast," *Washingtonian*, 1/96; Jeff Shesol, *Mutual Contempt: Lyndon Johnson, Robert Kennedy, and the Feud That Defined a Decade*, W. W. Norton (1997), 146–8; Dallek, *Flawed Giant*, 40–3; Caro, *Master of the Senate*, 392–3, 408.

28. AP, "Laird Protests LBJ Criticism," *Manitowoc Herald-Times*, 1/31/67.

29. MRL, letter to Bill Moyers, assistant to the president, 2/19/66.

30. Robert S. McNamara, memorandum for the president, 2/23/66.

31. Bill Gulley with Mary Ellen Reese, *Breaking Cover*, Simon and Shuster (1980), 22–3.

32. Gulley with Reese, *Breaking Cover*, 30.

33. MRL, news release, 4/18/64; MRL, "The Defense Appropriations Committee," *Your Washington Office Report*, 5/6/64.

34. "Window on Washington: Mel's Prediction Comes True," *Madison Capital Times*, 3/13/67.

35. AP, "Laird Censored," *Manitowoc Herald-Times*, 5/4/67.

36. As another example, the *Detroit Free Press* editorialized that it was a sad day for the administration when they found it necessary to censor a congressman who they categorized—in the Vietnam aviary—as "more of a hawk than a dove." "The Administration Now Is Censoring the Hawks," *Detroit Free Press*, 5/15/67.

37. "Absurd Action," *Milwaukee Sentinel*, 5/6/67.

38. MRL, "Remarks before the Lion's International Convention," Chicago Stadium, 7/8/67.

39. Evans and Novak, 8/15/67.

40. MRL, press release, "Keynote Address at Welcoming Luncheon of American Mining Congress' 70th Annual Convention," Denver (Colo.), Hilton ballroom, 9/11/67; "Laird Ends Viet Policy Support," *Denver Post*, 9/11/67; AP, "Rep. Laird Withdraws Johnson Policy Backing," *Washington Star*, 9/11/67; "Laird Ends GOP Support of Vietnam War," *Waukesha Daily Freeman*, 9/12/67; "Mr. Laird Changes Course," *Christian Science Monitor*, 9/16/67; John H. Averill, "Both Parties Watching as Laird Stirs Again; GOP's Gray Eminence Steps Up Criticism of Johnson's Policies on Vietnam, Taxes," *Los Angeles Times*, 9/18/67; Barry Goldwater, column, *Los Angeles Times* Syndicate, 9/20/67.

41. MRL, weekly news column, "The Long and the Short of It," 9/13/67.

42. Evans and Novak, "Dirksen Seen as Too Near LBJ," *Marshfield News-Herald*, 12/22/67.

43. MRL, "Shall We Watch Our Flag Burn?" *Wisconsin State Journal*, 7/4/67; "Flag Burning, Aid to Viet Cong," *1967 CQ Almanac*, 91.

44. "Laird Would Accept Coalition in Vietnam," *Milwaukee Journal*, 1/20/68; "Laird Proposes Direct Talks with Viet Cong," UPI, 1/20/68; Mary McGrory, "Laird, Nixon & Rocky," *New York Post*, 1/23/68; MRL, Chairman, HRC, "As the Other Side Sees It," *U.S. News & World Report*, 1/29/68; MRL, weekly news column, "Vietnam," 1/31/68.

45. Donald Oberdorfer, *Tet*, Doubleday & Company (1971); Stanley Karnow, *Vietnam: A History*, Viking Press (1983), 515–66; Adam Land, "Tet Offensive," *Encyclopedia of the Vietnam War*, Simon & Schuster and Prentice Hall International (1996), 536–41.

13 / THE RESURRECTION OF RICHARD NIXON

1. John Culver, interview, 10/5/00.

2. Nixon, letter to MRL, 11/16/62.

3. Nixon, *Memoirs*, 277.

4. "The Mood of Congress," *Dun's Review*, 4/68; MRL, press release, 6/28/68; MRL appearance on *Capitol Cloakroom*, CBS Radio Network, 7/24/68.

5. Mary McGrory, "Laird, Nixon & Rocky," *New York Post*, 1/23/68.

6. AP, "Laird Says (Wisconsin) Primary Ballot Should Have Rockefeller's Name," *Appleton Post-Crescent*, 2/13/68; "Aide Denies Laird Endorses Rocky," *Wisconsin State Journal*, 2/15/68; MRL, letter to Agatha Muehlenkamp, Milwaukee, Wis., 2/20/68; MRL, weekly news column, "The Wisconsin Presidential Primary," 2/28/68; "Romney Suddenly Quits; Rockefeller Reaffirms Availability to a Draft," *New York Times*, 2/29/68.

7. Derounian's Armenian parents had fled to Bulgaria from Turkey, just ahead of the country's World War I massacre of Armenians. Derounian was born in the capital of Sofia, and when the Balkans erupted in conflict, his family fled to the United States. Derounian was three when he was processed through Ellis Island. He distinguished himself as an American in World War II, winning the Bronze Star for valor.

8. Governor Nelson A. Rockefeller, telegram to MRL, 3/21/68.

9. Evans and Novak, *Washington Post*, 7/16/67; "Republican Parley Buzzes with Talk about Romney," *Milwaukee Journal*, 9/8/67; "Laird Wants Reagan off Ballot," *Madison Capital Times*, 10/4/67.

10. MRL, statement given to AP and UP, 4/4/68; "State's Leaders Express Sorrow," *Milwaukee Journal*, 4/5/68.

11. MRL, appearance, *Opinion: Washington*, 5/19/68; UPI, "Rockefeller Urged by Laird to Give Up," *New York Times*, 6/5/68.

12. "Laird Refutes Charges in Ripon Society Book," *Milwaukee Journal*, 10/9/66.

13. Goldwater, letter to MRL, 5/3/68; MRL, response to Goldwater, 5/10/68.

14. Daniel P. Moynihan, contributor, "Where Liberals Went Wrong," *Republican Papers*, 131.

15. MRL, statement before the full Committee on Resolutions (Platform Committee), Voltaire Room, Fontainebleau Hotel, Miami, Fla., 7/29/68.

16. Paul McCracken, letter to MRL, 12/5/72.

17. Paul McCracken, interview, 3/18/03.

18. The figure for the number killed by the time of the Republican convention is from Theodore H. White, *The Making of the President, 1968*, Atheneum Publishers (1969), 287. The total casualty figures and $1 million spent every twenty minutes are from the convention keynote address by Washington Gov. Dan Evans, Aug. 5, 1968, referring to a war that "we have not won in Saigon, cannot negotiate in Paris and will not explain to the American people."

19. "GOP Platform Debate Backs Anti-War Plank," *Baltimore Sun*, 7/30/68.

20. With Wisconsin, Nixon crossed the 667-vote line required for nomination. His final tally was 692. Rockefeller received 277, and Reagan 182.

21. "Wisconsinites Celebrate as Kingmakers," *Milwaukee Sentinel*, 8/9/68.

22. AP, "Laird Eyes Rock as No. 2 Man," *Marshfield News-Herald*, 8/5/68; "Laird Stays Offstage, but Tries to Play Influential Role," *Milwaukee Journal*, 8/7/68.

23. Richard M. Nixon, "Why I Chose Ted Agnew," *Where He Stands: The Life and Convictions of Spiro T. Agnew*, Hawthorn Books (1968), 1–4; White, *Making, 1968*, 269, 290–5.

24. Stephen E. Ambrose, *Nixon: The Triumph of a Politician 1962–1972*, Simon and Schuster (1989), 162–3.

25. "Badgers Angered by Choice of Agnew," *Madison Capital Times*, 8/9/68; "Agnew Splits State's Vote," *Green Bay Press-Gazette*, 8/9/68.

26. Richard M. Cohen and Jules Witcover, *A Heartbeat Away: The Investigation and Resignation of Vice President Spiro T. Agnew*, Viking Press (1974), 3–16, 91–6.

27. Hillary Rodham Clinton, interview, 1/20/98. Also interviews with other students of the Maine South High School Class of '65: Mike Andrews, 5/3/99; Ellen Press Murdock, 6/7/99; Penny Pullen, 6/7/99.

28. Dr. Alan Schechter, interview, 6/7/99.

29. Hillary Clinton, interview, 1/20/98.

30. Hillary Rodham Clinton, *Living History*, Simon & Schuster (2003), 34–5; "In '68, Hillary's Convention Time Was with GOP," *Chicago Tribune*, 9/18/95; "Good Old Days," *Washington Times*, 9/20/95.

31. Hillary Clinton, interview, 1/20/98.

32. Hillary Clinton, interview, 1/20/98.

33. Robert Pursley, interview, 10/28/97.

34. Laird, *Press Conference U.S.A.*

35. MRL, *Your Washington Office Report*, 9/11/68.

36. Tom Graham, interview, 10/26/99.

37. "Laird Reports Troop Cut Plan; Campaigning with Nixon, He Foresees 90,000 Reduction—Officials Voice Doubt," *New York Times*, 9/25/68; Don Oberdorfer, *Washington Post*, 9/25/68; White, *Making, 1968*, 389–91.

38. MRL, "Statement in Answer to a Question Concerning Humphrey's Troop Withdrawals (and) Vietnam Question Directed to Representative Mel Laird by *New York Times, Washington Post*, and *Los Angeles Times*," 9/24/68; AP, "Nixon Supports Laird on Troop Withdrawal Forecast,"

Wisconsin Rapids Tribune, 9/25/68; Orr Kelly, "2 Pullout Versions Offered by Laird," *Washington Star,* 12/1/71; Stephen Ambrose, *Nixon: The Triumph of a Politician,* Simon and Schuster (1989), 196–7.

39. *Washington Post,* 9/25/68.

40. "Clifford Denies Vietnam Cutback; Clarifies Rebuttal to Laird on Reducing Troop Level," *New York Times,* 9/26/68.

41. Transcript, Secretary of Defense Clark Clifford appearance on NBC News' *Meet the Press,* 9/29/68; "Clifford Doubts Early Cutback; Chides Those Who Forecast Day Troops Will Return," *New York Times,* 9/30/68; "Clifford Raps Guess on GI Withdrawal," *Milwaukee Journal,* 9/30/68; Secretary of Defense Clark Clifford, memorandum for the president, 10/3/68; "Laird Affirms Forecast of Troop Withdrawals," *Wisconsin State Journal,* 10/5/68.

42. "Nixon Vows to End War with a 'New Leadership,'" *New York Times,* 3/5/68; William Safire, "The Secret of Mr. Nixon's 'Secret Plan,'" *New York Times,* 9/12/72.

43. Godfrey Sperling, "Nixon's 'Secret Plan' That Never Was," *Christian Science Monitor,* 12/9/97.

44. Robert Pursley, interviews, 6/15, 7/17, 7/18, 10/3, and 11/6/00; Clifford with Holbrooke, *Counsel,* 581–4.

45. "Humphrey Vows Halt in Bombing if Hanoi Reacts," *New York Times,* 10/1/68; White, *Making, 1968,* 412–16; Nixon, *Memoirs,* 318–19.

46. Barefoot Sanders, memorandum for the president, Monday, 9 P.M., 9/30/68, Lyndon Baines Johnson Library, Austin, Texas.

47. Paul Nitze spoke to Laird and then reported the conversation to presidential aide Walt Rostow, who included in it a memorandum to the president, "Defense Report of Congressional Contacts," 11/2/68.

48. Secretary of Defense Donald Rumsfeld, interview, 2/28/01.

14 / CABINET MAKING

1. "Live Nixon Show Climaxes Cabinet Search," *Washington Post,* 12/12/68; "Getting to Know Them," *Time,* 12/20/68. "The Great Presentation: Day Starts Out Calmly," *New York Times,* 12/12/68.

2. "Mr. Nixon's National Security Team," *Washington Post,* 12/11/68.

3. "Pentagon Heir Apparent: Melvin Robert Laird," *New York Times,* 12/10/68.

4. Julie Nixon Eisenhower, *Special People,* Simon and Schuster (1977), 166–70.

5. The conversation with Eisenhower is reconstructed from Laird's memory of the visit. No presidential diaries or stenographer's notes exist of the hospital visits during this period. The author consulted with the following Eisenhower specialists in regard to these events: Barbara Constable, archivist, Eisenhower Library, National Archives, interview, 8/1/01; Carol Hegeman, supervisory historian, Eisenhower National Historic Site (Gettysburg, Pa.), interview, 12/18/01; Lillian (Rusty) Brown Black, Eisenhower's longtime secretary, interview, 1/11/02.

6. John Eisenhower, *Strictly Personal,* Doubleday (1974), 332–3.

7. Secretary of Defense Clark Clifford, letter to MRL, 12/12/68.

8. Clark Clifford with Richard Holbrooke, *Counsel to the President,* Random House (1991), 603–4.

9. Clifford with Holbrooke, *Counsel,* 603.

10. "Laird's Book Seen Sure Fuel for Forces," *Milwaukee Sentinel,* 12/19/68.

11. Edwin J. Feulner Jr., "Strategy," memorandum to Rep. Melvin Laird regarding *House Divided,* 12/10/68; also, Feulner's preface to the 1969 edition of *House Divided.*

12. Herb Klein, interview, 7/30/01; MRL, "News Conference at Pentagon," 4:00 to 4:35 P.M., 12/13/68; "Laird Plans Visit to the War Zone after He's Sworn," *New York Times,* 12/14/68; "Laird Vows Arms Policy Reappraisal; Blue-Ribbon Committee Is Planned," *Washington Post,* 12/14/68; "A New Administration Takes Shape," *Time,* 12/20/68.

13. Gulley with Reese, *Breaking Cover,* 95; "White House Kiss and Tell," *Newsweek,* 5/26/80.

14. "LBJ, Nixon Confer for Two Hours," *Washington Post,* 12/13/68.

15. President Lyndon B. Johnson, daily diary, entry for Monday, 12/23/68. Mike Parrish, researcher, Lyndon B. Johnson Library, interview, 7/25/01; "Rogers Joins Johnson for Report on Talks," *Washington Post,* 12/1/68

16. In one of his first meetings with top-level staff at the Pentagon, Laird referred to this

counsel: "President Johnson went out of his way to stress this point to Mr. Laird. He said that every effort would soon be made to divide the State Department and the White House, the State Department and Defense, and the White House and Defense. It was one of the biggest problems of his Administration. We would have to go out of our way to knock these efforts down." (Senior Staff Meeting minutes, 2/10/69.)

At the end of his second year in office, Laird recounted the LBJ advice in an interview with David Frost: "President Johnson ... recommended that we [Rogers and Laird] play golf once a week. We have played perhaps 20 times.... [T]his has been most worthwhile, I think, because the Department of State and the Department of Defense, in this Administration, are closer together and working for common goals as those two Departments never had. I think this is the best record. They never have been as close as they are today." ("Interview with Melvin Laird," *David Frost Show,* 12/2/70.)

17. Clifford with Holbrooke, *Counsel,* 603.

18. The 12/23/68 conversation between Laird and Johnson was reconstructed from Laird's memory. At a future date, the actual transcript may be available from the Lyndon B. Johnson Library, which is slowly, and chronologically, releasing the Johnson tapes.

19. Beschloss, *Taking Charge,* 547–550.

20. Interviews with Jack A. Albright, former head of the White House Communications Agency, by Robert Sherman in 1982. Sherman wrote extensively about White House bugging in the July 1982 issue of *Popular Mechanics* and for the Jack Anderson column, *Washington Post,* 7/12, 7/13/82.

21. Robert Seamans, former secretary of the air force, interview, 10/12/00; Dick Capen, interview, 8/8/00.

22. John Dressendorfer, interview, 7/20/00

23. Senator John Warner, interview, 11/10/99.

24. Paul Warnke, interview, 7/25/01.

25. Richard V. Allen, director of foreign policy research, Nixon Agnew Campaign Committee, memorandum, "Confidential Verbal Comment of the Joint Chiefs via Gen. McConnell," delivered to MRL after his appointment on 12/11/68.

26. Ambassador Richard Holbrooke, interview, 8/11/00.

27. Moot said, having voted for Eisenhower as well, he "switched back to Republicans" when Laird reappointed him, "and have been a Republican ever since." (Robert Moot, interview, 2/6/01.)

28. At first, Seamans said he couldn't serve as air force secretary until June 1969, but he became available sooner. Harold Brown served Laird only a month into the Nixon administration, until February 15. (Robert Seamans, interview, 10/12/00; Harold Brown, interview, 2/20/01.)

29. Stanley Resor, interview, 10/30/01.

30. Senator John Warner, interview, 11/10/99.

31. Nixon, *Memoirs,* 352.

32. Robert Frosch, interview, 7/31/01.

33. Robert F. Froehlke, "Memorandum for John C. Whitaker, Secretary to the Cabinet, the White House," 9/5/69.

34. David Packard, *The HP Way: How Bill Hewlett and I Built Our Company,* HarperBusiness (1996, paperback), 167–8.

35. Packard, *The HP Way,* 35–43.

36. Packard, *The HP Way,* 174–5.

37. John Gardner, interview, 4/30/01.

38. There was a precedent, which Laird cited: in 1967 the Senate Armed Services Committee had approved a similar trust arrangement involving oil stocks and leases held by former governor Price Daniel of Texas so that he could take the post of director of the Office of Emergency Planning.

39. This was Laird's recollection—that Packard and Nixon had never really met before. A *Washington Post* story the day after the press conference quoted "a Nixon source" as saying it was Nixon who suggested Packard to Laird, adding that Nixon "has known Packard for a long time." ("Electronics Tycoon to Be Laird Deputy," *Washington Post,* 12/31/68.)

Several years later, Laird told television correspondents, however, that Packard "had never met the President until I introduced him down at Key Biscayne in December of 1968." (MRL, "Remarks and Question-Answer Session at TV Correspondents' Breakfast," Harvard Club, New York City, 4/26/72.)

Later that year, President Nixon included a complimentary aside on this point in a letter to Laird: "Incidentally, your skill in getting top personnel to come into the Defense Department always amazed me. I recall trying to get Dave Packard to come into the government in a Cabinet position when I met him in New York at the Pierre Hotel before you and I met in Palm Springs. I struck out. I could not have been more amazed when you brought him down to Key Biscayne a few weeks later and told me that he had agreed to come aboard as your Deputy in the Sub-Cabinet. (Nixon, letter to MRL, 11/17/72.)

40. Laird and Packard, transcript, "Press Conference," 12/30/68.

41. Gerald Ford, interview, 8/28/97.

42. "Nixon Meets His Top Aides and Orders Vietnam Study," *New York Times*, 12/29/68.

43. Henry Kissinger, interview, 1/10/01. Kissinger also wrote in his memoirs about the visit he and Gen. Goodpaster made to Eisenhower. (Henry Kissinger, *White House Years*, Little, Brown, and Company [1979], 41–3.)

44. Lawrence Eagleburger, interview, 2/7/01.

45. Kissinger, *White House Years*, 44.

46. Robert Pursley, interviews, 8/7/97, 6/15/00, and 1/21/02.

15 / LOOKING FOR AN EXIT

1. Lewis Sorley, *A Better War*, Harcourt Brace & Company (1999), 94.

2. Robert Pursley, interview, 7/17, 11/6, 11/10/00; Jerry Friedheim, interview, 7/19/00; Thelma Stubbs Smith, interview, 4/23/01; Ann Waisbrot, New Visions Gallery, Marshfield, Wis., interview, 8/2/01. Jack Anderson, "Secretary of Defense Mel Laird's Pentagon Hideaway," *Parade*, 7/13/69; Vera Glaser and Malvina Stephenson, *Philadelphia Inquirer*, 5/23/71; UPI, 4/13/72; MRL, "Question-Answer Period following Remarks to AP Editors," Kansas City, Mo., 11/16/72.

3. Gen. William C. Westmoreland, *A Soldier Reports*, Doubleday & Company (1976), 467–473; Gen. Bruce Palmer Jr., *The 25-Year War: America's Military Role in Vietnam*, Touchstone (1984), 80; Mark Perry, *Four Stars*, Houghton Mifflin Co. (1989), 184+; Clifford with Holbrooke, *Counsel*, 479–501.

4. Lewis Sorley, *Thunderbolt: General Creighton Abrams and the Army of His Times*, Simon & Schuster (1992), 222.

5. U.S. Army, Office of Chief of Information, "Biography: General Earle G. Wheeler," ca. 1/69; MRL, "Remarks at Special Retirement Review for Gen. Earle G. Wheeler," Andrews AFB, Md., 7/2/70; Lawrence J. Korb, *The Joint Chiefs of Staff: The First Twenty-five Years*, Indiana University Press (1976), 42; Perry, *Four Stars*, 121, 134.

6. Robert Pursley, interview, 10/9/00; "Masterful Bureaucrat," *Newsweek*, 2/23/70; Perry, *Four Stars*, 132–5, 167–8; Clifford with Holbrooke, *Counsel*, 479–80.

7. The most thorough and accurate account of the August 1967 near-revolt is in Perry's *Four Stars*, 160–68.

8. Robert Pursley, interview, 10/9/00; Clifford with Holbrooke, *Counsel*, 479–80.

9. "Wheeler Reappointment," *CQ 1965–1968*, 858, 860.

10. Robert Pursley, interviews, 10/9, 11/10/00; Senior Staff Meeting Minutes, "Extension of General Wheeler's Term," 4/21/69; Perry, *Four Stars*, 201–3.

11. "Biography: General John P. McConnell," U.S. Air Force, 9/15/68; "Former Air Force Chief of Staff: Retired Gen. John Paul McConnell Dies," *Los Angeles Times*, 11/29/86; Perry, *Four Stars*, 132, 164, 166.

12. Details on "the Tank"—its history, location, appearance, and protocol—are found in the following sources, listed chronologically: "Pentagon's Inner Sanctum: An Ominous Clock and Lots of Candy," *New York Times*, 8/14/70; AP, "Newsmen Are Given a Peek at War Room in Pentagon," *Baltimore Sun*, 8/14/70; Lawrence J. Korb, *The Joint Chiefs of Staff: The First Twenty-five Years*, Indiana University Press (1976), 21–2; Palmer, *25-Year War*, 20–1; Admiral William J. Crowe Jr., with David Chanoff, *The Line of Fire*, Simon & Schuster (1993), 153; Chief of Naval Operations, *U.S. Navy Guidebook for Joint Actions*, 4/24/96; Chairman of the Joint Chiefs of Staff order, "Meetings in the JCS Conference Room," 3/31/01.

13. Perry, *Four Stars*, 212–17.

14. Zumwalt wrote that, at the beginning of 1973, "I was sorry to see Mel Laird go.... The last two paragraphs of the farewell letter I wrote Mel were from the heart." "Because of your loyalty up and down the chain of command and your evident concern for people, today's Navy man

and woman are better trained, better housed, better paid, and more motivated than any of their predecessors. You have been a fair and inspiring boss and a loyal and faithful friend, both to me and to the Navy. I believe the legacy of achievement which you will pass on to your successors is the stuff of which greatness is made.'" (Elmo R. Zumwalt Jr., *On Watch: A Memoir*, Quadrangle [1976] 267, 309–10.)

15. Robert Pursley, interview, 12/19/00.

16. Robert Pursley, interview, 10/12/00; Paul Warnke, interview, 7/25/01. "Nixon Meets His Top Aides and Orders Vietnam Study," *New York Times*, 12/29/68; " '69 Report to Nixon Was Split on War," *Washington Post*, 4/25/72; MRL, "Remarks and Question-Answer Session at TV Correspondents' Breakfast," Harvard Club, New York City, 4/26/72; Kissinger, *White House Years*, 237–8; Hersh, *Price of Power*, 46–50.

16 / OFF THE MENU

1. Paul Warnke, memorandum to MRL, 2/13/69.

2. Clifford with Holbrooke, *Counsel*, 539.

3. Paul Warnke, memorandum to MRL, 1/25/69.

4. "Nixon Cabinet Will Be Named Tomorrow," *Wall Street Journal*, 12/10/68; "Pentagon Gets a Tough Pragmatist," *Business Week*, 12/14/68.

5. Joint Chiefs of Staff, "Operations in SVN Involving Laos," Cable to CINCPAC, part of memorandum to MRL, 8/13/73.

6. William Hammond, *The Military and the Media*, Government Printing Office (1996), 61.

7. Sorley, *A Better War*, 115.

8. Hammond, *Military and the Media*, 73.

9. Hammond, *Military and the Media*, 74.

10. U.S. Senate hearing, 3/19 to 3/20/69.

11. Nixon, *Memoirs*, 392.

12. Kissinger memorandum to Nixon, 9/10/69; Lawrence Eagleburger, interview, 2/7/01.

13. Robert Pursley, interview, 9/11/97. In early 1969, among America's national security hierarchy, only Secretary of State Rogers and CIA Director Richard Helms supported Vietnamization. "The Nixon Administration wasn't going any place [before Laird came up with a plan]," Helms recalled. "We had to find some way out of Vietnam and, out of all the choices we had, Vietnamization was a pretty good choice." (Richard Helms, interview, 7/24/01.)

14. MRL, memorandum to chairman, JCS, 3/31/69.

15. Nixon, *Memoirs*, 375.

17 / TEMPLATE FOR A CRISIS

1. Pursley, memorandum to Kissinger, 4/15/69.

2. Department of Defense, options paper prepared for National Security Council Meeting, 4/16/69.

3. Perry, *Four Stars*, 221.

4. Kissinger, *White House Years*, 320.

5. Perry, *Four Stars*, 221.

6. MRL, memorandum to Kissinger, 6/24/69.

7. Gen. Earle Wheeler, Chairman, JCS, memorandum to MRL, 5/31/69.

8. *Washington Post*, 5/22/69; Sorley, *A Better War*, 140; Hammond, *Military and the Media*, 85.

9. *Washington Star*, 6/9/69.

10. U.S. Senate, Defense Subcommittee on Appropriations, 6/10/69.

11. Hammond, Military and the Media, 92–93.

18 / GOING PUBLIC

1. U.S. Embassy, Vientiane, Laos, cable to State Department, 7/18/69.

2. MRL, memorandum to Kissinger, 8/23/69.

3. Kissinger, memorandum to MRL, 10/22/69.

4. Vernon Davis, *The Long Road Home: U.S. Prisoner of War Policy and Planning in Southeast Asia*, Historical Office, Office of the Secretary of Defense (2000), 222+.

5. White House, press release, 12/12/69, attached to MRL, memorandum to Vice President Agnew, 12/22/69.

6. Adm. Thomas Moorer, Chairman, JCS, memorandum to MRL, 9/10/71.

7. MRL, memorandum for the record, 11/6/70.

8. Memorandum to MRL, cable to Adm. John McCain, CINCPAC, 6/19/72; Stuart Rochester, historian, Office of Secretary of Defense, 10/20/00; George Veith, *Code Name Bright Light*, Dell Publishing (1998).

19 / SLOWING THE ARMS RACE

1. Sen. Steven M. Young, letter to MRL, secretary-designate, 12/18/68.

2. Hearings before the U.S. Senate Committee on Armed Services, "Nominations of Laird, Packard, and Darden," 1/14/69.

3. Minutes, Senior Staff Meeting, 2/10/69.

4. MRL, memorandum for the assistant to the president for National Security Affairs, "Amendments to FY 1970 Defense Budget," 3/1/69.

5. The official renaming of the modified Sentinel program to "Safeguard" dates first to a March 19, 1969, memo in which Deputy Defense Secretary David Packard wrote Army Secretary Stan Resor: "As I am sure you have noted, the public and the press increasingly are identifying the modified Sentinel system as the Safeguard Program. I believe that in order to avoid confusion and to increase public understanding of this matter we should refer to it as the Safeguard Program." The next day, the administration publicly announced it would officially be "Safeguard" henceforth.

6. Mary McGrory, "Nixon Lost Chance on ABM," *Washington Star*, 3/16/69.

7. MRL, "Statement before the Subcommittee on International Organization and Disarmament Affairs of the Senate Foreign Relations Committee on the Ballistic Missile Defense System," 3/21/69; Hearings, U.S. Senate, Foreign Relations Subcommittee on International Organization and Disarmament Affairs, "Strategic and Foreign Policy Implications of ABM Systems," 165, 173, 175, 177–8, 187, 204–7, 213, 3/21/69; *1969 CQ Almanac*, 260–1.

8. One of those sticking to the old intelligence estimates that the Soviets were not interested in a first-strike capability was Air Force Gen. Joseph Carroll, whom Laird had inherited as the head of the Defense Intelligence Agency. Carroll was a McNamara loyalist who had served in the post for nearly eight years and whom Laird had planned to replace with someone whose loyalties would be with the new defense secretary. It was part of Laird's strategy to control the flow of intelligence information. General Carroll was reassigned in July 1969, in the middle of the ABM debate, and opted to retire instead after back surgery. His son, antiwar activist James Carroll, charged in a book he published in 2006 that Gen. Carroll had been "fired" because he dared to differ with Laird on the "first-strike capability" issue. James Carroll even implied that his father's health was permanently damaged because his spirit had been "broken" by Laird. (The general died in 1991 at the age of 80.) When those accusations were published in Carroll's book, a surprised Laird said he had no recollection of such a heated conflict with Gen. Carroll. "I told both Dick Helms (CIA director) and Gen. Carroll that their assessment was wrong based on my information which was later shared with them," Laird said. (James Carroll, *House of War*, Houghton Mifflin [2006], 331–337, 439.)

9. Laird did not remember his mother, Helen Laird, specifically saying, "You're scaring everybody," though he confirmed that she called and said she didn't like hearing the frightening things he was saying in the hearing. The specific remark was first reported in the *New York Times*, which no doubt got the story from a Laird aide paraphrasing what his boss had told him about the phone call. Laird later told interviewer David Frost that it seems to have become "a true story because it has been repeated so many times," and because it did summarize what Mrs. Laird said. (MRL, "Interview with David Frost," *David Frost Show*, 12/2/70.)

10. Hugh Carey, interview, 10/24/01.

11. "Laird Fails to Stop Talk against ABM," *Washington Post*, 4/4/69.

12. Minutes, Senior Staff Meeting, "Safeguard ABM," 4/7/69.

13. "Laird-Helms Confrontation on ABM Is Being Sanitized," *Washington Post*, 7/9/69.

14. At the time, the longest debate in Senate history had been the 1964 debate over the Civil Rights Act, which lasted 82 days. The ABM debate ranked as the sixth-longest debate in the Senate since the end of World War II. (*CQ*, "Longest Military Debate," 1434, 8/8/69.)

15. Dick Capen, interview, 8/8/00; James Lawrence, interview, 7/31/01.

16. Minutes, Senior Staff Meeting, 8/4/69.

17. *Congressional Record*, U.S. Senate, 22453, 8/6/69.

18 Nixon, *Memoirs*, 418.

19. Kissinger, *White House Years*, 212, 208. John Newhouse, in his 1973 book on SALT, *Cold Dawn*, came to the same conclusion independently. "Safeguard did help to promote the May [1972] agreement limiting ABMs because the Russians wanted to avoid a competition in modern ABMs and sought to discourage America's program by making a deal" (30–1). "Almost certainly, the misdirected ABM program has been a useful bargaining instrument at SALT" (78).

20. Richard Nixon, *Memoirs*, 615.

21. Henry Kissinger, speech at dedication of Laird Center, Marshfield, Wis., 9/12/97.

22. John Newhouse, *Cold Dawn: The Story of SALT*, Holt, Rinehart, and Winston (1973), 168.

23. Gerard Smith, *Doubletalk*, Doubleday & Company (1980), 29.

24. Robert Pursley, interview, 10/3/00.

25. Chalmers M. Roberts, "Nitze: Right Man for Geneva?" *Washington Post*, 1/12/82; "Paul Nitze, 97: Key Player in U.S. Foreign Policy during Cold War," *Los Angeles Times*, 10/21/04; "Paul H. Nitze, Missile Treaty Negotiator and Cold War Strategist, Dies at 97," *New York Times*, 10/21/04; "Architect of Cold War Had Role in Ending It," *Washington Post*, 10/21/04.

26. Kissinger, *White House Years*, 147.

27. MRL, memorandum for Secretary of State, "Control of the SALT Delegation," 6/1/70; William P. Rogers, letter to MRL, 6/2/70; MRL, letter and memorandum for secretary of state, "SALT," 6/5/70; MRL, memorandum for the president, 6/5/70; MRL, cable to Deputy Secretary of Defense Packard, "Breakfast Meeting with US SALT Delegation in Brussels on 11 June," 6/11/70; Rogers, letter to MRL, 6/16/70; Gerard Smith, letter to MRL, 6/17/70.

28. Harold Brown, interview, 2/20/01.

29. Nixon, *Memoirs*, 522–25.

30. MRL, memorandum for national security adviser (Kissinger), "SALT—Next Steps," 9/4/71. MRL, memorandum for national security advisor (Kissinger), "SALT," 10/29/71.

31. MRL, memorandum for the president, 1/18/72; Kissinger, *White House Years*, 1129–31, 1149–50.

32. Paul H. Nitze, *From Hiroshima to Glasnost: At the Center of Decision*, Grove Weidenfeld (1989), 295, 298–99.

33. Seymour M. Hersh, *The Price of Power*, Summit (1983), 535.

34. Assistant Secretary of Defense (Systems Analysis) Gardiner L. Tucker, memorandum for MRL, "Taking Stock," 1/30/73. Tucker's analyses and draft documents, as well as his participation in Washington interagency SALT meetings, were invaluable in helping Laird form his positions and plan his own SALT strategy.

35. The ABM Treaty limited each country to two sites, one to guard the capital city, and the other to guard a portion of the nation's offensive missile force; the United States chose Grand Forks, N.D., for the second site. Presidents Ford and Brezhnev signed a protocol in 1974 that limited each side to only one site. Russia has an active ABM system around Moscow, while the United States chose not to build an ABM system at any site. This treaty was the more significant of the two accords. As Nixon put it: "The ABM treaty stopped what inevitably would have become a defensive arms race, with untold billions of dollars being spent on each side for more and more ABM coverage." (Nixon, *Memoirs*, 617–18.)

Under SALT I, the total number of land-based intercontinental and submarine-launched ballistic missile launchers allowed was 1,710 for the United States and 2,238 for the Soviet Union. The numerical superiority accorded the Russians was partly offset by the American lead in intercontinental bombers, not covered by the treaties, by the superior accuracy of American missiles, and U.S. MIRV technology.

36. SALT II was signed in June 1979 by President Carter and Brezhnev but withdrawn from Senate ratification after the Soviets invaded Afghanistan.

Signed by Presidents Reagan and Gorbachev in December 1987, the Intermediate-Range Nuclear Forces Treaty eliminated a whole class of nuclear weapons, requiring more than 1,500 to be destroyed.

Each country was limited to a total of 6,000 warheads when START I (Strategic Arms Reduction Talks) took effect in July 1994, having been signed by Presidents George H.W. Bush and Mikhail Gorbachev in July 1991. The same pair signed START II in January 1993, which limited each country to 3,500 or fewer warheads. Though it was ratified by the governing bodies of both countries by 2000, it has not yet gone into effect.

START III was signed by Presidents Clinton and Boris Yeltsin in 1997 and would have limited each country to 2,500 or fewer nuclear warheads, but it has not been ratified by either country.

Presidents George W. Bush and Vladimir Putina signed the Strategic Offensive Reductions Treaty (SORT) on May 24, 2002, which limits each country to 2,200 nuclear warheads or fewer, but that agreement was not ratified either.

37. Robert Pursley, interview, 8/27/07.

20 / DUELING MACHIAVELLIS

1. Kissinger, *White House Years,* 32–3.
2. Kissinger, speech at Laird Center Dedication, 9/12/97; Kissinger, interview, 1/10/01.
3. "Pentagon Heir Apparent: Melvin Robert Laird," *New York Times,* 12/10/68.
4. George Shultz, interview, 2/6/01.
5. James Schlesinger, interview, 7/27/01.
6. Ivan Selin, interview, 2/19/01.
7. Dr. Johnny Foster, 6/21/01.
8. Entries for October 11, 15, 1969, and June 24, 1970, H. R. Haldeman, *The Haldeman Diaries: Inside the Nixon White House,* G. P. Putnam's Sons (1994), 98–100, 177.
9. Jack Mills, interview, 6/2/00.
10. Safire, *Before the Fall,* 396, 693.
11. Though he knows others described him as "devious," Laird does not believe that Eisenhower ever did so. As a man personally and painfully aware of Nixon's penchant for lying, Laird maintains that this is one more Nixon fabrication. The referenced quote comes from Nixon, *Memoirs,* 289.
12. Ehrlichman, *Witness to Power,* 95.
13. Caspar Weinberger, interview, 1/25/01.
14. Helmut Schmidt, interview, 2/4/01.
15. David Abshire, interview, 4/5/01.
16. Alexander Haig, interview, 1/21/02.
17. Kissinger, *White House Years,* 32.
18. Kissinger, *White House Years,* 32–3.
19. Robert Pursley, interviews, 8/7/97, 10/12/00.
20. Larry Eagleburger, interview, 2/7/01.
21. Kissinger, letter to MRL on the occasion of his 80th birthday, 9/1/02.
22. Kissinger, *White House Years,* 32–3; Kissinger speech, 9/12/97.
23. Barry Shillito, interview, 8/8/00.
24. Robert Pursley, interview, 10/12/00.
25. Ehrlichman, *Witness to Power,* 96–7.
26. Kissinger himself implied that the Nixon Doctrine was an outgrowth of his discussions with the president. (Kissinger, *White House Years,* 222–5.) Biographer Walter Isaacson suggested that the doctrine was a derivative of Kissinger's long fascination with the "doctrine of limits," which directs policy makers to recognize real-time boundaries that cannot be crossed in strategy development. (Isaacson, *Kissinger: A Biography,* Simon & Schuster [1992] 239–42.)
27. Laird gave several aides credit for Nixon Doctrine ideas, including Col. Robert Pursley, speech writers William Baroody and William Prendergast, public affairs chief Dan Henkin, Assistant Secretary of Defense (International Security Affairs) Warren Nutter, and Paul Warnke, the high-level Clark Clifford aide who stayed on for a few months at Laird's request.
28. MRL, "Remarks at the 'Salute to Mel Laird' Dinner,'" Milwaukee, Wis., 3/23/72; UPI report, 3/23/72; "Laird Has Quiet Visit at Home," *Marshfield News-Herald,* 3/27/72.
29. MRL, "Interview with Newsmen following Appearance before the House Committee on Foreign Affairs," 3/15/72.
30. Mel Cunningham, 12/93 and 12/95 issues of *Howgoesit,* the *Maddox* veterans' newsletter.
31. David Packard memorandum, 11/1/69.

32. Haldeman, *Haldeman Diaries*, 86.

33. Ehrlichman, *Witness to Power*, 95–7.

34. Col. Ralph Albertazzie, interviews, 4/2/01, 4/22/01; Lt. Gen. James D. Hughes, interview, 4/22/01; J. F. terHorst and Col. Ralph Albertazzie, *The Flying White House: The Story of Air Force One*, Coward, McCann & Geoghegan Inc. (1979), 275–95.

35. Robert Pursley, interviews, 8/7/97, 1/17/01; Henry Kissinger, interview, 1/10/01.

21 / BRIDGING THE GENERATION CAP

1. John Warner, interview, 11/10/99.

2. John Chafee, interview, 10/22/99.

3. Robert Froehlke, interview, 7/23/00.

4. Robert Seamans, interview, 10/12/00; Robert C. Seamans Jr., *Aiming at Targets: The Autobiography of Robert C. Seamans Jr.*, NASA History Office (1996), 183–4.

5. All quotes in this chapter from John Laird and Alison Laird-Large are from interviews with them, respectively, 2/27 and 3/2/01.

6. MRL, interviewed 11/17/70, "Interview with David Frost," *David Frost Show*, 12/2/70.

7. " 'Dove Kids' on Garde," *Washington News*, 1/26/70.

8. MRL, speech upon receiving Demolay Honorary Legion of Honor, New York City Masonic Temple, 4/15/71.

9. The directorate operated under Department of Defense Directive 3025.12, "Employment of Military Resources in the Event of Civil Disturbances," 6/8/68.

10. Public Law 90-331, passed in 1968 after the Robert F. Kennedy assassination, provided that federal troops could be used when needed to assist the Secret Service in the protection of the president.

11. Minutes, Senior Staff Meeting, 4/7/69.

12. Minutes, Senior Staff Meeting, 3/24/69.

13. Joe Zaice, interview, 7/16/01.

14. Julian Levine, interview, 8/1/01.

15. Transcript, "Address by the Honorable Melvin R. Laird, Secretary of Defense, at Commencement Exercises," St. Leo College, 4/26/69.

16. Transcript, "Remarks to the Press following Address," Saint Leo, Fl., 4/26/69.

17. *Tampa Times* and *St. Petersburg Times*, 4/28/69. The news accounts were based on details provided by officials at MacDill Air Force Base.

18. Joe Zaice, interviews, 7/16, 7/24/01.

19. Julian Levine, interview, 8/1/01.

20. "The Swelling War Moratorium," *Washington Post*, 11/2/69; Nancy Zaroulis and Gerald Sullivan, *Who Spoke Up? American Protest against the Vietnam War*, Holt, Rinehart and Winston (1984).

21. *Look*, 8/8/69.

22. " '70 Pullout Would Bring Bloodbath, Clifford Says," *Washington Star*, 10/15/69.

23. Transcript, "Question and Answer Session following Speech at National Press Club," Washington, D.C., 9/25/69.

24. Transcript, "Address by the Honorable Melvin R. Laird, Secretary of Defense, before the Eighth Convention of the AFL-CIO," Hotel Traymore, Atlantic City, N.J., 10/7/69.

25. "Laird Hails Nixon's Peace Bid; Labor Gives Support," *New York Times*, 10/8/69; "Laird Says Anti-War Forces Press for Capitulation to Hanoi," *Washington Post*, 10/8/69.

26. Nixon, memorandum to MRL, 10/8/69.

27. Transcript, "News Conference by Secretary of Defense MRL at Pentagon," 10/9/69.

28. *Janesville Gazette*, 10/9/69; AP, " 'Dad's Doing His Best'—Laird's Son to Protest War," *Washington Star*, 10/11/69.

29. "Laird Sees No 'Conflict With Father,' " *Washington Post*, 10/15/69.

30. Laird's daughter, Alison, was also an activist at the two colleges she attended. Though her primary energy was poured into a campus rape crisis center she founded, she did participate in the moratorium and other Vietnam war protests. "I was a little bit more guarded than John was," she explained.

31. "Forum Unique: Laird Plans to Face Wisconsin Students," *Washington Star*, 10/11/69.

32. "Mr. Laird Confronts the Students," *Wall Street Journal,* 11/3/69.

33. "Laird Hears Youths' Views," *Philadelphia Inquirer,* 10/28/69.

34. *Washington Post,* 10/28/69.

35. Vice President Agnew had used the term "silent majority" several times in May. White House speech writer William Safire, later a noted *New York Times* columnist and expert on language, says he coined the phrase, having gotten the general idea from a former senator's speech. Interestingly, Nixon must also have read the *Washington Star*'s October 15 editorial on the moratorium, which concluded: "Despite the tumult and the shouting on this Moratorium day, we think the *great, silent majority* of the American people want their President to stand firm for what he knows is right" (emphasis added).

36. "Gallup Finds 77% Support Nixon View," *New York Times,* 11/5/69.

37. Minutes, Senior Staff Meeting, 11/10/69.

38. "Laird Puts Protest Crowd at 119,000," *Washington Post,* 12/20/69; "Laird Erred on Antiwar Crowd Photo," 12/31/69; "Pentagon: Holes in the Head-Count," *Newsweek,* 1/5/70.

39. Senator Warner's account of that day came from an 11/10/99 interview, and from a memorial remembrance of Chafee that Warner offered on 10/25/99, *Congressional Record,* S13079.

22 / CROSSING THE LINE

1. "Thieu Doesn't Like the Word: 'Vietnamization' a No-no," *Christian Science Monitor,* 11/21/69.

2. *Los Angeles Times,* 2/26/70.

3. Palmer, *The 25-Year War,* 189+.

4. Gen. Earle G. Wheeler, Chairman, JCS, memorandum for MRL, "Force Planning," 8/12/69.

5. MRL, memorandum for the president, "Vietnamizing the War," NSSM 36, 9/4/69.

6. MRL, memorandum for the chairman, JCS, "Vietnamization—RVNAF Improvement and Modernization Aspects and Related U.S. Planning," 11/10/69.

7. Kissinger, *White House Years,* 304.

8. Nixon, *Memoirs,* 400.

9. *Washington Post,* 9/14/69.

10. *Newsweek,* 9/22/69.

11. Hersh, *The Price of Power,* 120.

12. Kissinger, *White House Years,* 307.

13. Haldeman, *Haldeman Diaries,* 104–5.

14. Sorley, *Thunderbolt,* 270.

15. Stanley Resor, interview, 10/30/01.

16. Rivers' involvement was originally reported in *Time* magazine, October 1969, and the congressman chose neither to confirm or deny the account. He maintained, however, that it was no secret that he had urged the Defense Department and the president, through Harlow, to drop the charges.

17. The case was dropped so swiftly that Edward Bennett Williams ended up doing little for his client, Col. Rheault, other than the intimidation his announced representation caused in Washington. Williams did fly to Saigon to meet with his client, but Secretary Resor's announcement came only three days into that trip, resolving the case. Nevertheless, Rheault, whose salary was $14,000 a year, was presented a bill from the lawyer for $25,000, according to Evan Thomas's biography, *The Man to See: Edward Bennett Williams,* Simon and Schuster (1991), 254–5. "Williams didn't do anything," Rheault was quoted. "We shouldn't have hired him, but my family hit the panic button."

18. *New York Times,* 10/1/69.

19. An incident related to the Green Beret murder case made Nixon and his top White House aides even more paranoid about their inability to outmaneuver Laird and keep him in the dark. At a Camp David dinner on September 12, 1969, Nixon asked an aide to quietly find out what Adm. John McCain in Hawaii thought about court-martialing the Green Berets involved. "Less than an hour later, Secretary Laird called to ask why the White House was trying to call McCain," Ehrlichman wrote in his memoir. "At that time Camp David's telephones went through an Army Signal Corps switchboard [whose operators] were all Army enlisted men and their supervisors were Army officers. The only question was: how closely did Mel Laird monitor the President and

the rest of us at Camp David when we called someone on his Army telephone system? Did he just keep track of whom we called, or did he also know what was said?" H. R. Haldeman confirmed the paranoia in his memoirs as well: "Tried to call Admiral McCain to get his view, and Laird found out, and called K[issinger], very upset that we hadn't gone to him instead. The fact that Laird apparently knew immediately of our attempt to call McCain from Camp David gave us something new to worry out. Were the Camp David phones tapped for the Defense Department?" (Ehrlichman, *Witness to Power*, 95–7; Haldeman, *The Haldeman Diaries*, 86.)

20. Minutes, Senior Staff Meeting, 9/15/69.

21. Dan Henkin memo to MRL, "News Items of Special Interest," 11/18/69.

22. Dan Henkin memo to MRL, "News Items of Special Interest," 11/25/69.

23. *New York Times*, 11/17/69.

24. Minutes, Senior Staff Meeting, 12/1/69; Hammond, *Military and the Media*, 224 and 228.

25. Dan Henkin to MRL, "News Items of Special Interest," 1/17/70.

26. Stanley Resor, interview, 10/30/01.

27. *Newsweek*, 4/12/71.

28. Stanley Resor, interview, 10/30/01. Columnists Evans and Novak reported that Nixon had gone around Laird and his staff, ordering Moorer to have Calley released, without telling Laird. However, Laird maintained that Nixon had discussed it with him.

29. Hammond, *Military and the Media*, 258.

30. MRL, memo to Henry Kissinger, 12/2/69.

31. MRL, memorandum for assistant to the president for National Security Affairs, "Force Planning," 12/12/69.

32. *Detroit Free Press*, 12/15/69.

33. Henry Kissinger, memorandum for MRL, "Vietnamization," 12/15/69.

23 / DEN OF IN-EQUITY

1. George Q. Flynn, *Lewis B. Hershey, Mr. Selective Service*, University of North Carolina Press (1985), 247, 254–5, 257.

2. Lawrence M. Baskir and William A. Strauss, *Chance and Circumstance: The Draft, the War and the Vietnam Generation*, Vintage Books (1968), 25–6.

3. Hershey, 1965 memorandum, "On Manpower Channeling," reprinted in *Ramparts* magazine, 12/66.

4. Roger T. Kelley, *Letters to My Children*, self-published (1999), 62.

5. Donald Rumsfeld, interview, 2/28/01; Pierre (Pete) du Pont, interview, 4/4/01; Barber Conable Jr., interview, 4/5/01; Roger Kelley, interview, 7/27/01; Alexander Haig, interview, 1/21/02; Baskir and Strauss, *Chance and Circumstance*, 6–10, 19–20, 23, 36; James Fallows, *Atlantic*, 4/80; Flynn, *Hershey*, 225–6, 234; "A Maverick's Rallying Cry," *Boston Globe*, 5/2/89.

6. Robert Pursley, interview, 10/23/00; Ivan Selin, interview, 2/19/01; Donald Rumsfeld, interview, 2/28/01; Roger Kelley, interview, 7/27/01; Colin Powell, interview, 12/18/01; Martin Anderson, interview, 5/6/02; Milton Friedman, interview, 5/7/02; Jack Anderson, "Should We Have a Professional Army?" *Parade*, 1/7/68.

7. Milton Friedman, interview, 5/7/02; Milton Friedman, "Why Not a Volunteer Army," *New Individual Review*, Spring 1967, 3–9; Martin Anderson, *The Making of the All-Volunteer Armed Force*, Hoover Institution (1991), 2–4; Ralph Pomeroy Witherspoon, "The Military Draft and the All-Volunteer Force: A Case Study of a Shift in Public Policy," doctoral dissertation, (hereafter Witherspoon dissertation) 320–3, 4/93.

8. Transcript, Richard Nixon radio address, "The All-Volunteer Armed Force," CBS radio network, 10/17/68; Safire, *Before the Fall*, 77–8; Anderson, *The Making*, 4; Witherspoon dissertation, 326–9.

9. Minutes, "Draft/All-Volunteer Force," Senior Staff Meeting, 2/3/69, 2/10/69; Witherspoon dissertation, 332–3.

10. Pres. Richard Nixon, letter to MRL, "My Dear Mr. Secretary," 2/6/69.

11. MRL, memorandum for the president, 2/7/69; Minutes, Senior Staff Meeting, 2/24/69; Minutes, Senior Staff Meeting, "All Volunteer Force," 3/10/69; "Nixon Names Advisory Panel to End the Draft," *Washington Post*, 3/28/69; Minutes, Senior Staff Meeting, "Defense Studies," 4/14/69; Anderson, *The Making*, 4–5; Witherspoon dissertation, 331–2, 336–41, 461.

12. Besides Gates, the panel included two former supreme allied commanders in Europe, the retired generals Alfred Gruenther and Lauris Norstad.

13. MRL, memorandum for secretaries of the military departments, chairman of the Joint Chiefs of Staff, and assistant secretaries of defense, "Project Volunteer," 4/10/69.

14. Minutes, Senior Staff Meeting, 2/10/69; Witherspoon dissertation, 335–6, 4/93.

15. Transcript, "Department of Defense Briefing on Manpower," 2/18/69.

16. Jack Star, "How Fair Is the Draft?", *Look*, 4/19/66; Witherspoon dissertation, 274–5.

Closer to the event, Laird recalled at a 1972 press conference: "People said we could never move toward random selection when I became Secretary of Defense—that Congress would never approve it." (MRL, "Press Conference," Milwaukee, Wis., 3/23/72.)

17. *Wall Street Journal*, 4/22/69; MRL, "Remarks to Press following St. Leo, Fla., Address," 4/26/69; Pres. Richard M. Nixon, "Message on the Draft Submitted to Congress on May 13," as published in *New York Times*, 5/14/69; Witherspoon dissertation, 341–3 and 461–3.

18. Minutes, Senior Staff Meeting, "Selective Service Legislation," 8/11/69.

19. MRL, memorandum for the president, "Draft Reform," 8/20/69; Minutes, Senior Staff Meeting, 9/8/69.

20. MRL, "Secretary of Defense Statement on the Draft," 9/19/69; "Congress Warned," *New York Times*, 9/20/69; "Congress Prodded on Reform," *Washington Post*, 9/20/69; "Draft Cuts and Reform," *Philadelphia Bulletin*, 9/22/69. *Time* reported: "President Nixon's demand last week for congressional action on his draft revision bill was adapted from a scenario inspired by Secretary of Defense Melvin Laird. More than anyone else in the Administration, Laird worries about the possible consequences of the autumnal unrest planned by student anti-Pentagon groups. With the opening of school approaching, Laird recently counseled the President to apply pressure for passage of the draft revision bill submitted to Congress last May." ("The Draft: Moving toward Equity," *Time*, 9/26/69.)

21. Roger Kelley, interview, 7/27/01; MRL, "Press Conference following Appearance before House Armed Services Committee," 9/30/69; "House Group Cool to Draft Changes," *New York Times*, 10/1/69; "Draft Evasion in High Places," *New York Times*, 10/10/69; MRL, "Press Conference," Pentagon, 10/16/69; "Nixon's Draft Lottery Plan Approved by House Panel," *New York Times*, 10/17/69.

22. Martin Anderson, interview, 5/6/02; "Hill to Act on Draft, Yields to Yale Head," *Washington Post*, 11/6/69; "News Items of Special Interest," 11/6/69; "Brewster Frees the Draft-Lottery Bill," *Washington Post*, 11/8/69; "The Brewster Compromise," *Washington Star*, 10/10/69.

23. "Draft Reformers Clear a Lottery for Senate Vote," *New York Times*, 11/12/69; "Senate Passage of Draft Bill Seen Certain," *Washington Post*, 11/12/69; "Congress Clears Bill Permitting a Draft Lottery," *New York Times*, 11/20/69; "Senate Approves Lottery Draft Plan, Sends It to Nixon," *Washington Star*, 11/20/69.

24. Bob Burke and Ralph G. Thompson, *Bryce Harlow: Mr. Integrity*, Oklahoma Heritage Association (2000), 197.

25. "Draft Evasion in High Places," *New York Times*, 10/10/69; "Answers to Frequently Asked Questions on New Lottery System for the Draft," *New York Times*, 12/6/69; "Laird Says Volunteer Plan Would Cut Forces a Third," *New York Times*, 1/30/70; Flynn, *Hershey*, 224, 276, 279–80; "Gen. Lewis Hershey, 83, Headed Selective Service," *Washington Post*, 5/21/77; John Whiteclay Chambers II, *To Raise an Army: The Draft Comes to Modern America*, Free Press (1987), 257; Witherspoon dissertation, 352–5.

26. "Draft Drawing Expected Soon," *Washington News*, 11/21/69; Minutes, Senior Staff Meeting, "Draft Lottery," 11/24/69; MRL, transcript, "Press Conference at the White House with Peter Flanigan," 10:20 A.M., 11/26/69; "Nixon Signs Draft Change; First Lottery Due Monday," *New York Times*, 11/27/69; "Lottery Is Held to Set the Order of Draft in 1970," *New York Times*, 12/2/69; "Sept. 14 Is No. 1 for Draft," *Washington Post*, 12/2/69; "Lottery Mood Is Low-Keyed," *Washington Post*, 12/2/69; Flynn, *Hershey*, 283.

27. "The Luck of the Draw," *Time*, 12/12/69; "Draft: The Numbers Game," *Newsweek*, 12/15/69.

28. "Groans and Quips Greet Draft Results," *New York Times*, 12/2/69; Max Lerner, "Draft Lottery Channels the Frustrations," *Washington Star*, 12/28/69; "Lessons and Legacies/25 Years after Vietnam," *Los Angeles Times*, 4/22/00.

29. Patrick Vann, Boulder, Colo., *Rocky Mountain News*, 10/5/98.

30. UPI, "David Eisenhower Is No. 30," *New York Times*, 12/2/69; "David Eisenhower Placed in Early Draft Callup Group," *Washington Post*, 12/2/69; "The Eisenhowers' Chronicles," *Washington Post*, 6/22/86; Ben Yagoda, "At Home with Julie and David," *Saturday Evening Post*, 3/87.

31. "Laird Takes Self Out of Race for Office in 1972," *Stevens Point Daily Journal,* 10/19/71; Nick Thimmesch, "Officials Visiting Campuses; It's Safe to Go Out Again," *Los Angeles Times,* 10/24/71.

32. "Lottery Is No. 1 Topic among the Nation's Youths," *New York Times,* 12/3/69.

33. "During War, Most Draft Boards Played by Own Rules," *Atlanta Journal and Constitution,* 2/7/92; "Vestiges of Vietnam," *St. Louis Post-Dispatch* 3/15/92; "ROTC Official Faults Clinton for Reneging," *Washington Times,* 9/28/92; "Days of the Draft Board Heading for History Books," *Chicago Tribune,* 7/4/93; "Clinton Waged War within Self," *Washington Post,* 2/5/95; David Maraniss, *First in His Class: The Biography of Bill Clinton,* Simon & Schuster (1995), 106, 118–20, 149, 168–205; "Lessons and Legacies/25 Years after Vietnam," *Los Angeles Times,* 4/22/00.

34. Tarr journal, 11/14, 11/24, 11/26, 12/13/69; Curtis W. Tarr, *By The Numbers: The Reform of the Selective Service System, 1970–1972,* National Defense University Press (1981), 3.

35. "News Items of Special Interest," 2/12/70; Tarr journal, 2/3, 2/19/70.

36. Tarr journal, 3/2/70; Tarr, *By the Numbers,* 1–3.

37. Curtis Tarr, interview, 3/13/02; Tarr journal, 3/30, 3/31, 4/10/70.

38. Tarr journal, 2/10/71; Flynn, *Hershey,* 297–309; Arlington National Cemetery Web site, "Lewis Blaine Hershey; General, United States Army."

24 / INTO CAMBODIA

1. "Vietnamization: Will It Work?" *Newsweek,* 2/9/70.

2. MRL, memorandum for the president, "Trip to Vietnam and CINCPAC, February 10–14, 1970," 2/17/70.

3. That may have sounded like wishful thinking, but Laird turned out to be right. The South Vietnamese army held its own with dwindling U.S. combat support. What it could not live without, however, was U.S. money, equipment, and supplies, and the loss of those would eventually prove its downfall two years after the troops were gone. It came as no surprise after many warnings from Laird.

4. MRL, memorandum for the chairman, JCS, "Contingency Plan for Attacks on North Vietnamese/VC Cambodian Sanctuaries," 3/26/70.

5. Kissinger, memorandum for MRL, "Operation against Enemy Base Camps in Cambodia," 3/26/70.

6. Hammond, *Military and the Media,* 287.

7. Sometimes classification markings themselves tell the story. Rogers stamped his memo the president "Secret." But he had his memo to Laird classified even higher, "Top Secret/Sensitive," adding "Exdis," so that only Rogers could say who could see it. (William Rogers, letter to MRL, 4/2/70; Rogers, memorandum for the president, "The Cambodian Situation and U.S. Initiative," 3/31/70.)

8. Robert Pursley, interview, 11/17/00.

9. Robert Pursley, interview, 11/22/00.

10. Hammond, *The Military and the Media,* 287.

11. Kissinger, *White House Years,* 481.

12. Kissinger, *White House Years,* 491.

13. Kissinger, *White House Years,* 496. Kissinger never wearied of game playing. He never told Nixon he had kept Laird in the loop and implied otherwise at the time. In an "Eyes Only" memo to prepare the president for the April 26 meeting, Kissinger cautioned: "Care should be exercised at today's meeting not to surface the fact that General Wheeler has been conducting intensified planning to implement the attacks on [Cambodian sanctuaries] without the full knowledge of the Secretary of Defense."

14. Nixon, "Actions to Protect U.S. Forces in South Vietnam," NSDM 57, 4/26/70.

15. Nixon, *Memoirs,* 450.

16. Nixon, "Actions to Protect U.S. Forces in South Vietnam," NSDM 58, 4/28/70.

17. MRL, memorandum for the president, "NSDM 57—Actions to Protect U.S. Forces in South Vietnam," 4/27/70.

18. Haldeman, memorandum for MRL, William P. Rogers, and Henry Kissinger, 4/30/70.

19. Nixon, *Memoirs,* 453.

20. Isaacson, *Kissinger,* 269.

21. Westmoreland, *A Soldier Reports*, 513.

22. Nixon, *Memoirs*, 454.

23. Robert Pursley, interview, 11/22/00.

24. Haldeman, *Haldeman Diaries*, 195.

25. Gen. Earle Wheeler, chairman, JCS, message to Adm. McCain and Gen. Abrams, "Completion of Individual Operations," 5/4/70.

26. Gen. Creighton Abrams, message to Gen. Earle Wheeler, Chairman, JCS, "Completion of Individual Operations," 5/5/70.

27. MRL, "Press Conference," Pentagon, 5/6/70.

28. The Godfrey Sperling "group" consisted of influential journalists whom the respected *Christian Science Monitor* reporter brought together, usually for background-only breakfasts and briefings. (MRL, "Press Briefing at Press Club for Godfrey Sperling Group," 5/14/70.)

29. MRL, appearance on *Meet the Press,* "Special Broadcast on Cambodia," 6/4/70.

·30. Robert Novak confirmed the episode, including that Laird had given him "a little hell afterwards" about it. Novak's take on it is that it demonstrates what a professional Laird was, and how he didn't hold grudges but took such minor setbacks in stride. "That's the kind of stuff that made Mel a lot of fun. Yes, it was serious business, but it was a great game, too." (Novak, interview, 10/2/00.)

31. MRL, memorandum for the president, "Cambodia Operations," 5/7/70.

32. MRL, "Press Conference," Detroit, Mich., 5/11/70.

33. Nixon, *Memoirs,* 467.

34. Robert Pursley, interview, 11/22/00.

35. G. Warren Nutter, ASD for International Security Affairs, memorandum for MRL, "Plan for SALEM HOUSE Operations after 30 June 1970," 5/21/70.

36. Hammond, *The Military and the Media,* 343.

37. Kissinger, memorandum for [State, Defense, JCS Chairman and CIA Director], "The President's Views on Cambodia," 6/17/70.

25 / SEA CHANGES

1. Robert Pursley, interviews, 11/22/00, 4/4/00.

2. Laird eventually did approve Gen. Cushman as the commandant of the Marine Corps in 1972. Cushman replaced Gen. Chapman and served in the post from January 1972 to July 1975.

3. Adm. Elmo Zumwalt Jr. and Lt. Elmo Zumwalt III, with John Pekkanen, *My Father, My Son,* Macmillan (1986), 41.

4. John Chafee, interview, 10/22/99.

5. Perry, *Four Stars,* 231.

6. MRL, memorandum for the president, "Trip to Vietnam and CINCPAC, February 10–14, 1970," 2/17/70.

7. "Fighting Slows Down, but Saigon's Woes Increase," *U.S. News & World Report,* 8/17/70.

8. MRL, memorandum for the president, "Vietnam," 4/4/70.

9. *U.S. News & World Report,* 8/17/70.

10. MRL, memorandum to assistant to the president for National Security Affairs (Henry Kissinger), "Economic Aspects of Southeast Asia Conflict," 5/15/70.

11. Kissinger, "Vietnam Economic Policy," NSDM 80, 8/13/70.

12. MRL, memorandum for chairman, JCS, "Military Strategy in Southeast Asia," 6/5/70.

13. Mason Freeman, Vice Director, Joint Staff, JCS, memorandum for MRL, "RVNAF Force Structure," 12/1/70

14. MRL, memorandum for the assistant to the president for National Security Affairs, "Tactical Air Operations in Southeast Asia," 6/5/70.

15. David Packard, memorandum for the president, "Air Operations in Southeast Asia," 6/18/70.

16. Adm. T. H. Moorer, acting chairman, JCS, memorandum for MRL, "Interdiction of North Vietnamese Supplies," 6/15/70.

17. The hijacking of a fourth plane on September 6, an El Al Airlines plane bound from Amsterdam, ended when security guards shot and killed one hijacker and wounded another. The dead commando was a twenty-seven-year-old American citizen who lived in Los Angeles and was

a UCLA graduate. The wounded hijacker was Leila Khaled, twenty-four, who had been involved in hijacking a TWA plane August 29. She was jailed in London and released as part of an exchange with the PFLP during the September 1970 crisis.

18. Minutes, Senior Staff Meeting, 9/8/70.

19. Kissinger, *White House Years,* 602.

20. Laird could not recall the exact date on which Nixon issued this order, but close analysis of the sequence of events, accounts of the crisis in various memoirs, and review of classified military histories places it on the evening of September 8, the day before a fourth airliner was hijacked.

21. A young National Security Council aide who was in and out of the Oval Office during this crisis told author Seymour Hersh, "I'd walk in and begin to give a specific listing of what'd happened overnight and Nixon would interject, 'Bomb the bastards,' or some other wild remark." Referenced in Hersh's *Price of Power,* 243–4.

22. Lt. Col. V.W. Martin Jr., Enclosure B, Fact Sheet, "The Jordan Crisis (August/September 1970)," 11/27/72.

23. MRL, memorandum for the president, "Proposed US Peace Initiative in the Middle East," 6/5/70.

24. G. Warren Nutter, ISA director, memorandum to MRL, 7/9/70.

25. MRL, memorandum for the president, "Follow-up Actions with Israel," 10/3/70.

26. Minutes, Senior Staff Meeting, 8/24/70.

27. MRL, memorandum for the president, "Visit of Israeli MOD Moshe Dayan," 12/10/70.

28. Minutes, Senior Staff Meeting, 12/14/70.

29. AP, "Held Greater Threat: Laird Says Sub Base Russian Goal in Cuba," *Monroe (Wis.) Evening Times,* 2/2/63.

30. According to the minutes of the 8/18/69 Senior Staff Meeting, presided over by David Packard in Laird's absence, Adm. Moorer "commented that the Soviets have the largest number of ships out of area to date. There are 30 combatants in the Mediterranean. There are more subs out and more . . . intelligence collectors. . . . Packard said we should possibly get information out to the press on the Soviet threat problems."

31. Admiral Moorer briefed the Senior Staff Meeting on 6/8/70, according to the minutes, on "Russian Naval Forces in the Gulf of Mexico." He noted that the naval task force, which had "been off of New Orleans and Miami" was "heading home." He added: "Noteworthy is the fact that an Echo Class Soviet nuclear-powered submarine put into Cienfuegos. This is the first time that the Soviets have found fit to send a nuclear powered submarine into a foreign port."

32. Transcript, "Press Conference," Pentagon, 9/2/70; Laird further issued a two-page press release, "Memorandum for Correspondents from Secretary Laird," 9/2/70.

33. Kissinger, *White House Years,* 643.

34. "Fulbright Warns on Cuba," *Washington Post,* 9/28/70; UPI, *Washington Star,* "Fulbright Hits Sub Base Talk as 'Hoodwink,'" 10/5/70.

35. Nixon, *Memoirs,* 488.

36. The press made a minor flap out of speculation that Laird had had to shuffle the three carriers in the Mediterranean so that Nixon would not be forced to spend time on the *John F. Kennedy.* But the Pentagon press office denied this report.

37. Lawrence Eagleburger, interview, 2/7/01.

38. Kissinger, *White House Years,* 924–5.

39 "Laird Meets Athens Leaders; Blast Shakes Downtown Area," *New York Times,* 10/4/70; Reuters, "Bomb Explodes Near Laird," *Washington Post,* 10/4/70.

40. Robert Froehlke, interview, 9/10/97.

41. "Laird Advocates Religious Values," *New York Times,* 5/24/70; Transcript, "Remarks by MRL at the Presbyterian General Assembly," Chicago, Ill., 7:15 A.M., 5/23/70; Transcript, "Question-Answer Period following Address to Presbyterian General Assembly," 5/23/70.

42. Transcript, "Address by MRL at the Dedication of Central Wisconsin Airport," Mosinee, Wisconsin, 11:30 A.M., 5/23/70.

43. "Censoring Agnew and Laird," *Milwaukee Journal,* 9/5/70.

44. At the request of the author, Carleton College Archivist Eric Hillemann and his staff made efforts to uncover records confirming the serious slight but failed. Laird knew the search would be futile, he said, because a college official once confided to him that all references to the faculty's threatened action had been destroyed.

45. The degree was bestowed on June 10, 2000, when Clinton gave his last commencement address as president to Carleton College. When the college president, Stephen R. Lewis, introduced

him, he used these words, intending to refer to Clinton's commitment to education and better race relations. Lewis was a long-time advisor to the African country of Botswana.

46. MAST had three rules: the assistance had to be requested, it had to be within one hundred miles of a military base, and the military could decline to help if the helicopters and crews were already busy with national security tasks. (MRL, press statement, 4/30/68; "Military Invades Civil Domain with MAST," *Armed Forces Journal*, 11/71; AP, "MAST," 2/4/72.)

47. Minutes, Senior Staff Meeting, "Hurricane Camille," 8/18, 8/25, 9/8/69; Minutes, Senior Staff Meeting, "Department of Defense Participation in Disaster Relief," 6/26/72; "Watch Out for Flood," *Newsweek*, 2/13/78.

48. UPI, "Clemente," 1/9/73; "Boggs Search Is Halted," *Washington Post*, 11/25/72; UPI, "Lindbergh," 4/1/72.

49. Billy Graham, interview, 8/28/01.

50. Transcript, "Remarks of MRL at the Dedication Ceremonies for the Meditation Room," Pentagon, 12/15/70.

26 / "JUST CALL ME MEL"

1. Laird flew to Florida for two reasons: to open the Defense Race Relations Institute at Patrick Air Force Base, and to be the NACDS's convention keynote speaker the morning after the Van Dyke–Benny show on the evening of 5/10/72. The request to appear before the association of drug stores came from the editor-in-chief of the *National Enquirer*, whose headquarters were in the same area. At the suggestion of special assistant Carl Wallace, Laird spent part of the afternoon at the *Enquirer*'s headquarters convincing them to support the all-volunteer force (AVF), and as a result the tabloid became one of the strongest supporters of ending the draft. Laird believed that with their huge circulation through drug and grocery stores, the *Enquirer* had a favorable impact regarding the creation of an AVF. (Joe Zaice, interview, 8/31/01; Vonda Van Dyke Scoates, interview, 5/8/05. Also, information from Miss America Pageant officials and web page; Program/ Annual Meeting, "The Challenge of Change," National Association of Chain Drug Stores, Palm Beach, Fla., 5/7 to 5/11/72.)

2. Laird's press chief, Dan Henkin, used the title in September 1969 after the *Washington Post* reported that "unsympathetic State Department wits have thought up" the derisive nomenclature CINCMINC for him. In a note to his boss, Henkin acknowledged that Laird was the original source of the title. "I have always preferred CINCMIC, but you have always used CINCMINC. Obviously, you have leaked [your version] to the State Department and they have been leaking to the press." ("Laird Is Given New 'Title,'" *Washington Post*, 9/15/69; Henkin, memorandum to MRL, "News Items of Special Interest," 9/15/69.)

3. Maj. James M. Fielding, Infantry, Adjutant, U.S. Army Service Center for the Armed Forces, *The Pentagon*, 6/1/66; AP, "The Pentagon at 50," 5/12/93.

4. Jerry Friedheim, interview, 7/19/00.

5. Thelma Stubbs Smith, interview, 4/23/01.

6. Kathy Weaver, interview, 7/11/02.

7. Richard A. Stubbing with Richard A. Mendel, *The Defense Game*, Harper & Row (1986), 292–3.

8. "DoD after Two Years of Laird," *Armed Forces Journal*, 12/21/70.

9. John Warner, interview, 11/10/99.

10. Ray Furlong, interview, 8/23/00; MRL and David Packard, transcript, "Press Conference," 12/30/68; "Mr. Packard Would Rather Listen," *Washington News*, 9/18/69; "Pentagon May See Return of Management by Politician-Industrialist Team," *Washington Post*, 3/11/89; MRL, "David Packard, 1912–1996," *Proceedings of the American Philosophical Society*, 147, 3/98.

11. James Schlesinger, interview, 7/27/01.

12. James Schlesinger, interview, 7/27/01.

13. Packard, *The HP Way*, 176–7, 184–5.

14. Ray Furlong, interview, 8/23/00; James Boatner, interview, 10/4/00; minutes, Senior Staff Meeting, 12/13/71.

15. Norman Augustine, interview, 11/7/00.

16. Atwood had been President-elect Bush's choice for the number two Pentagon position when he put forward Senator John Tower as his secretary of defense nominee. After Tower failed

to win Senate confirmation, Bush asked Cheney to serve as defense secretary. Thus Cheney "inherited" Atwood as his number two. (Vice President Richard Cheney, interview, 2/20/01; "Choice for Pentagon Deputy Seems to Be G.M. Executive," *New York Times*, 1/15/89; "GM Official Seen Headed For Senior Pentagon Post," *Washington Post*, 1/17/89; "Manager for Pentagon: Donald Jesse Atwood," *Washington Post*, 1/26/89; "Pentagon May See Return of Management by Politician-Industrialist Team," *Washington Post* 3/11/89.)

17. William Perry, interview, 1/18/02; Stuart Rochester, interview, 1/25/01; "Perry Moves to Erase Aspin's Marks upon Pentagon Organization," *Washington Post*, 2/17/94; "Perrypatetic," *Economist*, 4/9/94.

18. After Brown completed his tenure during the Carter administration, he offered a classic speech in March 1981 that summarized his management frustrations, entitled, " 'Managing' the Defense Department: Why It Can't Be Done." He said that, among other things, despite his best efforts there were still too many military bases and installations and "still 50-cent screws that cost $50." Most of the problem, he felt, traced directly to members of Congress who were less interested in Pentagon efficiency than the need to keep military activities in their districts to pacify their constituents. (Harold Brown, interview, 2/20/01; "Can the Defense Department Be Managed?" *National Journal*, 7/25/81.)

19. "McNamara Centralization in Retreat," *Washington Star*, 7/16/69.

20. "DoD Intelligence Management Faces Shakeup," *Armed Forces Management*, 10/69.

21. David Cooke, interview, 7/18/01.

22. Norman Augustine, interview, 11/7/00.

23. Robert C. Moot, memorandum for MRL, "How the Budget Battles Were Won, FY 1970–FY 1973," 12/4/72.

24. Robert Moot, interview, 2/6/01.

25. "The Inspector," *Washington Post*, 6/21/87.

26. MRL, remarks to the Washington Ridder Newspaper Group, Pentagon, 11/22/72.

27. Robert Froehlke, interview, 7/23/00; Philip N. Whittaker, former assistant secretary of the air force, interview, 7/24/01.

28. "Nuclear Submarine Sinks in 5 Minutes at Coast Yard," *New York Times*, 5/17/69.

29. "Military 'Mistakes' Scored By House Funds Chairman," *New York Times*, 5/21/69; "Mahon and Rivers Clash on Arms Cut," *Washington Post*, 5/21/69.

30. Richard Capen, interview, 8/8/00; minutes, Senior Staff Meeting, 5/19/69; :News Items of Special Interest" 5/29/69; UPI, "Sinking of A-Sub Blamed on an Avoidable Blunder," *Washington Post*, 5/29/69; "Navy Is Blamed in Sinking of Sub," *New York Times*, 5/30/69.

31. David Laird, MRL son, interview, 2/27/01.

32. Minutes, Senior Staff Meeting, "Meetings during the Week," 8/17/70.

33. James Boatner, interview, 10/4/00.

34. Jerry Friedheim, interview, 7/19/00; Rady Johnson, interview, 8/22/00.

35. John Gardner, interview, 4/30/01.

36. Susan Williams, interview, 10/24/01.

37. Colin L. Powell with Joseph E. Persico, *My American Journey*, Random House (1995).

38. Roger Kelley, interview, 7/27/01; Kelley, *Letters to My Children*, 65.

39. Richard Capen, interview, 8/8/00; Roger Kelley, interview, 7/27/01.

40. "Weekend in the Country Can Help," *Washington Star*, 9/15/71.

41. Stubbing with Mendel, *The Defense Game*, 293.

42. David Cooke, interview, 7/18/01.

27 / FINESSING CONGRESS

1. Governors Warren Knowles and Walter Kohler prided themselves on being members of this group.

2. Godfrey Sperling, interview, 5/7/02.

3. Robert Pursley, interview, 10/12/00; Gaylord Nelson, interview, 2/7/01; secretary's schedule, entry for July 28–29, 1971; "The Liberal Wilderness: Roasting Gaylord Nelson," *Washington Post*, 4/20/90; "Man behind Earthy Day Says Individual Action Can Turn Environmental Tide," *Los Angeles Times*, 4/17/90; "Another Gala for Gaylord," *Madison Capital Times*, 4/17/00; "Significance

of Earth Day Lives on through Awareness of Fragility, Founder Says," *Milwaukee Journal-Sentinel,* 4/22/00.

4. Richard Capen, interview, 8/8/00; minutes, Senior Staff Meetings: 3/23, 4/13, 11/16/70, 3/8/71; "Laird Clears Way for Bigger Budgets by Patching Pentagon Links with Congress," *National Journal,* 7/31/71; Seamans, *Aiming at Targets,* 168–9.

5. David Cooke, interview, 7/18/01; D. Douglas Blanke, memorandum for Dr. Prendergast, "Secretary Laird's Impact on Defense-Congressional Relations," 8/28/72.

6. Joe "Q" Quattrone, interview, 4/18/01.

7. Rady Johnson, interview, 8/22/00; Dick Capen, interview, 8/22/00; Capen, letter to MRL, 8/12/02.

8. George Dalferes, interview, 7/19/00.

9. Robert Pursley, interview, 6/15/00; Dick Capen, interviews, 7/15, 8/8, 9/29/00; Jerry Friedheim, interview, 7/19/00; Rady Johnson, interview, 8/22/00.

10. Jack Stempler, interview, 8/25/00; "Lobbyist Jack Stempler Doesn't Work for the Pentagon Anymore, but You'd Never Know It," *Washington Post Magazine,* 10/9/83; Seamans, *Aiming at Targets,* 158.

11. Richard Capen, interview, 8/8/00.

12. Carl Walske, interview, 4/23/01.

13. Robert Pursley, interview, 7/17/00; Rady Johnson, interview, 8/22/00; Richard Borda, interview, 4/2/01.

14. James Lawrence, interview, 7/31/01.

15. Thelma Stubbs Smith, interview, 4/23/01; AP, "Nixon Disposes of 2 Yachts," *Baltimore Sun,* 4/29/70; "All the President's Yachts," *Washington Post,* 4/2/77; "For Truman's Yacht, a 'Re-Berth,'" *Washington Post,* 10/23/80; Gulley with Reese, *Breaking Cover,* 36, 162–3; "Tracing Steps of Presidential Sea Legs," *Washington Times,* 8/5/96.

16. Bryce Harlow, "Congressional Report," Private Paper, Cabinet File for Thursday, 9/4/69.

17. Ehrlichman, *Witness to Power,* 96–7.

18. Robert Michel, interview, 4/19/01.

19. Richard Capen, interview, 8/8/00; Rady Johnson, interview, 8/22/00; minutes, Senior Staff Meetings, 4/20/70, 5/10/71, 3/6/72.

20. "Laird's Years: The Big Price for Keeping the Brass off His Back," *Washington Post,* 1/2/73.

21. Elmer Staats, interview, 1/29/02.

22. Burke and Thompson, *Bryce Harlow,*195, 197–8.

23. Prentiss Childs, CBS, *Face the Nation,* letter to MRL, 12/9/68.

24. Robert Pursley, interview, 10/28/97.

25. MRL, "Press Conference with Admiral Thomas Moorer," Brussels, Belgium, 5/28/71.

26. Minutes, Senior Staff Meeting, "Rockefeller Public Service Award to Mr. Robert C. Moot, Assistant Secretary of Defense," 11/15/71; "Six Career Public Servants Win $10,000 Service Awards," *Washington Post,* 11/16/71.

27. Seamans, *Aiming at Targets,* 165; John McLucas and Lawrence Benson, *Confessions of a Technocrat,* unpublished autobiography.

28. "Tough Decisions for a New Decade," *Newsweek,* 1/5/70.

29. Pres. Richard Nixon, "Defense Program Review Committee," NSDM 26, 10/11/69.

30. Zumwalt, *On Watch,* 314; Stubbing with Mendel, *Defense Game,* 301–2.

31. Zumwalt, *On Watch,* 314.

32. Joseph Kraft, "Laird Turns Around," *Washington Post,* 11/22/70.

33. Minutes, Senior Staff Meeting, "Budget," 1/5/70; minutes, Senior Staff Meeting, "Defense Budget," 2/2/70; minutes, Senior Staff Meeting, "FY 1972 Budget Briefing," 1/28/71; minutes, Senior Staff Meeting, "Beyond Vietnam," 4/26/71; "B-1 Essential to U.S. Security, Laird Says after Touring Plant" [which includes Laird's rule-of-thumb quote], *Los Angeles Times,* 8/25/72; MRL, "Interview with Newsmen Before Remarks to Civic Clubs," Oklahoma City, Okla., 9/27/72.

34. Minutes, Senior Staff Meeting, "Budget," 1/5/70; minutes, Senior Staff Meeting, "Budget Matters," 7/6/70; minutes, Senior Staff Meeting, "Budget Matters," 12/28/70; "House Passes Money Bill for HEW; With Trust Funds It Tops $77 Billion," *Washington Post,* 7/28/71; MRL, "Interview with Newsmen," Oklahoma City, Okla., 9/27/72.

35. Stubbing with Mendel, *Defense Game,* 299–301.

28 / LAIRD ON *DEEFENSE*

1. Minutes, Senior Staff Meetings: 4/7, 4/21/69.

2. AP, "Students Razz Moorer," *Washington Star*, 3/15/72; UPI, 3/15/72.

3. AP, 4/5/72; "Yale Melee Cancels Talk by Westmoreland," *New York Times*, 4/6/72.

4. Minutes, Senior Staff Meeting, 11/1/71.

5. Robert Froehlke, interview, 9/10/97; Dale Van Atta, "Froehlke Defends Army," BYU *Daily Universe* (student newspaper), 4/26/72.

6. Robert Froehlke, interview, 9/10/97; "Army Chief Seeks, Finds Boston Fight," *Boston Globe*, 12/3/72; "News Items of Special Interest," 12/9/72.

7. Minutes, Senior Staff Meeting, 1/31/72.

8. Orr Kelly, "Laird Leads as Talkingest Defense Secretary," *Washington Star*, 5/31/70.

9. MRL, "Remarks by the Honorable Melvin R. Laird at the Dedication of the Correspondents' Corridor, The Pentagon," 11/21/72.

10. David Cooke, interview, 7/18/01; minutes, Senior Staff Meeting, 2/24/70; MRL, keel-laying ceremony of USS *Eisenhower*, Newport News, Va., 8/15/70.

11. George Blanchard, interview, 10/24/01; "Omar Bradley Honored," *Washington Star*, 6/14/72; "Corridor for Bradley," *Baltimore Sun*, 6/15/72; "Salute to an Old Soldier," *Washington Post*, 6/15/72.

12. Lane VanderSteeg, interview, 10/25/01; "Penetrating the Pentagon," *New York Times*, 4/18/82; AP, "The Pentagon at 50," *The Record*, 5/12/93.

13. "Pentagon," 1/18/72; *Newsweek*, 1/31/72.

14. Excerpts from a luncheon speech as printed in "Notable & Quotable," *Wall Street Journal*, 12/1/72.

15. *New York Times*, 4/18/82.

16. MRL, "Remarks by the Honorable Melvin R. Laird at the Dedication of the Correspondents' Corridor, The Pentagon," 10 A.M., 11/21/72.

17. "PostScript," *Washington Post*, 5/7/79.

18. MRL, memorandum for secretaries of military departments; chairman, Joint Chiefs of Staff; director of Defense Research and Engineering; assistant secretaries of defense; assistants to the secretary of defense; directors of the defense agencies, "Public Information Principles"; 3/4/69; Dan Henkin, ASD (PA), news release, "Memorandum for Correspondents," 3/5/69.

19. David Heebner, interview, 8/28/00; Curtis Tarr journal, entry for 1/4/71.

20. MRL, "Question-Answer Period following Remarks to Associated Press Editors," Kansas City, Mo., 11/16/72.

21. Jack Anderson, "Secretary of Defense Mel Laird's Pentagon Hideaway," *Parade*, 7/69.

22. MRL, question-answer period, 11/16/72.

23. Jack Anderson, "AF Staff Car Used for Columnist," *Washington Post*, 4/18/72; "Tower Ticker," *Chicago Tribune*, 5/18/72.

24. Minutes, Senior Staff Meeting, 4/5/71; Robert F. Froehlke, "Unauthorized Disclosure of Classified Defense Information Appearing in the *Washington Post* Article Entitled, 'AF Rain Maker in Laos,' by Jack Anderson, Dated March 18, 1971," 4/16/71.

25. Jack Anderson with Daryl Gibson, *Peace, War, and Politics*, Forge (1999), 227–30; Hersh, *Price of Power*, 477–8.

26. Henry Kissinger, speech at dedication of Laird Center, Marshfield, Wis., 9/12/97.

27. David Broder, speech at the dedication of the Laird Center, Marshfield, Wis., 9/12/97.

28. Bob Schieffer, interview, 7/25/01.

29. Bob Novak, interview, 10/2/00; Henry Kissinger, interview, 1/10/01.

30. Pres. George H. W. Bush, interview, 10/14/97.

31. Jerry Friedheim, interview, 7/19/00; MRL, secretary of defense designate, "News Conference at Pentagon," 12/13/68.

32. Laird said "Kissinger thinks I leaked everything to Sy Hersh" for the latter's exhaustively reported book on Kissinger, *The Price of Power*. He confirmed he had helped Hersh on the book but not in a way "to undermine Kissinger." He confirmed facts Hersh had already gathered, as well as providing some new insights into the Nixon administration. ("News Items of Special Interest," 6/16/72; minutes, Senior Staff Meeting, 10/10/72.)

33. Democratic political guru Robert Strauss holds the record as Sperling's guest with eighty-nine appearances. Among the more notable meetings are one in which Senator Bobby Kennedy confided he was going to run for president, the 9/16/91 appearance of Bill and Hillary Clinton

addressing their marital problems for the first time, and Newt Gingrich's appearance when he complained about President Clinton snubbing him aboard Air Force One. (Godfrey Sperling, interview, 5/6/02; David Cook, Washington bureau Chief, *Christian Science Monitor*, interview, 5/8/02; Sperling, "It's Nixon in Primaries, Says Laird," *Christian Science Monitor*, 1/2/68; "Reporters' Breakfast and Lunch Groups——Good Reporting or 'Socialized Journalism'?" *National Journal*, 3/21/81; "20 Years on the Bacon and Egg Beat," *Washington Post*, 2/25/86; Sperling, "Curious Readers Want the Dish on Breakfast," *Christian Science Monitor*, 11/3/98.)

34. "News Items of Special Interest," 3/24/69.

35. "New Items of Special Interest," 1/17/70, 1/24/72, 11/20/72.

36. Henkin, "News Items of Special Interest," 3/24/71.

37. "Hebert Denounces C.B.S. Pentagon Show," *New York Times*, 2/26/71.

38. "DoD after Two Years of Laird," *Armed Forces Journal*, 12/21/70.

39. Jerry Friedheim, interview, 7/19/00; minutes, Senior Staff Meetings, 4/21, 4/28, 7/7/69, 9/27/72; Orr Kelly, "A New Era for Pentagon Press?" *Washington Star*, 5/13/69; "Briefings: A Ritual of Noncommunication," *Time*, 10/10/69.

40. "The Voice of the Pentagon: Jerry Warden Friedheim," *New York Times*, 1/5/73; UPI, "Friedheim," 1/8/73; "Obfuscation Revisited," *Aerospace Daily*, 1/8/73.

41. UPI, "Ball," a1/9/73; *New York Times*, 1/10/73; "People," *Sports Illustrated*, 1/73.

29 / LAOS

1. AP, "U.S. Enters Second Decade of Viet War," *Baltimore Sun*, 1/2/71.

2. AP, "Last U.S. Green Beret Camps Turned Over to S. Vietnamese," *Washington Post*, 1/5/71.

3. Kissinger, memorandum for secretaries of defense and state, CIA director, "Discussion of Troop Withdrawals and Vietnamization," 1/6/71.

4. MRL, "Press Conference," Paris, France, 1/6/71.

5. "Laird Sets Date, but . . . : White House Wary on Viet Phase-out," *Christian Science Monitor*, 1/8/71.

6. MRL, "Interview with Newsmen on Departure from Vietnam," Saigon, Vietnam, 1/11/71.

7. Joseph Alsop, "Vietnam Plan Sabotaged by Melvin Laird," *Washington Post*, 1/13/71.

8. UPI, "Hospitalized," 9/30/70; AP, "Gen. Abrams Suffers Dizzy Spell," 10/1/70.

9. MRL, memorandum of conversation, 1/11/71, included as part of MRL, memorandum for the president, 1/16/71.

10. The CIA also had a smaller sister company, Continental Air Services, which operated alongside Air America. It was not affiliated with Continental Airlines. According to Tammy Arbuckle, writing for the 1/17/70 *Washington Star*, Air America then employed 133 pilots, and Continental had 73 pilots. Together the two companies had about seventy aircraft and twenty helicopters.

11. Stanley I. Kutler, *Encyclopedia of the Vietnam War*, Simon & Schuster (1996), 561–2; Timothy N. Castle, *War in the Shadow of Vietnam: United States Military Aid to the Royal Lao Government, 1955–1975* (1993); Jane Hamilton-Merritt, *Tragic Mountains: The Hmong, the Americans, and the Secret Wars* (1993).

12. Robert Seamans, interview, 10/12/00.

13. Ivan Selin, interview, 2/19/01.

14. Kissinger, memorandum for MRL, 9/15/69.

15. "Fulbright Attacks U.S. Role in Laos," *Washington Post*, 10/29/69.

16. Jerry Friedheim, interview, 7/19/00.

17. MRL, "Operational Control Procedures, Laos," letter with attachment to Secretary of State William P. Rogers, 12/1/69.

18. Marquis Childs, "United States Unlikely to Slip into Another Vietnam in Laos," *Washington Post*, 3/11/70.

19. AP, "Senators Ask Facts on Role of U.S. in Laos," *Washington Star*, 2/26/70.

20. "Department of Defense Appropriations for 1971," Hearings before a Subcommittee of the Committee on Appropriations, House of Representatives, 2/26/70, pg. 359.

21. MRL, "Interview with Newsmen following Appearance before House Committee on Appropriations," 2/26/70.

22. Secretary of Air Force Robert C. Seamans Jr., memorandum for MRL, "U.S. Position in Southeast Asia," 2/27/70.

23. "The Secret War . . . ," *Wall Street Journal*, 12/18/69.

24. "Dilemma in Laos," *Newsweek,* 11/3/69.

25. MRL, memorandum for the president, with two attachments, "Draft Statement on Laos" and "Check List," 3/3/70.

26. Kissinger, memorandum for secretaries of defense and state, and CIA director, "Presidential Statement on Laos," 3/4/70.

27. MRL, memorandum for assistant to the president for national security affairs (Kissinger), "Presidential Statement on Laos," 3/5/70.

28. "News Items of Special Interest," 3/9/70.

29. "Deaths of 27 Americans in Laos Disclosed by U.S.," *New York Times,* 3/9/70.

30. MRL, memorandum for Kissinger, 3/13/70.

31. The fourteenth man, a sergeant, was not posthumously reinstated in the air force because, according to Laird's report, his "wife was not a U.S. citizen, and, therefore, not considered clearable. She was not briefed regarding the project on her husband's status vis-a-vis the U.S. Air Force. Therefore, his status remains that of a civilian."

32. The citation is for "extraordinary heroism in military operations against an opposing armed force on 11 March 1968." On that date Sgt. Etchberger was manning a defensive position when the rest of the northern Lao base was overrun by the enemy.

"The enemy was able to deliver sustained and withering fire directly upon this position from higher ground. His entire crew dead or wounded, Sgt. Etchberger managed to return the enemy's fire thus denying them access to his position. During this entire period, Sgt. Etchberger continued to direct air strikes and call for air rescue . . . enabling the air evacuation force to locate the surrounded friendly element. When air rescue arrived, Sgt. Etchberger deliberately exposed himself to enemy fire in order to place his three surviving wounded comrades in the rescue slings, permitting them to be airlifted to safety. As Sgt. Etchberger was finally being rescued, he was fatally wounded by enemy ground fire. His fierce defense, which culminated in the supreme sacrifice of his life, saved not only the lives of his three comrades but provided for the successful evacuation of the remaining survivors of the base."

33. Elliot Richardson, letter to Deputy Secretary of Defense David Packard, 5/29/70.

34. Deputy Secretary of Defense David Packard, memorandum for the chairman, JCS, "Prairie Fire Operations in Laos," 6/18/70.

35. John R. Stevenson, "Prairie Fire Operations—The President's Statement on the Church Amendment," opinion of the legal adviser, attached to 7/17/70, State Department letter to Deputy Secretary of Defense Packard.

36. Undersecretary of State for Political Affairs U. Alexis Johnson, State Department, letter to Deputy Secretary of Defense Packard, 7/17/70.

37. MRL, letter to Undersecretary of State for Political Affairs U. Alexis Johnson, State Department, 9/2/70.

38. Acting Secretary of State U. Alexis Johnson, letter to MRL, 9/5/70.

39. Kissinger, memorandum for secretaries of defense and state, with copy to CIA director, "Participation of U.S. Personnel in the Exploitation Phase of Prairie Fire Operations in Laos," 10/13/70.

40. MRL, memorandum for the president, "Participation of U.S. Personnel in the Exploitation Phase of PRAIRIE FIRE Operations in Laos," 12/7/70.

30 / THE HO CHI MINH TRAIL

1. "The two sides of this sign embody both the facts and the goal of the current action," Laird said. (MRL, "Address by the Honorable Melvin R. Laird, Secretary of Defense, before the Rotary Club of Phoenix," Phoenix, Ariz., 2/12/71; "Indochina: A Cavalry Man's Way Out," *Time,* 2/15/71.)

2. "Untold Story of the Ho Chi Minh Trail," *U.S. News & World Report,* 2/15/71.

3. According to Michael Maclear (*The Ten Thousand Day War: Vietnam, 1945–1975,* Avon Books [1981], 173), Hanoi strategist Ha Van Lau maintained after the war that "it was a road system of more than 13,000 kilometers," which is more than twice the size of the 5,645 kilometers (3,500 miles) that American military computers had mapped.

4. This is the figure used by North Vietnamese journalist Khanh Van, writing after the war in Hanoi's military newspaper, *Quan Doi Nhan Dan,* as cited by Maclear (*Ten Thousand Day War,* 186–7).

5. Minutes, JCS Chairman Thomas Moorer's briefing, Senior Staff Meeting, 2/1/71.

6. "Vietnam—Fencing in the North," *The New Republic*, 7/8/67; "McNamara's Gimmick," *Nation*, 9/25/67; "McNamara's Fence: Our Eyes and Ears along the Demilitarized Zone," *Army*, 8/68; William R. Corson, *The Betrayal* (1968); Paul Dickson, *The Electronic Battlefield* (1976); Willard Pearson, *The War in the Northern Provinces* (1978).

7. Maclear, *Ten Thousand Day War*, 185. Maclear asserts: "In World War II, two million tons of air ordnance were dropped. From 1965 to 1971, 2,235,918 tons of bombs were dropped over Laos infiltration routes."

8. Secretary of Defense schedule, 12/23/70; Kissinger, *White House Years*, 994.

9. MRL, memorandum of conversation, President Nguyen Van Thieu and MRL, 1/11/71.

10. Kissinger, memorandum for secretaries of state, defense, and CIA director, "Summary of the Pros and Cons of ARVN Operation in Southern Laos," 2/2/71; Kissinger, *White House Years*, 997–8.

11. "Reference is made to our meeting with highest authority on 27 January, in which approval was received to proceed with Phase I of the Tchepone Operation," JCS Chairman Moorer wrote in a memorandum for MRL, "Planning for Laos," 1/29/71; Kissinger (*White House Years*, 999) recounts that the Oval Office meeting included Nixon, Laird, Rogers, Helms, Moorer, Haig, and himself.

12. The American portion of the operation was called Dewey Canyon II. The first such operation in the Laotian panhandle had actually been misspelled, and that continued in 1971. It was supposed to be "*Dewy* Canyon," in reference to the dewlike mists that covered the Ho Chi Minh Trail. The evocation of the fifteenth-century Lam Son victory had such historic significance for the South Vietnamese that Admiral Moorer advised in a memo that U.S. military should not engage in "any action to terminate the use of the term Lam Son" in connection with any future RVNAF operations. (Adm. T. H. Moorer, Chairman, JCS, memorandum for MRL, "U.S. Support for RVNAF Cross-Border Operations," 4/1/71.)

13. He referred to his remarks during his weekly top-staff meeting held shortly after the Cabinet meeting on February 16, according to the minutes.

14. Hammond, *Military and the Media*, 428–30.

15. Vietnam Military History Institute, *History of the People's Army of Vietnam*.

16. MRL and Lt. Gen. John W. Vogt, Director, Joint Staff, JCS, "News Conference at Pentagon," 2/24/71.

17. "Laos Drive on Schedule, Laird Says," *Washington Post*, 2/25/71.

18. MRL, "Department of Defense Appropriations for 1972," hearing before a subcommittee of the Committee on Appropriations, House of Representatives, 209–212, 3/4/71.

19. Jerry Friedheim, interview, 7/19/00.

20. "Pentagon Pipe Dream," *Washington News*, 3/8/71.

21. Art Buchwald, "The Pentagon's Little Lies," *Washington Post*, 3/9/71.

22. "News Items of Special Interest," 3/9/71.

23. Minutes, Senior Staff Meeting, 3/1/71.

24. Minutes, Senior Staff Meeting, 3/1/71.

25. MRL, "Interview with Newsmen following Appearance before Defense Subcommittee of the House Committee on Appropriations," 3/5/71.

26. Senior Staff Meeting, Moorer briefing, 3/8/71.

27. Bernard C. Nalty, *Vietnam War*, Smithmark Publishers (1996), 253.

28. Minutes, Senior Staff Meeting, 3/29/71.

29. Henry Kissinger, interview, 1/10/71.

30. Alexander M. Haig Jr., with Charles McCarry, *Inner Circles: How America Changed the World, a Memoir*, Warner Books (1992), 273–8.

31. Nixon, *Memoirs*, 498–9.

32. Sorley, *A Better War*, 270.

33. Sorley, *A Better War*, 256, 261.

34. Gen. Bruce Palmer Jr., "U.S. Intelligence and Vietnam," *Studies in Intelligence*, CIA (1984), 90.

35. Minutes, Moorer briefing, Senior Staff Meeting, 3/29/71.

36. Minutes, Senior Staff Meeting, 7/12/71.

37. UPI, 1/28/71.

38. "Thousands in U.S. Protest on Laos," *New York Times*, 2/11/71.

39. Jack Vessey, interview, 2/25/02.

31 / WHEN THE HAWKS HAVE FLOWN

1. Minutes, Senior Staff Meeting, 4/5/71.

2. The account is from Laird's recollection of the evening, as well as a contemporary account in *Newsweek* that described Laird as being "alone in a roomful of friends." ("End of the Tunnel Remains Blurred," *Washington Post*, 4/8/71; "White House, Scott Split on Pullout Date," *Washington Post*, 4/9/71; " 'You Don't See Any Hawks around Here,'" *Newsweek*, 4/19/71.)

3. Jack Kemp, interview, 7/26/01.

4. This was a line Kemp would frequently repeat as a Congressman, presidential candidate, and when he was the first Bush administration's secretary of Housing and Urban Development. One reference to it is in "Jack Kemp: The JFK of the '80s?" *Washingtonian*, 5/81.

5. "Madison, Wis., Voters Favor Immediate War Pullout," *New York Times*, 4/8/71.

6. "Pressing for Peace: Antiwar Sentiment Increases in Congress Despite Nixon's Speech," *Wall Street Journal*, 4/9/71.

7. MRL, memorandum for the president, "Tempo of the War," 4/6/71.

8. "Ideas to End War Offered by Clifford," *Washington Star*, 4/3/71.

9. "Aiken Indicates Nixon Will Withdraw 18,000 GI's Monthly," *Baltimore Sun*, 4/7/71.

10. MRL, memorandum for the president, "Redeployment of U.S. Forces from Southeast Asia," 4/3/71.

11. "The President's War Report," *Washington Post*, 4/9/71.

12. "Eavesdropping Some More on Nixon in the Oval Office," *Chicago Tribune*, 10/31/99.

13. Pres. Richard Nixon, memorandum for the secretaries of state and defense, and CIA director, "Discussion of Vietnam Plans," 4/9/71.

14. Consider this contortionist exchange between Laird and the correspondents, according to the transcript of "News Conference by Secretary of Defense Melvin R. Laird at Pentagon," 4/13/71, 11:30 A.M.:

Question: Mr. Secretary, [the President apparently] has no intention of having a residual force in South Vietnam. Is that your understanding?

Secretary Laird: I think the President's statement and speech speaks for itself. I don't believe that it would serve any useful purpose to enlarge upon what the President has said.

Question: Mr. Secretary, would you enlarge on your own frequently-promised course that you're going to terminate American involvement in the war, and tell us whether terminate means what the dictionary says it means or whether we are going to continue to have—

Secretary Laird: It means exactly what the President said in his statement.

Question: What does it mean when you have used the term, sir?

Secretary Laird: Exactly the same as the President in his statement.

Question: Would you tell us what it means?

Secretary Laird: Well, I would be glad to give you a copy of the President's speech.

Question: [But] I heard that [speech].

Secretary Laird: I think there's a game going around here to try to divide the President from [others], and I am not going to get into that particular game....

Question: Mr. Secretary, can we get at it this way.... Do you plan a Korea-type solution in Vietnam, with leaving "X" number of Americans there as a support force indefinitely, or do you plan to get them completely out, period? Can you answer that?

Secretary Laird: I think the President made that very clear in his speech.

Question: What do you say, sir?

Secretary Laird: I support the President.

Question: I don't think that's an answer.

Secretary Laird: I think it is a pretty good answer and I will continue to support the President of the United States in his very historic policy pronouncement of April 7.

Question: Sir, he has never addressed himself on this question.

Secretary Laird: I think that anyone reading the speech would find the question is addressed.

Question: I did read it, and I listened to it.

15. "U.S. Plans Air, Sea Asia Role: Laird Cites 'Deterrent' after Pullout," *Washington Post*, 4/14/71.

16. John Kerry and Vietnam Veterans against the War, *The New Soldier*, Collier Books (1971), 12–24.

17. "Veterans Discard Medals in War Protest at Capitol," *New York Times*, 4/24/70; "Vets Leave; Mass March Slated Today," *Washington Post*, 4/24/71.

18. *Washington Post,* 2/21/85.

19. Barry Shillito, letter to MRL and Kathy Weaver, 6/13/07.

20. "Exclusive Interview with Defense Secretary Melvin R. Laird: U.S. Strategy beyond Vietnam," *U.S. News & World Report,* 5/17/71.

21. Haldeman, *Haldeman Diaries,* 278.

22. *Washington Post,* 2/21/85.

23. *New York Times,* 4/25/70.

24. Joe Zaice, interview, 8/31/01.

25. White House Tapes, Oval Office, Conversation No. 488-10, 7:55 to 8:04 A.M., 4/27/71.

26. MRL, "Press Conference with Secretary of Defense Melvin Laird, Secretary's Dining Room," Pentagon, 4/27/71.

27. "The Cost of the War after It's 'Over,'" *Time,* 4/19/71.

28. Laird told Vera Glaser and Malvina Stephenson of the calls during a 5/18/71 interview. Laird was hospitalized full-time for twelve days, and another four days "part-time," meaning he would go to his Pentagon office in the morning and return to Walter Reed in the afternoon.

29. Minutes, Senior Staff Meeting, 4/26/71.

30. Minutes, Senior Staff Meeting, 5/3/71; "Police Oust 15,000 from Camp in D.C.," *Baltimore Sun,* 5/3/71.

31. "7,000 Arrested in Capital War Protest; 150 Are Hurt as Clashes Disrupt Traffic," *New York Times,* 5/4/71.

32. "7,000 Arrested in Capital War Protest; 150 Are Hurt as Clashes Disrupt Traffic," *New York Times,* 5/4/71.

33. Kim Van Atta, former Vietnam War demonstrator, interview, 3/15/02.

34. White House Tapes, Conversation No. 2-86, Oval Office, 10:15 to 10:30 A.M., 5/5/71.

32 / DEFENDING THE PENTAGON

1. An Arlington, Va., FBI report of a 6/24/71 interview conducted with Pursley, dated the following day.

2. Pursley said that, prior to the 1971 controversy over the Pentagon Papers, he turned over his collection of handwritten notes to then Department of Defense General Counsel J. Fred Buzhardt. "I have never seen it since. It has the early notes of what Bob McNamara told me, what I thought, my memos back to him about how we were setting it up. The memos contain McNamara's initials for approval." (Pursley, interview, 7/17/00.) Until at least the time of the interview, Pursley had repeatedly tried with Pentagon officials to retrieve his notes from among the late Buzhardt's papers—and been refused.

3. Robert Pursley, interview, 10/9/00.

4. Minutes, Senior Staff Meeting, 6/14/71; both the *New York Times* and Secretary of State William Rogers, in June 1971, said that "thirty-six persons" authored the study.

5. Sanford J. Ungar, *The Papers & The Papers,* E.P. Dutton & Co. (1972), 31.

6. The title used by Pentagon officials in transmitting the documents to Congress was different: "United States–Vietnam Relations, 1945–1967."

7. "25 Years Later: Lessons from the Pentagon Papers," *New York Times,* 6/23/96.

8. At the 6/14/71 staff meeting, Laird generally outlined the location of the fifteen copies. A more detailed list was in "FBI Checking All Having Access to Known 15 Copies of Viet Study," *Washington Post,* 6/16/71. In a memo of the same day to Laird referring to the *Post* story, his spokesperson Dan Henkin called their list "rather complete." (Also, Ungar, *Papers and the Papers,* 40–1.)

9. The most complete account of the Fulbright-Laird exchanges is in Ungar, *Papers and the Papers,* 69–74. Numerous newspaper accounts in 1971 reported thoroughly on the exchange, including "Laird Refused '69 Fulbright Request for the Pentagon Study on Vietnam," *New York Times,* 6/17/71. Fulbright also published the full exchange of letters in the *Congressional Record.*

10. Bob Schieffer, interview, 7/25/01.

11. "New Items of Special Interest," 6/14/71.

12. National Archives, White House tapes, Conversation No. 519-1, 8:49 to 10:04 A.M., 6/14/71.

13. U.S. Senate hearings before the Committee on Foreign Relations, "Foreign Assistance Legislation, Fiscal Year 1972," 6/14/71, pgs. 341, 349–51.

14. National Archives, White House tapes, 6/14/71: Conversation No. 519-7, Alexander Haig, 12:27 to 1:09 P.M.; Conversation No. 521-7, Henry Kissinger, 3:19 to 3:31 P.M.; Conversation No. 521-9, John N. Mitchell and John D. Erlichman, 3:45 to 4:30 P.M.

15. Carl Walske, interview, 4/23/01.

16. Minutes, Senior Staff Meeting, 6/21/71.

17. "Pentagon Calls Study 'The McNamara Papers,'" *Washington Star*, 6/22/71.

18. Ungar, *Papers and the Papers*, 207, 229–30.

19. MRL, "Interview with Newsmen following Appearance before the Subcommittee on Foreign Operations of the Senate Committee on Appropriations," 1:30 P.M., 6/22/71.

20. "U.S. Declassifies Viet Papers, Rushes Volumes to Printer," *Chicago Tribune*, 9/22/71.

21. *The Pentagon Papers*, as published by *The New York Times*, based on investigative reporting by Neil Sheehan, written by Neil Sheehan, Hedrick Smith, E.W. Kenworthy, and Fox Butterfield, Bantam Books, Inc. (1971). Sales numbers come from Ungar, *Papers and The Papers*, 313–14.

22. Minutes, Senior Staff Meeting, 6/21/71.

23. "Ellsberg Yields, Is Indicted; Says He Gave Data to Press," *New York Times*, 6/29/71; "Patriot Motives Cited by Ellsberg," *Washington Post*, 6/29/71.

24. Minutes, Senior Staff Meeting, 6/28/71.

25. National Archives, White House tape, Conversation No. 533-1, 6/30/71.

26. Minutes, Senior Staff Meeting, 6/28/71.

27. All quotes except about Attorney General John Mitchell are from Conversation No. 534-3, White House tapes, National Archives, 10:28 to 11:49 A.M., 7/1/71, Oval Office, Nixon, Haldeman, and Colson. The John Mitchell reference is from an afternoon meeting that day, July 1, 1:38 to 2:05 P.M., between Nixon and Haldeman.

28. National Archives, White House tapes, Conversation No. 260-21, 5:39 to 6:29 P.M., 7/2/71, Old Executive Office Building; Nixon, Ehrlichman, and Haldeman.

29. National Archives, White House tape, 11:50 am. to 12:15 P.M., 7/6/71; Nixon, Mitchell, Ehrlichman, and Haldeman.

30. Minutes, Senior Staff Meeting, 7/12/71.

31. The survey was conducted July 9 and 12 and reported to Laird by Air Force Secretary Robert C. Seamans Jr., in a 7/15/71 memorandum.

32. Nixon, *Memoirs*, 511–13.

33. National Archives, Conversation No. 533-1, 6/30/71.

34. National Archives, White House tapes, 8:49 to 9:52 A.M., 7/1/71, Oval Office; Nixon, Haldeman, and Kissinger.

35. Gerald Ford, interview, 8/28/97.

36. "Hunt Was Denied Files from Pentagon," *Washington Post*, 5/10/73.

37. This dictum was so hard and fast that the Pentagon press corps was aware of it. Bob Schieffer, who was the CBS Pentagon correspondent from 1970 to 1974, recalled that even though Laird "never put out a press release on it, we all knew that Laird would not let anybody at the White House talk to anybody at the Pentagon unless they went through him." (Schieffer, interview, 7/25/01.)

38. John Chafee, interview, 10/22/99, two days before his death.

39. Barry Shillito, interview, 8/8/00; Johnny Foster, interview, 6/21/01; Stanley I. Kutler, interview, 7/14/00; Robert Pursley, interview, 3/30/01; John McLucas, interview, 7/31/01.

40. Minutes, Senior Staff Meeting, 8/31/70.

41. Jerry Friedheim, interview, 7/19/00.

42. Robert Seamans, interview, 10/12/00.

43. Bob Froehlke, interview, 7/23/00.

44. "Laird's Paper Barricade," *Washington Star*, 5/18/73.

45. Minutes, Senior Staff Meeting, 8/31/70.

46. MRL, memorandum for the president, 3/15/71.

47. Pres. Richard Nixon, memorandum for MRL, "Liaison between the Department of Defense and the White House," 4/8/71.

48. Richard Capen, interview, 8/8/00; Robert Pursley, interview, 10/28/97; Norman Augustine, interview, 11/7/00; Pierre Du Pont, interview, 4/4/01.

49. John Chafee, interview, 10/22/99.

50. John Warner, interview, 11/10/99; Laird also confirmed the conversation.

33 / FRIENDS IN HIGH PLACES

1. Helmut Schmidt, interview, 2/4/01; Col. J.E. Stannard, Department of Defense, memorandum for MRL, "Meeting with German MOD Schmidt," 11/4/69; "Leading from Strength," *Time,* 6/11/79; "Schmidt vs. Strauss: They're Using Bare Knuckles," *New York Times,* 7/27/80; "The Schmidt Factor," *New York Times,* 9/21/80; "A Talk," *New York Times,* 9/16/84; MRL, "My Friend Helmut Schmidt," unpublished article for *Reader's Digest,* 1990.

2. Headquarters, Department of the Army, "Employment of Atomic Demolition Munitions (ADM)," Field Manual, 8/71; Jack Anderson and Dale Van Atta, "Little Weapons with a Big Bang," *Washington Post,* 6/3/84.

3. Helmut Schmidt, interview, 2/4/01; State Department, memorandum of conversation, "Seventh Meeting of the Nuclear Planning Group," 6/8/70.

4. G. Warren Nutter, ASD (ISA), memorandum of 10/28/70 Ottawa conversation, "German/U.S. Bilateral," 11/9/70.

5. State Department, "Eighth Meeting of the Nuclear Planning Group," Ottawa, 10/29/70; "NATO Officials Draft Guidelines for Use of Nuclear Land Mines," *Washington Post,* 10/31/70.

6. Minutes, Senior Staff Meeting, "NATO," 5/25/70; MRL, "Secretary of Defense Presentation to NATO NPG, 8–9 June 1970," 6/8/70; State Department, "Seventh Meeting of the Nuclear Planning Group; Memorandum of Conversation," 6/8/70.

7. Minutes, Senior Staff Meeting, "NATO Meetings," 6/15/70.

8. Robert Pursley, interview, 1/31/01; Frederick S. Wyle, Deputy Assistant Secretary (ISA), memorandum of conversation, "US/FRG (West German) Meeting (of 10/12/68)," 10/23/68; *1968 CQ Almanac,* "National Security," pg. 82; MRL, memorandum for the president, "NATO Defense Issues," 2/20/69.

9. George Shultz, interview, 2/6/01; Lawrence Eagleburger, interview, 2/7/01; Donald Rumsfeld, interview, 2/28/01; G. Warren Nutter, ASD (ISA), memorandum of conversation, "Secretary Laird/Secretary General Brosio Meeting (Cape Kennedy, 3/18) during the NATO SATCOM Launch Program," 3/30/70.

10. G. Warren Nutter, ASD (ISA), memorandum of conversation, "Meeting of Mr. Laird with Minister Schroeder, February 1, 1969," 2/4/69; MRL, memorandum for the president, "NATO Defense Issues," 2/20/69.

11. Lawrence S. Kaplan, *NATO and the United States,* Twayne Publishers (1988), 131–2; Joan Hoff, *Nixon Reconsidered,* Basic Books (1995), 191–4.

12. Rear Adm. Daniel Murphy, military assistant to MRL, memorandum of (5/24) conversation, 5/26/71.

13. Murphy, memorandum of (5/25) conversation, 5/26/71.

14. Selden, "Summary Paper for the Record—Effect of Personal Rapport among MODs on Relations between US and Its Allies," 12/4/72.

15. John T. Mason, editor, *The Pacific War Remembered: An Oral History Collection,* U.S. Naval Institute Press (1986), 333; Humble, *Fighting Ships,* 26.

16. Kissinger, "Policy toward Japan," NSDM 13, 5/28/69.

17. Haldeman, *Haldeman Diaries,* 62–3.

18. Gen. Earle G. Wheeler, Chairman, JCS, memorandum for Deputy Secretary of Defense David Packard and MRL, "Okinawa Negotiating Strategy," 7/24/69.

19. Dick Capen, interview, 8/89/00; "Trip Report of Chemical Munition Safety Survey (of) Chibana Army Ammunition Depot," delivered to MRL and Secretary of the Army Stan Resor, 5/8/70.

20. Kennedy approved a total of 16,000 tons of chemical weapons for shipment to Okinawa, but the last 5,000 tons were held in the United States awaiting presidential approval for shipment from Kennedy's successors (Johnson and Nixon), which never came. (Ivan Selin, ASD, memorandum for MRL, "Storage of Chemical Warfare Weapons on Okinawa," 7/19/69; Gen. Earle Wheeler, chairman, JCS, memorandum for MRL, "Chemical Weapons on Okinawa," 9/12/69; MRL, memorandum for Gen. Wheeler, chairman, JCS, "Chemical Weapons on Okinawa," 10/24/69.)

21. Dan Henkin, memorandum to MRL, "News Items of Special Interest," 7/18/69; "24 Felled, Nerve Gas Is Blamed," *Washington Star,* 7/18/69.

22. "Okinawa Gas Leak Report Perils Sato's Treaty Plan," *Washington Post,* 7/20/69; "Okinawa Report on Gas Provides Windfall for Opposition in Japan," *New York Times,* 7/23/69; Minutes, Senior Staff Meeting, "CBW," 7/28/69.

23. Gen. Earle Wheeler, chairman, JCS, memorandum for MRL, "Overseas Storage of Toxic

Chemical Agents/Munitions," 8/28/69; MRL, memorandum for Army Secretary and ASD (I&L), "Chemical Weapons on Okinawa," 10/24/69.

24. The Johnston Atoll Chemical Agent Disposal System (JACADS) facility finished its mission in November 2000 after destroying nearly 7 percent of America's chemical weapons, including those previously based on Okinawa. (Secretary of Defense MRL Talking Paper, "Possible Alternate Location [Alaska] for RED HAT Munitions," 5/13/70; Adm. Flanagan, office memorandum to Warren Nutter, ASD (ISA), "Operation RED HAT," 5/13/70; AP, "U.S. to Start Moving War Gas on Okinawa to Atoll in January," *New York Times*, 12/5/70; "More Okinawa Turbulence Seen Despite Token Gas Removal," *Washington Post*, 1/14/71; Minutes, Senior Staff Meeting, "Operation RED HAT," 2/1/71; UPI, "U.S. Moving Okinawa Gas to Island in Mid-Pacific," *Washington Star*, 7/15/71.)

25. MRL, memorandum for Kissinger, 4/30/69; Kissinger, memorandum for MRL, "CBW Study," 5/9/69; Kissinger, "U.S. Policy on Chemical and Biological Warfare and Agents," NSSM 59, 5/28/69; MRL, memorandum for Warren Nutter, ASD (ISA), "NSSM 59," 8/6/69; "Laird Backs Senate Curb on Chemical War Agents," *New York Times*, 8/10/69; Minutes, Senior Staff Meeting, "Chemical Warfare/Biological Research," 8/11/69; MRL submission to NSC in response to NSSM 59, "Summary Report on Chemical Warfare Programs and Biological Research Programs," 10/8/69; Minutes, Senior Staff Meeting, "Chemical Warfare," 11/17/69.

26. "United States Policy on Chemical Warfare Program and Bacteriological/Biological Research Program," NSDM 35, 11/25/69; Transcript, "Remarks of the President on Announcing the Chemical and Biological Defense Policies and Programs," Roosevelt Room, White House, 11/25/69; *New York Times*, 11/26/69; "Joint Chiefs Lost Battle over Chemical Warfare," *Washington Star*, 11/27/69; Minutes, Senior Staff Meeting, "Chemical/Biological Warfare Resolution," 12/1/69; MRL, "Press Conference," Pentagon, 12/1/69.

27. Minutes, Senior Staff Meeting, "Okinawa," 11/3/69; MRL, memorandum for Kissinger, "Okinawa Reversion," 11/18/69.

28. "U.S. Says Japanese Bear Responsibility for Defense," *New York Times*, 8/24/70; "Japanese Seeking U.S. Nuclear Data," *New York Times*, 9/11/70.

29. Yasuhiro Nakasone, translated by Lesley Connors, *The Making of the New Japan: Reclaiming the Political Mainstream*, Curzon (1999), 26–41, 47–50.

30. Nakasone, *The Making*, 159.

31. Minutes, Senior Staff Meeting, "Visit of Japanese Director General for Defense Nakasone," 9/14/70; Transcript, MRL interview with *Asahi Shimbun*, 9/24/70; Minutes, Senior Staff Meeting, "Base Closure/Reduction Package," 11/16/70; UPI, "Japan Says U.S. Will Pull Out 15,000 of 40,000 GIs by June," *Washington Star*, 11/29/70; "U.S. Cutbacks Spur Move in Japan for Defense Buildup," *Washington Post*, 11/30/70; Minutes, Senior Staff Meeting, "Base Closures," 11/30/70; Nakasone, *The Making*, 159.

32. "Nakasone says Japan considered going nuclear," *Japan Economic Newswire*, 6/18/04; "Ex-Japanese Premier Once Challenged Japan's Non-Nuclear Taboo: Report," *Agence France Presse*, 6/18/04; "Japan Considered Developing Nukes: Nakasone," *Japan Times*, 6/19/04.

33. "Japan Won't Go Nuclear, Official Says," *Washington Post*, 10/12/71; *Asahai* News Service, "Ex-Prime Minister Nakasone Ok'd Nukes for Japan," 12/20/00.

34. "Japan Endorses Limited-Defense Concept," *Baltimore Sun*, 10/21/70; Reuter, "Japan's Military Forces Winning Public Approval," *New York Times*, 11/15/70; Reuter, "Japanese Defense Plan Doubles Expenditures," *Washington Post*, 4/28/71.

35. TerHorst and Albertazzie, *Flying White House*, 299–301.

36. Kissinger, *White House Years*, 729.

37. Henry Kissinger, interview, 1/10/01; Lawrence Eagleburger, interview, 2/7/01.

38. Yosuhiro Nakasone, interview, 10/9/01; Daniel Henkin, ASD, "News Release," 6/30/71; "Secretary Laird Arrives in Tokyo," *New York Times*, 7/5/71.

39. MRL, memorandum for the president, "Trip to Japan," 7/19/71.

40. Armistead I. Selden Jr., acting ASD, memorandum for MRL, "Summary Paper for the Record—Effect of Personal Rapport among MODs on Relations between US and Its Allies," 12/4/72; "Exemplary Envoy: Japanese Ambassador to U.S. Wins Friends, Helps Put Out Fires," *Wall Street Journal*, 1/2/85.

41. MRL, "Interview with Newsmen on Departing Japan," Tokyo, 7/11/71.

42. In September 1972 Sato's successor, Prime Minister Kakuei Tanaka, conducted summit talks in Peking at which it was agreed Japan and the PRC would establish diplomatic relations. ("Japan's Pro-U.S. Posture: Automatic No Longer," *Christian Science Monitor*, 7/30/71; "Japan:

Sato Role on China Assailed," *New York Times,* 10/27/71; William J. Baroody Jr., assistant to MRL, memorandum for MRL, "Far East Trip Report," 11/9/71.)

43. Minutes, Senior Staff Meeting, "South Asia," 5/24/71. Minutes, Senior Staff Meeting, "India/ Pakistan," 7/12/71. (The number of East Pakistan refugees would eventually peak at 9.5 million.)

44. Minutes quoted by columnist Jack Anderson, "U.S. Soviet Vessels in Bay of Bengal," *Washington Post,* 12/14/71.

45. Kissinger, *White House Years,* 900.

46. Minutes, Senior Staff Meeting, "India-Pakistan," 12/6/71.

47. J. Fred Buzhardt, memorandum for the secretary of defense, "Interim Report of Investigation of Recent Unauthorized Disclosure of Classified Material to Columnist Jack Anderson and the use of Unauthorized Communications Channels between the Nation Security Council Staff and the Office of the Joint Chiefs of Staff," 1/10/72.

48. Zumwalt, *On Watch,* 375–76.

34 / A FRIEND IN DEED

1. "Army Spied on 18,000 Civilians in 2-Year Operation," *New York Times,* 1/18/71.

2. MRL, "News Conference at the Pentagon," 12/28/70.

3. *Washington Monthly,* 1/70.

4. "Army Spy Shakeup Ordered," *Washington Post,* 12/24/70.

5. "Ex-Army Officer Says Unit Spied on Campuses in City," *New York Times,* 12/23/70.

6. "Ex-Agents Tell of Duplication and Competition in Army 'Watch' on Civilians," *New York Times,* 2/26/71; "Military Spying Overkill Described to Senate Panel," *Washington Post,* 2/26/71.

7. "Army Spied on Politicians, Ex-GI Says," *Washington Star,* 12/16/70; AP, "Ervin Says Army's Agents Spied on Illinois Politicians," *New York Times,* 12/17/70.

8. UPI, "Illinois Spying Denied by Army," *New York Times,* 12/18/70.

9. UPI, "Army Admits Snooping on Stevenson," *Washington News,* 3/3/71; "Senators Told Johnson Officials Began Army Check on Civilians," 3/3/71; "Army Admits Spying on Civilians," *Chicago Tribune,* 3/3/71.

10. MRL, memorandum for secretaries of the military departments, JCS chairman, directors of the defense agencies, "Department of Defense Intelligence and Counterintelligence," 12/23/70; minutes, Senior Staff Meeting, 12/28/70; "Laird Acts to Tighten Rule over Military Intelligence," *New York Times,* 12/24/70; "Army Spy Shakeup Ordered," *Washington Post,* 12/24/70.

11. "Laird Picks Panel to Curb American Spying on Civilians," *New York Times,* 2/19/71; AP, "Johnson Men Did Not Mean Army Spies to Cover Riots," *Baltimore Sun,* 2/20/71; "Ervin Views Army Spying as Illegal," *Washington Post,* 3/3/71; "Senators Told Johnson Officials Began Army Check on Civilians," *New York Times,* 3/3/71.

12. UPI, reporting on Laird's closed-door session the previous March 4, "Laird Parries Spy Blame," *Washington News,* 6/21/71.

13. Stanley Resor, interview, 10/30/01.

14. "Laird Backs Froehlke as Army Chief," *Washington Post,* 5/26/71.

15. *New York Times,* "New Civilian Chief . . . ," 6/16/71.

16. James Schlesinger, interview, 7/27/01.

17. "General-to-Be Is a Black Panther," *Washington Post,* 2/1/70 (the term "black panther" was a reference to an insignia he wore in Vietnam and Korea, not to the militant group); "Chappie James' Life Dedicated to Tenet 'Thou Shall Not Quit,' an American Success Story," *Washington Post,* 7/21/75; "Gen. Daniel (Chappie) James, Former NORAD Chief, Dies," *Washington Post,* 2/26/78; " 'Chappie' James, 1st Black 4-Star General, Dies," *Washington Star,* 2/26/78.

18. "U.S. to Abandon Wheelus by July," *Baltimore Sun,* 12/24/69; "Libyans Invite France to Wheelus," *Washington News,* 3/5/70; James R. McGovern, *Black Eagle: General Daniel "Chappie" James Jr.,* University of Alabama Press (1985), 109–116; J. Alfred Phelps, *Chappie: America's First Black Four-Star General,* Presidio (1991), 255–66; John McLucas and Lawrence Benson, *Confessions of a Technocrat,* unpublished manuscript autobiography.

19. UPI, "Pentagon Deputy," 2/3/70; AP, "Negro Pilot to Be PIO for Laird," *Washington Post,* 2/4/70; "Negro Gets Key Post at Pentagon," *Washington Star,* 2/4/70.

20. Phelps, *Chappie,* 277–8.

21. *Washington Post,* 7/21/75.

22. For quotes from James's speeches: McGovern, *Black Eagle,* 109–10, 269–78; Phelps, *Chappie,* 255–66, 279–88.

23. Alison Laird-Large, interview, 3/2/01; "Laird Opposes Club Race Bar," *Washington Post,* 12/21/68; "Laird Will Resign from Country Club," *Milwaukee Sentinel,* 12/21/68; "Laird Has Stayed Out of Club's Racial Rift," *Milwaukee Journal,* 12/23/68; "Rogers, Laird Quit Kenwood Country Club," *Washington Post,* 4/16/70.

24. Roger Kelley, interview, 7/27/01; MRL, "Address and Question-Answer Period," Fort Leavenworth, Kansas, 11/23/71.

25. MRL, "Press Conference," Pentagon, 11/17/71; MRL, interview on NBC-TV's *Today,* 11/30/72; minutes, Senior Staff Meeting, 12/4/72.

26. "Racial Climate Improving in Military," *Washington Star,* 6/15/71; Carl S. Wallace, special assistant, memorandum for Brig. James D. Hughes, USAF, military assistant to the president, "Information Regarding Accomplishments by the Department of Defense in the Area of Equal Opportunity During the Nixon Administration," 6/17/71.

27. "Richmond Man Selected as First Black Admiral," *Washington Post,* 4/28/71; "Blacks Named to Navy Posts," *Washington Star,* 4/29/71; "1st Black Admiral 'Won't Be the Last,'" *Chicago Tribune,* 4/29/71; "Rear Admiral, USN," *Christian Science Monitor,* 4/30/71.

28. UPI, "General," 4/19/72; UPI, "Black Generals," 7/27/72; "Black General Named to Command Ft. Carson," *Jet,* 9/21/72.

29. " 'Chappie' James, 1st Black 4-Star General, Dies," *Washington Star,* 2/26/78.

30. "Bias in Germany," *Parade,* 9/10/72.

31. AP, "James," 2/5/70; McGovern, *Black Eagle,* 133.

32. MRL, "Equal Opportunity within the Department of Defense," Department of Defense Directive #1100.15, 12/14/70; AP, "Anti-discrimination," 12/17/70; "Pentagon Widens Rules to Prevent Racial Inequities," *New York Times,* 12/18/70; minutes, Senior Staff meeting, "Equal Employment Opportunity," 12/21/70.

33. U.S. Civil Rights Commission, letter to MRL, 1/24/70; signed by Rev. Theodore M. Hesburgh, C.S.C., chairman; Stephen Horn, vice chairman; Frankie M. Freeman, Maurice B. Mitchell, Robert S. Rankin, and Manuel Ruiz, commissioners.

34. "Negroes an Issue in F-15 Contract; Air Force Prods Company to Comply on Hiring," *New York Times,* 1/31/70; "U.S. Pressing F-15 Contractor on Job Policy," *Washington Post,* 1/31/70; AP, "Laird Orders Close Checks on Job Bias by Contractors," *Washington Star,* 2/1/70.

35. Seamans, *Aiming at Targets,* 172; minutes, Senior Staff Meeting, "Equal Employment Opportunity and Contract Compliance," 2/9/70.

36. " 'I'll Bleed for Myself,' Says Black U.S. Soldier in Europe," *New York Times,* 10/11/70.

37. "Captain Shifted after Snub," *Washington Post,* 2/12/71; "7 Officers Said to Lost Posts in Rights Cases," *Washington Post,* 7/28/71; "Military Has Enforced Bias Rule, Aide Says," *Washington Star,* 7/29/71.

38. Secretary of the Navy John H. Chafee, memorandum for MRL, "Improved Communications with the Department of the Navy," 3/25/70; minutes, Senior Staff Meeting, "Minority Groups," 10/19/70; "200 Trainees at Ft. Dix Get Course in Race Relations," *New York Times,* 2/5/71; "Minorities Study Is Military 'Must' Now," *Chicago Tribune,* 3/3/71; "The Air Force Academy Blows Its Mind," *Ebony,* 3/72.

39. Roger Kelley, interview, 7/27/01; Frank Render, former assistant secretary of defense for civil rights, interview, 1/18/02; "Pentagon to Train 1,400 to Teach Race Relations," *Washington Star,* 3/5/71; Department of Defense news release, "Secretary of Defense Laird Establishes Equal Opportunity Education Program," 3/5/71; "Classes on Race Ordered for All in Armed Forces," *New York Times,* 3/6/71; "U.S. Struggles to Make Equality Work," *Washington Post,* 3/6/90.

40. David R. Segal, *Recruiting for Uncle Sam: Citizenship and Military Manpower Policy* (Modern War Series), University of Kansas Press (1992), 114.

41. Jeanne Holm, interview, 10/26/01.

42. Jerry Friedheim, interview, 7/19/00.

43. Jeanne Holm, interview, 10/26/01; Elizabeth P. Hoisington, interview, 10/28/01; Stan Resor, interview, 10/30/01; "First 2 Women Generals in U.S. Chosen by Nixon," *New York Times,* 5/16/70; MRL, memorandum for the president, "Making Greater Use of Women's Skills in High Level Positions," 6/6/71.

44. Jeanne Holm, interview, 10/26/01; AP, "Women's Rights," 3/31/70; AP, "Lady General," 1/22/73; UPI, "Lady General," 1/22/73; McLucas and Benson, *Confessions.*

45. Jerry Friedheim, interview, 7/19/00; Dick Capen, interview, 8/8/00; "Navy Set to Select a

Female Admiral," *Washington Post,* 3/23/72; minutes, Senior Staff Meeting, "DACOWITS," 4/10/72; "Woman Selected to Be 1st Admiral," *Washington Star,* 4/27/72; "First Woman Admiral: Alene Bertha Duerk," *New York Times,* 4/28/72; AP, "Navy Names First Woman Admiral," *Washington Post,* 4/28/72.

46. "Navy Would Put Gals Aboard Men o' War," *New York Daily News,* 8/9/72; Dan Henkin, memorandum to MRL, "New Items of Special Interest," 8/12/72.

47. During a June 1971 session of a special subcommittee of the Senate Government Operations Committee, Attorney General John Mitchell revealed the existence of this list.

48. Vera Glaser and Malvina Stephenson, "Secretary Laird's Future," *Washington Sunday Star,* 5/23/71.

49. In his book *A Better War* (296–8), Lewis Sorley noted that in one unit alone, the 173rd Airborne Brigade, "a study of about 1,000 men showed that 84 percent of drug users began use in the United States."

50. UPI, 3/24/70.

51. Department of Defense Drug Abuse Control Committee, "Fact Sheet," 1/5/70.

52. PBS, "Thirty Years of America's Drug War: A Chronology," *Frontline,* 2000.

53. MRL, memorandum for the president, "DoD Drug Abuse Control Program," 5/12/72.

54. PBS, "Thirty Years," *Frontline.*

55. Richard Nixon, memorandum for the secretary of defense, "Increased DoD Support for International Narcotics Control," 5/3/72.

35 / WITHDRAWAL SYMPTOMS

1. President Nixon was walking and waving, when about seventy-five of the marines came out of the bleachers and put him on their shoulders. He was carried for about fifteen yards before the Secret Service stepped in and forced them to let the president down, according to a Camp Pendleton spokesperson. ("Did Nixon Get a Ride on Marine Shoulders?" *Washington Star,* 5/2/71.)

2. MRL, "Press Conference," Fort Campbell, Ky., 9/2/71.

3. Adm. T.H. Moorer, chairman, JCS, memorandum for MRL, "U.S. Redeployments from Southeast Asia," 4/27/71.

4. MRL, "Address before the Rotary Club of Phoenix, Arizona," 2/12/71; minutes, Senior Staff Meeting, 11/29/71; minutes, Senior Staff Meeting, 12/27/71.

5. MRL, "Press Conference," Pentagon, 9/1/71.

6. Gen. William C. Westmoreland, acting chairman, JCS, memorandum for MRL, "RVNAF Improvement and Modernization Program," 4/6/71.

7. Hammond, *Military and the Media,* 503.

8. MRL, memorandum for Kissinger, "Your Memorandum of April 28, 1971," 5/4/71.

9. Minutes, Senior Staff Meeting, 11/29/71.

10. Kissinger, memorandum for MRL, "Air Activities over Southeast Asia: FY 1972 and FY 1973," 8/6/71.

11. Phil Odeen, ISA, "Vietnamization Meeting with Secretary Laird," 8/18/71.

12. This memo was referred to in the minutes of a Vietnam Task Force meeting. (Phil Odeen, ISA, memorandum for the record, "Vietnamization Meeting with Secretary Laird," 8/26/71.)

13. Minutes, Senior Staff Meeting, 5/3/71.

14. MRL, memorandum for the president, "Protective Reaction Strikes in North Vietnam," 2/26/71, with attachment: Adm. T.H. Moorer, chairman, JCS, "Protective Reaction Strikes in North Vietnam," 2/25/71.

15. MRL, memorandum for chairman, JCS, "Protective Reaction Strikes against North Vietnam," 3/6/71.

16. Adm. T.H. Moorer, chairman, JCS, memorandum for MRL, "Protective Reaction Strikes Against North Vietnam," 3/19/71.

17. Phil Odeen, ISA, memorandum for the record, "Vietnamization Meeting with Secretary Laird," 7/23/71.

18. MRL, memorandum for the chairman, JCS, "Request for Strikes," 10/21/71; Gen. John D. Ryan, acting chairman, JCS, memorandum for MRL, "Air Strikes against North Vietnam Air Defenses," 11/13/71; MRL, memorandum for the chairman, JCS, "Air Strikes against North Vietnam Air Defenses," 11/15/71; Adm. T.H. Moorer, chairman, JCS, memorandum for MRL, "Operations against Targets in North Vietnam," 11/30/71.

19. Adm. T.H. Moorer, chairman, JCS, cable to Gen. Holloway and Adm. John McCain, "Arc Light".

20. Adm. E.R. Zumwalt Jr., acting chairman, JCS, memorandum for the Deputy Secretary of Defense David Packard, "Reaction to MIG Activity——3 December 1971," 12/4/71.

21. MRL, memorandum for the president, "Air Strikes against North Vietnam," 12/9/71.

22. Adm. T.H. Moorer, chairman, JCS, cable to Adm. John McCain, "Proud Deep/Hai Cang Tudo II," 12/19/71.

23. UPI, "Christmas Truce Ends in Vietnam," *Baltimore Sun*, 12/27/71.

24. MRL, memorandum for the president, "Trip to Paris, Bangkok, South Vietnam, and CINCPAC, January 5–15, 1971," 1/16/71.

25. Hersh, *Price of Power*, 432–433.

26. Minutes, Senior Staff Meeting, 6/7/71.

27. Minutes, Senior Staff Meeting, 6/21/71, 7/12/71.

28. Phil Odeen, International Security Affairs, memorandum for the record, "Vietnamization Meeting with Secretary Laird," 7/30/71.

29. Phil Odeen, International Security Affairs, memorandum for the record, "Vietnamization Meeting with Secretary Laird," 8/10/71. In a private meeting later that day with Bunker, Laird additionally expressed discouragement over the one-sided campaign. He noted that the United States could give help to South Vietnam but could not give its people the will to save their democracy. (Memorandum of conversation between MRL and Amb. Ellsworth Bunker, U.S. Embassy Saigon, 8/10/71, as cited in Hammond, *Military and the Media*, 521.)

30. Frank Snepp, *Decent Interval: An Insider's Account of Saigon's Indecent End Told by the CIA's Chief Strategy Analyst in Vietnam*, Vintage Books (1978), 11.

31. Minutes, Senior Staff Meeting, 8/23/71.

32. Phil Odeen, memoranda for the record, "Vietnamization Meeting with Secretary Laird," 8/24/71, 8/26/71.

33. Phil Odeen, memorandum for the record, "Vietnamization Meeting with Secretary Laird," 9/10/71.

34. Minutes, Senior Staff Meeting, 10/4/71; "Thieu Gets 95% as 87% vote," *Washington Star*, 10/4/71.

35. "Laird Takes Self Out of Race for Office in 1972," *Stevens Point Daily Journal*, 10/19/71.

36. Phil Odeen, minutes, "Vietnamization Meeting with Secretary Laird," 10/13/71.

37. Minutes, Senior Staff Meeting, 6/21/71.

38. MRL, memorandum for chairman, JCS, "RVNAF Leadership," 6/23/71.

39. MRL, memorandum for the president, "Trip to Vietnam, November 2–8, 1971," 11/8/71.

40. Minutes, Senior Staff Meeting, 9/7/71.

41. Minutes, Senior Staff Meeting, 11/8/71.

42. Saigon police said McGovern was unwittingly meeting with Viet Cong agents, who were mingling with the South Vietnamese antiwar leaders at the school building. (Phil Odeen, memorandum for the record, "Vietnamization Meeting with Secretary Laird," 9/14/71; "McGovern Rescued after Saigon Riot," *New York Times*, 9/15/71.)

43. Phil Odeen, memoranda for the record, "Vietnamization Meeting with Secretary Laird," 10/5, 10/7/71.

44. Phil Odeen, memorandum for the record, "Vietnamization Meeting with Secretary Laird," 10/14/71.

45. MRL, memorandum for the chairman, JCS, "U.S. Force Planning, Southeast Asia," 8/26/71.

46. MRL, memorandum for the president, "Trip to Vietnam, November 2–8, 1971," 11/8/71.

47. MRL, "Memorandum of Conversation of November 5, 1971," President Thieu and Secretary of Defense Laird.

48. Sorley, *A Better War*, 282.

49. MRL, memorandum for the president, 11/8/71.

50. Transcript, NBC's *Meet the Press*, 11/14/71.

51. Adm. T.H. Moorer, chairman, JCS, memorandum for MRL, "U.S. Redeployments from the RVN," 12/30/71.

52. Minutes, Senior Staff Meeting, 12/13/71.

53. MRL and David Packard, "News Conference at Pentagon," 11:30 A.M., 12/13/71.

54. Sorley, *A Better War*, 282.

36 / DRAFTING THE VOLUNTEER ARMY

1. George Dalferes, interview, 7/19/00; "The Last Tyrant," *National Journal*, 1/19/80.

2. *Congressional Quarterly*, "For Better or Worse, Laird Left His Mark," *Los Angeles Times*, 12/10/72.

3. "News Items of Special Interest," 2/23/71.

4. Ralph Pomeroy Witherspoon, "The Military Draft and the All-Volunteer Force: A Case Study of a Shift in Public Policy," doctoral dissertation, 391–3, 4/93.

5. John Chafee, interview, 10/22/99; Milton Friedman, interview, 5/7/02; Witherspoon dissertation, 358–60; Milton and Rose D. Friedman, *Two Lucky People*, University of Chicago Press (1998), 380.

6. Stan Resor, interview, 10/30/01; Curtis Tarr, interview, 3/13/02; Tarr journal, 1/9/70; Tarr, *By the Numbers*, 4.

7. "How Much for a Volunteer Army?" *New York Times*, 1/4/70; "Nixon Panel Asks Volunteer Army by Middle of '71," *New York Times*, 2/22/70; "1971 End to Draft Is Urged," *Washington Post*, 2/23/70; "Panel Says Draft Could End in 1971," *Washington Star*, 2/23/70; Witherspoon dissertation, 360–5.

8. Minutes, Senior Staff Meeting, "Draft/All Volunteer Armed Force," 3/9/70; MRL, memorandum for the president, "Future of the Draft," 3/11/70; minutes, Senior Staff Meeting, "Zero Draft Call," 3/16/70.

9. Minutes, Senior Staff Meeting, "Draft" and "Draft Revisited," 8/10/70.

10. Colin Powell, interview, 12/18/01.

11. Martin Anderson, 5/6/02; Witherspoon dissertation, 385–6.

12. MRL, memorandum for secretaries of the military departments, and chairman, JCS, "Zero Draft Calls by July 1, 1973," 10/12/70.

13. Minutes, Senior Staff Meeting, "Zero Draft Calls," 10/12/70.

14. MRL, "News Briefing by MRL at Pentagon," 11:30 A.M., 10/12/70; "Laird Sets Mid-1973 Goal to End Draft," *Washington Post*, 10/13/70.

15. James Schlesinger, interview, 7/27/01; Roger Kelley, interview, 7/72/01; Alexander Haig, interview, 1/21/02; Robert Pursley, interview, 1/21/02; Tarr journal, 11/18/70.

16. Robert K. Griffith Jr., Ph.D., U.S. Army Center of Military History, unpublished paper, "Moving Mountains: The Army and the Transition from the Draft to the All Volunteer Force; A Preliminary Historical Inquiry," 6/83.

17. Bernard W. Rogers, interview, 1/22/05; David R. Hughes, interview, 1/22/05; also, by permission, Rogers's unpublished memoir chapter 18, *Ft. Carson, Colorado, 1969–1970*, hereafter, Rogers manuscript.

18. Jack Mills, interview, 6/2/00; Paul Martin, Fort Carson historian, interview, 7/25/01; Bernard Rogers, interview, 1/22/05; David Hughes, interview, 1/22/05; see also, *Red Diamond Brand and Mountaineer* (Fort Carson post newspaper) articles, "Secretary Laird Here Today," 10/3/69, and "Defense Secretary Laird Finds Carson Outstanding," 10/10/69.

19. UPI, "Pentagon to Allow Protest in Services," *New York Times*, 9/16/69; UPI, "Allow Protests within Limits, Military Told," *Washington Post*, 9/16/69; AP, "Laird Releases Guide about Post Protest Activity," *Baltimore Sun*, 9/16/69; UPI, "Politics," 10/1/69.

20. Bernard Rogers, interview, 1/22/05.

21. David Hughes, interview, 1/22/05.

22. "Humanizing the U.S. Military," *Time*, 12/21/70.

23. Bernard Rogers, interview, 1/22/05; Rogers manuscript.

24. Zumwalt, *On Watch*, 182–196.

25. Samuel Zaffiri, *Westmoreland: A Biography of General William C. Westmoreland*, William Morrow and Company (1994), 350–1.

26. Tarr journal, 1/7/71; "The Dump-the-Draft Talk Is Double-Talk," *Look*, 2/23/71.

27. "Draft Halts as Congress Snags on Bill," *Washington Post*, 7/1/71; "Tarr Keeps Draft Going," *Baltimore Sun*, 7/2/71; "Draft Lottery Is Scheduled for Aug. 5 as Deadlock in Congress Is Maintained on Extension of the Law," *New York Times*, 7/21/71; UPI, "Laird Fears Harm from Draft Delay," *New York Times*, 7/23/71; also, minutes, Senior Staff Meeting, "Legislative Affairs," 7/6, 7/12, 7/19/71.

28. MRL, "Memorandum for Correspondents Regarding Secretary of Defense Views on Draft Legislation," 9/14/71, "Laird Runs Lobby Blitz on Draft," *Washington Star*, 9/14/71; "Stennis Warns of a Crisis if Draft Bill Isn't Passed," *New York Times*, 9/15/71; "Draft Act Battle Shaping Up,"

Washington Post, 9/15/71; "Pentagon Presses Drive to Save the Draft," *Baltimore Sun*, 9/15/71; "Laird Plans Big Push on Draft Bill," *Chicago Tribune*, 9/15/71; "Pentagon Brass Comes to the Aid of Draft Bill," *Washington Star*, 9/15/71.

29. "Service Chiefs Press Senators for Draft," *New York Times*, 9/16/71; "Laird Says Draft Delay Signals U.S. Weakness," *Washington News*, 9/16/71; transcript of Nixon news conference published in *New York Times*, 9/17/71; "Antidraft Coalition in Senate Is Broken by Nixon Pressure," *New York Times*, 9/17/71; "Nixon Pay Pledge Revives Draft Bill," *Washington Post*, 9/17/71; AP, "Vermont Gets New Senator in Draft Fight," *Washington Post*, 9/17/71; "Senate Rejects a Delay on Draft by 47-to-36 Vote," *New York Times*, 9/18/71; "Draft Bill Survives in Senate," *Washington Post*, 9/18/71; "Doubts on Ending Draft," *Washington Post*, 9/18/71; "Senate Approves Draft Bill, 55–30; President to Sign," *New York Times*, 9/22/71; "Senate Votes Cloture, Passes Draft Measure," *Washington Post*, 9/22/71; "Nixon May Delay Military Raises," *New York Times*, 9/23/71; "President Signs Draft Extension, Delays Pay Increase for Military," *Washington Post*, 9/29/71.

30. AP, "Army Pay Forces Thousands onto Welfare," *Detroit News*, 10/13/69; Jack Anderson, *Parade*, 9/7/69; MRL, memorandum for the president, "Civilian and Military Pay Increases in 1970 and 1971," 12/11/69; "Thousands of Military on Relief," *Air Force Times*, 2/4/70; AP, "Service Families on Welfare Lists," *New York Times*, 2/7/70.

31. "House Unit Votes a Sharp Pay Rise for Servicemen," *New York Times*, 3/23/71; "Senate Votes $2.7 Billion GI Pay Boost," *Washington Post*, 6/9/71; MRL appearance on *Issues and Answers*, 1/30/72; MRL "Press Conference," Milwaukee, Wis., 3/23/72; MRL, interview with newsmen before address to National Association of Supervisors, Pensacola, Fla., 10/13/72; Robert C. Moot, ASD (Comptroller), memorandum for the secretary of defense, "Taking Stock: Financial Management," 12/12/72.

32. UPI, "Porpoise Ready to Fight for Navy," *Chicago Tribune*, 11/11/71.

37 / CARDINAL VIRTUES

1. Pres. Gerald R. Ford, speech at dedication of Laird Center, Marshfield, Wis., 9/12/97.

2. McNamara was secretary of defense for eighty-five months. The closest to his "record" was Ronald Reagan's defense secretary, Caspar Weinberger, who held the position for eighty-two months.

3. MRL, "Press Conference," Milwaukee, Wis., 3/23/72.

4. MRL, "Remarks and Question-Answer Session at TV Correspondents' Breakfast," Harvard Club, New York City, 4/26/72.

5. Dr. Alfred Goldberg, chief historian for the Office of the Secretary of Defense, agreed: "If McNamara had left in 1965, he would have been hailed as probably the most effective secretary of defense we had. If [Caspar] Weinberger had left several years earlier, he would have left with a better reputation. They overstayed." (Goldberg, interview, 10/19/99.)

6. MRL, "Interview with Hugh Downs on *Irving Kupcinet Show*," Chicago, Ill., 3/24/72.

7. Hearings before the Committee on Armed Services, U.S. Senate, "Fiscal Year 1973 Authorization for Military Procurement, Research and Development, Construction Authorization for the Safeguard ABM, and Active Duty and Selected Reserve Strengths," 2/15/72.

8. *Los Angeles Times*, 2/20/72.

9. Donald Rumsfeld, interview, 2/28/01.

10. Jerry Friedheim, interview, 7/19/00.

11. Pres. Richard Nixon, letter to Melvin Laird, 11/17/72.

12. Although the incident was vivid in Laird's memory, there is no independent confirmation of it. It was not recounted in Ginsberg's voluminous writings, nor in biographies on him. "That sounds like something Allen might have done," laughed the late poet's step-brother Harold Collen. "I really don't remember this particular incident. But knowing Allen, he could easily have peed on Melvin Laird's doorstep and followed it up with a defecation." Neither Collen, nor Ginsberg's most noted biographer, Michael Shumacher, nor Peter Hale of the Ginsberg Trust, could confirm the specific incident. On the other hand, they could not absolutely say that Ginsberg had *not* done it—especially if that's the way Laird remembered it. "Allen did a lot of things and it may just very well have gotten lost in all the other madness that was going on at the time," Collen added. (Harold Collen, interview, 8/31/01; Michael Shumacher, interview, 8/31/01; Peter Hale, interview, 8/31/01.)

13. John Laird, interview, 2/27/01.

14. David Laird, interview, 2/27/01; David Laird, speech in Marshfield, Wis., 9/12/97.

15. MRL at TV Correspondents' Breakfast, New York City, 4/26/72.

16. Minutes, Senior Staff Meeting, 12/13/71.

17. MRL, memorandum for the president, "Appointment of a Deputy Secretary of Defense," 1/6/72.

18. Laird recalled that Sen. John Tower, R-Texas, an influential member of the Senate Armed Services Committee, heavily pressured him to take Clements, too, and was quite disappointed when Laird discounted his candidate.

19. MRL, memorandum for the president, "U.S. Force Levels in the Republic of Vietnam," 1/11/72.

20. MRL, "Press Conference at the White House, following Announcement by President of Further Withdrawal of U.S. Troops from Vietnam," 1/13/72.

21. Minutes, Senior Staff Meeting, 1/17/72.

22. MRL, memorandum for Kissinger, "The Current Situation in SVN," 1/26/72.

23. Minutes, Senior Staff Meeting, 3/6/72.

24. On January 24, General Abrams had cabled his superiors that North Vietnamese prisoner interrogations had fixed on January 27 as the "kick-off date" for the invasion. At the March 13 Senior Staff Meeting, Admiral Moorer reported that General Abrams had "agent informants" who maintained that "enemy attacks had been scheduled for 20 and 21 February." After the invasion, in a 4/15 *New York Times* article, "U.S. Says Papers Show Enemy Planned a Trap," it was revealed that U.S. intelligence had two key top-level enemy directives to senior North Vietnamese officers dated as far back as the previous December that called for an early February launch date. Except for the date, the directives outlined an offensive that closely resembled the one that began, finally, on March 30.

25. Kissinger, "Additional Authorities for Southeast Asia," NSDM 149, 2/4/72.

26. Adm. T. H. Moorer, chairman, JCS, memorandum for MRL, "Urgent Request for Air Authorities," 3/9/72.

27. MRL, memorandum for the president, "Request for Operating Authorities to Counter the North Vietnamese Threat," 3/14/72.

28. Pres. Richard Nixon, memorandum for MRL, 3/18/72.

29. This timing was noted by Air Force Secretary Robert Seamans at the 6/12/72 Senior Staff Meeting.

30. MRL, memorandum for the record about the 3/27 meeting, dated 5/15/72.

31. Robert Pursley, interview, 11/28/00.

32. Ivan Selin, interview, 2/19/01.

33. MRL, memorandum for the chairman, JCS, "Rules of Engagement and 1968 Bombing Halt Understandings," 3/28/72.

34. MRL, memorandum for the chairman, JCS, "Command of Air Elements in Southeast Asia," 3/30/72.

35. Whether Congress was informed in a timely manner and adequately about the Lavelle "irregularities" became a minor controversy. General Ryan testified in June that he had recommended that he brief Congress about the episode, but Laird had turned him down. What Ryan didn't know was that Laird had already privately briefed Sens. Stuart Symington and Clifford P. Case. Laird informed the relevant committee chairs about the Lavelle matter over the following week. (Secretary of defense schedule for 4/6/72; "Hill Groups Got Private Briefing on Lavelle Raids," *Washington Star,* 9/26/72; MRL, "Interview on CBS Program *Capitol Cloakroom,*" 9/27/72.)

36. "Air Force Relieved Its Vietnam Chief for 'Irregularities,'" *New York Times,* 5/17/72.

37. The House Armed Services Committee chair, Rep. Edward Hebert, said in a 12/18/72 telephone interview with AP: "Lavelle fought the kind of war I was saying should be fought six years ago."

38. MRL, *Face the Nation,* 10/8/72.

39. *Capitol Cloakroom,* 9/27/72; MRL, "Interview with Newsmen before Remarks to Civic Clubs," Oklahoma City, Okla., 9/27/72; *Face the Nation,* 10/8/72.

40. MRL, letter to Sen. Stennis, 10/18/72; "Laird Tells of Moves to Bar Disobedient Military Acts," *New York Times,* 10/20/72.

38 / EASTER OFFENSIVE

1. "8 Bases near DMZ Heavily Attacked by North Vietnam," *New York Times*, 3/31/72; "Saigon's Forces Said to Abandon 6 Bases near DMZ," *New York Times*, 4/1/72; Adm. Thomas Moorer, Chairman, JCS, memorandum for MRL, "Daily Report, Enemy Land Campaign," 4/1/72; Sorley, *A Better War*, 321–2.

2. MRL, memorandum to chairman, JCS, 5/24/72.

3. Minutes, Senior Staff Meeting, 4/3/72.

4. MRL, "News Conference at Pentagon," 11 A.M., 4/7/72; "Laird Says Peace Rests with Soviet," *Washington Star*, 4/7/72; "Pull Out, Negotiate, Laird Warns Hanoi," *Washington Post*, 4/8/72; "Laird Adamant on Terms for Bombing Halt," *Baltimore Sun*, 4/8/72; "Nixon Maintains Silence," *New York Times*, 4/8/72; "Key Biscayne Calmly Views Viet Offensive," *Washington Post*, 4/8/72; "Laird's Frontal Attack," *Washington Post*, 4/8/72; "Nixon Indirectly Criticizes Soviet Arms Aid to Hanoi," *New York Times*, 4/11/72.

5. Pres. Richard Nixon, memorandum for MRL (and Secretary of State William Rogers), 4/15/72.

6. U.S. Senate, hearings before the Committee on Foreign Relations, "Foreign Assistance Act of 1972," 110–112, 114, 117–118, 4/18/72.

7. "Pentagon Official: On the Side of Restraint in Vietnam, an Aide Says," *New York Times*, 4/18/72.

8. MRL, memorandum for Kissinger, 4/21/72; Kissinger, memorandum for MRL, 4/28/72.

9. Kissinger, memorandum for MRL, 4/28/72.

10. Messages for CINCPAC (Adm. John McCain) from COMUSMACV (Gen. Creighton Abrams), "Redeployment of US Forces from the RVN," 4/16, 4/21/72.

11. MRL, memorandum to the president, "US Force Redeployments from SVN," 4/21/72; MRL, "US Force Deployments from SVN," 4/24/72.

12. The Abrams cable was quoted in MRL, memorandum for the president, "Personal Assessment of the Situation in RVN as of 26 April 1972," 4/26/72.

13. "U.S. Rushes Tank-Killer to Vietnam," *Washington Post*, 5/2/72; UPI, 5/5/72; Minutes, Senior Staff Meeting, 5/30/72; "U.S. Copter Aces 'Kill' Red Tanks with Missiles," *Chicago Tribune*, 6/5/72; Sorley, *A Better War*, 334–5.

14. Minutes, Senior Staff Meeting, 2/22/72.

15. Minutes, Senior Staff Meeting, "John Paul Vann," 6/12/72.

16. "America's Civilian Warrior in an Era of Vietnamization," *Washington Post*, 6/8/72; "Career Approached Legend," *New York Times*, 6/10/72; Neil Sheehan, *A Bright Shining Lie: John Paul Vann and America in Vietnam*, Random House (1988), 4–5, 7–33, 735–6, 739, 759 and 785–9; "Burial of the 'American Century,'" *Boston Globe*, 10/3/88; "The Soldier who Loved Reporters," *Los Angeles Times*, 10/9/88; "Trapped by Vietnam," *Los Angeles Times*, 10/12/88; "A Doomed Man and His War," *Newsday*, 10/17/88.

17. Minutes, Senior Staff Meeting, "General Westmoreland's Trip to the Far East," 2/22/72.

18. Phil Odeen, International Security Affairs, memoranda for the record, "Vietnamization Meeting(s) with Secretary Laird," 8/6, 8/10/71.

19. Quoted by MRL, memorandum for the president, "Personal Assessment of the Situation in RVN as of 1 May 1972," 5/1/72; "Saigon Weak in Military Leaders," *Christian Science Monitor*, 5/3/72; Sorley, *Thunderbolt*, 323.

20. "S. Vietnam Deserters Warned: 'Shoot on Sight' orders," *Washington News*, 5/4/72; minutes, Senior Staff Meeting, 5/8/72; Shillito, quoted by MRL, memorandum for the president, "Second Interim Report from Barry Shillito," 5/8/72; "The Commander in Hue: Ngo Quang Truong," *New York Times*, 5/9/72; Shillito, quoted by MRL, memorandum for the president, "Fourth Interim Report from Barry Shillito," 5/9/72; Sorley, *A Better War*, 331–3.

21. MRL, "News Conference," 5/10/72.

22. MRL statements and press releases, 6/14, 7/30, 8/21, 8/25, 9/8, 9/10/65. He continued to make similar pro-mining statements from 1966 to 1968.

23. MRL, memorandum for Kissinger, "Contingency Plans for Operations against North Vietnam," 4/6/72; Kissinger, *White House Years*, 1116; Jeffrey Kimball, *Nixon's Vietnam War*, University Press of Kansas (1998), 303.

24. U.S. Senate, hearings before the Committee on Foreign Relations, 158, 4/18/72; "Commanders Pick Targets: New Policy on Viet Bombing," *Washington Star*, 4/19/72; "U.S. Loads Blockade Explosives," *Washington Post*, 4/21/72.

25. "President Took Nearly a Week to Reach His Vietnam Decision," *New York Times*, 5/10/72; Zumwalt, *On Watch*, 384–7; Kissinger, *White House Years*, 1174–84; Haldeman, *Haldeman Diaries*, 453–6; Kimball, *Nixon's Vietnam War*, 314–15.

26. Kissinger, *White House Years*, 1180–5.

27. Safire, *Before the Fall*, 506; Kissinger, *White House Years*, 1185.

28. Safire, *Before the Fall*, 422–7.

29. Cdr. B. B. Traweek, USN, fact sheet (for MRL), "Mining of Haiphong Harbor," 11/28/72; Sorley, *A Better War*, 327.

30. Sorley, *Thunderbolt*, 324–5.

39 / THE VIEW FROM MAGGIE'S FARM

1. Bill Ayers, *Fugitive Days*, Beacon Press (2001), 223–4.

2. "Bomb Explodes inside Pentagon," *Washington Post*, 5/19/72; "Ho Chi Minh's Birthday Marked in Pentagon by Bomb," *ABC News*, 5/19/72; "Bombing Fails to Disrupt Pentagon," *Washington Post*, 5/20/72; "The Pentagon: Huge Building Is No Fortress," *Washington Post*, 5/20/72; "March Organizers Deny Knowledge of Pentagon Bombing," *Washington Post*, 5/20/72; "Who Are Weather People?—Ask FBI," *Washington Post*, 5/20/72; UPI, "F.B.I. Scanning Fingerprints for Clues to Pentagon Blast," *New York Times*, 5/21/72; "Protest: Blast at the Pentagon," *Newsweek*, 5/22/72.

3. "News Items of Special Interest," 5/19/71; minutes, Senior Staff Meeting, 5/22/72.

4. As Ayers went out on his ill-timed book tour after 9/11, he attempted to distance his former Weatherman revolutionary views from al Qaida rhetoric: "We weren't terrorists. The reason we weren't terrorists is because we did not commit random acts of terror against people. Terrorism was what was being practiced in the countryside of Vietnam by the United States." ("No Regrets for a Love of Explosives," *New York Times*, E-1, Arts, 9/11/01; "Radical on the Run," *Chicago Tribune*, 8/26/01; John Podhoretz, "A Reckoning for the Noisemakers," *New York Post*, 9/13/01; "The Calm after the Storm," *Chicago Tribune*, 9/16/01; AP, "Anti-War Radical Tells Story of Turbulent Times, Life as a Fugitive," 9/28/01; "The Left's Self-destructive Extremism," *The Chronicle of Higher Education*, 10/12/01; "Looking for Mr. Goodbomb," *The Nation*, 10/15/01; "The Academic al-Qaida; Hypocrites Hiding behind the Constitution," *Providence Journal*, 10/27/01; "Ex-Radicals on Faculty Rile Alumni, Professors," *Chicago Tribune*, 11/4/01; "Northwestern Alumni to End Donations if Ex-Radical Stays," *New York Times*, 11/4/01; "Enemy Within: Author Is Simply an American bin Laden," *Columbus Dispatch*, 11/12/01; "Author Defends Actions of 1960s Radical Group," *Daily Northwestern*, 11/16/01; "Former Radicals, Now Professors, Draw Ire of Alumni at 2 Universities," *The Chronicle of Higher Education*, 11/16/01; "No Regrets," *Commentary*.

5. "Laird May Aid Nixon Drive," *Washington Star*, 3/4/72.

6. AP, "Laird Climbs Off Perch," *Marshfield News Herald*, 1/14/72; Nixon, *Memoirs*, 513.

7. Rady Johnson, 8/22/00; "South Viet Pilots Fly 90 Pct. of Combat Missions, Laird Says," *Chicago Tribune*, 2/12/72; "Never Crawl to Negotiating Table—Laird" and "Laird Slips by Hecklers," *The Pantagraph*, Bloomington-Normal, Ill., 3/3/72.

8. George McGovern, interview, 3/5/03; "McGovern Offers a Plan to Cut Defense Outlays," *New York Times*, 1/20/72; "McGovern Asks Defense Cut of $33 Billion over 3 Years," *Washington Post*, 1/20/72.

9. UPI, 4/13/72; "Round 1: HHH Hits McGovern on Defense," *Washington Post*, 5/29/72; George McGovern, *Grassroots: The Autobiography of George McGovern*, Random House (1977), 184–5.

10. Minutes, Senior Staff Meeting, "Legislative Affairs," 5/30/72; AP, "Military Says McGovern Is in Error," *Washington Post*, 6/1/72.

11. U.S. Senate, hearings before a subcommittee of the Committee on Appropriations, "Foreign Assistance and Related Programs Appropriations for Fiscal Year 1973," 858–9, 898–901, 914, 6/5/72; "Laird Projects Big Rise in Cost of Vietnam War," *New York Times*, 6/6/72.

12. "Democrats Attacked on U.S. Spending: Laird Assails McGovern Cuts," *Washington Post*, 7/7/72; "McGovern Budget Called a Threat to U.S. by Laird," *New York Times*, 7/7/72; Stubbing with Mendel, *Defense Game*, (1986), 308; Ambrose, *Triumph of a Politician*, 581.

13. George McGovern, interview, 3/5/03; "McGovern Adopts Less Rigid Defense Plan but Still Specifies $30 Billion Opending Cut," *Wall Street Journal*, 9/22/72.

14. Herb Klein, interview, 7/30/01.

15. National Archives, White House tape, 9:44 to 10:40 A.M., 8/3/72; as transcribed by Stanley I. Kutler, *Abuse of Power,* Touchstone (1997), 113.

16. Tom Knock, McGovern biographer, interview, 3/3/03; Laurie Langland, McGovern Project archivist, Dakota Wesleyan University, interview, 3/3/03; George McGovern, interview, 3/5/03. UPI, 6/16/72; "M'Govern Defends His Service Record," *New York Times,* 6/17/72; "McGovern No Coward, Crew of Bomber Says," *Washington Post,* 6/17/72; Stephen E. Ambrose, *The Wild Blue: The Men and Boys Who Flew the B-24s over Germany,* Simon & Schuster (2001).

17. Adm. T. H. Moorer, chairman, JCS, memorandum to MRL, 6/21/72.

18. MRL, memorandum for the president, "Redeployments from SVN," 6/23/72.

19. Milton Friedman, University of Chicago, letter to MRL, 12/15/68; "War Is No Longer Business of Citizens," *Baltimore Sun,* 4/4/99.

20. MRL, memorandum for the president, "Volunteer Force in Vietnam," 2/8/70.

21. MRL, memorandum for the president, "Assignment of Draftees to Duty in Vietnam," 8/21/70.

22. MRL, memorandum for Kissinger, "An All-Volunteer/No Draftee Force in Vietnam," 5/6/71; Adm. T. H. Moorer, chairman, Joint Chiefs of Staff, memorandum for MRL, "All-Volunteer Force for Vietnam," 5/31/71.

23. "Pentagon Seems to Shelve Plan to Keep Draftees out of Vietnam," *Baltimore Sun,* 10/24/71; MRL, memorandum for Kissinger, "An All-Volunteer/No Draftee Force in Vietnam," 10/29/71; "Draftee Duty in Vietnam Falling Off," *Washington Post,* 1/10/72; Kenneth E. BeLieu, acting secretary of the army, memorandum for MRL, "All-Volunteer Force for Vietnam," 1/13/72; Robert F. Froehlke, secretary of the army, memorandum for MRL, "Draftees for Vietnam," 3/27/72; MRL, memorandum for the president, "Evaluation of a Policy to Stop Sending Draftees to Vietnam," 4/25/72; Kissinger, memorandum for MRL, "No Draftees to Vietnam," 5/10/72.

24. MRL, memorandum for the president, "US Force Redeployments from SVN," 6/23/72.

25. "Hanoi's Red River Dikes Called Underpinning of Nation's Life," *Washington Post,* 7/11/72; "Dikes in Hanoi Area Represent 2,000-Year Fight to Stem Floods," *New York Times,* 7/14/72; Reuter, "Dikes," 7/15/72.

26. Minutes, Senior Staff Meetings, 9/7, 9/27, 10/18, 11/1/71, as well as 8/21/72.

27. The DIA study was included as an attachment to a 7/3/72 memorandum from the chairman of the Joint Chiefs to Laird.

28. "News Items of Special Interest," 6/24/72; minutes, Senior Staff Meeting, 6/26/72; "Bombing Dikes Is Denied," *Baltimore Sun,* 6/27/72; "French Newsman and U.S. Differ on Bombing of Dikes," *New York Times,* 7/13/72.

29. MRL, "News Conference at the Pentagon," 7/6/72.

30. "Dikes Hit, Waldheim Says; Rogers Quickly Denies It," *New York Times,* 7/25/72; "U.N. Chief Says U.S. Hits Dikes," *Washington Post,* 7/25/72; "News Items of Special Interest," 7/25/72.

31. "U.S. Issues Report to Rebut Charges on Dike Bombings," *New York Times,* 7/29/72; "U.S. Admits 12 Areas Hit in North Vietnam's Dikes," *Washington Post,* 7/29/72.

32. Minutes, Senior Staff Meeting, "Alleged Bombing of Dikes and Dams in North Vietnam," 7/31/72; MRL, memorandum for the president, "Targeting in North Vietnam," 7/31/72.

33. "News Items of Special Interest," 8/1/72.

34. Jane Fonda, 2/16/98; Reuter, "Indochina-Fonda," 7/8/72; "News Items of Special Interest," 7/10/72.

35. Reuter, "State Dept. Reprimands Jane Fonda," *Washington Post,* 7/15/72; "Jane Fonda Hits U.S. on War," *New York Daily News,* 8/2/72; Jane Fonda, *My Life So Far,* Random House (2005), 291–324.

36. George McGovern, interview, 3/5/03; "News Items of Special Interest," 7/24/72; Fonda, *My Life So Far,* 291, 295, 314–18, 324.

37. North Vietnamese News Agency, "Hanoi Press Conference Statement," 7/20/72; "News Items of Special Interest," 7/29/72.

38. MRL, "News Conference at the Pentagon," 7/17/72; "Laird Again raps McGovern," *Washington Post,* 7/18/72; "U.S. Won't Prosecute Jane Fonda," *Washington Post,* 8/26/72; Fonda, *My Life So Far,* 304–6, 325.

39. Minutes, Senior Staff Meeting, 7/31/72.

40. MRL, "News Conference at the Pentagon," 5/10/72.

41. UPI, "Red Massacres in Church, An Loc Hospital Reported," 6/4/72; "Enemy Is Said to Execute Hundreds in South Vietnam," *New York Times,* 8/4/72; "Quangtri Refugees Shelled, U.S. Says," *New York Times,* 8/8/72; AP, "Massacre of Civilians Reported," *Baltimore Sun,* 8/8/72; "South

Vietnam: Campaign of Brutality," 8/21/72; "Defector Tells of Massacre by Enemy at Quangtri," *New York Times*, 9/9/72; Kissinger, *White House Years*, 1167–8.

40 / "PEACE IS AT HAND"

1. MRL, "Remarks at the Retirement Ceremonies for General William C. Westmoreland, U.S. Army," Fort Myer, Va., 6/30/72; "Westmoreland Gets Full-Dress Army Farewell," *Baltimore Sun*, 7/1/72; "Westmoreland Retires with All the Honors," *Washington Post*, 7/1/72.

2. "The General v. 'The System,'" *Time*, 2/15/71; AP, "Abrams Profile," 6/20/72.

3. MRL, "Unforgettable Creighton Abrams," *Reader's Digest*, 7/76.

4. MRL, undated memorandum of conversation, "Telephone Conversation (3/21/72) with General Creighton Abrams."

5. "Abrams Is Choice as Chief of Staff," *New York Times*, 6/1/72.

6. MRL, memorandum for the president, 6/15/72.

7. *New York Times*, 7/2/72.

8. "Abrams Leaves Vietnam after Transforming War," *New York Times*, 7/2/72.

9. Minutes, Senior Staff Meeting, 5/1/72.

10. Shillito, quoted by MRL in memoranda for the president, "Third" and "Fifth and Final Interim Report from Barry Shillito," 5/8, 5/9/72.

11. MRL, hearings before a subcommittee of the Committee on Appropriations, House of Representatives, "Department of Defense Appropriations for 1973: Strategic Arms Limitation Agreement and Vietnam War," 402–16, 6/5/72; "Lull in the Offensive," *New York Times*, 6/12/72.

12. Abrams, quoted by MRL in memorandum for the president, "Personal Assessment of the Situation in RVN as of 1 May 1972," 5/1/72; Adm. Thomas Moorer, chairman, JCS, memorandum to MRL, "Comparison of RVNAF and NVA Effectiveness," 5/4/72; "North Vietnam's Offensive Has Slowed," *Baltimore Sun*, 5/31/72; MRL, memorandum for the president, "Redeployments from SVN," 6/23/72; Maj. Gen. David E. Ott, memorandum for the record, "Visit by Sir Robert Thompson (with MRL)," 7/7/72; Kissinger, *White House Years*, 1196–1301; Sorley, *A Better War*, 336–7.

13. MRL, appearance on NBC-TV program *Today*, 7/20/72.

14. UPI, "Last American Ground Combat Unit Is Deactivated in South Vietnam," *New York Times*, 8/12/72; MRL, "Press Conference Prior to Luncheon Remarks," Sacramento, Cal., McClellan Air Force Base, 8/22/72; AP, "No U.S. Combat Deaths," *Washington Post*, 9/22/72.

15. After the Communists overran the South in 1975, Hanoi frequently used Kim Phuc for anti-American propaganda. In 1992 she defected during a refueling stop on a flight to Cuba and settled in Canada. In 1997 she became a goodwill ambassador for UNESCO. ("South Vietnamese Drop Napalm on Own Troops," *New York Times*, 6/9/72; "Bombing Error Takes Heavy Toll," *NBC News*, 6/9/72; "Napalm Misdirected at Civilians," *CBS News*, 6/9/72; "Bombing Error," *ABC News*, 6/9/72.)

16. CNN.com, "Nixon's Doubts over 'Napalm Girl' Photo," 2/28/02.

17. MRL, memorandum for Kissinger, "Enemy Activity Near the PRC," 7/21/72; MRL, memorandum for the president, "Strike Authorization," 7/25/72; "U.S. Aides Report Raids near China," *New York Times*, 8/25/72.

18. UPI, "Platform," 2/15/72; MRL, "News Conference by Secretary of Defense at Pentagon," 7/6/72.

19. Minutes, Senior Staff Meeting, "Security for the National Political Conventions" (6/26/72) and "Miami Convention" (7/10/72).

20. "McGovern Vows Total Pullout of Troops," *Washington Post*, 7/14/72.

21. "Freshman Senator Chosen as Others Turn Down Offer," *Washington Post*, 7/14/72.

22. MRL, "News Conference by Secretary of Defense at Pentagon," 7/17/72; "Laird Hits McGovern F-15 'Deal,'" *Washington Star*, 7/17/72; Mary McGrory, *Washington Star*, 7/18/72; "Laird Again Raps McGovern," *Washington Post*, 7/18/72.

23. MRL, "Remarks to Area Civilian Leaders," Clinton County Air Force Base, Wilmington, Ohio, 7/31/72; UPI, "Laird," 8/1/72.

24. Some criticized the defense secretary for this "partisan" appearance, but Laird reminded interrogators that when he was chairman of the GOP platform committee in 1964, he invited Defense Secretary Robert McNamara to speak to the group on defense spending. McNamara declined but later spoke before the Democratic platform committee. (MRL, Memorandum to Our

respondents," 8/15/72; "Laird Bids G.O.P. Back Nixon Policy," *New York Times,* 8/16/72; "Nixon's 'Dramatic Success' Recited," *Washington Post,* 8/16/72.)

25. Jerry Friedheim, interview, 7/19/00; "Colson: Power Mechanic," *Washington Post,* 12/6/72.

26. AP, "McGovern Calls Rogers, Laird 'fright mongers,'" *Baltimore Sun,* 8/13/72; David S. Broder, "McGovern Hits Nixon Letting 'Lackeys' Do His 'Dirty Work,'" *Washington Post,* 9/26/72.

27. Safire, *Before the Fall,* 651.

28. "Secretary of Defense Laird's Press Conference," *Bearcat Putt,* Henrietta, Tex., high school newspaper, 10/20/72.

29. AP, "POWs," 2/24/72; minutes, Senior Staff Meetings, 2/28, 3/6/72; UPI, "POWs," 2/28/72; MRL, hearings before the Committee on Foreign Relations, U.S. Senate, "Foreign Assistance Act of 1972," 129, 4/18/72.

30. UPI, "Clark, in Hanoi, Is Said to Find U.S. Prisoners in Good Health," *New York Times,* 8/13/72; "Ramsey Clark Says POWs Are Healthy," *Washington Post,* 8/13/72; MRL, "Press Conference," Miami, Fla., 8/15/72; MRL, "Press Conference Prior to Luncheon Remarks," McClellan Air Force Base, Sacramento, Cal., 8/22/72; "War Prisoners: Center of a Political Fight," *U.S. News & World Report,* 8/28/72.

31. "'Begging Is Better Than Bombing,'" *Washington Post,* 6/30/72; MRL, appearance on NBC's *Today* show, 7/20/72.

32. "Clark Sees Hanoi Ready to Free POWs if McGovern Is Elected," *Washington Post,* 8/15/72; Jack Anderson, "Hanoi Says It Prefers McGovern," *Washington Post,* 7/22/72; "McGovern's Peace View Held 'Positive' by Hanoi," *New York Times,* 7/30/72; MRL, "Interview with Newsmen," Chambersburg, Pa., 9/22/72.

33. MRL, "Interviewed on NBC's *Meet the Press,*" 9/24/72; MRL, "Statement on Senator McGovern's Comments Regarding Delay in Return of POW's," 9/24/72; "McGovern: Nixon 'Using' POWs," *Washington Post,* 9/25/72; UPI, "Laird Rips McGovern on POW Issue," *Washington Star,* 9/25/72.

34. Sorley, *A Better War,* 349.

35. MRL, memorandum to chairman, JCS, "Attack Sorties in North Vietnam," 10/14/72.

36. Minutes, Senior Staff Meeting, "General Abrams' Swearing In Ceremony," 10/16/72; "Abrams Sworn In, Sent to Vietnam," *New York Times,* 10/17/72; "Abrams Sent to Vietnam Again," *Baltimore Sun,* 10/17/72.

37. MRL, memorandum to chairman, JCS, "Changes in Existing Military Procedures in SEA," 11/2/72.

38. Major General David E. Ott, memorandum for the record, "Visit by Sir Robert Thompson (with MRL)," 7/7/72.

41 / THE MORNING AFTER

1. "Probe at Pentagon Got Out of Hand," *Washington Post,* 11/15/71.

2. Haldeman, *Haldeman Diaries,* 531–2.

3. MRL, letter to Pres. Richard Nixon, 11/8/72; Nixon, *Memoirs,* 717.

4. White House, memorandum, "Post-Election Activities," with attachments, 11/8/72.

5. Minutes, Senior Staff Meeting: "The Next Sixty Days," "Mr. Laird's Selection as Secretary of Defense," "*Pro Forma* Resignations of Statutory Appointees," and "*Pro Forma* Resignations of Non-Career Executive (Schedule C) Personnel," 11/9/72; also, Gardiner L. Tucker, handwritten notes of the same meeting, 11/9/72; Georgiana Sharp, interview, 1/16/02.

6. "A Two-Star General Is Favored for Second-Highest Army Post," *New York Times,* 9/2/72; "Haig, Kissinger Aide, Jumps to No. 2 Army Job," *Washington Post,* 9/8/72; UPI, "Generals," 9/8/72; "News Items of Special Interest," 9/8/72.

7. Robert Froehlke, interview, 7/23/00; Robert Pursley, interview, 10/3/00; Alexander Haig, interview, 1/21/02.

8. UPI, "Scowcroft," 1/5/73; "New Assistant to Kissinger in 'Soldier-Statesman' Mold," *Washington Star,* 1/7/73; Pres. Richard Nixon, letter to MRL, 1/10/73; MRL, letter to Pres. Nixon, 1/12/73.

9. AP, "U.S. Names New Pacific Commander," *Washington Post,* 3/15/72.

10. John Chafee, interview, 10/22/99; James Marshall, interview, 4/18/02; UPI, "Chafee," 3/23/72; "Chafee Resigns Post as Secretary of Navy," *Washington Post,* 4/5/72; "How John Chafee, Ex-Navy

Secretary, Runs against War," *Wall Street Journal*, 8/15/72; "Man in the Middle," *Providence Sunday Journal*, 9/12/93.

11. John Warner, interview, 11/10/99; "Surprising Senator: The New Warner Confounds Critics," *Washington Post*, 7/1/79; "Liz and John," *Washingtonian*, 11/82.

12. "Trail of Controversy Marks Warner's Past," *Washington Post*, 10/8/78; "John Warner's Charmed Life," *Washington Post*, 9/11/90.

13. The Taylor-Warner marriage lasted five years, ending in December 1981. While he was busy as a senator, she found it unfulfilling to be a political wife. (John Warner, Atoka Farm, letter to MRL, 4/20/78; "Liz and John," *Washingtonian*, 11/82.)

14. MRL, "Press Conference before Remarks to Secondary School Administration Association," Oshkosh, Wis., 11/2/72; "Laird Says Draft Will Call Fewer Than 10,000 in '73," *New York Times*, 11/29/72; "Final Draft Put at Fewer Than 10,000," *Baltimore Sun*, 11/29/72.

15. "Laird Indicates Rockefeller Is Choice for Post," *Baltimore Sun*, 8/2/72; "Laird Touts Rockefeller as Successor in Defense Post," *Washington Star*, 8/2/72; "Rocky Is Scratched from Cabinet Stakes," *New York Daily News*, 11/22/72; "Romney and Laird Leaving as Nixon Reshapes Cabinet," *New York Times*, 11/28/72.

16. Pres. Richard Nixon, letter to MRL, 11/17/72.

17. Richardson's successor in May 1973, James Schlesinger, named John McLucas as *his* secretary of the air force. (Rowland Evans and Robert Novak, "Richardson on the Defense," *Washington Post*, 11/30/72; minutes, Senior Staff Meetings, 12/4, 18/72; McLucas and Benson, *Confessions*.)

18. MRL, hearings before a subcommittee on the Committee on Appropriations, U.S. Senate, "Foreign Assistance and Related Programs Appropriations for Fiscal Year 1973," 850, 6/5/72; MRL, hearings before a subcommittee of the Committee on Appropriations, House of Representatives, "Department of Defense Appropriations for 1973: Strategic Arms Limitation Agreement and Vietnam War," 358, 362, 374–5, 379, 6/5/72.

19. MRL, memorandum for the president, "Approval of the TRIDENT System as a Program of Highest National Priority," 11/21/72; Kissinger, memorandum for MRL, "Approval of Trident as a Program of Highest National Priority," 12/3/72; "The Next Missile Gap: Trident Delays, Costs May Halve Undersea Missile Force in 1980s as Poseidons Retire," *Washington Post*, 3/19/78; "Depth Charge: Cost Overruns on America's New Trident Sub Make Wry History," *Washington Post*, 10/4/81.

20. "March 6 Starts '73 Draft List," *Washington Post*, 2/3/72; "50,000-Man Draft Limit Announced for All of '72," *New York Times*, 5/14/72.

21. MRL, report to the president, "Progress in Ending the Draft and Achieving the All-Volunteer Force," 7/28/72; MRL, memorandum for correspondents, "Secretary Laird's Remarks on the All-Volunteer Force," 8/28/72; "President to End Draft Next July if Pay Bill Wins," *New York Times*, 8/29/72; "President Sets End of Draft," *Washington Post*, 8/29/72; UPI, 8/29/72.

22. Minutes, Senior Staff Meeting, "All Volunteer Force," 8/21/72.

23. AP, "Uncertainties Cloud All-Volunteer Army," *Baltimore Sun*, 1/11/71; minutes, Senior Staff Meeting, "All Volunteer Force," 8/21/72, "FY 1973 Budget," 9/11/72, and "FY 1973 Budget Reclama," 9/18/72; "War Curb Vote Loses in House," *Washington Post*, 9/15/72; "House Votes to End K.P. Duty," *Chicago Tribune*, 9/15/72.

24. Dr. Richard Wilbur, former assistant secretary (Health and Environment), interview, 2/20, 10/28/01; MRL, report to the president, 7/28/72.

25. Richard Wilbur, interview, 2/20/01.

26. The American Medical Association also opposed the creation of a military medical academy. Laird hinted in his staff meetings that one of their former prominent officials, Dr. Richard Wilbur, who happened to be the Pentagon's chief medical official, now appeared to oppose it as well. With a wink and a smile, he teased Wilbur with the observation more than once that the good doctor had not personally supported the university during congressional testimony. Instead, Wilbur had carefully always quoted his boss Laird's statement of support when pressed by congressmen. (William K. Brehm, memorandum for Assistant Secretary of Defense Roger Kelly, "Ongoing, Planned and Other Actions to Reduce Reliance on the Draft," 7/12/69; William Raspberry, "Doctors for the Military," *Washington Post*, 10/27/71; minutes, Senior Staff Meeting, "H.R. 2—Military Medical Academy," 8/7/72; "Area Medical School for Military Gains," *Washington Post*, 9/24/72; "On the Way ... A 'West Point' for Doctors," *U.S. News & World Report*, 10/9/72.)

27. Harold Brown, interview, 2/20/01; MSgt. Gary Carpenter, Office of University Affairs, USU, interview, 11/1/01; "Military Medical School Appears to Be Aborted on Hill," *Washington Post*, 2/26/77; "A First-Class Federal Medical School," *Washington Post*, 3/19/95.

28. Gardiner Tucker, interview, 4/23/01; Roger Kelley, interview, 7/27/01; Project Volunteer Committee, report to MRL, "Plans and Actions to Move toward an All Volunteer Force," 8/14/70; "Pentagon to Cut Use of Draftees in Fast Build-Ups," *New York Times*, 9/9/70; Roger Kelley, summary essay for the record, memorandum for MRL, "Achieving the All-Volunteer Force," 12/11/72; "Taking Stock" memoranda to MRL from the Joint Chiefs of Staff, 12/12/72, Warren Nutter (International Security Affairs), 12/72, and Gardiner L. Tucker (Systems Analysis), 1/30/73.

29. MRL, memorandum for Henry Kissinger, "Accounting for US Servicemen Missing in Southeast Asia," 7/26/72; MRL, memorandum for Henry Kissinger, "Essential Negotiating Points" with attachment, "Essential Elements of Agreement," 11/10/72; minutes, Senior Staff Meeting, 11/20/72.

30. Laird explained that this was not his position alone, but that also held by Deputy Secretary Ken Rush and Adm. Thomas Moorer—with whom he "had long and detailed discussions" about the peace negotiations. In conclusion, he stated that together "Ken Rush, Tom Moorer and I strongly recommend" signing an agreement sooner than later. (MRL, memorandum for the president, "Ceasefire Agreement," 12/12/72.)

31. Deputy Secretary of Defense Kenneth Rush, on behalf of MRL, memorandum for the president, "North Vietnam Contingency Plan," 12/7/72.

32. Minutes, Senior Staff Meetings: 8/28, 9/5, 9/11, 9/18, 10/16, 11/27, 12/18/72; MRL, memoranda for the president, "Assessment of the Air and Naval Campaign against North Vietnam," 9/8, 10/25/72; Adm. T. H. Moorer, chairman, JCS, memorandum for MRL, "Objectives of the Linebacker/Pocket Money Campaign," 10/11/72; Cdr. B. B. Traweek, USN, fact sheet, "Mining in Haiphong Harbor," 11/28/72; Zumwalt, *On Watch*, 387–8.

33. MRL, memorandum for Kissinger, "US Military Actions to Sway President Thieu12/13/72.

34. MRL, memorandum for Henry Kissinger, "North Vietnam," 12/18/72; MRL, "News Conference at the Pearl Harbor (Hawaii) Enlisted Club," 12/29/72; minutes, Senior Staff Meeting, 1/2/73.

35. Robert Pierpont, *CBS Evening News*, 1/10/73; Reuter, "Indochina-Moorer," 1/11/73.

36. Pres. Richard Nixon, letter to MRL, 12/24/72.

37. "A 'Family' Farewell," *Washington Star*, 12/16/72.

38. "U.S. Could Now Quit Vietnam, Laird Says," *Washington Post*, 1/9/73.

39. MRL, "Press Conference at Pentagon," 1/19/73.

40. That afternoon Secretary Laird recounted the confidential morning conversation with Kissinger to *Milwaukee Journal* reporter John W. Kole during a ninety-minute end-of-service interview. ("Laird Was a Skillful Politician as Secretary," *Milwaukee Journal*, 2/4/73.) "Kissinger in Paris; Ceremonial Site Chosen for Talks," *New York Times*, 1/23/73.

41. Laird brought a typewritten statement he intended to paraphrase at the Cabinet meeting. Laird handwrote a note on the 1/23/72 document after the meeting: "Used substance but did not read—I spoke after Pres. paid special tribute to Vietnamization Program and how it made this night possible." Also, Nixon speech writer William Safire provided a detailed account of the Cabinet meeting in his memoirs (*Before the Fall*, 675–8).

42. The message was publicly announced in a 1/27/73 Department of Defense news release.

43. Gerald Ford, interview, 8/28/97; Richard Holbrooke, interview, 8/11/00; Dick Cheney, interview, 2/20/01.

44. Don Rumsfeld, one-page note to MRL, "Dear Mel," 1/27/73.

45. Pres. Richard Nixon, letter to MRL, 2/20/73.

42 / TRYING A MAN'S SOUL

1. *Green Bay Press-Gazette*, 2/7/73.

2. Rogers C. B. Morton, secretary of the interior, letter to MRL, 11/30/72; James R. Schlesinger, chairman, U.S. Atomic Energy Commission, letter to MRL, 1/29/73.

3. "Laird to Head N.Y. Stock Exchange?" *Washington Star*, 1/27/72; "Big Seat on the Big Board," *Newsweek*, 4/26/72; "Washington Whispers," *U.S. News & World Report*, 5/15/72; UPI, "Laird," 1/19/73.

4. "What's to Become of Laird?" *Washington Star*, 12/12/72.

5. " '74 Speculation Rises on Laird," *Milwaukee Sentinel*, 11/28/72.

6. David S. Broder, "The Domestic Vacuum," *Washington Post*, 11/21/72; "Mr. Laird's Past—and Future?" *Christian Science Monitor*, 11/29/72; "From Pentagon to White House?" *Chicago Tribune*,

12/7/72; UPI, 1/19/73; "Is Laird Looking at White House?" *Appleton Post-Crescent*, 1/23/73; Ehrlich-man, *Witness to Power*, 94

7. Pres. Richard Nixon, letter to MRL, 11/17/72. Nixon wrote Laird a steady stream of thank-you letters after Laird's resignation. A letter in March was accompanied by a gift. "The Cabinet chair of the Secretary of Defense has been filled by some of our country's great public servants. Few of them however, could match the record of dedicated, devoted service of my first Secretary of Defense whose selfless work for the past four years has meant so much to me. [Therefore,] I want you to have the chair you occupied with such distinction at the Cabinet table," Nixon wrote. (Pres. Richard Nixon, letter to MRL, 3/1/73.)

8. Jack Mills, interviews, 11/12/99, 10/6/00.

9. Nick Thimmesch, "Last 3 years Have Been Grueling for the Pentagon's Melvin Laird," *Baltimore Sun*, 10/24/72; "Laird: 'No Regrets,'" *Stevens Point Journal*, 3/30/73.

10. "Laird Denies He Will Take Nixon Job," *Wausau (Wis.) Record-Herald*, 4/26/73.

11. "Laird Says Nixon Musn't Be Tried, No Matter What," *Madison Capital Times*, 5/2/73.

12. "Packard May Be Next Defense Chief," *Chicago Daily News*, 5/1/73; "Packard Queried on Defense Job," *Washington Star*, 5/1/73; "Packard Is Undecided on Heading Pentagon," *Washington Post*, 5/4/73; UPI, "Packard Said to Reject Top Post at Pentagon," *Washington Post*, 5/10/73.

13. Cannon, *Time and Chance*, 171; Burke and Thompson, *Bryce Harlow*, 277–9.

14. Though more than one historical account suggests Laird *and* Harlow asked Nixon about his involvement, Harlow himself disputed that in a late 1970s interview with *Readers' Digest* senior editor Trevor Armbrister, who was working on Gerald Ford's autobiography. Armbrister asked Harlow if he, like Laird, made working at the White House conditional on Nixon's innocence regarding Watergate. "No," Harlow said, "I didn't ask him." And then Harlow expressed initial doubt that Laird had even asked the question.

"I don't want to challenge what Mel says to you at all, but I just find that amazing because Mel and I were talked to together by the President and Haig in an attempt to bring us in there.... We spent two or three hours up there at Camp David and I don't recall that we discussed that.... As far as I was concerned, I don't recall that." But then, vouching for his friend Laird's honesty, he added, however, that "if Mel says it was, it was."

The most likely thing is that Laird asked him when Harlow was out of the room. For more than three decades, Laird has maintained that he did ask the president pointedly about it. "Bryce didn't ask that question," he explained. "I did, because I told my wife I would." The fact that Laird soon referenced the "personal assurance [of] noninvolvement" from Nixon in his announcement press conference seems good evidence that it happened.

15. Alexander Haig, interview, 1/21/02.

16. Osborne's column was published 6/23/73 and reprinted in his book, *The Fifth Year of the Nixon Watch*, Liveright (1974), 104–5.

17. "Laird Takes Ehrlichman White House Job; Haig to Quit Army to Hold Haldeman Post as Civilian," *New York Times*, 6/7/73.

18. "Press Conference of MRL, Counsellor-Designate to the President for Domestic Affairs," Office of the White House Press Secretary, 6/6/73.

19. Rowland Evans and Robert Novak, "The Self-Bugging of Mr. Ehrlichman," *Washington Post*, 7/22/73.

20. Theodore H. White, *Breach of Faith: The Fall of Richard Nixon*, Atheneum Publishers (1975), 245–7.

21. "J. Fred Buzhardt: To the White House, Low Key, Experienced," *Washington Post*, 5/11/73.

22. Robert Froehlke, interview, 7/23/00.

23. Spiro T. Agnew, *Go Quietly ... Or Else*, William Morrow and Company (1980), 87.

24. Jack Mills, interview, 11/12/99.

25. Joseph Kraft, *Washington Post*, 7/22/72.

26. MRL, "Press Conference," Roosevelt Room, White House, 7/26/73.

27. MRL, "Remarks at the National Legislative Conference," Chicago, Ill., 8/10/73.

43 / ON THE ROPES

1. "Nixon Still Leans on 3 to Advise Him," *New York Times*, 7/23/73; Rowland Evans and Robert Novak, "Gen. Haig's White House," *Washington Post*, 7/23/73; "Laird's Leaving a Loss," *Chicago Sun-Times*, 12/21/73.

2. MRL, "Press Conference," Roosevelt Room, White House, 7/26/73.

3. MRL, appearance on NBC *Today Show*, 7/31/73.

4. Oval Office conversation between Nixon and Haig, 3:26–4 P.M., 7/12/73. (Kutler, *Abuse of Power*, 630–2.)

5. MRL, "Press Conference," 7/26/73; "Advice Ignored, Laird Suggests," *Washington Star*, 7/27/73; "Nixon Held Tapes over Advice of Laird, Harlow, Rep. Ford Says," *Washington Post*, 7/28/73; MRL, "Press Conference," Briefing Room, White House, 12/19/73.

6. Rowland Evans and Robert Novak, "Can Laird Decentralize The Power?" *Washington Post*, 6/25/73.

7. Caspar Weinberger, interview, 1/25/01.

8. George Shultz, interview, 2/6/01; "White House Weighs Plan for Tax Rise, with Refund When the Economy Slows," *New York Times*, 9/14/73; Reuter, "Shultz to Laird: 'Keep Hands Off' in Economic Area," *New York Times*, 9/14/73; "'Refundable' Increase in Taxes Considered," *Washington Post*, 9/14/73; "Proposal for Increase in Taxes Draws Stiff Opposition in the Administration," *New York Times*, 9/15/73; "Tax Raise Issue Clouded," *Washington Post*, 9/15/73; Rowland Evans and Robert Novak, "Tax Increase Turmoil," *Washington Post*, 9/19/73; MRL, *Washington Post* interview, 9/19/73; Rowland Evans and Robert Novak, "Mr. Nixon's Long, Cold Winter," *Washington Post*, 9/23/73.

9. Rady Johnson, interview, 8/22/00.

10. "Aides Say President Buoyed," *Washington Post*, 8/29/73; interview with MRL, "What's Ahead for the White House," *U.S. News & World Report*, 9/17//73; MRL, "Remarks before the Defense Credit Union Council," Washington, D.C., 9/11/73; MRL, *Washington Post* interview, 9/19/73; Earl L. Butz, Secretary of Agriculture, letter to MRL, 9/24/73.

11. Richard Wilbur, interview, 2/20/01.

12. MRL, "Press Conference," Briefing Room, White House, 8/13/73; "Nixon Signs $22 Billion Highway Bill," *Washington Post*, 8/14/73; MRL, "Meeting with Sarah McClendon Press Group," Roosevelt Room, White House, 11/29//73; "House Passes Budget for HEW and Labor," *Washington Post*, 12/6/73; "Nixon Gets $33 Billion HEW Money Bill," *Wall Street Journal*, 12/8/73.

13. "Congress vs. Nixon, How It Came Out," *Wall Street Journal*, 12/24/73.

14. "Congress in Mood to Defy President," *New York Times*, 7/13/73; MRL, "Press Conference," 7/26/73; "An Interview: MRL," *Investor*, a Wisconsin business magazine, 9/73; Kissinger, *Years of Upheaval*, Little, Brown, and Company (1982), 355–60.

15. Joseph Kraft, "Regrouping at the White House," *Washington Post*, 7/22/73.

16. Henry Kissinger, interview, 1/10/01; William Safire, "Let Henry and Al and George and Mel Do It: Who's What around the White House," *New York Times Magazine*, 11/11/73; Kissinger, *Years of Upheaval*, 370–2, 420.

17. Minutes, Senior Staff Meeting, "Letter Bombs," 9/25/72; "Israelis Intercept Letter-bombs Mailed to Nixon, Rogers and Laird," *New York Times*, 10/26/72; "Israel Says Syrian-Run Ring Mailed Letter Bomb to Nixon [and Laird, Rogers]," *New York Times*, 2/1/73; Reuter, "Israel Holding 14 as Spies for Syria," *New York Times*, 2/2/73.

18. Nixon, *Memoirs*, 922, 926–8; Seamans, *Aiming at Targets*, 167; McLucas and Benson, *Confessions*.

19. "Nixon to Reveal Stiff Fuel Curbs in Talk Tonight," *New York Times*, 11/25/73.

20. Cohen and Witcover, *A Heartbeat Away*, 3–11, 92–6, 116, 127–30, 214.

21. Program, "Launching *Glenard P. Lipscomb*," Groton, Conn., 8/4/73; passenger manifest, thirty-five-passenger SAM VC-131H, 8/4/73; Ford, *A Time to Heal*, 101; Cannon, *Time and Chance*, 189.

22. Cohen and Witcover, *A Heartbeat Away*, 158–9; Agnew, *Go Quietly*, 101–3.

23. Nixon, *Memoirs*, 913–14.

24. Rowland Evans and Robert Novak, "Laird's Warning about Agnew," *Washington Post*, 8/20/73; AP, "White House Reported Requesting Silence on Agnew," *New York Times*, 8/21/73; Cohen and Witcover, *A Heartbeat Away*, 203; Osborne, *The Fifth Year*, 168–9.

25. Agnew, *Go Quietly*, 27, 131–2, 151 and 191.

26. Carl Albert with Danney Goble, *The Life and Times of Speaker Carl Albert: Little Giant*, University of Oklahoma Press (1990), 359–60; Cannon, *Time and Chance*, 191–5.

27. No deal could be made, except between Richardson, representing the prosecution, and Agnew's lawyers. However, behind the scenes, Laird and Harlow—either personally or through their White House point man, special counsel Fred Buzhardt—effectively brought both sides closer to a compromise that Nixon also favored. Because Buzhardt delivered the bad news to Agnew, Laird was able to deny in a press conference that he had asked Agnew to resign. "I have been in communication with the Vice President," he told an inquiring reporter. "Matter of fact, I played golf with him last Tuesday and I can assure you that I am not the source of that particular (resignation) information because I had a long visit with the Vice President and do keep in touch with him, and the question of resigning has never been discussed with me." ("Some Aides Hint That Agnew Ought to Resign," *New York Times*, 9/19/73.) MRL, interview with *Washington Post* editors, 9/19/73; MRL, appearance on CBS's *Face the Nation*, 9/23/73; Burke and Thompson, *Bryce Harlow*, 233–6.

44 / CROWNING ACHIEVEMENTS

1. Hartmann, *Palace Politics*, 8–12.

2. A summary of the national coverage about Laird as Nixon's possible vice president was in his local newspaper, the *Marshfield News-Herald*, "Laird Rates High among Potentials," 10/11/73. Alexander Haig, interview, 1/21/02; James Reston, "A New Problem for President," *New York Times*, 10/11/73; "Congress to Vote," *New York Times*, 10/11/73.

3. Gerald R. Ford, interview, 8/28/97; George H. W. Bush, interview, 10/14/97; Alexander Haig, interview, 1/21/02; Safire, *Before the Fall*, 505–8.

4. Cannon, *Time and Chance*, 197–8.

5. Hartmann, *Palace Politics*, 15–16.

6. Albert with Goble, *Life and Times*, 361.

7. John Connally with Mickey Herskowitz, *In History's Shadow: An American Odyssey*, Hyperion Books (1993), 282–3, 288–9.

8. Cannon, *Time and Chance*, 203–5.

9. Gerald R. Ford, interviews, 8/28, 9/12/97; Ford, *A Time to Heal*, 103–4; Hartmann, *Palace Politics*, 17–18; Cannon, *Time and Chance*, 205–7.

10. Barber Conable, interview, 4/5/01.

11. Bryce Harlow interview with Trevor Armbrister, ca. 1978; Henry Kissinger, interview, 1/10/01; Alexander Haig, interview, 1/21/02.

12. While Ford was the first choice among the Republican representatives, he fell far behind in the Senate and Republican National Committee survey totals. Of the 142 members of the RNC, RNC Chair Bush tallied the following results: Rockefeller (30), Connally (27), Goldwater (22), Reagan (17), Bush (15), and Ford (4). Ford wasn't even among the top four—Rockefeller (6), Goldwater (5), Connally (4) and Reagan (4)—recommended by the Republican senators. Those results give a better idea of the uphill battle Laird had with his pro-Ford "campaign." (Cannon, *Time and Chance*, 207–10.)

13. Nixon, *Memoirs*, 925–6.

14. "How Richard Nixon Chose Gerald Ford," *Parade*, 1/12/75; Hartmann, *Palace Politics*, 21–3.

15. In his memoir Nixon maintained that during his morning meeting with Ford "I revealed nothing of my decision about the vice presidency." Ford's memoir says that he revealed everything. Ford's chief aide, Bob Hartmann, reported that his boss returned to the office unusually exuberant after the meeting, which was a tip-off to Hartmann that the nomination was Ford's. Nixon's memory may have been shaded by the factual arrangement he explained to Ford and others at the time that his final choice would get a call at 7:30 that evening. (Nixon, *Memoirs*, 926; Ford, *A Time to Heal*, 105–6; Hartmann, *Palace Politics*, 21–3.)

16. George H. W. Bush, interview, 10/14/97; Robert Novak, interview, 10/2/00; Henry Kissinger, interview, 1/10/01; Alexander Haig, interview, 1/21/02; Safire, *Before the Fall*, 508.

17. Gerald R. Ford, interview, 8/28/97.

18. Nixon, *Memoirs*, 909–11, 929–30.

19. MRL, appearance on *Meet the Press*, 10/21/73; "Nixon Defended," *New York Times*, 10/22/73;

Clifton Daniel, "White House Strategy," *New York Times*, 10/22/73; Rick Ball and NBC News, *Meet the Press: 50 Years of History in the Making*, McGraw-Hill (1998), 120.

20. William Archer, interview, 7/13/00; White House press release, "Leon Jaworski: Biographical Data," 11/1/73.

21. Connally with Herskowitz, *In History's Shadow*, 285–6.

22. Nixon, *Memoirs*, 929–30.

23. "Nixon Names Saxbe Attorney General; Jaworski Appointed Special Prosecutor," *New York Times*, 11/2/73; Leon Jaworski, *The Right and the Power: The Prosecution of Watergate*, Reader's Digest Press (1976), 1–7; James Doyle, *Not above the Law: The Battles of Watergate Prosecutors Cox and Jaworski*, William Morrow and Company (1977), 234–7.

24. Stanley I. Kutler, *The Wars of Watergate: The Last Crisis of Richard Nixon*, W.W. Norton & Company (1990), 426–9.

25. "Talk of Impeachment in Surprising Circles," *New York Times*, 10/21/73.

26. David S. Broder, "Laird Warns Nixon of Bid to Impeach," *Washington Post*, 10/17/73; Rowland Evans and Robert Novak, "Mr. Nixon: Determined to Defy the Supreme Court?" *Washington Post*, 10/17/73.

27. Clayton Fritchey, "Nixon and Laird: Breaking Off," *Washington Post*, 10/27/73.

28. "Doar to Direct Impeachment Inquiry," *New York Times*, 12/21/73; "Republican to Direct Hill Impeachment Study," *Washington Post*; "Doar to Head Probe," *Baltimore Sun*, 12/21/73; "Doar New Impeachment Kingpin," *Christian Science Monitor*, 12/21/73; MRL, "Remarks," Briefing Room, White House, 12/28/73; White, *Breach of Faith*, 280–4; Howard Fields, *High Crimes and Misdemeanors: The Dramatic Story of the Rodino Committee*, W.W. Norton (1978), 19–21.

29. Jaworski, *The Right and the Power*, 25–30; Nixon, *Memoirs*, 918–20, 948–51.

30. "Melvin Laird, Available for Comment," *Newsday*, 11/14/73.

31. Osborne, *Fifth Year*, 193.

32. Rowland Evans and Robert Novak, "Gerald Ford: A Political Threat to the President," *Washington Post*, 12/6/73.

33. "A Watershed for Nixon," *New York Times*, 12/7/73.

34. MRL, letter to Pres. Richard Nixon, 12/17/73.

35. MRL, "Press Conference," Briefing Room, White House, 12/19/73; "Laird Quits, Urges Speed on Impeachment Question," *New York Times*, 12/20/73; Peter Lisagor, "Departure of Laird Is Big Loss," *Denver Post*, 12/22/73.

36. Pres. Richard Nixon, letter to MRL, undated but ca. 12/17/73.

45 / ENDING THE NIGHTMARE

1. Class of '75, "Press Statement," 1/27/74; UPI, "Laird Praised by Ford for 'Perceptive Genius,'" *New York Times*, 1/28/74; "Vice President Ford Given Warm Welcome Despite Protesters," *Providence Journal-Bulletin*, 1/28/74; "Ford, Laird at PC: Elegance and Protest," *Providence Journal-Bulletin*, 1/28/74; "Protesters Hurl Eggs, Insults," *Pawtucket (R.I.) Times*, 1/28/74; news release, Providence College, 1/29/74; "Demonstrators Protest Laird's Credibility" and "Class of '75 Denounces Demonstration," *The Cowl* (Providence College student newspaper), 1/30/74; Maj. Stephen M. Maroney, acting chief of police, and The Attica Brigade, letters to the editor, *The Cowl*, 2/6/74.

2. Minutes, Senior Staff Meeting, "Europe," 1/15/73.

3. MRL, appearance on Maury Povich–hosted *Panorama* TV show, 1/15/74; "Schlesinger, Laird Differ on Vietnam," *Washington Post*, 1/17/74; "One Year Later, Peace in Vietnam Remains Elusive," *Washington Post*, 1/27/74; MRL, "Press Conference," Roosevelt Room, White House, 1/29/74; "Exit Mel Laird Firing a Few Parting Shots," *Philadelphia Inquirer*, 1/30/74.

4. "Laird Bars Amnesty on Draft Now," *Washington Post*, 2/4/72; MRL, "Question-Answer Period following Remarks to Rotary Club of Brooklyn," New York City, 4/26/72.

5. "Exchange of Remarks between the President and MRL, Counselor to the President, at the Presentation of the Medal of Freedom Award to MRL," 3/26/74; "Hail from the Chief," *Washington Post*, 3/27/74; AP, "Laird Is Beribboned," *Washington Star*, 3/27/74; *Washington Post*, 3/31/74.

6. Jaworski, *The Right and the Power*, 45–7, 57, 276–7.

7. "President Hands Over Transcripts," *Washington Post*, 5/1/74; Jaworski, *The Right and the Power*, 131–3; Bush, *All the Best*, 177.

8. Gulley with Reese, *Breaking Cover,* 226–7.

9. MRL, "The President I Know," *Reader's Digest,* 11/74; Cannon, *Time and Chance,* 275.

10. Ford, *A Time to Heal,* 119.

11. Jaworski, *The Right and the Power,* 203–4; Nixon, *Memoirs,* 1051–2; Cannon, *Time and Chance,* 282; Kutler, *Abuse of Power,* 639.

12. Albert Quie, interview, 4/5/01; "Ford and Friends Meet for Prayer," *New York Times,* 8/8/74; Ford, *A Time to Heal,* 26–7; Cannon, *Time and Chance,* 267, 275.

13. Jaworski, *The Right and the Power,* 17, 263–7, 286–7; Connally with Herskowitz, *In History's Shadow,* 271, 273, 281, 283–6.

14. MRL, manuscript, "The President I Know," 8/19/74, subsequently revised for publication in the 11/74 issue of *Reader's Digest.*

15. "Mel Laird's Friends Are Said to Be a Big and a Wary Group," *Wall Street Journal,* 5/11/76.

16. In recalling his side of the conversation to Robert Hartmann years after the fact, Rockefeller reportedly quoted Laird as saying: "My year is 1980"—meaning that he would become vice president or run for president if a Democrat won in 1976. Laird maintained that he neither uttered those words nor ever had such a plan. (Hartmann, *Palace Politics,* 222–3.)

17. Donald Rumsfeld, interview, 2/28/01; "What Happened to Our 'Wise Men'?" *U.S. News & World Report,* 11/10/75.

18. Dick Cheney, interview, 2/20/01; "A Ford Interview," *New York Times,* 8/8/74; "The 'Cronies' Ford Turns to When He Wants to Relax," *U.S. News & World Report,* 9/29/75; Ford, *A Time to Heal,* 188–9, 261–2.

19. Clarence Brown, interview, 8/1/01.

20. Jack Mills, interviews, 6/2/00, 2/13/01.

21. Evans and Novak, "The Man of the Ear," *New York.*

22. Ultimately, only 6 percent of the eligible persons ever applied for the program. It was easier for draft evaders and military deserters to turn themselves in to appropriate authorities and take their chances that they would not be prosecuted. Most weren't. Once the Vietnam war was over for Americans, neither the Justice nor the Defense department was interested in wasting resources on jailing draft dodgers and deserters. As one of his first acts in office, President Jimmy Carter in 1977 made amnesty *unconditional.* (Gerald Ford, interview, 8/28/97; Baskir and Strauss, *Chance and Circumstance,* 215; Ford, *A Time to Heal,* 181–2; Cannon, *Time and Chance,* 367.)

23. On the morning of Ford's first press conference, he received a memo from one of Nixon's lawyers, Leonard Garment, urging that he announce a pardon for the former president. Consistent with his conversation with Laird, Buchen counseled Ford: "I think it's premature, don't you?" "Yes," Ford agreed. "I'm going to say [at the press conference] we'll just let the matter go on for a while." (Cannon, *Time and Chance,* pg. 371.)

24 Ford, *A Time to Heal,* 157.

25. "Ford Says He Views Nixon as Punished Enough Now; Pardon Option Kept Open," *New York Times,* 8/29/74; Ford, *A Time to Heal,* 157–8.

26 Pres. Ford, interviews with Trevor Armbrister, 1977–79; Cannon, *Time and Chasnce,* 371–3.

27 Gerald Ford, interview, 8/28/97; Ford, *A Time to Heal,* 175–8; Kutler, *Wars of Watergate,* 567–8; Cannon, *Time and Chance,* 382–4.

28. "Ford's Gallup Rating Off 21 Points after Pardon," *New York Times,* 10/13/74; Jules Witcover, *Marathon: The Pursuit of the Presidency, 1972–1976,* Viking Press (1977), 43–4; Ford, *A Time to Heal,* 178–81; Kutler, *The Wars of Watergate,* 564–6; Cannon, *Time and Chance,* 384–6.

29. Bill Archer, interview, 7/13/00; Jaworski, *The Right and the Power,* 99–101, 108, 224–30, 237–8, 243–5; James Doyle, *Not Above the Law: The Battles of Watergate Prosecutors Cox and Jaworski,* Morrow (1977), 349–50; Kutler, *The Wars of Watergate,* 568–9.

46 / CITIZEN LAIRD

1. MRL, "Is *This* Detente?" *Reader's Digest,* 7/75; Secretary of State Henry Kissinger, memorandum for the president, "Mel Laird's *Reader's Digest* Article, 'Is *This* Detente?'" 7/75.

2. Nixon, *Memoirs,* 889; Snepp, *Decent Interval,* 146; Ford, *A Time to Heal,* 250; Cannon, *Time and Chance,* 275; Sorley, *A Better War,* 367.

3. Col. Bui Tin, though he was a journalist, was the highest-ranking officer on the scene in

Saigon on April 30 to accept Saigon's surrender. (Bui Tin, interview, "How North Vietnam Won the War," 8/3/95; Sorley, *A Better War,* 374.)

4. "Why Did the ARVN Break?" *Newsweek,* 4/7/75; "Reporter's Notebook," *New York Times,* 3/17/75.

5. AP, 5/27/06.

6. Ford, *A Time to Heal,* 233–5; Isaacson, *Kissinger,* 640–3.

7. William Shawcross, *Sideshow: Kissinger, Nixon, and the Destruction of Cambodia,* Simon and Schuster (1979), 365–9; Isaacson, *Kissinger,* 635–40.

8. Snepp, *Decent Interval,* 563.

9. Jeffrey Record, *The Wrong War: Why We Lost in Vietnam,* Naval Institute Press (1998); Sorley, *A Better War,* 383.

10. MRL, "Press Conference," Roosevelt Room, White House, 1/29/74.

11. "Exit Mel Laird Firing a Few Parting Shots," *Philadelphia Inquirer,* 1/30/74; "Laird Kisses Off Henry in Goodbye," New York *Daily News,* 1/30/74; Thimmesch, "Back-Room Master," 5/5/74.

12. MRL, "Let's Not Fool Ourselves about U.S.-Soviet Detente," *Reader's Digest,* 2/74.

13. "As I See It: An Interview with Melvin Laird," *Forbes,* 7/15/74.

14. Brent Scowcroft interview with Trevor Armbrister, ca. 1978; Hartmann, *Palace Politics,* 345–6.

15. MRL, "Hope for the West—and a Warning; A dialogue with West German Chancellor Helmut Schmidt," *Reader's Digest,* 9/75.

16. MRL, "Is *This* Detente?" *Reader's Digest,* 7/75.

17. Kissinger, memorandum for the president, "Mel Laird's *Reader's Digest* Article, 'Is *This* Detente?'" 7/75.

18. Kissinger, memorandum for the president, "Meeting with Melvin Laird," 7/75; Rowland Evans and Robert Novak, "A Tougher Stance on Arms Control?" *Washington Post,* 7/24/75.

19. Isaacson's chapter, "The Death of Detente" (*Kissinger,* 607–29), is a thorough exposition on the various antidétente forces. See also, "Big Push for Detente; Is U.S. Moving Too Fast?" *U.S. News & World Report,* 7/28/75.

20. Program, "AFL-CIO Banquet in Honor of Alexander Solzhenitsyn," Washington Hilton Hotel, Washington D.C., 6/30/75; Leslie H. Gelb, *New York Times,* 7/1/75; Mary McGrory, "Solzhenitsyn's Debut Is," *Washington Star,* 7/4/75; Ford, *A Time to Heal,* 297–8; Isaacson, *Kissinger,* 657–8.

21. Hugh Carey, interview, 10/24/01; Ford, *A Time to Heal,* 314–19, 331; Cannon, *Time and Chance,* 404.

22. John Heidenry, *Theirs Was the Kingdom: Lila and DeWitt Wallace and the Story of Reader's Digest,* W.W. Norton (1993), 13–18, 212.

23. Laurie Hawley, interview, 8/12/99; Kathy Weaver, interview, 7/11/02; *Wall Street Journal,* 5/11/76; Heidenry, *Theirs Was the Kingdom,* 98–100, 388–90; MRL, "Personal Notes on Life after Politics and Government," 2000.

24. Mills, 11/12/99, 6/2/00; "Seoul Gave Millions," *Washington Post,* 10/24/76; "Laird Says He Warned State Dept. about South Korea Lobby in 1976," *New York Times,* 11/11/76.

25. AP, "Laird Won't Head Ford's Campaign," 4/2/75; Ford, *A Time to Heal,* 295–7.

26. "Ready on the Right," *Newsweek,* 3/24/75; "Laird Expects Challenge to Rockefeller," *New York Times,* 5/14/75; "Laird Sees 'Dump Rocky' Bid in 1976," *Washington Post,* 5/14/75; Joseph Kraft, "Family Politics," *Washington Post,* 5/14/75; "Laird Moves to Assuage Reagan Wing," *Los Angeles Times,* 5/14/75; Mary McGrory, "Rockefeller, the Puzzle for 1976," *Washington Star,* 5/19/75; Rowland Evans and Robert Novak, "The Laird Ploy That Backfired," *Washington Post,* 5/21/75; Witcover, *Marathon,* 51.

27. "The Countdown," *Newsweek,* 11/17/75; Hartmann, *Palace Politics,* 360.

28. The conversation is as Laird remembered it. (John Walker, Air France representative who was on the Paris trip with Laird, interviews, 7/24, 7/25/01; "Detente Can Be U.S. Delusion, Former Defense Chief Warns," *Arizona Republic,* 12/5/75; "Mel Laird's Friends," *Wall Street Journal,* 5/11/76.)

29. "Enter Reagan, Stage Right," *Economist,* 11/15/75; "The Countdown," *Newsweek,* 11/17/75; "The Vice Presidency: With Rockefeller Out, a Wide-Open Choice," *U.S. News & World Report,* 11/17/75; Witcover, *Marathon,* 82–3.

30. Donald Rumsfeld, interview, 2/28/01; James Schlesinger, interview, 7/27/01.

31. Gerald Ford, interview, 8/28/97; Armbrister interviews with President Ford, 1977–79, which were referenced in Cannon, *Time and Chance,* 406–7.

32. Both Laird and Kissinger also thought that Nelson Rockefeller would make a good secretary

of state. Kissinger also mentioned Elliot Richardson as a good choice. ("Clouds over Kissinger," *Newsweek,* 12/8/75; "Pssst—Looks Like Henry May Be on the Way Out," *Chicago Tribune,* 3/7/76; John Osborne, "Kissinger's Future," *The New Republic,* 4/76; "Laird Slams Reagan on 'Demagogic' Speech," *Milwaukee Sentinel,* 4/2/76; "Talking with Beleaguered Henry K.," *Forbes,* 4/15/76; "If Republicans Win . . . What President's New Team Would Look Like," *U.S. News & World Report,* 8/30/76; "Laird Sees Rockefeller in Kissinger's Job," *Milwaukee Journal,* 10/26/76.)

33. "Kissinger Will Retire, Laird Says," *Wisconsin State Journal,* 4/1/76; "Diplomacy: Wall Posters," *Newsweek,* 4/19/76.

34. AP, "Rockefeller Backed as No. 2 (by Laird)," *New York Times,* 8/15/76.

35. "The Underdogs," *Newsweek,* 8/30/76; Cannon, *Time and Chance,* 407–8.

36. Ford, *A Time to Heal,* 440–41.

47 / BOARDROOM DRAMAS

1. Henry Kissinger, interview, 1/10/01; Reed Hall, interview, 5/8, 5/23/06; Meldon Maguire, interview, 5/22/06; AP, 9/12/97; *Marshfield News-Herald,* 9/13/97; *Madison Capital Times,* 19/4/97.

2. Quoted by Steve Hannah, columnist, "Secret of Fund-raising—Give Yourself," *Madison Capital Times,* 8/16/97.

3. "Laird Research Center Unveiled," *Marshfield News-Herald,* 10/25/94; PR Newswire, "Secretary Shalala Calls for Increased Commitment to Rural Health Care," 10/25/94.

4. Robert Froehlke, interview, 9/10/97; Reed Hall, interview, 5/23/06; "Big and Small, Donors Made It Happen," *Marshfield News-Herald,* 9/10/97.

5. Reed Hall, interview; 5/23/06; "Healing the World," *World Traveler,* Northwest Airlines magazine, 5/97; "Replanted in Larger Pot, Clinic Research Programs Ready to Take Off," *Marshfield News-Herald,* 9/10/97; program, "Dedication Ceremony: Melvin R. Laird Center," 9/12/97; brochure, "Laird Center for Medical Research," 1/06; Marshfield Clinic booklet, "The Strength of Our System: 2005 System Review," 4/06.

6. MRL, "Let's Stop Undermining the CIA," *Reader's Digest,* 5/76.

7. MRL, "Question and Answer Session Address following Address at the National Press Club," 9/25/69.

8. "Laird Collection Appraisal," Chestnut Court Appraisal Associates, 4/29/98.

9. Jeanne Dugan, *Business Week,* 7/14/97.

10. MRL, letter to PMG Preston R. Tisch, 12/1/87; Tisch, letter to MRL, 12/14/87.

11. MRL, letters to PMG Anthony M. Frank, 10/4/88, 11/1/88, 3/29/90, 4/19/90.

12. Monica Hand, publicist, Citizens' Stamp Advisory Committee, interview, 8/18/95; MRL, letter to Runyon, 9/15/94.

13. Melissa Dodge, U.S. Postal Service Headquarters, interviews, 5/9, 5/11/06.

14. "Executives," *New York Times,* 9/28/81; Jack Anderson, "Revolving Door," *Washington Post,* 10/7/82.

15. Allan Sloan, *Three Plus One Equals Billions,* Arbor House (1983), 163–4; Hope Lampert, *Till Death Do Us Part,* Harcourt Brace Jovanovich (1983), 193.

16. "High Noon: Showdown Time for Bendix," *Time,* 9/20/82"; "William Agee: Enigma of the Corporate World," *Washington Post,* 10/10/82; Mary Cunningham with Fran Schumer, *Power Play,* Linden Press (1984), 157–8.

17. " 'You're Going to Kill Us Both': Martin Marietta's Pownall Recalls His Epic Battle with Bendix," *Time,* 4/25/83; Cunningham, *Power Play,* 244.

18. Lampert, *Till Death,* 47–53.

19. Lampert, *Till Death,* 263–4;

20. Sloan, *Three Plus One,* 169.

21. "Mary, Mary, Quite Contrary; Two Post-mortems Dissect Last Year's Bendix Takeover Fiasco," *Time,* 7/4/83; Sloan, *Three Plus One,* 244–5; Cunningham, *Power Play,* 266–8.

22. "The William Agee Story: Getting Ahead by Failing," *Denver Post,* 2/4/95; "Agee in Exile," *Fortune,* 5/29/95.

23. "Thank You, Bill Agee," *Forbes,* 3/11/85; "Martin Marietta's Stunning Comeback," *Dun's Business Month,* 9/86, obituary, "Thomas Pownall, 83; Executive Popularized the 'Pac-Man Defense,'" *Los Angeles Times,* 7/1/05.

24. Thomas G. Pownall, letter to MRL, 4/28/92; Pownall, letter to Allan Sloan, *Newsweek,* 7/17/97.

25. Norman Augustine, interview, 11/7/00; Augustine, chairman and CEO, Martin Marietta, letter to MRL, 1/16/95.

26. *New York Times,* 2/25/75; *New York Times,* 2/19/76; "Phillips to Revamp Directorate," *Washington Post,* 2/20/76; "Outside Directors Take Over at Phillips," *Business Week,* 3/1/76; "A Year's Time Turns Phillips' Meeting from Jeers to Cheers," *Wall Street Journal,* 4/28/76; *United States of America, Plaintiff, v. Phillips Petroleum Company, Stanley Learned, William F. Martin, William W. Keeler, Defendants,* U.S. District Court ruling, 7/5/77; "Conspiracy Charge Voided," *Washington Post,* 7/6/77.

27. "Bartlesville, a 'Company Town' and Proud of It," *U.S. News & World Report,* 10/22/84; Michael Wallis, *Oil Man: The Story of Frank Phillips and the Birth of Phillips Petroleum,* Doubleday (1988); " 'Technology-Driven' Phillips to Celebrate 80 Years," *Daily Oklahoman,* 4/27/97; "Phillips Petroleum Timeline," *Tulsa World,* 8/31/02.

28. John Greenwald, "A Wily Raider Shakes Up Corporate America," *Time* 3/4/85; T. Boone Pickens Jr., *Boone,* Houghton Mifflin Company (1987), 181–217; Jeff Shear, "T. Boone Pickens: Reversal of Fortune Pending," *Insight,* 5/20/91.

29. AP, "Thousands Rally in Support of Oil Company," 12/13/84.

30. "Pickens Denies Move on Phillips Was 'Greenmail,'" *Washington Post,* 12/25/84; "Icahn's Bear Hug," *Time,* 2/18/85; "Test Case for the Raiders: The Battle for Phillips Petroleum," *Financial Times,* 2/22/85; "Bartlesville, Okla., Holds Its Breath," *Washington Post,* 2/23/85; Pickens, *Boone,* 217.

31. "The High Price of Freedom: Phillips Goes Deeply in Debt to Repulse Corporate Raiders," *Time,* 3/18/85.

32. UPI, "NWA Shareholders Re-elect Directors, Pan Am Encouraged to Bid for Northwest," 5/15/89; "NWA's Directors to Decide on Fate," *Journal of Commerce,* 5/30/89; PR Newswire, "NWA Invites Revised Proposals," 6/5/89.

33. PR Newswire, "Former Vice President Mondale Named to NWA Inc. Board; Laird Continues as Director," 8/11/89; Kevin R. Johnson, secretary, "Wings Holding Inc. Audit and Safety Committee Meeting," 7/24/91; MRL, chairman, Audit and Safety Committee, letter to Northwest Airlines Senior Vice President Herbert Ihle, 7/29/91.

34. "Executives See Finance Firm Opportunities: 'New' Commercial Credit Is Expected to Prosper," *Washington Post,* 11/3/86; "The *Post* One Hundred," *Washington Post,* 5/18/87; "American Express and Primerica; The Comeback Kid and the Hare," *Economist,* 10/2/93; Amey Stone and Mike Brewster, *King of Capital: Sandy Weill and the Making of Citigroup,* Wiley (2001); Monica Langley, *Tearing Down the Walls: How Sandy Weill Fought His Way to the Top of the Financial World . . . and Then Nearly Lost It All,* Free Press (2003).

35. David Heebner, interview, 8/28/00.

36. Arthur C. Clarke, essay, "A Short Pre-History of Comsats, Or: How I Lost a Billion Dollars in My Spare Time," included in Clarke's *Voices from the Sky,* Harper & Row (1961).

37. Joseph Charyk, 4/1/02; "Baldrige & Shultz Now Directly Involved in Commerce-State Feud," *Communications Daily,* 6/15/84.

38. MRL, letter to George P. Shultz, secretary of state, "Personal—Hand Delivered," 8/15/84.

39. MRL, letter to Shultz, 6/20/84; Kenneth W. Dam, acting secretary of state, letter to MRL, 8/7/84; MRL, letter to Robert C. McFarlane, assistant to the president for national security affairs, 8/21/84; MRL, letter to Dr. Joseph Charyk, chairman and CEO, COMSAT, 8/30/84; Shultz, letter to MRL, 9/6/84; MRL, "Should Intelsat Have Competition?" *Washington Post,* 12/30/84.

40. Colin Powell, interview, 12/18/01; "Gen. Roscoe Robinson Dies," *St. Louis Post-Dispatch,* 7/23/93; "Gen. Roscoe Robinson Jr., Ex-NATO Envoy, Dies at 64," 7/23/93; "Gen. Roscoe Robinson Jr.," *Los Angeles Times,* 7/24/73; PR Newswire, "COMSAT Corporation Establishes a Four-Year Scholarship in Memory of Gen. Roscoe Robinson," 12/10/93; Phillips, "A Loud Hurrah for an Unsung Member of our Military History," *Austin American-Statesman,* 2/23/03.

41. Dick Cheney, interview, 2/20/01.

42. "Mutombo Contemplates Search for Missing Parents in Zaire," *Chicago Tribune,* 3/14/93; "Mutombo relieved," *Boston Globe,* 3/18/93.

43. "Lockheed Martin Completes Acquisition of Comsat Corporation," *Space & Technology,* 8/7/00.

44. MRL, letter to James A. Michener, 6/9/92; "The Fine Art of Giving Away Money; Lila Wallace–Reader's Digest Fund Emerges as Top Cultural Supporter," *Washington Post,* 7/20/93;

"$11.3 Million . . . Digest That," *Los Angeles Times,* 6/9/96; MRL, letter to Postmaster General Marvin Runyon, 6/24/96.

45. MRL, letter to Sen. Edward M. Kennedy, D-Mass., 6/13/01.

46. "Fine Arts Grant Awarded to Center," *Marshfield News-Herald,* 8/13/92; press release, "$600,000 Pledged to the Laird Endowment Fund for the Arts at the University of Wisconsin Center–Marshfield/Wood County," 8/18/92; "Laird Gives 2 Big Gifts," *Marshfield News-Herald,* 8/19/92.

47. Kathy Weaver, interviews, 7/11/02, 5/15/03.

48 / WAR AND PEACE

1. "Reveille for the Reserves," *Newsweek,* 9/3/90; "Weekend to Full-Time Warriors," *Time,* 9/10/90.

2. "Meet Mr. Tomahawk," *Washington Times,* 1/24/91.

3. Robert C. Moot, ASD comptroller, memorandum for MRL, "How the Budget Battles Were Won, FY 1970–FY 1973," 12/4/72.

4. MRL, testimony, "Department of Defense Appropriations for 1970," House Appropriations Defense Subcommittee, 11/17/69.

5. MRL, "News Conference at Pentagon," 12/27/71; minutes, Secretary of Defense Staff Meeting, 1/19/70.

6. "Air War on Hill: 3 Planes for 1 Job?", *Washington Post,* 3/22/71.

7. David Packard, Deputy Secretary of Defense, memorandum for secretary of the army and secretary of the air force, "Systems for Air Delivered Fire Support of Ground Forces," 1/22/70.

8. Stanley R. Resor, secretary of the army, and Robert C. Seamans Jr., secretary of the air force, memorandum for Deputy Secretary of Defense Packard, "Systems for Air Delivered Fire Support of Ground Forces," 3/26/70.

9. Seamans, *Aiming at Targets,* 174–5.

10. David Heebner, interview, 8/28/00.

11. Minutes, Secretary of Defense Staff Meeting, "Close Air Support," 3/27/72; UPI, "Army Terminates Copter Program," *New York Times,* 8/10/72.

12. Dan Henkin, ASD (PA), news release, "A-X Proposals Received," 8/10/70; Robert C. Seamans Jr., memorandum for MRL, "A-X Source Selection Decision," 12/17/70; Henkin, ASD (PA), news release, "A-X Prototypes Designated," 3/1/71; Jack Anderson and Dale Van Atta, "The Hero That Almost Missed the War," *Washington Post,* 3/5/91; Seamans, *Aiming at Targets,* 175; McLucas and Benson, *Confessions,* 1/1/03.

13. "Saddam can hold on for months, Laird says," *Marshfield News-Herald,* 10/30/90; Rowland Evans and Robert Novak, columnists, *The Record* (N.J.), 11/8/90.

14. AP, "Seven Former Defense Secretaries Discuss Gulf Crisis," 12/1/90; "Mideast Tensions; Ex-Defense Secretaries Advise Patience in Gulf," *New York Times,* 12/3/90; AP, "Military Force Needed to Evict Iraq From Kuwait, Officials Say," 12/14/90.

15. George H. W. Bush, interview, 10/14/97.

16. Colin Powell, interview, 12/18/01.

17. Robert Pursley, interview, 12/19/00; "Singlaub's Fellow Officers Also Oppose Troop Pull-out," *Washington Post,* 5/21/77; MRL, "Statement at the Request of the White House in Support of President Carter's Comments at His Press Conference," 5/26/77; "President Defends His Korea Policy," *Washington Post,* 5/27/77; transcript, Carter news conference, *Washington Post,* 5/27/77.

18. Jimmy Carter, interview, 10/23/97.

19. Helmut Schmidt, interviews, 2/4/01, 6/29/01.

20. John Laird, interview, 2/27/01.

21. MRL, "Arms Control: The Russians Are Cheating!" *Reader's Digest,* 12/77.

22. Harold Brown, interview, 2/21/01.

23. Scripps-Howard News Service, "Laird Plans a Haven for Ex-GOPers," 8/2/71; "Ford Accepts Position with a Think Tank," *Washington Post,* 2/3/77; "The Dominant Washington Think Tanks—AEI and Brookings Institution—Are Widening Their Focus and Trying to Broaden Their Financial Support," *National Journal,* 2/25/78; "Conservative Brain Trust," *New York Times Magazine,* 1/81; "Right-of-Center Defense Groups—the Pendulum Has Swung Their Way," *National*

Journal, 1/24/81; James Allen Smith, *The Idea Brokers: Think Tanks and the Rise of the New Policy Elite,* Free Press (1991), 176–80.

24. David S. Broder, "Stumping Ford Unlikely to Run in '80," *Washington Post,* 9/29/78; Broder, "GOP Game: Will Ford Deal Himself In?" *Washington Post,* 3/6/80; "Ford's Stance Worries Friends, Rivals," *Washington Post,* 3/8/80.

25. For example, MRL, "Defense Secretaries Shouldn't Play Politics," *Washington Post,* 8/17/80.

26. "Shultz Thinks Weinberger Kept Him Out of Initial Reagan Cabinet," *Washington Post,* 7/4/82; "Shultz, At Swearing-in, Speaks of His Optimism," *New York Times,* 7/17/82.

27. MRL, "Not a Binge, but a Buildup," *Washington Post,* 11/19/80; MRL, "What Our Defense Really Needs," *Washington Post,* 4/12/82; "Military Costs Trouble Conservatives," *New York Times,* 4/19/82; MRL, "Defense: Bad Cuts," *Washington Post,* 2/21/83.

28. Caspar Weinberger, interview, 1/25/01.

29. "The Role of Political Parties in the Nomination Process," *Commonsense,* 1981; AP, "Another Reform Group Starts," 1/27/82; *Report of the Commission on the Presidential Nominating Process,* 3/82; AP, "Reduce Presidential Primaries, Commission Proposes," 3/17/82.

30. AP, "Reagan, with New Backing, Faces Foreign Policy Decisions," 10/31/83; *U.S. News & World Report,* 11/21/83; Rowland Evans and Robert Novak, "Laird Turned Down Job as Mideast Troubleshooter," 11/28/83.

31. Charles Bowsher, comptroller general of the United States, 1981–96, and later POB chairman, interview, 8/30/00; "Hill Unit Plans Probe Of Auditing Industry," *Washington Post,* 1/5/85; "Panel Calls for Tougher Auditing Standards," *Washington Post,* 3/5/93.

32. MRL, chairman, Diego C. Asencio, Richard M. Helms, and John W. Vessey Jr., *Report of the Assessment Review Panel for the United States Missions in the Soviet Union,* 7/87, 3–4; "At Moscow Embassy, Continuous Shadow War," *Washington Post,* 8/22/85; Ronald Kessler, *Moscow Station: How the KGB Penetrated the American Embassy* (1989), 4–5, 26–8, 92–7.

33. "President Orders Inquiry in Moscow into Embassy Site," *New York Times,* 4/8/87.

34. Jack Vessey, interview, 2/25/02.

35. State Department, "Action Taken," *The Laird Report Recommendations,* 9/17/87.

36. MRL, letter to Secretary of State George P. Shultz, 7/6/87; MRL et al., *Report,* 5–8; "Envoy Is Blamed in Moscow Spying," *New York Times,* 1/20/88; AP, "Ambassador, State Department Hit for Marine Spy Case," 2/25/88; Kessler, *Moscow Station,* 13–14, 84, 136, 262–3.

37. MRL et al., *Report,* 2, 5, 7, 22, 28.

38. "Reagan Decides to Raze New Moscow Embassy," *New York Times,* 10/28/88; "U.S. Embassy in Moscow to Be Razed," *Washington Post,* 12/21/89; "Moscow Embassy Opens after Years of Delay," *Philadelphia Inquirer,* 5/13/00; "Bug-Free U.S. Embassy Building in Moscow Opens for Business," *Baltimore Sun,* 7/7/00; "Brick, Bars, Art Adorn New U.S. Embassy in Moscow," *Boston Globe,* 7/7/00.

39. William Perry, interview, 1/18/02.

40. MRL, letter to Sen. John Warner, chairman, Senate Armed Services Committee, 2/17/98.

41. Donna Shalala, interview, 2/10/05.

42. Sen. John Warner, letter to MRL, 6/10/04.

49 / ANOTHER VIETNAM?

1. Much of the February 28 meeting, which Laird had arranged in part as an interview for this author, was taped. The author also accompanied Laird and Rumsfeld's aide, Susan Wallace, on the tour of the Pentagon.

2. Transcript, "Media Availability with Secretary of Defense Donald H. Rumsfeld," 1/26/01; UPI, " 'Time for Indecision Over,' New Defense Chief Says," 1/26/01.

3. MRL, "Why Scrap the ABM Treaty?" *Washington Post,* 8/23/01.

4. Transcript, "Secretary Rumsfeld Media Availability at the Pentagon," 8/23/01.

5. "Listen to Mr. Laird," *St. Louis Post-Dispatch,* 8/25/01.

6. Brown, Laird, and Perry, "Ratify, but Review," *New York Times,* 1/7/01.

7. "Executive Summary," *2005 Defense Base Closure and Realignment Commission (BRAC) Report,* 9/8/05.

8. The seven other signatory defenses secretaries were Harold Brown, Frank Carlucci, William

Cohen, Robert McNamara, William Perry, James Schlesinger, and Caspar Weinberger. (UPI, "Officials: Terror Warrants Base Closings," 10/16/01; *Washington Post*, 10/17/01.)

9. MRL, interview with MSBNC producer Andrew Franklin, 2/25/02.

10. Mel Cunningham, interview, 9/11/01.

11. Drew Lindsay, "71 People the President Should Listen To," *Washingtonian*, 11/01.

12. "Designing a Pentagon Tribute; Thousands Enter," *Washington Post*, 8/29/02; "Families Look to Memorial to Ease Grief," *Army Times*, 9/16/02; Department of Defense, news release, "Pentagon Memorial Design Selection Announced," 3/3/03.

13. MRL, letter to Gen. John W. Vessey Jr. (USA, Ret.), 1/8/04.

14. "Ex-Defense Chiefs Cautious on Iraq," *Atlanta Journal-Constitution*, 5/2/02.

15. Scowcroft confirmed some of the elements of his preinvasion efforts in interviews with reporter Jeffrey Goldberg. ("Breaking Ranks: What Turned Brent Scowcroft against the Bush Administration?" *The New Yorker*, 10/31/06.)

16. "Laird Remains Busy in Government, Still Going Strong at 81," *Stevens Point Journal*, 4/29/01.

17. MRL, memorandum (faxed) to Secretary of Defense Rumsfeld, 2/11/04.

18. Donald Rumsfeld, memorandum (faxed) to MRL, 6/6/04.

19. "Kissinger Tapes Describe Crises, War and Stark Photos of Abuse," *New York Times*, 5/27/04; "Weekend Edition," National Public Radio, 5/30/04; "This Atrocity Thing," *Harper's Magazine*, 8/1/04.

20. MRL, letter to Henry Kissinger, 1/8/02.

21. MRL, "Iraq: Learning the Lessons of Vietnam," *Foreign Affairs*, November/December 2005, 21–43. (Freelance writer Daryl Gibson collaborated with Laird on the article.)

22. Transcript, hearing of the Senate Foreign Relations Committee, "Iraq in United States Foreign Policy," 10/19/05; "Saving Face and How to Say Farewell," *New York Times*, 11/27/75; Helmut Schmidt, letter to MRL, 11/30/05.

23. "Visited by a Host of Administrations Past, Bush Hears Some Chastening Words," *New York Times*, 1/6/06; Maureen Dowd, "Reach Out and Touch No One," *New York Times*, 1/7/06.

24. "This Time Around, Bush Lets Former Secretaries Speak," *New York Times*, 5/13/06.

25. MRL, "Don't Downsize the Guard," *Washington Post*, 2/6/06.

26. MRL and Robert Pursley, "Why Are They Speaking Up Now?" *Washington Post*, 4/19/06.

27. Robert Novak, *Chicago Sun-Times*, 8/6/06; "Round 2 for Rumsfeld," *USA Today*, 9/25/06.

28. "Election 2006: Voters Side with Democrats," *Los Angeles Times*, 11/9/06.

29. MRL, "Purse Strings and Pragmatism," *Washington Post*, 1/17/07.

30. MRL, "A Model for Responsible Withdrawal; The Vietnam Plan Worked until Aid Was Cut Off," *Washington Post*, 6/29/07.

31. "President Compares Vietnam, Iraq wars; Innocents Would Perish if US Pulled Out, He Says," *Boston Globe*, 8/23/07.

32. AP, "As Iraq War Drags On, Comparisons with Vietnam Grow," 1/25/07.

EPILOGUE

1. Gerald R. Ford, speech at Laird Center dedication, Marshfield, Wis., 9/12/97.

2. David Broder, speech, Laird Center dedication, Marshfield, Wis., 9/12/97; Broder, " 'Fraternizing with the Enemy,' " *Washington Post*, 9/17/97.

BIBLIOGRAPHY

Ralph David Abernathy, *And the Walls Came Tumbling Down,* Harper and Row, 1989

Hans Christian Adamson and George Francis Kosco, *Halsey's Typhoons,* Crown Publishers, 1967

Spiro T. Agnew, *Where He Stands: The Life and Convictions of Spiro T. Agnew,* Hawthorn Books, 1968

Spiro T. Agnew, *Frankly Speaking: A Collection of Extraordinary Speeches,* Public Affairs Press, 1970

Spiro T. Agnew, *Go Quietly . . . Or Else,* William Morrow and Company, 1980

Carl Albert with Danney Goble, *Little Giant: The Life and Times of Speaker Carl Albert,* University of Oklahoma Press, 1990

Stephen E. Ambrose, *Eisenhower: Soldier, General of the Army, President-Elect,* Simon and Schuster, 1983

Stephen E. Ambrose, *Eisenhower: The President,* Simon and Schuster, 1984

Stephen E. Ambrose, *Nixon: The Education of a Politician 1913–1962,* Touchstone, 1987

Stephen E. Ambrose, *Nixon: The Triumph of a Politician 1962–1972,* Simon and Schuster, 1989

Stephen E. Ambrose, *The Wild Blue: The Men and Boys Who Flew the B-24s over Germany,* Simon and Schuster, 2001

Carl H. Amme Jr., *NATO without France: A Strategic Appraisal,* Hoover Institution, 1967

Jack Anderson and Ronald W. May, *McCarthy: The Man, the Senator, the "Ism,"* Beacon Press, 1952

Jack Anderson with Daryl Gibson, *Peace, War, and Politics,* Forge, 1999

Martin Anderson, *The Making of the All-Volunteer Armed Force,* Hoover Institution, 1991

Robert Sam Anson, *McGovern: A Biography,* Holt, Rinehart, and Winston, 1972

Frank Aukofer and William P. Lawrence: *America's Team: The Odd Couple; A Report on the Relationship between the Media and the Military,* Freedom Forum First Amendment Center, 1995

Bill Ayers, *Fugitive Days: A Memoir,* Beacon Press, 2001

Rick Ball and NBC News, *Meet the Press: Fifty Years of History in the Making,* McGraw-Hill, 1998

Lawrence Baskir and William Strauss, *Chance and Circumstance: The Draft, the War, and the Vietnam Generation,* Knopf, 1978

Tom Bates, *Rads: The 1970 Bombing of the Army Math Research Center at the University of Wisconsin and Its Aftermath,* HarperCollins, 1992

Kenneth E. BeLieu, *The Captains and the Kings,* Gateway Press, 1999

Ezra Taft Benson, *Cross Fire: The Eight Years with Eisenhower,* Doubleday and Company, 1962

Jason Berger, Editor, *The Military Draft,* H. W. Wilson Company, 1981

Michael R. Beschloss, *Taking Charge: The Johnson White House Tapes, 1963–1964,* Simon and Schuster, 1997

Michael R. Beschloss, *Reaching for Glory: Lyndon Johnson's Secret White House Tapes, 1964–1965,* Simon and Schuster, 2001

Michael R. Beschloss and Strobe Talbott, *At the Highest Levels: The Inside Story of the End of the Cold War,* Little, Brown, and Company, 1993

Don E. Beyer, The Marshfield Clinic: A History, 1916–1970, Master's Thesis, University of Wisconsin, 1975

Thomas D. Boettcher, *Vietnam: The Valor and the Sorrow,* Little, Brown, and Company, 1985

Richard Boyle, *GI Revolts: The Breakdown of the U.S. Army in Vietnam,* United Front Press, 1973

Walter J. Boyne, *Beyond the Horizons: The Lockheed Story,* St. Martin's Press, 1998

Harold Brayman, *The President Speaks Off-the-Record (Gridiron Club),* Dow Jones Books, 1976

Piers Brendon, *Ike: His Life and Times,* Harper and Row, 1986

Ted Brock and Larry Eldridge Jr., *Twenty-five Years: The NFL since 1960,* Simon and Schuster, 1985

David S. Broder, *Behind the Front Page,* Simon and Schuster, 1987

Fawn Brodie, *Richard Nixon: The Shaping of His Character,* W.W. Norton Publishing, 1981

Herbert Brownell with John P. Burke, *Advising Ike: The Memoirs of Attorney General Herbert Brownell,* University Press of Kansas, 1993

Patrick J. Buchanan, *The New Majority: President Nixon at Mid-Passage,* Girard Company, 1973

Patrick J. Buchanan, *Right from the Beginning,* Little, Brown, and Company, 1988

William Bundy, *A Tangled Web: The Making of Foreign Policy in the Nixon Presidency,* Hill and Wang, 1998

Robert F. Burk, *Dwight D. Eisenhower: Hero and Politician,* Twayne Publishers, 1986

Bob Burke and Ralph G. Thompson, *Bryce Harlow: Mr. Integrity,* Oklahoma Heritage Association, 2000

Diane L. Burns, *Cranberries: Fruit of the Bogs,* Carolrhoda Books, 1994

George Bush with Vic Gold, *Looking Forward,* Doubleday, 1987

George H.W. Bush, *All the Best, George Bush: My Life and Other Writings,* Scribner, 1999

Raymond Calhoun, *Typhoon: The Other Enemy; The Third Fleet and the Pacific Storm of December 1944,* United States Naval Institute, 1981

Shepherd Campbell and Peter Landau, *Presidential Lies: The Illustrated History of White House Golf,* Macmillan, 1996

James Cannon, *Time and Chance: Gerald Ford's Appointment with History,* HarperCollins, 1994

Robert A. Caro, *The Years of Lyndon Johnson: Means of Ascent,* Alfred A. Knopf, 1990

Robert A. Caro, *The Years of Lyndon Johnson: Master of the Senate,* Alfred A. Knopf, 2002

James Carroll, *An America Requiem: God, My Father, and the War That Came between Us,* Houghton Mifflin, 1996

James Carroll, *House of War,* Houghton Mifflin, 2006

Timothy N. Castle, *War in the Shadow of Vietnam: United States Military Aid to the Royal Lao Government, 1955–1975,* 1993

John Whiteclay Chambers II, *To Raise an Army: The Draft Comes to Modern America*, Free Press, 1987

Lewis Chester, Godfrey Hodgson, and Bruce Page, *An American Melodrama: The Presidential Campaign of 1968*, Viking Press, 1969

Clark Clifford with Richard Holbrooke, *Counsel to the President: A Memoir*, Random House, 1991

Hillary Rodham Clinton, *Living History*, Simon and Schuster, 2003

Richard M. Cohen and Jules Witcover, *A Heartbeat Away: The Investigation and Resignation of Vice President Spiro T. Agnew*, Viking Press, 1974

Len Colodny and Robert Gettlin, *Silent Coup*, St. Martin's Press, 1991

Timothy Conlan, *New Federalism: Intergovernmental Reform from Nixon to Reagan*, Brookings Institution, 1988

John Connally with Mickey Herskowitz, *In History's Shadow: An American Odyssey*, Hyperion Books, 1993

Adm. William J. Crowe with David Chanoff, *The Line of Fire*, Simon and Schuster, 1993

Monica Crowley, *Nixon Off the Record*, Random House, 1996

Mary Cunningham with Fran Schumer, *Power Play: What Really Happened at Bendix*, Simon and Schuster, 1984

Richard Curtis, *The Berrigan Brothers*, Hawthorn Books, 1974

Robert Dallek, *Flawed Giant: Lyndon Johnson and His Times 1961–1973*, Oxford University Press, 1998

Robert Dallek, *Nixon and Kissinger: Partners in Power*, HarperCollins, 2007

Clifton Daniel, *Lords, Ladies, and Gentlemen: A Memoir*, Arbor House, 1984

James Kirkpatrick Davis, *Assault on the Left: The FBI and the Sixties Antiwar Movement*, Praeger, 1997

Vernon E. Davis, *The Long Road Home: U.S. Prisoner of War Policy and Planning in Southeast Asia*, Historical Office, Office of the Secretary of Defense, 2000

John W. Dean III, *Blind Ambition*, Simon and Schuster, 1976

Department of Defense Key Officials 1947–1995, Historical Office, Office of the Secretary of Defense, 1995

John P. Dever and Maria C. Dever, *Women and the Military*, McFarland and Company, 1995

C. Dwight Dorough, *Mr. Sam*, Random House, 1962

James Doyle, *Not above the Law: The Battles of Watergate Prosecutors Cox and Jaworski*, William Morrow and Company, 1977

Lee Edwards, *Goldwater: The Man Who Made a Revolution*, Regnery Publishing, 1995

Lee Edwards, *The Power of Ideas: The Heritage Foundation at Twenty-five Years*, Jameson Books, 1997

John Ehrlichman, *Witness to Power*, Simon and Schuster, 1982

Dwight D. Eisenhower, Post-Presidential Appointment Books, unpublished manuscripts, 1961–1967

Dwight D. Eisenhower, *Mandate for Change*, Signet Books, 1963

Dwight D. Eisenhower, *Waging Peace*, Doubleday and Company, 1965

Dwight D. Eisenhower, *White House Years: Waging Peace, 1956–1961*, Doubleday and Company, 1965

Dwight D. Eisenhower, *At Ease: Stories I Tell to Friends*, Doubleday and Company, 1967

John S. D. Eisenhower, *Strictly Personal,* Doubleday and Company, 1974

Milton S. Eisenhower, *The President Is Calling,* Doubleday and Company, 1974

Fred Emery, *Watergate: The Corruption of American Politics and the Fall of Richard Nixon,* Simon and Schuster, 1994

Sen. Sam J. Ervin Jr., *Preserving the Constitution,* Michie Company, 1984

Elizabeth W. Etheridge, *Sentinel for Health: A History of the Centers for Disease Control,* University of California Press, 1992

Rowland Evans Jr., and Robert D. Novak, *Nixon in the White House: The Frustration of Power,* Random House, 1971

Adam Fairclough, *Better Day Coming: Blacks and Equality 1890–2000,* Viking, 2001

John A. Ferejohn and Barry R. Weingast, Editors, *The New Federalism: Can the States Be Trusted?* Hoover Institution Press, 1997

Robert H. Ferrell, Editor, *The Eisenhower Diaries,* W. W. Norton and Company, 1981

Howard Fields, *High Crimes and Misdemeanors: The Dramatic Story of the Rodino Committee,* W. W. Norton and Company, 1978

A. Ernest Fitzgerald, *The High Priests of Waste,* W. W. Norton and Company, 1972

Frances Fitzgerald, *Fire in the Lake: The Vietnamese and the Americans in Vietnam,* Vintage Books, 1972

Dan B. Fleming Jr., *Kennedy vs. Humphrey, West Virginia, 1960,* McFarland and Company, 1992

George Q. Flynn, *Lewis B. Hershey, Mr. Selective Service,* University of North Carolina Press, 1985

Jane Fonda, *My Life So Far,* Random House, 2005

Gerald R. Ford, *A Time to Heal,* Harper and Row, 1979

Verna Fowler, *The Menominee,* Raintree Steck-Vaughn Publishers, 2001

Milton Friedman and Rose D. Friedman, *Two Lucky People,* University of Chicago Press, 1998

Sen. J. W. Fulbright, *The Pentagon Propaganda Machine,* Liveright, 1970

John W. Gardner, *On Leadership,* Free Press, 1990

Raymond L. Garthoff, *Detente and Confrontation: American-Soviet Relations from Nixon to Reagan,* Brookings Institution, 1985

Irwin G. Gellman, *The Contender: Richard Nixon, The Congress Years: 1946–1952,* Free Press, 1999

David Gergen, *Eyewitness to Power: The Essence of Power: Nixon to Clinton,* Simon and Schuster, 2000

Marvin E. Gettleman, Jane Franklin, Marilyn B. Young, and H. Bruce Franklin, *Vietnam and America: A Documented History,* Grove Press, 1995

James A. Gibbs, *Shipwrecks of the Pacific Coast,* Binford and Mort Publishing, 1957

Joseph Godson, Editor, *Thirty-five Years of NATO,* Dodd, Mead, and Company, 1984

Sen. Barry M. Goldwater, *With No Apologies,* William Morrow and Company, 1979

Barry M. Goldwater with Jack Casserly, *Goldwater,* Doubleday, 1988

Richard A. Goodman, Karen L. Foster, and Michael B. Gregg, *Highlights in Public Health: Landmark Articles from the MMWR 1961–1996,* Centers for Disease Control and Prevention, 1996

Michael Gough, *Dioxin, Agent Orange: The Facts,* Plenum Press, 1986

Alberta Gould, *First Lady of the Senate: A Life of Margaret Chase Smith,* Windswept House Publishers, 1990

Phil G. Goulding, *Confirm or Deny: Informing the People on National Security,* Harper and Row, 1970

Fred I. Greenstein, *The Hidden-Hand Presidency: Eisenhower as Leader,* Basic Books, 1982

Sen. Ernest Gruening and Herbt Wilton Beaser, *Vietnam Folly,* National Press Inc., 1968

Bill Gulley with Mary Ellen Reese, *Breaking Cover,* Simon and Schuster, 1980

Col. David H. Hackworth and Julie Sherman, *About Face,* Simon and Schuster, 1989

Alexander M. Haig Jr. with Charles McCarry, *Inner Circles: How America Changed the World, a Memoir,* Warner Books, 1992

David Halberstam, *The Best and the Brightest,* Random House, 1969

H. R. Haldeman, *The Haldeman Diaries: Inside the Nixon White House,* G. P. Putnam's Sons, 1994

H. R. Haldeman with Joseph DiMona, *The Ends of Power,* Times Books, 1978

Jane Hamilton-Merritt, *Tragic Mountains: The Hmong, the Americans, and the Secret Wars,* 1993

William M. Hammond, *United States Army in Vietnam: Public Affairs: The Military and the Media, 1968–1973,* Government Printing Office, 1996

D. B. Hardeman and Donald C. Bacon, *Rayburn: A Biography,* Madison Books, 1987

Denis J. Harrington, *The Pro Football Hall of Fame: Players, Coaches, Team Owners, and League Officials, 1963–1991,* McFarland and Company, 1991

David Harris, *The League: The Rise and Decline of the NFL,* Bantam Books, 1986

Robert Hartmann, *Palace Politics,* McGraw-Hill, 1980

John Heidenry, *Theirs Was the Kingdom: Lila and DeWitt Wallace and the Story of Reader's Digest,* W. W. Norton, 1993

Paul Hendrickson, *The Living and the Dead: Robert McNamara and Five Lives of a Lost War,* Alfred A. Knopf, 1996

Seymour M. Hersh, *The Price of Power: Kissinger in the Nixon White House,* Summit Books, 1983

Hank Hillin, *Al Gore Jr.: His Life and Career,* Birch Lane Press, 1988

Joan Hoff, *Nixon Reconsidered,* Basic Books, 1994

Maj. Gen. Jeanne Holm, *Women in the Military: An Unfinished Revolution,* Presidio, 1992

R. Gordon Hoxie, *Command Decision and the Presidency: A Study in National Security Policy and Organization,* Reader's Digest Press, 1977

Richard Humble, *World War II Aircraft Carriers,* Franklin Watts, 1989

Hubert H. Humphrey, *The Education of a Public Man: My Life and Politics,* Doubleday and Company, 1976

Walter Isaacson, *Kissinger: A Biography,* Simon and Schuster, 1992

Leon Jaworski, *The Right and the Power: The Prosecution of Watergate,* Reader's Digest Press, 1976

Lyndon Baines Johnson, *The Vantage Point: Perspectives of the Presidency 1963–1969,* Holt, Rinehart, and Winston, 1971

Charles Kaiser, *1968 in America: Music, Politics, Chaos, Counterculture, and the Shaping of a Generation,* Weidenfeld and Nicholson, 1988

David Kaiser, *American Tragedy: Kennedy, Johnson, and the Origins of the Vietnam War,* Belknap Press, 2000

Marvin Kalb and Bernard Kalb, *Kissinger,* Little, Brown, and Company, 1974

Lawrence S. Kaplan, *NATO and the United States,* University Press of Kentucky, 1984

Stanley Karnow, *Vietnam: A History,* Viking Press, 1983

Roger Kelley, *Letters to My Children,* Roger Kelley, 1999

John Kerry and Vietnam Veterans against the War, *The New Soldier,* Collier Books, 1971

Ronald Kessler, *Moscow Station: How the KGB Penetrated the American Embassy,* Scribner, 1989

Jeffrey Kimball, *Nixon's Vietnam War,* University Press of Kansas, 1998

Jeffrey Kimball, *The Vietnam War Files: Uncovering the Secret History of Nixon-Era Strategy,* University Press of Kansas, 2004

Douglas Kinnard, *The Secretary of Defense,* University Press of Kentucky, 1980

Henry Kissinger, *White House Years,* Little, Brown, and Company, 1979

Henry Kissinger, *Years of Upheaval,* Little, Brown, and Company, 1982

Henry Kissinger, *Diplomacy,* Simon and Schuster, 1994

Henry Kissinger, *Ending the Vietnam War: A History of America's Involvement in and Extrication from the Vietnam War,* Simon and Schuster, 2003

Lawrence J. Korb, *The Joint Chiefs of Staff: The First Twenty-five Years,* Indiana University Press, 1976

Stanley I. Kutler, Editor, *Encyclopedia of the Vietnam War,* Simon and Schuster, 1990

Stanley I. Kutler, *The Wars of Watergate: The Last Crisis of Richard Nixon,* W. W Norton and Company, 1990

Stanley I. Kutler, *Abuse of Power: The New Nixon Tapes,* Simon and Schuster, 2000

Michael L. LaBlanc, Editor, *Professional Sports Team Histories,* Gale Research Inc., 1994

Helen Laird, *A Mind of Her Own: Helen Connor Laird and Family 1888–1982,* University of Wisconsin Press, 2006

Melvin R. Laird, *A House Divided,* Henry Regnery Company, 1962

Melvin R. Laird, Editor, *The Conservative Papers,* Quadrangle Books, 1964

Melvin R. Laird, Editor, *Republican Papers,* Frederick A. Praeger, 1968

Hope Lampert, *Till Death Do Us Part: Bendix vs. Martin Marietta,* Harcourt Brace Jovanovich, 1983

A. J. Langguth, *Our Vietnam: The War 1954–1975,* Simon and Schuster, 2000

Arthur Larson, *Eisenhower: The President Nobody Knew,* Charles Scribner's Sons, 1968

John Lehman, *Making War: The Two-Hundred-Year-Old Battle between the President and Congress over How America Goes to War,* Charles Scribner's Sons, 1992

Adam J. Lieberman and Simona C. Kwon, *Facts versus Fears: A Review of the Greatest Unfounded Health Scares of Recent Times,* American Council on Science and Health, 1997

Albert N. Link, *A Generosity of Spirit: The Early History of the Research Triangle Park,* Research Triangle Foundation, 1995

Carnes Lord, *The Presidency and the Management of National Security,* Free Press, 1988

Arnold S. Lott, *Brave Ship Brave Men,* United States Naval Institute, 1986

Peter Lyon, *Eisenhower: Portrait of the Hero,* Little, Brown, and Company, 1974

Michael Maclear, *The Ten Thousand Day War: Vietnam, 1945–1975,* Avon, 1981

Jeb Stuart Magruder, *An American Life: One Man's Road to Watergate,* Atheneum, 1974

Robert Mann, *Legacy to Power: Senator Russell Long of Louisiana,* Paragon House, 1992

David Maraniss, *When Pride Still Mattered: A Life of Vince Lombardi,* Simon and Schuster, 1999

David Maraniss and Ellen Nakashima, *The Prince of Tennessee: The Rise of Al Gore*, Simon and Schuster, 2000

Victor Marchetti and John D. Marks, *The CIA and the Cult of Intelligence*, Dell, 1974

Don Marshall, *Oregon Shipwrecks*, Binford and Mort Publishing, 1984

Marshfield History Project, *The Marshfield Story 1972–1997: Piecing Together Our Past*, Palmer Publications, 1997

Joe Martin, as told to Robert J. Donovan, *My First Fifty Years in Politics*, McGraw-Hill Book Company, 1960

John T. Mason, Editor, *The Pacific War Remembered: An Oral History Collection*, U.S. Naval Institute Press, 1986

John McCain with Mark Salter, *Faith of My Fathers*, Random House, 1999

Bill McCloud, *What Should We Tell Our Children about Vietnam?* University of Oklahoma Press, 1989

Joseph B. McCormick and Susan Fisher-Hoch with Leslie Alan Horvitz, *Level 4: Virus Hunters of the CDC*, Turner Publishing, 1996

George McGovern, *Grassroots: The Autobiography of George McGovern*, Random House, 1977

James R. McGovern, *Black Eagle: General Daniel "Chappie" James Jr.*, University of Alabama Press, 1985

John McLucas and Lawrence Benson, Confessions of a Technocrat, unpublished manuscript autobiography

H.R. McMaster, *Dereliction of Duty: Johnson, McNamara, the Joint Chiefs of Staff, and the Lies That Led to Vietnam*, HarperCollins, 1997

Robert S. McNamara with Brian VanDeMark, *In Retrospect: The Tragedy and Lessons of Vietnam*, Vintage Books, 1995

Golda Meir, *A Land of Our Own: An Oral Autobiography*, G.P. Putnam's Sons, 1973

Golda Meir, *My Life*, G.P. Putnam's Sons, 1975

Members of Congress for Peace through Law Military Spending Committee, *The Economics of Defense: A Bipartisan Review of Military Spending*, Praeger, 1971

James A. Michener, *Kent State: What Happened and Why*, Random House, 1971

Jack Mills, Caddy, unpublished memoir, 2007

Joyce Milton, *The First Partner: Hillary Rodham Clinton*, William Morrow and Company, 1990

Clark R. Mollenhoff, *George Romney: Mormon in Politics*, Meredith Press, 1968

Clark R. Mollenhoff, *The Man Who Pardoned Nixon*, St. Martin's Press, 1976

Arlene Bourgeois Molzahn, *The Green Bay Packers*, Enslow Publishers, 1999

Relman Morin, *Dwight D. Eisenhower: A Gauge of Greatness*, Associated Press, 1969

Samuel Eliot Morison, *History of United States Naval Operations in World War II*, Volumes IX, XII–XV, Little, Brown, and Company, 1954, 1958–1962

Roger Morris, *Haig: The General's Progress*, Playboy Press, 1982

David Murray, *Charles Percy of Illinois*, Harper and Row, 1968

Yasuhiro Nakasone, translated by Lesley Connors, *The Making of the New Japan: Reclaiming the Political Mainstream*, Curzon, 1999

Bernard C. Nalty, Editor, *Vietnam War: The History of America's Conflict in Southeast Asia*, Smithmark Publishers, 1996

National Football League, *The NFL's Official Encyclopedic History of Professional Football*, Macmillan Publishing, 1973

David S. Neft and Richard M. Cohen, *The Football Encyclopedia*, St. Martin's Press, 1991

W. Dale Nelson, *The President Is at Camp David,* Syracuse University Press, 1995

John Newhouse, *Cold Dawn: The Story of SALT,* Holt, Rinehart, and Winston, 1973

Paul H. Nitze with Ann M. Smith and Steven L. Rearden, *From Hiroshima to Glasnost: At the Center of Decision,* Grove Weidenfeld, 1989

Richard M. Nixon, *Six Crises,* Doubleday and Company, 1962

Richard Nixon, *RN: The Memoirs of Richard Nixon,* Grosset and Dunlap, 1978

Richard Nixon, *In the Arena: A Memoir of Victory, Defeat, and Renewal,* Simon and Schuster, 1990

Robert D. Novak, *The Prince of Darkness: Fifty Years of Reporting in Washington,* Crown Forum, 2007

G. Warren Nutter, *Kissinger's Grand Design,* American Enterprise Institute, 1975

Donald Oberdorfer, *Tet,* Doubleday and Company, 1971

Lawrence F. O'Brien, *No Final Victories: A Life in Politics—from John F. Kennedy to Watergate,* Doubleday and Company, 1974

Kenneth O'Donnell and David Powers with Joe McCarthy, *"Johnny, We Hardly Knew Ye": Memories of John Fitzgerald Kennedy,* Little, Brown, and Company, 1972

Peter J. Ognibene, *Scoop: The Life and Politics of Henry M. Jackson,* Stein and Day, 1975

James S. Olson and Randy Roberts, *Where the Domino Fell: America and Vietnam, 1945 to 1990,* St. Martin's Press, 1991

John Osborne, *The Second Year of the Nixon Watch,* Liveright, 1971

John Osborne, *The Fourth Year of the Nixon Watch,* Liveright, 1973

John Osborne, *The Fifth Year of the Nixon Watch,* Liveright, 1974

John Osborne, *White House Watch: The Ford Years,* New Republic Books, 1977

David Packard, *The HP Way: How Bill Hewlett and I Built Our Company,* HarperBusiness, 1995

Gen. Bruce Palmer Jr., *The Twenty-five-Year War: America's Military Role in Vietnam,* Simon and Schuster, 1984

Nicholas Peroff, *Menominee DRUMS: Tribal Termination and Restoration 1954–1974,* University of Oklahoma Press, 1982

Geoffrey Perret, *Eisenhower,* Random House, 1999

Mark Perry, *Four Stars,* Houghton Mifflin Company, 1989

J. Alfred Phelps, *Chappie: America's First Black Four-Star General,* Presidio, 1991

T. Boone Pickens Jr., *Boone,* Houghton Mifflin, 1987

Norman Polmar and Thomas B. Allen, *Rickover,* Simon and Schuster, 1982

Colin L. Powell with Joseph E. Persico, *My American Journey,* Random House, 1995

Thomas Powers, *The Man Who Kept the Secrets: Richard Helms and the CIA,* Alfred A. Knopf, 1979

Raymond Price, *With Nixon,* Viking Press, 1977

Albert Quie, *Riding the Divide,* Quie Publications, 2003

Dan Rather and Gary Paul Gates, *The Palace Guard,* Harper and Row, 1974

Marion Rivers Ravenel, *Rivers Delivers,* Wyrick and Company, 1995

Jeffrey Record, *Dark Victory: America's Second War against Iraq,* Naval Institute Press, 2004

Jeffrey Record, *The Wrong War: Why We Lost in Vietnam,* Naval Institute Press, 1998

Richard Reeves, *A Ford, Not a Lincoln,* Harcourt Brace Janovich, 1975

Richard Reeves, *President Nixon: Alone in the White House,* Simon and Schuster, 2001

Thomas C. Reeves, *The Life and Times of Joe McCarthy,* Stein and Day, 1982

Ed Regis, *Virus Ground Zero: Stalking the Killer Viruses with the Centers for Disease Control*, Pocket Books, 1996

Richard A. Rettig, *Cancer Crusade: The Story of the National Cancer Act of 1971*, Princeton University Press, 1977

Rep. Henry S. Reuss, *Revenue-Sharing: Crutch or Catalyst for State and Local Governments?* Praeger Publishers, 1970

Henry S. Reuss, *When Government Was Good: Memories of a Life in Politics*, University of Wisconsin Press, 1999

Elliot Richardson, *Reflections of a Radical Moderate*, Pantheon Books, 1996

George Richey, *Britain's Strategic Role in NATO*, Macmillan Press, 1986

Jason Richie, *Secretaries of War, Navy, and Defense: Ensuring National Security*, Oliver Press, 2002

Thomas E. Ricks, *Fiasco: The American Military Adventure in Iraq*, Penguin, 2006

Stuart I. Rochester and Frederick Kiley, *Honor Bound: The History of American Prisoners of War in Southeast Asia, 1961–73*, Historical Office, Office of the Secretary of Defense, 1998

David Rudenstine, *The Day the Presses Stopped: A History of the Pentagon Papers Case*, University of California Press, 1996

Harold P. Rusch, M.D., *Something Attempted, Something Done: A Personal History of Cancer Research at the University of Wisconsin, 1934–1979*, Wisconsin Medical Alumni Association, 1984

William Safire, *Before the Fall: An Inside View of the Pre-Watergate White House*, Doubleday and Company, 1975

Pierre Salinger, *With Kennedy*, Doubleday and Company, 1966

Jerrold L. Schecter and Nguyen Tien Hung, *The Palace File*, Harper and Row, 1986

Benjamin F. Schemmer, *The Raid*, Avon, 1976

Bob Schieffer, *This Just In: What I Couldn't Tell You on TV*, G.P. Putnam's Sons, 2003

Arthur M. Schlesinger Jr., *A Thousand Days: John F. Kennedy in the White House*, Houghton Mifflin, 1965

Helmut Schmidt, translated from German by Ruth Hein, *Men and Powers: A Political Retrospective*, Random House, 1989

Peter H. Schuck, *Agent Orange on Trial: Mass Toxic Disasters in the Courts*, Belknap Press, 1986

Robert C. Seamans Jr., *Aiming at Targets: The Autobiography of Robert C. Seamans Jr.*, NASA History Office, 1996

David R. Segal, *Recruiting for Uncle Sam: Citizenship and Military Manpower Policy*, University Press of Kansas, 1989

Deborah Shapley, *Promise and Power: The Life and Times of Robert McNamara*, Little, Brown, and Company, 1993

William Shawcross, *Sideshow: Kissinger, Nixon, and the Destruction of Cambodia*, Simon and Schuster, 1979

Neil Sheehan, *A Bright Shining Lie: John Paul Vann and America in Vietnam*, Random House,1988

Jeff Shesol, *Mutual Contempt: Lyndon Johnson, Robert Kennedy, and the Feud That Defined a Decade*, W.W. Norton, 1997

Barry J. Shillito, *A Memoir*, Shillito Publications, 1997

Edward Shorter, *The Health Century*, Doubleday, 1987

George P. Shultz, *Turmoil and Triumph: My Years as Secretary of State*, Charles Scribner's Sons, 1993

George P. Shultz and Kenneth W. Dam, *Economic Policy beyond the Headlines*, Stanford Alumni Association, 1977

Robert B. Sims, *The Pentagon Reporters*, National Defense University Press, 1983

Maj. Gen. John K. Singlaub with Malcolm McConnell, *Hazardous Duty: An American Soldier in the Twentieth Century*, Summit Books, 1991

Allan Sloan, *Three Plus One Equals Billions: The Bendix–Martin Marietta War*, Arbor House, 1983

James Allen Smith, *Brookings at Seventy-Five*, Brookings Institution, 1991

James Allen Smith, *The Idea Brokers: Think Tanks and the Rise of the New Policy Elite*, Free Press, 1991

James Allen Smith, *Strategic Calling: The Center for Strategic and International Studies 1962–1992*, CSIS, 1993

Kevin B. Smith, *The Iron Man: The Life and Times of Congressman Glenn R. Davis*, University Press of America, 1994

Frank Snepp, *Decent Interval: An Insider's Account of Saigon's Indecent End Told by the CIA's Chief Strategy Analyst in Vietnam*, Vintage Books, 1978

Theodore C. Sorensen, *Kennedy*, Harper and Row, 1965

Lewis Sorley, *Thunderbolt: General Creighton Abrams and the Army of His Times*, Simon and Schuster, 1992

Lewis Sorley, *A Better War: The Unexamined Victories and Final Tragedy of America's Last Years in Vietnam*, Harcourt Brace and Company, 1999

Donald Srull, Editor, *The Cost Analysis Improvement Group: A History*, Logistics Management Institute, 1998

Richard Stacewicz, *Winter Soldiers: An Oral History of the Vietnam Veterans against the War*, Twayne Publishers, 1997

Maurice H. Stans, *One of the Presidents' Men: Twenty Years with Eisenhower and Nixon*, Brassey's, 1995

Jim Stockdale and Sybil Stockdale, *In Love and War: The Story of a Family's Ordeal and Sacrifice during the Vietnam Years*, Naval Institute Press, 1990

Stephen P. Strickland, *Politics, Science, and Dread Disease*, Harvard University Press, 1972

Richard Stubbing, *The Defense Game*, HarperCollins, 1986

Cyrus Sulzberger, *An Age of Mediocrity*, Macmillan, 1973

Anthony Summers with Robbyn Swan, *The Arrogance of Power: The Secret World of Richard Nixon*, Viking, 2000

Strobe Talbott, *Endgame: The Inside Story of SALT II*, Harper and Row, 1979

Strobe Talbott, *The Master of the Game: Paul Nitze and the Nuclear Peace*, Vintage, 1988

Curtis W. Tarr, *By the Numbers: The Reform of the Selective Service System 1970–1972*, National Defense University Press, 1981

Anthony Michael Tedeschi, *Live Via Satellite: The Story of COMSAT and the Technology That Changed World Communication*, Acropolis Books, 1989

J. F. terHorst and Col. Ralph Albertazzie, *The Flying White House: The Story of Air Force One*, Coward, McCann, and Geoghegan Inc., 1979

Helen Thomas, *Dateline: White House*, Macmillan Publishing, 1975

Helen Thomas, *Front Row at the White House: My Life and Times*, Scribner, 1999

Lately Thomas, *When Even Angels Wept: The Senator Joseph McCarthy Affair—a Story without a Hero*, William Morrow and Company, 1973

Jack Todd, *Desertion in the Time of Vietnam*, Houghton Mifflin, 2001

John G. Tower, *Consequences: A Personal and Political Memoir*, Little, Brown, and Company, 1991

Roger R. Trask and Alfred Goldberg, *The Department of Defense 1947–1997: Organization and Leaders*, Historical Office, Office of the Secretary of Defense, 1997

Bill Turque, *Inventing Al Gore: A Biography*, Houghton Mifflin, 2000

Sanford J. Ungar, *The Papers and the Papers*, E. P. Dutton and Company, 1972

Richard Valeriani, *Travels with Henry*, Houghton Mifflin, 1979

Marlene Boyd Vallin, *Margaret Chase Smith: Model Public Servant*, Greenwood Press,1998

Frank E. Vandiver, *Shadows of Vietnam: Lyndon Johnson's Wars*, Texas A&M University Press, 1997

George Veith, *Code Name Bright Light*, Dell Publishing, 1998

Vamik Volkan, Norman Itzkowitz, and Andrew Dod, *Richard Nixon: A Psychobiography*, Columbia University Press, 1997

Samuel Walker, *In Defense of American Liberties: A History of the ACLU*, Southern Illinois University Press, 1990

Patricia Ward Wallace, *Politics of Conscience: A Biography of Margaret Chase Smith*, Praeger, 1995

Caspar W. Weinberger, *Fighting for Peace: Seven Critical Years in the Pentagon*, Warner Books, 1990

Tom Wells, *The War Within: America's Battle over Vietnam*, University of California Press, 1994

Gen. William C. Westmoreland, *A Soldier Reports*, Doubleday and Company, 1976

Ralph Wetterhahn, *The Last Battle: The Mayaguez Incident and the End of the Vietnam War*, Plume, 2002

Theodore H. White, *The Making of the President 1960*, Atheneum Publishers, 1961

Theodore H. White, *The Making of the President 1964*, Atheneum Publishers, 1965

Theodore H. White, *The Making of the President 1968*, Atheneum Publishers, 1969

Theodore H. White, *Breach of Faith: The Fall of Richard Nixon*, Atheneum Publishers, 1975

Tom Wicker, *One of Us: Richard Nixon and the American Dream*, Random House, 1991

Fred A. Wilcox, *Waiting for an Army to Die: The Tragedy of Agent Orange*, Vintage Books, 1983

James H. Willbanks, *Abandoning Vietnam: How America Left and South Vietnam Lost Its War*, University Press of Kansas, 2004

Jules Witcover, *Marathon: The Pursuit of the Presidency, 1972–1976*, Viking Press, 1977

Ralph Pomeroy Witherspoon, The Military Draft and the All-Volunteer Force: A Case Study of a Shift in Public Policy, Doctoral Dissertation, Virginia Polytechnic Institute and State University

Bob Woodward, *The Commanders*, Simon and Schuster, 1991

Bob Woodward, *Bush at War*, Simon and Schuster, 2002

Bob Woodward, *State of Denial*, Simon and Schuster, 2002

Bob Woodward, *Plan of Attack*, Simon and Schuster, 2004

Bob Woodward and Carl Bernstein, *All the President's Men*, Simon and Schuster, 1974

Bob Woodward and Carl Bernstein, *The Final Days*, Simon and Schuster, 1976

Harold Wool, *The Military Specialist: Skilled Manpower for the Armed Forces*, Johns Hopkins Press, 1968

Jim Wright, *Balance of Power: Presidents and Congress from the Era of McCarthy to the Age of Gingrich*, Turner Publishing, 1996

Samuel Zaffiri, *Hamburger Hill: May 11–20, 1969*, Presidio, 1988

Samuel Zaffiri, *Westmoreland*, William Morrow and Company, 1994

Nancy Zaroulis and Gerald Sullivan, *Who Spoke Up?: American Protest against the War in Vietnam 1963–1975*, Holt, Rinehart and Winston, 1984

Bob Zelnick, *Gore: A Political Life*, Regnery Publishing, 1999

Elmo R. Zumwalt Jr., *On Watch: A Memoir*, Quadrangle, 1976

Adm. Elmo Zumwalt Jr. and Lt. Elmo Zumwalt III with John Pekkanen, *My Father, My Son*, Macmillan, 1986

INDEX

opposition of military leadership to, 347,
524–26, 528–30, 533, 705
Rumsfeld and, 341, 709
as success, 696–97
women's military service and, 506
Alsop, Joseph, 424
Alvarez, Everett, Jr., 267–68
American Civil Liberties Union (ACLU),
54–55, 334
American Enterprise Institute for Public
Policy Research, 144–45, 342, 633, 700
American Express, 686–87, 689
American Film Institute, 690
American Football League, 139–40
American Red Cross, 272, 275–76, 608, 718
Amitrol (pesticide), 80
amnesty
from court martial for drug addicts, 509
for draft resisters, 641–42, 651, 653
Anderson, Clinton, 71
Anderson, Jack, 416–18, 493
Anderson, Martin, 342, 347, 527, 528
Andrus, Ethel Percy, 167
Annenberg, Walter, 6
anthrax, 129
antiballistic missiles (ABMs). See ABMs
(antiballistic missiles)
anti-Semitism, 76
antitank TOW missiles, 553–54
antitrust laws, 139–40
antiwar movement
bombing of the Pentagon by the
Weathermen, 562–63
bombing on UW-Madison campus, 384
CONUS Intelligence operation and surveillance of, 496–97
dissent within military and, 453
draft and, 163, 349
"fact finding" missions to North Vietnam,
570–72
Kent State University shootings and riots,
250, 362–63, 384
Laird and freedom of speech, 188, 385,
538–39
Laird as target of protests, 445, 454,
538–39, 563, 640
Laird's tolerance for, 319
March Against Death, 321
McGovern's candidacy and, 564–65, 576,
580–83
morale of forces and, 413
Moratorium Day protests, 315–20, 315–22,
332, 362
Nixon's reactions to, 311–12, 321, 356, 363,
538
numbers involved in, 319

numbers of participants in, 322
Pentagon and, 163, 562–63
Red River flood and, 568–69
ROTC as target of attacks, 362, 501
self-immolations, 103–4, 163
veterans as participants in protests,
451–53
Apache Snow, 260–61
Apollo program, 356
Arafat, Yasser, 374
Arbo, Paul, 29
Archer, William "Bill," 632–33, 654
Arends, Les, 153, 563, 612
arms control, 211, 215
ABM treaty, 290, 292–95, 710
Comprehensive Test Ban Treaty (CTBT),
710
Laird and, xi, 287, 290–91, 294–95,
699, 710
SALT (Strategic Arms Limitation Talks),
216, 290–95, 592–93, 659–60, 661, 699
arms race
CIA and intelligence gathering, 286–87
military spending and, 86, 100–102, 119,
303
"missile gap," 79–81, 83, 86, 100–101
with Soviet Union, xi, 83, 100–101, 119,
260, 284–87, 294, 303–4, 414, 710
Vietnam and drain on resources, 450
Armstrong, Anne, 633
Armstrong, Neil, 101
Army Corps of Engineers, 386
Army Intelligence Command, 312, 496
Arnaz, Desi, 130
arts, Laird's support of the, 690–91
Aspin, Les, 393, 705
assassination
attempt on Teddy Roosevelt, 36
attempt on Truman, 49
of Diem and Nhu, 104, 472
of double agent by Green Berets, 305,
329–32
Greek attempt on Laird and
Papadopoulos, 383
of Kennedy, 104, 105–6
Liddy and proposal to assassinate
Anderson, 472
of Medgar Evers, 635
of M.L. King, Jr., 312
of South Vietnamese after fall of Saigon,
658
Atomic Demolition Munitions (nuclear land
mines), 478–82
Atwood, Donald, 393
Augustine, Norman, 393, 394, 476, 683
Ayers, Bill, 562–63